TABLE II (cont.)
Areas under the standard normal curve

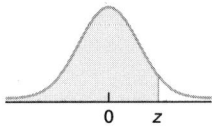

z	0.00	0.01	0.02	0.03	0.04	0.05	0.06	0.07	0.08	0.09
				Second decimal place in z						
0.0	0.5000	0.5040	0.5080	0.5120	0.5160	0.5199	0.5239	0.5279	0.5319	0.5359
0.1	0.5398	0.5438	0.5478	0.5517	0.5557	0.5596	0.5636	0.5675	0.5714	0.5753
0.2	0.5793	0.5832	0.5871	0.5910	0.5948	0.5987	0.6026	0.6064	0.6103	0.6141
0.3	0.6179	0.6217	0.6255	0.6293	0.6331	0.6368	0.6406	0.6443	0.6480	0.6517
0.4	0.6554	0.6591	0.6628	0.6664	0.6700	0.6736	0.6772	0.6808	0.6844	0.6879
0.5	0.6915	0.6950	0.6985	0.7019	0.7054	0.7088	0.7123	0.7157	0.7190	0.7224
0.6	0.7257	0.7291	0.7324	0.7357	0.7389	0.7422	0.7454	0.7486	0.7517	0.7549
0.7	0.7580	0.7611	0.7642	0.7673	0.7704	0.7734	0.7764	0.7794	0.7823	0.7852
0.8	0.7881	0.7910	0.7939	0.7967	0.7995	0.8023	0.8051	0.8078	0.8106	0.8133
0.9	0.8159	0.8186	0.8212	0.8238	0.8264	0.8289	0.8315	0.8340	0.8365	0.8389
1.0	0.8413	0.8438	0.8461	0.8485	0.8508	0.8531	0.8554	0.8577	0.8599	0.8621
1.1	0.8643	0.8665	0.8686	0.8708	0.8729	0.8749	0.8770	0.8790	0.8810	0.8830
1.2	0.8849	0.8869	0.8888	0.8907	0.8925	0.8944	0.8962	0.8980	0.8997	0.9015
1.3	0.9032	0.9049	0.9066	0.9082	0.9099	0.9115	0.9131	0.9147	0.9162	0.9177
1.4	0.9192	0.9207	0.9222	0.9236	0.9251	0.9265	0.9279	0.9292	0.9306	0.9319
1.5	0.9332	0.9345	0.9357	0.9370	0.9382	0.9394	0.9406	0.9418	0.9429	0.9441
1.6	0.9452	0.9463	0.9474	0.9484	0.9495	0.9505	0.9515	0.9525	0.9535	0.9545
1.7	0.9554	0.9564	0.9573	0.9582	0.9591	0.9599	0.9608	0.9616	0.9625	0.9633
1.8	0.9641	0.9649	0.9656	0.9664	0.9671	0.9678	0.9686	0.9693	0.9699	0.9706
1.9	0.9713	0.9719	0.9726	0.9732	0.9738	0.9744	0.9750	0.9756	0.9761	0.9767
2.0	0.9772	0.9778	0.9783	0.9788	0.9793	0.9798	0.9803	0.9808	0.9812	0.9817
2.1	0.9821	0.9826	0.9830	0.9834	0.9838	0.9842	0.9846	0.9850	0.9854	0.9857
2.2	0.9861	0.9864	0.9868	0.9871	0.9875	0.9878	0.9881	0.9884	0.9887	0.9890
2.3	0.9893	0.9896	0.9898	0.9901	0.9904	0.9906	0.9909	0.9911	0.9913	0.9916
2.4	0.9918	0.9920	0.9922	0.9925	0.9927	0.9929	0.9931	0.9932	0.9934	0.9936
2.5	0.9938	0.9940	0.9941	0.9943	0.9945	0.9946	0.9948	0.9949	0.9951	0.9952
2.6	0.9953	0.9955	0.9956	0.9957	0.9959	0.9960	0.9961	0.9962	0.9963	0.9964
2.7	0.9965	0.9966	0.9967	0.9968	0.9969	0.9970	0.9971	0.9972	0.9973	0.9974
2.8	0.9974	0.9975	0.9976	0.9977	0.9977	0.9978	0.9979	0.9979	0.9980	0.9981
2.9	0.9981	0.9982	0.9982	0.9983	0.9984	0.9984	0.9985	0.9985	0.9986	0.9986
3.0	0.9987	0.9987	0.9987	0.9988	0.9988	0.9989	0.9989	0.9989	0.9990	0.9990
3.1	0.9990	0.9991	0.9991	0.9991	0.9992	0.9992	0.9992	0.9992	0.9993	0.9993
3.2	0.9993	0.9993	0.9994	0.9994	0.9994	0.9994	0.9994	0.9995	0.9995	0.9995
3.3	0.9995	0.9995	0.9995	0.9996	0.9996	0.9996	0.9996	0.9996	0.9996	0.9997
3.4	0.9997	0.9997	0.9997	0.9997	0.9997	0.9997	0.9997	0.9997	0.9997	0.9998
3.5	0.9998	0.9998	0.9998	0.9998	0.9998	0.9998	0.9998	0.9998	0.9998	0.9998
3.6	0.9998	0.9998	0.9999	0.9999	0.9999	0.9999	0.9999	0.9999	0.9999	0.9999
3.7	0.9999	0.9999	0.9999	0.9999	0.9999	0.9999	0.9999	0.9999	0.9999	0.9999
3.8	0.9999	0.9999	0.9999	0.9999	0.9999	0.9999	0.9999	0.9999	0.9999	0.9999
3.9	1.0000†									

† For $z \geq 3.90$, the areas are 1.0000 to four decimal places.

INSTRUCTOR'S EDITION

FIFTH EDITION

Elementary Statistics

INSTRUCTOR'S EDITION

FIFTH EDITION
Elementary Statistics

Neil A. Weiss
ARIZONA STATE UNIVERSITY

Biographies by Carol A. Weiss

Boston San Francisco New York
London Toronto Sydney Tokyo Singapore Madrid
Mexico City Munich Paris Cape Town Hong Kong Montreal

 **On the cover:** Blue lobsters do exist, although they are extremely rare. According to the Northeast Fisheries Science Center, Woods Hole, MA, two components contribute to the existence of blue lobsters—one dietary and the other genetic. This fact helps explain why odds estimates for lobsters displaying a primary blue pigmentation vary considerably.

Care must be taken in obtaining and interpreting statistical results. Studying this book will provide you with the fundamental principles of gathering, analyzing, and interpreting data, such as those for blue lobsters.

Publisher: Greg Tobin
Sponsoring Editor: Deirdre Lynch
Project Editor: Rachel S. Reeve
Editorial Assistant: Anna Stillner
Executive Marketing Manager: Brenda L. Bravener
Marketing Coordinator: Julia Coen
Media Producer: Holly Rioux
Managing Editor: Karen Guardino
Production Project Editor: Jennifer Brownlow Bagdigian
Senior Designer: Barbara T. Atkinson
Copyeditor: Jerrold A. Moore
Interior Design: Silvers Design
Cover Photo: © IndexStock/Ed Bishop
Photo Research: Beth Anderson
Manufacturing Buyer: Evelyn Beaton
Composition and Art: Techsetters, Inc.

For permission to use copyrighted material, grateful acknowledgment is made to the copyright holders listed in the back of the book, following the Data Sources, which is hereby made part of this copyright page.

Many of the designations used by manufacturers and sellers to distinguish their products are claimed as trademarks. Where those designations appear in this book, and Addison-Wesley was aware of a trademark claim, the designations have been printed in initial caps or all caps.

The Library of Congress has already catalogued the student edition as follows:

Library of Congress Cataloging-in-Publication Data

Weiss, N. A. (Neil A.)
    Elementary statistics — 5th ed. / Neil A. Weiss; biographies by Carol Weiss.
       p. cm.
    Includes index.
    ISBN 0-201-71058-7
    1. Statistics. I. Title.

QA276.12.W445 2001
519.5–dc21

2001022685

Elementary Statistics Instructor's Edition, ISBN 0-201-73425-7

Copyright © 2002 by Pearson Education, Inc.

All rights reserved. No part of this publication may be reproduced, stored in a retrieval system, or transmitted, in any form or by any means, without the prior written permission of the publisher. Printed in the United States of America.

2 3 4 5 6 7 8 9 DOW 04030201

*To my father
and the memory
of my mother*

PREFACE

Using and understanding statistics and statistical procedures have become required skills in virtually every profession and academic discipline. The purpose of this book is to help students grasp basic statistical concepts and techniques, and to present real-life opportunities for applying them.

ABOUT THIS BOOK

The text is intended for a one-quarter or one-semester course. Instructors can easily fit the text to the pace and depth they prefer. Introductory high school algebra is a sufficient prerequisite.

Advances in technology and new insights into the practice of teaching statistics have inspired many of the changes in the Fifth Edition of *Elementary Statistics,* leading to more emphasis on conceptual understanding and less emphasis on computation. We made considerable improvements to the exercise sets, the clarity of the examples and explanations, the use of technology, and the real-world applications.

HIGHLIGHTS OF THE APPROACH

Several aspects of the approach and features used in the Fifth Edition give this text distinction and prominence among basic statistics books.

ASA/MAA-Guidelines Compliant. We followed ASA/MAA guidelines to stress the interpretation of statistical results, the contemporary applications of statistics, and the importance of critical thinking.

Consistent and Careful Interpretations. Throughout the book, we present consistent and careful interpretations of the results of statistical procedures. For emphasis, these interpretations are prominently displayed in colored boxes titled "What Does It Mean?".

Unique Variable-Centered Approach. This book is unique in its presentation of statistics through a variable-centered approach. By consistent and proper use of the terms *variable* and *population,* we unified and clarified the various statistical concepts.

Option for Brief Probability Coverage. We provide an authentic option for brief probability coverage, which is made possible by our unique variable-centered approach to statistics. The option for brief probability coverage is effected by omitting sections marked as optional (with an asterisk) in Chapter 5, as identified in the table of contents and in the chapter outline for that chapter.

Early Coverage of Regression/Correlation. The material on descriptive methods in regression and correlation occurs early in the text (Chapter 4). The placement is flexible; the chapter can also be postponed until later in the course.

Parallel Critical-Value/*P*-Value Approaches. We included parallel presentations of the critical-value and P-value approaches to hypothesis testing. Following introductions to each approach, our treatment makes it easy to cover one approach independently of the other approach. Both approaches can be covered and compared, if so desired.

Data Analysis and Exploration. We incorporated an extensive amount of data analysis and exploration in the text and exercises. Recognizing that not all readers will have access to technology, we provide ample opportunity to analyze and explore data without the use of a computer or statistical calculator.

Detailed and Careful Explanations. We included every step of explanation that we think a typical reader might need. Our guiding principle is to avoid cognitive jumps, making the learning process smooth and enjoyable. We believe that detailed and careful explanations result in better understanding.

Emphasis on Application. We concentrated on the application of statistical techniques to the analysis of data. Although statistical theory has been kept to a minimum, we provide a thorough explanation of the rationale for the use of each statistical procedure.

Real-World Examples. Because we believe that the majority of students learn by example, every concept discussed in the text is illustrated by at least one detailed example. The examples are based on real-life situations and were chosen for their interest as well as for their illustrative value.

Real-World Exercises. We made major improvements to the exercise sets. Now, more than ever, the exercises provide current, real-world applications. We constructed the exercises from an extensive variety of newspapers, magazines, statistical abstracts, journal articles, and Web sites; sources are explicitly cited. The exercises are designed to help the student learn the material and to show that statistics is a lively and relevant discipline. More than 1350 exercises are included in the book. For additional practice and for use on exams, over 500 supplementary exercises can be found on the WeissStats CD, which is supplied free with every new copy of the book.

The Technology Center. Within each chapter, we provided integrated, parallel treatments of Minitab, Excel, and TI-83 Plus in subsections titled The Technology Center. Our method of presentation makes it easy to cover one or more of these technologies, or none at all.

FEATURES

Following are notable features of the Fifth Edition. We have marked new and expanded features.

NEW! What Does It Mean? This feature presents the meaning and significance of statistical results in plain, everyday language. Instead of just obtaining the answers or results, students are shown the importance of interpretation.

NEW! Parallel Critical-Value/P-Value Approaches. For each hypothesis testing method, dual step-by-step procedures are given. One procedure provides the critical-value approach and the other the P-value approach. The illustrative example that follows the dual procedures is presented in parallel. Thus there is complete flexibility in the coverage of hypothesis testing: Either one or both approaches to hypothesis testing can be studied.

NEW! Supplementary Exercises. Besides the vast number of exercises presented in the text, we included more than 500 additional high-quality, section-by-section problems on the WeissStats CD.

NEW! All-New Design. We redesigned the text and now feature a four-color format for improved readability and understanding.

NEW! WeissStats CD. This CD, included with every new copy of the book, contains a wealth of resources. Among them are the following:

- More than 500 section-by-section supplementary exercises.

- All appropriate data sets in the book in relevant formats, including Minitab, Excel, SPSS, ASCII, and as a TI-83 Plus application.

- Data Desk/XL (DDXL) software, an Excel add-in from Data Description, Inc., that enhances Excel's statistics and graphics capabilities.

- Adobe Acrobat Reader software for reading the PDF-formatted supplementary exercises.

EXPANDED! Technology. We extended in-text coverage of statistical technology to include three of the most popular applications: Minitab, Excel, and TI-83 Plus. The technology sections, titled The Technology Center, are integrated as optional subsections immediately after the discussion of the particular statistical concepts under consideration. The Technology Centers usually include output and detailed instructions for obtaining the output. Also available are comprehensive technology supplements written explicitly to accompany the book: *Minitab Manual, Excel Manual, TI-83 Plus Manual,* and *SPSS Manual.*

Procedure Boxes. To help the student learn statistical procedures, we developed easy-to-follow, step-by-step methods for carrying out those procedures. A unique feature of this book is that each step in the procedure is highlighted and presented again within the example that illustrates the procedure. This approach serves a twofold purpose: It shows how the procedure is applied, and it helps the student master the steps in the procedure.

Procedure Index. Because of the numerous statistical procedures available, it is sometimes difficult to find a specific one. Consequently, we included a Procedure Index (located inside the back cover of the book), which provides a quick and easy way to find the right procedure for performing any particular statistical analysis.

EXPANDED! Case Studies. Each chapter begins with a classic or contemporary case study that highlights the real-world relevance of the material under consideration. At the end of the chapter, the case study is reviewed and discussed in light of the chapter's major points, and then problems are presented for the student to solve. Expanded case study explorations and resources are available on the Weiss Web site at www.aw.com/weiss.

Exercises. The exercise sets were extensively updated and revised, including the insertion of many new exercises obtained from journal articles and Internet resources. Most section exercise sets are divided into three categories.

- Statistical Concepts and Skills exercises help the student master the skills and concepts explicitly discussed in the section.

- Extending the Concepts and Skills exercises invite the student to extend his or her skills by examining material not necessarily covered in the text. Exercises that introduce new concepts are highlighted in blue.

- Using Technology exercises provide the student with an opportunity to apply and interpret the computing and statistical capabilities of Minitab, Excel, TI-83 Plus, SPSS, or any other statistical technology.

Review Tests. This comprehensive set of end-of-chapter review problems contains concept questions, basic-skill problems, and exercises using technology. Answers to the Review Tests are given in Appendix B.

Internet Projects. Each chapter includes an Internet Project. These projects, which are keyed to the text,

- engage the student in active and collaborative learning through simulations, demonstrations, and other activities, and
- guide the student through applications by using Internet links to access data and other information provided by the vast resources of the World Wide Web.

The Internet Projects can be completed individually or in a collaborative learning setting and are featured on the Weiss Web site at www.aw.com/weiss.

EXPANDED! Data Sets. In most examples and many exercises, we present both raw data and summary statistics. This practice gives a more realistic view of statistics and provides an opportunity for the student to solve problems by computer or statistical calculator, if so desired. Hundreds of new data sets were included and many more of the data sets were updated. All data sets, including large ones, are available in multiple formats on the WeissStats CD found in the back of each new book.

Computer Simulations. Computer simulations appear in both the text and the exercises. The simulations serve as pedagogical aids for understanding complex concepts such as sampling distributions.

General Objectives and Chapter Outlines. Included at the beginning of each chapter is a general description of the chapter, an explanation of how the chapter relates to the text as a whole, and an outline that lists the sections in the chapter.

Chapter Reviews. The end-of-chapter material begins with a Chapter Review. The review includes (1) chapter objectives, (2) a list of key terms with page references, and (3) a review test. These pedagogical aids provide the student with an organized method for reviewing and studying each chapter.

Focusing on Data Analysis. Included on the WeissStats CD is a collection of large data sets called the Focus Database. Through the Focusing on Data Analysis feature at the end of each chapter, the student can conduct various statistical analyses on these data sets, using his or her technology of choice. This feature gives the student an opportunity to work with large data sets, to practice using technology, and to discover the many methods of exploring and analyzing data.

Formula/Table Card. A detachable formula/table card (FTC) is provided with the book. This card contains all the formulas and many of the tables that appear in the text. The FTC is helpful for quick-reference purposes; many instructors also find it convenient for use with examinations.

Biographical Sketches. Each chapter ends with a brief biography of a famous statistician. Besides being of general interest, these biographies help the student obtain a perspective on the development of the science of statistics.

FLEXIBLE SYLLABUS

The text offers a great deal of flexibility in choosing material to cover. The flowchart on page xiv indicates chapter-coverage flexibility. Here are two additional noteworthy items.

Option for Brief Probability Coverage. The probability concepts that are required for statistical inference can now be covered in two or three class periods. Further probability concepts, provided in sections marked as optional, are available at the discretion of the instructor.

Option for Placement of Regression Coverage. The chapter discussing descriptive methods in regression and correlation (Chapter 4) was written so that it can be covered either early (immediately after Chapter 3 on descriptive measures) or later, say, directly before the chapter on inferential methods in regression and correlation (Chapter 14). Specifically, Chapter 4 can be covered at any time after Chapter 3 but before Chapter 14.

ORGANIZATION AND CHAPTER-BY-CHAPTER CHANGES

As we mentioned, the text offers a great deal of flexibility in choosing material to cover. Following is a brief chapter-by-chapter summary, including some important changes.

- Chapter 1 presents the nature of statistics, sampling designs, and an introduction to experimental designs. Chapters 2 and 3 discuss the fundamentals of descriptive statistics. Quartiles are now defined more intuitively and do not require interpolation.

- Chapter 4 gives an informal (but precise) treatment of regression and correlation, relying on intuitive and graphical presentation of important concepts. The placement is flexible—this chapter can be covered any time after Chapter 3 but before Chapter 14.

- Chapter 5 examines probability and optional material on discrete random variables. In this edition, only the first three sections of Chapter 5 are prerequisite to coverage of inferential statistics.

- Chapter 6 provides a concise discussion of the normal distribution. Chapter 7 introduces the concept of sampling distributions and presents an improved and simplified introduction to the sampling distribution of the sample mean.

- Chapters 8 and 9 give an easily accessible introduction to confidence intervals and hypothesis tests for one population mean by using the terminology of variables and avoiding formal probability. Both chapters employ the σ-known versus σ-unknown criterion for deciding which parametric procedure to use; this approach makes confidence intervals and hypothesis tests easier to understand and apply, and provides a method consistent with most statistical software, including Minitab, Excel (DDXL), and TI-83 Plus. We consider Chapters 1–9 to be the core of an elementary statistics course.

- Chapter 10 examines inferences for two population means. It contains a detailed discussion of the meaning of independent samples, including graphics for quick assimilation. The two-sample z-procedures are covered in the exercises so that the presentation can focus on the more practical two-sample t-procedures.

- Chapter 11 discusses inferences for one and two population proportions. Chapter 12 introduces the chi-square goodness-of-fit test and the chi-square independence test. Also included in Chapter 12 is a section on grouping bivariate data into contingency tables and an improved presentation of association.

- Chapter 13 presents one-way analysis-of-variance (ANOVA) by using the language of variables to simplify and unify assumptions. Chapter 14 examines inferential methods in regression and correlation.

The flowchart on the following page summarizes the preceding discussion and shows the interdependence among chapters. In the flowchart, the prerequisites for a given chapter consist of all chapters that have a path that leads to that chapter. Optional sections can be identified by consulting the table of contents.

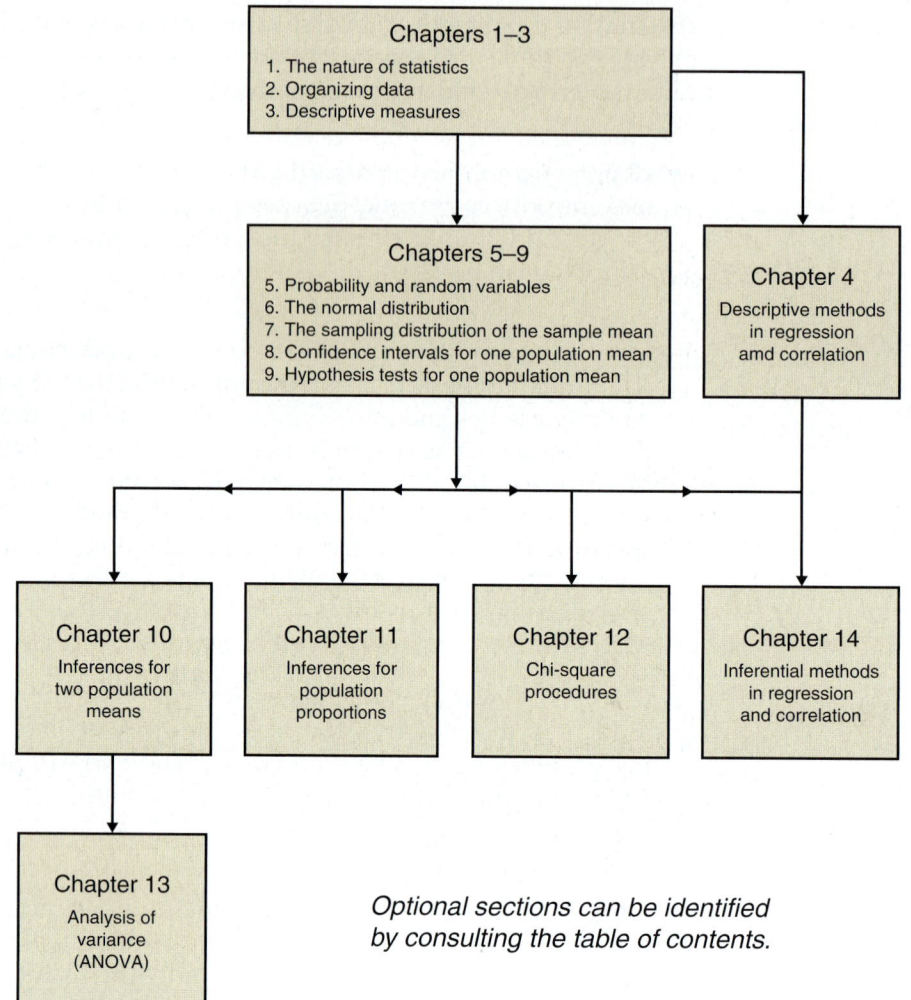

SUPPLEMENTS AND OTHER SUPPORT

The following supplements are designed specifically to accompany the Fifth Edition of *Elementary Statistics*.

FOR THE INSTRUCTOR

Instructor's Edition (0-201-73425-7). This version of the text includes answers to all appropriate exercises presented in the book.

Instructor's Solutions Manual (0-201-73470-2). Written by David Lund, University of Wisconsin, Eau Claire. This supplement contains detailed, worked-out solutions to all section exercises, review-test problems, Focusing on Data Analysis exercises, and case studies in the text. Also included are all the answers to the supplementary exercises found on the WeissStats CD.

PowerPoint Presentation Slides (0-201-73717-5). These slides, available on both a separate CD and the Weiss Web site, contain many of the book's figures, tables, definitions, formulas, key facts, and procedure boxes. The slides can be used with PowerPoint software or printed onto transparencies.

Printed Test Bank (0-201-73708-6). This supplement provides three printed examinations for each chapter of the text.

TestGen-EQ with QuizMaster-EQ (0-201-77475-5). TestGen-EQ is a computerized test generator with algorithmically defined problems organized specifically for this book. Its user-friendly graphical interface enables instructors to select, view, edit, and add test items and then print tests in a variety of fonts and forms. A built-in question editor gives the user the power to create graphs, import graphics, insert mathematical symbols and templates, and insert variable numbers or text. An "Export to HTML" feature lets instructors create practice tests that can be posted to a Web site. Tests created with TestGen-EQ can also be displayed on Web pages when the free TestGen-EQ plug-in has been installed with Internet Explorer or Netscape Navigator. Additionally, tests created with TestGen-EQ can be used with QuizMaster-EQ, which enables students to take exams on a computer network. QuizMaster-EQ automatically grades the exams, stores results on disk, and allows the instructor to view or print a variety of reports for individual students, classes, or courses. Contact your Addison-Wesley sales consultant.

FOR THE STUDENT

Minitab Manual (0-201-73712-4). Written by Peter W. Zehna, Naval Postgraduate School. This manual provides detailed Minitab instructions, examples from the book, and interpretations to complement those given in the book.

Excel Manual (0-201-73707-8). Written by Peter W. Zehna, Naval Postgraduate School. Correlated to examples in the book, this manual presents detailed Excel and DDXL instructions and interpretations to complement those given in the book.

TI-83 Plus Manual (0-201-73709-4). Written by Ellen Fischer, Georgia Southern University. This step-by-step guide for use of the TI-83 Plus calculator provides detailed instructions, examples from the book, and interpretations to complement those given in the book.

SPSS Manual (0-201-73713-2). Written by Roger Peck, California State University, Bakersfield. This manual examines the use of SPSS and gives step-by-step instructions for applying SPSS to conduct the statistical and data analyses discussed in the examples found in the book.

Student's Solutions Manual (0-201-73471-0). Written by David Lund, University of Wisconsin, Eau Claire. This manual includes detailed solutions to all odd-numbered section exercises and all Review-Test problems in the text. Also included are answers to the odd-numbered supplementary exercises on the WeissStats CD.

WeissStats CD. Provided free with every new copy of the book, this CD contains numerous resources, as discussed on page ix. In particular, the WeissStats CD allows for easy access to data sets without the user having to enter them manually.

MathXL, www.mathxl.com. The student text bundled with a 12-month registration coupon is 0-201-75976-4. With MathXL, the student can take diagnostic chapter tests correlated to the book, receive individualized study plans based on those test results, and take further tests to gauge progress. Instructors can customize tests or create their own, using TestGen-EQ testing software. All student test results are tracked in an online gradebook. For more information, contact your Addison-Wesley sales representative.

Weiss Web Sites. These Web sites include downloadable practice quizzes, PowerPoint slides, formula/table card, and more. They also provide access to the Internet projects and Case Study extensions, written and designed by Professor Kyle Siegrist of the University of Alabama at Huntsville. The URL is www.aw.com/weiss. Book specific WebCT and Course Compass Web sites are also available. For more information, contact your Addison-Wesley representative.

ActivStats (0-201-74114-8). Developed by Paul Velleman and Data Description, Inc., *ActivStats* presents a complete introductory statistics course on CD-ROM, using a full range of multimedia. Integrating video, simulation, animation, narration, text, interactive experiments, World Wide Web access, and Data Desk, a fully functioning statistics package, this product gives the student a rich learning environment. Also included are exercises for reinforcement of key concepts, an index, and a glossary. The list of topics and a number of homework problems taken directly from the Fifth Edition of *Elementary Statistics* make this program a strong complement to the text for use in both lecture- and Web-based courses. *ActivStats* is PC and Macintosh compatible. Also available are

- *ActivStats for Minitab* (PC) (0-201-74108-3),
- *ActivStats for Excel* (Mac and PC) (0-201-74110-5),
- *ActivStats for SPSS* (PC) (0-201-74111-3), and
- *ActivStats for JMP* (Mac and PC) (0-201-74653-0).

The Student Edition of Minitab for Windows 95/NT. This release of the Student Edition, Release 12 for Windows 95/NT (0-201-39715-3), allows for 5000 data points. It has improved graphing capabilities and increased functionality, including multiple regression and more. Also provided with the software are data sets drawn from business, the social sciences, and the physical sciences. In addition to the software, case studies and 16 tutorial sessions are featured in a tutorial manual.

AW Tutor Center. The Addison-Wesley Tutor Center is staffed by qualified statistics and mathematics instructors who provide students with tutoring on text examples and odd-numbered exercises. Tutoring assistance is provided by telephone, fax, and e-mail and is available five days a week, seven hours a day. For more information, contact your Addison-Wesley sales representative.

ACKNOWLEDGMENTS

First, we want to express our sincere appreciation to all reviewers of previous editions for their many contributions to the evolution of the book. For this edition, it is our pleasure to thank the following reviewers, whose comments and suggestions resulted in significant improvements.

James Albert
Bowling Green State University

Yvonne Brown
Pima Community College

Brant Deppa
Winona State University

Jacqueline Fesq
Raritan Valley Community College

Susan Herring
Sonoma State University

Christopher Lacke
Rowan University

Tze-San Lee
Western Illinois University

Ennis Donice McCune
Stephen F. Austin State University

Jacqueline B. Miller
Drury University

Bernard J. Morzuch
University of Massachusetts, Amherst

JoAnn Paderi
Lourdes College

Alan Polansky
Northern Illinois University

Kimberley A. Polly
Parkland College

Gina F. Reed
Gainesville College

Sharon Ross
Georgia Perimeter College

Arvind Shah
University of South Alabama

Brani Vidakovic
Georgia Institute of Technology

Marlene Will
Spalding University

Matthew Wood
University of Missouri, Columbia

Our thanks as well are extended to Professor Michael Driscoll for his help in selecting the statisticians for the biographical sketches; and Professors Charles Kaufman, Sharon Lohr, Kathy Prewitt, Walter Reid, and Bill Steed with whom we have had several illuminating discussions. Thanks also go to Professors Matthew Hassett and Ronald Jacobowitz for their many helpful comments and suggestions.

Several other people provided useful input and resources. They include Professor Thomas A. Ryan, Jr., Dr. William Feldman and Mr. Frank Crosswhite, Dr. George McManus and Mr. Gregory Weiss, Dr. Lawrence W. Harding, Jr., Professor Jeanne Sholl, Professor R. B. Campbell, Mr. Howard Blaut, Mr. Rick Hanna, Ms. Mary Neary, Ms. Alison Stern-Dunyak, Mr. Dale Philbrick, and Ms. Maureen Quinn. Our sincere thanks to all of them for their help in making a better book.

To Professor Larry Griffey, we convey our appreciation for his formula/table card. We are grateful to Professor Peter Zehna for preparing the *Minitab Manual* and *Excel Manual*, to Professor Ellen Fischer for the *TI-83 Manual*, and to Professor Roger Peck for the *SPSS Manual*. Our gratitude goes as well to Professor David Lund for writing the *Instructor's Solutions Manual* and *Student's Solutions Manual*.

We express our appreciation to Professor Dennis Young for his collaboration on numerous statistical and pedagogical issues. Thanks also go to Professor Kyle Siegrist for his Internet projects and case-study extensions. For their accuracy checking of the solutions to the examples and exercises, we extend our gratitude to Professors Christopher Lacke and Kimberley A. Polly.

Our thanks are extended to Gregory Weiss for his research in finding myriad new and interesting statistical studies and data for the examples and exercises and, as well, for compiling the data sets for the WeissStats CD and proofreading the book. We are also grateful to our copyeditor, Jerrold A. Moore, for his efforts that resulted in substantial improvements to the flow and style of the exposition.

Without the help of many people at Addison-Wesley, this book and its numerous ancillaries would not have been possible; to all of them go our heartfelt thanks. We would, however, like to give special thanks to Deirdre Lynch and to the following other people at Addison-Wesley: Rachel S. Reeve, Gary Merrill, Karen Guardino, Jenny Bagdigian, Brenda Bravener, Holly Rioux, Barbara

Atkinson, Beth Anderson, Caroline Fell, Evelyn Beaton, and Joan Flaherty. At this time, we would also like to recognize and thank Joe Vetere, our technical art consultant for more than 20 years—his extensive knowledge of art and graphics, both traditional and electronic, makes him an invaluable resource for issues concerning the many graphs, charts, and figures that appear in the book.

Finally, we convey our appreciation to Carol A. Weiss. Apart from writing the text, she was involved in every aspect of development and production. Moreover, Carol did a superb job of researching and writing the biographies.

Tempe, Arizona   *N.A.W.*

CONTENTS

PART I	**INTRODUCTION**	**1**
CHAPTER 1	**THE NATURE OF STATISTICS**	**2**

        General Objectives and Chapter Outline   2
        Case Study: Top Films of All Time   3
1.1   Two Kinds of Statistics   4
1.2   The Technology Center   10
1.3   Simple Random Sampling   10
1.4   Other Sampling Designs   17
1.5   Experimental Designs   22
        Chapter Review 30, Review Test 31, Internet Project 34, Focusing on Data Analysis 34, Case Study Discussion 35, Biography 35

PART II	**DESCRIPTIVE STATISTICS**	**37**
CHAPTER 2	**ORGANIZING DATA**	**38**

        General Objectives and Chapter Outline   38
        Case Study: Preventing Infant Mortality   39
2.1   Variables and Data   40
2.2   Grouping Data   44
2.3   Graphs and Charts   56
2.4   Stem-and-Leaf Diagrams   66
2.5   Distribution Shapes; Symmetry and Skewness   71
2.6   Misleading Graphs   78
        Chapter Review 82, Review Test 83, Internet Project 86, Focusing on Data Analysis 86, Case Study Discussion 86, Biography 87

indicates an optional section

CHAPTER 3 — DESCRIPTIVE MEASURES 88

General Objectives and Chapter Outline 88
Case Study: New York Yankees Y2K Salaries 89
3.1 Measures of Center 90
3.2 The Sample Mean 99
3.3 Measures of Variation; the Sample Standard Deviation 103
3.4 The Five-Number Summary; Boxplots 116
3.5 Descriptive Measures for Populations; Use of Samples 128
Chapter Review 140, Review Test 140, Internet Project 143, Focusing on Data Analysis 143, Case Study Discussion 144, Biography 145

CHAPTER 4 — DESCRIPTIVE METHODS IN REGRESSION AND CORRELATION 146

General Objectives and Chapter Outline 146
Case Study: Fat Consumption and Prostate Cancer 147
4.1 Linear Equations With One Independent Variable 148
4.2 The Regression Equation 153
4.3 The Coefficient of Determination 170
4.4 Linear Correlation 179
Chapter Review 189, Review Test 190, Internet Project 191, Focusing on Data Analysis 191, Case Study Discussion 192, Biography 192

PART III — PROBABILITY, RANDOM VARIABLES, AND SAMPLING DISTRIBUTIONS 195

CHAPTER 5 — PROBABILITY AND RANDOM VARIABLES 196

General Objectives and Chapter Outline 196
Case Study: The Powerball 197
5.1 Probability Basics 198
5.2 Events 205
5.3 Some Rules of Probability 213
*5.4 Discrete Random Variables and Probability Distributions 220
*5.5 The Mean and Standard Deviation of a Discrete Random Variable 227
*5.6 The Binomial Distribution 233
Chapter Review 249, Review Test 250, Internet Project 253, Focusing on Data Analysis 254, Case Study Discussion 254, Biography 255

indicates an optional section

CHAPTER 6	**THE NORMAL DISTRIBUTION** 256	

        General Objectives and Chapter Outline   256
        Case Study: Chest Sizes of Scottish Militiamen   257
6.1   Introducing Normally Distributed Variables   258
6.2   Areas Under the Standard Normal Curve   265
6.3   Working With Normally Distributed Variables   274
6.4   Assessing Normality; Normal Probability Plots   283
        Chapter Review 290, Review Test 291, Internet Project 293, Focusing on Data Analysis 293, Case Study Discussion 294, Biography 295

CHAPTER 7	**THE SAMPLING DISTRIBUTION OF THE SAMPLE MEAN** 296	

        General Objectives and Chapter Outline   296
        Case Study: The Chesapeake and Ohio Freight Study   297
7.1   Sampling Error; the Need for Sampling Distributions   298
7.2   The Mean and Standard Deviation of $\bar{x}$ 304
7.3   The Sampling Distribution of the Sample Mean   311
        Chapter Review 319, Review Test 320, Internet Project 322, Focusing on Data Analysis 322, Case Study Discussion 323, Biography 323

PART IV	**INFERENTIAL STATISTICS** 325	
CHAPTER 8	**CONFIDENCE INTERVALS FOR ONE POPULATION MEAN** 326	

        General Objectives and Chapter Outline   326
        Case Study: The Chips Ahoy! 1,000 Chips Challenge   327
8.1   Estimating a Population Mean   328
8.2   Confidence Intervals for One Population Mean When σ Is Known   334
8.3   Margin of Error   343
8.4   Confidence Intervals for One Population Mean When σ Is Unknown   349
        Chapter Review 361, Review Test 362, Internet Project 365, Focusing on Data Analysis 365, Case Study Discussion 366, Biography 367

* *indicates an optional section*

CHAPTER 9 — HYPOTHESIS TESTS FOR ONE POPULATION MEAN 368

General Objectives and Chapter Outline 368
Case Study: Sex and Sense of Direction 369
9.1 The Nature of Hypothesis Testing 370
9.2 Terms, Errors, and Hypotheses 378
9.3 Hypothesis Tests for One Population Mean When σ Is Known 386
9.4 P-Values 398
9.5 Hypothesis Tests for One Population Mean When σ Is Unknown 410
Chapter Review 424, Review Test 425, Internet Project 428, Focusing on Data Analysis 428, Case Study Discussion 428, Biography 429

CHAPTER 10 — INFERENCES FOR TWO POPULATION MEANS 430

General Objectives and Chapter Outline 430
Case Study: Breast Milk and IQ 431
10.1 The Sampling Distribution of the Difference Between Two Sample Means for Independent Samples 432
10.2 Inferences for Two Population Means, Using Independent Samples: Standard Deviations Assumed Equal 439
10.3 Inferences for Two Population Means, Using Independent Samples: Standard Deviations Not Assumed Equal 453
10.4 Inferences for Two Population Means, Using Paired Samples 468

Chapter Review 485, Review Test 485, Internet Project 489, Focusing on Data Analysis 489, Case Study Discussion 490, Biography 491

CHAPTER 11 — INFERENCES FOR POPULATION PROPORTIONS 492

General Objectives and Chapter Outline 492
Case Study: Double-Dipping ATM Fees 493
11.1 Confidence Intervals for One Population Proportion 494
11.2 Hypothesis Tests for One Population Proportion 508
11.3 Inferences for Two Population Proportions, Using Independent Samples 516
Chapter Review 531, Review Test 531, Internet Project 533, Focusing on Data Analysis 533, Case Study Discussion 534, Biography 534

indicates an optional section

CHAPTER 12	**CHI-SQUARE PROCEDURES** 536

          General Objectives and Chapter Outline   536
          Case Study: Road Rage   537
12.1   The Chi-Square Distribution   538
12.2   Chi-Square Goodness-Of-Fit Test   540
12.3   Contingency Tables; Association   549
12.4   Chi-Square Independence Test   558
          Chapter Review 571, Review Test 571, Internet Project 574, Focusing on Data Analysis 574, Case Study Discussion 575, Biography 575

CHAPTER 13	**ANALYSIS OF VARIANCE (ANOVA)** 576

          General Objectives and Chapter Outline   576
          Case Study: Heavy Drinking Among College Students   577
13.1   The F-Distribution   578
13.2   One-Way ANOVA: The Logic   580
13.3   One-Way ANOVA: The Procedure   587
          Chapter Review 602, Review Test 602, Internet Project 603, Focusing on Data Analysis 603, Case Study Discussion 604, Biography 605

CHAPTER 14	**INFERENTIAL METHODS IN REGRESSION AND CORRELATION** 606

          General Objectives and Chapter Outline   606
          Case Study: Fat Consumption and Prostate Cancer   607
14.1   The Regression Model; Analysis of Residuals   608
14.2   Inferences for the Slope of the Population Regression Line   622
14.3   Estimation and Prediction   632
14.4   Inferences in Correlation   642
          Chapter Review 650, Review Test 650, Internet Project 652, Focusing on Data Analysis 652, Case Study Discussion 653, Biography 654

* indicates an optional section

APPENDIXES A-1

APPENDIX A | STATISTICAL TABLES A-3

I	Random numbers	A-5
II	Areas under the standard normal curve	A-6
III	Normal scores	A-8
IV	Values of t_α	A-10
V	Values of χ^2_α	A-12
VI	Values of F_α	A-14

APPENDIX B | ANSWERS TO SELECTED EXERCISES A-23

INDEX I-1

DATA SOURCES I-8

* indicates an optional section

INSTRUCTOR'S EDITION

FIFTH EDITION

Elementary Statistics

part i

Introduction

CHAPTER 1 | **The Nature of Statistics**

chapter 1

The Nature of Statistics

CHAPTER OUTLINE

1.1 Two Kinds of Statistics

1.2 The Technology Center

1.3 Simple Random Sampling

1.4 Other Sampling Designs

1.5 Experimental Designs

GENERAL OBJECTIVES What does the word *statistics* bring to mind? Most people immediately think of numerical facts or data, such as unemployment figures, farm prices, or the number of marriages and divorces. *Webster's New World Dictionary* gives two definitions of the word *statistics*:

1. facts or data of a numerical kind, assembled, classified, and tabulated so as to present significant information about a given subject.
2. [construed as sing.], the science of assembling, classifying, and tabulating such facts or data.

But statistics encompasses much more than these definitions convey. Not only do statisticians assemble, classify, and tabulate data, but they also analyze data for the purpose of making generalizations and decisions. For example, a political analyst can use data from a portion of the voting population to predict the political preferences of the entire voting population. And a city council can decide where to build a new airport runway based on environmental impact statements and demographic reports that include a variety of statistical data.

In this chapter, we introduce some basic terminology so that the various meanings of the word *statistics* will become clear to you. We also examine two primary ways of producing data, namely, through sampling and experimentation. We discuss sampling designs in Sections 1.3 and 1.4, and experimental designs in Section 1.5.

case study

TOP FILMS OF ALL TIME

The American Film Institute (AFI) conducted a survey as part of a celebration of the 100th anniversary of cinema. AFI polled 1500 filmmakers, actors, critics, politicians, and film historians, asking them to pick their 100 favorite films from a list of 400. The films on the list were made between 1896 and 1996.

After tallying the responses, AFI compiled a list representing the top 100 films. *Citizen Kane*, made in 1941, finished in first place, followed by *Casablanca*, which was made in 1942. Following are the top 40 finishers in the poll.

Rank	Film	Year	Rank	Film	Year
1	Citizen Kane	1941	21	The Grapes of Wrath	1940
2	Casablanca	1942	22	2001: A Space Odyssey	1968
3	The Godfather	1972	23	The Maltese Falcon	1941
4	Gone With the Wind	1939	24	Raging Bull	1980
5	Lawrence of Arabia	1962	25	E.T. The Extra-Terrestrial	1982
6	The Wizard of Oz	1939	26	Dr. Strangelove	1964
7	The Graduate	1967	27	Bonnie & Clyde	1967
8	On the Waterfront	1954	28	Apocalypse Now	1979
9	Schindler's List	1993	29	Mr. Smith Goes to Washington	1939
10	Singin' in the Rain	1952	30	The Treasure of the Sierra Madre	1948
11	It's a Wonderful Life	1946	31	Annie Hall	1977
12	Sunset Blvd.	1950	32	The Godfather, Part II	1974
13	The Bridge on the River Kwai	1957	33	High Noon	1952
14	Some Like It Hot	1959	34	To Kill a Mockingbird	1962
15	Star Wars	1977	35	It Happened One Night	1934
16	All About Eve	1950	36	Midnight Cowboy	1969
17	The African Queen	1951	37	The Best Years of Our Lives	1946
18	Psycho	1960	38	Double Indemnity	1944
19	Chinatown	1974	39	Doctor Zhivago	1965
20	One Flew Over the Cuckoo's Nest	1975	40	North by Northwest	1959

Armed with the knowledge gained in this chapter, you will be asked to analyze further the AFI poll at the end of the chapter.

1.1 TWO KINDS OF STATISTICS

You probably already know something about statistics. If you read newspapers, surf the Web, watch the news on television, or follow sports, you see and hear the word *statistics* frequently. In this section, we use familiar examples such as baseball statistics and voter polls to introduce the two major types of statistics: **descriptive statistics** and **inferential statistics.** We also examine how to classify studies as either descriptive or inferential.

DESCRIPTIVE STATISTICS

Each spring in the late 1940s President Harry Truman officially opened the major league baseball season by throwing out the "first ball" at the opening game of the Washington Senators. Both President Truman and the Washington Senators had reason to be interested in statistics in 1948. We use the 1948 baseball season to illustrate the first major type of statistics, descriptive statistics, in Example 1.1.

Example 1.1 *Descriptive Statistics*

The 1948 Baseball Season In 1948, the Washington Senators played 153 games, winning 56 and losing 97. They finished seventh in the American League and were led in hitting by Bud Stewart, whose batting average was .279. These and many other statistics were compiled by baseball statisticians who took the complete records for each game of the season and organized that large mass of information effectively and efficiently.

Although baseball fans take baseball statistics for granted, a great deal of time and effort is required to gather and organize them. Moreover, without such statistics, baseball would be much harder to understand. For instance, picture yourself trying to select the best hitter in the American League with only the official score sheets for each game. (More than 600 games were played in 1948; the best hitter was Ted Williams, who led the league with a batting average of .369.) ◆

The work of baseball statisticians provides an excellent illustration of descriptive statistics. A formal definition of the term *descriptive statistics* follows.

DEFINITION 1.1 Descriptive Statistics

Descriptive statistics consists of methods for organizing and summarizing information.

Descriptive statistics includes the construction of graphs, charts, and tables and the calculation of various descriptive measures such as averages, measures of variation, and percentiles. We discuss descriptive statistics in detail in Chapters 2 and 3.

INFERENTIAL STATISTICS

We use the 1948 presidential election to introduce the other major type of statistics, inferential statistics, in Example 1.2.

Example 1.2 *Inferential Statistics*

The 1948 Presidential Election In the fall of 1948, President Truman was also concerned about statistics. The *Gallup Poll* taken just prior to the election predicted that he would win only 44.5% of the vote and be defeated by the Republican nominee, Thomas E. Dewey. But this time the statisticians had predicted incorrectly. Truman won more than 49% of the vote and, with it, the presidency. The Gallup Organization modified some of its procedures and has correctly predicted the winner ever since. ◆

Political polling provides an example of inferential statistics. Interviewing everyone of voting age in the United States on their voting preferences would be expensive and unrealistic. Statisticians who want to gauge the sentiment of the entire **population** of U.S. voters can afford to interview only a carefully chosen group of a few thousand voters. This group is called a **sample** of the population. Statisticians analyze the information obtained from a sample of the voting population to make inferences (draw conclusions) about the preferences of the entire voting population. Inferential statistics provides methods for making such inferences.

The terminology just introduced in the context of political polling is used in general in statistics. Specifically, the terms *population* and *sample* are defined as follows.

DEFINITION 1.2 Population and Sample

Population: The collection of all individuals or items under consideration in a statistical study.

Sample: That part of the population from which information is obtained.

Figure 1.1 depicts the relationship between a population and a sample from the population.

Now that we have discussed the terms *population* and *sample*, we can define *inferential statistics*.

DEFINITION 1.3 Inferential Statistics

Inferential statistics consists of methods for drawing and measuring the reliability of conclusions about a population based on information obtained from a sample of the population.

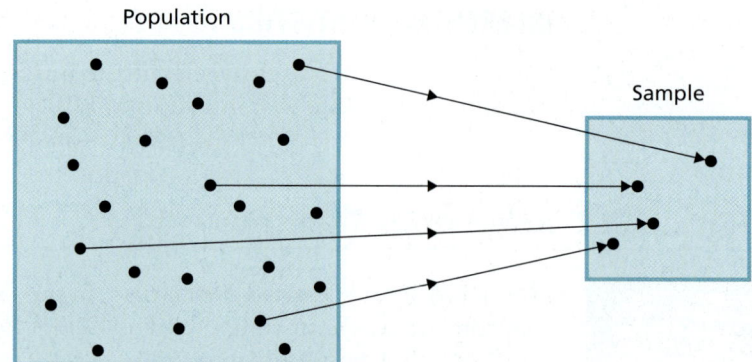

FIGURE 1.1
Relationship between population and sample

Descriptive statistics and inferential statistics are interrelated. You must almost always use techniques of descriptive statistics to organize and summarize the information obtained from a sample before carrying out an inferential analysis. Furthermore, the preliminary descriptive analysis of a sample often reveals features that lead you to the choice of (or to a reconsideration of the choice of) the appropriate inferential method.

CLASSIFYING STATISTICAL STUDIES

As you proceed through this book, you will obtain a thorough understanding of the principles of descriptive and inferential statistics. At this point, you should be able to classify statistical studies as either descriptive or inferential. In doing so, you should consider the intent of the study.

On the one hand, if the intent of the study is to examine and explore the information obtained for its own intrinsic interest only, the study is descriptive. On the other hand, if the information is obtained from a sample of a population and the intent of the study is to use that information to draw conclusions about the population, the study is inferential.

Thus a descriptive study may be performed on a sample as well as on a population. Only when an inference is made about the population, based on information obtained from the sample, does the study become inferential.

Examples 1.3 and 1.4 further illustrate the distinction between descriptive and inferential studies. In each example, we present the result of a statistical study and classify the study as either descriptive or inferential. Try to classify each study yourself before reading our explanation.

Example 1.3 *Classifying Statistical Studies*

The 1948 Presidential Election *The study* Table 1.1 displays the voting results for the 1948 presidential election.
Classification This study is descriptive. It is a summary of the votes cast by U.S. voters in the 1948 presidential election. No inferences are made. ◆

TABLE 1.1
Final results of the 1948 presidential election

Ticket	Votes	Percentage
Truman–Barkley (Democratic)	24,179,345	49.7
Dewey–Warren (Republican)	21,991,291	45.2
Thurmond–Wright (States Rights)	1,176,125	2.4
Wallace–Taylor (Progressive)	1,157,326	2.4
Thomas–Smith (Socialist)	139,572	0.3

Example 1.4 Classifying Statistical Studies

Testing Baseballs *The study* For the 101 years preceding 1977, baseballs used by the major leagues were purchased from the Spalding Company. In 1977, that company stopped manufacturing major league baseballs, and the major leagues arranged to buy their baseballs from the Rawlings Company.

Early in the 1977 season, pitchers began to complain that the Rawlings ball was "livelier" than the Spalding ball. They claimed it was harder, bounced farther and faster, and gave hitters an unfair advantage. There was some evidence for this claim: In the first 616 games of 1977, 1033 home runs were hit, compared to only 762 home runs hit in the first 616 games of 1976.

Sports Illustrated magazine sponsored a careful study of the liveliness question, and the results appeared in the article "They're Knocking the Stuffing Out of It" by Larry Keith (*Sports Illustrated*, June 13, 1977, pp. 23–27). In this study, an independent testing company randomly selected 85 baseballs from the current (1977) supplies of various major league teams. The bounce, weight, and hardness of the baseballs chosen were carefully measured. Those measurements were then compared with measurements obtained from similar tests on baseballs used in 1952, 1953, 1961, 1963, 1970, and 1973.

The conclusion, presented on page 24 of the *Sports Illustrated* issue, was that "… the 1977 Rawlings ball is livelier than the 1976 Spalding, but not as lively as it could be under big league rules, or as the ball has been in the past."

Classification This study is inferential. The independent testing company used a sample of 85 baseballs from the 1977 supplies of major league teams to make an inference about the population of all such baseballs. (An estimated 360,000 baseballs were used by the major leagues in 1977.)   ◆

The *Sports Illustrated* study also shows that it is often not feasible to obtain information for the entire population. Indeed, after the bounce and hardness tests, all of the baseballs sampled were taken to a butcher in Plainfield, New Jersey, to be sliced in half so that researchers could look inside them. Clearly, testing every baseball in this way would not have been practical.

THE DEVELOPMENT OF STATISTICS

According to the *Dictionary of Scientific Biography*, "The word *Statistik*, first printed in 1672, meant *Staatswissenschaft*, or, rather, a science concerning the states. It was cultivated at the German universities, where it consisted of more or less systematically collecting 'state curiosities' rather than quantitative material."

The modern science of statistics is much broader than just collecting "state curiosities." Historically, descriptive statistics appeared first. Censuses were taken as long ago as Roman times. Over the centuries, records of such things as births, deaths, marriages, and taxes led naturally to the development of descriptive statistics.

Inferential statistics is a newer arrival. Major developments began to occur with the research of Karl Pearson (1857–1936) and Ronald Fisher (1890–1962), who published their findings in the early years of the twentieth century. Since the work of Pearson and Fisher, inferential statistics has evolved rapidly and is now applied in a myriad of fields.

Familiarity with statistics will help you make sense of many things you read in newspapers and magazines and on the Internet. For instance, in the description of the *Sports Illustrated* baseball test (Example 1.4), you may have questioned whether a sample of only 85 baseballs could be used to draw a conclusion about a population of some 360,000 baseballs. By the time you complete Chapter 9, you will understand why such inferences are not unreasonable.

> **What Does it Mean?**
>
> An understanding of statistical reasoning and of the basic concepts of descriptive and inferential statistics has become mandatory for virtually everyone, in both their private and professional lives.

Exercises 1.1

Statistical Concepts and Skills

1.1 Define the following terms.
a. Population **b.** Sample

1.2 What are the two major types of statistics? Describe them in detail.

1.3 Identify some of the methods used in descriptive statistics.

1.4 Explain two ways in which descriptive statistics and inferential statistics are interrelated.

In Exercises 1.5–1.10, classify each of the studies as either descriptive or inferential.

1.5 TV Viewing Times. The A. C. Nielsen Company collects and publishes information on the television viewing habits of Americans. Data from a sample of Americans yielded the following estimates of average TV viewing time per week for all Americans. The times are in hours and minutes. [SOURCE: Nielsen Media Research, *Nielsen Report on Television*.]

Group (by age)		Time
Average all persons		30:14
Women	Total 18+	34:47
	18–24	28:54
	25–54	31:05
	55+	44:11
Men	Total 18+	30.41
	18–24	23:31
	25–54	28:44
	55+	38:47
Teens	12–17	21:50
Children	2–11	23:01

1.6 Professional Athlete Salaries. In the *Statistical Abstract of the United States, 1999*, average professional athletes' salaries in baseball, basketball, and football were compiled and compared for the years 1987 and 1997.

	Average Salary ($1000)	
Sport	**1987**	**1997**
Baseball (MLB)	412	1,337
Basketball (NBA)	440	2,200
Football (NFL)	203	725

1.7 Causes of Death. The U.S. National Center for Health Statistics published the following rate estimates for the leading causes of death in 1997 in *Vital Statistics of the United States*. The estimates are based on a 10% sampling of all 1997 U.S. death certificates. Rates are per 100,000 population.

Cause	Rate
Major cardiovascular diseases	352.2
Malignancies (cancers)	200.8
Chronic obstructive pulmonary diseases	41.3
Accidents	34.4
Pneumonia and influenza	33.0

1.8 Drug Use. The U.S. Substance Abuse and Mental Health Services Administration collects and publishes data on drug use, by type of drug and age group, in *National Household Survey on Drug Abuse*. The following table provides information for the years 1990 and 1997. The percentages shown are estimates obtained from national samples.

	Percentage, 12 years old and over			
Type of drug	**Ever used**		**Current user**	
	1990	**1997**	**1990**	**1997**
Marijuana	30.5	30.9	5.4	5.1
Cocaine	11.2	10.5	0.9	0.7
Inhalants	5.7	5.7	0.4	0.4
Hallucinogens	7.9	9.6	0.4	0.8
Heroin	0.8	0.9	—	0.2
Stimulants[1]	5.5	4.5	0.6	0.3
Sedatives[1]	2.8	1.9	0.2	0.1
Tranquilizers[1]	4.0	3.2	0.6	0.4
Analgesics[1]	6.3	4.9	0.9	0.7
Alcohol	82.2	81.9	52.6	51.4

1 = Nonmedical use.

1.9 Dow Jones Industrial Averages. The following table provides the closing values of the Dow Jones Industrial Averages as of the end of December for the years 1994–1999. [SOURCE: Global Financial Data.]

Year	Closing value
1994	3,834.4
1995	5,117.1
1996	6,448.3
1997	7,908.3
1998	9,181.4
1999	11,497.1

1.10 The Music People Buy. Results of monthly telephone surveys yielded the following percentage estimates of all music expenditures. These statistics were published in *1998 Consumer Profile*. [SOURCE: Recording Industry Association of America, Inc.]

Music Type	Expenditure (%)
Rock	25.7
Country	14.1
R&B	12.8
Pop	10.0
Rap	9.7
Oldies Gospel	6.3
Classical	3.3
Jazz	1.9
Soundtracks	1.7
New Age	0.6
Children's	0.4
Other	13.5

Extending the Concepts and Skills

1.11 Organically Grown Produce. A *Newsweek* poll of a sample of Americans revealed that "84% of those surveyed would choose organically grown produce over produce grown using chemical fertilizers, pesticides, and herbicides."
a. Is the statement in quotes an inferential or a descriptive statement?
b. Based on the same information, what if the statement had been "84% of Americans would choose organically grown produce over produce grown using chemical fertilizers, pesticides, and herbicides"?

1.12 Nuclear Weapons Test Ban. In a press release dated September 24, 1997, dateline Washington, D.C., the Mellman Group for the Coalition to Reduce Nuclear Dangers reported that "a new nationwide poll shows that 70.3% of Americans think the U.S. Senate should approve a treaty with 140 countries that would prohibit underground nuclear weapons explosions worldwide."

a. Do you think that the statement in the press release is inferential or descriptive? Can you be sure?

b. Actually, the Mellman Group conducted an opinion survey of 800 adults and determined that 70.3% of them thought that the U.S. Senate should approve a treaty with 140 countries to prohibit underground nuclear weapons explosions worldwide. How would you rephrase the statement in the press release to make clear that it is a descriptive statement?

1.2 THE TECHNOLOGY CENTER

Today, programs for conducting statistical and data analyses are available in dedicated statistical software packages, general-use spreadsheet software, and graphing calculators. In this book, we discuss three of the most popular technologies for doing statistics: Minitab, Excel, and the TI-83 Plus.

For the most part, for Excel we use Data Desk/XL (DDXL) from Data Description, Inc. This statistics add-in complements Excel's standard statistics capabilities; it is included on the WeissStats CD, which comes with your book. Further details of Minitab, Excel, the TI-83 Plus, and other statistical technologies are provided in supplements written specifically to accompany this book.

At the end of appropriate sections of the book, in subsections titled The Technology Center, we present and interpret output from the three technologies mentioned. The output from each technology addresses problems that were solved by hand earlier in the section. For this aspect of The Technology Center, you need neither a computer nor a graphing calculator, nor do you need any working knowledge of the technologies under discussion.

For those who want to learn how to obtain the output for one or more of the three technologies, step-by-step instructions are presented in subsections titled Obtaining the Output (Optional). When studying this material, you will get the best results by using your computer or graphing calculator to perform the steps described.

Each statistical technology has a slightly different method for data input and output. At this point, you should spend some time learning the method for each technology you want to study. The documentation or online help for your technology gives you the necessary details. For Minitab, Excel, and the TI-83 Plus, you can also find this information in the appropriate technology supplement to this book.

1.3 SIMPLE RANDOM SAMPLING

Throughout this book, we present examples of organizations or people conducting studies: A consumer group wants information about the gas mileage of a particular make of car, so it performs mileage tests on a sample of such cars and statistically analyzes the resulting data; or a teacher wants to know about the comparative merits of two teaching methods, so she tests those methods on two groups of students. This approach reflects a healthy attitude: To obtain information about a subject of interest, plan and conduct a study.

However, the possibility always exists that a study being considered has already been done. Repeating it would be a waste of time, energy, and money.

> **What Does it Mean?**
>
> You can often avoid the effort and expense of a study if someone else has already done that study and published the results.

Therefore, before a study is planned and conducted, a literature search should be made. Doing so does not require going through all the books in the library or making an extensive Internet search. Many information collection agencies specialize in finding studies on specific topics in specific areas.

CENSUS, SAMPLING, AND EXPERIMENTATION

If information required is not already available from a previous study, you can plan a new study to obtain the information. One method for acquiring information is to conduct a **census,** that is, obtain information on the entire population of interest. However, conducting a census is generally time consuming and costly, frequently impractical, and sometimes impossible.

Two methods other than a census for obtaining information are **sampling** and **experimentation.** In much of this book, we concentrate on sampling. However, we introduce experimentation in Section 1.5, discuss it sporadically throughout the text, and examine it in detail in the chapter *Design of Experiments and Analysis of Variance* on the WeissStats CD accompanying this book or on the Weiss Web site, www.aw.com/weiss.

If sampling is deemed appropriate, you must then decide how to select the sample; that is, you must choose the method for obtaining a sample from the population. In making that choice, keep in mind that the sample will be used to draw conclusions about the entire population. Consequently, the sample should be a **representative sample,** that is, it should reflect as closely as possible the relevant characteristics of the population under consideration.

For instance, it would not make sense to use the average weight of a sample of professional football players to make an inference about the average weight of all adult males. Nor would it be reasonable to estimate the median income of California residents by sampling the incomes of Beverly Hills residents.

To see what can happen when a sample is not representative, consider the presidential election of 1936. Before the election, the *Literary Digest* magazine conducted an opinion poll of the voting population. Its survey team asked a sample of the voting population whether they would vote for Franklin D. Roosevelt, the Democratic candidate, or for Alfred Landon, the Republican candidate.

Based on the results of the survey, the magazine predicted an easy win for Landon. But when the actual election results were in, Roosevelt won by the greatest landslide in the history of presidential elections! What happened? Here are two reasons given for the failure of the poll.

- The sample was obtained from among people who owned a car or had a telephone. In 1936, that group included only the more well-to-do people, and historically such people tend to vote Republican.
- The response rate was low (less than 25% of those polled responded), and there was a nonresponse bias (a disproportionate number of those who responded to the poll were Landon supporters).

Whatever the reason for the poll's failure, the sample obtained by the *Literary Digest* obviously was not representative.

Most modern sampling procedures involve the use of **probability sampling.** In probability sampling, a random device, such as tossing a coin or consulting a table of random numbers, is used to decide which members of the population will constitute the sample instead of leaving such decisions to human judgment.

The use of probability sampling may still yield a nonrepresentative sample. However, probability sampling eliminates unintentional selection bias and permits the researcher to control the chance of obtaining a nonrepresentative sample. Furthermore, the use of probability sampling guarantees that the techniques of inferential statistics can be applied. In this section and the next, we will examine the most important probability-sampling methods.

SIMPLE RANDOM SAMPLING

The inferential techniques considered in this book are intended for use with only one particular sampling procedure: **simple random sampling,** or just **random sampling,** which yields a **simple random sample.** Simple random sampling is the basic type of probability sampling and is also the foundation for the more complex types of probability sampling.

DEFINITION 1.4 Simple Random Sampling; Simple Random Sample

Simple random sampling: A sampling procedure for which each possible sample of a given size is equally likely to be the one obtained.

Simple random sample: A sample obtained by simple random sampling.

There are two types of simple random sampling. One is **simple random sampling with replacement,** whereby a member of the population can be selected more than once; the other is **simple random sampling without replacement,** whereby a member of the population can be selected at most once. *Unless we specify otherwise, assume that simple random sampling is done without replacement.*

In Example 1.5, we chose a very small population—the five top Oklahoma state officials—to illustrate simple random sampling. In practice, we would not sample from such a small population but would instead take a census. Using a small population here makes understanding the concept of simple random sampling easier.

Example 1.5 Simple Random Samples

TABLE 1.2
Five top Oklahoma state officials

Governor (G)
Lieutenant Governor (L)
Secretary of State (S)
Attorney General (A)
Treasurer (T)

Sampling Oklahoma State Officials As reported by *The World Almanac*, the top five state officials of Oklahoma are as shown in Table 1.2. Consider these five officials a population of interest.

a. List the possible samples (without replacement) of two officials from this population of five officials.
b. Describe a method for obtaining a simple random sample of two officials from this population of five officials.

c. For the sampling method described in part (b), what are the chances that any particular sample of two officials will be the one selected?
d. Repeat parts (a)–(c) for samples of size 4.

Solution For convenience, we use the letters in parentheses after the officials in Table 1.2 to represent them.

TABLE 1.3
The 10 possible samples of two officials

G, L	G, S	G, A	G, T
L, S	L, A	L, T	S, A
S, T	A, T		

TABLE 1.4
The five possible samples of four officials

G, L, S, A	G, L, S, T
G, L, A, T	G, S, A, T
L, S, A, T	

a. There are 10 possible samples of two officials from the population of five officials, as listed in Table 1.3.
b. To obtain a simple random sample of size 2 we could first write the letters that correspond to the five officials, G, L, S, A, and T, on separate pieces of paper. Next, we could place the five slips of paper in a box and shake it. Then, while blindfolded, we could pick two slips of paper.
c. The sampling procedure described in part (b) ensures that we are taking a simple random sample. Consequently, each of the possible samples of two officials is equally likely to be the one selected. There are 10 possible samples, so the chances are $\frac{1}{10}$ (1 in 10) that any particular sample will be the one selected.
d. There are five possible samples of four officials from the population of five officials, as listed in Table 1.4. In this case, a simple random sampling procedure, such as picking four slips of paper out of a box, gives each of the five possible samples in Table 1.4 a 1 in 5 chance of being the one selected. ◆

RANDOM-NUMBER TABLES

Obtaining a simple random sample by picking slips of paper out of a box is usually not practical, especially when the population to be sampled is large. But there are several practical procedures to get simple random samples. One common method is to use a **table of random numbers**—a table of randomly chosen digits. In Example 1.6, we explain how a table of random numbers can be used to obtain a simple random sample.

Example 1.6 *Random-Number Tables*

Sampling Student Opinions Student questionnaires, known as "teacher evaluations," gained widespread use in the late 1960s and early 1970s. Generally, student evaluations of teachers are not done at final exam time. More commonly, professors hand out evaluation forms a week or so before the final.

That practice, however, poses several problems. On some days, less than 60% of the students registered for a class may actually attend. Moreover, because many of those who are present have preparations to make for other classes, they often complete their teacher evaluation forms in a hurry so that they can leave class early. A better method, therefore, might be to select a sample of students from the class and interview them individually. In this kind of situation, a simple random sample is appropriate.

During one semester, Professor Hassett wanted to sample the attitudes of the students taking college algebra at his school. He decided to interview 15 of the 728 students enrolled in the course. Professor Hassett had a registration list on which the 728 students were numbered 1–728, so he could obtain a simple random sample of 15 students by randomly selecting 15 numbers between 1 and 728. To do so, he used a table of random numbers. The random-number table used by Professor Hassett is presented as Table I in Appendix A. For ease of reference, we repeat it here as Table 1.5.

TABLE 1.5
Random numbers

Line number	Column number				
	00–09	10–19	20–29	30–39	40–49
00	15544 80712	97742 21500	97081 42451	50623 56071	28882 28739
01	01011 21285	04729 39986	73150 31548	30168 76189	56996 19210
02	47435 53308	40718 29050	74858 64517	93573 51058	68501 42723
03	91312 75137	86274 59834	69844 19853	06917 17413	44474 86530
04	12775 08768	80791 16298	22934 09630	98862 39746	64623 32768
05	31466 43761	94872 92230	52367 13205	38634 55882	77518 36252
06	09300 43847	40881 51243	97810 18903	53914 31688	06220 40422
07	73582 13810	57784 72454	68997 72229	30340 08844	53924 89630
08	11092 81392	58189 22697	41063 09451	09789 00637	06450 85990
09	93322 98567	00116 35605	66790 52965	62877 21740	56476 49296
10	80134 12484	67089 08674	70753 90959	45842 59844	45214 36505
11	97888 31797	95037 84400	76041 96668	75920 68482	56855 97417
12	92612 27082	59459 69380	98654 20407	88151 56263	27126 63797
13	72744 45586	43279 44218	83638 05422	00995 70217	78925 39097
14	96256 70653	45285 26293	78305 80252	03625 40159	68760 84716
15	07851 47452	66742 83331	54701 06573	98169 37499	67756 68301
16	25594 41552	96475 56151	02089 33748	65289 89956	89559 33687
17	65358 15155	59374 80940	03411 94656	69440 47156	77115 99463
18	09402 31008	53424 21928	02198 61201	02457 87214	59750 51330
19	97424 90765	01634 37328	41243 33564	17884 94747	93650 77668

To select 15 random numbers between 1 and 728, we first pick a random starting point, say, by closing our eyes and placing a finger on Table 1.5. Then, beginning with the three digits under the finger, we go down the table and record the numbers as we go. Because we want numbers between 1 and 728 only, we discard the number 000 and numbers between 729 and 999. To avoid repetition, we also eliminate numbers that have occurred previously. If we have not found enough numbers by the time we reach the bottom of the table, we move over to the next column of three-digit numbers and go up.

Using this procedure, Professor Hassett obtained 069, circled in Table 1.5, as a starting point. Reading down from 069 to the bottom of Table 1.5 and then

1.3 Simple Random Sampling

FIGURE 1.2
Procedure used by Professor Hassett to obtain 15 random numbers between 1 and 728 from Table 1.5

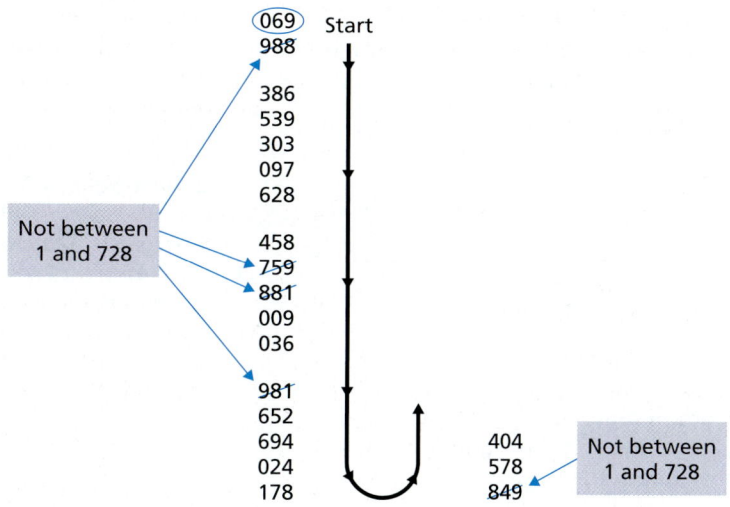

TABLE 1.6
Registration numbers of students interviewed

up the next column of three-digit numbers, he found the 15 random numbers displayed in Fig. 1.2 and in Table 1.6. Thus Professor Hassett interviewed the 15 students whose numbers on the registration list are shown in Table 1.6. ◆

The Technology Center

Nowadays, statistical software packages or graphing calculators, instead of random-number tables, are generally used to obtain random numbers. For instance, Minitab, Excel, and the TI-83 Plus all have built-in programs that can be utilized to generate random numbers within any specified range. See the technology manuals for details.

Exercises 1.3

Statistical Concepts and Skills

1.13 Explain why a census is often not the best way to obtain information about a population.

1.14 Identify two methods other than a census for obtaining information.

1.15 In sampling, why is obtaining a representative sample important?

1.16 Memorial Day Poll. An online poll conducted over Memorial Day Weekend (May 26–29, 2000) asked people what they were doing to observe Memorial Day. The choices were: (1) stay home and relax, (2) vacation outdoors over the weekend, or (3) visit a military cemetery. More than 22,000 people participated in the poll, with 86% selecting option 1. Discuss this poll with regard to its suitability.

1.17 Estimating Median Income. Explain why a sample of 30 dentists from Seattle taken to estimate the median income of all Seattle residents is not representative.

1.18 Provide a scenario of your own in which a sample is not representative.

1.19 Regarding probability sampling:
a. What is it?
b. Does probability sampling always yield a representative sample? Explain your answer.
c. Identify some advantages of probability sampling.

1.20 Regarding simple random sampling:
a. What is simple random sampling?
b. What is a simple random sample?
c. Identify two forms of simple random sampling and explain the difference between the two.

1.21 The inferential procedures discussed in this book are intended for use with only one particular sampling procedure. What sampling procedure is that?

1.22 Identify two methods for obtaining a simple random sample.

1.23 Oklahoma State Officials. The five top Oklahoma state officials are displayed in Table 1.2 on page 12. Use that table to solve the following problems.
a. List the 10 possible samples (without replacement) of size 3 that can be obtained from the population of five officials.
b. If a simple random sampling procedure is used to obtain a sample of three officials, what are the chances that it is the first sample on your list in part (a)? the second sample? the tenth sample?

1.24 Best-Selling Albums. *Billboard Online* provides data on the best-selling albums of all time. As of April, 2000, the top six best-selling albums of all time, by artist, are the Eagles (E), Michael Jackson (M), Pink Floyd (P), Led Zeppelin (L), Billy Joel (B), and Fleetwood Mac (F). [SOURCE: Record Industry Association of America, Inc.]
a. List the 15 possible samples (without replacement) of two artists that can be selected from the six. For brevity, use the initial provided.
b. Describe a procedure for taking a simple random sample of two artists from the six.
c. If a simple random sampling procedure is used to obtain two artists, what are the chances of selecting P and F? M and E?

1.25 Best-Selling Albums. Refer to Exercise 1.24.
a. List the 15 possible samples (without replacement) of four artists that can be selected from the six.
b. Describe a procedure for taking a simple random sample of four artists from the six.
c. If a simple random sampling procedure is used to obtain four artists, what are the chances of selecting E, F, L, and B? P, B, M, and F?

1.26 Best-Selling Albums. Refer to Exercise 1.24.
a. List the 20 possible samples (without replacement) of three artists that can be selected from the six.
b. Describe a procedure for taking a simple random sample of three artists from the six.
c. If a simple random sampling procedure is used to obtain three artists, what are the chances of selecting M, F, and L? P, L, and E?

1.27 The International 500. Each year, *Fortune Magazine* publishes an article titled "The International 500" that provides a ranking by sales of the top 500 firms outside the United States. Suppose that you want to examine various characteristics of successful firms. Further suppose that, for your study, you decide to take a simple random sample of 10 firms from *Fortune Magazine*'s list of "The International 500." Use Table I in Appendix A to obtain 10 random numbers that you can use to specify your sample.

1.28 Keno. In the game of keno, 20 balls are selected at random from 80 balls, numbered 1–80. Use Table I in Appendix A to simulate one game of keno by obtaining 20 random numbers between 1 and 80.

Extending the Concepts and Skills

1.29 Oklahoma State Officials. Refer to Exercise 1.23.
a. List the possible samples of size 1 that can be obtained from the population of five officials.
b. What is the difference between obtaining a simple random sample of size 1 and selecting one official at random?

1.30 Oklahoma State Officials. Refer to Exercise 1.23.
a. List the possible samples (without replacement) of size 5 that can be obtained from the population of five officials.
b. What is the difference between obtaining a simple random sample of size 5 and taking a census?

Using Technology

1.31 The International 500. Refer to Exercise 1.27. Use the technology of your choice to obtain 10 random numbers that you can use to specify your simple random sample of 10 firms.

1.32 Keno. Refer to Exercise 1.28. Use the technology of your choice to simulate one game of keno, that is, to obtain a simple random sample of 20 numbers between 1 and 80.

1.4 OTHER SAMPLING DESIGNS

Simple random sampling is the most natural and easily understood method of probability sampling—it corresponds to our intuitive notion of random selection by lot. However, simple random sampling does have drawbacks. For instance, it may fail to provide sufficient coverage when information about subpopulations is required and may be impractical when the members of the population are widely scattered geographically.

In this section, we examine some commonly used sampling procedures that are often more appropriate than simple random sampling. Remember, though, the inferential procedures discussed in this book must be modified before they can be applied to data that are obtained by sampling procedures other than simple random sampling.

SYSTEMATIC RANDOM SAMPLING

One method that takes less effort to implement than simple random sampling is **systematic random sampling.** Consider Example 1.7.

Example 1.7 Systematic Random Sampling

Sampling Student Opinions Let's return to the situation in Example 1.6 where Professor Hassett wanted to obtain a sample of 15 of the 728 students enrolled in college algebra at his school. Use systematic random sampling to obtain the sample.

Solution To begin, we divide the population size by the sample size and round the answer down to the nearest whole number: $\frac{728}{15} = 48$ (rounded down). Next, we select a number at random between 1 and 48 using, say, a table of random numbers. Suppose that we do so and obtain the number 22. Then, we list every 48th number, starting at 22, until we have 15 numbers. This method yields the 15 numbers displayed in Table 1.7.

Had Professor Hassett used systematic random sampling to obtain his sample of students and had he obtained the number 22 as his starting point, he would have interviewed the 15 students whose numbers on the registration list are shown in Table 1.7. ◆

TABLE 1.7
Numbers obtained by systematic random sampling

22	166	310	454	598
70	214	358	502	646
118	262	406	550	694

As illustrated in Example 1.7, we use the following procedure to implement systematic random sampling.

> **Procedure 1.1**
>
> **Systematic Random Sampling**
>
> **Step 1** Divide the population size by the sample size and round the result down to the nearest whole number, m.
>
> **Step 2** Use a random-number table (or a similar device) to obtain a number, k, between 1 and m.
>
> **Step 3** Select for the sample those members of the population that are numbered k, $k + m$, $k + 2m, \ldots$.

Systematic random sampling is not only easier to execute than simple random sampling, but it also usually provides results comparable to simple random sampling. The exception is the presence of some kind of cyclical pattern in the listing of the members of the population (e.g., male, female, male, female, …), a phenomenon that is relatively rare.

CLUSTER SAMPLING

Another sampling method is **cluster sampling.** It is particularly useful when the members of the population under consideration are widely scattered geographically. We illustrate this method in Example 1.8.

Example 1.8 Cluster Sampling

Bike Paths Survey Several years ago, the city council of Tempe, Arizona, was being pressured by citizens' groups to install bike paths in the city. The council members wanted to be sure they had the support of a majority of the taxpayers, so they decided to poll the city's homeowners.

Their first attempt at surveying public opinion was a questionnaire mailed out with the city's 18,000 homeowner water bills. Unfortunately, this method did not work very well. Only 19.4% of the questionnaires were returned, and a large number of those had written comments that indicated they came from avid bicyclists or from people who strongly resented bicyclists. The questionnaire generally had not been returned by the average voter, and the city council realized that.

The city had an employee in the planning department with sample survey experience, so the council asked her to do a survey. She was given two assistants to help interview a representative sample of voters and was instructed to report back within 10 days.

The planner thought about taking a simple random sample of 300 voters, 100 interviews for herself and for each of her two assistants. However, the simple random sample plan created some time problems. The city was so spread out that an interviewer with a list of 100 voters randomly scattered around the city would have to drive an average of 18 minutes from one interview to the next. Doing so would require approximately 30 hours of driving time for each interviewer and could delay completion of the report. Obviously, simple random sampling would not do.

To save time, the planner decided to use cluster sampling. The residential portion of the city was divided into 947 blocks, each containing approximately 20 houses, as shown in Fig. 1.3.

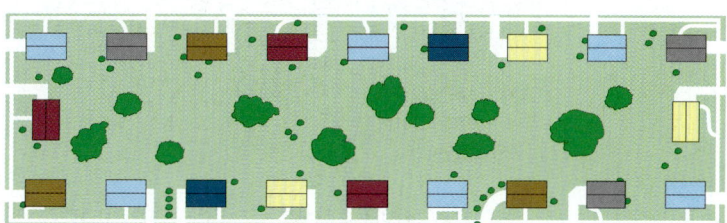

FIGURE 1.3
A typical block of homes

The planner numbered the blocks (clusters) on the city map from 1 to 947 and then used a table of random numbers to obtain a simple random sample of 15 of the 947 blocks. Each of the three interviewers was then assigned five of the 15 blocks obtained. This method gave each interviewer roughly 100 homes to visit but saved a great deal of travel time; an interviewer could work on a block for nearly a full day without having to drive to another neighborhood. The report was finished on time. ◆

In the simplest case, as illustrated by Example 1.8, cluster sampling is implemented by using the following procedure.

Procedure 1.2

Cluster Sampling

Step 1 Divide the population into groups (clusters).

Step 2 Obtain a simple random sample of the clusters.

Step 3 Use all the members of the clusters obtained in Step 2 as the sample.

Although cluster sampling can save time and money, it does have disadvantages. Ideally, each cluster should mirror the entire population. However, that is often not the case, as members of a cluster are frequently more homogeneous than the members of the population as a whole. This situation can cause problems.

For instance, consider a simplified small town, as depicted in Fig. 1.4 on the next page. The town council is thinking about building a town swimming pool. A planner for the town needs to sample voter opinion about using public funds to build the pool. Many upper-income and middle-income homeowners will probably say "No" because they own pools or can use a neighbor's. Many low-income voters will probably say "Yes" because they generally do not have access to pools.

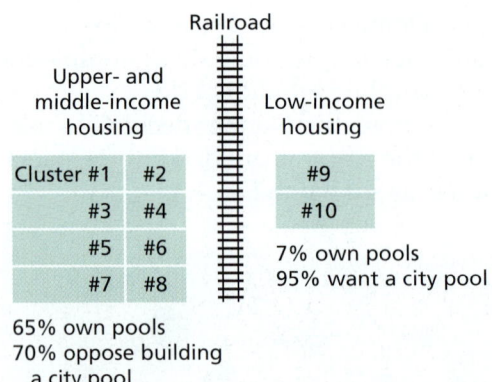

FIGURE 1.4
Clusters for a small town

If the planner uses cluster sampling and interviews the voters of, say, three randomly selected clusters, there is a good chance that no low-income voters will be interviewed.[1] And if no low-income voters are interviewed, the results of the survey will be misleading. Suppose, for instance, that the planner obtained clusters #3, #5, and #8. Then his survey would show that only about 30% of the voters want a pool. But that is not true because more than 40% of the voters actually want a pool. The clusters that most strongly support the town swimming pool would not have been included in the survey.

In this hypothetical example, the town is so small that common sense indicates that a cluster sample may not be representative. However, in situations where there are hundreds of clusters, such problems may be quite difficult to detect.

STRATIFIED SAMPLING

Another sampling method, known as **stratified sampling,** is often more reliable than cluster sampling. In stratified sampling the population is first divided into subpopulations, called **strata,** and then sampling is done from each stratum. Ideally, the members of each stratum should be homogeneous relative to the characteristic under consideration, as illustrated in Example 1.9.

Example 1.9 *Stratified Sampling*

Town Swimming Pool Consider again the town swimming pool situation. In stratified sampling, voters could be divided into three strata: upper income, middle income, and low income. A simple random sample could then be taken from each of the three strata.

This stratified sampling procedure would ensure that no income group is missed. It would also improve the precision of the statistical estimates (because the voters within each income group tend to be somewhat homogeneous) and would make it possible to estimate the separate opinions of each of the three strata. ◆

---

[1]There are 120 possible three-cluster samples, and 56 of those contain neither of the low-income clusters, #9 and #10. In other words, 46.7% of the possible three-cluster samples contain neither of the low-income clusters.

FORMULA/TABLE CARD FOR WEISS'S *ELEMENTARY STATISTICS, FIFTH EDITION*
Larry R. Griffey

TABLE II Areas under the standard normal curve

	Second decimal place in z										
	0.09	0.08	0.07	0.06	0.05	0.04	0.03	0.02	0.01	0.00	z
										0.0000†	−3.9
	0.0001	0.0001	0.0001	0.0001	0.0001	0.0001	0.0001	0.0001	0.0001	0.0001	−3.8
	0.0001	0.0001	0.0001	0.0001	0.0001	0.0001	0.0001	0.0001	0.0001	0.0001	−3.7
	0.0001	0.0001	0.0001	0.0001	0.0001	0.0001	0.0001	0.0001	0.0001	0.0002	−3.6
	0.0002	0.0002	0.0002	0.0002	0.0002	0.0002	0.0002	0.0002	0.0002	0.0002	−3.5
	0.0002	0.0003	0.0003	0.0003	0.0003	0.0003	0.0003	0.0003	0.0003	0.0003	−3.4
	0.0003	0.0004	0.0004	0.0004	0.0004	0.0004	0.0004	0.0005	0.0005	0.0005	−3.3
	0.0005	0.0005	0.0005	0.0006	0.0006	0.0006	0.0006	0.0006	0.0007	0.0007	−3.2
	0.0007	0.0007	0.0008	0.0008	0.0008	0.0008	0.0009	0.0009	0.0009	0.0010	−3.1
	0.0010	0.0010	0.0011	0.0011	0.0011	0.0012	0.0012	0.0013	0.0013	0.0013	−3.0
	0.0014	0.0014	0.0015	0.0015	0.0016	0.0016	0.0017	0.0018	0.0018	0.0019	−2.9
	0.0019	0.0020	0.0021	0.0021	0.0022	0.0023	0.0023	0.0024	0.0025	0.0026	−2.8
	0.0026	0.0027	0.0028	0.0029	0.0030	0.0031	0.0032	0.0033	0.0034	0.0035	−2.7
	0.0036	0.0037	0.0038	0.0039	0.0040	0.0041	0.0043	0.0044	0.0045	0.0047	−2.6
	0.0048	0.0049	0.0051	0.0052	0.0054	0.0055	0.0057	0.0059	0.0060	0.0062	−2.5
	0.0064	0.0066	0.0068	0.0069	0.0071	0.0073	0.0075	0.0078	0.0080	0.0082	−2.4
	0.0084	0.0087	0.0089	0.0091	0.0094	0.0096	0.0099	0.0102	0.0104	0.0107	−2.3
	0.0110	0.0113	0.0116	0.0119	0.0122	0.0125	0.0129	0.0132	0.0136	0.0139	−2.2
	0.0143	0.0146	0.0150	0.0154	0.0158	0.0162	0.0166	0.0170	0.0174	0.0179	−2.1
	0.0183	0.0188	0.0192	0.0197	0.0202	0.0207	0.0212	0.0217	0.0222	0.0228	−2.0
	0.0233	0.0239	0.0244	0.0250	0.0256	0.0262	0.0268	0.0274	0.0281	0.0287	−1.9
	0.0294	0.0301	0.0307	0.0314	0.0322	0.0329	0.0336	0.0344	0.0351	0.0359	−1.8
	0.0367	0.0375	0.0384	0.0392	0.0401	0.0409	0.0418	0.0427	0.0436	0.0446	−1.7
	0.0455	0.0465	0.0475	0.0485	0.0495	0.0505	0.0516	0.0526	0.0537	0.0548	−1.6
	0.0559	0.0571	0.0582	0.0594	0.0606	0.0618	0.0630	0.0643	0.0655	0.0668	−1.5
	0.0681	0.0694	0.0708	0.0721	0.0735	0.0749	0.0764	0.0778	0.0793	0.0808	−1.4
	0.0823	0.0838	0.0853	0.0869	0.0885	0.0901	0.0918	0.0934	0.0951	0.0968	−1.3
	0.0985	0.1003	0.1020	0.1038	0.1056	0.1075	0.1093	0.1112	0.1131	0.1151	−1.2
	0.1170	0.1190	0.1210	0.1230	0.1251	0.1271	0.1292	0.1314	0.1335	0.1357	−1.1
	0.1379	0.1401	0.1423	0.1446	0.1469	0.1492	0.1515	0.1539	0.1562	0.1587	−1.0
	0.1611	0.1635	0.1660	0.1685	0.1711	0.1736	0.1762	0.1788	0.1814	0.1841	−0.9
	0.1867	0.1894	0.1922	0.1949	0.1977	0.2005	0.2033	0.2061	0.2090	0.2119	−0.8
	0.2148	0.2177	0.2206	0.2236	0.2266	0.2296	0.2327	0.2358	0.2389	0.2420	−0.7
	0.2451	0.2483	0.2514	0.2546	0.2578	0.2611	0.2643	0.2676	0.2709	0.2743	−0.6
	0.2776	0.2810	0.2843	0.2877	0.2912	0.2946	0.2981	0.3015	0.3050	0.3085	−0.5
	0.3121	0.3156	0.3192	0.3228	0.3264	0.3300	0.3336	0.3372	0.3409	0.3446	−0.4
	0.3483	0.3520	0.3557	0.3594	0.3632	0.3669	0.3707	0.3745	0.3783	0.3821	−0.3
	0.3859	0.3897	0.3936	0.3974	0.4013	0.4052	0.4090	0.4129	0.4168	0.4207	−0.2
	0.4247	0.4286	0.4325	0.4364	0.4404	0.4443	0.4483	0.4522	0.4562	0.4602	−0.1
	0.4641	0.4681	0.4721	0.4761	0.4801	0.4840	0.4880	0.4920	0.4960	0.5000	−0.0

† For $z \leq -3.90$, the areas are 0.0000 to four decimal places.

TABLE II (cont.) Areas under the standard normal curve

z	Second decimal place in z									
	0.00	0.01	0.02	0.03	0.04	0.05	0.06	0.07	0.08	0.09
0.0	0.5000	0.5040	0.5080	0.5120	0.5160	0.5199	0.5239	0.5279	0.5319	0.5359
0.1	0.5398	0.5438	0.5478	0.5517	0.5557	0.5596	0.5636	0.5675	0.5714	0.5753
0.2	0.5793	0.5832	0.5871	0.5910	0.5948	0.5987	0.6026	0.6064	0.6103	0.6141
0.3	0.6179	0.6217	0.6255	0.6293	0.6331	0.6368	0.6406	0.6443	0.6480	0.6517
0.4	0.6554	0.6591	0.6628	0.6664	0.6700	0.6736	0.6772	0.6808	0.6844	0.6879
0.5	0.6915	0.6950	0.6985	0.7019	0.7054	0.7088	0.7123	0.7157	0.7190	0.7224
0.6	0.7257	0.7291	0.7324	0.7357	0.7389	0.7422	0.7454	0.7486	0.7517	0.7549
0.7	0.7580	0.7611	0.7642	0.7673	0.7704	0.7734	0.7764	0.7794	0.7823	0.7852
0.8	0.7881	0.7910	0.7939	0.7967	0.7995	0.8023	0.8051	0.8078	0.8106	0.8133
0.9	0.8159	0.8186	0.8212	0.8238	0.8264	0.8289	0.8315	0.8340	0.8365	0.8389
1.0	0.8413	0.8438	0.8461	0.8485	0.8508	0.8531	0.8554	0.8577	0.8599	0.8621
1.1	0.8643	0.8665	0.8686	0.8708	0.8729	0.8749	0.8770	0.8790	0.8810	0.8830
1.2	0.8849	0.8869	0.8888	0.8907	0.8925	0.8944	0.8962	0.8980	0.8997	0.9015
1.3	0.9032	0.9049	0.9066	0.9082	0.9099	0.9115	0.9131	0.9147	0.9162	0.9177
1.4	0.9192	0.9207	0.9222	0.9236	0.9251	0.9265	0.9279	0.9292	0.9306	0.9319
1.5	0.9332	0.9345	0.9357	0.9370	0.9382	0.9394	0.9406	0.9418	0.9429	0.9441
1.6	0.9452	0.9463	0.9474	0.9484	0.9495	0.9505	0.9515	0.9525	0.9535	0.9545
1.7	0.9554	0.9564	0.9573	0.9582	0.9591	0.9599	0.9608	0.9616	0.9625	0.9633
1.8	0.9641	0.9649	0.9656	0.9664	0.9671	0.9678	0.9686	0.9693	0.9699	0.9706
1.9	0.9713	0.9719	0.9726	0.9732	0.9738	0.9744	0.9750	0.9756	0.9761	0.9767
2.0	0.9772	0.9778	0.9783	0.9788	0.9793	0.9798	0.9803	0.9808	0.9812	0.9817
2.1	0.9821	0.9826	0.9830	0.9834	0.9838	0.9842	0.9846	0.9850	0.9854	0.9857
2.2	0.9861	0.9864	0.9868	0.9871	0.9875	0.9878	0.9881	0.9884	0.9887	0.9890
2.3	0.9893	0.9896	0.9898	0.9901	0.9904	0.9906	0.9909	0.9911	0.9913	0.9916
2.4	0.9918	0.9920	0.9922	0.9925	0.9927	0.9929	0.9931	0.9932	0.9934	0.9936
2.5	0.9938	0.9940	0.9941	0.9943	0.9945	0.9946	0.9948	0.9949	0.9951	0.9952
2.6	0.9953	0.9955	0.9956	0.9957	0.9959	0.9960	0.9961	0.9962	0.9963	0.9964
2.7	0.9965	0.9966	0.9967	0.9968	0.9969	0.9970	0.9971	0.9972	0.9973	0.9974
2.8	0.9974	0.9975	0.9976	0.9977	0.9977	0.9978	0.9979	0.9979	0.9980	0.9981
2.9	0.9981	0.9982	0.9982	0.9983	0.9984	0.9984	0.9985	0.9985	0.9986	0.9986
3.0	0.9987	0.9987	0.9987	0.9988	0.9988	0.9989	0.9989	0.9989	0.9990	0.9990
3.1	0.9990	0.9991	0.9991	0.9991	0.9992	0.9992	0.9992	0.9992	0.9993	0.9993
3.2	0.9993	0.9993	0.9994	0.9994	0.9994	0.9994	0.9994	0.9995	0.9995	0.9995
3.3	0.9995	0.9995	0.9995	0.9996	0.9996	0.9996	0.9996	0.9996	0.9996	0.9997
3.4	0.9997	0.9997	0.9997	0.9997	0.9997	0.9997	0.9997	0.9997	0.9997	0.9998
3.5	0.9998	0.9998	0.9998	0.9998	0.9998	0.9998	0.9998	0.9998	0.9998	0.9998
3.6	0.9998	0.9998	0.9999	0.9999	0.9999	0.9999	0.9999	0.9999	0.9999	0.9999
3.7	0.9999	0.9999	0.9999	0.9999	0.9999	0.9999	0.9999	0.9999	0.9999	0.9999
3.8	0.9999	0.9999	0.9999	0.9999	0.9999	0.9999	0.9999	0.9999	0.9999	0.9999
3.9	1.0000†									

† For $z \geq 3.90$, the areas are 1.0000 to four decimal places.

FORMULA/TABLE CARD FOR WEISS'S *ELEMENTARY STATISTICS, FIFTH EDITION*

Larry R. Griffey

- Two-sample z-interval for $p_1 - p_2$:

$$(\hat{p}_1 - \hat{p}_2) \pm z_{\alpha/2} \cdot \sqrt{\hat{p}_1(1-\hat{p}_1)/n_1 + \hat{p}_2(1-\hat{p}_2)/n_2}$$

(*Assumptions:* independent samples; $x_1, n_1 - x_1, x_2, n_2 - x_2$ are all 5 or greater)

- Margin of error for the estimate of $p_1 - p_2$:

$$E = z_{\alpha/2} \cdot \sqrt{\hat{p}_1(1-\hat{p}_1)/n_1 + \hat{p}_2(1-\hat{p}_2)/n_2}$$

- Sample size for estimating $p_1 - p_2$:

$$n_1 = n_2 = 0.5\left(\frac{z_{\alpha/2}}{E}\right)^2$$

or

$$n_1 = n_2 = \left(\hat{p}_{1g}(1-\hat{p}_{1g}) + \hat{p}_{2g}(1-\hat{p}_{2g})\right)\left(\frac{z_{\alpha/2}}{E}\right)^2$$

rounded up to the nearest whole number (g = "educated guess")

CHAPTER 12   Chi-Square Procedures

- Expected frequencies for a chi-square goodness-of-fit test:

$$E = np$$

- Test statistic for a chi-square goodness-of-fit test:

$$\chi^2 = \Sigma(O - E)^2/E$$

with df = $k - 1$, where k is the number of possible values for the variable under consideration.

- Expected frequencies for a chi-square independence test:

$$E = \frac{R \cdot C}{n}$$

where R = row total and C = column total.

- Test statistic for a chi-square independence test:

$$\chi^2 = \Sigma(O - E)^2/E$$

with df = $(r - 1)(c - 1)$, where r and c are the number of possible values for the two variables under consideration.

CHAPTER 13   Analysis of Variance (ANOVA)

- Notation in one-way ANOVA:

  k = number of populations
  n = total number of observations
  $\bar{x}$ = mean of all n observations
  n_j = size of sample from Population j
  $\bar{x}_j$ = mean of sample from Population j
  s_j^2 = variance of sample from Population j
  T_j = sum of sample data from Population j

- Defining formulas for sums of squares in one-way ANOVA:

$$SST = \Sigma(x - \bar{x})^2$$
$$SSTR = \Sigma n_j(\bar{x}_j - \bar{x})^2$$
$$SSE = \Sigma(n_j - 1)s_j^2$$

- One-way ANOVA identity: $SST = SSTR + SSE$

- Computing formulas for sums of squares in one-way ANOVA:

$$SST = \Sigma x^2 - (\Sigma x)^2/n$$
$$SSTR = \Sigma(T_j^2/n_j) - (\Sigma x)^2/n$$
$$SSE = SST - SSTR$$

- Mean squares in one-way ANOVA:

$$MSTR = \frac{SSTR}{k - 1}, \qquad MSE = \frac{SSE}{n - k}$$

- Test statistic for one-way ANOVA (independent samples, normal populations, and equal population standard deviations):

$$F = \frac{MSTR}{MSE}$$

with df = $(k - 1, n - k)$.

CHAPTER 14   Inferential Methods in Regression and Correlation

- Population regression equation: $y = \beta_0 + \beta_1 x$

- Standard error of the estimate: $s_e = \sqrt{\dfrac{SSE}{n - 2}}$

- Test statistic for H_0: $\beta_1 = 0$:

$$t = \frac{b_1}{s_e/\sqrt{S_{xx}}}$$

with df = $n - 2$.

- Confidence interval for β_1:

$$b_1 \pm t_{\alpha/2} \cdot \frac{s_e}{\sqrt{S_{xx}}}$$

with df = $n - 2$.

- Confidence interval for the conditional mean of the response variable corresponding to x_p:

$$\hat{y}_p \pm t_{\alpha/2} \cdot s_e \sqrt{\frac{1}{n} + \frac{(x_p - \Sigma x/n)^2}{S_{xx}}}$$

with df = $n - 2$.

- Prediction interval for an observed value of the response variable corresponding to x_p:

$$\hat{y}_p \pm t_{\alpha/2} \cdot s_e \sqrt{1 + \frac{1}{n} + \frac{(x_p - \Sigma x/n)^2}{S_{xx}}}$$

with df = $n - 2$.

- Test statistic for H_0: $\rho = 0$:

$$t = \frac{r}{\sqrt{\dfrac{1 - r^2}{n - 2}}}$$

with df = $n - 2$.

FORMULA/TABLE CARD FOR WEISS'S *ELEMENTARY STATISTICS*, FIFTH EDITION
Larry R. Griffey

NOTATION The following notation is used on this card:

- n = sample size
- $\bar{x}$ = sample mean
- s = sample stdev
- Q_j = jth quartile
- N = population size
- μ = population mean
- σ = population stdev
- d = paired difference
- $\hat{p}$ = sample proportion
- p = population proportion
- O = observed frequency
- E = expected frequency

CHAPTER 3 Descriptive Measures

- Sample mean: $\bar{x} = \dfrac{\Sigma x}{n}$
- Range: Range = Max − Min
- Sample standard deviation:

$$s = \sqrt{\frac{\Sigma(x - \bar{x})^2}{n-1}} \quad \text{or} \quad s = \sqrt{\frac{\Sigma x^2 - (\Sigma x)^2/n}{n-1}}$$

- Interquartile range: $\text{IQR} = Q_3 - Q_1$
- Lower limit = $Q_1 - 1.5 \cdot \text{IQR}$, Upper limit = $Q_3 + 1.5 \cdot \text{IQR}$
- Population mean (mean of a variable): $\mu = \dfrac{\Sigma x}{N}$
- Population standard deviation (standard deviation of a variable):

$$\sigma = \sqrt{\frac{\Sigma(x - \mu)^2}{N}} \quad \text{or} \quad \sigma = \sqrt{\frac{\Sigma x^2}{N} - \mu^2}$$

- Standardized variable: $z = \dfrac{x - \mu}{\sigma}$

CHAPTER 4 Descriptive Methods in Regression and Correlation

- S_{xx}, S_{xy}, and S_{yy}:

$$S_{xx} = \Sigma(x - \bar{x})^2 = \Sigma x^2 - (\Sigma x)^2/n$$
$$S_{xy} = \Sigma(x - \bar{x})(y - \bar{y}) = \Sigma xy - (\Sigma x)(\Sigma y)/n$$
$$S_{yy} = \Sigma(y - \bar{y})^2 = \Sigma y^2 - (\Sigma y)^2/n$$

- Regression equation: $\hat{y} = b_0 + b_1 x$, where

$$b_1 = \frac{S_{xy}}{S_{xx}} \quad \text{and} \quad b_0 = \frac{1}{n}(\Sigma y - b_1 \Sigma x) = \bar{y} - b_1 \bar{x}$$

- Total sum of squares: $SST = \Sigma(y - \bar{y})^2 = S_{yy}$
- Regression sum of squares: $SSR = \Sigma(\hat{y} - \bar{y})^2 = S_{xy}^2/S_{xx}$
- Error sum of squares: $SSE = \Sigma(y - \hat{y})^2 = S_{yy} - S_{xy}^2/S_{xx}$
- Regression identity: $SST = SSR + SSE$
- Coefficient of determination: $r^2 = \dfrac{SSR}{SST}$
- Linear correlation coefficient:

$$r = \frac{\frac{1}{n-1}\Sigma(x - \bar{x})(y - \bar{y})}{s_x s_y} \quad \text{or} \quad r = \frac{S_{xy}}{\sqrt{S_{xx} S_{yy}}}$$

CHAPTER 5 Probability and Random Variables

- Probability for equally likely outcomes:

$$P(E) = \frac{f}{N},$$

where f denotes the number of ways event E can occur and N denotes the total number of outcomes possible.

- Special addition rule:

$$P(A \text{ or } B \text{ or } C \text{ or } \cdots) = P(A) + P(B) + P(C) + \cdots$$

(A, B, C, ... mutually exclusive)

- Complementation rule: $P(E) = 1 - P(\text{not } E)$
- General addition rule: $P(A \text{ or } B) = P(A) + P(B) - P(A \& B)$
- Mean of a discrete random variable X: $\mu = \Sigma x P(X = x)$
- Standard deviation of a discrete random variable X:

$$\sigma = \sqrt{\Sigma(x - \mu)^2 P(X = x)} \quad \text{or} \quad \sigma = \sqrt{\Sigma x^2 P(X = x) - \mu^2}$$

- Factorial: $k! = k(k-1) \cdots 2 \cdot 1$
- Binomial coefficient: $\dbinom{n}{x} = \dfrac{n!}{x!(n-x)!}$
- Binomial probability formula:

$$P(X = x) = \binom{n}{x} p^x (1-p)^{n-x},$$

where n denotes the number of trials and p denotes the success probability.

- Mean of a binomial random variable: $\mu = np$
- Standard deviation of a binomial random variable: $\sigma = \sqrt{np(1-p)}$

CHAPTER 7 The Sampling Distribution of the Sample Mean

- Mean of the variable $\bar{x}$: $\mu_{\bar{x}} = \mu$
- Standard deviation of the variable $\bar{x}$: $\sigma_{\bar{x}} = \sigma/\sqrt{n}$

CHAPTER 8 Confidence Intervals for One Population Mean

- Standardized version of the variable $\bar{x}$:

$$z = \frac{\bar{x} - \mu}{\sigma/\sqrt{n}}$$

- z-interval for μ (σ known, normal population or large sample):

$$\bar{x} \pm z_{\alpha/2} \cdot \frac{\sigma}{\sqrt{n}}$$

- Margin of error for the estimate of μ: $E = z_{\alpha/2} \cdot \dfrac{\sigma}{\sqrt{n}}$
- Sample size for estimating μ:

$$n = \left(\frac{z_{\alpha/2} \cdot \sigma}{E}\right)^2,$$

rounded up to the nearest whole number.

FORMULA/TABLE CARD FOR WEISS'S *ELEMENTARY STATISTICS*, FIFTH EDITION
Larry R. Griffey

TABLE VI Values of F_α

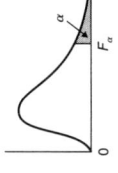

dfd	α	\	\	\	\	dfn	\	\	\	\
		1	2	3	4	5	6	7	8	9
1	0.10	39.86	49.50	53.59	55.83	57.24	58.20	58.91	59.44	59.86
	0.05	161.45	199.50	215.71	224.58	230.16	233.99	236.77	238.88	240.54
	0.025	647.79	799.50	864.16	899.58	921.85	937.11	948.22	956.66	963.28
	0.01	4052.2	4999.5	5403.4	5624.6	5763.6	5859.0	5928.4	5981.1	6022.5
	0.005	16211	20000	21615	22500	23056	23437	23715	23925	24091
2	0.10	8.53	9.00	9.16	9.24	9.29	9.33	9.35	9.37	9.38
	0.05	18.51	19.00	19.16	19.25	19.30	19.33	19.35	19.37	19.38
	0.025	38.51	39.00	39.17	39.25	39.30	39.33	39.36	39.37	39.39
	0.01	98.50	99.00	99.17	99.25	99.30	99.33	99.36	99.37	99.39
	0.005	198.50	199.00	199.17	199.25	199.30	199.33	199.36	199.37	199.39
3	0.10	5.54	5.46	5.39	5.34	5.31	5.28	5.27	5.25	5.24
	0.05	10.13	9.55	9.28	9.12	9.01	8.94	8.89	8.85	8.81
	0.025	17.44	16.04	15.44	15.10	14.88	14.73	14.62	14.54	14.47
	0.01	34.12	30.82	29.46	28.71	28.24	27.91	27.67	27.49	27.35
	0.005	55.55	49.80	47.47	46.19	45.39	44.84	44.43	44.13	43.88
4	0.10	4.54	4.32	4.19	4.11	4.05	4.01	3.98	3.95	3.94
	0.05	7.71	6.94	6.59	6.39	6.26	6.16	6.09	6.04	6.00
	0.025	12.22	10.65	9.98	9.60	9.36	9.20	9.07	8.98	8.90
	0.01	21.20	18.00	16.69	15.98	15.52	15.21	14.98	14.80	14.66
	0.005	31.33	26.28	24.26	23.15	22.46	21.97	21.62	21.35	21.14
5	0.10	4.06	3.78	3.62	3.52	3.45	3.40	3.37	3.34	3.32
	0.05	6.61	5.79	5.41	5.19	5.05	4.95	4.88	4.82	4.77
	0.025	10.01	8.43	7.76	7.39	7.15	6.98	6.85	6.76	6.68
	0.01	16.26	13.27	12.06	11.39	10.97	10.67	10.46	10.29	10.16
	0.005	22.78	18.31	16.53	15.56	14.94	14.51	14.20	13.96	13.77
6	0.10	3.78	3.46	3.29	3.18	3.11	3.05	3.01	2.98	2.96
	0.05	5.99	5.14	4.76	4.53	4.39	4.28	4.21	4.15	4.10
	0.025	8.81	7.26	6.60	6.23	5.99	5.82	5.70	5.60	5.52
	0.01	13.75	10.92	9.78	9.15	8.75	8.47	8.26	8.10	7.98
	0.005	18.63	14.54	12.92	12.03	11.46	11.07	10.79	10.57	10.39
7	0.10	3.59	3.26	3.07	2.96	2.88	2.83	2.78	2.75	2.72
	0.05	5.59	4.74	4.35	4.12	3.97	3.87	3.79	3.73	3.68
	0.025	8.07	6.54	5.89	5.52	5.29	5.12	4.99	4.90	4.82
	0.01	12.25	9.55	8.45	7.85	7.46	7.19	6.99	6.84	6.72
	0.005	16.24	12.40	10.88	10.05	9.52	9.16	8.89	8.68	8.51
8	0.10	3.46	3.11	2.92	2.81	2.73	2.67	2.62	2.59	2.56
	0.05	5.32	4.46	4.07	3.84	3.69	3.58	3.50	3.44	3.39
	0.025	7.57	6.06	5.42	5.05	4.82	4.65	4.53	4.43	4.36
	0.01	11.26	8.65	7.59	7.01	6.63	6.37	6.18	6.03	5.91
	0.005	14.69	11.04	9.60	8.81	8.30	7.95	7.69	7.50	7.34

TABLE VI (cont.) Values of F_α

dfd	α	\	\	\	\	dfn	\	\	\	\
		1	2	3	4	5	6	7	8	9
9	0.10	3.36	3.01	2.81	2.69	2.61	2.55	2.51	2.47	2.44
	0.05	5.12	4.26	3.86	3.63	3.48	3.37	3.29	3.23	3.18
	0.025	7.21	5.71	5.08	4.72	4.48	4.32	4.20	4.10	4.03
	0.01	10.56	8.02	6.99	6.42	6.06	5.80	5.61	5.47	5.35
	0.005	13.61	10.11	8.72	7.96	7.47	7.13	6.88	6.69	6.54
10	0.10	3.29	2.92	2.73	2.61	2.52	2.46	2.41	2.38	2.35
	0.05	4.96	4.10	3.71	3.48	3.33	3.22	3.14	3.07	3.02
	0.025	6.94	5.46	4.83	4.47	4.24	4.07	3.95	3.85	3.78
	0.01	10.04	7.56	6.55	5.99	5.64	5.39	5.20	5.06	4.94
	0.005	12.83	9.43	8.08	7.34	6.87	6.54	6.30	6.12	5.97
11	0.10	3.23	2.86	2.66	2.54	2.45	2.39	2.34	2.30	2.27
	0.05	4.84	3.98	3.59	3.36	3.20	3.09	3.01	2.95	2.90
	0.025	6.72	5.26	4.63	4.28	4.04	3.88	3.76	3.66	3.59
	0.01	9.65	7.21	6.22	5.67	5.32	5.07	4.89	4.74	4.63
	0.005	12.23	8.91	7.60	6.88	6.42	6.10	5.86	5.68	5.54
12	0.10	3.18	2.81	2.61	2.48	2.39	2.33	2.28	2.24	2.21
	0.05	4.75	3.89	3.49	3.26	3.11	3.00	2.91	2.85	2.80
	0.025	6.55	5.10	4.47	4.12	3.89	3.73	3.61	3.51	3.44
	0.01	9.33	6.93	5.95	5.41	5.06	4.82	4.64	4.50	4.39
	0.005	11.75	8.51	7.23	6.52	6.07	5.76	5.52	5.35	5.20
13	0.10	3.14	2.76	2.56	2.43	2.35	2.28	2.23	2.20	2.16
	0.05	4.67	3.81	3.41	3.18	3.03	2.92	2.83	2.77	2.71
	0.025	6.41	4.97	4.35	4.00	3.77	3.60	3.48	3.39	3.31
	0.01	9.07	6.70	5.74	5.21	4.86	4.62	4.44	4.30	4.19
	0.005	11.37	8.19	6.93	6.23	5.79	5.48	5.25	5.08	4.94
14	0.10	3.10	2.73	2.52	2.39	2.31	2.24	2.19	2.15	2.12
	0.05	4.60	3.74	3.34	3.11	2.96	2.85	2.76	2.70	2.65
	0.025	6.30	4.86	4.24	3.89	3.66	3.50	3.38	3.29	3.21
	0.01	8.86	6.51	5.56	5.04	4.69	4.46	4.28	4.14	4.03
	0.005	11.06	7.92	6.68	6.00	5.56	5.26	5.03	4.86	4.72
15	0.10	3.07	2.70	2.49	2.36	2.27	2.21	2.16	2.12	2.09
	0.05	4.54	3.68	3.29	3.06	2.90	2.79	2.71	2.64	2.59
	0.025	6.20	4.77	4.15	3.80	3.58	3.41	3.29	3.20	3.12
	0.01	8.68	6.36	5.42	4.89	4.56	4.32	4.14	4.00	3.89
	0.005	10.80	7.70	6.48	5.80	5.37	5.07	4.85	4.67	4.54
16	0.10	3.05	2.67	2.46	2.33	2.24	2.18	2.13	2.09	2.06
	0.05	4.49	3.63	3.24	3.01	2.85	2.74	2.66	2.59	2.54
	0.025	6.12	4.69	4.08	3.73	3.50	3.34	3.22	3.12	3.05
	0.01	8.53	6.23	5.29	4.77	4.44	4.20	4.03	3.89	3.78
	0.005	10.58	7.51	6.30	5.64	5.21	4.91	4.69	4.52	4.38

FORMULA/TABLE CARD FOR WEISS'S *ELEMENTARY STATISTICS*, FIFTH EDITION

Larry R. Griffey

- Studentized version of the variable $\bar{x}$:

$$t = \frac{\bar{x} - \mu}{s/\sqrt{n}}$$

- t-interval for μ (σ unknown, normal population or large sample):

$$\bar{x} \pm t_{\alpha/2} \cdot \frac{s}{\sqrt{n}}$$

with df $= n - 1$.

CHAPTER 9 Hypothesis Tests for One Population Mean

- z-test statistic for H_0: $\mu = \mu_0$ (σ known, normal population or large sample):

$$z = \frac{\bar{x} - \mu_0}{\sigma/\sqrt{n}}$$

- t-test statistic for H_0: $\mu = \mu_0$ (σ unknown, normal population or large sample):

$$t = \frac{\bar{x} - \mu_0}{s/\sqrt{n}}$$

with df $= n - 1$.

CHAPTER 10 Inferences for Two Population Means

- Pooled sample standard deviation:

$$s_p = \sqrt{\frac{(n_1 - 1)s_1^2 + (n_2 - 1)s_2^2}{n_1 + n_2 - 2}}$$

- Pooled t-test statistic for H_0: $\mu_1 = \mu_2$ (independent samples, normal populations or large samples, and equal population standard deviations):

$$t = \frac{\bar{x}_1 - \bar{x}_2}{s_p\sqrt{(1/n_1) + (1/n_2)}}$$

with df $= n_1 + n_2 - 2$.

- Pooled t-interval for $\mu_1 - \mu_2$ (independent samples, normal populations or large samples, and equal population standard deviations):

$$(\bar{x}_1 - \bar{x}_2) \pm t_{\alpha/2} \cdot s_p\sqrt{(1/n_1) + (1/n_2)}$$

with df $= n_1 + n_2 - 2$.

- Degrees of freedom for nonpooled-t procedures:

$$\Delta = \frac{\left[(s_1^2/n_1) + (s_2^2/n_2)\right]^2}{\frac{(s_1^2/n_1)^2}{n_1 - 1} + \frac{(s_2^2/n_2)^2}{n_2 - 1}},$$

rounded down to the nearest integer.

- Nonpooled t-test statistic for H_0: $\mu_1 = \mu_2$ (independent samples, and normal populations or large samples):

$$t = \frac{\bar{x}_1 - \bar{x}_2}{\sqrt{(s_1^2/n_1) + (s_2^2/n_2)}}$$

with df $= \Delta$.

- Nonpooled t-interval for $\mu_1 - \mu_2$ (independent samples, and normal populations or large samples):

$$(\bar{x}_1 - \bar{x}_2) \pm t_{\alpha/2} \cdot \sqrt{(s_1^2/n_1) + (s_2^2/n_2)}$$

with df $= \Delta$.

- Paired t-test statistic for H_0: $\mu_1 = \mu_2$ (paired sample, and normal differences or large sample):

$$t = \frac{\bar{d}}{s_d/\sqrt{n}}$$

with df $= n - 1$.

- Paired t-interval for $\mu_1 - \mu_2$ (paired sample, and normal differences or large sample):

$$\bar{d} \pm t_{\alpha/2} \cdot \frac{s_d}{\sqrt{n}}$$

with df $= n - 1$.

CHAPTER 11 Inferences for Population Proportions

- Sample proportion:

$$\hat{p} = \frac{x}{n},$$

where x denotes the number of members in the sample that have the specified attribute.

- One-sample z-interval for p:

$$\hat{p} \pm z_{\alpha/2} \cdot \sqrt{\hat{p}(1 - \hat{p})/n}$$

(*Assumption:* both x and $n - x$ are 5 or greater)

- Margin of error for the estimate of p:

$$E = z_{\alpha/2} \cdot \sqrt{\hat{p}(1 - \hat{p})/n}$$

- Sample size for estimating p:

$$n = 0.25\left(\frac{z_{\alpha/2}}{E}\right)^2 \quad \text{or} \quad n = \hat{p}_g(1 - \hat{p}_g)\left(\frac{z_{\alpha/2}}{E}\right)^2$$

rounded up to the nearest whole number (g = "educated guess")

- One-sample z-test statistic for H_0: $p = p_0$:

$$z = \frac{\hat{p} - p_0}{\sqrt{p_0(1 - p_0)/n}}$$

(*Assumption:* both np_0 and $n(1 - p_0)$ are 5 or greater)

- Pooled sample proportion: $\hat{p}_p = \dfrac{x_1 + x_2}{n_1 + n_2}$

- Two-sample z-test statistic for H_0: $p_1 = p_2$:

$$z = \frac{\hat{p}_1 - \hat{p}_2}{\sqrt{\hat{p}_p(1 - \hat{p}_p)}\sqrt{(1/n_1) + (1/n_2)}}$$

(*Assumptions:* independent samples; $x_1, n_1 - x_1, x_2, n_2 - x_2$ are all 5 or greater)

FORMULA/TABLE CARD FOR WEISS'S *ELEMENTARY STATISTICS, FIFTH EDITION*
Larry R. Griffey

TABLE I Random numbers

Line number	Column number 00–09		10–19		20–29		30–39		40–49	
00	15544	80712	97742	21500	97081	42451	50623	56071	28882	28739
01	01011	21285	04729	39986	73150	31548	30168	76189	56996	19210
02	47435	53308	40718	29050	74858	64517	93573	51058	68501	42723
03	91312	75137	86274	59834	69844	19853	06917	17413	44474	86530
04	12775	08768	80791	16298	22934	09630	98862	39746	64623	32768
05	31466	43761	94872	92230	52367	13205	38634	55882	77518	36252
06	09300	43847	40881	51243	97810	18903	53914	31688	06220	40422
07	73582	13810	57784	72454	68997	72229	30340	08844	53924	89630
08	11092	81392	58189	22697	41063	09451	09789	00637	06450	85990
09	93322	98567	00116	35605	66790	52965	62877	21740	56476	49296
10	80134	12484	67089	08674	70753	90959	45842	59844	45214	36505
11	97888	31797	95037	84400	76041	96668	75920	68482	56855	97417
12	92612	27082	59459	69380	98654	20407	88151	56263	27126	63797
13	72744	45586	43279	44218	83638	05422	00995	70217	78925	39097
14	96256	70653	45285	26293	78305	80252	03625	40159	68760	84716
15	07851	47452	66742	83331	54701	06573	98169	37499	67756	68301
16	25594	41552	96475	56151	02089	33748	65289	89956	89559	33687
17	65358	15155	59374	80940	03411	94656	69440	47156	77115	99463
18	09402	31008	53424	21928	02198	61201	02457	87214	59750	51330
19	97424	90765	01634	37328	41243	33564	17884	94747	93650	77668

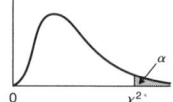

TABLE V Values of χ^2_α

$\chi^2_{0.10}$	$\chi^2_{0.05}$	$\chi^2_{0.025}$	$\chi^2_{0.01}$	$\chi^2_{0.005}$	df
2.706	3.841	5.024	6.635	7.879	1
4.605	5.991	7.378	9.210	10.597	2
6.251	7.815	9.348	11.345	12.838	3
7.779	9.488	11.143	13.277	14.860	4
9.236	11.070	12.833	15.086	16.750	5
10.645	12.592	14.449	16.812	18.548	6
12.017	14.067	16.013	18.475	20.278	7
13.362	15.507	17.535	20.090	21.955	8
14.684	16.919	19.023	21.666	23.589	9
15.987	18.307	20.483	23.209	25.188	10
17.275	19.675	21.920	24.725	26.757	11
18.549	21.026	23.337	26.217	28.300	12
19.812	22.362	24.736	27.688	29.819	13
21.064	23.685	26.119	29.141	31.319	14
22.307	24.996	27.488	30.578	32.801	15
23.542	26.296	28.845	32.000	34.267	16
24.769	27.587	30.191	33.409	35.718	17
25.989	28.869	31.526	34.805	37.156	18
27.204	30.143	32.852	36.191	38.582	19
28.412	31.410	34.170	37.566	39.997	20
29.615	32.671	35.479	38.932	41.401	21
30.813	33.924	36.781	40.290	42.796	22
32.007	35.172	38.076	41.638	44.181	23
33.196	36.415	39.364	42.980	45.559	24
34.382	37.653	40.647	44.314	46.928	25
35.563	38.885	41.923	45.642	48.290	26
36.741	40.113	43.195	46.963	49.645	27
37.916	41.337	44.461	48.278	50.994	28
39.087	42.557	45.722	49.588	52.336	29
40.256	43.773	46.979	50.892	53.672	30
51.805	55.759	59.342	63.691	66.767	40
63.167	67.505	71.420	76.154	79.490	50
74.397	79.082	83.298	88.381	91.955	60
85.527	90.531	95.023	100.424	104.213	70
96.578	101.879	106.628	112.328	116.320	80
107.565	113.145	118.135	124.115	128.296	90
118.499	124.343	129.563	135.811	140.177	100

TABLE III Normal scores

Ordered position	n = 5	6	7	8	9	10	11	12	13
1	−1.18	−1.28	−1.36	−1.43	−1.50	−1.55	−1.59	−1.64	−1.68
2	−0.50	−0.64	−0.76	−0.85	−0.93	−1.00	−1.06	−1.11	−1.16
3	0.00	−0.20	−0.35	−0.47	−0.57	−0.65	−0.73	−0.79	−0.85
4	0.50	0.20	0.00	−0.15	−0.27	−0.37	−0.46	−0.53	−0.60
5	1.18	0.64	0.35	0.15	0.00	−0.12	−0.22	−0.31	−0.39
6		1.28	0.76	0.47	0.27	0.12	0.00	−0.10	−0.19
7			1.36	0.85	0.57	0.37	0.22	0.10	0.00
8				1.43	0.93	0.65	0.46	0.31	0.19
9					1.50	1.00	0.73	0.53	0.39
10						1.55	1.06	0.79	0.60
11							1.59	1.11	0.85
12								1.64	1.16
13									1.68

TABLE IV Values of t_α

df	$t_{0.10}$	$t_{0.05}$	$t_{0.025}$	$t_{0.01}$	$t_{0.005}$
1	3.078	6.314	12.706	31.821	63.657
2	1.886	2.920	4.303	6.965	9.925
3	1.638	2.353	3.182	4.541	5.841
4	1.533	2.132	2.776	3.747	4.604
5	1.476	2.015	2.571	3.365	4.032
6	1.440	1.943	2.447	3.143	3.707
7	1.415	1.895	2.365	2.998	3.499
8	1.397	1.860	2.306	2.896	3.355
9	1.383	1.833	2.262	2.821	3.250
10	1.372	1.812	2.228	2.764	3.169
11	1.363	1.796	2.201	2.718	3.106
12	1.356	1.782	2.179	2.681	3.055
13	1.350	1.771	2.160	2.650	3.012
14	1.345	1.761	2.145	2.624	2.977
15	1.341	1.753	2.131	2.602	2.947
16	1.337	1.746	2.120	2.583	2.921
17	1.333	1.740	2.110	2.567	2.898
18	1.330	1.734	2.101	2.552	2.878
19	1.328	1.729	2.093	2.539	2.861
20	1.325	1.725	2.086	2.528	2.845
21	1.323	1.721	2.080	2.518	2.831
22	1.321	1.717	2.074	2.508	2.819
23	1.319	1.714	2.069	2.500	2.807
24	1.318	1.711	2.064	2.492	2.797
25	1.316	1.708	2.060	2.485	2.787
26	1.315	1.706	2.056	2.479	2.779
27	1.314	1.703	2.052	2.473	2.771
28	1.313	1.701	2.048	2.467	2.763
29	1.311	1.699	2.045	2.462	2.756
30	1.310	1.697	2.042	2.457	2.750
31	1.309	1.696	2.040	2.453	2.744
32	1.309	1.694	2.037	2.449	2.738
33	1.308	1.692	2.035	2.445	2.733
34	1.307	1.691	2.032	2.441	2.728
35	1.306	1.690	2.030	2.438	2.724
36	1.306	1.688	2.028	2.434	2.719
37	1.305	1.687	2.026	2.431	2.715
38	1.304	1.686	2.024	2.429	2.712
39	1.304	1.685	2.023	2.426	2.708
40	1.303	1.684	2.021	2.423	2.704
41	1.303	1.683	2.020	2.421	2.701
42	1.302	1.682	2.018	2.418	2.698
43	1.302	1.681	2.017	2.416	2.695
44	1.301	1.680	2.015	2.414	2.692
45	1.301	1.679	2.014	2.412	2.690
46	1.300	1.679	2.013	2.410	2.687
47	1.300	1.678	2.012	2.408	2.685
48	1.299	1.677	2.011	2.407	2.682
49	1.299	1.677	2.010	2.405	2.680

$z_{0.10}$	$z_{0.05}$	$z_{0.025}$	$z_{0.01}$	$z_{0.005}$
1.282	1.645	1.960	2.326	2.576

In stratified sampling, the strata are often sampled in proportion to their size, which is called **proportional allocation.** For instance, suppose that the strata consisting of the three income groups (upper, middle, and low) in Example 1.9 comprise, respectively, 10%, 70%, and 20% of the town. Then, for a sample size of, say, 50, the number of upper-income, middle-income, and low-income individuals sampled would be, respectively, 5 (10% of 50), 35 (70% of 50), and 10 (20% of 50).

The simplest type of stratified sampling, called **stratified random sampling with proportional allocation,** is implemented by using the following procedure.

Procedure 1.3 — Stratified Random Sampling with Proportional Allocation

Step 1 Divide the population into subpopulations (strata).

Step 2 From each stratum, obtain a simple random sample of size proportional to the size of the stratum; that is, the sample size for a stratum equals the total sample size times the stratum size divided by the population size.

Step 3 Use all the members obtained in Step 2 as the sample.

MULTISTAGE SAMPLING

Most large-scale surveys combine one or more of simple random sampling, systematic random sampling, cluster sampling, and stratified sampling in ways that can be quite complex. Such **multistage sampling** is used frequently by pollsters and government agencies.

For instance, the U.S. National Center for Health Statistics conducts surveys of the civilian noninstitutional U.S. population to obtain information on illnesses, injuries, and other health issues. Data collection is by a multistage probability sample of approximately 42,000 households. Information obtained from the surveys is published in the *National Health Interview Survey*.

Exercises 1.4

Statistical Concepts and Skills

1.33 The International 500. In Exercise 1.27 on page 16, you used simple random sampling to obtain a sample of 10 firms from *Fortune Magazine*'s list of "The International 500."
a. Use systematic random sampling to accomplish that same task.
b. Which method is easier: simple random sampling or systematic random sampling?
c. Does it seem reasonable to use systematic random sampling to obtain a representative sample? Explain your answer.

1.34 Keno. In the game of keno, 20 balls are selected at random from 80 balls, numbered 1–80. In Exercise 1.28 on page 16, you used simple random sampling to simulate one game of keno.
a. Use systematic random sampling to obtain a sample of 20 of the 80 balls.

b. Which method is easier: simple random sampling or systematic random sampling?

c. Does it seem reasonable to use systematic random sampling to simulate one game of Keno? Explain your answer.

1.35 Sampling Dorm Residents. Students in the dormitories of a university in the state of New York live in clusters of four double rooms, called *suites*. There are 48 suites, with eight students per suite.

a. Describe a cluster sampling procedure for obtaining a sample of 24 dormitory residents.

b. Students typically choose friends from their classes as suitemates. With that in mind, do you think cluster sampling is a good procedure for obtaining a representative sample of dormitory residents? Explain your answer.

c. The university housing office has separate lists of dormitory residents by class level. The number of dormitory residents in each class level is as follows.

Class level	Number of dorm residents
Freshman	128
Sophomore	112
Junior	96
Senior	48

Use the table to design a procedure for obtaining a stratified sample of 24 dormitory residents. Use stratified random sampling with proportional allocation.

1.5 EXPERIMENTAL DESIGNS

Extending the Concepts and Skills

1.36 In simple random sampling, all samples of a given size are equally likely. Is that true in systematic random sampling? Explain your answer.

1.37 White House Ethics. On June 27, 1996, an article appeared in *The Wall Street Journal* presenting the results of a nationwide poll regarding the White House procurement of FBI files on prominent Republicans and related ethical controversies. The article was headlined "White House Assertions on FBI Files Are Widely Rejected, Survey Shows." At the end of the article, the following explanation of the sampling procedure was given. Discuss the different aspects of sampling that appear in this explanation.

> The Wall Street Journal/NBC News poll was based on nationwide telephone interviews of 2,010 adults, including 1,637 registered voters, conducted Thursday to Tuesday by the polling organizations of Peter Hart and Robert Teeter. Questions related to politics were asked only of registered voters; questions related to economics and health were asked of all adults.
>
> The sample was drawn from 520 randomly selected geographic points in the continental U.S. Each region was represented in proportion to its population. Households were selected by a method that gave all telephone numbers, listed and unlisted, an equal chance of being included.
>
> One adult, 18 years or older, was selected from each household by a procedure to provide the correct number of male and female respondents.
>
> Chances are 19 of 20 that if all adults with telephones in the U.S. had been surveyed, the finding would differ from these poll results by no more than 2.2 percentage points in either direction among all adults and 2.5 among registered voters. Sample tolerances for subgroups are larger.

As we mentioned earlier, two methods for obtaining information other than a census are sampling and experimentation. In Sections 1.3 and 1.4, we discussed some of the basic principles and techniques of sampling. Now, we do the same for experimentation. To begin, we introduce some important terminology that further helps us differentiate among types of studies.

OBSERVATIONAL STUDIES AND DESIGNED EXPERIMENTS

Often the purpose of a statistical study is to investigate whether a relationship exists between two characteristics, such as smoking and lung cancer, height and weight, or educational attainment and annual income. For these kinds of studies, it is essential to distinguish between two types of procedures: observational studies and designed experiments.

In an **observational study,** researchers simply observe characteristics and take measurements, as in a sample survey. In a **designed experiment,** researchers impose treatments and controls and then observe characteristics and take measurements. Observational studies can reveal only *association*, whereas designed experiments can help establish *causation*. Examples 1.10 and 1.11 illustrate some major differences between observational studies and designed experiments.

Example 1.10 *An Observational Study*

Vasectomies and Prostate Cancer Approximately 450,000 vasectomies are performed each year in the United States. In this surgical procedure for contraception, the tube carrying sperm from the testicles is cut and tied.

Several studies have been conducted to analyze the relationship between vasectomies and prostate cancer. The results of one such study by E. Giovannucci et al. appeared in the paper "A Retrospective Cohort Study of Vasectomy and Prostate Cancer in U.S. Men" (*The Journal of the American Medical Association*, 1993, Vol. 269(7), pp. 878–882).

Dr. Edward Giovannucci, leader of the study and epidemiologist at Harvard-affiliated Brigham and Women's Hospital, said that "...we found 113 cases of prostate cancer among 22,000 men who had a vasectomy. This compares to a rate of 70 cases per 22,000 among men who didn't have a vasectomy."

The study shows about a 60% elevated risk of prostate cancer for men who have had a vasectomy, thereby revealing an association between vasectomy and prostate cancer. But does it establish causation: that having a vasectomy causes an increased risk of prostate cancer?

The answer is no, because the study is observational. The researchers simply observed two groups of men, one with vasectomies and the other without. Thus, although an association was established between vasectomy and prostate cancer, the association might be due to other factors (e.g., temperament) that make some men more likely to have vasectomies and also put them at greater risk of prostate cancer.

In the words of Dr. Stuart Howards, a urology professor at the University of Virginia Medical School who did not participate in the study, "...[these results] have to be considered seriously but do not prove that vasectomy causes prostate cancer." ◆

Example 1.11 *A Designed Experiment*

Folic Acid and Birth Defects For several years, evidence had been mounting that folic acid reduces major birth defects. An issue of *The Arizona Republic* reported on a Hungarian study that provided the strongest evidence to date. The results of the study, directed by Drs. Andrew E. Czeizel and Istvan Dudas of the National Institute of Hygiene in Budapest, were published in the paper "Prevention of the First Occurrence of Neural-Tube Defects by Periconceptional Vitamin Supplementation" (*The New England Journal of Medicine*, 1992, Vol. 327(26), p. 1832).

For the study, the doctors enrolled 4753 women prior to conception. The women were divided randomly into two groups. One group took daily multivitamins containing 0.8 mg of folic acid, whereas the other group received only trace elements. A drastic reduction in the rate of major birth defects occurred among the women who took folic acid: 13 per 1000 as compared to 23 per 1000 for those women who did not take folic acid.

In contrast to the observational study considered in Example 1.10, this is a designed experiment and does help establish causation. The researchers did not simply observe two groups of women but, instead, randomly assigned one group to take daily doses of folic acid and the other group to take only trace elements. ◆

The study presented in Example 1.11 illustrates three basic principles of experimental design: control, randomization, and replication.

- *Control:* The doctors compared the rate of major birth defects for the women who took folic acid to that for the women who took only trace elements. This comparison controlled for such things as the *placebo effect* where subjects respond to the idea of a specific treatment rather than to the treatment itself.
- *Randomization:* The women were divided randomly into two groups to avoid unintentional selection bias in constituting the groups and thereby help eliminate the problem of potential confounding factors such as lifestyle and emotional state.
- *Replication:* A large number of women were recruited for the study to make it likely that the two groups created by randomization would be similar and also to increase the chances of detecting an effect due to the folic acid if such an effect exists.

In the folic acid study, both dosages of folic acid (0.8 mg and essentially none) are called *treatments* in the context of experimental design. Generally, each experimental condition is called a **treatment,** of which there may be several. Key Fact 1.1 summarizes our discussion about the principles of experimental design.

Key Fact 1.1 Principles of Experimental Design

The following principles of experimental design enable a researcher to conclude that differences in the results of an experiment not reasonably attributable to chance are likely caused by the treatments.

- **Control:** Some method should be used to control for effects due to factors other than the ones of primary interest.
- **Randomization:** Subjects should be randomly divided into groups to avoid unintentional selection bias in constituting the groups, that is, to make the groups as similar as possible.
- **Replication:** A sufficient number of subjects should be used to ensure that randomization creates groups that resemble each other closely and to increase the chances of detecting differences among the treatments when such differences actually exist.

An important method of control is to compare several treatments. In fact, one of the most common experimental situations involves a specified treatment and *placebo*, an inert or innocuous medical substance. Technically, both the specified treatment and placebo are treatments. The group receiving the specified treatment is called the **treatment group**, and the group receiving placebo is called the **control group**. In the folic acid study, the women who took folic acid constituted the treatment group and those who took only trace elements constituted the control group.

TERMINOLOGY OF EXPERIMENTAL DESIGN

We now introduce some additional terminology used in experimental design. Each woman in the folic acid study is, in the language of experimental design, an **experimental unit,** or a **subject.** More generally, we have the following definition.

DEFINITION 1.5 **Experimental Units; Subjects**

In a designed experiment, the individuals or items on which the experiment is performed are called *experimental units.* When the experimental units are human beings, the term *subject* is often used in place of experimental unit.

In the folic acid study, the researchers were interested in the effect of folic acid on major birth defects. Birth-defect classification (major or not) is the **response variable** for this study. The daily dosage of folic acid is called the **factor**. In this case, the factor has two **levels,** namely, 0.8 mg and essentially none.

When there is only one factor, as in the folic acid study, the treatments are the same as the levels of the factor. But, if there is more than one factor, each treatment is a combination of levels of the various factors. Example 1.12 presents an experiment in which there are two factors.

Example 1.12 *Experimental Design*

Weight Gain of Golden Torch Cacti   The Golden Torch Cactus (botanical name, *Trichocereus spachianus*), a columnar cactus native to Argentina, has excellent landscape potential. William Feldman and Frank Crosswhite, two researchers at the Boyce Thompson Southwestern Arboretum, conducted a thorough investigation of the optimal method for producing these cacti.

The researchers examined, among other things, the effects of a hydrophilic polymer and irrigation regime on weight gain. Hydrophilic polymers are used as soil additives to keep moisture in the root zone. For this study, the researchers chose Broadleaf P-4 polyacrylamide, abbreviated P4. The hydrophilic polymer was either used or not used, and five irrigation regimes were employed: none, light, medium, heavy, and very heavy. Identify the

a. experimental units.
b. response variable.

c. factors.
d. levels of each factor.
e. treatments.

Solution a. The experimental units are the cacti used in the study.
b. The response variable is weight gain.
c. The factors are hydrophilic polymer and irrigation regime.
d. Hydrophilic polymer has two levels: with and without. Irrigation regime has five levels: none, light, medium, heavy, and very heavy.
e. Each treatment is a combination of a level of hydrophilic polymer and a level of irrigation regime. Table 1.8 depicts the treatments. In the table, we abbreviated "very heavy" as "Xheavy."

TABLE 1.8
Schematic for the 10 treatments in the cactus study

		\multicolumn{5}{c}{Irrigation regime}			
		None	Light	Medium	Heavy	Xheavy
Polymer	No P4	No water No P4 (Treatment 1)	Light water No P4 (Treatment 2)	Medium water No P4 (Treatment 3)	Heavy water No P4 (Treatment 4)	Xheavy water No P4 (Treatment 5)
	With P4	No water With P4 (Treatment 6)	Light water With P4 (Treatment 7)	Medium water With P4 (Treatment 8)	Heavy water With P4 (Treatment 9)	Xheavy water With P4 (Treatment 10)

Note that there are 10 different treatments for this experiment. ◆

We now present formal definitions of several important terms used in experimental design that we introduced earlier.

DEFINITION 1.6 **Response Variable, Factors, Levels, and Treatments**

Response variable: The characteristic of the experimental outcome that is to be measured or observed.

Factor: A variable whose effect on the response variable is of interest in the experiment.

Levels: The possible values of a factor.

Treatment: Each experimental condition. For one-factor experiments, the treatments are the levels of the single factor. For multifactor experiments, each treatment is a combination of levels of the factors.

STATISTICAL DESIGNS

Once we have chosen the treatments, we must decide how the experimental units are to be assigned to the treatments (or vice versa). The women in the folic acid study were randomly divided into two groups; one group received folic acid and the other only trace elements. In the cactus study, 40 cacti were divided randomly into 10 groups of four cacti each and then each group was assigned a different treatment from among the 10 depicted in Table 1.8. Both of these experiments involved the use of a **completely randomized design.**

DEFINITION 1.7 **Completely Randomized Design**

In a *completely randomized design,* all the experimental units are assigned randomly among all the treatments.

The completely randomized design is one of the most commonly used and simplest designs, but it is not always the best design. There are several alternatives to the completely randomized design.

For instance, in a **randomized block design,** experimental units that are similar in ways that are expected to affect the response variable are grouped in **blocks.** Then the random assignment of experimental units to the treatments is made block by block.

DEFINITION 1.8 **Randomized Block Design**

In a *randomized block design,* the experimental units are assigned randomly among all the treatments separately within each block.

In Example 1.13, we contrast completely randomized designs and randomized block designs.

Example 1.13 Statistical Designs

Golf Ball Driving Distances Suppose that we want to compare the driving distances for five different brands of golf ball. For 40 golfers, discuss a method of comparison based on

a. a completely randomized design.   **b.** a randomized block design.

Solution Here the experimental units are the golfers, the response variable is driving distance, the factor is brand of golf ball, and the levels (and treatments) are the five brands.

  a. For a completely randomized design, we would randomly divide the 40 golfers into five groups of 8 golfers each and then randomly assign each group to drive a different brand of ball, as illustrated in Fig. 1.5 on the next page.
  b. As driving distance is affected by gender, using a randomized block design, with blocking by gender, is probably a better approach. We could do so with 40 golfers, say, 20 men and 20 women. We would randomly divide the 20 men into five groups of 4 men each and then randomly assign each group of men to drive a different brand of ball. Likewise, we would randomly divide the 20 women into five groups of 4 women each and then randomly

28 CHAPTER 1 The Nature of Statistics

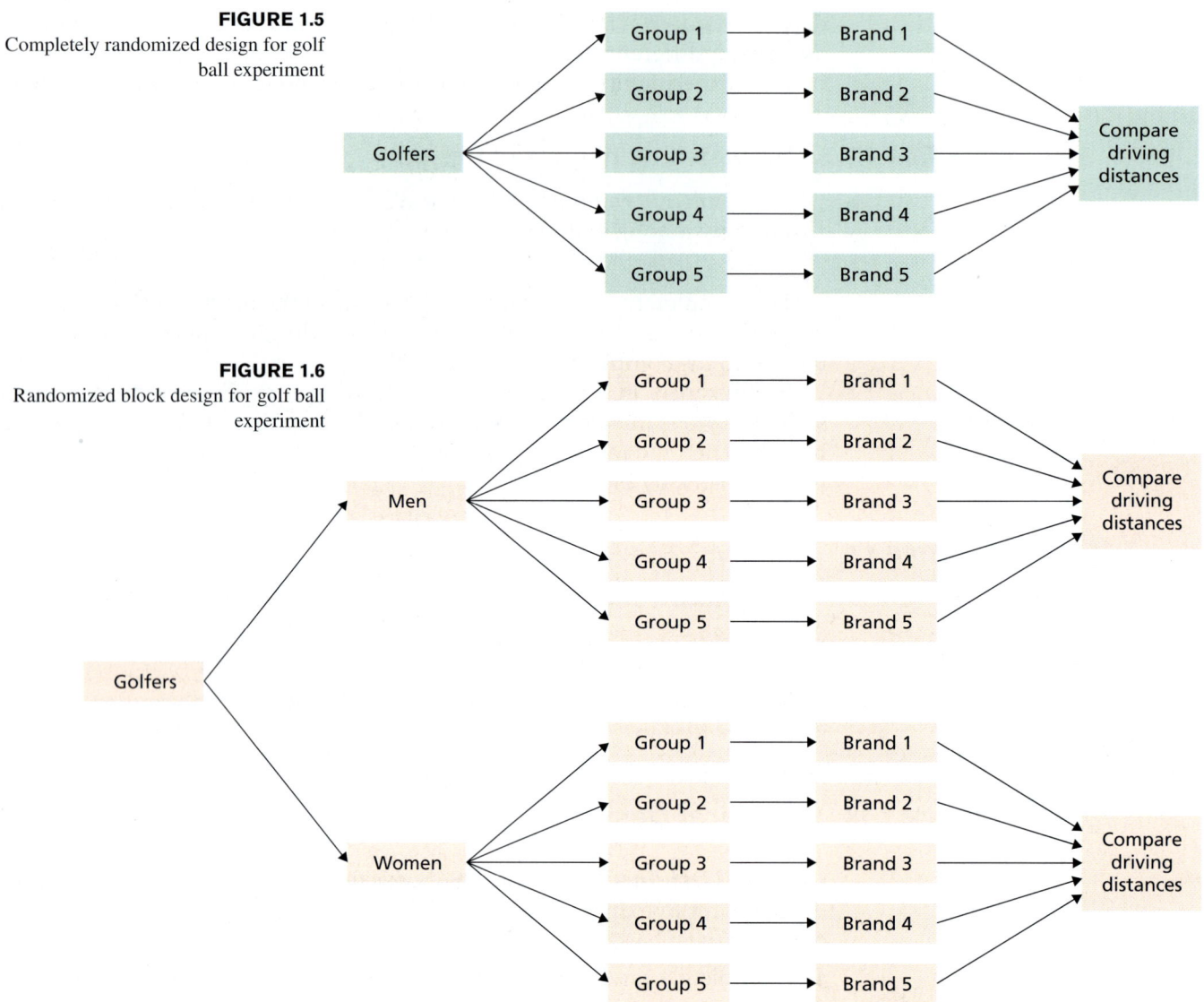

FIGURE 1.5
Completely randomized design for golf ball experiment

FIGURE 1.6
Randomized block design for golf ball experiment

assign each group of women to drive a different brand of ball, as shown in Fig. 1.6.

By blocking, we can isolate and remove the variation in driving distances between men and women and thereby make it easier to detect differences in driving distances among the five brands of golf ball, if such differences exist. Additionally, blocking permits us to analyze separately the differences in driving distances among the five brands for men and women. ◆

As illustrated in Example 1.13, blocking can be used to isolate and remove systematic differences among blocks, thereby making differences among treatments easier to detect when such differences exist. Blocking also makes possible the separate analysis of treatment effects on each block.

The simplest and one of the most common randomized block designs occurs when there is only one factor; the number of experimental units in each block equals the number of treatments; and, within each block, each experimental unit is assigned to a different treatment.

In this section, we introduced some of the basic terminology and principles of experimental design. However, we have just scratched the surface of this vast and important topic to which entire courses and books are devoted. Further discussion of experimental design is provided in the chapter *Design of Experiments and Analysis of Variance* on the WeissStats CD accompanying this book or on the Weiss Web site, www.aw.com/weiss.

Exercises 1.5

Statistical Concepts and Skills

1.38 Define
a. observational study.
b. designed experiment.

1.39 Fill in the following blank. Observational studies can reveal only association, whereas designed experiments can help establish _____.

1.40 State and explain the significance of the three basic principles of experimental design.

1.41 Folic Acid and Birth Defects. In the folic acid study, 4753 women were enrolled by the doctors. Explain how a table of random numbers could be used to divide the women randomly into two groups, one of size 2376 and the other of size 2377.

1.42 Vasectomies and Prostate Cancer. Refer to the vasectomy/prostate cancer study discussed in Example 1.10 on page 23.
a. How could the study be modified to make it a designed experiment?
b. Comment on the feasibility of the designed experiment that you described in part (a).

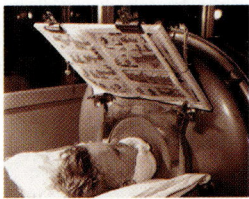

1.43 The Salk Vaccine. In the 1940s and early 1950s, there was great public concern over epidemics of polio. In an attempt to alleviate this serious problem, Jonas Salk of the University of Pittsburgh developed a vaccine for polio. Various preliminary experiments indicated that the vaccine was safe and potentially effective. Nonetheless, a large-scale study was needed to determine whether the vaccine would truly work. A test involving nearly 2 million grade-school children was devised. All the children were inoculated, but only half received the Salk vaccine; the other half were given placebo, in this case an injection of salt dissolved in water. Neither the children nor the doctors performing the diagnoses knew which children belonged to which group. Instead, an evaluation center kept records of who received the Salk vaccine and who did not. The center found that the incidence of polio was far less among the children inoculated with the Salk vaccine. From that information, the researchers concluded that the Salk vaccine would be effective in preventing polio for all U.S. schoolchildren and, consequently, it was then made available for general use. Was this investigation an observational study or a designed experiment? Justify your answer.

1.44 Do Left-Handers Die Earlier? According to a study published in the *Journal of the American Public Health Association*, left-handed people do not die at an earlier age than right-handed people, contrary to the conclusion of a highly publicized report done 2 years earlier. The investigation involved a 6-year study of 3800 people in East Boston older than age 65. Researchers at Harvard University and the National Institute of Aging found that the "lefties" and "righties" died at exactly the same rate. "There was no difference, period," said Dr. Jack Guralnik, an epidemiologist at the institute and one of the coauthors of the report. Was this investigation an observational study or a designed experiment? Justify your answer.

1.45 In a designed experiment
a. what are the experimental units?
b. if the experimental units are human beings, what term is often used in place of experimental unit?

1.46 Adverse Effects of Prozac. Prozac (fluoxetine hydrochloride), a product of Eli Lilly and Company, is used for the treatment of depression, obsessive–compulsive disorder (OCD), and bulimia nervosa. A 1998 issue of the magazine *Arthritis Today* contained an advertisement reporting on the "... treatment-emergent adverse events that occurred in 2% or more patients treated with Prozac and with incidence greater than placebo in the treatment of depression, OCD, or bulimia." In the study, 2444 patients took Prozac and 1331 patients were given a placebo. Identify the
a. treatment group.   b. control group.
c. treatments.

In Exercises 1.47–1.50, we present descriptions of designed experiments. In each case, identify the
a. experimental units.
b. response variable.
c. factor(s).
d. levels of each factor.
e. treatments.

1.47 Lifetimes of Flashlight Batteries. To compare the lifetimes of four brands of flashlight battery, 20 flashlights were used. The 20 flashlights were randomly divided into four groups of 5 flashlights each. Then each group of flashlights was equipped with a different brand of battery.

1.48 Storage of Perishable Items. Storage of perishable items is an important concern for many companies. One study examined the effects of storage time and storage temperature on the deterioration of a particular item. Three different storage temperatures and five different storage times were used.

1.49 Increasing Unit Sales. Supermarkets are interested in strategies to increase temporarily the unit sales of a product. In one study, researchers compared the effect of display type and price on unit sales for a particular product. The following display types and pricing schemes were employed.

- Display types: normal display space interior to an aisle, normal display space at the end of an aisle, and enlarged display space.
- Pricing schemes: regular price, reduced price, and cost.

1.50 Oat Yield and Manure. In a classic study, described by F. Yates in *The Design and Analysis of Factorial Experiments*, the effect on oat yield was compared for three different varieties of oats and four different concentrations of manure (0, 0.2, 0.4, and 0.6 cwt per acre).

1.51 Lifetimes of Flashlight Batteries. Refer to Exercise 1.47. Did this study utilize a completely randomized design or a randomized block design? Explain your answer.

1.52 Lifetimes of Flashlight Batteries. Refer to Exercise 1.47. Suppose that we compare the lifetimes of the four brands of flashlight battery by using 20 flashlights, five different brands of 4 flashlights each. Each of the 4 flashlights of a given brand uses a different brand of battery. Does this study utilize a completely randomized design or a randomized block design? Explain your answer.

Extending the Concepts and Skills

1.53 The Salk Vaccine. In Exercise 1.43, we discussed the Salk vaccine experiment. The experiment utilized a technique called *double-blinding* because neither the children nor the doctors involved knew which children had been given the vaccine and which had been given placebo. Explain the advantages of using double-blinding in the Salk vaccine experiment.

1.54 In sampling from a population, state which type of sampling design corresponds to each of the following experimental designs:
a. completely randomized design.
b. randomized block design.

Using Technology

1.55 Folic Acid and Birth Defects. Use the technology of your choice to carry out the process described in Exercise 1.41.

Chapter Review

You Should Be Able To

1. classify statistical studies as either descriptive or inferential.

2. identify the population and the sample in an inferential study.

3. explain what is meant by a representative sample.

4. describe simple random sampling, systematic random sampling, cluster sampling, and stratified sampling.

5. use a table of random numbers to obtain a simple random sample.

6. explain the difference between an observational study and a designed experiment.

7. classify a study concerning the relationship between two variables or characteristics as either an observational study or a designed experiment.

8. state the three basic principles of experimental design.

9. identify the treatment group and control group in a study.

10. identify the experimental units, response variable, factor(s), levels of each factor, and treatments in a designed experiment.

11. distinguish between a completely randomized design and a randomized block design.

Key Terms

blocks, 27
census, 11
cluster sampling, 18
completely randomized design, 27
control, 24
control group, 25
descriptive statistics, 4
designed experiment, 22
experimental unit, 25
experimentation, 11
factor, 26
inferential statistics, 5
levels, 26
multistage sampling, 21

observational study, 22
population, 5
probability sampling, 12
proportional allocation, 21
random sampling, 12
randomization, 24
randomized block design, 27
replication, 24
representative sample, 11
response variable, 26
sample, 5
sampling, 11
simple random sample, 12
simple random sampling, 12

simple random sampling
   with replacement, 12
simple random sampling
   without replacement, 12
strata, 20
stratified random sampling with
   proportional allocation, 21
stratified sampling, 20
subject, 25
systematic random sampling, 17
table of random numbers, 13
treatment, 26
treatment group, 25

Review Test

Statistical Concepts and Skills

1. In a newspaper or magazine, or on the Internet, find an example of
a. a descriptive study. **b.** an inferential study.

2. Almost any inferential study involves aspects of descriptive statistics. Explain why.

3. Baseball Scores. On April 18, 2000, the following baseball scores were posted on *USA TODAY*'s Web site. Is this study descriptive or inferential? Explain your answer.

NATIONAL LEAGUE BASEBALL			
Giants	13	Expos	4
Reds	9	Cubs	3
Marlins	12	Mets	10
Pirates	5	Brewers	7
Braves	4	Diamondbacks	7
Phillies	3	Rockies	1
Cardinals	5	Dodgers	5
Padres	4	Astros	3

4. Columbine High School Tragedy. As a response to the Columbine High School tragedy, *USA WEEKEND*'s 13th annual *Teen Survey* asked 129,593 students about school safety. Over 20% of the students surveyed said that they have felt afraid at school since Columbine. Also, 30% said that they have been physically threatened, and over 75% said that they would be happier in general if they felt safer at school. Is this study descriptive or inferential? Explain your answer.

5. Before planning and conducting a study to obtain information, what should be done?

6. Explain the meaning of
a. a representative sample.
b. probability sampling.
c. simple random sampling.

7. Incomes of College Students' Parents. A researcher wants to estimate the average income of parents of college students. To accomplish that, he surveys a sample of 250 students at Yale. Is this a representative sample? Explain your answer.

8. Which of the following sampling procedures involve the use of probability sampling?
a. A college student is hired to interview a sample of voters in her town. She stays on campus and interviews 100 students in the cafeteria.
b. A pollster wants to interview 20 gas station managers in Baltimore. He posts a list of all such managers on his wall, closes his eyes, and tosses a dart at the list 20 times. He interviews the people whose names the dart hits.

9. On-Time Airlines. According to the Office of General Counsel, U.S. Department of Transportation, the five airlines with the highest percentage of on-time arrivals for 1998 were Southwest (SW), American (AA), Delta (DL), US Airways (US), and Alaska (AK).
a. List the 10 possible samples (without replacement) of size 3 that can be obtained from the population of five airlines.
b. If a simple random sampling procedure is used to obtain a sample of three of these five airlines, what are the chances that it is the first sample on your list in part (a)? the second sample? the tenth sample?

10. Top North American Athletes. As part of ESPN's *SportsCenturyRetrospective*, a panel chosen by ESPN ranked the top 100 North American athletes of the twentieth century. For a class project, you are to obtain a simple random sample of 15 of these 100 athletes and briefly describe their athletic feats.
a. Explain how you can use Table I in Appendix A to obtain the simple random sample.

b. Starting at the three-digit number in line number 10 and column numbers 7–9 of Table I, read down the column, up the next, and so on, to find 15 numbers that you can use to identify the athletes to be considered.

11. Describe each of the following sampling methods and indicate conditions under which each is appropriate.
a. Systematic random sampling
b. Cluster sampling
c. Stratified random sampling with proportional allocation

12. Top North American Athletes. Refer to Problem 10.
a. Use systematic random sampling to obtain a sample of 15 athletes.
b. In this case, is systematic random sampling an appropriate alternative to simple random sampling? Explain your answer.

13. Surveying the Faculty. The faculty of a college consists of 820 members. A new president has just been appointed. The president wants to get an idea of what the faculty considers the most important issues currently facing the school. She does not have time to interview all the faculty members and so decides to stratify the faculty by rank and use stratified random sampling with proportional allocation to obtain a sample of 40 faculty members. There are 205 full professors, 328 associate professors, 246 assistant professors, and 41 instructors.
a. How many faculty members of each rank should be selected for interviewing?
b. Use Table I in Appendix A to obtain the required sample. Explain your procedure in detail.

14. QuickVote. *TalkBack Live* conducts online surveys on various issues. The following photo shows the result of a *quickvote* taken on July 5, 2000, that asked whether a person would vote for a third-party candidate. Beneath the vote tally is a statement regarding the sampling procedure. Discuss this statement in light of what you have learned in this chapter.

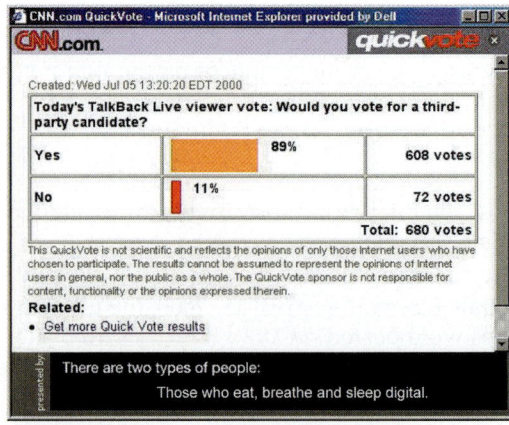

15. Regarding observational studies and designed experiments,
   a. describe each type of study.
   b. with respect to possible conclusions, what important difference exists between the two types of study?

16. Persistent Poverty and IQ. An article appearing in an issue of *The Arizona Republic* reported on a study conducted by Greg Duncan of the University of Michigan. According to the report, "Persistent poverty during the first 5 years of life leaves children with IQs 9.1 points lower at age 5 than children who suffer no poverty during that period...." Is this an observational study or is it a designed experiment? Explain your answer.

17. AVONEX and MS. The Spring 1998 issue of *Inside MS* contained an article describing AVONEX (Interferon beta-1a), a drug used in the treatment of relapsing forms of multiple sclerosis. Included in the article was a report on "... adverse events and selected laboratory abnormalities that occurred at an incidence of 2% or more among the 158 multiple sclerosis patients treated with 30 mcg of AVONEX once weekly by IM injection. In the study, 158 patients took AVONEX and 143 patients were given placebo.
   a. Is this study observational or is it a designed experiment?
   b. Identify the treatment group, control group, and treatments.

18. Identify and explain the significance of the three basic principles of experimental design.

19. Doughnuts and Fat. A classic study, conducted in 1935 by B. Lowe, analyzed differences in the amount of fat absorbed by doughnuts in cooking with four different fats. For the experiment, 24 batches of doughnuts were randomly divided into four groups of 6 batches each. The four groups were then randomly assigned to the four fats. Identify the
   a. experimental units.   **b.** response variable.
   c. factor(s).   **d.** levels of each factor.
   e. treatments.

20. Plant Density and Tomato Yield. In the paper "Effects of Plant Density on Tomato Yields in Western Nigeria" (*Experimental Agriculture*, 1976, Vol. 12(1), pp. 43–47), B. Adelana reported on the effect of tomato variety and planting density on yield. Identify the
   a. experimental units.   **b.** response variable.
   c. factor(s).   **d.** levels of each factor.
   e. treatments.

21. Comparing Gas Mileages. An experiment is to be conducted to compare four different brands of gasoline for gas mileage.
   a. Suppose that you randomly divide 24 cars into four groups of 6 cars each and then randomly assign the four groups to the four brands of gasoline, one group per brand. Is this experimental design a completely randomized design or a randomized block design? If it is the latter, what are the blocks?
   b. Suppose, instead, that you use six different models of car whose varying characteristics (e.g., weight and horsepower) affect gas mileage. Four cars of each model are randomly assigned to the four different brands of gasoline. Is this experimental design a completely randomized design or a randomized block design? If it is the latter, what are the blocks?
   c. Which design is better, the one in part (a) or the one in part (b)? Explain your answer.

22. *USA Today* Polls. The following explanation of *USA TODAY* polls and surveys, effective April 19, 1999, was obtained from the *USA TODAY* Web site. Discuss the explanation in detail.

> USATODAY.com frequently publishes the results of both scientific opinion polls and online reader surveys. Sometimes the topics of these two very different types of public opinion sampling are similar but the results appear very different. It is important that readers understand the difference between the two.
>
> USA TODAY/CNN/Gallup polling is a scientific phone survey taken from a random sample of U.S. residents and weighted to reflect the population at large. This is a process that has been used and refined for more than 50 years. Scientific polling of this type has been used to predict the outcome of elections with considerable accuracy.
>
> Online surveys, such as USATODAY.com's "Quick Question," are not scientific and reflect the views of a self-selected slice of the population. People using the Internet and answering online surveys tend to have different demographics than the nation as a whole and as such, results will differ---sometimes dramatically---from scientific polling.
>
> USATODAY.com will clearly label results from the various types of surveys for the convenience of our readers.

Using Technology

23. Top North American Athletes. Refer to Problem 10. Use the technology of your choice to obtain 15 random numbers that can be used to specify a simple random sample of 15 athletes.

Internet Project

The Internet Projects Page for your book, *Elementary Statistics*, 5th ed., is a location on the Internet designed to help you understand statistics. The starting Internet address (URL) for the page is www.aw.com/weiss. From this Web page, you can reach the Internet Projects Page. We suggest that you bookmark the Internet Projects Page for easy access in the future.

Each chapter in the book includes an Internet project that provides a set of simulations, demonstrations, and other activities as a supplement to those found in the text. The material comes from universities, individuals, and companies from all over the world.

The Titanic Disaster

In this first Internet project, you will become acquainted with the controversy and data surrounding the Titanic disaster. You will visit Web sites at several locations, viewing and thinking about the data and facts presented there. You will also see statistical demonstrations and animations that illustrate the concepts you have covered in class.

In 1912, the Titanic was the largest, most luxurious, and most technologically advanced liner in the world. At 11:40 P.M. on Sunday, April 14 of that year, the Titanic struck an iceberg. In $2\frac{1}{2}$ hours, the liner that many thought unsinkable went down. Only 705 of her 2224 passengers and crew were saved.

Some believe that the rescue procedures used that night unfairly favored the wealthier passengers. In this project, you will use statistical thinking to explore the data from the disaster to arrive at your own (statistically informed) conclusion.

Focusing on Data Analysis

The Focus Database

The file Focus.txt in the Focus Database folder of the WeissStats CD contains information on 500 randomly selected Arizona State University (ASU) sophomores. Seven variables are considered for each student: sex, high school GPA, SAT math score, cumulative GPA, SAT verbal score, age, and total hours completed. Because this database was created from the *ASU Focus Student Database*, we will call it the Focus database.

You will examine the data in the Focus database in sections titled *Focusing on Data Analysis* at the end of each chapter. Large data sets are almost always analyzed by computer, and that is how you should handle the data sets in the *Focusing on Data Analysis* sections.

Once you have input the Focus database into your chosen technology, you should, if possible, name each data set as indicated in Table 1.9.

TABLE 1.9 Names for data sets in the Focus database

Data set	Name
Sex	SEX
High school GPA	HS GPA
SAT math score	SAT MATH
Cumulative GPA	CUM GPA
SAT verbal score	SAT VERB
Age	AGE
Total hours completed	HOURS

Now that you have the data sets in the Focus database stored and named in your chosen technology, save the worksheet to a file named Focus with an appropriate file extension. Consult the documentation for your technology as required. Now, any time you want to analyze the Focus database, you can simply retrieve the Focus worksheet.

case study discussion

Top Films of All Time

At the beginning of this chapter, we discussed the results of a survey by the American Film Institute (AFI). Now that you have learned some of the basic terminology of statistics, we want you to examine that survey in greater detail.

Answer each of the following questions pertaining to the survey. In doing so, you may want to reread the description of the survey given on page 3.

a. Identify the population.
b. Identify the sample.
c. Is the sample representative of the population of all U.S. moviegoers? Explain your answer.
d. Consider the following statement: "Among the 1500 filmmakers, actors, critics, politicians, and film historians polled by AFI, the top-ranking film was *Citizen Kane*." Is this statement descriptive or inferential? Explain your answer.
e. Suppose that the statement in part (d) is changed to: "Based on the AFI poll, *Citizen Kane* is the top-ranking film among all filmmakers, actors, critics, politicians, and film historians." Is this statement descriptive or inferential? Explain your answer.

Internet Resources: Visit the Weiss Web site www.aw.com/weiss for additional discussion, exercises, and resources related to this case study.

Biography

Florence Nightingale: Lady of the Lamp

FLORENCE NIGHTINGALE (1820–1910), the founder of modern nursing, was born in Florence, Italy, into a wealthy English family. In 1849, over the objections of her parents, she entered the Institution of Protestant Deaconesses at Kaiserswerth, Germany, which "...trained country girls of good character to nurse the sick."

The Crimean War began in March, 1854, when England and France declared war on Russia. After serving as superintendent of the Institution for the Care of Sick Gentlewomen in London, Nightingale was appointed by the English Secretary of State at War, Sidney Herbert, to be in charge of 38 nurses who were to be stationed at military hospitals in Turkey.

Nightingale found the conditions in the hospitals appalling—overcrowded, filthy, and without sufficient facilities. In addition to the administrative duties she undertook to alleviate those conditions, she spent many hours tending patients. After 8:00 P.M. she allowed none of her nurses in the wards, but made rounds herself every night, a deed that earned her the epithet Lady of the Lamp.

Nightingale was an ardent believer in the power of statistics and used statistics extensively to gain an understanding of social and health issues. She lobbied to introduce statistics into the curriculum at Oxford and invented the coxcomb chart, a type of pie chart. Nightingale felt that charts and diagrams were a means of making statistical information understandable to people who would otherwise be unwilling to digest the dry numbers.

In May 1857, as a result of Nightingale's interviews with officials ranging from the Secretary of State to Queen Victoria herself, the Royal Commission on the Health of the Army was established. Under the auspices of the commission, the Army Medical School was founded. In 1860, Nightingale used a fund set up by the public to honor her work in the Crimea to create the Nightingale School for Nurses at St. Thomas's Hospital. During that same year, at the International Statistical Congress in London, she authored one of the three papers discussed in the Sanitary Section and also met Adolphe Quetelet (see Chapter 2 biography) who had greatly influenced her work.

After 1857, Nightingale lived as an invalid, although it has never been determined that she had any specific illness. In fact, many speculated that her invalidism was a stratagem she employed to devote herself to her work.

Nightingale was elected an Honorary Member of the American Statistical Association in 1874. In 1907, she was presented the Order of Merit for meritorious service by King Edward VII; she was the first woman to receive that award.

Florence Nightingale died in 1910. An offer of a national funeral and burial at Westminster Abbey was declined, and, according to her wishes, Nightingale was buried in the family plot in East Mellow, Hampshire, England.

part ii

Descriptive Statistics

CHAPTER 2	**Organizing Data**
CHAPTER 3	**Descriptive Measures**
CHAPTER 4	**Descriptive Methods in Regression and Correlation**

chapter 2

Organizing Data

CHAPTER OUTLINE

- **2.1** Variables and Data
- **2.2** Grouping Data
- **2.3** Graphs and Charts
- **2.4** Stem-and-Leaf Diagrams
- **2.5** Distribution Shapes; Symmetry and Skewness
- **2.6** Misleading Graphs

GENERAL OBJECTIVES In Chapter 1, we introduced two major interrelated branches of statistics: *descriptive statistics* and *inferential statistics*. As you discovered there, descriptive statistics consists of methods for organizing and summarizing information clearly and effectively.

In this chapter, you begin your study of descriptive statistics. As a prerequisite, in Section 2.1, we show you how to classify data by type. Data type is often an important factor in selecting the correct statistical method, both in descriptive statistics and inferential statistics.

In Section 2.2, we explain how to group data so that they are easier to work with and understand. In Section 2.3, we demonstrate various classical ways to portray data graphically, thus providing a "picture" of the data. In Section 2.4, we introduce stem-and-leaf diagrams—one of an arsenal of statistical tools known collectively as *exploratory data analysis*.

In Section 2.5, we discuss the identification of the shape of a data set, an important aspect of both descriptive and inferential statistics. And, in Section 2.6, we present some tips for avoiding confusion when you read and interpret graphical displays.

case study

PREVENTING INFANT MORTALITY

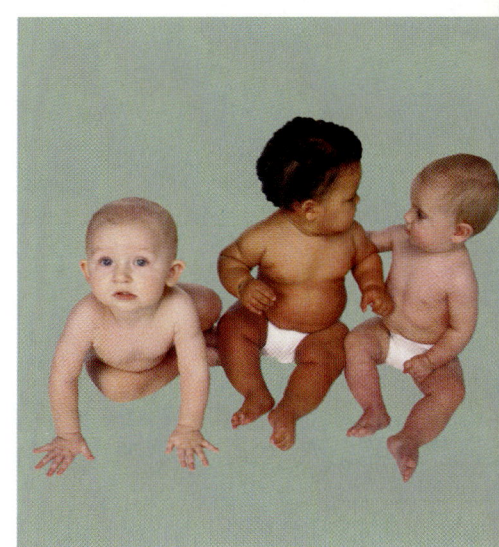

Infant mortality is concerned with infant deaths during the first year of life. Generally, the infant mortality rate provides the number of such deaths per 1000 live births during a calendar year. In 1987, the U.S. Congress established the National Commission to Prevent Infant Mortality, whose charge is to create a national strategy for reducing the infant mortality rate of the United States.

From the *Statistical Abstract of the United States*, we obtained information on 1999 infant mortality rates for nations that had a 1999 population of 10 million people or more. If we rank those nations according to their infant mortality rates, the 24 with the lowest rates are as shown in the following table.

Rank	Country	Infant mortality	Rank	Country	Infant mortality
1	Japan	4.1	13	Czech Republic	6.7
2	Australia	5.1	14	Greece	7.1
3	Germany	5.1	15	South Korea	7.6
4	Netherlands	5.1	16	Cuba	7.8
5	Canada	5.5	17	Hungary	9.5
6	France	5.6	18	Chile	10.0
7	United Kingdom	5.8	19	Poland	12.8
8	Taiwan	6.0	20	Belarus	14.4
9	Belgium	6.2	21	Sri Lanka	16.1
10	**United States**	**6.3**	22	Serbia	16.5
11	Italy	6.3	23	Romania	18.1
12	Spain	6.4	24	Argentina	18.4

As the table reveals, even among nations with the lowest rates, infant mortality varies considerably, from a low of 4.1 (Japan) to a high of 18.4 (Argentina). Although the United States made a relatively poor showing, its infant mortality rate dropped by roughly one-third since 1989.

At the end of this chapter, you will be asked to revisit the information presented here and apply some of your newly learned statistical skills to identify and analyze various aspects of these infant mortality rates.

2.1 VARIABLES AND DATA

A characteristic that varies from one person or thing to another is called a **variable.** Examples of variables for human beings are height, weight, number of siblings, sex, marital status, and eye color. The first three of these variables yield numerical information and are examples of **quantitative variables;** the last three yield nonnumerical information and are examples of **qualitative variables,** also called **categorical variables.**

Quantitative variables can be classified as either *discrete* or *continuous.* A **discrete variable** is a variable whose possible values can be listed, even though the list may continue indefinitely. Mathematically, the numbers that make sense for values of a discrete variable form a finite or countably infinite set, usually some collection of whole numbers. "Number of siblings" is an example of a discrete variable. A discrete variable usually involves a count of something.

A **continuous variable** is a variable whose possible values form some interval of numbers—all numbers within the interval make sense for values of the variable. "Height" is an example of a continuous variable. Typically, a continuous variable involves a measurement of something.

The preceding discussion is summarized graphically in Fig. 2.1 and verbally in the following definition.

DEFINITION 2.1

Variables

Variable: A characteristic that varies from one person or thing to another.

Qualitative variable: A nonnumerically valued variable.[1]

Quantitative variable: A numerically valued variable.

Discrete variable: A quantitative variable whose possible values form a finite (or countably infinite) set of numbers.

Continuous variable: A quantitative variable whose possible values form some interval of numbers.

FIGURE 2.1
Types of variables

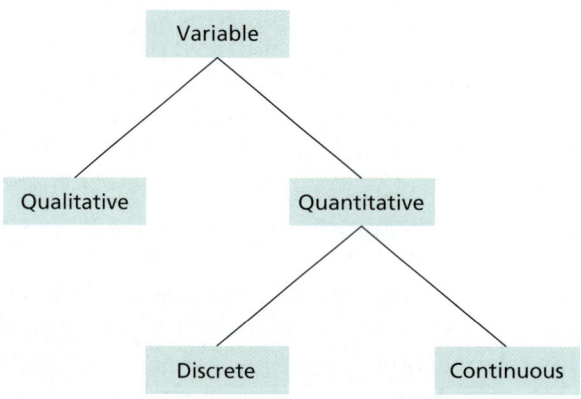

---

[1] Values of a qualitative variable are sometimes coded with numbers—for example, zip codes, which represent geographical locations. Note that it is not meaningful to do arithmetic with such numbers, in contrast to numbers obtained from a quantitative variable.

2.1 Variables and Data

Observing the values of a variable for one or more people or things yields **data.** Thus the information collected, organized, and analyzed by statisticians is data. As for variables, data can be classified as **qualitative data, quantitative data, discrete data,** and **continuous data.**

DEFINITION 2.2 **Data**

Data: Information obtained by observing values of a variable.

Qualitative data: Data obtained by observing values of a qualitative variable.

Quantitative data: Data obtained by observing values of a quantitative variable.

Discrete data: Data obtained by observing values of a discrete variable.

Continuous data: Data obtained by observing values of a continuous variable.

Each individual piece of data is called an **observation,** and the collection of all observations for a particular variable is called a **data set.**[2] In Examples 2.1–2.4, we illustrate various types of variables and data.

Example 2.1 *Variables and Data*

The 104th Boston Marathon At noon on April 17, 2000, almost 18,000 men and women set out to run from Hopkinton Center to the John Hancock Building in Boston. Their run, covering 26 miles and 385 yards, would be watched by thousands of people lining the streets leading into Boston and by millions more on television. It was the 104th running of the Boston Marathon.

A great deal of information was accumulated and recorded that afternoon by the Boston Athletic Association. The men's competition was won by Elijah Lagat of Kenya with a time of 2 hours, 9 minutes, and 47 seconds. The winner of the women's competition was Catherine Ndereba, also of Kenya, with a time of 2 hours, 26 minutes, and 11 seconds. According to *The Boston Globe*'s Marathon Central Web page, "Kenya's domination in Boston extended to a record 10 consecutive victories Monday, as Elijah Lagat outkicked Ethiopia's Gezahenge Abera and Kenya's Moses Tanui in the closest finish in the race's 104-year history."

The Boston Marathon provides examples of different types of variables and data. The simplest type of variable is illustrated by the classification of each entrant as either male or female. "Sex" is a qualitative variable because its possible values (male or female) are nonnumerical. Thus, for instance, the information that Elijah Lagat is a male is qualitative data—data obtained by observing the value of the variable "sex" for Elijah Lagat.

---

[2]Sometimes *data set* is used to refer to all the data for all the variables under consideration.

Most racing fans are interested in the places of the finishers. "Place of finish" is a quantitative variable, which is also a discrete variable because it makes sense to talk only about first place, second place, and so on—there are only a finite number of possible finishing places. The information that, among the women, Catherine Ndereba and Irina Bogacheva finished first and second, respectively, and Melissa Moon and Kristin Schwartz finished 19th and 20th, respectively, is discrete, quantitative data—data obtained by observing the values of the variable "place of finish" for the four runners.

More can be learned about what happened in a race by looking at the times of the finishers. For instance, Catherine Ndereba beat Irina Bogacheva by only 16 seconds, whereas Melissa Moon finished 2 minutes and 3 seconds ahead of Kristin Schwartz. "Finishing time" is a quantitative variable, which is also a continuous variable because the finishing time of a runner can conceptually be any positive number. The information that Elijah Lagat ran his race in 2:09:47 and Catherine Ndereba ran hers in 2:26:11 is continuous, quantitative data—data obtained by observing the values of the variable "finishing time" for Elijah Lagat and Catherine Ndereba. ◆

Example 2.2 Variables and Data

Human Blood Types Human beings have one of four blood types: A, B, AB, or O. What kind of data do you receive when you are told your blood type?

Solution Your blood type is qualitative data—data obtained by observing your value of the variable "blood type." ◆

Example 2.3 Variables and Data

Household Size The U.S. Bureau of the Census collects data on household size and publishes the information in *Current Population Reports*. What kind of data is the number of people in your household?

Solution The number of people in your household is discrete, quantitative data—data obtained by observing the value of the variable "household size" for your particular household. ◆

Example 2.4 Variables and Data

The World's Highest Waterfalls The *Information Please Almanac* lists the world's highest waterfalls. The list shows that Angel Falls in Venezuela is 3281 feet high, or more than twice as high as Ribbon Falls in Yosemite, California, which is 1612 feet high. What kind of data are these heights?

Solution The waterfall heights are continuous, quantitative data—data obtained by observing the values of the variable "height" for the two waterfalls. ◆

CLASSIFICATION AND THE CHOICE OF A STATISTICAL METHOD

Some of the descriptive and inferential procedures that you will study are valid for only certain types of data. This limitation is one reason why you must be able to correctly classify data. Statisticians use other classifications besides the ones presented here. But the types we have discussed are sufficient for the majority of applications.

Data classification is difficult sometimes; even statisticians occasionally disagree over data type. For example, some classify amounts of money as discrete data, whereas others classify amounts of money as continuous data. In most cases, however, the appropriate classification of data is fairly clear and may help you choose the correct statistical method for analyzing the data.

Exercises 2.1

Statistical Concepts and Skills

2.1 Give an example, other than those presented in this section, of a
a. qualitative variable.
b. discrete, quantitative variable.
c. continuous, quantitative variable.

2.2 Explain the meaning of
a. qualitative variable.
b. discrete, quantitative variable.
c. continuous, quantitative variable.

2.3 Explain the meaning of
a. qualitative data.
b. discrete, quantitative data.
c. continuous, quantitative data.

2.4 Give a reason why the classification of data is important.

2.5 Of the variables you have studied so far, which type yields nonnumerical data?

For each part of Exercises 2.6–2.9, classify the data as either qualitative or quantitative; if quantitative, further classify it as discrete or continuous. Also, identify the variable under consideration.

2.6 Languages of the World. According to Professor Sidney S. Culbert of the University of Washington, the principal languages of the world in 1998 were as follows.

Rank	Language	Speakers (millions)
1	Mandarin	1052
2	English	508
3	Hindi	487
4	Spanish	417
5	Russian	277
6	Arabic	246
7	Bengali	211

a. What type of data is presented in the first column of the table?
b. What type of data is provided by the information that Sally Ride speaks English?
c. What type of data is provided by the information in the third column of the table?

2.7 How Hot Does It Get? The highest temperatures on record for selected cities are collected by the U.S. National Oceanic and Atmospheric Administration and published in *Comparative Climatic Data*. The following table displays data for years through 1997.

City	Rank	Highest temperature (°F)
Phoenix, AZ	1	122
Sacramento, CA	2	115
El Paso, TX	3	114
Omaha, NE	3	114
Dallas–Fort Worth	5	113
Wichita, KS	5	113
Boise, ID	7	111
San Diego, CA	7	111
Los Angeles, CA	9	110
Bismarck, ND	10	109

a. What type of data is presented in the second column of the table?
b. What type of data is provided in the third column of the table?
c. What type of data is provided by the information that Phoenix is in Arizona.

2.8 Prime-Time Favorites. According to Nielsen Media Research, the favorite prime-time television programs for the years 1997–1998 are as shown in the following table. Average audience percentage, or ratings, are estimates of the percentage of all TV-owning households that are watching a particular program.

Rank	Program	Average audience (%)
1	Seinfeld	22.0
2	E.R.	20.7
3	Veronica's Closet	16.8
4	Friends	16.4
5	NFL Monday Night Football	15.0
6	Touched by an Angel	14.4
7	60 Minutes	13.9
8	Union Square	13.6
9	CBS Sunday Night Movie	13.3

a. What type of data is presented in the first column of the table?
b. What type of data is provided by the information in the third column of the table?

Album	Artist/Group	Sold (millions)
Millennium	Back Street Boys	9.3
Baby One More Time	Britney Spears	8.2
Ricky Martin	Ricky Martin	5.9
Come on Over	Shania Twain	5.5
Significant Other	Limp Bizkit	4.8
Supernatural	Santana	4.5
FanMail	TLC	4.2
Devil Without a Cause	Kid Rock	4.1
Christina Aguilera	Christina Aguilera	3.4
Wide Open Spaces	Dixie Chicks	3.4

a. What type of data is provided by the information in the third column of the table?
b. What type of data is given by the information that *Supernatural* was performed by Santana?

Extending the Concepts and Skills

2.10 Ordinal data. Another important type of data is *ordinal data*, which is data about order or rank given on a scale such as 1, 2, 3, … or A, B, C, …. Following are several variables. Which, if any, yield ordinal data? Explain your answer.

a. Height
b. Weight
c. Age
d. Sex
e. Number of siblings
f. Religion
g. Place of birth
h. High school class rank

2.9 Best-Selling Albums. According to *Entertainment Weekly*, the best-selling albums of 1999 and the numbers sold are as follows.

2.2 GROUPING DATA

The amount of data collected in real-world situations can sometimes be overwhelming. For example, a list of U.S. colleges and universities with information on enrollment, number of teachers, highest degree offered, and governing official can be found in *The World Almanac*. These data occupy 28 pages of small type!

By suitably organizing data, we can often make a large and complicated set of data more compact and easier to understand. In this section, we discuss **grouping**, which involves, as the term implies, putting data into groups rather than treating each observation individually. Grouping is one of the most common methods of organizing data.

We first consider the grouping of quantitative data, both continuous and discrete. Later in this section, we examine the grouping of qualitative (categorical) data.

GROUPING QUANTITATIVE DATA

To begin, consider the grouping of quantitative data presented in Example 2.5.

Example 2.5   Grouping Quantitative Data

Days to Maturity for Short-Term Investments Table 2.1 displays the number of days to maturity for 40 short-term investments. The data are from *Barron's National Business and Financial Weekly*.

Getting a clear picture of the data in Table 2.1 is difficult. By grouping the data into categories, or **classes,** we can make the data much easier to comprehend. The first step is to decide on the classes. One convenient way to group these data is by 10s.

Because the shortest maturity period is 36 days, our first class is for maturity periods from 30 days up to, but not including, 40 days. We use the symbol $\prec$ as a shorthand for "up to, but not including," so our first class is denoted $30 \prec 40$.[3] The longest maturity period is 99 days, so grouping by 10s results in the seven classes given in the first column of Table 2.2.

The final step for grouping the data is to determine the number of investments in each class. We do so by placing a tally mark for each investment from Table 2.1 on the appropriate line of Table 2.2. For instance, the first investment in Table 2.1 has a 70-day maturity period, calling for a tally mark on the line for the class $70 \prec 80$. The results of the tallying procedure are shown in the second column of Table 2.2. Now we count the tallies for each class and record each total in the third column of Table 2.2.

By simply glancing at Table 2.2, we can easily obtain various pieces of useful information. For instance, more investments are in the 60s range than in any other. Comparing Tables 2.1 and 2.2 clearly shows that grouping the data makes the data much easier to read and understand.   ◆

TABLE 2.1 Days to maturity for 40 short-term investments

70	64	99	55	64	89	87	65
62	38	67	70	60	69	78	39
75	56	71	51	99	68	95	86
57	53	47	50	55	81	80	98
51	36	63	66	85	79	83	70

TABLE 2.2 Classes and counts for the days-to-maturity data in Table 2.1

Days to maturity	Tally	Number of investments
$30 \prec 40$	III	3
$40 \prec 50$	I	1
$50 \prec 60$	ШН III	8
$60 \prec 70$	ШН ШН	10
$70 \prec 80$	ШН II	7
$80 \prec 90$	ШН II	7
$90 \prec 100$	IIII	4
		40

In Example 2.5, we used a commonsense approach to grouping data into classes. Some of that common sense can be used as guidelines for grouping. Three of the most important guidelines are the following.

1. *The number of classes should be small enough to provide an effective summary but large enough to display the relevant characteristics of the data.*

   In Example 2.5, we used seven classes. Usually the number of classes should be between 5 and 20, but that is only a rule of thumb.

2. *Each observation must belong to one, and only one, class.*

   Careless planning in Example 2.5 could have led to classes such as 30–40, 40–50, 50–60, and so on. Then, for instance, to which class would the investment with a 50-day maturity period belong? The classes in Table 2.2 do not cause such confusion; they cover all maturity periods and do not overlap.

---

[3]The symbol $\prec$ is obtained by superimposing a less-than symbol over a dash. Using the notation $30 \prec 40$ is less awkward than using the notation 30–< 40 or 30–under 40.

> **What Does it Mean?**
>
> Always keep in mind that the reason for grouping is to organize the data into a sensible number of classes to make the data more accessible and understandable.

3. *Whenever feasible, all classes should have the same width.*

The classes in Table 2.2 all have a width of 10 days. Among other things, choosing classes of equal width facilitates the graphical display of the data.

The list could go on, but for our purposes these three guidelines provide a solid basis for grouping data.

FREQUENCY AND RELATIVE-FREQUENCY DISTRIBUTIONS

The number of observations that fall into a particular class is called the **frequency** (or **count**) of that class. For instance, in Table 2.2, the frequency of the class $50 \leq 60$ is 8 because eight investments are in the 50s days-to-maturity range. A table that provides all classes and their frequencies is called a **frequency distribution**. The first and third columns of Table 2.2 constitute a frequency distribution for the days-to-maturity data.

In addition to the frequency of a class, we are often interested in the **percentage** of a class. We find the percentage by first dividing the frequency of the class by the total number of observations and then multiplying the result by 100. From Table 2.2, the percentage of investments in the class $50 \leq 60$ is

$$\frac{8}{40} = 0.20 \quad \text{or} \quad 20\%.$$

Thus 20% of the investments have a number of days to maturity in the 50s.

The percentage of a class, expressed as a decimal, is called the **relative frequency** of the class. For the class $50 \leq 60$, the relative frequency is 0.20. A table that provides all classes and their relative frequencies is called a **relative-frequency distribution**. Table 2.3 displays a relative-frequency distribution for the days-to-maturity data. Note that the relative frequencies sum to 1 (100%).

Relative-frequency distributions are better than frequency distributions for comparing two data sets. The reason is that relative frequencies always fall between 0 and 1 and hence provide a standard for comparison. Two data sets that have identical frequency distributions have identical relative-frequency distributions. But two data sets that have identical relative-frequency distributions have identical frequency distributions only if both data sets have the same number of observations.

TABLE 2.3
Relative-frequency distribution for the days-to-maturity data in Table 2.1

Days to maturity	Relative frequency		
30 ≤ 40	0.075	←	3/40
40 ≤ 50	0.025	←	1/40
50 ≤ 60	0.200	←	8/40
60 ≤ 70	0.250	←	10/40
70 ≤ 80	0.175	←	7/40
80 ≤ 90	0.175	←	7/40
90 ≤ 100	0.100	←	4/40
	1.000		

GROUPING TERMINOLOGY

To be adept at grouping, you need to become familiar with and understand the various terms associated with grouping. We have already discussed several of these terms. To introduce some additional ones, let's return to the days-to-maturity data.

Consider, for example, the class $50 \leq 60$. The smallest maturity period that could go in this class is 50; this value is called the **lower cutpoint** of the class. The smallest maturity period that could go in the next higher class is 60; this value is called the **upper cutpoint** of the class and, of course, is also the lower cutpoint of the next higher class, $60 \leq 70$.

The number in the middle of the class 50 ≤ 60 is (50 + 60)/2 = 55 and is called the **midpoint** of the class. Midpoints provide single numbers for representing classes and are often used in graphical displays and for computing descriptive measures. The **width** of the class 50 ≤ 60, obtained by subtracting its lower cutpoint from its upper cutpoint, is 60 − 50 = 10. We summarize the terminology of grouping as follows.

DEFINITION 2.3 **Terms Used in Grouping**

Classes: Categories for grouping data.

Frequency: The number of observations that fall in a class.

Frequency distribution: A listing of all classes and their frequencies.

Relative frequency: The ratio of the frequency of a class to the total number of observations.

Relative-frequency distribution: A listing of all classes and their relative frequencies.

Lower cutpoint: The smallest value that could go in a class.

Upper cutpoint: The smallest value that could go in the next higher class. The upper cutpoint of a class is the same as the lower cutpoint of the next higher class.

Midpoint: The middle of a class, obtained by taking the average of its lower and upper cutpoints.

Width: The difference between the upper and lower cutpoints of a class.

A table that provides the classes, frequencies, relative frequencies, and midpoints of a data set is called a **grouped-data table.** Table 2.4 is a grouped-data table for the days-to-maturity data. Construction of a grouped-data table from raw data is further illustrated in Example 2.6.

TABLE 2.4
Grouped-data table for the days-to-maturity data

Days to maturity	Frequency	Relative frequency	Midpoint
30 ≤ 40	3	0.075	35
40 ≤ 50	1	0.025	45
50 ≤ 60	8	0.200	55
60 ≤ 70	10	0.250	65
70 ≤ 80	7	0.175	75
80 ≤ 90	7	0.175	85
90 ≤ 100	4	0.100	95
	40	1.000	

Example 2.6 Grouped-Data Tables

Weights of 18–24-Year-Old Males The U.S. National Center for Health Statistics publishes data on weights and heights by age and sex in *Vital and Health Statistics*. The weights shown in Table 2.5, given to the nearest tenth of a pound, were obtained from a sample of 18–24-year-old males. Construct a grouped-data table for these weights. Use a class width of 20 and a first cutpoint of 120.

Solution Because we are to use a class width of 20 and a first cutpoint of 120, the first class will be $120 \le 140$. In Table 2.5, the largest weight is 278.8 lb. Thus we choose the classes displayed in the first column of Table 2.6.

Applying the tallying procedure to the data in Table 2.5, we obtain the frequencies in the second column of Table 2.6. To illustrate some typical computations for the third and fourth columns of Table 2.6, we use the class $160 \le 180$:

$$\text{relative frequency} = \frac{14}{37} = 0.378$$

and

$$\text{midpoint} = \frac{160 + 180}{2} = 170.$$

The other entries in the third and fourth columns are computed similarly.

TABLE 2.5
Weights of 37 males, aged 18–24 years

129.2	185.3	218.1	182.5	142.8
155.2	170.0	151.3	187.5	145.6
167.3	161.0	178.7	165.0	172.5
191.1	150.7	187.0	173.7	178.2
161.7	170.1	165.8	214.6	136.7
278.8	175.6	188.7	132.1	158.5
146.4	209.1	175.4	182.0	173.6
149.9	158.6			

TABLE 2.6
Grouped-data table for the weights of 37 males, aged 18–24 years

Weight (lb)	Frequency	Relative frequency	Midpoint
$120 \le 140$	3	0.081	130
$140 \le 160$	9	0.243	150
$160 \le 180$	14	0.378	170
$180 \le 200$	7	0.189	190
$200 \le 220$	3	0.081	210
$220 \le 240$	0	0.000	230
$240 \le 260$	0	0.000	250
$260 \le 280$	1	0.027	270
	37	0.999	

Recall that relative frequencies must always sum to 1. However, the sum of the relative frequencies in the third column of Table 2.6 is given as 0.999. The reason for this discrepancy is as follows. Each relative frequency is rounded to three decimal places and, in this case, the resulting sum differs from 1 by a little. Such a result is usually referred to as *rounding error* or *roundoff error*. ◆

AN ALTERNATE METHOD FOR DEPICTING CLASSES

An alternate method is often used to depict classes, especially when the data are expressed as whole numbers. For instance, the third class for the days-to-maturity data, $50 \le 60$, is for maturity periods from 50 days up to, but not including, 60 days. In this case the maturity periods are expressed to the nearest whole day, so the third class can also be characterized as being for maturity periods from 50 days up to, and including, 59 days.

Thus, as an alternative to depicting the third class by 50 ≤ 60, we can use 50–59. The smallest maturity period that could go in this class is 50 and, in this context, is called the **lower limit** of the class. The largest maturity period that can go in this class is 59 and, in this context, is called the **upper limit** of the class.

When utilizing class limits to depict classes, we generally use *marks* instead of midpoints as representatives for the classes. The **mark** of a class is the average of its lower and upper limits. For example, the mark of the class 50–59 is $(50 + 59)/2 = 54.5$.

An alternate grouped-data table for the days-to-maturity data—one that uses class limits and class marks instead of class cutpoints and class midpoints—is displayed in Table 2.7. Compare Tables 2.4 and 2.7.

TABLE 2.7
Grouped-data table for the days-to-maturity data, using class limits and class marks

Days to maturity	Frequency	Relative frequency	Mark
30–39	3	0.075	34.5
40–49	1	0.025	44.5
50–59	8	0.200	54.5
60–69	10	0.250	64.5
70–79	7	0.175	74.5
80–89	7	0.175	84.5
90–99	4	0.100	94.5
	40	1.000	

The weight data in Table 2.5 are presented to one decimal place. Consequently, the alternate method for depicting the classes shown in the first column of Table 2.6 would be 120–139.9, 140–159.9, 160–179.9, and so on. The marks for these classes are, respectively, 129.95, 149.95, 169.95, and so on.

Both of these methods of depicting classes and their representatives are commonly used, and each has its advantages and disadvantages. We freely use both methods throughout this book. So, be sure that you have a clear understanding of the two approaches.

SINGLE-VALUE GROUPING

Up to this point, each class that we have used for grouping data represents a range of possible values. For instance, in Table 2.6, the first class, 120 ≤ 140, is for weights from 120 lb up to, but not including, 140 lb. In some cases, however, using classes that each represent a single possible value is more appropriate. This remark is particularly true for discrete data in which there are only relatively few distinct observations. Consider, for instance, Example 2.7.

Example 2.7 Single-Value Grouping

TVs per Household *Trends in Television*, published by the Television Bureau of Advertising, contains information on the number of television sets owned by U.S. households. Data on the number of TV sets per household for 50 randomly selected households are displayed in Table 2.8. Use classes based on a single value to construct a grouped-data table for these data.

Solution We first note that, because each class is to represent a single numerical value, the classes are 0, 1, 2, 3, 4, 5, and 6. These classes are displayed in the first column of Table 2.9.

Tallying the data in Table 2.8, we obtain the frequencies in the second column of Table 2.9. Dividing each frequency by the total number of observations, 50, we get the relative frequencies shown in the third column of Table 2.9. The table indicates, for example, that 14 of the 50 households, or 0.280 (28.0%), have two television sets.

Because each class is based on a single value, the midpoint (and mark) of each class is the same as the class. For instance, the midpoint (and mark) of the class 3 is 3. Therefore a midpoint (or mark) column in Table 2.9 is unnecessary, as such a column would be identical to the first column. In other words, Table 2.9 can serve as a grouped-data table.[4]

TABLE 2.8 Number of TV sets in each of 50 randomly selected households

1	1	1	2	6	3	3	4	2	4
3	2	1	5	2	1	3	6	2	2
3	1	1	4	3	2	2	2	2	3
0	3	1	2	1	2	3	1	1	3
3	2	1	2	1	3	1	5	1	

TABLE 2.9 Grouped-data table for number of TV sets

Number of TVs	Frequency	Relative frequency
0	1	0.020
1	16	0.320
2	14	0.280
3	12	0.240
4	3	0.060
5	2	0.040
6	2	0.040
	50	1.000

GROUPING QUALITATIVE DATA

The concepts of cutpoints and midpoints are not appropriate for qualitative data. For instance, with data that categorize people as male or female, the classes are "male" and "female." To consider cutpoints or midpoints for such data makes no sense.

We can, of course, still group qualitative data and compute frequencies and relative frequencies for the classes. For qualitative data, the classes coincide with the observed values of the corresponding variable, as illustrated in Example 2.8.

Example 2.8 Grouping Qualitative Data

Political Party Affiliations Professor Weiss asked his introductory statistics students to state their political party affiliations as Democratic (D), Republican (R), or Other (O). The responses are given in Table 2.10. Determine the frequency and relative-frequency distributions for these data.

Solution The classes for grouping the data are "Democratic," "Republican," and "Other." Tallying the data in Table 2.10, we obtain the frequency distribution displayed in the first two columns of Table 2.11.

---

[4]For single-value grouped data, the upper and lower limits of each class are also identical to the class. And, although it is generally unnecessary, we can also obtain the cutpoints. For the grouped data in Table 2.9, the cutpoints are −0.5, 0.5, 1.5, 2.5, 3.5, 4.5, 5.5, and 6.5.

TABLE 2.10
Political party affiliations of the students in introductory statistics

D	R	O	R	R	R	R
D	O	R	D	O	O	R	D
D	R	O	D	R	R	O	R
D	O	D	D	D	R	O	D
O	R	D	R	R	R	D

TABLE 2.11
Frequency and relative-frequency distributions for political party affiliations

Party	Frequency	Relative frequency
Democratic	13	0.325
Republican	18	0.450
Other	9	0.225
	40	1.000

Dividing each frequency in the second column of Table 2.11 by the total number of students, 40, we get the relative frequencies in the third column. The first and third columns of Table 2.11 provide the relative-frequency distribution for the data. ◆

The Technology Center

Grouping data can be tedious if done by hand. You can avoid the tedium by using a computer or graphing calculator. In this subsection, we present output and optional step-by-step instructions for grouping data into single-value classes. Refer to the technology manuals for other grouping methods.

Minitab and Excel have dedicated programs for single-value grouping of quantitative data or for grouping of qualitative (categorical) data. At the time of this writing, the TI-83 Plus does not have such a program. Example 2.9 illustrates the use of Minitab and Excel to group quantitative data. You can use the same steps to group qualitative data.

Example 2.9 Using Technology to Obtain a Grouped-Data Table

TVs per Household Table 2.8 displays data on the number of TV sets per household for 50 randomly selected households. Use Minitab or Excel to obtain a grouped-data table for these data, based on single-value classes.

Solution Printout 2.1 shows the output obtained by applying the grouping programs to the data on the number of TV sets per household.

Compare the output in Printout 2.1 to the grouped-data table we obtained by hand in Table 2.9. Note, in particular, that both technologies use percents instead of relative frequencies. ◆

PRINTOUT 2.1
Grouped-data table output for the data on the number of TVs per household

MINITAB

Tally for Discrete Variables: TVs

```
TVs  Count   Percent
  0      1      2.00
  1     16     32.00
  2     14     28.00
  3     12     24.00
  4      3      6.00
  5      2      4.00
  6      2      4.00
N=      50
```

EXCEL

Summary of TVs

```
          Total Cases    50
Number of Categories      7
```

TVs Frequency Table

Group	Count	%
0	1	2
1	16	32
2	14	28
3	12	24
4	3	6
5	2	4
6	2	4

Obtaining the Output (Optional)

Printout 2.1 provides output from Minitab and Excel for a grouped-data table based on single-value grouping. Here are detailed instructions for obtaining that output. First, we store the data from Table 2.8 in a column (Minitab) or range (Excel) named TVs. Then, we proceed as follows.

MINITAB

1. Choose **Stat ➤ Tables ➤ Tally...**
2. Specify TVs in the **Variables** text box
3. Select the **Counts** and **Percents** check boxes
4. Click **OK**

EXCEL

1. Choose **DDXL ➤ Tables**
2. Select **Frequency Table** from the **Function type** drop-down box
3. Specify TVs in the **Categorical Variable** text box
4. Click **OK**

TI-83 PLUS

SEE THE TI-83 PLUS MANUAL

Exercises 2.2

Statistical Concepts and Skills

2.11 Identify an important reason for grouping data.

2.12 Do the concepts of cutpoints and midpoints make sense for qualitative data? Explain your answer.

2.13 State three of the most important guidelines in choosing the classes for grouping a data set.

2.14 Explain the difference between
a. frequency and relative frequency.
b. percentage and relative frequency.

2.15 Are frequency distributions or relative-frequency distributions better for comparing two data sets? Explain your answer.

2.16 What are the four elements of a grouped-data table? Explain the meaning of each element.

2.17 With regard to grouping quantitative data into classes that each represent a range of possible values, we discussed two methods for depicting the classes. Identify the two methods and explain the relative advantages and disadvantages of each.

2.18 For grouping quantitative data, we examined three types of classes: (1) $a < b$, (2) $a-b$, and (3) single-value grouping. For each type of data given, decide which of these three types is usually best. Explain your answers.
a. Continuous data displayed to one or more decimal places
b. Discrete data in which there are relatively few distinct observations

2.19 When you group quantitative data into classes that each represent a single possible numerical value, why is it unnecessary to include a midpoint column in the grouped-data table?

2.20 Residential Energy Consumption. The U.S. Energy Information Administration collects data on residential energy consumption and expenditures. Results are published in the document *Residential Energy Consumption Survey: Consumption and Expenditures*. The following table gives 1 year's energy consumptions for a sample of 50 households in the South. Data are in millions of BTUs.

130	55	45	64	155	66	60	80	102	62
58	101	75	111	151	139	81	55	66	90
97	77	51	67	125	50	136	55	83	91
54	86	100	78	93	113	111	104	96	113
96	87	129	109	69	94	99	97	83	97

Use classes of equal width beginning with $40 < 50$ to construct a grouped-data table for these data.

2.21 Clocking the Cheetah. The Cheetah (*Acinonyx jubatus*) is the fastest land mammal on earth and is highly specialized to run down prey. According to the Cheetah Conservation of Southern Africa *Trade Environment Database*, the cheetah often exceeds speeds of 60 mph and has been clocked at speeds of more than 70 mph. The following table, based on information in the database, gives the speeds, in miles per hour, over a 1/4 mile for 35 cheetahs.

57.3	57.5	59.0	56.5	61.3	57.6	59.2
65.0	60.1	59.7	62.6	52.6	60.7	62.3
65.2	54.8	55.4	55.5	57.8	58.7	57.8
60.9	75.3	60.6	58.1	55.9	61.6	59.6
59.8	63.4	54.7	60.2	52.4	58.3	66.0

Use 52 as the first cutpoint and classes of equal width 2 to construct a grouped-data table for these speeds.

2.22 Residential Energy Consumption. Redo Exercise 2.20 by using the alternative method for grouping data based on class limits and class marks.

2.23 Clocking the Cheetah. Redo Exercise 2.21 by using the alternative method for grouping data based on class limits and class marks.

2.24 Household Size. The U.S. Bureau of the Census conducts nationwide surveys on characteristics of U.S. households and publishes the results in *Current Population Reports*. Following are data on the number of people per household for a sample of 40 households. Construct a grouped-data table for these household sizes. Use classes based on a single value.

2	5	2	1	1	2	3	4
1	4	4	2	1	4	3	3
7	1	2	2	3	4	2	2
6	5	2	5	1	3	2	5
2	1	3	3	2	2	3	3

54 CHAPTER 2 Organizing Data

2.25 The Great White Shark. In a recent article entitled "Great White, Deep Trouble" (*National Geographic*, 2000, Vol. 197(4), pp. 2–29), Peter Benchley—the author of *JAWS*—discussed various aspects of the Great White Shark (*Carcharodon carcharias*). The following table, based on information in that article, provides data on the number of pups borne in a lifetime by each of 80 Great White Shark females. Construct an appropriate grouped-data table for these data.

3	5	4	5	5	9	8	7	5	8
9	8	7	6	7	9	4	7	6	8
7	5	8	9	8	8	7	4	5	9
10	4	5	10	8	8	7	7	8	12
7	9	6	9	6	7	7	9	8	9
6	7	11	8	8	8	7	7	10	6
6	8	4	6	5	5	9	7	8	3
6	5	8	7	11	10	7	9	6	6

2.26 Road Rage. The report *Controlling Road Rage: A Literature Review and Pilot Study*, dated June 9, 1999, was prepared for the AAA Foundation for Traffic Safety by Daniel B. Rathbone, Ph.D., and Jorg C. Huckabee, MSCE. The authors discuss the results of a literature review and pilot study on how to prevent aggressive driving and road rage. As described in the study, road rage is criminal behavior by motorists characterized by uncontrolled anger that results in violence or threatened violence on the road. One of the goals of the study was to determine when road rage occurs most often. The following table provides the days on which 69 road rage incidents occurred. Construct a frequency distribution and a relative-frequency distribution for these data.

F	Sa	W	M	Tu	F	Th	M
Tu	F	Tu	F	Su	W	Th	F
Th	W	Th	Sa	W	W	F	F
Tu	Su	Tu	Th	W	Sa	Tu	Th
F	W	F	F	Su	F	Th	Tu
F	Tu	Tu	Tu	Sa	W	W	Sa
F	Sa	Th	W	F	Th	F	M
F	M	F	Su	W	Th	M	Tu
Sa	Th	F	Su	W			

2.27 All-Time Top TV Programs. According to *The World Almanac*, the all-time top television programs by rating (percentage of TV-owning households tuned in to the program)
are as follows. [SOURCE: Nielsen Media Research, January 1961–May 1998.]

Program	Telecast date	Network	Rating (%)	Audience (millions)
M*A*S*H (last episode)	02/28/83	CBS	60.2	50.2
Dallas (Who shot J.R.?)	11/21/80	CBS	53.3	41.5
Roots—Pt. 8	01/30/77	ABC	51.1	36.4
Super Bowl XVI	01/24/82	CBS	49.1	40.0
Super Bowl XVII	01/30/83	NBC	48.6	40.5
XVII Winter Olympics—2d Wed.	02/23/94	CBS	48.5	45.7
Super Bowl XX	01/26/86	NBC	48.3	41.5
Gone With the Wind—Pt. 1	11/07/76	NBC	47.7	34.0
Gone With the Wind—Pt. 2	11/08/76	NBC	47.4	33.8
Super Bowl XII	01/15/78	CBS	47.2	34.4
Super Bowl XIII	01/21/79	NBC	47.1	35.1
Bob Hope Christmas Show	01/15/70	NBC	46.6	27.3
Super Bowl XVIII	01/22/84	CBS	46.4	38.8
Super Bowl XIX	01/20/85	ABC	46.4	39.4
Super Bowl XIV	01/20/80	CBS	46.3	35.3
Super Bowl XXX	01/28/96	NBC	46.0	44.2
ABC Theatre (The Day After)	11/20/83	ABC	46.0	38.6
Roots—Pt. 6	01/28/77	ABC	45.9	32.7
The Fugitive	08/29/67	ABC	45.9	25.7
Super Bowl XXI	01/25/87	CBS	45.8	40.0

Construct frequency and relative-frequency distributions for the network data. (*Hint:* The classes are "ABC," "CBS," and "NBC.")

Extending the Concepts and Skills

The table at the top of the following column gives the closing Dow Jones Industrial Averages (Dow) on April 26, 2000. Use these data in Exercises 2.28–2.30.

2.28 Dow Closing Prices. The column headed "Last" in the Dow table gives the closing price per share, in dollars, for each of the Dow stocks. Construct a grouped-data table for these closing prices. Use equal-width classes and begin with the class $20 \leq 40$.

2.29 Dow Volume. The column headed "Volume" in the Dow table shows the number of shares sold, in hundreds, for each of the Dow stocks.

Symbol	Last	Change	Volume (100s)
AA	65 5/8	-2 7/8	19,185
AXP	164 5/8	-3 3/8	23,266
BA	39 15/16	+15/16	53,383
C	62 1/2	-2	84,208
CAT	39 3/4	-3/8	22,722
DD	49 1/8	-2 1/2	86,721
DIS	42 3/8	+1 7/8	59,216
EK	57 3/4	-1 1/2	17,803
GE	163 1/4	-2 3/4	71,111
GM	92	+2 9/16	83,319
HD	60 1/2	+1 1/2	44,694
HON	55 11/16	-2 1/8	22,325
HWP	140 9/16	+1 1/4	40,317
IBM	110 1/2	-2	61,828
INTC	120 13/16	-4 3/16	237,860
IP	37 3/8	+1/8	41,884
JNJ	82 3/4	-1 9/16	27,400
JPM	134 9/16	-3 3/8	12,554
KO	49 7/16	-1 1/16	47,681
MCD	38 7/8	+1/8	34,793
MMM	88 15/16	-4 7/8	34,783
MO	22 5/16	+1/8	96,863
MRK	71 15/16	-1/2	46,194
MSFT	68	-1 3/8	535,457
PG	60 3/4	-3 1/2	123,028
SBC	44	-15/16	74,473
T	51	-7/8	119,184
UTX	60 5/8	-3 15/16	18,646
WMT	58 3/4	-15/16	52,020
XOM	80 1/8	-7/8	42,090

a. Construct a grouped-data table for these sales volumes. Use the classes 1 < 2, 2 < 3, ..., 9 < 10, and "10 & over," where the values are in millions of sales.
b. Why is there no midpoint for the last class?

2.30 Dow Gains and Losses. The column headed "Change" in the Dow table provides the difference, in dollars, between the closing price per share given in the second column of the table and the closing price per share on the previous trading day. Construct a grouped-data table for the changes, using classes of your choice. Explain your choice of classes.

2.31 Exam Scores. The exam scores for the students in an introductory statistics class are as follows.

88	82	89	70	85
63	100	86	67	39
90	96	76	34	81
64	75	84	89	96

a. Group these exam scores, using the classes 30–39, 40–49, 50–59, 60–69, 70–79, 80–89, and 90–100.
b. What are the widths of the classes?
c. If you wanted all the classes to have the same width, what classes would you use?

Contingency Tables. The methods presented in this section apply to grouping data obtained from observing values of one variable of a population. Such data are called *univariate data*. For instance, in Example 2.6 on page 48, we examined data obtained from observing the values of the variable "weight" for a sample of 18–24-year-old males; those data are univariate. We could have considered not only the weights of the males but also their heights. Then, we would have data on two variables, height and weight. Data obtained from observing values of two variables of a population are called *bivariate data*. Tables called *contingency tables* can be used to group bivariate data, as explained in Exercise 2.32.

2.32 Age and Sex. The following bivariate data on age (in years) and sex were obtained from the students in a freshman calculus course. The data show, for example, that the first student on the list is 21 years old and is a male.

Age	Sex	Age	Sex	Age	Sex	Age	Sex	Age	Sex
21	M	29	F	22	M	23	F	21	F
20	M	20	M	23	M	44	M	28	F
42	F	18	F	19	F	19	M	21	F
21	M	21	M	21	M	21	F	21	F
19	F	26	M	21	F	19	M	24	F
21	F	24	F	21	F	25	M	24	F
19	F	19	M	20	F	21	M	24	F
19	M	25	M	20	F	19	M	23	M
23	M	19	F	20	F	18	F	20	F
20	F	23	M	22	F	18	F	19	M

a. Group these data in the following contingency table. For the first student, place a tally mark in the box labeled by the "21–25" column and the "Male" row, as indicated. Tally the data for the other 49 students.

	Age (yr)			
		Under 21	21–25	Over 25	Total
Sex	Male				
	Female				
	Total				

b. Construct a table like the one in part (a) but with frequencies replacing the tally marks. Add the frequencies in each row and column of your table and record the sums in the proper "Total" boxes.
c. What do the row and column totals in your table in part (b) represent?
d. Add the row totals and add the column totals. Why are those two sums equal, and what does their common value represent?

e. Construct a table that shows the relative frequencies for the data. (*Hint:* Divide each frequency obtained in part (b) by the total of 50 students.)
f. Interpret the entries in your table in part (e) as percentages.

Using Technology

2.33 Clocking the Cheetah. Use the technology of your choice to obtain the grouped-data table required in Exercise 2.21.

2.34 The Great White Shark. Use the technology of your choice to obtain the grouped-data table required in Exercise 2.25.

2.35 All-Time Top TV Programs. Use the technology of your choice to obtain the frequency and relative-frequency distributions required in Exercise 2.27.

2.3 GRAPHS AND CHARTS

Besides grouping, another method for organizing and summarizing data is to draw a picture of some kind. The old saying "a picture is worth a thousand words" has particular relevance in statistics—a graph or chart of a data set often provides the simplest and most efficient display. In this section, we examine various techniques for organizing and summarizing data with graphs and charts. We first discuss histograms, beginning with an illustration of their use in Example 2.10.

Example 2.10 *Histograms*

Days to Maturity for Short-Term Investments Table 2.4 in Section 2.2 shows a grouped-data table for the number of days to maturity for 40 short-term investments. The first three columns of that table are repeated here in Table 2.12. Obtain graphical displays for these grouped data.

Solution One way to display these grouped data pictorially is to construct a graph, called a **frequency histogram,** that depicts the classes on the horizontal axis and the frequencies on the vertical axis. A frequency histogram for the days-to-maturity data is shown in Fig. 2.2(a).

Here are some important observations about Fig. 2.2(a).

- The height of each bar is equal to the frequency of the class it represents.
- The bar for each class extends from the lower cutpoint of the class to the upper cutpoint of the class.[5]

---

[5]This method is only one of several that can be used to depict the classes on the horizontal axis. Another common method is to use midpoints instead of cutpoints to label the horizontal axis. In that case, each bar is centered over the midpoint of the class it represents.

FIGURE 2.2
Days-to-maturity:
(a) frequency histogram;
(b) relative-frequency histogram

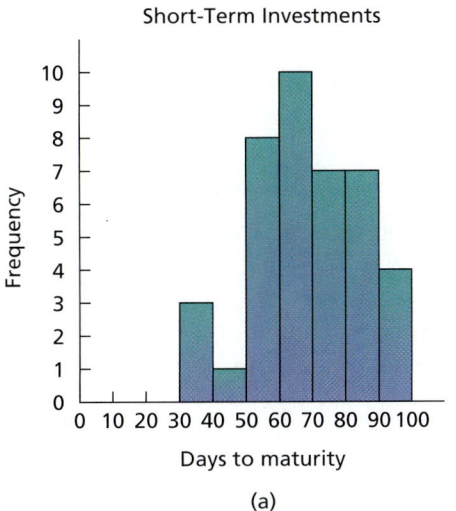
(a)

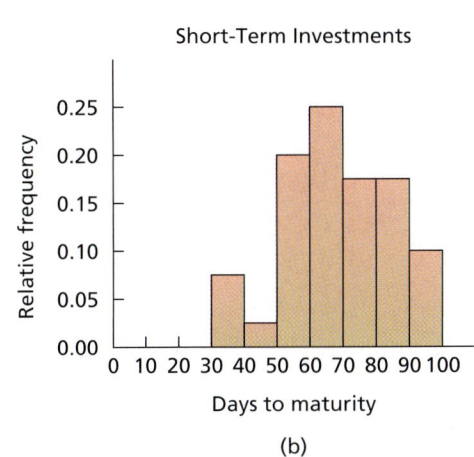
(b)

TABLE 2.12
Frequency and relative-frequency distributions for the days-to-maturity data

Days to maturity	Frequency	Relative frequency
30 ≤ 40	3	0.075
40 ≤ 50	1	0.025
50 ≤ 60	8	0.200
60 ≤ 70	10	0.250
70 ≤ 80	7	0.175
80 ≤ 90	7	0.175
90 ≤ 100	4	0.100
	40	1.000

- Each axis of the frequency histogram has a label, and the frequency histogram as a whole has a title.

A frequency histogram displays the frequencies of the classes. To display the relative frequencies (or percentages), we use a **relative-frequency histogram**, which is similar to a frequency histogram. The only difference is that the height of each bar in a relative-frequency histogram is equal to the relative frequency of the class instead of the frequency of the class. A relative-frequency histogram for the days-to-maturity data is shown in Fig. 2.2(b).

Note that the shapes of the relative-frequency histogram in Fig. 2.2(b) and the frequency histogram in Fig. 2.2(a) are identical. The reason is that the frequencies and relative frequencies are proportional.

DEFINITION 2.4 **Frequency and Relative-Frequency Histograms**

Frequency histogram: A graph that displays the classes on the horizontal axis and the frequencies of the classes on the vertical axis. The frequency of each class is represented by a vertical bar whose height is equal to the frequency of the class.

Relative-frequency histogram: A graph that displays the classes on the horizontal axis and the relative frequencies of the classes on the vertical axis. The relative frequency of each class is represented by a vertical bar whose height is equal to the relative frequency of the class.

For purposes of visually comparing the distributions of two data sets, relative-frequency histograms are better than frequency histograms. The same vertical scale is used for all relative-frequency histograms—a minimum of 0 and a maximum of 1—making direct comparison easy. In contrast, the vertical scale of a frequency histogram depends on the number of observations, making comparison more difficult.

HISTOGRAMS FOR SINGLE-VALUE GROUPING

For the days-to-maturity data, each class represents a range of possible days to maturity, and in Figs. 2.2(a) and 2.2(b) the histogram bar for each class extends over that range. When data are grouped into classes based on a single value, the procedure is somewhat different. In that case, each bar is centered over the only possible value in the class, as illustrated in Example 2.11.

Example 2.11 Histograms for Single-Value Grouped Data

TVs per Household In Example 2.7, we considered data on the number of television sets per household for 50 randomly selected U.S. households. We used classes based on a single value to group those data. The frequency and relative-frequency distributions are given in Table 2.9 in Section 2.2 and are repeated here in Table 2.13. Construct a frequency histogram and a relative-frequency histogram for these grouped data.

TABLE 2.13
Frequency and relative-frequency distributions for number of TV sets

Number of TVs	Frequency	Relative frequency
0	1	0.020
1	16	0.320
2	14	0.280
3	12	0.240
4	3	0.060
5	2	0.040
6	2	0.040
	50	1.000

Solution For single-value grouping, we place the middle of each histogram bar directly over the single value represented by the class. Hence the frequency and relative-frequency histograms for the grouped data in Table 2.13 are those depicted in Figs. 2.3(a) and (b).

Note the symbol // on the horizontal axes in Figs. 2.3(a) and (b). This symbol indicates that the zero point on that axis is not in its usual position at the intersection of the horizontal and vertical axes. Whenever any such modification is made, whether on the horizontal axis or vertical axis, the symbol // or some similar symbol should be used to indicate that fact.

2.3 Graphs and Charts

FIGURE 2.3
Number of TVs per household:
(a) frequency histogram;
(b) relative-frequency histogram

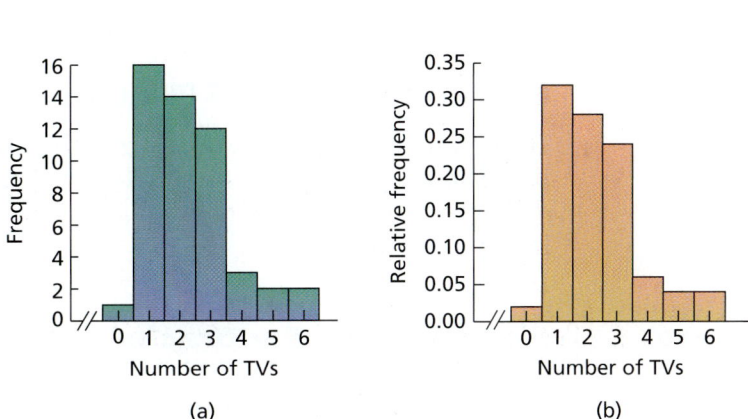

DOTPLOTS

Another type of graphical display for quantitative data is the **dotplot.** Dotplots are particularly useful for showing the relative positions of the data in a data set or for comparing two or more data sets. We introduce dotplots in Example 2.12.

Example 2.12 Dotplots

TABLE 2.14
Prices, in dollars, of 16 DVD players

210	212	209	199	197	199
224	219	212	215	199	210
208	219	214	219		

Prices of DVD Players One of Professor Weiss's sons was interested in adding a new DVD player to his home theater system. He decided to use the Internet to shop and went to Price Watch U.S.A. There he found 16 quotes on different brands and styles of DVD players. The prices, in dollars, are listed in Table 2.14. Construct a dotplot for these data.

Solution To construct a dotplot for the data in Table 2.14, we begin by drawing a horizontal axis that displays the possible prices. Then we record each price by placing a dot over the appropriate value on the horizontal axis. For instance, the first price is $210, which calls for a dot over the "210" on the horizontal axis. The dotplot for the data in Table 2.14 is shown in Fig. 2.4.

FIGURE 2.4
Dotplot for prices of DVD players

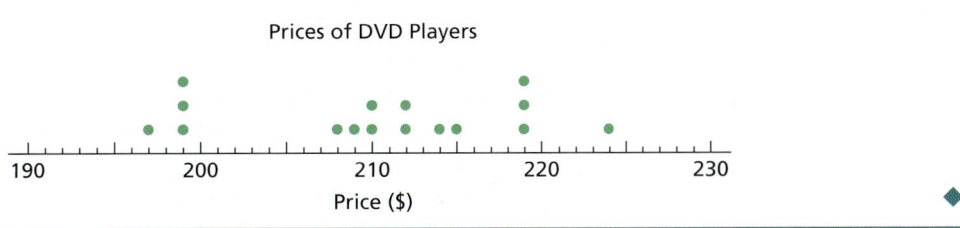

Note that dotplots are similar to histograms. In fact, when data are grouped in classes based on a single value, a dotplot and a frequency histogram are essentially identical. However, for single-value grouped data that involve decimals, dotplots are generally preferable to histograms because they are easier to construct and use.

GRAPHICAL DISPLAYS FOR QUALITATIVE DATA

Histograms and dotplots are designed for use with quantitative data. Qualitative data are portrayed with different techniques. Two common methods for displaying qualitative data graphically are *pie charts* and *bar graphs,* as illustrated in Example 2.13.

Example 2.13 Pie Charts and Bar Graphs

Political Party Affiliations In Example 2.8, we obtained frequency and relative-frequency distributions for the political party affiliations of the students in Professor Weiss's introductory statistics class. We repeat those distributions in Table 2.15. Display the relative-frequency distribution of these qualitative data with a

a. pie chart.
b. bar graph.

TABLE 2.15
Frequency and relative-frequency distributions for political party affiliations

Party	Frequency	Relative frequency
Democratic	13	0.325
Republican	18	0.450
Other	9	0.225
	40	1.000

Solution a. A **pie chart** is a disk divided into wedge-shaped pieces that are proportional to the relative frequencies. In this case, we need to divide a disk into three wedge-shaped pieces that comprise 32.5%, 45.0%, and 22.5% of the disk. We do so by using a protractor and the fact that there are 360° in a circle. Thus, for instance, the first piece of the disk is obtained by marking off 117° (32.5% of 360°). The pie chart for the relative-frequency distribution in Table 2.15 is shown in Fig. 2.5(a).
b. A **bar graph** is like a histogram. However, to avoid confusing bar graphs and histograms, we position the bars in a bar graph so that they do not touch each other. The bar graph for the relative-frequency distribution in Table 2.15 is shown in Fig. 2.5(b). ◆

Histograms, dotplots, pie charts, and bar graphs are only a few of the countless ways that data can be portrayed pictorially. We will consider some additional graphical displays in the exercises for this section.

2.3 Graphs and Charts 61

FIGURE 2.5
Political party affiliations:
(a) pie chart;
(b) bar graph

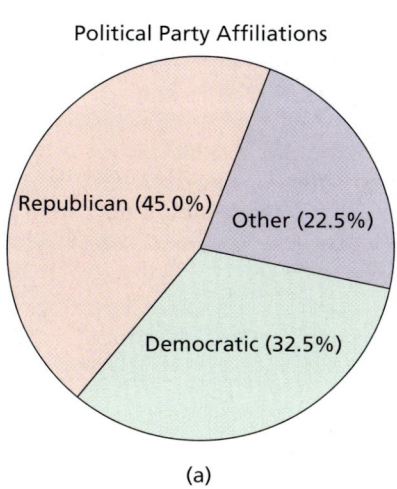

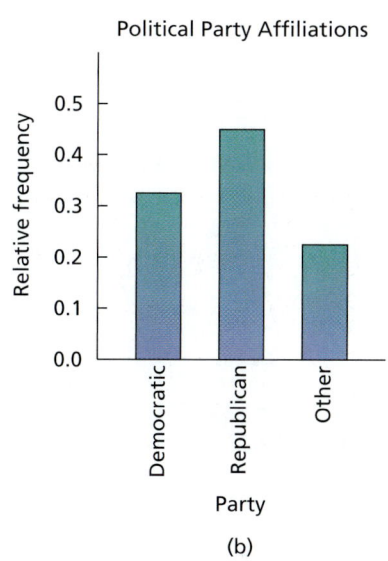

The Technology Center

Most statistical software packages and some graphing calculators have built-in programs for constructing histograms, dotplots, pie charts, and bar graphs. In this subsection, we present output and optional step-by-step instructions for obtaining a frequency histogram. Refer to the technology manuals for producing dotplots, pie charts, and bar graphs.

Example 2.14 **Using Technology to Obtain Histograms**

Days to Maturity for Short-Term Investments Use Minitab, Excel, or the TI-83 Plus to obtain a frequency histogram of the days-to-maturity data displayed in Table 2.1 on page 45.

Solution Printout 2.2 on the next page shows the output obtained by applying the histogram programs to the days-to-maturity data.

Some technologies require the user to specify the classes that are used for the construction of a histogram; others (e.g., Excel) automatically choose the classes; and still others (e.g., Minitab and the TI-83 Plus) give the user the choice of either specifying the classes or letting the program do it.

We obtained all three histograms in Printout 2.2 by letting the programs automatically choose the classes. This choice explains why the three histograms differ from each other and from the histogram we constructed by hand in Fig. 2.2(a) on page 57. Refer to the technology manuals for instructions to obtain histograms that are based on user-specified classes.

If the option is available, letting the technology automatically choose the classes for construction of a histogram is fast and easy. For most of our applications of histograms, the automatic method is sufficient for the required tasks. ◆

Obtaining the Output (Optional)

Printout 2.2 provides output from Minitab, Excel, and the TI-83 Plus for a histogram of the days-to-maturity data. Here are detailed instructions for obtaining that output. First, we store the data from Table 2.1 in a column (Minitab), range (Excel), or list (TI-83 Plus) named DAYS. Then, we proceed as follows.

MINITAB	EXCEL	TI-83 PLUS
1 Choose **Graph ➤ Histogram...** 2 Specify DAYS in the **X** text box for **Graph 1** 3 Click **OK**	1 Choose **DDXL ➤ Charts and Plots** 2 Select **Histogram** from the **Function type** drop-down box 3 Specify DAYS in the **Quantitative Variable** text box 4 Click **OK**	1 Press **2nd ➤ STAT PLOT** and then press **ENTER** twice 2 Arrow to the third graph icon and press **ENTER** 3 Press the down-arrow key 4 Press **2nd ➤ LIST** 5 Arrow down to DAYS and press **ENTER** 6 Press **ZOOM** and then **9** (and then **TRACE**, if desired)

PRINTOUT 2.2
Histogram output for the days-to-maturity data

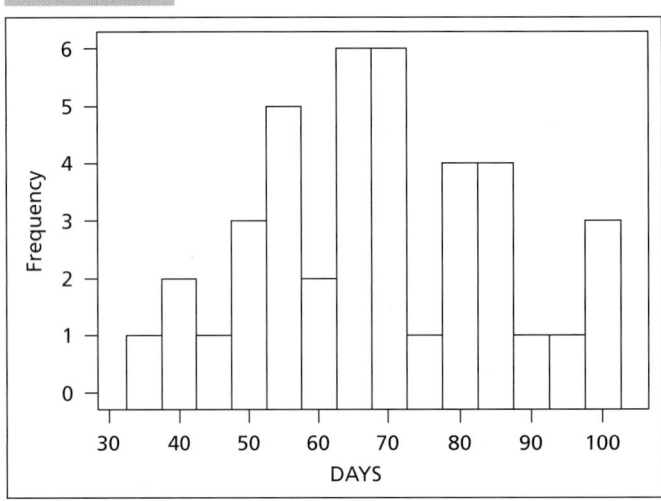

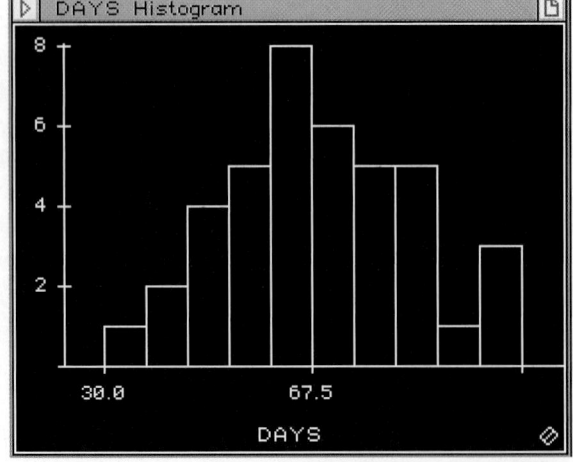

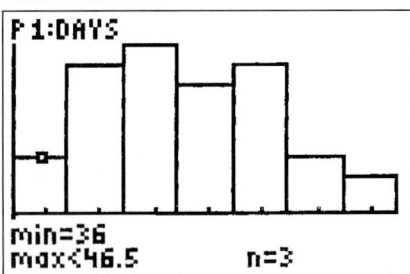

Exercises 2.3

Statistical Concepts and Skills

2.36 Explain the advantages and disadvantages of histograms relative to grouped-data tables.

2.37 Explain the difference between a frequency histogram and a relative-frequency histogram.

2.38 For data that are grouped in classes based on more than a single value, cutpoints are used on the horizontal axis of a histogram for depicting the classes. But, midpoints can also be used, in which case each bar is centered over the midpoint of the class it represents. Explain the advantages and disadvantages of each method.

2.39 In a bar graph, unlike in a histogram, the bars do not abut. Give a reason for that.

2.40 Some users of statistics prefer pie charts to bar graphs because people are accustomed to having the horizontal axis of a graph show order. For example, someone might infer from Fig. 2.5(b) on page 61 that "Republican" is less than "Other" because "Republican" is shown to the left of "Other" on the horizontal axis. Pie charts do not lead to such inferences. Give other advantages and disadvantages of each method.

2.41 DVD Players. Refer to Example 2.12 on page 59.
a. Explain why a frequency histogram of the DVD prices with classes based on a single value would be essentially identical to the dotplot shown in Fig. 2.4.
b. Would the dotplot and a frequency histogram be essentially identical if the classes for the histogram are not each based on a single value? Explain your answer.

2.42 Residential Energy Consumption. Shown in the following table are frequency and relative-frequency distributions for the data given in Exercise 2.20 on 1 year's energy consumptions for a sample of 50 households in the South.

Energy consumption (millions of BTU)	Frequency	Relative frequency
40 < 50	1	0.02
50 < 60	7	0.14
60 < 70	7	0.14
70 < 80	3	0.06
80 < 90	6	0.12
90 < 100	10	0.20
100 < 110	5	0.10
110 < 120	4	0.08
120 < 130	2	0.04
130 < 140	3	0.06
140 < 150	0	0.00
150 < 160	2	0.04

a. Construct a frequency histogram.
b. Construct a relative-frequency histogram.

2.43 Clocking the Cheetah. The following table provides frequency and relative-frequency distributions for the data presented in Exercise 2.21 on the speeds in miles per hour for a sample of 35 cheetahs.

Speed (mph)	Frequency	Relative frequency
52 < 54	2	0.057
54 < 56	5	0.143
56 < 58	6	0.171
58 < 60	8	0.229
60 < 62	7	0.200
62 < 64	3	0.086
64 < 66	2	0.057
66 < 68	1	0.029
68 < 70	0	0.000
70 < 72	0	0.000
72 < 74	0	0.000
74 < 76	1	0.029

a. Construct a frequency histogram.
b. Construct a relative-frequency histogram.

2.44 Household Size. The following table gives frequency and relative-frequency distributions for the data given in Exercise 2.24 on the number of people per household for a sample of 40 U.S. households.

Number of people	Frequency	Relative frequency
1	7	0.175
2	13	0.325
3	9	0.225
4	5	0.125
5	4	0.100
6	1	0.025
7	1	0.025

a. Construct a frequency histogram.
b. Construct a relative-frequency histogram.

2.45 The Great White Shark. The following table presents frequency and relative-frequency distributions for the data presented in Exercise 2.25 on the number of pups borne in a lifetime by each of 80 Great White Shark females.

Number of pups	Frequency	Relative frequency
3	2	0.025
4	5	0.063
5	10	0.125
6	11	0.138
7	17	0.213
8	17	0.213
9	11	0.138
10	4	0.050
11	2	0.025
12	1	0.013

a. Construct a frequency histogram.
b. Construct a relative-frequency histogram.

2.46 Exam Scores. Construct a dotplot for the following exam scores of the students in an introductory statistics class.

88	82	89	70	85
63	100	86	67	39
90	96	76	34	81
64	75	84	89	96

2.47 Ages of Trucks. The Motor Vehicle Manufacturers Association of the United States publishes information in *Motor Vehicle Facts and Figures* on the ages of cars and trucks currently in use. A sample of 37 trucks provided the ages, in years, displayed in the following table. Construct a dotplot for the ages.

8	12	14	16	15	5	11	13
4	12	12	15	12	3	10	9
11	3	18	4	9	11	17	
7	4	12	12	8	9	10	
9	9	1	7	6	9	7	

2.48 Road Rage. The following table shows frequency and relative-frequency distributions for the data given in Exercise 2.26 on the days on which 69 road rage incidents occurred.

Day	Frequency	Relative frequency
Su	5	0.072
M	5	0.072
Tu	11	0.159
W	12	0.174
Th	11	0.159
F	18	0.261
Sa	7	0.101

a. Draw a pie chart for the relative frequencies.
b. Construct a bar graph for the relative frequencies.

2.49 All-Time Top TV Programs. The following table presents frequency and relative-frequency distributions for the network data presented in Exercise 2.27 on the all-time top television programs by rating (percentage of TV-owning households tuned in to the program) as of May 1998.

Network	Frequency	Relative frequency
CBS	8	0.40
ABC	5	0.25
NBC	7	0.35

a. Draw a pie chart for the relative frequencies.
b. Construct a bar graph for the relative frequencies.

2.50 Adjusted Gross Incomes. The Internal Revenue Service (IRS) publishes data on adjusted gross incomes in *Statistics of Income, Individual Income Tax Returns*. The following relative-frequency histogram shows 1 year's individual income tax returns for adjusted gross incomes of less than $50,000.

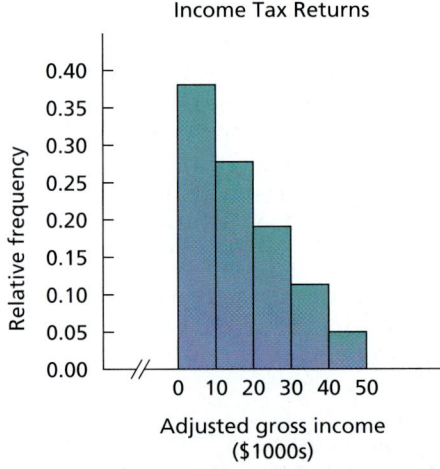

Use the histogram and the fact that adjusted gross incomes are expressed to the nearest whole dollar to answer each of the following questions.
a. Approximately what percentage of the individual income tax returns had an adjusted gross income between $10,000 and $19,999, inclusive?
b. Approximately what percentage had an adjusted gross income of less than $30,000?
c. The IRS reported that 89,928,000 individual income tax returns had an adjusted gross income of less than $50,000. Approximately how many had an adjusted gross income between $30,000 and $49,999, inclusive?

2.51 Cholesterol Levels. A pediatrician who tested the cholesterol levels of several young patients was alarmed to find that many had levels higher than 200 mg per 100 mL. The following relative-frequency histogram shows the readings for some patients who had high cholesterol levels.

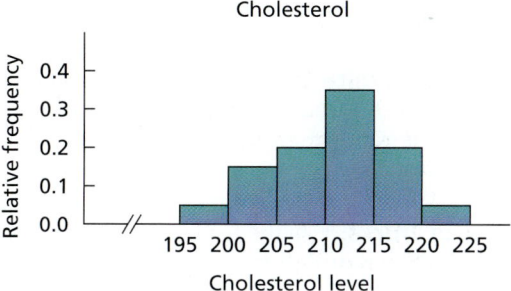

Use the graph to answer the following questions. Note that cholesterol levels are always expressed as whole numbers.
a. What percentage of the patients have cholesterol levels between 205 and 209, inclusive?
b. What percentage of the patients have levels of 215 or higher?
c. If the number of patients is 20, how many have levels between 210 and 214, inclusive?

Extending the Concepts and Skills

Relative-Frequency Polygons. Another graphical display commonly used is the relative-frequency polygon. In a *relative-frequency polygon*, a point is plotted above each class midpoint at a height equal to the relative frequency of the class. Then the points are connected with lines. For instance, the days-to-maturity data given in Table 2.4 on page 47 yield the following relative-frequency polygon.

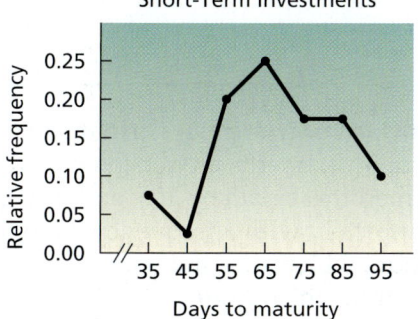

2.52 Residential Energy Consumption. Construct a relative-frequency polygon for the energy-consumption data given in Exercise 2.42.

Ogives. Cumulative information can be portrayed using a graph called an *ogive* (ō′jīv). To construct an ogive, first make a table that displays cumulative frequencies and cumulative relative frequencies, as shown in Table 2.16 for the days-to-maturity data.

TABLE 2.16
Cumulative information for days-to-maturity data

Less than	Cumulative frequency	Cumulative relative frequency
30	0	0.000
40	3	0.075
50	4	0.100
60	12	0.300
70	22	0.550
80	29	0.725
90	36	0.900
100	40	1.000

The first column of Table 2.16 gives the cutpoints of the classes and the second column gives the cumulative frequencies. A *cumulative frequency* is obtained by summing the frequencies of all classes representing values less than the specified cutpoint. For instance, by referring to Table 2.12 on page 57, we can find the cumulative frequency of investments with a maturity period of less than 50 days:

$$\text{Cumulative frequency} = 3 + 1 = 4.$$

That is, four of the investments have a maturity period of less than 50 days.

The third column of Table 2.16 gives the cumulative relative frequencies. A *cumulative relative frequency* is found by dividing the corresponding cumulative frequency by the total number of observations which, in this case, is 40. For instance, the cumulative relative frequency of investments with a maturity period of less than 50 days is

$$\text{cumulative relative frequency} = \frac{4}{40} = 0.100.$$

That is, 10% of the investments have a maturity period of less than 50 days.

Using Table 2.16, we can now construct an ogive for the days-to-maturity data. In an ogive, a point is plotted above each cutpoint at a height equal to the cumulative relative frequency. Then the points are connected with lines. The ogive for the days-to-maturity data is as follows.

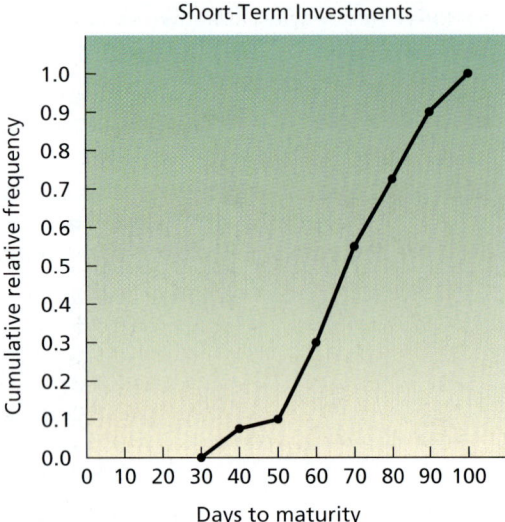

2.53 Residential Energy Consumption. Refer to Exercise 2.42.
a. Construct a table similar to Table 2.16 for the energy-consumption data. Interpret your results.
b. Draw an ogive for the data.

Using Technology

2.54 Clocking the Cheetah. Use the technology of your choice to obtain a frequency histogram and a relative-frequency (or percent) histogram, as required in Exercise 2.43. The raw (ungrouped) data are given in Exercise 2.21 on page 53.

2.55 The Great White Shark. Use the technology of your choice to obtain the frequency histogram required in Exercise 2.45. The raw (ungrouped) data are given in Exercise 2.25 on page 54.

2.56 Ages of Trucks. Use the technology of your choice to obtain the dotplot required in Exercise 2.47.

2.57 All-Time Top TV Programs. Use the technology of your choice to obtain the pie chart and bar graph required in Exercise 2.49. The raw data are given in Exercise 2.27 on page 54.

2.4 STEM-AND-LEAF DIAGRAMS

New ways of displaying data are constantly being invented. One method, developed in the 1960s by the late Professor John Tukey of Princeton University, is called a *stem-and-leaf diagram,* or *stemplot.* This ingenious diagram is often easier to construct than either a frequency distribution or a histogram and generally displays more information. Returning once more to the days-to-maturity data, we illustrate stem-and-leaf diagrams in Example 2.15.

Example 2.15 Stem-and-Leaf Diagrams

Days to Maturity for Short-Term Investments The data on the number of days to maturity for 40 short-term investments are repeated in Table 2.17.

In Table 2.2 on page 45, we grouped these data by 10s, and in Fig. 2.2(a) on page 57, we portrayed the data graphically with a frequency histogram. Now we construct a stem-and-leaf diagram, which simultaneously groups the data and yields a graphical display similar to a histogram.

First, we select the leading digits from the data in Table 2.17, or 3, 4, ..., 9. Next, we list those leading digits in a column, as shown to the left of the vertical rule in Fig. 2.6(a).

Then we write the final digit of each number from Table 2.17 to the right of the appropriate leading digit: The first investment has a maturity period of 70 days, which calls for a 0 to the right of the leading digit, 7. Reading down the

TABLE 2.17
Days to maturity for 40 short-term investments

70	64	99	55	64	89	87	65
62	38	67	70	60	69	78	39
75	56	71	51	99	68	95	86
57	53	47	50	55	81	80	98
51	36	63	66	85	79	83	70

first column of Table 2.17, we find that the second investment has a maturity period of 62 days, which calls for a 2 to the right of the leading digit, 6.

Continuing in this manner, we obtain the diagram displayed in Fig. 2.6(a). As indicated in the figure, the leading digits are called **stems** and the final digits **leaves;** the entire diagram is called a **stem-and-leaf diagram.**

FIGURE 2.6
Diagrams for days-to-maturity data: (a) stem-and-leaf; (b) shaded stem-and-leaf; (c) ordered stem-and-leaf

Stems	Leaves
3	8 6 9
4	7
5	7 1 6 3 5 1 0 5
6	2 4 7 3 6 4 0 9 8 5
7	0 5 1 0 9 8 0
8	5 9 1 7 0 3 6
9	9 9 5 8

(a)

3	8 6 9
4	7
5	7 1 6 3 5 1 0 5
6	2 4 7 3 6 4 0 9 8 5
7	0 5 1 0 9 8 0
8	5 9 1 7 0 3 6
9	9 9 5 8

(b)

3	6 8 9
4	7
5	0 1 1 3 5 5 6 7
6	0 2 3 4 4 5 6 7 8 9
7	0 0 0 1 5 8 9
8	0 1 3 5 6 7 9
9	5 8 9 9

(c)

The stem-and-leaf diagram for the days-to-maturity data is similar to a frequency histogram for those data because the length of the row of leaves for a class equals the frequency of the class. [Turn the stem-and-leaf diagram 90° counterclockwise, and compare it to the frequency histogram shown in Fig. 2.2(a) on page 57.]

By shading each row of leaves, as in Fig. 2.6(b), we get a diagram that looks even more like a frequency histogram of the data. It is called a **shaded stem-and-leaf diagram.** Because the numbers in it are still visible under the shading, a shaded stem-and-leaf diagram exhibits the raw (ungrouped) data in addition to providing a graphical display of a frequency distribution. Although a frequency histogram provides a graphical display of a frequency distribution, recovering the raw data from a frequency histogram generally is not possible.

Another form of stem-and-leaf diagram is called an **ordered stem-and-leaf diagram,** in which the leaves in each row are ordered from smallest to largest. Ordering makes the data easier to comprehend and facilitates computation of descriptive measures such as the median (discussed in Chapter 3). The ordered stem-and-leaf diagram for the days-to-maturity data is presented in Fig. 2.6(c). ◆

In Example 2.16, we describe use of the stem-and-leaf diagram for three-digit numbers.

Example 2.16 *Stem-and-Leaf Diagrams*

Cholesterol Levels A pediatrician tested the cholesterol levels of several young patients and was alarmed to find that many had levels higher than 200 mg per 100 mL. The readings of 20 patients with high levels are presented in Table 2.18. Construct a stem-and-leaf diagram for these data.

TABLE 2.18 Cholesterol levels for 20 high-level patients

210	209	212	208	217	207	210
203	208	210	210	199	215	221
213	218	202	218	200	214	

Solution Because these data are three-digit numbers, we use the first two digits as the stems and the third digit as the leaves. A stem-and-leaf diagram for the cholesterol levels is displayed in Fig. 2.7(a).

FIGURE 2.7 Stem-and-leaf diagram for cholesterol levels:
(a) one line per stem;
(b) two lines per stem

```
19 | 9                          19 |
20 | 8 2 9 7 0 8 3              19 | 9
21 | 0 7 5 0 8 2 0 0 3 8 4      20 | 2 0 3
22 | 1                          20 | 8 9 7 8
                                21 | 0 0 2 0 0 3 4
                                21 | 7 5 8 8
                                22 | 1
                                22 |
         (a)                           (b)
```

The stem-and-leaf diagram in Fig. 2.7(a) is only moderately helpful because there are so few stems. We can construct a better stem-and-leaf diagram by using two lines for each stem, with the first line for the leaf digits 0–4 and the second line for the leaf digits 5–9. This stem-and-leaf diagram is shown in Fig. 2.7(b). ◆

Although stem-and-leaf diagrams have several advantages over the more classical techniques for grouping and graphing, they do have some drawbacks. For instance, they are generally not useful with large data sets and can be awkward with data containing many digits; histograms are usually preferable to stem-and-leaf diagrams in such cases.

The Technology Center

Some technologies (e.g., Minitab) have built-in programs for constructing stem-and-leaf diagrams, but others (e.g., Excel and the TI-83 Plus) do not. Refer to the technology manuals for detailed instructions on obtaining stem-and-leaf diagrams—provided, of course, such plots are available in the technology under consideration. See Exercise 2.70 on page 70 for an example of a stem-and-leaf diagram generated by Minitab.

Exercises 2.4

Statistical Concepts and Skills

2.58 Discuss the relative advantages and disadvantages of stem-and-leaf diagrams and frequency histograms.

2.59 Suppose that you have a data set that contains a large number of observations. Which graphical display is generally preferable: a histogram or a stem-and-leaf diagram? Explain your answer.

2.60 Explain why the raw data generally cannot be recovered from a frequency histogram. Under what circumstances is recovering the raw data possible?

2.61 Suppose that you have constructed a stem-and-leaf diagram and discover that it is only moderately useful because there are too few stems. How can you remedy the problem?

2.62 Contents of Soft Drinks. A soft-drink bottler fills bottles with soda. For quality assurance purposes, filled bottles are sampled to ensure that they contain close to the content indicated on the label. A sample of 30 "one-liter" bottles of soda contain the amounts, in milliliters, shown in the following table.

1025	977	1018	975	977
990	959	957	1031	964
986	914	1010	988	1028
989	1001	984	974	1017
1060	1030	991	999	997
996	1014	946	995	987

Using the stems 91, 92, ..., 106,
a. construct a stem-and-leaf diagram.
b. construct an ordered stem-and-leaf diagram.

2.63 Stressed-Out Bus Drivers. Frustrated passengers, congested streets, time schedules, and air and noise pollution are just some of the physical and social pressures that lead many urban bus drivers to retire prematurely with disabilities such as coronary heart disease and stomach disorders. An intervention program designed by the Stockholm Transit District was implemented to improve the work conditions of the city's bus drivers. Improvements were evaluated by Evans et al., who collected physiological and psychological data for bus drivers who drove the improved routes (intervention) and for drivers who were assigned the normal routes (control). Their findings were published in the article "Hassles on the Job: A Study of a Job Intervention with Urban Bus Drivers" (*Journal of Organizational Behavior*, 1999, Vol. 20, pp. 199–208). Following are data based on the results of the study for the heart rates, in beats per minute, of the control drivers.

74	52	67	63	77	57	80	77
53	76	54	73	54	60	77	63
60	68	64	66	71	66	55	71
84	63	73	59	68	64	82	

a. Construct a stem-and-leaf diagram having one line per stem.
b. Construct an ordered stem-and-leaf diagram having one line per stem.
c. Repeat parts (a) and (b) for two lines per stem.

2.64 High School Completion Rates. As reported by the U.S. Bureau of the Census in *Current Population Reports*, the percentage of adults in each state and the District of Columbia who have completed high school is as follows.

State	Percent	State	Percent	State	Percent
AL	79	KY	78	ND	84
AK	91	LA	79	OH	86
AZ	82	ME	87	OK	85
AR	77	MD	85	OR	86
CA	80	MA	86	PA	84
CO	90	MI	85	RI	81
CT	84	MN	89	SC	79
DE	85	MS	77	SD	86
DC	84	MO	83	TN	77
FL	82	MT	89	TX	78
GA	80	NE	88	UT	89
HI	85	NV	89	VT	87
ID	83	NH	84	VA	83
IL	84	NJ	87	WA	92
IN	84	NM	80	WV	76
IA	88	NY	82	WI	88
KS	89	NC	81	WY	90

Construct a stem-and-leaf diagram for these percentages with
a. one line per stem.
b. two lines per stem.
c. five lines per stem.
d. Which stem-and-leaf diagram do you consider most useful? Explain your answer.

2.65 Crime Rates. The U.S. Federal Bureau of Investigation published the following annual crime rates in *Crime in the United States*. Rates are per 1000 population.

State	Rate	State	Rate	State	Rate
AL	49	LA	64	OH	45
AK	52	ME	31	OK	55
AZ	72	MD	57	OR	63
AR	47	MA	37	PA	34
CA	49	MI	49	RI	37
CO	47	MN	44	SC	61
CT	40	MS	46	SD	32
DE	51	MO	48	TN	55
FL	73	MT	44	TX	55
GA	58	NE	43	UT	60
HI	60	NV	60	VT	28
ID	39	NH	26	VA	39
IL	51	NJ	41	WA	59
IN	45	NM	69	WV	25
IA	38	NY	39	WI	37
KS	46	NC	55	WY	41
KY	31	ND	27		

Construct a stem-and-leaf diagram for these crime rates with
a. one line per stem.
b. two lines per stem.
c. five lines per stem.
d. Which stem-and-leaf diagram do you consider most useful? Explain your answer.

Extending the Concepts and Skills

Further Stem-and-Leaf Techniques. We mentioned earlier that the use of stem-and-leaf diagrams can be awkward with data that contain many digits. In such cases, we can either round or truncate each observation to a suitable number of digits. Exercises 2.66 and 2.67 involve rounding and truncating numbers for use in stem-and-leaf diagrams.

2.66 Weights of Males. The U.S. National Center for Health Statistics publishes data on weights and heights by age and sex in *Vital and Health Statistics*. The following weights, to the nearest tenth of a pound, were obtained from a sample of 18–24-year-old males.

129.2	185.3	218.1	182.5	142.8
155.2	170.0	151.3	187.5	145.6
167.3	161.0	178.7	165.0	172.5
191.1	150.7	187.0	173.7	178.2
161.7	170.1	165.8	214.6	136.7
278.8	175.6	188.7	132.1	158.5
146.4	209.1	175.4	182.0	173.6
149.9	158.6			

a. Round each observation to the nearest pound and then construct a stem-and-leaf diagram of the rounded data.
b. Truncate each observation by dropping the decimal part and then construct a stem-and-leaf diagram of the truncated data.
c. Compare the stem-and-leaf diagrams obtained in parts (a) and (b).

2.67 Contents of Soft Drinks. Refer to Exercise 2.62.
a. Round each observation to the nearest 10 mL, drop the terminal 0s, and then obtain a stem-and-leaf diagram of the resulting data.
b. Truncate each observation by dropping the units digit and then construct a stem-and-leaf diagram of the truncated data.
c. Compare the stem-and-leaf diagrams that you obtained in parts (a) and (b) with each other and with the one obtained in Exercise 2.62.

Using Technology

2.68 High School Completion Rates. Use the technology of your choice to construct the stem-and-leaf diagrams required in Exercise 2.64.

2.69 Crime Rates. Use the technology of your choice to construct the stem-and-leaf diagrams required in Exercise 2.65.

2.70 NBA Leading Scorers. The National Basketball Association (NBA) provides information on average points per game for leading scorers on the Web site www.nba.com. A random sample of 24 NBA scoring leaders for the 1999–2000 season gave the following data on average points per game (PPG).

Player	PPG	Player	PPG
Grant Hill	25.8	Eddie Jones	20.1
Alonzo Mourning	21.7	Mitch Richmond	17.4
Jerry Stackhouse	23.6	Allen Iverson	28.4
Derrick Coleman	16.7	Tim Duncan	23.2
Steve Smith	14.9	Antonio McDyess	19.1
Darrell Armstrong	16.2	Cliff Robinson	18.5
Shaquille O'Neal	29.7	Steve Francis	18.0
Gary Payton	24.2	Tracy McGrady	15.4
Michael Finley	22.6	Chris Webber	24.5
Vince Carter	25.7	Kobe Bryant	22.5
Sam Cassell	18.6	Ray Allen	22.1
Larry Hughes	15.0	Rasheed Wallace	16.4

The following Minitab printout displays a stem-and-leaf diagram for the data on average number of points per game.

The second column gives the stems and the third column gives the leaves.

```
Stem-and-leaf of PPG       N  = 24
Leaf Unit = 1.0

    3    1 455
    7    1 6667
   11    1 8889
   (2)   2 01
   11    2 22233
    6    2 4455
    2    2
    2    2 89
```

Did Minitab use rounding or truncation to obtain this stem-and-leaf diagram? Explain your answer.

2.5 DISTRIBUTION SHAPES; SYMMETRY AND SKEWNESS

In this section, we discuss distributions and their associated properties. To begin, we present a formal definition for the **distribution of a data set.**

DEFINITION 2.5   **Distribution of a Data Set**

The *distribution of a data set* is a table, graph, or formula that provides the values of the observations and how often they occur.

Up to now, we have portrayed distributions of data sets by frequency distributions, relative-frequency distributions, frequency histograms, relative-frequency histograms, dotplots, stem-and-leaf diagrams, pie charts, and bar graphs.

An important aspect of the distribution of a quantitative data set is its shape. Indeed, as we demonstrate in later chapters, the shape of a distribution frequently plays a role in determining the appropriate method of statistical analysis. To identify the shape of a distribution, the best approach usually is to use a smooth curve that approximates the overall shape.

For instance, Fig. 2.8 on the following page displays a relative-frequency histogram for the heights of the 3264 female students who attend a midwestern college. Also included in Fig. 2.8 is a smooth curve that approximates the overall shape of the distribution. Both the histogram and the smooth curve show that this distribution of heights is bell-shaped (or mound-shaped), but the smooth curve makes seeing the shape a little easier.

Another advantage of using smooth curves to identify distribution shapes is that we need not worry about minor differences in shape. Instead we can

FIGURE 2.8
Relative-frequency histogram and approximating smooth curve for the distribution of heights

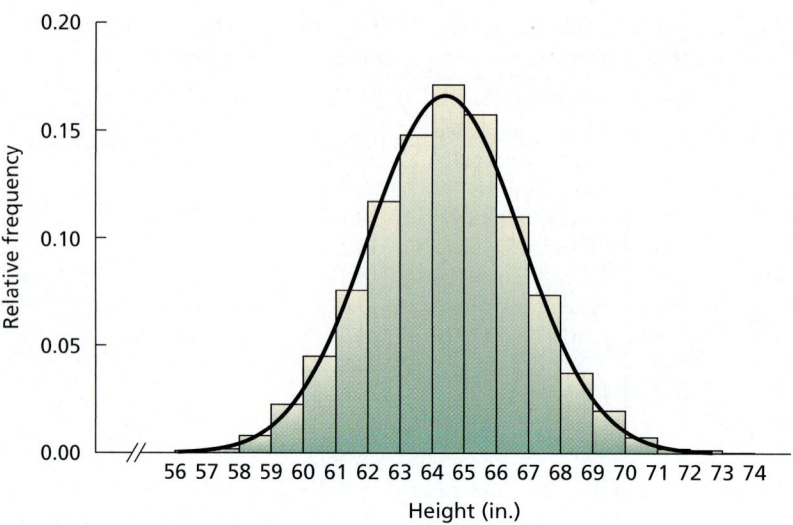

concentrate on overall patterns, which, in turn, allows us to classify most distributions by designating relatively few shapes.

DISTRIBUTION SHAPES

Figure 2.9 displays some common distribution shapes: **bell-shaped, triangular, uniform, reverse J-shaped, J-shaped, right skewed, left skewed, bimodal,** and **multimodal**. These shapes are idealized forms; in practice, distributions rarely have these exact shapes. Consequently, in identifying the shape of a distribution, exact conformance is not required, especially when we are considering small data sets. So, for example, we describe the distribution of heights displayed in Fig. 2.8 as bell-shaped, even though the histogram does not form a perfect bell. In Example 2.17, we illustrate how to identify a distribution shape.

Example 2.17 Identifying Distribution Shapes

Household Size The relative-frequency histogram for household size in the United States shown in Fig. 2.10(a) is based on data contained in *Current Population Reports*, a publication of the U.S. Bureau of the Census.[6] Identify the distribution shape for sizes of U.S. households.

Solution First, we draw a smooth curve through the histogram shown in Fig. 2.10(a) to get Fig. 2.10(b). Then, by referring to Fig. 2.9, we find that the distribution of household sizes is right skewed. ◆

There are distribution shapes other than those represented in Fig. 2.9. However, the types shown in Fig. 2.9 comprise the most commonly encountered distribution shapes and suffice for our purposes in this book.

---

[6] Actually, the class 7 portrayed in Fig. 2.10 is for seven or more people.

2.5 Distribution Shapes; Symmetry and Skewness

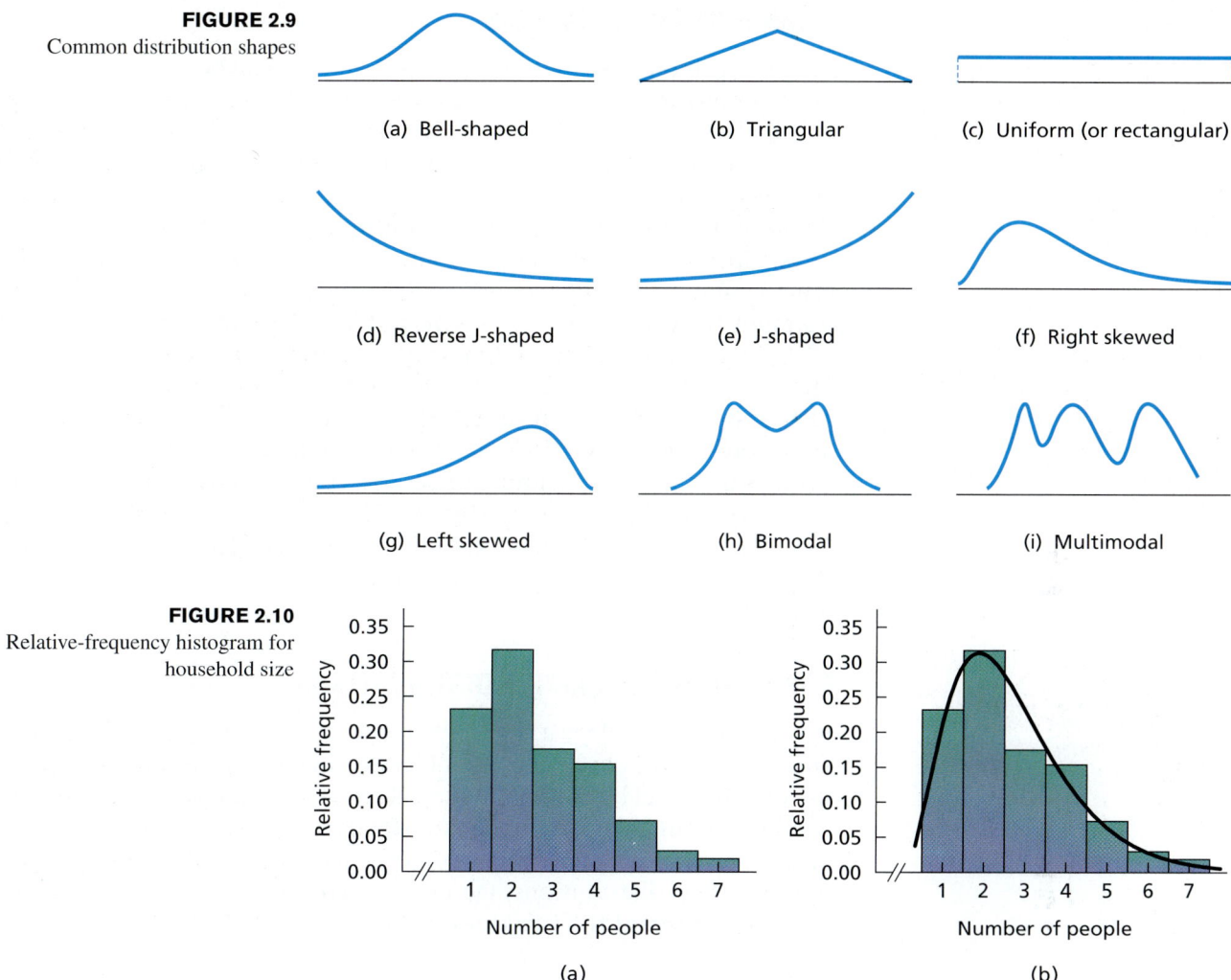

FIGURE 2.9 Common distribution shapes

(a) Bell-shaped (b) Triangular (c) Uniform (or rectangular)
(d) Reverse J-shaped (e) J-shaped (f) Right skewed
(g) Left skewed (h) Bimodal (i) Multimodal

FIGURE 2.10 Relative-frequency histogram for household size

What Does it Mean?

Technically, a distribution is bimodal or multimodal only if the peaks are the same height. However, in practice, distributions with pronounced but not necessarily equal-height peaks are often called bimodal or multimodal.

MODALITY

When considering the shape of a distribution, you should observe the number of peaks (highest points). A distribution is said to be **unimodal** if it has one peak; **bimodal** if it has two peaks; and **multimodal** if it has three or more peaks.

The distribution of heights in Fig. 2.8 is unimodal. More generally, we see from Fig. 2.9 that bell-shaped, triangular, reverse J-shaped, J-shaped, right-skewed, and left-skewed distributions are unimodal. Representations of bimodal and multimodal distributions are displayed in Figs. 2.9(h) and (i), respectively.[7]

---

[7] A uniform distribution has either no peaks or infinitely many peaks, depending on how you look at it. In any case, we do not classify a uniform distribution according to modality.

SYMMETRY AND SKEWNESS

Each of the three distributions in Figs. 2.9(a)–(c) can be divided into two pieces that are mirror images of one another. A distribution that has that property is called **symmetric**. Therefore bell-shaped, triangular, and uniform distributions are symmetric. The bimodal distribution pictured in Fig. 2.9(h) also is symmetric, but that is not always true for bimodal or multimodal distributions. Figure 2.9(i) shows an asymmetric multimodal distribution.

Again, when classifying distributions, we must be somewhat flexible. Thus exact symmetry is not required to classify a distribution as symmetric. For example, the distribution of heights in Fig. 2.8 is considered symmetric.

A unimodal distribution that is not symmetric is either right skewed, as in Fig. 2.9(f), or left skewed, as in Fig. 2.9(g). On the one hand, a right-skewed distribution rises to its peak rapidly and comes back toward the horizontal axis more slowly—its "right tail" is longer than its "left tail." On the other hand, a left-skewed distribution rises to its peak slowly and comes back toward the horizontal axis more rapidly—its "left tail" is longer than its "right tail." Note that reverse J-shaped distributions (Fig. 2.9(d)) and J-shaped distributions (Fig. 2.9(e)) are special types of right-skewed and left-skewed distributions, respectively.

POPULATION AND SAMPLE DISTRIBUTIONS

Recall that a variable is a characteristic that varies from one person or thing to another and that observing one or more values of a variable yields data. The data set obtained by observing the values of a variable for an entire population is called **population data** or **census data;** a data set obtained by observing the values of a variable for a sample of the population is called **sample data**. To distinguish their distributions, we use the terminology **population distribution** (or **distribution of the variable**) and **sample distribution**.

> **DEFINITION 2.6** **Population and Sample Distributions; Distribution of a Variable**
>
> The distribution of population data is called the *population distribution,* or the *distribution of the variable.*
>
> The distribution of sample data is called a *sample distribution.*

For a particular population and variable, sample distributions vary from sample to sample. However, there is only one population distribution, namely, the distribution of the variable under consideration on the population under consideration. Example 2.18 illustrates this point and some others as well.

Example 2.18 *Population and Sample Distributions*

Household Size In Example 2.17, we considered the distribution of household size for U.S. households. Here the variable is household size, and the

2.5 Distribution Shapes; Symmetry and Skewness

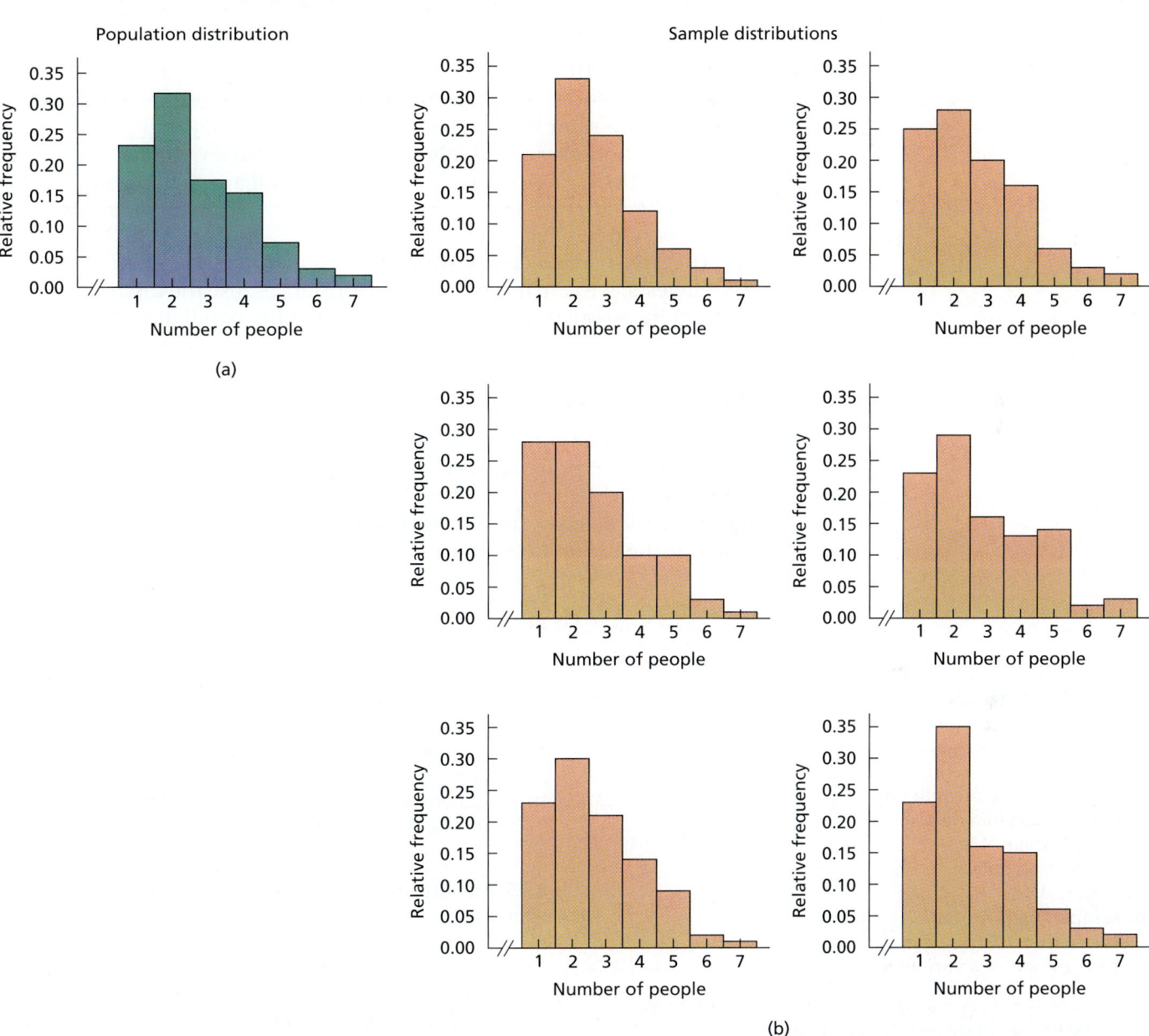

FIGURE 2.11
Population distribution and six sample distributions for household size

population consists of all U.S. households. Figure 2.10(a) on page 73 provides a relative-frequency histogram of household size for the population of all U.S. households—this graph gives the population distribution or, equivalently, the distribution of the variable "household size." For ease in reference, we repeat Fig. 2.10(a) as Fig. 2.11(a).

We obtained six random samples of 100 households each from the population of all U.S. households. Figure 2.11(b) shows relative-frequency histograms of household size for all six samples. Compare the six sample distributions in Fig. 2.11(b) to each other and to the population distribution in Fig. 2.11(a).

Solution As shown in Fig. 2.11(b), the distributions of the six samples, although similar, have definite differences. This result is not surprising because we would expect variation from one sample to another. Nonetheless, the overall shapes of the six sample distributions are roughly the same and also are similar in shape to the population distribution shown in Fig. 2.11(a)—all are right skewed. ◆

In practice, we usually do not know the population distribution. As Example 2.18 suggests, we can, under those circumstances, use the distribution of a sample from the population to get a rough idea of the population distribution.

Key Fact 2.1 **Population and Sample Distributions**

The distribution of a random sample from a population approximates the population distribution. In other words, if a random sample is taken from a population, the distribution of the observed values of the variable under consideration will approximate the distribution of the variable. The larger the sample, the better the approximation tends to be.

Exercises 2.5

Statistical Concepts and Skills

2.71 Explain the meaning of
a. distribution of a data set.
b. sample data.
c. population data.
d. census data.
e. sample distribution.
f. population distribution.
g. distribution of a variable.

2.72 Give two reasons why the use of smooth curves to describe shapes of distributions is helpful.

2.73 Suppose that a variable of a population has a bell-shaped distribution. If you take a large sample from the population, roughly what shape would you expect the distribution of the sample to be?

2.74 Suppose that a variable of a population has a reverse J-shaped distribution and that two samples are taken from the population.

a. Would you expect the distributions of the two samples to have roughly the same shape? If so, what shape?
b. Would you expect some variation in shape for the distributions of the two samples? Explain your answer.

2.75 Identify and sketch three distribution shapes that are symmetric.

In each of Exercises 2.76–2.81, we have provided a graphical display of a data set. For each exercise,
a. *identify the overall shape of the distribution by referring to Fig. 2.9 on page 73.*
b. *state whether the distribution is (roughly) symmetric, right skewed, or left skewed.*

2.76 Children of U.S. Presidents. The *Information Please Almanac* provides the number of children of each of the U.S. presidents. A frequency histogram for number of children by president, through President Clinton, is as follows.

2.5 Distribution Shapes; Symmetry and Skewness

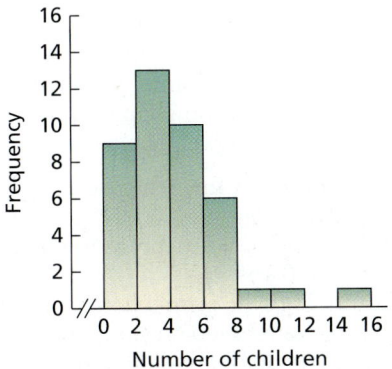

2.77 The Great White Shark. Refer to Exercise 2.25 on page 54. The following frequency histogram was obtained from data on the number of pups borne in a lifetime by each of 80 Great White Shark females.

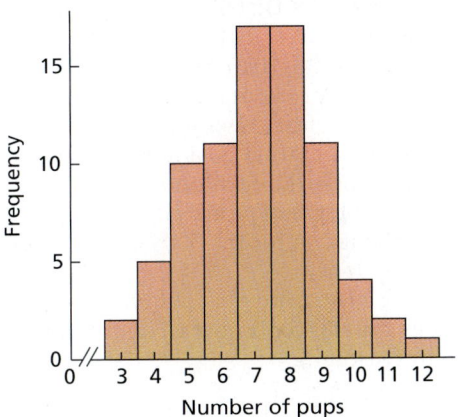

2.78 Adjusted Gross Incomes. Refer to Exercise 2.50 on page 64. The following relative-frequency histogram shows 1 year's individual income tax returns for adjusted gross incomes of less than $50,000.

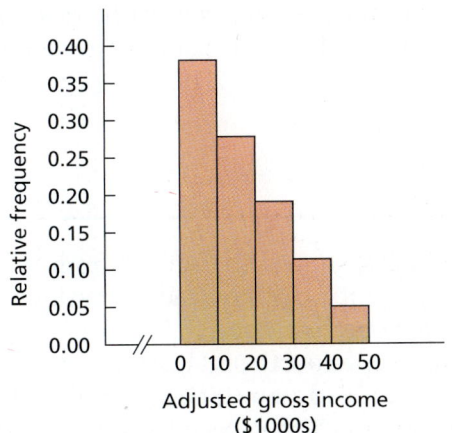

2.79 Cholesterol Levels. Refer to Exercise 2.51 on page 65. The following relative-frequency histogram shows the readings of some patients having high cholesterol levels.

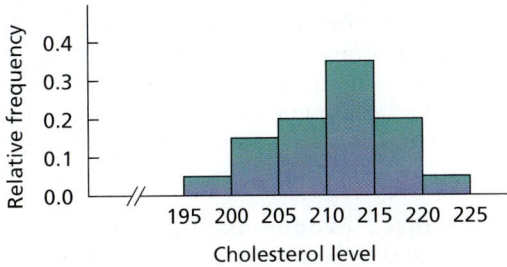

2.80 High School Completion Rates. Refer to Exercise 2.64 on page 69. The following stem-and-leaf diagram displays the completion rates.

7	6 7 7 7
7	8 8 9 9 9
8	0 0 0 1 1
8	2 2 2 3 3 3
8	4 4 4 4 4 4 5 5 5 5 5
8	6 6 6 6 7 7 7
8	8 8 8 9 9 9 9 9
9	0 0 1
9	2

2.81 Stays in Europe and the Mediterranean. The Bureau of Economic Analysis gathers information on the length of stay in Europe and the Mediterranean by U.S. travelers. Data are published in *Survey of Current Business*. The following stem-and-leaf diagram portrays the length of stay, in days, of a sample of 36 U.S. residents who traveled to Europe and the Mediterranean last year.

0	5 3 3 1 6 2 1 1 8 5 3
1	6 3 1 5 4 0 2 7 8 0 2 2 0
2	1 0 1 7 1
3	1 2
4	1 4 8
5	6
6	4

Extending the Concepts and Skills

2.82 Class Project: Number of Siblings. This exercise is a class project and works best in relatively large classes.
a. Determine the number of siblings for each student in the class.
b. Obtain a relative-frequency histogram of the number of siblings. Use single-value grouping.

c. Obtain a simple random sample of about one-third of the students in the class.
d. Determine the number of siblings for each student in the sample.
e. Obtain a relative-frequency histogram of the number of siblings for the sample. Use single-value grouping.
f. Repeat parts (c)–(e) three more times.
g. Compare the histograms for the samples to each other and to that for the entire population. Relate your observations to Key Fact 2.1.

2.83 Class Project: Random Digits. This exercise can be done individually or, better yet, as a class project.
a. Use a table of random numbers or a random-number generator to obtain 50 random integers between 0 and 9.
b. Without graphing the distribution of the 50 numbers you obtained, guess its shape. Explain your reasoning.
c. Construct a relative-frequency histogram based on single-value grouping for the 50 numbers that you obtained in part (a). Is its shape about what you expected?
d. If your answer to part (c) was "no," provide an explanation.
e. What would you do to make getting a "yes" answer to part (c) more plausible?
f. If you are doing this exercise as a class project, repeat parts (a)–(c) for 1000 random integers.

Using Technology

Simulation. For purposes of both understanding and research, simulating variables is often useful. Simulating a variable involves the use of a computer or statistical calculator to generate observations of the variable. In Exercises 2.84 and 2.85, the use of simulation will enhance your understanding of distribution shapes and the relation between population and sample distributions.

2.84 Random Digits. In this exercise, use technology to work Exercise 2.83, as follows.
a. Use the technology of your choice to obtain 50 random integers between 0 and 9.
b. Use the technology of your choice to get a relative-frequency histogram based on single-value grouping for the numbers that you obtained in part (a).
c. Repeat parts (a) and (b) five more times.
d. Are the shapes of the distributions that you obtained in parts (a)–(c) about what you expected?
e. Repeat parts (a)–(d), but generate 1000 random integers each time instead of 50.

2.85 Standard Normal Distribution. One of the most important distributions in statistics is the *standard normal distribution*. We discuss this distribution in detail in Chapter 6.
a. Use the technology of your choice to generate a sample of 3000 observations from a variable that has the standard normal distribution, that is, a normal distribution with mean 0 and standard deviation 1.
b. Use the technology of your choice to get a relative-frequency histogram for the 3000 observations that you obtained in part (a).
c. Based on the histogram you obtained in part (b), what shape does the standard normal distribution have? Explain your reasoning.

2.6 MISLEADING GRAPHS

Graphs and charts are frequently constructed in a manner that causes them to be misleading. Sometimes the misleading is intentional, and sometimes it is inadvertent. Regardless of intent, graphs and charts must be read and interpreted with a great deal of care. In this section, we examine some misleading graphs and charts, beginning with one in Example 2.19.

Example 2.19 *Truncated Graphs*

Unemployment Rates Figure 2.12(a) shows a bar graph from an article in a major metropolitan newspaper. The graph displays the unemployment rates in the United States from September of one year through March of the next year.

Because the bar for March is about one-fourth smaller than the bar for January, a quick look at Fig. 2.12(a) might lead you to conclude that the unemployment rate dropped by roughly one-fourth between January and March. In

FIGURE 2.12
Unemployment rates: (a) truncated graph; (b) nontruncated graph

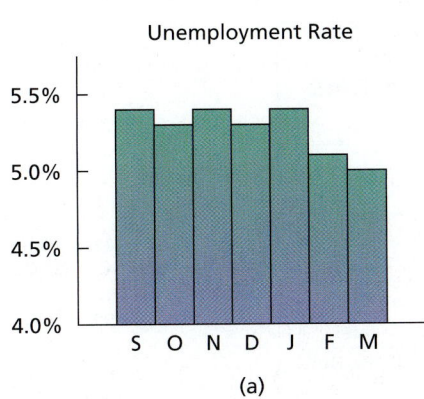

reality, however, the unemployment rate dropped by less than one-thirteenth, from 5.4% to 5.0%. Consequently, you must analyze the graph more carefully to discover what it truly represents.

Figure 2.12(a) is an example of a **truncated graph** because the vertical axis, which should start at 0%, starts at 4% instead. Thus the part of the graph from 0% to 4% has been cut off, or truncated. This truncation causes the bars to be out of correct proportion and hence creates a misleading impression.

The graph would be even more deceptive if it started at 4.5%. To see this result, slide a piece of paper over the bottom of Fig. 2.12(a) so that the bars begin at 4.5%. By how much does it now appear that the unemployment rate dropped between January and March?

Although the truncated graph in Fig. 2.12(a) is potentially misleading, the truncation probably was done to present a picture of the "ups" and "downs" in the unemployment rate pattern rather than to mislead the reader intentionally.

A nontruncated version of Fig. 2.12(a) is shown in Fig. 2.12(b). Figure 2.12(b) provides a correct graphical display of the unemployment rate data, but the "ups" and "downs" are not so easy to spot as they are in the truncated graph in Fig. 2.12(a). ◆

Truncated graphs have long been a target of statisticians, and many statistics books warn against their use. Nonetheless, as illustrated by Example 2.19, truncated graphs are still used today, even in reputable publications.

However, Example 2.19 also suggests that cutting off part of the vertical axis of a graph may be desirable. Doing so may allow relevant information, such as the "ups" and "downs" of the monthly unemployment rates, to be conveyed more easily. In such cases, though, a truncated graph should not be used. Instead, a special symbol, such as //, should be utilized to signify that the vertical axis has been modified.

The two graphs shown in Fig. 2.13 provide an excellent illustration. Both portray the number of new single-family homes sold per month over several months. The graph shown in Fig. 2.13(a) is truncated—most likely in an attempt to present a clear visual display of the variation in sales. The graph shown in Fig. 2.13(b) accomplishes the same result but is less subject to misinterpretation;

FIGURE 2.13
New single-family home sales

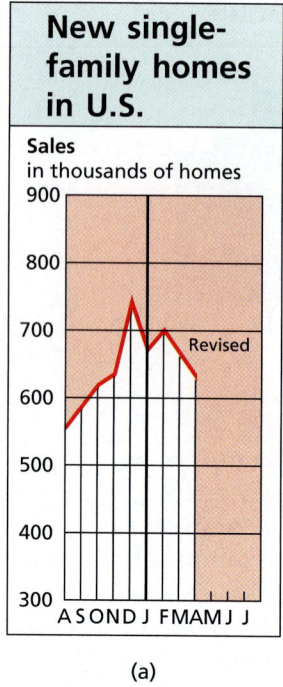

(a)

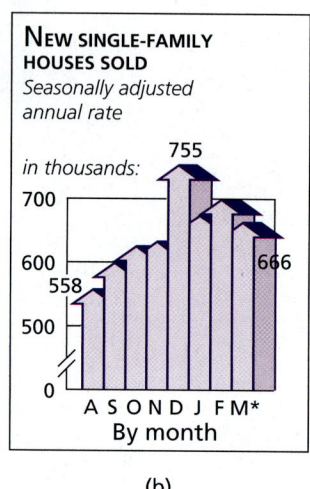

(b)

SOURCES: Figure 2.13(a) reprinted by permission of Tribune Media Services. Figure 2.13(b) data from U.S. Department of Commerce and U.S. Department of Housing and Urban Development.

you are aptly warned by the slashes that part of the vertical axis between 0 and 500 has been removed.

IMPROPER SCALING

Misleading graphs and charts can also result from **improper scaling.** In Example 2.20, we show how that can happen.

Example 2.20 Improper Scaling

FIGURE 2.14
Pictogram for home building

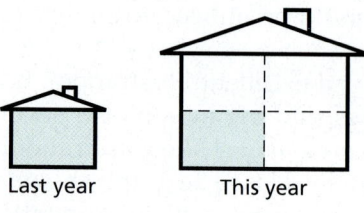

Home Building A developer is preparing a brochure to attract investors for a new shopping center to be built in an area of Denver, Colorado. The area is growing rapidly; this year twice as many homes will be built there as last year. To illustrate that fact, the developer draws a **pictogram,** as shown in Fig. 2.14.

The house on the left represents the number of homes built last year. Because the number of homes that will be built this year is double the number built last year, the developer makes the house on the right twice as tall and twice as wide as the house on the left. However, this scaling is improper as it gives the visual impression that four times as many homes will be built this year as last. Thus the developer's brochure may mislead the unwary investor. ◆

2.6 Misleading Graphs

Graphs and charts can be misleading in countless ways besides the two that we discussed. Many more examples of misleading graphs can be found in the entertaining and classic book *How to Lie with Statistics* by Darrell Huff (New York: Norton, 1955). The main purpose of this section has been to show you that graphs and charts should be constructed and read carefully.

Exercises 2.6

Statistical Concepts and Skills

2.86 Give one reason why constructing and reading graphs and charts carefully is important.

2.87 This exercise deals with truncated graphs.
a. What is a truncated graph?
b. Give a legitimate motive for truncating the axis of a graph.
c. If you have a legitimate motive for truncating the axis of a graph, how can you correctly obtain that objective without creating the possibility of misinterpretation?

2.88 In a current newspaper or magazine, find two examples of graphs that might be misleading. Explain why you think the graphs are potentially misleading.

2.89 Reading Skills. Each year the director of the reading program in a school district administers a standard test of reading skills. Then the director compares the average score for his district with the national average. Figure 2.15 was presented to the school board in the year 2000.

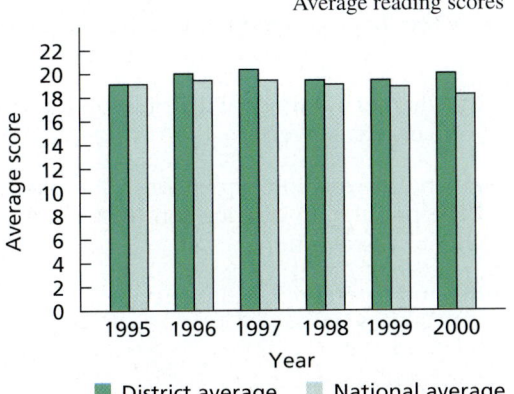

FIGURE 2.15
Average reading scores

a. Obtain a truncated version of Fig. 2.15 by sliding a piece of paper over the bottom of the graph so that the bars start at 16.
b. Repeat part (a) but have the bars start at 18.

c. What misleading impression about the year 2000 scores is given by the truncated graphs obtained in parts (a) and (b)?

2.90 America's Melting Pot. The following bar graph is based on a newspaper article entitled "Immigrants add seasoning to America's melting pot." [Used with permission from American Demographics, Ithaca, NY.]

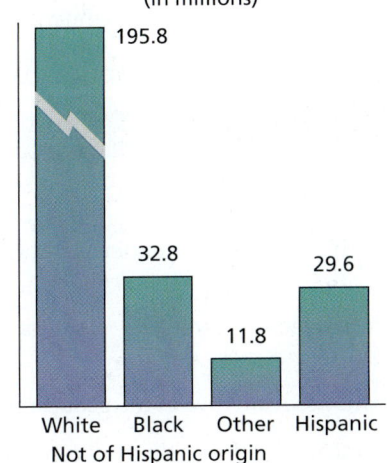

a. Explain why a break is shown in the first bar.
b. Why was the graph constructed with a broken bar?
c. Is this graph potentially misleading? Explain your answer.

2.91 M2 Money Supply. The following bar graph, taken from *The Arizona Republic*, provides data on the M2 money supply over several months. M2 consists of cash in circulation, deposits in checking accounts, nonbank traveler's checks, accounts such as savings deposits, and money-market mutual funds.

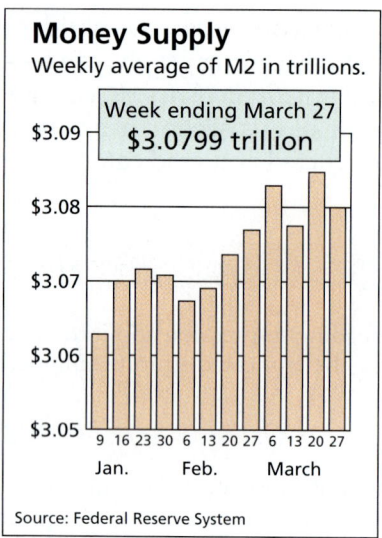

a. What is wrong with the bar graph?
b. Construct a version of the bar graph with a nontruncated and unmodified vertical axis.
c. Construct a version of the bar graph in which the vertical axis is modified in an acceptable manner.

Extending the Concepts and Skills

2.92 Home Building. Refer to Example 2.20 on page 80. Suggest a way in which the developer can accurately illustrate that twice as many homes will be built in the area this year as last.

2.93 Marketing Golf Balls. A golf ball manufacturer has determined that a newly developed process results in a ball that lasts roughly twice as long as a ball produced by the current process. To illustrate this advance graphically, she designs a brochure showing a "new" ball having twice the radius of the "old" ball.

Old ball   New ball

a. What is wrong with this depiction?
b. How can the manufacturer accurately illustrate the fact that the "new" ball lasts twice as long as the "old" ball?

Chapter Review

You Should Be Able To

1. classify variables and data as either qualitative or quantitative.

2. distinguish between discrete and continuous variables and data.

3. identify terms associated with the grouping of data.

4. group data into a frequency distribution and a relative-frequency distribution.

5. construct a grouped-data table.

6. draw a frequency histogram and a relative-frequency histogram.

7. construct a dotplot.

8. draw a pie chart and a bar graph.

9. construct stem-and-leaf, shaded stem-and-leaf, and ordered stem-and-leaf diagrams.

10. identify the shape and modality of the distribution of a data set.

11. specify whether a unimodal distribution is symmetric, right skewed, or left skewed.

12. understand the relationship between sample distributions and the population distribution (distribution of the variable under consideration).

13. identify and correct misleading graphs.

Key Terms

bar graph, 60
bell-shaped, 72
bimodal, 72, 73
categorical variables, 40

census data, 74
classes, 47
continuous data, 41
continuous variable, 40

count, 46
data, 41
data set, 41
discrete data, 41

discrete variable, 40
distribution of a data set, 71
distribution of a variable, 74
dotplot, 59
frequency, 47
frequency distribution, 47
frequency histogram, 57
grouped-data table, 47
grouping, 44
improper scaling, 80
J-shaped, 72
leaves, 67
left skewed, 72
lower cutpoint, 47
lower limit, 49
mark, 49

midpoint, 47
multimodal, 72, 73
observation, 41
ordered stem-and-leaf diagram, 67
percentage, 46
pictogram, 80
pie chart, 60
population data, 74
population distribution, 74
qualitative data, 41
qualitative variables, 40
quantitative data, 41
quantitative variables, 40
relative frequency, 47
relative-frequency distribution, 47
relative-frequency histogram, 57

reverse J-shaped, 72
right skewed, 72
sample data, 74
sample distribution, 74
shaded stem-and-leaf diagram, 67
stem-and-leaf diagram, 67
stems, 67
symmetric, 74
triangular, 72
truncated graph, 79
uniform, 72
unimodal, 73
upper cutpoint, 47
upper limit, 49
variable, 40
width, 47

Review Test

Statistical Concepts and Skills

1. This problem is about variables and data.
   a. What is a variable?
   b. Identify two main types of variables.
   c. Identify the two types of quantitative variables.
   d. What are data?
   e. How is data type determined?

2. Explain why grouping data is important.

3. To which type of data do the concepts of cutpoints and midpoints not apply? Explain your answer.

4. A quantitative data set has been grouped into a grouped-data table with equal-width classes of width 8.
   a. If the midpoint of the first class is 10, what are its lower and upper cutpoints?
   b. What is the midpoint of the second class?
   c. What are the lower and upper cutpoints of the third class?
   d. Into which class would an observation of 22 go?

5. A quantitative data set has been grouped into a grouped-data table with equal-width classes.
   a. If the lower and upper cutpoints of the first class are 5 and 15, respectively, what is the common class width?
   b. What is the midpoint of the second class?
   c. What are the lower and upper cutpoints of the third class?

6. When is the use of single-value grouping particularly appropriate?

7. In each of the following cases, explain the relative positioning of the bars in a histogram to the numbers that label the horizontal axis.
   a. Cutpoints are used to label the horizontal axis.
   b. Midpoints are used to label the horizontal axis.

8. Identify two main types of graphical displays that are used for qualitative data.

9. Which is preferable as a graphical display for a large, quantitative data set: a histogram or a stem-and-leaf diagram? Explain your answer.

10. Sketch the curve corresponding to each of the following distribution shapes.
    a. Bell-shaped
    b. Right skewed
    c. Reverse J-shaped
    d. Uniform

11. Make an educated guess as to the distribution shape of each of the following variables. Explain your answers.
    a. Height of American adult males
    b. Annual income of U.S. households
    c. Age of full-time college students
    d. Cumulative GPA of college seniors

12. A variable of a population has a left-skewed distribution.
    a. If a large random sample is taken from the population, roughly what shape will the distribution of the sample have? Explain your answer.
    b. If two random samples are taken from the population, would you expect the two sample distributions to have identical shapes? Explain your answer.

c. If two random samples are taken from the population, would you expect the two sample distributions to have similar shapes? If so, what shape would that be? Explain your answers.

13. Largest Hydroelectric Plants. The world's five largest hydroelectric plants, based on ultimate capacity, are as shown in the following table. Capacities are in megawatts. [SOURCE: T. W. Mermel, *Intl. Waterpower & Dam Construction Handbook*.]

Rank	Name	Country	Capacity
1	Turukhansk	Russia	20,000
2	Three Gorges	China	18,200
3	Itaipu	Brazil/Para.	13,320
4	Grand Coulee	U.S.A.	10,830
5	Guri	Venezuela	10,300

a. What type of data is given in the first column of the table?
b. What type of data is given in the fourth column?
c. What type of data is given in the third column?

14. Inauguration Ages. The ages at inauguration for the first 42 presidents of the United States are as follows.

President	Age at inaug.	President	Age at inaug.
G. Washington	57	G. Cleveland	47
J. Adams	61	B. Harrison	55
T. Jefferson	57	G. Cleveland	55
J. Madison	57	W. McKinley	54
J. Monroe	58	T. Roosevelt	42
J. Q. Adams	57	W. Taft	51
A. Jackson	61	W. Wilson	56
M. Van Buren	54	W. Harding	55
W. Harrison	68	C. Coolidge	51
J. Tyler	51	H. Hoover	54
J. Polk	49	F. Roosevelt	51
Z. Taylor	64	H. Truman	60
M. Fillmore	50	D. Eisenhower	62
F. Pierce	48	J. Kennedy	43
J. Buchanan	65	L. Johnson	55
A. Lincoln	52	R. Nixon	56
A. Johnson	56	G. Ford	61
U. Grant	46	J. Carter	52
R. Hayes	54	R. Reagan	69
J. Garfield	49	G. Bush	64
C. Arthur	50	W. Clinton	46

a. Construct a grouped-data table for the inauguration ages in the preceding table. Use equal-width classes and begin with the class 40–44.
b. Identify the lower and upper cutpoints of the first class. (*Hint:* Be careful!)
c. Identify the common class width.
d. Draw a frequency histogram for the inauguration ages based on your grouping in part (a).

15. Inauguration Ages. Refer to Problem 14. Construct a dotplot for the ages at inauguration of the first 42 presidents of the United States.

16. Inauguration Ages. Refer to Problem 14. Construct an ordered stem-and-leaf diagram for the inauguration ages of the first 42 presidents of the United States. Use
a. one line per stem.
b. two lines per stem.
c. Which of the two stem-and-leaf diagrams that you just constructed corresponds to the frequency distribution of Problem 14(a)?

17. Busy Bank Tellers. The Prescott National Bank has six tellers available to serve customers. The data in the following table provide the number of busy tellers observed during 25 spot checks.

6	5	4	1	5
6	1	5	5	5
3	5	2	4	3
4	5	0	6	4
3	4	2	3	6

a. Construct a grouped-data table for these data. Use single-value grouping.
b. Draw a relative-frequency histogram for the data based on the grouping in part (a).

18. Student Class Levels. The class levels of the students in Professor Weiss's introductory statistics course are shown in the following table. The abbreviations Fr, So, Ju, and Se represent Freshman, Sophomore, Junior, and Senior, respectively.

Fr	So	Ju	So	Ju	Ju	Se	Ju
Se	So	Fr	Ju	So	Ju	So	Se
So	So	Se	So	So	Se	So	Fr
Ju	So	Ju	Fr	Fr	Ju	Ju	Fr
So	Se	Ju	Ju	So	So	So	Se

a. Obtain frequency and relative-frequency distributions for these data.
b. Draw a pie chart of the data that displays the percentage of students at each class level.
c. Draw a bar graph of the data that displays the relative frequency of students at each class level.

19. Dow Jones Annual Highs. According to *The World Almanac*, the highs for the Dow Jones Industrial Averages for 1964–1999 are as follows.

Year	High	Year	High
1964	891.71	1982	1071.55
1965	969.26	1983	1287.20
1966	995.15	1984	1286.64
1967	943.08	1985	1553.10
1968	985.21	1986	1955.57
1969	968.85	1987	2722.42
1970	842.00	1988	2183.50
1971	950.82	1989	2791.41
1972	1036.27	1990	2999.75
1973	1051.70	1991	3168.83
1974	891.66	1992	3413.21
1975	881.81	1993	3794.33
1976	1014.79	1994	3978.36
1977	999.75	1995	5216.47
1978	907.74	1996	6560.91
1979	897.61	1997	8259.31
1980	1000.17	1998	9547.94
1981	1024.05	1999	11568.80

a. Construct a grouped-data table for the highs. Use classes of equal width and start with the class $0 \leq 1000$.
b. Draw a relative-frequency histogram for the highs based on your result in part (a).

20. Identify the distribution shapes of each of the following data sets.
a. The inauguration ages of the first 42 presidents of the United States (from Problem 14).
b. The number of tellers busy with customers at Prescott National Bank during 25 spot checks (from Problem 17).

21. Draw a smooth curve that represents a symmetric tri-modal (three-peak) distribution.

22. Reshaping the Labor Force. The following graph is based on one that appeared in a newspaper article entitled "Hand that rocked cradle turns to work as women reshape U.S. labor force." The graph depicts the labor force participation rates for the years 1960, 1980, and 2000.

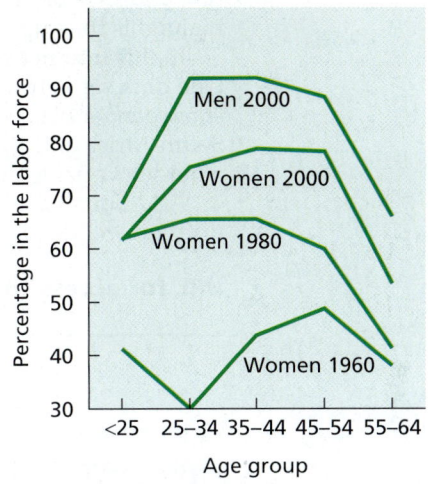
Working Men and Women by Age, 1960–2000

a. Cover the numbers on the vertical axis of the graph with a piece of paper.
b. Look at the 1960 and 2000 graphs for women, focusing on the 35–44-year-old age group. What impression does the graph convey regarding the ratio of the percentages of women in the labor force for 1960 and 2000?
c. Now remove the piece of paper from the graph. Use the vertical scale to find the actual ratio of the percentages of 35–44-year-old women in the labor force for 1960 and 2000.
d. Why is the graph potentially misleading?
e. What can be done to make the graph less potentially misleading?

Using Technology

23. Inauguration Ages. Refer to the age data in Problem 14. Use the technology of your choice to obtain a
a. frequency histogram of the data similar to the one found in Problem 14(d).
b. dotplot of the data.
c. stem-and-leaf diagram similar to the one constructed in Problem 16(b).

24. Student Class Levels. Refer to Problem 18. Use the technology of your choice to obtain a
a. pie chart of the data.
b. bar graph of the data.

Internet Project

Simpson's Paradox

One of the most important and basic of all statistical questions is whether there is a relationship (or association) between variables. Sometimes two variables may appear to be related in a certain way, but when a third, hidden variable is taken into consideration, the association vanishes or even reverses direction! This behavior is known as *Simpson's paradox* and highlights the importance of looking for hidden or confounding variables.

In this Internet project, you will explore two data sets that illustrate Simpson's paradox. One data set is from a famous study of graduate admissions at a university and seems to show gender bias. The other data set comes from a recent study of healthcare for children in South Africa and appears to reveal a surprising association. In both cases, you will discover a hidden variable that significantly changes the apparent association.

Additionally, this project will provide an opportunity for further practice with the organization and display of data.

URL for access to Internet Projects Page: www.aw.com/weiss

Focusing on Data Analysis

Age, Sex, GPA, and SAT Scores

Recall from Chapter 1 (see page 34) that the Focus database contains information on 500 randomly selected Arizona State University sophomores. Use the technology of your choice to solve the following problems.

a. Obtain a histogram for the ages of the sophomores in the sample.
b. Obtain individual histograms for the ages of the female sophomores and the male sophomores in the sample. Compare the two histograms and discuss the differences you observe.
c. Construct a stem-and-leaf diagram for the cumulative GPAs of the sophomores in the sample. Use five lines per stem.
d. Construct individual stem-and-leaf diagrams for the cumulative GPAs of the female sophomores and the male sophomores in the sample. Use five lines per stem for both diagrams. Compare the two diagrams and discuss any differences you observe.
e. Obtain dotplots for both the SAT math and SAT verbal scores of the sophomores in the sample. Compare the two dotplots.
f. Identify the shapes of the distributions in parts (a)–(e). Which distributions are symmetric?

case study discussion

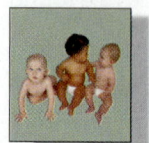

Preventing Infant Mortality

Recall that the infant mortality rate of a nation represents the number of deaths of children under 1 year of age per 1000 live births in a calendar year. At the beginning of this chapter, we presented data on infant mortality for nations with 10 million or more population having the lowest rates. Refer to that data table on page 39 and solve each of the following problems.

a. What type of data is displayed in the second column of the table?
b. What type of data is given by the statement that the United States ranks 10th in infant mortality rate among nations with 10 million or more population?

c. Construct a grouped-data table for the infant mortality rates. Use classes of equal width and start with the class 4 ≤ 6.
d. Construct a frequency histogram for the infant mortality rates based on your grouping in part (c).
e. Construct an ordered stem-and-leaf diagram for the infant mortality rates.
f. Use the technology of your choice to solve parts (c)–(e).

Internet Resources: Visit the Weiss Web site www.aw.com/weiss for additional discussion, exercises, and resources related to this case study.

Biography
Adolphe Quetelet: On "The Average Man"

LAMBERT ADOLPHE JACQUES QUETELET was born in Ghent, Belgium, on February 22, 1796. He attended school locally and, in 1819, received the first doctorate of science degree granted at the newly established University of Ghent. In that same year, he obtained a position as a professor of mathematics at the Brussels Athenaeum.

Quetelet was elected to the Belgian Royal Academy in 1820 and served as its secretary from 1834 until his death in 1874. He was founder and director of the Royal Observatory in Brussels, founder and a major contributor to the journal *Correspondance Mathématique et Physique*, and, according to Stephen M. Stigler in *The History of Statistics*, was "…active in the founding of more statistical organizations than any other individual in the nineteenth century." Among the organizations he established was the International Statistical Congress, initiated in 1853.

In 1835, Quetelet wrote a two-volume set titled *A Treatise on Man and the Development of His Faculties,* the publication in which he introduced his concept of the "average man" and that firmly established his international reputation as a statistician and sociologist. A review in the *Athenaeum* stated, "We consider the appearance of these volumes as forming an epoch in the literary history of civilization."

In 1855, Quetelet suffered a stroke that limited his work but not his popularity. He died on February 17, 1874. His funeral was attended by royalty and famous scientists from around the world. A monument to his memory was erected in Brussels in 1880.

chapter 3

Descriptive Measures

CHAPTER OUTLINE

3.1 Measures of Center

3.2 The Sample Mean

3.3 Measures of Variation; The Sample Standard Deviation

3.4 The Five-Number Summary; Boxplots

3.5 Descriptive Measures for Populations; Use of Samples

GENERAL OBJECTIVES In Chapter 2, you began your study of descriptive statistics. There you learned how to organize data into tables and summarize data with graphs. Another method of summarizing data is to compute numbers, such as averages and percentiles, that describe the data set. Numbers that are used to describe data sets are called **descriptive measures.** In this chapter, we continue our discussion of descriptive statistics by examining some of the most commonly used descriptive measures.

In Section 3.1, we present *measures of center*—descriptive measures that indicate the center, or most typical value, in a data set. A particularly important measure of center is the mean; we discuss the mean of a sample in Section 3.2. Next, we examine *measures of variation*—descriptive measures that indicate the amount of variation or spread in a data set. In Section 3.3, we introduce two important measures of variation, the range and standard deviation.

The five-number summary, which we discuss in Section 3.4, includes descriptive measures that can be used to obtain both measures of center and measures of variation. That summary also provides the basis for a widely used graphical display, the boxplot.

In Section 3.5, we apply descriptive measures to populations. We also suggest how sample data can be used to provide estimates of descriptive measures of populations when census data are unavailable.

case study

NEW YORK YANKEES Y2K SALARIES

As boisterous fans waved yellow plastic brooms, symbolizing an astounding World Series sweep, the New York Yankees claimed the 1999 World Series title. The Bronx Bombers have won a Major League record 25 championships and finished the 1990s with their third Series title and second sweep. Sports analysts around the country predicted a threepeat with the solid roster of the 2000 Yankees squad. As we now know, they predicted correctly.

A great team commands great salaries. Here are the New York Yankees roster and players' salaries for the 2000 season, as reported online by *CBS Sportsline*.

Player	2000 Salary	Player	2000 Salary
Bernie Williams	$12,357,143	Jorge Posada	$1,250,000
David Cone	12,000,000	Jim Leyritz	1,000,000
Derek Jeter	10,000,000	Roberto Kelly	800,000
Mariano Rivera	7,250,000	Jason Grimsley	750,000
Andy Pettitte	7,000,000	Lance Johnson	350,000
Paul O'Neill	6,500,000	Shane Spencer	250,000
Roger Clemens	6,350,000	Ricky Ledee	240,000
Chuck Knoblauch	6,000,000	Wilson Delgado	213,000
Scott Brosius	5,250,000	Clay Bellinger	206,650
Tino Martinez	4,800,000	Todd Erdos	203,800
Mike Stanton	2,400,000	Ted Lilly	201,000
Orlando Hernandez	1,950,000	Luis De Los Santos	200,000
Jeff Nelson	1,916,667	D'Angelo Jimenez	200,000
Ramiro Mendoza	1,400,000	Nick Johnson	200,000
Allen Watson	1,300,000		

In this chapter, we demonstrate several additional techniques to help you analyze data. At the end of the chapter, after you have mastered those techniques, we ask you to apply them in analyzing the salaries for the New York Yankees players in the 2000 season.

3.1 MEASURES OF CENTER

Descriptive measures that indicate where the center or most typical value of a data set lies are called **measures of central tendency** or, more simply, **measures of center**. Measures of center are often referred to as *averages*.

In this section, we discuss the three most important measures of center: the *mean*, *median*, and *mode*. The mean and median apply only to quantitative data, whereas the mode can be used with either quantitative or qualitative (categorical) data.

THE MEAN

The most commonly used measure of center is the **mean**. When people speak of taking an average, they are most often referring to the mean.

DEFINITION 3.1 **Mean of a Data Set**

The *mean* of a data set is the sum of the observations divided by the number of observations.

Example 3.1 illustrates calculation of the mean for data sets.

Example 3.1 The Mean

TABLE 3.1 Data Set I

$300	300	300	940	300
300	400	300	400	
450	800	450	1050	

TABLE 3.2 Data Set II

$300	300	940	450	400
400	300	300	1050	300

Weekly Salaries Professor Hassett spent one summer working for a small mathematical consulting firm. The firm employed a few senior consultants, who made between $800 and $1050 per week; a few junior consultants, who made between $400 and $450 per week; and several clerical workers, who made $300 per week.

Because the first half of the summer was busier than the second half, more employees were required during the first half. Tables 3.1 and 3.2 display typical lists of weekly earnings for the two halves of the summer. Find the mean of each of the two data sets.

Solution According to Definition 3.1, the mean of a data set is obtained by summing all the observations and then dividing that sum by the total number of observations. Data Set I has 13 observations. The sum of those observations is $6290, so

$$\text{Mean of Data Set I} = \frac{\$6290}{13} = \$483.85 \text{ (rounded to the nearest cent).}$$

Similarly,

$$\text{Mean of Data Set II} = \frac{\$4740}{10} = \$474.00.$$

What Does it Mean?

On average, the employees who worked in the first half of the summer earned more than those who worked in the second half of the summer.

Thus the mean salary of the 13 employees in Data Set I is $483.85 and that of the 10 employees in Data Set II is $474.00.

THE MEDIAN

Another frequently used measure of center is the median. Essentially, the **median** of a data set is the number that divides the bottom 50% of the data from the top 50%. To obtain the median of a data set, we arrange the data in increasing order and then determine the middle value in the ordered list. A more precise definition of the median follows.

DEFINITION 3.2 Median of a Data Set

Arrange the data in increasing order.

- If the number of observations is odd, then the *median* is the observation exactly in the middle of the ordered list.
- If the number of observations is even, then the *median* is the mean of the two middle observations in the ordered list.

In both cases, if we let n denote the number of observations, then the median is at position $(n+1)/2$ in the ordered list.

Example 3.2 shows how to find the median of data sets.

Example 3.2 The Median

Weekly Salaries Consider again the two sets of salary data shown in Tables 3.1 and 3.2. Determine the median of each of the two data sets.

Solution To find the median of Data Set I, we apply Definition 3.2. First, we arrange the data in increasing order:

300 300 300 300 300 300 **400** 400 450 450 800 940 1050

The number of observations in Data Set I is 13, which is an odd number. Because $n = 13$, we have $(n+1)/2 = (13+1)/2 = 7$. Consequently, the median is the seventh observation in the ordered list, which is 400 (shown in boldface). The median salary of the 13 employees in Data Set I is $400.

To find the median of Data Set II, we again apply Definition 3.2. First, we arrange the data in increasing order:

300 300 300 300 **300 400** 400 450 940 1050

The number of observations in Data Set II is 10, which is an even number. Because $n = 10$, we have $(n+1)/2 = (10+1)/2 = 5.5$. Consequently, the median is halfway between the fifth and sixth observations (shown in boldface) in the ordered list. In other words, the median salary of the 10 employees in Data Set II is $(300 + 400)/2 = 350.

What Does it Mean?

Again, the analysis shows that the employees who worked in the first half of the summer tended to earn more than those who worked in the second half of the summer.

To determine the median of a data set, you must first arrange the data in increasing order. Constructing a stem-and-leaf diagram as a preliminary step to ordering the data is often helpful.

THE MODE

The final measure of center that we discuss here is the mode. Basically, the **mode** is the value that occurs most frequently in a data set. A more exact definition of the mode is the following.

DEFINITION 3.3 Mode of a Data Set

Obtain the frequency of occurrence of each value and note the greatest frequency.

- If the greatest frequency is 1 (i.e., no value occurs more than once), then the data set has no mode.
- If the greatest frequency is 2 or greater, then any value that occurs with that greatest frequency is called a *mode* of the data set.

To obtain the mode(s) of a data set, we first construct a frequency distribution for the data with classes based on a single value. The mode(s) can then be determined easily from the frequency distribution, as explained in Example 3.3.

Example 3.3 The Mode

Weekly Salaries Determine the mode(s) of each of the two sets of salary data given in Tables 3.1 and 3.2.

Solution First, we consider the salary data in Data Set I. Referring to Table 3.1, we obtain the frequency distribution of the data with classes based on a single value, as shown in Table 3.3.

TABLE 3.3
Frequency distribution for Data Set I, using single-value grouping

Salary	300	400	450	800	940	1050
Frequency	6	2	2	1	1	1

What Does it Mean?

The most frequent salary was $300 both for the employees who worked in the first half of the summer and those who worked in the second half of the summer.

From Table 3.3, the greatest frequency of occurrence is 6, and 300 is the only value that occurs with that frequency. So the mode of the 13 salaries in Data Set I is $300.

Proceeding in the same way, we find that, for Data Set II, the greatest frequency of occurrence is 5 and that 300 is the only value that occurs with that frequency. So the mode of the 10 salaries in Data Set II is $300. ◆

A data set can have more than one mode if there is more than one value that occurs with the greatest frequency. For instance, suppose that two of the clerical workers in Data Set I, who make $300 per week, were promoted to $400-per-week jobs. Then both the value 300 and the value 400 would occur with greatest frequency, 4. This new data set would thus have two modes, $300 and $400.

COMPARISON OF THE MEAN, MEDIAN, AND MODE

The mean, median, and mode of a data set are often different. Table 3.4 summarizes the definitions of these three measures of center and gives their values for Data Set I and Data Set II, which we computed in Examples 3.1–3.3.

TABLE 3.4
Means, medians, and modes of salaries in Data Set I and Data Set II

Measure of center	Definition	Data Set I	Data Set II
Mean	Sum of observations / Number of observations	$483.85	$474.00
Median	Middle value in ordered list	$400.00	$350.00
Mode	Most frequent value	$300.00	$300.00

In both Data Sets I and II, the mean is larger than the median. The reason is that the mean is strongly affected by the few large salaries in each data set. In general, the mean is sensitive to extreme (very large or very small) observations, whereas the median is not. Consequently, when the choice for the measure of center is between the mean and the median, the median is usually preferred for data sets that have extreme observations.

Figure 3.1 shows the relative positions of the mean and median for right-skewed, symmetric, and left-skewed distributions. Note that the mean is pulled in the direction of skewness, that is, in the direction of the extreme observations. For a right-skewed distribution, the mean is greater than the median; for a symmetric distribution, the mean and the median are equal; and, for a left-skewed distribution, the mean is less than the median.

FIGURE 3.1
Relative positions of the mean and median for (a) right-skewed, (b) symmetric, and (c) left-skewed distributions

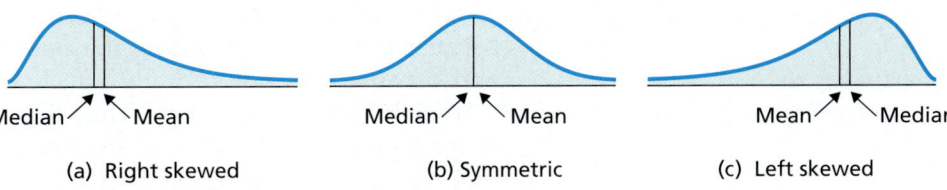

(a) Right skewed (b) Symmetric (c) Left skewed

A **resistant measure** is not sensitive to the influence of a few extreme observations. Thus the median is a resistant measure of center, whereas the mean is not. The resistance of the mean can be improved by using **trimmed means**, whereby a specified percentage of the smallest and largest observations are removed before computing the mean. In Exercise 3.16, we discuss trimmed means in more detail.

The mode for each of Data Sets I and II differs from both the mean and the median. Whereas the mean and the median are aimed at finding the center of a data set, the mode is really not—the value that occurs most frequently may not be near the center.

It should now be clear that the mean, median, and mode generally provide different information. There is no simple rule for deciding which measure of center to use in a given situation. Although skill in making such decisions is attained through practice, even experts may disagree about the most suitable measure of center for a particular data set. In Example 3.4, we discuss three data sets and suggest the most appropriate measure of center for each.

Example 3.4 Selecting an Appropriate Measure of Center

a. A student takes four exams in a biology class. His grades are 88, 75, 95, and 100. If asked for his average, which measure of center is the student likely to report?

b. The National Association of REALTORS publishes data on resale prices of U.S. homes. Which measure of center is most appropriate for such resale prices?

c. In the 2000 Boston Marathon, there were two categories of official finishers: male and female. The following table provides a frequency distribution for those data. Which measure of center should be used here?

Sex	Frequency
Male	11,442
Female	6,371

Solution a. Chances are that the student would report the mean of his four exam scores, which is 89.5. The mean is probably the most suitable measure of center for the student to use because it takes into account the numerical value of each score and therefore indicates total overall performance.

b. The most appropriate measure of center for resale home prices is the median because it is aimed at finding the center of the data on resale home prices and because it is not strongly affected by the relatively few homes with extremely high resale prices. Thus the median provides a better indication of the "typical" resale price than either the mean or the mode.

c. The only suitable measure of center for these data is the mode, which is "male." Each observation in this data set is either "male" or "female." There is no way to compute a mean or median for such data. Of the mean, median, and mode, the mode is the only measure of center that can be used for qualitative data.

Many measures of center that appear in newspapers or that are reported by government agencies are medians, as is the case for household income and number of years of school completed. In an attempt to provide a clearer picture, some reports include both the mean and the median. For instance, the National Center for Health Statistics does so for daily intake of nutrients in the publication *Vital and Health Statistics*.

POPULATION MEAN AND SAMPLE MEAN

Recall that a variable is a characteristic that varies from one person or thing to another and that observing one or more values of a variable yields data. The data set obtained by observing the values of a variable for an entire population is called *population data;* a data set obtained by observing the values of a variable for a sample of the population is called *sample data.*

The mean of population data is called the *population mean* or the *mean of the variable;* the mean of sample data is called a *sample mean.* The same terminology is used for the median and mode and, for that matter, any descriptive measure. Figure 3.2 shows the two ways in which the mean of a data set can be interpreted.

FIGURE 3.2
Possible interpretations for the mean of a data set

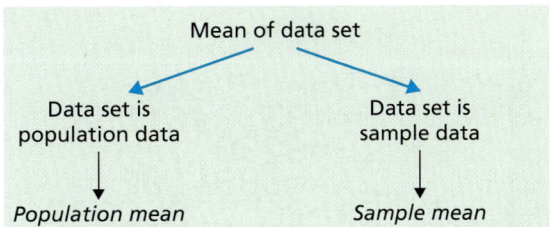

In Sections 3.2–3.4, we concentrate on descriptive measures of samples. Then, in Section 3.5, we discuss descriptive measures of populations and their relationship to descriptive measures of samples.

The Technology Center

For small data sets, such as the two sets of salary data in Tables 3.1 and 3.2, obtaining the mean, median, and mode by hand is easy. However, for even moderately large data sets, determining these descriptive measures by hand is tedious and prone to error.

All statistical software packages and most graphing calculators have built-in procedures for obtaining commonly used descriptive measures. Some offer individual descriptive measures, others provide related groups of descriptive measures, and still others supply both.

In Example 3.5, we present output for descriptive measures from three different technologies. Then we give (optional) step-by-step instructions for obtaining that output. Refer to the technology manuals for more details and other options.

Example 3.5 Using Technology to Obtain Descriptive Measures

Weekly Salaries Use Minitab, Excel, or the TI-83 Plus to obtain the mean and median of the salary data for Data Set I, displayed in Table 3.1 on page 90.

Solution Printout 3.1 shows output from Minitab, Excel, and the TI-83 Plus that provides several descriptive measures. At this point, we want to concentrate on the mean and median.

PRINTOUT 3.1
Output giving descriptive measures for Data Set I

MINITAB

```
Descriptive Statistics: SETI

Variable         N        Mean     Median    TrMean     StDev    SE Mean
SETI            13       483.8      400.0     449.1     265.8       73.7

Variable   Minimum    Maximum        Q1        Q3
SETI         300.0     1050.0     300.0     625.0
```

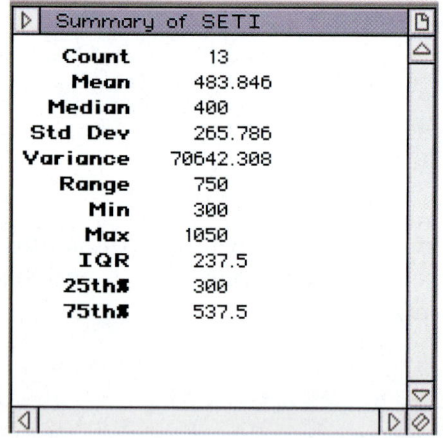

EXCEL

```
Summary of SETI
Count           13
Mean       483.846
Median         400
Std Dev    265.786
Variance 70642.308
Range          750
Min            300
Max           1050
IQR          237.5
25th%          300
75th%        537.5
```

TI-83 PLUS

```
1-Var Stats
x̄=483.8461538
Σx=6290
Σx²=3891100
Sx=265.7862067
σx=255.3591276
↓n=13
```

```
1-Var Stats
↑n=13
minX=300
Q₁=300
Med=400
Q₃=625
maxX=1050
```

All three outputs shown in Printout 3.1 reveal that the mean and median of Data Set I are 483.8 and 400, respectively. *Note:* The TI-83 Plus uses $\bar{x}$ to denote the mean, a notation that we discuss in Section 3.2. ◆

Obtaining the Output (Optional)

Here are detailed instructions for obtaining descriptive measures for Data Set I by using Minitab, Excel, and the TI-83 Plus. First, store the data from Table 3.1 in a column (Minitab), range (Excel), or list (TI-83 Plus) named SETI. Then proceed as follows.

MINITAB	EXCEL	TI-83 PLUS
1 Choose **Stat** ➤ **Basic Statistics** ➤ **Display Descriptive Statistics...** 2 Specify SETI in the **Variables** text box 3 Click **OK**	1 Choose **DDXL** ➤ **Summaries** 2 Select **Summary of One Variable** from the **Function type** drop-down box 3 Specify SETI in the **Quantitative Variable** text box 4 Click **OK**	1 Press **STAT** 2 Arrow over to **CALC** 3 Press **1** 4 Press **2nd** ➤ **LIST** 5 Arrow down to SETI and press **ENTER** twice

Exercises 3.1

Statistical Concepts and Skills

3.1 Explain in detail the purpose of a measure of center.

3.2 Name and describe the three most important measures of center.

3.3 Of the mean, median, and mode, which is the only one appropriate for use with qualitative data?

3.4 True or false: The mean, median, and mode can all be used with quantitative data.

3.5 Consider the data set 1, 2, 3, 4, 5, 6, 7, 8, 9.
a. Obtain the mean and median of the data.
b. Replace the 9 in the data set by 99 and again compute the mean and median. Decide which measure of center works better here and explain your answer.
c. For the data set in part (b), the mean is neither central nor typical for the data. The lack of what property of the mean accounts for this result?

3.6 Complete the following statement: A descriptive measure is *resistant* if ....

3.7 Floor Space. The U.S. Department of Housing and Urban Development and the U.S. Bureau of the Census compile information on new, privately owned single-family houses. According to the document *Characteristics of New Housing*, in 1998 the mean floor space of such homes was 2190 sq ft and the median was 2000 sq ft. Which measure of center do you think is more appropriate? Justify your answer.

3.8 Net Worth. The Board of Governors of the Federal Reserve System publishes information on family net worth in the *Federal Reserve Bulletin*. In 1998, the mean net worth of families in the United States was $208.1 thousand and the median net worth was $55.6 thousand. Which measure of center do you think is more appropriate? Explain your answer.

In Exercises 3.9–3.12, determine the mean, median, and mode(s) for each of the data sets by hand, that is, using only basic calculator functions. For the mean and the median, round each answer to one more decimal place than that used for the observations.

3.9 College Libraries. The National Center for Education Statistics surveys college and university libraries to obtain information on the number of volumes held. The number of volumes, in thousands, for a sample of seven public colleges and universities are as follows.

79	516	24	265	41	15	411

3.10 Hurricanes. A recent article by D. Schaefer et al. (*Journal of Tropical Ecology*, 2000, Vol. 16, pp. 189–207) reported on a long-term study of the effects of hurricanes on tropical streams of the Luquillo Experimental Forest in Puerto Rico. The study shows that Hurricane Hugo had a significant impact on stream water chemistry. The following is a sample of 10 ammonia fluxes in the first year after Hugo. Data are in kilograms per hectare per year.

96	66	147	147	175
116	57	154	88	154

3.11 Tornado Touchdowns. Each year, tornadoes that touch down are recorded by the Storm Prediction Center and published in *Monthly Tornado Statistics*. The following table gives the number of tornadoes that touched down in the United States during each month of 1998. [SOURCE: National Oceanic and Atmospheric Administration.]

| 47 | 72 | 72 | 182 | 308 | 373 |
| 82 | 60 | 104 | 86 | 25 | 6 |

3.12 Hospital Stays. The U.S. National Center for Health Statistics compiles data on the length of stay by patients in short-term hospitals and publishes its findings in *Vital and Health Statistics*. A random sample of nine patients yielded the following data on length of stay, in days.

| 4 | 12 | 18 | 9 | 12 | 6 | 7 | 3 | 55 |

3.13 All-Time Top TV Programs. According to *The World Almanac*, the all-time top television programs by rating (percentage of TV-owning households tuned into the program) are as shown in the following table. [SOURCE: Nielsen Media Research, January 1961–May 1998.]

Program	Telecast date	Network	Rating (%)	Audience (millions)
M*A*S*H (last episode)	02/28/83	CBS	60.2	50.2
Dallas (Who shot J.R.?)	11/21/80	CBS	53.3	41.5
Roots—Pt. 8	01/30/77	ABC	51.1	36.4
Super Bowl XVI	01/24/82	CBS	49.1	40.0
Super Bowl XVII	01/30/83	NBC	48.6	40.5
XVII Winter Olympics—2d Wed.	02/23/94	CBS	48.5	45.7
Super Bowl XX	01/26/86	NBC	48.3	41.5
Gone With the Wind —Pt. 1	11/07/76	NBC	47.7	34.0
Gone With the Wind —Pt. 2	11/08/76	NBC	47.4	33.8
Super Bowl XII	01/15/78	CBS	47.2	34.4
Super Bowl XIII	01/21/79	NBC	47.1	35.1
Bob Hope Christmas Show	01/15/70	NBC	46.6	27.3
Super Bowl XVIII	01/22/84	CBS	46.4	38.8
Super Bowl XIX	01/20/85	ABC	46.4	39.4
Super Bowl XIV	01/20/80	CBS	46.3	35.3
Super Bowl XXX	01/28/96	NBC	46.0	44.2
ABC Theatre (The Day After)	11/20/83	ABC	46.0	38.6
Roots—Pt. 6	01/28/77	ABC	45.9	32.7
The Fugitive	08/29/67	ABC	45.9	25.7
Super Bowl XXI	01/25/87	CBS	45.8	40.0

a. Determine the mode of the network data.
b. Would it be appropriate to use either the mean or the median here? Explain your answer.

3.14 Road Rage. The report *Controlling Road Rage: A Literature Review and Pilot Study*, dated June 9, 1999, was prepared for the AAA Foundation for Traffic Safety by Daniel B. Rathbone, Ph.D., and Jorg C. Huckabee, MSCE. The authors discuss the results of a literature review and pilot study on how to prevent aggressive driving and road rage. As described in the report, *road rage* is criminal behavior by motorists characterized by uncontrolled anger that results in violence or threatened violence on the road. One of the goals of the study was to determine when road rage occurs most often. The following data provide the days on which 69 road-rage incidents occurred.

F	Sa	W	M	Tu	F	Th	M
Tu	F	Tu	F	Su	W	Th	F
Th	W	Th	Sa	W	W	F	F
Tu	Su	Tu	Th	W	Sa	Tu	Th
F	W	F	F	Su	F	Th	Tu
F	Tu	Tu	Tu	Sa	W	W	Sa
F	Sa	Th	W	F	Th	F	M
F	M	F	Su	W	Th	M	Tu
Sa	Th	F	Su	W			

a. Determine the mode of the road-rage data.
b. Would it be appropriate to use either the mean or the median here? Explain your answer.

Extending the Concepts and Skills

3.15 Food Choice. As you discovered earlier, *ordinal data* are data about order or rank given on a scale such as 1, 2, 3, ... or A, B, C, ... Most statisticians recommend using the median to indicate the center of an ordinal data set, but some researchers also use the mean. In the paper "Measurement of Ethical Food Choice Motives" (*Appetite*, 2000, Vol. 34, pp. 55–59), research psychologists M. Lindeman and M. Väänänen of the University of Helsinki published a study on the factors that most influence people's choice of food. One of the questions asked of the participants was how important, on a scale of 1 to 4 (1 = not at all important, 4 = very important), is ecological welfare in food choice motive, where ecological welfare includes animal welfare and environmental protection. Here are the ratings given by 14 of the participants.

2	4	1	2	4	3	3
2	2	1	2	4	2	3

a. Compute the mean of the data.
b. Compute the median of the data.
c. Decide which of the two measures of center is best.

3.16 Outliers and Trimmed Means. Some data sets contain *outliers*, observations that fall well outside the overall pattern of the data. (We discuss outliers in more detail in Section 3.4.) Suppose, for instance, that you are interested in the ability of high school algebra students to compute square roots. You decide to give a square-root exam to 10 of these students. Unfortunately, one of the students had a fight with his girlfriend and cannot concentrate—he gets a 0. The 10 scores are displayed in increasing order in the following table. The score of 0 is an outlier.

0	58	61	63	67	69	70	71	78	80

Statisticians have a systematic method for avoiding extreme observations and outliers when they calculate means. They compute *trimmed means*, in which high and low observations are deleted or "trimmed off" before the mean is calculated. For instance, to compute the 10% trimmed mean of the test-score data, we first delete both the bottom 10% and the top 10% of the ordered data, that is, 0 and 80. Then we calculate the mean of the remaining data. Thus the 10% trimmed mean of the test-score data is

$$\frac{58 + 61 + 63 + 67 + 69 + 70 + 71 + 78}{8} = 67.1.$$

The following table displays a set of scores for a 40-question algebra final exam.

2	15	16	16	19	21	21	25	26	27
4	15	16	17	20	21	24	25	27	28

a. Do any of the scores look like outliers?
b. Compute the usual mean of the data.
c. Compute the 5% trimmed mean of the data.
d. Compute the 10% trimmed mean of the data.
e. Compare the means you obtained in parts (b)–(d). Which of the three means provides the best measure of center for the data?

Using Technology

3.17 Tornado Touchdowns. Use the technology of your choice to determine the mean and median of the tornado data in Exercise 3.11.

3.18 Hospital Stays. Use the technology of your choice to determine the mean and median of the length-of-stay data in Exercise 3.12.

3.19 Body Temperature. A study by researchers at the University of Maryland addressed the question of whether the mean body temperature of humans is 98.6°F. The results of the study by P. Mackowiak, S. Wasserman, and M. Levine appeared in the article "A Critical Appraisal of 98.6°F, the Upper Limit of the Normal Body Temperature, and Other Legacies of Carl Reinhold August Wunderlich" (*Journal of the American Medical Association*, 1992, Vol 268, pp. 1578–1580). The researchers obtained the body temperatures of 93 healthy humans. We have supplied these temperatures on the the WeissStats CD. Use the technology of your choice to determine the mean and median of the temperature data. Interpret your results.

3.20 Sex and Direction. In the paper "The Relation of Sex and Sense of Direction to Spatial Orientation in an Unfamiliar Environment" (*Journal of Environmental Psychology*, 2000, Vol. 20, pp. 17–28), Sholl et al. published the results of examining the sense of direction of 30 male and 30 female students. After being taken to an unfamiliar wooded park, the students were given a number of spatial orientation tests, including pointing to south, which tested their absolute frame of reference. Pointing to south was done by moving a pointer attached to a 360° protractor. We have supplied on the WeissStats CD the absolute pointing errors, in degrees, for both the male and female participants.
a. Use the technology of your choice to obtain the mean and median of each of the two data sets.
b. Use your results from part (a) to compare the two data sets.

3.2 THE SAMPLE MEAN

In this section, we discuss the sample mean in more detail. We also introduce some mathematical notation that is useful for expressing the formula for the sample mean and many other descriptive measures.

To begin, we note that in statistics, as in algebra, we use letters such as x, y, and z to denote variables. So, for instance, if we are studying heights and weights of college students, we might let x denote the variable "height" and y denote the variable "weight."

In Definition 3.1, we defined the mean of a data set in words: *The mean of a data set is the sum of the observations divided by the number of observations.* Using mathematical notation, we can express such definitions concisely. First, we introduce the mathematical notation for "sum of the observations" in Example 3.6.

Example 3.6 Introducing Summation Notation

Exam Scores The exam scores for the student in Example 3.4(a) are 88, 75, 95, and 100.

a. Use mathematical notation to represent the individual exam scores.
b. Use summation notation to express the sum of the four exam scores.

Solution Let x denote the variable "exam score."

a. We use the symbol x_i to represent the ith observation of the variable x. Thus, for the exam scores, we have

$$x_1 = \text{score on Exam 1} = 88;$$
$$x_2 = \text{score on Exam 2} = 75;$$
$$x_3 = \text{score on Exam 3} = 95;$$
$$x_4 = \text{score on Exam 4} = 100.$$

More simply, we can just write $x_1 = 88$, $x_2 = 75$, $x_3 = 95$, and $x_4 = 100$. The numbers 1, 2, 3, and 4 written below the xs are called **subscripts.**

b. Using the notation introduced in part (a), we can express the sum of the exam-score data symbolically as

$$x_1 + x_2 + x_3 + x_4.$$

We can use **summation notation** to obtain a shorthand description for this sum. This notation is the uppercase Greek letter Σ (sigma). That letter, which corresponds to the English letter S, is an abbreviation for the phrase "the sum of." So, in place of the lengthy expression $x_1 + x_2 + x_3 + x_4$, we can use Σx, read as "summation x" or "the sum of the observations of the variable x." For the exam-score data,

$$\Sigma x = x_1 + x_2 + x_3 + x_4 = 88 + 75 + 95 + 100 = 358.$$

In words, the sum of the four exam scores is 358. ◆

For clarity, we sometimes incorporate subscripts into the summation notation. We do so by writing Σx_i instead of Σx. The subscript i is a generic subscript. To be even more precise, we can use *indices* and write $\sum_{i=1}^{n} x_i$, read as "the sum of x_i from i equals 1 to n," where n denotes the number of observations.

NOTATION FOR A SAMPLE MEAN

Recall that a data set obtained by observing the values of a variable for a sample of a population is called *sample data* and that the mean of sample data is called a *sample mean*. The symbol used for a sample mean is a bar over the letter representing the variable.

So, for a variable x, a sample mean is denoted $\bar{x}$, read as "x bar." If we also use the letter n to denote the **sample size** or, equivalently, the number of observations, we can express the definition of a sample mean concisely.

DEFINITION 3.4 Sample Mean

For a variable x, the mean of the observations for a sample is called a *sample mean* and is denoted $\bar{x}$. Symbolically,

$$\bar{x} = \frac{\Sigma x}{n},$$

where n is the sample size.

We illustrate calculation of the sample mean in Example 3.7.

Example 3.7 The Sample Mean

AML and the Cost of Labor Active Management of Labor (AML) was introduced in the 1960s to reduce the amount of time a woman spends in labor during the birth process. Recently, R. Rogers et al. conducted a study to determine whether AML also translates into a reduction in delivery cost to the patient. They reported their findings in the paper "Active Management of Labor: A Cost Analysis of a Randomized Controlled Trial" (*Western Journal of Medicine*, 2000, Vol. 172, pp. 240–243).

Table 3.5 displays the costs, in dollars, of eight randomly sampled AML deliveries. Determine the sample mean of these delivery costs.

TABLE 3.5 Costs ($) of eight AML deliveries

3141.09	2873.28
2115.64	1683.61
3470.08	1798.89
2539.48	3092.56

Solution Let x denote the variable "cost" for AML deliveries. We want to obtain the mean, $\bar{x}$, of the eight observations of the variable x shown in Table 3.5. Summing those observations, we obtain $\Sigma x = 20{,}714.63$. Because the sample size (number of observations) is 8, we have $n = 8$. Thus

$$\bar{x} = \frac{\Sigma x}{n} = \frac{20{,}714.63}{8} = \$2{,}589.329.$$

In Chapter 9, we return to the AML study and decide whether it provides sufficient evidence to conclude that, on average, AML reduces delivery cost to the patient.

What Does it Mean?

The mean cost of the sample of eight AML deliveries is $2589.329.

OTHER IMPORTANT SUMS

We must often find sums other than the sum of the observations, Σx. One such sum is the sum of the squares of the observations, Σx^2. In Section 3.3, we need to obtain Σx, Σx^2, and various other sums. So that we can concentrate on the concepts presented there instead of the computations, we discuss computing those sums now, in Example 3.8.

Example 3.8 Other Important Sums

Exam Scores The exam-score data from Example 3.6 are repeated in the first column of Table 3.6. The remaining columns of the table contain some related quantities whose significance will become apparent in Section 3.3.

In Example 3.6, we found that the sum of the exam-score data is 358, a fact that we record at the bottom of the first column of Table 3.6. The second column of Table 3.6 displays the squares, x^2, of the exam scores. The sum of those squares is 32,394; that is, $\Sigma x^2 = 32{,}394$.

To obtain the third column of Table 3.6, we must first compute the mean, $\bar{x}$, of the four exam scores. Because $n = 4$ and $\Sigma x = 358$,

$$\bar{x} = \frac{\Sigma x}{n} = \frac{358}{4} = 89.5.$$

Subtracting 89.5 from each of the four exam scores in the first column of Table 3.6, we get the $x - \bar{x}$ values shown in the third column. The sum of those values is 0; that is, $\Sigma(x - \bar{x}) = 0$. The fourth column of Table 3.6 gives the squares, $(x - \bar{x})^2$, of the $x - \bar{x}$ values. The sum of those squares is 353; that is, $\Sigma(x - \bar{x})^2 = 353$.

TABLE 3.6
Exam-score data and related quantities

x	x^2	$x - \bar{x}$	$(x - \bar{x})^2$
88	7,744	−1.5	2.25
75	5,625	−14.5	210.25
95	9,025	5.5	30.25
100	10,000	10.5	110.25
358	32,394	0	353.00

Exercises 3.2

Statistical Concepts and Skills

3.21 Explain in your own words why mathematical notation is useful.

3.22 Explain what each symbol represents.
a. Σ b. n c. $\bar{x}$

3.23 For a given population, is the population mean a variable? What about a sample mean?

3.24 Let $x_1 = 1$, $x_2 = 7$, $x_3 = 4$, $x_4 = 5$, and $x_5 = 10$.
a. Compute Σx. b. Find n. c. Determine $\bar{x}$.

3.25 Let $x_1 = 12$, $x_2 = 8$, $x_3 = 9$, and $x_4 = 17$.
a. Compute Σx. b. Find n. c. Determine $\bar{x}$.

3.26 Honeymoons. Popular destinations for the newlyweds of today are the Caribbean and Hawaii. According to *Bride's Magazine*, a honeymoon, on average, lasts 9 days and costs $3657. A sample of 12 newlyweds reported the following lengths of stay of their honeymoons.

| 5 | 14 | 7 | 10 | 6 | 8 |
| 12 | 9 | 10 | 9 | 7 | 11 |

a. Compute Σx. b. Find n.
c. Determine the sample mean. Round your answer to one more decimal place than that used for the observations.

3.27 Sleep. In 1908, W. S. Gosset published the article "The Probable Error of a Mean" (*Biometrika*, Vol. 6, pp. 1–25). It is in this pioneering paper, written under the pseudonym "Student," that Gosset introduced what later became known as Student's t-distribution, which we discuss in Chapter 8. Gosset used the following data set, which shows the additional sleep in hours obtained by a sample of 10 patients given laevohysocyamine hydrobromide.

1.9	0.8	1.1	0.1	−0.1
4.4	5.5	1.6	4.6	3.4

a. Compute Σx. b. Find n.
c. Determine the sample mean. Round your answer to one more decimal place than that used for the observations.

3.28 Acute Postoperative Days. Several neurosurgeons wanted to see whether a dynamic system (Z-plate) reduced the number of acute postoperative days in the hospital relative to a static system (ALPS plate). R. Jacobowitz, Ph.D., an Arizona State University professor, along with G. Vishteh, M.D., and other neurosurgeons, obtained the following data on the number of acute postoperative days in the hospital for the static system.

6	18	9	7	14	9

a. Compute $\bar{x}$.
b. Compute Σx^2, $\Sigma(x - \bar{x})$, and $\Sigma(x - \bar{x})^2$ by constructing a table similar to Table 3.6.

3.29 NBA Champs. The winner of the 1999–2000 National Basketball Association (NBA) championship was the Los Angeles Lakers. The following table lists the starting players and their positions and heights.

Player	Position	Height (in.)
Ron Harper	Guard	78
Kobe Bryant	Guard	79
Robert Horry	Forward	82
A. C. Green	Forward	81
Shaquille O'Neal	Center	85

For the height data,
a. Compute $\bar{x}$.
b. Compute Σx^2, $\Sigma(x - \bar{x})$, and $\Sigma(x - \bar{x})^2$ by constructing a table similar to Table 3.6.

Extending the Concepts and Skills

3.30 Explain the difference between the quantities $(\Sigma x)^2$ and Σx^2. Construct an example to show that, in general, those two quantities are unequal.

3.31 Explain the difference between the quantities Σxy and $\Sigma x \Sigma y$. Provide an example to show that, in general, those two quantities are unequal.

3.32 For the exam-score data in Example 3.8, we found that $\Sigma(x - \bar{x}) = 0$. Explain why this result holds for any data set. (Hint: Write out the sum and use the fact that $\Sigma x = n\bar{x}$.)

3.3 MEASURES OF VARIATION; THE SAMPLE STANDARD DEVIATION

Up to this point, we have discussed only descriptive measures of center, specifically, the mean, median, and mode. However, two data sets can have the same mean, median, or mode and yet still be quite different in other respects. For example, consider the heights of the five starting players on each of two men's college basketball teams, as shown in Fig. 3.3 on the following page.

The two teams have the same mean heights, 75 inches (6' 3"); the same median heights, 76 inches (6' 4"); and the same modes, 76 inches (6' 4"). Nonetheless, the two data sets clearly differ. In particular, the heights of the players on Team II vary much more than those on Team I. To describe that difference quantitatively, we use a descriptive measure that indicates the amount of variation, or spread, in a data set. Such descriptive measures are referred to as **measures of variation** or **measures of spread**.

FIGURE 3.3
Five starting players on each of two men's college basketball teams and their heights

	Team I					Team II				
Feet and inches	6'	6'1"	6'4"	6'4"	6'6"	5'7"	6'	6'4"	6'4"	7'
Inches	72	73	76	76	78	67	72	76	76	84

Just as there are several different measures of center, there are also several different measures of variation. In this section, we examine two of the most frequently used measures of variation: the *range* and *sample standard deviation*. We begin with the range because it is the simplest to understand and compute.

THE RANGE

The contrast between the heights of the two teams shown in Fig. 3.3 becomes clear if we place the shortest player on each team next to the tallest, as shown in Fig. 3.4.

FIGURE 3.4
Shortest and tallest starting players on each of two men's college basketball teams and their heights

	Team I		Team II	
Feet and inches	6'	6'6"	5'7"	7'
Inches	72	78	67	84

> **What Does it Mean?**
> The heights of the players on Team II vary more than the heights of the players on Team I.

The **range** of a data set is obtained by computing the difference between the maximum (largest) and minimum (smallest) observations. From Fig. 3.4,

$$\text{Team I: Range} = 78 - 72 = 6 \text{ inches,}$$
$$\text{Team II: Range} = 84 - 67 = 17 \text{ inches.}$$

DEFINITION 3.5 **Range of a Data Set**

The *range* of a data set is the difference between its maximum and minimum observations: Range = Max − Min.

3.3 Measures of Variation; The Sample Standard Deviation

The range of a data set is quite easy to compute. However, when we use the range, a great deal of information is ignored: Only the largest and smallest observations are considered; the other observations are disregarded.

For that reason, two other measures of variation, the *standard deviation* and the *interquartile range*, are generally favored over the range. The standard deviation is the preferred measure of variation when the mean is used as the measure of center; the interquartile range is preferred when the median is used as the measure of center. We discuss the standard deviation in this section and consider the interquartile range in Section 3.4.

THE SAMPLE STANDARD DEVIATION

In contrast to the range, the standard deviation takes into account all the observations. The calculations required to determine a standard deviation are more involved than those needed to obtain a range. However, this problem is not serious because almost all computers and statistical calculators have built-in functions to do the necessary computations.

Roughly speaking, the **standard deviation** measures variation by indicating how far, on average, the observations are from the mean. For a data set with a large amount of variation, the observations will, on average, be far from the mean; hence the standard deviation will be large. For a data set with a small amount of variation, the observations will, on average, be close to the mean; consequently, the standard deviation will be small.

To compute the standard deviation of a data set, we need to know whether the set is population data or sample data. This information is necessary because the formulas for the standard deviations of sample data and population data differ slightly. In this section, we concentrate on the sample standard deviation. We discuss the population standard deviation in Section 3.5.

The first step in computing a sample standard deviation is to find how far each observation is from the mean, that is, the **deviations from the mean**. We show how to calculate them in Example 3.9.

Example 3.9 The Deviations From the Mean

Heights of Starting Players The heights, in inches, of the five starting players on Team I are 72, 73, 76, 76, and 78, as shown in Fig. 3.3. Find the deviations from the mean.

Solution The mean height of the starting players on Team I is

$$\bar{x} = \frac{\Sigma x}{n} = \frac{72 + 73 + 76 + 76 + 78}{5} = \frac{375}{5} = 75 \text{ inches.}$$

To obtain the deviation from the mean for a particular observation, we subtract the mean from it; that is, we compute $x - \bar{x}$. For instance, the deviation from the mean for the height of 72 inches is $x - \bar{x} = 72 - 75 = -3$. The deviations from the mean for all five observations are given in the second column of Table 3.7 and are displayed graphically in Fig. 3.5.

TABLE 3.7 Deviations from the mean

Height x	Deviation from mean $x - \bar{x}$
72	−3
73	−2
76	1
76	1
78	3

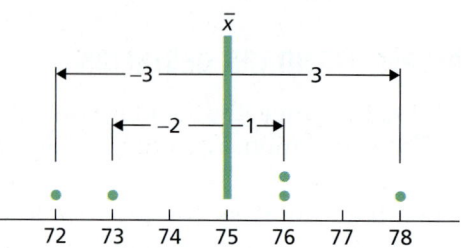

FIGURE 3.5 Graphical display of the deviations from the mean (dots represent observations)

The second step in computing a sample standard deviation is to obtain a measure of the total deviation from the mean for all the observations. Although the quantities $x - \bar{x}$ represent deviations from the mean, adding them to get a total deviation from the mean is of no value because their sum, $\Sigma(x-\bar{x})$, always equals zero. Summing the data in the second column of Table 3.7 shows this result to be true for the height data of Team I but, in fact, it is true in general.

In computing a sample standard deviation, the deviations from the mean, $x - \bar{x}$, are squared to obtain quantities that do not sum to zero. The sum of the squared deviations from the mean, $\Sigma(x - \bar{x})^2$, is called the **sum of squared deviations** and provides a measure of total deviation from the mean for all the observations. We show how to calculate it in Example 3.10.

Example 3.10 The Sum of Squared Deviations

Heights of Starting Players Compute the sum of squared deviations for the heights of the starting players on Team I.

Solution To get Table 3.8, we added a column for $(x - \bar{x})^2$ to Table 3.7.

TABLE 3.8 Table for computing the sum of squared deviations for the heights of Team I

Height x	Deviation from mean $x - \bar{x}$	Squared deviation $(x - \bar{x})^2$
72	−3	9
73	−2	4
76	1	1
76	1	1
78	3	9
		24

From the third column of Table 3.8, $\Sigma(x - \bar{x})^2 = 24$. The sum of squared deviations is 24 inches².

◆

The third step in computing a sample standard deviation is to take an average of the squared deviations. We do so by dividing the sum of squared deviations by $n - 1$, or 1 less than the sample size. The resulting quantity is called a **sample variance** and is denoted s_x^2 or, when no confusion can arise, s^2. In symbols,

$$s^2 = \frac{\Sigma(x - \bar{x})^2}{n - 1}.$$

Note: If we divided by n instead of by $n - 1$, the sample variance would be the mean of the squared deviations. Although dividing by n seems more natural, we divide by $n - 1$ for the following reason. One of the main uses of the sample variance is to estimate the population variance (defined in Section 3.5). Division by n tends to underestimate the population variance, whereas division by $n - 1$ gives, on average, the correct value.

The computation of the sample variance is shown in Example 3.11.

Example 3.11 The Sample Variance

Heights of Starting Players Obtain the sample variance of the heights of the starting players on Team I.

Solution From Example 3.10, the sum of squared deviations is 24 inches². Because $n = 5$,

$$s^2 = \frac{\Sigma(x - \bar{x})^2}{n - 1} = \frac{24}{5 - 1} = 6.$$

The sample variance is 6 inches².

◆

A sample variance is in units that are the square of the original units, the result of squaring the deviations from the mean. For instance, as we determined in Example 3.11, the sample variance of the heights of the players on Team I is 6 inches². Because descriptive measures should be expressed in the original units, the final step in computing a sample standard deviation is to take the square root of the sample variance. In other words, the **sample standard deviation**, denoted s_x or s, is

$$s = \sqrt{\frac{\Sigma(x - \bar{x})^2}{n - 1}},$$

which, for the heights of the players on Team I, is computed in Example 3.12.

Example 3.12 The Sample Standard Deviation

Heights of Starting Players Determine the sample standard deviation of the heights of the starting players on Team I.

108 CHAPTER 3 Descriptive Measures

Solution From Example 3.11, the sample variance is 6 inches². Thus the sample standard deviation is

$$s = \sqrt{\frac{\Sigma(x - \bar{x})^2}{n - 1}} = \sqrt{6} = 2.4 \text{ inches},$$

rounded to the nearest tenth of an inch. ◆

> **What Does it Mean?**
>
> Roughly speaking, on average, the heights of the players on Team I vary from the mean height of 75 inches by 2.4 inches.

The following definition summarizes our discussion of the sample standard deviation.

> **DEFINITION 3.6** **Sample Standard Deviation**
>
> For a variable x, the standard deviation of the observations for a sample is called a *sample standard deviation*. It is denoted s_x or, when no confusion will arise, simply s. We have
>
> $$s = \sqrt{\frac{\Sigma(x - \bar{x})^2}{n - 1}},$$
>
> where n is the sample size.

We performed the computations required to obtain a sample standard deviation in four separate examples to explain the sample standard deviation and the calculations involved. Now that we have done that, we can present a simple procedure for computing a sample standard deviation, which we illustrate in Example 3.13.

Step 1 Calculate the sample mean, $\bar{x}$.

Step 2 Construct a table to obtain the sum of squared deviations, $\Sigma(x - \bar{x})^2$.

Step 3 Apply Definition 3.6 to determine the sample standard deviation, s.

Example 3.13 **The Sample Standard Deviation**

Heights of Starting Players The heights, in inches, of the five starting players on Team II are 67, 72, 76, 76, and 84. Obtain the sample standard deviation of these heights.

Solution We apply the three-step procedure just described.

Step 1 Calculate the sample mean, $\bar{x}$.

We have

$$\bar{x} = \frac{\Sigma x}{n} = \frac{67 + 72 + 76 + 76 + 84}{5} = \frac{375}{5} = 75 \text{ inches}.$$

Step 2 Construct a table to obtain the sum of squared deviations, $\Sigma(x - \bar{x})^2$.

Table 3.9 provides columns for x, $x - \bar{x}$, and $(x - \bar{x})^2$. From the third column, $\Sigma(x - \bar{x})^2 = 156$ inches².

TABLE 3.9
Table for computing the sum of squared deviations for the heights of Team II

x	$x - \bar{x}$	$(x - \bar{x})^2$
67	−8	64
72	−3	9
76	1	1
76	1	1
84	9	81
		156

Step 3 Apply Definition 3.6 to determine the sample standard deviation, s.

We have $n = 5$ and $\Sigma(x - \bar{x})^2 = 156$. Consequently, the sample standard deviation of the heights for Team II is

$$s = \sqrt{\frac{\Sigma(x - \bar{x})^2}{n - 1}} = \sqrt{\frac{156}{5 - 1}} = \sqrt{39} = 6.2 \text{ inches},$$

rounded to the nearest tenth of an inch. ◆

> **What Does it Mean?**
>
> Roughly speaking, on average, the heights of the players on Team II vary from the mean height of 75 inches by 6.2 inches.

In Examples 3.12 and 3.13, we found that the sample standard deviations of the heights of the starting players on Teams I and II are 2.4 inches and 6.2 inches, respectively. Hence Team II, which has more variation in height than Team I, also has a larger standard deviation. That is the way a measure of variation is supposed to work.

Key Fact 3.1 **Variation and the Standard Deviation**

The more variation there is in a data set, the larger is its standard deviation.

Key Fact 3.1 shows that the standard deviation satisfies the basic criterion for a measure of variation; in fact, the standard deviation is the most commonly used measure of variation. However, the standard deviation does have its drawbacks. For instance, it is not resistant: Its value can be strongly affected by a few extreme observations.

A COMPUTING FORMULA FOR s

Next, we present an alternative formula for obtaining a sample standard deviation. Thus we need a name for the original formula given in Definition 3.6 to distinguish it from the alternative formula. Because the original formula was used to define the sample standard deviation, we call it the *defining formula* for s. The alternative formula for obtaining a sample standard deviation is given in Formula 3.1, which we call the *computing formula* for s.

FORMULA 3.1 Computing Formula for a Sample Standard Deviation

A sample standard deviation can be computed using the formula

$$s = \sqrt{\frac{\Sigma x^2 - (\Sigma x)^2/n}{n-1}},$$

where n is the sample size.

The computing formula for s is equivalent to the defining formula—both formulas give the same answer, although differences owing to roundoff error are possible. However, the computing formula is usually faster and easier for doing calculations by hand and also reduces the chance for roundoff error.

Before illustrating the computing formula for s in Example 3.14, we need to comment on the similar-looking expressions, Σx^2 and $(\Sigma x)^2$, that occur in that formula. The expression Σx^2 represents the sum of the squares of the data; it is obtained by first squaring each observation and then summing those squared values. The expression $(\Sigma x)^2$ represents the square of the sum of the data; it is obtained by first summing the observations and then squaring that sum.

In the numerator of the computing formula, the division of $(\Sigma x)^2$ by n should be performed before the subtraction from Σx^2. In other words, first compute $(\Sigma x)^2/n$ and then subtract the result from Σx^2.

Example 3.14 Computing Formula for s

Heights of Starting Players In Example 3.13, we obtained the sample standard deviation of the heights for the five starting players on Team II by using the defining formula for s. Obtain that sample standard deviation by using the computing formula.

Solution To apply the computing formula for s, we need the sums Σx and Σx^2. They are determined in Table 3.10.

We know that $n = 5$ and the bottom row of Table 3.10 shows that $\Sigma x = 375$ and $\Sigma x^2 = 28,281$. Thus, by Formula 3.1,

TABLE 3.10
Table for computation of s, using the computing formula

x	x^2
67	4,489
72	5,184
76	5,776
76	5,776
84	7,056
375	28,281

$$s = \sqrt{\frac{\Sigma x^2 - (\Sigma x)^2/n}{n-1}} = \sqrt{\frac{28,281 - (375)^2/5}{5-1}}$$

$$= \sqrt{\frac{28,281 - 28,125}{4}} = \sqrt{\frac{156}{4}} = \sqrt{39} = 6.2 \text{ inches},$$

rounded to the nearest tenth of an inch.

We have now obtained the sample standard deviation of the heights of the players on Team II in two ways—using the defining formula and using the computing formula. Both formulas give the same value, 6.2 inches, for the sample standard deviation. For these height data, either formula is relatively easy to apply. However, for most data sets—especially for those in which the mean is not a whole number—the computing formula is preferable.

Here is an important rule to remember when you use only basic calculator functions to obtain a sample standard deviation or any other descriptive measure.

> **Rounding Rule:** Do not perform any rounding until the computation is complete; otherwise, substantial roundoff error can result.

Another common rounding rule is to round final answers that contain units to one more decimal place than the raw data. Although we usually abide by this convention, occasionally we vary from it for pedagogical reasons. In general, you should stick to this rounding rule as well.

FURTHER INTERPRETATION OF THE STANDARD DEVIATION

Again, the standard deviation is a measure of variation—the more variation there is in a data set, the larger is its standard deviation. Table 3.11 displays two data sets, each with 10 observations. A brief inspection of the table reveals that Data Set II has more variation than Data Set I.

TABLE 3.11 Data sets that have different variation

Data Set I	41	44	45	47	47	48	51	53	58	66
Data Set II	20	37	48	48	49	50	53	61	64	70

TABLE 3.12 Means and standard deviations of the data sets in Table 3.11

Data Set I	Data Set II
$\bar{x} = 50.0$	$\bar{x} = 50.0$
$s = 7.4$	$s = 14.2$

We computed the sample mean and sample standard deviation of each data set and summarized the results in Table 3.12. As expected, the standard deviation of Data Set II is larger than that of Data Set I.

To enable you to compare visually the variations in the two data sets, we produced the graphs shown in Figs. 3.6 and 3.7, located on the following page. On each graph, we marked the observations with dots. In addition, we located the sample mean, $\bar{x} = 50$, and measured intervals equal in length to the standard deviation: 7.4 for Data Set I and 14.2 for Data Set II.

In Fig. 3.6, note that the horizontal position labeled $\bar{x} + 2s$ represents the number that is two standard deviations to the right of the mean, which in this case is

$$\bar{x} + 2s = 50.0 + 2 \cdot 7.4 = 50.0 + 14.8 = 64.8.[1]$$

Likewise, the horizontal position labeled $\bar{x} - 3s$ represents the number that is

---

[1] Recall that, for an expression of the form $a + b \cdot c$, the multiplication should be done before the addition. Thus $50.0 + 2 \cdot 7.4 = 50.0 + 14.8 = 64.8$. Similarly, for an expression of the form $a - b \cdot c$, the multiplication should be done before the subtraction.

FIGURE 3.6
Data Set I; $\bar{x} = 50$, $s = 7.4$

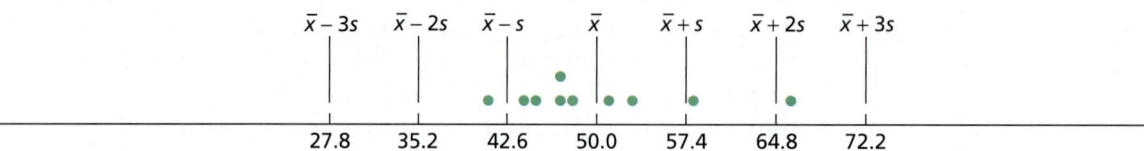

FIGURE 3.7
Data Set II; $\bar{x} = 50$, $s = 14.2$

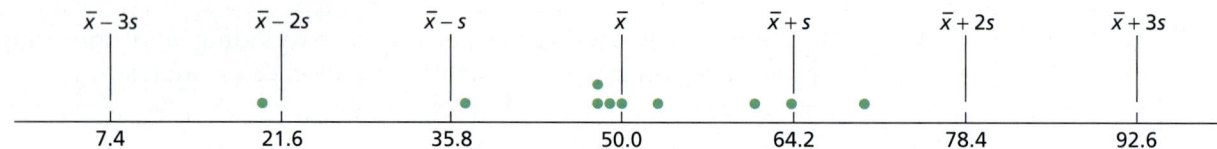

three standard deviations to the left of the mean, which in this case is

$$\bar{x} - 3s = 50.0 - 3 \cdot 7.4 = 50.0 - 22.2 = 27.8.$$

Figure 3.7 is interpreted in a similar manner.

The graphs shown in Figs. 3.6 and 3.7 vividly illustrate that Data Set II has more variation than Data Set I. They also show that for each data set all observations lie within a few standard deviations to either side of the mean. This result is no accident.

Key Fact 3.2 **Three-Standard-Deviations Rule**

Almost all the observations in any data set lie within three standard deviations to either side of the mean.

A data set with a great deal of variation has a large standard deviation, so three standard deviations to either side of its mean will be extensive, as shown in Fig. 3.7. A data set with little variation has a small standard deviation, and hence three standard deviations to either side of its mean will be narrow, as shown in Fig. 3.6.

The three-standard-deviations rule is somewhat vague—what does "almost all" mean? It can be made more precise in several ways, two of which we now briefly describe. We can apply **Chebychev's rule,** which is valid for all data sets and implies, in particular, that at least 89% of the observations lie within three standard deviations to either side of the mean. If the distribution of the data set is approximately bell-shaped, we can apply the **empirical rule** which implies, in particular, that roughly 99.7% of the observations lie within three standard deviations to either side of the mean.

We discuss both Chebychev's rule and the empirical rule in greater detail in the supplementary exercises for Section 3.3. These exercises can be found in the Supplementary Exercises folder on the WeissStats CD, which comes with your book.

3.3 Measures of Variation; The Sample Standard Deviation

The Technology Center

In this section, we discussed two measures of variation: the range and the sample standard deviation. For learning purposes, calculating a few of these and other descriptive measures by hand is essential. However, in practice, because such calculations are usually tedious and prone to error, you should use a computer or statistical calculator to obtain descriptive measures whenever possible.

In Section 3.1, we described a method for using technology to determine simultaneously several descriptive measures. Printout 3.1 on page 96—the outputs from Minitab, Excel, and the TI-83 Plus—contains the sample standard deviation, labeled StDev, Std Dev, and S_x, respectively.

These outputs also contain the maximum and minimum observations. From these two descriptive measures, we can easily obtain the range by subtraction: Range = Max − Min. Refer to the technology manuals for more details and other options.

Exercises 3.3

Statistical Concepts and Skills

3.33 Explain the purpose of a measure of variation.

3.34 Why is the standard deviation preferable to the range as a measure of variation?

3.35 When you use the standard deviation as a measure of variation, what is the reference point?

3.36 Discuss one major drawback to the standard deviation as a measure of variation.

3.37 Consider the data set 1, 2, 3, 4, 5, 6, 7, 8, 9.
a. Use the defining formula to obtain the sample standard deviation.
b. Replace the 9 in the data set by 99 and again use the defining formula to compute the sample standard deviation.
c. Compare your answers in parts (a) and (b). The lack of what property of the standard deviation accounts for its extreme sensitivity to the change of 9 to 99?

3.38 Consider the following four data sets.

Data Set I		Data Set II		Data Set III		Data Set IV	
1	5	1	9	5	5	2	4
1	8	1	9	5	5	4	4
2	8	1	9	5	5	4	4
2	9	1	9	5	5	4	10
5	9	1	9	5	5	4	10

a. Compute the mean of each data set.
b. Although the four data sets have the same means, they are quite different in another respect. How are they different?
c. Which data set appears to have the least variation? the greatest variation?
d. Compute the range of each data set.
e. Use the defining formula to compute the sample standard deviation of each data set.
f. From your answers to parts (d) and (e), which measure of variation better distinguishes the spread in the four data sets: the range or the standard deviation? Explain your answer.
g. Are your answers from parts (c) and (e) consistent?

3.39 IQ Scores. Below are 10 IQ scores.

| 110 | 122 | 132 | 107 | 101 |
| 97 | 115 | 91 | 125 | 142 |

Time each of the following calculations.
a. Use the defining formula to obtain the sample standard deviation of the 10 IQs.
b. Use the computing formula to obtain the sample standard deviation of the 10 IQs.
c. Did the computing formula save time? Explain why it did or did not.

3.40 Consider the data set 3, 3, 3, 3, 3, 3.
a. Guess the value of the sample standard deviation without calculating it. Explain your reasoning.
b. Use the defining formula to calculate the sample standard deviation.
c. Complete the following statement and explain your reasoning: If all observations in a data set are equal, the sample standard deviation is ___.
d. Complete the following statement and explain your reasoning: If the sample standard deviation of a data set is 0, ….

In Exercises 3.41–3.44, we repeat the essential data from Exercises 3.9–3.12 on pages 97–98. For each exercise, using only basic calculator functions, obtain the
a. range of the data.
b. sample standard deviation of the data from the defining formula.
c. sample standard deviation of the data from the computing formula.
d. State which formula you found easier to use in obtaining s.

Note: In parts (b) and (c), round your final answers to one more decimal place than that used for the data.

3.41 College Libraries. The number of volumes, in thousands, for a sample of seven public college and university libraries are as follows.

| 79 | 516 | 24 | 265 | 41 | 15 | 411 |

3.42 Hurricanes. Hurricane Hugo had a significant impact on stream water chemistry of streams in the Luquillo Experimental Forest in Puerto Rico. The following are a sample of 10 ammonia fluxes in the first year after Hugo. Data are in kilograms per hectare per year.

| 96 | 66 | 147 | 147 | 175 |
| 116 | 57 | 154 | 88 | 154 |

3.43 Tornado Touchdowns. The following table gives the number of tornadoes that touched down in the United States during each month of the year 1998.

| 47 | 72 | 72 | 182 | 308 | 373 |
| 82 | 60 | 104 | 86 | 25 | 6 |

3.44 Hospital Stays. A random sample of nine patients yielded the following data on length of stay, in days, by patients in short-term hospitals.

| 4 | 12 | 18 | 9 | 12 | 6 | 7 | 3 | 55 |

Extending the Concepts and Skills

3.45 Outliers. In Exercise 3.16 on page 99, we discussed *outliers*, or observations that fall well outside the overall pattern of the data. The following table contains two data sets. Data Set II was obtained by removing the outliers from Data Set I.

Data Set I					Data Set II			
0	12	14	15	23	10	14	15	17
0	14	15	16	24	12	14	15	
10	14	15	17		14	15	16	

a. Compute the sample standard deviation of each of the two data sets.
b. Compute the range of each of the two data sets.
c. What effect do outliers have on variation? Explain your answer.

Grouped-Data Formulas. When data are grouped in a frequency distribution, we use the following formulas to obtain the sample mean and sample standard deviation.

> **Grouped-Data Formulas.**
> $$\bar{x} = \frac{\Sigma xf}{n} \quad \text{and} \quad s = \sqrt{\frac{\Sigma(x-\bar{x})^2 f}{n-1}},$$
> where x denotes class midpoint, f denotes class frequency, and $n\ (=\Sigma f)$ denotes sample size.

In general, these formulas yield only approximations to the actual sample mean and sample standard deviation. We ask you to apply the grouped-data formulas in Exercises 3.46 and 3.47.

3.46 Weekly Salaries. In the following table, we repeat the salary data in Data Set II from Example 3.1.

300	300	940	450	400
400	300	300	1050	300

a. Use Definitions 3.4 and 3.6 on pages 101 and 108, respectively, to obtain the sample mean and sample standard deviation of this (ungrouped) data set.
b. A frequency distribution for Data Set II, based on single-value grouping, is presented in the first two columns of the following table. The third column of the table is for the xf-values, that is, class midpoint (which here is the same as the class) times class frequency.

Salary x	Frequency f	Salary · Frequency xf
300	5	1500
400	2	
450	1	
940	1	
1050	1	
	10	

Complete the missing entries in the table and then use the grouped-data formula to obtain the sample mean.
c. Compare the answers that you obtained for the sample mean in parts (a) and (b). Explain why the grouped-data formula always yields the actual sample mean when the data are grouped in classes that are each based on a single value. (*Hint:* What does xf represent for each class?)
d. Construct a table similar to the one in part (b) but with columns for $x, f, x - \bar{x}, (x - \bar{x})^2$, and $(x - \bar{x})^2 f$. Use the table and the grouped-data formula to obtain the sample standard deviation.
e. Compare your answers for the sample standard deviation in parts (a) and (d). Explain why the grouped-data formula always yields the actual sample standard deviation when the data are grouped in classes that are each based on a single value.

3.47 Days to Maturity. Following is a grouped-data table for the days to maturity for 40 short-term investments, as found in *Barron's National Business and Financial Weekly*.

Days to maturity	Frequency f	Relative frequency	Midpoint x
30 < 40	3	0.075	35
40 < 50	1	0.025	45
50 < 60	8	0.200	55
60 < 70	10	0.250	65
70 < 80	7	0.175	75
80 < 90	7	0.175	85
90 < 100	4	0.100	95
	40	1.000	

a. Use the grouped-data formulas to estimate the sample mean and sample standard deviation of the days-to-maturity data. Round your final answers to one decimal place.
b. The following table gives the raw days-to-maturity data.

70	64	99	55	64	89	87	65
62	38	67	70	60	69	78	39
75	56	71	51	99	68	95	86
57	53	47	50	55	81	80	98
51	36	63	66	85	79	83	70

Using Definitions 3.4 and 3.6 on pages 101 and 108, respectively, gives the true sample mean and sample standard deviation of the days-to-maturity data as 68.3 and 16.7, rounded to one decimal place. Compare these actual values of $\bar{x}$ and s to the estimates from part (a). Explain why the grouped-data formulas generally yield only approximations to the sample mean and sample standard deviation for non–single value grouping.

Using Technology

3.48 Tornado Touchdowns. Use the technology of your choice to determine the range and sample standard deviation of the tornado occurrence data in Exercise 3.43.

3.49 Hospital Stays. Use the technology of your choice to determine the range and sample standard deviation of the length-of-stay data in Exercise 3.44.

3.50 Body Temperature. Refer to Exercise 3.19 on page 99. Use the technology of your choice to determine the range and sample standard deviation of the temperature data which we have supplied on the WeissStats CD. Interpret your results.

3.51 Sex and Direction. Refer to Exercise 3.20 on page 99 and do the following.
a. Use the technology of your choice to obtain the range and sample standard deviation of each of the two data sets which we have supplied on the WeissStats CD.

b. Use your results from part (a) to compare the two data sets.

3.4 THE FIVE-NUMBER SUMMARY; BOXPLOTS

So far, we have focused on the mean and standard deviation to measure center and variation. We now examine several descriptive measures based on percentiles.

Unlike the mean and standard deviation, descriptive measures based on percentiles are *resistant*—they are not sensitive to the influence of a few extreme observations. For this reason, descriptive measures based on percentiles are often preferred over those based on the mean and standard deviation.

QUARTILES

As you learned in Section 3.1, the median of a data set divides the data into two equal parts: the bottom 50% and the top 50%. The **percentiles** of a data set divide it into hundredths, or 100 equal parts. A data set has 99 percentiles, denoted $P_1, P_2, \ldots, P_{99}$. Roughly speaking, the first percentile, P_1, is the number that divides the bottom 1% of the data from the top 99%; the second percentile, P_2, is the number that divides the bottom 2% of the data from the top 98%; and so on. Note that the median is also the 50th percentile.

Certain percentiles are particularly important: the **deciles** divide a data set into tenths (10 equal parts), the **quintiles** divide a data set into fifths (five equal parts), and the **quartiles** divide a data set into quarters (four equal parts).

Quartiles are the most commonly used percentiles. A data set has three quartiles, which we denote Q_1, Q_2, and Q_3. Roughly speaking, the **first quartile, Q_1,** is the number that divides the bottom 25% of the data from the top 75%; the **second quartile, Q_2,** is the median, which, as you know, is the number that divides the bottom 50% of the data from the top 50%; and the **third quartile, Q_3,** is the number that divides the bottom 75% of the data from the top 25%. Note that the first and third quartiles are the 25th and 75th percentiles, respectively.

Figure 3.8 depicts the quartiles for uniform, bell-shaped, right-skewed, and left-skewed distributions.

To determine the quartiles of a data set, we first obtain the set's median. Then we find the median of each of the two parts formed by the median of the entire data set. The resulting three numbers are the quartiles because they divide the data set into four parts that each contain (approximately) 25% of the data.

3.4 The Five-Number Summary; Boxplots

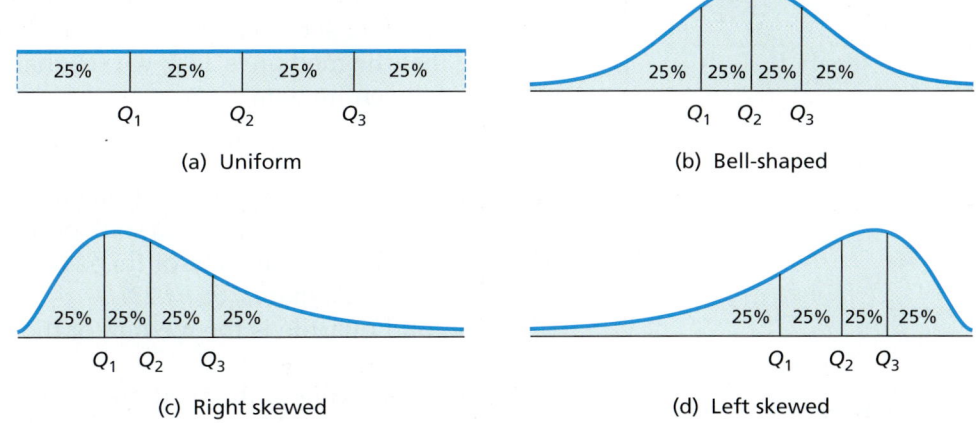

FIGURE 3.8
Quartiles for (a) uniform, (b) bell-shaped, (c) right-skewed, and (d) left-skewed distributions

DEFINITION 3.7

Quartiles

Arrange the data in increasing order and determine the median.

- The *first quartile* is the median of the data set that lies at or below the median of the entire data set.
- The *second quartile* is the median of the entire data set.
- The *third quartile* is the median of the data set that lies at or above the median of the entire data set.

Note: Not all statisticians define quartiles in exactly the same way. Other definitions may lead to different values but, in practice, the differences tend to be small with large data sets.

In Example 3.15, we demonstrate how to find quartiles.

Example 3.15 Quartiles

Weekly TV-Viewing Times The A. C. Nielsen Company publishes data on the TV-viewing habits of Americans by various characteristics in *Nielsen Report on Television*. A sample of 20 people yielded the weekly viewing times, in hours, displayed in Table 3.13. Determine and interpret the quartiles for these data.

Solution To find the quartiles, we apply Definition 3.7. First, we arrange the data in Table 3.13 in increasing order:

5 15 16 20 21 25 26 27 30 **30 31** 32 32 34 35 38 38 41 43 66

Next, we determine the median of the entire data set. The number of observations is 20, so the position of the median is at $(20 + 1)/2 = 10.5$, halfway between the tenth and eleventh observations (shown in boldface) in the ordered list. Thus, the median of the entire data set is $(30 + 31)/2 = 30.5$.

TABLE 3.13
Weekly TV-viewing times

25	41	27	32	43
66	35	31	15	5
34	26	32	38	16
30	38	30	20	21

The first quartile is the median of the data set that lies at or below the median of the entire data set. Referring to the ordered list of the entire data set and recalling that the median is 30.5, we see that the data set lying at or below the median of the entire data set is

$$5 \; 15 \; 16 \; 20 \; \mathbf{21} \; \mathbf{25} \; 26 \; 27 \; 30 \; 30$$

This data set has 10 observations. Its median is therefore at position $(10+1)/2 = 5.5$, halfway between the fifth and sixth observations (shown in boldface) in the ordered list. Thus the median of this data set—and hence the first quartile—is $(21 + 25)/2 = 23$; that is, $Q_1 = 23$.

The second quartile is the median of the entire data set, or 30.5. Therefore $Q_2 = 30.5$.

The third quartile is the median of the data set that lies at or above the median of the entire data set. Referring to the ordered list of the entire data set and recalling that the median is 30.5, we see that the data set lying at or above the median of the entire data set is

$$31 \; 32 \; 32 \; 34 \; \mathbf{35} \; \mathbf{38} \; 38 \; 41 \; 43 \; 66$$

This data set has 10 observations. Its median is therefore at position $(10+1)/2 = 5.5$, halfway between the fifth and sixth observations (shown in boldface) in the ordered list. Thus the median of this data set—and hence the third quartile—is $(35 + 38)/2 = 36.5$; that is, $Q_3 = 36.5$.

In summary, the three quartiles for the TV-viewing times in Table 3.13 are $Q_1 = 23$ hours, $Q_2 = 30.5$ hours, and $Q_3 = 36.5$ hours. ◆

> **What Does it Mean?**
>
> 25% of the TV-viewing times are less than 23 hours, 25% are between 23 hours and 30.5 hours, 25% are between 30.5 hours and 36.5 hours, and 25% are greater than 36.5 hours.

In Example 3.15, the number of observations is 20, which is even. To illustrate the determination of quartiles when the number of observations is odd, we consider the TV-viewing-time data again, but this time without the largest observation, 66. In this case, the ordered list of the entire data set is

$$5 \; 15 \; 16 \; 20 \; 21 \; 25 \; 26 \; 27 \; 30 \; \mathbf{30} \; 31 \; 32 \; 32 \; 34 \; 35 \; 38 \; 38 \; 41 \; 43$$

The median of the entire data set (also the second quartile) is 30, shown in boldface. The first quartile is the median of the data set that lies at or below the median of the entire data set, or the median of the 10 observations from 5 through the boldfaced 30, which is $(21 + 25)/2 = 23$. The third quartile is the median of the data set that lies at or above the median of the entire data set, or the median of the 10 observations from the boldfaced 30 through 43, which is $(34 + 35)/2 = 34.5$. Thus for this data set we have $Q_1 = 23$ hours, $Q_2 = 30$ hours, and $Q_3 = 34.5$ hours.

THE INTERQUARTILE RANGE

Next, we discuss the **interquartile range,** or **IQR.** Because quartiles are used to define the interquartile range, it is the preferred measure of variation when the median is used as the measure of center. Like the median, the interquartile range is a resistant measure.

3.4 The Five-Number Summary; Boxplots

DEFINITION 3.8 **Interquartile Range**

The *interquartile range*, or **IQR,** is the difference between the first and third quartiles; that is,

$$IQR = Q_3 - Q_1.$$

Roughly speaking, the IQR gives the range of the middle 50% of the observations.

In Example 3.16, we show how to obtain the interquartile range.

Example 3.16 *The Interquartile Range*

Weekly TV-Viewing Times Obtain the IQR for the TV-viewing-time data displayed in Table 3.13 on page 117.

Solution As we discovered in Example 3.15, the first and third quartiles are 23 and 36.5, respectively. Therefore the interquartile range is

$$Q_3 - Q_1 = 36.5 - 23 = 13.5 \text{ hours.}$$

In symbols, IQR = 13.5 hours. ◆

What Does it Mean?

The middle 50% of the TV-viewing times are spread out over a 13.5 hour interval, roughly.

THE FIVE-NUMBER SUMMARY

From the three quartiles, we can obtain a measure of center (the median, Q_2) and measures of variation of the two middle quarters of the data, $Q_2 - Q_1$ for the second quarter and $Q_3 - Q_2$ for the third quarter. But the three quartiles don't tell us anything about the variation of the first and fourth quarters.

To gain that information, we need only include the minimum and maximum observations as well. Then the variation of the first quarter can be measured as the difference between the minimum and the first quartile, $Q_1 - $ Min, and the variation of the fourth quarter can be measured as the difference between the third quartile and the maximum, Max $- Q_3$.

Thus the minimum, maximum, and quartiles together provide, among other things, information on center and variation. Written in increasing order, they comprise the **five-number summary** of a data set.

DEFINITION 3.9 **Five-Number Summary**

The *five-number summary* of a data set consists of the minimum, maximum, and quartiles written in increasing order: Min, Q_1, Q_2, Q_3, Max.

In Example 3.17, we show how to obtain and interpret the five-number summary of a set of data.

Example 3.17 The Five-Number Summary

Weekly TV-Viewing Times Obtain and interpret the five-number summary for the TV-viewing-time data given in Table 3.13 on page 117.

Solution From the ordered list of the entire data set (page 117), Min = 5 and Max = 66. Furthermore, as we showed earlier, $Q_1 = 23$, $Q_2 = 30.5$, and $Q_3 = 36.5$. Consequently, the five-number summary of the data on TV-viewing times is given by 5, 23, 30.5, 36.5, and 66 hours.

From the five-number summary, the variations of the four quarters of the TV-viewing-time data are 18, 7.5, 6, and 29.5 hours, respectively. Interpreting this information, we get the statement shown in the margin. ◆

> **What Does it Mean?**
>
> There is less variation in the middle two quarters of the TV-viewing times than in the first and fourth quarters, and the fourth quarter has the greatest variation of all.

OUTLIERS

In data analysis, the identification of **outliers,** or observations that fall well outside the overall pattern of the data, is important. An outlier requires special attention. It may be the result of a measurement or recording error, an observation from a different population, or an unusual extreme observation. Note that an extreme observation need not be an outlier; it may instead be an indication of skewness.

As an example of an outlier, consider the data set consisting of the individual wealths (in dollars) of all U.S. residents. For this data set, the wealth of Bill Gates is an outlier—in this case, an unusual extreme observation.

When an outlier is observed, you should always try to determine its cause. If an outlier is caused by a measurement or recording error, or for some other reason it clearly does not belong in the data set, the outlier can simply be removed. However, if no explanation for the outlier is apparent, the decision whether to retain it in the data set can often be a difficult judgment call.

We can use quartiles and the IQR to identify potential outliers, that is, as a diagnostic tool for spotting observations that may be outliers. To do so, we define the **lower limit** and the **upper limit** as the numbers that lie 1.5 IQRs below the first quartile and 1.5 IQRs above the third quartile, respectively.

DEFINITION 3.10 Lower and Upper Limits

The *lower limit* and *upper limit* are defined as follows:

$$\text{Lower limit} = Q_1 - 1.5 \cdot \text{IQR};$$

$$\text{Upper limit} = Q_3 + 1.5 \cdot \text{IQR}.$$

Observations that lie outside the lower and upper limits—either below the lower limit or above the upper limit—are potential outliers. Further data analysis should be done (using histograms, stem-and-leaf diagrams, or other methods) to find out whether such observations are truly outliers. In Example 3.18, we demonstrate this process.

Example 3.18 Outliers

Weekly TV-Viewing Times For the TV-viewing-time data in Table 3.13 on page 117,

a. obtain the lower and upper limits.
b. determine potential outliers, if any.

Solution a. As before, $Q_1 = 23$, $Q_3 = 36.5$, and IQR $= 13.5$. Therefore

$$\text{Lower limit} = Q_1 - 1.5 \cdot \text{IQR} = 23 - 1.5 \cdot 13.5 = 2.75 \text{ hours};$$

$$\text{Upper limit} = Q_3 + 1.5 \cdot \text{IQR} = 36.5 + 1.5 \cdot 13.5 = 56.75 \text{ hours}.$$

These limits are portrayed graphically in Fig. 3.9.

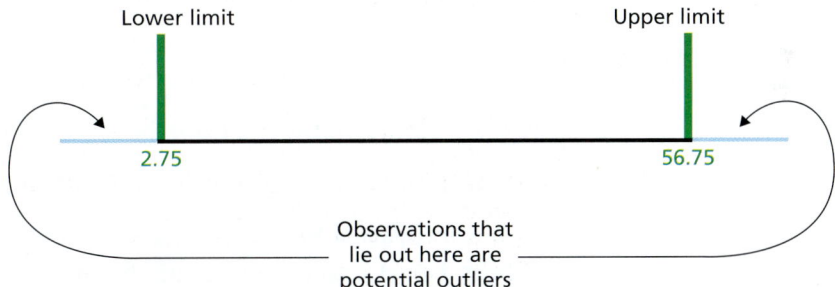

FIGURE 3.9
Lower and upper limits for TV-viewing times

What Does it Mean?

The weekly viewing time of 66 hours lies outside the overall pattern of the other 19 viewing times in the data set.

b. The ordered list of the entire data set on page 117 reveals one observation, 66, that lies outside the lower and upper limits—specifically, above the upper limit. Consequently, 66 is a potential outlier. A histogram and a stem-and-leaf diagram both indicate that the observation of 66 hours is truly an outlier. ◆

BOXPLOTS

A **boxplot,** also called a **box-and-whisker diagram,** is based on the five-number summary and can be used to provide a graphical display of the center and variation of a data set. These diagrams, like stem-and-leaf diagrams, were invented by Professor John Tukey.

Actually, two types of boxplots are in common use. One is simply called a boxplot; the other is called a **modified boxplot.** The main difference between the two types of boxplots is that potential outliers are plotted individually in a modified boxplot, but not in a boxplot. Thus, when outliers are of concern, modified boxplots are the preferred type of boxplot. Procedures 3.1 and 3.2 provide step-by-step instructions for constructing boxplots and modified boxplots, respectively.

Procedure 3.1

To Construct a Boxplot

Step 1 Determine the five-number summary.

Step 2 Draw a horizontal axis on which the numbers obtained in Step 1 can be located. Above this axis, mark the quartiles and the minimum and maximum with vertical lines.

Step 3 Connect the quartiles to make a box and then connect the box to the minimum and maximum with lines.

To construct a modified boxplot, we need to use the concept of *adjacent values*. The **adjacent values** of a data set are the most extreme observations that still lie within the lower and upper limits, that is, the most extreme observations that are not potential outliers. Note that, if a data set has no potential outliers, the adjacent values are just the minimum and maximum observations.

Procedure 3.2

To Construct a Modified Boxplot

Step 1 Determine the quartiles.

Step 2 Determine potential outliers and the adjacent values.

Step 3 Draw a horizontal axis on which the numbers obtained in Steps 1 and 2 can be located. Above this axis, mark the quartiles and the adjacent values with vertical lines.

Step 4 Connect the quartiles to make a box and then connect the box to the adjacent values with lines.

Step 5 Plot each potential outlier with an asterisk.

Note:

- If a data set has no potential outliers, its boxplot and modified boxplot are identical.
- In both types of boxplots, the two lines emanating from the box are called **whiskers**.
- Boxplots are frequently drawn vertically instead of horizontally.
- Symbols other than an asterisk are often used to plot potential outliers.

In Example 3.19, we demonstrate the use of Procedures 3.1 and 3.2 in obtaining a boxplot and a modified boxplot for a set of data.

Example 3.19 *Boxplots and Modified Boxplots*

Weekly TV-Viewing Times The weekly TV-viewing times for a sample of 20 people are displayed in Table 3.13 on page 117. Construct a boxplot and, if appropriate, a modified boxplot.

3.4 The Five-Number Summary; Boxplots

Solution To obtain a boxplot for the TV-viewing times, we apply the step-by-step method presented in Procedure 3.1.

Step 1 Determine the five-number summary.

We have already obtained the five-number summary for the TV-viewing times: Min = 5, $Q_1 = 23$, $Q_2 = 30.5$, $Q_3 = 36.5$, and Max = 66.

Step 2 Draw a horizontal axis on which the numbers obtained in Step 1 can be located. Above this axis, mark the quartiles and the minimum and maximum with vertical lines.

See Fig. 3.10(a).

Step 3 Connect the quartiles to make a box and then connect the box to the minimum and maximum with lines.

See Fig. 3.10(a).

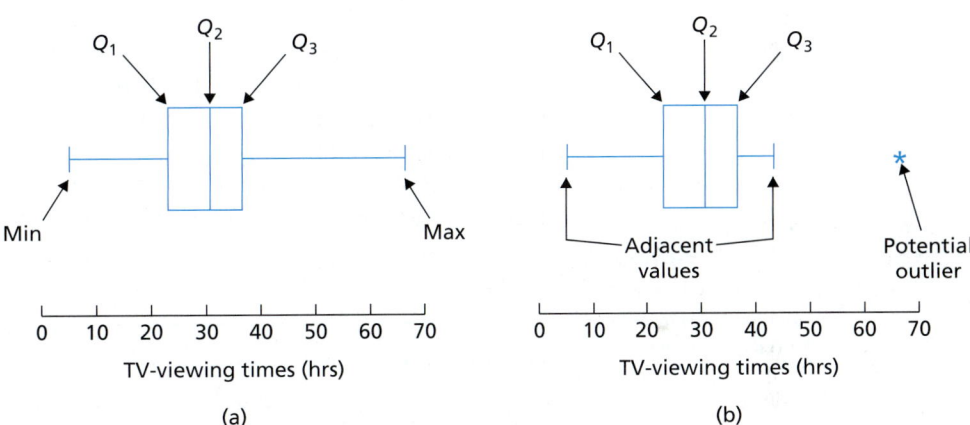

FIGURE 3.10
(a) Boxplot for TV-viewing times;
(b) modified boxplot for TV-viewing times

What Does it Mean?

There is less variation in the middle two quarters of the TV-viewing times than in the first and fourth quarters, and the fourth quarter has the greatest variation of all.

Figure 3.10(a) is a boxplot for the data on TV-viewing times. Because the ends of the combined box are at the quartiles, the width of that box equals the interquartile range, IQR. Observe that the two boxes in the boxplot indicate the spread of the second and third quarters of the data and that the two whiskers indicate the spread of the first and fourth quarters.

We discovered earlier that the TV-viewing times contain a potential outlier. Therefore it is appropriate to construct a modified boxplot because it will be different from the boxplot that we just obtained. To do so, we apply Procedure 3.2.

Step 1 Determine the quartiles.

The quartiles for the TV-viewing times were found in Example 3.15: $Q_1 = 23$, $Q_2 = 30.5$, and $Q_3 = 36.5$.

Step 2 Determine the potential outliers and the adjacent values.

The TV-viewing times contain one potential outlier, 66. From the ordered list of the entire data set on page 117, the adjacent values are 5 and 43.

Step 3 Draw a horizontal axis on which the numbers obtained in Steps 1 and 2 can be located. Above this axis, mark the quartiles and the adjacent values with vertical lines.

See Fig. 3.10(b).

Step 4 Connect the quartiles to make a box and then connect the box to the adjacent values with lines.

See Fig. 3.10(b).

Step 5 Plot each potential outlier with an asterisk.

As we noted in Step 2, this data set contains one potential outlier—namely, 66. It is plotted with an asterisk in Fig. 3.10(b). ◆

OTHER USES OF BOXPLOTS

Boxplots are especially suited to comparing two or more data sets. In doing so, you should use the same scale for all the boxplots. We introduce this use of boxplots in the exercises for this section and, later, when we discuss inferential statistics, we further apply this use of boxplots as an exploratory tool preliminary to inference.

We can also use a boxplot to identify the approximate shape of the distribution of a data set. Figure 3.11 displays some common distribution shapes and

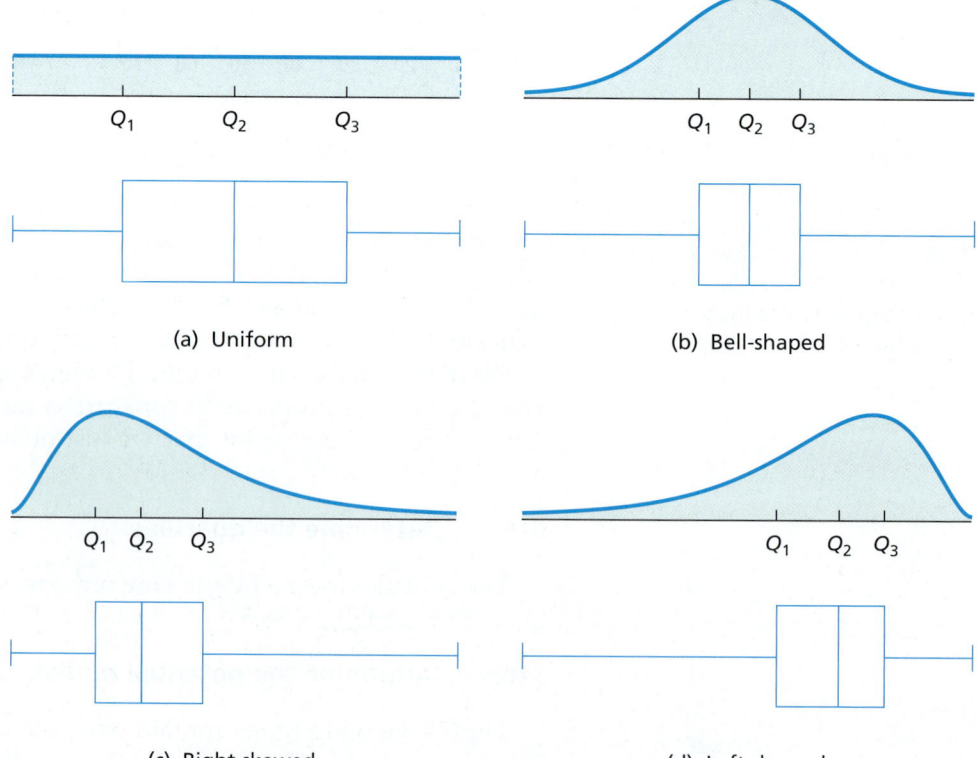

FIGURE 3.11
Distribution shapes and boxplots for (a) uniform, (b) bell-shaped, (c) right-skewed, and (d) left-skewed distributions

(a) Uniform

(b) Bell-shaped

(c) Right skewed

(d) Left skewed

their corresponding boxplots. Study Fig. 3.11 carefully, noting especially how box width and whisker length relate to skewness and symmetry.

Employing boxplots to identify the shape of a distribution is most useful with large data sets. For small data sets, boxplots can be unreliable in identifying distribution shape; using a stem-and-leaf diagram or dotplot is generally a better way to ascertain distribution shape for a small data set.

The Technology Center

In Section 3.1, we discussed a method for using technology to determine simultaneously several descriptive measures. Printout 3.1 on page 96—the output from Minitab, Excel, and the TI-83 Plus—includes the five-number summary.

Minitab, Excel, and the TI-83 have built-in programs for obtaining modified boxplots. Both Minitab and the TI-83 Plus also provide programs for boxplots. Here we discuss the use of these three technologies to get modified boxplots. For other options, refer to the technology manuals.

Example 3.20 Using Technology to Obtain a Modified Boxplot

Weekly TV-Viewing Times   Use Minitab, Excel, or the TI-83 Plus to obtain a modified boxplot for the TV-viewing times displayed in Table 3.13 on page 117.

Solution   Printout 3.2 on the following page shows the output obtained by applying the modified-boxplot programs to the TV-viewing-time data.

As we mentioned earlier and as Printout 3.2 shows, boxplots are frequently drawn vertically instead of horizontally. Compare the modified boxplots in Printout 3.2 to the one in Fig. 3.10(b) on page 123.   ◆

Obtaining the Output (Optional)

Here are detailed instructions for obtaining a modified boxplot for the TV-viewing times, using Minitab, Excel, and the TI-83 Plus. First, store the data from Table 3.13 on page 117 in a column (Minitab), range (Excel), or list (TI-83 Plus) named TIMES. Then proceed as follows.

MINITAB	EXCEL	TI-83 PLUS
1 Choose **Graph ➤ Boxplot...** 2 Specify TIMES in the **Y** text box for **Graph 1** 3 Click **OK**	1 Choose **DDXL ➤ Charts and Plots** 2 Select **Boxplot** from the **Function type** drop-down box 3 Specify TIMES in the **Quantitative Variables** text box 4 Click **OK**	1 Press **2nd ➤ STAT PLOT** and then press **ENTER** twice 2 Arrow to the fourth graph icon and press **ENTER** 3 Press the down-arrow key 4 Press **2nd ➤ LIST** 5 Arrow down to TIMES and press **ENTER** 6 Press **ZOOM** and then **9** (and then **TRACE**, if desired)

PRINTOUT 3.2
Modified-boxplot output for the TV-viewing times

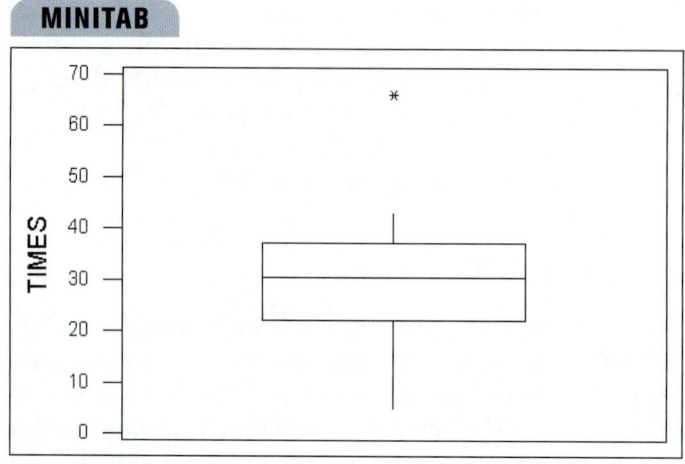

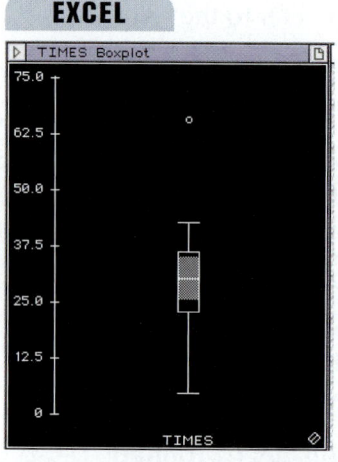

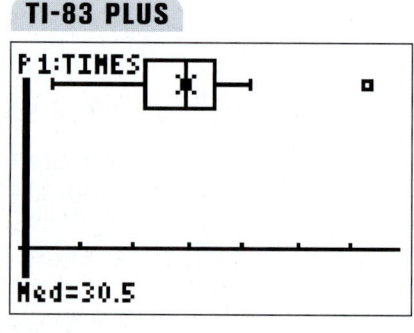

Exercises 3.4

Statistical Concepts and Skills

3.52 Identify by name three important groups of percentiles.

3.53 Identify an advantage that the median and interquartile range have over the mean and standard deviation, respectively.

3.54 Explain why the minimum and maximum observations are added to the three quartiles to describe better the variation in a data set.

3.55 Is an extreme observation necessarily an outlier? Explain your answer.

3.56 Under what conditions are boxplots useful for identifying the shape of a distribution?

3.57 Regarding the interquartile range,
a. what type of descriptive measure is it?
b. what does it measure?

3.58 Identify a use of the lower and upper limits.

3.59 When is a modified boxplot the same as a boxplot? Explain your answer.

3.60 Which measure of variation is preferred when
a. the mean is used as a measure of center?
b. the median is used as a measure of center?

In Exercises 3.61–3.64, use only basic calculator functions to determine the quartiles.

3.61 Traveling Salmon. The Pacific salmon (*Oncorhynchus spp.*) spends part of its life in freshwater and the other in saltwater. A fisheries scientist at the University of Washington was interested in the distance that salmon travel per day while at sea. She radio-tagged 16 salmon and determined the miles traveled per day. Her findings are given in the following table. [SOURCE: Public Broadcasting System.]

31	16	29	13
21	23	38	30
44	51	38	22
35	30	18	28

3.62 Unemployment Benefits. The U.S. Employment and Training Administration reports figures on average weekly unemployment benefits in the *Unemployment Insurance Financial Handbook*. A random sample of 14 currently unemployed individuals in Nevada gave the following amounts of their weekly unemployment checks, in dollars.

200	195	215	205	180	212	190
210	220	205	198	202	225	210

3.63 Hospital Stays. The U.S. National Center for Health Statistics compiles data on the length of stay by patients in short-term hospitals and publishes its findings in *Vital and Health Statistics*. A random sample of 21 patients yielded the following data on length of stay, in days.

4	4	12	18	9	6	12
3	6	15	7	3	55	1
10	13	5	7	1	23	9

3.64 Miles Driven. The U.S. Federal Highway Administration conducts studies on motor vehicle travel by type of vehicle. Results are published annually in *Highway Statistics*. A sample of 15 cars yields the following data on number of miles driven, in thousands, for last year.

13.2	13.3	11.9	15.7	11.3
12.2	16.7	10.7	3.3	13.6
14.8	9.6	11.6	8.7	15.0

In Exercises 3.65–3.68,
a. *determine the interquartile range.*
b. *obtain the five-number summary.*
c. *identify potential outliers, if any.*
d. *construct and interpret a boxplot and, if appropriate, a modified boxplot.*

3.65 Traveling Salmon. The miles traveled by the 16 radio-tagged salmon, as given in Exercise 3.61.

3.66 Unemployment Benefits. The amounts of the weekly unemployment checks of 14 currently unemployed individuals in Nevada, as given in Exercise 3.62.

3.67 Hospital Stays. The lengths of stay in short-term hospitals by 21 randomly selected patients, as given in Exercise 3.63.

3.68 Miles Driven. The number of thousands of miles 15 cars were driven last year, as given in Exercise 3.64.

3.69 Nicotine Patches. In the paper "The Smoking Cessation Efficacy of Varying Doses of Nicotine Patch Delivery Systems 4 to 5 Years Post-Quit Day" (*Preventative Medicine*, 1999, 28, pp. 113–118), D. Daughton et al. discussed the long-term effectiveness of transdermal nicotine patches on participants who had previously smoked at least 20 cigarettes per day. A sample of 15 participants in the Transdermal Nicotine Study Group (TNSG) reported that they now smoke the following number of cigarettes per day.

10	9	10	8	7
6	10	9	10	8
9	10	8	8	10

a. Determine the quartiles for these data.
b. Remark on the usefulness of quartiles with respect to this data set.

Extending the Concepts and Skills

3.70 Starting Salaries. Surveys are conducted by the Northwestern University Placement Center, Evanston, Illinois, on starting salaries for college graduates. Results of the surveys can be found in *The Northwestern Lindquist-Endicott Report*. The following diagram shows boxplots for the starting annual salaries, in thousands of dollars, obtained from samples of 32 computer-science graduates (top boxplot) and 35 accounting graduates (bottom boxplot). Use the boxplots to compare the starting salaries of the computer-science and accounting graduates sampled.

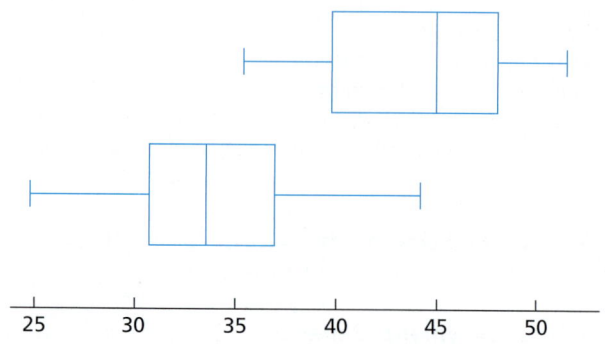

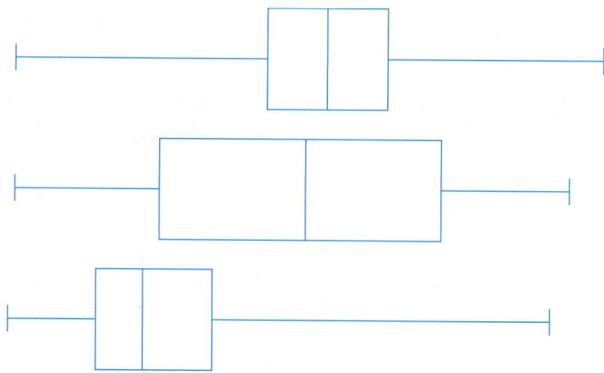

3.71 Obesity. Researchers in obesity wanted to compare the effectiveness of dieting with exercise against dieting without exercise. Seventy-three patients were randomly divided into two groups. Group 1, composed of 37 patients, was put on a program of dieting with exercise. Group 2, composed of 36 patients, dieted only. The results for weight loss, in pounds, after 2 months are summarized in the following boxplots. The top boxplot is for Group 1 and the bottom boxplot is for Group 2. Use the boxplots to compare the weight losses for the two groups.

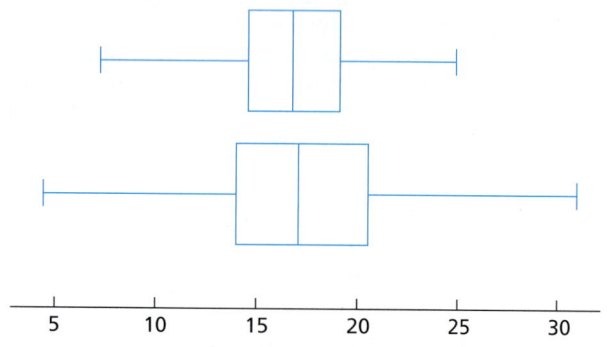

3.72 Each of the following boxplots was obtained from a very large data set. Use the boxplots to identify the approximate shape of the distribution of each data set.

3.73 What can you say about the boxplot of a symmetric distribution?

Using Technology

3.74 Traveling Salmon. Refer to the miles-traveled data for the 16 radio-tagged salmon, as given in Exercise 3.61. Use the technology of your choice to
a. obtain a boxplot for the data.
b. determine the five-number summary of the data.

3.75 Unemployment Benefits. Refer to the data on the amounts of the weekly unemployment checks of 14 currently unemployed individuals in Nevada, as given in Exercise 3.62. Use the technology of your choice to
a. obtain a boxplot for the data.
b. determine the five-number summary of the data.

3.76 Body Temperature. Refer to Exercise 3.19 on page 99. Use the technology of your choice to determine a boxplot and the five-number summary of the temperature data, which we have supplied on the WeissStats CD. Interpret your results.

3.77 Sex and Direction. Refer to Exercise 3.20 on page 99 and do the following.
a. Use the technology of your choice to obtain side-by-side boxplots of the two data sets, which we have supplied on the WeissStats CD.
b. Use the boxplots that you obtained in part (a) to compare the two data sets.

3.5 DESCRIPTIVE MEASURES FOR POPULATIONS; USE OF SAMPLES

In this section, we discuss several descriptive measures for *population data*—the data obtained by observing the values of a variable for an entire population. Although, in reality, we often don't have access to population data, it is nonetheless helpful to become familiar with the notation and formulas used for descriptive measures of such data.

THE POPULATION MEAN

Recall that, for a variable x and a sample of size n from a population, the sample mean is

$$\bar{x} = \frac{\Sigma x}{n}.$$

First, we sum the observations of the variable for the sample, and then we divide by the size of the sample.

The mean of a finite population is obtained similarly: First, we sum all possible observations of the variable for the entire population, and then we divide by the size of the population. However, to distinguish the **population mean** from a sample mean, we use the Greek letter μ (pronounced "mew") to denote the population mean. We also use the uppercase English letter N to represent the size of the population.

Table 3.14 summarizes the notation used for both a sample and the population.

TABLE 3.14 Notation used for a sample and for the population

	Size	Mean
Sample	n	$\bar{x}$
Population	N	μ

DEFINITION 3.11 Population Mean (Mean of a Variable)

For a variable x, the mean of all possible observations for the entire population is called the *population mean* or *mean of the variable x*. It is denoted μ_x or, when no confusion will arise, simply μ. For a finite population,

$$\mu = \frac{\Sigma x}{N},$$

where N is the population size.

Example 3.21 illustrates calculation of the population mean.

Example 3.21 The Population Mean

U.S. Women's World Cup Soccer Team On Saturday, July 10, 1999, in front of the largest crowd ever to see a women's soccer game, the United States beat China in a thrilling 120-minute match that was ultimately decided in a penalty-kick shootout. The 1999 U.S. Women's World Cup team became world champions.

According to *CNN/Sports Illustrated Online*, data for the players on that team are as shown in Table 3.15 on the next page. The weights are rounded to the nearest 5 pounds. Obtain the population mean weight of these soccer players.

Solution The variable under consideration here is weight, and the population of interest consists of the players on the 1999 U.S. Women's World Cup soccer team. The sum of the weights in Table 3.15 is 2695 pounds. Because there are 20 players, $N = 20$. Consequently,

$$\mu = \frac{\Sigma x}{N} = \frac{2695}{20} = 134.75 \text{ lb}.$$

What Does it Mean?

The population mean weight of the players on the 1999 U.S. Women's World Cup soccer team is 134.75 pounds.

TABLE 3.15
U.S. Women's World Cup soccer team, 1999

Name	Position	Height	Weight (lb)	College
Briana Scurry	G	5'8"	145	UMass
Lorrie Fair	D	5'3"	125	UNC
Christie Pearce	D	5'6"	140	Monmouth
Carla Overbeck	D	5'7"	125	UNC
Tiffany Roberts	M	5'4"	120	UNC
Brandi Chastain	D	5'7"	130	Santa Clara
Sara Whalen	D	5'5"	130	UConn
Shannon MacMillan	F	5'5"	130	Portland
Mia Hamm	F	5'5"	130	UNC
Michelle Akers	M	5'10"	150	Central Florida
Julie Foudy	M	5'6"	130	Stanford
Cindy Parlow	F	5'11"	145	UNC
Kristine Lilly	M	5'4"	130	UNC
Joy Fawcett	D	5'5"	130	California
Tisha Venturini	M	5'6"	125	UNC
Tiffeny Milbrett	F	5'2"	125	Portland
Danielle Fotopoulos	F	5'11"	165	Florida
Saskia Webber	G	5'9"	135	Rutgers
Tracy Ducar	G	5'7"	145	UNC
Kate Sobrero	D	5'9"	140	Notre Dame

USING A SAMPLE MEAN TO ESTIMATE A POPULATION MEAN

In inferential studies, we analyze sample data. Nonetheless, the objective is to describe the entire population. The reason for resorting to a sample is that its use is generally more practical. We illustrate this point in Example 3.22.

Example 3.22 A Use of a Sample Mean

Estimating Mean Household Income The U.S. Bureau of the Census reports the mean (annual) income of U.S. households in the publication *Current Population Reports*. To obtain the population data—the incomes of all U.S. households—would be extremely expensive and time-consuming. It is also unnecessary because accurate estimates of the mean income of all U.S. households can be obtained from the mean income of a sample of such households. In reality, the Census Bureau samples 60,000 households from a total of more than 100 million U.S. households.

The variable under consideration here is household income; the population of interest is all U.S. households; the mean income of all U.S. households is the population mean, μ. The sample consists of the 60,000 households obtained by the Census Bureau; the mean income of those households is a sample mean, $\bar{x}$. Figure 3.12 summarizes this discussion graphically.

After the sample has been taken, the Census Bureau can compute the sample mean income, $\bar{x}$, of the 60,000 households obtained. Using the value of $\bar{x}$, the Census Bureau can then estimate the population mean income, μ, of all U.S. households. We discuss these types of inferences in Chapter 8. ◆

FIGURE 3.12
Population and sample for incomes of U.S. households

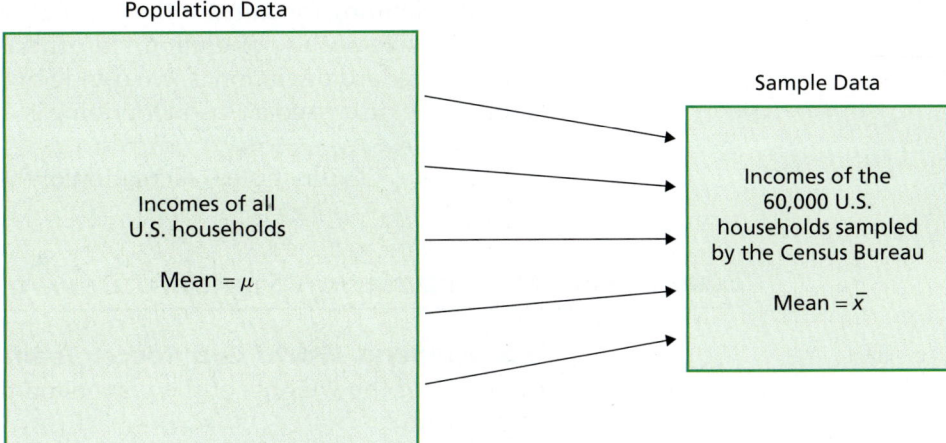

THE POPULATION STANDARD DEVIATION

Recall that, for a variable x and a sample of size n from a population, the sample standard deviation is

$$s = \sqrt{\frac{\Sigma(x-\bar{x})^2}{n-1}}.$$

The standard deviation of a finite population is obtained in a similar but slightly different way. To distinguish the **population standard deviation** from a sample standard deviation, we use the Greek letter σ (pronounced "sigma") to denote the population standard deviation.

DEFINITION 3.12 Population Standard Deviation (Standard Deviation of a Variable)

For a variable x, the standard deviation of all possible observations for the entire population is called the *population standard deviation* or *standard deviation of the variable x*. It is denoted σ_x or, when no confusion will arise, simply σ. For a finite population,

$$\sigma = \sqrt{\frac{\Sigma(x-\mu)^2}{N}},$$

where N is the population size. The population standard deviation can also be obtained from the computing formula

$$\sigma = \sqrt{\frac{\Sigma x^2}{N} - \mu^2}.$$

Note: Just as s^2 is called a sample variance, σ^2 is called the **population variance**.

In the defining formula for the population standard deviation, σ, we divide by N, the size of the population. In contrast, in the defining formula for the sample standard deviation, s, we divide by $n - 1$, or 1 less than the size of the sample. We discussed a reason for doing so in the note preceding Example 3.11 on page 107.

Example 3.23 illustrates calculation of the population standard deviation.

Example 3.23 The Population Standard Deviation

U.S. Women's World Cup Soccer Team Obtain the population standard deviation of the weights of the players on the 1999 U.S. Women's World Cup soccer team.

Solution We apply the computing formula given in Definition 3.12. To do so, we need the sum of the squares of the weights and the population mean weight, μ. From Example 3.21, $\mu = 134.75$ pounds. Squaring each weight in Table 3.15 and adding the results yields $\Sigma x^2 = 365{,}425$. Recalling that there are 20 players, we have

$$\sigma = \sqrt{\frac{\Sigma x^2}{N} - \mu^2} = \sqrt{\frac{365{,}425}{20} - (134.75)^2} = 10.7 \text{ lb.,}$$

rounded to one decimal place.

What Does it Mean?

The population standard deviation of the weights of the players on the 1999 U.S. Women's World Cup soccer team is 10.7 pounds.

USING A SAMPLE STANDARD DEVIATION TO ESTIMATE A POPULATION STANDARD DEVIATION

We have shown that a sample mean can be used to estimate a population mean. Likewise, a sample standard deviation can be used to estimate a population standard deviation, as demonstrated in Example 3.24.

Example 3.24 A Use of a Sample Standard Deviation

Estimating Variation in Bolt Diameters A hardware manufacturer produces "10-millimeter (mm)" bolts. The manufacturer knows that the diameters of the bolts produced vary somewhat from 10 mm and also from each other. But even if he is willing to accept some variation in bolt diameters, he cannot tolerate too much variation—if the variation is too large, too many of the bolts will be unusable (too narrow or too wide).

To evaluate the variation in bolt diameters, the manufacturer needs to know the population standard deviation, σ, of bolt diameters. Because, in this case, σ cannot be determined exactly (do you know why?), the manufacturer must use the standard deviation of the diameters of a sample of bolts to estimate σ. He decides to take a sample of 20 bolts.

The variable under consideration here is bolt diameter; the population of interest consists of all 10-mm bolts that have been or ever will be produced by the manufacturer; the standard deviation of the diameters of all such bolts is the population standard deviation, σ. The sample consists of the 20 bolts obtained by the manufacturer; the standard deviation of the diameters of those bolts is a sample standard deviation, s. Figure 3.13 summarizes this discussion graphically.

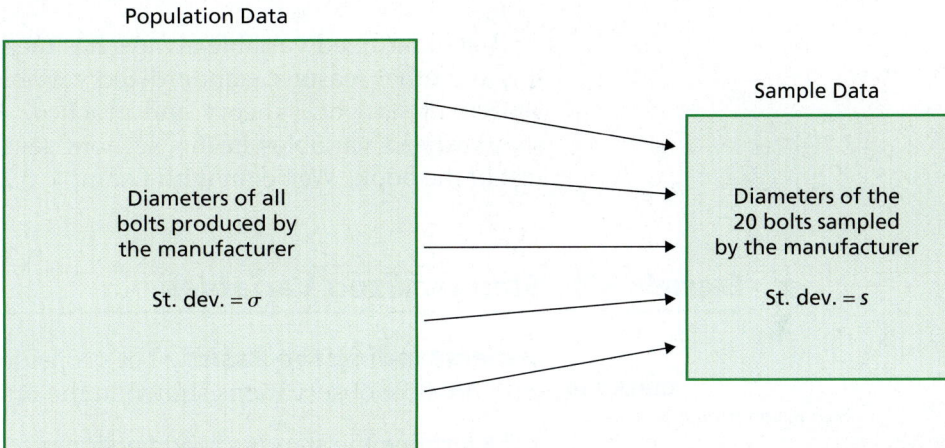

FIGURE 3.13
Population and sample for bolt diameters

After the sample has been taken, the manufacturer can compute the sample standard deviation, s, of the diameters of the 20 bolts obtained. Using the value of s, he can then estimate the population standard deviation, σ, of the diameters of all bolts being produced. ◆

PARAMETER AND STATISTIC

The following definition provides statistical terminology that helps us distinguish between a descriptive measure for a population—a **parameter**—and a descriptive measure for a sample—a **statistic**.

DEFINITION 3.13 **Parameter and Statistic**

Parameter: A descriptive measure for a population.

Statistic: A descriptive measure for a sample.

Thus, for example, μ and σ are parameters, whereas $\bar{x}$ and s are statistics.

STANDARDIZED VARIABLES

We can associate with any variable x a new variable z, obtained by first subtracting from x its mean and then dividing by its standard deviation. This new variable is the **standardized version** of x, or the **standardized variable**.

DEFINITION 3.14 Standardized Variable

For a variable x, the variable

$$z = \frac{x - \mu}{\sigma}$$

is called the *standardized version* of x or the *standardized variable* corresponding to the variable x.

A standardized variable always has mean 0 and standard deviation 1. For this and other reasons, standardized variables play an important role in many aspects of statistical theory and practice. We present a few applications of standardized variables in this section; several others appear throughout the rest of the book. We begin with Example 3.25.

Example 3.25 Standardized Variables

Understanding the Basics Let's consider a simple variable x—namely, one with possible observations shown in the first row of Table 3.16.

TABLE 3.16
Possible observations of x and z

x	−1	3	3	3	5	5
z	−2	0	0	0	1	1

a. Determine the standardized version of x.
b. Determine the observed value of z corresponding to an observed value of x of 5.
c. Obtain all possible observations of z.
d. Find the mean and standard deviation of z using Definitions 3.11 and 3.12. Was it necessary to do these calculations to obtain the mean and standard deviation?
e. Obtain dotplots of the distributions of both x and z. Interpret the results.

Solution a. Using Definitions 3.11 and 3.12, we find that the mean and standard deviation of x are $\mu = 3$ and $\sigma = 2$. Consequently, the standardized version of x is

$$z = \frac{x - 3}{2}.$$

b. The observed value of z corresponding to an observed value of x of 5 is

$$z = \frac{x - 3}{2} = \frac{5 - 3}{2} = 1.$$

c. Applying the formula $z = (x - 3)/2$ to each of the possible observations of the variable x shown in the first row of Table 3.16, we obtain the possible observations of the standardized variable z shown in the second row of Table 3.16.

d. From the second row of Table 3.16,

$$\mu_z = \frac{\Sigma z}{N} = \frac{0}{6} = 0$$

and

$$\sigma_z = \sqrt{\frac{\Sigma(z - \mu_z)^2}{N}} = \sqrt{\frac{6}{6}} = 1.$$

The results of these two computations illustrate something that we mentioned earlier: The mean of a standardized variable is always 0 and its standard deviation is always 1. Thus we really didn't need to perform the calculations to obtain the mean and standard deviation of the variable z.

e. Figures 3.14(a) and 3.14(b) show dotplots of the distributions of x and z, respectively.

> **What Does it Mean?**
>
> The two dotplots in Fig. 3.14 illustrate visually something that we already know: Standardizing shifts a distribution so that the new mean is 0, and it changes the scale so that the new standard deviation is 1.

FIGURE 3.14
Dotplots of the distributions of x and its standardized version z

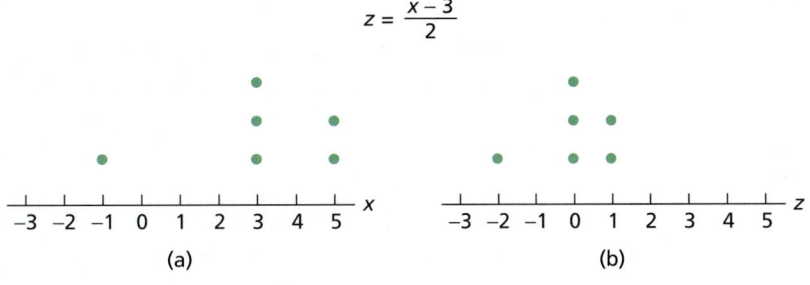

z-SCORES

An important concept associated with standardized variables is that of the **z-score**, or **standard score**, which we now define.

DEFINITION 3.15 **z-Score**

For an observed value of a variable x, the corresponding value of the standardized variable z is called the **z-score** of the observation. The term **standard score** is often used instead of **z-score**.

The z-score of an observation tells us the number of standard deviations that the observation is from the mean, that is, how far the observation is from the mean in units of standard deviation. A negative z-score indicates that the observation is below (less than) the mean, whereas a positive z-score indicates that the observation is above (greater than) the mean. Example 3.26 illustrates calculation and interpretation of z-scores.

Example 3.26 z-Scores

U.S. Women's World Cup Soccer Team The weight data for the 1999 U.S. Women's World Cup soccer team is given in the fourth column of Table 3.15 on page 130. We determined earlier that the mean and standard deviation of the weights are 134.75 pounds and 10.7 pounds, respectively. So, in this case, the standardized variable is

$$z = \frac{x - 134.75}{10.7}.$$

a. Find and interpret the z-score of Tiffany Roberts's weight of 120 pounds.
b. Find and interpret the z-score of Danielle Fotopoulos's weight of 165 pounds.
c. Construct a graph showing the results obtained in parts (a) and (b).

Solution a. The z-score for Tiffany Roberts's weight of 120 pounds is

$$z = \frac{x - 134.75}{10.7} = \frac{120 - 134.75}{10.7} = -1.38.$$

Thus Tiffany Roberts's weight is 1.38 standard deviations below the mean.

b. The z-score for Danielle Fotopoulos's weight of 165 pounds is

$$z = \frac{x - 134.75}{10.7} = \frac{165 - 134.75}{10.7} = 2.83.$$

Thus Danielle Fotopoulos's weight is 2.83 standard deviations above the mean.

c. In Fig. 3.15, we marked Tiffany Roberts's weight of 120 pounds with a color dot and Danielle Fotopoulos's weight of 165 pounds with a black dot. Additionally, we located the mean, $\mu = 134.75$ pounds, and measured intervals equal in length to the standard deviation, $\sigma = 10.7$ pounds.

FIGURE 3.15
Graph showing Tiffany Roberts's weight (color dot) and Danielle Fotopoulos's weight (black dot)

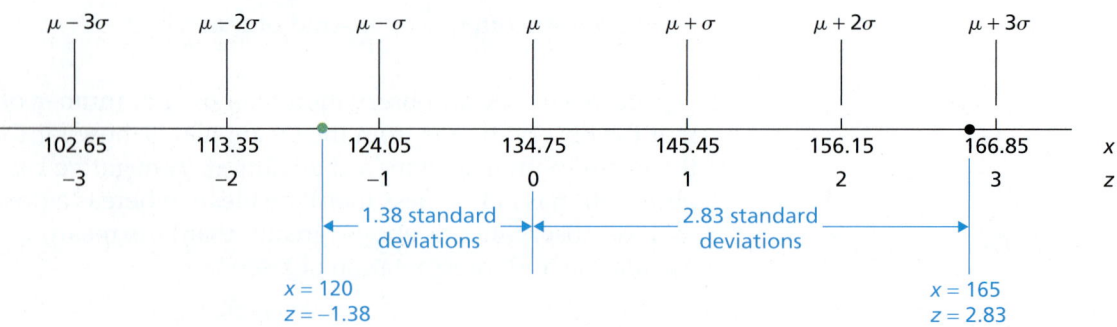

In Fig. 3.15, the numbers in the row labeled x represent weights in pounds and the numbers in the row labeled z represent z-scores (i.e., number of standard deviations from the mean). ◆

THE z-SCORE AS A MEASURE OF RELATIVE STANDING

The three-standard-deviations rule states that almost all the observations in any data set lie within three standard deviations to either side of the mean. Thus, for any variable, almost all possible observations have z-scores between −3 and 3.

Consequently, the z-score of an observation can be used as a measure of its relative standing among all the observations comprising a data set. A large positive z-score (i.e., a z-score roughly 3 or more) indicates that the observation is larger than most of the other observations; a large negative z-score (i.e., a z-score roughly −3 or less) indicates that the observation is smaller than most of the other observations; and a z-score near 0 indicates that the observation is located near the mean.

We can refine and make more precise the preceding statements by applying Chebychev's rule, as discussed in the supplementary exercises for this section found on the WeissStats CD. And, if the distribution of the variable is roughly bell-shaped, then, as we show in Chapter 6, we can do even better by applying the empirical rule.

We can also use z-scores to compare the relative standings of two observations from different populations. For example, we could use z-scores to compare the exam scores of two students in different sections of a beginning English course.

OTHER DESCRIPTIVE MEASURES FOR POPULATIONS

Up to this point, we have concentrated on the mean and standard deviation in our discussion of descriptive measures for populations. The reason is that many of the classical inference procedures for center and variation concern those two parameters.

However, modern statistical analyses also rely heavily on descriptive measures based on percentiles. Quartiles, the IQR, and other descriptive measures based on percentiles are defined in the same way for (finite) populations as they are for samples. For simplicity and with one exception, we use the same notation for descriptive measures based on percentiles whether we are considering a sample or a population. The exception is: We use M to denote a sample median and η (eta) to denote a population median.

Exercises 3.5

Statistical Concepts and Skills

3.78 Identify each quantity as a parameter or a statistic.
a. μ **b.** s **c.** $\bar{x}$ **d.** σ

3.79 Although, in practice, sample data are generally analyzed in inferential studies, what is the ultimate objective of such studies?

3.80 A standardized variable always has mean _____ and standard deviation _____.

3.81 Complete the following sentences.
a. The z-score corresponding to an observed value of a variable tells you _____.

b. A positive z-score indicates that the observation is _____ the mean, whereas a negative z-score indicates that the observation is _____ the mean.

3.82 Identify the statistic that is used to estimate
a. a population mean.
b. a population standard deviation.

3.83 Earlier in this section, we found that the population mean weight of the players on the 1999 U.S. Women's World Cup soccer team is 134.75 lb. In this context, is the number 134.75 a parameter or a statistic? Explain your answer.

3.84 Heights of Basketball Players. In Section 3.3, we analyzed the heights of the starting five players on each of two men's college basketball teams. The heights, in inches, of the players on Team II are 67, 72, 76, 76, and 84. Regarding the five players as a sample of all male starting college basketball players,
a. compute the sample mean height, $\bar{x}$.
b. compute the sample standard deviation, s.

Regarding the players now as a population,
c. compute the population mean height, μ.
d. compute the population standard deviation, σ.

Comparing your answers from parts (a) and (c) and from parts (b) and (d),
e. why are the values for $\bar{x}$ and μ equal?
f. why are the values for s and σ different?

3.85 Hurricane Hunters. The Air Force Reserve's 53rd Weather Reconnaissance Squadron, better known as the *Hurricane Hunters*, fly into the eye of tropical cyclones in their WC-130 Hercules aircraft to collect and report vital meteorological data for advance storm warnings. The data are relayed to the National Hurricane Center in Miami, Florida, for broadcasting emergency storm warnings on land. Over the Atlantic, 1999 was the third busiest year ever for the Hurricane Hunters with 12 tropical cyclones, 8 of which were hurricanes. The maximum winds, in miles per hour, were recorded for each cyclone, and are shown in the following table, where TS = tropical storm and Hu = hurricane. [SOURCE: U.S. Air Force, National Oceanic and Atmospheric Administration.]

Cyclone	Date	Maximum wind (mph)
TS Arlene	Jun 11–18	60
Hu Bret	Aug 18–25	140
Hu Cindy	Aug 19–31	140
Hu Dennis	Aug 24–Sep 5	105
TS Emily	Aug 24–28	50
Hu Floyd	Sep 7–17	155
Hu Gert	Sep 11–23	150
TS Harvey	Sep 19–22	60
Hu Irene	Oct 13–19	110
Hu Jose	Oct 17–25	100
TS Katrina	Oct 28–Nov 1	40
Hu Lenny	Nov 13–22	155

Using only basic calculator functions, obtain the following parameters for the population of maximum wind speeds. Use the appropriate mathematical notation for the parameters to express your answers.
a. Mean **b.** Standard deviation
c. Median **d.** Mode **e.** IQR

3.86 Corn Harvest. As reported by the U.S. Department of Agriculture in *Crop Production*, the acreages (in thousands) of corn harvested in 1998 by the leading corn-producing states are as follows.

State	IA	IL	NE	MN	IN	OH
Acreage	12.2	10.5	8.6	6.8	5.6	3.3

Using only basic calculator functions,
a. obtain the population mean of the corn harvests.
b. obtain the population standard deviation of the corn harvests.

3.87 Doing Time. According to *Statistical Report*, published by the U.S. Bureau of Prisons, the mean time served by prisoners released from federal institutions for the first time is 16.3 months. Assume the standard deviation of the times served is 17.9 months. Let x denote time served by a prisoner released for the first time from a federal institution.
a. Find the standardized version of x.
b. Find the mean and standard deviation of the standardized variable.
c. Determine the z-scores for prison times served of 64.7 months and 4.2 months. Round your answers to two decimal places.
d. Interpret your answers in part (c).
e. Construct a graph similar to Fig. 3.15 on page 136 that depicts your results from parts (b) and (c).

3.88 Gestation Periods of Humans. Gestation periods of humans have a mean of 266 days and a standard deviation of 16 days. Let y denote the variable "gestation period" for humans.
a. Find the standardized variable corresponding to y.
b. What are the mean and standard deviation of the standardized variable?
c. Obtain the z-scores for gestation periods of 227 days and 315 days. Round your answers to two decimal places.
d. Interpret your answers in part (c).
e. Construct a graph similar to Fig. 3.15 on page 136 that shows your results from parts (b) and (c).

3.89 Exam Scores. Suppose that you take an exam with 400 possible points and are told that the mean score is 280 and that the standard deviation is 20. You are also told that you got 350. Did you do well on the exam? Explain your answer.

Extending the Concepts and Skills

3.90 SAT Scores. Each year, thousands of high school students bound for college take the Scholastic Assessment Test, or SAT. The test measures the verbal and mathematical abilities of prospective college students. Student scores are reported on a scale that ranges from a low of 200 to a high of 800. In one high school graduating class, the mean mathematics score on the SAT was 493 and the standard deviation was 105; the mean verbal score was 420 and the standard deviation was 98. A student in the graduating class scored 703 on the math and 665 on the verbal. Relative to the other students in the graduating class, on which test did the student do better? Explain your answer.

Population and Sample Standard Deviations. In Exercises 3.91 and 3.92, you examine the numerical relationship between the population standard deviation and the sample standard deviation computed from the same data. This relationship is helpful when the computer or statistical calculator being used has a built-in program for sample standard deviation but not for population standard deviation.

3.91 Consider the following three data sets.

Data Set 1	Data Set 2	Data Set 3
2 4	7 5 5 3	4 7 8 9 7
7 3	9 8 6	4 5 3 4 5

a. Assuming that each of these data sets is sample data, compute the standard deviations. (Round your final answers to two decimal places.)
b. Assuming that each of these data sets is population data, compute the standard deviations. (Round your final answers to two decimal places.)
c. Using your results from parts (a) and (b), make an educated guess about the answer to the question: If both s and σ are computed for the same data set, will they tend to be closer together if the data set is large or if it is small?

3.92 Consider a data set with m observations. If the data are sample data, you compute the sample standard deviation, s, whereas if the data are population data, you compute the population standard deviation, σ.
a. Derive a mathematical formula that gives σ in terms of s when both are computed for the same data set. (Hint: First note that, numerically, the values of $\bar{x}$ and μ are identical. Consider the ratio of the defining formula for σ to the defining formula for s.)
b. Refer to the three data sets in Exercise 3.91. Verify that your formula in part (a) works for each of the three data sets.
c. Suppose that a data set consists of 15 observations. You compute the sample standard deviation of the data and obtain $s = 38.6$. Then you realize that the data are actually population data and that you should have obtained the population standard deviation instead. Use your formula from part (a) to obtain σ.

Using Technology

Note: Some statistical software packages and calculators have a built-in program for obtaining a sample standard deviation but do not have one for obtaining a population standard deviation. You can deal with this lack by using the following formula that expresses the population standard deviation in terms of the sample standard deviation when both are computed for the same data set:

$$\sigma = \sqrt{\frac{m-1}{m}} \cdot s,$$

where m is the number of observations.

3.93 Women's Soccer. Refer to the heights of the 1999 U.S. Women's World Cup soccer team in the third column of Table 3.15 on page 130. Use the technology of your choice to obtain
a. the population mean height, in inches. *Note:* You must first convert the heights to inches.
b. the population standard deviations of the heights. *Note:* Depending on the technology that you're using, you may need to refer to the formula given in the note preceding this exercise.

3.94 Hurricane Hunters. Refer to Exercise 3.85. Use the technology of your choice to obtain the population mean and population standard deviation of the maximum wind speeds. See the note in Exercise 3.93(b).

CHAPTER 3 Descriptive Measures

Chapter Review

You Should Be Able To

1. use and understand the formulas presented in this chapter.
2. explain the purpose of a measure of center.
3. obtain and interpret the mean, the median, and the mode(s) of a data set.
4. choose an appropriate measure of center for a data set.
5. use and understand summation notation.
6. define, compute, and interpret a sample mean.
7. explain the purpose of a measure of variation.
8. define, compute, and interpret the range of a data set.
9. define, compute, and interpret a sample standard deviation.
10. define percentiles, deciles, and quartiles.
11. obtain and interpret the quartiles, IQR, and five-number summary of a data set.
12. obtain the lower and upper limits of a data set and identify potential outliers.
13. construct and interpret a boxplot and a modified boxplot.
14. use a boxplot to identify distribution shape for large data sets.
15. define the population mean (mean of a variable).
16. define the population standard deviation (standard deviation of a variable).
17. compute the population mean and population standard deviation of a finite population.
18. distinguish between a parameter and a statistic.
19. understand how and why statistics are used to estimate parameters.
20. obtain and interpret z-scores.

Key Terms

adjacent values, 122
box-and-whisker diagram, 121
boxplot, 121
Chebychev's rule, 112
deciles, 116
descriptive measures, 88
deviations from the mean, 105
empirical rule, 112
first quartile (Q_1), 117
five-number summary, 119
interquartile range (IQR), 119
lower limit, 120
mean, 90
mean of a variable (μ), 129
measures of center, 90
measures of central tendency, 90
measures of spread, 103
measures of variation, 103
median, 91
mode, 92
modified boxplot, 121
outliers, 120
parameter, 133
percentiles, 116
population mean (μ), 129
population standard deviation (σ), 131
population variance (σ^2), 131
quartiles, 116
quintiles, 116
range, 104
resistant measure, 93
sample mean ($\bar{x}$), 101
sample size (n), 101
sample standard deviation (s), 108
sample variance (s^2), 107
second quartile (Q_2), 117
standard deviation, 105
standard deviation of a variable (σ), 131
standard score, 135
standardized variable, 134
standardized version, 134
statistic, 133
subscripts, 100
sum of squared deviations, 106
summation notation, 100
third quartile (Q_3), 117
trimmed means, 93
upper limit, 120
whiskers, 122
z-score, 135

Review Test

Statistical Concepts and Skills

1. Define
a. descriptive measures.
b. measures of center.
c. measures of variation.

2. Identify the two most commonly used measures of center for quantitative data. Explain the relative advantages and disadvantages of each.

3. Among the measures of center discussed, which is the only one appropriate for qualitative data?

4. Identify the most appropriate measure of variation corresponding to each of the following measures of center.
a. Mean
b. Median

5. Specify the mathematical symbol used for each of the following descriptive measures.
a. Sample mean
b. Sample standard deviation
c. Population mean
d. Population standard deviation

6. Data Set A has more variation than Data Set B. Decide which of the following statements are necessarily true.
a. Data Set A has a larger mean than Data Set B.
b. Data Set A has a larger standard deviation than Data Set B.

7. Complete the statement: Almost all the observations in any data set lie within _____ standard deviations to either side of the mean.

8. Regarding the five-number summary:
a. Identify its components.
b. How can it be employed to describe center and variation?
c. What graphical display is based on it?

9. Regarding outliers:
a. What is an outlier?
b. Explain how you can identify potential outliers, using only the first and third quartiles.

10. Regarding z-scores:
a. How is a z-score obtained?
b. What is the interpretation of a z-score?
c. An observation has a z-score of 2.9. Roughly speaking, what is the relative standing of the observation?

11. Party Time. An integral part of doing business in the dot-com culture is frequenting the party circuit centered in San Francisco. Here high-tech companies throw as many as five parties a night to recruit or retain talented workers in a highly competitive job market. With as many as 700 guests at a single party, the food and booze flow with an average alcohol cost per guest of $15–$18 and average food bill of $75–$150. A sample of a recent dot-com party yielded the following data on number of alcoholic drinks consumed per person. [SOURCE: *USA TODAY* Online, May 17, 2000]

4	4	1	0	5
1	1	2	4	3
1	5	3	0	2
2	2	1	2	4

a. Find the mean, median, and mode of these data.
b. Which measure of center do you think is best here? Explain your answer.

12. Duration of Marriages. The National Center for Health Statistics publishes information on the duration of marriages in *Vital Statistics of the United States*. Which measure of center is more appropriate for data on the duration of marriages, the mean or the median? Explain your answer.

13. Causes of Death. Death certificates provide data on the causes of death. Which of the three main measures of center is appropriate here? Explain your answer.

14. Road Patrol. In the paper "Injuries and Risk Factors in a 100-Mile (161 km) Infantry Road March" (*Preventative Medicine*, 1999, Vol. 28, pp. 167–173), Reynolds et al. reported on a study commissioned by the U.S. Army. The purpose of the study was to improve medical planning and identify risk factors during multiple-day road patrols by examining the acute effects of long-distance marches by light-infantry soldiers. Each soldier carried a standard U.S. Army rucksack, Meal-Ready-to-Eat packages, and other field equipment. A sample of 10 participating soldiers revealed the following data on total load mass, in kilograms.

| 48 | 50 | 45 | 49 | 44 |
| 47 | 37 | 54 | 40 | 43 |

a. Obtain the sample mean of these 10 load masses.
b. Obtain the range of the load masses.
c. Obtain the sample standard deviation of the load masses.

15. Millionaires. Dr. Thomas Stanley of Georgia State University has collected information on millionaires, including their ages, since 1973. A sample of 36 millionaires has a mean age of 58.5 years and a standard deviation of 13.4 years.
a. Complete the following graph.

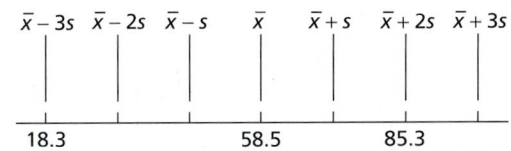

b. Fill in the blanks: Almost all the 36 millionaires are between _____ and _____ years old.

16. Millionaires. Refer to Problem 15. The ages of the 36 millionaires sampled are arranged in increasing order in the following table.

31	38	39	39	42	42	45	47	48
48	48	52	52	53	54	55	57	59
60	61	64	64	66	66	67	68	68
69	71	71	74	75	77	79	79	79

a. Determine the quartiles for the data.
b. Obtain and interpret the interquartile range.
c. Find and interpret the five-number summary.
d. Calculate the lower and upper limits.
e. Identify potential outliers, if any.
f. Construct and interpret a boxplot and, if appropriate, a modified boxplot.

17. UC Enrollment. According to *Peterson's Guide to Four-Year Colleges 2000*, the Fall 1998 enrollment figures for the University of California campuses were as follows.

Campus	Enrollment (1000s)
Berkeley	31.0
Davis	24.7
Irvine	18.1
Los Angeles	35.8
Riverside	10.6
San Diego	19.4
San Francisco	3.5
Santa Barbara	19.3
Santa Cruz	10.9

a. Compute the population mean enrollment, μ, of the UC campuses. (Round your answer to two decimal places.)
b. Compute σ. (Round your answer to two decimal places.)
c. Letting x denote enrollment, specify the standardized variable, z, corresponding to x.
d. Without performing any calculations, give the mean and standard deviation of z. Explain your answers.
e. Construct dotplots for the distributions of both x and z. Interpret your graphs.
f. Obtain and interpret the z-scores for the enrollments at the Los Angeles and Riverside campuses.

18. Gasoline Prices. The U.S. Energy Information Administration reports figures on retail gasoline prices in the *Monthly Energy Review*. Data are obtained by sampling 10,000 gasoline service stations from a total of more than 185,000. For the 10,000 stations sampled in August 2000, the mean price per gallon for unleaded regular gasoline was $1.51.
a. Is the mean price given here a sample mean or a population mean? Explain your answer.
b. What letter would you use to designate the mean of $1.51?
c. Is the mean price given here a statistic or a parameter? Explain your answer.

Using Technology

19. Millionaires. Use the technology of your choice to determine the following statistics for the age data in Problem 16.
a. Mean   b. Median   c. Range
d. Sample standard deviation

20. Millionaires. Refer to the data in Problem 16. Use the technology of your choice to obtain
a. a (modified) boxplot for the data.
b. the five-number summary of the data.

21. Millionaires. Refer to Problem 16.
a. Printout 3.3 shows a boxplot generated by Minitab for the age data. Use the boxplot to discuss the variation in the data set.
b. Are there potential outliers in the data? If so, identify them approximately and provide a possible explanation for their cause.

PRINTOUT 3.3
Minitab output for Problem 21(a)

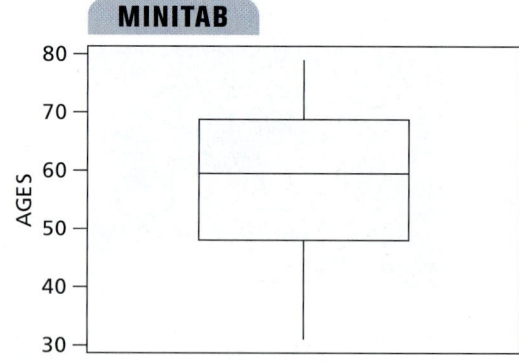

Internet Project

Old Faithful Geyser and a Survey of Wages

In this Internet project, you are to explore two topics. The first involves the Old Faithful Geyser. Specifically, you will examine data on the duration of eruptions and the times between successive eruptions.

The second is a survey of wages. Wages provide an example in which the use of different descriptive measures is important to help in understanding and explaining data. The statistic you choose can make a striking difference in the conclusions you draw; in this case, the difference is between using the mean and the median.

In each part of the project, you will see how certain measures can help describe the data and how some measures work better than others. As usual, you will look at several different views of the data to understand better the true nature of the phenomenon that the data describes.

URL for access to Internet Projects Page: www.aw.com/weiss

Focusing on Data Analysis

SAT Scores

Recall from Chapter 1 (see page 34) that the Focus database contains information on 500 randomly selected Arizona State University sophomores. Use the technology of your choice to solve the following problems. For both the SAT math scores and the SAT verbal scores:

a. Determine the means and medians. Use these measures of center to compare the two sets of scores.
b. Find the ranges, sample standard deviations, and interquartile ranges. Use these measures of variation to compare the two sets of scores.
c. Construct boxplots. Use the boxplots to compare the two sets of scores. Be sure to consider variation, distribution shape, and outliers.

case study discussion

New York Yankees Y2K Salaries

The table on page 89 displays the New York Yankees roster and players' salaries for the 2000 season, as reported online by *CBS Sportsline.* Refer to that table and solve the following problems.

a. Determine the mean and median of the salaries. Explain any difference between these two measures of center.
b. Obtain the range and population standard deviation of the salaries.
c. Find and interpret the z-scores for the salaries of David Cone and Lance Johnson.
d. Determine and interpret the quartiles of the salaries.
e. Find and interpret the five-number summary of the data.
f. Find the lower and upper limits. Use them to identify potential outliers.
g. Construct a boxplot for the salaries and interpret your result in terms of the variation in the data.
h. Use the technology of your choice to solve parts (a)–(g).

Internet Resources: Visit the Weiss Web site www.aw.com/weiss for additional discussion, exercises, and resources related to this case study.

Biography

John Tukey: A Pioneer of EDA

JOHN WILDER TUKEY was born on June 16, 1915, in New Bedford, Massachusetts. After earning bachelor's and master's degrees in chemistry from Brown University in 1936 and 1937, respectively, he enrolled in the mathematics program at Princeton University, where he received a master's degree in 1938 and a doctorate in 1939.

After graduating, Tukey was appointed Henry B. Fine Instructor in Mathematics at Princeton; 10 years later he was advanced to a full professorship. In 1965, Princeton established a department of statistics, and Tukey was named its first chairperson. In addition to his position at Princeton, he was a member of the Technical Staff at AT&T Bell Laboratories where he served as Associate Executive Director, Research in the Information Sciences Division, from 1945 until his retirement in 1985.

Tukey was among the leaders in the field of exploratory data analysis (EDA), which provides techniques such as stem-and-leaf diagrams for effectively investigating data. He also made fundamental contributions to the areas of robust estimation and time series analysis. Tukey wrote numerous books and more than 350 technical papers on mathematics, statistics, and other scientific subjects. Additionally, he coined the word *bit,* a contraction of *binary digit* (a unit of information, often as processed by a computer).

Tukey's participation in educational, public, and government service was most impressive. He was appointed to serve on the President's Science Advisory Committee by President Eisenhower; was chairperson of the committee that prepared "Restoring the Quality of our Environment" in 1965; helped develop the National Assessment of Educational Progress; and was a member of the Special Advisory Panel on the 1990 Census of the U.S. Department of Commerce, Bureau of the Census—to name only a few of his involvements.

Among many honors, Tukey received the National Medal of Science, the IEEE Medal of Honor, Princeton University's James Madison Medal, and Foreign Member, The Royal Society (London). He was the first recipient of the Samuel S. Wilks Award of the American Statistical Association. Until his death, Tukey remained on the faculty at Princeton as Donner Professor of Science, Emeritus; Professor of Statistics, Emeritus; and Senior Research Statistician. Tukey died of a heart attack on July 26, 2000, after a short illness. He was 85 years old.

chapter 4

Descriptive Methods in Regression and Correlation

CHAPTER OUTLINE

4.1 Linear Equations with One Independent Variable

4.2 The Regression Equation

4.3 The Coefficient of Determination

4.4 Linear Correlation

GENERAL OBJECTIVES We often want to know whether two or more variables are related and, if they are, how they are related. In Chapter 12, we examine relationships between two variables where each variable is either a qualitative (categorical) variable or a quantitative variable whose possible values constitute or have been grouped into a finite number of categories. In this chapter, we discuss relationships between two quantitative variables.

Some commonly used methods for examining the relationship between two or more quantitative variables and for making predictions are *linear regression* and *correlation.* We discuss descriptive methods in linear regression and correlation in this chapter and consider inferential methods in Chapter 14.

In preparation for our discussion of linear regression, we review linear equations with one independent variable in Section 4.1. In Section 4.2, we explain how to determine the *regression equation,* the equation of the line that best fits a set of data points.

In Section 4.3, we examine the coefficient of determination, a descriptive measure of the utility of the regression equation for making predictions. In Section 4.4, we discuss the linear correlation coefficient, which provides a descriptive measure of the strength of the linear relationship between two quantitative variables.

case study

FAT CONSUMPTION AND PROSTATE CANCER

Researchers have asked whether there is a relationship between nutrition and cancer, and many studies have shown that there is. In fact, one of the conclusions of a study by B. Reddy et al., "Nutrition and Its Relationship to Cancer," *Advances in Cancer Research*, Vol. 32, pp. 237–345, was that "…none of the risk factors for cancer is probably more significant than diet and nutrition."

One dietary factor that has been studied for its relationship with prostate cancer is fat consumption. The data in the following table were obtained from a graph—adapted from information in the article mentioned—in John Robbins's classic book *Diet for a New America* (Walpole, N.H.: Stillpoint, 1987).

Country	Dietary fat (grams/day)	Death rate (per 100,000)	Country	Dietary fat (grams/day)	Death rate (per 100,000)
El Salvador	38	0.9	Spain	97	10.1
Philippines	29	1.3	Portugal	73	11.4
Japan	42	1.6	Finland	112	11.1
Mexico	57	4.5	Hungary	100	13.1
Greece	96	4.8	United Kingdom	143	12.4
Colombia	47	5.4	Germany	134	12.9
Bulgaria	67	5.5	Canada	142	13.4
Yugoslavia	72	5.6	Austria	119	13.9
Poland	93	6.4	France	137	14.4
Panama	58	7.8	Netherlands	152	14.4
Israel	95	8.4	Australia	129	15.1
Romania	67	8.8	Denmark	156	15.9
Venezuela	62	9.0	United States	147	16.3
Czechoslovakia	96	9.1	Norway	133	16.8
Italy	86	9.4	Sweden	132	18.4

After studying the techniques of regression and correlation, you will be asked to investigate how fat consumption is related to the death rate from prostate cancer among various nations of the world.

4.1 LINEAR EQUATIONS WITH ONE INDEPENDENT VARIABLE

As an aid to understanding linear regression, we first need to review linear equations with one independent variable. The general form of a **linear equation** with one independent variable can be written as

$$y = b_0 + b_1 x,$$

where b_0 and b_1 are constants (fixed numbers), x is the independent variable, and y is the dependent variable.[1]

The graph of a linear equation with one independent variable is a **straight line**; furthermore, any nonvertical straight line can be represented by such an equation. Examples of linear equations with one independent variable are $y = 4 + 0.2x$, $y = -1.5 - 2x$, and $y = -3.4 + 1.8x$. Figure 4.1 depicts the straight-line graphs of these three linear equations.

FIGURE 4.1
Straight-line graphs of three linear equations

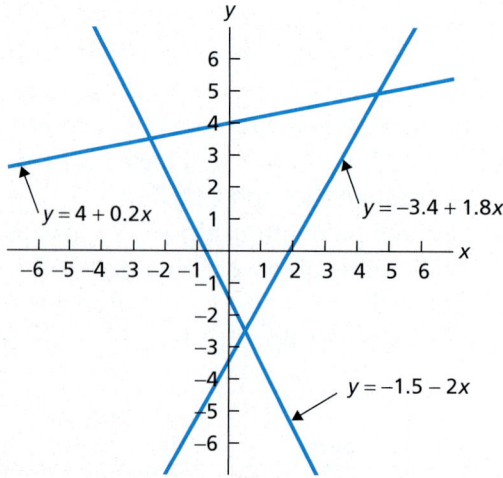

Linear equations with one independent variable occur frequently in applications of mathematics to many different fields, including the management, life, and social sciences, as well as the physical and mathematical sciences. In Examples 4.1 and 4.2, we illustrate the use of linear equations in a simple business application.

Example 4.1 Linear Equations

Word Processing Costs CJ² Business Services does word processing as one of its basic functions. Its rate is $20/hr plus a $25 disk charge. The total cost to a customer depends, of course, on the number of hours needed to complete

---

[1] You may be familiar with the form $y = mx + b$ instead of the form $y = b_0 + b_1 x$. In statistics, the latter form is preferred because it allows a smoother transition to multiple regression, in which there is more than one independent variable. Material on multiple regression is provided in the chapters *Multiple Regression Analysis* and *Model Building in Regression* on the WeissStats CD accompanying this book or on the Weiss Web site.

the job. Find the equation that expresses the total cost in terms of the number of hours required to complete the job.

Solution Let x denote the number of hours required to complete the job, and let y denote the total cost to the customer. Because the rate for word processing is \$20/hr, a job that takes x hours will cost \$20x plus the \$25 disk charge. Hence the total cost, y, of a job that takes x hours is $y = 25 + 20x$. ◆

The equation, $y = 25 + 20x$, for the total cost of a word processing job is a linear equation; here $b_0 = 25$ and $b_1 = 20$. Using the equation, we can find the exact cost for a job once we know the number of hours required. For instance, a job that takes 5 hours will cost $y = 25 + 20 \cdot 5 = \$125$; a job that takes 7.5 hours will cost $y = 25 + 20 \cdot 7.5 = \$175$. Table 4.1 displays these costs and a few others.

TABLE 4.1
Times and costs for five word processing jobs

Time (hr) x	5.0	7.5	15.0	20.0	22.5
Cost (\$) y	125	175	325	425	475

As we have already mentioned, a linear equation, such as $y = 25 + 20x$, has a straight-line graph. We can obtain the graph of $y = 25 + 20x$ by plotting the points displayed in Table 4.1 and connecting them with a straight line, as shown in Fig. 4.2.

FIGURE 4.2
Graph of $y = 25 + 20x$, obtained from the points displayed in Table 4.1

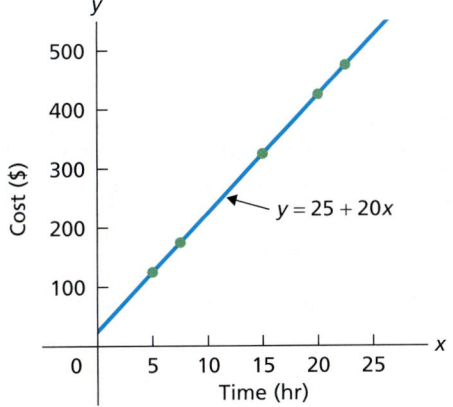

The graph in Fig. 4.2 is useful for quickly estimating cost. For example, a glance at the graph shows that a 10-hour job will cost somewhere between \$200 and \$300. The exact cost is $y = 25 + 20 \cdot 10 = \$225$.

INTERCEPT AND SLOPE

For a linear equation $y = b_0 + b_1 x$, the numbers b_0 and b_1 have an important geometric interpretation. The number b_0 is the y-value where the straight-line graph of the linear equation intersects the y-axis. The number b_1 measures the steepness of the straight line; more precisely, b_1 indicates how much the y-value on the straight line changes when the x-value increases by 1 unit. Figure 4.3 illustrates these relationships.

FIGURE 4.3
Graph of $y = b_0 + b_1 x$

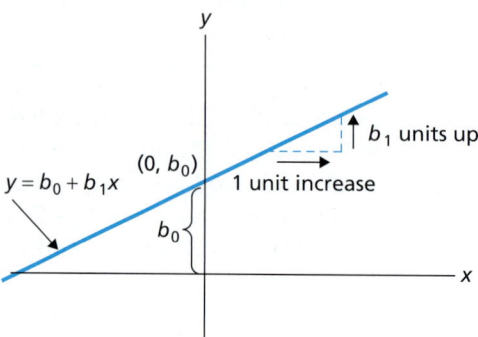

Because of the geometric interpretation of the numbers b_0 and b_1, they have special names that reflect that interpretation: the **y-intercept** and the **slope** of the line, respectively.

DEFINITION 4.1 **y-Intercept and Slope**

For a linear equation $y = b_0 + b_1 x$, the number b_0 is called the *y-intercept* and the number b_1 is called the *slope*.

Example 4.2 y-Intercept and Slope

Word Processing Costs In Example 4.1, we obtained the linear equation that expresses the total cost, y, of a word processing job in terms of the number of hours, x, required to complete the job. The equation is $y = 25 + 20x$.

a. Find the y-intercept and slope of that linear equation.
b. Interpret the y-intercept and slope in terms of the graph of the equation.
c. Interpret the y-intercept and slope in terms of word processing costs.

Solution
a. The y-intercept for the equation is $b_0 = 25$, and the slope is $b_1 = 20$.
b. The y-intercept $b_0 = 25$ is the y-value where the straight line $y = 25 + 20x$ intersects the y-axis. The slope $b_1 = 20$ indicates that the y-value increases by 20 units for every increase in x of 1 unit, as shown in Fig. 4.4.
c. In terms of word processing costs, the y-intercept $b_0 = 25$ represents the total cost of a job that takes 0 hours. In other words, the y-intercept of $25 is a fixed cost that is charged no matter how long the job takes. The slope $b_1 = 20$ represents the cost per hour of $20; it is the amount that the total cost, y, goes up for every increase of 1 hour in the time, x, required to complete the job.

FIGURE 4.4
Graph of $y = 25 + 20x$

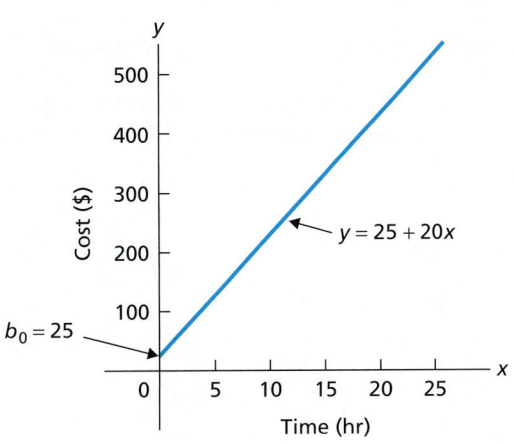

A straight line is determined by any two distinct points that lie on the line. Thus the straight-line graph of a linear equation, $y = b_0 + b_1 x$, can be obtained by first substituting two different x-values into the equation to get two distinct points and then connecting those two points with a straight line.

For example, to graph the linear equation $y = 5 - 3x$, we can use the x-values 1 and 3 (or any other two x-values). The y-values corresponding to those two x-values are $y = 5 - 3 \cdot 1 = 2$ and $y = 5 - 3 \cdot 3 = -4$, respectively. Therefore the graph of the linear equation $y = 5 - 3x$ is the straight line that passes through the two points $(1, 2)$ and $(3, -4)$, as depicted in Fig. 4.5.

FIGURE 4.5
Graph of $y = 5 - 3x$

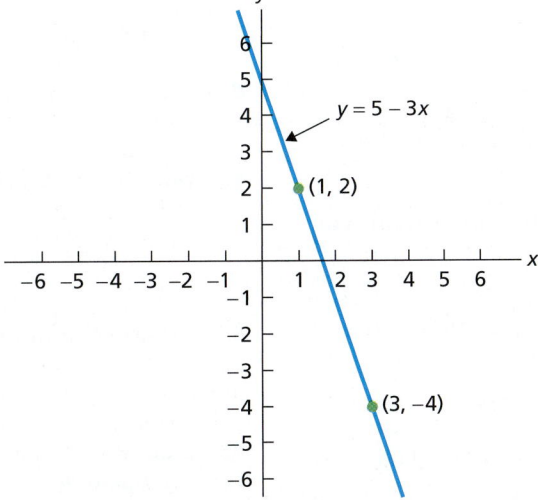

Note that the line in Fig. 4.5 slopes downward—the y-values decrease as x increases—because the slope of the line is negative: $b_1 = -3 < 0$. Now look at the line in Fig. 4.4, the graph of the linear equation $y = 25 + 20x$. That line slopes upward—the y-values increase as x increases—because the slope of the line is positive: $b_1 = 20 > 0$. In general, we have Key Fact 4.1.

Key Fact 4.1 Graphical Interpretation of Slope

The straight-line graph of the linear equation $y = b_0 + b_1 x$ slopes upward if $b_1 > 0$, slopes downward if $b_1 < 0$, and is horizontal if $b_1 = 0$, as shown in Fig. 4.6.

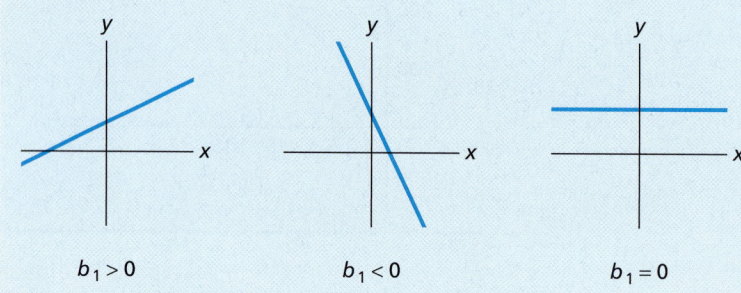

FIGURE 4.6 Graphical interpretation of slope

Exercises 4.1

Statistical Concepts and Skills

4.1 Regarding linear equations with one independent variable:
a. Write the general form of such an equation.
b. In your expression in part (a), which letters represent constants and which represent variables?
c. In your expression in part (a), which letter represents the independent variable and which represents the dependent variable?

4.2 Fill in the blank. The graph of a linear equation with one independent variable is a _____.

4.3 Consider the linear equation $y = b_0 + b_1 x$.
a. Identify and give the geometric interpretation of b_0.
b. Identify and give the geometric interpretation of b_1.

4.4 Answer true or false to each statement and explain your answers.
a. The straight-line graph of a linear equation slopes upward unless the slope is 0.
b. The value of the y-intercept has no effect on the direction that the straight-line graph of a linear equation slopes.

4.5 Car Rentals. On October 2, 2000, the Avis Rent-A-Car rate for renting a full-size, four-door, Chevrolet Impala in Mobile, Alabama, was $120 per day plus $0.25 per mile. For a 1-day rental, let x denote the number of miles driven and y the total cost.

a. Obtain the equation that expresses y in terms of x.
b. Find b_0 and b_1.
c. Construct a table similar to Table 4.1 on page 149 for the x-values 50, 100, and 250 miles.
d. Draw the graph of the equation that you obtained in part (a) by plotting the points from part (c) and connecting them with a straight line.
e. Apply the graph from part (d) to estimate visually the cost of driving the car 150 miles. Then calculate that cost exactly by using the equation from part (a).

4.6 Air-Conditioning Repairs. Encore Air Conditioning charges $36 per hour plus a $30 service charge. Let x denote the number of hours required for a job and y the total cost to the customer.

a. Obtain the equation that expresses y in terms of x.
b. Find b_0 and b_1.
c. Construct a table similar to Table 4.1 on page 149 for the x-values 0.5, 1, and 2.25 hours.
d. Draw the graph of the equation that you obtained in part (a) by plotting the points from part (c) and connecting them with a straight line.
e. Apply the graph from part (d) to estimate visually the cost of a job that takes 1.75 hours. Then calculate that cost exactly by using the equation from part (a).

4.7 Measuring Temperature. The two most commonly used scales for measuring temperature are the Fahrenheit and Celsius scales. If you let y denote Fahrenheit temperature and x denote Celsius temperature, you can express the relationship between those two scales with the linear equation $y = 32 + 1.8x$.
a. Determine b_0 and b_1.
b. Find the Fahrenheit temperatures corresponding to the Celsius temperatures $-40°, 0°, 20°$, and $100°$.
c. Graph the linear equation $y = 32 + 1.8x$, using the four points found in part (b).
d. Apply the graph obtained in part (c) to estimate visually the Fahrenheit temperature corresponding to a Celsius temperature of $28°$. Then calculate that temperature exactly by using the linear equation $y = 32 + 1.8x$.

4.8 A Law of Physics. A ball is thrown straight up in the air with an initial velocity of 64 feet per second (ft/sec). According to the laws of physics, if you let y denote the velocity of the ball after x seconds, $y = 64 - 32x$.
a. Determine b_0 and b_1 for this linear equation.
b. Determine the velocity of the ball after 1, 2, 3, and 4 sec.
c. Graph the linear equation $y = 64 - 32x$, using the four points obtained in part (b).
d. Use the graph from part (c) to estimate visually the velocity of the ball after 1.5 sec. Then calculate that velocity exactly by using the linear equation $y = 64 - 32x$.

In Exercises 4.9–4.12,
a. *determine the y-intercept and slope of the specified linear equation.*
b. *explain what the y-intercept and slope represent in terms of the graph of the equation.*
c. *explain what the y-intercept and slope represent in terms relating to the application.*

4.9 Car Rentals. $y = 120 + 0.25x$ (from Exercise 4.5)

4.10 Air-Conditioning Repairs. $y = 30 + 36x$ (from Exercise 4.6)

4.11 Measuring Temperature. $y = 32 + 1.8x$ (from Exercise 4.7)

4.12 A Law of Physics. $y = 64 - 32x$ (from Exercise 4.8)

In Exercises 4.13–4.22, we give linear equations. For each equation,
a. *find the y-intercept and slope.*
b. *determine whether the line slopes upward, slopes downward, or is horizontal, without graphing the equation.*
c. *use two points to graph the equation.*

4.13 $y = 3 + 4x$
4.14 $y = -1 + 2x$
4.15 $y = 6 - 7x$
4.16 $y = -8 - 4x$
4.17 $y = 0.5x - 2$
4.18 $y = -0.75x - 5$
4.19 $y = 2$
4.20 $y = -3x$
4.21 $y = 1.5x$
4.22 $y = -3$

In Exercises 4.23–4.30, we identify the y-intercepts and slopes, respectively, of straight lines. For each line,
a. *determine whether it slopes upward, slopes downward, or is horizontal, without graphing the equation.*
b. *find its equation.*
c. *use two points to graph the equation.*

4.23 5 and 2
4.24 -3 and 4
4.25 -2 and -3
4.26 0.4 and 1
4.27 0 and -0.5
4.28 -1.5 and 0
4.29 3 and 0
4.30 0 and 3

Extending the Concepts and Skills

4.31 In this section, we stated that any nonvertical straight line can be described by an equation of the form $y = b_0 + b_1 x$.
a. Explain why a vertical straight line can't be expressed in this form.
b. What is the form of the equation of a vertical straight line?
c. Does a vertical straight line have a slope? Explain your answer.

4.2 THE REGRESSION EQUATION

In Examples 4.1 and 4.2, we discussed the linear equation $y = 25 + 20x$, which expresses the total cost, y, of a word processing job in terms of the time in hours, x, required to complete it. Given the amount of time required, x, we can use the equation to determine the *exact* cost of the job, y.

TABLE 4.2
Age and price data for a sample of 11 Orions

Car	Age (yr) x	Price ($100) y
1	5	85
2	4	103
3	6	70
4	5	82
5	5	89
6	5	98
7	6	66
8	6	95
9	2	169
10	7	70
11	7	48

Real-life applications are frequently not so simple as the word processing example, in which one variable (cost) can be predicted exactly in terms of another variable (time required). Rather, we must often be content with rough predictions. For instance, we cannot predict the exact price, y, of a particular make and model of car just by knowing its age, x. Indeed, even for a fixed age, say, 3 years old, price varies from car to car. We must be content with making a rough prediction for the price of a 3-year-old car of the particular make and model or with an estimate of the mean price of all such 3-year-old cars.

Table 4.2 displays data on age and price for a sample of cars of a particular make and model. We refer to the car as the Orion, but the data, obtained from the *Asian Import* edition of the *Auto Trader* magazine, is for a real car. Ages are in years; prices are in hundreds of dollars, rounded to the nearest hundred dollars.

Plotting the data helps us visualize any apparent relationships between age and price. Such a plot is called a **scatter diagram** (or **scatterplot**). The scatter diagram for the data in Table 4.2 is depicted in Fig. 4.7.

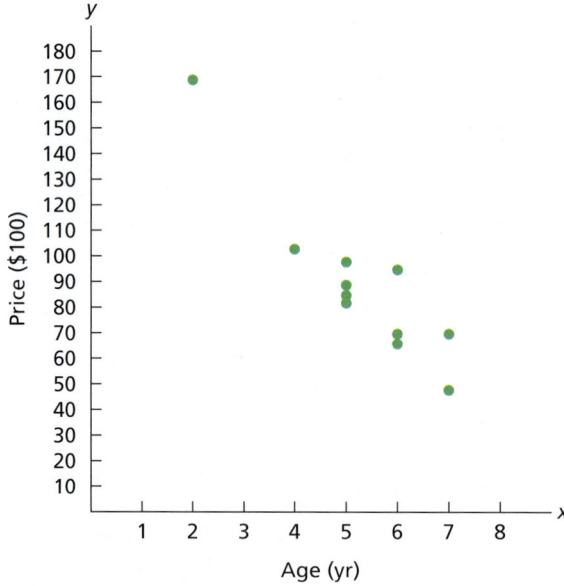

FIGURE 4.7
Scatter diagram for the age and price data of Orions from Table 4.2

Clearly, the data points do not lie on a straight line, but they appear to cluster about a straight line. We want to fit a straight line to the data points and use that line to predict the price of an Orion based on its age.

Because we could draw many different straight lines through the cluster of data points, we need a method to choose the "best" line. The method, called the **least-squares criterion**, is based on an analysis of the errors made in using a straight line to fit the data points. To introduce the least-squares criterion, we use a very simple data set in Example 4.3. We return to the Orion data shortly.

Example 4.3 Introducing the Least-Squares Criterion

TABLE 4.3 Four data points

x	y
1	1
1	2
2	2
4	6

Consider the problem of fitting a straight line to the four data points displayed in Table 4.3. A scatter diagram for those data is depicted in Fig. 4.8.

Many (in fact, infinitely many) straight lines can be fit to the data points in Table 4.3. Two possibilities are shown in Fig. 4.9(a) and Fig. 4.9(b).

To avoid confusion, we use $\hat{y}$ to denote the y-value predicted by a straight line for a value of x. For instance, the y-value predicted by Line A for $x = 2$ is

$$\hat{y} = 0.50 + 1.25 \cdot 2 = 3,$$

and the y-value predicted by Line B for $x = 2$ is

$$\hat{y} = -0.25 + 1.50 \cdot 2 = 2.75.$$

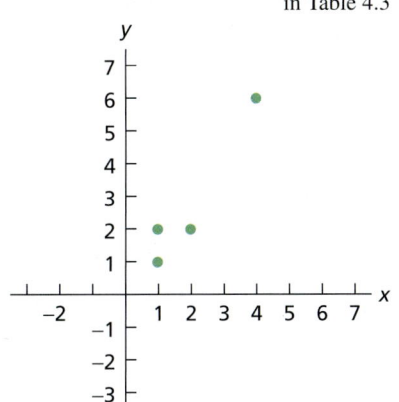

FIGURE 4.8 Scatter diagram for the data points in Table 4.3

To measure quantitatively how well a line fits the data, we first consider the errors, e, made in using the line to predict the y-values of the data points. For instance, as we have just demonstrated, Line A predicts a y-value of $\hat{y} = 3$ when $x = 2$. The actual y-value for $x = 2$ is $y = 2$ (see Table 4.3). So, the error made in using Line A to predict the y-value of the data point $(2, 2)$ is

$$e = y - \hat{y} = 2 - 3 = -1,$$

as seen in Fig. 4.9(a).

The fourth column of Table 4.4(a), located on the following page, shows the errors made by Line A for all four data points; the fourth column of Table 4.4(b) shows the same for Line B.

To decide which line, Line A or Line B, fits the data better, we first compute the sum of the squared errors, Σe^2, in the final column of Table 4.4(a) and Table 4.4(b). The line having the smaller sum of squared errors, in this case Line B, is the one that fits the data better. And, among all straight lines, the least-squares criterion is that the line having the smallest sum of squared errors is the one that fits the data best.

FIGURE 4.9 Two possible straight-line fits to the data points in Table 4.3

Line A: $y = 0.50 + 1.25x$

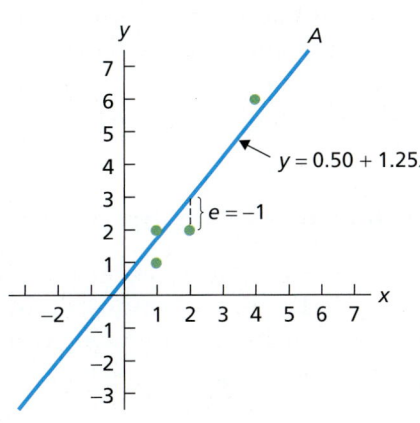

(a)

Line B: $y = -0.25 + 1.50x$

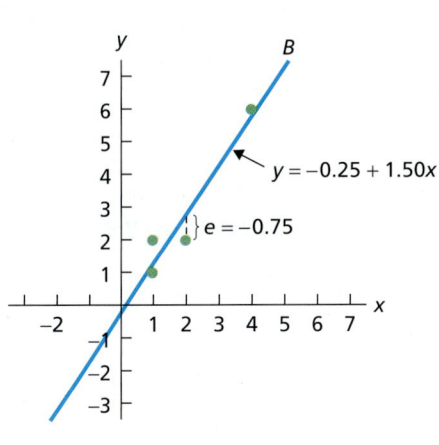

(b)

TABLE 4.4 Determining how well the data points in Table 4.3 are fit by (a) Line A and (b) Line B

(a) Line A: $y = 0.50 + 1.25x$

x	y	$\hat{y}$	e	e^2
1	1	1.75	−0.75	0.5625
1	2	1.75	0.25	0.0625
2	2	3.00	−1.00	1.0000
4	6	5.50	0.50	0.2500
				1.8750

(b) Line B: $y = -0.25 + 1.50x$

x	y	$\hat{y}$	e	e^2
1	1	1.25	−0.25	0.0625
1	2	1.25	0.75	0.5625
2	2	2.75	−0.75	0.5625
4	6	5.75	0.25	0.0625
				1.2500

With the results of Example 4.3 in mind, we can now state the least-squares criterion—as Key Fact 4.2—for the straight line that best fits a set of data points. Following that, we present definitions of the terminology used for the line that best fits the data—the **regression line**—and the equation that represents it—the **regression equation.**

Key Fact 4.2   Least-Squares Criterion

The straight line that best fits a set of data points is the one having the smallest possible sum of squared errors.

DEFINITION 4.2   Regression Line and Regression Equation

Regression line: The straight line that best fits a set of data points according to the least-squares criterion.

Regression equation: The equation of the regression line.

Although the least-squares criterion states the property that the regression line for a set of data points must satisfy, it does not tell us how to find that line. This task is accomplished by Formula 4.1, which provides formulas for obtaining the regression line. In preparation, we introduce some notation that will be used throughout our study of regression and correlation.

DEFINITION 4.3   Notation Used in Regression and Correlation

We define S_{xx}, S_{xy}, and S_{yy} by $S_{xx} = \Sigma(x - \bar{x})^2$, $S_{xy} = \Sigma(x - \bar{x})(y - \bar{y})$, and $S_{yy} = \Sigma(y - \bar{y})^2$. For hand computations, these three quantities are most easily obtained by using the following computing formulas:

$$S_{xx} = \Sigma x^2 - (\Sigma x)^2/n, \quad S_{xy} = \Sigma xy - (\Sigma x)(\Sigma y)/n, \quad S_{yy} = \Sigma y^2 - (\Sigma y)^2/n.$$

FORMULA 4.1 Regression Equation

The regression equation for a set of n data points is $\hat{y} = b_0 + b_1 x$, where

$$b_1 = \frac{S_{xy}}{S_{xx}} \quad \text{and} \quad b_0 = \frac{1}{n}(\Sigma y - b_1 \Sigma x) = \bar{y} - b_1 \bar{x}.$$

Example 4.4 illustrates use of the regression equation.

Example 4.4 The Regression Equation

Age and Price of Orions Table 4.2 displays data on age and price for a sample of 11 Orions. We repeat that data in the first two columns of Table 4.5.

a. Determine the regression equation for the data.
b. Graph the regression equation and the data points.
c. Describe the apparent relationship between age and price of Orions.
d. Interpret the slope of the regression line in terms of prices for Orions.
e. Use the regression equation to predict the price of a 3-year-old Orion and a 4-year-old Orion.

Solution a. To determine the regression equation, we first need to compute b_1 and b_0 by using Formula 4.1. We did so by constructing a table of values for x (age), y (price), xy, x^2, and their sums in Table 4.5.

The slope of the regression line therefore is

$$b_1 = \frac{S_{xy}}{S_{xx}} = \frac{\Sigma xy - (\Sigma x)(\Sigma y)/n}{\Sigma x^2 - (\Sigma x)^2/n} = \frac{4732 - (58)(975)/11}{326 - (58)^2/11} = -20.26.$$

TABLE 4.5
Table for computing the regression equation for the Orion data

Age (yr) x	Price ($100) y	xy	x^2
5	85	425	25
4	103	412	16
6	70	420	36
5	82	410	25
5	89	445	25
5	98	490	25
6	66	396	36
6	95	570	36
2	169	338	4
7	70	490	49
7	48	336	49
58	975	4732	326

The y-intercept is

$$b_0 = \frac{1}{n}(\Sigma y - b_1 \Sigma x) = \frac{1}{11}\big[975 - (-20.26) \cdot 58\big] = 195.47.$$

So the regression equation is $\hat{y} = 195.47 - 20.26x$.

Note: The usual warnings about rounding apply. When computing the slope, b_1, of the regression line, do not round until the computation is finished. And when computing the y-intercept, b_0, do not use the rounded value of b_1; instead, keep full calculator accuracy.

b. To graph the regression equation, we need to substitute two different x-values in the regression equation to obtain two distinct points. Let's use the x-values 2 and 8. The corresponding y-values are

$$\hat{y} = 195.47 - 20.26 \cdot 2 = 154.95 \quad \text{and} \quad \hat{y} = 195.47 - 20.26 \cdot 8 = 33.39.$$

Hence the regression line passes through the two points $(2, 154.95)$ and $(8, 33.39)$. In Fig. 4.10, we plotted these two points with hollow dots. Drawing a straight line through the two hollow dots yields the regression line, or the graph of the regression equation.

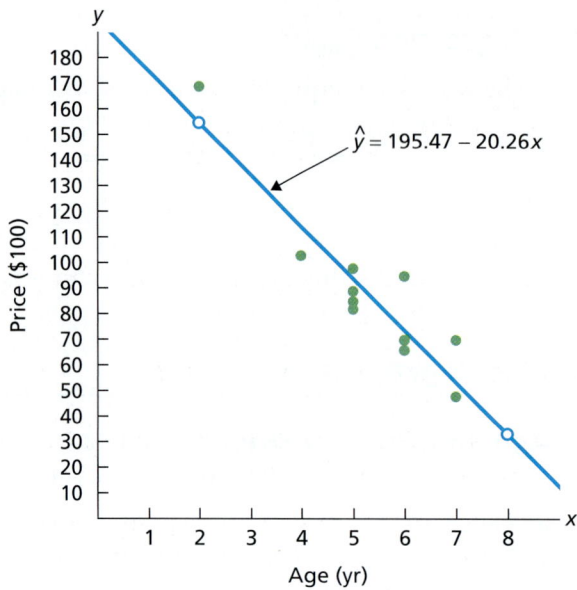

FIGURE 4.10
Regression line and data points for Orion data

Also shown in Fig. 4.10 are the data points from the first two columns of Table 4.5. The regression line in Fig. 4.10 thus is the straight line that best fits the data points according to the least-squares criterion; that is, it is the straight line that has the smallest possible sum of squared errors.

c. Because the slope of the regression line is negative, price tends to decrease as age increases—no particular surprise.

d. Because x represents age, in years, and y represents price, in hundreds of dollars, the slope of -20.26 indicates that Orions depreciate an estimated $2026 per year, at least in the 2- to 7-year-old range.

e. For a 3-year-old Orion, $x = 3$, and the regression equation yields the predicted price of

$$\hat{y} = 195.47 - 20.26 \cdot 3 = 134.69,$$

or $13,469.
  Similarly, the predicted price for a 4-year-old Orion is

$$\hat{y} = 195.47 - 20.26 \cdot 4 = 114.43,$$

or $11,443. We discuss questions concerning the accuracy and reliability of such predictions later in this chapter and also in Chapter 14. ◆

What Does it Mean?

We estimate that the price of a 3-year-old Orion is $13,469.

What Does it Mean?

We estimate that the price of a 4-year-old Orion is $11,443.

PREDICTOR VARIABLE AND RESPONSE VARIABLE

For a linear equation $y = b_0 + b_1 x$, y is the dependent variable and x is the independent variable. However, in the context of regression analysis, we more customarily call y the **response variable** and x the **predictor variable** or **explanatory variable** (because it is used to predict or explain the values of the response variable). For the Orion example, then, age is the predictor variable and price is the response variable.

EXTRAPOLATION

If a scatter diagram indicates a linear relationship between two variables, we can reasonably use the regression equation to make predictions for values of the predictor variable within the range of the observed values of the predictor variable. However, to do so for values of the predictor variable outside that range may not be reasonable because the linear relationship between the variables may not hold there.

Using the regression equation to make predictions for values of the predictor variable outside the range of the observed values of the predictor variable is called **extrapolation.** Grossly incorrect predictions can result from extrapolation.

The Orion example provides an excellent illustration of extrapolation leading to grossly incorrect predictions. The regression equation for the sample of Orions is $\hat{y} = 195.47 - 20.26x$, and the observed ages (values of the predictor variable) range from 2 to 7 years old.

Suppose that we extrapolate by using the regression equation to predict the price of an 11-year-old Orion. The predicted price is

$$\hat{y} = 195.47 - 20.26 \cdot 11 = -27.39,$$

or −$2739. Clearly, this result is ridiculous—no one is going to pay us $2739 to take away their 11-year-old Orion.

Consequently, although the relationship between age and price of Orions appears to be linear in the range from 2 to 7 years old, it is definitely not so in the range from 2 to 11 years old. Figure 4.11 on the next page summarizes the discussion on extrapolation as it applies to age and price of Orions.

To help avoid extrapolation, some researchers include the range of the observed values of the predictor variable with the regression equation. For the Orion example, we would write

$$\hat{y} = 195.47 - 20.26x, \quad 2 \leq x \leq 7.$$

Writing the regression equation in this way makes clear that using it to predict price for ages outside the range from 2 to 7 years old is extrapolation.

OUTLIERS AND INFLUENTIAL OBSERVATIONS

Recall that an outlier is an observation that lies outside the overall pattern of the data. In the context of regression, an **outlier** is a data point that lies far from the regression line, relative to the other data points. Figure 4.10 shows that the Orion data has no outliers.

An outlier can sometimes have a significant effect on a regression analysis. Thus, as usual, we need to identify outliers and remove them from the analysis when appropriate—for example, if we find the outlier to be a measurement or recording error.

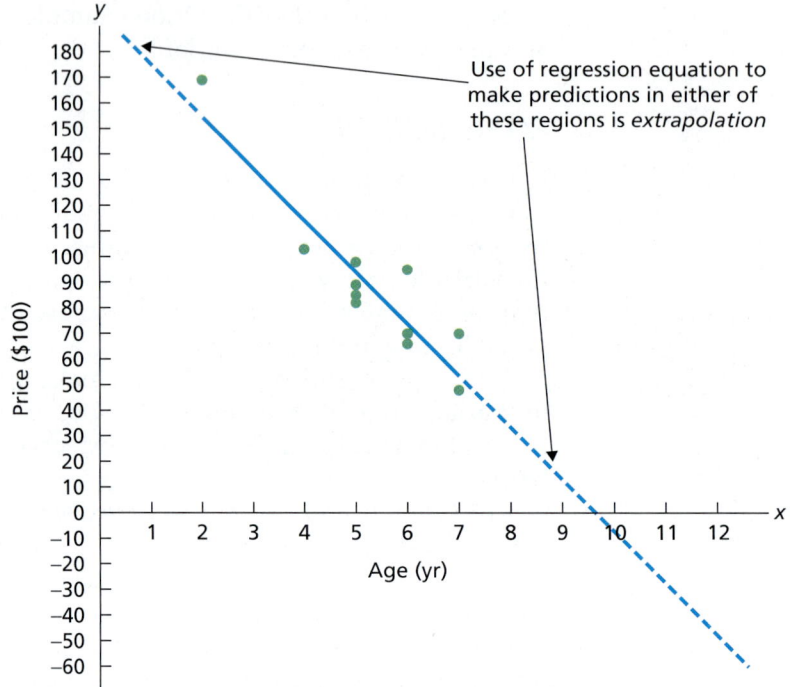

FIGURE 4.11
Extrapolation in the Orion example

We must also watch for influential observations. In regression analysis, an **influential observation** is a data point whose removal causes the regression equation (and line) to change considerably. A data point separated in the x-direction from the other data points is often an influential observation because the regression line is "pulled" toward such a data point without counteraction by other data points.

As with an outlier, we must try to determine the reason for an influential observation. If an influential observation is due to a measurement or recording error or for some other reason it clearly does not belong in the data set, it can be removed without further consideration. However, if no explanation for the influential observation is apparent, the decision whether to retain it is often difficult and calls for a judgment by the researcher.

For the Orion data, Fig. 4.10 on page 158 (or Table 4.5 on page 157) shows that the data point (2, 169) is potentially an influential observation because the age of 2 years appears separated from the other observed ages. When we remove that data point and recalculate the regression equation, the result is $\hat{y} = 160.33 - 14.24x$. Figure 4.12 reveals that this equation differs markedly from the regression equation, $\hat{y} = 195.47 - 20.26x$, based on the full data set. The data point (2, 169) is indeed an influential observation.

The influential observation (2, 169) is not a recording error; it is a legitimate data point. Nonetheless, we may need either to remove it—thus limiting the analysis to Orions between 4 and 7 years old—or to obtain additional data on 2-year-old (and 3-year-old) Orions so that the regression analysis is not so dependent on one data point.

FIGURE 4.12
Regression lines with and without the influential observation removed

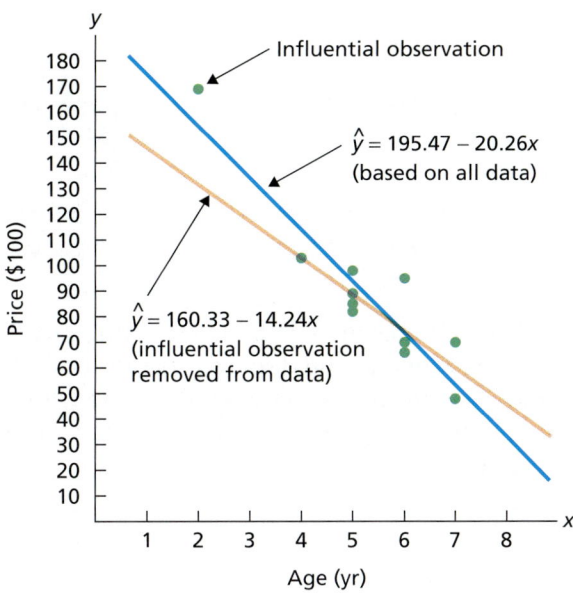

We added data for one 2-year-old and three 3-year-old Orions and obtained the regression equation $\hat{y} = 193.63 - 19.93x$. This regression equation differs little from our original regression equation, $\hat{y} = 195.47 - 20.26x$. Therefore we could justify using the original regression equation to analyze the relationship between age and price of Orions between 2 and 7 years of age, even though the corresponding data set contains an influential observation.

An outlier may or may not be an influential observation; and an influential observation may or may not be an outlier. Many statistical software packages identify potential outliers and influential observations.

A WARNING ON THE USE OF LINEAR REGRESSION

The idea behind finding a regression line is based on the assumption that the data points are scattered about a straight line.[2] Frequently, the data points are scattered about a curve instead of a straight line, as depicted in Fig. 4.13(a) on the next page. The formulas for b_0 and b_1 will still work for this data set and fit an inappropriate straight line, as shown in Fig. 4.13(b), instead of a curve. That would lead us to predict that y-values in Fig. 4.13(a) will keep increasing when they have actually begun to decrease. Key Fact 4.3 summarizes the criterion for finding a regression line.

Key Fact 4.3 **Criterion for Finding a Regression Line**

Before finding a regression line for a set of data points, draw a scatter diagram. If the data points do not appear to be scattered about a straight line, do not determine a regression line.

---

[2] We discuss this assumption in detail and make it more precise in Section 14.1.

FIGURE 4.13
(a) Data points scattered about a curve; (b) inappropriate straight line fit to the data points

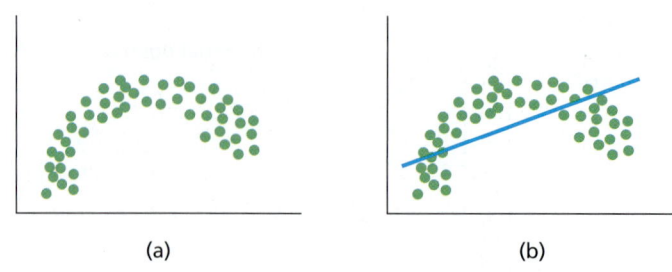

Techniques are available for fitting curves to data points showing a curved pattern, such as the data points plotted in Fig. 4.13(a). We discuss those techniques, referred to as **curvilinear regression,** in the chapter *Model Building in Regression* on the WeissStats CD accompanying this book or on the Weiss Web site.

The Technology Center

Almost all statistical technologies have programs that automatically obtain a scatter diagram and a regression line for a set of data points. In this subsection, we present output and (optional) step-by-step instructions to carry out these two procedures.

Again, before determining a regression line, you should look at a scatter diagram of the data to determine whether the data points appear to be scattered about a straight line. Consider Example 4.5.

Example 4.5 Using Technology to Obtain a Scatter Diagram

Age and Price of Orions Use Minitab, Excel, or the TI-83 Plus to obtain a scatter diagram for the age and price data presented in Table 4.2 on page 154.

Solution Printout 4.1 shows output obtained by applying the scatter diagram programs to the age and price data presented in Table 4.2.

These outputs show that the data points are scattered about a straight line and hence that we can reasonably find a regression line for these data. Compare the scatter diagrams in Printout 4.1 to the scatter diagram we drew by hand in Fig. 4.7 on page 154. ◆

Now consider Example 4.6.

Example 4.6 Using Technology to Obtain a Regression Line

Age and Price of Orions Use Minitab, Excel, or the TI-83 Plus to obtain the regression equation for the age and price data displayed in Table 4.2 on page 154.

Solution Printout 4.2 on page 164 shows output obtained by applying the regression programs to the age and price data displayed in Table 4.2.

PRINTOUT 4.1
Scatter diagrams for the age and price data of 11 Orions

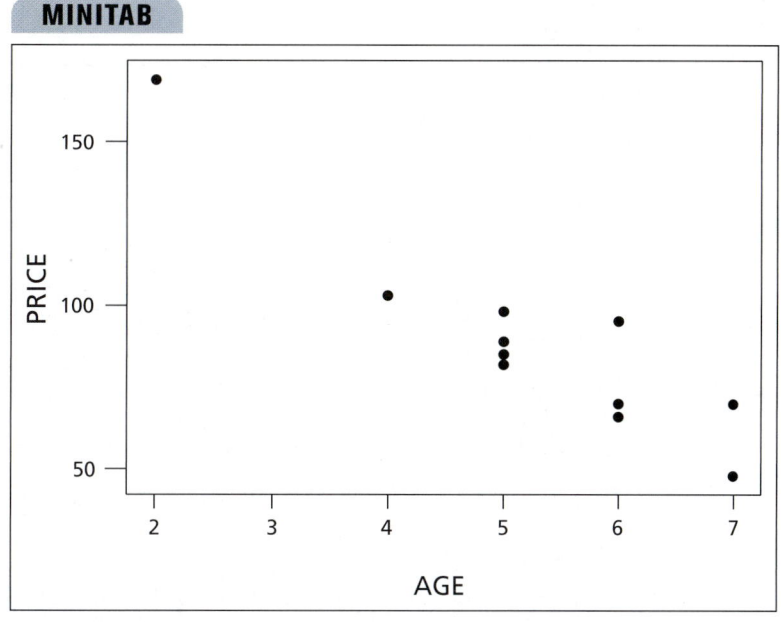

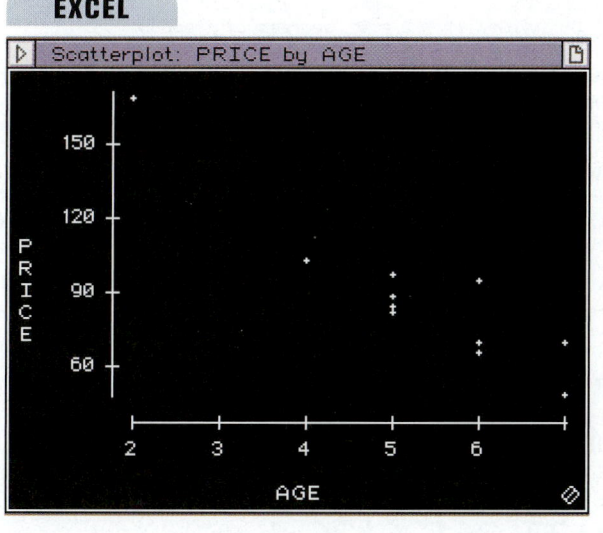

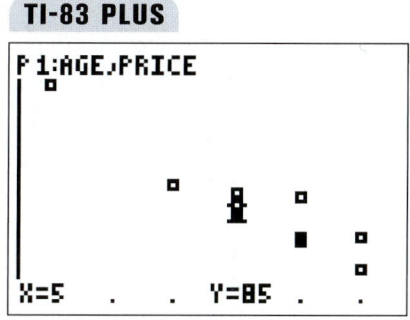

The outputs in Printout 4.2 show that the regression equation for the age and price data is $\hat{y} = 195.47 - 20.26x$. (In the Minitab and Excel outputs, the y-intercept and slope of the regression line are displayed as the first and second entries in the column labeled Coef in Minitab and the column labeled Coefficient in Excel, respectively.)

PRINTOUT 4.2

Regression output for the age and price data of 11 Orions

MINITAB

```
The regression equation is
PRICE = 195 - 20.3 AGE

Predictor        Coef      SE Coef         T         P
Constant       195.47        15.24     12.83     0.000
AGE            -20.261        2.800     -7.24     0.000

S = 12.58      R-Sq = 85.3%     R-Sq(adj) = 83.7%

Analysis of Variance

Source           DF          SS          MS         F         P
Regression        1      8285.0      8285.0     52.38     0.000
Residual Error    9      1423.5       158.2
Total            10      9708.5
```

EXCEL

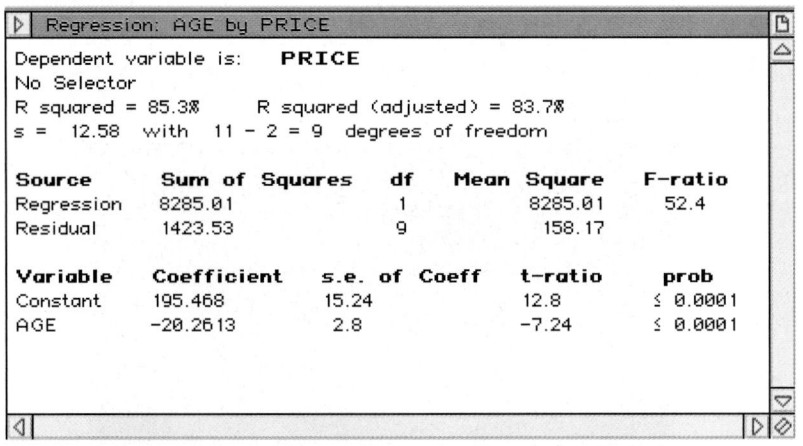

TI-83 PLUS

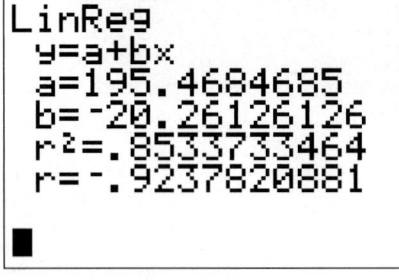

We can also use Minitab, Excel, or the TI-83 Plus to obtain a scatter diagram of the data with the regression line superimposed. We show output from the three technologies in Printout 4.3. Compare the scatter diagrams and superimposed regression lines in Printout 4.3 to those we drew by hand in Fig. 4.10 on page 158.

PRINTOUT 4.3
Scatter diagrams with superimposed regression lines for the age and price data of 11 Orions

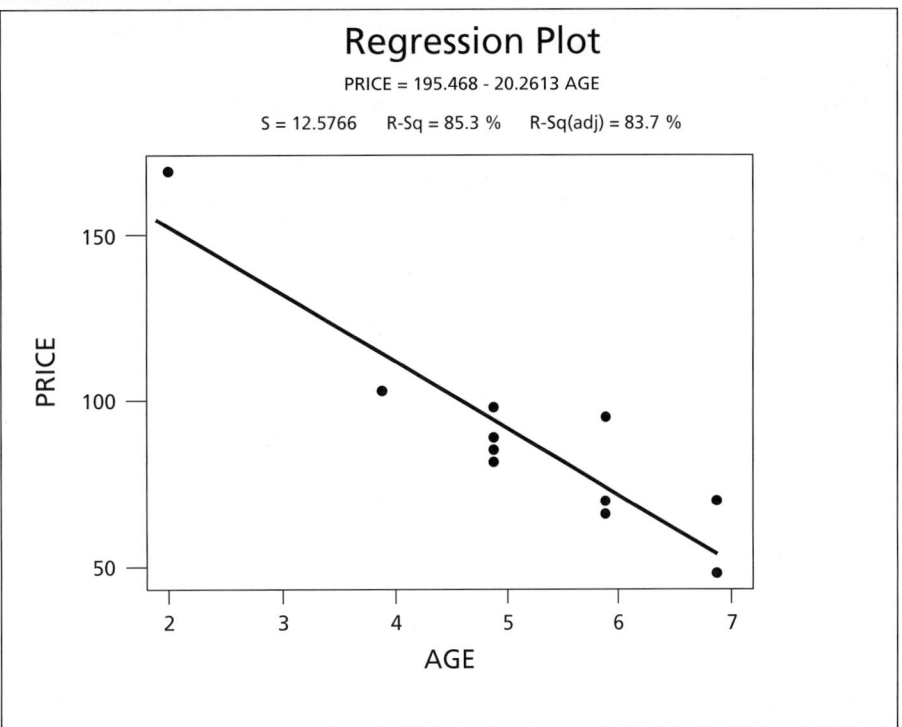

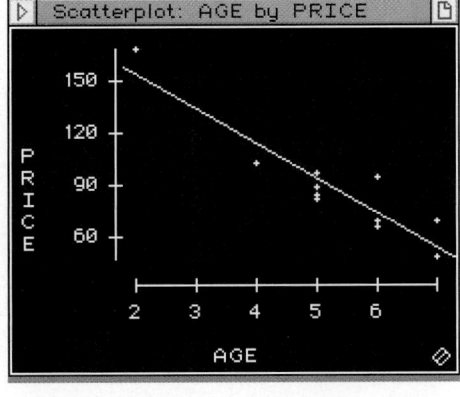

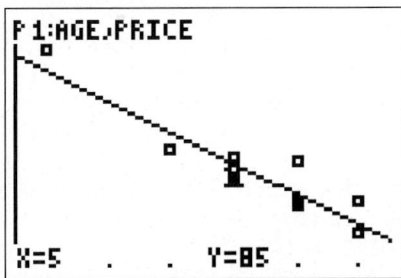

Obtaining the Output (Optional)

Printout 4.1 provides output from Minitab, Excel, and the TI-83 Plus for a scatter diagram for the age and price data of 11 Orions given in Table 4.2 on page 154. The following are detailed instructions for obtaining that output. First, we store the age and price data in columns (Minitab), ranges (Excel), or lists (TI-83 Plus) named AGE and PRICE, respectively. Then, we proceed as follows.

MINITAB	EXCEL	TI-83 PLUS
1 Choose **Graph ➤ Plot...** 2 Specify PRICE in the **Y** text box for **Graph 1** 3 Specify AGE in the **X** text box for **Graph 1** 4 Click **OK**	1 Choose **DDXL ➤ Charts and Plots** 2 Select **Scatterplot** from the **Function type** drop-down list box 3 Specify AGE in the **x-Axis Variable** text box 4 Specify PRICE in the **y-Axis Variable** text box 5 Click **OK**	1 Press **2nd ➤ STAT PLOT** and then press **ENTER** twice 2 Arrow to the first graph icon and press **ENTER** 3 Press the down-arrow key 4 Press **2nd ➤ LIST**, arrow down to AGE, and press **ENTER** twice 5 Press **2nd ➤ LIST**, arrow down to PRICE, and press **ENTER** twice 6 Press **ZOOM** and then **9** (and then **TRACE**, if desired)

Printout 4.2 provides output from Minitab, Excel, and the TI-83 Plus for the regression equation for the age and price data in Table 4.2. The following are detailed instructions for obtaining that output. First, we store the age and price data in columns (Minitab), ranges (Excel), or lists (TI-83 Plus) named AGE and PRICE, respectively. Then, we proceed as follows.

MINITAB	EXCEL	TI-83 PLUS
1 Choose **Stat ➤ Regression ➤ Regression...** 2 Specify PRICE in the **Response** text box 3 Specify AGE in the **Predictors** text box 4 Click the **Results...** button 5 Select the **Regression equation, table of coefficients, s, R-squared, and basic analysis of variance** option button 6 Click **OK** 7 Click **OK**	1 Choose **DDXL ➤ Regression** 2 Select **Simple Regression** from the **Function type** drop-down list box 3 Specify PRICE in the **Response Variable** text box 4 Specify AGE in the **Explanatory Variable** text box 5 Click **OK**	1 Press **2nd ➤ CATALOG** and then press **D** 2 Arrow down to **DiagnosticOn** and press **Enter** twice 3 Press **STAT**, arrow over to **CALC**, and press **8** 4 Press **2nd ➤ LIST**, arrow down to AGE, and press **ENTER** 5 Press **, ➤ 2nd ➤ LIST**, arrow down to PRICE, and press **ENTER** 6 Press **, ➤ VARS**, arrow over to **Y-VARS**, and press **ENTER** three times

The Excel output in Printout 4.3 is part of the DDXL output that results from applying the steps in the previous Excel instructions. To obtain the TI-83 Plus output in Printout 4.3, simply press **GRAPH** and then **TRACE** after executing the steps in the previous TI-83 Plus instructions. The Minitab output in Printout 4.3 is easily obtained by using Minitab's **Stat ➤ Regression ➤ Fitted Line Plot...** program. See the technology manuals for details.

Exercises 4.2

Statistical Concepts and Skills

4.32 Regarding a scatter diagram,
a. identify one of its uses.
b. what property should it have to obtain a regression line for the data?

4.33 Regarding the criterion used to decide on the line that best fits a set of data points,
a. what is that criterion called?
b. specifically, what is the criterion?

4.34 Regarding the line that best fits a set of data points,
a. what is that line called?
b. what is the equation of that line called?

4.35 Regarding the two variables under consideration in a regression analysis,
a. what is the dependent variable called?
b. what is the independent variable called?

4.36 Using the regression equation to make predictions for values of the predictor variable outside the range of the observed values of the predictor variable is called _____.

4.37 Fill in the blanks.
a. In the context of regression, an _____ is a data point that lies far from the regression line, relative to the other data points.
b. In regression analysis, an _____ is a data point whose removal causes the regression equation to change considerably.

In Exercises 4.38 and 4.39,
a. graph the linear equations and data points.
b. construct tables for x, y, $\hat{y}$, e, and e^2 similar to Table 4.4 on page 156.
c. determine which line fits the set of data points better, according to the least-squares criterion.

4.38 Line A: $y = 1.5 + 0.5x$
Line B: $y = 1.125 + 0.375x$

x	1	1	5	5
y	1	3	2	4

4.39 Line A: $y = 3 - 0.6x$
Line B: $y = 4 - x$

x	0	2	2	5	6
y	4	2	0	-2	1

For Exercises 4.40–4.45, be sure to save your work. You will need it in later sections.

4.40 Refer to Exercise 4.38.
a. Find the regression equation for the data points.
b. Graph the regression equation and the data points.

4.41 Refer to Exercise 4.39.
a. Find the regression equation for the data points.
b. Graph the regression equation and the data points.

4.42 Tax Efficiency. *Tax efficiency* is a measure—ranging from 0 to 100—of how much tax due to capital gains stock or mutual fund investors pay on their investments each year; the higher the tax efficiency, the lower is the tax. The paper "At the Mercy of the Manager" (*Financial Planning*, 2000, Vol. 30(5), pp. 54–56) by Craig Israelsen examined the relationship between investments in mutual fund portfolios and their associated tax efficiencies. The following table shows percentage of investments in energy securities (x) and tax efficiency (y) for 10 mutual fund portfolios.

x	3.1	3.2	3.7	4.3	4.0	5.5	6.7	7.4	7.4	10.6
y	98.1	94.7	92.0	89.8	87.5	85.0	82.0	77.8	72.1	53.5

a. Determine the regression equation for the data.
b. Graph the regression equation and the data points.
c. Describe the apparent relationship between percent of investments in energy securities and tax efficiency for mutual fund portfolios.
d. What does the slope of the regression line represent in terms of percent of investments in energy securities and tax efficiency for mutual fund portfolios?
e. Use the regression equation that you obtained in part (a) to predict the tax efficiency of a mutual fund portfolio with 5.0% of its investments in energy securities; with 7.4% of its investments in energy securities.
f. Identify the predictor and response variables.
g. Identify outliers and potential influential observations.

4.43 Corvette Prices. The *Kelley Blue Book* provides information on wholesale and retail prices of cars. Following are age and price data for 10 randomly selected Corvettes between 1 and 6 years old. Here, x denotes age, in years, and y denotes price, in hundreds of dollars.

x	6	6	6	2	2	5	4	5	1	4
y	205	195	210	340	299	230	270	243	340	240

a. Determine the regression equation for the data.
b. Graph the regression equation and the data points.
c. Describe the apparent relationship between age and price for Corvettes.
d. What does the slope of the regression line represent in terms of Corvette age and price?
e. Use the regression equation that you obtained in part (a) to predict the price of a 2-year-old Corvette; a 3-year-old Corvette.
f. Identify the predictor and response variables.
g. Identify outliers and potential influential observations.

4.44 Custom Homes. Hanna Properties specializes in custom-home resales in the Equestrian Estates, an exclusive subdivision in Phoenix, Arizona. A random sample of nine custom homes currently listed for sale provided the following information on size and price. Here, x denotes size, in hundreds of square feet, rounded to the nearest hundred, and y denotes price, in thousands of dollars, rounded to the nearest thousand.

x	26	27	33	29	29	34	30	40	22
y	259	274	294	296	325	380	457	523	215

a. Determine the regression equation for the data.
b. Graph the regression equation and the data points.
c. Describe the apparent relationship between square footage and price for custom homes in the Equestrian Estates.
d. What does the slope of the regression line represent in terms of size and price of custom homes in the Equestrian Estates?
e. Use the regression equation determined in part (a) to predict the price of a custom home in the Equestrian Estates that has 2600 sq ft.
f. Identify the predictor and response variables.
g. Identify outliers and potential influential observations.

4.45 Plant Emissions. Plants emit gases that trigger the ripening of fruit, attract pollinators, and cue other physiological responses. N. G. Agelopolous, K. Chamberlain, and J. A. Pickett examined factors that affect the emission of volatile compounds by the potato plant *Solanum tuberosom* and published their findings in the *Journal of Chemical Ecology* (2000, Vol. 26(2), pp. 497–511). The volatile compounds analyzed were hydrocarbons used by other plants and animals. Following are data on plant weight (x), in grams, and quantity of volatile compounds emitted (y), in hundreds of nanograms, for 11 potato plants.

x	57	85	57	65	52	67	62	80	77	53	68
y	8.0	22.0	10.5	22.5	12.0	11.5	7.5	13.0	16.5	21.0	12.0

a. Determine the regression equation for the data.
b. Graph the regression equation and the data points.
c. Describe the apparent relationship between potato plant weight and quantity of volatile compounds emitted.
d. What does the slope of the regression line represent in terms of potato plant weight and quantity of volatile compounds emitted?
e. Use the regression equation determined in part (a) to predict the quantity of volatile compounds emitted by a potato plant that weighs 75 grams.
f. Identify the predictor and response variables.
g. Identify outliers and potential influential observations.

4.46 For which of the following sets of data points can you reasonably determine a regression line? Explain your answer.

4.47 For which of the following sets of data points can you reasonably determine a regression line? Explain your answer.

4.48 Tax Efficiency. In Exercise 4.42, you determined a regression equation that relates the variables percentage of investments in energy securities and tax efficiency for mutual fund portfolios.
a. Should that regression equation be used to predict the tax efficiency of a mutual fund portfolio with 6.4% of its investments in energy securities? with 15% of its investments in energy securities? Explain your answers.
b. For which percentages of investments in energy securities is use of the regression equation to predict tax efficiency reasonable?

4.49 Corvette Prices. In Exercise 4.43, you determined a regression equation that can be used to predict the price of a Corvette, given its age.
a. Should that regression equation be used to predict the price of a 4-year-old Corvette? a 10-year-old Corvette? Explain your answers.
b. For which ages is use of the regression equation to predict price reasonable?

4.50 Palm Beach Fiasco. The 2000 U.S. presidential election brought great controversy to the election process. Many voters in Palm Beach, Florida, claimed that they were confused by the ballot format and may have accidentally voted for Pat Buchanan when they intended to vote for Al Gore. Professors Greg D. Adams of Carnegie Mellon University and Chris Fastnow of Chatham College compiled and analyzed data on election votes in Florida, by county, for both 1996 and 2000. What conclusions would you draw from the following scatter diagrams constructed by the researchers? Explain your answers.

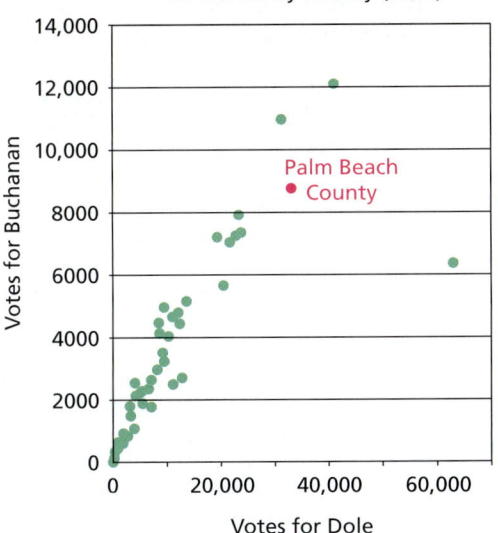

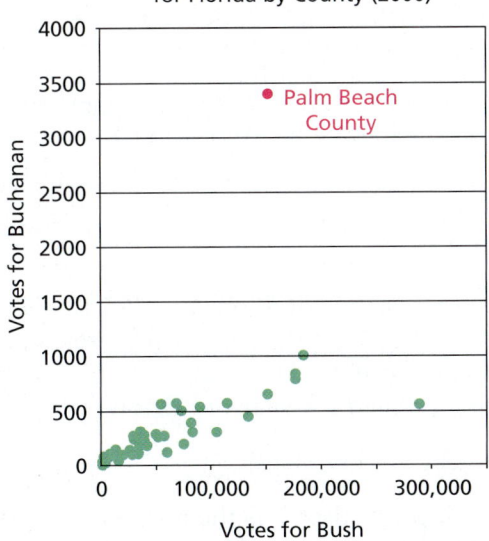

Source: Prof. Greg D. Adams, Dept. of Social & Decision Sciences, Carnegie Mellon University, and Prof. Chris Fastnow, Director, Center for Women in Politics in Pennsylvania, Chatham College

Extending the Concepts and Skills

4.51 Sample Covariance. For n pairs of observations from two variables, x and y, the *sample covariance*, s_{xy}, is defined by

$$s_{xy} = \frac{\Sigma(x - \bar{x})(y - \bar{y})}{n - 1}. \qquad (4.1)$$

a. Determine the sample covariance of the data points in Exercise 4.39.

The sample covariance can be used as an alternative method for obtaining the slope and y-intercept of the regression line for a set of data points. The formulas are

$$b_1 = s_{xy}/s_x^2 \quad \text{and} \quad b_0 = \bar{y} - b_1\bar{x}, \qquad (4.2)$$

where s_x denotes the sample standard deviation of the x-values.

b. Use Equations (4.1) and (4.2) to find the regression equation for the data points in Exercise 4.39. Compare your answer to the answer you obtained in part (a) of Exercise 4.41.

Using Technology

In Exercises 4.52–4.58, use the technology of your choice to:
a. *Obtain a scatter diagram for the data.*
b. *Decide whether finding a regression line for the data is reasonable. If so, then also do parts (c) and (d).*
c. *Determine and interpret the regression equation for the data.*
d. *Identify potential outliers and influential observations.*

4.52 Batting and Scoring. Is the number of runs a baseball team scores in a season related to its team batting average? ESPN compiles end-of-season statistics for Major League Baseball and maintains them on its Web site. The following table provides season team batting averages and total runs scored for a sample of major league baseball teams.

Average	Runs	Average	Runs
.294	968	.267	793
.278	938	.265	792
.278	925	.256	764
.270	887	.254	752
.274	825	.246	740
.271	810	.266	738
.263	807	.262	731
.257	798	.251	708

4.53 Body Fat. In the paper "Total Body Composition by Dual-Photon (^{153}Gd) Absorptiometry" (*American Journal of Clinical Nutrition*, 1984, Vol. 40, pp. 834–839), R. B. Mazess et al. studied methods for quantifying body composition. Eighteen randomly selected adults were measured for percentage of body fat, using dual-photon absorptiometry. Each adult's age and percentage of body fat are shown in the following table.

Age	%Fat	Age	%Fat	Age	%Fat
23	9.5	45	27.4	56	32.5
23	27.9	49	25.2	57	30.3
27	7.8	50	31.1	58	33.0
27	17.8	53	34.7	58	33.8
39	31.4	53	42.0	60	41.1
41	25.9	54	29.1	61	34.5

4.54 PCBs and Pelicans. Polychlorinated biphenyls (PCBs), an industrial pollutant, are known to be a great danger to natural ecosystems. In a study by R. W. Risebrough titled "Effects of Environmental Pollutants Upon Animals Other Than Man" (*Proceedings of the 6th Berkeley Symposium on Mathematics and Statistics, VI*, 1972, University of California Press, pp. 443–463), 60 Anacapa pelican eggs were collected and measured for their shell thickness, in millimeters (mm), and concentration of PCBs, in parts per million (ppm). The data are on the WeissStats CD.

4.55 More Money More Beer? Does a higher state per capita income equate to a higher per capita beer consumption? Data downloaded from *The Beer Institute Online* on per capita income, in dollars, and per capita beer consumption, in gallons, for the 50 states and Washington, D.C., are provided on the WeissStats CD.

4.56 Gas Guzzlers. The magazine *Consumer Reports* publishes information on automobile gas mileage and variables that affect gas mileage. In the April 1999 issue, data on gas mileage (in miles per gallon) and engine displacement (in liters) were published for 121 vehicles. Those data are available on the WeissStats CD.

4.57 Estriol Level and Birth Weight. J. Greene and J. Touchstone conducted a study on the relationship between the estriol levels of pregnant women and the birth weights of their children. Their findings, "Urinary Tract Estriol: An Index of Placental Function," were published in the *American Journal of Obstetrics and Gynecology* (1963, Vol. 85(1), pp. 1–9). The data from the study are provided on the WeissStats CD, where estriol levels are in mg/24 hr and birth weights are in hectograms.

4.58 Shortleaf Pines. The ability to estimate the volume of a tree based on a simple measurement, such as the tree's diameter, is important to the lumber industry, ecologists, and conservationists. Data on volume, in cubic feet, and diameter at breast height, in inches, for 70 shortleaf pines was reported in C. Bruce and F. X. Schumacher's *Forest Mensuration* (New York: McGraw-Hill, 1935) and analyzed by A. C. Akinson in the article "Transforming Both Sides of a Tree" (*The American Statistician*, 1994, Vol. 48, pp. 307–312). The data are presented on the WeissStats CD.

4.3 THE COEFFICIENT OF DETERMINATION

In Example 4.4, we determined the regression equation, $\hat{y} = 195.47 - 20.26x$, for data on age and price of a sample of 11 Orions, where x represents age, in years, and $\hat{y}$ represents predicted price, in hundreds of dollars. We also applied the regression equation to predict the price of a 4-year-old Orion,

$$\hat{y} = 195.47 - 20.26 \cdot 4 = 114.43,$$

or $11,443. But how valuable are such predictions? Is the regression equation useful for predicting price, or could we do just as well by ignoring age?

In general, the utility of a regression equation for making predictions can be evaluated in several ways. One way is to determine the percentage of variation in the observed values of the response variable explained by the regression (or predictor variable). To illustrate, we return to the data on age and price of Orions in Example 4.7.

Example 4.7 Introduces the Coefficient of Determination

Age and Price of Orions The scatter diagram and regression line for the age and price data of 11 Orions are repeated in Fig. 4.14.

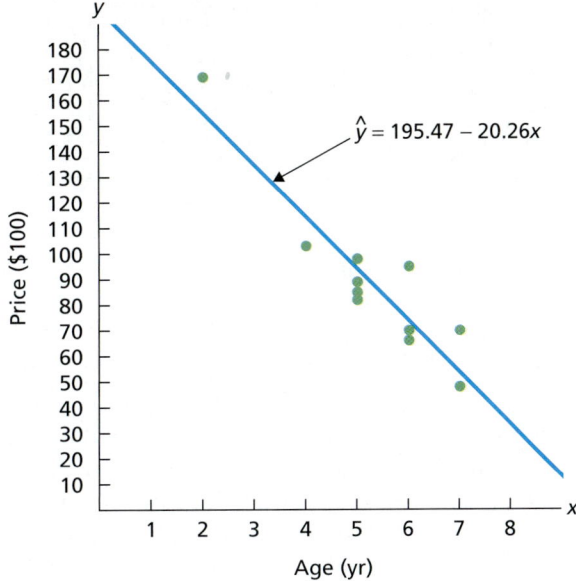

FIGURE 4.14
Scatter diagram and regression line for Orion data

The scatter diagram reveals that the prices of the 11 Orions vary widely, ranging from a low of 48 ($4800) to a high of 169 ($16,900). But Fig. 4.14 also shows that much of the price variation is "explained" by the regression (or age); that is, the regression line, with age as the predictor variable, predicts a sizeable portion of the type of variation found in the prices.

To describe quantitatively how much of the variation in the observed prices is explained by the regression, we need to define two measures of variation: (1) the total variation in the observed prices and (2) the amount of variation in the observed prices explained by the regression.

As a measure of total variation in the observed prices, we use the sum of squared deviations of the observed prices from the mean price. This measure is called the **total sum of squares, SST**; in symbols, $SST = \Sigma(y - \bar{y})^2$. If we divide SST by $n - 1$, we get the sample variance of the observed prices, so SST really is a measure of total variation.

To compute the total sum of squares, we must first find the sample mean price:

$$\bar{y} = \frac{\Sigma y}{n} = \frac{975}{11} = 88.64.$$

Now, using Table 4.6, we obtain the total sum of squares for the Orion price data.[3]

TABLE 4.6
Table for computing SST for the Orion price data

Age (yr) x	Price ($100) y	$y - \bar{y}$	$(y - \bar{y})^2$
5	85	−3.64	13.2
4	103	14.36	206.3
6	70	−18.64	347.3
5	82	−6.64	44.0
5	89	0.36	0.1
5	98	9.36	87.7
6	66	−22.64	512.4
6	95	6.36	40.5
2	169	80.36	6458.3
7	70	−18.64	347.3
7	48	−40.64	1651.3
	975		9708.5

From the final column of Table 4.6,

$$SST = \Sigma(y - \bar{y})^2 = 9708.5,$$

which is the measure of total variation in the observed prices.

To obtain the amount of variation in the observed prices explained by the regression, let's first look at a particular observed price—say, $y = 98$—corresponding to the data point $(5, 98)$. In Fig. 4.15, we magnified the portion of Fig. 4.14 that shows that data point and included the mean of the observed prices ($\bar{y} = 88.64$) and the predicted price for a 5-year-old Orion ($\hat{y} = 94.16$).

The total variation in the observed prices is based on the deviation of each observed price from the mean price, $y - \bar{y}$. As illustrated in Fig. 4.15, each such deviation can be decomposed into two parts: the deviation explained by the regression line, $\hat{y} - \bar{y}$, and the remaining unexplained deviation, $y - \hat{y}$. Hence the amount of variation (squared deviation) in the observed prices explained by the regression is $\Sigma(\hat{y} - \bar{y})^2$. This measure is called the **regression sum of squares, SSR.**

To compute SSR, we need the predicted prices, $\hat{y}$, and the mean of the observed prices, $\bar{y}$. We have already computed the mean of the observed prices, and each predicted price is obtained by substituting the age of the Orion in question for x in the regression equation $\hat{y} = 195.47 - 20.26x$. The third column of Table 4.7 shows the predicted prices for all 11 Orions.

Recalling that $\bar{y} = 88.64$, we construct the fourth column of Table 4.7. We then calculate the entries for the fifth column and obtain the regression sum of squares, SSR:

$$SSR = \Sigma(\hat{y} - \bar{y})^2 = 8285.0.$$

---

[3] Values in Table 4.6 and all other tables in this section are displayed to various numbers of decimal places, but computations were done with full calculator accuracy.

4.3 The Coefficient of Determination 173

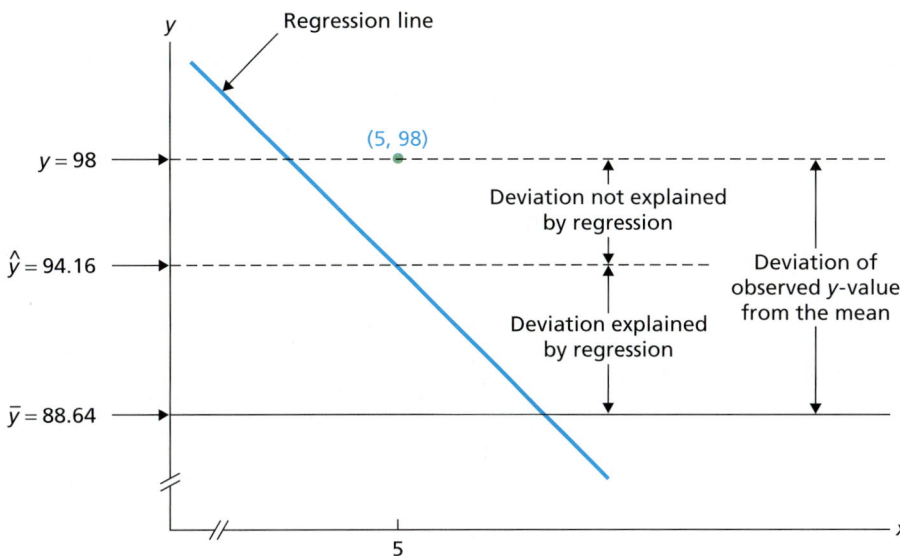

FIGURE 4.15
Magnification of a portion of Fig. 4.14 showing only the data point (5, 98)

TABLE 4.7
Table for computing SSR for the Orion data

Age (yr) x	Price ($100) y	$\hat{y}$	$\hat{y} - \bar{y}$	$(\hat{y} - \bar{y})^2$
5	85	94.16	5.53	30.5
4	103	114.42	25.79	665.0
6	70	73.90	−14.74	217.1
5	82	94.16	5.53	30.5
5	89	94.16	5.53	30.5
5	98	94.16	5.53	30.5
6	66	73.90	−14.74	217.1
6	95	73.90	−14.74	217.1
2	169	154.95	66.31	4397.0
7	70	53.64	−35.00	1224.8
7	48	53.64	−35.00	1224.8
				8285.0

This measure is the amount of variation in the observed prices explained by the regression.

Using the values of *SST* and *SSR*, we can now determine the percentage of variation in the observed prices explained by the regression, which is called the **coefficient of determination**, or r^2. We have

$$r^2 = \frac{SSR}{SST} = \frac{8285.0}{9708.5} = 0.853,$$

or 85.3%.

What Does it Mean?

Evidently, age is quite useful for predicting price because 85.3% of the variation in the observed prices is explained by the regression of price on age.

Now let's consider the remaining deviation portrayed in Fig. 4.15—the deviation not explained by the regression, $y - \hat{y}$. The amount of variation (squared deviation) in the observed prices not explained by the regression is $\Sigma(y - \hat{y})^2$, called the **error sum of squares, SSE**.

To compute SSE, we need the observed prices, y, and the predicted prices, $\hat{y}$. Both quantities are displayed in Table 4.7 and are repeated in the second and third columns of Table 4.8.

TABLE 4.8
Table for computing SSE for the Orion data

Age (yr) x	Price ($100) y	$\hat{y}$	$y - \hat{y}$	$(y - \hat{y})^2$
5	85	94.16	−9.16	83.9
4	103	114.42	−11.42	130.5
6	70	73.90	−3.90	15.2
5	82	94.16	−12.16	147.9
5	89	94.16	−5.16	26.6
5	98	94.16	3.84	14.7
6	66	73.90	−7.90	62.4
6	95	73.90	21.10	445.2
2	169	154.95	14.05	197.5
7	70	53.64	16.36	267.7
7	48	53.64	−5.64	31.8
				1423.5

From the final column of Table 4.8, we obtain the error sum of squares:

$$SSE = \Sigma(y - \hat{y})^2 = 1423.5.$$

This measure is the amount of variation in the observed prices not explained by the regression. Because the regression line is the line that best fits the data according to the least squares criterion, SSE is also the smallest possible sum of squared errors among all straight lines.

We now summarize our discussion of the three sums of squares and the coefficient of determination in the following two definitions.

DEFINITION 4.4 **Sums of Squares in Regression**

Total sum of squares, SST: The variation in the observed values of the response variable: $SST = \Sigma(y - \bar{y})^2$.

Regression sum of squares, SSR: The variation in the observed values of the response variable explained by the regression: $SSR = \Sigma(\hat{y} - \bar{y})^2$.

Error sum of squares, SSE: The variation in the observed values of the response variable not explained by the regression: $SSE = \Sigma(y - \hat{y})^2$.

4.3 The Coefficient of Determination

DEFINITION 4.5 **Coefficient of Determination**

The *coefficient of determination*, r^2, is the proportion of variation in the observed values of the response variable explained by the regression, or

$$r^2 = \frac{SSR}{SST}.$$

The coefficient of determination always lies between 0 and 1 and is a descriptive measure of the utility of the regression equation for making predictions. A value of r^2 near 0 indicates that the regression equation is not very useful for making predictions, whereas a value of r^2 near 1 indicates that the regression equation is extremely useful for making predictions.

THE REGRESSION IDENTITY

For the Orion data, we have determined that $SST = 9708.5$, $SSR = 8285.0$, and $SSE = 1423.5$. As $9708.5 = 8285.0 + 1423.5$, we see that $SST = SSR + SSE$. This equation is always true and is called the **regression identity,** which we state as Key Fact 4.4.

Key Fact 4.4 **Regression Identity**

The total sum of squares equals the regression sum of squares plus the error sum of squares, or $SST = SSR + SSE$.

Because of the regression identity, we can also express the coefficient of determination in terms of the total sum of squares and the error sum of squares:

$$r^2 = \frac{SSR}{SST} = \frac{SST - SSE}{SST} = 1 - \frac{SSE}{SST}.$$

This formula shows that we can also interpret the coefficient of determination as the percentage reduction obtained in the total squared error by using the regression equation instead of the mean, $\bar{y}$, to predict the observed values of the response variable. We examine this interpretation in Exercise 4.69.

COMPUTING FORMULAS FOR THE SUMS OF SQUARES

Calculating the three sums of squares—SST, SSR, and SSE—with the defining formulas is time-consuming and can lead to significant roundoff error unless full accuracy is retained. For those reasons, we usually use computing formulas or a computer to obtain the sums of squares. The computing formulas are stated in Formula 4.2 and applied in Example 4.8.

FORMULA 4.2 Computing Formulas for the Sums of Squares

The three sums of squares, SST, SSR, and SSE, can be obtained by using the following computing formulas.

$$\text{Total sum of squares: } SST = S_{yy}$$

$$\text{Regression sum of squares: } SSR = S_{xy}^2/S_{xx}$$

$$\text{Error sum of squares: } SSE = S_{yy} - S_{xy}^2/S_{xx}$$

The formulas for S_{yy}, S_{xy}, and S_{xx} are given in Definition 4.3 on page 156.

Example 4.8 Computing Formulas for the Sums of Squares

Age and Price of Orions The age and price data for a sample of 11 Orions are repeated in the first two columns of Table 4.9. Use the computing formulas in Formula 4.2 to determine the three sums of squares.

Solution To apply the computing formulas, we need a table of values for x (age), y (price), xy, x^2, y^2, and their sums, as shown in Table 4.9.

TABLE 4.9 Table for obtaining the three sums of squares for the Orion data by using the computing formulas

Age (yr) x	Price ($100) y	xy	x^2	y^2
5	85	425	25	7,225
4	103	412	16	10,609
6	70	420	36	4,900
5	82	410	25	6,724
5	89	445	25	7,921
5	98	490	25	9,604
6	66	396	36	4,356
6	95	570	36	9,025
2	169	338	4	28,561
7	70	490	49	4,900
7	48	336	49	2,304
58	975	4732	326	96,129

Using the last row of Table 4.9 and Formula 4.2, we can now obtain the three sums of squares for the Orion data. The total sum of squares is

$$SST = S_{yy} = \Sigma y^2 - (\Sigma y)^2/n = 96{,}129 - (975)^2/11 = 9708.5;$$

the regression sum of squares is

$$SSR = \frac{S_{xy}^2}{S_{xx}} = \frac{[\Sigma xy - (\Sigma x)(\Sigma y)/n]^2}{\Sigma x^2 - (\Sigma x)^2/n} = \frac{[4732 - (58)(975)/11]^2}{326 - (58)^2/11} = 8285.0;$$

and, from the two preceding results, the error sum of squares is

$$SSE = S_{yy} - \frac{S_{xy}^2}{S_{xx}} = 9708.5 - 8285.0 = 1423.5.$$

The values that we obtained for the three sums of squares by applying the computing formulas are, of course, the same as the values we found earlier by using the defining formulas. However, when the computing formulas are used, the computations are much simpler and less subject to roundoff error. ◆

The Technology Center

Most statistical technologies have programs to compute the coefficient of determination, r^2, and the three sums of squares, SST, SSR, and SSE. In fact, many statistical technologies present those four statistics as part of the output for a regression equation. In Example 4.9, we concentrate on the coefficient of determination. Refer to the technology manuals for a discussion of the three sums of squares.

Example 4.9 **Using Technology to Obtain a Coefficient of Determination**

Age and Price of Orions The age and price data for a sample of 11 Orions is given in Table 4.2 on page 154. Use Minitab, Excel, or the TI-83 Plus to obtain the coefficient of determination, r^2, for those data.

Solution In Section 4.2, we used Minitab, Excel, and the TI-83 Plus to find the regression equation for the age and price data. The results are shown in Printout 4.2 on page 164. The outputs in Printout 4.2 also display the coefficient of determination: `R-Sq = 85.3%` (Minitab), `R Squared = 85.3%` (Excel), and r^2=`.8533733464` (TI-83 Plus). Thus, to three decimal places, $r^2 = 0.853$. ◆

Exercises 4.3

Statistical Concepts and Skills

4.59 In this section, we introduced a descriptive measure of the utility of the regression equation for making predictions.
a. Identify the term and symbol for that descriptive measure.
b. Provide an interpretation of that descriptive measure.

4.60 Fill in the blanks.
a. A measure of total variation in the observed values of the response variable is the _____. The mathematical abbreviation for it is _____.
b. A measure of the amount of variation in the observed values of the response variable explained by the regression is the _____. The mathematical abbreviation for it is _____.
c. A measure of the amount of variation in the observed values of the response variable not explained by the regression is the _____. The mathematical abbreviation for it is _____.

4.61 For a particular regression analysis, $SST = 8291.0$ and $SSR = 7626.6$.
a. Obtain and interpret the coefficient of determination.
b. Determine SSE.

In Exercises 4.62 and 4.63, we repeat the data from Exercises 4.38 and 4.39, respectively. We also provide the regression equations for those data from Exercises 4.40 and 4.41, respectively. For each exercise here,
a. compute the three sums of squares, SST, SSR, and SSE, using the defining formulas (page 174).
b. verify the regression identity, $SST = SSR + SSE$.
c. compute the coefficient of determination.
d. determine the percentage of variation in the observed values of the response variable that is explained by the regression.
e. state how useful the regression equation appears to be for making predictions. (Answers for this part may vary, owing to differing interpretations.)

4.62 Following are the data from Exercise 4.38.

x	1	1	5	5
y	1	3	2	4

The regression equation is $\hat{y} = 1.75 + 0.25x$.

4.63 Following are the data from Exercise 4.39.

x	0	2	2	5	6
y	4	2	0	−2	1

The regression equation is $\hat{y} = 2.875 - 0.625x$.

For Exercises 4.64–4.67,
a. compute SST, SSR, and SSE, using Formula 4.2 on page 176.
b. compute the coefficient of determination, r^2.
c. determine the percentage of variation in the observed values of the response variable explained by the regression, and interpret your answer.
d. state how useful the regression equation appears to be for making predictions.

4.64 Tax Efficiency. Following are the data on percentage of investments in energy securities and tax efficiency from Exercise 4.42.

x	3.1	3.2	3.7	4.3	4.0	5.5	6.7	7.4	7.4	10.6
y	98.1	94.7	92.0	89.8	87.5	85.0	82.0	77.8	72.1	53.5

4.65 Corvette Prices. Following are the age and price data for Corvettes from Exercise 4.43.

x	6	6	6	2	2	5	4	5	1	4
y	205	195	210	340	299	230	270	243	340	240

4.66 Custom Homes. Following are the size and price data for custom homes from Exercise 4.44.

x	26	27	33	29	29	34	30	40	22
y	259	274	294	296	325	380	457	523	215

4.67 Plant Emissions. Following are the data on plant weight and quantity of volatile emissions from Exercise 4.45.

x	57	85	57	65	52	67	62	80	77	53	68
y	8.0	22.0	10.5	22.5	12.0	11.5	7.5	13.0	16.5	21.0	12.0

Extending the Concepts and Skills

4.68 What can you say about SSE, SSR, and the utility of the regression equation for making predictions if
a. $r^2 = 1$?   b. $r^2 = 0$?

4.69 On page 175, we noted that, because of the regression identity, we can also express the coefficient of determination in terms of the total sum of squares and the error sum of squares as

$$r^2 = 1 - \frac{SSE}{SST}.$$

a. Explain why this formula shows that the coefficient of determination can also be interpreted as the percentage reduction obtained in the total squared error by using the regression equation instead of the mean, $\bar{y}$, to predict the observed values of the response variable.
b. Refer to Exercise 4.65. What percentage reduction is obtained in the total squared error by using the regression equation instead of the mean of the observed prices to predict the observed prices?

Using Technology

In Exercises 4.70–4.75, use the technology of your choice to
a. obtain the coefficient of determination.
b. determine the percentage of variation in the observed values of the response variable explained by the regression and interpret your answer.
c. state how useful the regression equation appears to be for making predictions.

4.70 Batting and Scoring. Following are the data on season team batting average and total runs scored for a sample of major league baseball teams from Exercise 4.52.

Average	Runs	Average	Runs
.294	968	.267	793
.278	938	.265	792
.278	925	.256	764
.270	887	.254	752
.274	825	.246	740
.271	810	.266	738
.263	807	.262	731
.257	798	.251	708

4.71 Body Fat. Following are the age and body fat data for 18 randomly selected adults from Exercise 4.53.

Age	%Fat	Age	%Fat	Age	%Fat
23	9.5	45	27.4	56	32.5
23	27.9	49	25.2	57	30.3
27	7.8	50	31.1	58	33.0
27	17.8	53	34.7	58	33.8
39	31.4	53	42.0	60	41.1
41	25.9	54	29.1	61	34.5

4.72 PCBs and Pelicans. The data for shell thickness and concentration of PCBs for 60 Anacapa pelican eggs from Exercise 4.54 are on the WeissStats CD.

4.73 More Money More Beer? The data for per capita income and per capita beer consumption for the 50 states and Washington, D.C., from Exercise 4.55 are on the WeissStats CD.

4.74 Gas Guzzlers. The data for gas mileage and engine displacement for 121 vehicles from Exercise 4.56 are on the WeissStats CD.

4.75 Estriol Level and Birth Weight. The data for estriol levels of pregnant women and birth weights of their children from Exercise 4.57 are on the WeissStats CD.

4.4 LINEAR CORRELATION

We often hear statements pertaining to the correlation or lack of correlation between two variables: "There is a positive correlation between advertising expenditures and sales" or "IQ and alcohol consumption are uncorrelated." In this section, we explain the meaning of such statements.

Several statistics can be used to measure the correlation between two variables. The statistic most commonly used is the **linear correlation coefficient**, r, which is a descriptive measure of the strength of the linear (straight-line) relationship between two variables.[4] The following are the defining and computing formulas for the linear correlation coefficient.

DEFINITION 4.6 **Linear Correlation Coefficient**

The *linear correlation coefficient*, r, of n data points is defined by

$$r = \frac{\frac{1}{n-1}\Sigma(x-\bar{x})(y-\bar{y})}{s_x s_y}.$$

It can also be obtained from the computing formula

$$r = \frac{S_{xy}}{\sqrt{S_{xx}S_{yy}}},$$

where S_{xx}, S_{xy}, and S_{yy} are given in Definition 4.3 on page 156.

The computing formula presented in Definition 4.6 is almost always preferred for hand calculations, but the defining formula reveals the meaning and basic properties of the linear correlation coefficient. For instance, because of the division by the sample standard deviations, s_x and s_y, in the defining formula for r, we can conclude that *r is independent of the choice of units and always lies between −1 and 1*.

UNDERSTANDING THE LINEAR CORRELATION COEFFICIENT

We now discuss some other important properties of the linear correlation coefficient, r. Keep in mind that r measures the strength of the *linear* relationship between two variables and that the following properties of r are meaningful only when the data points are scattered about a straight line.

- *r reflects the slope of the scatter diagram.* The linear correlation coefficient is positive when the scatter diagram shows a positive slope and is negative when the scatter diagram shows a negative slope. To demonstrate why this property is true, we refer to the defining formula in Definition 4.6 and to Fig. 4.16, where we have drawn a coordinate system with a second set of axes centered at point $(\bar{x},\bar{y})$.

    If the scatter diagram shows a positive slope, the data points, on average, will lie either in Region I or Region III. For such a data point, the deviations from the means, $x-\bar{x}$ and $y-\bar{y}$, will either both be positive or both be negative. This condition implies that, on average, the product $(x-\bar{x})(y-\bar{y})$ will be positive and consequently that the correlation coefficient will be positive.

    If the scatter diagram shows a negative slope, the data points, on average, will lie either in Region II or Region IV. For such a data point, one of the deviations from the mean will be positive and the other negative. This condition implies that, on average, the product $(x-\bar{x})(y-\bar{y})$ will be negative and consequently that the correlation coefficient will be negative.

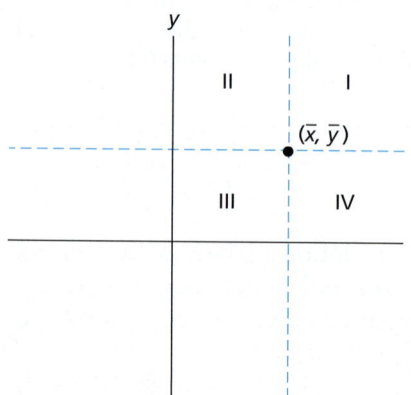

FIGURE 4.16
Coordinate system with a second set of axes centered at $(\bar{x},\bar{y})$

---

[4]The *linear correlation coefficient* is also referred to as the **Pearson product moment correlation coefficient** in honor of its developer, Karl Pearson.

- *The magnitude of r indicates the strength of the linear relationship.* A value of r close to -1 or to 1 indicates a strong linear relationship between the variables and that the variable x is a good linear predictor of the variable y (i.e., the regression equation is extremely useful for making predictions). A value of r near 0 indicates at most a weak linear relationship between the variables and that the variable x is a poor linear predictor of the variable y (i.e., the regression equation is either useless or not very useful for making predictions).
- *The sign of r suggests the type of linear relationship.* A positive value of r suggests that the variables are **positively linearly correlated variables,** meaning that y tends to increase linearly as x increases, with the tendency being greater the closer that r is to 1. A negative value of r suggests that the variables are **negatively linearly correlated variables,** meaning that y tends to decrease linearly as x increases, with the tendency being greater the closer that r is to -1.
- *The sign of r and the direction of the regression line are identical.* If r is positive, so is the slope of the regression line (i.e., the regression line slopes upward); if r is negative, so is the slope of the regression line (i.e., the regression line slopes downward).

To graphically portray the meaning of the linear correlation coefficient, we present various degrees of linear correlation in Fig. 4.17 on the next page.

If r is close to ± 1, the data points are clustered closely about the regression line, as shown in Fig. 4.17(b) and (e). If r is farther from ± 1, the data points are more widely scattered about the regression line, as shown in Fig. 4.17(c) and (f). And, if r is near 0, the data points are essentially scattered about a horizontal line (i.e., the slope of the regression line is near 0), as shown in Fig. 4.17(g), indicating at most a weak linear relationship between the variables.

COMPUTING AND INTERPRETING THE LINEAR CORRELATION COEFFICIENT

We demonstrate how to compute and interpret the linear correlation coefficient of a set of data points by returning to the data on age and price for a sample of Orions in Example 4.10.

Example 4.10 The Linear Correlation Coefficient

Age and Price of Orions The age and price data for a sample of 11 Orions are repeated in the first two columns of Table 4.10 on the next page.

a. Compute the linear correlation coefficient, r, of the data.
b. Interpret the value of r obtained in part (a) in terms of the linear relationship between the variables age and price of Orions.
c. Discuss the graphical implications of the value of r.

Solution First recall that the scatter diagram shown in Fig. 4.7 on page 154 indicates that the data points are scattered about a straight line. Hence it is meaningful to obtain the linear correlation coefficient of these data.

FIGURE 4.17 Various degrees of linear correlation

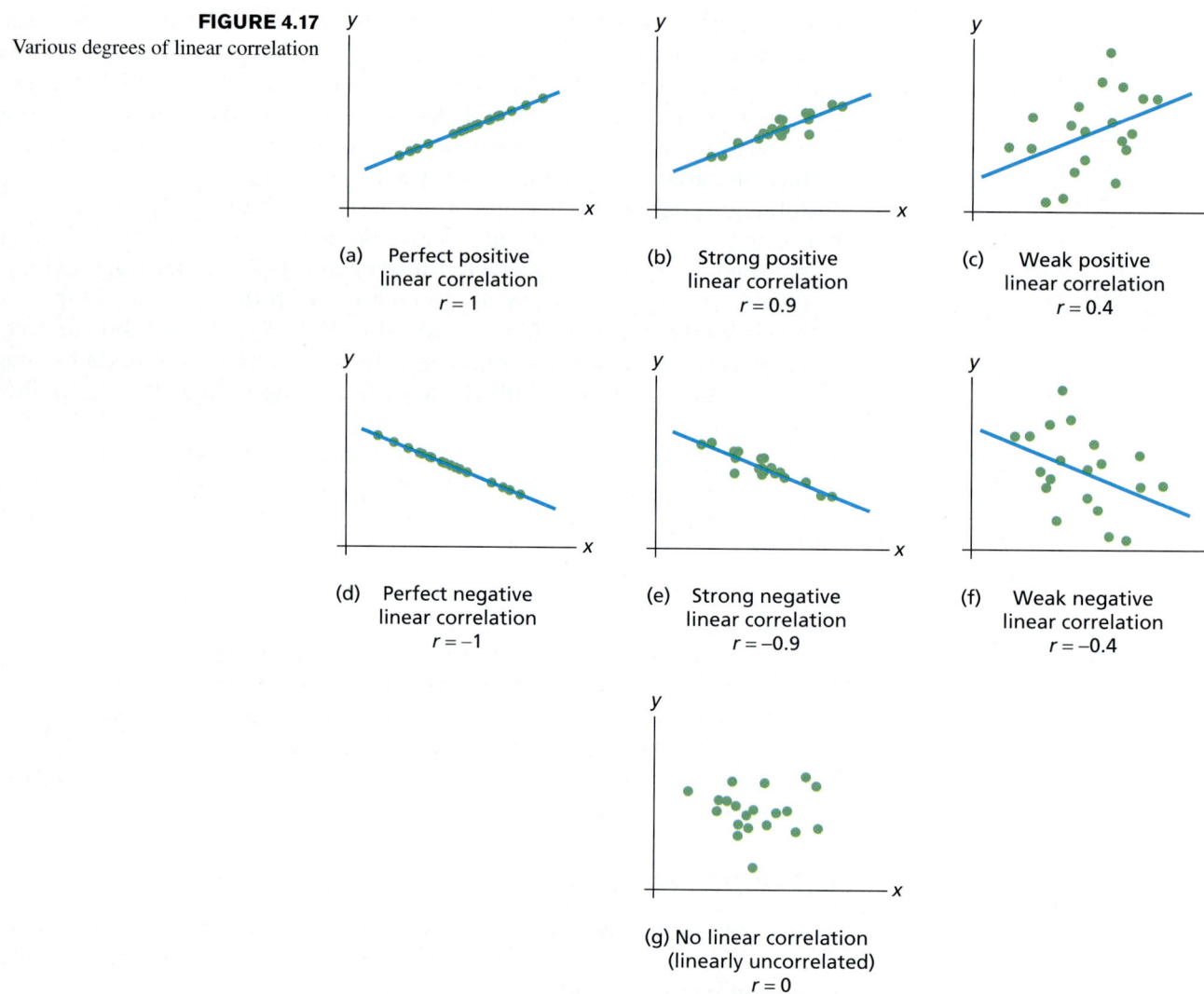

TABLE 4.10 Table for obtaining the linear correlation coefficient for the Orion data by using the computing formula

Age (yr) x	Price ($100) y	xy	x^2	y^2
5	85	425	25	7,225
4	103	412	16	10,609
6	70	420	36	4,900
5	82	410	25	6,724
5	89	445	25	7,921
5	98	490	25	9,604
6	66	396	36	4,356
6	95	570	36	9,025
2	169	338	4	28,561
7	70	490	49	4,900
7	48	336	49	2,304
58	975	4732	326	96,129

a. We apply the computing formula in Definition 4.6 on page 180 to obtain the linear correlation coefficient. To do so, we need a table of values for x, y, xy, x^2, y^2, and their sums, as shown in Table 4.10.

Referring to the last row of Table 4.10, we get

$$r = \frac{S_{xy}}{\sqrt{S_{xx}S_{yy}}} = \frac{\Sigma xy - (\Sigma x)(\Sigma y)/n}{\sqrt{\left[\Sigma x^2 - (\Sigma x)^2/n\right]\left[\Sigma y^2 - (\Sigma y)^2/n\right]}}$$

$$= \frac{4732 - (58)(975)/11}{\sqrt{\left[326 - (58)^2/11\right]\left[96{,}129 - (975)^2/11\right]}} = -0.924.$$

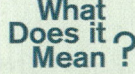

b. The linear correlation coefficient, $r = -0.924$, suggests a strong negative linear correlation between age and price of Orions. In particular, it indicates that as age increases there is a strong tendency for price to decrease, which is not surprising. It also implies that the regression equation, $\hat{y} = 195.47 - 20.26x$, is extremely useful for making predictions.

c. Because the correlation coefficient, $r = -0.924$, is quite close to -1, the data points should be clustered rather closely about the regression line. Figure 4.14 on page 171 shows that to be the case. ◆

RELATIONSHIP BETWEEN THE CORRELATION COEFFICIENT AND THE COEFFICIENT OF DETERMINATION

In Section 4.3, we discussed the coefficient of determination, r^2, a descriptive measure of the utility of the regression equation for making predictions. In this section, we introduced the linear correlation coefficient, r, as a descriptive measure of the strength of the linear relationship between two variables.

We expect the strength of the linear relationship also to indicate the usefulness of the regression equation for making predictions. In other words, there should be a relationship between the linear correlation coefficient and the coefficient of determination—and there is. The relationship is precisely the one suggested by the notation used, as stated in Key Fact 4.5.

Key Fact 4.5 **Relationship Between the Correlation Coefficient and the Coefficient of Determination**

The coefficient of determination is the square of the linear correlation coefficient.

In Example 4.10, we found that the linear correlation coefficient for the data on age and price of a sample of 11 Orions is $r = -0.924$. From this result and Key Fact 4.5, we can easily obtain the coefficient of determination: $r^2 = (-0.924)^2 = 0.854$. As expected, this value is the same (except for roundoff error) as the value we found for r^2 on page 173 by using the defining formula $r^2 = SSR/SST$. In general, we can obtain the coefficient of determination either by using the defining formula or by first finding the linear correlation coefficient and then squaring the result.

Likewise, we can obtain the linear correlation coefficient either by using Definition 4.6 or from the coefficient of determination, provided we also know the direction of the regression line. Specifically, the square root of the coefficient of determination gives the magnitude of the linear correlation coefficient; the sign of the linear correlation coefficient is the same as that of the slope of the regression line.

WARNINGS ON THE USE OF THE LINEAR CORRELATION COEFFICIENT

As we mentioned in Section 4.2, an assumption for finding the regression line for a set of data points is that the data points are scattered about a straight line. Similarly, because the linear correlation coefficient is used to describe the strength of the *linear* relationship between two variables, it should be used as a descriptive measure only when a scatter diagram indicates that the data points are scattered about a straight line.

For instance, in general, we cannot say that a value of r near 0 implies that there is no relationship between the two variables under consideration, nor can we say that a value of r near ± 1 implies that a linear relationship exists between the two variables. Such statements are meaningful only when a scatter diagram indicates that the data points are scattered about a straight line. See Exercise 4.91 for more on these issues.

When using the linear correlation coefficient, you must also watch for outliers and influential observations. Such data points can sometimes unduly affect r because sample means and sample standard deviations are not resistant to outliers and other extreme values.

CORRELATION AND CAUSATION

Two variables may have a high correlation without being causally related. For example, Table 4.11 displays data on total pari-mutuel turnover (money wagered) at U.S. racetracks and college enrollment for five randomly selected years. [SOURCE: National Association of State Racing Commissioners and U.S. National Center for Education Statistics.]

The linear correlation coefficient of the data points in Table 4.11 is $r = 0.931$, suggesting a strong positive linear correlation between pari-mutuel wagering and college enrollment. But this result doesn't mean that a causal relationship exists between the two variables, such as that when people go to racetracks they are somehow inspired to go to college. On the contrary, we can only infer that the two variables have a strong tendency to increase (or decrease) simultaneously and that total pari-mutuel turnover is a good predictor of college enrollment.

TABLE 4.11
Pari-mutuel turnover and college enrollment for five randomly selected years

Pari-mutuel turnover ($millions) x	College enrollment (thousands) y
5,977	8,581
7,862	11,185
10,029	11,260
11,677	12,372
11,888	12,426

Two variables may be strongly correlated because they are both associated with other variables, called **lurking variables,** that cause changes in the two variables under consideration. For example, a study showed that teachers' salaries and the dollar amount of liquor sales are positively linearly correlated. A possible explanation for this curious fact might be that both variables are tied to other variables, such as the rate of inflation, that pull them along together.

The Technology Center

Almost all statistical technologies have programs that automatically obtain the linear correlation coefficient for a set of data points. In this subsection, we present output and (optional) step-by-step instructions for obtaining a linear correlation coefficient.

Example 4.11 Using Technology to Obtain a Linear Correlation Coefficient

Age and Price of Orions Use Minitab, Excel, or the TI-83 Plus to obtain the linear correlation coefficient of the age and price data displayed in Table 4.10 on page 182, for a sample of 11 Orions.

Solution Printout 4.4 on the next page shows output obtained by applying the linear correlation coefficient programs to the age and price data.

These outputs show that the linear correlation coefficient for the age and price data is -0.924. ◆

We can also obtain the linear correlation coefficient for the age and price data from the output of the linear regression programs shown in Printout 4.2 on page 164. For the TI-83 Plus, r is the last item in the output. For Minitab and Excel, we find r by first taking the square root of the coefficient of determination, r^2, and then using the sign of the slope of the regression line, b_1, for r. From the Minitab and Excel outputs in Printout 4.2, $r^2 = 0.853$ and $b_1 = -20.261$. Therefore $r = -\sqrt{r^2} = -\sqrt{0.853} = -0.924$.

Obtaining the Output (Optional)

Printout 4.4 provides output from Minitab, Excel, and the TI-83 Plus for the linear correlation coefficient of the age and price data for a sample of 11 Orions,

PRINTOUT 4.4
Linear correlation coefficient for the age
and price data of 11 Orions

MINITAB

Correlations: AGE, PRICE

Pearson correlation of AGE and PRICE = -0.924
P-Value = 0.000

EXCEL

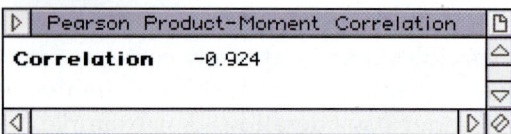

Pearson Product-Moment Correlation	
Correlation	-0.924

TI-83 PLUS

LinReg
y=a+bx
a=195.4684685
b=-20.26126126
r²=.8533733464
r=-.9237820881

displayed in Table 4.10 on page 182. The following are detailed instructions for obtaining that output. First, we store the age and price data in columns (Minitab), ranges (Excel), or lists (TI-83 Plus) named AGE and PRICE, respectively. Then, we proceed as follows.

MINITAB
1. Choose **Stat** ➤ **Basic Statistics** ➤ **Correlation...**
2. Specify AGE and PRICE in the **Variables** text box
3. Click **OK**

EXCEL
1. Choose **DDXL** ➤ **Regression**
2. Select **Correlation** from the **Function type** drop-down list box
3. Specify AGE in the **x-Axis Quantitative Variable** text box
4. Specify PRICE in the **y-Axis Quantitative Variable** text box
5. Click **OK**

TI-83 PLUS
1. Press **2nd** ➤ **CATALOG** and then press **D**
2. Arrow down to **DiagnosticOn** and press **Enter** twice
3. Press **STAT**, arrow over to **CALC**, and press **8**
4. Press **2nd** ➤ **LIST**, arrow down to AGE, and press **ENTER**
5. Press **,** ➤ **2nd** ➤ **LIST**, arrow down to PRICE, and press **ENTER** twice

Exercises 4.4

Statistical Concepts and Skills

4.76 What is one purpose of the linear correlation coefficient?

4.77 The linear correlation coefficient is also known by another name. What is it?

4.78 Fill in the blanks.
a. The symbol used for the linear correlation coefficient is _____.
b. A value of r close to ±1 indicates that there is a _____ linear relationship between the variables.
c. A value of r close to _____ indicates that there is either no linear relationship between the variables or a weak one.

4.79 Fill in the blanks.
a. A value of r close to _____ indicates that the regression equation is extremely useful for making predictions.
b. A value of r close to 0 indicates that the regression equation is either useless or _____ for making predictions.

4.80 Fill in the blanks.
a. If y tends to increase linearly as x increases, the variables are _____ linearly correlated.
b. If y tends to decrease linearly as x increases, the variables are _____ linearly correlated.
c. If there is no linear relationship between x and y, the variables are linearly _____.

4.81 Answer true or false to the following statement and provide a reason for your answer: If there is a very strong positive correlation between two variables, a causal relationship exists between the two variables.

4.82 The linear correlation coefficient of a set of data points is 0.846.
a. Is the slope of the regression line positive or negative? Explain your answer.
b. Determine the coefficient of determination.

4.83 The coefficient of determination of a set of data points is 0.709 and the slope of the regression line is -3.58. Determine the linear correlation coefficient of the data.

In Exercises 4.84 and 4.85, we repeat data from exercises in Section 4.2. For each exercise here, obtain the linear correlation coefficient by using the defining formula in Definition 4.6 on page 180.

4.84 Following are the data from Exercise 4.38.

x	1	1	5	5
y	1	3	2	4

4.85 Following are the data from Exercise 4.39.

x	0	2	2	5	6
y	4	2	0	-2	1

In Exercises 4.86–4.89, we repeat data from exercises in Section 4.2. For each exercise here,
a. *obtain the linear correlation coefficient by using the computing formula in Definition 4.6 on page 180.*
b. *interpret the value of r in terms of the linear relationship between the two variables in question.*
c. *discuss the graphical interpretation of the value of r and verify that it is consistent with the graph you obtained in the corresponding exercise in Section 4.2.*
d. *square r and compare the result with the value of the coefficient of determination you obtained in the corresponding exercise in Section 4.3.*

4.86 Tax Efficiency. Following are the data on percentage of investments in energy securities and tax efficiency from Exercise 4.42.

x	3.1	3.2	3.7	4.3	4.0	5.5	6.7	7.4	7.4	10.6
y	98.1	94.7	92.0	89.8	87.5	85.0	82.0	77.8	72.1	53.5

Refer to the graph you obtained in Exercise 4.42 and your answer to Exercise 4.64(b).

4.87 Corvette Prices. Following are the age and price data for Corvettes from Exercise 4.43.

x	6	6	6	2	2	5	4	5	1	4
y	205	195	210	340	299	230	270	243	340	240

Refer to the graph you obtained in Exercise 4.43 and your answer to Exercise 4.65(b).

4.88 Custom Homes. Following are the size and price data for custom homes from Exercise 4.44.

x	26	27	33	29	29	34	30	40	22
y	259	274	294	296	325	380	457	523	215

Refer to the graph you obtained in Exercise 4.44 and your answer to Exercise 4.66(b).

4.89 Plant Emissions. Following are the data on plant weight and quantity of volatile emissions from Exercise 4.45.

x	57	85	57	65	52	67	62	80	77	53	68
y	8.0	22.0	10.5	22.5	12.0	11.5	7.5	13.0	16.5	21.0	12.0

Refer to the graph you obtained in Exercise 4.45 and your answer to Exercise 4.67(b).

4.90 Height and Score. A random sample of 10 students was taken from an introductory statistics class. The following data were obtained, where x denotes height, in inches, and y denotes score on the final exam.

x	71	68	71	65	66	68	68	64	62	65
y	87	96	66	71	71	55	83	67	86	60

a. What sort of value of r would you expect to find for these data? Explain your answer.
b. Compute r.

4.91 Consider the following set of data points.

x	-3	-2	-1	0	1	2	3
y	9	4	1	0	1	4	9

a. Compute the linear correlation coefficient, r.
b. Can you conclude from your answer in part (a) that the variables x and y are unrelated? Explain your answer.
c. Draw a scatter diagram for the data.
d. Is use of the linear correlation coefficient as a descriptive measure for the data appropriate? Explain your answer.
e. Show that the data are related by the quadratic equation $y = x^2$. Graph that equation and the data points.

Now consider the following set of data points.

x	-3	-2	-1	0	1	2	3
y	-27	-8	-1	0	1	8	27

f. Compute the linear correlation coefficient, r.
g. Can you conclude from your answer in part (f) that the variables x and y are linearly related? Explain your answer.
h. Draw a scatter diagram for the data.
i. Is use of the linear correlation coefficient as a descriptive measure for the data appropriate? Explain your answer.
j. Show that the data are related by the cubic equation $y = x^3$. Graph that equation and the data points.

4.92 Determine whether r is positive, negative, or zero for each of the following data sets.

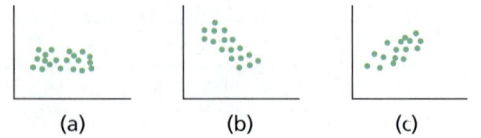

(a)   (b)   (c)

Extending the Concepts and Skills

4.93 The coefficient of determination of a set of data points is 0.716.
a. Can you determine the linear correlation coefficient? If yes, obtain it. If no, why not?
b. Can you determine whether the slope of the regression line is positive or negative? Why or why not?

c. If we tell you that the slope of the regression line is negative, can you determine the linear correlation coefficient? If yes, obtain it. If no, why not?
d. If we tell you that the slope of the regression line is positive, can you determine the linear correlation coefficient? If yes, obtain it. If no, why not?

4.94 Country Music Blues. A Knight-Ridder News Service article in the November 27, 1992, issue of the *Wichita Eagle* discussed a study on the relationship between country music and suicide. The results of the study, coauthored by Steven Stack and James Gundlach, appeared as the paper "The Effect of Country Music on Suicide" (*Social Forces*, 1992, Vol. 71(1), pp. 211–218). According to the article, "...analysis of 49 metropolitan areas shows that the greater the airtime devoted to country music, the greater the white suicide rate." (Suicide rates in the black population were found to be uncorrelated with the amount of country music airtime.)
a. Use the terminology introduced in this section to describe the statement quoted.
b. One of the conclusions stated in the journal article was that country music "nurtures a suicidal mood" by dwelling on marital status and alienation from work. Is this conclusion warranted solely on the basis of the positive correlation found between airtime devoted to country music and white suicide rate? Explain your answer.

Using Technology

In Exercises 4.95–4.100, use the technology of your choice to
a. *obtain the linear correlation coefficient.*
b. *interpret the value of r in terms of the linear relationship between the two variables in question.*

4.95 Batting and Scoring. Following are the data on season team batting average and total runs scored for a sample of major league baseball teams from Exercise 4.52.

Average	Runs	Average	Runs
.294	968	.267	793
.278	938	.265	792
.278	925	.256	764
.270	887	.254	752
.274	825	.246	740
.271	810	.266	738
.263	807	.262	731
.257	798	.251	708

4.96 Body Fat. Following are the age and body fat data for 18 randomly selected adults from Exercise 4.53.

Age	%Fat	Age	%Fat	Age	%Fat
23	9.5	45	27.4	56	32.5
23	27.9	49	25.2	57	30.3
27	7.8	50	31.1	58	33.0
27	17.8	53	34.7	58	33.8
39	31.4	53	42.0	60	41.1
41	25.9	54	29.1	61	34.5

4.97 PCBs and Pelicans. The data on shell thickness and concentration of PCBs for 60 Anacapa pelican eggs from Exercise 4.54 are on the WeissStats CD.

4.98 More Money More Beer? The data for per capita income and per capita beer consumption for the 50 states and Washington, D.C., from Exercise 4.55 are on the WeissStats CD.

4.99 Gas Guzzlers. The data for gas mileage and engine displacement for 121 vehicles from Exercise 4.56 are on the WeissStats CD.

4.100 Estriol Level and Birth Weight. The data for estriol levels of pregnant women and birth weights of their children from Exercise 4.57 are on the WeissStats CD.

Chapter Review

You Should Be Able To

1. use and understand the formulas presented in this chapter.

2. define and apply the concepts related to linear equations with one independent variable.

3. explain the least-squares criterion.

4. obtain and graph the regression equation for a set of data points, interpret the slope of the regression line, and use the regression equation to make predictions.

5. define and use the terminology *predictor variable* and *response variable*.

6. understand the concept of extrapolation.

7. identify outliers and influential observations.

8. know when obtaining a regression line for a set of data points is appropriate.

9. calculate and interpret the three sums of squares, SST, SSE, and SSR, and the coefficient of determination, r^2.

10. determine and interpret the linear correlation coefficient, r.

11. explain and apply the relationship between the linear correlation coefficient and the coefficient of determination.

Key Terms

coefficient of determination (r^2), *175*
curvilinear regression, *162*
error sum of squares (SSE), *174*
explanatory variable, *158*
extrapolation, *159*
influential observation, *160*
least-squares criterion, *156*
linear correlation coefficient (r), *180*
linear equation, *148*
lurking variables, *185*

negatively linearly correlated variables, *181*
outlier, *159*
Pearson product moment correlation coefficient, *180*
positively linearly correlated variables, *181*
predictor variable, *158*
regression equation, *156, 157*
regression identity, *175*

regression line, *156*
regression sum of squares (SSR), *174*
response variable, *158*
scatter diagram, *154*
scatterplot, *154*
slope, *150*
straight line, *148*
total sum of squares (SST), *174*
y-intercept, *150*

Review Test

Statistical Concepts and Skills

1. For a linear equation $y = b_0 + b_1 x$, identify the
   a. independent variable.   b. dependent variable.
   c. slope.   d. y-intercept.

2. Consider the linear equation $y = 4 - 3x$.
   a. At what y-value does its graph intersect the y-axis?
   b. At what x-value does its graph intersect the y-axis?
   c. What is its slope?
   d. By how much does the y-value on the line change when the x-value increases by 1 unit?
   e. By how much does the y-value on the line change when the x-value decreases by 2 units?

3. Answer true or false to each statement and explain your answers.
   a. The y-intercept of a straight line has no effect on the steepness of the line.
   b. A horizontal line has no slope.
   c. If a line has a positive slope, y-values on the line decrease as the x-values decrease.

4. What kind of plot is useful for deciding whether finding a regression line for a set of data points is reasonable?

5. Identify one use of a regression equation.

6. Regarding the variables in a regression analysis,
   a. what is the independent variable called?
   b. what is the dependent variable called?

7. Fill in the blanks.
   a. Based on the least-squares criterion, the line that best fits a set of data points is the one having the _____ possible sum of squared errors.
   b. The line that best fits a set of data points according to the least-squares criterion is called the _____ line.
   c. Using a regression equation to make predictions for values of the predictor variable outside the range of the observed values of the predictor variable is called _____.

8. In the context of regression analysis, what is an
   a. outlier?   b. influential observation?

9. Identify a use of the coefficient of determination as a descriptive measure.

10. For each of the sums of squares in regression, state its name and what it measures.
    a. SST   b. SSR   c. SSE

11. Fill in the blanks.
    a. One use of the linear correlation coefficient is as a descriptive measure of the strength of the _____ relationship between two variables.
    b. A positive linear relationship between two variables means that one variable tends to increase linearly as the other _____.
    c. A value of r close to -1 suggests a strong _____ linear relationship between the variables.
    d. A value of r close to _____ suggests at most a weak linear relationship between the variables.

12. Answer true or false to the statement: A strong correlation between two variables does not necessarily mean that they are causally related.

13. **Equipment Depreciation.** A small company has purchased a microcomputer system for $7200 and plans to depreciate the value of the equipment by $1200 per year for 6 years. Let x denote the age of the equipment, in years, and y denote the value of the equipment, in hundreds of dollars.
    a. Find the equation that expresses y in terms of x.
    b. Find the y-intercept, b_0, and slope, b_1, of the linear equation in part (a).
    c. Without graphing the equation in part (a), decide whether the line slopes upward, slopes downward, or is horizontal.
    d. Find the value of the computer equipment after 2 years; after 5 years.
    e. Obtain the graph of the equation in part (a) by plotting the points from part (d) and connecting them with a straight line.
    f. Use the graph from part (e) to visually estimate the value of the equipment after 4 years. Then calculate that value exactly, using the equation from part (a).

14. **Graduation Rates.** Graduation rate—the percentage of entering freshmen, attending full time and graduating within 5 years—and what influences it have become a concern in U.S. colleges and universities. *U.S. News and World Report*'s "College Guide" provides data on graduation rates for colleges and universities as a function of the percentage of freshmen in the top 10% of their high school class, total spending per student, and student-to-faculty ratio. A random sample of 10 universities gave the following data on student-to-faculty ratio (S/F ratio) and graduation rate (grad rate).

S/F ratio x	Grad rate y	S/F ratio x	Grad rate y
16	45	17	46
20	55	17	50
17	70	17	66
19	50	10	26
22	47	18	60

a. Draw a scatter diagram of the data.
b. Is finding a regression line for the data reasonable? Explain your answer.
c. Determine the regression equation for the data and draw its graph on the scatter diagram you drew in part (a).
d. Describe the apparent relationship between student-to-faculty ratio and graduation rate.
e. What does the slope of the regression line represent in terms of student-to-faculty ratio and graduation rate?
f. Use the regression equation to predict the graduation rate of a university having a student-to-faculty ratio of 17.
g. Identify outliers and potential influential observations.

15. Graduation Rates. Refer to Problem 14.
a. Determine SST, SSR, and SSE by using the computing formulas.
b. Obtain the coefficient of determination.
c. Obtain the percentage of the total variation in the observed graduation rates that is explained by student-to-faculty ratio (i.e., by the regression line).
d. State how useful the regression equation appears to be for making predictions.

16. Graduation Rates. Refer to Problem 14.
a. Compute the linear correlation coefficient, r.
b. Interpret your answer from part (a) in terms of the linear relationship between student-to-faculty ratio and graduation rate.
c. Discuss the graphical implications of the value of the linear correlation coefficient, r.
d. Use your answer from part (a) to obtain the coefficient of determination.

Using Technology

17. Graduation Rates. Refer to Problem 14. Use the technology of your choice to
a. obtain a scatter diagram of the data.
b. determine the regression equation for the data.
c. find the coefficient of determination, r^2, and the three sums of squares, SST, SSR, and SSE.
d. identify potential outliers and influential observations.
e. obtain the regression equation with the potential influential observation removed.
f. Is the potential influential observation actually an influential observation? That is, does its removal markedly change the regression equation?

18. Graduation Rates. Use the technology of your choice to obtain the linear correlation coefficient of the data in Problem 14.

Internet Project

Assisted Reproductive Technology

Since 1981, assisted reproductive technology (ART) has been used in the United States to help women achieve pregnancy. Many U.S. women have received some type of fertility service, such as in vitro fertilization (IVF) or egg transfer.

Several factors can influence the chance of having a child by using ART, one of the most important being the age of the prospective mother. In this Internet project, you are to examine how a woman's age can influence the chance for success in assisted reproductive technology. Specifically, you are to consider the relationship between the variables reproductive success rate and age.

URL for access to Internet Projects Page: www.aw.com/weiss

SAT Scores and GPA

Recall from Chapter 1 (see page 34) that the Focus database contains information on 500 randomly selected Arizona State University sophomores. For these database exercises, you should eliminate all cases (students) in which one or more of the four variables, cumulative GPA, high school GPA, SAT math score, and SAT verbal score, equal 0. Use the technology of your choice to solve the following problems.

First, you are to perform a correlation analysis to choose the best predictor of cumulative GPA from the variables high school GPA, SAT math score, and SAT verbal score as follows.

a. Determine the linear correlation coefficient between cumulative GPA and each of high school GPA, SAT math score, and SAT verbal score.
b. Among the variables high school GPA, SAT math score, and SAT verbal score, identify the one that appears to be the best predictor of cumulative GPA for Arizona State University sophomores. Explain your answer.

Next, you are to perform a regression analysis on cumulative GPA, using the predictor variable identified in part (b), as follows.

c. Obtain the regression equation for cumulative GPA.
d. Find the coefficient of determination and interpret your answer.
e. Determine and interpret the sums of squares SSR, SSE, and SST.

case study discussion

Fat Consumption and Prostate Cancer

At the beginning of this chapter, we presented data on fat consumption and prostate cancer death rate for various nations of the world. Now that you have studied regression and correlation, you can analyze the relationship between those two variables. Refer to the table on page 147 and solve each of the following problems.

a. Draw a scatter diagram for the data on dietary fat and prostate cancer death rate. What does the scatter diagram tell you?
b. Does obtaining a regression equation for the data appear reasonable? Explain your answer.
c. Find the regression equation for the data, using dietary fat as the predictor variable.
d. Interpret the slope of the regression line.
e. Compute the correlation coefficient of the data and interpret your result.
f. Identify outliers and potential influential observations, if any.
g. Use the technology of your choice to solve parts (a), (c), (e) and (f).

Internet Resources: Visit the Weiss Web site www.aw.com/weiss for additional discussion, exercises, and resources related to this case study.

Biography

Adrien Legendre: Introducing the Method of Least-Squares

ADRIEN-MARIE LEGENDRE was born in Paris, France, on September 18, 1752, the son of a moderately wealthy family. He studied at the Collège Mazarin and received degrees in mathematics and physics in 1770 at the age of 18.

Although Legendre's financial assets were sufficient to allow him to devote himself to research, he took a position teaching mathematics at the École Militaire in Paris from 1775 to 1780. In March 1783, he was elected to the Academie des Sciences in Paris and, in 1787, he was assigned to a project undertaken jointly by the observatories at Paris and at Greenwich, England. At that time, he became a fellow of the Royal Society.

As a result of the French Revolution, which began in 1789, Legendre lost his "small fortune" and was forced to find work. He held various positions during the early 1790s as, for example, commissioner of astronomical operations for the Academie des Sciences, professor of pure mathematics at the Institut de Marat, and head of the National Executive Commission of Public Instruction. During this same period, Legendre wrote a geometry book that became the major text used in elementary geometry courses for nearly a century.

Legendre's major contribution to statistics was the publication, in 1805, of the first statement and the first application of the most widely used, nontrivial technique of statistics: the method of least squares. In his book, *The History of Statistics: The Measurement of Uncertainty Before 1900* (Cambridge, Mass.: Belknap Press of Harvard University Press, 1986), Stephen M. Stigler writes "[Legendre's] presentation ... must be counted as one of the clearest and most elegant introductions of a new statistical method in the history of statistics."

Because Gauss also claimed the method of least squares, there was strife between the two men. Although evidence shows that Gauss was not successful in any communication of the method prior to 1805, his development of the method was crucial to its usefulness.

In 1813, Legendre was appointed Chief of the Bureau des Longitudes. He remained in that position until his death, following a long illness, in Paris on January 10, 1833.

part iii

Probability, Random Variables, and Sampling Distributions

CHAPTER 5	**Probability and Random Variables**
CHAPTER 6	**The Normal Distribution**
CHAPTER 7	**The Sampling Distribution of the Sample Mean**

chapter 5

Probability and Random Variables

CHAPTER OUTLINE

- 5.1 Probability Basics
- 5.2 Events
- 5.3 Some Rules of Probability
- 5.4 Discrete Random Variables and Probability Distributions*
- 5.5 The Mean and Standard Deviation of a Discrete Random Variable*
- 5.6 The Binomial Distribution*

GENERAL OBJECTIVES Until now, we have concentrated on *descriptive statistics*, or methods for organizing and summarizing data. Another important aspect of this book is to present the fundamentals of *inferential statistics*, or methods of drawing conclusions about a population based on information obtained from a sample of the population.

Because inferential statistics involves using information obtained from part of a population (a sample) to draw conclusions about the entire population, you can never be certain that your conclusions are correct. And, because uncertainty is inherent in inferential statistics, you need to become familiar with uncertainty before you can understand, develop, and apply the methods of inferential statistics.

The science of uncertainty is called **probability theory.** It enables you to evaluate and control the likelihood that a statistical inference is correct. More generally, probability theory provides the mathematical basis for inferential statistics.

The theory of probability also allows us to extend concepts that apply to variables of finite populations—such as relative-frequency distribution, mean, and standard deviation—to other types of variables. In doing so, we are led to the notion of a *random variable* and its *probability distribution*.

In Sections 5.1–5.3, we present the fundamentals of probability and, in Sections 5.4–5.6, we discuss and apply the basics of discrete random variables and their probability distributions.

case study

THE POWERBALL

The Powerball is a lottery sold in Arizona, Connecticut, Delaware, District of Columbia, Idaho, Indiana, Iowa, Kansas, Kentucky, Louisiana, Minnesota, Missouri, Montana, Nebraska, New Hampshire, New Mexico, Oregon, Rhode Island, South Dakota, West Virginia, and Wisconsin. It was introduced in April 1992 and took its present form in November 1997.

Although the Powerball is a multistate lottery game, it isn't the first. That distinction goes to Lotto*America, which was created in 1988 when Iowa and six other states joined forces to offer a game with a large jackpot. The more people that play, the bigger the jackpots tend to be, so multistate lotteries offer larger prizes than those of individual states.

A Powerball jackpot starts at $10 million and grows if no one wins it. Because the chance of winning a jackpot is small, the jackpot often grows to huge amounts, sometimes as much as $300 million. When there are multiple winners, the jackpot is divided equally among them. Drawings take place on Wednesday and Saturday evenings at 9:59 P.M. and can be watched during the 10:00 P.M. news.

To play the Powerball, a player first selects five numbers from the numbers 1–49 and then chooses a Powerball number, which can be any number between 1 and 42. A ticket costs $1. In the drawing, five white balls are drawn randomly from 49 white balls numbered 1–49; then one red Powerball is drawn randomly from 42 red balls numbered 1–42.

To win the jackpot, a ticket must match all the balls drawn; smaller prizes are awarded for matching some but not all the balls drawn. What are the chances of winning the jackpot? What are the chances of winning any prize at all? After studying probability, you will be able to answer these and similar questions. You will be asked to do so when you revisit the Powerball at the end of this chapter.

5.1 PROBABILITY BASICS

Although most applications of probability theory to statistical inference involve large populations, the fundamental concepts of probability are most easily illustrated and explained with relatively small populations and games of chance. So, keep in mind that many of the examples in this chapter are designed expressly to demonstrate clearly the principles of probability.

THE EQUAL-LIKELIHOOD MODEL

We discussed an important aspect of probability when we examined probability sampling in Chapter 1. In Example 5.1, we return to the illustration of simple random sampling given in Example 1.5 on page 12.

Example 5.1 Introducing Probability

Oklahoma State Officials As reported by *The World Almanac*, the top five state officials of Oklahoma are as shown in Table 5.1.

Suppose that we take a simple random sample without replacement of two officials from the five officials.

a. Determine the probability that we obtain the governor and treasurer.
b. Determine the probability that the attorney general is included in the sample.

Solution For convenience, we use the letters in parentheses after the titles in Table 5.1 to represent the officials. As we discovered in Example 1.5, there are 10 possible samples of two officials from the population of five officials. They are listed in Table 5.2. If we take a simple random sample of size 2, each of the possible samples of two officials is equally likely to be the one selected.

TABLE 5.1
Five top Oklahoma state officials

Governor (G)
Lieutenant Governor (L)
Secretary of State (S)
Attorney General (A)
Treasurer (T)

a. Because there are 10 possible samples, the probability is $\frac{1}{10}$, or 0.1, of selecting the governor and treasurer (G, T). Another way of looking at this result is that one out of 10, or 10%, of the samples include both the governor and treasurer; hence the probability of obtaining such a sample is 10%, or 0.1. The same goes for any other two particular officials.

b. Table 5.2 shows that the attorney general (A) is included in four of the 10 possible samples of size 2. As each of the 10 possible samples is equally likely to be the one selected, the probability is $\frac{4}{10}$, or 0.4, that the attorney general is included in the sample. Another way of looking at this result is that four out of 10, or 40%, of the samples include the attorney general; hence the probability of obtaining such a sample is 40%, or 0.4.

TABLE 5.2
The 10 possible samples of two officials

G, L	G, S	G, A	G, T	L, S
L, A	L, T	S, A	S, T	A, T

The essential idea in Example 5.1 is that when outcomes are equally likely, probabilities are nothing more than percentages (relative frequencies). In other words, we can use a simple formula, which we refer to as the ***f/N* rule,** to compute probabilities.

DEFINITION 5.1 Probability for Equally Likely Outcomes

Suppose that an experiment has N possible outcomes, all equally likely. Then the probability that a specified event occurs equals the number of ways, f, that the event can occur, divided by the total number of possible outcomes. In symbols,

$$\text{Probability of an event} = \frac{f}{N}.$$

where f = Number of ways event can occur and N = Total number of possible outcomes.

In stating Definition 5.1, we used the terms *experiment* and *event* in their intuitive sense. Basically, by an **experiment**, we mean an action whose outcome cannot be predicted with certainty. By an **event**, we mean some specified result that may or may not occur when an experiment is performed.

For instance, in Example 5.1 the experiment consists of taking a random sample of size 2 from the five officials. It has 10 possible outcomes ($N = 10$), all equally likely. In part (b), the event is that the sample obtained includes the attorney general, which can occur in four ways ($f = 4$); hence its probability equals

$$\frac{f}{N} = \frac{4}{10} = 0.4,$$

as we noted in Example 5.1(b). Examples 5.2 and 5.3 provide two additional illustrations of Definition 5.1. These examples further indicate the varied contexts under which the equal-likelihood model applies.

Example 5.2 Probability for Equally Likely Outcomes

Family Income The U.S. Bureau of the Census compiles data on family income and publishes its findings in *Current Population Reports*. Table 5.3 gives a frequency distribution of annual income for U.S. families in 1998.

TABLE 5.3 Frequency distribution of annual income for U.S. families

Income	Frequency (1000s)
Under $10,000	4,187
$10,000–$14,999	3,653
$15,000–$24,999	8,639
$25,000–$34,999	8,996
$35,000–$49,999	12,192
$50,000–$74,999	15,676
$75,000 & over	18,192
	71,535

A 1998 U.S. family is selected **at random,** meaning that each family is equally likely to be the one obtained (simple random sample of size 1). Determine the probability that the family selected has an annual income of

a. between $50,000 and $74,999, inclusive.
b. between $25,000 and $74,999, inclusive.
c. under $15,000.

Solution The second column of Table 5.3 shows that, in 1998, there were 71,535 thousand U.S. families; so $N = 71{,}535$ thousand.

a. The event in question is that the family selected makes between $50,000 and $74,999. Table 5.3 shows that the number of such families is 15,676 thousand, so $f = 15{,}676$ thousand. Applying the f/N rule, we find that the probability the family selected makes between $50,000 and $74,999 is

$$\frac{f}{N} = \frac{15{,}676}{71{,}535} = 0.219,$$

to three decimal places.

b. The event in question is that the family selected makes between $25,000 and $74,999. Table 5.3 reveals that the number of such families is $8{,}996 + 12{,}192 + 15{,}676$, or 36,864 thousand. Consequently, $f = 36{,}864$ thousand, so the required probability is

$$\frac{f}{N} = \frac{36{,}864}{71{,}535} = 0.515,$$

to three decimal places.

c. Proceeding as in parts (a) and (b), we find that the probability that the family selected makes under $15,000 is

$$\frac{f}{N} = \frac{4{,}187 + 3{,}653}{71{,}535} = \frac{7{,}840}{71{,}535} = 0.110,$$

to three decimal places. ◆

> **What Does it Mean?**
>
> In terms of percentages, our results show that for U.S. families in 1998 (a) 21.9% made between $50,000 and $74,999, (b) 51.5% made between $25,000 and $74,999, and (c) 11.0% made under $15,000.

Example 5.3 Probability for Equally Likely Outcomes

Dice When a pair of balanced dice are rolled, 36 equally likely outcomes are possible, as depicted in Fig. 5.1. Find the probability that

a. the sum of the dice is 11.
b. doubles are rolled; that is, both dice come up the same number.

Solution For this experiment, $N = 36$.

a. The sum of the dice can be 11 in two ways, as is apparent from Fig. 5.1. Hence the probability that the sum of the dice is 11 equals $f/N = 2/36 = 0.056$.

FIGURE 5.1
Possible outcomes for rolling a pair of dice

What Does it Mean?

When a pair of balanced dice are rolled, there is a 5.6% chance of a sum of 11 and a 16.7% chance of doubles.

b. Figure 5.1 also shows that doubles can be rolled in six ways. Consequently, the probability of rolling doubles equals $f/N = 6/36 = 0.167$. ◆

THE MEANING OF PROBABILITY

Essentially, probability is a generalization of the concept of percentage. When we select a member at random from a finite population, as we did in Example 5.2, probability is nothing more than percentage. But, in general, how do we interpret probability? For instance, what do we mean when we say that

- the probability is 0.314 that the gestation period of a woman will exceed 9 months or
- the probability is 0.667 that the favorite in a horse race finishes in the money (first, second, or third place) or
- the probability is 0.40 that a traffic fatality involves an intoxicated or alcohol-impaired driver or nonoccupant?

Some probabilities are easy to interpret: A probability near 0 indicates that the event in question is very unlikely to occur when the experiment is performed, whereas a probability near 1 (100%) suggests that the event is quite likely to occur. To gain further insight into the meaning of probability, it is useful to consider the **frequentist interpretation of probability,** which construes the probability of an event to be the proportion of times it occurs in a large number of repetitions of the experiment.

Consider, for instance, the simple experiment of tossing a balanced coin once. Because the coin is balanced, we reason that there is a 50–50 chance the coin will land with heads facing up. Consequently, we attribute a probability of 0.5 to that event. The frequentist interpretation is that in a large number of tosses, the coin will land with heads facing up about half the time.

We used a computer to perform two simulations of tossing a balanced coin 100 times. The results are displayed in Fig. 5.2 on the next page. Each graph shows the number of tosses of the coin versus the proportion of heads. Both graphs seem to corroborate the frequentist interpretation.

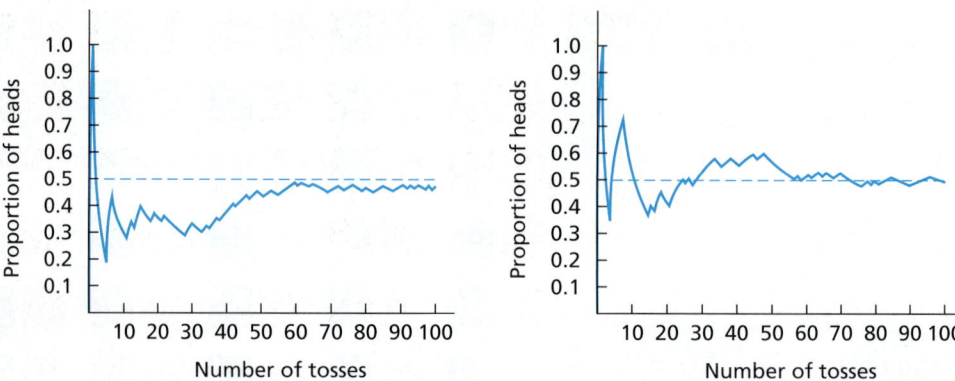

FIGURE 5.2
Two computer simulations of tossing a balanced coin 100 times

Although the frequentist interpretation is helpful for understanding the meaning of probability, it cannot be used as a definition of probability. One common way to define probabilities is to specify a **probability model**—a mathematical description of the experiment based on certain primary aspects and assumptions.

The **equal-likelihood model** discussed earlier in this section is an example of a probability model. Its primary aspect and assumption are that all possible outcomes are equally likely to occur. We discuss other probability models later in this and subsequent chapters.

BASIC PROPERTIES OF PROBABILITIES

Probabilities have some simple but basic properties, as listed in Key Fact 5.1.

> **Key Fact 5.1** **Basic Properties of Probabilities**
>
> *Property 1:* The probability of an event is always between 0 and 1, inclusive.
>
> *Property 2:* The probability of an event that cannot occur is 0. (An event that cannot occur is called an **impossible event**.)
>
> *Property 3:* The probability of an event that must occur is 1. (An event that must occur is called a **certain event**.)

Property 1 indicates that numbers such as 5 or -0.23 could not possibly be probabilities. Thus, if you calculate a probability and get an answer such as 5 or -0.23, you made an error. Example 5.4 illustrates Properties 2 and 3.

Example 5.4 *Basic Properties of Probabilities*

Dice Let's return to Example 5.3, wherein a pair of balanced dice are rolled. Determine the probability that

a. the sum of the dice is 1.
b. the sum of the dice is 12 or less.

Solution a. Figure 5.1 on page 201 shows that the sum of the dice must be no less than 2. Thus the probability that the sum of the dice is 1 equals $f/N = 0/36 = 0$. This result illustrates Property 2 of Key Fact 5.1.

b. Again, in Fig. 5.1 the sum of the dice is always 12 or less. Thus the probability of that event equals $f/N = 36/36 = 1$. This result illustrates Property 3 of Key Fact 5.1.

Exercises 5.1

Statistical Concepts and Skills

5.1 Roughly speaking, what is an experiment? an event?

5.2 Concerning the equal-likelihood model of probability,
a. what is it?
b. how is the probability of an event found?

5.3 What is the difference between selecting a member at random from a finite population and taking a simple random sample of size 1?

5.4 If a member is selected at random from a finite population, probabilities are identical to _____.

5.5 State the frequentist interpretation of probability.

5.6 Interpret each of the following probability statements, using the frequentist interpretation of probability.
a. The probability is 0.487 that a newborn baby will be a girl.
b. The probability of a single ticket winning a prize in the Powerball lottery is 0.029.
c. If a balanced dime is tossed three times, the probability that it will come up heads all three times is 0.125.

5.7 Which of the following numbers could not possibly be probabilities? Justify your answer.
a. 0.462   b. −0.201   c. 1
d. $\frac{5}{6}$ e. 3.5   f. 0

5.8 Oklahoma State Officials. Refer to Table 5.1 on page 198.
a. List the possible samples without replacement of size 3 that can be obtained from the population of five officials. (*Hint:* There are 10 possible samples.)
If a simple random sample without replacement of three officials is taken from the five officials, determine the probability that
b. the governor, attorney general, and treasurer are obtained.
c. the governor and treasurer are included in the sample.
d. the governor is included in the sample.

In the following exercises, express your probability answers as a decimal rounded to three places.

5.9 Housing Units. The U.S. Bureau of the Census publishes data on housing units in *American Housing Survey in the United States*. The following table provides a frequency distribution for the number of rooms in U.S. housing units. The frequencies are in thousands.

Rooms	No. of units
1	471
2	1,470
3	11,715
4	23,468
5	24,476
6	21,327
7	13,782
8+	15,647

A U.S. housing unit is selected at random. Find the probability that the housing unit obtained has
a. four rooms.   b. more than four rooms.
c. one or two rooms.   d. fewer than one room.
e. one or more rooms.

5.10 Murder Victims. As reported by the Federal Bureau of Investigation in *Crime in the United States*, the age distribution of murder victims between 20 and 59 years old is as shown in the following table.

Age	Frequency
20–24	2916
25–29	2175
30–34	1842
35–39	1581
40–44	1213
45–49	888
50–54	540
55–59	372

A murder case in which the person murdered was between 20 and 59 years old is selected at random. Find the probability that the murder victim was
a. between 40 and 44 years old, inclusive.
b. at least 25 years old, that is, 25 years old or older.

c. between 45 and 59 years old, inclusive.
d. under 30 or over 54.

5.11 Graduate Students. According to the *Survey of Graduate Science Engineering Students and Postdoctorates*, published by the National Science Foundation, the distribution of full-time graduate science and engineering students with U.S. citizenship in doctorate-granting institutions is as follows. Frequencies are in thousands.

Field	Frequency
Physical sciences	24.1
Engineering	33.6
Mathematical sciences	6.8
Computer sciences	7.6
Agricultural sciences	6.3
Biological sciences	35.0
Psychology	27.3
Social sciences	39.3

If one of these graduate students is selected at random, determine the probability that the field of this student is
a. psychology.   b. physical or social science.
c. not computer science.

5.12 Nobel Prize Winners. The National Science Foundation collects data on Nobel Prize Laureates in the field of science and the date and location of their award-winning research. A frequency distribution for the number of winners, by country, for the years 1901–1997 are as follows.

Country	Winners
United States	190
United Kingdom	71
Germany	61
France	25
Soviet Union	10
Japan	4
Other Countries	87

Suppose that a recipient of a Nobel Prize in science between 1901–1997 is selected at random. Find the probability that the Nobel Laureate is from
a. Japan.   b. either France or Germany.
c. any country other than the United States.

5.13 Dice. Two balanced dice are rolled. Refer to Fig. 5.1 on page 201 and determine the probability that the sum of the dice is
a. 6.   b. even.   c. 7 or 11.   d. 2, 3, or 12.

5.14 Coin Tossing. A balanced dime is tossed three times. The possible outcomes can be represented as follows.

| HHH | HTH | THH | TTH |
| HHT | HTT | THT | TTT |

Here, for example, HHT means that the first two tosses come up heads and the third tails. Find the probability that
a. exactly two of the three tosses come up heads.
b. the last two tosses come up tails.
c. all three tosses come up the same.
d. the second toss comes up heads.

5.15 Housing Units. Refer to Exercise 5.9. Which, if any, of the events in parts (a)–(e) are certain? impossible?

Extending the Concepts and Skills

5.16 Explain what is wrong with the argument: When two balanced dice are rolled, the sum of the dice can be 2, 3, 4, 5, 6, 7, 8, 9, 10, 11, or 12, giving 11 possibilities. Therefore the probability is $\frac{1}{11}$ that the sum is 12.

5.17 We stated in this section that the frequentist interpretation cannot be used as a definition of probability. Why is that so?

Odds. Closely related to probabilities are *odds*. Newspapers, magazines, and other popular publications often express likelihood in terms of odds instead of probabilities, and odds are used much more than probabilities in gambling contexts. If the probability that an event occurs is p, the odds that the event occurs are p to $1 - p$. This fact is also expressed by saying that the odds are p to $1 - p$ *in favor of the event* or that the odds are $1 - p$ to p *against the event*. Conversely, if the odds in favor of an event are a to b (or, equivalently, the odds against it are b to a), the probability the event occurs is $a/(a + b)$. For example, if an event has probability 0.75 of occurring, the odds that the event occurs are 0.75 to 0.25, or 3 to 1; if the odds against an event are 3 to 2, the probability that the event occurs is $2/(2 + 3)$, or 0.4. We examine odds in Exercises 5.18–5.20.

5.18 Roulette. An American roulette wheel contains 38 numbers, of which 18 are red, 18 are black, and 2 are green. When the roulette wheel is spun, the ball is equally likely to land on any of the 38 numbers. For a bet on red, the house pays even odds (i.e., 1 to 1). What should the odds actually be to make the bet fair?

5.19 Cyber Affair. As found in *USA TODAY*, results of a survey by International Communications Research revealed that roughly 75% of adult women believe that a romantic relationship over the Internet while in an exclusive relationship in the real world is cheating. What are the odds against randomly selecting an adult female Internet user who believes that having a "cyber affair" is cheating?

Solution The first event—that the card selected is the king of hearts—consists of the single outcome "king of hearts." This event is pictured in Fig. 5.4.

The second event—that the card selected is a king—consists of the four outcomes "king of spades," "king of hearts," "king of clubs," and "king of diamonds." This event is depicted in Fig. 5.5.

Thirteen outcomes comprise the third event—that the card selected is a heart—namely, the outcomes "ace of hearts," "two of hearts,"..., "king of hearts." This event is shown in Fig. 5.6.

The fourth event—that the card selected is a face card—consists of 12 outcomes, namely, the 12 face cards shown in Fig. 5.7.

When the experiment of selecting a card from the deck is performed, an event *occurs* if it includes the card selected. For instance, if the card selected turns out to be the king of spades, the second and fourth events (Figs. 5.5 and 5.7) occur, whereas the first and third events (Figs. 5.4 and 5.6) do not.

FIGURE 5.4
The event the king of hearts is selected

FIGURE 5.5
The event a king is selected

FIGURE 5.6
The event a heart is selected

FIGURE 5.7
The event a face card is selected

The term *sample space* reflects the fact that, in statistics, the collection of possible outcomes often consists of the possible samples of a given size, as displayed in Table 5.2 on page 198. The following definition summarizes the terminology discussed so far in this section.

DEFINITION 5.2 **Sample Space and Event**

Sample space: The collection of all possible outcomes for an experiment.

Event: A collection of outcomes for the experiment, that is, any subset of the sample space.

NOTATION AND GRAPHICAL DISPLAYS FOR EVENTS

For convenience, we use letters such as $A, B, C, D, \ldots$ to represent events. In the card-selection experiment of Example 5.5, for instance, we might let

A = event the card selected is the king of hearts,
B = event the card selected is a king,
C = event the card selected is a heart, and
D = event the card selected is a face card.

5.20 The Triple Crown. Fusaichi Pegasus, the winner of the 2000 Kentucky Derby, was the heavy favorite to win the Preakness on May 20, 2000, with odds at 3 to 5 (against). The second favorite and actual winner, Red Bullet, posted odds at 9 to 2 to win the race. Based on the posted odds, determine the probability that Fusaichi Pegasus would win the race; that Red Bullet would win the race.

5.2 EVENTS

Before continuing, we need to discuss events in greater detail. In Section 5.1, we used the word *event* intuitively. To be more precise, as used in probability, an event consists of a collection of outcomes, as illustrated in Example 5.5.

Example 5.5 Introducing Events

Playing Cards A deck of playing cards contains 52 cards, as displayed in Fig. 5.3. When we perform the experiment of randomly selecting one card from the deck, one of these 52 cards will be obtained. The collection of all 52 cards—the possible outcomes—is called the **sample space** for this experiment.

FIGURE 5.3 A deck of playing cards

Many different events can be associated with this card-selection experiment. Let's consider four:

1. The event that the card selected is the king of hearts.
2. The event that the card selected is a king.
3. The event that the card selected is a heart.
4. The event that the card selected is a face card.

List the outcomes comprising each of these four events.

Graphical displays of events are useful for explaining and understanding probability. **Venn diagrams,** named after English logician John Venn (1834–1923), are one of the best ways to portray events and relationships among events visually. The sample space is depicted as a rectangle, and the various events are drawn as disks (or other geometric shapes) inside the rectangle. In the simplest case, only one event is displayed, as shown in Fig. 5.8, with the colored portion representing the event.

FIGURE 5.8
Venn diagram for event E

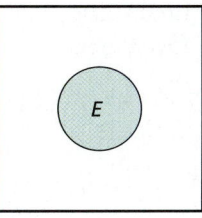

RELATIONSHIPS AMONG EVENTS

Each event E has a corresponding event defined by the condition that "E does not occur." That event is called the **complement** of E and is denoted **(not E)**. Event (not E) consists of all outcomes not in E. A Venn diagram clarifies this idea, as shown in Fig. 5.9(a), clarifies this idea.

FIGURE 5.9
Venn diagrams for (a) event (not E), (b) event (A & B), and (c) event (A or B)

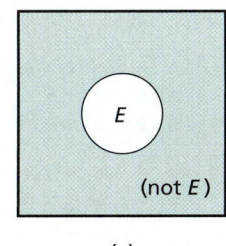
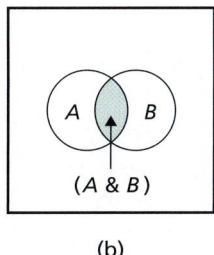
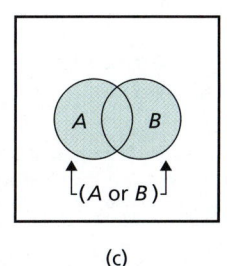

(a)   (b)   (c)

With any two events, say, A and B, we can associate two new events. One new event is defined by the condition that "both event A and event B occur" and is denoted **(A & B)**. Event (A & B) consists of all outcomes common to both event A and event B, as illustrated in Fig. 5.9(b).

The other new event associated with A and B is defined by the condition that "either event A or event B or both occur" or, equivalently, that "at least one of events A and B occurs." That event is denoted **(A or B)** and consists of all outcomes in either event A or event B or both, as Fig. 5.9(c) shows.

DEFINITION 5.3   **Relationships Among Events**

(not E): The event "E does not occur."
(A & B): The event "both A and B occur."
(A or B): The event "either A or B or both occur."

Note: Because the event "both A and B occur" is the same as the event "both B and A occur," event (A & B) is the same as event (B & A). Similarly, event (A or B) is the same as event (B or A).

In Example 5.6, we demonstrate relationships among events.

Example 5.6 Relationships Among Events

Playing Cards For the experiment of randomly selecting one card from a deck of 52, let

A = event the card selected is the king of hearts,
B = event the card selected is a king,
C = event the card selected is a heart, and
D = event the card selected is a face card.

We showed the outcomes for each of those four events in Figs. 5.4–5.7, respectively, in Example 5.5. Determine the following events.

a. (not D) **b.** (B & C) **c.** (B or C) **d.** (C & D)

Solution **a.** (not D) is the event D does not occur—the event that a face card is not selected. Event (not D) consists of the 40 cards in the deck that are not face cards, as depicted in Fig. 5.10.

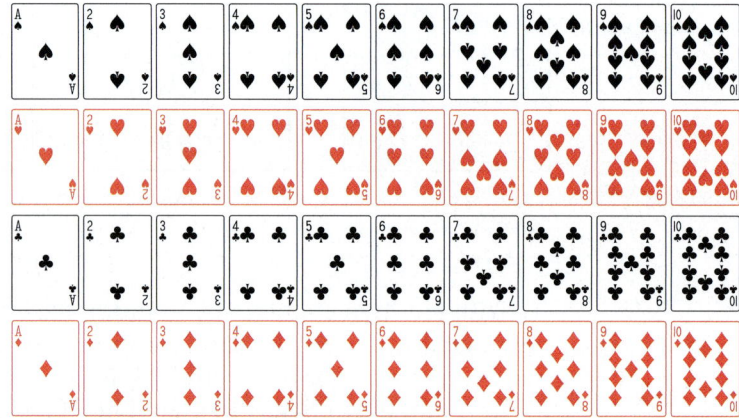

FIGURE 5.10 Event (not D)

b. (B & C) is the event both B and C occur—the event that the card selected is both a king and a heart. This event can occur only if the card selected is the king of hearts. Consequently, (B & C) is the event that the card selected is the king of hearts and consists of the single outcome shown in Fig. 5.11.

FIGURE 5.11 Event (B & C)

Note: Event (B & C) is the same as event A, so we can write $A = (B$ & $C)$.

c. (B or C) is the event either B or C or both occur—the event that the card selected is either a king or a heart or both. Event (B or C) consists of 16 outcomes—namely, the 4 kings and the 12 non-king hearts—as illustrated in Fig. 5.12.

Note: Event (B or C) can occur in 16, not 17, ways because the outcome "king of hearts" is common to both event B and event C.

d. (C & D) is the event both C and D occur—the event that the card selected is both a heart and a face card. For that event to occur, the card selected must

FIGURE 5.12
Event (B or C)

FIGURE 5.13
Event (C & D)

be the jack, queen, or king of hearts. Thus event (C & D) consists of the three outcomes displayed in Fig. 5.13. These three outcomes are those common to events C and D.

In Example 5.6, we described each of four events by listing their outcomes (Figs. 5.10–5.13). Sometimes, describing events verbally, as in Example 5.7, is more appropriate.

Example 5.7 Relationships Among Events

Student Ages A frequency distribution for the ages of the 40 students in Professor Weiss's introductory statistics class is presented in Table 5.4.

TABLE 5.4
Frequency distribution for students' ages

Age (yrs)	17	18	19	20	21	22	23	24	26	35	36
Frequency	1	1	9	7	7	5	3	4	1	1	1

One student is selected at random. Let

A = event the student selected is under 21,
B = event the student selected is over 30,
C = event the student selected is in his or her 20s, and
D = event the student selected is over 18.

Determine the following events.

a. (not D)   **b.** (A & D)   **c.** (A or D)   **d.** (B or C)

Solution **a.** (not D) is the event D does not occur—the event that the student selected is not over 18, that is, is 18 or under. From Table 5.4, (not D) comprises the two students in the class who are 18 or under.
b. (A & D) is the event both A and D occur—the event that the student selected is both under 21 and over 18, that is, is either 19 or 20. Event (A & D) comprises the 16 students in the class who are 19 or 20.
c. (A or D) is the event either A or D or both occur—the event that the student selected is either under 21 or over 18 or both. But every student in the class is either under 21 or over 18. Consequently, event (A or D) comprises all 40 students in the class and is certain to occur.

d. (*B* or *C*) is the event either *B* or *C* or both occur—the event that the student selected is either over 30 or in his or her 20s. Table 5.4 shows that (*B* or *C*) comprises the 29 students in the class who are 20 or over. ◆

MUTUALLY EXCLUSIVE EVENTS

Next, we introduce the concept of **mutually exclusive events**.

DEFINITION 5.4 Mutually Exclusive Events

Two or more events are said to be *mutually exclusive events* if at most one of them can occur when the experiment is performed, that is, if no two of them have outcomes in common.

The Venn diagrams shown in Fig. 5.14 portray the difference between two events that are mutually exclusive and two events that are not mutually exclusive. In Fig. 5.15, we show three mutually exclusive events and two cases of three events that are not mutually exclusive.

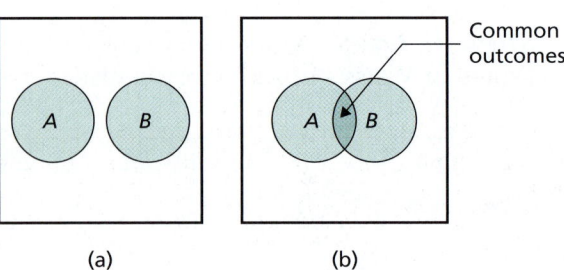

FIGURE 5.14
(a) Two mutually exclusive events; (b) two non–mutually exclusive events

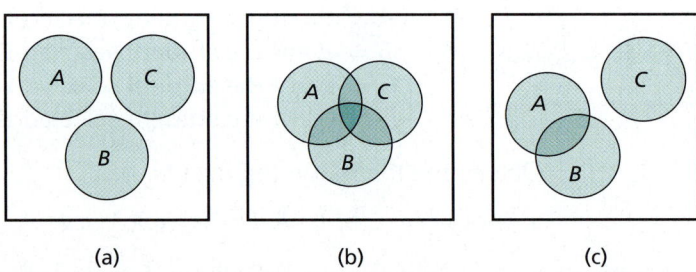

FIGURE 5.15
(a) Three mutually exclusive events; (b) three non–mutually exclusive events; (c) three non–mutually exclusive events

In Example 5.8, we show how to determine whether events are mutually exclusive.

Example 5.8 *Mutually Exclusive Events*

Playing Cards For the experiment of randomly selecting one card from a deck of 52, let

C = event the card selected is a heart,
D = event the card selected is a face card,

E = event the card selected is an ace,
F = event the card selected is an 8, and
G = event the card selected is a 10 or a jack.

Which of the following collections of events are mutually exclusive?

a. C and D **b.** C and E **c.** D and E
d. D, E, and F **e.** D, E, F, and G

Solution
a. Event C and event D are not mutually exclusive because they have the common outcomes "king of hearts," "queen of hearts," and "jack of hearts." Both events occur if the card selected is the king, queen, or jack of hearts.
b. Event C and event E are not mutually exclusive because they have the common outcome "ace of hearts." Both events occur if the card selected is the ace of hearts.
c. Event D and event E are mutually exclusive because they have no common outcomes. They cannot both occur when the experiment is performed because selecting a card that is both a face card and an ace is impossible.
d. Events D, E, and F are mutually exclusive because no two of them can occur simultaneously.
e. Events D, E, F, and G are not mutually exclusive because event D and event G both occur if the card selected is a jack.

Exercises 5.2

Statistical Concepts and Skills

5.21 What type of graphical displays are useful for portraying events and relationships among events?

5.22 Construct a Venn diagram representing each event.
a. (not E)   **b.** (A or B)   **c.** (A & B)
d. (A & B & C)   **e.** (A or B or C)
f. ((not A) & B)

5.23 What does it mean for two events to be mutually exclusive? for three events?

5.24 Answer true or false to each statement, and give reasons for your answers.
a. If event A and event B are mutually exclusive, so are events A, B, and C for every event C.
b. If event A and event B are not mutually exclusive, neither are events A, B, and C for every event C.

5.25 Dice. When one die is rolled, the following six outcomes are possible:

List the outcomes comprising

A = event the die comes up even,
B = event the die comes up 4 or more,
C = event the die comes up at most 2, and
D = event the die comes up 3.

5.26 Horse Racing. In a horse race, the odds against winning are as shown in the following table. For example, the odds against winning are 8 to 1 for horse #1.

Horse	#1	#2	#3	#4	#5	#6	#7	#8
Odds	8	15	2	3	30	5	10	5

List the outcomes comprising

A = event one of the top two favorites wins (the top two favorites are the two horses with the lowest odds against winning),
B = event the winning horse's number is above 5,
C = event the winning horse's number is at most 3, that is, 3 or less, and
D = event one of the two long shots wins (the two long shots are the two horses with the highest odds against winning).

5.27 Dice. Refer to Exercise 5.25. For each of the following events, list the outcomes that constitute the event and describe the event in words.
a. (not A)   b. (A & B)   c. (B or C)

5.28 Horse Racing. Refer to Exercise 5.26. For each of the following events, list the outcomes that constitute the event and describe the event in words.
a. (not C)   b. (C & D)   c. (A or C)

5.29 Housing Units. The U.S. Bureau of the Census publishes data on housing units in *American Housing Survey in the United States*. The following table provides a frequency distribution for the number of rooms in U.S. housing units. The frequencies are in thousands.

Rooms	No. of units
1	471
2	1,470
3	11,715
4	23,468
5	24,476
6	21,327
7	13,782
8+	15,647

For a U.S. housing unit selected at random, let
A = event the unit has at most four rooms,
B = event the unit has at least two rooms,
C = event the unit has between five and seven rooms, inclusive, and
D = event the unit has more than seven rooms.
Describe each of the following events in words and determine the number of outcomes (housing units) that comprise each event.
a. (not A)   b. (A & B)   c. (C or D)

5.30 Biological Control. Recent research by Schidt et al. (*African Entomology*, 1999, 7, pp. 107–112) describes the effectiveness of a seed-eating weevil on the population control of a nonnative, invasive species of tree in South Africa, called *Paraserianates lophantha*. A frequency distribution of percent seed damage caused by the weevil in a sample of 39 trees is provided in the following table.

Percent seed damage	Number of trees
0 < 10	19
10 < 20	2
20 < 30	5
30 < 40	3
40 < 50	6
50 < 60	2
60 < 70	2

Suppose that one of these 39 trees is selected at random. Let
A = event the tree has less than 40% seed damage,
B = event the tree has at least 20% seed damage,
C = event the tree has at least 30% but less than 60% seed damage, inclusive, and
D = event the tree has at least 50% seed damage.

Describe each of the following events in words and find the number of outcomes (trees) that comprise each event.
a. (not B)
b. (C & D)
c. (A or D)
d. (not C)
e. (A & D)

5.31 Dice. Refer to Exercise 5.25.
a. Are events A and B mutually exclusive?
b. Are events B and C mutually exclusive?
c. Are events A, C, and D mutually exclusive?
d. Are there three mutually exclusive events among A, B, C, and D? four?

5.32 Horse Racing. Each part of this exercise contains events from Exercise 5.26. In each case, decide whether the events are mutually exclusive.
a. A and B
b. B and C
c. A, B, and C
d. A, B, and D
e. A, B, C, and D

5.33 Housing Units. Refer to Exercise 5.29. Among the events A, B, C, and D, identify the collections of events that are mutually exclusive.

5.34 Biological Control. Refer to Exercise 5.30. Among the events A, B, C, and D, identify the collections of events that are mutually exclusive.

5.35 Draw a Venn diagram portraying four mutually exclusive events.

Extending the Concepts and Skills

5.36 Construct a Venn diagram that portrays four events, A, B, C, and D that have the following properties: Events A, B, and C are mutually exclusive; events A, B, and D are mutually exclusive; no other three of the four events are mutually exclusive.

5.37 Suppose that A, B, and C are three events that cannot all occur simultaneously. Does this condition necessarily imply that A, B, and C are mutually exclusive? Justify your answer and illustrate it with a Venn diagram.

5.3 SOME RULES OF PROBABILITY

In this section, we discuss several rules of probability. Before beginning, however, we need to introduce additional notation used in probability, **P(E)**, which we do in Example 5.9.

Example 5.9 Probability Notation

Dice When a balanced die is rolled once, six equally likely outcomes are possible, as shown in Fig. 5.16. Use probability notation to express the probability that the die comes up an even number.

FIGURE 5.16
Sample space for rolling a die once

Solution The event that the die comes up an even number can occur in three ways—namely, if 2, 4, or 6 is rolled. Because $f/N = 3/6 = 0.5$, *the probability that the die comes up even is 0.5.* We want to express the italicized phrase using probability notation.

Let A denote the event that the die comes up even. We use the notation $P(A)$ to represent the probability that event A occurs. Hence we can rewrite the italicized statement simply as $P(A) = 0.5$, which is read "the probability of A is 0.5."

What Does it Mean?

Keep in mind that A refers to the event that the die comes up even, whereas $P(A)$ refers to the probability of that event occurring.

DEFINITION 5.5 Probability Notation

If E is an event, then $P(E)$ represents the probability that event E occurs. It is read "the probability of E."

THE SPECIAL ADDITION RULE

The first rule of probability that we present is the **special addition rule,** which states that, for mutually exclusive events, the probability that one or another of the events occurs equals the sum of the individual probabilities. We use a Venn diagram to show the validity of the special addition rule. Figure 5.17 shows two mutually exclusive events, event A and event B.

FIGURE 5.17
Two mutually exclusive events

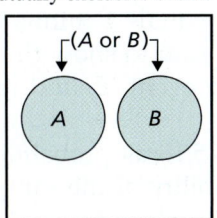

If you think of the colored regions shown in Fig. 5.17 as probabilities, the colored disk on the left is $P(A)$, the colored disk on the right is $P(B)$, and the total colored region is $P(A \text{ or } B)$. Because event A and event B are mutually exclusive, the total colored region equals the sum of the two colored disks; that is, $P(A \text{ or } B) = P(A) + P(B)$. We express this result and a more general result as the following formula.

FORMULA 5.1 The Special Addition Rule

If event A and event B are mutually exclusive, then

$$P(A \text{ or } B) = P(A) + P(B).$$

More generally, if events A, B, C, ... are mutually exclusive, then

$$P(A \text{ or } B \text{ or } C \text{ or } \cdots) = P(A) + P(B) + P(C) + \cdots.$$

In words, for mutually exclusive events, the probability that one or another of the events occurs equals the sum of the individual probabilities.

Example 5.10 illustrates use of the special addition rule.

Example 5.10 The Special Addition Rule

TABLE 5.5
Size of farms in the United States

Size (acres)	Relative frequency	Event
Under 10	0.082	A
10 ⩽ 50	0.215	B
50 ⩽ 100	0.154	C
100 ⩽ 180	0.156	D
180 ⩽ 260	0.086	E
260 ⩽ 500	0.124	F
500 ⩽ 1000	0.092	G
1000 ⩽ 2000	0.054	H
2000 & over	0.037	I

Size of Farms The U.S. Bureau of the Census compiles information about farms and publishes its findings in the *Census of Agriculture*. From that publication, we present a relative-frequency distribution for the size of farms in the United States in the first two columns of Table 5.5.

In the third column of Table 5.5, we introduce events that correspond to the size classes. For example, if a farm is selected at random, D denotes the event that the farm has between 100 and 180 acres. The probabilities of the events in the third column of Table 5.5 equal the relative frequencies displayed in the second column. Thus, for instance, the probability is 0.156 that a randomly selected farm has between 100 and 180 acres: $P(D) = 0.156$.

Use Table 5.5 and the special addition rule to determine the probability that a randomly selected farm has between 100 and 500 acres.

Solution The event that the farm selected has between 100 and 500 acres can be expressed as (D or E or F). Events D, E, and F are mutually exclusive and hence by the special addition rule,

$$P(D \text{ or } E \text{ or } F) = P(D) + P(E) + P(F)$$
$$= 0.156 + 0.086 + 0.124 = 0.366.$$

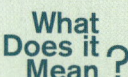

What Does it Mean?

The probability that a randomly selected farm has between 100 and 500 acres is 0.366.

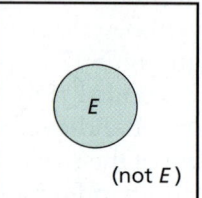

FIGURE 5.18
An event and its complement

THE COMPLEMENTATION RULE

The second rule of probability that we discuss is the **complementation rule**. It states that the probability an event occurs equals 1 minus the probability the event does not occur. We use a Venn diagram to show the validity of the complementation rule. Figure 5.18 shows an event, E, and its complement, (not E).

If you think of the regions shown in Fig. 5.18 as probabilities, the entire region enclosed by the rectangle is the probability of the sample space, or 1.

5.3 Some Rules of Probability

Furthermore, the colored region is $P(E)$ and the uncolored region is $P(\text{not } E)$. Thus, $P(E) + P(\text{not } E) = 1$ or, equivalently, $P(E) = 1 - P(\text{not } E)$, which we express as the following formula.

FORMULA 5.2 **The Complementation Rule**

For any event E,
$$P(E) = 1 - P(\text{not } E).$$

In words, the probability that an event occurs equals 1 minus the probability that the event does not occur.

The complementation rule is useful because sometimes computing the probability that an event does not occur is easier than computing the probability that it does occur. In such cases, we can, because of the complementation rule, obtain the probability that the event occurs by first computing the probability that it does not occur and then subtracting the result from 1. Example 5.11 illustrates this approach.

Example 5.11 *The Complementation Rule*

Size of Farms The first two columns of Table 5.5 provide a relative-frequency distribution for the size of U.S. farms. For a randomly selected farm, find the probability that the farm has

a. less than 2000 acres.   b. 50 acres or more.

Solution a. Let

$J =$ event the farm selected has less than 2000 acres.

To determine $P(J)$, we apply the complementation rule because $P(\text{not } J)$ is easier to compute than $P(J)$. Note that (not J) is the event the farm obtained has 2000 or more acres, which is event I in Table 5.5. Therefore $P(\text{not } J) = P(I) = 0.037$. Applying the complementation rule yields

$$P(J) = 1 - P(\text{not } J) = 1 - 0.037 = 0.963.$$

b. Let

$K =$ event the farm selected has 50 acres or more.

We apply the complementation rule to find $P(K)$. Now, (not K) is the event the farm obtained has less than 50 acres. From Table 5.5, event (not K) is the same as event (A or B). Because event A and event B are mutually exclusive, the special addition rule implies that

$$P(\text{not } K) = P(A \text{ or } B) = P(A) + P(B) = 0.082 + 0.215 = 0.297.$$

Using this result and the complementation rule, we conclude that

$$P(K) = 1 - P(\text{not } K) = 1 - 0.297 = 0.703.$$

What Does it Mean?

The probability that a randomly selected farm has less than 2000 acres is 0.963.

What Does it Mean?

The probability that a randomly selected farm has 50 acres or more is 0.703.

THE GENERAL ADDITION RULE

The special addition rule (Formula 5.1) allows us to find the probability of event (A or B) from the probabilities of event A and event B, provided that event A and event B are mutually exclusive. For events that are not mutually exclusive, we must use a different rule—the *general addition rule.* To introduce it, we use the Venn diagram shown in Fig. 5.19.

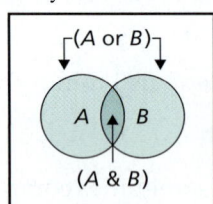

FIGURE 5.19
Non–mutually exclusive events

If you think of the colored regions shown in Fig. 5.19 as probabilities, the colored disk on the left is $P(A)$, the colored disk on the right is $P(B)$, and the total colored region is $P(A$ or $B)$. To obtain the total colored region, $P(A$ or $B)$, we first sum the two colored disks, $P(A)$ and $P(B)$. When we do so, the common colored region, $P(A \ \& \ B)$, is counted twice. Thus, we must subtract $P(A \ \& \ B)$ from the sum. So, we see that $P(A$ or $B) = P(A) + P(B) - P(A \ \& \ B)$. This formula is the **general addition rule,** which we express as the following formula.

FORMULA 5.3 The General Addition Rule

If A and B are any two events, then

$$P(A \text{ or } B) = P(A) + P(B) - P(A \ \& \ B).$$

In words, for any two events, the probability that one or the other (or both) occurs equals the sum of the individual probabilities less the probability that both occur.

In Example 5.12, we compute the probability of selecting either a spade or a face card in two ways: first without using the general addition rule and then using it.

Example 5.12 *The General Addition Rule*

Playing Cards Consider again the experiment of selecting one card at random from a deck of 52 playing cards. Find the probability that the card selected is either a spade or a face card

a. without using the general addition rule.
b. using the general addition rule.

Solution **a.** Let

$E = $ event the card selected is either a spade or a face card.

Event E consists of 22 cards—namely, the 13 spades plus the other nine face cards that are not spades—as shown in Fig. 5.20. Consequently, by the f/N rule,

$$P(E) = \frac{f}{N} = \frac{22}{52} = 0.423.$$

FIGURE 5.20
Event E

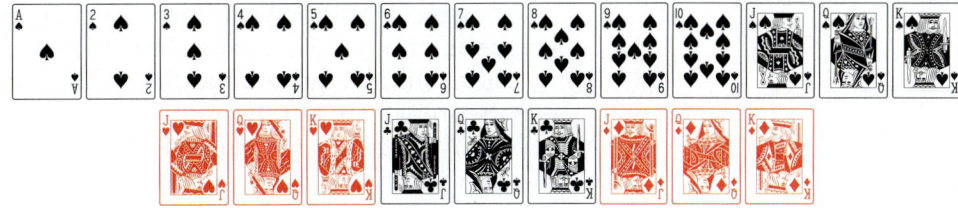

b. To determine $P(E)$ using the general addition rule, we first note that we can write $E = (C \text{ or } D)$, where

C = event the card selected is a spade, and
D = event the card selected is a face card.

Event C consists of the 13 spades, and event D consists of the 12 face cards. Also, event $(C \ \& \ D)$ consists of the three spades that are face cards—the jack, queen, and king of spades. Applying the general addition rule gives

$$P(E) = P(C \text{ or } D) = P(C) + P(D) - P(C \ \& \ D)$$
$$= \frac{13}{52} + \frac{12}{52} - \frac{3}{52} = 0.250 + 0.231 - 0.058 = 0.423,$$

which agrees with the answer obtained in part (a). ◆

In Example 5.12, computing the probability was simpler without using the general addition rule. Frequently, however, the general addition rule is the easier or even the only way to compute a probability, as illustrated in Example 5.13.

Example 5.13 The General Addition Rule

Characteristics of People Arrested Data on people arrested are published by the U.S. Federal Bureau of Investigation in *Crime in the United States*. Records for one year showed that 79.6% of the people arrested were male, 18.3% were under 18 years of age, and 13.5% were males under 18 years of age. If a person arrested that year is selected at random, what is the probability that the person obtained is either male or under 18?

Solution Let

M = event the person obtained is male, and
E = event the person obtained is under 18.

The event that the person obtained is either male or under 18 can be expressed as $(M \text{ or } E)$. We want to determine $P(M \text{ or } E)$. From the percentage data provided, we know that $P(M) = 0.796$, $P(E) = 0.183$, and $P(M \ \& \ E) = 0.135$. Applying the general addition rule, we conclude that

$$P(M \text{ or } E) = P(M) + P(E) - P(M \ \& \ E)$$
$$= 0.796 + 0.183 - 0.135 = 0.844.$$

The probability that the person obtained is either male or under 18 is 0.844. ◆

What Does it Mean?

In terms of percentages, this result means that 84.4% of those arrested during the year in question were either male or under 18 years of age (or both).

Exercises 5.3

Statistical Concepts and Skills

5.38 A Lottery. Suppose that you hold 20 out of a total of 500 tickets sold for a lottery. The grand-prize winner is determined by the random selection of one of the 500 tickets. Let G be the event that you win the grand prize. Find the probability that you win the grand prize. Express your answer in probability notation.

5.39 Ages of Senators. According to the *Congressional Directory*, the age distribution for senators in the 104th U.S. Congress is as follows.

Age (yrs)	No. of senators
Under 40	1
40–49	14
50–59	41
60–69	27
70 and over	17
	100

Suppose that a senator from the 104th U.S. Congress is selected at random. Let

A = event the senator is under 40,
B = event the senator is in his or her 40s,
C = event the senator is in his or her 50s, and
S = event the senator is under 60.

a. Use the table and the f/N rule to find $P(S)$.
b. Express event S in terms of events A, B, and C.
c. Determine $P(A)$, $P(B)$, and $P(C)$.
d. Compute $P(S)$, using the special addition rule and your answers from parts (b) and (c). Compare your answer with that in part (a).

5.40 Home Internet Access. The online publication *CyberStats*, by Mediamark Research, Inc., reports Internet access and usage. The following is a percentage distribution of household income for households with home Internet access only.

Household income	Percentage	Event
Under $50,000	27.2	A
$50,000 < $75,000	27.3	B
$75,000 < $150,000	37.2	C
$150,000 or above	8.3	D

Suppose that a household with home Internet access only is selected at random. Let A denote the event the household has an income under $50,000, B denote the event the household has an income between $50,000 and $75,000, and so on (see the third column of the table). Apply the special addition rule to find the probability that the household obtained has an income
a. under $75,000.   b. $50,000 or above.
c. between $50,000 and $150,000.
d. Interpret each of your answers in parts (a)–(c) in terms of percentages.

5.41 Oil Spills. The U.S. Coast Guard maintains a database of the number, source, and location of oil spills in U.S. navigable and territorial waters. The following is a probability distribution for location of oil spill events. [SOURCE: *Statistical Abstract of the United States*.]

Location	Probability
Atlantic Ocean	0.011
Pacific Ocean	0.059
Gulf of Mexico	0.271
Great Lakes	0.018
Other lakes	0.003
Rivers and canals	0.211
Bays and sounds	0.094
Harbors	0.099
Other	0.234

Apply the special addition rule to find the percentage of oil spills in U.S. navigable and territorial waters that
a. occur in an ocean.
b. occur in a lake or harbor.
c. do not occur in a lake, ocean, river, or canal.

5.42 Explain why the complementation rule is often useful.

5.43 Ages of Senators. Refer to Exercise 5.39. Use the complementation rule to find the probability that a randomly selected senator in the 104th Congress is
a. 40 years old or older.   b. under 60 years old.

5.44 Home Internet Access. Solve part (b) of Exercise 5.40 by using the complementation rule. Compare your work here to that in Exercise 5.40(b) where you used the special addition rule.

5.45 Craps. In the game of *craps*, a player rolls two balanced dice. Thirty-six equally likely outcomes are possible, as shown in Fig. 5.1 on page 201. Let

A = event the sum of the dice is 7,
B = event the sum of the dice is 11,
C = event the sum of the dice is 2,
D = event the sum of the dice is 3,
E = event the sum of the dice is 12,
F = event the sum of the dice is 8, and
G = event doubles are rolled.

a. Compute the probability of each of the seven events.
b. The player wins on the first roll if the sum of the dice is 7 or 11. Find the probability of that event by using the special addition rule and your answers from part (a).
c. The player loses on the first roll if the sum of the dice is 2, 3, or 12. Determine the probability of that event by using the special addition rule and your answers from part (a).
d. Compute the probability that either the sum of the dice is 8 or doubles are rolled, without using the general addition rule.
e. Compute the probability that either the sum of the dice is 8 or doubles are rolled by using the general addition rule and compare your answer to the one you obtained in part (d).

5.46 Sex and Divorce. According to the *Current Population Reports*, published by the Census Bureau, 51.0% of U.S. adults are female, 7.1% are divorced, and 4.1% are divorced females. For a U.S. adult selected at random, let

F = event the person is female, and
D = event the person is divorced.

a. Obtain $P(F)$, $P(D)$, and $P(F \& D)$.
b. Determine $P(F \text{ or } D)$ and interpret your answer in terms of percentages.
c. Find the probability that a randomly selected adult is male.

5.47 Let A and B be events such that $P(A) = \frac{1}{4}$, $P(B) = \frac{1}{3}$, and $P(A \text{ or } B) = \frac{1}{2}$.
a. Are events A and B mutually exclusive? Explain your answer.
b. Determine $P(A \& B)$.

5.48 Suppose that A and B are events such that $P(A) = \frac{1}{3}$, $P(A \text{ or } B) = \frac{1}{2}$, and $P(A \& B) = \frac{1}{10}$. Find $P(B)$.

Extending the Concepts and Skills

5.49 Suppose that A and B are mutually exclusive events.
a. Use the special addition rule to express $P(A \text{ or } B)$ in terms of $P(A)$ and $P(B)$.
b. Show that the general addition rule gives the same answer.

5.50 Secrets of Success. Gerald Kushel, Ed.D., was interviewed by *Bottom Line/Personal* on the secrets of successful people. To study success, Kushel questioned 1200 people, among whom were lawyers, artists, teachers, and students. He found that 15% enjoy neither their jobs nor their personal lives, 80% enjoy their jobs but not their personal lives, and 4% enjoy both their jobs and their personal lives. Determine the percentage of the 1200 people interviewed who
a. enjoy either their jobs or their personal lives.
b. enjoy their personal lives but not their jobs.

5.4 DISCRETE RANDOM VARIABLES AND PROBABILITY DISTRIBUTIONS

In this section, we introduce discrete random variables and probability distributions. As you will discover, these concepts are natural extensions of the ideas of variables and relative-frequency distributions. Example 5.14 introduces random variables.

Example 5.14 Introducing Random Variables

Number of Siblings Professor Weiss asked his introductory statistics students to state how many siblings they have. Table 5.6 presents a grouped-data table for that information. The table shows, for instance, that 11 of the 40 students, or 27.5%, have two siblings. Discuss the "number of siblings" in the context of randomness.

Solution Because the "number of siblings" varies from student to student, it is a variable. Suppose now that a student is selected at random. Then the "number of siblings" of the student obtained is called a **random variable** because its value depends on chance—namely, on which student is selected. ◆

DEFINITION 5.6 Random Variable

A *random variable* is a quantitative variable whose value depends on chance.

TABLE 5.6
Grouped-data table for number of siblings for students in introductory statistics

Siblings x	Frequency f	Relative frequency
0	8	0.200
1	17	0.425
2	11	0.275
3	3	0.075
4	1	0.025
	40	1.000

Example 5.14 shows how random variables arise naturally as quantitative variables of finite populations in the context of randomness. But random variables occur in many other ways. Four examples are

- the sum of the dice when a pair of fair dice are rolled,
- the number of puppies in a litter,
- the return on an investment, and
- the lifetime of a flashlight battery.

As you learned in Chapter 2, a *discrete variable* is a variable whose possible values form a finite or countably infinite set of numbers. The variable "number of siblings" in Example 5.14 is a discrete variable, its possible values being 0, 1, 2, 3, and 4. We use the adjective *discrete* for random variables in the same way that we do for variables—hence the term **discrete random variable.**

DEFINITION 5.7 Discrete Random Variable

A *discrete random variable* is a random variable whose possible values can be listed, even though the list may continue indefinitely. Mathematically, the numbers that make sense for values of a discrete random variable form a finite or countably infinite set, usually some collection of whole numbers.

5.4 Discrete Random Variables and Probability Distributions

RANDOM-VARIABLE NOTATION

Recall that we use letters near the end of the alphabet, such as x, y, and z, to denote variables. We also use such letters to represent random variables but, in this context, we usually make the letters uppercase. For instance, we could use x to denote the variable "number of siblings"; in the context of randomness, however, we would generally use X.

By utilizing random-variable notation, we can develop useful shorthands for discussing and analyzing random variables. For example, suppose that we use X to denote the number of siblings of a randomly selected student. Then we can represent the event that the student selected has, say, two siblings by $\{X = 2\}$, read "X equals two." And we can express the probability of that event as $P(X = 2)$, read "the probability that X equals two."

PROBABILITY DISTRIBUTIONS AND HISTOGRAMS

Recall that the relative-frequency distribution of a variable gives the possible values of the variable and the proportion of times each value occurs. Using the language of probability, we can extend the notion of relative-frequency distribution—a concept applying to variables of finite populations—to any random variable. In doing so, we use the terms **probability distribution** and **probability histogram** to describe the values and probabilities of a discrete random variable.

DEFINITION 5.8 **Probability Distribution and Probability Histogram**

Probability distribution: A listing of the possible values and corresponding probabilities of a discrete random variable, or a formula for the probabilities.

Probability histogram: A graph of the probability distribution that displays the possible values of a discrete random variable on the horizontal axis and the probabilities of those values on the vertical axis. The probability of each value is represented by a vertical bar whose height equals the probability. A probability histogram provides a quick and easy way to visualize how the probabilities of a random variable are distributed.

Example 5.15 illustrates probability distributions and probability histograms.

Example 5.15 *Probability Distributions and Histograms*

Number of Siblings Refer to Example 5.14 and let X denote the number of siblings of a randomly selected student.

  a. Determine the probability distribution of the random variable X.
  b. Construct a probability histogram for the random variable X.

Solution **a.** We want to determine the probability of each of the possible values of the random variable X. To obtain, for instance, $P(X = 2)$, the probability that

TABLE 5.7
Probability distribution of the random variable X, the number of siblings of a randomly selected student

Siblings x	Probability $P(X = x)$
0	0.200
1	0.425
2	0.275
3	0.075
4	0.025
	1.000

the student selected has two siblings, we apply the f/N rule. From Table 5.6 on page 220, we find that

$$P(X = 2) = \frac{f}{N} = \frac{11}{40} = 0.275.$$

The other probabilities are found in the same way. Table 5.7 displays these probabilities and provides the probability distribution of the random variable X.

b. To construct a probability histogram for X, we plot its possible values on the horizontal axis and display the corresponding probabilities as vertical bars. Referring to Table 5.7, we get the probability histogram shown in Fig. 5.21.

FIGURE 5.21
Probability histogram for the random variable X, the number of siblings of a randomly selected student

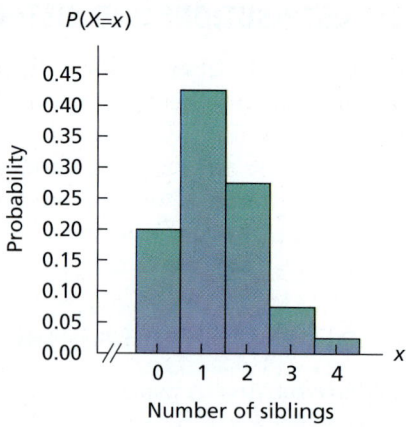

The variable "number of siblings" is a variable of a finite population, so its probabilities are identical to relative frequencies. As a consequence, its probability distribution, given in the first and second columns of Table 5.7, is the same as its relative-frequency distribution, shown in the first and third columns of Table 5.6. Apart from labeling, the variable's probability histogram is identical to its relative-frequency histogram. These statements hold for any variable of a finite population.

Note also that the probabilities in the second column of Table 5.7 sum to 1, which is always the case for discrete random variables. We express this fact as follows.

Key Fact 5.2 **Sum of the Probabilities of a Discrete Random Variable**

For any discrete random variable, X, the sum of the probabilities of its possible values equals 1; in symbols, $\Sigma P(X = x) = 1$.

Examples 5.16 and 5.17 provide additional illustrations of random-variable notation and probability distributions.

Example 5.16 Random Variables and Probability Distributions

Elementary-School Enrollment The U.S. National Center for Education Statistics compiles enrollment data on U.S. public schools and publishes the results in the *Digest of Education Statistics*. Table 5.8 displays a frequency distribution for the enrollment by grade level in public elementary schools, where 0 = kindergarten, 1 = first grade, and so on. Frequencies are in thousands of students.

For a randomly selected student in elementary school, let Y denote the grade level of the student obtained. Then Y is a discrete random variable whose possible values are $0, 1, 2, \ldots, 8$.

a. Use random-variable notation to represent the event that the student selected is in the fifth grade.
b. Determine $P(Y = 5)$ and express the result in terms of percentages.
c. Determine the probability distribution of Y.

Solution a. The event that the student selected is in the fifth grade can be represented as $\{Y = 5\}$.

> **What Does it Mean?**
>
> In terms of percentages, 10.7% of elementary-school students are in the fifth grade.

b. $P(Y = 5)$ is the probability that the student selected is in the fifth grade. Using Table 5.8 and the f/N rule, we get

$$P(Y = 5) = \frac{f}{N} = \frac{3{,}447}{32{,}326} = 0.107.$$

c. The probability distribution of Y is obtained by computing $P(Y = y)$ for $y = 0, 1, 2, \ldots, 8$. We have already done that for $y = 5$. The other probabilities are computed similarly and are displayed in Table 5.9.

TABLE 5.8
Frequency distribution for enrollment by grade level in U.S. public elementary schools

Grade level y	Frequency f
0	4,208
1	3,769
2	3,596
3	3,518
4	3,447
5	3,447
6	3,486
7	3,457
8	3,398
	32,326

TABLE 5.9
Probability distribution of the random variable Y, the grade level of a randomly selected elementary-school student

Grade level y	Probability $P(Y = y)$
0	0.130
1	0.117
2	0.111
3	0.109
4	0.107
5	0.107
6	0.108
7	0.107
8	0.105
	1.001

Note: In Table 5.9, the sum of the probabilities is given as 1.001. However, Key Fact 5.2 states that the sum of the probabilities must be exactly 1. Our computation is off slightly because we rounded the probabilities for Y to three decimal places.

Once we have the probability distribution of a discrete random variable, we can easily determine any probability involving that random variable. The basic tool for accomplishing this is the special addition rule (Formula 5.1 on page 214).

Example 5.17 Random Variables and Probability Distributions

TABLE 5.10
Possible outcomes

HHH	HTH	THH	TTH
HHT	HTT	THT	TTT

Coin Tossing When a balanced dime is tossed three times, eight equally likely outcomes are possible, as shown in Table 5.10. Here, for instance, HHT means that the first two tosses are heads and the third is tails. Let X denote the total number of heads obtained in the three tosses. Then X is a discrete random variable whose possible values are 0, 1, 2, and 3.

a. Use random-variable notation to represent the event that exactly two heads are tossed.
b. Determine $P(X = 2)$.
c. Find the probability distribution of X.
d. Use random-variable notation to represent the event that at most two heads are tossed.
e. Find $P(X \leq 2)$.

Solution

TABLE 5.11
Probability distribution of the random variable X, the number of heads obtained in three tosses of a balanced dime

No. of heads x	Probability $P(X = x)$
0	0.125
1	0.375
2	0.375
3	0.125
	1.000

a. The event that exactly two heads are tossed can be represented as $\{X = 2\}$.
b. $P(X = 2)$ is the probability that exactly two heads are tossed. Table 5.10 indicates there are three ways to get a total of two heads and that there are eight possible outcomes altogether. So, by the f/N rule,

$$P(X = 2) = \frac{f}{N} = \frac{3}{8} = 0.375.$$

c. The remaining probabilities for X are computed as in part (b) and are shown in Table 5.11.
d. The event that at most two heads are tossed can be represented as $\{X \leq 2\}$, read as "X is less than or equal to two."
e. $P(X \leq 2)$ is the probability that at most two heads are tossed. The event that at most two heads are tossed can be expressed as

$$\{X \leq 2\} = (\{X = 0\} \text{ or } \{X = 1\} \text{ or } \{X = 2\}).$$

Because the three events on the right are mutually exclusive, we use the special addition rule and Table 5.11 to conclude that

$$P(X \leq 2) = P(X = 0) + P(X = 1) + P(X = 2)$$
$$= 0.125 + 0.375 + 0.375 = 0.875.$$

What Does it Mean?

The probability is 0.875 that at most two heads are tossed.

INTERPRETATION OF PROBABILITY DISTRIBUTIONS

Recall that the frequentist interpretation of probability construes the probability of an event to be the proportion of times it occurs in a large number of (independent) repetitions of the experiment. Using that interpretation, we clarify the meaning of a probability distribution in Example 5.18.

Example 5.18 Interpreting a Probability Distribution

Coin Tossing Consider once again the random variable X discussed in Example 5.17: the number of heads obtained in three tosses of a balanced dime. Suppose that we repeat the experiment of observing the number of heads obtained in three tosses of a balanced dime a large number of times. Then the proportion of those times in which, say, no heads are obtained (i.e., $X = 0$) should approximately equal the probability of that event [i.e., $P(X = 0)$]. The same statement holds for the other three possible values of the random variable X. Use simulation to verify these facts.

Solution Simulating a random variable means that we use a computer or statistical calculator to generate observations of the random variable. In this instance, we used a computer to simulate 1000 observations of the random variable X, the number of heads obtained in three tosses of a balanced dime.

Table 5.12 shows the frequencies and proportions for the numbers of heads obtained in the 1000 observations. For example, 136 of the 1000 observations resulted in no heads out of three tosses, which gives a proportion of 0.136.

As expected, the proportions in the third column of Table 5.12 are fairly close to the true probabilities in the second column of Table 5.11. This result is more easily seen if we compare the histogram for the proportions to the probability histogram of the random variable X, as shown in Fig. 5.22.

If we simulated, say, 10,000 observations instead of 1000, the proportions that would appear in the third column of Table 5.12 would most likely be even closer to the true probabilities listed in the second column of Table 5.11.

TABLE 5.12
Frequencies and proportions for the numbers of heads obtained in three tosses of a balanced dime for 1000 observations

No. of heads x	Frequency f	Proportion $f/1000$
0	136	0.136
1	377	0.377
2	368	0.368
3	119	0.119
	1000	1.000

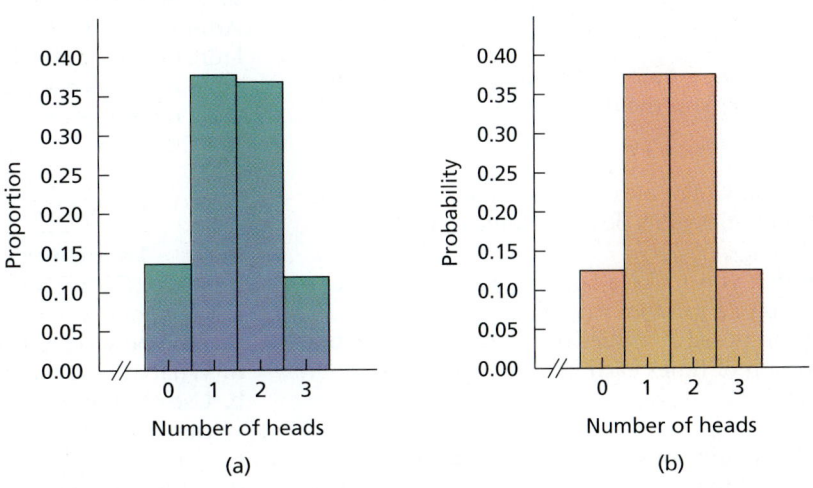

FIGURE 5.22
(a) Histogram of proportions for the numbers of heads obtained in three tosses of a balanced dime for 1000 observations; (b) probability histogram for the number of heads obtained in three tosses of a balanced dime

In light of Example 5.18, we can make the following statement concerning the interpretation of a probability distribution.

Key Fact 5.3 Interpretation of a Probability Distribution

In a large number of independent observations of a random variable X, the proportion of times each possible value occurs will approximate the probability distribution of X; or, equivalently, a histogram of the proportions will approximate the probability histogram for X.

The Technology Center

Most statistical software packages and some graphing calculators have built-in procedures to simulate observations of specified random variables. For instance, both Minitab and Excel can be used to conduct the simulation described in Example 5.18. Refer to the technology manuals for details.

Exercises 5.4

Statistical Concepts and Skills

5.51 Fill in the blanks.
a. A relative-frequency distribution is to a variable as a _____ distribution is to a random variable.
b. A relative-frequency histogram is to a variable as a _____ histogram is to a random variable.

5.52 Provide an example (other than one discussed in the text) of a random variable that does not arise from a quantitative variable of a finite population in the context of randomness.

5.53 Let X denote the number of siblings of a randomly selected student. Explain the difference between $\{X = 3\}$ and $P(X = 3)$.

5.54 Fill in the blank. For a discrete random variable, the sum of the probabilities of its possible values equals _____.

5.55 Suppose that you make a large number of independent observations of a random variable and then construct a table giving the possible values of the random variable and the proportion of times each value occurs. What will this table resemble?

5.56 What rule of probability permits you to obtain any probability for a discrete random variable by simply knowing its probability distribution?

5.57 Space Shuttles. The National Aeronautics and Space Administration (NASA) compiles data on space-shuttle launches and publishes them on its Web site. The following table displays a frequency distribution for the number of crew members on each shuttle mission from April 1981 to July 2000.

Crew Size	2	3	4	5	6	7	8
Frequency	4	1	2	36	18	33	2

Let X denote the crew size of a randomly selected shuttle mission between April 1981 and July 2000.
a. What are the possible values of the random variable X?
b. Use random-variable notation to represent the event that the shuttle mission obtained has a crew size of 7.
c. Find $P(X = 4)$; interpret in terms of percentages.
d. Obtain the probability distribution of X.
e. Construct a probability histogram for X.

5.58 Dice. When two balanced dice are rolled, 36 equally likely outcomes are possible, as depicted in Fig. 5.1 on page 201. Let Y denote the sum of the dice.
a. What are the possible values of the random variable Y?
b. Use random-variable notation to represent the event that the sum of the dice is 7.
c. Find $P(Y = 7)$.
d. Find the probability distribution of Y. Leave your probabilities in fraction form.
e. Construct a probability histogram for Y.

5.59 Busy Tellers. Prescott National Bank has six tellers available to serve customers. The number of tellers busy with customers at, say, 1:00 P.M. varies from day to day and depends on chance, so it is a random variable, say, X. Past records indicate that the probability distribution of X is as shown in the following table.

x	0	1	2	3	4	5	6
$P(X = x)$	0.029	0.049	0.078	0.155	0.212	0.262	0.215

For example, the probability is 0.262 that exactly five of the tellers will be busy with customers at 1:00 P.M.; that is, about 26.2% of the time, exactly five tellers are busy with customers at 1:00 P.M. Use random-variable notation to represent each of the following events. At 1:00 P.M.,
a. exactly four tellers are busy.
b. at least two tellers are busy.
c. fewer than five tellers are busy.
d. at least two but fewer than five tellers are busy.

Use the special addition rule and the probability distribution to determine
e. $P(X = 4)$. f. $P(X \geq 2)$. g. $P(X < 5)$. h. $P(2 \leq X < 5)$.

5.60 Solar Eclipses. The *World Almanac* provides information on past and projected total solar eclipses from 1955–2015. Unlike total lunar eclipses, observing a total solar eclipse from Earth is rare because it can be seen along only a very narrow path and for only a short period of time.
a. Let X denote the duration, in minutes, of a total solar eclipse. Is X a discrete random variable? Explain your answer.

b. Let Y denote the duration, to the nearest minute, of a total solar eclipse. Is Y a discrete random variable? Explain your answer.

Extending the Concepts and Skills

5.61 Suppose that Z is a random variable and that $P(Z > 1.96) = 0.025$. Find $P(Z \leq 1.96)$. (*Hint:* Use the complementation rule.)

5.62 Suppose that T and Z are random variables.
a. If $P(T > 2.02) = 0.05$ and $P(T < -2.02) = 0.05$, obtain $P(-2.02 \leq T \leq 2.02)$.
b. Suppose that $P(-1.64 \leq Z \leq 1.64) = 0.90$ and that $P(Z > 1.64) = P(Z < -1.64)$. Find $P(Z > 1.64)$.

5.63 Let $c > 0$ and $0 \leq \alpha \leq 1$. Also let X, Y, and T be random variables.
a. If $P(X > c) = \alpha$, determine $P(X \leq c)$ in terms of α.
b. If $P(Y > c) = \alpha/2$ and $P(Y < -c) = P(Y > c)$, find $P(-c \leq Y \leq c)$ in terms of α.
c. Suppose that $P(-c \leq T \leq c) = 1 - \alpha$ and, moreover, that $P(T < -c) = P(T > c)$. Find $P(T > c)$ in terms of α.

Using Technology

5.64 Simulation. Refer to the probability distribution displayed in Table 5.11 on page 224.
a. Use the technology of your choice to repeat the simulation done in Example 5.18 on page 225.
b. Obtain the proportions for the number of heads in three tosses and compare it to the probability distribution in Table 5.11.
c. Obtain a histogram of the proportions and compare it to the probability histogram in Fig. 5.22(b) on page 225.
d. What do parts (b) and (c) illustrate?

5.5 THE MEAN AND STANDARD DEVIATION OF A DISCRETE RANDOM VARIABLE

In this section, we introduce the mean and standard deviation of a discrete random variable. As you will see, the mean and standard deviation of a discrete random variable are analogous to the population mean and population standard deviation.

MEAN OF A DISCRETE RANDOM VARIABLE

Recall that, for a variable x, the mean of all possible observations for the entire population is called the *population mean* or *mean of the variable x*. In Section 3.5, we gave a formula for the mean of a variable x:

$$\mu = \frac{\Sigma x}{N}.$$

Although this formula applies only to variables of finite populations, we can use it and the language of probability to extend the concept of the mean to any discrete variable. We show how to do so in Example 5.19.

Example 5.19 Introducing the Mean of a Discrete Random Variable

TABLE 5.13 Ages of eight students

19	20	20	19
21	27	20	21

Student Ages Consider a population of eight students whose ages are those given in Table 5.13. The variable under consideration here is age, and the population consists of the eight students. Let X denote the age of a randomly selected student. In light of Table 5.13, the probability distribution of the random variable X is as shown in Table 5.14. Express the mean age of the eight students in terms of the probability distribution of the random variable X.

Solution Referring first to Table 5.13 and then to Table 5.14, we get

$$\mu = \frac{\Sigma x}{N} = \frac{19 + 20 + 20 + 19 + 21 + 27 + 20 + 21}{8}$$

TABLE 5.14 Probability distribution of X, the age of a randomly selected student

Age x	Probability $P(X = x)$	
19	0.250	← 2/8
20	0.375	← 3/8
21	0.250	← 2/8
27	0.125	← 1/8

$$= \frac{\overbrace{19 + 19}^{2} + \overbrace{20 + 20 + 20}^{3} + \overbrace{21 + 21}^{2} + \overbrace{27}^{1}}{8}$$

$$= \frac{19 \cdot 2 + 20 \cdot 3 + 21 \cdot 2 + 27 \cdot 1}{8}$$

$$= 19 \cdot \frac{2}{8} + 20 \cdot \frac{3}{8} + 21 \cdot \frac{2}{8} + 27 \cdot \frac{1}{8}$$

$$= 19 \cdot P(X = 19) + 20 \cdot P(X = 20) + 21 \cdot P(X = 21) + 27 \cdot P(X = 27)$$

$$= \Sigma x P(X = x).$$

◆

Example 5.19 shows that we can express the mean of a variable of a finite population in terms of the probability distribution of the corresponding random variable: $\mu = \Sigma x P(X = x)$. Because the expression on the right of this equation is meaningful for any discrete random variable, we can define the **mean of a discrete random variable** as follows, along with the synonyms **expected value** and **expectation** for *mean*.

5.5 The Mean and Standard Deviation of a Discrete Random Variable

DEFINITION 5.9 **Mean of a Discrete Random Variable**

The *mean of a discrete random variable* X is denoted μ_X or, when no confusion will arise, simply μ. It is defined by

$$\mu = \Sigma x P(X = x).$$

The terms *expected value* and *expectation* are commonly used in place of *mean*.

We now have a definition of *mean* consistent with that for variables of finite populations and applicable to any discrete random variable. In other words, we have extended the concept of population mean to any discrete variable.[1]

As you learned in Chapter 3, constructing appropriate tables provides an efficient way to compute descriptive measures by hand. In Example 5.20, we apply this technique to obtain the mean of a discrete random variable.

Example 5.20 The Mean of a Discrete Random Variable

Busy Tellers Prescott National Bank has six tellers available to serve customers. The number of tellers busy with customers at, say, 1:00 P.M. varies from day to day and depends on chance; hence it is a random variable, say, X. Past records indicate that the probability distribution of X is as shown in the first two columns of Table 5.15. For instance, the probability is 0.262 that exactly five tellers will be busy with customers at 1:00 P.M. Find the mean of the random variable X.

TABLE 5.15
Table for computing the mean of the random variable X, the number of tellers busy with customers

x	$P(X = x)$	$xP(X = x)$
0	0.029	0.000
1	0.049	0.049
2	0.078	0.156
3	0.155	0.465
4	0.212	0.848
5	0.262	1.310
6	0.215	1.290
		4.118

Solution To obtain the mean of the random variable X, we append a column for the product of x with $P(X = x)$, shown as the third column in Table 5.15, and apply Definition 5.9. Summing the entries in the third column, we find that

$$\mu = \Sigma x P(X = x) = 4.118.$$

The mean number of tellers busy with customers is 4.118.

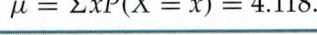
[1]We can also extend the concept of population mean to any continuous variable and, using integral calculus, develop a formula analogous to the one given in Definition 5.9 for discrete variables. We do not present the formula for the mean of a continuous variable because it is not needed in this book.

INTERPRETATION OF THE MEAN OF A RANDOM VARIABLE

Recall that the mean of a variable of a finite population is the arithmetic average of all possible observations. A similar interpretation holds for the mean of a random variable.

For instance, in Example 5.20 the random variable X is the number of tellers busy with customers at 1:00 P.M., and the mean of that random variable is 4.118. Of course, there never will be a day when 4.118 tellers are busy with customers at 1:00 P.M. The mean of 4.118 simply indicates that, over many days, the average number of busy tellers at 1:00 P.M. will be about 4.118.

This interpretation holds in all cases. It is commonly known as the **law of averages** and in mathematical circles as the **law of large numbers**. We restate this interpretation as the following fact.

Key Fact 5.4

Interpretation of the Mean of a Random Variable

In a large number of independent observations of a random variable X, the average value of those observations will approximately equal the mean, μ, of X. The larger the number of observations, the closer the average tends to be to μ.

We used a computer to simulate the number of busy tellers at 1:00 P.M. on 100 randomly selected days; that is, we obtained 100 independent observations of the random variable X. The data are displayed in Table 5.16.

TABLE 5.16
One hundred observations of the random variable X, the number of tellers busy with customers

5	3	5	3	4	3	4	3	6	5	6	4	5	4	3	5	4	5	6	3
4	1	6	5	3	6	3	5	5	4	6	4	1	6	5	3	3	6	4	5
3	4	2	5	5	6	5	4	6	2	4	5	4	6	4	5	5	3	4	6
1	5	4	6	4	4	4	5	6	2	5	4	5	1	3	3	6	4	6	4
5	6	5	5	3	2	4	6	6	1	5	1	3	6	5	3	5	4	3	6

The average value of the 100 observations in Table 5.16 is 4.25. This value is quite close to the mean, $\mu = 4.118$, of the random variable X. If we made, say, 1000 observations instead of 100, the average value of those 1000 observations would most likely be even closer to 4.118.

Figure 5.23(a) shows a plot of the average number of busy tellers versus the number of observations for the data in Table 5.16. The dashed line is at $\mu = 4.118$. Figure 5.23(b) depicts a plot for a different simulation of the number of busy tellers at 1:00 P.M. on 100 randomly selected days. Both plots suggest that, as the number of observations increases, the average number of busy tellers approaches the mean, $\mu = 4.118$, of the random variable X.

STANDARD DEVIATION OF A DISCRETE RANDOM VARIABLE

Similar reasoning also lets us extend the concept of population standard deviation (standard deviation of a variable) to any discrete variable. When we do so, we have the **standard deviation of a discrete random variable,** which we define as follows.

FIGURE 5.23
Graphs showing the average number of busy tellers versus the number of observations for two simulations of 100 observations each

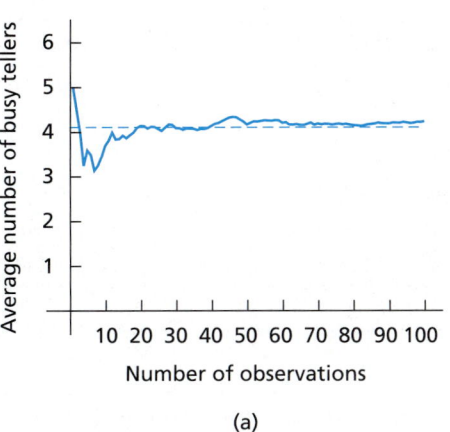
(a)

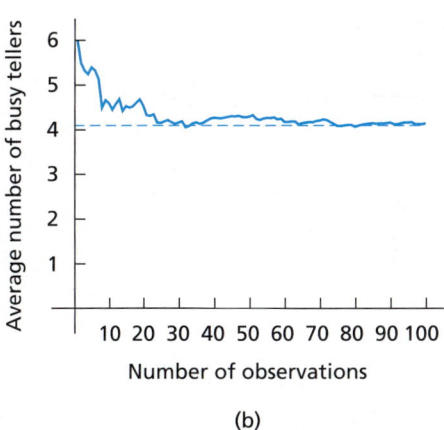
(b)

DEFINITION 5.10 **Standard Deviation of a Discrete Random Variable**

The *standard deviation of a discrete random variable* X is denoted σ_X or, when no confusion will arise, simply σ. It is defined as

$$\sigma = \sqrt{\Sigma(x-\mu)^2 P(X=x)}.$$

The standard deviation of a discrete random variable can also be obtained from the computing formula

$$\sigma = \sqrt{\Sigma x^2 P(X=x) - \mu^2}.$$

Note: The square of the standard deviation, σ^2, is called the **variance** of the random variable X.

In Example 5.21, we demonstrate computing the standard deviation of a discrete random variable.

Example 5.21 The Standard Deviation of a Discrete Random Variable

Busy Tellers Refer to Example 5.20, where X denotes the number of tellers busy with customers at 1:00 P.M. Find the standard deviation of the random variable X.

Solution We apply the computing formula given in Definition 5.10. To use that formula, we need the mean of X, which we found in Example 5.20, and columns for x^2 and $x^2 P(X=x)$, which are presented in the last two columns of Table 5.17 on the next page. From the final column of Table 5.17, $\Sigma x^2 P(X=x) = 19.438$. Recalling that $\mu = 4.118$, we can now obtain the standard deviation of X,

$$\sigma = \sqrt{\Sigma x^2 P(X=x) - \mu^2} = \sqrt{19.438 - 4.118^2} = 1.6,$$

rounded to one decimal place.

What Does it Mean?

The standard deviation of the number of tellers busy with customers is 1.6.

TABLE 5.17
Table for computing the standard deviation of the random variable X, the number of tellers busy with customers

x	$P(X = x)$	x^2	$x^2 P(X = x)$
0	0.029	0	0.000
1	0.049	1	0.049
2	0.078	4	0.312
3	0.155	9	1.395
4	0.212	16	3.392
5	0.262	25	6.550
6	0.215	36	7.740
			19.438

Recall that the standard deviation of a variable of a finite population indicates the variation of all possible observations by, roughly speaking, measuring how far the possible observations are from the mean, on average. A similar interpretation can be given to the standard deviation of a random variable. In particular, the smaller the standard deviation of a random variable X, the more likely it is that an observed value of X will be close to the mean.

Exercises 5.5

Statistical Concepts and Skills

5.65 What concept does the mean of a discrete random variable X generalize?

5.66 Comparing Investments. Suppose that the random variables X and Y represent the amount of return on two different investments. Further suppose that the mean of X equals the mean of Y but that the standard deviation of X is greater than the standard deviation of Y.
a. On average, is there a difference between the returns of the two investments? Explain your answer.
b. Which investment is more conservative? Why?

5.67 Space Shuttles. In Exercise 5.57 on page 226, you were asked to determine the probability distribution of the crew size, X, of a randomly selected shuttle mission between April 1981 and July 2000. That probability distribution is as follows.

x	2	3	4	5	6	7	8
$P(X = x)$	0.042	0.010	0.021	0.375	0.188	0.344	0.021

a. Find and interpret the mean of the random variable X.
b. Obtain the standard deviation of X by using one of the formulas given in Definition 5.10 on page 231.
c. Draw a probability histogram for the random variable; locate the mean; and show one, two, and three standard-deviation intervals.

5.68 Dice. In Exercise 5.58 on page 227, you were asked to determine the probability distribution of the sum of the dice, Y, when two balanced dice are rolled. That probability distribution is as follows.

y	2	3	4	5	6	7	8	9	10	11	12
$P(Y = y)$	$\frac{1}{36}$	$\frac{1}{18}$	$\frac{1}{12}$	$\frac{1}{9}$	$\frac{5}{36}$	$\frac{1}{6}$	$\frac{5}{36}$	$\frac{1}{9}$	$\frac{1}{12}$	$\frac{1}{18}$	$\frac{1}{36}$

a. Find and interpret the mean of Y.
b. Obtain the standard deviation of Y by using one of the formulas given in Definition 5.10 on page 231.
c. Draw a probability histogram for the random variable; locate the mean; and show one, two, and three standard-deviation intervals.

Expected Value. As noted in Definition 5.9 on page 229, the mean of a random variable is also called its *expected value*. This terminology is especially useful in gambling and decision theory, as illustrated in Exercises 5.69 and 5.70.

5.69 Roulette. An American roulette wheel contains 38 numbers: 18 are red, 18 are black, and 2 are green. When the roulette wheel is spun, the ball is equally likely to land on any of the 38 numbers. Suppose that you bet $1 on red. If the ball lands on a red number, you win $1; otherwise you lose your $1. Let X be the amount you win on your $1 bet. Then X is a random variable whose probability distribution is as follows.

x	1	−1
$P(X = x)$	0.474	0.526

a. Verify that the probability distribution shown in the table is correct.
b. Find the expected value of the random variable X.
c. On average, how much will you lose per play?
d. Approximately how much would you expect to lose if you bet $1 on red 100 times? 1000 times?
e. Is roulette a profitable game to play? Explain.

5.70 Evaluating Investments. An investor plans to put $50,000 in one of four investments. The return on each investment depends on whether next year's economy is strong or weak. The following table summarizes the possible payoffs, in dollars, for the four investments.

Investment	Next year's economy	
	Strong	Weak
Certificate of deposit	6,000	6,000
Office complex	15,000	5,000
Land speculation	33,000	−17,000
Technical school	5,500	10,000

Let V, W, X, and Y denote the payoffs for the certificate of deposit, office complex, land speculation, and technical school, respectively. Then V, W, X, and Y are random variables. Assume that next year's economy has a 40% chance of being strong and a 60% chance of being weak.
a. Find the probability distribution of each random variable V, W, X, and Y.
b. Determine the expected value of each random variable.
c. Which investment has the best expected payoff? Which has the worst?

d. Which investment would you select? Explain your answer.

5.71 Equipment Breakdowns. A factory manager collected data on the number of equipment breakdowns per day. From those data, she derived the probability distribution shown in the following table, where W denotes the number of breakdowns on a given day.

w	0	1	2
$P(W = w)$	0.80	0.15	0.05

a. Determine μ_W and σ_W.
b. On average, how many breakdowns occur per day?
c. About how many breakdowns are expected during a 1-year period, assuming 250 work days per year?

Using Technology

5.72 Queueing Simulation. Benny's Barber Shop in Cleveland has five chairs for waiting customers. The number of customers waiting is a random variable Y that, based on previous records, has the following probability distribution.

y	0	1	2	3	4	5
$P(Y = y)$	0.424	0.161	0.134	0.111	0.093	0.077

a. Compute the mean number of customers waiting, μ.
b. In a large number of independent observations, how many customers will be waiting, on average?
c. Use the technology of your choice to simulate 100 observations of the number of customers waiting.
d. Obtain the mean of the observations in part (c) and compare it to μ.
e. What does part (d) illustrate?

5.6 THE BINOMIAL DISTRIBUTION

Many problems in probability and statistics concern the repetition of an experiment that has two possible outcomes. In such contexts, each repetition of the experiment is called a **trial**. Here are three examples.

- Testing the effectiveness of a drug: Several patients take the drug (the trials), and for each patient the drug is either effective or not effective (the two possible outcomes).
- Weekly sales of a car salesperson: The salesperson has several customers during the week (the trials), and for each customer the salesperson either makes a sale or does not make a sale (the two possible outcomes).
- Taste tests for colas: A number of people taste two different colas (the trials), and for each person the preference is either for the first cola or for the second cola (the two possible outcomes).

To analyze repeated trials of an experiment that has two possible outcomes requires knowledge of factorials, binomial coefficients, Bernoulli trials, and the binomial distribution. We begin with factorials.

FACTORIALS

Factorials are defined as follows.

DEFINITION 5.11 Factorials

The product of the first k positive integers is called k *factorial* and is denoted $k!$. In symbols,

$$k! = k(k-1) \cdots 2 \cdot 1.$$

We also define $0! = 1$.

Example 5.22 Factorials

Doing the Calculations Determine $3!$, $4!$, and $5!$.

Solution Applying Definition 5.11, we obtain $3! = 3 \cdot 2 \cdot 1 = 6$, $4! = 4 \cdot 3 \cdot 2 \cdot 1 = 24$, and $5! = 5 \cdot 4 \cdot 3 \cdot 2 \cdot 1 = 120$. ◆

Note, for instance, that $6! = 6 \cdot 5!$, $6! = 6 \cdot 5 \cdot 4!$, $6! = 6 \cdot 5 \cdot 4 \cdot 3!$, and so on. In general, if $j \leq k$, then $k! = k(k-1) \cdots (k-j+1)(k-j)!$.

BINOMIAL COEFFICIENTS

You may have already encountered binomial coefficients in algebra when you studied the binomial expansion, the expansion of $(a+b)^n$. Here is the definition of binomial coefficients.

5.6 The Binomial Distribution

DEFINITION 5.12 Binomial Coefficients

If n is a positive integer and x is a nonnegative integer less than or equal to n, then the *binomial coefficient* $\binom{n}{x}$ is defined as

$$\binom{n}{x} = \frac{n!}{x!\,(n-x)!}.$$

Example 5.23 Binomial Coefficients

Doing the Calculations Determine the value of each binomial coefficient.

a. $\binom{6}{1}$ b. $\binom{5}{3}$ c. $\binom{7}{3}$ d. $\binom{4}{4}$

Solution We apply Definition 5.12.

a. $\binom{6}{1} = \dfrac{6!}{1!\,(6-1)!} = \dfrac{6!}{1!\,5!} = \dfrac{6 \cdot 5!}{1!\,5!} = \dfrac{6}{1} = 6$

b. $\binom{5}{3} = \dfrac{5!}{3!\,(5-3)!} = \dfrac{5!}{3!\,2!} = \dfrac{5 \cdot 4 \cdot 3!}{3!\,2!} = \dfrac{5 \cdot 4}{2} = 10$

c. $\binom{7}{3} = \dfrac{7!}{3!\,(7-3)!} = \dfrac{7!}{3!\,4!} = \dfrac{7 \cdot 6 \cdot 5 \cdot 4!}{3!\,4!} = \dfrac{7 \cdot 6 \cdot 5}{6} = 35$

d. $\binom{4}{4} = \dfrac{4!}{4!\,(4-4)!} = \dfrac{4!}{4!\,0!} = \dfrac{4!}{4!\,0!} = \dfrac{1}{1} = 1$

◆

BERNOULLI TRIALS

Next we define **Bernoulli trials**, the trial outcomes—**success** and **failure**—and the **success probability**.

DEFINITION 5.13 Bernoulli Trials

Repeated identical trials are called *Bernoulli trials* if three conditions are satisfied:

1. each trial has two possible outcomes, denoted generically s, for *success*, and f, for *failure*;
2. the trials are independent; and
3. the probability of a success remains the same from trial to trial, called the *success probability* and denoted p.

INTRODUCING THE BINOMIAL DISTRIBUTION

The **binomial distribution** is the probability distribution for the number of successes in a sequence of Bernoulli trials. We introduce this concept in Example 5.24.

Example 5.24 Introducing the Binomial Distribution

Mortality Mortality tables enable actuaries to obtain the probability that a person at any particular age will live a specified number of years. Such probabilities, in turn, permit the determination of life-insurance premiums, retirement pensions, annuity payments, and related items of importance to insurance companies and others.

According to tables provided by the U.S. National Center for Health Statistics in *Vital Statistics of the United States*, there is about an 80% chance that a person aged 20 will be alive at age 65. Suppose that three people aged 20 are selected at random.

a. Formulate the process of observing which people are alive at age 65 as a sequence of three Bernoulli trials.
b. Obtain the possible outcomes of the three Bernoulli trials.
c. Determine the probability of each outcome in part (b).
d. Find the probability that exactly two of the three people will be alive at age 65.
e. Obtain the probability distribution of the number of people of the three that are alive at age 65.

Solution a. Each trial consists of observing whether a person currently aged 20 is alive at age 65 and has two possible outcomes: alive or dead. The trials are independent. If we let a success, s, correspond to being alive at age 65, the success probability is 0.8 (80%); that is, $p = 0.8$.

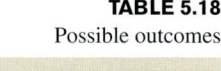
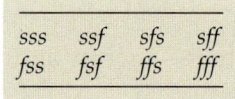

TABLE 5.18
Possible outcomes

| sss | ssf | sfs | sff |
| fss | fsf | ffs | fff |

b. The possible outcomes of the three Bernoulli trials are shown in Table 5.18 (s = success = alive, f = failure = dead). For instance, ssf represents the outcome that at age 65 the first two people are alive and the third is not.

c. As Table 5.18 indicates, eight outcomes are possible. However, because these eight outcomes are not equally likely, we cannot use the f/N rule to determine their probabilities; instead, we must proceed as follows. First of all, by part (a), the success probability equals 0.8, or

$$P(s) = p = 0.8.$$

Therefore the failure probability is

$$P(f) = 1 - p = 1 - 0.8 = 0.2.$$

Because the trials are independent, we can obtain the probability of each three-trial outcome by multiplying the probabilities for each trial.[2] For in-

---

[2]Mathematically, this procedure is expressed by the *special multiplication rule* of probability. See, for example, *Introductory Statistics*, 6th edition, by Neil A. Weiss (Boston: Addison-Wesley, 2002).

5.6 The Binomial Distribution

stance, the probability of the outcome *ssf* is

$$P(ssf) = P(s) \cdot P(s) \cdot P(f) = 0.8 \cdot 0.8 \cdot 0.2 = 0.128.$$

Similar computations yield the probabilities of the other seven possible outcomes. All eight possible outcomes and their probabilities are shown in Table 5.19. Note that outcomes containing the same number of successes have the same probability. For instance, three outcomes contain exactly two successes: *ssf*, *sfs*, and *fss*. Each of those three outcomes has the same probability: 0.128. The reason is that each probability is obtained by multiplying two success probabilities of 0.8 and one failure probability of 0.2.

A tree diagram is useful for organizing and summarizing the possible outcomes of this experiment and their probabilities. The tree diagram corresponding to Table 5.19 is presented in Fig. 5.24.

TABLE 5.19
Outcomes and probabilities for observing whether each of three people is alive at age 65

Outcome	Probability
sss	(0.8)(0.8)(0.8) = 0.512
ssf	(0.8)(0.8)(0.2) = 0.128
sfs	(0.8)(0.2)(0.8) = 0.128
sff	(0.8)(0.2)(0.2) = 0.032
fss	(0.2)(0.8)(0.8) = 0.128
fsf	(0.2)(0.8)(0.2) = 0.032
ffs	(0.2)(0.2)(0.8) = 0.032
fff	(0.2)(0.2)(0.2) = 0.008

FIGURE 5.24
Tree diagram corresponding to Table 5.19

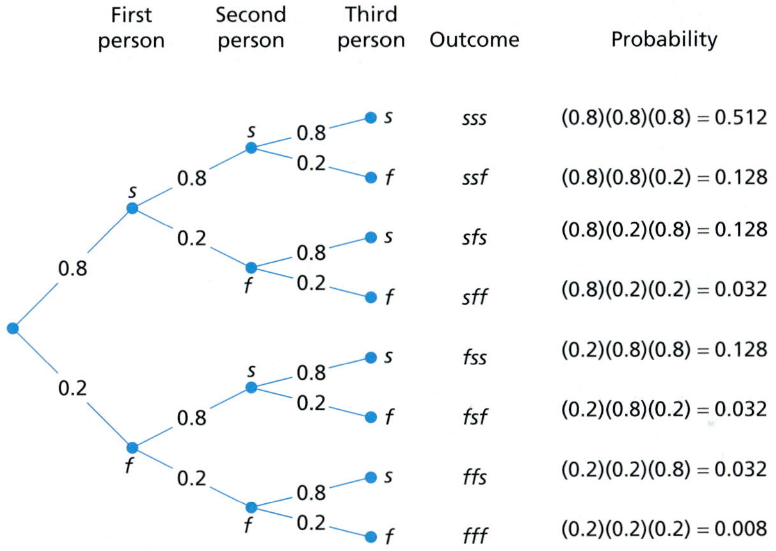

d. Table 5.19 shows that the event that exactly two of the three people are alive at age 65 consists of three outcomes: *ssf*, *sfs*, and *fss*. It also shows that each of those three outcomes has the same probability, 0.128. So, by the special addition rule (Formula 5.1 on page 214), we have

$$P(\text{Exactly two will be alive}) = P(ssf) + P(sfs) + P(fss)$$

$$= \underbrace{0.128 + 0.128 + 0.128}_{3 \text{ times}} = 3 \cdot 0.128 = 0.384.$$

The probability that exactly two of the three people will be alive at age 65 is 0.384.

e. Let X denote the number of people of the three that are alive at age 65. In part (d), we found $P(X = 2)$. Proceeding in the same way, we can determine the remaining three probabilities: $P(X = 0)$, $P(X = 1)$, and $P(X = 3)$. The results are displayed in Table 5.20. A probability histogram for the

TABLE 5.20
Probability distribution of the random variable X, the number of people out of three that are alive at age 65

Number alive x	Probability $P(X = x)$
0	0.008
1	0.096
2	0.384
3	0.512

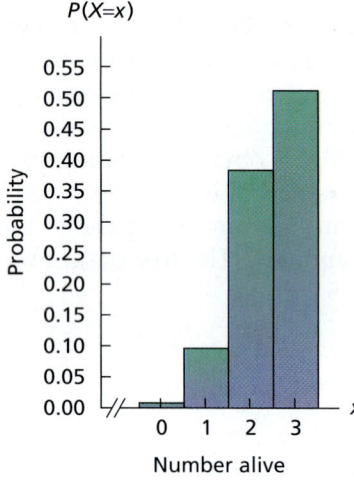

FIGURE 5.25
Probability histogram for the random variable X, the number of people out of three that are alive at age 65

distribution in Table 5.20 is given in Fig. 5.25. Note for future reference that the probability distribution is left skewed. ◆

THE BINOMIAL PROBABILITY FORMULA

Table 5.20 displays the probability distribution of the random variable "number alive at age 65" for three people currently aged 20. To obtain that probability distribution, we used a tabulation method (Table 5.19), which required a significant amount of work.

In most practical applications, the amount of work required would be considerably more and often would be prohibitive because the number of trials is generally much larger than 3. For instance, for twenty 20-year-olds instead of three 20-year-olds, there would be over one million possible outcomes. In that case, the tabulation method certainly would not be feasible.

The good news is that there is a relatively simple formula for obtaining binomial probabilities. A first step in developing that formula is the following fact.

Key Fact 5.5 | **Number of Outcomes Containing a Specified Number of Successes**

In n Bernoulli trials, the number of outcomes that contain exactly x successes equals the binomial coefficient $\binom{n}{x}$.

We won't stop to prove Key Fact 5.5, but let's quickly see whether it is consistent with the results obtained in Example 5.24. For instance, the direct listing in Table 5.18 shows that there are three outcomes in which exactly two of the three people are alive at age 65—namely, *ssf*, *sfs*, and *fss*. Using binomial coefficients, we can determine that fact without resorting to a direct listing. Applying Key Fact 5.5, we have

$$\begin{bmatrix} \text{Number of outcomes} \\ \text{comprising the event} \\ \text{exactly two alive} \end{bmatrix} = \binom{3}{2} = \frac{3!}{2!\,(3-2)!} = \frac{3!}{2!\,1!} = 3.$$

We can now develop a probability formula for the number of successes in Bernoulli trials. We indicate briefly how that formula is derived by referring to Example 5.24. For instance, to determine the probability that exactly two of the three people will be alive at age 65, $P(X = 2)$, we reason as follows.

1. Any particular outcome in which exactly two of the three people are alive at age 65 (e.g., *sfs*) has probability

5.6 The Binomial Distribution

$$\underset{\substack{\uparrow \\ \text{Probability} \\ \text{alive}}}{\underset{\downarrow}{\overset{\text{Two alive}}{(0.8)^2}}} \cdot \underset{\substack{\uparrow \\ \text{Probability} \\ \text{dead}}}{\underset{\downarrow}{\overset{\text{One dead}}{(0.2)^1}}} = 0.64 \cdot 0.2 = 0.128,$$

obtained by multiplying two success probabilities of 0.8 and one failure probability of 0.2.

2. By Key Fact 5.5, the number of outcomes in which exactly two of the three people are alive at age 65 is

$$\underset{\substack{\uparrow \\ \text{Number alive}}}{\binom{\overset{\text{Number of trials}}{\downarrow}{3}}{2}} = \frac{3!}{2!\,(3-2)!} = 3.$$

3. By the special addition rule, the probability that exactly two of the three people will be alive at age 65 is

$$P(X = 2) = \binom{3}{2} \cdot (0.8)^2 (0.2)^1 = 3 \cdot 0.128 = 0.384.$$

Of course, this result is the same as that obtained in Example 5.24(d). However, this time we determined the probability quickly and easily—no tabulation and no listing were required. More important, the reasoning we used applies to any sequence of Bernoulli trials and leads to the **binomial probability formula,** which we express as follows.

FORMULA 5.4   **Binomial Probability Formula**

Let X denote the total number of successes in n Bernoulli trials with success probability p. Then the probability distribution of the random variable X is given by

$$P(X = x) = \binom{n}{x} p^x (1-p)^{n-x}.$$

The random variable X is called a *binomial random variable* and is said to have the *binomial distribution* with parameters n and p.

To determine a binomial probability formula in specific problems, having a well-organized strategy, such as the one presented in Procedure 5.1 on the next page, is useful.

In Example 5.25, we illustrate Procedure 5.1 by applying it to the random variable considered in Example 5.24.

Procedure 5.1 — To Find a Binomial Probability Formula

Assumptions

1. n identical trials are to be performed.
2. Two outcomes, success or failure, are possible for each trial.
3. The trials are independent.
4. The success probability, p, remains the same from trial to trial.

Step 1 Identify a success.

Step 2 Determine p, the success probability.

Step 3 Determine n, the number of trials.

Step 4 The binomial probability formula for the number of successes, X, is

$$P(X = x) = \binom{n}{x} p^x (1-p)^{n-x}.$$

Example 5.25 Obtaining Binomial Probabilities

Mortality According to tables provided by the U.S. National Center for Health Statistics in *Vital Statistics of the United States*, there is about an 80% chance that a person aged 20 will be alive at age 65. Suppose that three people aged 20 are selected at random. Find the probability that the number alive at age 65 will be

a. exactly two. b. at most one. c. at least one.
d. Determine the probability distribution of the number alive at age 65.

Solution Let X denote the number of people of the three that are alive at age 65. To solve parts (a)–(d), we first apply Procedure 5.1.

Step 1 Identify a success.

A success is that a person currently aged 20 will be alive at age 65.

Step 2 Determine p, the success probability.

The probability that a person currently aged 20 will be alive at age 65 is 80%, so $p = 0.8$.

Step 3 Determine n, the number of trials.

The number of trials is the number of people in the study, which is three, so $n = 3$.

Step 4 The binomial probability formula for the number of successes, X, is

$$P(X = x) = \binom{n}{x} p^x (1-p)^{n-x}.$$

As $n = 3$ and $p = 0.8$, the formula becomes

$$P(X = x) = \binom{3}{x}(0.8)^x(0.2)^{3-x}.$$

Now that we have applied Procedure 5.1, solving parts (a)–(d) is relatively easy.

a. Applying the binomial probability formula with $x = 2$ yields

$$P(X = 2) = \binom{3}{2}(0.8)^2(0.2)^{3-2} = \frac{3!}{2!\,(3-2)!}(0.8)^2(0.2)^1 = 0.384.$$

> **What Does it Mean?**
>
> Chances are 38.4% that exactly two of the three people will be alive at age 65.

b. The probability that at most one person will be alive at age 65 is

$$P(X \leq 1) = P(X = 0) + P(X = 1)$$

$$= \binom{3}{0}(0.8)^0(0.2)^{3-0} + \binom{3}{1}(0.8)^1(0.2)^{3-1}$$

$$= 0.008 + 0.096 = 0.104.$$

> **What Does it Mean?**
>
> Chances are only 10.4% that one or fewer of the three people will be alive at age 65.

c. The probability that at least one person will be alive at age 65 is $P(X \geq 1)$, which we can obtain by first using the fact that

$$P(X \geq 1) = P(X = 1) + P(X = 2) + P(X = 3)$$

and then applying the binomial probability formula to calculate each of the three individual probabilities. However, using the complementation rule is easier:

$$P(X \geq 1) = 1 - P(X < 1) = 1 - P(X = 0)$$

$$= 1 - \binom{3}{0}(0.8)^0(0.2)^{3-0} = 1 - 0.008 = 0.992.$$

> **What Does it Mean?**
>
> Chances are 99.2% that one or more of the three people will be alive at age 65.

d. To obtain the probability distribution of the random variable X, we need to use the binomial probability formula to compute $P(X = x)$, for $x = 0, 1, 2$, and 3. We have already done so for $x = 0, 1$, and 2 in parts (a) and (b). For $x = 3$, we have

$$P(X = 3) = \binom{3}{3}(0.8)^3(0.2)^{3-3} = (0.8)^3 = 0.512.$$

Thus the probability distribution of X is as shown in Table 5.20 on page 237. But this time we computed the probabilities quickly and easily by using the binomial probability formula. ◆

SHAPE OF A BINOMIAL DISTRIBUTION

Figure 5.25 on page 238 shows that, for three people currently 20 years old, the probability distribution of the number that will be alive at age 65 is left skewed. The reason is that the success probability, $p = 0.8$, exceeds 0.5.

More generally, *a binomial distribution is right skewed if $p < 0.5$, is symmetric if $p = 0.5$, and is left skewed if $p > 0.5$.* Figure 5.26 illustrates these facts for three different binomial distributions with $n = 6$.

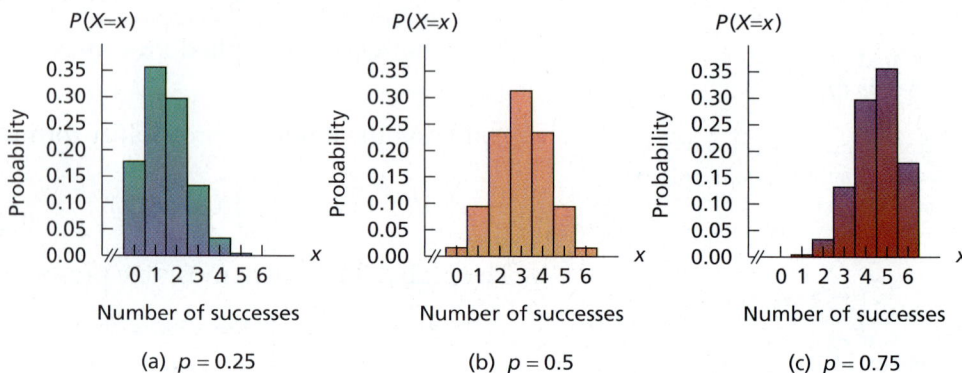

FIGURE 5.26
Probability histograms for binomial distributions with parameters $n = 6$ and (a) $p = 0.25$, (b) $p = 0.5$, and (c) $p = 0.75$

MEAN AND STANDARD DEVIATION OF A BINOMIAL RANDOM VARIABLE

In Section 5.5, we discussed the mean and standard deviation of a discrete random variable. We presented formulas to compute these parameters in Definition 5.9 on page 229 and Definition 5.10 on page 231.

Because these formulas apply to any discrete random variable, they work for a binomial random variable. Hence we can determine the mean and standard deviation of a binomial random variable by first using the binomial probability formula to obtain its probability distribution and then applying Definitions 5.9 and 5.10.

But there is an easier way. If we substitute the binomial probability formula into the formulas for the mean and standard deviation of a discrete random variable and then simplify mathematically, we obtain the following.

> **FORMULA 5.5** **Mean and Standard Deviation of a Binomial Random Variable**
>
> The mean and standard deviation of a binomial random variable with parameters n and p are
>
> $$\mu = np \quad \text{and} \quad \sigma = \sqrt{np(1-p)},$$
>
> respectively.

In Example 5.26, we apply these formulas.

Example 5.26 Mean and Standard Deviation of a Binomial Random Variable

Mortality For three randomly selected 20-year-olds, let X denote the number that are still alive at age 65. Obtain the mean and standard deviation of the random variable X.

Solution As we previously found, X is a binomial random variable with parameters $n = 3$ and $p = 0.8$. Applying Formula 5.5, we get

$$\mu = np = 3 \cdot 0.8 = 2.4$$

and

$$\sigma = \sqrt{np(1-p)} = \sqrt{3 \cdot 0.8 \cdot 0.2} = 0.69.$$

The number expected to be alive at age 65 is 2.4; that is, on average, 2.4 of every three 20-year-olds will still be alive at age 65.   ◆

BINOMIAL APPROXIMATION TO THE HYPERGEOMETRIC DISTRIBUTION

Many statistical studies are concerned with the proportion (percentage) of members of a finite population that have a specified attribute. For instance, we might be interested in the proportion of U.S. adults that have Internet access. Here the population consists of all U.S. adults, and the specified attribute is "has Internet access." Or we might want to know the proportion of U.S. businesses that are minority owned. In this case, the population consists of all U.S. businesses, and the specified attribute is "minority owned."

Generally, the population under consideration is large, and it is therefore usually impractical and often impossible to determine the population proportion by taking a census; for instance, imagine trying to interview every U.S. adult to ascertain the proportion who have Internet access. So, in practice, we rely mostly on sampling and use the sample data to estimate the population proportion.

Suppose that a simple random sample of size n is taken from a population in which the proportion of members that have a specified attribute is p. Then a random variable of primary importance in the estimation of p is the number of members sampled that have the specified attribute, which we denote X. The exact probability distribution of X depends on whether the sampling is done with or without replacement.

If sampling is done with replacement, the sampling process constitutes Bernoulli trials: Each selection of a member from the population corresponds to a trial. A success occurs on a trial if the member selected in that trial has the specified attribute; otherwise, a failure occurs. The trials are independent because the sampling is done with replacement. The success probability remains the same from trial to trial—it always equals the proportion of the population that has the specified attribute. Therefore the random variable X has the binomial distribution with parameters n (the sample size) and p (the population proportion).

In reality, however, sampling is ordinarily done without replacement. Under these circumstances, the sampling process does not constitute Bernoulli trials because the trials are not independent and the success probability varies from trial to trial. In other words, the random variable X does not have a binomial distribution. Its distribution is important, however, and is referred to as a **hypergeometric distribution.**

We won't present the hypergeometric probability formula here because, in practice, a hypergeometric distribution can usually be approximated by a binomial distribution. The reason is that, if the sample size does not exceed 5% of the population size, there is little difference between sampling with and without replacement. We summarize the previous discussion as follows.

Key Fact 5.6 — Sampling and the Binomial Distribution

Suppose that a simple random sample of size n is taken from a finite population in which the proportion of members that have a specified attribute is p. Then the number of members sampled that have the specified attribute has

- exactly a binomial distribution with parameters n and p if the sampling is done with replacement and
- approximately a binomial distribution with parameters n and p if the sampling is done without replacement and the sample size does not exceed 5% of the population size.

For example, according to the U.S. Bureau of the Census publication *Current Population Reports*, 81.7% of U.S. adults have completed high school. Suppose that eight U.S. adults are to be randomly selected without replacement. Let X denote the number of those sampled that have completed high school. Then, as the sample size does not exceed 5% of the population size, the random variable X has approximately a binomial distribution with parameters $n = 8$ and $p = 0.817$.

OTHER DISCRETE PROBABILITY DISTRIBUTIONS

The binomial distribution is the most important and most widely used discrete probability distribution. However, many other discrete probability distributions are often used in practice.

In addition to the hypergeometric distribution are the Poisson, discrete uniform, geometric, negative binomial, and multinomial distributions. We briefly discuss the Poisson, hypergeometric, and geometric distributions in the exercises of this section.

The Technology Center

Almost all statistical technologies provide programs for determining binomial probabilities. In this subsection, we present output and (optional) step-by-step instructions to obtain individual binomial probabilities. For other options, refer to the technology manuals.

Example 5.27 Using Technology to Obtain Binomial Probabilities

Mortality Consider once again the mortality illustration discussed in Example 5.25(a). Use Minitab, Excel, or the TI-83 Plus to determine the probability that exactly two of the three people will be alive at age 65.

Solution Recall that of three randomly selected people aged 20, the number, X, that are alive at age 65 has a binomial distribution with parameters $n = 3$ and $p = 0.8$. We want the probability that exactly two of the three people will be alive at age 65, that is, $P(X = 2)$. Printout 5.1 shows output obtained for this probability by applying the binomial probability programs from Minitab, Excel, and the TI-83 Plus.

PRINTOUT 5.1
Output giving the probability that exactly two of the three people will be alive at age 65

MINITAB

Probability Density Function

Binomial with n = 3 and p = 0.800000

```
     x        P( X = x )
  2.00           0.3840
```

TI-83 PLUS

```
binompdf(3,0.8,2
)
            .384
```

EXCEL

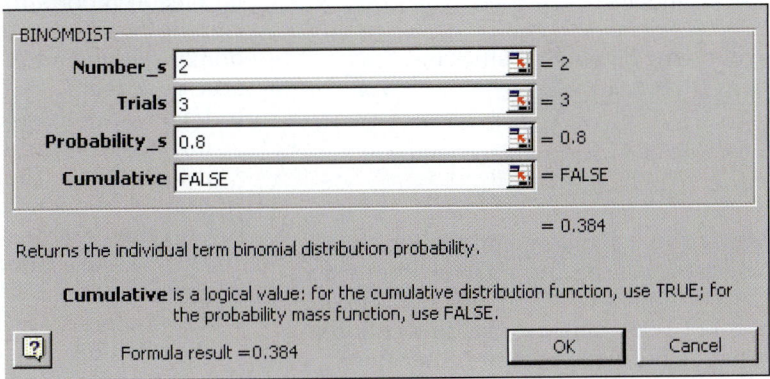

From any of these outputs, we find that the required probability is 0.384. This result, of course, agrees with the result that we obtained in part (a) of Example 5.25.

Obtaining the Output (Optional)

Printout 5.1 displays the probability that a binomial random variable with parameters $n = 3$ and $p = 0.8$ will be 2. Here are detailed instructions for obtaining that output.

MINITAB	EXCEL	TI-83 PLUS
1 Choose **Calc ▸ Probability Distributions ▸ Binomial...** 2 Select the **Probability** option button 3 Click in the **Number of trials** text box and type 3 4 Click in the **Probability of success** text box and type 0.8 5 Select the **Input constant** option button 6 Click in the **Input constant** text box and type 2 7 Click **OK**	1 Click f_x on the button bar 2 Select **Statistical** from the **Function category** list 3 Select **BINOMDIST** from the **Function name** list 4 Click **OK** 5 Type 2 in the **Number_s** text box 6 Click in the **Trials** text box and type 3 7 Click in the **Probability_s** text box and type 0.8 8 Click in the **Cumulative** text box and type FALSE	1 Press **2nd ▸ DISTR** 2 Arrow down to **binompdf(** and press **ENTER** 3 Type 3,0.8,2) and press **ENTER**

Exercises 5.6

Statistical Concepts and Skills

5.73 Give two examples of Bernoulli trials other than those presented in the text.

5.74 What does the "bi" in "binomial" signify?

5.75 Compute 3!, 7!, 8!, and 9!.

5.76 Evaluate the following binomial coefficients.
a. $\binom{4}{1}$ b. $\binom{6}{2}$ c. $\binom{8}{3}$ d. $\binom{9}{6}$

5.77 Determine the value of each binomial coefficient.
a. $\binom{5}{3}$ b. $\binom{10}{0}$ c. $\binom{10}{10}$ d. $\binom{9}{5}$

5.78 Pinworm Infestation. Pinworm infestation, commonly found in children, can be treated with the drug pyrantel pamoate. According to the *Merck Manual*, the treatment is effective in 90% of cases. Suppose that three children with pinworm infestation are given pyrantel pamoate.
a. Considering a success in a given case to be "a cure," formulate the process of observing which children are cured and which children are not cured as a sequence of three Bernoulli trials.
b. Construct a table similar to Table 5.19 on page 237 for the three cases. Display the probabilities to three decimal places.
c. Draw a tree diagram for this problem similar to the one shown in Fig. 5.24 on page 237.
d. List the outcomes in which exactly two of the three children are cured.
e. Find the probability of each outcome in part (d). Why are those probabilities all the same?
f. Use parts (d) and (e) to determine the probability that exactly two of the three children will be cured.
g. Without using the binomial probability formula, obtain the probability distribution of the random variable X, the number of children out of three that are cured.

5.79 Psychiatric Disorders. The National Institute of Mental Health reports that there is a 20% chance of an adult American suffering from a psychiatric disorder. Four randomly selected adult Americans are examined for psychiatric disorders.
a. If you let a success correspond to an adult American having a psychiatric disorder, what is the success probability, p? (*Note:* The use of the word *success* in Bernoulli trials need not reflect its usually positive connotation.)
b. Construct a table similar to Table 5.19 on page 237 for the four people examined. Display the probabilities to four decimal places.
c. Draw a tree diagram for this problem similar to the one shown in Fig. 5.24 on page 237.
d. List the outcomes in which exactly three of the four people examined have a psychiatric disorder.
e. Find the probability of each outcome in part (d). Why are those probabilities all the same?
f. Use parts (d) and (e) to determine the probability that exactly three of the four people examined have a psychiatric disorder.
g. Without using the binomial probability formula, obtain the probability distribution of the random variable Y, the number of adults out of four that have a psychiatric disorder.

5.80 Use Procedure 5.1 on page 240 to solve part (g) of Exercise 5.78.

5.81 Use Procedure 5.1 on page 240 to solve part (g) of Exercise 5.79.

5.82 For each of the following probability histograms of binomial distributions, specify whether the success probability is less than, equal to, or greater than 0.5. Explain your answers.

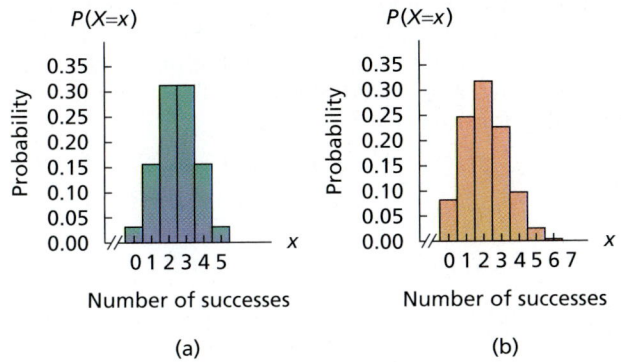

(a)   (b)

In Exercises 5.83–5.85, use Procedure 5.1 on page 240 to obtain the required probabilities. Express each probability answer as a decimal rounded to three places.

5.83 Horse Racing. According to the *Daily Racing Form*, the probability is about 0.67 that the favorite in a horse race will finish in the money (first, second, or third place). In the next five races, what is the probability that the favorite finishes in the money
a. exactly twice?
b. exactly four times?
c. at least four times?
d. between two and four times, inclusive?
e. Determine the probability distribution of the random variable X, the number of times the favorite finishes in the money in the next five races.
f. Identify the probability distribution of X as right skewed, symmetric, or left skewed without consulting its probability distribution or drawing its probability histogram.
g. Draw a probability histogram for X.
h. Use your answer from part (e) and Definitions 5.9 and 5.10 on pages 229 and 231, respectively, to obtain the mean and standard deviation of the random variable X.
i. Use Formula 5.5 on page 242 to obtain the mean and standard deviation of the random variable X.
j. Interpret your answer for the mean in words.

5.84 Households with VCRs. As reported by Television Bureau of Advertising, Inc., in *Trends in Television*, 84.2% of U.S. households have a VCR. If six households are randomly selected without replacement, what is the (approximate) probability that the number of households sampled that have a VCR will be

a. exactly four?
b. at least four?
c. at most five?
d. between two and five, inclusive?
e. Determine the (approximate) probability distribution of the random variable Y, the number of households of the six sampled that have a VCR.
f. Determine and interpret the mean of the random variable Y.
g. Obtain the standard deviation of Y.
h. Strictly speaking, why is the probability distribution that you obtained in part (e) only approximately correct? What is the exact distribution called?

5.85 Teen Pregnancy. According to the periodical *Zero Population Growth* (Spring 2000, Vol. 32, No. 2, p. 18), the United States leads the fully industrialized world in teen pregnancy rates, with 40% of U.S. females getting pregnant at least once before reaching the age of 20. Suppose that 10 U.S. 20-year-old females are selected at random. Find the probability that the number who have been pregnant at least once before the age of 20 will be
a. exactly five.
b. between three and five, inclusive.
c. less than 20% of those surveyed.
d. more than one.

Extending the Concepts and Skills

5.86 Roulette. A success, s, in Bernoulli trials is often derived from a collection of outcomes. For example, an American roulette wheel consists of 38 numbers, of which 18 are red, 18 are black, and 2 are green. When the roulette wheel is spun, the ball is equally likely to land on any one of the 38 numbers. If you are interested in which number the ball lands on, each play at the roulette wheel has 38 possible outcomes. Suppose, however, that you are betting on red. Then you are interested only in whether the ball lands on a red number. From this point of view, each play at the wheel has only two possible outcomes—either the ball lands on a red number or it doesn't. Hence successive bets on red constitute a sequence of Bernoulli trials with success probability $\frac{18}{38}$. In four plays at a roulette wheel, what is the probability that the ball lands on red
a. exactly twice?   b. at least once?

5.87 Lotto. A previous Arizona state lottery, called *Lotto*, is played as follows: The player selects six numbers from the numbers 1–42 and buys a ticket for $1. There are six winning numbers, which are selected at random from the numbers 1–42. To win a prize, a *Lotto* ticket must contain three or more of the winning numbers. A probability distribution for the number of winning numbers for a single ticket is shown in the following table.

Number of winning numbers	Probability
0	0.3713060
1	0.4311941
2	0.1684352
3	0.0272219
4	0.0018014
5	0.0000412
6	0.0000002

a. If you buy one *Lotto* ticket, determine the probability that you win a prize. Round your answer to three decimal places.
b. If you buy one *Lotto* ticket per week for a year, determine the probability that you win a prize at least once in the 52 tries.

5.88 Sickle Cell Anemia. Sickle cell anemia is an inherited blood disease that occurs primarily in blacks. In the United States, about 15 of every 10,000 black children have sickle cell anemia. The red blood cells of an affected person are abnormal; the result is severe chronic anemia (inability to carry the required amount of oxygen), which causes headaches, shortness of breath, jaundice, increased risk of pneumococcal pneumonia and gallstones, and other severe problems. Sickle cell anemia occurs in children who inherit an abnormal type of hemoglobin, called hemoglobin S, from both parents. If hemoglobin S is inherited from only one parent, the person is said to have sickle cell trait and is generally free from symptoms. There is a 50% chance that a person who has sickle cell trait will pass hemoglobin S to an offspring.
a. Obtain the probability that a child of two people who have sickle cell trait will have sickle cell anemia.
b. If two people who have sickle cell trait have five children, determine the probability that at least one of the children will have sickle cell anemia.
c. If two people who have sickle cell trait have five children, find the probability distribution of the number of those children who will have sickle cell anemia.
d. Construct a probability histogram for the probability distribution in part (c).
e. If two people who have sickle cell trait have five children, how many can they expect will have sickle cell anemia?

5.89 Sampling and the Binomial Distribution. Refer to the discussion on the binomial approximation to the hypergeometric distribution that begins on page 243.
a. If sampling is with replacement, explain why the trials are independent and the success probability remains the same from trial to trial—always the proportion of the population that has the specified attribute.
b. If sampling is without replacement, explain why the trials are not independent and the success probability varies from trial to trial.

5.90 The Hypergeometric Distribution. In this exercise, we discuss the *hypergeometric distribution* in more detail. When sampling is done without replacement from a finite population, the hypergeometric distribution is the exact probability distribution for the number of members sampled that have a specified attribute. The hypergeometric probability formula is

$$P(X = x) = \frac{\binom{Np}{x}\binom{N(1-p)}{n-x}}{\binom{N}{n}},$$

where X denotes the number of members sampled that have the specified attribute, N is the population size, n is the sample size, and p is the population proportion.

To illustrate, suppose that a customer purchases 4 fuses from a shipment of 250, of which 94% are not defective. Let a success correspond to a fuse that is not defective.
a. Determine N, n, and p.
b. Use the hypergeometric probability formula to find the probability distribution of the number of nondefective fuses the customer gets.

Key Fact 5.6 shows that a hypergeometric distribution can be approximated by a binomial distribution provided the sample size does not exceed 5% of the population size. In particular, you can use the binomial probability formula

$$P(X = x) = \binom{n}{x}p^x(1-p)^{n-x},$$

with $n = 4$ and $p = 0.94$, to approximate the probability distribution of the number of nondefective fuses that the customer gets.
c. Obtain the binomial distribution with parameters $n = 4$ and $p = 0.94$.
d. Compare the hypergeometric distribution that you obtained in part (b) with the binomial distribution that you obtained in part (c).

5.91 The Geometric Distribution. In this exercise, we discuss the *geometric distribution*, the probability distribution for the number of trials until the first success in Bernoulli trials. The geometric probability formula is

$$P(X = x) = p(1-p)^{x-1},$$

where X denotes the number of trials until the first success and p the success probability. Using the geometric probability formula and Definition 5.9 on page 229, we can show that the mean of the random variable X is $1/p$.

To illustrate, again consider the Arizona state lottery, *Lotto*, as described in Exercise 5.87. Suppose that you buy one *Lotto* ticket per week. Let X denote the number of weeks until you win a prize.

a. Find and interpret the probability formula for the random variable X. (*Note:* The appropriate success probability was obtained in Exercise 5.87(a).)
b. Compute the probability that the number of weeks until you win a prize is exactly 3; at most 3; at least 3.
c. On average, how long will it be until you win a prize?

5.92 The Poisson Distribution. Another important discrete probability distribution is the *Poisson distribution*, named in honor of the French mathematician and physicist Simeon Poisson (1781–1840). This probability distribution is often used to model the frequency with which a specified event occurs during a particular period of time. The Poisson probability formula is

$$P(X = x) = e^{-\lambda} \frac{\lambda^x}{x!},$$

where X is the number of times the event occurs and λ is a parameter equal to the mean of X. The number e is the base of natural logarithms and is approximately equal to 2.7183.

To illustrate, consider the following problem: Desert Samaritan Hospital, located in Mesa, Arizona, keeps records of emergency room traffic. Those records reveal that the number of patients who arrive between 6:00 P.M. and 7:00 P.M. has a Poisson distribution with parameter $\lambda = 6.9$. Determine the probability that, on a given day, the number of patients who arrive at the emergency room between 6:00 P.M. and 7:00 P.M. will be
a. exactly four.
b. at most two.
c. between four and 10, inclusive.

Using Technology

5.93 Horse Racing. Use the technology of your choice to obtain the required probability or probabilities in parts (a)–(e) of Exercise 5.83.

5.94 Households with VCRs. Use the technology of your choice to obtain the required probability or probabilities in parts (a)–(e) of Exercise 5.84.

Chapter Review

You Should Be Able To

1. use and understand the formulas presented in this chapter.

2. compute probabilities for experiments having equally likely outcomes.

3. interpret probabilities, using the frequentist interpretation of probability.

4. state and understand the basic properties of probability.

5. construct and interpret Venn diagrams.

6. find and describe (not E), (A & B), and (A or B).

7. determine whether two or more events are mutually exclusive.

8. understand and use probability notation.

9. state and apply the special addition rule.

10. state and apply the complementation rule.

11. state and apply the general addition rule.

*12. determine the probability distribution of a discrete random variable.

*13. construct a probability histogram.

*14. describe events using random-variable notation, when appropriate.

*15. use the frequentist interpretation of probability to understand the meaning of the probability distribution of a random variable.

*16. find and interpret the mean and standard deviation of a discrete random variable.

*17. compute factorials and binomial coefficients.

*18. define and apply the concept of Bernoulli trials.

*19. assign probabilities to the outcomes in a sequence of Bernoulli trials.

*20. obtain binomial probabilities.

*21. compute the mean and standard deviation of a binomial random variable.

---

*An asterisk indicates material from optional sections.

Key Terms

(A & B), 207
(A or B), 207
at random, 200
Bernoulli trials,* 235
binomial coefficients,* 235
binomial distribution,* 236, 239
binomial probability formula,* 239
binomial random variable,* 239
certain event, 202
complement, 207
complementation rule, 215
discrete random variable,* 220
equal-likelihood model, 202
event, 199, 206
expectation,* 229
expected value,* 229

experiment, 199
factorials,* 234
failure,* 235
f/N rule, 199
frequentist interpretation of probability, 201
general addition rule, 216
hypergeometric distribution,* 243
impossible event, 202
law of averages,* 230
law of large numbers,* 230
mean of a discrete random variable,* 229
mutually exclusive events, 210
(not E), 207
P(E), 213

probability distribution,* 221
probability histogram,* 221
probability model, 202
probability theory, 196
random variable,* 220
sample space, 206
special addition rule, 214
standard deviation of a discrete random variable,* 231
success,* 235
success probability,* 235
trial,* 233
variance of a discrete random variable,* 231
Venn diagrams, 207

Review Test

Statistical Concepts and Skills

1. Why is probability theory important to statistics?

2. Regarding the equal-likelihood model,
   a. what is it?
   b. how are probabilities computed?

3. What meaning is given to the probability of an event by the frequentist interpretation of probability?

4. Decide which of these numbers could not possibly be probabilities. Explain your answers.
   a. 0.047   b. −0.047   c. 3.5   d. 1/3.5

5. Identify a commonly used graphical technique for portraying events and relationships among events.

6. What does it mean for two or more events to be mutually exclusive?

7. Suppose that E is an event. Use probability notation to represent
   a. the probability that event E occurs.
   b. the probability that event E occurs is 0.436.

8. Answer true or false to each statement and explain your answers.
   a. For any two events, the probability that one or the other occurs equals the sum of the two individual probabilities.
   b. For any event, the probability that it occurs equals 1 minus the probability that it doesn't occur.

9. Identify one reason why the complementation rule is useful.

10. **Adjusted Gross Incomes.** The U.S. Internal Revenue Service compiles data on income tax returns and summarizes its findings in *Statistics of Income*. The first two columns of Table 5.21 show a frequency distribution (number of returns) for adjusted gross income (AGI) from federal individual income tax returns, where K = thousand.

TABLE 5.21
Adjusted gross incomes

Adjusted gross income	Frequency (1000s)	Event	Probability
Under $10K	28,269	A	
$10K ⩽ 20K	24,568	B	
$20K ⩽ 30K	18,010	C	
$30K ⩽ 40K	12,967	D	
$40K ⩽ 50K	9,788	E	
$50K ⩽ 100K	21,635	F	
$100K & over	7,186	G	
	122,423		

A federal individual income tax return is selected at random.
a. Determine $P(A)$, the probability that the return selected shows an AGI under $10K.

b. Find the probability that the return selected shows an AGI between $30K and $100K (i.e., at least $30K but less than $100K).
c. Compute the probability of each of the seven events in the third column of Table 5.21, and record those probabilities in the fourth column.

11. Adjusted Gross Incomes. Refer to Problem 10. A federal individual income tax return is selected at random. Let

H = event the return shows an AGI between $20K and $100K,

I = event the return shows an AGI of less than $50K,

J = event the return shows an AGI of less than $100K, and

K = event the return shows an AGI of at least $50K.

Describe each of the following events in words and determine the number of outcomes (returns) that comprise each event.
a. (not J)
b. (H & I)
c. (H or K)
d. (H & K)

12. Adjusted Gross Incomes. For the following groups of events from Problem 11, determine which are mutually exclusive.
a. H and I
b. I and K
c. H and (not J)
d. H, (not J), and K

13. Adjusted Gross Incomes. Refer to Problems 10 and 11.
a. Use the second column of Table 5.21 and the f/N rule to compute the probability of each of the events H, I, J, and K.
b. Express each of the events H, I, J, and K in terms of the mutually exclusive events displayed in the third column of Table 5.21.
c. Compute the probability of each of the events H, I, J, and K, using your answers from part (b), the special addition rule, and the fourth column of Table 5.21, which you completed in Problem 10(c).

14. Adjusted Gross Incomes. Consider the events (not J), (H & I), (H or K), and (H & K) discussed in Problem 11.
a. Find the probability of each of those four events, using the f/N rule and your answers from Problem 11.
b. Compute $P(J)$, using the complementation rule and your answer for P (not J) from part (a).
c. In Problem 13(a), you found that $P(H) = 0.510$ and $P(K) = 0.235$; and, in part (a) of this problem, you found that $P(H \& K) = 0.177$. Using those probabilities and the general addition rule, find $P(H$ or $K)$.
d. Compare the answers that you obtained for $P(H$ or $K)$ in parts (a) and (c).

*__15.__ Fill in the blanks.
a. A _____ is a quantitative variable whose value depends on chance.
b. A discrete random variable is a random variable whose possible values form a _____ (or _____) set of numbers.

*__16.__ What does the probability distribution of a discrete random variable tell you?

*__17.__ How do you graphically portray the probability distribution of a discrete random variable?

*__18.__ If you sum the probabilities of the possible values of a discrete random variable, the result always equals _____.

*__19.__ A random variable X equals 2 with probability 0.386.
a. Use probability notation to express that fact.
b. If you make repeated independent observations of the random variable X, in approximately what percentage of those observations will you observe the value 2?
c. Roughly how many times would you expect to observe the value 2 in 50 observations? 500 observations?

*__20.__ A random variable X has mean 3.6. If you make a large number of repeated independent observations of the random variable X, the average value of those observations will be approximately _____.

*__21.__ Two random variables, X and Y, have standard deviations 2.4 and 3.6, respectively. Which one is more likely to take a value close to its mean? Explain your answer.

*__22.__ List the three requirements for repeated trials to constitute Bernoulli trials.

*__23.__ What is the relationship between Bernoulli trials and the binomial distribution?

*24. In 10 Bernoulli trials, how many outcomes contain exactly three successes?

*25. Explain how the special formulas for the mean and standard deviation of a binomial random variable are derived.

*26. Suppose that a simple random sample of size n is taken from a finite population in which the proportion of members having a specified attribute is p. Let X be the number of members sampled that have the specified attribute.
  a. If the sampling is done with replacement, identify the probability distribution of X.
  b. If the sampling is done without replacement, identify the probability distribution of X.
  c. Under what conditions is it acceptable to approximate the probability distribution in part (b) by the probability distribution in part (a)? Why is it acceptable?

*27. **ASU-Main Enrollment.** According to the *Arizona State University Main Facts Book*, a frequency distribution for the number of undergraduate students attending the main campus in the fall of 1998, by class level, is as shown in the following table. Here, 1 = freshman, 2 = sophomore, 3 = junior, and 4 = senior.

Class level	1	2	3	4
No. of students	6,159	6,790	8,141	11,220

Let X denote the class level of a randomly selected ASU undergraduate.
  a. What are the possible values of the random variable X?
  b. Use random-variable notation to represent the event that the student selected is a junior (class-level 3).
  c. Determine $P(X = 3)$ and interpret your answer in terms of percentages.
  d. Determine the probability distribution of the random variable X.
  e. Construct a probability histogram for the random variable X.

*28. **Busy Phone Lines.** An accounting office has six incoming telephone lines. The probability distribution of the number of busy lines, Y, is as follows.

y	$P(Y = y)$
0	0.052
1	0.154
2	0.232
3	0.240
4	0.174
5	0.105
6	0.043

Use random-variable notation to express each of the following events. The number of busy lines is
  a. exactly four.   b. at least four.
  c. between two and four, inclusive.
  d. at least one.
Apply the special addition rule and the probability distribution to determine
  e. $P(Y = 4)$.   f. $P(Y \geq 4)$.
  g. $P(2 \leq Y \leq 4)$.   h. $P(Y \geq 1)$.

*29. **Busy Phone Lines.** Refer to the probability distribution displayed in the table in Problem 28.
  a. Find the mean of the random variable Y.
  b. On average, how many lines are busy?
  c. Compute the standard deviation of Y.
  d. Construct a probability histogram for Y; locate the mean; and show one, two, and three standard deviation intervals.

*30. Determine 0!, 3!, 4!, and 7!.

*31. Determine the value of each binomial coefficient.
  a. $\binom{8}{3}$ b. $\binom{8}{5}$ c. $\binom{6}{6}$ d. $\binom{10}{2}$
  e. $\binom{40}{4}$ f. $\binom{100}{0}$

*32. **DUI Fatalities.** According to *Reader's Digest*, there is a 40% chance that a traffic fatality involves an intoxicated or alcohol-impaired driver or nonoccupant. For brevity, the word *drinker* is used to designate an intoxicated or alcohol-impaired driver or nonoccupant. For a given traffic fatality, regard a success, s, to be that a drinker is involved.
  a. Identify the success probability, p.
  b. Construct a table showing the possible success–failure results and their probabilities for three traffic fatalities.
  c. Draw a tree diagram for part (b).
  d. List the outcomes in which exactly two of the three traffic fatalities involve a drinker.
  e. Determine the probability of each of the outcomes in part (d). Explain why those probabilities are equal.
  f. Find the probability that exactly two of the three traffic fatalities involve a drinker.
  g. Without using the binomial probability formula, obtain the probability distribution of the random variable Y, the number of traffic fatalities of the three that involve a drinker.
  h. Identify the probability distribution in part (g).

*33. **Booming Pet Business.** The pet industry has undergone a surge in recent years, surpassing even the $20 billion a year toy industry. According to *U.S. News & World Report*, 60% of U.S. households live with one or more pets. If four U.S. households are selected at random without replacement, determine the (approximate) probability that the number living with one or more pets will be
  a. exactly three.   b. at least three.
  c. at most three.

d. Find the probability distribution of the random variable X, the number of U.S. households in a random sample of four that live with one or more pets.
e. Without referring to the probability distribution obtained in part (d) or constructing a probability histogram, decide whether the probability distribution is right skewed, symmetric, or left skewed. Explain your answer.
f. Draw a probability histogram for X.
g. Strictly speaking, why is the probability distribution that you obtained in part (d) only approximately correct? What is the exact distribution called?
h. Determine and interpret the mean of the random variable X.
i. Determine the standard deviation of X.

*34. Following are two probability histograms of binomial distributions. For each, specify whether the success probability is less than, equal to, or greater than 0.5.

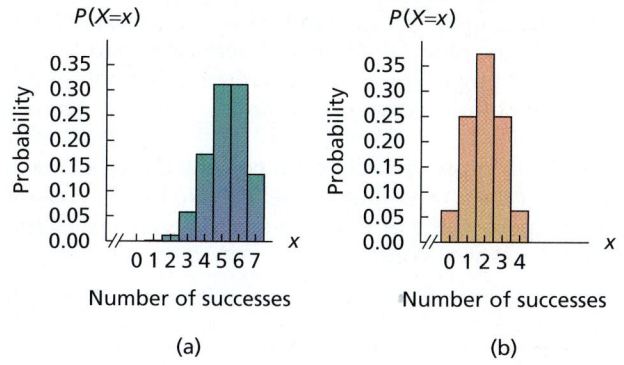

Using Technology

*35. **ASU-Main Enrollment.** Refer to the probability distribution obtained in Problem 27(d).
   a. Use the technology of your choice to simulate 2500 observations of the class level of a randomly selected undergraduate at ASU.
   b. Obtain the proportions for the 2500 class levels simulated in part (a), and compare it to the probability distribution you obtained in Problem 27(d).
   c. Construct a histogram of the proportions and compare it to the probability histogram you obtained in Problem 27(e).
   d. What do parts (b) and (c) illustrate?

*36. **Busy Phone Lines.** Refer to the probability distribution displayed in the table in Problem 28.
   a. Use the technology of your choice to simulate 200 observations of the number of busy lines.
   b. Obtain the mean of the observations in part (a), and compare it to μ, which you determined in Problem 29(a).
   c. What is part (b) illustrating?

*37. **Booming Pet Business.** Use the technology of your choice to obtain the required probability or probabilities in parts (a)–(d) of Problem 33.

 **Internet Project**

The Space Shuttle Challenger

In this Internet project, you are to interactively explore the concepts of probability. The animations and demonstrations can help you understand how these concepts actually work.

On January 20, 1986, the 25th flight of the National Aeronautics and Space Administration's (NASA) space shuttle program took off. Just after liftoff, a puff of gray smoke could be seen coming from the right solid rocket booster. Seventy-three seconds into the flight, the space shuttle Challenger had climbed 10 miles and then exploded into a fireball, killing all aboard.

The cause of the explosion was found to be an O-ring failure in the right solid rocket booster. Cold weather was a contributing factor. In this project, you are to examine the data concerning temperature and its effect on the Challenger's O-rings.

When you studied the theory and concepts of probability in this chapter, you saw that everyday events follow probabilistic rules. The importance of learning how probability works is related to the significance of the events. As you will see in this project, sometimes those events have momentous consequences indeed.

URL for access to Internet Projects Page: www.aw.com/weiss

Focusing on Data Analysis

Sex and Age

Recall from Chapter 1 (see page 34) that the Focus database contains information on 500 randomly selected Arizona State University sophomores. Use the technology of your choice to solve the following problems.

a. Obtain a relative-frequency distribution for the sex data.
b. Using your answer from part (a), determine the probability that a randomly selected sophomore from the sample of 500 is a female.
c. Consider the experiment of selecting a sophomore at random from the sample of 500 and observing the sex of the person obtained. Simulate that experiment 1000 times. (*Hint:* The simulation is equivalent to taking a random sample of size 1000 with replacement.)
d. Referring to the simulation performed in part (c), in approximately what percentage of the 1000 experiments would you expect a female to be selected? Compare that percentage to the actual percentage of the 1000 experiments in which a female was selected.
e. Let X denote the age of a randomly selected sophomore from the sample of 500. Obtain the probability distribution of the random variable X.
f. Obtain a probability histogram or similar graphic for the random variable in part (e).
g. Find the mean and standard deviation of the random variable X defined in part (e).
h. Consider the experiment of randomly selecting 10 sophomores with replacement from the sample of 500 and observing the number of those selected who are 21 years old. Simulate that experiment 2000 times.
i. Referring to the simulation from part (h), in approximately what percentage of the 2000 experiments would you expect exactly 3 of the 10 sophomores selected to be 21 years old? Compare that percentage to the actual percentage of the 2000 experiments in which exactly 3 of the 10 sophomores selected are 21 years old.

case study discussion

The Powerball

At the beginning of this chapter on page 197, we discussed the Powerball lottery and described some of its rules. Recall that, for a single ticket, a player first selects five numbers from the numbers 1–49 and then chooses a Powerball number, which can be any number between 1 and 42. A ticket costs $1. In the drawing, five white balls are drawn randomly from 49 white balls numbered 1–49, and one red Powerball is drawn randomly from 42 red balls numbered 1–42.

To win the jackpot, a ticket must match all the balls drawn. Prizes are also given for matching some but not all the balls drawn. Table 5.22 displays the number of matches, the prizes given, and the probabilities of winning.

TABLE 5.22 Powerball winning combinations, prizes, and probabilities

Matches	Prize	Probability
5 + 1	Jackpot	0.00000001
5	$100,000	0.00000051
4 + 1	$5,000	0.00000275
4	$100	0.00011262
3 + 1	$100	0.00011812
3	$7	0.00484285
2 + 1	$7	0.00165366
1 + 1	$4	0.00847500
0 + 1	$3	0.01355999

Here are some things to note about Table 5.22.

- In the first column, an entry of the form $w+1$ indicates w matches out of the five plus the Powerball; one of the form w indicates w matches out of the five and no Powerball.
- The prize amount for the jackpot depends on how recently it has been won, how many people win it, and choice of jackpot payment.
- Each probability in the third column is given to eight decimal places and can be obtained by using the f/N rule and special counting techniques, as discussed in Section 4.8 of *Introductory Statistics*, 6th edition, by Neil A. Weiss (Boston: Addison-Wesley, 2002).

Let E be an event having probability p. In independent repetitions of the experiment, it takes, on average, $1/p$ times until event E occurs. We apply this fact to the Powerball.

Suppose that you were to purchase one Powerball ticket per week. How long should you expect to wait before winning the jackpot? The third column of Table 5.22 shows that, for the jackpot, $p = 0.00000001$, and therefore we have $1/0.00000001 = 100,000,000$. So, if you purchased one Powerball ticket per week, you should expect to wait approximately 100 million weeks, or roughly 1.92 million years, before winning the jackpot.[3]

a. If you purchase one ticket, what is the probability that you win a prize?
b. If you purchase one ticket, what is the probability that you don't win a prize?
c. If you were to buy one ticket per week, approximately how long should you expect to wait before getting a ticket with exactly three winning numbers and no Powerball?
d. If you were to buy one ticket per week, approximately how long should you expect to wait before winning a prize?

Internet Resources: Visit the Weiss Web site www.aw.com/weiss for additional discussion, exercises, and resources related to this case study.

Biography

Andrei Kolmogorov: Father of Modern Probability Theory

ANDREI NIKOLAEVICH KOLMOGOROV was born on April 25, 1903, in Tambov, Russia. At the age of 17, Kolmogorov entered Moscow State University, from which he graduated in 1925. His contributions to the world of mathematics, many of which appear in his numerous articles and books, encompass a formidable range of subjects.

Kolmogorov revolutionized probability theory with the introduction of the modern axiomatic approach to probability and by proving many of the fundamental theorems that are a consequence of that approach. He also developed two systems of partial differential equations, which bear his name. Those systems extended the development of probability theory and allowed its broader application to the fields of physics, chemistry, biology, and civil engineering.

Kolmogorov became a member of the faculty at Moscow State University in 1925, at the age of 22. In 1931, he was promoted to professor; in 1933, he was appointed a director of the Institute of Mathematics of the university; and in 1937, he became Head of the University.

In addition to his work in higher mathematics, Kolmogorov was interested in the mathematical education of schoolchildren. He was chairman of the Commission for Mathematical Education under the Presidium of the Academy of Sciences of the U.S.S.R. During his tenure as chairman, he was instrumental in the development of a new mathematics training program that was introduced into Soviet schools. Kolmogorov remained on the faculty at Moscow State University until his death in Moscow on October 20, 1987.

---

[3]The probability 0.00000001 for winning the jackpot is approximate. Using a more exact value, we find that you should expect to wait "only" about 1.54 million years before winning the jackpot.

chapter 6

The Normal Distribution

CHAPTER OUTLINE

6.1 Introducing Normally Distributed Variables

6.2 Areas Under the Standard Normal Curve

6.3 Working With Normally Distributed Variables

6.4 Assessing Normality; Normal Probability Plots

GENERAL OBJECTIVES In this chapter, we discuss the most important distribution in statistics—the *normal distribution*. As you will see, its importance lies in the fact that it appears again and again in both theory and practice.

A variable is said to be *normally distributed* or to have a *normal distribution* if its distribution has the shape of a normal curve, a special type of bell-shaped curve. In Section 6.1, we introduce normally distributed variables, show that percentages (or probabilities) for such a variable are equal to areas under its associated normal curve, and explain how all normal distributions can be converted to a single normal distribution—the *standard normal distribution*.

In Section 6.2, we demonstrate how to obtain areas under the *standard normal curve*, the normal curve corresponding to a variable that has the standard normal distribution. Then, in Section 6.3, we provide an efficient procedure for finding percentages (or probabilities) for any normally distributed variable from areas under the standard normal curve. We present a method for graphically assessing whether a variable is normally distributed—*the normal probability plot*—in Section 6.4.

case study

CHEST SIZES OF SCOTTISH MILITIAMEN

In 1817, an article entitled "Statement of the Sizes of Men in Different Counties of Scotland, Taken from the Local Militia" appeared in the *Edinburgh Medical and Surgical Journal* (Vol. 13, pp. 260–264). Included in the article were data on chest circumference for 5732 Scottish militiamen. The data were collected by an army contractor who was responsible for providing clothing for the militia. A frequency distribution for the chest circumferences is given in the following table.

Chest size	Frequency	Chest size	Frequency
33	3	41	935
34	19	42	646
35	81	43	313
36	189	44	168
37	409	45	50
38	753	46	18
39	1062	47	3
40	1082	48	1

In his book *Lettres à S.A.R. le Duc Régnant de Saxe-Cobourg et Gotha sur la théorie des probabilités appliquée aux sciences morales et politiques* (Brussels: Hayez, 1846), Adolphe Quetelet discussed a procedure for fitting a normal curve to the data on chest circumferences. The method he used was based on the binomial distribution. At the end of this chapter, you will be asked to fit a normal curve to the data, using a different technique.

6.1 INTRODUCING NORMALLY DISTRIBUTED VARIABLES

In everyday life, people deal with and use a wide variety of variables, many of which are intrinsically different. But some—such as aptitude-test scores, heights of women, and wheat yield—share an important characteristic: Their distributions have roughly the shape of a **normal curve,** that is, a special type of bell-shaped curve like the one shown in Fig. 6.1. Such a variable is called a **normally distributed variable** and is said to have a **normal distribution.**

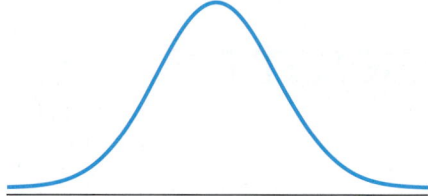

FIGURE 6.1
A normal curve

DEFINITION 6.1 **Normally Distributed Variable**

A variable is said to be a *normally distributed variable* or to have a *normal distribution* if its distribution has the shape of a normal curve.

Here is some important terminology associated with normal distributions.

- If a variable of a population is normally distributed and is the only variable under consideration, common practice is to say that the **population is normally distributed** or that it is a **normally distributed population.**
- In practice, a distribution is unlikely to have exactly the shape of a normal curve. If a variable's distribution is shaped roughly like a normal curve, we say that the variable is an **approximately normally distributed variable** or that it has **approximately a normal distribution.**

A normal distribution (and hence a normal curve) is completely determined by the mean and standard deviation; that is, two normally distributed variables having the same mean and standard deviation must have the same distribution. We often identify a normal curve by stating the corresponding mean and standard deviation and calling those the **parameters** of the normal curve.[1]

A normal distribution is symmetric about and centered at the mean of the variable, and its spread depends on the standard deviation of the variable—the larger the standard deviation, the flatter and more spread out is the distribution. Figure 6.2 displays three normal distributions.

The three standard–deviations rule, when applied to a variable, states that almost all the possible observations of the variable lie within three standard deviations to either side of the mean. This rule is illustrated by the three normal distributions in Fig. 6.2: Each normal curve is close to the horizontal axis outside the range of three standard deviations to either side of the mean.

---

[1]The equation of the normal curve with parameters μ and σ is $y = e^{-(x-\mu)^2/2\sigma^2}/\sqrt{2\pi}\sigma$, where $e \approx 2.718$ and $\pi \approx 3.142$.

FIGURE 6.2
Three normal distributions

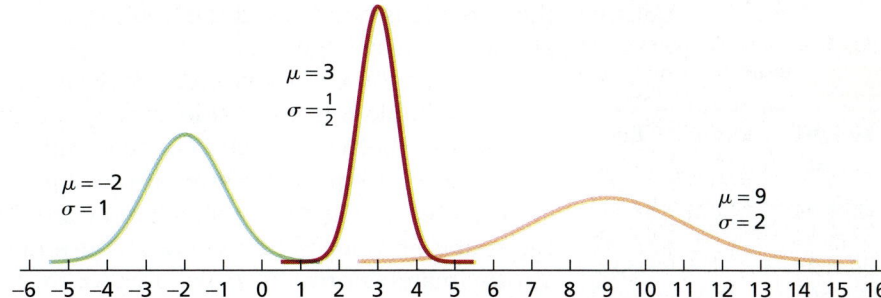

For instance, the third normal distribution in Fig. 6.2 has mean $\mu = 9$ and standard deviation $\sigma = 2$. Three standard deviations below (to the left of) the mean is

$$\mu - 3\sigma = 9 - 3 \cdot 2 = 3,$$

and three standard deviations above (to the right of) the mean is

$$\mu + 3\sigma = 9 + 3 \cdot 2 = 15.$$

As shown in Fig. 6.2, the corresponding normal curve is close to the horizontal axis outside the range from 3 to 15.

In summary, the normal curve associated with a normal distribution is

- bell-shaped,
- centered at μ, and
- close to the horizontal axis outside the range from $\mu - 3\sigma$ to $\mu + 3\sigma$,

as depicted in Figs. 6.2 and 6.3. This information helps us sketch a normal distribution.

FIGURE 6.3
Graph of generic normal distribution

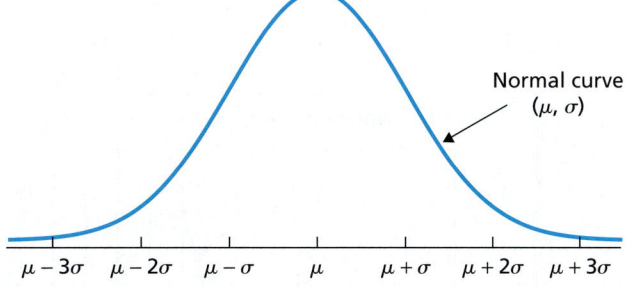

Example 6.1 illustrates a normally distributed variable and discusses some additional properties of such variables.

Example 6.1 *A Normally Distributed Variable*

Heights of Female College Students A midwestern college has an enrollment of 3264 female students. Records show that the mean height of these students is 64.4 inches and that the standard deviation is 2.4 inches. Here

TABLE 6.1 Frequency and relative-frequency distributions for heights

Height (inches)	Freq. f	Rel. freq.
56 – < 57	3	0.0009
57 – < 58	6	0.0018
58 – < 59	26	0.0080
59 – < 60	74	0.0227
60 – < 61	147	0.0450
61 – < 62	247	0.0757
62 – < 63	382	0.1170
63 – < 64	483	0.1480
64 – < 65	559	0.1713
65 – < 66	514	0.1575
66 – < 67	359	0.1100
67 – < 68	240	0.0735
68 – < 69	122	0.0374
69 – < 70	65	0.0199
70 – < 71	24	0.0074
71 – < 72	7	0.0021
72 – < 73	5	0.0015
73 – < 74	1	0.0003
	3264	1.0000

the variable is height, and the population consists of the 3264 female students attending the college.

Frequency and relative-frequency distributions for these heights are presented in Table 6.1. The table shows, for instance, that 7.35% (0.0735) of the students are between 67 and 68 inches tall.

A relative-frequency histogram for the heights of the 3264 female students is presented in Fig. 6.4. It shows that the distribution of heights has roughly the shape of a normal curve and, consequently, that the variable "height" is approximately normally distributed for this population. The associated normal curve, the one with parameters $\mu = 64.4$ and $\sigma = 2.4$, is superimposed on the histogram in Fig. 6.4.

Figure 6.4 illustrates another important point—namely, that the percentage of female students whose heights lie within any specified range can be approximated by the corresponding area under the normal curve. For instance, consider the percentage of female students who are between 67 and 68 inches tall. According to Table 6.1, the exact percentage is 7.35% (0.0735). Note that 0.0735 also equals the area of the cross-hatched bar in Fig. 6.4 because the bar has height 0.0735 and width 1.

Now look at the area under the normal curve between 67 and 68, the area shaded in Fig. 6.4. This area approximates the area of the cross-hatched bar which, as we have noted, equals the percentage of students who are between 67 and 68 inches tall. Thus we can approximate the percentage of students who are between 67 and 68 inches tall by the area under the normal curve between 67 and 68.

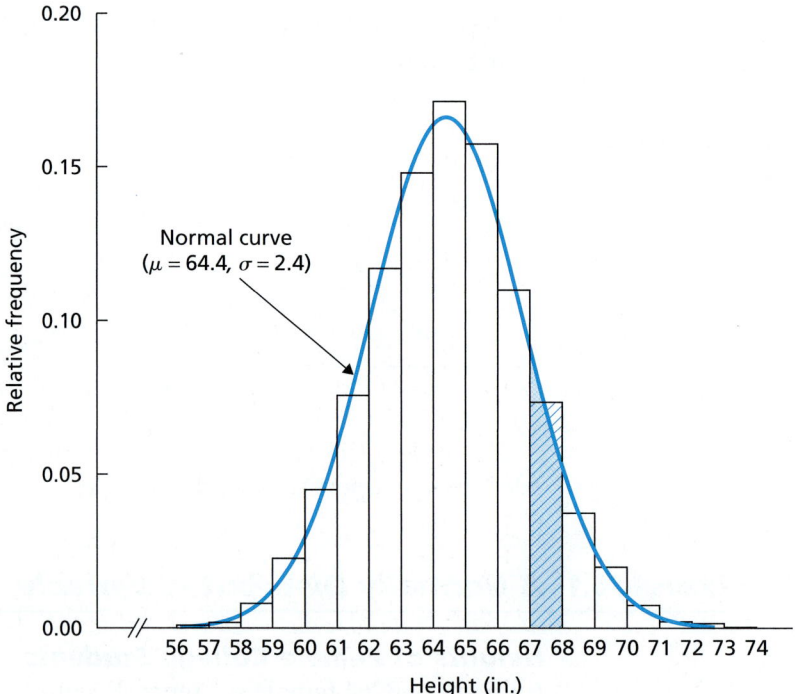

FIGURE 6.4 Relative-frequency histogram for heights with superimposed normal curve

In Key Fact 6.1, we summarize the important relationship established in Example 6.1 between percentages for a normally distributed variable and areas under its associated normal curve.

> **Key Fact 6.1** **Normally Distributed Variables and Normal-Curve Areas**
>
> For a normally distributed variable, the percentage of all possible observations that lie within any specified range equals the corresponding area under its associated normal curve, expressed as a percentage. This result holds approximately for a variable that is approximately normally distributed.

Note: For brevity, we often paraphrase the content of Key Fact 6.1 with the statement "percentages for a normally distributed variable are equal to areas under its associated normal curve."

STANDARDIZING A NORMALLY DISTRIBUTED VARIABLE

Let's summarize two essential facts about normally distributed variables and their associated normal curves.

- Once we know the mean and standard deviation of a normally distributed variable, we know its distribution and associated normal curve.
- Percentages for a normally distributed variable are equal to areas under its associated normal curve.

Consequently, once we know the mean and standard deviation of a normally distributed variable, we can obtain the percentage of all possible observations that lie within any specified range by determining the corresponding area under its associated normal curve. Now the question is: How do we find areas under a normal curve?

Conceptually, we need a table of areas for each normal curve. This, of course, is not possible because there are infinitely many different normal curves—one for each choice of μ and σ. The way out of this difficulty is standardizing, which transforms every normal distribution into one particular normal distribution, the **standard normal distribution**.

> **DEFINITION 6.2** **Standard Normal Distribution; Standard Normal Curve**
>
> A normally distributed variable having mean 0 and standard deviation 1 is said to have the *standard normal distribution*. Its associated normal curve is called the *standard normal curve*, which is shown in Fig. 6.5.

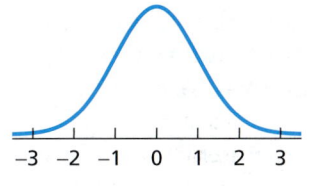

FIGURE 6.5 Standard normal distribution

Recall that we standardize a variable x by subtracting its mean and then dividing by its standard deviation. The resulting variable, $z = (x - \mu)/\sigma$, is called the *standardized version* of x or the *standardized variable* corresponding to x.

As you learned in Chapter 3, the standardized version of any variable has mean 0 and standard deviation 1. For a normally distributed variable, we can say even more: If a variable is normally distributed, then so is its standardized version. In other words, we have the following essential fact.

Key Fact 6.2 Standardized Normally Distributed Variable

The standardized version of a normally distributed variable x,

$$z = \frac{x - \mu}{\sigma},$$

has the standard normal distribution.

We can interpret Key Fact 6.2 in several ways. Theoretically, it says that standardizing converts all normal distributions to the standard normal distribution, as depicted in Fig. 6.6.

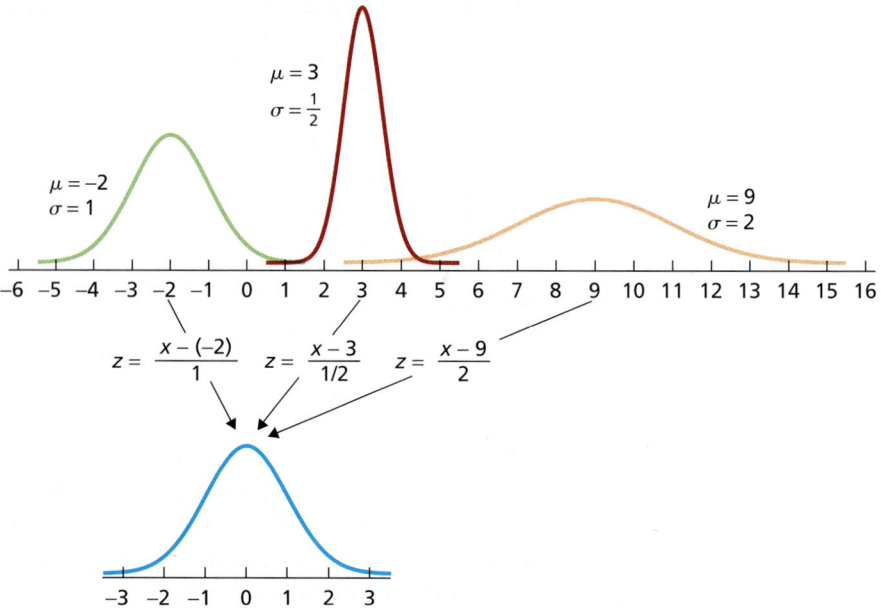

FIGURE 6.6
Standardizing normal distributions

But we need a more practical interpretation of Key Fact 6.2. Let x be a normally distributed variable and let a and b be real numbers with $a < b$. The percentage of all possible observations of x that lie between a and b is the same as the percentage of all possible observations of z that lie between $(a - \mu)/\sigma$ and $(b - \mu)/\sigma$. And, in light of Key Fact 6.2, this latter percentage equals the area under the standard normal curve between $(a - \mu)/\sigma$ and $(b - \mu)/\sigma$. We summarize these ideas graphically in Fig. 6.7.

Consequently, for a normally distributed variable, we can find the percentage of all possible observations that lie within any specified range by

1. expressing the range in terms of z-scores, and
2. obtaining the corresponding area under the standard normal curve.

FIGURE 6.7
Finding percentages for a normally distributed variable from areas under the standard normal curve

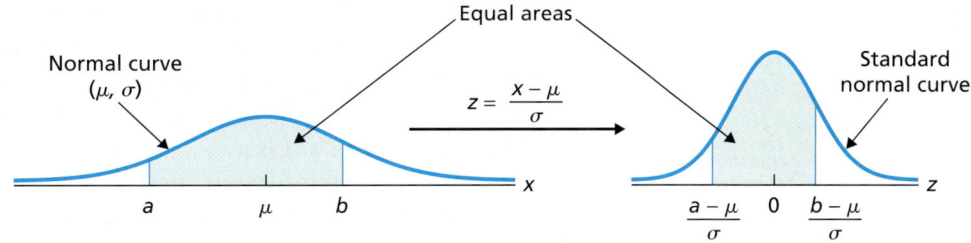

You already know how to convert to z-scores. Therefore you need only learn how to find areas under the standard normal curve, which we demonstrate in Section 6.2.

SIMULATING A NORMAL DISTRIBUTION

Both for purposes of understanding and research, simulating a variable is often useful. Doing so involves use of a computer or statistical calculator to generate observations of the variable. In Example 6.2, we conduct and interpret a simulation of a normally distributed variable.

Example 6.2 Simulating a Normally Distributed Variable

Gestation Periods of Humans Gestation periods of humans are normally distributed with a mean of 266 days and a standard deviation of 16 days. Simulate 1000 human gestation periods, obtain a histogram of the simulated data, and interpret the results.

Solution Here the variable x is gestation period and, for humans, it is normally distributed with mean $\mu = 266$ days and standard deviation $\sigma = 16$ days. We used a computer to simulate 1000 observations of the variable x for humans. A histogram for those observations is shown in Printout 6.1. For purposes of comparison, we have superimposed the normal curve associated with the variable—namely, the normal curve with parameters $\mu = 266$ and $\sigma = 16$.

PRINTOUT 6.1
Histogram of 1000 simulated human gestation periods with superimposed normal curve

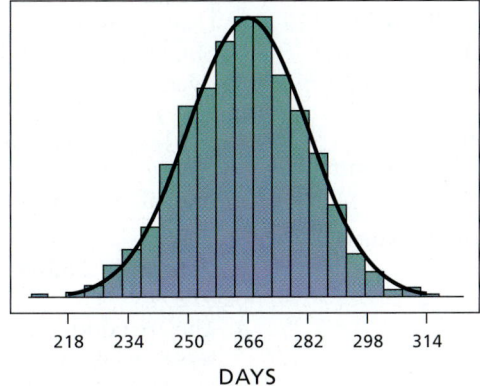

As expected, the histogram in Printout 6.1 is shaped roughly like the normal curve associated with the variable. Because we have only sample data here, we would not expect the histogram to be shaped exactly like the normal curve. But, because the sample size is large, we would expect the histogram to be close to that shape, which it is.

If you do the simulation, you will (almost) certainly obtain different results than those depicted in Printout 6.1. However, your results should be similar.

The Technology Center

Most statistical software packages and some graphing calculators have built-in procedures to simulate observations of normally distributed variables. In Example 6.2, we used Minitab but, for instance, Excel can also be used to conduct that simulation and obtain the histogram. Refer to the technology manuals for details.

Exercises 6.1

Statistical Concepts and Skills

6.1 A variable is approximately normally distributed. If you draw a histogram of the distribution of the variable, roughly what shape will it have?

6.2 Precisely what is meant by the statement that a population is normally distributed?

6.3 Two normally distributed variables have the same means and the same standard deviations. What can you say about their distributions? Explain your answer.

6.4 Which normal distribution has a wider spread: the one with mean 1 and standard deviation 2 or the one with mean 2 and standard deviation 1? Explain your answer.

6.5 Consider two normal distributions, one with mean -4 and standard deviation 3 and the other with mean 6 and standard deviation 3. Answer true or false to each statement and explain your answers.
a. The two normal distributions have the same shape.
b. The two normal distributions are centered at the same place.

6.6 True or false: The mean of a normal distribution has no effect on its shape. Explain your answer.

6.7 What are the parameters for a normal curve?

6.8 Sketch the normal distribution with
a. $\mu = 3$ and $\sigma = 3$.   b. $\mu = 1$ and $\sigma = 3$.
c. $\mu = 3$ and $\sigma = 1$.

6.9 For a normally distributed variable, what is the relationship between the percentage of all possible observations that lie between 2 and 3 and the area under the associated normal curve between 2 and 3? What if the variable is only approximately normally distributed?

6.10 The area under a particular normal curve between 10 and 15 is 0.6874. A normally distributed variable has the same mean and standard deviation as the parameters for this normal curve. What percentage of all possible observations of the variable lie between 10 and 15? Explain your answer.

6.11 Female College Students. Refer to Example 6.1 on page 259.
a. Use the relative-frequency distribution in Table 6.1 to obtain the percentage of female students who are between 60 and 65 inches tall.
b. Use your answer from part (a) to estimate the area under the normal curve having parameters $\mu = 64.4$ and $\sigma = 2.4$ that lies between 60 and 65. Why do you get only an estimate of the true area?

6.12 Female College Students. Refer to Example 6.1 on page 259.
a. The area under the standard normal curve with parameters $\mu = 64.4$ and $\sigma = 2.4$ that lies to the left of 61 is 0.0783. Use this information to estimate the percentage of female students who are shorter than 61 inches.

b. Use the relative-frequency distribution in Table 6.1 to obtain the exact percentage of female students who are shorter than 61 inches.
c. Compare your answers from parts (a) and (b).

6.13 New York City 10 km Run. As reported in *Runner's World* magazine, the times of the finishers in the New York City 10 km run are normally distributed with a mean of 61 minutes and a standard deviation of 9 minutes. Let x denote finishing time for the finishers.
a. Sketch the distribution of the variable x.
b. Obtain the standardized version, z, of x.
c. Identify and sketch the distribution of z.
d. The percentage of finishers with times between 50 and 70 minutes is equal to the area under the standard normal curve between ____ and ____.
e. The percentage of finishers with times exceeding 75 minutes is equal to the area under the standard normal curve that lies to the ____ of ____.

6.14 Polychaete Worms. *Opisthotrochopodus n. sp.* is a polychaete worm that inhabits deep sea hydrothermal vents along the Mid-Atlantic Ridge. According to an article by Van Dover et al. in *Marine Ecology Progress Series* (1999, Vol. 181, pp. 201–214), the lengths of female polychaete worms are normally distributed with mean 6.1 mm and standard deviation 1.3 mm. Let x denote length for female polychaete worms.
a. Sketch the distribution of the variable x.
b. Obtain the standardized version, z, of x.
c. Identify and sketch the distribution of z.
d. The percentage of female polychaete worms that have lengths between 7 inches and 8 inches is equal to the area under the standard normal curve between ____ and ____.
e. The percentage of female polychaete worms that have lengths less than 3 inches is equal to the area under the standard normal curve that lies to the ____ of ____.

Extending the Concepts and Skills

6.15 Chips Ahoy! 1,000 Chips Challenge. Students in an introductory statistics course at the U.S. Air Force Academy participated in Nabisco's "Chips Ahoy! 1,000 Chips Challenge" by confirming that there were at least 1000 chips in every 18-ounce bag of cookies that they examined. As part of their assignment, they concluded that the number of chips per bag is approximately normally distributed. Could the number of chips per bag be exactly normally distributed? Explain your answer. [SOURCE: Brad Warner and Jim Rutledge, "Checking the Chips Ahoy! Guarantee," *Chance*, 1999, Vol. 12(1), pp. 10–14]

6.16 Use the footnote on page 258 to write the equation of
a. the associated normal curve for a normally distributed variable with mean 5 and standard deviation 2.
b. the standard normal curve.

Using Technology

6.17 Using any technology available to you, graph the normal distribution with mean 5 and standard deviation 2.

6.18 Gestation Periods of Humans. Refer to the simulation of human gestation periods discussed in Example 6.2 on page 263.
a. Sketch the normal curve for human gestation periods.
b. Simulate 1000 human gestation periods. (*Note:* Users of the TI-83 Plus should simulate 500 human gestation periods.)
c. Approximately what values would you expect for the sample mean and sample standard deviation of the 1000 observations? Explain your answers.
d. Obtain the sample mean and sample standard deviation of the 1000 observations and compare your answers to your estimates in part (c).
e. Roughly what would you expect a histogram of the 1000 observations to look like? Explain your answer.
f. Obtain a histogram of the 1000 observations and compare your result to your expectation in part (e).

6.2 AREAS UNDER THE STANDARD NORMAL CURVE

In Section 6.1, we introduced normally distributed variables. There we demonstrated, among other things, that we can obtain the percentage of all possible observations of a normally distributed variable that lie within any specified range by (1) expressing the range in terms of z-scores and (2) determining the corresponding area under the standard normal curve.

You already know how to convert to z-scores. Now, in this section, you will discover how to implement the second step—determining areas under the standard normal curve.

BASIC PROPERTIES OF THE STANDARD NORMAL CURVE

Before we show how to find areas under the standard normal curve, we need to discuss some of the basic properties of the standard normal curve. Recall that the standard normal curve is the curve associated with the standard normal distribution, that is, the normal distribution having mean 0 and standard deviation 1. Figure 6.8 again depicts the standard normal distribution and the standard normal curve.

In Section 6.1, we showed that a normal curve is bell-shaped, is centered at μ, and is close to the horizontal axis outside the range from $\mu - 3\sigma$ to $\mu + 3\sigma$. Applied to the standard normal curve, these characteristics mean that it is bell-shaped, is centered at 0, and is close to the horizontal axis outside the range from -3 to 3. Thus the standard normal curve is symmetric about 0. All of these properties are reflected in Fig. 6.8.

One property of the standard normal curve that is not obvious from Fig. 6.8 is that the total area under the curve is 1. This property is not unique to the standard normal curve; in fact, the total area under any curve that represents the distribution of a variable is equal to 1. Key Fact 6.3 summarizes our discussion about the properties of the standard normal curve.

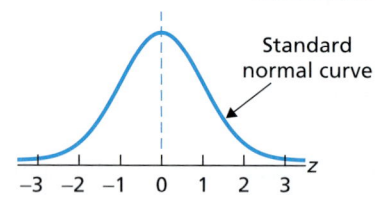

FIGURE 6.8
Standard normal distribution and standard normal curve

Key Fact 6.3 — Basic Properties of the Standard Normal Curve

Property 1: The total area under the standard normal curve is 1.

Property 2: The standard normal curve extends indefinitely in both directions, approaching, but never touching, the horizontal axis as it does so.

Property 3: The standard normal curve is symmetric about 0; that is, the part of the curve to the left of the dashed line in Fig. 6.8 is the mirror image of the part of the curve to the right of it.

Property 4: Almost all the area under the standard normal curve lies between -3 and 3.

Because the standard normal curve is the associated normal curve for a standardized normally distributed variable, we labeled the horizontal axis in Fig. 6.8 with the letter z and refer to numbers on that axis as z-scores. For these reasons, the standard normal curve is sometimes called the **z-curve**.

USING THE STANDARD NORMAL TABLE (TABLE II)

Because of the importance of areas under the standard normal curve, tables of those areas have been constructed. Such a table is Table II, which can be found inside the front cover of this book and in Appendix A.

A typical four decimal–place number in the body of Table II gives the area under the standard normal curve that lies to the left of a specified z-score. The left page of Table II is for negative z-scores and the right page is for positive z-scores. In Example 6.3, we show how to find the area to the left of a z-score.

Example 6.3 Finding the Area to the Left of a Specified z-Score

Determine the area under the standard normal curve that lies to the left of 1.23, as shown in Fig. 6.9(a).

FIGURE 6.9
Finding the area under the standard normal curve to the left of 1.23

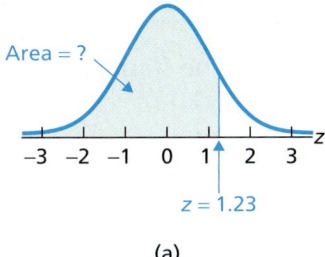
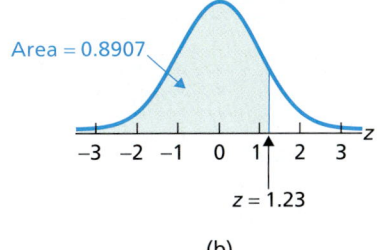

Solution We use Table II, specifically the portion on the right page because 1.23 is positive. First, we go down the left-hand column, labeled z, to "1.2." Then, we go across that row to "0.03" in the top row. The number in the body of the table there, 0.8907, is the area under the standard normal curve that lies to the left of 1.23, as shown in Fig. 6.9(b). ◆

Finding the area under the standard normal curve that lies to the left of a specified z-score is one important use of Table II. Two other important uses of that table are finding the area to the right of a specified z-score and finding the area between two specified z-scores. We illustrate these two uses in Examples 6.4 and 6.5, respectively.

Example 6.4 Finding the Area to the Right of a Specified z-Score

Determine the area under the standard normal curve that lies to the right of 0.76, as shown in Fig. 6.10(a).

FIGURE 6.10
Finding the area under the standard normal curve to the right of 0.76

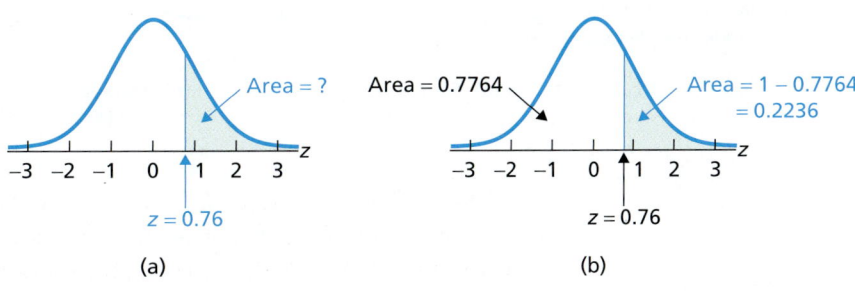

Solution Because the total area under the standard normal curve is 1 (Property 1 of Key Fact 6.3), the area to the right of 0.76 equals 1 minus the area to the left of 0.76. This latter area can be found in Table II, as explained in Example 6.3.

First, we go down the left-hand column, labeled z, to "0.7." Then, we go across that row to "0.06" in the top row. The number in the body of the table there, 0.7764, is the area under the standard normal curve that lies to the left of 0.76. Consequently, the area under the standard normal curve that lies to the right of 0.76 is $1 - 0.7764 = 0.2236$, as shown in Fig. 6.10(b). ◆

Example 6.5 Finding the Area Between Two Specified z-Scores

Determine the area under the standard normal curve that lies between -0.68 and 1.82, as shown in Fig. 6.11(a).

FIGURE 6.11
Finding the area under the standard normal curve that lies between -0.68 and 1.82

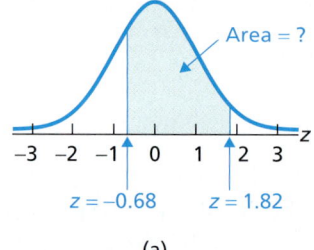
(a)

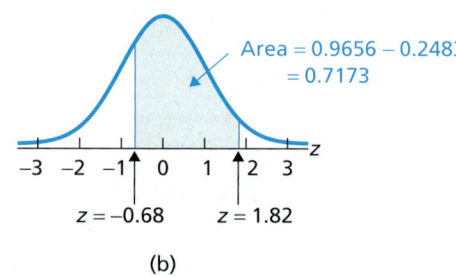
(b)

Solution The area under the standard normal curve that lies between -0.68 and 1.82 equals the area to the left of 1.82 minus the area to the left of -0.68. Table II shows that the area to the left of 1.82 is 0.9656 and that the area to the left of -0.68 is 0.2483. So the area under the standard normal curve that lies between -0.68 and 1.82 is $0.9656 - 0.2483 = 0.7173$, as depicted in Fig. 6.11(b). ◆

The discussion presented in Examples 6.3–6.5 is summarized by the three graphs in Fig. 6.12. Each graph shows how Table II, which gives areas to the left of a specified z-score, can be used to obtain a required area.

FIGURE 6.12
Using Table II to find the area under the standard normal curve that lies (a) to the left of a specified z-score, (b) to the right of a specified z-score, and (c) between two specified z-scores

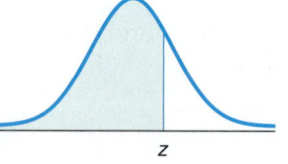

(a) Shaded area:
Area to left of z

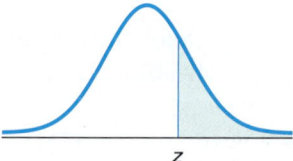

(b) Shaded area:
$1 -$ (Area to left of z)

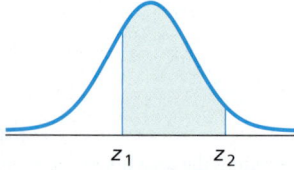

(c) Shaded area:
(Area to left of z_2)
$-$ (Area to left of z_1)

Obtaining the area to the left of a specified z-score requires one table look-up, as shown in Fig. 6.12(a). Obtaining the area to the right of a specified z-score requires one table look-up and one subtraction (from 1), as shown in Fig. 6.12(b).

Obtaining the area between two specified z-scores requires two table look-ups and one subtraction, as shown in Fig. 6.12(c).

A NOTE CONCERNING TABLE II

The first area given in Table II is for $z = -3.90$. According to the table, the area under the standard normal curve that lies to the left of -3.90 is 0.0000. This entry does not mean that the area under the standard normal curve that lies to the left of -3.90 is exactly 0, but only that it is 0 to four decimal places (the area is 0.0000481 to seven decimal places). Indeed, as the standard normal curve extends indefinitely to the left without ever touching the axis, the area to the left of any z-score is greater than 0.

The last area given in Table II is for $z = 3.90$. According to the table, the area under the standard normal curve that lies to the left of 3.90 is 1.0000. This entry does not mean that the area under the standard normal curve that lies to the left of 3.90 is exactly 1, but only that it is 1 to four decimal places (the area is 0.9999519 to seven decimal places). Indeed, as the total area under the standard normal curve is exactly 1 and the curve extends indefinitely to the right without ever touching the axis, the area to the left of any z-score is less than 1.

FINDING THE z-SCORE FOR A SPECIFIED AREA

So far, we have used Table II to find areas under the standard normal curve to the left of a specified z-score, to the right of a specified z-score, and between two specified z-scores. Now, in Example 6.6, we show how to use Table II to find the z-score(s) corresponding to a specified area under the standard normal curve.

Example 6.6 Finding the z-Score Having a Specified Area to Its Left

Determine the z-score having an area of 0.04 to its left under the standard normal curve, as depicted in Fig. 6.13(a).

FIGURE 6.13
Finding the z-score having an area of 0.04 to its left

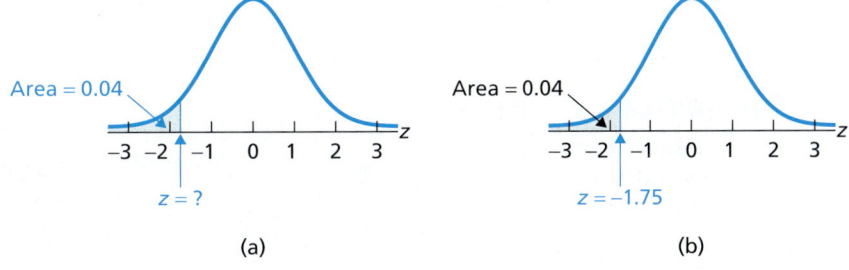

Solution We use Table II to obtain the z-score corresponding to the area 0.04. For ease of reference, we have reproduced a portion of Table II as Table 6.2.

TABLE 6.2
Areas under the standard normal curve

	Second decimal place in z									
0.09	0.08	0.07	0.06	0.05	0.04	0.03	0.02	0.01	0.00	z
.	.	.	.	.	.	.	.	.	.	.
.	.	.	.	.	.	.	.	.	.	.
.	.	.	.	.	.	.	.	.	.	.
0.0233	0.0239	0.0244	0.0250	0.0256	0.0262	0.0268	0.0274	0.0281	0.0287	−1.9
0.0294	0.0301	0.0307	0.0314	0.0322	0.0329	0.0336	0.0344	0.0351	0.0359	−1.8
0.0367	0.0375	0.0384	0.0392	0.0401	0.0409	0.0418	0.0427	0.0436	0.0446	−1.7
0.0455	0.0465	0.0475	0.0485	0.0495	0.0505	0.0516	0.0526	0.0537	0.0548	−1.6
0.0559	0.0571	0.0582	0.0594	0.0606	0.0618	0.0630	0.0643	0.0655	0.0668	−1.5
.	.	.	.	.	.	.	.	.	.	.
.	.	.	.	.	.	.	.	.	.	.
.	.	.	.	.	.	.	.	.	.	.

We search the body of Table 6.2 (or Table II) for the area 0.04. Because we find no such area, we use the area closest to 0.04, which is 0.0401. As we see from Table 6.2, the z-score corresponding to that area is −1.75. Figure 6.13(b) summarizes our results. ◆

In Example 6.6, we were to determine the z-score having an area of 0.04 to its left. Because we were unable to find an area entry of 0.04 in Table II, we selected the area closest to 0.04 and took the z-score corresponding to that area as an approximation of the required z-score.

This approach illustrates what we do in the most typical case: When no area entry in Table II equals the one desired, but there is one area entry closest to the one desired, we take the z-score corresponding to the closest area entry as an approximation of the required z-score.

Two other cases are possible. One is when an area entry in Table II equals the one desired; nothing more need be done. The other is when no area entry in Table II equals the one desired, but two area entries are equally closest to the one desired; in this case, we take the mean of the two corresponding z-scores as an approximation of the required z-score. Both of these cases are illustrated in Example 6.7, which we present momentarily.

Finding the z-score having a specified area to its right is often necessary. We have to make this determination so frequently that a special notation, z_α, is required.

DEFINITION 6.3

FIGURE 6.14
The z_α notation

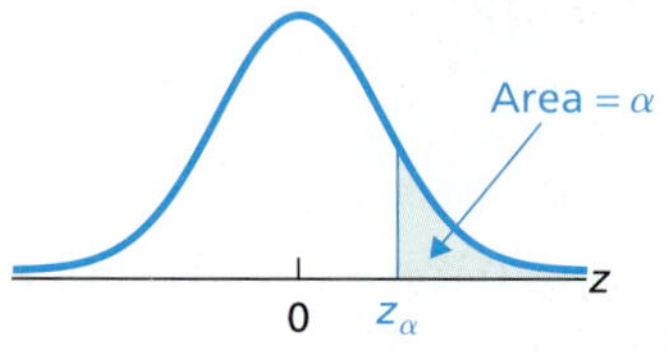

The z_α Notation

The symbol z_α is used to denote the z-score having an area of α (alpha) to its right under the standard normal curve, as illustrated in Fig. 6.14. Read "z_α" as "z sub α" or more simply as "z α."

Example 6.7 Finding z_α

Use Table II to find
a. $z_{0.025}$.   **b.** $z_{0.05}$.

Solution **a.** $z_{0.025}$ is the z-score having an area of 0.025 to its right under the standard normal curve, as shown in Fig. 6.15(a).

FIGURE 6.15
Finding $z_{0.025}$

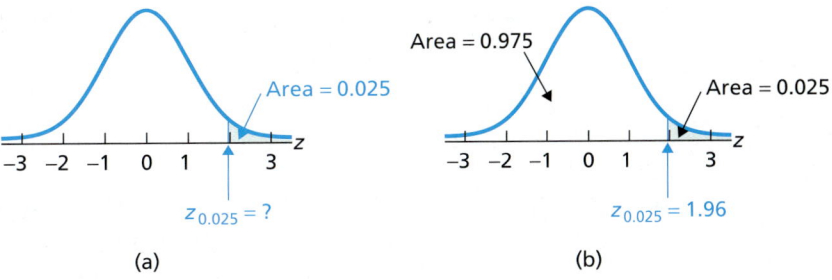

(a) (b)

Because the area under the standard normal curve to the right of $z_{0.025}$ is 0.025, the area to its left is $1 - 0.025 = 0.975$, as shown in Fig. 6.15(b). We search the body of Table II for the area 0.975 and find that entry. Its corresponding z-score is 1.96. Thus, $z_{0.025} = 1.96$, as shown in Fig. 6.15(b).

b. $z_{0.05}$ is the z-score having an area of 0.05 to its right under the standard normal curve, as shown in Fig. 6.16(a).

FIGURE 6.16
Finding $z_{0.05}$

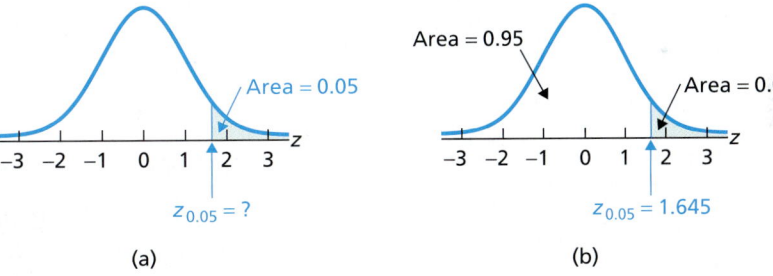

(a) (b)

Because the area under the standard normal curve to the right of $z_{0.05}$ is 0.05, the area to its left is $1 - 0.05 = 0.95$, as shown in Fig. 6.16(b). We search the body of Table II for the area 0.95 but find no such area. Instead, we find two areas are equally closest to 0.95—namely, 0.9495 and 0.9505. The z-scores corresponding to those two areas are 1.64 and 1.65, respectively. So our approximation of $z_{0.05}$ is the z-score halfway between 1.64 and 1.65; that is, $z_{0.05} = 1.645$, as shown in Fig. 6.16(b). ◆

In Example 6.8, we show how to find the two z-scores that divide the area under the standard normal curve into a specified middle area and two outside areas.

Example 6.8 Finding the z-Scores for a Specified Area

Find the two z-scores that divide the area under the standard normal curve into a middle 0.95 area and two outside 0.025 areas, as depicted in Fig. 6.17(a).

FIGURE 6.17
Finding the two z-scores that divide the area under the standard normal curve into a middle 0.95 area and two outside 0.025 areas

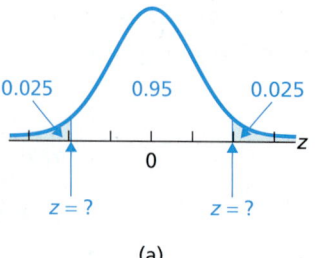
(a)

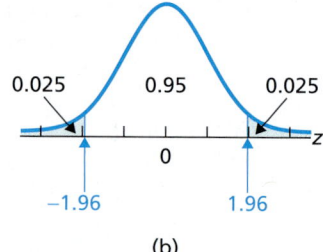
(b)

Solution In Fig. 6.17(a), the area of the shaded region on the right is 0.025, which means that the z-score on the right is $z_{0.025}$. In Example 6.7(a), we found that $z_{0.025} = 1.96$. Thus the z-score on the right is 1.96. The standard normal curve is symmetric about 0, so the z-score on the left is -1.96. Therefore the two required z-scores are ± 1.96, as shown in Fig. 6.17(b). ◆

Note: We could also solve Example 6.8 by first using Table II to find the z-score on the left in Fig. 6.17(a), which is -1.96, and then applying the symmetry property to obtain the z-score on the right, which is 1.96. Can you think of a third way to solve the problem?

Exercises 6.2

Statistical Concepts and Skills

6.19 Explain why being able to obtain areas under the standard normal curve is important.

6.20 With which normal distribution is the standard normal curve associated?

6.21 Without consulting Table II, explain why the area under the standard normal curve that lies to the right of 0 is 0.5.

6.22 According to Table II, the area under the standard normal curve that lies to the left of -2.08 is 0.0188. Without further consulting Table II, determine the area under the standard normal curve that lies to the right of 2.08. Explain your reasoning.

6.23 According to Table II, the area under the standard normal curve that lies to the left of 0.43 is 0.6664. Without further consulting Table II, determine the area under the standard normal curve that lies to the right of 0.43. Explain your reasoning.

6.24 According to Table II, the area under the standard normal curve that lies to the left of 1.96 is 0.975. Without further consulting Table II, determine the area under the standard normal curve that lies to the left of -1.96. Explain your reasoning.

6.25 Property 4 of Key Fact 6.3 states that most of the area under the standard normal curve lies between -3 and 3. Use Table II to determine precisely the percentage of the area under the standard normal curve that lies between -3 and 3.

6.26 Why is the standard normal curve sometimes referred to as the z-curve?

6.27 Explain how Table II is used to determine the area under the standard normal curve that lies
a. to the left of a specified z-score.
b. to the right of a specified z-score.
c. between two specified z-scores.

6.28 The area under the standard normal curve that lies to the left of a z-score is always strictly between _____ and _____.

Use Table II to obtain the areas under the standard normal curve required in Exercises 6.29–6.32. Sketch a standard normal curve and shade the area of interest in each problem.

6.29 Determine the area under the standard normal curve that lies to the left of
a. 2.24.   b. −1.56.   c. 0.   d. −4.

6.30 Find the area under the standard normal curve that lies to the right of
a. −1.07.   b. 0.6.   c. 0.   d. 4.2.

6.31 Determine the area under the standard normal curve that lies between
a. −2.18 and 1.44.   b. −2 and −1.5.
c. 0.59 and 1.51.   d. 1.1 and 4.2.

6.32 Find the area under the standard normal curve that lies
a. either to the left of −2.12 or to the right of 1.67.
b. either to the left of 0.63 or to the right of 1.54.

6.33 Use Table II to obtain each shaded area under the standard normal curve.

a.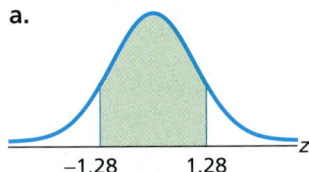
b.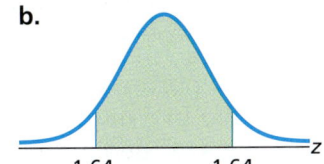
c.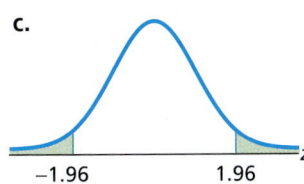
d.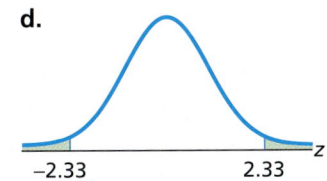

6.34 In each part, find the area under the standard normal curve that lies between the specified z-scores, sketch a standard normal curve, and shade the area of interest.
a. −1 and 1   b. −2 and 2   c. −3 and 3

6.35 The total area under the following standard normal curve is divided into eight regions.

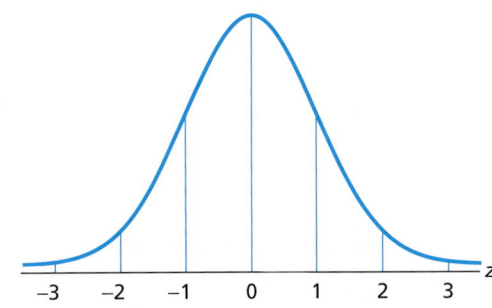

a. Determine the area of each region.
b. Complete the following table.

Region	Area	Percentage of total area
−∞ to −3	0.0013	0.13
−3 to −2		
−2 to −1		
−1 to 0		
0 to 1	0.3413	34.13
1 to 2		
2 to 3		
3 to ∞		
	1.0000	100.00

In Exercises 6.36–6.42, use Table II to obtain the required z-scores. Illustrate your work with graphs.

6.36 Obtain the z-score for which the area under the standard normal curve to its left is 0.025.

6.37 Find the z-score that has an area of 0.75 to its left under the standard normal curve.

6.38 Obtain the z-score that has an area of 0.95 to its right.

6.39 Determine $z_{0.33}$.

6.40 Find the following z-scores.
a. $z_{0.03}$ b. $z_{0.005}$

6.41 Determine the two z-scores that divide the area under the standard normal curve into a middle 0.90 area and two outside 0.05 areas.

6.42 Complete the following table.

$z_{0.10}$	$z_{0.05}$	$z_{0.025}$	$z_{0.01}$	$z_{0.005}$
1.28				

Extending the Concepts and Skills

6.43 In this section, we mentioned that the total area under any curve representing the distribution of a variable equals 1. Explain why.

6.44 Let $0 < \alpha < 1$. Determine the

a. z-score having an area of α to its right in terms of z_α.
b. z-score having an area of α to its left in terms of z_α.
c. two z-scores that divide the area under the curve into a middle $1 - \alpha$ area and two outside areas of $\alpha/2$.
d. Draw graphs to illustrate your results in parts (a)–(c).

6.3 WORKING WITH NORMALLY DISTRIBUTED VARIABLES

You have now learned everything required to obtain the percentage of all possible observations of a normally distributed variable that lie within any specified range. To do so, first express the range in terms of z-scores and then determine the corresponding area under the standard normal curve. More formally, use Procedure 6.1.

> **Procedure 6.1**
>
> **To Determine a Percentage or Probability for a Normally Distributed Variable**
>
> **Step 1** Sketch the normal curve associated with the variable.
>
> **Step 2** Shade the region of interest and mark the delimiting x-values.
>
> **Step 3** Compute the z-scores for the delimiting x-values found in Step 2.
>
> **Step 4** Use Table II to obtain the area under the standard normal curve delimited by the z-scores found in Step 3.

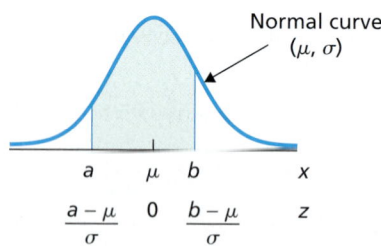

FIGURE 6.18
Graphical portrayal of Procedure 6.1

The steps in Procedure 6.1 are portrayed graphically in Fig. 6.18, with the specified range lying between the two numbers a and b. When the specified range is to the left (or right) of a specified number, it is represented similarly. However, there will be only one x-value, and the shaded region will be the area under the normal curve that lies to the left (or right) of that x-value.

Note: When computing z-scores in Step 3 of Procedure 6.1, round to two decimal places because that is the precision provided in Table II.

Procedure 6.1 applies to probabilities as well as to percentages. In other words, if a member of a population is selected at random, the probability that the observed value of a variable will lie within any specified range equals the percentage of all possible observations of the variable lying within that range. In Example 6.9, we apply Procedure 6.1 to obtain a percentage result.

Example 6.9 *Percentages for a Normally Distributed Variable*

Intelligence Quotients Intelligence quotients (IQs) measured on the Stanford Revision of the Binet–Simon Intelligence Scale are normally distributed with a mean of 100 and a standard deviation of 16. Obtain the percentage of people who have IQs between 115 and 140.

Solution Here the variable is IQ, and the population consists of all people. Because IQs are normally distributed, we can determine the required percentage by applying Procedure 6.1.

Step 1 Sketch the normal curve associated with the variable.

Here $\mu = 100$ and $\sigma = 16$. The normal curve associated with the variable is presented in Fig. 6.19. Note that the tick marks are 16 units apart; that is, the distance between successive tick marks is equal to the standard deviation.

FIGURE 6.19
Determination of the percentage of people having IQs between 115 and 140

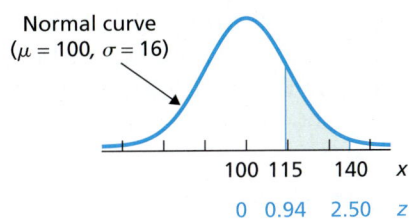

z-score computations:

$x = 115 \longrightarrow z = \dfrac{115 - 100}{16} = 0.94 \qquad 0.8264$

$x = 140 \longrightarrow z = \dfrac{140 - 100}{16} = 2.50 \qquad 0.9938$

Area to the left of z:

Shaded area = 0.9938 − 0.8264 = 0.1674

Step 2 Shade the region of interest and mark the delimiting x-values.

See the shaded region and delimiting x-values in Fig. 6.19.

Step 3 Compute the z-scores for the delimiting x-values found in Step 2.

We need to obtain the z-scores for the x-values 115 and 140:

$$x = 115 \longrightarrow z = \frac{115 - \mu}{\sigma} = \frac{115 - 100}{16} = 0.94,$$

and

$$x = 140 \longrightarrow z = \frac{140 - \mu}{\sigma} = \frac{140 - 100}{16} = 2.50.$$

These z-scores are marked beneath the x-values in Fig. 6.19.

Step 4 Use Table II to obtain the area under the standard normal curve delimited by the z-scores found in Step 3.

The area under the standard normal curve to the left of 0.94 is 0.8264 and that to the left of 2.50 is 0.9938. Consequently, the required area, the area shaded in Fig. 6.19, is 0.9938 − 0.8264 = 0.1674. ◆

What Does it Mean?

16.74% of all people have IQs between 115 and 140. Equivalently, the probability is 0.1674 that a randomly selected person will have an IQ between 115 and 140.

Note: Procedure 6.1 can be accomplished efficiently by performing all four steps in a "picture," as illustrated in Fig. 6.19.

VISUALIZING A NORMAL DISTRIBUTION

We now present a rule that permits us quickly and easily to visualize and obtain useful information about a normally distributed variable. The rule gives the percentages of all possible observations that lie within one, two, and three standard deviations to either side of the mean.

Recall that the z-score of an observation tells us how many standard deviations the observation is from the mean. Thus the percentage of all possible observations that lie within one standard deviation to either side of the mean equals the percentage of all observations whose z-scores lie between -1 and 1. For a normally distributed variable, that percentage is the same as the area under the standard normal curve between -1 and 1, which is 0.6826 or 68.26%. Proceeding in the same way, we get the **68.26-95.44-99.74 rule**, expressed as the following fact.

Key Fact 6.4 68.26-95.44-99.74 Rule

Any normally distributed variable has the following properties.

Property 1: 68.26% of all possible observations lie within one standard deviation to either side of the mean, that is, between $\mu - \sigma$ and $\mu + \sigma$.

Property 2: 95.44% of all possible observations lie within two standard deviations to either side of the mean, that is, between $\mu - 2\sigma$ and $\mu + 2\sigma$.

Property 3: 99.74% of all possible observations lie within three standard deviations to either side of the mean, that is, between $\mu - 3\sigma$ and $\mu + 3\sigma$.

These properties are displayed graphically in Fig. 6.20.

FIGURE 6.20
68.26-95.44-99.74 rule

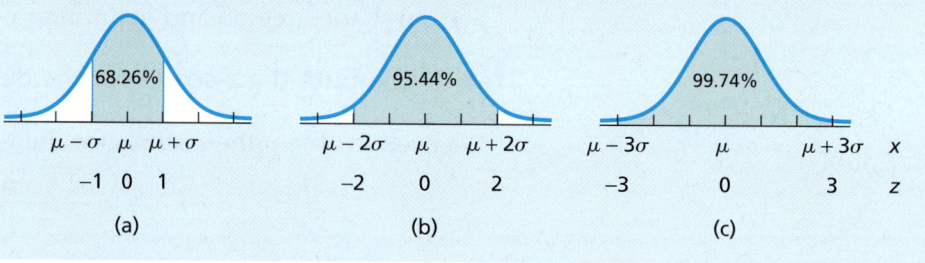

In Example 6.10, we apply this rule to IQs.

Example 6.10 68.26-95.44-99.74 Rule

Intelligence Quotients Apply the 68.26-95.44-99.74 rule to IQs.

Solution Recall that IQs (measured on the Stanford Revision of the Binet–Simon Intelligence Scale) are normally distributed with a mean of 100 and a standard deviation of 16. In particular, we have $\mu = 100$ and $\sigma = 16$.

From Property 1 of the 68.26-95.44-99.74 rule, 68.26% of all people have IQs within one standard deviation to either side of the mean. One standard deviation below the mean is $\mu - \sigma = 100 - 16 = 84$; one standard deviation above the mean is $\mu + \sigma = 100 + 16 = 116$.

6.3 Working With Normally Distributed Variables 277

> **What Does it Mean?**
>
> 68.26% of all people have IQs between 84 and 116; 95.44% of all people have IQs between 68 and 132; 99.74% of all people have IQs between 52 and 148, as illustrated in Fig. 6.21.

From Property 2 of the 68.26-95.44-99.74 rule, 95.44% of all people have IQs within two standard deviations to either side of the mean. Two standard deviations below the mean is $\mu - 2\sigma = 100 - 2 \cdot 16 = 100 - 32 = 68$; two standard deviations above the mean is $\mu + 2\sigma = 100 + 2 \cdot 16 = 100 + 32 = 132$.

From Property 3 of the 68.26-95.44-99.74 rule, 99.74% of all people have IQs within three standard deviations to either side of the mean. Three standard deviations below the mean is $\mu - 3\sigma = 100 - 3 \cdot 16 = 100 - 48 = 52$; three standard deviations above the mean is $\mu + 3\sigma = 100 + 3 \cdot 16 = 100 + 48 = 148$.

FIGURE 6.21
Graphical display of the 68.26-95.44-99.74 rule for IQs

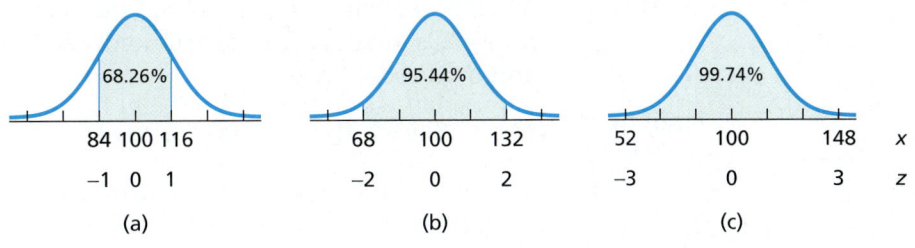

As illustrated in Example 6.10, the 68.26-95.44-99.74 rule allows us to obtain useful information about a normally distributed variable quickly and easily. Note, however, that similar facts are obtainable for any number of standard deviations. For instance, Table II reveals that, for any normally distributed variable, 86.64% of all possible observations lie within 1.5 standard deviations to either side of the mean.

Experience has shown that the 68.26-95.44-99.74 rule works reasonably well for any variable having approximately a bell-shaped distribution—normal or not. This fact is called the **empirical rule**. See page 10 of the supplementary exercises for Chapter 3 (on the WeissStats CD) for more on the empirical rule.

FINDING THE OBSERVATIONS FOR A SPECIFIED PERCENTAGE

Procedure 6.1 shows how to determine the percentage of all possible observations of a normally distributed variable that lie within any specified range. Frequently, however, we want to carry out the reverse procedure, that is, to find the observations corresponding to a specified percentage. Procedure 6.2 allows us to do that.

> **Procedure 6.2**
>
> **To Determine the Observations Corresponding to a Specified Percentage or Probability for a Normally Distributed Variable**
>
> **Step 1** Sketch the normal curve associated with the variable.
>
> **Step 2** Shade the region of interest.
>
> **Step 3** Use Table II to obtain the z-scores delimiting the region found in Step 2.
>
> **Step 4** Obtain the x-values having the z-scores found in Step 3.

Among other things, we can use Procedure 6.2 to obtain quartiles, deciles, or any other percentile for a normally distributed variable. Example 6.11 shows how to find percentiles by this method.

Example 6.11 Obtaining Percentiles for a Normally Distributed Variable

Intelligence Quotients Obtain the 90th percentile for IQs.

Solution The 90th percentile, P_{90}, is the IQ that is higher than those of 90% of all people. As IQs are normally distributed, we can determine the 90th percentile by applying Procedure 6.2.

Step 1 Sketch the normal curve associated with the variable.

Here $\mu = 100$ and $\sigma = 16$. The normal curve associated with IQs is shown in Fig. 6.22.

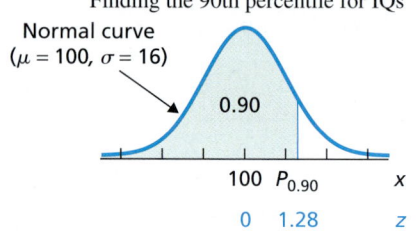

FIGURE 6.22
Finding the 90th percentile for IQs

Step 2 Shade the region of interest.

See the shaded region in Fig. 6.22.

Step 3 Use Table II to obtain the z-scores delimiting the region found in Step 2.

The z-score corresponding to P_{90} is the one having an area of 0.90 to its left under the standard normal curve. From Table II, that z-score is 1.28, approximately, as illustrated in Fig. 6.22.

Step 4 Obtain the x-values having the z-scores found in Step 3.

We must find the x-value having the z-score 1.28—the IQ that is 1.28 standard deviations above the mean. It is $100 + 1.28 \cdot 16 = 100 + 20.48 = 120.48$. ◆

What Does it Mean?

The 90th percentile for IQs is 120.48. In other words, 90% of people have IQs below 120.48 and 10% have IQs above 120.48.

The Technology Center

Almost all statistical technologies provide programs to implement automatically the procedures that we discussed in this section—namely, to obtain for a normally distributed variable

- the percentage of all possible observations that lie within any specified range and
- the observations corresponding to a specified percentage.

In this subsection, we present output and (optional) step-by-step instructions to carry out these two procedures.

Example 6.12 Using Technology to Obtain Normal Percentages

Intelligence Quotients Use Minitab, Excel, or the TI-83 Plus to determine the percentage of people who have IQs between 115 and 140.

6.3 Working With Normally Distributed Variables

Solution Each of the three technologies provides a program for obtaining the area under the associated normal curve of a normally distributed variable that lies to the left of a specified value. Such an area corresponds to a **cumulative probability,** the probability that the variable will be less than or equal to the specified value.

Recall that IQs are normally distributed with a mean of 100 and a standard deviation of 16. We want to find the percentage of people who have IQs between 115 and 140. Printout 6.2 shows output that can be easily used to obtain this percentage.

PRINTOUT 6.2
Output for obtaining the percentage of people who have IQs between 115 and 140

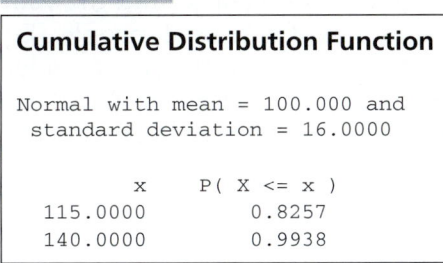

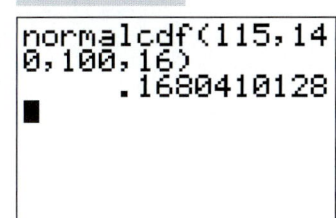

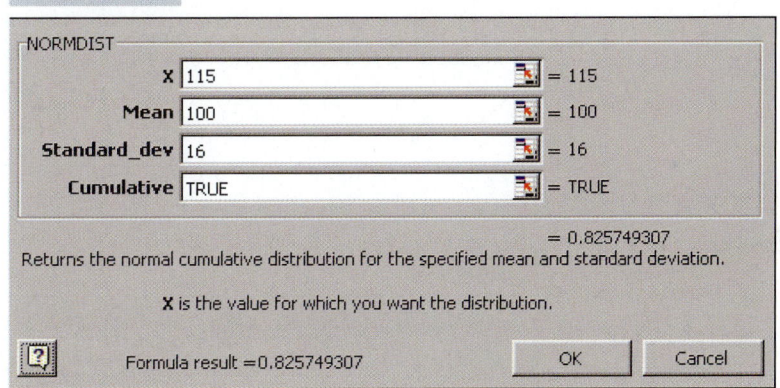

NOTE: Replacing 115 by 140 in the **X** text box yields 0.99379032.

We get the required percentage from the Minitab output in Printout 6.2 by subtracting the two cumulative probabilities: $0.9938 - 0.8257 = 0.1681$, or 16.81%. Similarly, in Printout 6.2, Excel gives the required percentage as $0.99379032 - 0.825749307 = 0.168041013$, or 16.80%. Printout 6.2 shows that the TI-83 Plus does the subtraction for us and presents the required percentage as 0.1680410128, or 16.80%.

Note that the percentages obtained by the three technologies differ slightly from the percentage of 16.74% that we found in Example 6.9. The differences reflect the fact that the technologies retain more accuracy than we can get from Table II.

Example 6.13 Using Technology to Obtain Normal Percentiles

Intelligence Quotients Use Minitab, Excel, or the TI-83 Plus to find the 90th percentile for IQs.

Solution Each of the three technologies provides a program for obtaining the observation that has a specified area to its left under the associated normal curve of a normally distributed variable. Such an observation corresponds to an **inverse cumulative probability,** the observation whose cumulative probability is the specified area.

Recall that IQs are normally distributed with a mean of 100 and a standard deviation of 16. We want to find the 90th percentile for IQs, the IQ that is higher than those of 90% of all people. Equivalently, we want to find the x-value that has an area of 0.90 to its left under the normal curve with parameters $\mu = 100$ and $\sigma = 16$. Printout 6.3 shows output obtained for this x-value by applying the inverse cumulative probability programs from Minitab, Excel, and the TI-83 Plus.

PRINTOUT 6.3
Output for obtaining the 90th percentile for IQs

```
MINITAB

Inverse Cumulative Distribution Function

Normal with mean = 100.000 and
 standard deviation = 16.0000

P( X <= x )            x
    0.9000        120.5048
```

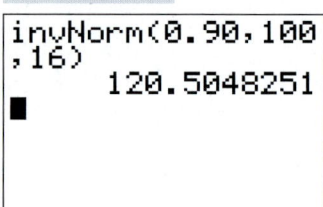

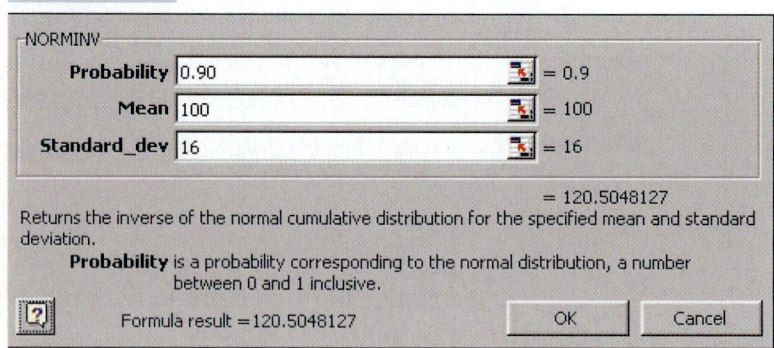

From any of the three outputs in Printout 6.3, the 90th percentile for IQs is 120.5048. Note that this value differs slightly from the value of 120.48 that we obtained in Example 6.11. The difference again reflects the fact that the three technologies retain more accuracy than we can get from Table II.

6.3 Working With Normally Distributed Variables

Obtaining the Output (Optional)

Printout 6.2 provides output that can be easily used to determine the percentage of people who have IQs between 115 and 140. Here are detailed instructions for obtaining that output.

MINITAB	EXCEL	TI-83 PLUS
1 Store the delimiting IQs, 115 and 140, in a column named IQ 2 Choose **Calc ➤ Probability Distributions ➤ Normal...** 3 Select the **Cumulative probability** option button 4 Click in the **Mean** text box and type 100 5 Click in the **Standard deviation** text box and type 16 6 Select the **Input column** option button 7 Click in the **Input column** text box and specify IQ 8 Click **OK**	1 Click f_x on the button bar 2 Select **Statistical** from the **Function category** list 3 Select **NORMDIST** from the **Function name** list 4 Click **OK** 5 Type 115 in the **X** text box 6 Click in the **Mean** text box and type 100 7 Click in the **Standard_dev** text box and type 16 8 Click in the **Cumulative** text box and type TRUE 9 To obtain the cumulative probability for 140, replace 115 by 140 in the **X** text box	1 Press **2nd ➤ DISTR** 2 Arrow down to **normalcdf(** and press **ENTER** 3 Type 115,140,100,16) and press **ENTER**

Printout 6.3 provides output that gives the 90th percentile for IQs. Here are detailed instructions for obtaining that output.

MINITAB	EXCEL	TI-83 PLUS
1 Choose **Calc ➤ Probability Distributions ➤ Normal...** 2 Select the **Inverse cumulative probability** option button 3 Click in the **Mean** text box and type 100 4 Click in the **Standard deviation** text box and type 16 5 Select the **Input constant** option button 6 Click in the **Input constant** text box and type 0.90 7 Click **OK**	1 Click f_x on the button bar 2 Select **Statistical** from the **Function category** list 3 Select **NORMINV** from the **Function name** list 4 Click **OK** 5 Type 0.90 in the **Probability** text box 6 Click in the **Mean** text box and type 100 7 Click in the **Standard_dev** text box and type 16	1 Press **2nd ➤ DISTR** 2 Arrow down to **invNorm(** and press **ENTER** 3 Type 0.90,100,16) and press **ENTER**

Exercises 6.3

Statistical Concepts and Skills

6.45 Briefly, for a normally distributed variable, how do you obtain the percentage of all possible observations that lie within a specified range?

6.46 Explain why the percentage of all possible observations of a normally distributed variable that lie within two standard deviations to either side of the mean equals the area under the standard normal curve between −2 and 2.

6.47 Drive for Show, Putt for Dough. An article by Scott M. Berry titled "Drive for Show and Putt for Dough" (*Chance*, 1999, Vol. 12(4), pp. 50–54) discussed driving distances of PGA players. The mean distance for tee shots on the 1999 men's PGA tour is 272.2 yards with a standard deviation of 8.12 yards. Assuming that the 1999 tee-shot distances are normally distributed, find the percentage of such tee shots that went
a. between 260 and 280 yards.
b. more than 300 yards.

6.48 Brain Weights. In 1905, R. Pearl published the article "Biometrical Studies on Man. I. Variation and Correlation in Brain Weight" (*Biometrika*, Vol. 4, pp. 13–104). According to the study, brain weights of Swedish men are normally distributed with a mean of 1.40 kilograms (kg) and a standard deviation of 0.11 kg. Obtain the percentage of Swedish men who have brain weights
a. between 1.50 kg and 1.70 kg.
b. less than 1.6 kg.

6.49 New York City 10 km Run. As reported in *Runner's World* magazine, the times of the finishers in the New York City 10 km run are normally distributed with a mean of 61 minutes and a standard deviation of 9 minutes. Let X be the time of a randomly selected finisher. Find
a. $P(X > 75)$.
b. $P(X < 50 \text{ or } X > 70)$.

6.50 Polychaete Worms. *Opisthotrochopodus n. sp.* is a polychaete worm that inhabits deep sea hydrothermal vents along the Mid-Atlantic Ridge. According to an article by Van Dover et al. in *Marine Ecology Progress Series* (1999, Vol. 181, pp. 201–214) the lengths of female polychaete worms are normally distributed with mean 6.1 mm and standard deviation 1.3 mm. Let X denote the length of a randomly selected female polychaete worm. Determine
a. $P(X \leq 3)$.
b. $P(5 < X < 7)$.

6.51 Gibbon Song Duration. A preliminary behavioral study of the Jingdong black gibbon, a primate endemic to the Wuliang Mountains in China, found that the mean song bout duration in the wet season is 12.59 minutes with a standard deviation of 5.31 minutes. [SOURCE: Lori K. Sheeran, Zhang Yongzu, Frank E. Poirier, and Yang Dehua, "Preliminary Report on the Behavior of the Jingdong Black Gibbon (*Hylobates concolor jingdongensis*)," *Tropical Biodiversity*, 1998, Vol. 5(2), pp. 113-125] Assume that song bout is normally distributed and apply the 68.26-95.44-99.74 rule to determine the percentage of song bouts that have durations within
a. 1 standard deviation to either side of the mean.
b. 2 standard deviations to either side of the mean.
c. 3 standard deviations to either side of the mean.

6.52 Children Watching TV. The A. C. Nielsen Company reports in the *Nielsen Report on Television* that the mean weekly television viewing time for children aged 2–11 years is 24.50 hours. Assume that the weekly television viewing times of such children are normally distributed with a standard deviation of 6.23 hours and apply the 68.26-95.44-99.74 rule to fill in the blanks.
a. 68.26% of all such children watch between _____ and _____ hours of TV per week.
b. 95.44% of all such children watch between _____ and _____ hours of TV per week.
c. 99.74% of all such children watch between _____ and _____ hours of TV per week.
d. Draw graphs similar to those in Fig. 6.21 on page 277 to portray your results.

6.53 Drive for Show, Putt for Dough. Refer to Exercise 6.47.
a. Determine the quartiles of the driving distances.
b. Find the 95th percentile.
c. Obtain the third decile.
d. Interpret your answers for parts (a)–(c).

6.54 Brain Weights. Refer to Exercise 6.48.
a. Determine the quartiles of the brain weights.

b. Obtain the 20th percentile.
c. Find the seventh decile.
d. Interpret your answers for parts (a)–(c).

Extending the Concepts and Skills

6.55 For a normally distributed variable, fill in the blanks.
a. ____% of all possible observations lie within 1.96 standard deviations to either side of the mean.
b. ____% of all possible observations lie within 1.64 standard deviations to either side of the mean.

6.56 For a normally distributed variable, fill in the blanks.
a. ____% of all possible observations lie within 1.28 standard deviations to either side of the mean.
b. ____% of all possible observations lie within 2.33 standard deviations to either side of the mean.

6.57 Heights of Female Students. Refer to Example 6.1 on page 259. The heights of the 3264 female students attending a midwestern college are approximately normally distributed with mean 64.4 inches and standard deviation 2.4 inches. Thus we can use the normal distribution with $\mu = 64.4$ and $\sigma = 2.4$ to approximate the percentage of these students having heights within any specified range. In each part, (i) obtain the exact percentage from Table 6.1, (ii) use the normal distribution to approximate the percentage, and (iii) compare your answers.
a. The percentage of female students with heights between 62 and 63 inches.
b. The percentage of female students with heights between 65 and 70 inches.

6.58 Let $0 < \alpha < 1$. For a normally distributed variable, show that $100(1-\alpha)\%$ of all possible observations lie within $z_{\alpha/2}$ standard deviations to either side of the mean, that is, between $\mu - z_{\alpha/2} \cdot \sigma$ and $\mu + z_{\alpha/2} \cdot \sigma$.

6.59 Let x be a normally distributed variable with mean μ and standard deviation σ.
a. Express the quartiles, Q_1, Q_2, and Q_3, in terms of μ and σ.
b. Express the kth percentile, P_k, in terms of μ, σ, and k.

Using Technology

6.60 Drive for Show, Putt for Dough. Use the technology of your choice to solve Exercises 6.47 and 6.53.

6.61 Polychaete Worms. Use the technology of your choice to solve Exercise 6.50.

6.4 ASSESSING NORMALITY; NORMAL PROBABILITY PLOTS

You have now seen how to work with normally distributed variables. For instance, you know how to determine the percentage of all possible observations that lie within any specified range and how to obtain the observations corresponding to a specified percentage.

Another problem involves deciding whether a variable is normally distributed, or at least approximately so, based on a sample of observations. Such decisions often play a major role in subsequent analyses—from percentage or percentile calculations to statistical inferences.

From Key Fact 2.1, if a random sample is taken from a population, the distribution of the observed values of a variable will approximate the distribution of the variable—and the larger the sample, the better the approximation tends to be. We can use this fact to help decide whether a variable is normally distributed.

On the one hand, if a variable is normally distributed, then, for a large sample, a histogram of the observations should be roughly bell-shaped; for a very large sample, even moderate departures from a bell shape cast doubt on the normality of the variable. On the other hand, for a relatively small sample, ascertaining a clear shape in a histogram and, in particular, whether it is bell-shaped is often difficult. These comments also hold for stem-and-leaf diagrams and dotplots.

Thus, for relatively small samples, a more sensitive graphical technique than the ones we have presented so far is required for assessing normality. Normal probability plots provide such a technique.

The idea behind a normal probability plot is simple: Compare the observed values of the variable to the observations expected for a normally distributed variable. More precisely, a **normal probability plot** is a plot of the observed values of the variable versus the **normal scores**—the observations expected for a variable having the standard normal distribution. If the variable is normally distributed, the normal probability plot should be roughly linear (i.e., fall roughly in a straight line) and vice versa.

When you use a normal probability plot to assess the normality of a variable, you must remember two things: (1) that the decision of whether a normal probability plot is roughly linear is a subjective one and (2) that you are using the observations of the variable for a sample to make a judgment about all possible observations of the variable (i.e., the distribution of the variable). With these considerations in mind, the following guidelines can be used to assess normality.

Key Fact 6.5 — Guidelines for Assessing Normality Using a Normal Probability Plot

To assess the normality of a variable using sample data, construct a normal probability plot.

- If the plot is roughly linear, accept as reasonable that the variable is approximately normally distributed.
- If the plot shows systematic deviations from linearity (e.g., if it displays significant curvature), conclude that the variable probably is not approximately normally distributed.

These guidelines should be interpreted loosely for small samples, but they can be interpreted rather strictly for large samples.

In practice, normal probability plots are obtained by computer. However, for purposes of understanding, constructing a few by hand is helpful. Table III in Appendix A provides the normal scores for sample sizes from 5 to 30. In Example 6.14, we explain how to use Table III to obtain a normal probability plot.

Example 6.14 *Normal Probability Plots*

TABLE 6.3 Adjusted gross incomes ($1000s)

9.7	93.1	33.0	21.2
81.4	51.1	43.5	10.6
12.8	7.8	18.1	12.7

Adjusted Gross Incomes The Internal Revenue Service publishes data on federal individual income tax returns in *Statistics of Income, Individual Income Tax Returns*. A random sample of 12 returns from last year revealed the adjusted gross incomes, in thousands of dollars, shown in Table 6.3. Construct a normal probability plot for these data, and use the plot to assess the normality of adjusted gross incomes.

Solution Here the variable is adjusted gross income, and the population consists of all last year's federal individual income tax returns. To construct a normal probability plot, we first arrange the data in increasing order and obtain the normal scores

6.4 Assessing Normality; Normal Probability Plots 285

TABLE 6.4
Ordered data and normal scores

Adjusted gross income	Normal score
7.8	−1.64
9.7	−1.11
10.6	−0.79
12.7	−0.53
12.8	−0.31
18.1	−0.10
21.2	0.10
33.0	0.31
43.5	0.53
51.1	0.79
81.4	1.11
93.1	1.64

from Table III. The ordered data are shown in the first column of Table 6.4; the normal scores, from the $n = 12$ column of Table III, are shown in the second column of Table 6.4.

Next, we plot the points in Table 6.4, using the horizontal axis for the adjusted gross incomes and the vertical axis for the normal scores. For instance, the first point plotted has a horizontal coordinate of 7.8 and a vertical coordinate of −1.64.

Figure 6.23 shows all 12 points from Table 6.4, the normal probability plot for the sample of adjusted gross incomes. Note that the normal probability plot in Fig. 6.23 has significant curvature.

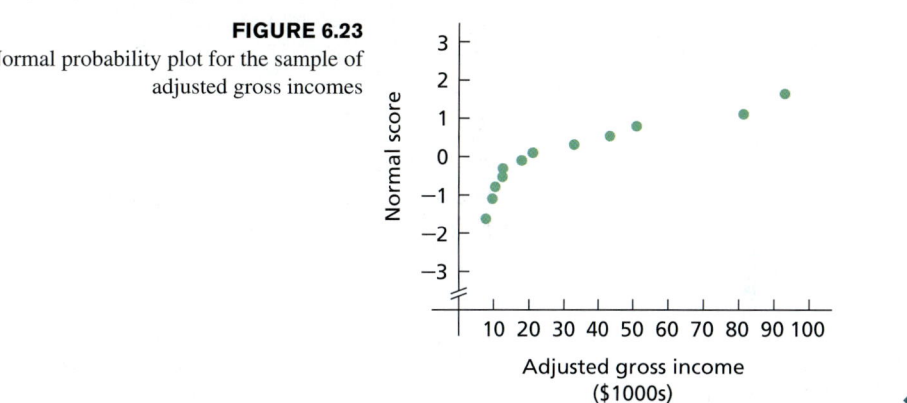

FIGURE 6.23
Normal probability plot for the sample of adjusted gross incomes

What Does it Mean?

In light of Key Fact 6.5, last year's adjusted gross incomes apparently are not (approximately) normally distributed.

In some books and statistical technologies, you may encounter one or both of the following differences in normal probability plots:

- The vertical axis is used for the data and the horizontal axis for the normal scores.
- A probability scale is used instead of normal scores.

DETECTING OUTLIERS WITH NORMAL PROBABILITY PLOTS

Recall that outliers are observations that fall well outside the overall pattern of the data. We can use normal probability plots to detect outliers, as explained in Example 6.15.

Example 6.15 *Using Normal Probability Plots to Detect Outliers*

TABLE 6.5
Sample of last year's chicken consumption (lb)

47	39	62	49	50	70
59	53	55	0	65	63
53	51	50	72	45	

Chicken Consumption The U.S. Department of Agriculture publishes data on U.S. chicken consumption in *Food Consumption, Prices, and Expenditures*. Last year's chicken consumption, in pounds, for 17 randomly selected people are displayed in Table 6.5. A normal probability plot for these observations is presented in Fig. 6.24(a) on the next page. Use the plot to discuss the distribution of chicken consumption and to detect any outliers.

FIGURE 6.24
Normal probability plots for chicken consumption: (a) original data; (b) data with outlier removed

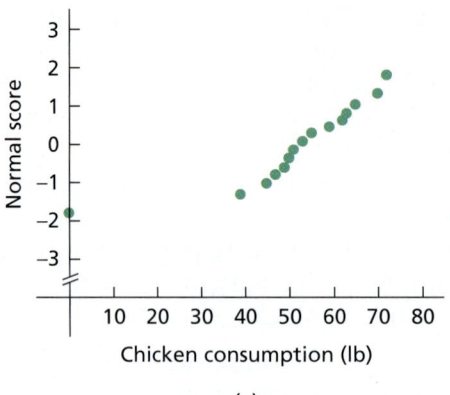
(a)

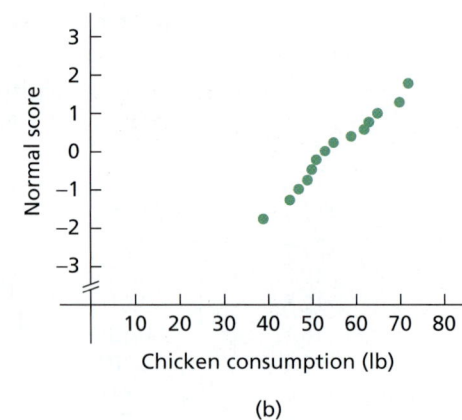
(b)

Solution Figure 6.24(a) reveals that the normal probability plot falls roughly in a straight line except for the point corresponding to the consumption of 0 lb. That point falls well outside the overall pattern of the plot and hence 0 lb is an outlier. This outlier might be a recording error or due to a person in the sample who does not eat chicken for some reason (e.g., a vegetarian).

If we remove the outlier 0 lb from the sample data and draw a normal probability plot for the abridged data, Fig. 6.24(b) shows that this normal probability plot is quite linear. It appears plausible that, among people who eat chicken, the amounts they consume annually are (approximately) normally distributed. ◆

Note: There appear to be only 15 points (instead of 17) in Fig. 6.24(a). The reason is that we, as do many statistical software packages, use an averaging process to assign identical normal scores to identical observations; keep this fact in mind when you examine normal probability plots in figures and printouts. Thus, in Example 6.15, the two observations of 50 are assigned identical normal scores as are the two observations of 53. So, there really are 17 points in the graph, but only 15 are distinguishable because there are two sets of two identical points. An alternative procedure is to treat identical observations as being slightly different; then no averaging is required.

In this section, you learned how a normal probability plot for a sample of observations of a variable can be used as an aid for deciding whether the variable is (approximately) normally distributed. Although this visual assessment of normality is subjective, it is sufficient for most statistical analyses.

The Technology Center

Most statistical technologies have programs that automatically construct normal probability plots. In this subsection, we present output and (optional) step-by-step instructions to implement such programs.

Example 6.16 Using Technology to Obtain Normal Probability Plots

Adjusted Gross Incomes Use Minitab, Excel, or the TI-83 Plus to obtain a normal probability plot for the adjusted gross incomes displayed in Table 6.3 on page 284.

Solution Printout 6.4 shows the output obtained by applying the normal probability–plot programs to the data on adjusted gross incomes.

PRINTOUT 6.4
Normal probability–plot output for the sample of adjusted gross incomes

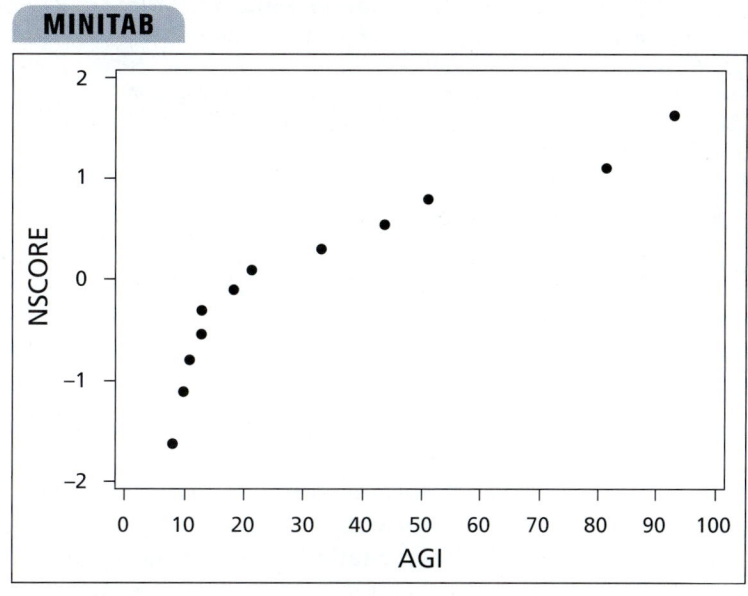

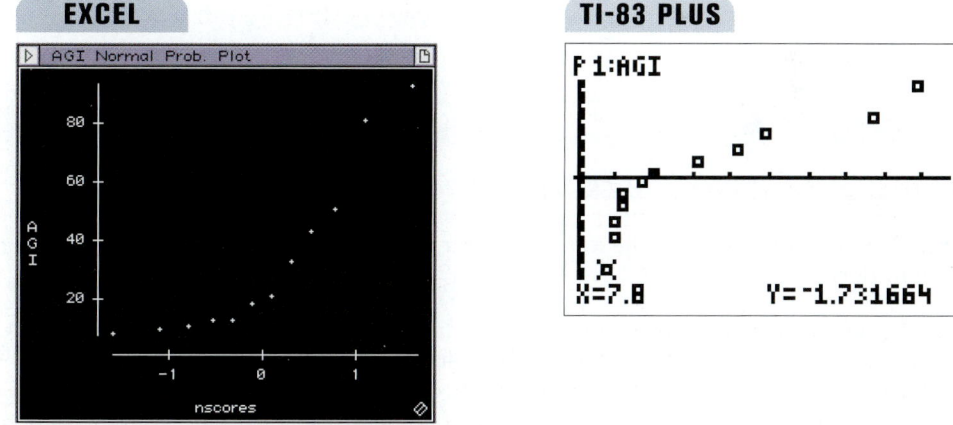

As we mentioned earlier and as you can see from the Excel output in Printout 6.4, normal probability plots are sometimes drawn with the vertical axis used for the data and the horizontal axis for the normal scores. Compare the normal probability plots in Printout 6.4 to the one in Fig. 6.23 on page 285. ◆

Obtaining the Output (Optional)

Here are detailed instructions for obtaining a normal probability plot for the sample of adjusted gross incomes using Minitab, Excel, and the TI-83 Plus.

First, we store the data from Table 6.3 on page 284 in a column (Minitab), range (Excel), or list (TI-83 Plus) named AGI. Then, we proceed as follows.

MINITAB
1. Choose **Calc ➤ Calculator...**
2. Type NSCORE in the **Store result in variable** text box
3. Select **Normal scores** from the **Functions** list box
4. Specify AGI for **number** in the **Expression** text box
5. Click **OK**
6. Choose **Graph ➤ Plot...**
7. Specify NSCORE in the **Y** text box for **Graph 1**
8. Click in the **X** text box for **Graph 1** and specify AGI
9. Click **OK**

EXCEL
1. Choose **DDXL ➤ Charts and Plots**
2. Select **Normal Probability Plot** from the **Function type** drop-down box
3. Specify AGI in the **Quantitative Variable** text box
4. Click **OK**

TI-83 PLUS
1. Press **2nd ➤ STAT PLOT** and then press **ENTER** twice
2. Arrow to the sixth graph icon and press **ENTER**
3. Press the down-arrow key
4. Press **2nd ➤ LIST**
5. Arrow down to AGI and press **ENTER**
6. Press **ZOOM** and then **9** (and then **TRACE**, if desired)

Note to Minitab users: Minitab has several programs for obtaining normal probability plots. In the instructions, we provided for getting a normal probability plot with normal scores on the vertical axis. A quicker procedure, but one that yields a plot with cumulative probabilities on the vertical axis, is to choose **Stat ➤ Basic Statistics ➤ Normality Test...**, specify AGI in the **Variable** text box, and click **OK**.

Exercises 6.4

Statistical Concepts and Skills

6.62 Explain why assessing the normality of a variable is often important.

6.63 Under what circumstances is using a normal probability plot to assess the normality of a variable usually better than using a histogram, stem-and-leaf diagram, or dotplot?

6.64 Regarding normal probability plots,
a. explain in detail what a normal probability plot is and how it is used to assess the normality of a variable.
b. how is a normal probability plot used to detect outliers?

In Exercises 6.65–6.68,
a. use Table III in Appendix A to construct a normal probability plot of the given data. For simplicity, treat equal observations as being slightly different when obtaining normal scores.
b. use part (a) to identify any outliers.

c. use part (a) to assess the normality of the variable under consideration.

6.65 Exam Scores. A sample of the final exam scores in a large introductory statistics course is as follows.

88	67	64	76	86
85	82	39	75	34
90	63	89	90	84
81	96	100	70	96

6.66 Law Periodicals. As reported in *Library Journal* by the R. R. Bowker Company of New York, the mean annual subscription rate of law periodicals was $138.78 in 1998. A sample of this year's law periodicals yielded the following subscription rates to the nearest dollar.

147	163	161	164
159	155	179	172
169	165	160	171

6.67 Miles Driven. The U.S. Federal Highway Administration conducts studies on motor vehicle travel by type of vehicle. Results are published annually in *Highway Statistics*. A sample of 15 cars gave the following data on number of miles driven, in thousands, for last year.

13.2	13.3	11.9	15.7	11.3
12.2	16.7	10.7	6.3	13.6
14.8	9.6	11.6	8.7	15.0

6.68 Beverage Expenditures. The Bureau of Labor Statistics publishes information on average annual expenditures by consumers in the *Consumer Expenditure Survey*. In 1997, the mean amount spent by consumers on nonalcoholic beverages was $245. A random sample of 12 consumers yielded the following data, in dollars, on last year's expenditures on nonalcoholic beverages.

361	176	184	265
259	281	240	273
259	249	194	258

Using Technology

6.69 Exam Scores. Use the technology of your choice to obtain a normal probability plot for the exam scores in Exercise 6.65.

6.70 Law Periodicals. Use the technology of your choice to obtain a normal probability plot for the subscription rates in Exercise 6.66.

6.71 Fat Consumption in Vegetarians. A paper by Shao-Chun Lu et al., titled "LDL of Taiwanese Vegetarians are Less Oxidizable Than Those of Omnivores" (*Human Nutrition and Metabolism*, 2000, Vol. 130(6), pp. 1591–1596) compared fat consumption by vegetarians and omnivores. The following table displays the amount of fat consumed, in grams per day, for 28 vegetarians in the study.

20.5	31.4	35.7	52.8	27.0	40.3	45.7
19.7	32.5	33.5	58.5	30.1	61.4	33.3
35.3	54.7	54.1	56.7	35.9	58.8	25.7
66.3	35.9	35.7	47.1	38.7	16.4	42.0

a. Use the technology of your choice to obtain a normal probability plot of the data.

b. Identify outliers, if any.
c. Assess the normality of fat consumption for Taiwanese vegetarians.

6.72 Chips Ahoy! 1,000 Chips Challenge. Students in an introductory statistics course at the U.S. Air Force Academy participated in Nabisco's "Chips Ahoy! 1,000 Chips Challenge" by confirming that there were at least 1000 chips in every 18-ounce bag of cookies that they examined. As part of their assignment, they concluded that the number of chips per bag is approximately normally distributed. Their conclusion was based on the following data, which gives the number of chips per bag for 42 bags. Do you agree with the conclusion of the students? Explain your answer. [SOURCE: Brad Warner and Jim Rutledge, "Checking the Chips Ahoy! Guarantee," *Chance*, 1999, Vol. 12(1), pp. 10–14]

1200	1219	1103	1213	1258	1325	1295
1247	1098	1185	1087	1377	1363	1121
1279	1269	1199	1244	1294	1356	1137
1545	1135	1143	1215	1402	1419	1166
1132	1514	1270	1345	1214	1154	1307
1293	1546	1228	1239	1440	1219	1191

6.73 Finger Length of Criminals. In 1902, W. R. Macdonell published the article "On Criminal Anthropometry and the Identification of Criminals" (*Biometrika*, 1, pp. 177–227). Among other things, the author presented data on the left middle finger length, in centimeters. The following table provides the midpoints and frequencies of the finger length classes used.

Midpoint (cm)	Frequency	Midpoint (cm)	Frequency
9.5	1	11.6	691
9.8	4	11.9	509
10.1	24	12.2	306
10.4	67	12.5	131
10.7	193	12.8	63
11.0	417	13.1	16
11.3	575	13.4	3

Use these data and the technology of your choice to assess the normality of middle finger length of criminals by using
a. a histogram.
b. a normal probability plot. Explain your procedure and reasoning in detail.

6.74 Gestation Periods of Humans. For humans, gestation periods are normally distributed with a mean of 266 days and a standard deviation of 16 days.
a. Use the technology of your choice to simulate four random samples of 50 human gestation periods each.

b. Obtain a normal probability plot of each sample in part (a).

c. Are the normal probability plots in part (b) what you expected? Explain your answer.

6.75 Emergency Room Traffic. Desert Samaritan Hospital in Mesa, Arizona, keeps records of emergency room traffic. Those records reveal that the times between arriving patients have a special type of reverse J-shaped distribution called an *exponential distribution*. The records also show that the mean time between arriving patients is 8.7 minutes.

a. Use the technology of your choice to simulate four random samples of 75 interarrival times each.

b. Obtain a normal probability plot of each sample in part (a).

c. Are the normal probability plots in part (b) what you expected? Explain your answer.

Chapter Review

You Should Be Able To

1. use and understand the formulas presented in this chapter.

2. explain what it means for a variable to be normally distributed or approximately normally distributed.

3. explain the meaning of the parameters for a normal curve.

4. identify the basic properties of and sketch a normal curve.

5. identify the standard normal distribution and the standard normal curve.

6. use Table II to find areas under the standard normal curve.

7. use Table II to find the z-score(s) corresponding to a specified area under the standard normal curve.

8. use and understand the z_α notation.

9. determine a percentage or probability for a normally distributed variable.

10. state and apply the 68.26-95.44-99.74 rule.

11. determine the observations corresponding to a specified percentage or probability for a normally distributed variable.

12. explain how to assess the normality of a variable with a normal probability plot.

13. construct a normal probability plot with the aid of Table III.

14. use a normal probability plot to detect outliers.

Key Terms

68.26-95.44-99.74 rule, *276*
approximately normally distributed variable, *258*
cumulative probability, *279*
empirical rule, *277*
inverse cumulative probability, *280*
normal curve, *258*

normal distribution, *258*
normal probability plot, *284*
normal scores, *284*
normally distributed population, *258*
normally distributed variable, *258*
parameters, *258*
standard normal curve, *261*

standard normal distribution, *261*
standardized normally distributed variable, *262*
z_α, *270*
z-curve, *266*

Review Test

Statistical Concepts and Skills

1. State two of the main reasons for studying the normal distribution.

2. Define
   a. normally distributed variable.
   b. normally distributed population.
   c. parameters for a normal curve.

3. Answer true or false to each statement. Give reasons for your answers.
   a. Two variables that have the same mean and standard deviation have the same distribution.
   b. Two normally distributed variables that have the same mean and standard deviation have the same distribution.

4. Explain the relationship between percentages for a normally distributed variable and areas under the corresponding normal curve.

5. Identify the distribution of the standardized version of a normally distributed variable.

6. Answer true or false to each statement. Explain your answers.
   a. Two normal distributions that have the same mean are centered at the same place, regardless of the relationship between their standard deviations.
   b. Two normal distributions that have the same standard deviation have the same shape, regardless of the relationship between their means.

7. Consider the normal curves that have the parameters $\mu = 1.5$ and $\sigma = 3$; $\mu = 1.5$ and $\sigma = 6.2$; $\mu = -2.7$ and $\sigma = 3$; $\mu = 0$ and $\sigma = 1$.
   a. Which curve has the largest spread?
   b. Which curves are centered at the same place?
   c. Which curves have the same shape?
   d. Which curve is centered farthest to the left?
   e. Which curve is the standard normal curve?

8. What key fact permits you to determine percentages for a normally distributed variable by first converting to z-scores and then determining the corresponding area under the standard normal curve?

9. Explain how to use Table II to determine the area under the standard normal curve that lies
   a. to the left of a specified z-score.
   b. to the right of a specified z-score.
   c. between two specified z-scores.

10. Explain how to use Table II to determine the z-score that has a specified area to its
    a. left under the standard normal curve.
    b. right under the standard normal curve.

11. What does the symbol z_α signify?

12. State the 68.26-95.44-99.74 rule.

13. Roughly speaking, what are the normal scores corresponding to a sample of observations?

14. If you observe the values of a normally distributed variable for a sample, a normal probability plot should be roughly _____.

15. Sketch the normal curve having the parameters
    a. $\mu = -1$ and $\sigma = 2$.   b. $\mu = 3$ and $\sigma = 2$.
    c. $\mu = -1$ and $\sigma = 0.5$.

16. **Forearm Length.** In 1903, K. Pearson and A. Lee published a paper entitled "On the Laws of Inheritance in Man. I. Inheritance of Physical Characters" (*Biometrika*, Vol. 2, pp. 357–462). From information presented in that paper, forearm lengths of men, measured from the elbow to the middle fingertip, are (roughly) normally distributed with a mean of 18.8 inches and a standard deviation of 1.1 inches. Let x denote forearm length, in inches, for men.
    a. Sketch the distribution of the variable x.
    b. Obtain the standardized version, z, of x.
    c. Identify and sketch the distribution of z.
    d. The area under the normal curve with parameters 18.8 and 1.1 that lies between 17 and 20 is 0.8115. Determine the probability that a randomly selected man will have a forearm length between 17 inches and 20 inches.
    e. The percentage of men who have forearm lengths less than 16 inches equals the area under the standard normal curve that lies to the _____ of _____.

17. According to Table II, the area under the standard normal curve that lies to the left of 1.05 is 0.8531. Without further reference to Table II, determine the area under the standard normal curve that lies
    a. to the right of 1.05.
    b. to the left of -1.05.
    c. between -1.05 and 1.05.

18. Determine and sketch the area under the standard normal curve that lies
    a. to the left of -3.02.
    b. to the right of 0.61.
    c. between 1.11 and 2.75.
    d. between -2.06 and 5.02.
    e. between -4.11 and -1.5.
    f. either to the left of 1 or to the right of 3.

19. For the standard normal curve, find the z-score(s)
a. that has area 0.30 to its left.
b. that has area 0.10 to its right.
c. $z_{0.025}$, $z_{0.05}$, $z_{0.01}$, and $z_{0.005}$.
d. that divide the area under the curve into a middle 0.99 area and two outside 0.005 areas.

20. **GRE Scores.** Each year, thousands of college seniors take the Graduate Record Examination (GRE). The scores are transformed so they have a mean of 500 and a standard deviation of 100. Furthermore, the scores are known to be normally distributed. Determine the percentage of students that score
a. between 350 and 625.   b. 375 or greater.
c. below 750.

21. **GRE Scores.** Use the 68.26-95.44-99.74 rule to fill in the blanks with regard to Problem 20.
a. 68.26% of students who take the GRE score between _____ and _____.
b. 95.44% of students who take the GRE score between _____ and _____.
c. 99.74% of students who take the GRE score between _____ and _____.

22. **GRE Scores.** Refer to Problem 20. Solve the following problems and interpret your answers.
a. Obtain the quartiles for GRE scores.
b. Find the 99th percentile for GRE scores.

23. **Costly Gas.** According to the *AAA Daily Fuel Gauge Report*, the national average price for unleaded gasoline in June 2000 was $1.58. A random sample of 12 gas stations across the country yielded the following unleaded gas prices.

1.59	1.65	1.97	1.69
1.45	1.42	1.73	1.45
1.31	1.57	1.39	1.65

a. Use Table III to construct a normal probability plot for the data. For simplicity, treat equal observations as being slightly different when obtaining the normal scores.
b. Use part (a) to identify any outliers.
c. Use part (a) to assess normality.

Using Technology

24. **GRE Scores.** Refer to Problem 20. Use the technology of your choice to do the following.
a. Sketch the normal curve for GRE scores.
b. Simulate 1000 GRE scores. (*Note:* Users of the TI-83 Plus should simulate 500 GRE scores.)
c. Approximately what values would you expect for the sample mean and sample standard deviation of the 1000 GRE scores obtained in part (b)? Explain your answers.
d. Determine the sample mean and sample standard deviation of the 1000 GRE scores obtained in part (b), and compare your answers to your answers in part (c).
e. Roughly what would you expect a histogram of the 1000 GRE scores obtained in part (b) to look like? Explain your answer.
f. Obtain a histogram of the 1000 GRE scores from part (b), and compare your result to your expectation in part (e).

25. **GRE Scores.** Use the technology of your choice to solve Problem 20. Comment on any discrepancies between the answers obtained here and those in Problem 20.

26. **GRE Scores.** Use the technology of your choice to solve Problem 22. Comment on any discrepancies between the answers obtained here and those in Problem 22.

27. **Costly Gas.** Use the technology of your choice to obtain a normal probability plot for the gasoline prices in Problem 23. Comment on any differences between the plot obtained here and the one in Problem 23.

Internet Project

IQ of Boys and Girls

In this Internet project, you are to interact with several simulations and animations that show why and how the normal distribution is useful. You also are to explore a real data set containing the intelligence quotient (IQ) scores for boys and girls in primary school. In general, are boys and girls equally smart? Although most people believe there is no difference in IQ between the sexes, some believe there is.

IQ is a measure constructed to be normally distributed with a mean of 100 and a standard deviation of 16. Earlier in this chapter, we calculated probabilities for IQs based on this normal distribution model. In this Internet project, you will discover how well the model fits the real data.

URL for access to Internet Projects Page: www.aw.com/weiss

Focusing on Data Analysis

GPA, SAT Scores, Age, and Hours

Recall from Chapter 1 (see page 34) that the Focus database contains information on 500 randomly selected Arizona State University sophomores. Use the technology of your choice to solve the following problems.

a. Obtain a histogram and a dotplot for each of the data sets high school GPA, SAT math score, cumulative GPA, SAT verbal score, age, and total hours.

b. Based on part (a), which of the six variables for ASU sophomores—high school GPA, SAT math score, cumulative GPA, SAT verbal score, age, and total hours—appear to be approximately normally distributed?

c. Obtain a normal probability plot for each of the data sets high school GPA, SAT math score, cumulative GPA, SAT verbal score, age, and total hours.

d. Based on part (c), which of the six variables for ASU sophomores—high school GPA, SAT math score, cumulative GPA, SAT verbal score, age, and total hours—appear to be approximately normally distributed?

case study discussion

Chest Sizes of Scottish Militiamen

On page 257, we presented a frequency distribution for data on chest circumference for 5732 Scottish militiamen. As mentioned there, Adolphe Quetelet used a procedure for fitting a normal curve to the data based on the binomial distribution. Here you are to accomplish that task by using techniques that you studied in this chapter.

a. Construct a relative-frequency histogram for the chest circumference data, using classes based on a single value.
b. Find the population mean and population standard deviation of the data.
c. Identify the normal curve that should be used for the chest circumferences.
d. Use the table on page 257 to find the percentage of militiamen in the survey with chest circumferences between 36 and 41 inches, inclusive. *Note:* As the circumferences were rounded to the nearest inch, you are actually finding the percentage of militiamen in the survey with chest circumferences between 35.5 and 41.5 inches.
e. Use the normal curve you identified in part (c) to obtain an approximation to the percentage of militiamen in the survey having chest circumferences between 35.5 and 41.5 inches. Compare your answer to the exact percentage found in part (d).
f. Use the technology of your choice to solve parts (a), (b), (d), and (e).

Internet Resources: Visit the Weiss Web site www.aw.com/weiss for additional discussion, exercises, and resources related to this case study.

Biography
Carl Friedrich Gauss: Child Prodigy

Born on April 30, 1777, in Brunswick, Germany, the only son in a poor, semiliterate peasant family, Carl Friedrich Gauss taught himself to calculate before he could talk. At the age of 3, he pointed out an error in his father's calculations of wages. In addition to his arithmetic experimentation, he taught himself to read. At the age of 8, Gauss instantly solved the summing of all numbers from 1 to 100. His father was persuaded to allow him to stay in school and to study after school instead of working to help support the family.

Impressed by Gauss's brilliance, the Duke of Brunswick supported him monetarily from the ages of 14 to 30. This patronage permitted Gauss to pursue his studies exclusively. He conceived most of his mathematical discoveries by the time he was 17. Gauss was granted a doctorate in absentia from the university at Helmstedt; his doctoral thesis developed the concept of complex numbers and proved the fundamental theorem of algebra, which had previously been only partially established. Shortly thereafter, Gauss published his theory of numbers, which is considered one of the most brilliant achievements in mathematics.

Gauss made important discoveries in mathematics, physics, astronomy, and statistics. Two of his major contributions to statistics were the development of the least-squares method and fundamental work with the normal distribution, often called the *Gaussian distribution* in his honor.

In 1807, Gauss accepted the directorship of the observatory at the University of Göttingen which ended his dependence on the Duke of Brunswick. He remained there the rest of his life. In 1833, Gauss and a colleague, Wilhelm Weber, invented a working electric telegraph, 5 years before Samuel Morse. Gauss died in Göttingen in 1855.

chapter 7

The Sampling Distribution of the Sample Mean

CHAPTER OUTLINE

7.1 Sampling Error; the Need for Sampling Distributions

7.2 The Mean and Standard Deviation of $\bar{x}$

7.3 The Sampling Distribution of the Sample Mean

GENERAL OBJECTIVES In the preceding chapters, you have studied sampling, descriptive statistics, probability, and the normal distribution. Now you will learn how these seemingly diverse topics can be integrated to lay the groundwork for inferential statistics.

In Section 7.1, we introduce the concepts of *sampling error* and *sampling distribution* and explain the essential role these concepts play in the design of inferential studies. The *sampling distribution* of a statistic is simply the distribution of the statistic, that is, the distribution of all possible observations of the statistic for samples of a given size from a population. In this chapter, we concentrate on the sampling distribution of the sample mean.

In Sections 7.2 and 7.3, we provide the required background for applying the sampling distribution of the sample mean. Specifically, in Section 7.2, we present formulas for the mean and standard deviation of the sample mean. Then, in Section 7.3, we indicate that, under certain general conditions, the sampling distribution of the sample mean is a normal distribution, or at least approximately so.

We apply this momentous fact in Chapters 8 and 9 to develop two important statistical-inference procedures: using the mean, $\bar{x}$, of a sample from a population to estimate and to draw conclusions about the mean, μ, of the entire population.

case study

THE CHESAPEAKE AND OHIO FREIGHT STUDY

Can relatively small samples really provide results that are nearly as accurate as those obtained from a census? Although statisticians have shown mathematically that such is the case, a real study in which the results of a sample are compared with those of a census might make this assertion even more credible.

When a freight shipment travels over several railroads, the freight charge is divided among them according to prearranged agreements. With each shipment of freight, a document called a *waybill* is issued that provides information on the goods, route, and total charges. From the waybill of any particular freight shipment, the amount due each railroad can be calculated.

For a large number of shipments, the computations required for allocating the shares properly among the railroads are time-consuming and costly. Consequently, if the division of total revenue among the railroads in question could be done accurately on the basis of a sample—as statisticians contend—considerable savings could be realized in accounting and clerical costs.

To convince themselves of the validity of the sampling approach, officials of the Chesapeake and Ohio Railroad Company (C&O) undertook a study of freight shipments that had traveled over its Pere Marquette district and another railroad during a 6-month period. The total number of waybills for that period was known (22,984), as was the total freight revenue.

Statistical theory was applied to determine the smallest number of waybills required to obtain an estimate of the total revenue due C&O with a prescribed accuracy. In all, 2072 of the 22,984 waybills, roughly 9%, were sampled. For each waybill in the sample, the necessary calculations were performed to find the amount of freight revenue for that shipment belonging to C&O. From those amounts the total revenue due C&O for all shipments was estimated to be $64,568.

How close was the estimate of $64,568, based on a sample of only 2072 waybills, to the total revenue actually due C&O for the 22,984 waybills? Take a guess! We'll discuss the answer at the end of this chapter.

7.1 SAMPLING ERROR; THE NEED FOR SAMPLING DISTRIBUTIONS

We have already demonstrated that using a sample to acquire information about a population is often preferable to conducting a census, where data for the entire population are collected. Generally, sampling is less costly and can be done more quickly than a census; it is often the only practical way to gather information.

But now we need to deal with the following problem: Because a sample from a population provides data for only a portion of the entire population, we cannot expect the sample to yield perfectly accurate information about the population. Thus we should anticipate that a certain amount of error will result simply because we are sampling, which we call **sampling error** and define as follows.

DEFINITION 7.1 **Sampling Error**

Sampling error is the error resulting from using a sample to estimate a population characteristic.

Example 7.1 illustrates sampling error and the need for determining sampling distributions.

Example 7.1 *Sampling Error and the Need for Sampling Distributions*

Household Income The U.S. Bureau of the Census publishes annual figures on the mean income of U.S. households in *Current Population Reports*. Actually, the Census Bureau reports the mean income of a sample of about 60,000 households out of a total of more than 103 million households. For instance, in 1998, the mean income of U.S. households was reported to be $51,855. This amount is really the sample mean income, $\bar{x}$, of the 60,000 households surveyed, not the (population) mean income, μ, of all U.S. households.

We certainly cannot expect the mean income, $\bar{x}$, of the 60,000 households sampled by the Census Bureau to be exactly the same as the mean income, μ, of all U.S. households—some sampling error is to be anticipated. But how much sampling error should we expect; that is, how accurate are such estimates likely to be? For instance, is the sample mean household income reported by the Census Bureau likely to be within $1000 of the population mean household income?

To answer such questions, we need to know the distribution of all possible sample means that could be obtained by sampling the incomes of 60,000 households. That distribution is called the *sampling distribution of the sample mean.* ◆

The distribution of a statistic (i.e., of all possible observations of the statistic for samples of a given size) is called the **sampling distribution** of the statistic. In this chapter, we concentrate on the **sampling distribution of the sample mean,** that is, of the statistic $\bar{x}$.

DEFINITION 7.2 Sampling Distribution of the Sample Mean

For a variable x and a given sample size, the distribution of the variable $\bar{x}$—that is, the distribution of all possible sample means—is called the *sampling distribution of the sample mean*.

In statistics, the following terms and phrases are synonymous.

- Sampling distribution of the sample mean
- Distribution of the variable $\bar{x}$
- Distribution of all possible sample means of a given sample size

Therefore, in this book, we use these three terms interchangeably.

Introducing the sampling distribution of the sample mean with an example that is both realistic and concrete is difficult because even for moderately large populations the number of possible samples is enormous, thus prohibiting an actual listing of the possibilities.[1] Consequently, in Example 7.2, we use an unrealistically small population to introduce the sampling distribution of the sample mean. Keep in mind, however, that populations are much larger in real-life applications.

Example 7.2 Sampling Distribution of the Sample Mean

Heights of Starting Players Suppose that the population of interest consists of the five starting players on a men's basketball team whom, for convenience, we will call A, B, C, D, and E. Further suppose that the variable of interest is height, in inches. Table 7.1 lists the players and their heights.

TABLE 7.1
Heights, in inches, of the five starting players

Player	A	B	C	D	E
Height	76	78	79	81	86

a. Obtain the sampling distribution of the sample mean for samples of size 2.
b. Make some observations about sampling error when the mean height of a random sample of two players is used to estimate the population mean height.[2]
c. Find the probability that, for a random sample of size 2, the sampling error made in estimating the population mean by the sample mean will be 1 inch or less; that is, determine the probability that $\bar{x}$ will be within 1 inch of μ.

Solution For future reference we first compute the population mean height:

$$\mu = \frac{\Sigma x}{N} = \frac{76 + 78 + 79 + 81 + 86}{5} = 80 \text{ inches.}$$

---

[1] For example, the number of possible samples of size 50 from a population of size 10,000 is approximately equal to 3×10^{135}, a 3 followed by 135 zeros.
[2] As we mentioned in Section 1.3, the statistical-inference techniques considered in this book are intended for use only with simple random sampling. Therefore, unless otherwise specified, when we say *sample* or *random sample*, we mean *simple random sample*. Furthermore, we assume that sampling is without replacement unless explicitly stated otherwise.

TABLE 7.2
Possible samples and sample means for samples of size 2

Sample	Heights	$\bar{x}$
A, B	76, 78	77.0
A, C	76, 79	77.5
A, D	76, 81	78.5
A, E	76, 86	81.0
B, C	78, 79	78.5
B, D	78, 81	79.5
B, E	78, 86	82.0
C, D	79, 81	80.0
C, E	79, 86	82.5
D, E	81, 86	83.5

a. The population under consideration here is so small that we can list the possibilities directly. There are 10 possible samples of size 2. The first column of Table 7.2 displays the 10 possible samples, the second column the corresponding heights (i.e., values of the variable "height"), and the third column the sample means. As a visual aid, we have also drawn a dotplot in Fig. 7.1 to portray the distribution of the sample means, that is, the sampling distribution of the sample mean for samples of size 2.

b. Referring to Table 7.2 or Fig. 7.1, we can make some simple but significant observations about sampling error when the mean height of a random sample of two players is used to estimate the population mean height.

For instance, the mean height of the two players selected isn't likely to equal the population mean of 80 inches. In fact, only one of the 10 samples has a mean of 80 inches, the eighth sample in Table 7.2. Thus, in this case, the chances are only $\frac{1}{10}$, or 10%, that $\bar{x}$ will equal μ; some sampling error is likely.

c. Figure 7.1 shows that exactly 3 of the 10 samples have means within 1 inch of the population mean of 80 inches. So the probability is $\frac{3}{10}$, or 0.3, that the sampling error made in estimating μ by $\bar{x}$ will be 1 inch or less. In other words, there is a 30% chance that the mean height of the two players selected will be within 1 inch of the population mean.

FIGURE 7.1
Dotplot for the sampling distribution of the sample mean for samples of size 2 ($n = 2$)

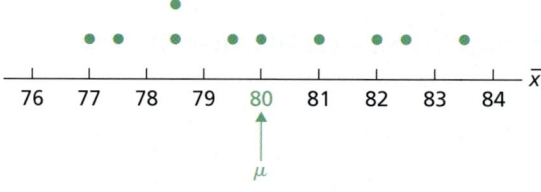

In Example 7.2, we determined the sampling distribution of the sample mean for samples of size 2. If we consider samples of another size—say, of size 4—we obtain a different sampling distribution of the sample mean, as demonstrated in Example 7.3.

Example 7.3 Sampling Distribution of the Sample Mean

Heights of Starting Players The heights of the five starting players on a men's basketball team are presented in Table 7.1 (previous page).

a. Obtain the sampling distribution of the sample mean for samples of size 4.
b. Make some observations about sampling error when the mean height of a random sample of four players is used to estimate the population mean height.
c. Find the probability that, for a random sample of size 4, the sampling error made in estimating the population mean by the sample mean will be 1 inch or less; that is, determine the probability that $\bar{x}$ will be within 1 inch of μ.

Solution

TABLE 7.3
Possible samples and sample means for samples of size 4

Sample	Heights	$\bar{x}$
A, B, C, D	76, 78, 79, 81	78.50
A, B, C, E	76, 78, 79, 86	79.75
A, B, D, E	76, 78, 81, 86	80.25
A, C, D, E	76, 79, 81, 86	80.50
B, C, D, E	78, 79, 81, 86	81.00

a. There are five possible samples of size 4. The first column of Table 7.3 displays the possible samples, the second column the corresponding heights (i.e., values of the variable "height"), and the third column the sample means. As a visual aid, we have also drawn a dotplot in Fig. 7.2 to portray the distribution of the sample means, that is, the sampling distribution of the sample mean for samples of size 4.

b. Referring to Table 7.3 or Fig. 7.2, we observe that none of the samples of size 4 has a mean equal to the population mean of 80 inches. Thus, when the mean height of a random sample of four players is used to estimate the population mean height, some sampling error is certain.

c. Figure 7.2 shows that exactly four of the five samples have means within 1 inch of the population mean of 80 inches. So the probability is $\frac{4}{5}$, or 0.8, that the sampling error made in estimating μ by $\bar{x}$ will be 1 inch or less. In other words, there is an 80% chance that the mean height of the four players selected will be within 1 inch of the population mean.

FIGURE 7.2
Dotplot for the sampling distribution of the sample mean for samples of size 4 ($n = 4$)

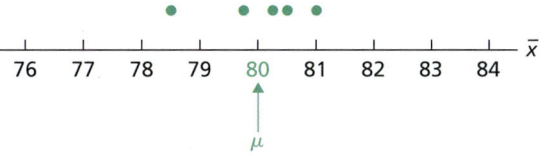

SAMPLE SIZE AND SAMPLING ERROR

In Figs. 7.1 and 7.2, we drew dotplots for the sampling distributions of the sample mean for samples of sizes 2 and 4, respectively. Those two dotplots and dotplots for samples of sizes 1, 3, and 5 are displayed in Fig. 7.3 (next page).

Figure 7.3 vividly shows that the possible sample means cluster more closely around the population mean as the sample size increases. This result, in turn, implies that sampling error tends to (although may not) be smaller for large samples than for small samples.

For example, Fig. 7.3 reveals that, for samples of size 1, two of five, or 40%, of the possible sample means lie within 1 inch of μ. For samples of size 2, three of ten, or 30%, of the possible sample means lie within 1 inch of μ. For samples of size 3, five of ten, or 50%, of the possible sample means lie within 1 inch of μ. For samples of size 4, four of five, or 80%, of the possible sample means lie within 1 inch of μ. And for samples of size 5, one of one, or 100%, of the possible sample means lie within 1 inch of μ.

Table 7.4 (next page) summarizes these results and also provides another sampling-error illustration easily obtained from Fig. 7.3.

More generally, we can make the following qualitative statement.

Key Fact 7.1 **Sample Size and Sampling Error**

The possible sample means cluster more closely around the population mean as the sample size increases. Thus the larger the sample size, the smaller the sampling error tends to be in estimating a population mean, μ, by a sample mean, $\bar{x}$.

FIGURE 7.3
Dotplots for the sampling distributions of the sample mean for samples of sizes 1, 2, 3, 4, and 5

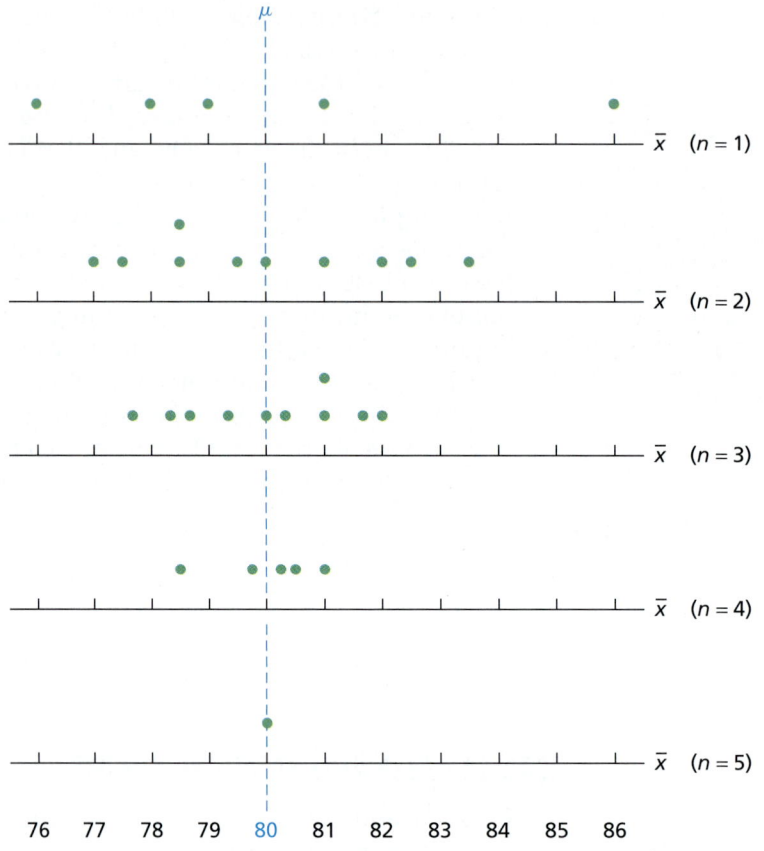

TABLE 7.4
Sample size and sampling error illustrations for the heights of the basketball players

Sample size n	No. possible samples	No. within 1" of μ	% within 1" of μ	No. within 0.5" of μ	% within 0.5" of μ
1	5	2	40%	0	0%
2	10	3	30%	2	20%
3	10	5	50%	2	20%
4	5	4	80%	3	60%
5	1	1	100%	1	100%

WHAT WE DO IN PRACTICE

We have used the heights of a population of five basketball players to illustrate and explain the importance of the sampling distribution of the sample mean. For that small population, we can easily obtain the sampling distribution of the sample mean for any sample size by listing all of the possible sample means.

However, as we have noted, in practice, we usually deal with large populations. For such populations, obtaining the sampling distribution of the sample mean by a direct listing is not feasible. A more serious practical problem is that, in reality, we do not even know the population data (i.e., the distribution of the variable)—if we did, there would be no need to sample! Realistically then, we could not list the possible sample means to determine the sampling distribution of the sample mean even if we were willing to expend the effort.

So, what can we do in the usual case of a large and unknown population? Fortunately, mathematical relationships exist that allow us to determine, at least approximately, the sampling distribution of the sample mean for any specified sample size, which we discuss in Sections 7.2 and 7.3.

Exercises 7.1

Statistical Concepts and Skills

7.1 Why is sampling often preferable to conducting a census for the purpose of obtaining information about a population?

7.2 Why should you generally expect some error when estimating a parameter (e.g., a population mean) by a statistic (e.g., a sample mean)? What is this kind of error called?

Exercises 7.3–7.15 are intended solely to provide concrete illustrations of the sampling distribution of the sample mean. For that reason, the populations considered are unrealistically small. In each exercise, assume that sampling is without replacement.

7.3 NBA Champs. The winner of the 1999–2000 National Basketball Association (NBA) championship was the Los Angeles Lakers. The following table provides the starting players and their positions and heights.

Player	Position	Height (in.)
Ron Harper (HG)	Guard	78
Kobe Bryant (BG)	Guard	79
Robert Horry (HF)	Forward	82
A.C. Green (GF)	Forward	81
Shaquille O'Neal (OC)	Center	85

a. Find the population mean height of the five players.
b. For samples of size 2, construct a table similar to Table 7.2 on page 300. Use the letters in parentheses after each player's name to represent the players.
c. Draw a dotplot for the sampling distribution of the sample mean for samples of size 2 like the one shown in Fig. 7.1 on page 300.
d. For a random sample of size 2, what is the chance that the sample mean will equal the population mean? That is, determine $P(\bar{x} = \mu)$.
e. For a random sample of size 2, obtain the probability that the sampling error made in estimating the population mean by the sample mean will be 1 inch or less; that is, determine the probability that $\bar{x}$ will be within 1 inch of μ. Interpret your result in terms of percentages.

7.4 NBA Champs. Repeat parts (b)–(e) of Exercise 7.3 for samples of size 1.

7.5 NBA Champs. Repeat parts (b)–(e) of Exercise 7.3 for samples of size 3.

7.6 NBA Champs. Repeat parts (b)–(e) of Exercise 7.3 for samples of size 4.

7.7 NBA Champs. Repeat parts (b)–(e) of Exercise 7.3 for samples of size 5.

7.8 NBA Champs. This exercise requires that you have done Exercises 7.3–7.7.
a. Draw a graph similar to that shown in Fig. 7.3 for sample sizes of 1, 2, 3, 4, and 5.
b. What does your graph in part (a) illustrate about the impact of increasing sample size on sampling error?
c. Construct a table similar to Table 7.4 for some values of your choice.

7.9 World's Richest. Each year, *Forbes* magazine publishes a list of the world's richest people. In 2000, the six richest people and their wealth, to the nearest billion dollars, are as shown in the following table. Consider these six people a population of interest.

Person	Wealth ($billions)
William H. Gates III (G)	60
Lawrence J. Ellison (E)	47
King Fahd Bin Abdulaziz Alsaud (K)	30
Paul G. Allen (A)	28
Warren Buffet (B)	28
Sheikh Zayed Al Nahyan (N)	23

a. Calculate the mean wealth, μ, of the six people.
b. For samples of size 2, construct a table similar to Table 7.2 on page 300. (There are 15 possible samples of size 2.)
c. Draw a dotplot for the sampling distribution of the sample mean for samples of size 2.
d. For a random sample of size 2, what is the chance that the sample mean will equal the population mean? That is, determine $P(\bar{x} = \mu)$.
e. For a random sample of size 2, determine the probability that the mean wealth of the two people obtained will be within 2 (i.e., $2 billion) of the population mean. Interpret your result in terms of percentages.

7.10 World's Richest. Repeat parts (b)–(e) of Exercise 7.9 for samples of size 1.

7.11 World's Richest. Repeat parts (b)–(e) of Exercise 7.9 for samples of size 3. (There are 20 possible samples.)

7.12 World's Richest. Repeat parts (b)–(e) of Exercise 7.9 for samples of size 4. (There are 15 possible samples.)

7.13 World's Richest. Repeat parts (b)–(e) of Exercise 7.9 for samples of size 5. (There are six possible samples.)

7.14 World's Richest. Repeat parts (b)–(e) of Exercise 7.9 for samples of size 6. What is the relationship between the only possible sample here and the population?

7.15 World's Richest. Explain what the dotplots in part (c) of Exercises 7.9–7.14 illustrate about the impact of increasing sample size on sampling error.

Extending the Concepts and Skills

7.16 Suppose that a sample is to be taken without replacement from a finite population of size N. If the sample size is the same as the population size,
a. how many possible samples are there?
b. what are the possible sample means?
c. what is the relationship between the only possible sample and the population?

7.17 Suppose that a random sample of size 1 is to be taken from a finite population of size N.
a. How many possible samples are there?
b. Identify the relationship between the possible sample means and the possible observations of the variable under consideration.
c. What is the difference between taking a random sample of size 1 from a population and selecting a member at random from the population?

7.2 THE MEAN AND STANDARD DEVIATION OF $\bar{x}$

In Section 7.1, we discussed the sampling distribution of the sample mean—the distribution of all possible sample means for any specified sample size or, equivalently, the distribution of the variable $\bar{x}$. We use the sampling distribution of the sample mean to make inferences about a population mean based on the mean of a sample from the population.

As we said earlier, we generally do not know the sampling distribution of the sample mean exactly. Fortunately, however, we can often approximate that sampling distribution by a normal distribution; that is, under certain conditions, the variable $\bar{x}$ is approximately normally distributed.

Recall that a variable is normally distributed if its distribution has the shape of a normal curve and that a normal distribution is determined by the mean and standard deviation. Hence a first step in learning how to approximate the sampling distribution of the sample mean by a normal distribution is to obtain the mean and standard deviation of $\bar{x}$. We describe how to do that in this section.

To begin, let's review the notation used for the mean and standard deviation of a variable. Recall that the mean of a variable is denoted μ, subscripted if necessary with the letter representing the variable. So the mean of x is written as μ_x, the mean of y as μ_y, and so on. In particular, then, the mean of $\bar{x}$ is written as $\mu_{\bar{x}}$; similarly, the standard deviation of $\bar{x}$ is written as $\sigma_{\bar{x}}$.

THE MEAN OF $\bar{x}$

There is a simple relationship between the mean of the variable $\bar{x}$ and the mean of the variable under consideration: They are equal, or $\mu_{\bar{x}} = \mu$. In other words, for any particular sample size, the mean of all possible sample means equals the population mean. This equality holds regardless of the size of the sample. In Example 7.4, we illustrate the relationship $\mu_{\bar{x}} = \mu$ by returning to the heights of the basketball players considered in Section 7.1.

Example 7.4 The Relation $\mu_{\bar{x}} = \mu$

Heights of Starting Players The heights, in inches, of the five starting players on a men's basketball team are repeated in Table 7.5. Here the population of interest consists of the five players, and the variable under consideration is height.

TABLE 7.5
Heights of the five starting players

Player	A	B	C	D	E
Height	76	78	79	81	86

a. Determine the population mean, μ.
b. Obtain the mean, $\mu_{\bar{x}}$, of the variable $\bar{x}$ for samples of size 2. Verify that the relation $\mu_{\bar{x}} = \mu$ holds.
c. Repeat part (b) for samples of size 4.

Solution a. To determine the population mean (i.e., the mean of the variable "height"), we apply Definition 3.11 on page 129 to the heights in Table 7.5:

$$\mu = \frac{\Sigma x}{N} = \frac{76 + 78 + 79 + 81 + 86}{5} = 80 \text{ inches.}$$

Thus the mean height of the five players is 80 inches.

b. To obtain the mean of the variable $\bar{x}$ for samples of size 2, we again apply Definition 3.11, but this time to $\bar{x}$. Referring to the third column of Table 7.2 on page 300, we get

$$\mu_{\bar{x}} = \frac{77.0 + 77.5 + \cdots + 83.5}{10} = 80 \text{ inches.}$$

By part (a), $\mu = 80$ inches. So, for samples of size 2, $\mu_{\bar{x}} = \mu$.

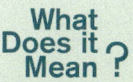

What Does it Mean?

For samples of size 2, the mean of all possible sample means equals the population mean.

c. Proceeding as in part (b), but this time referring to the third column of Table 7.3 on page 301, we obtain the mean of the variable $\bar{x}$ for samples of size 4:

$$\mu_{\bar{x}} = \frac{78.50 + 79.75 + 80.25 + 80.50 + 81.00}{5} = 80 \text{ inches,}$$

which again is the same as μ.

> **What Does it Mean?**
>
> For samples of size 4, the mean of all possible sample means equals the population mean.

For emphasis, we restate the relationship $\mu_{\bar{x}} = \mu$ as the following formula.

FORMULA 7.1 Mean of the Variable $\bar{x}$

For samples of size n, the mean of the variable $\bar{x}$ equals the mean of the variable under consideration:

$$\mu_{\bar{x}} = \mu.$$

In other words, for each sample size, the mean of all possible sample means equals the population mean.

THE STANDARD DEVIATION OF $\bar{x}$

Next, we investigate the standard deviation of the variable $\bar{x}$. We want to discover any apparent relationship of the standard deviation of $\bar{x}$ to the standard deviation of the variable under consideration. To begin our investigation, in Example 7.5, we return to the basketball players.

Example 7.5 Relation Between $\sigma_{\bar{x}}$ and σ

Heights of Starting Players Refer to Table 7.5 on the previous page.

a. Determine the population standard deviation, σ.
b. Obtain the standard deviation, $\sigma_{\bar{x}}$, of the variable $\bar{x}$ for samples of size 2. Indicate any apparent relationship between $\sigma_{\bar{x}}$ and σ.
c. Repeat part (b) for samples of sizes 1, 3, 4, and 5.
d. Summarize and discuss the results obtained in parts (a)–(c).

Solution a. To determine the population standard deviation (i.e., the standard deviation of the variable "height"), we apply Definition 3.12 on page 131 to the heights in Table 7.5. Recalling that $\mu = 80$ inches, we have

$$\sigma = \sqrt{\frac{\Sigma(x-\mu)^2}{N}}$$

$$= \sqrt{\frac{(76-80)^2 + (78-80)^2 + (79-80)^2 + (81-80)^2 + (86-80)^2}{5}}$$

$$= \sqrt{\frac{16 + 4 + 1 + 1 + 36}{5}} = \sqrt{11.6} = 3.41 \text{ inches.}$$

Thus the standard deviation of the heights of the five players is 3.41 inches.

TABLE 7.6
The standard deviation of $\bar{x}$ for sample sizes 1, 2, 3, 4, and 5

Sample size n	Standard deviation of $\bar{x}$ $\sigma_{\bar{x}}$
1	3.41
2	2.09
3	1.39
4	0.85
5	0.00

What Does it Mean?

Figure 7.3 indicates graphically that the variation, and hence the standard deviation, of all possible sample means decreases with increasing sample size. Table 7.6 indicates that same thing numerically.

b. To obtain the standard deviation of the variable $\bar{x}$ for samples of size 2, we again apply Definition 3.12, but this time to $\bar{x}$. Referring to the third column of Table 7.2 on page 300 and recalling that $\mu_{\bar{x}} = \mu = 80$ inches, we have

$$\sigma_{\bar{x}} = \sqrt{\frac{(77.0 - 80)^2 + (77.5 - 80)^2 + \cdots + (83.5 - 80)^2}{10}}$$

$$= \sqrt{\frac{9.00 + 6.25 + \cdots + 12.25}{10}} = \sqrt{4.35} = 2.09 \text{ inches},$$

to two decimal places. Note that this result is not the same as the population standard deviation, which is $\sigma = 3.41$ inches. Also note that $\sigma_{\bar{x}}$ is smaller than σ.

c. Using the same procedure as in part (b), we compute $\sigma_{\bar{x}}$ for samples of sizes 1, 3, 4, and 5 and summarize the results in Table 7.6.

d. Table 7.6 suggests that the standard deviation of $\bar{x}$ gets smaller as the sample size gets larger. We could have predicted this result from the dotplots shown in Fig. 7.3 on page 302 and from the fact that the standard deviation of a variable measures the variation of its possible values. ◆

Example 7.5 provides evidence that the standard deviation of $\bar{x}$ gets smaller as the sample size gets larger; that is, the variation of all possible sample means decreases as the sample size increases. The question now is whether there is a formula that relates the standard deviation of $\bar{x}$ to the sample size and standard deviation of the population. The answer is yes! In fact, two different formulas express the precise relationship.

When sampling is done without replacement from a finite population, as in Example 7.5, the appropriate formula is

$$\sigma_{\bar{x}} = \sqrt{\frac{N-n}{N-1}} \cdot \frac{\sigma}{\sqrt{n}},$$

where, as usual, n denotes the sample size and N the population size. When sampling is done with replacement from a finite population or when it is done from an infinite population, the appropriate formula is

$$\sigma_{\bar{x}} = \frac{\sigma}{\sqrt{n}}.$$

When the sample size is small relative to the population size, there is little difference between sampling with and without replacement.[3] So, in such cases, it is not surprising that the two formulas for $\sigma_{\bar{x}}$ yield almost the same numbers. In most practical applications, the sample size is in fact small relative to the population size, so with the understanding that the equality may be only approximate, we use the second formula, denoted Formula 7.2, exclusively in this book.

---

[3] As a rule of thumb, we say that the sample size is small relative to the population size if $n \leq 0.05N$, that is, if the size of the sample does not exceed 5% of the size of the population.

CHAPTER 7 The Sampling Distribution of the Sample Mean

FORMULA 7.2 **Standard Deviation of the Variable $\bar{x}$**

For samples of size n, the standard deviation of the variable $\bar{x}$ equals the standard deviation of the variable under consideration divided by the square root of the sample size:

$$\sigma_{\bar{x}} = \frac{\sigma}{\sqrt{n}}.$$

In other words, for each sample size, the standard deviation of all possible sample means equals the population standard deviation divided by the square root of the sample size.

APPLYING THE FORMULAS

We have shown that simple formulas relate the mean and standard deviation of $\bar{x}$ to the mean and standard deviation of the population: $\mu_{\bar{x}} = \mu$ and $\sigma_{\bar{x}} = \sigma/\sqrt{n}$ (at least approximately). We apply those formulas in Example 7.6.

Example 7.6 The Mean and Standard Deviation of $\bar{x}$

Living Space of Homes As reported by the U.S. Bureau of the Census in *Current Housing Reports*, the mean living space for single-family detached homes is 1742 square feet. The standard deviation is 568 square feet.

a. For samples of 25 single-family detached homes, determine the mean and standard deviation of the variable $\bar{x}$.
b. Repeat part (a) for a sample of size 500.

Solution Here the variable is living space, and the population consists of all single-family detached homes in the United States. We know that $\mu = 1742$ sq. ft. and $\sigma = 568$ sq. ft.

a. The sample size is 25, so $\bar{x}$ denotes the mean living space of a sample of 25 single-family detached homes. We want to obtain the mean and standard deviation of all such possible sample means. Applying Formula 7.1 on page 306, we get

$$\mu_{\bar{x}} = \mu = 1742 \text{ sq. ft.}$$

As $n = 25$, we conclude from Formula 7.2 that

$$\sigma_{\bar{x}} = \frac{\sigma}{\sqrt{n}} = \frac{568}{\sqrt{25}} = 113.6 \text{ sq. ft.}$$

b. Proceeding as in part (a), we find that

$$\mu_{\bar{x}} = \mu = 1742 \text{ sq. ft.},$$

What Does it Mean?

For samples of 25 single-family detached homes, the mean and standard deviation of all possible sample mean living spaces are 1742 sq. ft. and 113.6 sq. ft., respectively.

> **What Does it Mean?**
>
> For samples of 500 single-family detached homes, the mean and standard deviation of all possible sample mean living spaces are 1742 sq. ft. and 25.4 sq. ft., respectively.

and, as $n = 500$,

$$\sigma_{\bar{x}} = \frac{\sigma}{\sqrt{n}} = \frac{568}{\sqrt{500}} = 25.4 \text{ sq. ft.}$$

SAMPLE SIZE AND SAMPLING ERROR (REVISITED)

Key Fact 7.1 states that the possible sample means cluster more closely around the population mean as the sample size increases, and therefore the larger the sample size, the smaller the sampling error tends to be in estimating a population mean by a sample mean. Here is why that key fact is true.

- The larger the sample size, the smaller is the standard deviation of $\bar{x}$.
- The smaller the standard deviation of $\bar{x}$, the more closely the possible values of $\bar{x}$ (the possible sample means) cluster around the mean of $\bar{x}$.
- The mean of $\bar{x}$ equals the population mean.

Because the standard deviation of $\bar{x}$ determines the amount of sampling error to be expected when a population mean is estimated by a sample mean, it is often referred to as the **standard error of the sample mean**. In general, the standard deviation of a statistic used to estimate a parameter is called the **standard error (SE)** of the statistic.

Exercises 7.2

Statistical Concepts and Skills

7.18 Although, in general, you cannot know the sampling distribution of the sample mean exactly, by what distribution can you often approximate it?

7.19 Why is obtaining the mean and standard deviation of $\bar{x}$ a first step in approximating the sampling distribution of the sample mean by a normal distribution?

7.20 Does the sample size have an effect on the mean of all possible sample means? Explain your answer.

7.21 Does the sample size have an effect on the standard deviation of all possible sample means? Explain your answer.

7.22 Explain why increasing the sample size tends to result in a smaller sampling error when a sample mean is used to estimate a population mean.

7.23 What is another name for the standard deviation of the variable $\bar{x}$? What is the reason for that name?

7.24 In this section, we stated that, when the sample size is small relative to the population size, there is little difference between sampling with and without replacement. Explain in your own words why that statement is true.

Exercises 7.25–7.29 require that you have done Exercises 7.3–7.7.

7.25 NBA Champs. The winner of the 1999–2000 National Basketball Association (NBA) championship was the Los Angeles Lakers. The following table provides the starting players and their positions and heights.

Player	Position	Height (in.)
Ron Harper (HG)	Guard	78
Kobe Bryant (BG)	Guard	79
Robert Horry (HF)	Forward	82
A.C. Green (GF)	Forward	81
Shaquille O'Neal (OC)	Center	85

a. Determine the population mean height, μ, of the five players.

b. Consider samples of size 2 without replacement. Use your answer to Exercise 7.3(b) on page 303 and Definition 3.11 on page 129 to find the mean of the variable $\bar{x}$.
c. Find $\mu_{\bar{x}}$, using only the result of part (a).

7.26 NBA Champs. Repeat parts (b) and (c) of Exercise 7.25 for samples of size 1. For part (b), use your answer to Exercise 7.4(b).

7.27 NBA Champs. Repeat parts (b) and (c) of Exercise 7.25 for samples of size 3. For part (b), use your answer to Exercise 7.5(b).

7.28 NBA Champs. Repeat parts (b) and (c) of Exercise 7.25 for samples of size 4. For part (b), use your answer to Exercise 7.6(b).

7.29 NBA Champs. Repeat parts (b) and (c) of Exercise 7.25 for samples of size 5. For part (b), use your answer to Exercise 7.7(b).

7.30 Working at Home. According to the U.S. Bureau of Labor Statistics publication *News*, self-employed persons with home-based businesses work a mean of 23 hours per week at home with a standard deviation of 10 hours.
a. Identify the population and variable under consideration.
b. For samples of size 100, find the mean and standard deviation of all possible sample mean hours worked per week at home.
c. Repeat part (b) for samples of size 1000.

7.31 Baby Weight. The 1999 paper "Are Babies Normal?" by Traci Clemons and Marcello Pagano (*The American Statistician*, Vol. 53, No. 4, pp. 298–302) focused on babies born in 1991. According to the article, the mean birth weight is 3369 grams (7 pounds 6.5 ounces) with a standard deviation of 581 grams.
a. Identify the population and variable under consideration.
b. For samples of size 200, find the mean and standard deviation of all possible sample mean weights.
c. Repeat part (b) for samples of size 400.

7.32 Hospital Stays. The U.S. National Center for Health Statistics publishes information on the length of stay by patients in short-stay hospitals in *Vital and Health Statistics*. According to that publication, the mean stay of female patients in short-stay hospitals is $\mu = 5.8$ days. The standard deviation is $\sigma = 4.3$ days. Let $\bar{x}$ denote the mean length of stay for a sample of discharged female patients.
a. For a sample size of 75, find the mean and standard deviation of $\bar{x}$. Interpret your results in words.
b. Repeat part (a) with $n = 500$.

7.33 Mobile Homes. According to the U.S. Census Bureau publication *Current Construction Reports*, the mean price of new mobile homes is $43,800. The standard deviation of the prices is $7200. Let $\bar{x}$ denote the mean price of a sample of new mobile homes.
a. For samples of size 50, find the mean and standard deviation of $\bar{x}$. Interpret your results in words.
b. Repeat part (a) with $n = 100$.

7.34 Earthquakes. According to *The Earth: Structure, Composition and Evolution* (The Open University, S237, 1981), for earthquakes with a magnitude of 7.5 or greater on the Richter scale, the time between successive earthquakes has a mean of 437 days and a standard deviation of 399 days. Suppose that you observe a sample of four times between successive earthquakes that have a magnitude of 7.5 or greater on the Richter scale.
a. On average, what would you expect to be the mean of the four times?
b. How much variation would you expect from your answer in part (a)? (*Hint:* Use the three-standard-deviations rule.)

Extending the Concepts and Skills

7.35 Unbiased and Biased Estimators. A statistic is said to be an *unbiased estimator* of a parameter if the mean of all its possible values equals the parameter; otherwise, it is said to be a *biased estimator*. An unbiased estimator yields, on average, the correct value of the parameter, whereas a biased estimator does not.
a. Is the sample mean an unbiased estimator of the population mean? Explain your answer.
b. Is the sample median an unbiased estimator of the population median? (*Hint:* Refer to Example 7.2 on page 299. Consider samples of size 2.)

7.36 Class Project Simulation. This exercise can be done individually or, better yet, as a class project.
a. Use a random-number table or random-number generator to obtain a sample (with replacement) of four digits

between 0 and 9. Do so a total of 50 times and compute the mean of each sample.
b. Theoretically, what are the mean and standard deviation of all possible sample means for samples of size 4?
c. Roughly what would you expect the mean and standard deviation of the 50 sample means you obtained in part (a) to be? Explain your answers.
d. Determine the mean and standard deviation of the 50 sample means you obtained in part (a).
e. Compare your answers in parts (c) and (d). Why are they different?

Using Technology

7.37 Gestation Periods of Humans. For humans, gestation periods are normally distributed with a mean of 266 days and a standard deviation of 16 days. Suppose that you observe the gestation periods for a sample of nine humans.
a. Theoretically, what are the mean and standard deviation of all possible sample means?
b. Use the technology of your choice to simulate 2000 samples of nine human gestation periods each.
c. Determine the mean of each of the 2000 samples you obtained in part (b).
d. Roughly what would you expect the mean and standard deviation of the 2000 sample means you obtained in part (c) to be? Explain your answers.
e. Determine the mean and standard deviation of the 2000 sample means you obtained in part (c).
f. Compare your answers in parts (d) and (e). Why are they different?

7.38 Emergency Room Traffic. Desert Samaritan Hospital in Mesa, Arizona, keeps records of emergency room traffic. Those records reveal that the times between arriving patients have a special type of reverse J-shaped distribution called an *exponential distribution*. They also indicate that the mean time between arriving patients is 8.7 minutes, as is the standard deviation. Suppose that you observe a sample of 10 interarrival times.
a. Theoretically, what are the mean and standard deviation of all possible sample means?
b. Use the technology of your choice to simulate 1000 samples of 10 interarrival times each.
c. Determine the mean of each of the 1000 samples you obtained in part (b).
d. Roughly what would you expect the mean and standard deviation of the 1000 sample means you obtained in part (c) to be? Explain your answers.
e. Determine the mean and standard deviation of the 1000 sample means you obtained in part (c).
f. Compare your answers in parts (d) and (e). Why are they different?

7.3 THE SAMPLING DISTRIBUTION OF THE SAMPLE MEAN

In Section 7.2, we took the first step in describing the sampling distribution of the sample mean, that is, the distribution of the variable $\bar{x}$. There, we showed that the mean and standard deviation of $\bar{x}$ can be expressed in terms of the sample size and the population mean and standard deviation: $\mu_{\bar{x}} = \mu$ and $\sigma_{\bar{x}} = \sigma/\sqrt{n}$.

In this section, we take the final step in describing the sampling distribution of the sample mean. In doing so, we distinguish between the case in which the variable under consideration is normally distributed and the case in which it may not be so.

SAMPLING DISTRIBUTION OF THE SAMPLE MEAN FOR NORMALLY DISTRIBUTED VARIABLES

Although it is by no means obvious, if the variable under consideration is normally distributed, so is the variable $\bar{x}$. The proof of this fact requires advanced mathematics, but we can make it plausible by simulation, as demonstrated in Example 7.7.

Example 7.7 Sampling Distribution of the Sample Mean for a Normally Distributed Variable

Intelligence Quotients Intelligence quotients (IQs) measured on the Stanford Revision of the Binet–Simon Intelligence Scale are normally distributed with a mean of 100 and a standard deviation of 16. For a sample size of, say, 4, use simulation to make plausible the fact that $\bar{x}$ is normally distributed, that is, that the possible sample mean IQs for samples of four people have a normal distribution.

Solution First, we apply Formula 7.1 (page 306) and Formula 7.2 (page 308) to conclude that $\mu_{\bar{x}} = \mu = 100$ and $\sigma_{\bar{x}} = \sigma/\sqrt{n} = 16/\sqrt{4} = 8$; that is, the variable $\bar{x}$ has a mean of 100 and a standard deviation of 8. We simulated 1000 samples of four IQs each, determined the sample mean ($\bar{x}$) of each of the 1000 samples, and obtained a histogram of the 1000 sample means.

Printout 7.1 displays the histogram. For purposes of comparison, we superimposed on the histogram the normal distribution with a mean of 100 and a standard deviation of 8. Note that the histogram is shaped roughly like a normal curve—specifically, like the normal curve with parameters 100 and 8.

> **What Does it Mean?**
>
> The histogram in Printout 7.1 indicates that $\bar{x}$ is normally distributed, that is, that the possible sample mean IQs for samples of four people have a normal distribution.

PRINTOUT 7.1
Histogram of the sample means for 1000 samples of four IQs with superimposed normal curve

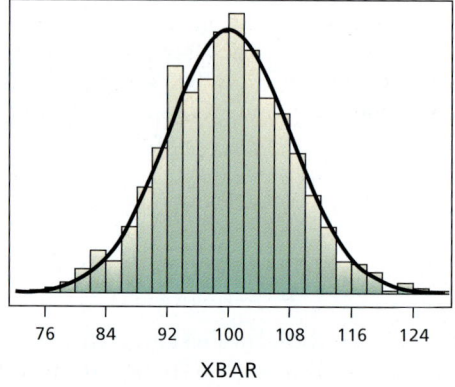

Key Fact 7.2 summarizes our discussion and simulation of the sampling distribution of the sample mean when the variable under consideration is normally distributed.

Key Fact 7.2 Sampling Distribution of the Sample Mean for a Normally Distributed Variable

Suppose that a variable x of a population is normally distributed with mean μ and standard deviation σ. Then, for samples of size n, the variable $\bar{x}$ is also normally distributed and has mean μ and standard deviation $\sigma/\sqrt{n}$.

In Example 7.8, we compare the sampling distribution of the sample mean for two sample sizes to the normal distribution for IQs.

Example 7.8 Sampling Distribution of the Sample Mean for a Normally Distributed Variable

Intelligence Quotients Consider again the variable IQ, which is normally distributed with mean 100 and standard deviation 16. Obtain the sampling distribution of the sample mean for samples of size
 a. 4.   b. 16.

Solution The normal distribution for IQs is shown in Fig. 7.4(a). Because IQs are normally distributed, Key Fact 7.2 implies that, for any particular sample size n, the variable $\bar{x}$ is also normally distributed and has mean $\mu = 100$ and standard deviation $\sigma/\sqrt{n} = 16/\sqrt{n}$.

a. For samples of size 4, we have $16/\sqrt{n} = 16/\sqrt{4} = 8$, and therefore the sampling distribution of the sample mean is a normal distribution with a mean of 100 and a standard deviation of 8. This normal distribution is shown in Fig. 7.4(b).

b. For samples of size 16, we have $16/\sqrt{n} = 16/\sqrt{16} = 4$, and therefore the sampling distribution of the sample mean is a normal distribution with a mean of 100 and a standard deviation of 4. This normal distribution is shown in Fig. 7.4(c).

FIGURE 7.4
(a) Normal distribution for IQs; (b) sampling distribution of the sample mean for $n = 4$; (c) sampling distribution of the sample mean for $n = 16$

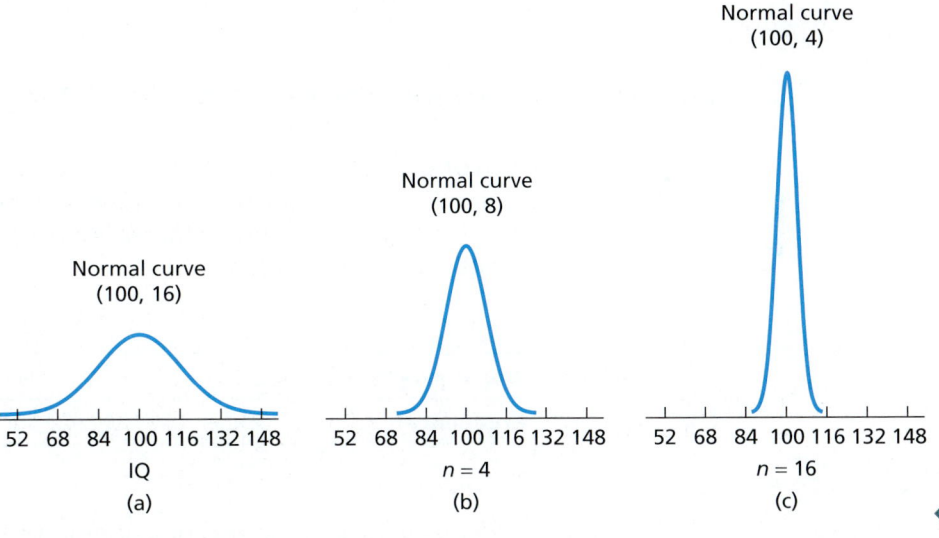

The normal curves in Figs. 7.4(b) and 7.4(c) are drawn to scale so that you can compare them visually and observe two important things that you already know: Both curves are centered at the population mean ($\mu_{\bar{x}} = \mu$), and the spread becomes less extensive as the sample size increases ($\sigma_{\bar{x}} = \sigma/\sqrt{n}$).

Figure 7.4 also illustrates something else that you already know: The possible sample means cluster more closely around the population mean as the sample size increases, and therefore the larger the sample size, the smaller the sampling error tends to be in estimating a population mean by a sample mean.

CHAPTER 7 The Sampling Distribution of the Sample Mean

CENTRAL LIMIT THEOREM

According to Key Fact 7.2, if the variable x under consideration is normally distributed, so is the variable $\bar{x}$. Remarkably, that key fact holds approximately regardless of the distribution of x, provided only that the sample size is relatively large. This extraordinary fact, presented in the following key fact, is called the **central limit theorem** and is one of the most important theorems in statistics.

> **Key Fact 7.3** **The Central Limit Theorem (CLT)**
>
> For a relatively large sample size, the variable $\bar{x}$ is approximately normally distributed, regardless of the distribution of the variable under consideration. The approximation becomes better and better with increasing sample size.

Roughly speaking, the farther the variable under consideration is from being normally distributed, the larger the sample size must be for a normal distribution to provide an adequate approximation to the distribution of $\bar{x}$. Usually, however, a sample size of 30 or more ($n \geq 30$) is large enough.

The proof of the central limit theorem is quite difficult. But we can make it plausible by simulation, as shown in Example 7.9.

Example 7.9 Checking the Plausibility of the CLT by Simulation

Household Size According to the U.S. Bureau of the Census publication *Current Population Reports*, a frequency distribution for the number of people per household in the United States is as displayed in Table 7.7. Frequencies are in millions of households.

TABLE 7.7
Frequency distribution for U.S. household size

No. of people	1	2	3	4	5	6	7
Frequency	19.4	26.5	14.6	12.9	6.1	2.5	1.6

Here, the variable under consideration is household size, and the population consists of all U.S. households. From Table 7.7, we find that the mean household size is $\mu = 2.685$ persons and the standard deviation is $\sigma = 1.47$ persons. Consequently, for samples of size n, $\mu_{\bar{x}} = \mu = 2.685$ and $\sigma_{\bar{x}} = \sigma/\sqrt{n} = 1.47/\sqrt{n}$.

In Fig. 7.5, we present a relative-frequency histogram for household size, obtained from Table 7.7.

Note that the variable household size is far from being normally distributed; it is clearly right skewed. Nonetheless, according to the central limit theorem, the sampling distribution of the sample mean can be approximated by a normal

FIGURE 7.5
Relative-frequency histogram for household size

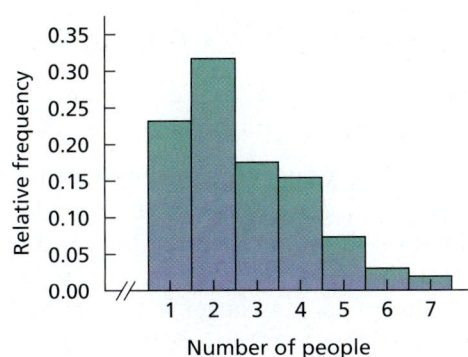

distribution when the sample size is relatively large. Use simulation to make that fact plausible for a sample size of 30.

Solution For a sample size of 30, the variable $\bar{x}$ has mean 2.685 and standard deviation $1.47/\sqrt{30} = 0.27$. We simulated 1000 samples of 30 household sizes each, determined the sample mean ($\bar{x}$) of each of the 1000 samples, and obtained a histogram of the 1000 sample means.

Printout 7.2 displays the histogram. For purposes of comparison, we superimposed on the histogram the normal distribution with a mean of 2.685 and a standard deviation of 0.27. Note that the histogram is shaped roughly like a normal curve—namely, like the normal curve with parameters 2.685 and 0.27.

> **What Does it Mean?**
>
> The histogram in Printout 7.2 indicates that $\bar{x}$ is approximately normally distributed, as guaranteed by the central limit theorem.

PRINTOUT 7.2
Histogram of the sample means for 1000 samples of 30 household sizes with superimposed normal curve

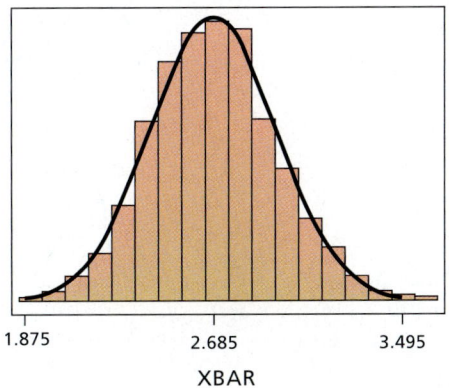

THE SAMPLING DISTRIBUTION OF THE SAMPLE MEAN

We now summarize in Key Fact 7.4 the important facts that we have learned about the sampling distribution of the sample mean. We use Key Fact 7.4 frequently in the remainder of this book.

Key Fact 7.4 Sampling Distribution of the Sample Mean

Suppose that a variable x of a population has mean μ and standard deviation σ. Then, for samples of size n,

- the mean of $\bar{x}$ equals the population mean, or $\mu_{\bar{x}} = \mu$;
- the standard deviation of $\bar{x}$ equals the population standard deviation divided by the square root of the sample size, or $\sigma_{\bar{x}} = \sigma/\sqrt{n}$;
- if x is normally distributed, so is $\bar{x}$, regardless of sample size; and
- if the sample size is large, $\bar{x}$ is approximately normally distributed, regardless of the distribution of x.

Thus, if either the variable under consideration is normally distributed or the sample size is large, the distribution of all possible sample means is, at least approximately, a normal distribution with mean μ and standard deviation $\sigma/\sqrt{n}$.

The content of Key Fact 7.4 is illustrated graphically in Fig. 7.6 for normal, reverse-J-shaped, and uniform variables.

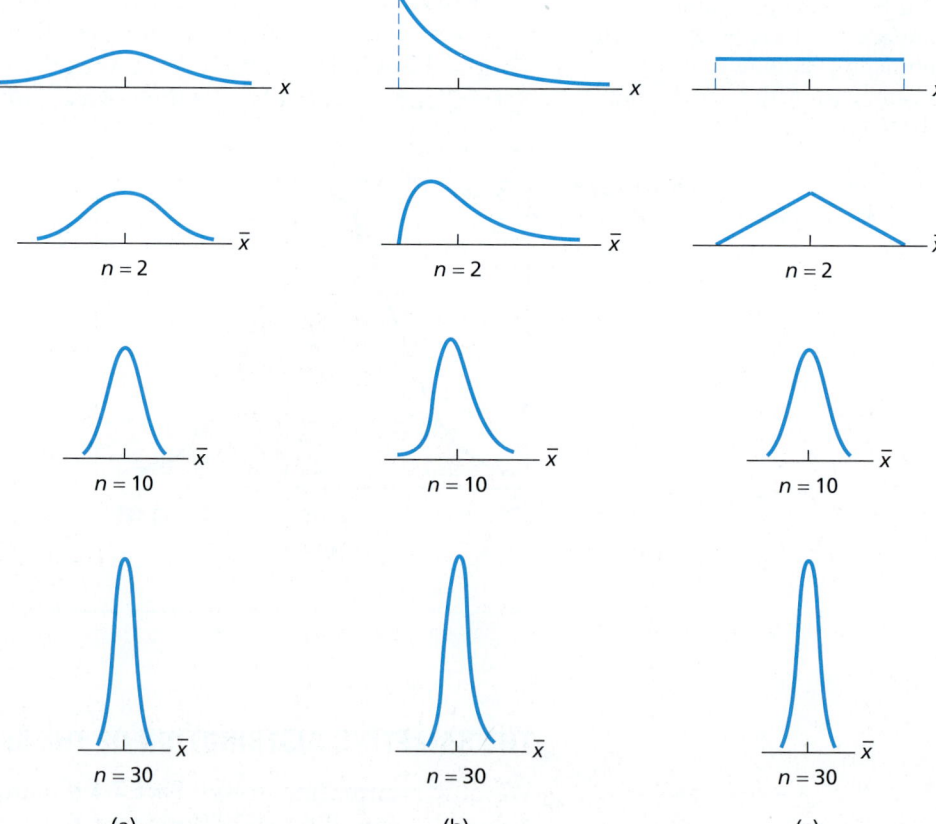

FIGURE 7.6
Sampling distributions for (a) normal, (b) reverse-J-shaped, and (c) uniform variables

We know that, if the variable under consideration is normally distributed, so is the variable $\bar{x}$, regardless of sample size, as illustrated by Fig. 7.6(a). Additionally, we know that, if the sample size is large, the variable $\bar{x}$ is approximately normally distributed, regardless of the distribution of the variable under consideration. Figures 7.6(b) and 7.6(c) illustrate this fact for two nonnormal variables, one having a reverse-J-shaped distribution and the other having a uniform distribution.

In each of these latter two cases, for samples of size 2, the variable $\bar{x}$ is far from being normally distributed; for samples of size 10, it is already somewhat normally distributed; and for samples of size 30, it is very close to being normally distributed.

Exercises 7.3

Statistical Concepts and Skills

7.39 A variable of a population has a mean of $\mu = 100$ and a standard deviation of $\sigma = 28$.
a. Identify the sampling distribution of the sample mean for samples of size 49.
b. In answering part (a), what assumptions did you make about the distribution of the variable under consideration?
c. Can you answer part (a) if the sample size is 16 instead of 49? Why or why not?

7.40 A variable of a population has a mean of $\mu = 35$ and a standard deviation of $\sigma = 42$.
a. If the variable is normally distributed, identify the sampling distribution of the sample mean for samples of size 9.
b. Can you answer part (a) if the distribution of the variable under consideration is unknown? Explain your answer.
c. Can you answer part (a) if the distribution of the variable under consideration is unknown but the sample size is 36 instead of 9? Why or why not?

7.41 A variable of a population is normally distributed with mean μ and standard deviation σ.
a. Identify the distribution of $\bar{x}$.
b. Does your answer to part (a) depend on the sample size? Explain your answer.
c. Identify the mean and the standard deviation of $\bar{x}$.
d. Does your answer to part (c) depend on the assumption that the variable under consideration is normally distributed? Why or why not?

7.42 A variable of a population has mean μ and standard deviation σ. For a large sample size n, answer the following questions.
a. Identify the distribution of $\bar{x}$.
b. Does your answer to part (a) depend on n being large? Explain your answer.
c. Identify the mean and the standard deviation of $\bar{x}$.

d. Does your answer to part (c) depend on the sample size being large? Why or why not?

7.43 Refer to Fig. 7.6.
a. Why are the four graphs in Fig. 7.6(a) all centered at the same place?
b. Why does the spread of the graphs diminish with increasing sample size? How does this result affect the sampling error when you estimate a population mean, μ, by a sample mean, $\bar{x}$?
c. Why are the graphs in Fig. 7.6(a) bell-shaped?
d. Why do the graphs in Figs. 7.6(b) and (c) become bell-shaped as the sample size increases?

7.44 According to the central limit theorem, for a relatively large sample size, the variable $\bar{x}$ is approximately normally distributed.
a. What rule of thumb is used for deciding whether the sample size is relatively large?
b. Roughly speaking, what property of the distribution of the variable under consideration determines how large the sample size must be for a normal distribution to provide an adequate approximation to the distribution of $\bar{x}$?

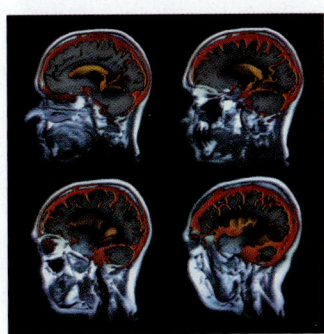

7.45 Brain Weights. In 1905, R. Pearl published the article "Biometrical Studies on Man. I. Variation and Correlation in Brain Weight" (*Biometrika*, Vol. 4, pp. 13–104). According to the study, brain weights of Swedish men are normally

distributed with a mean of 1.40 kg and a standard deviation of 0.11 kg.
a. Determine the sampling distribution of the sample mean for samples of size 3. Interpret your answer in terms of the distribution of all possible sample mean brain weights for samples of three Swedish men.
b. Repeat part (a) for samples of size 12.
c. Construct graphs similar to those shown in Fig. 7.4 on page 313.

7.46 Teacher Salaries. Data on salaries in the public school system are published annually in *National Survey of Salaries and Wages in Public Schools*. The mean annual salary for classroom teachers is $40,133. Assume a standard deviation of $8000.
a. Determine the sampling distribution of the sample mean for samples of size 64. Interpret your answer in terms of the distribution of all possible sample mean salaries for samples of 64 teachers.
b. Repeat part (a) for samples of size 256.
c. Do you need to assume that public school teacher salaries are normally distributed to answer parts (a) and (b)? Explain your answer.

7.47 Drive for Show, Putt for Dough. An article by Scott M. Berry entitled "Drive for Show and Putt for Dough" (*Chance*, 1999, Vol. 12(4), pp. 50–54) discussed driving distances of PGA players. The mean distance for tee shots in the 1999 men's PGA tour was 272.2 yards with a standard deviation of 8.12 yards.
a. Determine the sampling distribution of the sample mean for samples of size 100.
b. Repeat part (a) for samples of size 200.
c. Must you assume that the tee-shot distances are normally distributed to answer parts (a) and (b)? Explain your answer.

7.48 New York City 10 km Run. As reported by *Runner's World* magazine, the times of the finishers in the New York City 10 km run are normally distributed with a mean of 61 minutes and a standard deviation of 9 minutes.
a. Determine the sampling distribution of the sample mean for samples of size 4.
b. Repeat part (a) for samples of size 9.
c. Construct graphs similar to those shown in Fig. 7.4 on page 313.

7.49 Brain Weights. Refer to Exercise 7.45.
a. Determine the percentage of all samples of three Swedish men that have mean brain weights within 0.1 kg of the population mean brain weight of 1.40 kg. Interpret your answer in terms of sampling error.
b. Repeat part (a) for samples of size 12.

7.50 Teacher Salaries. Refer to Exercise 7.46.

a. Determine the percentage of all samples of 64 public school teachers that have mean salaries within $1000 of the population mean salary of $40,133. Interpret your answer in terms of sampling error.
b. Repeat part (a) for samples of size 256.

7.51 Drive for Show, Putt for Dough. Refer to Exercise 7.47.
a. What is the probability that the sampling error made in estimating the population mean tee-shot distance by that of a random sample of 100 tee-shot distances will be at most 1 yard?
b. Repeat part (a) for samples of size 200.

7.52 New York City 10 km Run. Refer to Exercise 7.48.
a. What is the probability that the sampling error made in estimating the population mean finishing time by that of a random sample of four finishing times will be no more than 5 minutes?
b. Repeat part (a) for samples of size 9.

7.53 Air Conditioning Service Contracts. An air conditioning contractor is preparing to offer service contracts on the brand of compressor used in all of the units her company installs. Before she can work out the details, she must estimate how long those compressors last, on average. The contractor anticipated this need and has kept detailed records on the lifetimes of a random sample of 250 compressors. She plans to use the sample mean lifetime, $\bar{x}$, of those 250 compressors as her estimate for the population mean lifetime, μ, of all such compressors. If the lifetimes of this brand of compressor have a standard deviation of 40 months, what is the probability that the contractor's estimate will be within 5 months of the true mean?

Extending the Concepts and Skills

Use the 68.26-95.44-99.74 rule (page 276) to answer the questions posed in parts (a)–(c) of Exercises 7.54 and 7.55.

7.54 A variable of a population is normally distributed with mean μ and standard deviation σ. For samples of size n, fill in the blanks. Justify your answers.
a. 68.26% of all possible samples have means that lie within _____ of the population mean, μ.
b. 95.44% of all possible samples have means that lie within _____ of the population mean, μ.
c. 99.74% of all possible samples have means that lie within _____ of the population mean, μ.
d. $100(1-\alpha)$% of all possible samples have means that lie within _____ of the population mean, μ. (*Hint*: Draw a graph for the distribution of $\bar{x}$ and determine the z-scores dividing the area under the normal curve into a middle $1-\alpha$ area and two outside areas of $\alpha/2$.)

7.55 A variable of a population has mean μ and standard deviation σ. For a large sample size n, fill in the blanks. Justify your answers.
a. Approximately ____% of all possible samples have means within $\sigma/\sqrt{n}$ of the population mean, μ.
b. Approximately ____% of all possible samples have means within $2\sigma/\sqrt{n}$ of the population mean, μ.
c. Approximately ____% of all possible samples have means within $3\sigma/\sqrt{n}$ of the population mean, μ.
d. Approximately ____% of all possible samples have means within $z_{\alpha/2}$ of the population mean, μ.

7.56 Testing for Content Accuracy. A brand of water-softener salt comes in packages marked "net weight 40 lb." The company that packages the salt claims that the bags contain an average of 40 lb of salt and that the standard deviation of the weights is 1.5 lb. Assume that the weights are normally distributed.
a. Obtain the probability that the weight of one randomly selected bag of water-softener salt will be 39 lb or less, if the company's claim is true.
b. Determine the probability that the mean weight of 10 randomly selected bags of water-softener salt will be 39 lb or less, if the company's claim is true.
c. If you bought one bag of water-softener salt and it weighed 39 lb, would you consider this evidence that the company's claim is incorrect? Explain your answer.
d. If you bought 10 bags of water-softener salt and their mean weight was 39 lb, would you consider this evidence that the company's claim is incorrect? Explain your answer.

Using Technology

7.57 Gestation Periods of Humans. For humans, gestation periods are normally distributed with a mean of 266 days and a standard deviation of 16 days. Suppose that you observe the gestation periods for a sample of nine humans.
a. Use the technology of your choice to simulate 2000 samples of nine human gestation periods each.
b. Find the sample mean of each of the 2000 samples.
c. Obtain the mean, the standard deviation, and a histogram of the 2000 sample means.
d. Theoretically, what are the mean, standard deviation, and distribution of all possible sample means for samples of size 9?
e. Compare your results from parts (c) and (d).

7.58 Emergency Room Traffic. A variable is said to have an *exponential distribution* or to be *exponentially distributed* if its distribution has the shape of an exponential curve, that is, a curve of the form $y = e^{-x/\mu}/\mu$ for $x > 0$, where μ is the mean of the variable. The standard deviation of such a variable also equals μ. At the emergency room at Desert Samaritan Hospital in Mesa, Arizona, the time from the arrival of one patient to the next, called an interarrival time, has an exponential distribution with a mean of 8.7 minutes.
a. Sketch the exponential curve for the distribution of the variable "interarrival time." Note that this variable is far from being normally distributed. What shape does its distribution have?
b. Use the technology of your choice to simulate 1000 samples of four interarrival times each.
c. Find the sample mean of each of the 1000 samples.
d. Determine the mean and standard deviation of the 1000 sample means.
e. Theoretically, what are the mean and the standard deviation of all possible sample means for samples of size 4? Compare your answers to those you obtained in part (d).
f. Obtain a histogram of the 1000 sample means. Is the histogram bell-shaped? Would you necessarily expect it to be?
g. Repeat parts (b)-(f) for a sample size of 40.

Chapter Review

You Should Be Able To

1. use and understand the formulas presented in this chapter.

2. define sampling error and explain the need for sampling distributions.

3. find the mean and standard deviation of the variable $\bar{x}$, given the mean and standard deviation of the population and the sample size.

4. state and apply the central limit theorem.

5. determine the sampling distribution of the sample mean when the variable under consideration is normally distributed.

6. determine the sampling distribution of the sample mean when the sample size is relatively large.

Key Terms

central limit theorem, *314*
sampling distribution, *298*
sampling distribution of the sample mean, *299*
sampling error, *298*
standard error (SE), *309*
standard error of the sample mean, *309*

Review Test

Statistical Concepts and Skills

1. Define sampling error.

2. What is the sampling distribution of a statistic? Why is it important?

3. Provide two synonyms for "the distribution of all possible sample means for samples of a given size."

4. Relative to the population mean, what happens to the possible sample means for samples of the same size as the sample size increases? Explain the relevance of this property in estimating a population mean by a sample mean.

5. **Income Tax and the IRS.** In 1998, the Internal Revenue Service (IRS) sampled approximately 125,000 tax returns to obtain estimates of various parameters. Data were published in *Statistics of Income, Individual Income Tax Returns*. According to that document, the mean income tax per return for the returns sampled was $8426.
    a. Explain the meaning of sampling error in this context.
    b. If, in reality, the population mean income tax per return in 1998 was $8514, how much sampling error was made in estimating that parameter by the sample mean of $8426?
    c. If the IRS had sampled 250,000 returns instead of 125,000, would the sampling error necessarily have been smaller? Explain your answer.
    d. In future surveys, how can the IRS increase the likelihood of small sampling error?

6. **Officer Salaries.** The following table gives the monthly salaries (in $1000s) of the six officers of a company.

Officer	A	B	C	D	E	F
Salary	8	12	16	20	24	28

a. Calculate the population mean monthly salary, μ. There are 15 possible samples of size 4 from the population of six officers. They are listed in the first column of the following table.

Sample	Salaries	$\bar{x}$
A, B, C, D	8, 12, 16, 20	14
A, B, C, E	8, 12, 16, 24	15
A, B, C, F	8, 12, 16, 28	16
A, B, D, E	8, 12, 20, 24	16
A, B, D, F	8, 12, 20, 28	17
A, B, E, F	8, 12, 24, 28	18
A, C, D, E		
A, C, D, F		
A, C, E, F		
A, D, E, F		
B, C, D, E		
B, C, D, F		
B, C, E, F		
B, D, E, F		
C, D, E, F		

b. Complete the second and third columns of the table.
c. Complete the following dotplot for the sampling distribution of the sample mean for samples of size 4. Locate the population mean on the graph.

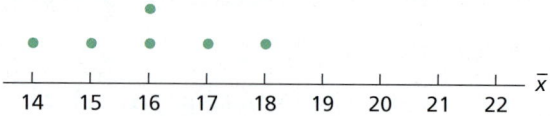

d. Obtain the probability that the mean of a random sample of four salaries will be within 1 (i.e., $1000) of the population mean.
e. Use the answer you obtained in part (b) and Definition 3.11 on page 129 to find the mean of the variable $\bar{x}$. Interpret your answer.
f. Can you obtain the mean of the variable $\bar{x}$ without doing the calculation in part (e)? Explain your answer.

7. **New Car Passion.** The U.S. Bureau of Economic Analysis publishes data on sales of cars and trucks in *Survey of Current Business*. The year 1999 set a record for new car and truck sales with Americans spending an average of $21,022 for a new vehicle. Assume a standard deviation of $10,200.
   a. Identify the population and variable under consideration.
   b. For samples of 50 new vehicle sales in 1999, determine the mean and standard deviation of all possible sample mean prices.
   c. Repeat part (b) for samples of size 100.
   d. For samples of size 1000, answer the following question without doing any computations: Will the standard deviation of all possible sample mean prices be larger, smaller, or the same as that in part (c)? Explain your answer.

8. **Hours Actually Worked.** An article by Daniel Hecker in the *Monthly Labor Review* discussed the number of hours actually worked as opposed to the number of hours paid for. The study examined both full-time men and full-time women in 87 different occupations. According to the study, the mean number of hours (actually) worked by female marketing and advertising managers is $\mu = 45$ hours. Assuming a standard deviation of $\sigma = 7$ hours, decide whether each of the following statements is true or false or whether the information is insufficient for you to decide. Give a reason for each of your answers.
   a. For a random sample of 196 female marketing and advertising managers, chances are roughly 95.44% that the sample mean number of hours worked will be between 31 hours and 59 hours.
   b. 95.44% of all possible observations of the number of hours worked by female marketing and advertising managers lie between 31 hours and 59 hours.
   c. For a random sample of 196 female marketing and advertising managers, chances are roughly 95.44% that the sample mean number of hours worked will be between 44 hours and 46 hours.

9. **Hours Actually Worked.** Repeat Problem 8, assuming that the number of hours worked by female marketing and advertising managers is normally distributed.

10. **Antarctic Krill.** In the Southern Ocean food web, the krill species *Euphausia superba* is the most important prey species for many marine predators, from seabirds to the largest whales. Body lengths of the species are normally distributed with a mean of 40 mm and a standard deviation of 12 mm. [SOURCE: K. Reid, J. Watkins, J. Croxall, E. Murphy, "Krill Population Dynamics at South Georgia 1991–1997 Based on Data From Predators and Nets," *Marine Ecology Progress Series*, 1999, Vol. 177, pp. 103–114]
   a. Sketch the normal curve for the krill lengths.
   b. Find the sampling distribution of the sample mean for samples of size 4. Draw a graph of the normal curve associated with $\bar{x}$.
   c. Repeat part (b) for samples of size 9.

11. **Antarctic Krill.** Refer to Problem 10.
    a. Determine the percentage of all samples of four krill that have mean lengths within 9 mm of the population mean length of 40 mm.
    b. Obtain the probability that the mean length of four randomly selected krill will be within 9 mm of the population mean length of 40 mm.
    c. Interpret the probability you obtained in part (b) in terms of sampling error.
    d. Repeat parts (a)–(c) for samples of size 9.

12. The following graph shows the curve for a normally distributed variable. Superimposed are the curves for the sampling distributions of the sample mean for two different sample sizes.

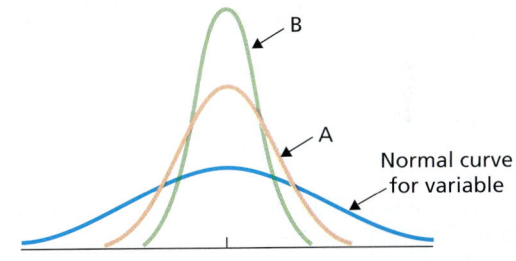

   a. Explain why all three curves are centered at the same place.
   b. Which curve corresponds to the larger sample size? Explain your answer.
   c. Why is the spread of each curve different?
   d. Which of the two sampling-distribution curves corresponds to the sample size that will tend to produce less sampling error? Explain your answer.
   e. Why are the two sampling-distribution curves normal curves?

13. **Life Insurance in Force.** The American Council of Life Insurance reports the mean life insurance in force per covered family in the *Life Insurance Fact Book*. Assume that the standard deviation of life insurance in force is $50,900.
    a. Determine the probability that the sampling error made in estimating the population mean life insurance in force by that of a sample of 500 covered families will be $2000 or less.
    b. Must you assume that life-insurance amounts are normally distributed in order to answer part (a)? What if the sample size is 20 instead of 500?
    c. Repeat part (a) for a sample size of 5000.

14. **Paint Durability.** A paint manufacturer in Pittsburgh claims that his paint will last an average of 5 years. Assuming that paint life is normally distributed and has a standard deviation of 0.5 year, answer the following questions.

a. Suppose that you paint one house with the paint and that the paint lasts 4.5 years. Would you consider that evidence against the manufacturer's claim? (*Hint:* Assuming that the manufacturer's claim is correct, determine the probability that the paint life for a randomly selected house painted with the paint is 4.5 years or less.)
b. Suppose that you paint 10 houses with the paint and that the paint lasts an average of 4.5 years for the 10 houses. Would you consider that evidence against the manufacturer's claim?
c. Repeat part (b) if the paint lasts an average of 4.9 years for the 10 houses painted.

Using Technology

15. GRE Scores. Each year, thousands of college seniors take the Graduate Record Examination (GRE). The scores are transformed so that they have a mean of 500 and a standard deviation of 100. The scores are known to be normally distributed.
a. Use the technology of your choice to simulate 1000 samples of four GRE scores each.
b. Find the sample mean of each of the 1000 samples obtained in part (a).
c. Obtain the mean, the standard deviation, and a histogram of the 1000 sample means.
d. Theoretically, what are the mean, standard deviation, and distribution of all possible sample means for samples of size 4?

e. Compare your answers from parts (c) and (d).

16. Random Numbers. A variable is said to be *uniformly distributed* or to have a *uniform distribution* with parameters a and b if its distribution has the shape of the horizontal line segment $y = 1/(b - a)$, for $a < x < b$. The mean and standard deviation of such a variable are $(a + b)/2$ and $(b - a)/\sqrt{12}$, respectively. The basic random-number generator on a computer or calculator, which returns a number between 0 and 1, simulates a variable having a uniform distribution with parameters 0 and 1.
a. Sketch the distribution of a uniformly distributed variable with parameters 0 and 1. Observe from your sketch that such a variable is far from being normally distributed.
b. Use the technology of your choice to simulate 2000 samples of two random numbers between 0 and 1.
c. Find the sample mean of each of the 2000 samples obtained in part (b).
d. Determine the mean and standard deviation of the 2000 sample means.
e. Theoretically, what are the mean and the standard deviation of all possible sample means for samples of size 2? Compare your answers to those you obtained in part (d).
f. Obtain a histogram of the 2000 sample means. Is the histogram bell-shaped? Would you expect it to be?
g. Repeat parts (b)–(f) for a sample size of 35.

Internet Project

Simulations

The sampling distribution of the mean and the properties of this distribution are essential concepts in statistics. They are, at first, often difficult concepts to grasp, as well.

This Internet project uses several simulation applets to illustrate these concepts in a dynamic and interactive way that may help you understand them. Through these simulations, you are to explore the distribution of the sample mean, the mean and standard deviation of the sample mean, and the central limit theorem by using a variety of different population distributions.

URL for access to Internet Projects Page: www.aw.com/weiss

Focusing on Data Analysis

Simple Random Sampling

Recall from Chapter 1 (see page 34) that the Focus database contains information on 500 randomly selected Arizona State University sophomores. Suppose that you want to conduct extensive interviews on college life with 25 of the 500 sophomores. Use the technology of your choice to obtain a simple random sample of 25 of the 500 sophomores in the Focus database.

case study discussion

The Chesapeake and Ohio Freight Study

At the beginning of this chapter, we discussed a freight study commissioned by the Chesapeake and Ohio Railroad Company (C&O). A sample of 2072 waybills from a population of 22,984 waybills was used to estimate the total revenue due C&O. The estimate arrived at was $64,568.

Because all 22,984 waybills were available, a census could be taken to determine exactly the total revenue due C&O and thereby reveal the accuracy of the estimate obtained by sampling. The exact amount due C&O was found to be $64,651.

a. What percentage of the waybills constituted the sample?
b. What percentage error was made by using the sample to estimate the total revenue due C&O?
c. At the time, the cost of a complete examination was approximately $5000, whereas the cost of the sampling was only $1000. Knowing this information and your answers to parts (a) and (b), do you think that sampling was preferable to a census? Explain your answer.
d. In the study, the $83 error was against C&O. Would it necessarily have to be that way?

Internet Resources: Visit the Weiss Web site www.aw.com/weiss for additional discussion, exercises, and resources related to this case study.

Biography

Pierre-Simon Laplace: The Newton of France

PIERRE-SIMON LAPLACE was born on March 23, 1749, at Beaumount-en-Auge, Normandy, France, the son of a peasant farmer. His early schooling was at the military academy at Beaumount, where he developed his mathematical abilities. At the age of 18, he went to Paris. Within 2 years he was recommended for a professorship at the École Militaire by the French mathematician and philosopher Jean d'Alembert. (It is said that Laplace examined and passed Napoleon Bonaparte there in 1785.) In 1773 Laplace was granted membership in the Academy of Sciences.

Laplace held various positions in public life: He was president of the Bureau des Longitudes, professor at the École Normale, Minister of the Interior under Napoleon for 6 weeks (at which time he was replaced by Napoleon's brother), and Chancellor of the Senate; he was also made a marquis.

Laplace's professional interests were also varied. He published several volumes on celestial mechanics (which the Scottish geologist and mathematician John Playfair said were "the highest point to which man has yet ascended in the scale of intellectual attainment"), a book entitled *Théorie analytique des probabilités* (Analytic Theory of Probability), and other works on physics and mathematics. Laplace's primary contribution to the field of probability and statistics was the remarkable and all-important central limit theorem, which appeared in an 1809 publication and was read to the Academy of Sciences on April 9, 1810.

Astronomy was Laplace's major work; approximately half of his publications were concerned with the solar system and its gravitational interactions. These interactions were so complex that even Sir Isaac Newton had concluded "divine intervention was periodically required to preserve the system in equilibrium." Laplace, however, proved that planets' average angular velocities are invariable and periodic, and thus made the most important advance in physical astronomy since Newton.

When Laplace died in Paris on March 5, 1827, he was eulogized by the famous French mathematician and physicist Simeon Poisson as "the Newton of France."

part iv

Inferential Statistics

CHAPTER 8	**Confidence Intervals for One Population Mean**
CHAPTER 9	**Hypothesis Tests for One Population Mean**
CHAPTER 10	**Inferences for Two Population Means**
CHAPTER 11	**Inferences for Population Proportions**
CHAPTER 12	**Chi-Square Procedures**
CHAPTER 13	**Analysis of Variance (ANOVA)**
CHAPTER 14	**Inferential Methods in Regression and Correlation**

chapter 8

Confidence Intervals for One Population Mean

CHAPTER OUTLINE

8.1 Estimating a Population Mean

8.2 Confidence Intervals for One Population Mean When σ Is Known

8.3 Margin of Error

8.4 Confidence Intervals for One Population Mean When σ Is Unknown

GENERAL OBJECTIVES In this chapter, you begin your study of inferential statistics by examining methods for estimating the mean of a population. As you might suspect, the statistic used to estimate the population mean, μ, is a sample mean, $\bar{x}$. Because of sampling error, you cannot expect $\bar{x}$ to equal μ exactly. Thus providing information about the accuracy of the estimate is important, which leads to a discussion of confidence intervals, the main topic of this chapter.

In Section 8.1, we provide the intuitive foundation for confidence intervals. Then, in Section 8.2, we present confidence intervals for one population mean when the population standard deviation, σ, is known. Although, in practice, σ is usually unknown, we first consider the case where σ is known to set the stage for handling the case where σ is unknown.

In Section 8.3, we investigate in detail how sample size affects the precision of estimating the population mean by a sample mean. In doing so, we introduce a salient quantity in that regard: the *margin of error.*

In Section 8.4, we discuss confidence intervals for one population when the population standard deviation is unknown. As a prerequisite to that topic, we introduce and describe one of the most important distributions in inferential statistics—*Student's t-distribution.*

case study

THE CHIPS AHOY! 1,000 CHIPS CHALLENGE

Nabisco, the maker of Chips Ahoy! cookies, challenged students across the nation to confirm the cookie maker's claim that there are [at least] 1000 chocolate chips in every 18-ounce bag of Chips Ahoy! cookies. According to the folks at Nabisco, a chocolate chip is defined as "…any distinct piece of chocolate that is baked into or on top of the cookie dough regardless of whether or not it is 100% whole." Students competed for $25,000 in scholarships and other prizes for participating in the Challenge.

As reported by Brad Warner and Jim Rutledge in the paper "Checking the Chips Ahoy! Guarantee" (*Chance*, 1999, Vol. 12(1), pp. 10–14), one such group that participated in the Challenge was an introductory statistics class at the United States Air Force Academy. With chocolate chips on their minds, cadets and faculty accepted the Challenge. Friends and families of the cadets sent 275 bags of Chips Ahoy! cookies from all over the country. From the 275 bags, 42 were randomly selected for the study, while the other bags were used to keep cadet morale high during counting.

For each of the 42 bags selected for the study, the cookies were first dissolved in water to separate the chips, and then the chips were counted. The following are the number of chips per bag for the 42 bags of Chips Ahoy! analyzed by the cadets in the introductory statistics class.

1200	1219	1103	1213	1258	1325	1295
1247	1098	1185	1087	1377	1363	1121
1279	1269	1199	1244	1294	1356	1137
1545	1135	1143	1215	1402	1419	1166
1132	1514	1270	1345	1214	1154	1307
1293	1546	1228	1239	1440	1219	1191

After studying confidence intervals in this chapter, you will be asked to analyze these data for the purpose of estimating the mean number of chips per bag for all bags of Chips Ahoy! cookies.

CHAPTER 8 Confidence Intervals for One Population Mean

8.1 ESTIMATING A POPULATION MEAN

A common problem in statistics is to obtain information about the mean, μ, of a population. For example, we might want to know

- the mean age of people in the civilian labor force,
- the mean cost of a wedding,
- the mean gas mileage of a new-model car, or
- the mean starting salary of liberal-arts graduates.

If the population is small, we can ordinarily determine μ exactly by first taking a census and then computing μ from the population data. But if the population is large, as it often is in practice, taking a census is generally impractical, extremely expensive, or impossible. Nonetheless, we can usually obtain sufficiently accurate information about μ by taking a sample from the population, as illustrated in Example 8.1.

Example 8.1 Point Estimate of a Population Mean

Prices of New Mobile Homes The U.S. Bureau of the Census publishes annual price figures for new mobile homes in *Current Construction Reports*. The figures are obtained from sampling, not from a census. A random sample of 36 new mobile homes yielded the prices, in thousands of dollars, shown in Table 8.1. Use the data to estimate the population mean price, μ, of all new mobile homes.

TABLE 8.1
Prices ($1000s) of 36 randomly selected new mobile homes

46.8	42.9	41.6	36.7	47.4	41.2	46.1	45.7	38.2
34.6	52.4	40.7	35.9	51.9	42.7	34.5	28.3	50.2
34.9	55.7	51.9	38.1	30.3	55.8	28.9	43.3	32.7
39.6	35.5	43.0	35.0	53.5	36.9	49.4	42.8	56.9

Solution We estimate the population mean price, μ, of all new mobile homes by the sample mean price, $\bar{x}$, of the 36 new mobile homes sampled. From Table 8.1,

$$\bar{x} = \frac{\Sigma x}{n} = \frac{1522.0}{36} = 42.28.$$

Therefore, based on the sample data, we estimate the mean price, μ, of all new mobile homes to be approximately $42.28 thousand, that is, $42,280. An estimate of this kind is called a *point estimate* for μ because it consists of a single number, or point. ◆

As indicated in the following definition, the term **point estimate** applies to the use of a statistic to estimate any parameter, not just a population mean.

8.1 Estimating a Population Mean

DEFINITION 8.1 **Point Estimate**

A *point estimate* of a parameter is the value of a statistic used to estimate the parameter.

As you learned in Chapter 7, expecting a sample mean to exactly equal the population mean is unreasonable; some sampling error is to be anticipated. Therefore, in addition to reporting a point estimate for μ, we need to provide information that indicates the accuracy of the estimate. We do so by giving a **confidence-interval estimate** for μ. With a confidence-interval estimate for μ, we use the mean of a sample to construct an interval of numbers and state how confident we are that μ lies in that interval, called the **confidence level**.

DEFINITION 8.2 **Confidence-Interval Estimate; Confidence Level**

A *confidence-interval estimate* of a parameter consists of an interval of numbers obtained from a point estimate of the parameter and a percentage that specifies how confident we are that the parameter lies in the interval. The confidence percentage is called the *confidence level*.

Note: The term *confidence interval* is often abbreviated as CI.

In Example 8.2, we obtain a 95.44% confidence interval for the mean price of all new mobile homes. In doing so, we discuss in detail the logic behind determining confidence intervals. We present a general procedure based on this logic for obtaining confidence intervals at any prescribed confidence level in Section 8.2.

Example 8.2 Introducing Confidence Intervals

Prices of New Mobile Homes We refer to Example 8.1 and continue to work in thousands of dollars. As a normal probability plot of the data in Table 8.1 shows, a reasonable presumption is that prices of new mobile homes are normally distributed. We assume that the population standard deviation of all such prices is $7.2 thousand, that is, $7200.[1]

a. Identify the distribution of the variable $\bar{x}$, that is, the sampling distribution of the sample mean for samples of size 36.
b. Use part (a) to show that 95.44% of all samples of 36 new mobile homes have the property that the interval from $\bar{x} - 2.4$ to $\bar{x} + 2.4$ contains μ.
c. Use part (b) and the sample data in Table 8.1 to obtain a 95.44% confidence interval for the mean price of all new mobile homes.

Solution a. Because $n = 36$, $\sigma = 7.2$, and prices of new mobile homes are normally distributed, Key Fact 7.4 on page 316 implies that

---

[1] We might know the population standard deviation from previous research or from a preliminary study of prices. We examine the more usual case, where σ is unknown, in Section 8.4.

- $\mu_{\bar{x}} = \mu$ (which we don't know),
- $\sigma_{\bar{x}} = \sigma/\sqrt{n} = 7.2/\sqrt{36} = 1.2$, and
- $\bar{x}$ is normally distributed.

In other words, for samples of size 36, the variable $\bar{x}$ is normally distributed with mean μ and standard deviation 1.2.

b. The "95.44" part of the 68.26-95.44-99.74 rule states that, for a normally distributed variable, 95.44% of all possible observations lie within two standard deviations to either side of the mean. Applying this rule to the variable $\bar{x}$ and referring to part (a), we see that 95.44% of all samples of 36 new mobile homes have mean prices within $2 \cdot 1.2 = 2.4$ of μ. Or, equivalently, 95.44% of all samples of 36 new mobile homes have the property that the interval from $\bar{x} - 2.4$ to $\bar{x} + 2.4$ contains μ.

c. From part (b), we can be 95.44% confident that the sample of 36 new mobile homes whose prices are shown in Table 8.1 has the property that the interval from $\bar{x} - 2.4$ to $\bar{x} + 2.4$ contains μ. For that sample, $\bar{x} = 42.28$, so

$$\bar{x} - 2.4 = 42.28 - 2.4 = 39.88 \quad \text{and} \quad \bar{x} + 2.4 = 42.28 + 2.4 = 44.68.$$

Consequently, our 95.44% confidence interval is from 39.88 to 44.68; we can be 95.44% confident that the mean price, μ, of all new mobile homes is somewhere between $39,880 and $44,680.

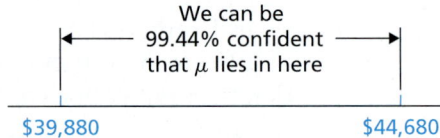

Note: Although this or any other 95.44% confidence interval may or may not contain μ, we can be 95.44% confident that it does. ◆

A confidence interval for a population mean depends on the sample mean, $\bar{x}$, which, in turn, depends on the sample selected. For example, suppose that the prices of the 36 new mobile homes sampled were as shown in Table 8.2 instead of as in Table 8.1.

TABLE 8.2
Prices ($1000s) of another sample of 36 randomly selected new mobile homes

52.0	51.1	40.2	32.0	43.1	39.6	45.5	43.7	51.0
54.5	42.8	35.0	54.7	41.5	40.3	41.1	47.0	47.8
44.7	32.2	45.6	44.3	58.2	48.2	47.0	39.2	43.3
47.9	37.4	48.1	44.8	51.1	33.9	45.1	43.1	56.9

Then we would have $\bar{x} = 44.83$ so that

$$\bar{x} - 2.4 = 44.83 - 2.4 = 42.43 \quad \text{and} \quad \bar{x} + 2.4 = 44.83 + 2.4 = 47.23.$$

In this case, the 95.44% confidence interval for μ would be from 42.43 to 47.23. We could be 95.44% confident that the mean price, μ, of all new mobile homes is somewhere between $42,430 and $47,230.

INTERPRETING CONFIDENCE INTERVALS

Example 8.3 stresses the importance of interpreting a confidence interval correctly. It also illustrates that the population mean, μ, may or may not lie in the confidence interval obtained.

Example 8.3 Interpreting Confidence Intervals

Prices of New Mobile Homes Consider again the prices of new mobile homes. As demonstrated in part (b) of Example 8.2, 95.44% of all samples of 36 new mobile homes have the property that the interval from $\bar{x} - 2.4$ to $\bar{x} + 2.4$ contains μ. In other words, if 36 new mobile homes are selected at random and their mean price, $\bar{x}$, is computed, the interval from

$$\bar{x} - 2.4 \quad \text{to} \quad \bar{x} + 2.4 \tag{8.1}$$

will be a 95.44% confidence interval for the mean price of all new mobile homes.

To illustrate that the mean price, μ, of all new mobile homes may or may not lie in the 95.44% confidence interval obtained, we used a computer to simulate 20 samples of 36 new mobile home prices each. For the simulation, we assumed that $\mu = 44$ (i.e., $44 thousand) and $\sigma = 7.2$ (i.e., $7.2 thousand). In reality, we don't know μ; we are assuming a value for μ to illustrate a point.

For each of the 20 samples of 36 new mobile home prices, we did three things: computed the sample mean price, $\bar{x}$; used Equation (8.1) to obtain the 95.44% confidence interval for μ based on the sample; and noted whether the population mean, $\mu = 44$, actually lies in the confidence interval.

Figure 8.1 on the next page summarizes our results. For each sample, we have drawn a graph on the right-hand side of Fig. 8.1. The dot represents the sample mean, $\bar{x}$, in thousands of dollars, and the horizontal line represents the corresponding 95.44% confidence interval. Note that the population mean, μ, lies in the confidence interval only when the horizontal line crosses the dashed line.

Figure 8.1 reveals that μ lies in the 95.44% confidence interval in 19 of the 20 samples, that is, in 95% of the samples. If, instead of 20 samples, we simulated, say, 1000 samples, we would most likely find that the percentage of those 1000 samples for which μ lies in the 95.44% confidence interval would be even closer to 95.44%. Hence we can be 95.44% confident that any computed 95.44% confidence interval will contain μ. ◆

In Example 8.2, we obtained a 95.44% confidence interval for the mean price of all new mobile homes based on a sample of size 36. In doing so, we assumed the prices to be normally distributed, which we used to conclude that $\bar{x}$ is normally distributed.

If the prices are not normally distributed, then, because of the central limit theorem, we can still say that $\bar{x}$ is approximately normally distributed. The impact on the resulting 95.44% confidence interval would be that it is only approximately correct; that is, the true confidence level would only approximately equal 95.44%.

FIGURE 8.1
Twenty confidence intervals for the mean price of all new mobile homes, each based on a sample of 36 new mobile homes

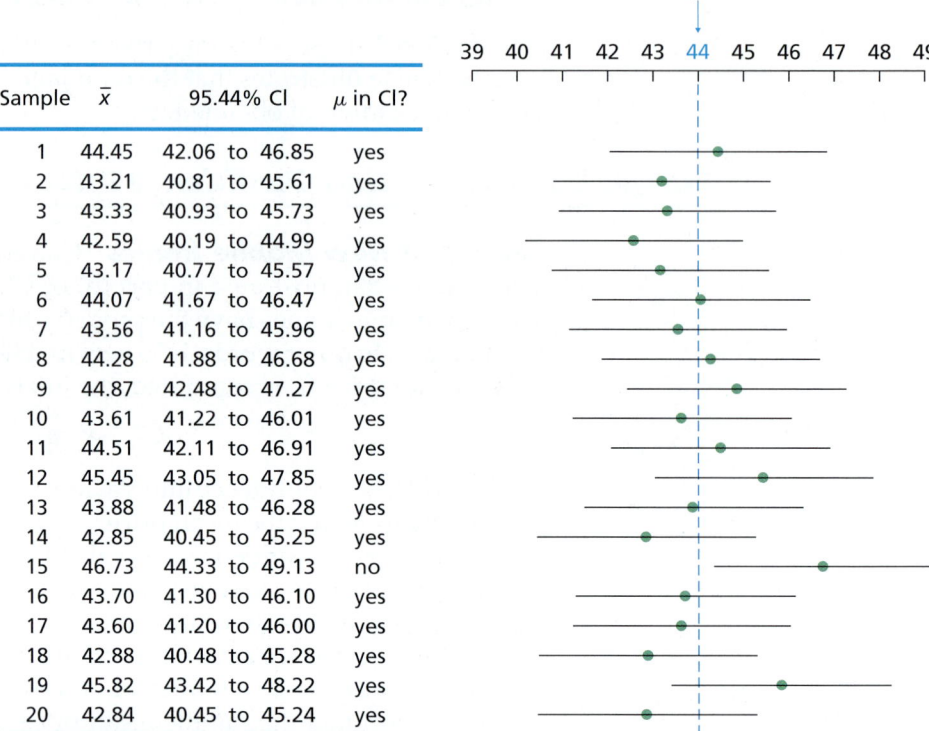

Sample	$\bar{x}$	95.44% CI	μ in CI?
1	44.45	42.06 to 46.85	yes
2	43.21	40.81 to 45.61	yes
3	43.33	40.93 to 45.73	yes
4	42.59	40.19 to 44.99	yes
5	43.17	40.77 to 45.57	yes
6	44.07	41.67 to 46.47	yes
7	43.56	41.16 to 45.96	yes
8	44.28	41.88 to 46.68	yes
9	44.87	42.48 to 47.27	yes
10	43.61	41.22 to 46.01	yes
11	44.51	42.11 to 46.91	yes
12	45.45	43.05 to 47.85	yes
13	43.88	41.48 to 46.28	yes
14	42.85	40.45 to 45.25	yes
15	46.73	44.33 to 49.13	no
16	43.70	41.30 to 46.10	yes
17	43.60	41.20 to 46.00	yes
18	42.88	40.48 to 45.28	yes
19	45.82	43.42 to 48.22	yes
20	42.84	40.45 to 45.24	yes

Exercises 8.1

Statistical Concepts and Skills

8.1 The value of a statistic used to estimate a parameter is called a _____ of the parameter.

8.2 What is a confidence-interval estimate of a parameter? Why is such an estimate superior to a point estimate?

8.3 Wedding Costs. According to *Bride's Magazine*, getting married these days can be expensive when the costs of the reception, engagement ring, bridal gown, and pictures—just to name a few—are included. A random sample of 20 recent U.S. weddings yielded the following data on wedding costs, in dollars.

12,113	16,406	10,929	7,171	11,077
20,423	13,820	21,905	26,698	20,513
22,715	5,977	25,795	35,263	16,670
24,886	33,023	27,667	13,700	12,127

a. Use the data to obtain a point estimate for the population mean wedding cost, μ, of all recent U.S. weddings. (*Note:* The sum of the data is $378,878.)
b. Is your point estimate in part (a) likely to equal μ exactly? Explain your answer.

8.4 Cottonmouth Litter Size. A study published by Blem and Blem in the *Journal of Herpetology* (1995, Vol. 29, pp. 391–398) examined the reproductive characteristics of the eastern cottonmouth, a once widely distributed snake whose numbers have decreased recently due to encroachment by humans. A random sample of 44 female cottonmouths yielded the following data on number of young per litter.

5	12	7	7	6	8	12	9	7
4	9	6	12	7	5	6	10	3
10	8	8	12	5	6	10	11	3
8	4	5	7	6	11	7	6	8
8	14	8	7	11	7	5	4

a. Use the data to obtain a point estimate for the mean number of young per litter, μ, of all female eastern cottonmouths. (*Note:* $\Sigma x = 334$.)
b. Is your point estimate in part (a) likely to equal μ exactly? Explain your answer.

For Exercises 8.5–8.8, you may want to review Example 8.2, which begins on page 329.

8.5 Wedding Costs. Refer to Exercise 8.3. Assume that recent wedding costs in the United States are normally distributed with a standard deviation of $8100.
a. Determine a 95.44% confidence interval for the mean cost, μ, of all recent U.S. weddings.
b. Interpret your result in part (a).
c. Does the mean cost of all recent U.S. weddings lie in the confidence interval you obtained in part (a)? Explain your answer.

8.6 Cottonmouth Litter Size. Refer to Exercise 8.4. Assume that $\sigma = 2.4$.
a. Obtain an approximate 95.44% confidence interval for the mean number of young per litter of all female eastern cottonmouths.
b. Interpret your result in part (a).
c. Why is the 95.44% confidence interval that you obtained in part (a) not necessarily exact?

8.7 Business Travel. As business travelers pile up frequent flyer miles, business travel has increased steadily over the past decade. Information on number of miles traveled per business flight within the United States is published online by the U.S. Bureau of Transportation Statistics. Following are the number of miles traveled for 30 randomly sampled business flights within the United States during 1999.

763	1769	935	1427	628	444
1025	1271	716	1140	1200	1585
1311	1427	1576	1447	788	1039
1760	1057	1373	1576	896	1609
942	561	380	1773	2026	1187

a. Find a point estimate for the population mean number of miles traveled per business flight in 1999. Interpret your answer in words. (*Note:* $\Sigma x = 35{,}631$.)
b. Determine a 95.44% confidence interval for the population mean number of miles traveled per business flight in 1999 and interpret your result in words. Assume that $\sigma = 450$ miles.
c. How would you decide whether the number of miles traveled per business flight in 1999 is approximately normally distributed?
d. Must the number of miles traveled per business flight in 1999 be exactly normally distributed for the confidence interval that you obtained in part (b) to be approximately correct? Explain your answer.

8.8 Home Improvements. The 2000 American Express Retail Index provides information on budget amounts for home improvements. The following table displays the budgets, in dollars, of 45 randomly sampled home improvement jobs in the United States.

3179	1032	1822	4093	2285
1478	955	2773	514	3915
4800	3843	5265	2467	2353
4200	3146	551	2659	4660
3570	1598	2605	3643	2816
3125	3104	4503	2911	3605
2948	1421	1910	5145	4557
2026	2750	2069	3056	2550
631	4550	5069	2124	1573

a. Determine a point estimate for the population mean budget, μ, for such home improvement jobs. Interpret your answer in words. (*Note:* The sum of the data is $129,849.)
b. Obtain a 95.44% confidence interval for the population mean budget, μ, for such home improvement jobs and interpret your result in words. Assume that the population standard deviation of budgets for home improvement jobs is $1350.
c. How would you decide whether budgets for such home improvement jobs are approximately normally distributed?
d. Must the budgets for such home improvement jobs be exactly normally distributed for the confidence interval that you obtained in part (b) to be approximately correct? Explain your answer.

Extending the Concepts and Skills

8.9 New Mobile Homes. Refer to Examples 8.1 and 8.2. Use the data in Table 8.1 on page 328 to obtain a 99.74% confidence interval for the mean price of all new mobile homes. (*Hint:* Proceed as in Example 8.2 but use the "99.74" part of the 68.26-95.44-99.74 rule instead of the "95.44" part.)

8.10 New Mobile Homes. Refer to Examples 8.1 and 8.2. Use the data in Table 8.1 on page 328 to obtain a 68.26% confidence interval for the mean price of all new mobile homes. (*Hint:* Proceed as in Example 8.2 but use the "68.26" part of the 68.26-95.44-99.74 rule instead of the "95.44" part.)

8.2 CONFIDENCE INTERVALS FOR ONE POPULATION MEAN WHEN σ IS KNOWN

In Section 8.1, we showed how to find a 95.44% confidence interval for a population mean, that is, a confidence interval at a confidence level of 95.44%. In this section, we generalize the arguments used there to obtain a confidence interval for a population mean at any prescribed confidence level.

To begin, we introduce some general notation used with confidence intervals. Frequently, we want to write the confidence level in the form $1 - \alpha$, where α is a number between 0 and 1; that is, if the confidence level is expressed as a decimal, α is the number that must be subtracted from 1 to get the confidence level. To find α, we simply subtract the confidence level from 1. If the confidence level is 95.44%, then $\alpha = 1 - 0.9544 = 0.0456$; if the confidence level is 90%, then $\alpha = 1 - 0.90 = 0.10$; and so on.

Next, recall from Section 6.2 that the symbol z_α is used to denote the z-score that has area α to its right under the standard normal curve. So, for example, $z_{0.05}$ denotes the z-score that has area 0.05 to its right, $z_{0.025}$ denotes the z-score that has area 0.025 to its right, and $z_{\alpha/2}$ denotes the z-score that has area $\alpha/2$ to its right.

OBTAINING CONFIDENCE INTERVALS FOR A POPULATION MEAN WHEN σ IS KNOWN

We now develop a simple step-by-step procedure for obtaining a confidence interval for a population mean when the population standard deviation is known. In doing so, we assume that the variable under consideration is normally distributed. But keep in mind that, because of the central limit theorem, the procedure also applies to obtaining an approximately correct confidence interval for a population mean when the sample size is large, regardless of the distribution of the variable.

The basis of our confidence-interval procedure is stated in Key Fact 7.4: If x is a normally distributed variable with mean μ and standard deviation σ, then, for samples of size n, the variable $\bar{x}$ is also normally distributed and has mean μ and standard deviation $\sigma/\sqrt{n}$. In Section 8.1, we used this fact and the "95.44" part of the 68.26-95.44-99.74 rule to conclude that 95.44% of all samples of size n have means within $2 \cdot \sigma/\sqrt{n}$ of μ, as depicted in Fig. 8.2(a).

More generally, we can say that $100(1 - \alpha)\%$ of all samples of size n have means within $z_{\alpha/2} \cdot \sigma/\sqrt{n}$ of μ, as depicted in Fig. 8.2(b). Equivalently, we can say that $100(1 - \alpha)\%$ of all samples of size n have the property that the interval

8.2 Confidence Intervals for One Population Mean When σ Is Known 335

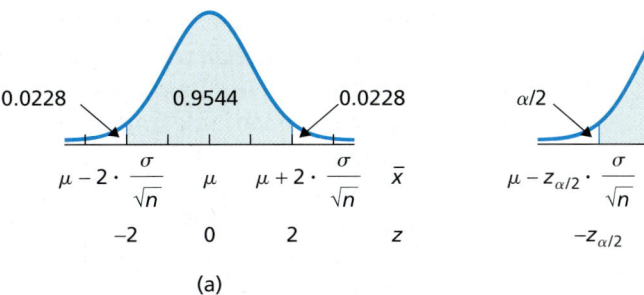

FIGURE 8.2
(a) 95.44% of all samples have means within 2 standard deviations of μ;
(b) $100(1 - \alpha)\%$ of all samples have means within $z_{\alpha/2}$ standard deviations of μ

from

$$\bar{x} - z_{\alpha/2} \cdot \frac{\sigma}{\sqrt{n}} \quad \text{to} \quad \bar{x} + z_{\alpha/2} \cdot \frac{\sigma}{\sqrt{n}}$$

contains μ. Consequently, we have Procedure 8.1, sometimes referred to as the **one-sample z-interval procedure**, or, more briefly, as the **z-interval procedure**.

Procedure 8.1

The One-Sample z-Interval Procedure for a Population Mean

Assumptions
1. Normal population or large sample
2. σ known

Step 1 For a confidence level of $1 - \alpha$, use Table II to find $z_{\alpha/2}$.

Step 2 The confidence interval for μ is from

$$\bar{x} - z_{\alpha/2} \cdot \frac{\sigma}{\sqrt{n}} \quad \text{to} \quad \bar{x} + z_{\alpha/2} \cdot \frac{\sigma}{\sqrt{n}},$$

where $z_{\alpha/2}$ is found in Step 1, n is the sample size, and $\bar{x}$ is computed from the sample data.

Step 3 Interpret the confidence interval.

The confidence interval is exact for normal populations and is approximately correct for large samples from nonnormal populations.

Note: By saying that the confidence interval is *exact*, we mean that the true confidence level equals $1 - \alpha$; by saying that the confidence interval is *approximately correct*, we mean that the true confidence level only approximately equals $1 - \alpha$.

Before applying Procedure 8.1, we need to make several comments. In Chapter 6, we mentioned that, if a variable of a population is normally distributed and is the only variable under consideration, common statistical practice is to say that the population is normally distributed. In Assumption 1 of Procedure 8.1, we have abbreviated this statement as *normal population*. But remember, *normal population* really means that the variable under consideration is normally distributed on the population of interest. Similarly, *nonnormal population* means that the variable under consideration is not normally distributed on the population of interest.

Assumption 1 of Procedure 8.1 read in full means that the variable under consideration is normally distributed or that the sample size is large. Actually, the procedure works reasonably well even when the variable is not normally distributed and the sample size is small or moderate, provided the variable is not too far from being normally distributed. Procedures that are insensitive to departures from the assumptions on which they are based are called **robust procedures.** Thus the z-interval procedure is robust to moderate violations of the normality assumption.

When considering the z-interval procedure, you must also watch for outliers because their presence calls into question the normality assumption. Moreover, even for large samples, outliers can sometimes unduly affect a z-interval because the sample mean is not resistant to outliers. Key Fact 8.1 lists some general guidelines for use of the z-interval procedure.

Key Fact 8.1   When to Use the z-Interval Procedure[2]

- For small samples—say, of size less than 15—the z-interval procedure should be used only when the variable under consideration is normally distributed or very close to being so.
- For samples of moderate size—say, between 15 and 30—the z-interval procedure can be used unless the data contain outliers or the variable under consideration is far from being normally distributed.
- For large samples—say, of size 30 or more—the z-interval procedure can be used essentially without restriction. However, if outliers are present and their removal is not justified, the effect of the outliers on the confidence interval should be examined; that is, you should compare the confidence intervals obtained with and without the outliers. If the effect is substantial, using a different procedure or taking another sample probably is best.
- If outliers are present but their removal is justified and results in a data set for which the z-interval procedure is appropriate (as previously stated), the procedure can be used.

Key Fact 8.1 makes it clear that you should conduct preliminary data analyses before applying the z-interval procedure. Normal probability plots, boxplots, stem-and-leaf diagrams, and histograms are often useful in this regard.

---

[2] We can refine these guidelines further by considering the impact of skewness. Roughly speaking, the more skewed the distribution of the variable under consideration, the larger is the sample size required for the validity of the z-interval procedure. See, for instance, the paper "How Large Does n Have to be for Z and t Intervals?" by Dennis D. Boos and Jacqueline M. Hughes-Oliver (*The American Statistician*, 2000, Vol. 54, No. 2, pp. 121–128).

8.2 Confidence Intervals for One Population Mean When σ Is Known

More generally, the following fundamental principle of data analysis is relevant to all inferential procedures.

Key Fact 8.2   A Fundamental Principle of Data Analysis

Before performing a statistical-inference procedure, examine the sample data. If any of the conditions required for using the procedure appear to be violated, do not apply the procedure. Instead use a different, more appropriate procedure, or, if you are unsure of one, consult a statistician.

Even for small samples, where graphical displays must be interpreted carefully, examining the data is still far better than not doing so. Even for very small samples, graphical displays can sometimes detect violations of assumptions required for inferential procedures. Remember to proceed cautiously when conducting graphical analyses of small samples, especially very small samples—say, of size 10 or less.

In Example 8.4, we apply Procedure 8.1, in the process checking the guidelines presented in Key Fact 8.1.

Example 8.4   The One-Sample z-Interval Procedure

Age of the Civilian Labor Force The U.S. Bureau of Labor Statistics collects information on the ages of people in the civilian labor force and publishes the results in *Employment and Earnings*. Fifty people in the civilian labor force are randomly selected; their ages are displayed in Table 8.3. Find a 95% confidence interval for the mean age, μ, of all people in the civilian labor force. Assume that the population standard deviation of the ages is 12.1 years.

Solution We constructed (not shown) a normal probability plot, histogram, stem-and-leaf diagram, and boxplot for these data. The boxplot indicated potential outliers, but in view of the other three graphs, we concluded that, in fact, the data contain no outliers. As the sample size is 50, which is large, and the population standard deviation, σ, is known, we can apply Procedure 8.1 to obtain the required confidence interval.

TABLE 8.3
Ages of 50 randomly selected people in the civilian labor force

22	58	40	42	43
32	34	45	38	19
33	16	49	29	30
43	37	19	21	62
60	41	28	35	37
51	37	65	57	26
27	31	33	24	34
28	39	43	26	38
42	40	31	34	38
35	29	33	32	33

Step 1 For a confidence level of $1 - \alpha$, use Table II to find $z_{\alpha/2}$.

We want a 95% confidence interval, so $\alpha = 1 - 0.95 = 0.05$. From Table II, $z_{\alpha/2} = z_{0.05/2} = z_{0.025} = 1.96$.

Step 2 The confidence interval for μ is from

$$\bar{x} - z_{\alpha/2} \cdot \frac{\sigma}{\sqrt{n}} \quad \text{to} \quad \bar{x} + z_{\alpha/2} \cdot \frac{\sigma}{\sqrt{n}}.$$

We have $\sigma = 12.1$, $n = 50$, and, from Step 1, $z_{\alpha/2} = 1.96$. To compute $\bar{x}$ for the data in Table 8.3, we apply the usual formula:

$$\bar{x} = \frac{\Sigma x}{n} = \frac{1819}{50} = 36.4,$$

to one decimal place. Consequently, a 95% confidence interval for μ is from

$$36.4 - 1.96 \cdot \frac{12.1}{\sqrt{50}} \quad \text{to} \quad 36.4 + 1.96 \cdot \frac{12.1}{\sqrt{50}},$$

or 33.0 to 39.8.

Step 3 Interpret the confidence interval.

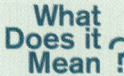
We can be 95% confident that the mean age, μ, of all people in the civilian labor force is somewhere between 33.0 years and 39.8 years.

CONFIDENCE AND PRECISION

On the one hand, the confidence level of a confidence interval for a population mean, μ, signifies the confidence of the estimate, that is, the confidence we have that μ actually lies in the confidence interval. On the other hand, the length of the confidence interval indicates the precision of the estimate, that is, how well we have "pinned down" μ; long confidence intervals indicate poor precision, whereas short confidence intervals indicate good precision.

How does the confidence level affect the length of the confidence interval? To answer this question, let's return to Example 8.4, where we found a 95% confidence interval for the mean age, μ, of all people in the civilian labor force. The confidence level there is 0.95, and the confidence interval we computed is from 33.0 to 39.8 years. If we change the confidence level from 0.95 to, say, 0.90, then $z_{\alpha/2}$ changes from $z_{0.05/2} = z_{0.025} = 1.96$ to $z_{0.10/2} = z_{0.05} = 1.645$. The resulting confidence interval, using the same sample data (Table 8.3), is from

$$36.4 - 1.645 \cdot \frac{12.1}{\sqrt{50}} \quad \text{to} \quad 36.4 + 1.645 \cdot \frac{12.1}{\sqrt{50}},$$

or from 33.6 to 39.2 years. We show both the 90% and 95% confidence intervals in Fig. 8.3.

FIGURE 8.3
90% and 95% confidence intervals for μ, using the data in Table 8.3

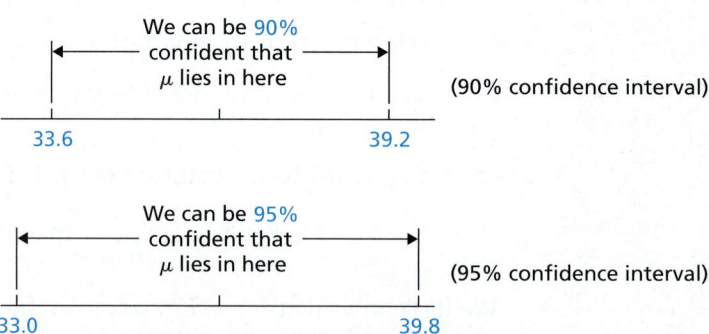

Thus, decreasing the confidence level decreases the length of the confidence interval, and vice-versa, which makes sense: If we are willing to settle for less confidence that μ lies in our confidence interval, we can obtain a shorter interval. However, if we want to be more confident that μ lies in our confidence interval, we must settle for a greater interval. In other words, confidence and precision are related as stated in the following key fact.

Key Fact 8.3 Confidence and Precision

For a fixed sample size, decreasing the confidence level increases the precision, and vice-versa.

The Technology Center

Procedure 8.1 on page 335 provides a step-by-step method for obtaining a confidence interval for a population mean when the population standard deviation is known. Most statistical technologies have programs that automatically determine this type of confidence interval. In this subsection, we present output and (optional) step-by-step instructions to implement such programs.

Example 8.5 Using Technology to Obtain a z-Interval

Age of the Civilian Labor Force Table 8.3 on page 337 displays the ages of 50 randomly selected people in the civilian labor force. Use Minitab, Excel, or the TI-83 Plus to determine a 95% confidence interval for the mean age, μ, of all people in the civilian labor force. Assume that the population standard deviation of the ages is 12.1 years.

Solution Printout 8.1 at the top of the next page shows the output obtained by applying the one-sample z-interval programs to the age data in Table 8.3.

As shown in the three outputs in Printout 8.1, the required 95% confidence interval is from 33.03 to 39.73. Hence we can be 95% confident that the mean age, μ, of all people in the civilian labor force is somewhere between 33.03 years and 39.73 years. Compare this confidence interval to the one obtained in Example 8.4. Can you explain the slight discrepancy? ◆

Obtaining the Output (Optional)

Printout 8.1 provides output from Minitab, Excel, and the TI-83 Plus for a one-sample z-interval with a 95% confidence level based on the sample of ages presented in Table 8.3. The following are detailed instructions for obtaining that output. First, we store the age data in a column (Minitab), range (Excel), or list (TI-83 Plus) named AGE. Then, we proceed as indicated on the bottom of the next page.

340 CHAPTER 8 Confidence Intervals for One Population Mean

PRINTOUT 8.1
One-sample z-interval output for the sample of ages

MINITAB

```
One-Sample Z: AGE

The assumed sigma = 12.1
Variable       N      Mean     StDev    SE Mean        95.0% CI
AGE           50     36.38     11.07       1.71   (  33.03,   39.73)
```

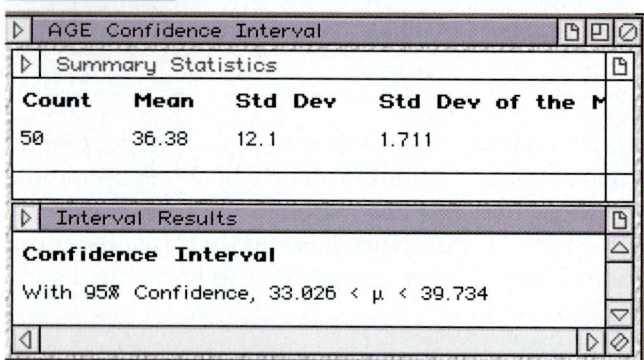

MINITAB

1. Choose **Stat ➤ Basic Statistics ➤ 1-Sample Z...**
2. Specify AGE in the **Variables** text box
3. Click in the **Sigma** text box and type 12.1
4. Click the **Options...** button
5. Type 95 in the **Confidence level** text box
6. Click the arrow button at the right of the **Alternative** drop-down list box and select **not equal**
7. Click **OK**
8. Click **OK**

EXCEL

1. Choose **DDXL ➤ Confidence Intervals**
2. Select **1 Var z Interval** from the **Function type** drop-down box
3. Specify AGE in the **Quantitative Variable** text box
4. Click **OK**
5. Click the **95%** button
6. Click in the **Type in the population standard deviation** text box and type 12.1
7. Click the **Compute Interval** button

TI-83 PLUS

1. Press **STAT**, arrow over to **TESTS**, and press **7**
2. Highlight **Data** and press **ENTER**
3. Press the down-arrow key, type 12.1 for σ, and press **ENTER**
4. Press **2nd ➤ LIST**
5. Arrow down to AGE and press **ENTER** three times
6. Type .95 for **C-Level** and press **ENTER** twice

Exercises 8.2

Statistical Concepts and Skills

8.11 Find the confidence level and α for
a. a 90% confidence interval.
b. a 99% confidence interval.

8.12 What is meant by saying that a $1-\alpha$ confidence interval is
a. exact?   b. approximately correct?

8.13 In developing Procedure 8.1, we assumed that the variable under consideration is normally distributed.
a. Explain why we needed that assumption.
b. Explain why the procedure yields an approximately correct confidence interval for large samples, regardless of the distribution of the variable under consideration.

8.14 What does the abbreviation *normal population* stand for?

8.15 Refer to Procedure 8.1.
a. Explain in detail the assumptions required for using the z-interval procedure.
b. How important is the normality assumption? Explain your answer.

8.16 What is meant by saying that a statistical procedure is robust?

8.17 In each part, assume that the population standard deviation is known. Decide whether use of the z-interval procedure to obtain a confidence interval for the population mean is reasonable. Explain your answers.
a. The variable under consideration is very close to being normally distributed, and the sample size is 10.
b. The variable under consideration is very close to being normally distributed, and the sample size is 75.
c. The sample data contain outliers, and the sample size is 20.
d. The sample data contain no outliers, the variable under consideration is roughly normally distributed, and the sample size is 20.
e. The distribution of the variable under consideration is highly skewed, and the sample size is 20.
f. The sample data contain no outliers, the sample size is 250, and the variable under consideration is far from being normally distributed.

8.18 Suppose that you have obtained data by taking a random sample from a population. Before performing a statistical inference, what should you do?

8.19 Suppose that you have obtained data by taking a random sample from a population and that you intend to find a confidence interval for the population mean, μ. Which confidence level, 95% or 99%, will result in the confidence interval's giving a more precise estimate of μ?

Preliminary data analyses indicate that you can reasonably apply the z-interval procedure (Procedure 8.1 on page 335) in Exercises 8.20–8.23.

8.20 Smelling Out the Enemy. Snakes deposit chemical trails as they travel through their habitats. These trails are often detected and recognized by lizards, which are potential prey. The ability to recognize their predators via tongue flicks can often mean life or death for lizards. Scientists from the University of Antwerp were interested in quantifying the responses of juveniles of the common lizard (*Lacerta vivipara*) to natural predator cues to determine whether the behavior is learned or congenital. Seventeen juvenile common lizards were exposed to the chemical cues of the viper snake. Their responses, in number of tongue flicks per 20 minutes, are presented in the following table. [SOURCE: Van Damme et al., "Responses of Naïve Lizards to Predator Chemical Cues," *Journal of Herpetology*, 1995, Vol. 29(1), pp. 38–43.]

425	510	629	236	654	200
276	501	811	332	424	674
676	694	710	662	633	

a. Find a 90% confidence interval for the mean number of tongue flicks per 20 minutes for all juvenile common lizards. Assume a population standard deviation of 190.0. (*Note:* The sum of the data is 9047.)
b. Interpret your answer from part (a).

8.21 Venture Capital Investments. Data on investments in the high-tech industry by venture capitalists are compiled by VentureOne Corporation and published in *America's Network Telecom Investor Supplement*. A random sample of 18 venture capital investments in the fiber optics business sector yielded the following data, in millions of dollars.

5.60	6.27	5.96	10.51	2.04	5.48
5.74	5.58	4.13	8.63	5.95	6.67
4.21	7.71	9.21	4.98	8.64	6.66

a. Determine a 95% confidence interval for the mean amount, μ, of all venture capital investments in the fiber optics business sector. Assume that the population standard deviation is $2.04 million. (*Note:* The sum of the data is $113.97 million.)
b. Interpret your answer from part (a).

8.22 Political Prisoners. Ehlers, Maercker, and Boos studied various characteristics of political prisoners from the former East Germany and presented their findings in the paper "Posttraumatic Stress Disorder (PTSD) Following Political Imprisonment: The Role of Mental Defeat, Alienation, and Perceived Permanent Change" (*Journal of Abnormal Psychology*, 2000, Vol. 109, pp. 45–55). According to the article, the mean duration of imprisonment for 32 patients with chronic PTSD was 33.4 months. Assuming that $\sigma = 42$ months, determine a 95% confidence interval for the mean duration of imprisonment, μ, of all East German political prisoners with chronic PTSD. Interpret your answer in words.

8.23 Keep on Rolling. The Rolling Stones, a rock group formed in the 1960s, has toured extensively in support of new albums. *Pollstar* has collected data on the earnings from the Stones's North American tours. For 30 randomly selected Rolling Stones concerts, the mean gross earnings is $2.27 million. Assuming a population standard deviation gross earnings of $0.5 million, obtain a 99% confidence interval for the mean gross earnings of all Rolling Stones concerts. Interpret your answer in words.

8.24 Smelling Out the Enemy. Refer to Exercise 8.20.
a. Find a 99% confidence interval for μ.
b. Why is the confidence interval you found in part (a) longer than the one in Exercise 8.20?
c. Draw a graph similar to that shown in Fig. 8.3 on page 338 to display both confidence intervals.

d. Which confidence interval yields a more precise estimate of μ? Explain your answer.

8.25 Venture Capital Investments. Refer to Exercise 8.21.
a. Determine an 80% confidence interval for μ.
b. Why is the confidence interval you found in part (a) shorter than the one in Exercise 8.21?
c. Draw a graph similar to that shown in Fig. 8.3 on page 338 to display both confidence intervals.
d. Which confidence interval yields a more precise estimate of μ? Explain your answer.

Extending the Concepts and Skills

8.26 Family Size. The U.S. Bureau of the Census compiles data on family size and presents its findings in *Current Population Reports*. Suppose that 500 U.S. families are randomly selected to estimate the mean size, μ, of all U.S. families. Further suppose that the results are as shown in the following frequency distribution.

Size	2	3	4	5	6	7	8	9
Frequency	198	118	101	59	12	3	8	1

a. If the population standard deviation of family sizes is 1.3, determine a 95% confidence interval for the mean size, μ, of all U.S. families. (*Hint:* To find the sample mean, use the grouped-data formulas on page 114.)
b. Interpret your answer from part (a).

8.27 Key Fact 8.3 states that, for a fixed sample size, decreasing the confidence level increases the precision of the confidence-interval estimate of μ and vice-versa.
a. Suppose that you want to increase the precision without reducing the level of confidence. What can you do?
b. Suppose that you want to increase the level of confidence without reducing the precision. What can you do?

Using Technology

In Exercises 8.28 and 8.29, use the technology of your choice to
a. *obtain a normal probability plot, boxplot, histogram, and stem-and-leaf diagram of the data, and*
b. *construct the required confidence interval.*
c. *Justify the use of your procedure in part (b).*

8.28 The data set and confidence interval in Exercise 8.20.

8.29 The data set and confidence interval in Exercise 8.21.

8.30 Ages of Diabetics. A research physician wants to estimate the average age of people with diabetes. She takes a random sample of 35 diabetics and obtains the following ages.

48	41	57	83	41	55	59
61	38	48	79	75	77	7
54	23	47	56	79	68	61
64	45	53	82	68	38	70
10	60	83	76	21	65	47

Use the technology of your choice to
a. find a 95% confidence interval for the mean age, μ, of people with diabetes. Assume that $\sigma = 21.2$ years.
b. obtain a normal probability plot, boxplot, histogram, and stem-and-leaf diagram of the data.
c. Remove the outliers (if any) from the data and then repeat part (a).
d. Comment on the advisability of using the z-interval procedure here.

8.31 Farm Children. A sociologist wants information on the number of children per farm family in her native state of Nebraska. Twenty-two randomly selected farm families have the following number of children.

1	2	1	2	0	2
1	5	4	1	0	2
1	3	1	0	1	
0	1	8	0	1	

Use the technology of your choice to
a. determine a 90% confidence interval for the mean number of children, μ, per farm family in Nebraska. Assume that $\sigma = 1.95$ children.
b. obtain a normal probability plot, boxplot, histogram, and stem-and-leaf diagram of the data.
c. Remove the outliers (if any) from the data and then repeat part (a).
d. Comment on the advisability of using the z-interval procedure here.

8.32 Gestation Periods of Humans. This exercise can be done individually or, better yet, as a class project. Gestation periods of humans are normally distributed with a mean of 266 days and a standard deviation of 16 days.
a. Simulate 100 samples of nine human gestation periods each.
b. For each sample in part (a), obtain a 95% confidence interval for the population mean gestation period.
c. For the 100 confidence intervals that you obtained in part (b), roughly how many would you expect to contain the population mean gestation period of 266 days?
d. For the 100 confidence intervals that you obtained in part (b), determine the number that contain the population mean gestation period of 266 days.
e. Compare your answers from parts (c) and (d) and comment on any observed difference.

8.3 MARGIN OF ERROR

In this section, we examine in detail how sample size affects the precision of estimating a population mean by a sample mean. Recall Key Fact 7.1, which states that the larger the sample size, the smaller the sampling error tends to be. Now that you have studied confidence intervals, you can determine exactly how sample size affects the accuracy of the estimate. We begin by introducing the concept of the *margin of error* in Example 8.6.

Example 8.6 Introducing Margin of Error

Age of the Civilian Labor Force In Example 8.4, we applied the one-sample z-interval procedure to the ages of a sample of 50 people in the civilian labor force to obtain a 95% confidence interval for the mean age, μ, of all people in the civilian labor force. Discuss the precision with which $\bar{x}$ estimates μ.

Solution Recalling that $z_{\alpha/2} = z_{0.05/2} = z_{0.025} = 1.96$, $n = 50$, $\sigma = 12.1$, and $\bar{x} = 36.4$, we found that a 95% confidence interval for μ is from

$$\bar{x} - z_{\alpha/2} \cdot \frac{\sigma}{\sqrt{n}} \quad \text{to} \quad \bar{x} + z_{\alpha/2} \cdot \frac{\sigma}{\sqrt{n}}$$

or

$$36.4 - 1.96 \cdot \frac{12.1}{\sqrt{50}} \quad \text{to} \quad 36.4 + 1.96 \cdot \frac{12.1}{\sqrt{50}}$$

or

$$36.4 - 3.4 \quad \text{to} \quad 36.4 + 3.4$$

or

$$33.0 \quad \text{to} \quad 39.8.$$

We can be 95% confident that the mean age, μ, of all people in the civilian labor force is somewhere between 33.0 years and 39.8 years.

The confidence interval that we obtained provides a rather wide range for the possible values of μ. In other words, the precision of the estimate is poor. To improve the precision, we need to decrease the length of the confidence interval.

As demonstrated in Section 8.2, we can decrease the length of the confidence interval and thereby increase the precision of the estimate by decreasing the confidence level from 95% to some lower level. But suppose that we want to retain the same level of confidence and still narrow the confidence interval. How can we do so? To answer that question, we first look more closely at the confidence interval by displaying it graphically in Fig. 8.4.

FIGURE 8.4
95% confidence interval for the mean age, μ, of all people in the civilian labor force

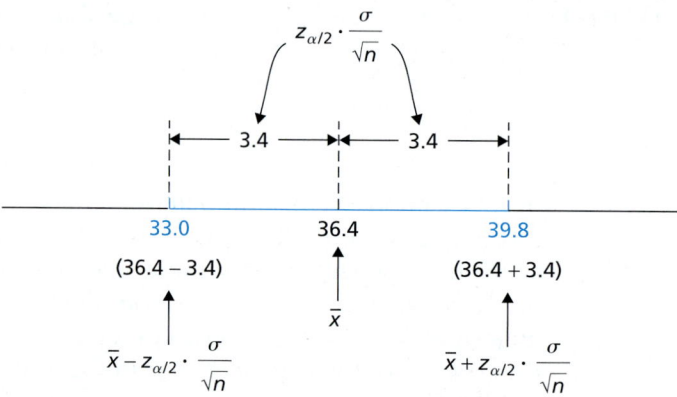

From Fig. 8.4 or the computations preceding it, we find that the length of the confidence interval is determined by the quantity

$$E = z_{\alpha/2} \cdot \frac{\sigma}{\sqrt{n}},$$

which is half the length of the confidence interval, or 3.4 in this case. The quantity E is called the **margin of error**, also known as the **maximum error of the estimate.** We use this terminology because, at the specified level of confidence (in this case, 95%), we are confident that our error in estimating μ by $\bar{x}$ is at most 3.4 years, as shown in Fig. 8.4. In newspapers and magazines, this fact is often expressed as "The poll has a margin of error of 3.4 years." Or as "Theoretically, in 95 out of 100 such polls the margin of error will be 3.4 years."

In any case, to narrow the confidence interval and thereby increase the precision of the estimate, we need only decrease the margin of error, E. As the sample size, n, occurs in the denominator of the formula for E, we can decrease E by increasing the sample size. This fact makes sense, of course, because we expect to get more precise information from larger samples. ◆

In Example 8.6, we introduced some concepts and terminology important in confidence-interval analysis. We summarize that discussion in the following definition and in Key Fact 8.4.

DEFINITION 8.3 Margin of Error for the Estimate of μ

The *margin of error* for the estimate of μ is

$$E = z_{\alpha/2} \cdot \frac{\sigma}{\sqrt{n}}.$$

The margin of error is equal to half the length of the confidence interval, as depicted in Fig. 8.5.

FIGURE 8.5
Margin of error, $E = z_{\alpha/2} \cdot \dfrac{\sigma}{\sqrt{n}}$

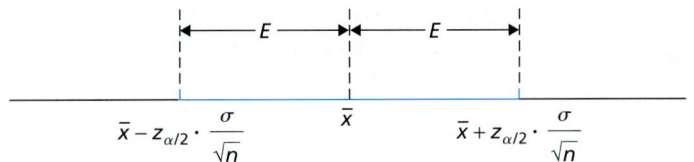

Key Fact 8.4 Margin of Error, Precision, and Sample Size

The length of a confidence interval for a population mean, μ, and hence the precision with which $\bar{x}$ estimates μ, is determined by the margin of error, E. For a fixed confidence level, increasing the sample size increases the precision, and vice-versa.

DETERMINING THE REQUIRED SAMPLE SIZE

The margin of error and confidence level of a confidence interval are often specified in advance. We must then determine the sample size required to meet the specifications. The formula for the required sample size can be obtained by solving for n in the formula for the margin of error, $E = z_{\alpha/2} \cdot \sigma/\sqrt{n}$. The result is Formula 8.1, which we apply in Example 8.7.

FORMULA 8.1 Sample Size for Estimating μ

The sample size required for a $(1 - \alpha)$-level confidence interval for μ with a specified margin of error, E, is given by the formula

$$n = \left(\frac{z_{\alpha/2} \cdot \sigma}{E}\right)^2,$$

rounded up to the nearest whole number.

Example 8.7 Sample Size for Estimating μ

Age of the Civilian Labor Force Consider again the problem of estimating the mean age, μ, of all people in the civilian labor force.

a. Determine the sample size required to ensure that we can be 95% confident that μ is within 0.5 year of the estimate, $\bar{x}$. Recall that $\sigma = 12.1$ years.
b. Find a 95% confidence interval for μ if a sample of the size determined in part (a) has a mean age of 38.8 years.

Solution a. To determine the required sample size, we apply Formula 8.1. In doing so, we must identify σ, E, and $z_{\alpha/2}$. We know that $\sigma = 12.1$ years; the margin of error, E, is specified at 0.5 year; and the confidence level is stipulated as 0.95, which means that $\alpha = 0.05$ and $z_{\alpha/2} = z_{0.05/2} = z_{0.025} = 1.96$. Thus the required sample size is

$$n = \left(\frac{z_{\alpha/2} \cdot \sigma}{E}\right)^2 = \left(\frac{1.96 \cdot 12.1}{0.5}\right)^2 = 2249.79.$$

Obviously, we cannot take a fractional sample size, so, to be conservative, we round up to 2250.

b. We are to find a 95% confidence interval for the mean age of all people in the civilian labor force if a sample of the size determined in part (a) has a mean age of 38.8 years. Applying Procedure 8.1 with $\alpha = 0.05$, $\sigma = 12.1$, $\bar{x} = 38.8$, and $n = 2250$, we obtain the confidence interval:

$$\bar{x} - z_{\alpha/2} \cdot \frac{\sigma}{\sqrt{n}} \quad \text{to} \quad \bar{x} + z_{\alpha/2} \cdot \frac{\sigma}{\sqrt{n}}$$

or

$$38.8 - 1.96 \cdot \frac{12.1}{\sqrt{2250}} \quad \text{to} \quad 38.8 + 1.96 \cdot \frac{12.1}{\sqrt{2250}}$$

or

$$38.8 - 0.5 \quad \text{to} \quad 38.8 + 0.5$$

or

$$38.3 \quad \text{to} \quad 39.3.$$

What Does it Mean?

If 2250 people in the civilian labor force are randomly selected, we can be 95% confident that the mean age, μ, of all people in the civilian labor force is within 0.5 year of the mean age, $\bar{x}$, of the people in the sample.

What Does it Mean?

We can be 95% confident that the mean age, μ, of all people in the civilian labor force is somewhere between 38.3 years and 39.3 years.

Note: The sample size of 2250 was determined in part (a) of Example 8.7 to guarantee a margin of error of 0.5 year for a 95% confidence interval. Therefore, in light of Fig. 8.5 on page 345, we could have obtained the 95% confidence interval required in part (b) of Example 8.7 simply by computing

$$\bar{x} \pm E = 38.8 \pm 0.5.$$

Doing so would give the same confidence interval, 38.3 to 39.3, that we got in part (b) of Example 8.7 but with much less work. However, because the sample size is a rounded value, the simpler method we just used might have incorrectly yielded a slightly wider confidence interval. In practice, the simpler method is acceptable because, at worst, it provides a slightly conservative estimate.

The formula for finding the required sample size, Formula 8.1, involves the population standard deviation, σ. If σ is unknown, which is usually the case in practice, and we want to apply the formula, we must first estimate σ. One way to do so is to take a preliminary large sample, say, of size 30 or more. The sample standard deviation, s, of the sample obtained provides an estimate of σ and can be used in place of σ in Formula 8.1.

Exercises 8.3

Statistical Concepts and Skills

8.33 Discuss the relationship between the margin of error and the standard error of the mean.

8.34 Explain why the margin of error determines the precision with which a sample mean estimates a population mean.

8.35 In each part, explain the effect on the margin of error and hence the effect on the precision of estimating a population mean by a sample mean.
a. Increasing the confidence level while keeping the same sample size.
b. Increasing the sample size while keeping the same confidence level.

8.36 A confidence interval for a population mean has a margin of error of 3.4.
a. Determine the length of the confidence interval.
b. If the sample mean is 52.8, obtain the confidence interval.

8.37 A confidence interval for a population mean has length 20.
a. Determine the margin of error.
b. If the sample mean is 60, obtain the confidence interval.

8.38 Answer true or false to each statement concerning a confidence interval for a population mean. Give reasons for your answers.
a. The length of a confidence interval can be determined if you know only the margin of error.
b. The margin of error can be determined if you know only the length of the confidence interval.
c. The confidence interval can be obtained if you know only the margin of error.
d. The confidence interval can be obtained if you know only the margin of error and the sample mean.
e. The margin of error can be determined if you know only the confidence level.
f. The confidence level can be determined if you know only the margin of error.
g. The margin of error can be determined if you know only the confidence level, population standard deviation, and sample size.
h. The confidence level can be determined if you know only the margin of error, population standard deviation, and sample size.

8.39 Formula 8.1 provides a method for computing the sample size required to obtain a confidence interval with

a specified confidence level and margin of error. The number resulting from the formula should be rounded up to the nearest whole number.
a. Why do you want a whole number?
b. Why do you round up instead of down?

8.40 Explain how to apply Formula 8.1 if σ is unknown.

8.41 Fuel Expenditures. In estimating the mean monthly fuel expenditure, μ, per household vehicle, the U.S. Energy Information Administration takes a sample of size 6841. Assuming that $\sigma = \$20.65$, determine the margin of error in estimating μ at the 95% level of confidence.

8.42 Smelling Out the Enemy. In Exercise 8.20, you found a 90% confidence interval for the mean number of tongue flicks per 20 minutes for all juvenile common lizards to be from 456.4 to 608.0. Obtain the margin of error by
a. taking half the length of the confidence interval.
b. using the formula in Definition 8.3 on page 345. (Recall that $n = 17$ and $\sigma = 190.0$.)

8.43 Venture Capital Investments. In Exercise 8.21, you found a 95% confidence interval for the mean amount of all venture capital investments in the fiber optics business sector to be from $5.39 million to $7.27 million. Obtain the margin of error by
a. taking half the length of the confidence interval.
b. using the formula in Definition 8.3 on page 345. (Recall that $n = 18$ and $\sigma = \$2.04$ million.)

8.44 Political Prisoners. In Exercise 8.22, you found a 95% confidence interval of 18.8 months to 48.0 months for the mean duration of imprisonment, μ, of all East German political prisoners with chronic PTSD.
a. Determine the margin of error, E.
b. Explain the meaning of E in this context in terms of the accuracy of the estimate.
c. Find the sample size required to have a margin of error of 12 months and a 99% confidence level. (Recall that $\sigma = 42$ months.)

d. Determine a 99% confidence interval for the mean duration of imprisonment, μ, if a sample of the size determined in part (c) has a mean of 36.2 months.

8.45 Keep on Rolling. In Exercise 8.23, you found a 99% confidence interval of $2.03 million to $2.51 million for the mean gross earnings of all Rolling Stones concerts.
a. Determine the margin of error, E.
b. Explain the meaning of E in this context in terms of the accuracy of the estimate.
c. Find the sample size required to have a margin of error of $0.1 million and a 95% confidence level. (Recall that $\sigma = \$0.5$ million.)
d. Obtain a 95% confidence interval for the mean gross earnings if a sample of the size determined in part (c) has a mean of $2.35 million.

Extending the Concepts and Skills

8.46 Millionaires. Professor Thomas Stanley of Georgia State University has surveyed millionaires since 1973. Among other information, Professor Stanley obtains estimates for the mean age, μ, of all U.S. millionaires. Suppose that one year's study involved a random sample of 36 U.S. millionaires whose mean age was 58.53 years with a sample standard deviation of 13.36 years.
a. If, for next year's study, a confidence interval for μ is to have a margin of error of 2 years and a confidence level of 95%, determine the required sample size.
b. Why did you use the sample standard deviation, $s = 13.36$, in place of σ in your solution to part (a)? Why is it permissible to do so?

8.47 Corporate Farms. The U.S. Bureau of the Census estimates the mean value of the land and buildings per corporate farm. Those estimates are published in the *Census of Agriculture*. Suppose that an estimate, $\bar{x}$, is obtained and that the margin of error is $1000. Does this result imply that the true mean, μ, is within $1000 of the estimate? Explain your answer.

8.48 Suppose that a random sample is taken from a normal population having a standard deviation of 10 for the purpose of obtaining a 95% confidence interval for the mean of the population.
a. If the sample size is 4, obtain the margin of error.
b. Repeat part (a) for a sample size of 16.
c. Can you guess the margin of error for a sample size of 64? Explain your reasoning.

8.49 For a fixed confidence level, show that (approximately) quadrupling the sample size is necessary to halve the margin of error. (*Hint:* Use Formula 8.1.)

8.4 CONFIDENCE INTERVALS FOR ONE POPULATION MEAN WHEN σ IS UNKNOWN

In Section 8.2, you learned how to determine a confidence interval for a population mean, μ, when the population standard deviation, σ, is known. The basis of the procedure is in Key Fact 7.4: If x is a normally distributed variable with mean μ and standard deviation σ, then, for samples of size n, the variable $\bar{x}$ is also normally distributed and has mean μ and standard deviation $\sigma/\sqrt{n}$; equivalently, the **standardized version of $\bar{x}$**,

$$z = \frac{\bar{x} - \mu}{\sigma/\sqrt{n}}, \tag{8.2}$$

has the standard normal distribution.

But what if, as is usually the case in practice, the population standard deviation is unknown? Then we cannot base our confidence-interval procedure on the standardized version of $\bar{x}$. The best we can do is estimate the population standard deviation, σ, by the sample standard deviation, s; in other words, we replace σ by s in Equation (8.2) and base our confidence-interval procedure on the resulting variable,

$$t = \frac{\bar{x} - \mu}{s/\sqrt{n}}, \tag{8.3}$$

called the **studentized version of $\bar{x}$.**

Unlike the standardized version, the studentized version of $\bar{x}$ does not have a normal distribution. To get an idea of how their distributions differ, we used statistical software to simulate each variable for samples of size 4, assuming that $\mu = 15$ and $\sigma = 0.8$. (Any sample size, population mean, and population standard deviation will do.)

1. We simulated 5000 samples of size 4 each.
2. For each of the 5000 samples, we obtained the sample mean and sample standard deviation.
3. For each of the 5000 samples, we determined the observed values of both the standardized and studentized versions of $\bar{x}$, as given by Equations (8.2) and (8.3), respectively.
4. We obtained histograms of both the 5000 observed values of the standardized version of $\bar{x}$ and the 5000 observed values of the studentized version of $\bar{x}$, as shown in Printout 8.2 on the following page.

The two histograms shown in Printout 8.2 suggest that the distributions of the standardized version of $\bar{x}$—the variable z in Equation (8.2)—and the studentized version of $\bar{x}$—the variable t in Equation (8.3)—have things in common; both are bell-shaped and symmetric about 0. But there is an important difference: The distribution of the studentized version has more spread than the standardized version. This difference is not surprising because the variation in the possible values of the standardized version is due solely to the variation of sample means, whereas that of the studentized version is due to the variation of both sample means and sample standard deviations.

PRINTOUT 8.2

Histograms of z (standardized version of $\bar{x}$) and t (studentized version of $\bar{x}$) for 5000 samples of size 4

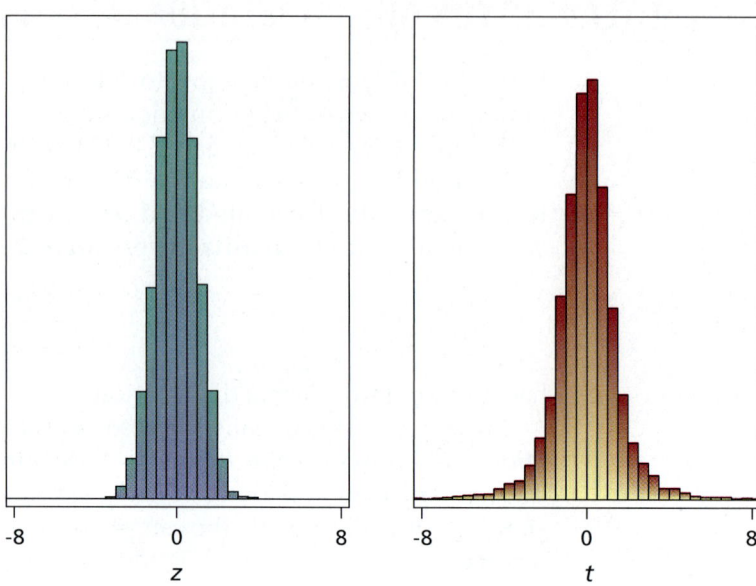

As we know, the standardized version of $\bar{x}$ has the standard normal distribution. In 1908, William Gosset determined the distribution of the studentized version of $\bar{x}$, a distribution now called **Student's t-distribution** or, simply, the **t-distribution.** (See the Biography on page 367 for more on Gosset and the story of Student's t-distribution.)

t-DISTRIBUTIONS AND t-CURVES

Actually, there is a different t-distribution for each sample size. We identify a particular t-distribution by giving its **degrees of freedom (df).** For the studentized version of $\bar{x}$, the degrees of freedom is 1 less than the sample size, which we indicate symbolically by df = $n - 1$. Later, we encounter t-statistics other than the studentized version of $\bar{x}$ whose degrees of freedom are different. But for now, we summarize what we have presented about the studentized version of $\bar{x}$ as Key Fact 8.5.

Key Fact 8.5 | **Studentized Version of the Sample Mean**

Suppose that a variable x of a population is normally distributed with mean μ. Then, for samples of size n, the studentized version of $\bar{x}$,

$$t = \frac{\bar{x} - \mu}{s/\sqrt{n}},$$

has the t-distribution with $n - 1$ degrees of freedom.

Like normally distributed variables, a variable having a t-distribution has an associated curve, called a **t-curve.** In this book, you don't need to know the equation of a *t*-curve, but you do need to understand the basic properties of a *t*-curve.

Although there is a different *t*-curve for each number of degrees of freedom, all *t*-curves are similar and resemble the standard normal curve. Figure 8.6 shows the standard normal curve and two *t*-curves. As illustrated in Fig. 8.6, *t*-curves have the properties delineated in Key Fact 8.6.

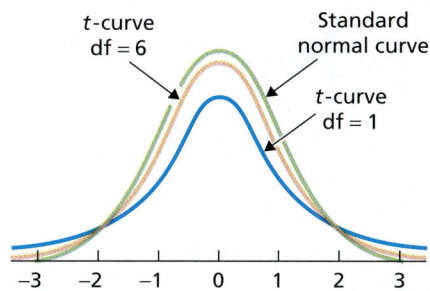

FIGURE 8.6
Standard normal curve and two *t*-curves

Key Fact 8.6

Basic Properties of *t*-Curves

Property 1: The total area under a *t*-curve equals 1.

Property 2: A *t*-curve extends indefinitely in both directions, approaching, but never touching, the horizontal axis as it does so.

Property 3: A *t*-curve is symmetric about 0.

Property 4: As the number of degrees of freedom becomes larger, *t*-curves look increasingly like the standard normal curve.

USING THE *t*-TABLE

Percentages (and probabilities) for a variable having a *t*-distribution equal areas under the variable's associated *t*-curve. For our purposes, one of which is obtaining confidence intervals for a population mean, we don't need a complete *t*-table for each *t*-curve; only certain areas will be important. Table IV, which appears in Appendix A and in abridged form on the inside back cover, is sufficient for our purposes.

The two outside columns of Table IV, labeled df, display the number of degrees of freedom. As expected, the symbol t_α denotes the *t*-value having area α to its right under a *t*-curve. Thus the column headed $t_{0.10}$ contains *t*-values having area 0.10 to their right; the column headed $t_{0.05}$ contains *t*-values having area 0.05 to their right; and so on. We illustrate a use of Table IV in Example 8.8.

Example 8.8 Finding the t-Value Having a Specified Area to Its Right

For a *t*-curve with 13 degrees of freedom, determine $t_{0.05}$; that is, find the *t*-value having area 0.05 to its right, as shown in Fig. 8.7(a).

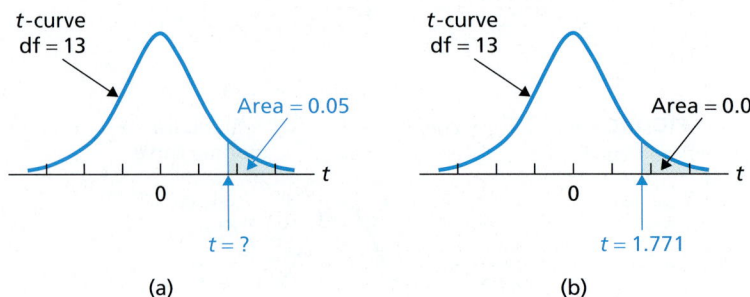

FIGURE 8.7 Finding the *t*-value having area 0.05 to its right

(a) *t*-curve df = 13, Area = 0.05, t = ?
(b) *t*-curve df = 13, Area = 0.05, t = 1.771

Solution To find the *t*-value in question, we use Table IV. For ease of reference, we have repeated a portion of Table IV as Table 8.4.

TABLE 8.4 Values of t_α

df	$t_{0.10}$	$t_{0.05}$	$t_{0.025}$	$t_{0.01}$	$t_{0.005}$	df
.	.	.	.	.	.	.
.	.	.	.	.	.	.
.	.	.	.	.	.	.
12	1.356	1.782	2.179	2.681	3.055	12
13	1.350	1.771	2.160	2.650	3.012	13
14	1.345	1.761	2.145	2.624	2.977	14
15	1.341	1.753	2.131	2.602	2.947	15
.	.	.	.	.	.	.
.	.	.	.	.	.	.
.	.	.	.	.	.	.

The number of degrees of freedom is 13, so we first go down the outside columns, labeled df, to "13." Then we go across that row to the column headed $t_{0.05}$. The number in the body of the table there, 1.771, is the required *t*-value; that is, for a *t*-curve with df = 13, the *t*-value having area 0.05 to its right is $t_{0.05} = 1.771$, as shown in Fig. 8.7(b). ◆

Note that Table IV in Appendix A contains degrees of freedom from 1 to 75 consecutively, but then contains only selected degrees of freedom. If you need a value of t_α with a degrees of freedom not included in Table IV, you have several options: Find a more detailed *t*-table, use technology, or use linear interpolation and Table IV. A less exact option, but one that usually suffices, is to use the degrees of freedom in Table IV closest to the one required.

As we noted earlier, *t*-curves look increasingly like the standard normal curve as the number of degrees of freedom gets larger. For degrees of freedom greater than 1000, a *t*-curve and the standard normal curve are virtually indistinguishable. Consequently, we stopped the *t*-table at df = 1000 and supplied the corresponding values of z_α beneath. These values can be used not only for the standard normal distribution, but also for any t-distribution having degrees of freedom greater than 1000.[3]

OBTAINING CONFIDENCE INTERVALS FOR A POPULATION MEAN WHEN σ IS UNKNOWN

Having discussed t-distributions and t-curves, we can now develop a procedure for obtaining a confidence interval for a population mean when the population standard deviation is unknown. We proceed in essentially the same way as we did when the population standard deviation is known, except now we invoke a t-distribution instead of the standard normal distribution.

Hence we use $t_{\alpha/2}$ instead of $z_{\alpha/2}$ in the formula for the confidence interval. As a result, we have Procedure 8.2, which we refer to as the **one-sample t-interval procedure** or, simply, as the **t-interval procedure.**

Procedure 8.2

The One-Sample t-Interval Procedure for a Population Mean

Assumptions

1. Normal population or large sample
2. σ unknown

Step 1 For a confidence level of $1 - \alpha$, use Table IV to find $t_{\alpha/2}$ with df $= n - 1$, where n is the sample size.

Step 2 The confidence interval for μ is from

$$\bar{x} - t_{\alpha/2} \cdot \frac{s}{\sqrt{n}} \quad \text{to} \quad \bar{x} + t_{\alpha/2} \cdot \frac{s}{\sqrt{n}},$$

where $t_{\alpha/2}$ is found in Step 1 and $\bar{x}$ and s are computed from the sample data.

Step 3 Interpret the confidence interval.

The confidence interval is exact for normal populations and is approximately correct for large samples from nonnormal populations.

Before applying Procedure 8.2, we need to make several comments. Although the t-interval procedure is based on the assumption that the variable under consideration is normally distributed (normal population), it also applies approximately for large samples, regardless of the distribution of the variable under consideration, as noted at the bottom of Procedure 8.2.

Actually, like the z-interval procedure, the t-interval procedure works reasonably well even when the variable under consideration is not normally

---

[3]The values of z_α given at the bottom of Table IV are accurate to three decimal places and, because of that, some differ slightly from what you get by applying the method you learned for using Table II.

distributed and the sample size is small or moderate, provided the variable is not too far from being normally distributed. In other words, the *t*-interval procedure is robust to moderate violations of the normality assumption.

When considering the *t*-interval procedure, we also have to watch for outliers. Again, the presence of outliers calls into question the normality assumption. In addition, even for large samples, outliers can sometimes unduly affect a *t*-interval because the sample mean and sample standard deviation are not resistant to outliers.

Guidelines for use of the *t*-interval procedure are the same as those for the *z*-interval procedure (Key Fact 8.1 on page 336). Remember always to examine the data before applying the *t*-interval procedure to ensure that its use is reasonable. Examples 8.9 and 8.10 illustrate use of Procedure 8.2.

Example 8.9 The One-Sample t-Interval Procedure

Pick-Pocket Offenses The U.S. Federal Bureau of Investigation (FBI) compiles data on robbery and property crimes and publishes the information in *Population-at-Risk Rates and Selected Crime Indicators*. A sample of a recent year's pick-pocket offenses yielded the values lost shown in Table 8.5. Use the data to obtain a 95% confidence interval for the mean value lost, μ, of all the year's pick-pocket offenses.

Solution Because the sample size, $n = 25$, is moderate, we first need to consider questions of normality and outliers. (See the second bulleted item in Key Fact 8.1 on page 336.) To do that, we constructed a normal probability plot for the data in Table 8.5, as shown in Fig. 8.8.

The normal probability plot in Fig. 8.8 shows no outliers and falls roughly in a straight line. Thus we can apply Procedure 8.2 to obtain the required confidence interval.

TABLE 8.5
Value lost ($) for a sample of 25 pick-pocket offenses

447	207	627	430	883
313	844	253	397	214
217	768	1064	26	587
833	277	805	653	549
649	554	570	223	443

Step 1 For a confidence level of $1 - \alpha$, use Table IV to find $t_{\alpha/2}$ with df $= n - 1$, where *n* is the sample size.

We want a 95% confidence interval, so $\alpha = 1 - 0.95 = 0.05$. For $n = 25$, df $= 25 - 1 = 24$. From Table IV, $t_{\alpha/2} = t_{0.05/2} = t_{0.025} = 2.064$.

Step 2 The confidence interval for μ is from

$$\bar{x} - t_{\alpha/2} \cdot \frac{s}{\sqrt{n}} \quad \text{to} \quad \bar{x} + t_{\alpha/2} \cdot \frac{s}{\sqrt{n}}.$$

From Step 1, $t_{\alpha/2} = 2.064$. Applying the usual formulas for $\bar{x}$ and *s* to the data in Table 8.5, we get $\bar{x} = 513.32$ and $s = 262.23$. Consequently, a 95% confidence interval for μ is from

$$513.32 - 2.064 \cdot \frac{262.23}{\sqrt{25}} \quad \text{to} \quad 513.32 + 2.064 \cdot \frac{262.23}{\sqrt{25}},$$

or 405.07 to 621.57.

8.4 Confidence Intervals for One Population Mean When σ is Unknown 355

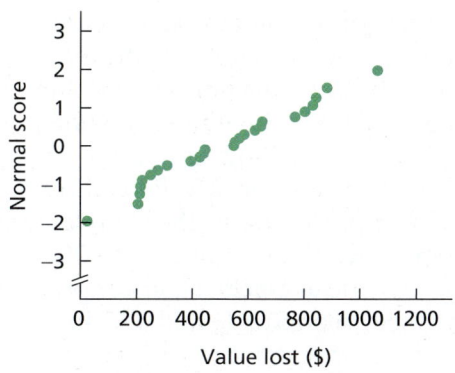

FIGURE 8.8
Normal probability plot of the value-lost data in Table 8.5

Step 3 Interpret the confidence interval.

> **What Does it Mean?** We can be 95% confident that the mean value lost, μ, of all the year's pick-pocket offenses is somewhere between $405.07 and $621.57.

Example 8.10 The One-Sample t-Interval Procedure

TABLE 8.6
Sample of year's chicken consumption (lb)

47	39	62	49	50	70
59	53	55	0	65	63
53	51	50	72	45	

Chicken Consumption The U.S. Department of Agriculture publishes data on chicken consumption in *Food Consumption, Prices, and Expenditures*. A recent year's chicken consumption, in pounds, for 17 randomly selected people is displayed in Table 8.6. Use the data to obtain a 90% confidence interval for the year's mean chicken consumption, μ.

Solution A normal probability plot of the data in Table 8.6 is displayed in Fig. 8.9(a). The plot reveals an outlier—the observation of 0 lb. Because the sample size is only moderate, applying Procedure 8.2 to the data in Table 8.6 is inappropriate.

FIGURE 8.9
Normal probability plots for chicken consumption: (a) original data and (b) data with outlier removed

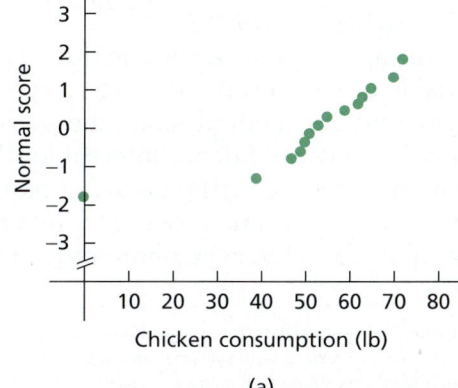
(a)

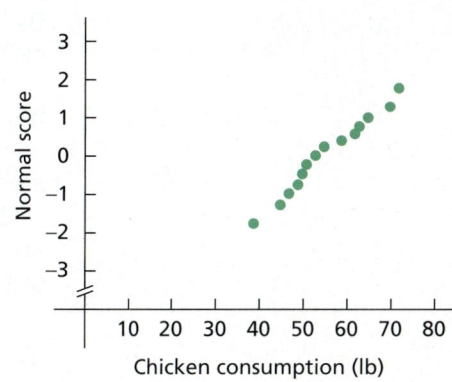
(b)

The outlier of 0 lb might be a recording error or it might reflect a person in the sample who does not eat chicken (e.g., a vegetarian). If we remove the outlier from the data, the normal probability plot for the abridged data shows no outliers and is roughly linear, as shown in Fig. 8.9(b).

Thus, if we are willing to take as our population of interest only people who eat chicken, we can use Procedure 8.2 to obtain a confidence interval. Applying that procedure to the sample data with the outlier removed yields a 90% confidence interval of 51.2 to 59.2. That is, we can be 90% confident that the year's mean chicken consumption, among people who eat chicken, is somewhere between 51.2 lb and 59.2 lb. ◆

> **What Does it Mean?**
>
> Performing preliminary data analyses to check assumptions before applying inferential procedures is essential.

By making our population of interest in Example 8.10 only those people who eat chicken, we were justified in removing the outlier of 0 lb. Generally, an outlier should not be removed without careful consideration. *Simply removing an outlier because it is an outlier is unacceptable statistical practice.*

In Example 8.10, if we had been careless in our analysis by blindly finding a confidence interval without first examining the data, our result would have been invalid and misleading.

WHAT IF THE ASSUMPTIONS ARE NOT SATISFIED?

We have now described two methods for obtaining a confidence interval for a population mean. If the population standard deviation is known, you can use the z-interval procedure (Procedure 8.1 on page 335); if the population standard deviation is unknown, you can use the t-interval procedure (Procedure 8.2 on page 353).

However, use of both procedures is based on an assumption: The variable under consideration should be approximately normally distributed or the sample size should be relatively large and, for small samples, both procedures should be avoided in the presence of outliers. (Again, refer to Key Fact 8.1 on page 336 for general guidelines.)

Suppose that you want to obtain a confidence interval for a population mean based on a small sample but that preliminary data analyses indicate either the presence of outliers or that the variable under consideration is far from normally distributed. As neither the z-interval procedure nor the t-interval procedure is appropriate, what can you do?

Under certain conditions, you can use a *nonparametric method*.[4] For example, if the variable under consideration has a symmetric distribution, then you can use a nonparametric method called the *one-sample Wilcoxon confidence-interval procedure* to obtain a confidence interval for the population mean.

Most nonparametric methods do not require even approximate normality, are resistant to outliers and other extreme values, and can be applied regardless of sample size. However, parametric methods, such as the z-interval and

---

[4]Recall that descriptive measures for a population, such as μ and σ, are called parameters. Technically, inferential methods concerned with parameters are called **parametric methods;** those that are not are called **nonparametric methods.** However, common practice is to refer to most methods that can be applied without assuming normality (regardless of sample size) as nonparametric. Thus the term *nonparametric method* as used in contemporary statistics is somewhat of a misnomer.

t-interval procedures, tend to give more accurate results than nonparametric methods when the normality assumption and other requirements for their use are met.

Although we will not cover nonparametric methods in this book, many basic statistics books do discuss them. See, for example, *Introductory Statistics* by Neil A. Weiss (Boston: Addison-Wesley, 2002).

Example 8.11 illustrates the use of preliminary data analysis to decide which confidence-interval procedure to use.

Example 8.11 Choosing a Confidence Interval Procedure

TABLE 8.7
Adjusted gross incomes ($1000)

Adjusted Gross Incomes The U.S. Internal Revenue Service (IRS) publishes data on federal individual income tax returns in *Statistics of Income, Individual Income Tax Returns*. A sample of 12 returns from a recent year revealed the adjusted gross incomes, in thousands of dollars, shown in Table 8.7. Which procedure should be used to obtain a confidence interval for the mean adjusted gross income, μ, of all the year's individual income tax returns?

Solution Because the sample size is small ($n = 12$), we must first consider questions of normality and outliers. A normal probability plot of the sample data, as shown in Fig. 6.23 on page 285, suggests that adjusted gross incomes are far from being normally distributed. Consequently, neither the *z*-interval procedure nor the *t*-interval procedure should be used; instead, some nonparametric confidence interval procedure should be applied. ◆

The Technology Center

Procedure 8.2 on page 353 provides a step-by-step method for obtaining a confidence interval for a population mean when the population standard deviation is unknown. Most statistical technologies have programs that automatically determine this type of confidence interval. In this subsection, we present output and (optional) step-by-step instructions to implement such programs.

Example 8.12 Using Technology to Obtain a t-Interval

Pick-Pocket Offenses The values lost, in dollars, of 25 randomly selected pick-pocket offenses from a recent year are displayed in Table 8.5 on page 354. Use Minitab, Excel, or the TI-83 Plus to obtain a 95% confidence interval for the mean value lost, μ, of all the year's pick-pocket offenses.

Solution Printout 8.3 on the next page shows the output obtained by applying the one-sample *t*-interval programs to the value-lost data in Table 8.5.

As shown in the three outputs in Printout 8.3, the required 95% confidence interval is from 405.1 to 621.6. Hence we can be 95% confident that the mean value lost, μ, of all the year's pick-pocket offenses is somewhere between $405.1 and $621.6. Compare this confidence interval to the one obtained in Example 8.9. ◆

358 CHAPTER 8 Confidence Intervals for One Population Mean

PRINTOUT 8.3
One-sample *t*-interval output for the sample of values lost

MINITAB

```
One-Sample T: LOST

Variable      N      Mean      StDev     SE Mean          95.0% CI
LOST         25     513.3      262.2        52.4     (   405.1,    621.6)
```

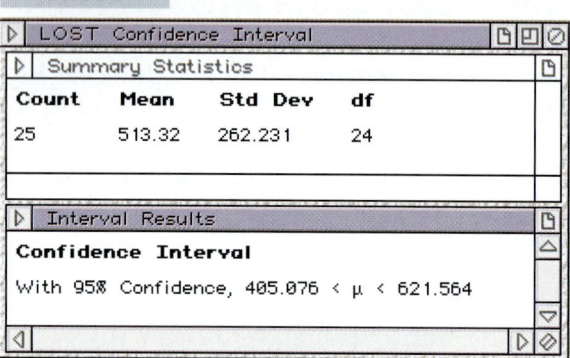

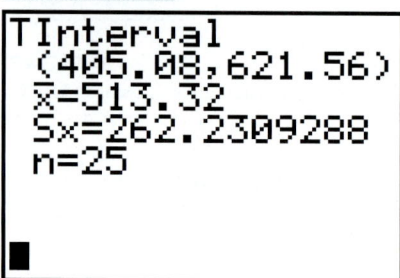

Obtaining the Output (Optional)

Printout 8.3 provides output from Minitab, Excel, and the TI-83 Plus for a one-sample *t*-interval with a 95% confidence level based on the sample of values lost presented in Table 8.5. The following are detailed instructions for obtaining that output. First, we store the values-lost data in a column (Minitab), range (Excel), or list (TI-83 Plus) named LOST. Then, we proceed as follows.

MINITAB
1. Choose **Stat ➤ Basic Statistics ➤ 1-Sample t...**
2. Specify LOST in the **Variables** text box
3. Click the **Options...** button
4. Type 95 in the **Confidence level** text box
5. Click the arrow button at the right of the **Alternative** drop-down list box and select **not equal**
6. Click **OK**
7. Click **OK**

EXCEL
1. Choose **DDXL ➤ Confidence Intervals**
2. Select **1 Var t Interval** from the **Function type** drop-down box
3. Specify LOST in the **Quantitative Variable** text box
4. Click **OK**
5. Click the **95%** button
6. Click the **Compute Interval** button

TI-83 PLUS
1. Press **STAT**, arrow over to **TESTS**, and press **8**
2. Highlight **Data** and press **ENTER**
3. Press the down-arrow key
4. Press **2nd ➤ LIST**
5. Arrow down to LOST and press **ENTER** three times
6. Type .95 for **C-Level** and press **ENTER** twice

Exercises 8.4

Statistical Concepts and Skills

8.50 Explain the difference in the formulas for the standardized and studentized versions of $\bar{x}$.

8.51 Why do you need to consider the studentized version of $\bar{x}$ to develop a confidence-interval procedure for a population mean when the population standard deviation is unknown?

8.52 A variable has a mean of 100 and a standard deviation of 16. Four observations of this variable have a mean of 108 and a sample standard deviation of 12. Determine the observed value of the
a. standardized version of $\bar{x}$.
b. studentized version of $\bar{x}$.

8.53 A variable of a population has a normal distribution. Suppose that you want to find a confidence interval for the population mean.
a. If you know the population standard deviation, which procedure would you use?
b. If you do not know the population standard deviation, which procedure would you use?

8.54 Batting Averages. An issue of *Scientific American* reveals that the batting averages of major-league baseball players are normally distributed and have a mean of .270 and a standard deviation of .031. For samples of 20 batting averages, identify the distribution of each variable.

a. $\dfrac{\bar{x} - .270}{.031/\sqrt{20}}$ b. $\dfrac{\bar{x} - .270}{s/\sqrt{20}}$

8.55 Explain why there is more variation in the possible values of the studentized version of $\bar{x}$ than in the possible values of the standardized version of $\bar{x}$.

8.56 Two *t*-curves have degrees of freedom 12 and 20, respectively. Which one more closely resembles the standard normal curve? Explain your answer.

8.57 For a *t*-curve with df = 6, use Table IV to find each *t*-value.
a. $t_{0.10}$ b. $t_{0.025}$ c. $t_{0.01}$

8.58 For a *t*-curve with df = 17, use Table IV to find each *t*-value.
a. $t_{0.05}$ b. $t_{0.025}$ c. $t_{0.005}$

8.59 For a *t*-curve with df = 21, find each *t*-value and illustrate your results graphically.
a. The *t*-value having area 0.10 to its right
b. $t_{0.01}$
c. The *t*-value having area 0.025 to its left (*Hint:* A *t*-curve is symmetric about 0.)

d. The two *t*-values that divide the area under the curve into a middle 0.90 area and two outside areas of 0.05

8.60 For a *t*-curve with df = 8, find each *t*-value and illustrate your results graphically.
a. The *t*-value having area 0.05 to its right
b. $t_{0.10}$
c. The *t*-value having area 0.01 to its left (*Hint:* A *t*-curve is symmetric about 0.)
d. The two *t*-values that divide the area under the curve into a middle 0.95 area and two outside 0.025 areas

8.61 A random sample of size 100 is taken from a population with unknown standard deviation. A normal probability plot of the data displays significant curvature but no outliers. Can you reasonably apply the *t*-interval procedure? Explain your answer.

8.62 A random sample of size 17 is taken from a population with unknown standard deviation. A normal probability plot of the data reveals an outlier but is otherwise roughly linear. Can you reasonably apply the *t*-interval procedure? Explain your answer.

Preliminary data analyses indicate the reasonableness of applying the t-interval procedure (Procedure 8.2 on page 353) in Exercises 8.63–8.66.

8.63 Family Fun? Taking the family to an amusement park has become increasingly costly according to the industry publication *Amusement Business*, which provides figures on the cost for a family of four to spend the day at one of America's amusement parks. A random sample of 25 families of four that attended amusement parks yielded the following costs, rounded to the nearest dollar.

122	166	171	148	135
173	137	163	119	144
164	153	162	140	142
158	130	167	173	186
92	170	126	163	172

a. Determine a 95% confidence interval for the mean cost of a family of four to spend the day at an American amusement park. (Note: $\bar{x} = \$151.04$; $s = \$22.01$.)
b. Interpret your answer from part (a).

8.64 Northeast Commutes. According to Scarborough Research, more than 85% of working adults commute by car. Of all U.S. cities, Washington, D.C., and New York City have the longest commute times. A sample of 30 commuters in the Washington, D.C., area yielded the following commute times, in minutes.

24	28	31	29	54	28
27	38	24	14	46	38
31	16	21	11	21	15
30	29	17	23	27	18
29	44	19	35	34	38

a. Find a 90% confidence interval for the mean commute time of all commuters in Washington, D.C. (Note: $\bar{x} = 27.97$ minutes; $s = 10.04$ minutes.)
b. Interpret your answer from part (a).

8.65 The Coruro's Burrow. The subterranean coruro (*Spalacopus cyanus*) is a social rodent that lives in large colonies in underground burrows that can reach lengths of up to 600 meters. Zoologists Sabine Begall and Milton H. Gallardo studied the characteristics of the burrow systems of the subterranean coruro in central Chile and published their findings in the *Journal of Zoology, London*, (2000, Vol. 251, pp. 53–60). A sample of 51 burrows had the following depths, in centimeters (cm).

15.1	16.0	18.3	18.8	13.9	15.8	14.2
12.3	11.8	12.1	17.9	16.6	16.5	16.0
12.8	14.7	15.9	13.9	17.2	12.2	18.2
16.9	13.3	14.4	15.0	12.1	11.0	16.7
17.4	8.2	19.3	17.4	15.3	15.6	19.7
14.5	12.5	12.8	13.3	16.8	17.5	14.0
14.9	16.7	12.0	15.0	16.2	9.7	15.4
18.9	14.9					

a. Obtain a 90% confidence interval for the mean depth of all subterranean coruro burrows. (Note: $\bar{x} = 15.05$ cm; $s = 2.50$ cm.)
b. Interpret your answer from part (a).

8.66 Sleep. In 1908, W. S. Gosset published the article "The Probable Error of a Mean" (*Biometrika*, Vol. 6, pp. 1–25). In this pioneering paper, written under the pseudonym "Student," Gosset introduced what later became known as Student's *t*-distribution. Gosset used the following data set, which gives the additional sleep in hours obtained by a sample of 10 patients using laevohysocyamine hydrobromide.

1.9	0.8	1.1	0.1	−0.1
4.4	5.5	1.6	4.6	3.4

a. Find a 95% confidence interval for the additional sleep that would be obtained on average for all people using laevohysocyamine hydrobromide. (Note: $\bar{x} = 2.33$ hr; $s = 2.002$ hr.)
b. Was the drug effective in increasing sleep? Explain your answer.

Extending the Concepts and Skills

8.67 Bicycle Commuting Times. A city planner working on bikeways designs a questionaire to obtain information about local bicycle commuters. One of the questions asks how long it takes the rider to pedal from home to his or her destination. A sample of local bicycle commuters yields the following times, in minutes.

22	19	24	31	29	29
21	15	27	23	37	31
30	26	16	26	12	
23	48	22	29	28	

a. Find a 90% confidence interval for the mean commuting time of all local bicycle commuters in the city. (Note: The sample mean and sample standard deviation of the data are 25.82 minutes and 7.71 minutes, respectively.)
b. Interpret your result in part (a).
c. Graphical analyses of the data indicate that the time of 48 minutes may be an outlier. Remove this potential outlier and repeat part (a). (Note: The sample mean and sample standard deviation of the abridged data are 24.76 and 6.05, respectively.)
d. Should you have used the procedure that you did in part (a)? Explain your answer.

8.68 Table IV in Appendix A contains degrees of freedom from 1 to 75 consecutively but then contains only selected degrees of freedom.
a. Why couldn't we provide entries for all possible degrees of freedom?

b. Why did we construct the table so that consecutive entries appear for smaller degrees of freedom but that only selected entries occur for larger degrees of freedom?

c. If you had only Table IV, what value would you use for $t_{0.05}$ with df = 87? with df = 125? with df = 650? with df = 2000? Explain your answers.

8.69 As we mentioned earlier in this section, we stopped the t-table at df = 1000 and supplied the corresponding values of z_α beneath. Explain why that makes sense.

8.70 A variable of a population has mean μ and standard deviation σ. For a sample of size n, under what conditions are the observed values of the studentized and standardized versions of $\bar{x}$ equal? Explain your answer.

8.71 Let $0 < \alpha < 1$. For a t-curve, determine
a. the t-value having area α to its right in terms of t_α.
b. the t-value having area α to its left in terms of t_α.
c. the two t-values that divide the area under the curve into a middle $1 - \alpha$ area and two outside $\alpha/2$ areas.
d. Draw graphs to illustrate your results in parts (a)–(c).

Using Technology

8.72 Forearm Length. In 1903, K. Pearson and A. Lee published a paper entitled "On the Laws of Inheritance in Man. I. Inheritance of Physical Characters" (*Biometrika*, Vol. 2, pp. 357–462). The article examined and presented data on forearm length, in inches, for a random sample of 140 men. The data are contained on the WeissStats CD.
a. Import the data into the technology of your choice.
b. Use the technology of your choice to obtain a normal probability plot, boxplot, and histogram of the data.
c. Is it reasonable to apply the t-interval procedure to the data? Explain your answer.
d. If you answered "yes" to part (c), obtain a 95% confidence interval for the mean forearm length of men. Interpret your result.

8.73 Family Fun? Refer to Exercise 8.63.
a. Use the technology of your choice to obtain a normal probability plot, boxplot, histogram, and stem-and-leaf diagram of the data.
b. Use the technology of your choice to construct the required confidence interval.
c. Justify the use of your procedure in part (b).

8.74 Northeast Commutes. Refer to Exercise 8.64.
a. Use the technology of your choice to obtain a normal probability plot, boxplot, histogram, and stem-and-leaf diagram of the data.
b. Use the technology of your choice to construct the required confidence interval.
c. Justify the use of your procedure in part (b).

8.75 Batting Averages. An issue of *Scientific American* reveals that the batting averages of major-league baseball players are normally distributed with mean .270 and standard deviation .031.
a. Simulate 2000 samples of five batting averages each.
b. Determine the sample mean and sample standard deviation of each of the 2000 samples.
c. For each of the 2000 samples, determine the observed value of the standardized version of $\bar{x}$.
d. Obtain a histogram of the 2000 observations in part (c).
e. Theoretically, what is the distribution of the standardized version of $\bar{x}$?
f. Compare your results from parts (d) and (e).
g. For each of the 2000 samples, determine the observed value of the studentized version of $\bar{x}$.
h. Obtain a histogram of the 2000 observations in part (g).
i. Theoretically, what is the distribution of the studentized version of $\bar{x}$?
j. Compare your results from parts (h) and (i).
k. Compare your histograms from parts (d) and (h). How and why do they differ?

Chapter Review

You Should Be Able To

1. use and understand the formulas presented in this chapter.

2. obtain a point estimate for a population mean.

3. find and interpret a confidence interval for a population mean when the population standard deviation is known.

4. compute and interpret the margin of error for the estimate of μ.

5. understand the relationship between sample size, standard deviation, confidence level, and margin of error for a confidence interval for μ.

6. determine the sample size required for a specified confidence level and margin of error for the estimate of μ.

7. understand the difference between the standardized and studentized versions of $\bar{x}$.

8. state the basic properties of t-curves.

9. use Table IV to find $t_{\alpha/2}$ for df $= n - 1$ and selected values of α.

10. find and interpret a confidence interval for a population mean when the population standard deviation is unknown.

11. decide whether it is appropriate to use the z-interval procedure, t-interval procedure, or neither.

Key Terms

confidence-interval estimate, 329
confidence level, 329
degrees of freedom (df), 350
margin of error (E), 345
maximum error of the estimate, 344
nonparametric methods, 356
one-sample t-interval procedure, 353

one-sample z-interval procedure, 335
parametric methods, 356
point estimate, 329
robust procedures, 336
standardized version of $\bar{x}$, 349
studentized version of $\bar{x}$, 349
Student's t-distribution, 350

t_α, 351
t-curve, 350
t-distribution, 350
t-interval procedure, 353
z_α, 334
z-interval procedure, 335

Review Test

Statistical Concepts and Skills

1. Explain the difference between a point estimate of a parameter and a confidence-interval estimate of a parameter.

2. Answer true or false to the following statement and give a reason for your answer: If a 95% confidence interval for a population mean, μ, is from 33.8 to 39.0, the mean of the population must lie somewhere between 33.8 and 39.0.

3. Must the variable under consideration be normally distributed for you to use the z-interval procedure or t-interval procedure? Explain your answer.

4. If you obtained one thousand 95% confidence intervals for a population mean, μ, roughly how many of the intervals would actually contain μ?

5. Suppose that you have obtained a sample with the intent of performing a particular statistical-inference procedure. What should you do before applying the procedure to the sample data? Why?

6. Suppose that you intend to find a 95% confidence interval for a population mean by applying the one-sample z-interval procedure to a sample of size 100.
   a. What would happen to the precision of the estimate if you used a sample of size 50 instead but kept the same confidence level of 0.95?
   b. What would happen to the precision of the estimate if you changed the confidence level to 0.90 but kept the same sample size of 100?

7. A confidence interval for a population mean has a margin of error of 10.7.
   a. Obtain the length of the confidence interval.
   b. If the mean of the sample is 75.2, determine the confidence interval.

8. Suppose that you plan to apply the one-sample z-interval procedure to obtain a 90% confidence interval for a population mean, μ. You know that $\sigma = 12$ and that you are going to use a sample of size 9.
   a. What will be your margin of error?
   b. What else do you need to know in order to obtain the confidence interval?

9. A variable of a population has a mean of 266 and a standard deviation of 16. Ten observations of this variable have

a mean of 262.1 and a sample standard deviation of 20.4. Obtain the observed value of the
a. standardized version of $\bar{x}$.
b. studentized version of $\bar{x}$.

10. Baby Weight. The paper "Are Babies Normal?" by Traci Clemons and Marcello Pagano (*The American Statistician*, 1999, Vol. 53, No. 4, pp. 298–302) focused on babies born in 1991. According to the article, for babies born within the "normal" gestational range of 37–43 weeks, birth weights are normally distributed with a mean of 3432 grams (7 pounds 9 ounces) and a standard deviation of 482 grams (1 pound 1 ounce). For samples of 15 such birth weights, identify the distribution of each variable.

a. $\dfrac{\bar{x} - 3432}{482/\sqrt{15}}$ b. $\dfrac{\bar{x} - 3432}{s/\sqrt{15}}$

11. The following figure shows the standard normal curve and two *t*-curves. Which of the two *t*-curves has the larger degrees of freedom? Explain your answer.

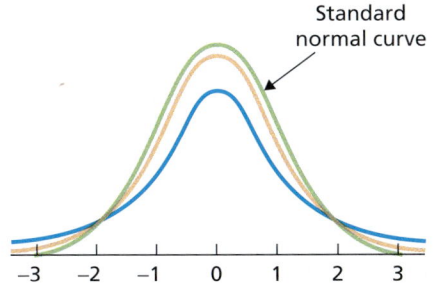

12. In each part of this problem, we have provided a scenario for a confidence interval. Decide whether the appropriate method for obtaining the confidence interval is the *z*-interval procedure, the *t*-interval procedure, or neither.
a. A random sample of size 17 is taken from a population. A normal probability plot of the sample data is found to be very close to linear (straight line). The population standard deviation is unknown.
b. A random sample of size 50 is taken from a population. A normal probability plot of the sample data is found to be roughly linear. The population standard deviation is known.
c. A random sample of size 25 is taken from a population. A normal probability plot of the sample data shows three outliers but is otherwise roughly linear. Checking reveals that the outliers are due to recording errors. The population standard deviation is known.
d. A random sample of size 20 is taken from a population. A normal probability plot of the sample data shows three outliers but is otherwise roughly linear. Removal of the outliers is questionable. The population standard deviation is unknown.
e. A random sample of size 128 is taken from a population. A normal probability plot of the sample data shows no outliers but has significant curvature. The population standard deviation is known.
f. A random sample of size 13 is taken from a population. A normal probability plot of the sample data shows no outliers but has significant curvature. The population standard deviation is unknown.

13. Millionaires. Dr. Thomas Stanley of Georgia State University has surveyed millionaires since 1973. Among other information, Stanley obtains estimates for the mean age, μ, of all U.S. millionaires. Suppose that 36 randomly selected U.S. millionaires are the following ages.

31	45	79	64	48	38	39	68	52
59	68	79	42	79	53	74	66	66
71	61	52	47	39	54	67	55	71
77	64	60	75	42	69	48	57	48

Determine a 95% confidence interval for the mean age, μ, of all U.S. millionaires. Assume that the standard deviation of ages of all U.S. millionaires is 13.0 years. (*Note:* The mean of the data is 58.53 years.)

14. Millionaires. From Problem 13, we know that "a 95% confidence interval for the mean age of all U.S. millionaires is from 54.3 years to 62.8 years." Decide which of the following sentences provide a correct interpretation of the statement in quotes. Justify your answers.
a. 95% of all U.S. millionaires are between the ages of 54.3 years and 62.8 years.
b. There is a 95% chance that the mean age of all U.S. millionaires is between 54.3 years and 62.8 years.
c. We can be 95% confident that the mean age of all U.S. millionaires is between 54.3 years and 62.8 years.
d. The probability is 0.95 that the mean age of all U.S. millionaires is between 54.3 years and 62.8 years.

15. Sea Shell Morphology. In a 1903 paper, Abigail Camp Dimon discussed the effect of environment on the shape and

form of two sea snail species, *Nassa obsoleta* and *Nassa trivittata*. One of the variables that Dimon considered was length of shell. She found the mean shell length of 461 randomly selected specimens of *N. trivittata* to be 11.9 mm. [SOURCE: "Quantitative Study of the Effect of Environment Upon the Forms of *Nassa obsoleta* and *Nassa trivittata* from Cold Spring Harbor, Long Island," *Biometrika*, Vol. 2, pp. 24–43.]
a. Assuming that $\sigma = 2.5$ mm, obtain a 90% confidence interval for the mean length, μ, of all *N. trivittata*.
b. Interpret your answer from part (a).
c. What properties should a normal probability plot of the data have for it to be permissible to apply the procedure that you used in part (a)?

16. **Sea Shell Morphology.** Refer to Problem 15.
a. Find the margin of error, E.
b. Explain the meaning of E as far as the accuracy of the estimate is concerned.
c. Determine the sample size required to have a margin of error of 0.1 mm and a 90% confidence level.
d. Find a 90% confidence interval for μ if a sample of the size determined in part (c) yields a mean of 12.0 mm.

17. For a t-curve with df $= 18$, obtain the t-value and illustrate your results graphically.
a. The t-value having area 0.025 to its right
b. $t_{0.05}$
c. The t-value having area 0.10 to its left
d. The two t-values that divide the area under the curve into a middle 0.99 area and two outside 0.005 areas

18. **Children of Diabetic Mothers.** A paper by Cho et al. in the May 2000 issue of *The Journal of Pediatrics* (Vol. 136(5), pp. 587–592) presented the results of research on various characteristics in children of diabetic mothers. Past studies have shown that maternal diabetes results in obesity, blood pressure, and glucose tolerance complications in the offspring. Following are the arterial blood pressures, in millimeters of mercury (mm Hg), for a random sample of 16 children of diabetic mothers.

81.6	84.1	87.6	82.8
82.0	88.9	86.7	96.4
84.6	104.9	90.8	94.0
69.4	78.9	75.2	91.0

a. A normal probability plot of these sample data shows no outliers and is roughly linear. Find a 95% confidence interval for the mean arterial blood pressure for all children of diabetic mothers. (Note: $\bar{x} = 86.2$ mm Hg; $s = 8.5$ mm Hg.)
b. Interpret your answer from part (a).

Using Technology

19. **Millionaires.** Use the technology of your choice to obtain the confidence interval required in Problem 13.

20. **Children of Diabetic Moms.** Refer to Problem 18. Use the technology of your choice to
a. obtain and interpret a normal probability plot of the sample data.
b. find the required confidence interval.

21. **Delaying Adulthood.** The convict surgeonfish is a common tropical reef fish that has been found to delay metamorphosis into adult by extending its larval phase. This delay often leads to enhanced survivorship in the species by increasing the chances of finding suitable habitat. In the 1999 paper, "Delayed Metamorphosis of a Tropical Reef Fish (*Acanthurus triostegus*): A Field Experiment" (*Marine Ecology Progress Series*, Vol. 176, pp. 25–38), Mark I. McCormick published data that he obtained on the larval duration, in days, of 90 convict surgeonfish. The data are contained on the WeissStats CD.
a. Import the data into the technology of your choice.
b. Use the technology of your choice to obtain a normal probability plot, boxplot, and histogram of the data.
c. Is it reasonable to apply the t-interval procedure to the data? Explain your answer.
d. If you answered "yes" to part (c), obtain a 99% confidence interval for the mean larval duration of convict surgeonfish. Interpret your result.

22. **GRE Scores.** Each year, thousands of college seniors take the Graduate Record Examination (GRE). The scores are transformed so that they have a mean of 500 and a standard deviation of 100. Furthermore, the scores are known to be normally distributed.
a. Simulate 3000 samples of four GRE scores each.
b. Determine the sample mean and sample standard deviation of each of the 3000 samples.
c. For each of the 3000 samples, determine the observed value of the standardized version of $\bar{x}$.
d. Obtain a histogram of the 3000 observations in part (c).
e. Theoretically, what is the distribution of the standardized version of $\bar{x}$?
f. Compare your results from parts (d) and (e).
g. For each of the 3000 samples, determine the observed value of the studentized version of $\bar{x}$.
h. Obtain a histogram of the 3000 observations in part (g).
i. Theoretically, what is the distribution of the studentized version of $\bar{x}$?
j. Compare your results from parts (h) and (i).
k. Compare your histograms from parts (d) and (h). How and why do they differ?

Internet Project

Famous Data Sets

In 1797, British scientist Henry Cavendish performed a famous experiment to measure the density of the earth. In 1879, German–American physicist Albert Michelson performed an equally famous experiment to measure the velocity of light.

In both cases, the experiments were repeated many times, giving slightly different results each time. The variations were due, of course, to measurement errors and other factors beyond the control of the scientists. Thus these famous experiments were inherently statistical, and the fundamental problem in each case was to estimate the true value of the physical constant (the unknown parameter).

In this project, you are to study these experiments in some detail to understand their design and the possible sources of error. You are to compute a variety of confidence intervals for the physical constants. Because the true values of these constants are now known with great accuracy, you will be able to see how well your confidence intervals work.

URL for access to Internet Projects Page: www.aw.com/weiss

Focusing on Data Analysis

GPA, SAT Scores, Age, and Hours

Recall from Chapter 1 (see page 34) that the Focus database contains information on 500 randomly selected Arizona State University sophomores. Among the variables considered are high school GPA, SAT math score, cumulative GPA, SAT verbal score, age, and total hours. Use the technology of your choice to solve the following problems.

a. Obtain a 99% confidence interval for the mean high school GPA of all Arizona State University sophomores.
b. Repeat part (a) for the other five variables mentioned.
c. Justify your use of the confidence-interval procedures in parts (a) and (b).

case study discussion

The Chips Ahoy! 1,000 Chips Challenge

At the beginning of this chapter, on page 327, we presented data on the number of chocolate chips per bag for 42 bags of Chips Ahoy! cookies. These data were obtained by the students in an introductory statistics class at the United States Air Force Academy in response to the Chips Ahoy! 1,000 Chips Challenge sponsored by Nabisco, the makers of Chips Ahoy! cookies. Use the data collected by the students to answer the questions and conduct the analyses required in each part.

a. Obtain and interpret a point estimate for the mean number of chocolate chips per bag for all bags of Chips Ahoy! cookies. (*Note:* The sum of the data is 52,986.)
b. Construct and interpret a normal probability plot, boxplot, and histogram of the data.
c. Use the graphs in part (b) to identify outliers, if any.
d. Is it reasonable to use the one-sample *t*-interval procedure to obtain a confidence interval for the mean number of chocolate chips per bag for all bags of Chips Ahoy! cookies? Explain your answer.
e. Determine a 95% confidence interval for the mean number of chips per bag for all bags of Chips Ahoy! cookies, and interpret your result in words. (*Note:* $\bar{x} = 1261.6$; $s = 117.6$.)
f. Use the technology of your choice to solve parts (a), (b), and (e).

Internet Resources: Visit the Weiss Web site www.aw.com/weiss for additional discussion, exercises, and resources related to this case study.

Biography

William Gosset: The "Student" in Student's *t*-Distribution

WILLIAM SEALY GOSSET was born in Canterbury, England, on June 13, 1876, the eldest son of Colonel Frederic Gosset and Agnes Sealy. He studied mathematics and chemistry at Winchester College and New College, Oxford, receiving a first-class degree in natural sciences in 1899.

After graduation Gosset began work with Arthur Guinness and Sons, a brewery in Dublin, Ireland. He saw the need for accurate statistical analyses of various brewing processes ranging from barley production to yeast fermentation, and pressed the firm to solicit mathematical advice. In 1906, the brewery sent him to work under Karl Pearson (see Biography in Chapter 12) at University College in London.

During the next few years, Gosset developed what has come to be known as Student's *t*-distribution. This distribution has proved to be fundamental in statistical analyses involving normal distributions. In particular, Student's *t*-distribution is used in performing inferences for a population mean when the population being sampled is (approximately) normally distributed and the population standard deviation is unknown. Although the statistical theory for large samples had been completed in the early 1800s, no small-sample theory was available before Gosset's work.

Because Guinness's brewery prohibited its employees from publishing any of their research, Gosset published his contributions to statistical theory under the pseudonym "Student"—thus the name "Student" in Student's *t*-distribution.

Gosset remained with Guinness his entire working life. In 1935, he moved to London to take charge of a new brewery. But his tenure there was short-lived; he died in Beaconsfield, England, on October 16, 1937.

chapter 9

Hypothesis Tests for One Population Mean

CHAPTER OUTLINE

9.1 The Nature of Hypothesis Testing

9.2 Terms, Errors, and Hypotheses

9.3 Hypothesis Tests for One Population Mean When σ Is Known

9.4 P-Values

9.5 Hypothesis Tests for One Population Mean When σ Is Unknown

GENERAL OBJECTIVES In Chapter 8, we examined methods for obtaining confidence intervals for one population mean. We know that a confidence interval for a population mean, μ, is based on a sample mean, $\bar{x}$. Now we show how that statistic can be used to make decisions about hypothesized values of a population mean.

For example, suppose that we want to decide whether the mean prison sentence, μ, of all people imprisoned last year for drug offenses exceeds the 1994 mean of 80.1 months. To make that decision, we can take a random sample of people imprisoned last year for drug offenses, compute their sample mean sentence, $\bar{x}$, and then apply a statistical-inference technique called a *hypothesis test*.

In Sections 9.1 and 9.2, we present generic information about the nature, notation, and terminology of hypothesis testing. Then, in the remainder of the chapter, we consider two different hypothesis testing procedures for one population mean—the *one-sample z-test* (Sections 9.3 and 9.4) and the *one-sample t-test* (Section 9.5). These two procedures are the hypothesis-test analogues of the one-sample z-interval and one-sample t-interval confidence-interval procedures, respectively, discussed in Chapter 8.

We also examine two different approaches to hypothesis testing, the *critical-value approach*—which we introduce and apply in Sections 9.2, 9.3, and 9.5—and the *P-value approach*—which we introduce and apply in Sections 9.4 and 9.5.

case study

SEX AND SENSE OF DIRECTION

Many of you have been there, a classic scene: mom yelling at dad to turn left while dad decides to do just the opposite. Well, who made the right call? And, more generally, who has a better sense of direction, women or men?

Dr. Jeanne Sholl et al. considered these and other questions in a recent paper entitled "The Relation of Sex and Sense of Direction to Spatial Orientation in an Unfamiliar Environment" (*Journal of Environmental Psychology*, 2000, Vol. 20, pp. 17–28). These researchers defined sense of direction as "…the knowledge of the location and orientation of the body with respect to large stationary objects, or landmarks, attached to the surface of the earth."

In their study, the spatial orientation skills of 30 male students and 30 female students from Boston College were challenged in Houghton Garden Park, a wooded park near the BC campus in Newton, Massachusetts. Before driving to the park, the participants were asked to rate their own sense of direction as either good or poor.

In the park, students were instructed to point to predesignated target landmarks and also to the direction of south. Pointing was carried out by students moving a pointer attached to a 360° protractor; the angle of the pointing response was then recorded to the nearest degree. For the female students who had rated their sense of direction to be good, the table at the right provides the absolute pointing errors (in degrees) when they attempted to point south.

14	122	128	109	12
91	8	78	31	36
27	68	20	69	18

Based on these data, can you conclude that, in general, women who consider themselves to have a good sense of direction really do better, on average, than they would by just randomly guessing at the direction of south? To answer that question, you need to conduct a hypothesis test, which you will do after you study hypothesis testing in this chapter. In Chapter 10, you will decide whether there is a difference in sense of direction between women and men.

9.1 THE NATURE OF HYPOTHESIS TESTING

We often use inferential statistics to make decisions or judgments about the value of a parameter, such as a population mean. For example, we might need to decide whether the mean weight, μ, of all bags of pretzels packaged by a particular company differs from the advertised weight of 454 grams (g); or, we might want to determine whether the mean age, μ, of all cars in use has increased from the 1995 mean of 8.5 years (yr).

One of the most commonly used methods for making such decisions or judgments is to perform a **hypothesis test.** A **hypothesis** is a statement that something is true. For example, the statement "the mean weight of all bags of pretzels packaged differs from the advertised weight of 454 g" is a hypothesis.

Typically, a hypothesis test involves two hypotheses: the **null hypothesis** and the **alternative hypothesis** (or **research hypothesis**), which we define as follows.

> **DEFINITION 9.1** Null and Alternative Hypotheses
>
> *Null hypothesis:* A hypothesis to be tested. We use the symbol H_0 to represent the null hypothesis.
>
> *Alternative hypothesis:* A hypothesis to be considered as an alternative to the null hypothesis. We use the symbol H_a to represent the alternative hypothesis.

For instance, in the pretzel packaging example, the null hypothesis might be "the mean weight of all bags of pretzels packaged equals the advertised weight of 454 g," and the alternative hypothesis might be "the mean weight of all bags of pretzels packaged differs from the advertised weight of 454 g."

Originally, the word *null* in *null hypothesis* stood for "no difference" or "the difference is null." Over the years, however, *null hypothesis* has come to mean simply a hypothesis to be tested. The problem in a hypothesis test is to decide whether the null hypothesis should be rejected in favor of the alternative hypothesis.

CHOOSING THE HYPOTHESES

The first step in setting up a hypothesis test is to decide on the null hypothesis and the alternative hypothesis. The following are some guidelines for choosing these two hypotheses. Although the guidelines refer specifically to hypothesis tests for one population mean, μ, they apply to any hypothesis test concerning one parameter.

NULL HYPOTHESIS

In this book, the null hypothesis for a hypothesis test concerning a population mean, μ, always specifies a single value for that parameter. Hence the null hypothesis always takes the form $\mu = \mu_0$, where μ_0 is some number. In other words, an equals sign (=) should appear in the null hypothesis. We can therefore express the null hypothesis concisely as

$$H_0: \mu = \mu_0.$$

ALTERNATIVE HYPOTHESIS

The choice of the alternative hypothesis depends on and should reflect the purpose of the hypothesis test. Three choices are possible for the alternative hypothesis.

- If the primary concern is deciding whether a population mean, μ, is *different from* a specified value μ_0, the alternative hypothesis should be $\mu \neq \mu_0$. In other words, a does-not-equal sign ($\neq$) should appear in the alternative hypothesis. We express such an alternative hypothesis as

$$H_a: \mu \neq \mu_0.$$

A hypothesis test whose alternative hypothesis has this form is called a **two-tailed test**.

- If the primary concern is deciding whether a population mean, μ, is *less than* a specified value μ_0, the alternative hypothesis should be $\mu < \mu_0$. In other words, a less-than sign (<) should appear in the alternative hypothesis. We express such an alternative hypothesis as

$$H_a: \mu < \mu_0.$$

A hypothesis test whose alternative hypothesis has this form is called a **left-tailed test**.

- If the primary concern is deciding whether a population mean, μ, is *greater than* a specified value μ_0, the alternative hypothesis should be $\mu > \mu_0$. In other words, a greater-than sign (>) should appear in the alternative hypothesis. We express such an alternative hypothesis as

$$H_a: \mu > \mu_0.$$

A hypothesis test whose alternative hypothesis has this form is called a **right-tailed test**.

A hypothesis test is called a **one-tailed test** if it is either left-tailed or right-tailed, that is, if it is not two-tailed. In Section 9.2, we explain the relevance of the term *tailed*. But for now let's consider Examples 9.1–9.3, which illustrate the preceding discussion.

Example 9.1 *Choosing the Null and Alternative Hypotheses*

Quality Assurance A snack-food company produces a 454 g bag of pretzels. Although the actual net weights deviate slightly from 454 g and vary from one bag to another, the company insists that the mean net weight of the bags be kept at 454 g. Indeed, if the mean net weight is less than 454 g, the company will be short-changing its customers; and if the mean net weight exceeds 454 g, the company will be unnecessarily overfilling the bags.

As part of its program, the quality assurance department periodically performs a hypothesis test to decide whether the packaging machine is working properly, that is, to decide whether the mean net weight of all bags packaged is 454 g.

a. Determine the null hypothesis for the hypothesis test.
b. Determine the alternative hypothesis for the hypothesis test.
c. Classify the hypothesis test as two-tailed, left-tailed, or right-tailed.

Solution Let μ denote the mean net weight of all bags packaged.

a. The null hypothesis for this hypothesis test is that the packaging machine is working properly, that is, that the mean net weight, μ, of all bags packaged *equals* 454 g. In symbols, $H_0: \mu = 454$ g.
b. The alternative hypothesis for this hypothesis test is that the packaging machine is not working properly, that is, that the mean net weight, μ, of all bags packaged is *different from* 454 g. In symbols, $H_a: \mu \neq 454$ g.
c. This hypothesis test is two-tailed because a does-not-equal sign ($\neq$) appears in the alternative hypothesis. ◆

Example 9.2 Choosing the Null and Alternative Hypotheses

Prices of History Books The R. R. Bowker Company of New York collects information on the retail prices of books and publishes the data in *Publishers Weekly*. In 1997, the mean retail price of history books was $43.50. Suppose that we want to perform a hypothesis test to decide whether this year's mean retail price of history books has increased from the 1997 mean.

a. Determine the null hypothesis for the hypothesis test.
b. Determine the alternative hypothesis for the hypothesis test.
c. Classify the hypothesis test as two-tailed, left-tailed, or right-tailed.

Solution Let μ denote this year's mean retail price of history books.

a. The null hypothesis for this hypothesis test is that this year's mean retail price of history books *equals* the 1997 mean of $43.50; that is, $H_0: \mu = \$43.50$.
b. The alternative hypothesis for this hypothesis test is that this year's mean retail price of history books is *greater than* $43.50; that is, $H_a: \mu > \$43.50$.
c. This hypothesis test is right-tailed because a greater-than sign ($>$) appears in the alternative hypothesis. ◆

Example 9.3 Choosing the Null and Alternative Hypotheses

Poverty and Calcium Calcium is the most abundant mineral in the body and also one of the most important. It works with phosphorus to build and maintain bones and teeth. According to the Food and Nutrition Board of the National Academy of Sciences, the recommended daily allowance (RDA) of calcium for adults is 800 milligrams (mg). Suppose that we want to perform a hypothesis test to decide whether the average person with an income below the poverty level gets less than the RDA of 800 mg.

a. Determine the null hypothesis for the hypothesis test.
b. Determine the alternative hypothesis for the hypothesis test.
c. Classify the hypothesis test as two-tailed, left-tailed, or right-tailed.

Solution Let μ denote the mean calcium intake (per day) of all people with incomes below the poverty level.

a. The null hypothesis for this hypothesis test is that the mean calcium intake of all people with incomes below the poverty level *equals* 800 mg per day; that is, H_0: $\mu = 800$ mg.
b. The alternative hypothesis for this hypothesis test is that the mean calcium intake of all people with incomes below the poverty level is *less than* the RDA of 800 mg per day; that is, H_a: $\mu < 800$ mg.
c. This hypothesis test is left-tailed because a less-than sign ($<$) appears in the alternative hypothesis.

THE LOGIC OF HYPOTHESIS TESTING

After we have chosen appropriate null and alternative hypotheses for a hypothesis test, the next question is: How do we decide which of the two hypotheses is true; that is, how do we decide whether to reject the null hypothesis in favor of the alternative hypothesis? Very roughly, the procedure for deciding is as follows.

> **Basic Logic of Hypothesis Testing**
> Take a random sample from the population. If the sample data are consistent with the null hypothesis, do not reject the null hypothesis; if the sample data are inconsistent with the null hypothesis (in the direction of the alternative hypothesis), reject the null hypothesis and conclude that the alternative hypothesis is true.

In practice, of course, we must have a precise criterion for deciding whether to reject the null hypothesis. Example 9.4 illustrates how such a criterion can be devised for a two-tailed hypothesis test about a population mean. The example also introduces the logic and some of the terminology of hypothesis testing.

Later in this chapter we give general procedures for performing hypothesis tests.

Example 9.4 The Logic of Hypothesis Testing

Quality Assurance A company that produces snack foods uses a machine to package 454 g bags of pretzels. We assume that the net weights are normally distributed and that the population standard deviation of all such weights is 7.8 g.[1] A random sample of 25 bags of pretzels has the net weights, in grams, displayed in Table 9.1.

Do the data provide sufficient evidence to conclude that the packaging machine is not working properly? We use the following steps in order to answer the question.

TABLE 9.1 Weights, in grams, of 25 randomly selected bags of pretzels

465	456	438	454	447
449	442	449	446	447
468	433	454	463	450
446	447	456	452	444
447	456	456	435	450

a. State the null and alternative hypotheses for the hypothesis test.
b. Discuss the logic behind carrying out the hypothesis test.
c. Identify the distribution of the variable $\bar{x}$, that is, the sampling distribution of the mean for samples of size 25.
d. Obtain a precise criterion for deciding whether to reject the null hypothesis in favor of the alternative hypothesis.
e. Apply the criterion in part (d) to the sample data and state the conclusion.

Solution Let μ denote the mean net weight of all bags packaged.

a. The null and alternative hypotheses for the hypothesis test, as stated in Example 9.1, are

H_0: $\mu = 454$ g (the packaging machine is working properly)

H_a: $\mu \neq 454$ g (the packaging machine is not working properly).

b. Basically, the logic behind carrying out the hypothesis test is this: If the null hypothesis is true, that is, if $\mu = 454$ g, the mean weight, $\bar{x}$, of the sample of 25 bags of pretzels should approximately equal 454 g. We say "approximately equal" because we cannot expect a sample mean to equal exactly the population mean; some sampling error is to be anticipated. However, if the sample mean weight differs "too much" from 454 g, we would be inclined to reject the null hypothesis and conclude that the alternative hypothesis is true. As we show in part (d), we can use our knowledge of the sampling distribution of the mean to decide how much difference is "too much."

c. Because $n = 25$, $\sigma = 7.8$, and the weights are normally distributed, Key Fact 7.4 on page 316 implies that

- $\mu_{\bar{x}} = \mu$ (which we don't know),
- $\sigma_{\bar{x}} = \sigma/\sqrt{n} = 7.8/\sqrt{25} = 1.56$, and
- $\bar{x}$ is normally distributed.

---

[1] We might know the population standard deviation from previous research or from a preliminary study of net weights. In Section 9.5, we consider the more usual case of an unknown σ.

In other words, for samples of size 25, the variable $\bar{x}$ is normally distributed with mean μ and a standard deviation of 1.56 g.

d. The "95.44" part of the 68.26-95.44-99.74 rule states that, for a normally distributed variable, 95.44% of all possible observations lie within two standard deviations to either side of the mean. Applying this part of the rule to the variable $\bar{x}$ and referring to part (c), we see that 95.44% of all samples of 25 bags of pretzels have mean weights within $2 \cdot 1.56 = 3.12$ g of μ. Or, equivalently, only 4.56% of all samples of 25 bags of pretzels have mean weights that are not within 3.12 g of μ, as illustrated in Fig. 9.1.

Consequently, if the mean weight, $\bar{x}$, of the 25 bags of pretzels sampled is not within two standard deviations (3.12 g) of 454 g, we have evidence against the null hypothesis. Why? Because observing such a sample mean would occur by chance only 4.56% of the time if the null hypothesis, $\mu = 454$ g, is true.

In summary, then, we have obtained the following precise criterion for deciding whether to reject the null hypothesis:

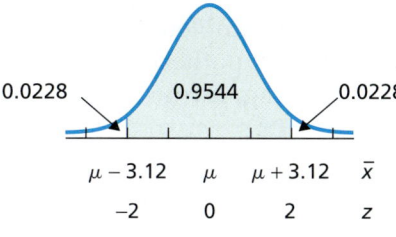

FIGURE 9.1
95.44% of all samples of 25 bags of pretzels have mean weights within two standard deviations (3.12 g) of μ

If the mean weight, $\bar{x}$, of the 25 bags of pretzels sampled is more than two standard deviations from 454 g, reject the null hypothesis, $\mu = 454$ g, and conclude that the alternative hypothesis, $\mu \neq 454$ g, is true. Otherwise, do not reject the null hypothesis.

This criterion is portrayed graphically in Fig. 9.2(a). If the null hypothesis is true, the normal curve associated with $\bar{x}$ is the one with parameters 454 and 1.56; that normal curve is superimposed on Fig. 9.2(a) in Fig. 9.2(b).

FIGURE 9.2
(a) Criterion for deciding whether to reject the null hypothesis; (b) normal curve associated with $\bar{x}$ if the null hypothesis is true, superimposed on the decision criterion

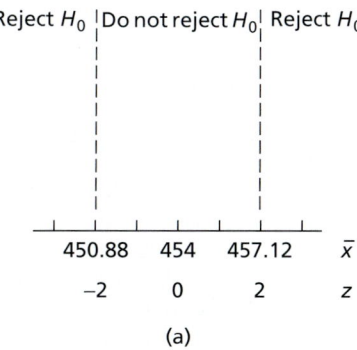
(a)

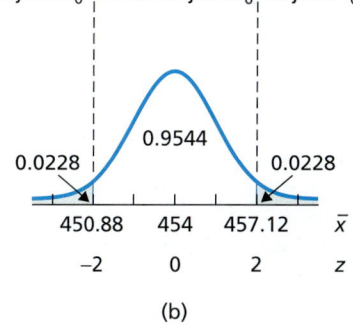
(b)

e. The mean weight, $\bar{x}$, of the sample of 25 bags of pretzels whose weights are given in Table 9.1 is 450 g. Therefore

$$z = \frac{\bar{x} - 454}{1.56} = \frac{450 - 454}{1.56} = -2.56.$$

That is, the sample mean of 450 g is 2.56 standard deviations below the null-hypothesis population mean of 454 g, as shown in Fig. 9.3.

FIGURE 9.3 Graph showing the number of standard deviations that the sample mean of 450 g is from the null-hypothesis population mean of 454 g

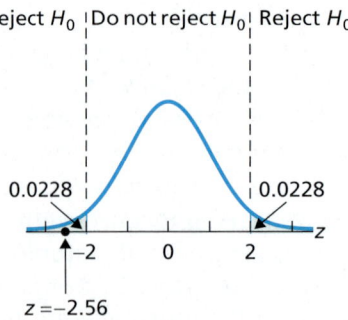

What Does it Mean?

The data provide sufficient evidence to conclude that the packaging machine is not working properly.

Because the mean weight of the 25 bags of pretzels sampled is more than two standard deviations from 454 g, we reject the null hypothesis, $\mu = 454$ g, and conclude that the alternative hypothesis, $\mu \neq 454$ g, is true. ◆

Example 9.4 contains all the elements of a hypothesis test, including the necessary theory, but don't worry too much about the details at this point. What you should understand now is how to choose the null and alternative hypotheses for a hypothesis test and the logic behind performing the test.

Exercises 9.1

Statistical Concepts and Skills

9.1 Explain the meaning of the term *hypothesis* as used in inferential statistics.

9.2 What role does the decision criterion play in a hypothesis test?

9.3 Suppose that you want to perform a hypothesis test for a population mean μ.
a. Express the null hypothesis both in words and in symbolic form.
b. Express each of the three possible alternative hypotheses in words and in symbolic form.

9.4 Suppose that you are considering a hypothesis test for a population mean, μ. In each part, express the alternative hypothesis symbolically and identify the hypothesis test as two-tailed, left-tailed, or right-tailed.
a. You want to decide whether the population mean is different from a specified value μ_0.
b. You want to decide whether the population mean is less than a specified value μ_0.
c. You want to decide whether the population mean is greater than a specified value μ_0.

In Exercises 9.5–9.10, hypothesis tests are proposed. For each hypothesis test,
a. *determine the null hypothesis.*
b. *determine the alternative hypothesis.*
c. *classify the hypothesis test as two-tailed, left-tailed, or right-tailed.*

9.5 Toxic Mushrooms? Cadmium, a heavy metal, is toxic to animals. Mushrooms, however, are able to absorb and accumulate cadmium at high concentrations. The Czech and Slovak governments have set a safety limit for cadmium in dry vegetables at 0.5 part per million (ppm). M. Melgar et al. measured the cadmium levels in a random sample of the edible mushroom *Boletus pinicola* and published the results in the *Journal of Environmental Science and Health* (1998, Vol. B33(4), pp. 439–455). A hypothesis test is to be performed to decide whether the mean cadmium level in *Boletus pinicola* mushrooms is greater than the government's recommended limit.

9.6 Body Temperature. A study by researchers at the University of Maryland addressed the question of whether the mean body temperature of humans is 98.6°F. The results of the study by P. Mackowiak, S. Wasserman, and M. Levine appeared in the article "A Critical Appraisal of 98.6°F, the Upper Limit of the Normal Body Temperature, and Other Legacies of Carl Reinhold August Wunderlich" (*Journal of the American Medical Association*, 1992, Vol. 268, pp. 1578–1580). Among other data, the researchers obtained the body temperatures of some 100 healthy humans. Suppose that you want to use that data to decide whether the mean body temperature of healthy humans differs from 98.6°F.

9.7 Cell Phones. The number of cell phone users has increased exponentially since 1987. The increase in cell phone use should bring a reduction in customer phone bills because of heightened competition. According to *The World of Wireless Communication*, in 1996, the mean local monthly bill for cell phone users in the United States was $47.70. A hypothesis test is to be performed to determine whether last year's mean local monthly bill for cell phone users has decreased from the 1996 mean of $47.70.

9.8 Iron Deficiency? The Food and Nutrition Board of the National Academy of Sciences states that the recommended daily allowance (RDA) of iron for adult females under the age of 51 is 18 mg. A hypothesis test is to be performed to decide whether adult females under the age of 51 are, on average, getting less than the RDA of 18 mg of iron.

9.9 Beer Drinking. According to The Beer Institute, the mean annual consumption of beer per person in the United States is 22.0 gallons (roughly 235 twelve-ounce bottles). You want to perform a hypothesis test to decide whether the mean for the nation's capital differs from the national mean.

9.10 Hospital Costs. The American Hospital Association reports in *Hospital Stat* that the mean cost to community hospitals per patient per day in U.S. hospitals was $1033 in 1997. In that same year, a random sample was obtained of 30 daily costs in Ohio hospitals. A hypothesis test was then performed to decide whether the mean cost in Ohio hospitals exceeded the national mean.

Extending the Concepts and Skills

9.11 Energy Use. The U.S. Energy Information Administration compiles data on energy consumption and publishes its findings in *Residential Energy Consumption Survey: Consumption and Expenditures*. One year, the mean energy consumed per U.S. household was 103.6 million British thermal units (BTU). For that same year, 20 randomly selected households in the West had the following energy consumptions, in millions of BTU.

104	84	72	95	69
80	78	74	76	81
82	61	94	65	100
70	65	83	76	84

Do the data provide sufficient evidence to conclude that the mean energy consumed by western households differed from that of all U.S. households? Assume that the standard deviation of energy consumptions of all western households was 15 million BTU. Use the following steps to answer the question. You may want to refer to Example 9.4, which begins on page 374.
a. State the null and alternative hypotheses.
b. Discuss the logic of conducting the hypothesis test.
c. Identify the distribution of the variable $\bar{x}$, that is, the sampling distribution of the mean for samples of size 20.
d. Obtain a precise criterion for deciding whether to reject the null hypothesis in favor of the alternative hypothesis.
e. Apply the criterion in part (d) to the sample data and state your conclusion.

9.12 Quality Assurance. Refer to Example 9.4, which begins on page 374. Suppose that, in the solution to part (d), we use the "99.74" part of the 68.26-95.44-99.74 rule.
a. Determine the resulting decision criterion and portray it graphically, using a graph similar to the one shown in Fig. 9.2(a) on page 375.
b. Construct a graph similar to the one shown in Fig. 9.2(b) that illustrates the implications of the decision criterion in part (a) if in fact the null hypothesis is true.
c. Apply the criterion from part (a) to the sample data in Table 9.1 on page 374 and state your conclusion.

9.13 Quality Assurance. Refer to Example 9.4, which begins on page 374. In that example, we rejected the null hypothesis that the mean net weight of all bags packaged is 454 g in favor of the alternative hypothesis that the mean net weight of all bags packaged differs from 454 g. If in fact the null hypothesis is true, what is the chance of incorrectly rejecting it using a sample of 25 bags of pretzels? (*Hint:* Refer to Fig. 9.2(b).)

9.2 TERMS, ERRORS, AND HYPOTHESES

To explain fully the nature of hypothesis testing, we need some additional terms and concepts. In this section, we define several more terms used in hypothesis testing, discuss the two types of errors that can occur in a hypothesis test, and interpret the possible conclusions for a hypothesis test.

SOME ADDITIONAL TERMINOLOGY

To introduce some additional terminology used in hypothesis testing, we refer to the pretzel packaging hypothesis test of Example 9.4 on page 374. Recall that the null and alternative hypotheses for that hypothesis test are

H_0: $\mu = 454$ g (the packaging machine is working properly)

H_a: $\mu \neq 454$ g (the packaging machine is not working properly),

where μ is the mean net weight of all bags of pretzels packaged.

As a basis for deciding whether to reject the null hypothesis, in part (e) of Example 9.4 we utilized the variable

$$z = \frac{\bar{x} - \mu_0}{\sigma/\sqrt{n}} = \frac{\bar{x} - 454}{1.56},$$

which tells us how many standard deviations the sample mean is from the null hypothesis population mean of 454 g. That variable is called the **test statistic** for the hypothesis test.

Figure 9.3 includes a graph portraying the criterion used to decide whether the null hypothesis should be rejected. For ease of reference, we repeat that graph in Fig. 9.4.

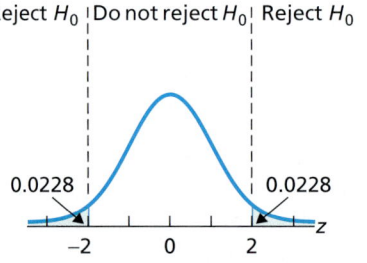

FIGURE 9.4
Criterion used to decide whether to reject the null hypothesis

The set of values for the test statistic that leads us to reject the null hypothesis is called the **rejection region.** In this case, the rejection region consists of all z-scores that lie either to the left of −2 or to the right of 2—that part of the horizontal axis under the shaded areas in Fig. 9.4.

The set of values for the test statistic that leads us not to reject the null hypothesis is called the **nonrejection region,** or **acceptance region.** In this case, the nonrejection region consists of all z-scores that lie between −2 and 2—that part of the horizontal axis under the unshaded area in Fig. 9.4.

The values of the test statistic that separate the rejection and nonrejection regions are called the **critical values.** In this case, the critical values are $z = \pm 2$, as shown in Fig. 9.4. We summarize the preceding discussion in Fig. 9.5.

The terminology introduced so far in this section, and defined formally as follows, applies to any hypothesis test, not just to hypothesis tests for a population mean.

DEFINITION 9.2 Test Statistic, Rejection Region, Nonrejection Region, Critical Values

Test statistic: The statistic used as a basis for deciding whether the null hypothesis should be rejected.

Rejection region: The set of values for the test statistic that leads to rejection of the null hypothesis.

Nonrejection region: The set of values for the test statistic that leads to nonrejection of the null hypothesis.

Critical values: The values of the test statistic that separate the rejection and nonrejection regions. A critical value is considered part of the rejection region.

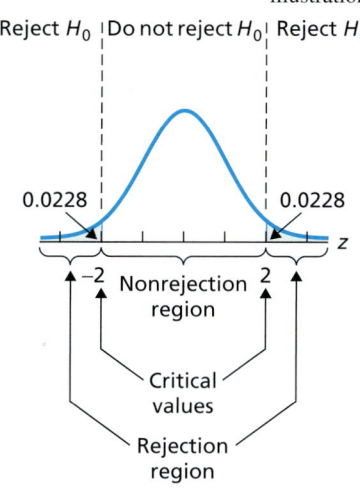

FIGURE 9.5
Rejection region, nonrejection region, and critical values for the pretzel packaging illustration

For a two-tailed test, as in the pretzel packaging illustration, the null hypothesis is rejected when the test statistic is either too small or too large. Thus the rejection region for such a test consists of two parts: one on the left and one on the right, as shown in Fig. 9.5 and Fig. 9.6(a).

For a left-tailed test, as in Example 9.3 on page 373 (the calcium intake illustration), the null hypothesis is rejected only when the test statistic is too small. Thus the rejection region for such a test consists of only one part, and that part is on the left, as shown in Fig. 9.6(b).

For a right-tailed test, as in Example 9.2 on page 372 (the history book illustration), the null hypothesis is rejected only when the test statistic is too large. Thus the rejection region for such a test consists of only one part, and that part is on the right, as shown in Fig. 9.6(c).

Table 9.2 and Fig. 9.6 summarize our discussion. Figure 9.6 shows why the term *tailed* is used: The rejection region is in both tails for a two-tailed test, in the left tail for a left-tailed test, and in the right tail for a right-tailed test.

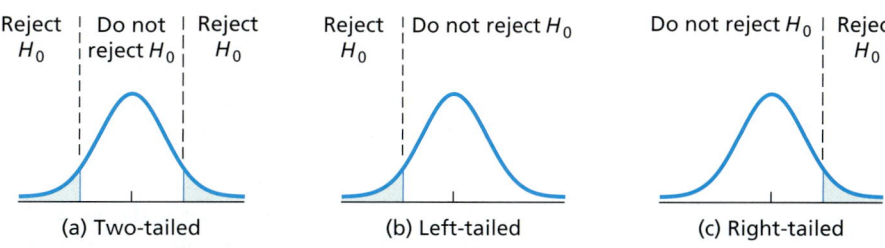

FIGURE 9.6
Graphical display of rejection regions for two-tailed, left-tailed, and right-tailed tests

TABLE 9.2
Rejection regions for two-tailed, left-tailed, and right-tailed tests

	Two-tailed test	Left-tailed test	Right-tailed test
Sign in H_a	$\neq$	$<$	$>$
Rejection region	Both sides	Left side	Right side

TYPE I AND TYPE II ERRORS

Whenever we conduct a hypothesis test, any decision that we make may be incorrect. The reason is that partial information, obtained from a sample, is used to draw conclusions about the entire population.

There are two types of incorrect decisions—**Type I error,** or rejection of a true null hypothesis, and **Type II error,** or nonrejection of a false null hypothesis, as indicated in Table 9.3 and the following definition.

TABLE 9.3
Correct and incorrect decisions for a hypothesis test

	H_0 is: True	H_0 is: False
Do not reject H_0	Correct decision	Type II error
Reject H_0	Type I error	Correct decision

DEFINITION 9.3 Type I and Type II Errors

Type I error: Rejecting the null hypothesis when it is in fact true.
Type II error: Not rejecting the null hypothesis when it is in fact false.

Example 9.5 illustrates Type I and Type II errors and the consequences of these two types of errors.

Example 9.5 Type I and Type II Errors

Quality Assurance Consider once again the pretzel packaging hypothesis test. The null and alternative hypotheses are

H_0: $\mu = 454$ g (the packaging machine is working properly)
H_a: $\mu \neq 454$ g (the packaging machine is not working properly),

where μ is the mean net weight of all bags of pretzels packaged. Explain what each of the following would mean.
 a. Type I error   b. Type II error   c. Correct decision

Recall from Example 9.4 that the results of sampling 25 bags of pretzels led to rejection of the null hypothesis, $\mu = 454$ g, that is, to the conclusion that $\mu \neq 454$ g. Classify that conclusion by error type or as a correct decision if
 d. the mean net weight, μ, is in fact 454 g.
 e. the mean net weight, μ, is in fact not 454 g.

Solution a. A Type I error occurs when a true null hypothesis is rejected. In this case, a Type I error would occur if in fact $\mu = 454$ g but the results of the sampling lead to the conclusion that $\mu \neq 454$ g—in words, if we conclude that the packaging machine is not working properly when in fact it is working properly.

b. A Type II error occurs when a false null hypothesis is not rejected. In this case, a Type II error would occur if in fact $\mu \neq 454$ g but the results of the sampling fail to lead to that conclusion—in words, if we fail to conclude that the packaging machine is not working properly when in fact it is not working properly.

c. A correct decision can occur in either of two ways.

- A true null hypothesis is not rejected. That would happen if in fact $\mu = 454$ g and the results of the sampling do not lead to the rejection of that fact—in words, if we fail to conclude that the packaging machine is not working properly when in fact it is working properly.
- A false null hypothesis is rejected. That would happen if in fact $\mu \neq 454$ g and the results of the sampling lead to that conclusion—in words, if we conclude that the packaging machine is not working properly when in fact it is not working properly.

d. If in fact $\mu = 454$ g, the null hypothesis is true. Consequently, by rejecting the null hypothesis, $\mu = 454$ g, a Type I error has been made—a true null hypothesis has been rejected.

e. If in fact $\mu \neq 454$ g, the null hypothesis is false. Consequently, by rejecting the null hypothesis, $\mu = 454$ g, a correct decision has been made—a false null hypothesis has been rejected. ◆

PROBABILITIES OF TYPE I AND TYPE II ERRORS

Part of evaluating the effectiveness of a hypothesis test involves an analysis of the chances of making an incorrect decision. A Type I error occurs if the test statistic falls in the rejection region when in fact the null hypothesis is true. The probability of that happening, the **Type I error probability,** commonly called the **significance level** of the hypothesis test, is denoted α (the Greek letter alpha).

Figure 9.4 on page 378 shows the rejection and nonrejection regions for the pretzel packaging hypothesis test in Example 9.4. It also shows the normal curve for the test statistic

$$z = \frac{\bar{x} - 454}{1.56},$$

under the assumption that the null hypothesis, $\mu = 454$ g, is true. Figure 9.4 reveals that, if the null hypothesis is true, the probability is $0.0228 + 0.0228$, or 0.0456, that the test statistic, z, will fall in the rejection region. Thus, for this hypothesis test, the significance level is 0.0456; in symbols, $\alpha = 0.0456$. In other words, there is only a 4.56% chance of concluding that $\mu \neq 454$ g when in fact $\mu = 454$ g.

DEFINITION 9.4 Significance Level

The probability of making a Type I error, that is, of rejecting a true null hypothesis, is called the *significance level*, α, of a hypothesis test.

A Type II error occurs if the test statistic falls in the nonrejection region when in fact the null hypothesis is false. The probability of that happening, the **Type II error probability,** is denoted β (the Greek letter beta). It depends on the true value of μ.

A concept closely related to that of Type II error probability is *power*. The **power** of a hypothesis test is the probability of not making a Type II error, that is, the probability of rejecting a false null hypothesis. We have

$$\text{Power} = 1 - P(\text{Type II error}) = 1 - \beta.$$

The power of a hypothesis test is between 0 and 1 and measures the ability of the hypothesis test to detect a false null hypothesis. If the power is near 0, the hypothesis test is not very good at detecting a false null hypothesis; if the power is near 1, the hypothesis test is extremely good at detecting a false null hypothesis.

Calculation of Type II error probabilities and power is examined briefly in Exercise 9.29. For a detailed discussion, refer to the text *Introductory Statistics*, 6th edition, by Neil A. Weiss (Boston: Addison-Wesley, 2002).

Ideally, both Type I and Type II errors should have small probabilities. Then the chance of making an incorrect decision would be small, regardless of whether the null hypothesis is true or false. As we demonstrate in Section 9.3, we can design a hypothesis test to have any specified significance level. So, for instance, if not rejecting a true null hypothesis is important, we should specify a small value for α. However, in making our choice for α, we must keep Key Fact 9.1 in mind.

Key Fact 9.1 Relation Between Type I and Type II Error Probabilities

For a fixed sample size, the smaller we specify the significance level, α, the larger will be the probability, β, of not rejecting a false null hypothesis.

Consequently, we must always assess the risks involved in committing both types of errors and use that assessment as a method for balancing the Type I and Type II error probabilities.

POSSIBLE CONCLUSIONS FOR A HYPOTHESIS TEST

The significance level, α, is the probability of making a Type I error, that is, of rejecting a true null hypothesis. Therefore, if the hypothesis test is conducted at a small significance level (e.g., $\alpha = 0.05$), the chance of rejecting a true null hypothesis will be small. In this text, we generally specify a small significance level, so we can make the following statement concerning a hypothesis test: If we do reject the null hypothesis in a hypothesis test, we can be reasonably confident that the null hypothesis is false and therefore that the alternative hypothesis is true.

However, we usually do not know the probability, β, of making a Type II error, that is, of not rejecting a false null hypothesis. Consequently, if we do not reject the null hypothesis in a hypothesis test, we simply reserve judgment about which hypothesis is true. In other words, if we do not reject the null hypothesis, we conclude only that the data did not provide sufficient evidence to support the alternative hypothesis; we do not conclude that the data provided sufficient evidence to support the null hypothesis. Key Fact 9.2 summarizes this discussion.

Key Fact 9.2 Possible Conclusions for a Hypothesis Test

Suppose that a hypothesis test is conducted at a small significance level.

- If the null hypothesis is rejected, we conclude that the alternative hypothesis is true.
- If the null hypothesis is not rejected, we conclude that the data do not provide sufficient evidence to support the alternative hypothesis.

When the null hypothesis is rejected in a hypothesis test performed at the significance level α, we frequently express that fact with the phrase "the test results are **statistically significant** at the α level." Similarly, when the null hypothesis is not rejected in a hypothesis test performed at the significance level α, we often express that fact with the phrase "the test results are **not statistically significant** at the α level."

Exercises 9.2

Statistical Concepts and Skills

9.14 Decide whether each statement is true or false. Explain your answers.
a. If it is important not to reject a true null hypothesis, the hypothesis test should be performed at a small significance level.
b. For a fixed sample size, decreasing the significance level of a hypothesis test results in an increase in the probability of making a Type II error.

9.15 Identify the two types of incorrect decisions in a hypothesis test. For each incorrect decision, what symbol is used to represent the probability of making that type of error?

Exercises 9.16–9.18 contain graphs portraying the decision criterion for a hypothesis test for a population mean, μ. The null hypothesis for each test is $H_0: \mu = \mu_0$; the test statistic is

$$z = \frac{\bar{x} - \mu_0}{\sigma/\sqrt{n}}.$$

The curve in each graph is the normal curve for the test statistic under the assumption that the null hypothesis is true. For each exercise, determine the
a. rejection region. b. nonrejection region.
c. critical value(s). d. significance level.
e. Construct a graph similar to Fig. 9.5 on page 379 that depicts your results from parts (a)–(d).
f. Identify the hypothesis test as two-tailed, left-tailed, or right-tailed.

9.16 A graphical display of the decision criterion is:

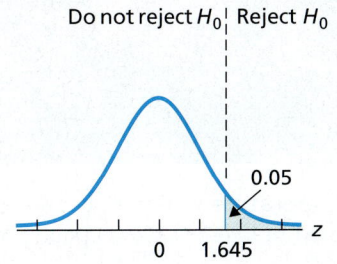

9.17 A graphical display of the decision criterion is:

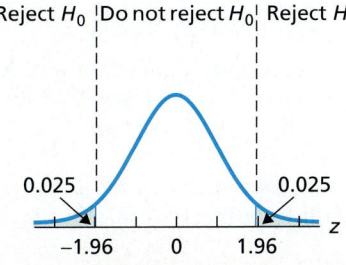

9.18 A graphical display of the decision criterion is:

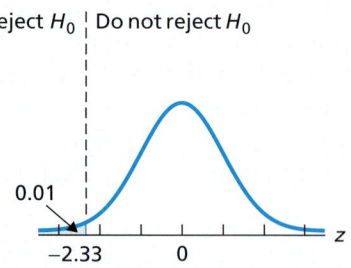

9.19 Toxic Mushrooms? The null and alternative hypotheses obtained in Exercise 9.5 on page 376 are

$$H_0: \mu = 0.5 \text{ ppm}$$
$$H_a: \mu > 0.5 \text{ ppm},$$

where μ is the mean cadmium level in *Boletus pinicola* mushrooms. Explain what each outcome would mean.
a. Type I error   b. Type II error
c. Correct decision
Now suppose that the results of carrying out the hypothesis test lead to nonrejection of the null hypothesis. Classify that conclusion by error type or as a correct decision if in fact the mean cadmium level in *Boletus pinicola* mushrooms
d. equals 0.5 ppm.
e. is greater than 0.5 ppm.

9.20 Body Temperature. The null and alternative hypotheses obtained in Exercise 9.6 on page 376 are

$$H_0: \mu = 98.6°F$$
$$H_a: \mu \neq 98.6°F,$$

where μ is the mean body temperature of all healthy humans. Explain what each outcome would mean.
a. Type I error   b. Type II error
c. Correct decision
Now suppose that the sample of temperatures leads to rejection of the null hypothesis. Classify that conclusion by error type or as a correct decision if in fact the mean body temperature, μ, of all healthy humans is
d. 98.6°F.   e. not 98.6°F.

9.21 Cell Phones. The null and alternative hypotheses obtained in Exercise 9.7 on page 377 are

$$H_0: \mu = \$47.70$$
$$H_a: \mu < \$47.70$$

where μ is last year's mean local monthly bill for cell phone users. Explain what each outcome would mean.
a. Type I error   b. Type II error
c. Correct decision
Now suppose that the results of performing the hypothesis test lead to nonrejection of the null hypothesis. Classify that conclusion by error type or as a correct decision if in fact last year's mean local monthly bill for cell phone users
d. equals the 1996 mean of $47.70.
e. is less than the 1996 mean of $47.70.

9.22 Iron Deficiency? The null and alternative hypotheses obtained in Exercise 9.8 on page 377 are

$$H_0: \mu = 18 \text{ mg}$$
$$H_a: \mu < 18 \text{ mg},$$

where μ is the mean iron intake (per day) of all adult females under the age of 51. Explain what each outcome would mean.
a. Type I error   b. Type II error
c. Correct decision
Now suppose that the results of carrying out the hypothesis test lead to rejection of the null hypothesis, $\mu = 18$ mg, that is, to the conclusion that $\mu < 18$ mg. Classify that conclusion by error type or as a correct decision if in fact the mean iron intake, μ, of all adult females under the age of 51
d. equals the RDA of 18 mg per day.
e. is less than the RDA of 18 mg per day.

9.23 Beer Drinking. The null and alternative hypotheses obtained in Exercise 9.9 on page 377 are

$$H_0: \mu = 22.0 \text{ gallons}$$
$$H_a: \mu \neq 22.0 \text{ gallons},$$

where μ is the mean annual consumption of beer per person for the nation's capital. Explain what each outcome would mean.
a. Type I error   b. Type II error
c. Correct decision
Now suppose that the results of carrying out the hypothesis test lead to rejection of the null hypothesis. Classify that conclusion by error type or as a correct decision if in fact the mean annual consumption of beer per person for the nation's capital

d. equals 22.0 gallons.
e. does not equal 22.0 gallons.

9.24 Hospital Costs. The null and alternative hypotheses obtained in Exercise 9.10 on page 377 are

$$H_0: \mu = \$1033$$
$$H_a: \mu > \$1033,$$

where μ is the 1997 mean cost to community hospitals per patient per day in Ohio. Explain what each outcome would mean.
a. Type I error   b. Type II error
c. Correct decision

Now suppose that the results of the sampling led to nonrejection of the null hypothesis. Classify that conclusion by error type or as a correct decision if in fact the 1997 mean cost to community hospitals per patient per day in Ohio
d. equaled the national mean of \$1033.
e. exceeded the national mean of \$1033.

Extending the Concepts and Skills

9.25 Suppose that you choose the significance level of a hypothesis test to be 0.
a. What is the probability of a Type I error?
b. What is the probability of a Type II error?

9.26 Identify an exercise in this section for which it is important to have
a. a small α probability.
b. a small β probability.
c. both α and β probabilities small.

9.27 Approving Nuclear Reactors. Suppose that you are performing a statistical test to decide whether a nuclear reactor should be approved for use. Further suppose that failing to reject the null hypothesis corresponds to approval. What property would you want the Type II error probability, β, to have?

9.28 Guilty or Innocent? In the U.S. court system, a defendant is assumed innocent until proven guilty. Suppose that you regard a court trial as a hypothesis test with null and alternative hypotheses

$$H_0: \text{Defendant is innocent}$$
$$H_a: \text{Defendant is guilty.}$$

a. Explain the meaning of a Type I error.
b. Explain the meaning of a Type II error.
c. If you were the defendant, would you want α to be large or small? Explain your answer.
d. If you were the prosecuting attorney, would you want β to be large or small? Explain your answer.
e. What are the consequences to the court system if you make $\alpha = 0$? $\beta = 0$?

9.29 Type II Error Probabilities and Power. For the pretzel packaging hypothesis test (Example 9.4, page 374), the null and alternative hypotheses are

$$H_0: \mu = 454 \text{ g (machine is working properly)}$$
$$H_a: \mu \neq 454 \text{ g (machine is not working properly)},$$

where μ is the mean net weight of all bags of pretzels packaged. Recall that the net weights are normally distributed with a standard deviation of 7.8 g. Figure 9.2(a) on page 375 portrays the decision criterion for a hypothesis test at the 4.56% significance level ($\alpha = 0.0456$) using a sample size of 25.
a. Identify the probability of a Type I error.
b. Assuming that the mean net weight being packaged is in fact 447 g, identify the distribution of the variable $\bar{x}$, that is, the sampling distribution of the mean for samples of size 25.
c. Use part (b) to determine the probability, β, of a Type II error if in fact the mean net weight being packaged is 447 g. (*Hint:* Referring to Fig. 9.2(a), note that β equals the percentage of all samples of 25 bags of pretzels whose mean weights are between 450.88 g and 457.12 g.)
d. Repeat parts (b) and (c) if in fact the mean net weight being packaged is 448 g, 449 g, 450 g, 451 g, 452 g, 453 g, 455 g, 456 g, 457 g, 458 g, 459 g, 460 g, and 461 g.
e. Use your answers from parts (b)–(d) to draw and interpret a graph of β versus the true value of μ. This type of graph is called an *operating characteristic (OC) curve*.
f. Use your answers from parts (b)–(d) to draw and interpret a graph of power versus the true value of μ. This type of graph is called a *power curve*.

Using Technology

9.30 Class Project: Quality Assurance. This exercise can be done individually or, better yet, as a class project. For the pretzel packaging hypothesis test in Example 9.4, the null and alternative hypotheses are

H_0: $\mu = 454$ g (machine is working properly)

H_a: $\mu \neq 454$ g (machine is not working properly),

where μ is the mean net weight of all bags of pretzels packaged. Recall that the net weights are normally distributed with a standard deviation of 7.8 g. Figure 9.4 on page 378 portrays the decision criterion for a test at the 4.56% significance level ($\alpha = 0.0456$). For a sample size of 25, the test statistic is

$$z = \frac{\bar{x} - \mu_0}{\sigma/\sqrt{n}} = \frac{\bar{x} - 454}{1.56}.$$

a. Assuming that H_0: $\mu = 454$ g is true, simulate 100 samples of 25 net weights each.
b. Determine the mean of each sample in part (a).
c. Use part (b) to determine the value of the test statistic, z, for each sample in part (a).
d. For the 100 samples obtained in part (a), roughly how many would you expect to lead to rejection of the null hypothesis? Explain your answer.
e. For the 100 samples obtained in part (a), determine the number that lead to rejection of the null hypothesis. (*Hint:* Refer to part (c) and Fig. 9.4.)
f. Compare your answers from parts (d) and (e) and comment on any observed difference.

9.3 HYPOTHESIS TESTS FOR ONE POPULATION MEAN WHEN σ IS KNOWN

In this section, we describe how to conduct a hypothesis test for a population mean at any prescribed significance level. You have already learned most of what you need to know in order to do that. What remains is to discuss how to obtain the critical value(s) when the significance level is specified in advance.

Recall that the significance level of a hypothesis test is the probability of rejecting a true null hypothesis or, equivalently, the probability that the test statistic will fall in the rejection region when the null hypothesis is true. With this fact in mind, we state Key Fact 9.3, which applies to any hypothesis test.

Key Fact 9.3 **Obtaining Critical Values**

Suppose that a hypothesis test is to be performed at a specified significance level, α. Then the critical value(s) must be chosen so that, if the null hypothesis is true, the probability is α that the test statistic will fall in the rejection region.

HYPOTHESIS TESTS FOR A POPULATION MEAN WHEN σ IS KNOWN

We now develop a simple step-by-step procedure for performing a hypothesis test for a population mean when the population standard deviation is known. In doing so, we assume that the variable under consideration is normally distributed. But keep in mind that, because of the central limit theorem, the procedure will work reasonably well when the sample size is large, regardless of the distribution of the variable.

As you have seen, the null hypothesis for a hypothesis test concerning one population mean, μ, has the form H_0: $\mu = \mu_0$, where μ_0 is some number. Recall, also, that the test statistic for the hypothesis test is

$$z = \frac{\bar{x} - \mu_0}{\sigma/\sqrt{n}},$$

which tells you how many standard deviations the observed sample mean, $\bar{x}$, is from μ_0 (the value specified for the population mean in the null hypothesis).

The basis of the hypothesis testing procedure is in Key Fact 7.4: If x is a normally distributed variable with mean μ and standard deviation σ, for samples of size n, the variable $\bar{x}$ is also normally distributed and has mean μ and standard deviation $\sigma/\sqrt{n}$. This fact implies that, if the null hypothesis is true, the test statistic z has the standard normal distribution.

Consequently, in light of Key Fact 9.3, for a specified significance level, α, we need to choose the critical value(s) so that the area under the standard normal curve that lies above the rejection region equals α. In Example 9.6, we demonstrate how to choose these critical values.

Example 9.6 Obtaining the Critical Values

Determine the critical value(s) for a hypothesis test at the 5% significance level ($\alpha = 0.05$) if the test is

a. two-tailed.   **b.** left-tailed.   **c.** right-tailed.

Solution As $\alpha = 0.05$, we need to choose the critical value(s) so that the area under the standard normal curve that lies above the rejection region equals 0.05.

a. For a two-tailed test, the rejection region is on both the left and right. So, in this case, the critical values are the two z-scores that divide the area under the standard normal curve into a middle 0.95 area and two outside areas of 0.025. In other words, the critical values are $\pm z_{0.025}$. From Table II in Appendix A, $\pm z_{0.025} = \pm 1.96$, as shown in Fig. 9.7(a).

FIGURE 9.7
Critical value(s) for a hypothesis test at the 5% significance level if the test is (a) two-tailed, (b) left-tailed, or (c) right-tailed

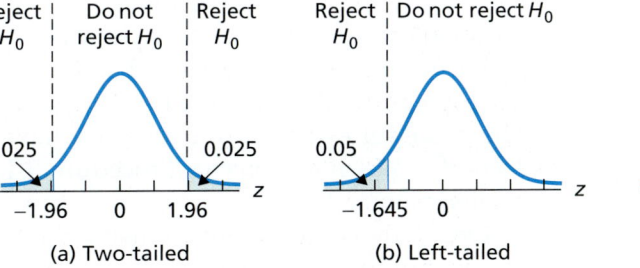
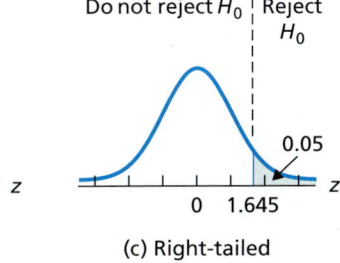

(a) Two-tailed   (b) Left-tailed   (c) Right-tailed

b. For a left-tailed test, the rejection region is on the left. So, in this case, the critical value is the z-score having area 0.05 to its left under the standard normal curve, which is $-z_{0.05}$. From Table II, $-z_{0.05} = -1.645$, as shown in Fig. 9.7(b).

c. For a right-tailed test, the rejection region is on the right. So, in this case, the critical value is the z-score having area 0.05 to its right under the standard normal curve, which is $z_{0.05}$. From Table II, $z_{0.05} = 1.645$, as shown in Fig. 9.7(c).

By reasoning as we did in Example 9.6, we can obtain the critical value(s) for any specified significance level, α. As depicted in Fig. 9.8, for a two-tailed test, the critical values are $\pm z_{\alpha/2}$; for a left-tailed test, the critical value is $-z_\alpha$; and for a right-tailed test, the critical value is z_α.

FIGURE 9.8
Critical value(s) for a hypothesis test at the significance level α if the test is (a) two-tailed, (b) left-tailed, or (c) right-tailed

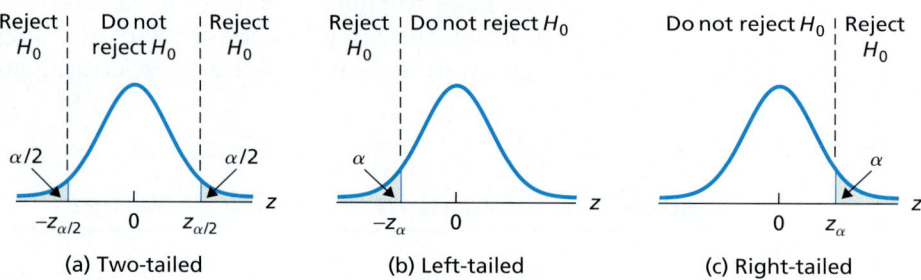

(a) Two-tailed   (b) Left-tailed   (c) Right-tailed

The most commonly used significance levels are 0.10, 0.05, and 0.01. If we consider both one-tailed and two-tailed tests, these three significance levels give rise to five "tail areas." Using the standard-normal table, Table II, we obtained the value of z_α corresponding to each of those five tail areas, as displayed in Table 9.4.

TABLE 9.4
Some important values of z_α

$z_{0.10}$	$z_{0.05}$	$z_{0.025}$	$z_{0.01}$	$z_{0.005}$
1.28	1.645	1.96	2.33	2.575

Alternatively, these five values of z_α can be found at the bottom of the t-table, Table IV, where they are displayed to three decimal places. Can you explain the slight discrepancy between the values given for $z_{0.005}$ in the two tables?

We now present Procedure 9.1, a simple method for performing a hypothesis test for a population mean when the population standard deviation is known. The procedure summarizes what we have done in this and the previous two sections. We often refer to Procedure 9.1 as the **one-sample z-test** or, more briefly, as the **z-test**.

One of the assumptions for using the z-test is that either the variable under consideration is normally distributed or the sample size is large. But, as with the z-interval procedure, the z-test is robust to moderate violations of the normality assumption. Thus the z-test works reasonably well even when the sample size is small or moderate and the variable is not normally distributed, provided the variable is not too far from being normally distributed.

Again, as with the z-interval procedure, you must watch for outliers when considering the z-test. Recall that the presence of outliers calls into question the normality assumption; and that, even for large samples, outliers can sometimes unduly affect a z-test because the sample mean is not resistant to outliers.

Procedure 9.1 — The One-Sample z-Test for a Population Mean (Critical-Value Approach)

Assumptions
1. Normal population or large sample
2. σ known

Step 1 The null hypothesis is $H_0: \mu = \mu_0$, and the alternative hypothesis is

$$H_a: \mu \neq \mu_0 \qquad H_a: \mu < \mu_0 \qquad H_a: \mu > \mu_0$$
$$\text{(Two-tailed)} \quad \text{or} \quad \text{(Left-tailed)} \quad \text{or} \quad \text{(Right-tailed)}$$

Step 2 Decide on the significance level, α.

Step 3 Compute the value of the test statistic

$$z = \frac{\bar{x} - \mu_0}{\sigma/\sqrt{n}}.$$

Step 4 The critical value(s) are

$$\pm z_{\alpha/2} \qquad -z_\alpha \qquad z_\alpha$$
$$\text{(Two-tailed)} \quad \text{or} \quad \text{(Left-tailed)} \quad \text{or} \quad \text{(Right-tailed)}$$

Use Table II to find the critical value(s).

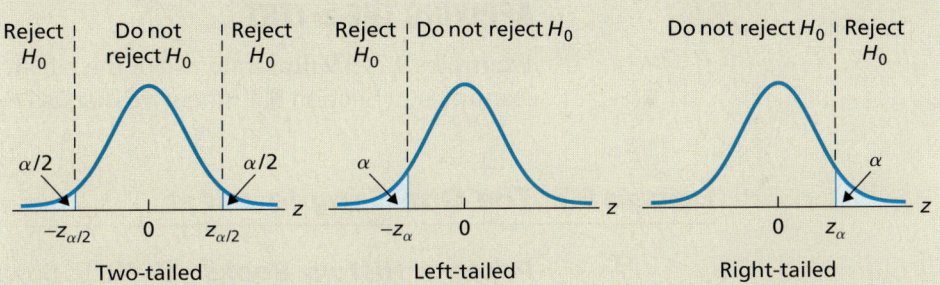

Step 5 If the value of the test statistic falls in the rejection region, reject H_0; otherwise, do not reject H_0.

Step 6 Interpret the results of the hypothesis test.

The hypothesis test is exact for normal populations and is approximately correct for large samples from nonnormal populations.

Note: By saying that the hypothesis test is *exact*, we mean that the true significance level equals α; by saying that it is *approximately correct*, we mean that the true significance level only approximately equals α.

In Key Fact 9.4, we present guidelines for the use of Procedure 9.1.

Key Fact 9.4 — **When to Use the z-Test[2]**

- For small samples—say, of size less than 15—the z-test should be used only when the variable under consideration is normally distributed or very close to being so.
- For samples of moderate size—say, between 15 and 30—the z-test can be used unless the data contain outliers or the variable under consideration is far from being normally distributed.
- For large samples—say, of size 30 or more—the z-test can be used essentially without restriction. However, if outliers are present and their removal is not justified, the effect of the outliers on the hypothesis test should be examined; that is, you should perform the hypothesis test, once with the outliers and once without them. If the conclusion remains the same either way, you may be content to take that as your conclusion and close the investigation. But if the conclusion is affected, you probably should make the more conservative conclusion, use a different procedure, or take another sample.
- If outliers are present but their removal is justified and results in a data set for which the z-test is appropriate (as previously stated), the procedure can be used.

APPLYING THE z-TEST

Examples 9.7–9.9 illustrate use of the z-test, Procedure 9.1. We reexamine these examples in Section 9.4 when we discuss P-values.

Example 9.7 — *The One-Sample z-Test*

Prices of History Books The R. R. Bowker Company of New York collects information on the retail prices of books and publishes its findings in *Publishers Weekly*. In 1997, the mean retail price of all history books was $43.50. This year's retail prices for 40 randomly selected history books are shown in Table 9.5. At the 1% significance level, do the data provide sufficient evidence to conclude that this year's mean retail price of all history books has increased from the 1997 mean of $43.50? Assume that the standard deviation of prices for this year's history books is $7.61.

Solution We constructed (not shown) a normal probability plot, a histogram, a stem-and-leaf diagram, and a boxplot for these data. The boxplot indicated potential outliers, but in view of the other three graphs, we concluded that in fact the

---

[2] We can refine these guidelines further by considering the impact of skewness. Roughly speaking, the more skewed the distribution of the variable under consideration, the larger is the sample size required to use the z-test.

TABLE 9.5
This year's prices ($) for 40 history books

48.04	38.29	39.38	46.03
45.75	39.92	46.86	47.77
43.04	53.74	39.07	54.72
39.84	42.93	44.40	42.99
43.32	42.98	52.74	64.42
39.74	48.20	44.37	43.74
45.84	42.94	55.78	44.91
33.12	56.97	49.48	46.13
67.41	48.52	61.08	34.75
45.80	64.21	53.30	34.69

data contain no outliers. As the sample size is 40, which is large, and the population standard deviation is known, we can apply Procedure 9.1 to perform the required hypothesis test.

Step 1 State the null and alternative hypotheses.

Let μ denote this year's mean retail price of all history books. We stated the null and alternative hypotheses in Example 9.2 as

H_0: $\mu = \$43.50$ (mean price has not increased)
H_a: $\mu > \$43.50$ (mean price has increased).

Note that the hypothesis test is right-tailed because a greater-than sign (>) appears in the alternative hypothesis.

Step 2 Decide on the significance level, α.

We are to perform the test at the 1% significance level, or $\alpha = 0.01$.

Step 3 Compute the value of the test statistic

$$z = \frac{\bar{x} - \mu_0}{\sigma/\sqrt{n}}.$$

We have $\mu_0 = 43.50$, $\sigma = 7.61$, and $n = 40$. The mean of the sample data in Table 9.5 is $\bar{x} = 46.93$. Thus the value of the test statistic is

$$z = \frac{46.93 - 43.50}{7.61/\sqrt{40}} = 2.85.$$

This value of z is marked with a dot in Fig. 9.9.

Step 4 The critical value for a right-tailed test is z_α.

As $\alpha = 0.01$, the critical value is $z_{0.01}$. From Table II (or Table 9.4 on page 388), $z_{0.01} = 2.33$, as shown in Fig. 9.9.

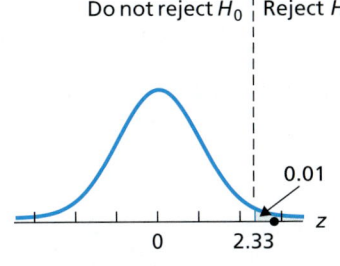

FIGURE 9.9
Criterion for deciding whether to reject the null hypothesis

Step 5 If the value of the test statistic falls in the rejection region, reject H_0; otherwise, do not reject H_0.

The value of the test statistic, found in Step 3, is $z = 2.85$. Figure 9.9 reveals that this value falls in the rejection region, so we reject H_0. The test results are statistically significant at the 1% level.

Step 6 Interpret the results of the hypothesis test.

What Does it Mean? At the 1% significance level, the data provide sufficient evidence to conclude that this year's mean retail price of all history books has increased from the 1997 mean of $43.50.

Example 9.8 The One-Sample z-Test

Poverty and Calcium Calcium is the most abundant mineral in the body and also one of the most important. It works with phosphorus to build and maintain bones and teeth. According to the Food and Nutrition Board of the National Academy of Sciences, the recommended daily allowance (RDA) of calcium for adults is 800 milligrams (mg).

A random sample of 18 people with incomes below the poverty level gives the daily calcium intakes shown in Table 9.6. At the 5% significance level, do the data provide sufficient evidence to conclude that the mean calcium intake of all people with incomes below the poverty level is less than the RDA of 800 mg? Assume that $\sigma = 188$ mg.

TABLE 9.6
Daily calcium intakes (mg) for 18 people with incomes below the poverty level

686	433	743	647	734	641
993	620	574	634	850	858
992	775	1113	672	879	609

Solution As the sample size, $n = 18$, is moderate, we first need to consider questions of normality and outliers. (See the second bulleted item in Key Fact 9.4 on page 390.) Hence we constructed a normal probability plot (not shown) for the data. The plot reveals no outliers and falls roughly in a straight line. Thus we can apply Procedure 9.1 to perform the required hypothesis test.

Step 1 State the null and alternative hypotheses.

Let μ denote the mean calcium intake (per day) of all people with incomes below the poverty level. We obtained the null and alternative hypotheses in Example 9.3 as

$H_0: \mu = 800$ mg (mean calcium intake is not less than the RDA)

$H_a: \mu < 800$ mg (mean calcium intake is less than the RDA).

Note that the hypothesis test is left-tailed because a less-than sign (<) appears in the alternative hypothesis.

Step 2 Decide on the significance level, α.

We are to perform the test at the 5% significance level, or $\alpha = 0.05$.

Step 3 Compute the value of the test statistic

$$z = \frac{\bar{x} - \mu_0}{\sigma/\sqrt{n}}.$$

We have $\mu_0 = 800$, $\sigma = 188$, and $n = 18$. From the data in Table 9.6, we find that $\bar{x} = 747.4$. Thus the value of the test statistic is

$$z = \frac{747.4 - 800}{188/\sqrt{18}} = -1.19.$$

This value of z is marked with a dot in Fig. 9.10.

Step 4 The critical value for a left-tailed test is $-z_\alpha$.

As $\alpha = 0.05$, the critical value is $-z_{0.05}$. From Table II (or Table 9.4 or Table IV), $z_{0.05} = 1.645$. Hence the critical value is $-z_{0.05} = -1.645$, as shown in Fig. 9.10.

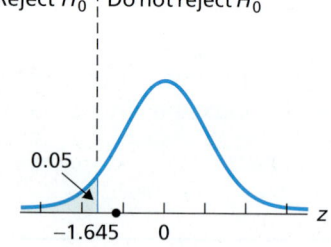

FIGURE 9.10
Criterion for deciding whether to reject the null hypothesis

Step 5 If the value of the test statistic falls in the rejection region, reject H_0; otherwise, do not reject H_0.

The value of the test statistic, found in Step 3, is $z = -1.19$. Figure 9.10 reveals that this value does not fall in the rejection region, and so we do not reject H_0. The test results are not statistically significant at the 5% level.

Step 6 Interpret the results of the hypothesis test.

At the 5% significance level, the data do not provide sufficient evidence to conclude that the mean calcium intake of all people with incomes below the poverty level is less than the RDA of 800 mg.

◆

Example 9.9 The One-Sample z-Test

Clocking the Cheetah The Cheetah (*Acinonyx jubatus*) is the fastest land mammal on earth and is highly specialized to run down prey. According to the Cheetah Conservation of Southern Africa *Trade Environment Database*, the cheetah often exceeds speeds of 60 miles per hour (mph) and has been clocked at speeds of more than 70 mph.

One common estimate of mean top speed for cheetahs is 60 mph. Table 9.7 gives the top speeds, in miles per hour, over a quarter mile for a sample of 35 cheetahs. Do the data provide sufficient evidence to conclude that the mean top speed of all cheetahs differs from 60 mph? Assume that the population standard deviation of top speeds is 3.2 mph.

TABLE 9.7
Top speeds, in miles per hour, for a sample of 35 cheetahs

57.3	57.5	59.0	56.5	61.3	57.6	59.2
65.0	60.1	59.7	62.6	52.6	60.7	62.3
65.2	54.8	55.4	55.5	57.8	58.7	57.8
60.9	75.3	60.6	58.1	55.9	61.6	59.6
59.8	63.4	54.7	60.2	52.4	58.3	66.0

Solution A frequency histogram for the data in Table 9.7, displayed in Fig. 9.11 on the next page, suggests that the top speed of 75.3 mph (second entry in the fourth row) is an outlier.

Thus, as suggested in the third bulleted item in Key Fact 9.4 (page 390), we first apply Procedure 9.1 to the full data set in Table 9.7 and then examine the effect on the test results when we remove the outlier, 75.3 mph.

Step 1 State the null and alternative hypotheses.

The null and alternative hypotheses are

H_0: $\mu = 60$ mph (mean top speed of cheetahs is 60 mph)

H_a: $\mu \neq 60$ mph (mean top speed of cheetahs is not 60 mph),

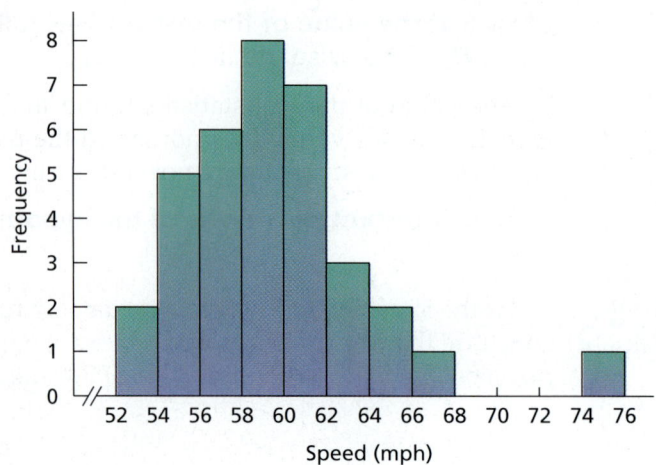

FIGURE 9.11
Frequency histogram for the top speeds in Table 9.7

where μ denotes the mean top speed of all cheetahs. Note that the hypothesis test is two-tailed because a does-not-equal sign ($\neq$) appears in the alternative hypothesis.

Step 2 Decide on the significance level, α.

We are to perform the hypothesis test at the 5% significance level, or $\alpha = 0.05$.

Step 3 Compute the value of the test statistic

$$z = \frac{\bar{x} - \mu_0}{\sigma/\sqrt{n}}.$$

We have $\mu_0 = 60$, $\sigma = 3.2$, and $n = 35$. From the data in Table 9.7, we find that $\bar{x} = 59.526$. Thus the value of the test statistic is

$$z = \frac{59.526 - 60}{3.2/\sqrt{35}} = -0.88.$$

This value of z is marked with a solid dot in Fig. 9.12.

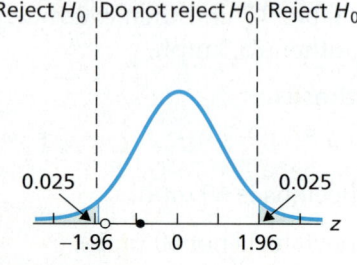

FIGURE 9.12
Criterion for deciding whether to reject the null hypothesis

Step 4 The critical values for a two-tailed test are $\pm z_{\alpha/2}$.

As $\alpha = 0.05$, we obtain from Table II (or Table 9.4 or Table IV) the critical values of $\pm z_{0.05/2} = \pm z_{0.025} = \pm 1.96$, as shown in Fig. 9.12.

Step 5 If the value of the test statistic falls in the rejection region, reject H_0; otherwise, do not reject H_0.

From Step 3, the value of the test statistic is $z = -0.88$. This value does not fall in the rejection region shown in Fig. 9.12. Hence we do not reject H_0. The test results are not statistically significant at the 5% level.

Step 6 Interpret the results of the hypothesis test.

> **What Does it Mean?** At the 5% significance level, the (complete) data do not provide sufficient evidence to conclude that the mean top speed of all cheetahs differs from 60 mph.

We have now completed the hypothesis test, using all 35 top speeds in Table 9.7. However, recall that the top speed of 75.3 mph is an outlier. For this problem, although we don't actually know whether removing this outlier is justified (a common situation), we can still remove it from the sample data and assess the effect on the hypothesis test.

Doing so, we find that the value of the test statistic for the abridged data is $z = -1.71$, which we have marked with a hollow dot in Fig. 9.12. This value still lies in the nonrejection region, although it is much closer to the rejection region than the value of the test statistic for the unabridged data, $z = -0.88$.

> **What Does it Mean?** In this case, removing the outlier therefore does not affect the conclusion of the hypothesis test. We can probably accept that the mean top speed of all cheetahs is roughly 60 mph.

◆

STATISTICAL SIGNIFICANCE VERSUS PRACTICAL SIGNIFICANCE

Recall that the results of a hypothesis test are *statistically significant* if the null hypothesis is rejected at the chosen level of α. Statistical significance means that the data provide sufficient evidence to conclude that the truth is different from the stated null hypothesis. However, it does not necessarily mean that the difference is important in any practical sense.

For example, the manufacturer of a new car, the Orion, claims that a typical car gets 26 miles per gallon—that is, the mean gas mileage of all Orions is $\mu = 26$ mpg. Suppose that the mean gas mileage of a sample of 1000 Orions is 25.9 mpg. Assuming that the standard deviation of gas mileages for all Orions is 1.4 mpg, the value of the test statistic for a z-test of

H_0: $\mu = 26$ mpg (mean gas mileage is 26 mpg)

H_a: $\mu < 26$ mpg (mean gas mileage is less than 26 mpg)

is $z = -2.26$. This result is statistically significant at the 5% level (and even at the 1.19% level). Thus we can easily reject the null hypothesis, that is, the manufacturer's claim that the mean gas mileage of all Orions is 26 mpg.

Because the sample size, 1000, is so large, the sample mean, $\bar{x} = 25.9$ mpg, is probably nearly the same as the population mean. As a result, we rejected the manufacturer's claim because μ is about 25.9 mpg instead of 26 mpg. From a practical point of view, however, the difference between 25.9 mpg and 26 mpg is not important.

> **What Does it Mean?** Statistical significance does not necessarily imply practical significance!

THE RELATION BETWEEN HYPOTHESIS TESTS AND CONFIDENCE INTERVALS

Hypothesis tests and confidence intervals are closely related. Consider, for example, a two-tailed hypothesis test for a population mean at the significance level α. In this case, the null hypothesis will be rejected if and only if the value μ_0 given for the mean in the null hypothesis lies outside the $(1 - \alpha)$-level confidence interval for μ. Exercises 9.42 and 9.43 deal with this relation between hypothesis tests and confidence intervals in greater detail.

Exercises 9.3

Statistical Concepts and Skills

In Exercises 9.31–9.33, suppose that a hypothesis test is to be performed for a population mean, μ, with a null hypothesis of $H_0: \mu = \mu_0$. Further suppose that the test statistic to be used is

$$z = \frac{\bar{x} - \mu_0}{\sigma/\sqrt{n}}.$$

For each exercise, obtain the required critical value(s) and draw a graph that illustrates your answers.

9.31 A left-tailed test with $\alpha = 0.05$.

9.32 A right-tailed test with $\alpha = 0.01$.

9.33 A two-tailed test with $\alpha = 0.05$.

9.34 Explain why considering outliers is important when you are conducting a one-sample z-test.

Preliminary data analyses indicate that applying the z-test (Procedure 9.1 on page 389) in Exercises 9.35–9.40 is reasonable. Comment on the practical significance of all hypothesis tests whose results are statistically significant.

9.35 Toxic Mushrooms? Refer to Exercise 9.5 on page 376. Here are the data obtained by the researchers.

0.24	0.59	0.62	0.16	0.77	1.33
0.92	0.19	0.33	0.25	0.59	0.32

At the 5% significance level, do the data provide sufficient evidence to conclude that the mean cadmium level in *Boletus pinicola* mushrooms is greater than the government's recommended limit of 0.5 ppm? Assume that the population standard deviation of cadmium levels in *Boletus pinicola* mushrooms is 0.37 ppm. (*Note:* The sum of the data is 6.31 ppm.)

9.36 Body Temperature. Refer to Exercise 9.6 on page 376. The researchers obtained the following body temperatures of 93 healthy humans.

98.0	97.6	98.8	98.0	98.8	98.8	97.6	98.6	98.6
98.8	98.0	98.2	98.0	98.0	97.0	97.2	98.2	98.1
98.2	98.5	98.5	99.0	98.0	97.0	97.3	97.3	98.1
97.8	99.0	97.6	97.4	98.0	97.4	98.0	98.6	98.6
98.4	97.0	98.4	99.0	98.0	99.4	97.8	98.2	99.2
99.0	97.7	98.2	98.2	98.8	98.1	98.5	97.2	98.5
99.2	98.3	98.7	98.8	98.6	98.0	99.1	97.2	97.6
97.9	98.8	98.6	98.6	99.3	97.8	98.7	99.3	97.8
98.4	97.7	98.3	97.7	97.1	98.4	98.6	97.4	96.7
96.9	98.4	98.2	98.6	97.0	97.4	98.4	97.4	96.8
98.2	97.4	98.0						

At the 1% significance level, do the data provide sufficient evidence to conclude that the mean body temperature of healthy humans differs from 98.6°F? Assume that $\sigma = 0.63$°F. (*Note:* The sum of the 93 temperatures is 9125.5°F.)

9.37 Cell Phones. Refer to Exercise 9.7 on page 377. Following are last year's local monthly bills, in dollars, for a random sample of 50 cell phone users.

33.21	31.42	16.46	104.53	47.98
117.29	62.30	44.07	13.85	15.70
30.42	14.95	27.43	29.13	42.37
17.26	61.64	15.83	32.81	22.76
45.00	35.97	20.28	29.28	46.87
28.41	89.28	23.78	31.93	48.65
65.01	50.81	46.57	35.93	24.86
16.50	16.74	42.13	25.07	77.54
28.37	16.89	49.68	45.15	15.45
58.00	13.81	81.49	51.95	127.17

At the 1% significance level, do the data provide sufficient evidence to conclude that last year's mean local monthly bill for cell phone users has decreased from the 1996 mean of $47.70? Assume that $\sigma = \$25$. (*Note:* The sum of the 50 cell phone bills is $2069.98.)

9.38 Iron Deficiency? Refer to Exercise 9.8 on page 377. The following iron intakes, in milligrams, were obtained during a 24-hour period for 45 randomly selected adult females under the age of 51.

15.0	18.1	14.4	14.6	10.9	18.1	18.2	18.3	15.0
16.0	12.6	16.6	20.7	19.8	11.6	12.8	15.6	11.0
15.3	9.4	19.5	18.3	14.5	16.6	11.5	16.4	12.5
14.6	11.9	12.5	18.6	13.1	12.1	10.7	17.3	12.4
17.0	6.3	16.8	12.5	16.3	14.7	12.7	16.3	11.5

At the 1% significance level, do the data suggest that adult females under the age of 51 are, on average, getting less than the RDA of 18 mg of iron? Assume that the population standard deviation is 4.2 mg. (*Note:* $\bar{x} = 14.68$ mg.)

9.39 Beer Drinking. From Exercise 9.9, the mean annual consumption of beer per person in the United States is 22.0 gallons (roughly 235 twelve-ounce bottles). A random sample of 300 Washington, D.C., residents yielded a mean annual beer consumption of 27.8 gallons. At the 10% significance level, do the data provide sufficient evidence to conclude that the mean annual consumption of beer per person for the nation's capital differs from the national mean? Assume that the standard deviation of annual beer consumptions for Washington, D.C., residents is 55 gallons.

9.40 Hospital Costs. From Exercise 9.10, the mean cost to community hospitals per patient per day in U.S. hospitals was $1033 in 1997. In that same year, a random sample of 30 daily costs in Ohio hospitals had a mean of $1123. Assuming a population standard deviation of $350 for Ohio hospitals, do the data provide sufficient evidence to conclude that, in 1997, the mean cost in Ohio hospitals exceeded the national mean of $1033? Perform the required hypothesis test at the 5% significance level.

Extending the Concepts and Skills

9.41 Each part of this exercise provides a scenario for a hypothesis test. Decide whether the z-test is an appropriate method for conducting the hypothesis test. Assume that the population standard deviation is known in each case.
a. Preliminary analyses reveal that the sample data contain no outliers but that the distribution of the variable under consideration is probably highly skewed. The sample size is 20.
b. A normal probability plot reveals an outlier but is otherwise roughly linear. It is determined that the outlier is a legitimate observation and should not be removed. The sample size is 15.
c. Preliminary analyses reveal that the sample data contain no outliers but that the distribution of the variable under consideration is probably mildly skewed. The sample size is 70.

In Exercises 9.42 and 9.43, you are to examine the relationship between hypothesis tests and confidence intervals for one population mean.

9.42 How Far People Drive. In 1996, the average passenger vehicle in the United States was driven 11.3 thousand miles, as reported by the U.S. Federal Highway Administration in *Highway Statistics*. A random sample of 500 passenger vehicles revealed a mean of 11.1 thousand miles driven for last year. Let μ denote last year's mean distance driven for all passenger vehicles.
a. Use Procedure 9.1 on page 389 to perform the hypothesis test

$$H_0: \mu = 11.3 \text{ thousand miles}$$
$$H_a: \mu \neq 11.3 \text{ thousand miles}$$

at the 5% significance level. Assume that last year's standard deviation of distances driven for all passenger vehicles is 6.0 thousand miles.
b. Use Procedure 8.1 on page 335 to find a 95% confidence interval for μ.
c. Does the value of 11.3 thousand miles, hypothesized for the mean, μ, in the null hypothesis of part (a), lie within your confidence interval from part (b)?
d. Repeat parts (a)–(c) for a sample of 500 passenger vehicles driven a mean of 11.9 thousand miles last year.
e. Based on your observations in parts (a)–(d), complete the following statements concerning the relationship between a two-tailed hypothesis test,

$$H_0: \mu = \mu_0$$
$$H_a: \mu \neq \mu_0,$$

at the significance level α and a $(1 - \alpha)$-level confidence interval for μ.
i. If μ_0 lies within the $(1 - \alpha)$-level confidence interval for μ, the null hypothesis *(will, will not)* be rejected.
ii. If μ_0 lies outside the $(1 - \alpha)$-level confidence interval for μ, the null hypothesis *(will, will not)* be rejected.

9.43 In this exercise, you are to examine the general relationship between a two-tailed hypothesis test for a population mean and a confidence-interval estimate for a population mean.

a. Show that the inequalities

$$\bar{x} - z_{\alpha/2} \cdot \frac{\sigma}{\sqrt{n}} < \mu_0 < \bar{x} + z_{\alpha/2} \cdot \frac{\sigma}{\sqrt{n}}$$

are equivalent to

$$-z_{\alpha/2} < \frac{\bar{x} - \mu_0}{\sigma/\sqrt{n}} < z_{\alpha/2}.$$

b. Deduce the following fact from part (a): For a two-tailed hypothesis test,

$$H_0: \mu = \mu_0$$
$$H_a: \mu \neq \mu_0,$$

at the significance level α, the null hypothesis will not be rejected if μ_0 lies within the $(1 - \alpha)$-level confidence interval for μ, and conversely, the null hypothesis will be rejected if μ_0 does not lie within the $(1 - \alpha)$-level confidence interval for μ.

9.4 P-VALUES

In Section 9.3, we presented Procedure 9.1, a step-by-step method for performing a hypothesis test for a population mean when the population standard deviation is known. Step 4 of that procedure requires us to obtain critical values. Because of that requirement, Procedure 9.1 is said to use the **critical-value approach** to hypothesis testing.

In this section, we discuss another approach to hypothesis testing, called the **P-value approach**. Very roughly speaking, the P-value indicates how likely (or unlikely) observation of the value obtained for the test statistic would be if the null hypothesis is true. In particular, a small P-value (close to 0) indicates that observation of the value obtained for the test statistic would be unlikely if the null hypothesis is true.

We can define the **P-value** (also called the **observed significance level** or the **probability value**) as the percentage of samples that would yield a value of the test statistic as extreme or more extreme than that observed if the null hypothesis is true. But, more commonly, the P-value is defined in the language of probability as follows.

> **What Does it Mean?**
>
> Small P-values provide evidence against the null hypothesis; larger P-values do not. The smaller (closer to 0) the P-value, the stronger the evidence is against the null hypothesis.

DEFINITION 9.5 **P-Value**

To obtain the **P-value** of a hypothesis test, we assume that the null hypothesis is true and compute the probability of observing a value of the test statistic as extreme or more extreme than that observed. By *extreme* we mean "far from what we would expect to observe if the null hypothesis is true." We use the letter P to denote the P-value.

In this section, we concentrate on P-values and the P-value approach for the one-sample z-test. But much of what we say here applies to P-values and the P-value approach for any hypothesis test.

OBTAINING P-VALUES FOR A ONE-SAMPLE z-TEST

Recall that the test statistic for a one-sample z-test for a population mean with null hypothesis $H_0: \mu = \mu_0$ is

$$z = \frac{\bar{x} - \mu_0}{\sigma/\sqrt{n}}.$$

If the null hypothesis is true, this test statistic has the standard normal distribution, and its probabilities equal areas under the standard normal curve.

If we let z_0 be the observed value of the test statistic z, we obtain the P-value as follows.

- *Two-tailed test:* The P-value is the probability of observing a value of the test statistic z at least as large in magnitude as the value actually observed, which is the area under the standard normal curve that lies outside the interval from $-|z_0|$ to $|z_0|$, as illustrated in Fig. 9.13(a).
- *Left-tailed test:* The P-value is the probability of observing a value of the test statistic z as small as or smaller than the value actually observed, which is the area under the standard normal curve that lies to the left of z_0, as illustrated in Fig. 9.13(b).
- *Right-tailed test:* The P-value is the probability of observing a value of the test statistic z as large as or larger than the value actually observed, which is the area under the standard normal curve that lies to the right of z_0, as illustrated in Fig. 9.13(c).

FIGURE 9.13
P-value for a z-test if the test is (a) two-tailed, (b) left-tailed, or (c) right-tailed

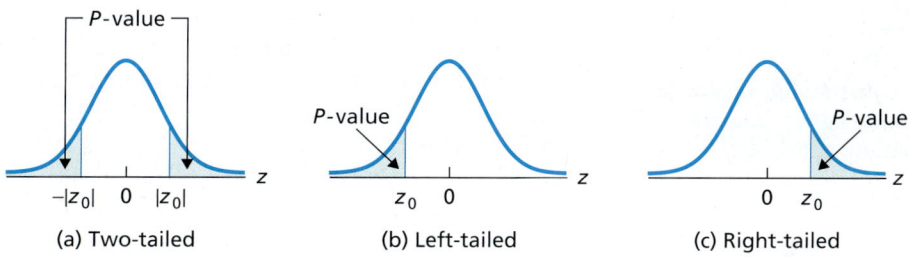

(a) Two-tailed (b) Left-tailed (c) Right-tailed

The best way to understand P-values is to examine several examples. In Examples 9.10 and 9.11, we obtain the P-values for two of the hypothesis tests we conducted in Section 9.3.

Example 9.10 *P-Values*

Prices of History Books Consider again the history book hypothesis test of Example 9.7 where we wanted to decide whether this year's mean cost of all history books has increased from the 1997 mean of $43.50. Recall that the null and alternative hypotheses are

$$H_0: \mu = \$43.50 \text{ (mean price has not increased)}$$

$$H_a: \mu > \$43.50 \text{ (mean price has increased)},$$

where μ is this year's mean retail price of all history books. Note that the test is right-tailed because a greater-than sign (>) appears in the alternative hypothesis.

Table 9.5 on page 391 displays this year's prices for 40 randomly selected history books, for which the mean price is $\bar{x} = \$46.93$. Using that sample mean and $\sigma = \$7.61$, we found the value of the test statistic to be 2.85. Obtain and interpret the P-value of the hypothesis test.

Solution Because the hypothesis test is a right-tailed z-test, the P-value is the probability of observing a value of z of 2.85 or greater if the null hypothesis is true. That probability equals the area under the standard normal curve to the right of 2.85, the shaded area shown in Fig. 9.14. From Table II, we find that area to be $1 - 0.9978 = 0.0022$.

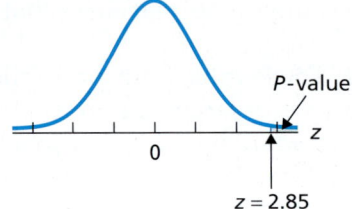

FIGURE 9.14
P-value for the history book hypothesis test

What Does it Mean?

The data provide very strong evidence against the null hypothesis.

Therefore the P-value of this hypothesis test is 0.0022. If the null hypothesis is true, we would observe a value of the test statistic z of 2.85 or greater only about 2 times in 1000. In other words, if the null hypothesis is true, a random sample of 40 history books would have a mean of $46.93, or greater, about 0.2% of the time. ◆

Example 9.11 P-Values

Clocking the Cheetah In Example 9.9, we conducted a hypothesis test to decide whether the mean top speed of all cheetahs differs from 60 mph. Recall that the null and alternative hypotheses are

H_0: $\mu = 60$ mph (mean top speed of cheetahs is 60 mph)

H_a: $\mu \neq 60$ mph (mean top speed of cheetahs is not 60 mph),

where μ denotes the mean top speed of all cheetahs. Note that the hypothesis test is two-tailed because a does-not-equal sign ($\neq$) appears in the alternative hypothesis.

Table 9.7 on page 393 shows the top speeds of a random sample of 35 cheetahs. Recall that the top speed of 75.3 mph is an outlier.

a. Obtain and interpret the P-value of the hypothesis test, using the unabridged data (i.e., including the outlier).
b. Obtain and interpret the P-value of the hypothesis test, using the abridged data (i.e., with the outlier removed).

9.4 P-Values

c. Comment on the effect that removing the outlier has on the evidence against the null hypothesis.

Solution a. In Example 9.9, we found the value of the test statistic for the unabridged data to be -0.88. Because the test is a two-tailed z-test, the P-value is the probability of observing a value of z of 0.88 or greater in magnitude if the null hypothesis is true. That probability, as depicted in Fig. 9.15(a), equals 0.3788.

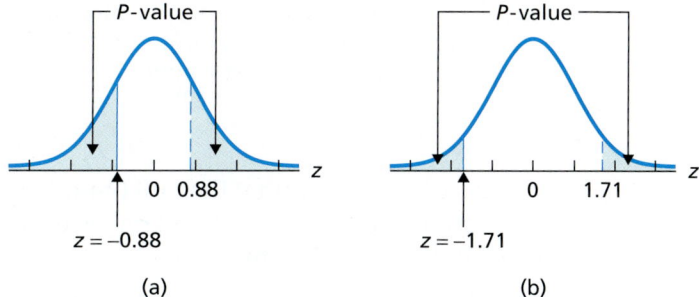

FIGURE 9.15
P-value for the cheetah speed hypothesis test (a) including the outlier, and (b) with the outlier removed

What Does it Mean?

The unabridged data do not provide evidence against the null hypothesis.

What Does it Mean?

The abridged data provide moderate evidence against the null hypothesis.

Thus, if the null hypothesis is true, we would observe a value of the test statistic z of 0.88 or greater in magnitude more than 37 times in 100. In other words, if the null hypothesis is true, a random sample of 35 cheetahs would have a mean top speed at least as far from 60 mph as that of our sample more than 37% of the time.

b. In Example 9.9, we found the value of the test statistic to be -1.71. In this case, the P-value, shown in Fig. 9.15(b), equals 0.0872. Thus, if the null hypothesis is true, we would observe a value of the test statistic z of 1.71 or greater in magnitude less than 9 times in 100. In other words, if the null hypothesis is true, a random sample of 34 cheetahs would have a mean top speed at least as far from 60 mph as that of our abridged sample less than 9% of the time.

c. Parts (a) and (b) indicate that the strength of the evidence against the null hypothesis depends on whether the outlier is retained or removed. If the outlier is retained, there is virtually no evidence against the null hypothesis; if the outlier is removed, there is moderate evidence against the null hypothesis.

THE P-VALUE APPROACH TO HYPOTHESIS TESTING

The P-value can be interpreted as the *observed significance level* of a hypothesis test. To illustrate, suppose that the value of the test statistic for a right-tailed z-test turns out to be 1.88. Then the P-value of the hypothesis test is 0.03 (actually 0.0301), as depicted by the shaded area in Fig. 9.16.

FIGURE 9.16
P-value as the observed significance level

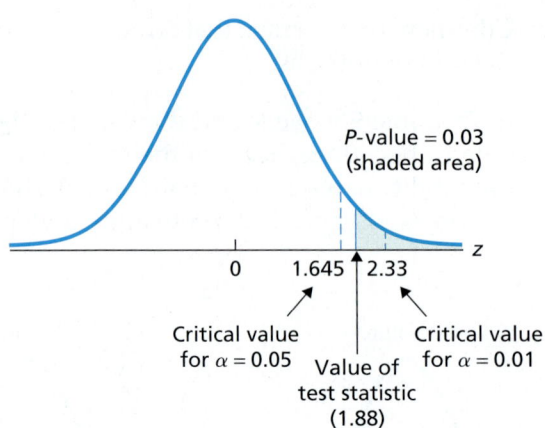

Figure 9.16 reveals that the null hypothesis would be rejected for a test at the 0.05 significance level but would not be rejected for a test at the 0.01 significance level. In fact, Fig. 9.16 makes it clear that the P-value is precisely the smallest significance level at which the null hypothesis would be rejected, which we restate as Key Fact 9.5.

Key Fact 9.5   P-Value as the Observed Significance Level

The P-value of a hypothesis test equals the smallest significance level at which the null hypothesis can be rejected, that is, the smallest significance level for which the observed sample data results in rejection of H_0.

In view of Key Fact 9.5, we have the following criterion, expressed as Key Fact 9.6, for deciding whether the null hypothesis should be rejected in favor of the alternative hypothesis.

Key Fact 9.6   Decision Criterion for a Hypothesis Test Using the P-Value

If the P-value is less than or equal to the specified significance level, reject the null hypothesis; otherwise, do not reject the null hypothesis.

Key Fact 9.6 provides a foundation for the P-value approach to hypothesis testing. For the one-sample z-test, then, we have Procedure 9.2.

In Example 9.8, we performed a one-sample z-test to decide whether the mean calcium intake of all people with incomes below the poverty level is less than the RDA of 800 mg. To carry out that hypothesis test, we used Procedure 9.1 on page 389, which involves the critical-value approach. We now perform that same test, using the P-value approach, in Example 9.12.

Procedure 9.2

The One-Sample z-Test for a Population Mean (P-Value Approach)

Assumptions
1. Normal population or large sample
2. σ known

Step 1 The null hypothesis is H_0: $\mu = \mu_0$, and the alternative hypothesis is

H_a: $\mu \neq \mu_0$	or	H_a: $\mu < \mu_0$	or	H_a: $\mu > \mu_0$
(Two-tailed)		(Left-tailed)		(Right-tailed)

Step 2 Decide on the significance level, α.

Step 3 Compute the value of the test statistic

$$z = \frac{\bar{x} - \mu_0}{\sigma/\sqrt{n}}$$

and denote that value z_0.

Step 4 Use Table II to obtain the P-value.

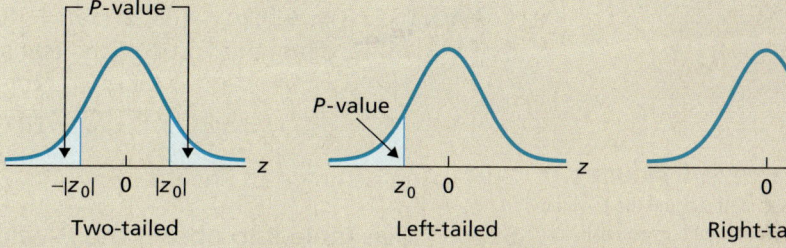

Step 5 If $P \leq \alpha$, reject H_0; otherwise, do not reject H_0.

Step 6 Interpret the results of the hypothesis test.

The hypothesis test is exact for normal populations and is approximately correct for large samples from nonnormal populations.

Example 9.12 The One-Sample z-Test (P-Value Approach)

Poverty and Calcium A random sample of 18 people with incomes below the poverty level gives the daily calcium intakes shown in Table 9.8. At the 5% significance level, do the data provide sufficient evidence to conclude that the mean calcium intake of all people with incomes below the poverty level is less than the RDA of 800 mg? Assume that $\sigma = 188$ mg.

Solution Recall that a normal probability plot of the data in Table 9.8 reveals no outliers and falls roughly in a straight line. So, for this moderate sample size, we can apply Procedure 9.2 to perform the hypothesis test.

TABLE 9.8
Daily calcium intakes (mg) for 18 people with incomes below the poverty level

686	433	743	647	734	641
993	620	574	634	850	858
992	775	1113	672	879	609

Step 1 State the null and alternative hypotheses.

Let μ denote the mean calcium intake (per day) of all people with incomes below the poverty level. The null and alternative hypotheses are

H_0: $\mu = 800$ mg (mean calcium intake is not less than the RDA)

H_a: $\mu < 800$ mg (mean calcium intake is less than the RDA).

Note that the hypothesis test is left-tailed because a less-than sign (<) appears in the alternative hypothesis.

Step 2 Decide on the significance level, α.

We are to perform the test at the 5% significance level, or $\alpha = 0.05$.

Step 3 Compute the value of the test statistic

$$z = \frac{\bar{x} - \mu_0}{\sigma/\sqrt{n}}.$$

We have $\mu_0 = 800$, $\sigma = 188$, and $n = 18$. From the data in Table 9.8, we find that $\bar{x} = 747.4$. Thus the value of the test statistic is

$$z = \frac{747.4 - 800}{188/\sqrt{18}} = -1.19.$$

This value is shown in Fig. 9.17.

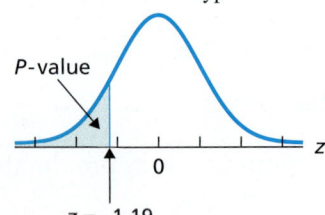

FIGURE 9.17
Value of the test statistic and the P-value for the calcium intake hypothesis test

Step 4 Use Table II to obtain the P-value.

The test is left-tailed, so the P-value is the probability of observing a value of z of -1.19 or less if the null hypothesis is true. That probability equals the shaded area in Fig. 9.17, which by Table II is 0.1170. Hence $P = 0.1170$.

Step 5 If $P \leq \alpha$, reject H_0; otherwise, do not reject H_0.

From Step 4, $P = 0.1170$. Because this P-value exceeds the specified significance level of 0.05, we do not reject H_0. The test results are not statistically significant at the 5% level.

Step 6 Interpret the results of the hypothesis test.

What Does it Mean? At the 5% significance level, the data do not provide sufficient evidence to conclude that the mean calcium intake of all people with incomes below the poverty level is less than the RDA of 800 mg.

COMPARISON OF THE CRITICAL-VALUE AND P-VALUE APPROACHES

We have now discussed both the critical-value and P-value approaches to hypothesis testing, but we have done so only in terms of the one-sample z-test. For future reference, we now list the general steps involved in each approach in Table 9.9.

TABLE 9.9 Comparison of critical-value and P-value approaches

Critical-Value Approach	P-Value Approach
Step 1 State the null and alternative hypotheses.	**Step 1** State the null and alternative hypotheses.
Step 2 Decide on the significance level, α.	**Step 2** Decide on the significance level, α.
Step 3 Compute the value of the test statistic.	**Step 3** Compute the value of the test statistic.
Step 4 Determine the critical value(s).	**Step 4** Determine the P-value.
Step 5 If the value of the test statistic falls in the rejection region, reject H_0; otherwise, do not reject H_0.	**Step 5** If $P \leq \alpha$, reject H_0; otherwise, do not reject H_0.
Step 6 Interpret the result of the hypothesis test.	**Step 6** Interpret the result of the hypothesis test.

USING THE P-VALUE TO ASSESS THE EVIDENCE AGAINST THE NULL HYPOTHESIS

Key Fact 9.5 asserts that the P-value is the smallest significance level at which the null hypothesis can be rejected. Consequently, knowing the P-value allows us to assess significance at any level we desire. For instance, if the P-value of a hypothesis test is 0.03, the null hypothesis can be rejected at any significance level larger than 0.03 (e.g., $\alpha = 0.05$) and it cannot be rejected at any significance level smaller than 0.03 (e.g., $\alpha = 0.01$).

Knowing the P-value, we can also evaluate the strength of the evidence against the null hypothesis—the smaller the P-value, the stronger will be the evidence against the null hypothesis. Table 9.10 presents guidelines for interpreting the P-value of a hypothesis test.

In Example 9.10 (page 399) and Example 9.11 (page 400), we used the P-value to evaluate the strength of the evidence against the null hypothesis without reference to critical values or significance levels. This practice is common among researchers.

TABLE 9.10 Guidelines for using the P-value to assess the evidence against the null hypothesis

P-value	Evidence against H_0
$P > 0.10$	Weak or none
$0.05 < P \leq 0.10$	Moderate
$0.01 < P \leq 0.05$	Strong
$P \leq 0.01$	Very strong

> **Hypothesis Tests Without Significance Levels:** Many researchers do not explicitly refer to significance levels or critical values. Instead, they simply obtain the P-value of the hypothesis test and use it (or let the reader use it) to assess the strength of the evidence against the null hypothesis.

The Technology Center

Most statistical technologies have programs that automatically perform a one-sample z-test for a population mean. In this subsection, we present output and (optional) step-by-step instructions to implement such programs.

Example 9.13 Using Technology to Conduct a z-Test

Poverty and Calcium Table 9.8 on page 404 displays the calcium intakes for a sample of 18 people with incomes below the poverty level. Use Minitab, Excel, or the TI-83 Plus to perform the hypothesis test in Example 9.12 on page 403.

Solution Let μ denote the mean calcium intake (per day) of all people with incomes below the poverty level. You are to perform the hypothesis test

$H_0: \mu = 800$ mg (mean calcium intake is not less than the RDA)

$H_a: \mu < 800$ mg (mean calcium intake is less than the RDA)

at the 5% significance level ($\alpha = 0.05$). Note that the hypothesis test is left-tailed because a less-than sign (<) appears in the alternative hypothesis. Also, recall that $\sigma = 188$ mg.

Printout 9.1 on the next page shows the output obtained by applying the one-sample z-test programs to the calcium intake data in Table 9.8.

The three outputs in Printout 9.1 show that the P-value for the hypothesis test is 0.118. Because the P-value exceeds the specified significance level of 0.05, we do not reject H_0. The test results are not statistically significant at the 5% level; that is, at the 5% significance level, the data do not provide sufficient evidence to conclude that the mean calcium intake of all people with incomes below the poverty level is less than the RDA of 800 mg. ◆

Obtaining the Output (Optional)

Printout 9.1 provides output from Minitab, Excel, and the TI-83 Plus for a one-sample z-test based on the sample of calcium intakes displayed in Table 9.8. The following are detailed instructions for obtaining that output. First, we store the calcium intake data in a column (Minitab), range (Excel), or list (TI-83 Plus) named CALCI. Then, we proceed as follows.

MINITAB	EXCEL	TI-83 PLUS
1 Choose **Stat ➤ Basic Statistics ➤ 1-Sample Z...**	1 Choose **DDXL ➤ Hypothesis Tests**	1 Press **STAT**, arrow over to **TESTS**, and press **1**
2 Specify CALCI in the **Variables** text box	2 Select **1 Var z Test** from the **Function type** drop-down box	2 Highlight **Data** and press **ENTER**
3 Click in the **Sigma** text box and type <u>188</u>	3 Specify CALCI in the **Quantitative Variable** text box	3 Press the down-arrow key, type <u>800</u> for μ_0, and press **ENTER**
4 Click in the **Test mean** text box and type <u>800</u>	4 Click **OK**	4 Type <u>188</u> for σ and press **ENTER**
5 Click the **Options...** button	5 Click the **Set μ0 and sd** button	5 Press **2nd ➤ LIST**
6 Click the arrow button at the right of the **Alternative** drop-down list box and select **less than**	6 Click in the **Hypothesized μ0** text box and type <u>800</u>	6 Arrow down to CALCI and press **ENTER** three times
7 Click **OK**	7 Click in the **Population std dev** text box and type <u>188</u>	7 Highlight **< μ_0** and press **ENTER**
8 Click **OK**	8 Click **OK**	8 Press the down-arrow key, highlight **Calculate** or **Draw**, and press **ENTER**
	9 Click the **0.05** button	
	10 Click the **$\mu < \mu$0** button	
	11 Click the **Compute** button	

PRINTOUT 9.1
One-sample z-test output for the sample of calcium intakes

MINITAB

```
One-Sample Z: CALCI

Test of mu = 800  vs mu < 800
The assumed sigma = 188

Variable            N         Mean      StDev    SE Mean
CALCI              18        747.4      172.0       44.3

Variable     95.0% Upper Bound          Z          P
CALCI                   820.3       -1.19      0.118
```

EXCEL

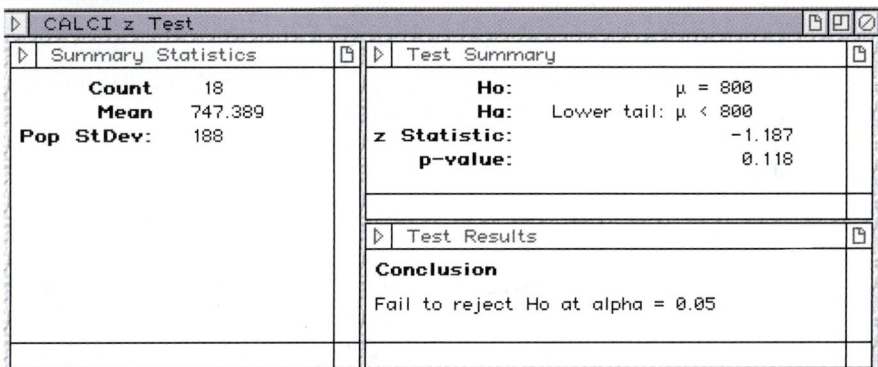

TI-83 PLUS

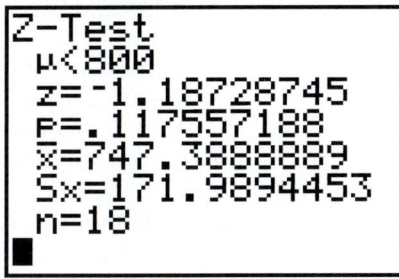
Using **Calculate**

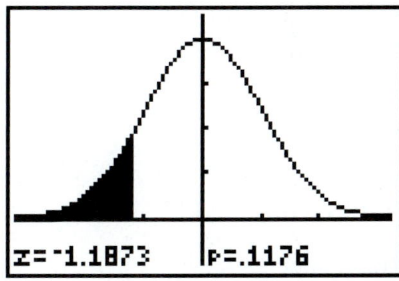
Using **Draw**

Exercises 9.4

Statistical Concepts and Skills

9.44 What is the *P*-value of a hypothesis test? When does it provide evidence against the null hypothesis?

9.45 We presented two different approaches to hypothesis testing. Identify and compare these two approaches.

9.46 Explain how the P-value is obtained for a one-sample z-test in case the hypothesis test is
a. left-tailed.   **b.** right-tailed.   **c.** two-tailed.

9.47 True or false: The P-value is the smallest significance level for which the observed sample data results in rejection of the null hypothesis.

9.48 In each part, we have given the significance level and P-value for a hypothesis test. For each case, decide whether the null hypothesis should be rejected.
a. $\alpha = 0.05$, $P = 0.06$
b. $\alpha = 0.10$, $P = 0.06$
c. $\alpha = 0.06$, $P = 0.06$

9.49 Which provides stronger evidence against the null hypothesis, a P-value of 0.02 or a P-value of 0.03? Explain your answer.

9.50 In each part, we have given the P-value for a hypothesis test. For each case, determine the strength of the evidence against the null hypothesis.
a. $P = 0.06$ **b.** $P = 0.35$
c. $P = 0.027$ **d.** $P = 0.004$

In Exercises 9.51–9.54, we have given the value obtained for the test statistic

$$z = \frac{\bar{x} - \mu_0}{\sigma/\sqrt{n}}$$

in a one-sample z-test for a population mean. We have also specified whether the test is two-tailed, left-tailed, or right-tailed. Determine the P-value in each case.

9.51 Right-tailed test:
a. $z = 2.03$ **b.** $z = -0.31$

9.52 Left-tailed test:
a. $z = -1.84$ **b.** $z = 1.25$

9.53 Two-tailed test:
a. $z = 3.08$ **b.** $z = -2.42$

9.54 Right-tailed test:
a. $z = 1.24$ **b.** $z = -0.69$

In Exercises 9.35–9.40 of Section 9.3, you were asked to use Procedure 9.1, which employs the critical-value approach to hypothesis testing, to perform a one-sample z-test for a population mean. Now, in Exercises 9.55–9.60, you are asked to use Procedure 9.2 on page 403, which employs the P-value approach to hypothesis testing, to perform those same hypothesis tests. In addition, use Table 9.10 on page 405 to assess the strength of the evidence against the null hypotheses.

9.55 Toxic Mushrooms? Refer to Exercise 9.5 on page 376. Here are the data obtained by the researchers.

| 0.24 | 0.59 | 0.62 | 0.16 | 0.77 | 1.33 |
| 0.92 | 0.19 | 0.33 | 0.25 | 0.59 | 0.32 |

At the 5% significance level, do the data provide sufficient evidence to conclude that the mean cadmium level in *Boletus pinicola* mushrooms is greater than the government's recommended limit of 0.5 ppm? Assume that the population standard deviation of cadmium levels in *Boletus pinicola* mushrooms is 0.37 ppm. (*Note:* The sum of the data is 6.31 ppm.)

9.56 Body Temperature. Refer to Exercise 9.6 on page 376. The researchers obtained the following body temperatures of 93 healthy humans.

98.0	97.6	98.8	98.0	98.8	98.8	97.6	98.6	98.6
98.8	98.0	98.2	98.0	98.0	97.0	97.2	98.2	98.1
98.2	98.5	98.5	99.0	98.0	97.0	97.3	97.3	98.1
97.8	99.0	97.6	97.4	98.0	97.4	98.0	98.6	98.6
98.4	97.0	98.4	99.0	98.0	99.4	97.8	98.2	99.2
99.0	97.7	98.2	98.2	98.8	98.1	98.5	97.2	98.5
99.2	98.3	98.7	98.8	98.6	98.0	99.1	97.2	97.6
97.9	98.8	98.6	98.6	99.3	97.8	98.7	99.3	97.8
98.4	97.7	98.3	97.7	97.1	98.4	98.6	97.4	96.7
96.9	98.4	98.2	98.6	97.0	97.4	98.4	97.4	96.8
98.2	97.4	98.0						

At the 1% significance level, do the data provide sufficient evidence to conclude that the mean body temperature of healthy humans differs from 98.6°F? Assume that $\sigma = 0.63$°F. (*Note:* The sum of the 93 temperatures is 9125.5°F.)

9.57 Cell Phones. Refer to Exercise 9.7 on page 377. Following are last year's local monthly bills, in dollars, for a random sample of 50 cell phone users.

33.21	31.42	16.46	104.53	47.98
117.29	62.30	44.07	13.85	15.70
30.42	14.95	27.43	29.13	42.37
17.26	61.64	15.83	32.81	22.76
45.00	35.97	20.28	29.28	46.87
28.41	89.28	23.78	31.93	48.65
65.01	50.81	46.57	35.93	24.86
16.50	16.74	42.13	25.07	77.54
28.37	16.89	49.68	45.15	15.45
58.00	13.81	81.49	51.95	127.17

At the 1% significance level, do the data provide sufficient evidence to conclude that last year's mean local monthly bill for cell phone users has decreased from the 1996 mean of $47.70? Assume that $\sigma = \$25$. (*Note:* The sum of the 50 cell phone bills is $2069.98.)

9.58 Iron Deficiency? Refer to Exercise 9.8 on page 377. The following iron intakes, in milligrams, were obtained during a 24-hour period for 45 randomly selected adult females under the age of 51.

15.0	18.1	14.4	14.6	10.9	18.1	18.2	18.3	15.0
16.0	12.6	16.6	20.7	19.8	11.6	12.8	15.6	11.0
15.3	9.4	19.5	18.3	14.5	16.6	11.5	16.4	12.5
14.6	11.9	12.5	18.6	13.1	12.1	10.7	17.3	12.4
17.0	6.3	16.8	12.5	16.3	14.7	12.7	16.3	11.5

At the 1% significance level, do the data suggest that adult females under the age of 51 are, on average, getting less than the RDA of 18 mg of iron? Assume that the population standard deviation is 4.2 mg. (*Note:* $\bar{x} = 14.68$ mg.)

9.59 Beer Drinking. From Exercise 9.9, the mean annual consumption of beer per person in the United States is 22.0 gallons (roughly 235 twelve-ounce bottles). A random sample of 300 Washington, D.C., residents yielded a mean annual beer consumption of 27.8 gallons. At the 10% significance level, do the data provide sufficient evidence to conclude that the mean annual consumption of beer per person for the nation's capital differs from the national mean? Assume that the standard deviation of annual beer consumptions for Washington, D.C., residents is 55 gallons.

9.60 Hospital Costs. From Exercise 9.10, the mean cost to community hospitals per patient per day in U.S. hospitals was $1033 in 1997. In that same year, a random sample of 30 daily costs in Ohio hospitals had a mean of $1123. Assuming a population standard deviation of $350 for Ohio hospitals, do the data provide sufficient evidence to conclude that, in 1997, the mean cost in Ohio hospitals exceeded the national mean of $1033? Perform the required hypothesis test at the 5% significance level.

Extending the Concepts and Skills

9.61 Consider a one-sample z-test for a population mean. Denote z_0 as the observed value of the test statistic z. If the test is right-tailed, then the P-value can be expressed as $P(z \geq z_0)$. Determine the corresponding expression for the P-value if the test is
a. left-tailed.   **b.** two-tailed.

9.62 The symbol $\Phi(z)$ is often used to denote the area under the standard normal curve that lies to the left of a specified value of z. Consider a one-sample z-test for a population mean. Denote z_0 as the observed value of the test statistic z. Express the P-value of the hypothesis test in terms of Φ if the test is
a. left-tailed.   **b.** right-tailed.   **c.** two-tailed.

9.63 Obtaining the P-value. Let x denote the test statistic for a hypothesis test and x_0 its observed value. Then the P-value of the hypothesis test equals
a. $P(x \geq x_0)$ for a right-tailed test,
b. $P(x \leq x_0)$ for a left-tailed test,
c. $2 \cdot \min\{P(x \leq x_0), P(x \geq x_0)\}$ for a two-tailed test,
where the probabilities are computed under the assumption that the null hypothesis is true. Suppose that you are considering a one-sample z-test for a population mean. Verify that the probability expressions in parts (a)–(c) are equivalent to those obtained in Exercise 9.61.

9.64 Discuss the relative advantages and disadvantages of using the P-value approach to hypothesis testing instead of the critical-value approach.

Using Technology

9.65 Use the technology of your choice to perform the hypothesis test in Exercise 9.55.

9.66 Use the technology of your choice to perform the hypothesis test in Exercise 9.56.

9.67 A 1998 issue of *Habitat World*, the publication of Habitat for Humanity International, contains an article on housing affordability. Included in the article is a table of 1997 fair market rents (FMR) for two-bedroom units, by state, obtained from the National Low Income Housing Coalition. According to the table, the 1997 FMR for Maine is $590. A sample of 32 randomly selected two-bedroom units in Maine yielded the following data on monthly rents.

289	597	648	669	745	577	626	661
657	595	604	739	598	545	696	450
521	669	656	565	610	503	589	472
675	586	663	609	560	507	643	749

At the 5% significance level, do the data provide sufficient evidence to conclude that the mean monthly rent for two-bedroom units in Maine differs from the FMR of $590? Assume that the standard deviation of monthly rents for two-bedroom units in Maine is $73.10.
a. Use the technology of your choice to identify potential outliers, if any.

b. Use the technology of your choice to perform the required hypothesis test, using the unabridged sample data.

c. Remove observations that are potential outliers, if any, and perform the required hypothesis test, using the abridged sample data.

d. Comment on the effect that removing the potential outliers has on the hypothesis test.

e. State your conclusion regarding the hypothesis test and explain your answer.

9.5 HYPOTHESIS TESTS FOR ONE POPULATION MEAN WHEN σ IS UNKNOWN

In Section 9.3, you learned how to perform a hypothesis test for one population mean when the population standard deviation, σ, is known. However, as we have mentioned, the population standard deviation is usually not known.

To develop a hypothesis-testing procedure for a population mean when σ is unknown, we begin by recalling Key Fact 8.5: If a variable x of a population is normally distributed with mean μ, then, for samples of size n, the studentized version of $\bar{x}$,

$$t = \frac{\bar{x} - \mu}{s/\sqrt{n}},$$

has the t-distribution with $n - 1$ degrees of freedom.

Because of Key Fact 8.5, we can perform a hypothesis test for a population mean when the population standard deviation is unknown by proceeding in essentially the same way as when it is known. The only difference is that we invoke a t-distribution instead of the standard normal distribution—that is, we employ the variable

$$t = \frac{\bar{x} - \mu_0}{s/\sqrt{n}}$$

as our test statistic and use the t-table, Table IV, to obtain the critical value(s) or P-value. We refer to this hypothesis-testing procedure as the **one-sample t-test** or, simply, as the **t-test**.

P-VALUES FOR A t-TEST

Before presenting a step-by-step procedure for conducting a (one-sample) t-test, we need to discuss P-values for such a test. P-values for a t-test are obtained in a manner similar to that for a z-test.

As we have just shown, the test statistic for a one-sample t-test for a population mean with null hypothesis H_0: $\mu = \mu_0$ is

$$t = \frac{\bar{x} - \mu_0}{s/\sqrt{n}}.$$

If the null hypothesis is true, this test statistic has the t-distribution with $n - 1$ degrees of freedom, and its probabilities equal areas under the t-curve with df $= n - 1$.

If we let t_0 be the observed value of the test statistic t, we obtain the P-value as follows.

9.5 Hypothesis Tests for One Population Mean When σ is Unknown

- *Two-tailed test:* The P-value is the probability of observing a value of the test statistic t at least as large in magnitude as the value actually observed, which is the area under the t-curve that lies outside the interval from $-|t_0|$ to $|t_0|$, as shown in Fig. 9.18(a).
- *Left-tailed test:* The P-value is the probability of observing a value of the test statistic t as small as or smaller than the value actually observed, which is the area under the t-curve that lies to the left of t_0, as shown in Fig. 9.18(b).
- *Right-tailed test:* The P-value is the probability of observing a value of the test statistic t as large as or larger than the value actually observed, which is the area under the t-curve that lies to the right of t_0, as shown in Fig. 9.18(c).

FIGURE 9.18
P-value for a t-test if the test is (a) two-tailed, (b) left-tailed, or (c) right-tailed

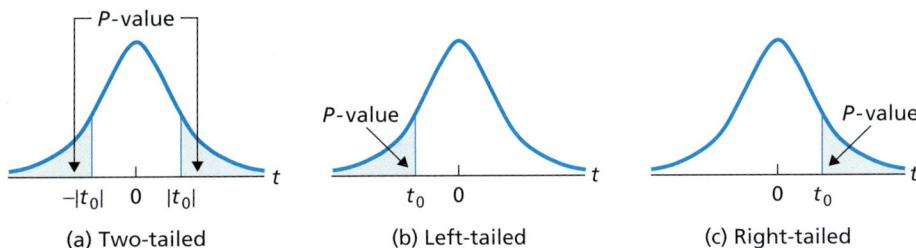

ESTIMATING THE P-VALUE OF A t-TEST

To obtain the exact P-value of a t-test, we need to use a computer with statistical software or a statistical calculator. However, we can use t-tables, such as Table IV, to estimate the P-value of a t-test, and an estimate of the P-value is usually sufficient for deciding whether to reject the null hypothesis.

For instance, consider a right-tailed t-test with $n = 15$, $\alpha = 0.05$, and a value of the test statistic of $t = 3.458$. For df $= 15 - 1 = 14$, the t-value 3.458 is larger than any t-value in Table IV, the largest one being $t_{0.005} = 2.977$ (which means that the area under the t-curve that lies to the right of 2.977 equals 0.005). This fact, in turn, implies that the area to the right of 3.458 is less than 0.005; in other words, $P < 0.005$. Because the P-value is less than the designated significance level of 0.05, we reject H_0.

Example 9.14 provides two more illustrations of how Table IV can be used to estimate the P-value of a t-test.

Example 9.14 Using Table IV to Estimate the P-Value of a t-Test

Use Table IV to estimate the P-value of each t-test.

a. Left-tailed test, $n = 12$, and $t = -1.938$
b. Two-tailed test, $n = 25$, and $t = -0.895$

Solution **a.** Because the test is left-tailed, the P-value is the area under the t-curve with df $= 12 - 1 = 11$ that lies to the left of -1.938, as depicted in Fig. 9.19(a).

A t-curve is symmetric about 0, so the area to the left of -1.938 equals the area to the right of 1.938, and we can use Table IV to estimate this latter area. Concentrating on the df $= 11$ row of Table IV, we search for the two t-values that straddle 1.938; we find that they are $t_{0.05} = 1.796$ and $t_{0.025} = 2.201$.

FIGURE 9.19
Estimating the P-value of a left-tailed t-test with a sample size of 12 and test statistic $t = -1.938$

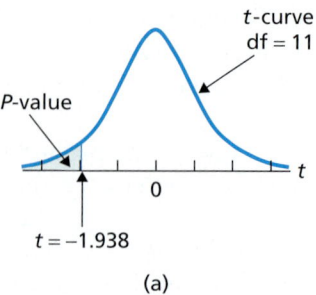
(a)

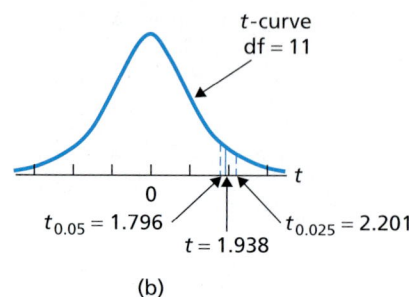
(b)

These values imply that the area under the t-curve that lies to the right of 1.938 is somewhere between 0.025 and 0.05, as depicted in Fig. 9.19(b).

Consequently, the area under the t-curve that lies to the left of -1.938 is also somewhere between 0.025 and 0.05, which means that $0.025 < P < 0.05$. Hence we can reject H_0 at any significance level of 0.05 or larger, and we cannot reject H_0 at any significance level of 0.025 or smaller. For significance levels between 0.025 and 0.05, Table IV is not sufficiently detailed to help us to decide whether to reject H_0.[3]

b. Because the test is two-tailed, the P-value is the area under the t-curve with $df = 25 - 1 = 24$ that lies either to the left of -0.895 or to the right of 0.895, as depicted in Fig. 9.20(a).

FIGURE 9.20
Estimating the P-value of a two-tailed t-test with a sample size of 25 and test statistic $t = -0.895$

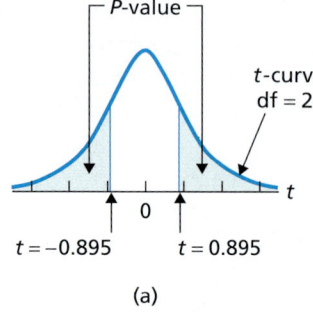
(a)

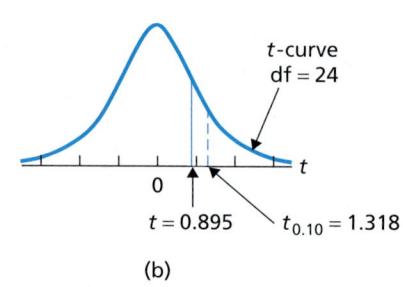
(b)

Because a t-curve is symmetric about 0, the area to the left of -0.895 and the area to the right of 0.895 are equal. Concentrating on the $df = 24$ row of Table IV, we find that 0.895 is smaller than any t-value in the table, the smallest being $t_{0.10} = 1.318$. This fact implies that the area under the t-curve that lies to the right of 0.895 is greater than 0.10, as depicted in Fig. 9.20(b).

Consequently, the area under the t-curve that lies either to the left of -0.895 or to the right of 0.895 is greater than 0.20, which means that $P > 0.20$. Hence we cannot reject H_0 at any significance level of 0.20 or smaller. For significance levels larger than 0.20, Table IV is not sufficiently detailed to help us to decide whether to reject H_0. ◆

We now present two step-by-step procedures for performing a one-sample t-test. Procedure 9.3A covers the critical-value approach, and Procedure 9.3B covers the P-value approach.

---

[3]This latter case provides an example of a P-value estimate that is not good enough. In such cases, use a computer with statistical software or a statistical calculator to obtain the exact P-value.

Procedure 9.3A The One-Sample t-Test for a Population Mean (Critical-Value Approach)

Assumptions
1. Normal population or large sample
2. σ unknown

Step 1 The null hypothesis is $H_0: \mu = \mu_0$, and the alternative hypothesis is

$$H_a: \mu \neq \mu_0 \quad \text{or} \quad H_a: \mu < \mu_0 \quad \text{or} \quad H_a: \mu > \mu_0$$
$$\text{(Two-tailed)} \qquad\qquad \text{(Left-tailed)} \qquad\qquad \text{(Right-tailed)}$$

Step 2 Decide on the significance level, α.

Step 3 Compute the value of the test statistic

$$t = \frac{\bar{x} - \mu_0}{s/\sqrt{n}}.$$

Step 4 The critical value(s) are

$$\pm t_{\alpha/2} \quad \text{or} \quad -t_\alpha \quad \text{or} \quad t_\alpha$$
$$\text{(Two-tailed)} \qquad \text{(Left-tailed)} \qquad \text{(Right-tailed)}$$

with df $= n - 1$. Use Table IV to find the critical value(s).

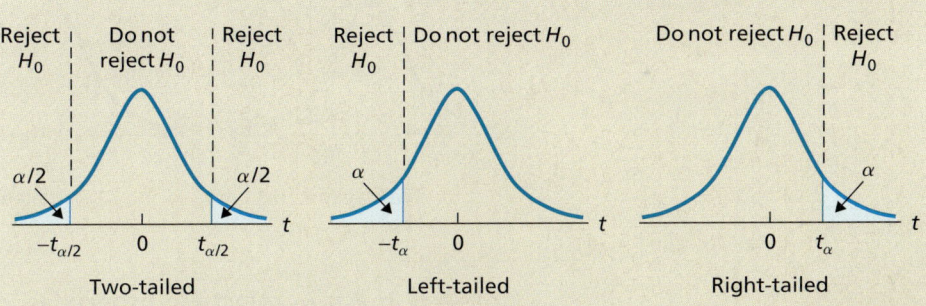

Step 5 If the value of the test statistic falls in the rejection region, reject H_0; otherwise, do not reject H_0.

Step 6 Interpret the results of the hypothesis test.

The hypothesis test is exact for normal populations and is approximately correct for large samples from nonnormal populations.

Before applying Procedure 9.3 (A or B), we need to make several comments. Although derivation of the t-test is based on the assumption that the variable under consideration is normally distributed (normal population), it also applies

Procedure 9.3B The One-Sample t-Test for a Population Mean (P-Value Approach)

Assumptions
1. Normal population or large sample
2. σ unknown

Step 1 The null hypothesis is $H_0: \mu = \mu_0$, and the alternative hypothesis is

$H_a: \mu \neq \mu_0$ or $H_a: \mu < \mu_0$ or $H_a: \mu > \mu_0$
(Two-tailed)   (Left-tailed)   (Right-tailed)

Step 2 Decide on the significance level, α.

Step 3 Compute the value of the test statistic

$$t = \frac{\bar{x} - \mu_0}{s/\sqrt{n}}$$

and denote that value t_0.

Step 4 The t-statistic has df $= n - 1$. Use Table IV to estimate the P-value, or obtain it exactly by using technology.

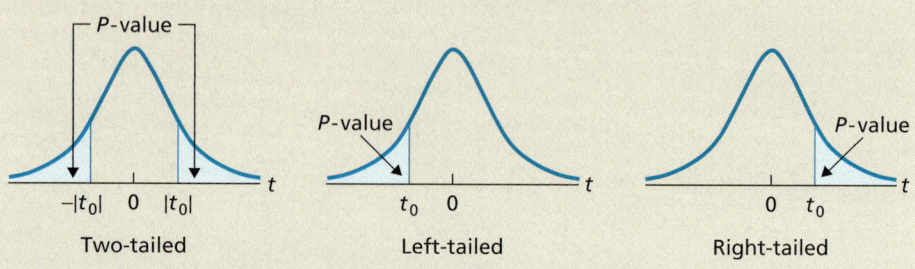

Step 5 If $P \leq \alpha$, reject H_0; otherwise, do not reject H_0.

Step 6 Interpret the results of the hypothesis test.

The hypothesis test is exact for normal populations and is approximately correct for large samples from nonnormal populations.

approximately for large samples regardless of the distribution of the variable under consideration, as noted at the end of Procedure 9.3.

Actually, like the z-test, the t-test works reasonably well even when the variable under consideration is not normally distributed and the sample size is small or moderate, provided the variable is not too far from being normally distributed. In other words, the t-test is robust to moderate violations of the normality assumption.

9.5 Hypothesis Tests for One Population Mean When σ is Unknown

When considering the *t*-test, you must also watch for outliers. Again, the presence of outliers calls into question the normality assumption. Moreover, even for large samples, outliers can sometimes unduly affect a *t*-test because the sample mean and sample standard deviation are not resistant to outliers.

Guidelines for use of the *t*-test are the same as those given for the *z*-test in Key Fact 9.4 on page 390. Remember, always look at the data before applying the *t*-test to ensure that it is reasonable to use it. Example 9.15 illustrates use of Procedure 9.3.

Example 9.15 The One-Sample t-Test

Acid Rain and Lake Acidity Acid rain from the burning of fossil fuels has caused many of the lakes around the world to become acidic. The biology in these lakes often collapses because of the rapid and unfavorable changes in water chemistry. A lake is classified as nonacidic if it has a pH greater than 6.

Aldo Marchetto and Andrea Lami measured the pH of high mountain lakes in the Southern Alps and reported their findings in the paper "Reconstruction of pH by Chrysophycean Scales in Some Lakes of the Southern Alps (*Hydrobiologia*, 1994, Vol. 274, pp. 83–90). Table 9.11 shows the pH levels obtained by the researchers for 15 lakes. At the 5% significance level, do the data provide sufficient evidence to conclude that, on average, high mountain lakes in the Southern Alps are nonacidic?

Solution A normal probability plot (not shown) of the data in Table 9.11 reveals no outliers and is quite linear. Consequently, we can apply Procedure 9.3 to conduct the required hypothesis test.

TABLE 9.11
pH levels for 15 lakes

7.2	7.3	6.1	6.9	6.6
7.3	6.3	5.5	6.3	6.5
5.7	6.9	6.7	7.9	5.8

Step 1 State the null and alternative hypotheses.

Let μ denote the mean pH level of all high mountain lakes in the Southern Alps. Then the null and alternative hypotheses are

$H_0: \mu = 6$ (mean pH level is not greater than 6)

$H_a: \mu > 6$ (mean pH level is greater than 6).

Note that the hypothesis test is right-tailed because a greater-than sign ($>$) appears in the alternative hypothesis.

Step 2 Decide on the significance level, α.

We are to perform the test at the 5% significance level, so $\alpha = 0.05$.

Step 3 Compute the value of the test statistic

$$t = \frac{\bar{x} - \mu_0}{s/\sqrt{n}}.$$

We have $\mu_0 = 6$ and $n = 15$ and calculate the mean and standard deviation of the sample data in Table 9.11 as 6.6 and 0.672, respectively. Hence the value of the test statistic is

$$t = \frac{6.6 - 6}{0.672/\sqrt{15}} = 3.458.$$

Critical-Value Approach

Step 4 The critical value for a right-tailed test is t_α, with df $= n - 1$.

We have $n = 15$ and $\alpha = 0.05$. Table IV shows that for df $= 15 - 1 = 14$, $t_{0.05} = 1.761$, as shown in Fig. 9.21A.

FIGURE 9.21A

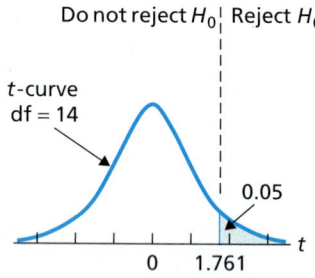

Step 5 If the value of the test statistic falls in the rejection region, reject H_0; otherwise, do not reject H_0.

The value of the test statistic, found in Step 3, is $t = 3.458$. Figure 9.21A reveals that it falls in the rejection region. Consequently, we reject H_0. The test results are statistically significant at the 5% level.

P-Value Approach

Step 4 The t-statistic has df $= n - 1$. Use Table IV to estimate the P-value, or obtain it exactly by using technology.

From Step 3, the value of the test statistic is $t = 3.458$. The test is right-tailed, so the P-value is the probability of observing a value of t of 3.458 or greater if the null hypothesis is true. That probability equals the shaded area in Fig. 9.21B.

FIGURE 9.21B

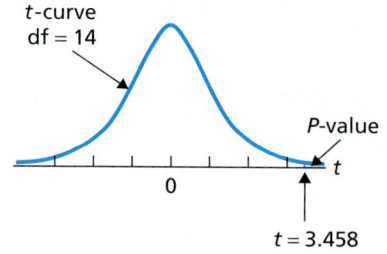

We have $n = 15$, and so df $= 15 - 1 = 14$. From Fig. 9.21B and Table IV, $P < 0.005$. (Using technology, we obtain $P = 0.00192$.)

Step 5 If $P \leq \alpha$, reject H_0; otherwise, do not reject H_0.

From Step 4, $P < 0.005$. Because the P-value is less than the specified significance level of 0.05, we reject H_0. The test results are statistically significant at the 5% level and (see Table 9.10 on page 405) provide very strong evidence against the null hypothesis.

Step 6 Interpret the results of the hypothesis test.

What Does it Mean? At the 5% significance level, the data provide sufficient evidence to conclude that, on average, high mountain lakes in the Southern Alps are nonacidic.

WHAT IF THE ASSUMPTIONS ARE NOT SATISFIED?

You have now learned two methods for performing a hypothesis test for a population mean. If the population standard deviation is known, you can use the z-test; if the population standard deviation is unknown, you can use the t-test.

But both of these procedures have another assumption for their use—the variable under consideration should be approximately normally distributed or the sample size should be relatively large and, for small samples, both procedures should be avoided in the presence of outliers. (Refer to Key Fact 9.4 on page 390 for general guidelines.)

So, then, suppose that you want to perform a hypothesis test for a population mean based on a small sample but that preliminary data analyses indicate either the presence of outliers or that the variable under consideration is far from being normally distributed. As neither the z-test nor the t-test is appropriate, what can you do?

Under certain conditions, you can use a nonparametric method. For instance, if the variable under consideration has a symmetric distribution, then you can use a nonparametric method called the *one-sample Wilcoxon signed-rank test* to perform a hypothesis test for the mean of the population.

As we said earlier, although most nonparametric methods have some assumptions for their use, they do not require even approximate normality, are resistant to outliers and other extreme values, and can be applied regardless of sample size. However, parametric methods (such as the z-test and t-test) tend to give more accurate results than nonparametric methods when the normality assumption and other requirements for their use are met.

We will not cover nonparametric methods in this book. But many basic statistics books do discuss them. See, for example, *Introductory Statistics*, 6th edition, by Neil A. Weiss (Boston: Addison-Wesley, 2002).

The Technology Center

Most statistical technologies have programs that automatically perform a one-sample t-test for a population mean. In this subsection, we present output and (optional) step-by-step instructions to implement such programs.

Example 9.16 Using Technology to Conduct a t-Test

Acid Rain and Lake Acidity Table 9.11 on page 415 displays the pH levels of a sample of 15 lakes in the Southern Alps. Use Minitab, Excel, or the TI-83 Plus to perform the hypothesis test in Example 9.15 on page 415.

Solution Let μ denote the mean pH level of all high mountain lakes in the Southern Alps. The problem is to perform the hypothesis test

$$H_0: \mu = 6 \text{ (mean pH level is not greater than 6)}$$

$$H_a: \mu > 6 \text{ (mean pH level is greater than 6)}$$

at the 5% significance level ($\alpha = 0.05$). Note that the hypothesis test is right-tailed because a greater-than sign (>) appears in the alternative hypothesis.

PRINTOUT 9.2
One-sample t-test output for the sample of pH levels

MINITAB

One-Sample T: PH

Test of mu = 6 vs mu > 6

Variable	N	Mean	StDev	SE Mean
PH	15	6.600	0.672	0.173

Variable	95.0% Lower Bound	T	P
PH	6.294	3.46	0.002

EXCEL

PH t Test

Summary Statistics
- Count 15
- Mean 6.6
- Std Dev 0.672
- Std Error 0.173

Test Summary
- Ho: $\mu = 6$
- Ha: Upper tail: $\mu > 6$
- df: 14
- t Statistic: 3.459
- p-value: 0.00192

Test Results
Conclusion
Reject Ho at alpha = 0.05

TI-83 PLUS

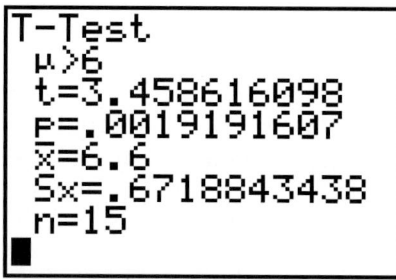

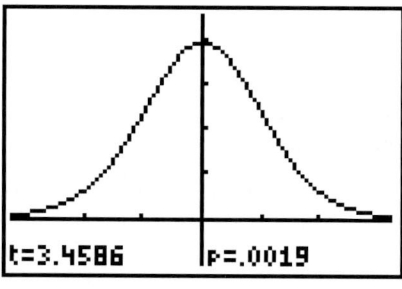

Using **Calculate**   Using **Draw**

Printout 9.2 shows the output obtained by applying the one-sample t-test programs to the pH data contained in Table 9.11.

From the outputs in Printout 9.2, the P-value for the hypothesis test is 0.002. The P-value is less than the specified significance level of 0.05, so we reject H_0. The test results are statistically significant at the 5% level. That is, at the 5% significance level, the data provide sufficient evidence to conclude that, on average, high mountain lakes in the Southern Alps are nonacidic. ◆

9.5 Hypothesis Tests for One Population Mean When σ is Unknown

Obtaining the Output (Optional)

Printout 9.2 provides output from Minitab, Excel, and the TI-83 Plus for a one-sample *t*-test based on the sample of pH levels presented in Table 9.11. The following are detailed instructions for obtaining that output. First, we store the pH data in a column (Minitab), range (Excel), or list (TI-83 Plus) named PH. Then, we proceed as follows.

MINITAB
1. Choose **Stat ➤ Basic Statistics ➤ 1-Sample t...**
2. Specify PH in the **Variables** text box
3. Click in the **Test mean** text box and type 6
4. Click the **Options...** button
5. Click the arrow button at the right of the **Alternative** drop-down list box and select **greater than**
6. Click **OK**
7. Click **OK**

EXCEL
1. Choose **DDXL ➤ Hypothesis Tests**
2. Select **1 Var t Test** from the **Function type** drop-down box
3. Specify PH in the **Quantitative Variable** text box
4. Click **OK**
5. Click the **Set μ_0** button and type 6
6. Click **OK**
7. Click the **0.05** button
8. Click the **$\mu > \mu_0$** button
9. Click the **Compute** button

TI-83 PLUS
1. Press **STAT**, arrow over to **TESTS**, and press 2
2. Highlight **Data** and press **ENTER**
3. Press the down-arrow key, type 6 for μ_0, and press **ENTER**
4. Press **2nd ➤ LIST**
5. Arrow down to PH and press **ENTER** three times
6. Highlight $> \mu_0$ and press **ENTER**
7. Press the down-arrow key, highlight **Calculate** or **Draw**, and press **ENTER**

Exercises 9.5

Statistical Concepts and Skills

9.68 What is the difference in assumptions between the one-sample *t*-test and the one-sample *z*-test?

Preliminary data analyses indicate that you can reasonably use a t-test to conduct each of the hypothesis tests required in Exercises 9.69–9.74. Perform each t-test, using either the critical-value approach or the P-value approach. Comment on the practical significance of those tests whose results are statistically significant.

9.69 Apparel and Services. According to the document *Consumer Expenditures*, a publication of the U.S. Bureau of Labor Statistics, the average consumer unit spent $1729 on apparel and services in 1997. That same year, 36 consumer units in the Midwest had the following annual expenditures, in dollars, on apparel and services.

2220	1646	2072	2172	2125	2036
1310	1540	2182	1842	1470	973
1624	1882	1419	1644	1896	1783
1854	1280	1397	1602	1599	1742
1067	1697	2118	1276	1843	2297
1555	1691	1323	1003	1483	1353

At the 5% significance level, do the data provide sufficient evidence to conclude that the 1997 mean annual expenditure on apparel and services for consumer units in the Midwest differed from the national mean of $1729? (*Note:* The sample mean and sample standard deviation of the data are $1667.11 and $351.69, respectively.)

9.70 Stressed-Out Bus Drivers. Previous studies have shown that urban bus drivers have an extremely stressful job and that a large proportion of drivers retire prematurely with disabilities due to occupational stress. These stresses come from a combination of physical and social sources such as traffic congestion, incessant time pressure, and unruly passengers. A recent paper, "Hassles on the Job: A Study of a Job Intervention With Urban Bus Drivers" by G. Evans et al. (*Journal of Organizational Behavior*, 1999, Vol. 20, pp. 199–208), examined the effects of an intervention program to improve the conditions of urban bus drivers. Among other variables, the researchers monitored diastolic blood pressure of bus drivers in downtown Stockholm, Sweden. The following data, in millimeters of mercury (mm Hg), are based on the blood pressures obtained prior to intervention for the 41 bus drivers in the study.

95	58	99	81	85	81	84
77	79	100	83	89	73	79
80	70	90	74	79	76	65
91	88	83	90	93	69	89
95	80	70	66	90	94	93
77	81	75	95	73	63	

At the 10% significance level, do the data provide sufficient evidence to conclude that the mean diastolic blood pressure of bus drivers in Stockholm, Sweden exceeds the normal diastolic blood pressure of 80 mm Hg? (*Note:* The sample mean and sample standard deviation of the data are 81.76 mm Hg and 10.32 mm Hg, respectively.)

9.71 Brewery Effluent and Crops. Because many industrial wastes contain nutrients that enhance crop growth, efforts are being made for environmental purposes to use such wastes on agricultural soils. Two researchers, Mohammad Ajmal and Ahsan Ullah Khan, reported their findings on experiments with brewery wastes used for agricultural purposes in the article "Effects of Brewery Effluent on Agricultural Soil and Crop Plants" (*Environmental Pollution (Series A)*, 33, pp. 341–351). The researchers studied the physico-chemical properties of effluent from Mohan Meakin Breweries Ltd. (MMBL), Ghazibad, UP, India, and "…its effects on the physico-chemical characteristics of agricultural soil, seed germination pattern, and the growth of two common crop plants." They assessed the impact of using different concentrations of the effluent: 25%, 50%, 75%, and 100%. The following data, based on the results of the study, provide the percentages of limestone in the soil obtained by using 100% effluent.

2.41	2.31	2.54	2.28	2.72
2.60	2.51	2.51	2.42	2.70

Do the data provide sufficient evidence to conclude, at the 1% level of significance, that the mean available limestone in soil treated with 100% MMBL effluent exceeds 2.30%, the percentage ordinarily found? (*Note:* $\bar{x} = 2.5$ and $s = 0.149$.)

9.72 TV Viewing. According to Nielsen Media Research, in 1998, during the time slot from 8:00 P.M. to 11:00 P.M., the average person watched 7 hours and 43 minutes of TV per week. A random sample of 40 women in the age group 18–24 years yielded the following TV-viewing times, rounded to the nearest 10 minutes, during that same time slot.

0	110	790	450	0	750	550	510
130	160	510	70	740	550	350	120
710	310	580	260	240	130	190	240
120	240	240	540	430	350	50	240
680	400	450	340	10	440	330	420

Do the data provide sufficient evidence to conclude that, during the time slot from 8:00 P.M. to 11:00 P.M., women in the age group 18–24 years watched less TV on average than people in general? Perform the hypothesis test at the 1% significance level. (*Note:* $\bar{x} = 343.25$ and $s = 222.2$.)

9.73 Banana Prices. The average retail price for bananas in 1998 was 51.0 cents per pound, as reported by the U.S. Department of Agriculture in *Food Cost Review*. Recently, a random sample of 15 markets gave the following prices for bananas in cents per pound.

56	53	55	53	50
57	58	54	48	47
50	57	57	51	55

Can you conclude that the current mean retail price for bananas is different from the 1998 mean of 51.0 cents per pound? Use $\alpha = 0.05$. (*Note:* $\bar{x} = 53.4$ and $s = 3.5$.)

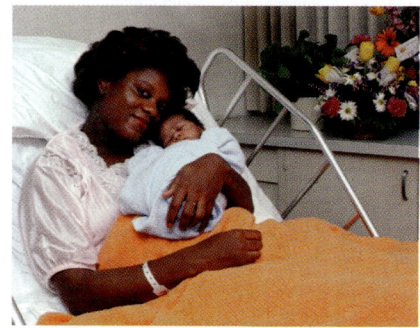

9.74 Active Management of Labor. Having a baby in a U.S. hospital costs $2528, on average. Active management of labor (AML) is a group of interventions designed to help reduce the length of labor and the rate of cesarean deliveries. Physicians from the Department of Obstetrics and Gynecology at the University of New Mexico Health Sciences Center were interested in determining whether AML would also translate into a reduced cost for delivery. The results of their study can be found in Rogers et al., "Active Management of Labor: A Cost Analysis of a Randomized Controlled Trial" *Western Journal of Medicine*, 2000, Vol. 172, pp. 240–243). According to the article, 200 AML deliveries had a mean cost of $2480 with a standard deviation of $766.

At the 5% significance level, do the data provide sufficient evidence to conclude that, on average, AML reduces the cost of having a baby in a U.S. hospital?

Each of Exercises 9.75–9.82 includes a normal probability plot and either a stem-and-leaf diagram or a frequency histogram for a set of sample data. The intent is to employ the sample data to perform a hypothesis test for the mean of the population from which the data were obtained. In each case, consult the graphs provided to decide whether it is reasonable to use the z-test, the t-test, or neither. Explain your answers.

9.75 The normal probability plot and stem-and-leaf diagram of the data are shown in Fig. 9.22. σ is known.

9.76 The normal probability plot and histogram of the data are shown in Fig. 9.23. σ is known.

9.77 The normal probability plot and histogram of the data are shown in Fig. 9.24. σ is unknown.

9.78 The normal probability plot and stem-and-leaf diagram of the data are shown in Fig. 9.25. σ is unknown.

9.79 The normal probability plot and stem-and-leaf diagram of the data are shown in Fig. 9.26. σ is unknown.

9.80 The normal probability plot and stem-and-leaf diagram of the data are shown in Fig. 9.27. σ is unknown. (*Note:* The decimal parts of the observations were removed before the stem-and-leaf diagram was constructed.)

9.81 The normal probability plot and stem-and-leaf diagram of the data are shown in Fig. 9.28. σ is known.

9.82 The normal probability plot and stem-and-leaf diagram of the data are shown in Fig. 9.29. σ is known.

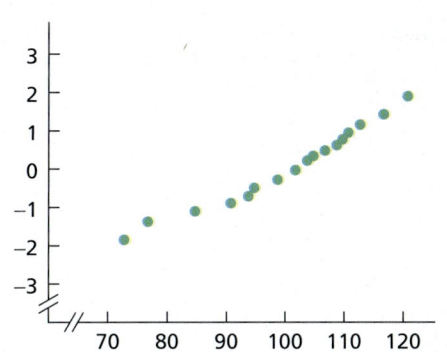
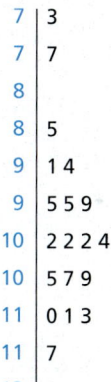

FIGURE 9.22
Normal probability plot and stem-and-leaf diagram for Exercise 9.75

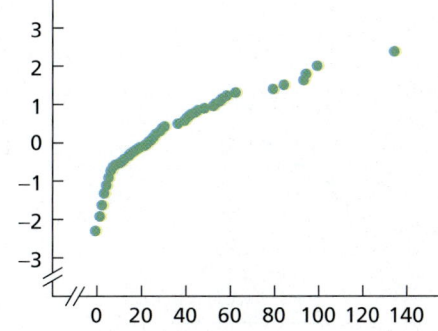
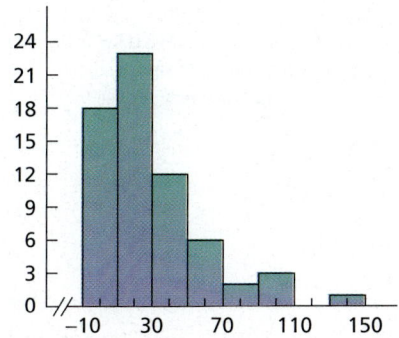

FIGURE 9.23
Normal probability plot and histogram for Exercise 9.76

FIGURE 9.24
Normal probability plot and histogram for Exercise 9.77

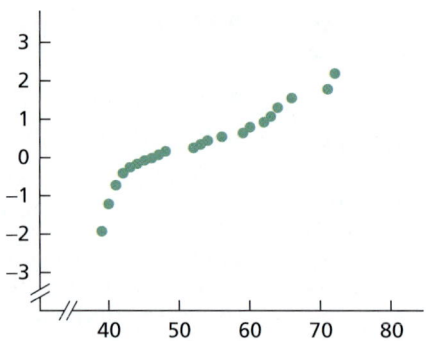 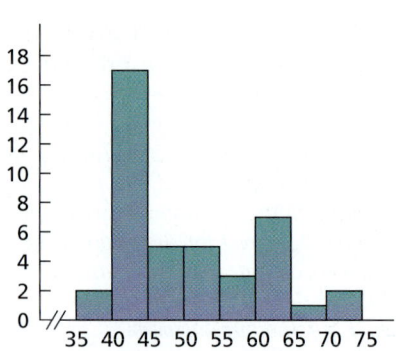

FIGURE 9.25
Normal probability plot and stem-and-leaf diagram for Exercise 9.78

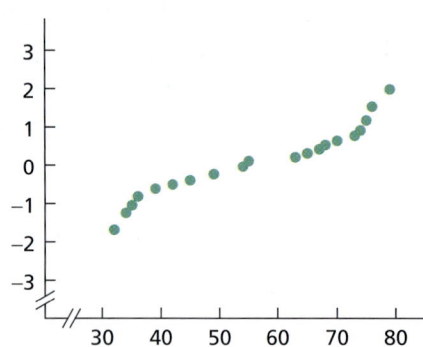 

FIGURE 9.26
Normal probability plot and stem-and-leaf diagram for Exercise 9.79

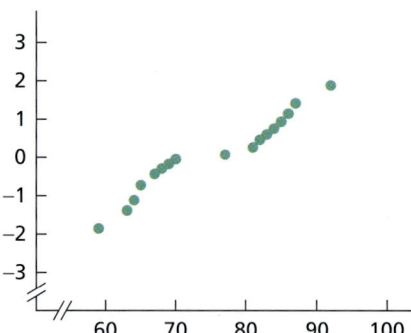 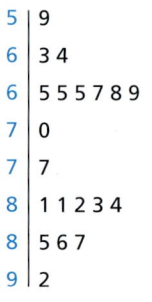

FIGURE 9.27
Normal probability plot and stem-and-leaf diagram for Exercise 9.80

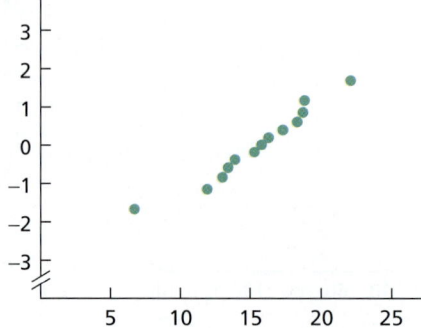 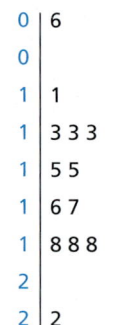

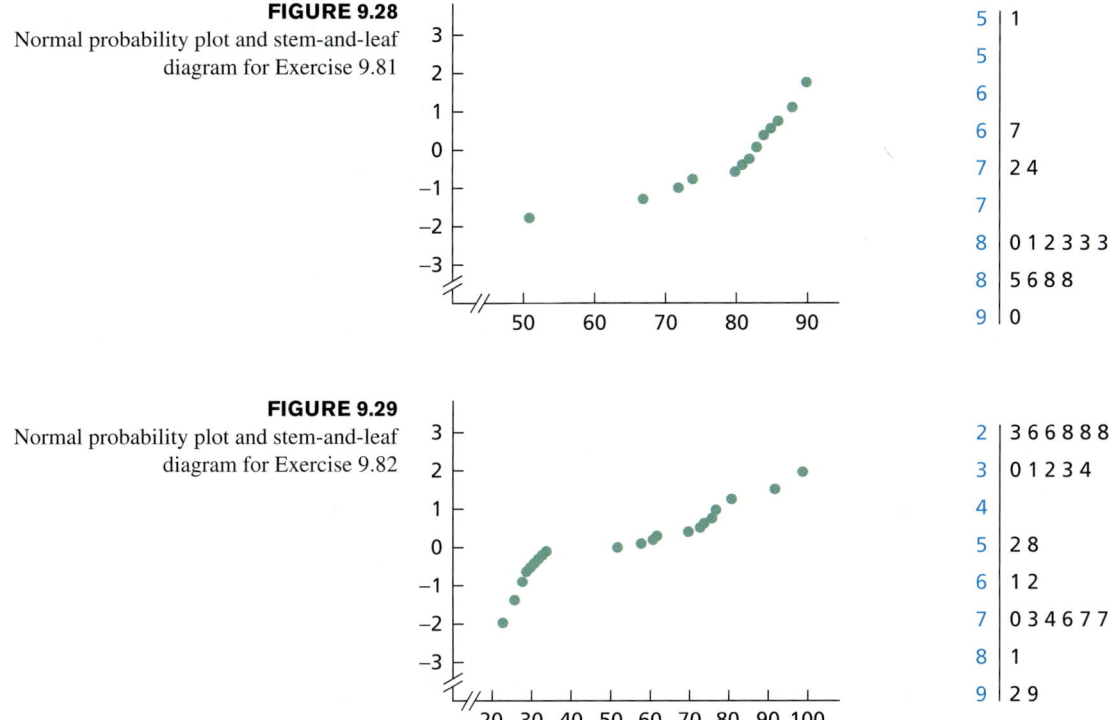

FIGURE 9.28
Normal probability plot and stem-and-leaf diagram for Exercise 9.81

```
5 | 1
5 |
6 |
6 | 7
7 | 2 4
7 |
8 | 0 1 2 3 3 3 4
8 | 5 6 8 8
9 | 0
```

FIGURE 9.29
Normal probability plot and stem-and-leaf diagram for Exercise 9.82

```
2 | 3 6 6 8 8 8 9
3 | 0 1 2 3 4
4 |
5 | 2 8
6 | 1 2
7 | 0 3 4 6 7 7
8 | 1
9 | 2 9
```

Extending the Concepts and Skills

9.83 Refer to Exercises 9.75–9.82. In each case, consult the graphs provided to decide whether it is reasonable to use the one-sample Wilcoxon signed-rank test to perform a hypothesis test for the mean of the population from which the data were obtained. Explain your answers.

9.84 Suppose that you want to perform a hypothesis test for a population mean. Assume that the variable under consideration is normally distributed and that the population standard deviation is unknown.
a. Is it permissible to use the t-test to perform the hypothesis test? Explain your answer.
b. Is it permissible to use the one-sample Wilcoxon signed-rank test to perform the hypothesis test? Explain your answer.
c. Which procedure is better to use, the t-test or the one-sample Wilcoxon signed-rank test? Explain your answer.

9.85 Suppose that you want to perform a hypothesis test for a population mean. Assume that the variable under consideration has a symmetric nonnormal distribution and that the population standard deviation is unknown. Further assume that the sample size is large and that no outliers are present in the sample data.
a. Is it permissible to use the t-test to perform the hypothesis test? Explain your answer.
b. Is it permissible to use the one-sample Wilcoxon signed-rank test to perform the hypothesis test? Explain your answer.
c. Which procedure is better to use, the t-test or the one-sample Wilcoxon signed-rank test? Explain your answer.

9.86 Beef Consumption. According to *Food Consumption, Prices, and Expenditures*, published by the U.S. Department of Agriculture, the mean consumption of beef per person in 1997 was 64 lb (boneless, trimmed weight). A sample of 40 people taken this year yielded the following data, in pounds, on last year's beef consumption.

77	65	57	54	68	79	56	0
50	49	51	56	56	78	63	72
0	62	74	61	61	60	56	37
76	77	67	67	62	89	56	75
69	73	75	62	8	71	20	47

a. Use the sample data to decide, at the 5% significance level, whether last year's mean beef consumption is less than the 1997 mean of 64 lb. (*Note:* The mean and standard deviation of the sample data are 58.40 lb and 20.42 lb, respectively.)
b. The sample data contain four potential outliers: 0, 0, 8, and 20. Remove those four observations and repeat the

hypothesis test in part (a). (*Note:* The mean and standard deviation of the abridged sample data are 64.11 lb and 11.02 lb, respectively.)
c. Compare your results in parts (a) and (b).
d. Assuming that the four potential outliers are not recording errors, comment on the advisability of removing them from the sample data before performing the hypothesis test.
e. What action would you take regarding this hypothesis test?

9.87 Suppose that you want to perform a hypothesis test for a population mean based on a small sample but that preliminary data analyses indicate either the presence of outliers or that the variable under consideration is far from normally distributed.
a. Is either the *z*-test or *t*-test appropriate?
b. If not, what type of procedure might be appropriate?

Using Technology

9.88 Apparel and Services. Refer to Exercise 9.69. Use the technology of your choice to
a. obtain a normal probability plot, a boxplot, a histogram, and a stem-and-leaf diagram of the data.
b. perform the required hypothesis test.
c. Is the use of your procedure in part (b) justified? Explain your answer.

9.89 Stressed-Out Bus Drivers. Refer to Exercise 9.70. Use the technology of your choice to
a. obtain a normal probability plot, a boxplot, a histogram, and a stem-and-leaf diagram of the data.
b. perform the required hypothesis test.
c. Is the use of your procedure in part (b) justified? Explain your answer.

9.90 Beef Consumption. Refer to Exercise 9.86. Use the technology of your choice to
a. identify the potential outliers.
b. perform the hypothesis test considered in part (a) of Exercise 9.86.
c. perform the hypothesis test considered in part (b) of Exercise 9.86.
d. Compare the results obtained in parts (b) and (c).

Chapter Review

You Should Be Able To

1. use and understand the formulas presented in this chapter.
2. define the terms associated with hypothesis testing.
3. choose the null and alternative hypotheses for a hypothesis test.
4. explain the logic behind hypothesis testing.
5. identify the test statistic, rejection region, nonrejection region, and critical value(s) for a hypothesis test.
6. define and apply the concepts of Type I and Type II errors.
7. state and interpret the possible conclusions for a hypothesis test.
8. obtain the critical value(s) for a specified significance level.
9. perform a hypothesis test for a population mean when the population standard deviation is known.
10. obtain the *P*-value of a hypothesis test.
11. state and apply the steps for performing a hypothesis test, using the critical-value approach to hypothesis testing.
12. state and apply the steps for performing a hypothesis test, using the *P*-value approach to hypothesis testing.
13. perform a hypothesis test for a population mean when the population standard deviation is unknown.

Key Terms

acceptance region, *378*
alternative hypothesis, *370*
critical-value approach to hypothesis testing, *398*
critical values, *379*
hypothesis, *370*
hypothesis test, *370*
left-tailed test, *371*
nonrejection region, *379*
not statistically significant, *383*
null hypothesis, *370*
observed significance level, *398*
one-sample *t*-test, *413, 414*
one-sample *z*-test, *389, 403*
one-tailed test, *371*
P-value (*P*), *398*
P-value approach to hypothesis testing, *398*
power, *382*
probability value, *398*
rejection region, *379*
research hypothesis, *370*
right-tailed test, *371*
significance level (α), *382*

statistically significant, 383
t-test, 410
test statistic, 379

two-tailed test, 371
Type I error, 380
Type I error probability (α), 381

Type II error, 380
Type II error probability (β), 382
z-test, 388

Review Test

Statistical Concepts and Skills

1. Explain the meaning of each term.
   a. Null hypothesis
   b. Alternative hypothesis
   c. Test statistic
   d. Rejection region
   e. Nonrejection region
   f. Critical value(s)

2. The following statement appeared on a box of Tide laundry detergent: "Individual packages of Tide may weigh slightly more or less than the marked weight due to normal variations incurred with high speed packaging machines, but each day's production of Tide will average slightly above the marked weight."
   a. Explain in statistical terms what the statement means.
   b. Describe in words a hypothesis test for checking the statement.
   c. Suppose that the marked weight is 76 ounces. State in words the null and alternative hypotheses for the hypothesis test. Then express those hypotheses in statistical terminology.

3. Regarding a hypothesis test,
   a. what is the procedure, generally, for deciding whether the null hypothesis should be rejected?
   b. how can the procedure identified in part (a) be made objective and precise?

4. There are three possible alternative hypotheses in a hypothesis test for a population mean. Identify them and explain when each is used.

5. Two types of incorrect decisions can be made in a hypothesis test: a Type I error and a Type II error.
   a. Explain the meaning of each type of error.
   b. Identify the letter used to represent the probability of each type of error.
   c. If the null hypothesis is in fact true, only one type of error is possible. Which type is that? Explain your answer.
   d. If you fail to reject the null hypothesis, only one type of error is possible. Which type is that? Explain your answer.

6. Suppose that you want to conduct a right-tailed hypothesis test at the 5% significance level. How must the critical value be chosen?

7. In each part, we have identified a hypothesis testing procedure for a population mean. State the assumptions required and the test statistic used in each case.

   a. One-sample t-test
   b. One-sample z-test

8. What is meant when we say that a hypothesis test is
   a. exact?   b. approximately correct?

9. Discuss the difference between statistical significance and practical significance.

10. For a fixed sample size, what happens to the probability of a Type II error if the significance level is decreased from 0.05 to 0.01?

11. Regarding the P-value of a hypothesis test,
    a. what is the P-value of a hypothesis test?
    b. answer true or false: A P-value of 0.02 provides more evidence against the null hypothesis than a P-value of 0.03. Explain your answer.
    c. answer true or false: A P-value of 0.74 provides essentially no evidence against the null hypothesis. Explain your answer.
    d. explain why the P-value of a hypothesis test is also referred to as the observed significance level.

12. Discuss the differences between the critical-value and P-value approaches to hypothesis testing.

13. **Cheese Consumption.** The U.S. Department of Agriculture reports in *Food Consumption, Prices, and Expenditures* that the average American consumed 28.0 lb of cheese in 1997. Cheese consumption has increased steadily since 1960 when the average American ate only 8.3 lb of cheese annually. Suppose that you want to decide whether last year's mean cheese consumption is greater than the 1997 mean.
    a. Identify the null hypothesis.
    b. Identify the alternative hypothesis.
    c. Classify the hypothesis test as two-tailed, left-tailed, or right-tailed.

14. The following graph portrays the decision criterion for a hypothesis test about a population mean, μ. The null hypothesis for the test is $H_0: \mu = \mu_0$, and the test statistic is

$$z = \frac{\bar{x} - \mu_0}{\sigma/\sqrt{n}}.$$

The curve shown in the graph reveals the implications of the decision criterion if in fact the null hypothesis is true.

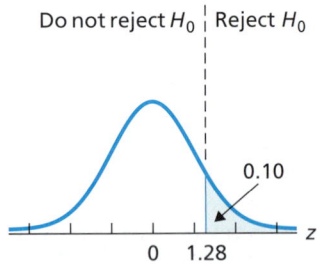

Determine the
a. rejection region.
b. nonrejection region.
c. critical value(s).
d. significance level.
e. Draw a graph that depicts the answers you obtained in parts (a)–(d).
f. Classify the hypothesis test as two-tailed, left-tailed, or right-tailed.

15. Cheese Consumption. The null and alternative hypotheses for the hypothesis test in Problem 13 are

H_0: $\mu = 28.0$ lb (mean has not increased)

H_a: $\mu > 28.0$ lb (mean has increased),

where μ is last year's mean cheese consumption for all Americans. Explain what each of the following would mean.
a. Type I error
b. Type II error
c. Correct decision

Now suppose that the results of carrying out the hypothesis test lead to nonrejection of the null hypothesis. Classify that decision by error type or as a correct decision if in fact last year's mean cheese consumption
d. has not increased from the 1997 mean of 28.0 lb.
e. has increased from the 1997 mean of 28.0 lb.

16. Cheese Consumption. Refer to Problem 13. The following table provides last year's cheese consumption, in pounds, for 35 randomly selected Americans.

40	23	27	32	36	34	28
27	26	30	22	41	20	36
30	26	39	18	33	22	27
38	27	20	31	21	25	30
31	31	30	16	38	30	23

a. At the 10% significance level, do the data provide sufficient evidence to conclude that last year's mean cheese consumption for all Americans has increased over the 1997 mean? Assume that $\sigma = 6.9$ lb. For your hypothesis test, use a z-test and the critical-value approach. (*Note:* The sum of the data is 1008 lb.)
b. Given the conclusion in part (a), if an error has been made, what type must it be? Explain your answer.

17. Cheese Consumption. Refer to Problem 16.
a. Repeat the hypothesis test, using the P-value approach to hypothesis testing.
b. Use Table 9.10 on page 405 to assess the strength of the evidence against the null hypothesis.

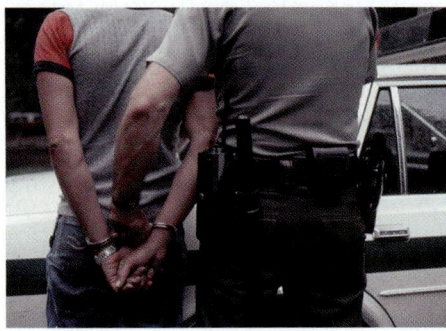

18. Purse Snatching. According to *Crime in the United States*, a publication of the FBI, the mean value lost to purse snatching was $362 in 1998. For last year, 12 randomly selected purse-snatching offenses yielded the following values lost, to the nearest dollar.

| 237 | 452 | 302 | 392 | 195 | 299 |
| 267 | 256 | 235 | 378 | 296 | 460 |

Use a t-test with either the critical-value approach or the P-value approach to decide, at the 5% significance level, whether last year's mean value lost to purse snatching has decreased from the 1998 mean. The mean and standard deviation of the data are $314.1 and $86.9, respectively.

19. Betting the Spreads. College basketball, and particularly the NCAA basketball tournament, is a popular venue for gambling, from novices in office betting pools to the high-roller. To encourage uniform betting across teams, Las Vegas oddsmakers assign a point spread to each game. The *point spread* is the oddsmakers' prediction for the number of points by which the favored team will win. If you bet on the favorite, you win the bet provided the favorite wins by more than the point spread; otherwise, you lose the bet. Is the point spread a good measure of the relative ability of the two

teams? Hal S. Stern and Barbara Mock addressed this question in the paper "College Basketball Upsets: Will a 16-Seed Ever Beat a 1-Seed?" (*Chance*, 1998, Vol. 11(1), pp. 27–31). They obtained the difference between the actual margin of victory and the point spread, called the *point-spread error*, for 2109 college basketball games. The mean point-spread error was found to be −0.2 point with a standard deviation of 10.9 points. For a particular game, a point-spread error of 0 indicates that the point spread was a perfect estimate of the two teams' relative abilities.
a. If, on average, the oddsmakers are estimating correctly, what is the (population) mean point-spread error?
b. Use the data to decide, at the 5% significance level, whether the (population) mean point-spread error differs from 0.
c. Interpret your answer in part (b).

Problems 20 and 21 each include a normal probability plot and either a frequency histogram or a stem-and-leaf diagram for a set of sample data. The intent is to use the sample data to perform a hypothesis test for the mean of the population from which the data were obtained. In each case, consult the graphs provided to decide whether to use the z-test, the t-test, or neither. Explain your answer.

20. The normal probability plot and histogram of the data are depicted in Fig. 9.30; σ is known.

21. The normal probability plot and stem-and-leaf diagram of the data are depicted in Fig. 9.31; σ is unknown.

Using Technology

22. Cheese Consumption. Refer to Problems 16 and 17. Use the technology of your choice to
a. obtain a normal probability plot of the data.
b. perform the required hypothesis test.
c. Justify the use of your procedure in part (b).

23. Purse Snatching. Refer to Problem 18. Use the technology of your choice to
a. obtain a normal probability plot of the data.
b. perform the required hypothesis test.
c. Justify the use of your procedure in part (b).

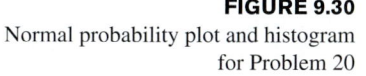

FIGURE 9.30
Normal probability plot and histogram for Problem 20

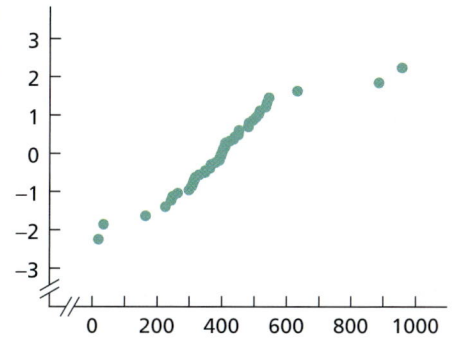
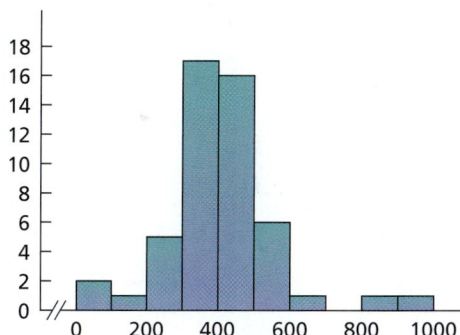

FIGURE 9.31
Normal probability plot and stem-and-leaf diagram for Problem 21

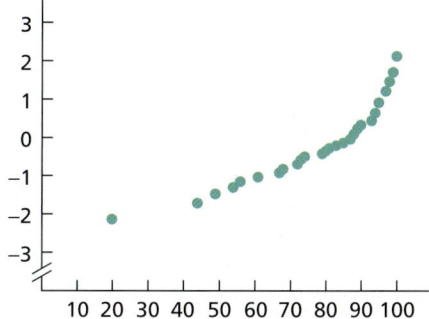
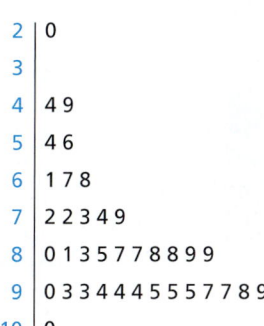

Internet Project

The Ozone Hole

Ozone is a molecule made up of three atoms of oxygen. It plays many roles in the ecosystem, but one of the most important for every life form on Earth is the protection it provides from the harmful effects of the Sun's ultraviolet light.

For years, humans have used chemicals that only recently have been discovered to be harmful to the protective ozone layer. Humankind is beginning to see the possible effects of that damage. For example, the depletion of ozone in the stratosphere may increase the rate of skin cancer and cataracts, and it can harm crops and ocean life.

In this Internet project, you are to explore data collected worldwide on the decrease of ozone in the Earth's atmosphere. You also have the opportunity to investigate the possible consequences of ozone depletion: the amount of solar ultraviolet light reaching the Earth's surface and the effects it may have on humans.

URL for access to Internet Projects Page: www.aw.com/weiss

Focusing on Data Analysis

SAT Scores

Recall from Chapter 1 (see page 34) that the Focus database contains information on 500 randomly selected Arizona State University sophomores. Use the technology of your choice to solve the following problems.

a. In 1995, the (nonrecentered) mean SAT math score was 482 nationally. Do the Focus data on SAT math scores provide sufficient evidence to conclude that the mean SAT math score of Arizona State University sophomores exceeds the 1995 national mean? Use $\alpha = 0.05$.
b. In 1995, the (nonrecentered) mean SAT verbal score was 428 nationally. Do the Focus data on SAT verbal scores provide sufficient evidence to conclude that the mean SAT verbal score of Arizona State University sophomores exceeds the 1995 national mean? Use $\alpha = 0.05$.
c. Justify your use of the specific hypothesis testing procedures in parts (a) and (b).

case study discussion

Sex and Sense of Direction

At the beginning of this chapter, we discussed research by Jeanne Sholl et. al on the relationship between sex and sense of direction. Recall that, in their study, the spatial orientation skills of 30 male students and 30 female students from Boston College were challenged in Houghton Garden Park, a wooded park near the BC campus in Newton, Massachusetts. Before driving out to the park, the participants were asked to rate their own sense of direction as either good or poor.

In the park, students were instructed to point to predesignated target landmarks and also to the direction of south. Pointing was carried out by moving a pointer attached to a 360° protractor; the angle of the pointing response was then recorded to the nearest degree.

For the female students who had rated their sense of direction to be good, the table on page 369 provides the absolute pointing errors (in degrees) when they attempted to point south.

a. If, on average, women who consider themselves to have a good sense of direction do no better than they would by just randomly guessing at the direction of south, what would be their mean absolute pointing error?
b. At the 1% significance level, do the data provide sufficient evidence to conclude that women who consider themselves to have a good sense of direction really do better, on average, than they would by just randomly guessing at the direction of south? Use a one-sample *t*-test.
c. Obtain a normal probability plot, boxplot, and stem-and-leaf diagram of the data. Based on these plots, is use of the *t*-test reasonable? Explain your answer.
d. Use the technology of your choice to perform the data analyses in parts (b) and (c).

Internet Resources: Visit the Weiss Web site www.aw.com/weiss for additional discussion, exercises, and resources related to this case study.

Biography

Jerzy Neyman: A Principal Founder of Modern Statistical Theory

JERZY NEYMAN was born on April 16, 1894, in Bendery, Russia. His father, Czeslaw, was a member of the Polish nobility, a lawyer, a judge, and an amateur archaeologist. Because Russian authorities prohibited the family from living in Poland, Jerzy Neyman grew up in various cities in Russia. He entered the university in Kharkov in 1912. At Kharkov he was at first interested in physics, but, because of his clumsiness in the laboratory, he decided to pursue mathematics.

After World War I, when Russia was at war with Poland over borders, Neyman was jailed as an enemy alien. In 1921, as a result of a prisoner exchange, he went to Poland for the first time. In 1924, he received his doctorate from the University of Warsaw. Between 1924 and 1934, Neyman worked with Karl Pearson (see Biography in Chapter 12) and his son Egon Pearson and held a position at the University of Kraków. In 1934, Neyman took a position in Karl Pearson's statistical laboratory at University College in London. He stayed in England, where he worked with Egon Pearson until 1938, at which time he accepted an offer to join the faculty at the University of California at Berkeley.

When the United States entered World War II, Neyman set aside development of a statistics program and did war work. After the war ended, Neyman organized a symposium to celebrate its end and "the return to theoretical research." That symposium, held in August 1945, and succeeding ones, held every 5 years until 1970, were instrumental in establishing Berkeley as a preeminent statistical center.

Neyman was a principal founder of the theory of modern statistics. His work on hypothesis testing, confidence intervals, and survey sampling transformed both the theory and the practice of statistics. His achievements were acknowledged by the granting of many honors and awards, including election to the United States National Academy of Sciences, the Guy Medal in Gold of the Royal Statistical Society, and the United States National Medal of Science.

Neyman remained active until his death of heart failure on August 5, 1981, at the age of 87, in Oakland, California.

chapter 10

Inferences for Two Population Means

CHAPTER OUTLINE

10.1 The Sampling Distribution of the Difference Between Two Sample Means for Independent Samples

10.2 Inferences for Two Population Means, Using Independent Samples: Standard Deviations Assumed Equal

10.3 Inferences for Two Population Means, Using Independent Samples: Standard Deviations Not Assumed Equal

10.4 Inferences for Two Population Means, Using Paired Samples

GENERAL OBJECTIVES In Chapters 8 and 9, you learned how to obtain confidence intervals and perform hypothesis tests for one population mean. Frequently, however, inferential statistics is used to compare the means of two or more populations.

For example, we might want to perform a hypothesis test to decide whether the mean age of buyers of new domestic cars is greater than the mean age of buyers of new imported cars; or, we might want to find a confidence interval for the difference between the two mean ages.

Broadly speaking, in this chapter we examine two types of inferential procedures for comparing the means of two populations. The first type applies when the samples from the two populations are *independent*, meaning that the sample selected from one of the populations has no effect or bearing on the sample selected from the other population. We present such inferences in Sections 10.2 and 10.3.

The second type of inferential procedure for comparing the means of two populations applies when the samples from the two populations are *paired*. A paired sample may be appropriate when there is a natural pairing of the members of the two populations such as husband and wife. We present such inferences in Section 10.4.

case study

BREAST MILK AND IQ

Considerable controversy exists over whether long-term neurodevelopment is affected by nutritional factors in early life. Five researchers summarized their findings on that question for preterm babies in the paper "Breast Milk and Subsequent Intelligence Quotient in Children Born Preterm" (*The Lancet*, 339, pp. 261–264). Their study was a continuation of work begun in January, 1982.

Previously, these researchers had showed that a mother's decision to provide breast milk for preterm infants is associated with higher developmental scores for the children at age 18 months. In the article mentioned, they analyzed IQ data on the same children at age $7\frac{1}{2}$–8 years. IQ was measured for 300 children, using an abbreviated form of the Weschler Intelligence Scale for Children (revised Anglicized version: WISC-R UK).

The mothers of the children in the study had chosen whether to provide their infants with breast milk within 72 hours of delivery; 90 did not and 210 did. Of those 210 who chose to provide their infants with breast milk, 193 succeeded and 17 did not.

The children whose mothers declined to provide breast milk were designated by the researchers as Group I; those whose mothers had chosen but were unable to provide breast milk were designated as Group IIa; and those whose mothers had chosen and were able to provide breast milk were designated as Group IIb. The following table displays statistics for all three groups.

Group	Sample size	Mean IQ	St. Dev.
I	90	92.8	15.2
IIa	17	94.8	19.0
IIb	193	103.7	15.3

After studying the inferential methods discussed in this chapter, you will be able to conduct statistical analyses to examine how breast feeding affects subsequent IQ for children age $7\frac{1}{2}$–8 years who were born preterm.

10.1 THE SAMPLING DISTRIBUTION OF THE DIFFERENCE BETWEEN TWO SAMPLE MEANS FOR INDEPENDENT SAMPLES

In this section, we lay the groundwork for making statistical inferences to compare the means of two populations. The methods that we first consider require not only that the samples selected from the two populations be random but also that they be **independent samples.** That is, the sample selected from one of the populations has no effect or bearing on the sample selected from the other population.

With independent random samples, each possible pair of samples—one from one population and one from the other—is equally likely to be the pair of samples selected. Example 10.1 provides an unrealistically simple illustration of independent samples, but it will help you understand the concept.

Example 10.1 Introducing Independent Random Samples

Males and Females   Let's consider two small populations, one consisting of three men and the other of four women, as shown in the following figure.

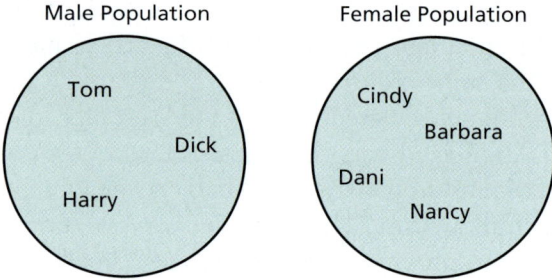

Suppose that we take a sample of size 2 from the male population and a sample of size 3 from the female population.

a. List the possible pairs of independent samples.
b. If the samples are selected at random, determine the chance that any particular pair of samples will be the pair of independent samples obtained.

Solution   For convenience, we use the first letter of each name as an abbreviation for the actual name.

a. The possible samples of size 2 from the male population are listed on the left in Table 10.1. The possible samples of size 3 from the female population are listed on the right in Table 10.1.

To obtain the possible pairs of independent samples, we list each possible male sample of size 2 with each possible female sample of size 3, as shown in Table 10.2. There are 12 possible pairs of independent samples of two men and three women.

10.1 Sampling Distribution of the Difference Between Two Means

TABLE 10.1
Possible samples of size 2 from the male population and possible samples of size 3 from the female population

Male sample of size 2	Female sample of size 3
T, D	C, B, D
T, H	C, B, N
D, H	C, D, N
	B, D, N

TABLE 10.2
Possible pairs of independent samples of two men and three women

Male sample of size 2	Female sample of size 3
T, D	C, B, D
T, D	C, B, N
T, D	C, D, N
T, D	B, D, N
T, H	C, B, D
T, H	C, B, N
T, H	C, D, N
T, H	B, D, N
D, H	C, B, D
D, H	C, B, N
D, H	C, D, N
D, H	B, D, N

b. For independent random samples, each of the 12 possible pairs of samples shown in Table 10.2 is equally likely to be the pair selected. Therefore the chances are $\frac{1}{12}$ (1 in 12) that any particular pair of samples will be the one obtained. ◆

The purpose of Example 10.1 is to provide a concrete illustration of independent samples and to emphasize that, for independent random samples of any given sizes, each possible pair of independent samples is equally likely to be the one selected. In practice, we neither obtain the number of possible pairs of independent samples nor explicitly compute the chance of selecting a particular pair of independent samples. But these concepts underlie the methods we do use.

COMPARING TWO POPULATION MEANS, USING INDEPENDENT SAMPLES

Now we are ready to examine the process for comparing the means of two populations based on independent samples. Example 10.2 introduces the pertinent ideas.

Example 10.2 Comparing Two Population Means, Using Independent Samples

Faculty Salaries The American Association of University Professors (AAUP) conducts salary studies of college professors and publishes its findings in *AAUP Annual Report on the Economic Status of the Profession*. Suppose that we want to decide whether the mean salaries of college faculty in public and private institutions are different.

To formulate the problem statistically, we first note that we have one variable (salary) and two populations (faculty in public institutions and faculty in private institutions). Let the two populations in question be designated Populations 1 and 2, respectively:

Population 1: Faculty in public institutions

Population 2: Faculty in private institutions

Next, we denote the means of the variable "salary" for the two populations μ_1 and μ_2, respectively:

μ_1 = mean salary of faculty in public institutions;

μ_2 = mean salary of faculty in private institutions.

Then, we can state the hypothesis test we want to perform as

H_0: $\mu_1 = \mu_2$ (mean salaries are the same)

H_a: $\mu_1 \neq \mu_2$ (mean salaries are different).

Roughly speaking, we can carry out the hypothesis test as follows.

1. Independently and randomly take a sample of faculty members from public institutions (Population 1) and a sample of faculty members from private institutions (Population 2).
2. Compute the mean salary, $\bar{x}_1$, of the sample of faculty members from public institutions and the mean salary, $\bar{x}_2$, of the sample of faculty members from private institutions.
3. Reject the null hypothesis if the sample means, $\bar{x}_1$ and $\bar{x}_2$, differ by too much; otherwise, do not reject the null hypothesis.

This process is depicted in Fig. 10.1.

Suppose that we randomly and independently sample 30 faculty members from public institutions (Population 1) and 35 faculty members from private institutions (Population 2) and that the salaries of these faculty members are as displayed in Table 10.3, in thousands of dollars rounded to the nearest hundred.

The means of the two samples in Table 10.3 are

$$\bar{x}_1 = \frac{\Sigma x}{n_1} = \frac{1724.4}{30} = 57.48 \quad \text{and} \quad \bar{x}_2 = \frac{\Sigma x}{n_2} = \frac{2323.8}{35} = 66.39.$$

The question now is: Can the difference of 8.91 ($8910) between these two sample means be reasonably attributed to sampling error or is the difference

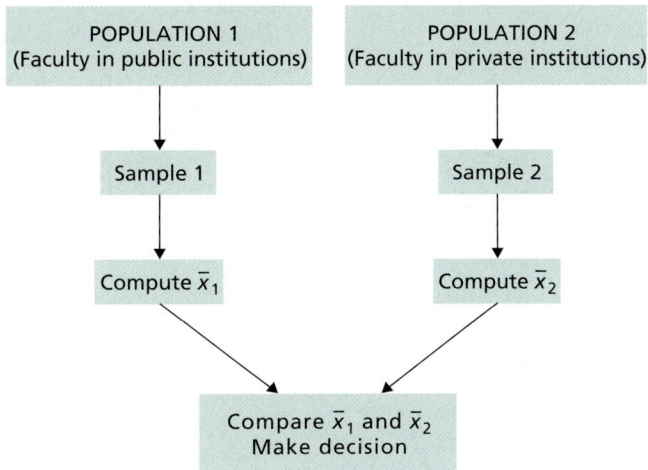

FIGURE 10.1
Process for comparing two population means, using independent samples

TABLE 10.3
Annual salaries ($1000s) for 30 faculty members in public institutions and 35 faculty members in private institutions

Sample 1 (public institutions)						Sample 2 (private institutions)					
34.2	63.6	24.4	79.4	33.8	88.2	92.9	102.2	51.5	77.6	71.1	59.3	71.0
90.0	56.8	56.0	42.2	40.2	44.6	52.0	62.9	46.4	61.6	73.5	97.5	97.3
100.4	41.4	58.2	81.8	51.2	64.4	63.1	53.8	45.2	78.3	67.6	27.2	92.6
24.6	35.0	76.8	29.2	41.2	74.0	118.5	101.0	76.0	66.3	52.4	81.2	56.0
107.4	54.2	84.2	15.8	60.2	71.0	37.7	68.6	56.1	31.1	47.2	24.8	62.3

large enough to indicate that the two populations have different means? To answer that question, we need to know the distribution of the difference between two sample means—the *sampling distribution of the difference between two sample means*. We examine that sampling distribution in this section and complete the hypothesis test in the next section. ◆

THE SAMPLING DISTRIBUTION OF THE DIFFERENCE BETWEEN TWO SAMPLE MEANS FOR INDEPENDENT SAMPLES

First, we need to discuss the notation used for parameters and statistics when we are analyzing two populations. Let's call the two populations under consideration Population 1 and Population 2. Then, as indicated in Example 10.2, we use a subscript 1 when referring to parameters or statistics for Population 1 and a subscript 2 when referring to them for Population 2. We present the notation in Table 10.4 on the next page.

Armed with this notation, we describe in Key Fact 10.1 the **sampling distribution of the difference between two sample means.** In doing so, we assume that the variable under consideration is normally distributed on each population. But keep in mind that, because of the central limit theorem, consequences of Key Fact 10.1 will still apply approximately for large samples regardless of distribution type.

TABLE 10.4 Notation for parameters and statistics when considering two populations

	Population 1	Population 2
Population mean	μ_1	μ_2
Population std. dev.	σ_1	σ_2
Sample mean	$\bar{x}_1$	$\bar{x}_2$
Sample std. dev.	s_1	s_2
Sample size	n_1	n_2

Understanding Key Fact 10.1 is also aided by recalling Key Fact 7.2: Suppose that a variable x of a population is normally distributed and has mean μ and standard deviation σ. Then, for samples of size n,

- $\mu_{\bar{x}} = \mu$,
- $\sigma_{\bar{x}} = \sigma/\sqrt{n}$, and
- $\bar{x}$ is normally distributed.

Key Fact 10.1 The Sampling Distribution of the Difference Between Two Sample Means for Independent Samples

Suppose that x is a normally distributed variable on each of two populations. Then, for independent samples of sizes n_1 and n_2 from the two populations,

- $\mu_{\bar{x}_1 - \bar{x}_2} = \mu_1 - \mu_2$,
- $\sigma_{\bar{x}_1 - \bar{x}_2} = \sqrt{(\sigma_1^2/n_1) + (\sigma_2^2/n_2)}$, and
- $\bar{x}_1 - \bar{x}_2$ is normally distributed.

In words, the first bulleted item says that the mean of all possible differences between the two sample means equals the difference between the two population means. The second bulleted item indicates that the standard deviation of all possible differences between the two sample means equals the square root of the sum of the population variances each divided by the corresponding sample size.

The formulas for the mean and standard deviation of $\bar{x}_1 - \bar{x}_2$ given in the first and second bulleted items, respectively, hold regardless of the distributions of the variable on the two populations. The assumption that the variable is normally distributed on each of the two populations is needed only to conclude that $\bar{x}_1 - \bar{x}_2$ is normally distributed (third bulleted item) and, as we noted, that too holds approximately for large samples, regardless of distribution type.

THE TWO-SAMPLE z-PROCEDURES

Under the conditions of Key Fact 10.1, the standardized version of $\bar{x}_1 - \bar{x}_2$,

$$z = \frac{(\bar{x}_1 - \bar{x}_2) - (\mu_1 - \mu_2)}{\sqrt{(\sigma_1^2/n_1) + (\sigma_2^2/n_2)}},$$

has the standard normal distribution. Using that fact, we can develop hypothesis testing and confidence-interval procedures for comparing two population means when the population standard deviations are known. These procedures are often called the *two-sample z-test* and the *two-sample z-interval procedure*, respectively, or, collectively, as the *two-sample z-procedures*.

Because population standard deviations are usually unknown, however, we won't discuss the two-sample z-procedures in detail. Instead we relegate them to the exercises and concentrate on the more useful two-sample t-procedures, which apply in the case of unknown population standard deviations. In Sections 10.2 and 10.3, we examine the two-sample t-procedures, specifically, the pooled t- and nonpooled t-procedures, respectively.

Exercises 10.1

Statistical Concepts and Skills

10.1 Age of Car Buyers. In the introduction to this chapter, we mentioned comparing the mean age of buyers of new domestic cars to the mean age of buyers of new imported cars.
a. Identify the variable that would be considered.
b. Identify the two populations that would be considered.
c. Suppose that we want to perform a hypothesis test to decide whether the mean age of buyers of new domestic cars is greater than the mean age of buyers of new imported cars. State the null and alternative hypotheses for the hypothesis test.

10.2 Spending at the Mall. An issue of *USA TODAY* compared the mean amounts spent by teens and adults at shopping malls.
a. Identify the variable under consideration.
b. Identify the two populations.
c. Suppose that we want to perform a hypothesis test to decide whether the mean amount spent by teens is less than the mean amount spent by adults. State the null and alternative hypotheses for the hypothesis test.

10.3 Give an example of interest to you for comparing two population means. Identify the variable under consideration and the two populations.

10.4 Define the phrase *independent samples*.

10.5 Consider the quantities $\mu_1, \sigma_1, \bar{x}_1, s_1, \mu_2, \sigma_2, \bar{x}_2$, and s_2.
a. Which quantities represent parameters and which represent statistics?
b. Which quantities are fixed numbers and which are variables?

10.6 Discuss the basic strategy for performing a hypothesis test to compare the means of two populations, based on independent samples.

10.7 Why do you need to know the sampling distribution of the difference between two sample means in order to perform a hypothesis test to compare two population means?

10.8 Identify the assumption for using the two-sample z-procedures that renders those procedures generally impractical.

10.9 A variable of two populations has a mean of 40 and a standard deviation of 12 for one of the populations and a mean of 40 and a standard deviation of 6 for the other population.
a. For independent samples of sizes 9 and 4, respectively, find the mean and standard deviation of $\bar{x}_1 - \bar{x}_2$.
b. Must the variable under consideration be normally distributed on each of the two populations for you to answer part (a)? Explain your answer.
c. Can you conclude that the variable $\bar{x}_1 - \bar{x}_2$ is normally distributed? Explain your answer.

10.10 A variable of two populations has a mean of 40 and a standard deviation of 12 for one of the populations and a mean of 40 and a standard deviation of 6 for the other population. Moreover, the variable is normally distributed on each of the two populations.
a. For independent samples of sizes 9 and 4, respectively, determine the mean and standard deviation of $\bar{x}_1 - \bar{x}_2$.
b. Can you conclude that the variable $\bar{x}_1 - \bar{x}_2$ is normally distributed? Explain your answer.
c. Determine the percentage of all pairs of independent samples of sizes 9 and 4, respectively, from the two populations that have the property that the difference between the sample means is between -10 and 10.

Extending the Concepts and Skills

The Two-Sample z-Procedures. Using Key Fact 10.1, we can derive the following two-sample z-procedures.

Two-Sample z-Procedures

ASSUMPTIONS

1. Independent samples
2. Normal populations or large samples
3. Known population standard deviations

- **Two-sample z-test.** The test statistic for a hypothesis test with null hypothesis $H_0: \mu_1 = \mu_2$ (population means are equal) is

$$z = \frac{\bar{x}_1 - \bar{x}_2}{\sqrt{(\sigma_1^2/n_1) + (\sigma_2^2/n_2)}}.$$

- **Two-sample z-interval procedure.** The endpoints of a $(1-\alpha)$-level confidence interval for the difference, $\mu_1 - \mu_2$, between the two population means are

$$(\bar{x}_1 - \bar{x}_2) \pm z_{\alpha/2} \cdot \sqrt{(\sigma_1^2/n_1) + (\sigma_2^2/n_2)}.$$

Exercises 10.11 and 10.12 illustrate use of the two-sample z-procedures.

10.11 Starting Salaries. The Northwestern University Placement Center at Evanston, Illinois, conducts surveys on starting salaries for college graduates and publishes its observations in *The Northwestern Lindquist–Endicott Report*. The following table gives the starting annual salaries obtained from independent random samples of 35 liberal arts graduates and 32 accounting graduates. Data are in thousands of dollars.

Liberal arts					Accounting			
33.0	29.8	34.3	33.6	34.0	35.9	31.4	34.3	31.9
31.7	36.8	31.3	30.7	31.0	34.4	36.3	37.8	33.6
32.1	34.1	32.6	32.0	31.7	35.0	33.0	32.7	34.0
33.8	33.4	30.1	32.5		37.2	36.9	35.8	36.3
32.9	32.2	32.1	30.2		36.5	31.4	33.4	35.5
31.3	35.7	33.0	32.2		35.9	36.4	36.8	35.2
33.9	32.1	33.8	33.5		33.2	33.1	32.0	35.7
34.4	29.3	29.3	33.5		32.5	33.5	36.4	37.6

a. At the 5% significance level, can you conclude that the mean starting salaries of liberal arts and accounting graduates differ? Assume that the population standard deviations of starting salaries are 1.82 ($1820) for liberal arts graduates and 1.73 ($1730) for accounting graduates. (*Note:* The sum of the liberal arts data is 1137.9, and the sum of the accounting data is 1111.6.)

b. Determine a 95% confidence interval for the difference, $\mu_1 - \mu_2$, between the mean starting annual salaries of liberal arts and accounting graduates.

10.12 Hospital Stays. The U.S. National Center for Health Statistics compiles data on the length of stay by patients in short-term hospitals and publishes its findings in *Vital and Health Statistics*. Independent samples of 39 male patients and 35 female patients gave the following data on length of stay, in days.

Male					Female			
4	4	12	18	9	14	7	15	1	12
6	12	10	3	6	1	3	7	21	4
15	7	3	13	1	1	5	4	4	3
2	10	13	5	7	5	18	12	5	1
1	23	9	2	1	7	7	2	15	4
17	2	24	11	14	9	10	7	3	6
6	2	1	8	1	5	9	6	2	14
3	19	3	1						

a. At the 5% significance level, do the data provide sufficient evidence to conclude that, on average, the lengths of stay in short-term hospitals by males and females differ? Assume that $\sigma_1 = 5.4$ days and $\sigma_2 = 4.6$ days. (*Note:* The sum of the male data is 308 days, and the sum of the female data is 249 days.)

b. Determine a 95% confidence interval for the difference, $\mu_1 - \mu_2$, between the mean lengths of stay in short-term hospitals by males and females.

10.13 Hypothesis Tests and Confidence Intervals. Use the results obtained in Exercises 10.11 and 10.12 to complete the statement: A hypothesis test of $H_0: \mu_1 = \mu_2$ versus $H_a: \mu_1 \neq \mu_2$ at the significance level α will lead to rejection of the null hypothesis if and only if the number _____ does not lie in the $(1-\alpha)$-level confidence interval for $\mu_1 - \mu_2$.

Using Technology

10.14 To obtain the sampling distribution of the difference between two sample means for independent samples, as stated in Key Fact 10.1 on page 436, we need to know that, for independent observations, the difference of two normally distributed variables is also a normally distributed variable. In this exercise, you are to perform a computer simulation to make that fact plausible.

a. Simulate 2000 observations from a normally distributed variable with a mean of 100 and a standard deviation of 16.
b. Repeat part (a) for a normally distributed variable with a mean of 120 and a standard deviation of 12.
c. Determine the difference between each pair of observations in parts (a) and (b).
d. Obtain a histogram of the 2000 differences found in part (c). Why is the histogram bell-shaped?

10.15 In this exercise, you are to perform a computer simulation to illustrate the sampling distribution of the difference between two sample means for independent samples, as stated in Key Fact 10.1.

a. Simulate 1000 samples of size 12 from a normally distributed variable with a mean of 640 and a standard deviation of 70. Obtain the sample mean of each of the 1000 samples.
b. Simulate 1000 samples of size 15 from a normally distributed variable with a mean of 715 and a standard deviation of 150. Obtain the sample mean of each of the 1000 samples.
c. Obtain the difference, $\bar{x}_1 - \bar{x}_2$, for each of the 1000 pairs of sample means obtained in parts (a) and (b).
d. Obtain the mean, the standard deviation, and a histogram of the 1000 differences found in part (c).
e. Theoretically, what are the mean, standard deviation, and distribution of all possible differences, $\bar{x}_1 - \bar{x}_2$?
f. Compare your answers from parts (d) and (e).

10.2 INFERENCES FOR TWO POPULATION MEANS, USING INDEPENDENT SAMPLES: STANDARD DEVIATIONS ASSUMED EQUAL

In Section 10.1, we took the first steps required to develop inferential procedures based on independent samples for comparing the means of two populations. Armed with that information, we can derive two inferential methods. One requires that the two populations have equal standard deviations; the other does not. We develop the first method in this section and the second method in Section 10.3.

HYPOTHESIS TESTS FOR THE MEANS OF TWO POPULATIONS WITH EQUAL STANDARD DEVIATIONS, USING INDEPENDENT SAMPLES

We now develop a procedure for performing a hypothesis test based on independent samples to compare the means of two populations with equal, but unknown, standard deviations. Our immediate goal is to find a test statistic for such a test. In doing so, we assume that the variable under consideration is normally distributed on each population. As we demonstrate later, the resulting hypothesis testing procedure is approximately correct for large samples, regardless of the type of distribution.

Let's use σ to denote the common standard deviation of the two populations. We know from Key Fact 10.1 on page 436 that, for independent samples, the standardized version of $\bar{x}_1 - \bar{x}_2$,

$$z = \frac{(\bar{x}_1 - \bar{x}_2) - (\mu_1 - \mu_2)}{\sqrt{(\sigma_1^2/n_1) + (\sigma_2^2/n_2)}},$$

has the standard normal distribution. Replacing σ_1 and σ_2 in that expression with their common value σ and using some algebra, we obtain the variable

$$z = \frac{(\bar{x}_1 - \bar{x}_2) - (\mu_1 - \mu_2)}{\sigma\sqrt{(1/n_1) + (1/n_2)}}. \tag{10.1}$$

However, we cannot use this variable as a basis for the required test statistic because σ is unknown.

Consequently, we need to use sample information to estimate the unknown population standard deviation, σ. We do so by first obtaining an estimate of the unknown population variance, σ^2. The best way to do that is to regard the sample variances, s_1^2 and s_2^2, as two estimates of σ^2 and then **pool** those estimates by weighting them according to sample size (actually by degrees of freedom). Thus our estimate of σ^2 is

$$s_p^2 = \frac{(n_1 - 1)s_1^2 + (n_2 - 1)s_2^2}{n_1 + n_2 - 2}$$

and hence that of σ is

$$s_p = \sqrt{\frac{(n_1 - 1)s_1^2 + (n_2 - 1)s_2^2}{n_1 + n_2 - 2}}.$$

The subscript "p" stands for "pooled," and the quantity s_p is called the **pooled sample standard deviation.**

Replacing σ in Equation (10.1) with its estimate, s_p, we get the variable

$$\frac{(\bar{x}_1 - \bar{x}_2) - (\mu_1 - \mu_2)}{s_p\sqrt{(1/n_1) + (1/n_2)}},$$

which we can use as a basis for the required test statistic. Unlike the variable in Equation (10.1), this one does not have the standard normal distribution. However, its distribution is one with which you are already familiar—a t-distribution—which we describe in Key Fact 10.2.

Key Fact 10.2 Distribution of the Pooled t-Statistic

Suppose that x is a normally distributed variable on each of two populations and that the population standard deviations are equal. Then, for independent samples of sizes n_1 and n_2 from the two populations, the variable

$$t = \frac{(\bar{x}_1 - \bar{x}_2) - (\mu_1 - \mu_2)}{s_p\sqrt{(1/n_1) + (1/n_2)}}$$

has the t-distribution with $df = n_1 + n_2 - 2$.

In light of Key Fact 10.2, for a hypothesis test that has null hypothesis $H_0: \mu_1 = \mu_2$ (population means are equal), we can use the variable

$$t = \frac{\bar{x}_1 - \bar{x}_2}{s_p\sqrt{(1/n_1) + (1/n_2)}}$$

as the test statistic and obtain the critical value(s) from the t-table, Table IV in Appendix A. Again, we have alternative procedures, Procedure 10.1A (critical-value approach on page 442) and Procedure 10.1B (P-value approach on page 443), both of which we often refer to as the **pooled t-test.**

Before we apply the pooled t-test, several comments are in order. In Step 3 of Procedure 10.1 (A or B), we need to calculate the pooled sample standard deviation, s_p. The pooled sample standard deviation always lies between the two sample standard deviations, s_1 and s_2, which is useful as a check when s_p is calculated by hand.

Next, we need to discuss the three assumptions for the pooled t-test. Assumption 1 (independent samples) is essential; the samples must be independent or the procedure does not apply.

Regarding Assumption 2, although the pooled t-test was derived under the condition that the variable under consideration is normally distributed on each of the two populations (normal populations), it also applies approximately for large samples regardless of distribution type, as noted at the bottom of Procedure 10.1.

Actually, the pooled t-test works reasonably well even for small samples or samples of moderate size from nonnormal populations provided the populations are not too nonnormal. In other words, the pooled t-test is robust to moderate violations of the normality assumption. The pooled t-test is also robust to moderate violations of Assumption 3 (equal population standard deviations) provided the sample sizes are roughly equal. We have more to say about the robustness of the pooled t-test at the end of Section 10.3.

As before, we can check normality with normal probability plots. The equal-standard-deviations assumption is more difficult to check, especially when the sample sizes are small. We recommend checking it by informally comparing the standard deviations of the two samples and by comparing their stem-and-leaf diagrams, histograms, or boxplots. Be sure to use the same scales for each pair of graphs.

The equal-standard-deviations assumption is sometimes checked by performing a formal hypothesis test, called an F-test for the equality of two standard deviations. We don't recommend this procedure because, although the pooled t-test is robust to moderate violations of normality, the F-test is extremely nonrobust to such violations. As the noted statistician George E. P. Box remarked: "To make a preliminary test on variances [standard deviations] is rather like putting to sea in a rowing boat to find out whether conditions are sufficiently calm for an ocean liner to leave port!"

When considering the pooled t-test, you must also watch for outliers. Again, the presence of outliers calls into question the normality assumption. Moreover, even for large samples, outliers can sometimes unduly affect a pooled t-test because the sample mean and sample standard deviation are not resistant to them.

Example 10.3 illustrates use of the pooled t-test.

Procedure 10.1A The Pooled t-Test for Two Population Means (Critical-Value Approach)

Assumptions
1. Independent samples
2. Normal populations or large samples
3. Equal population standard deviations

Step 1 The null hypothesis is $H_0: \mu_1 = \mu_2$, and the alternative hypothesis is

$H_a: \mu_1 \neq \mu_2$	or	$H_a: \mu_1 < \mu_2$	or	$H_a: \mu_1 > \mu_2$
(Two-tailed)		(Left-tailed)		(Right-tailed)

Step 2 Decide on the significance level, α.

Step 3 Compute the value of the test statistic

$$t = \frac{\bar{x}_1 - \bar{x}_2}{s_p\sqrt{(1/n_1) + (1/n_2)}},$$

where

$$s_p = \sqrt{\frac{(n_1 - 1)s_1^2 + (n_2 - 1)s_2^2}{n_1 + n_2 - 2}}.$$

Step 4 The critical value(s) are

$\pm t_{\alpha/2}$	or	$-t_\alpha$	or	t_α
(Two-tailed)		(Left-tailed)		(Right-tailed)

with df $= n_1 + n_2 - 2$. Use Table IV to find the critical value(s).

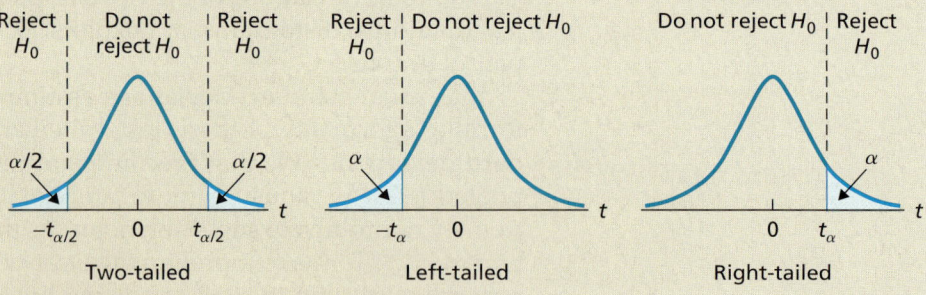

Step 5 If the value of the test statistic falls in the rejection region, reject H_0; otherwise, do not reject H_0.

Step 6 Interpret the results of the hypothesis test.

The hypothesis test is exact for normal populations and is approximately correct for large samples from nonnormal populations.

Procedure 10.1B The Pooled t-Test for Two Population Means (P-Value Approach)

Assumptions
1. Independent samples
2. Normal populations or large samples
3. Equal population standard deviations

Step 1 The null hypothesis is $H_0: \mu_1 = \mu_2$, and the alternative hypothesis is

$H_a: \mu_1 \neq \mu_2$ $H_a: \mu_1 < \mu_2$ $H_a: \mu_1 > \mu_2$
(Two-tailed)   or   (Left-tailed)   or   (Right-tailed)

Step 2 Decide on the significance level, α.

Step 3 Compute the value of the test statistic

$$t = \frac{\bar{x}_1 - \bar{x}_2}{s_p\sqrt{(1/n_1) + (1/n_2)}},$$

where

$$s_p = \sqrt{\frac{(n_1 - 1)s_1^2 + (n_2 - 1)s_2^2}{n_1 + n_2 - 2}}.$$

Denote the value of the test statistic t_0.

Step 4 The t-statistic has df $= n_1 + n_2 - 2$. Use Table IV to estimate the P-value or obtain it exactly by using technology.

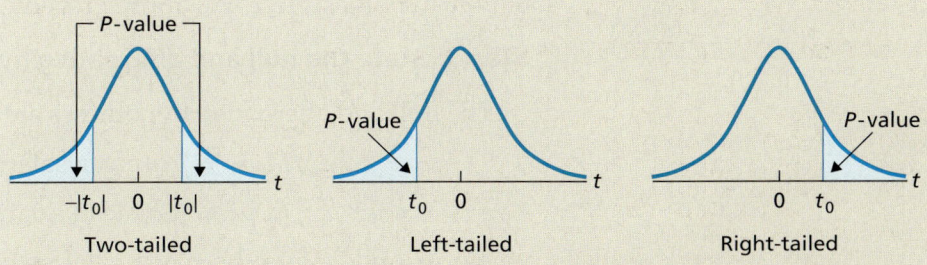

Two-tailed | Left-tailed | Right-tailed

Step 5 If $P \leq \alpha$, reject H_0; otherwise, do not reject H_0.

Step 6 Interpret the results of the hypothesis test.

The hypothesis test is exact for normal populations and is approximately correct for large samples from nonnormal populations.

Example 10.3 The Pooled t-Test

Faculty Salaries We now return to the salary problem posed in Example 10.2. Recall that we want to perform a hypothesis test to decide whether there is a difference between the mean salaries of faculty in public and private institutions.

Independent random samples of 30 faculty members in public institutions and 35 faculty members in private institutions yielded the data in Table 10.5. At the 5% significance level, do the data provide sufficient evidence to conclude that mean salaries for faculty in public and private institutions differ?

TABLE 10.5 Annual salaries ($1000s) for 30 faculty members in public institutions and 35 faculty members in private institutions

Sample 1 (public institutions)						Sample 2 (private institutions)					
34.2	63.6	24.4	79.4	33.8	88.2	92.9	102.2	51.5	77.6	71.1	59.3	71.0
90.0	56.8	56.0	42.2	40.2	44.6	52.0	62.9	46.4	61.6	73.5	97.5	97.3
100.4	41.4	58.2	81.8	51.2	64.4	63.1	53.8	45.2	78.3	67.6	27.2	92.6
24.6	35.0	76.8	29.2	41.2	74.0	118.5	101.0	76.0	66.3	52.4	81.2	56.0
107.4	54.2	84.2	15.8	60.2	71.0	37.7	68.6	56.1	31.1	47.2	24.8	62.3

Solution First, we present in Table 10.6 the required summary statistics for the two samples in Table 10.5. These statistics are obtained in the usual way.

Next, we check the three conditions required for using the pooled t-test. As the samples are independent, Assumption 1 is satisfied. To check Assumption 2, we first note that the sample sizes are large. Thus we need only be concerned with the presence of outliers. Careful graphical analysis (not shown) suggests no outliers for either sample, so we can consider Assumption 2 satisfied. From Table 10.6, the sample standard deviations are 23.95 and 22.26; these are certainly close enough for us to consider Assumption 3 satisfied.

The preceding paragraph suggests that the pooled t-test can be used to carry out the hypothesis test. We apply Procedure 10.1.

TABLE 10.6 Summary statistics for the samples in Table 10.5

Public institutions	Private institutions
$\bar{x}_1 = 57.48$	$\bar{x}_2 = 66.39$
$s_1 = 23.95$	$s_2 = 22.26$
$n_1 = 30$	$n_2 = 35$

Step 1 State the null and alternative hypotheses.

The null and alternative hypotheses are

$$H_0: \mu_1 = \mu_2 \text{ (mean salaries are the same)}$$

$$H_a: \mu_1 \neq \mu_2 \text{ (mean salaries are different),}$$

where μ_1 and μ_2 are the mean salaries of all faculty in public and private institutions, respectively. Note that the hypothesis test is two-tailed because a does-not-equal sign ($\neq$) appears in the alternative hypothesis.

Step 2 Decide on the significance level, α.

The test is to be performed at the 5% significance level, or $\alpha = 0.05$.

Step 3 Compute the value of the test statistic

$$t = \frac{\bar{x}_1 - \bar{x}_2}{s_p\sqrt{(1/n_1)+(1/n_2)}},$$

where

$$s_p = \sqrt{\frac{(n_1-1)s_1^2 + (n_2-1)s_2^2}{n_1+n_2-2}}.$$

We first determine the pooled sample standard deviation, s_p. Using the summary statistics in Table 10.6, we find that

$$s_p = \sqrt{\frac{(30-1)\cdot(23.95)^2 + (35-1)\cdot(22.26)^2}{30+35-2}} = 23.05.$$

Referring again to Table 10.6, we obtain the value of the test statistic:

$$t = \frac{\bar{x}_1 - \bar{x}_2}{s_p\sqrt{(1/n_1)+(1/n_2)}} = \frac{57.48 - 66.39}{23.05\sqrt{(1/30)+(1/35)}} = -1.554.$$

Critical-Value Approach

Step 4 The critical values for a two-tailed test are $\pm t_{\alpha/2}$ with $df = n_1 + n_2 - 2$.

From Table 10.6, $n_1 = 30$ and $n_2 = 35$, so $df = 30 + 35 - 2 = 63$. Also, from Step 2, $\alpha = 0.05$. In Table IV with $df = 63$, we find that the critical values are $\pm t_{\alpha/2} = \pm t_{0.05/2} = \pm t_{0.025} = \pm 1.998$, as shown in Fig. 10.2A.

FIGURE 10.2A

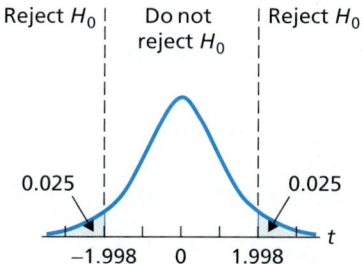

Step 5 If the value of the test statistic falls in the rejection region, reject H_0; otherwise, do not reject H_0.

From Step 3, the value of the test statistic is $t = -1.554$, which does not fall in the rejection region (see Fig. 10.2A). Thus we do not reject H_0. The test results are not statistically significant at the 5% level.

P-Value Approach

Step 4 The t-statistic has $df = n_1 + n_2 - 2$. Use Table IV to estimate the P-value or obtain it exactly by using technology.

From Step 3, the value of the test statistic is $t = -1.554$. As the test is two-tailed, the P-value is the probability of observing a value of t of 1.554 or greater in magnitude if the null hypothesis is true. That probability equals the shaded area shown in Fig. 10.2B.

FIGURE 10.2B

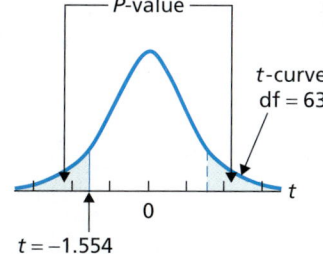

From Table 10.6, $n_1 = 30$ and $n_2 = 35$, so $df = 30 + 35 - 2 = 63$. Referring to Fig. 10.2B and to Table IV with $df = 63$, we find that $0.10 < P < 0.20$. (Using technology, we obtain $P = 0.125$.)

Step 5 If $P \leq \alpha$, reject H_0; otherwise, do not reject H_0.

From Step 4, $0.10 < P < 0.20$. Because the P-value exceeds the specified significance level of 0.05, we do not reject H_0. The test results are not statistically significant at the 5% level and (see Table 9.10 on page 405) provide at most weak evidence against the null hypothesis.

Step 6 Interpret the results of the hypothesis test.

> **What Does it Mean?** At the 5% significance level, the data do not provide sufficient evidence to conclude that a difference exists between the mean salaries of faculty in public and private institutions.

CONFIDENCE INTERVALS FOR THE DIFFERENCE BETWEEN THE MEANS OF TWO POPULATIONS WITH EQUAL STANDARD DEVIATIONS

We can also use Key Fact 10.2 on page 440 to derive a confidence-interval procedure, Procedure 10.2, for the difference between two population means, which we often refer to as the **pooled t-interval procedure.** We demonstrate its use in Example 10.4.

Procedure 10.2 — **The Pooled t-Interval Procedure for Two Population Means**

Assumptions
1. Independent samples
2. Normal populations or large samples
3. Equal population standard deviations

Step 1 For a confidence level of $1-\alpha$, use Table IV to find $t_{\alpha/2}$ with $df = n_1 + n_2 - 2$.

Step 2 The endpoints of the confidence interval for $\mu_1 - \mu_2$ are

$$(\bar{x}_1 - \bar{x}_2) \pm t_{\alpha/2} \cdot s_p \sqrt{(1/n_1)+(1/n_2)}.$$

Step 3 Interpret the confidence interval.

The confidence interval is exact for normal populations and is approximately correct for large samples from nonnormal populations.

Example 10.4 The Pooled t-Interval Procedure

Faculty Salaries Determine a 95% confidence interval for the difference, $\mu_1 - \mu_2$, between the mean salaries of faculty in public and private institutions.

Solution We apply Procedure 10.2.

Step 1 For a confidence level of $1-\alpha$, use Table IV to find $t_{\alpha/2}$ with $df = n_1 + n_2 - 2$.

For a 95% confidence interval, $\alpha = 0.05$. From Table 10.6, $n_1 = 30$ and $n_2 = 35$, so df $= n_1 + n_2 - 2 = 30 + 35 - 2 = 63$. In Table IV, we find that with df $= 63$, $t_{\alpha/2} = t_{0.05/2} = t_{0.025} = 1.998$.

Step 2 The endpoints of the confidence interval for $\mu_1 - \mu_2$ are

$$(\bar{x}_1 - \bar{x}_2) \pm t_{\alpha/2} \cdot s_p \sqrt{(1/n_1) + (1/n_2)}.$$

From Step 1, $t_{\alpha/2} = 1.998$. Also, $n_1 = 30$, $n_2 = 35$, and, from Example 10.3, we know that $\bar{x}_1 = 57.48$, $\bar{x}_2 = 66.39$, and $s_p = 23.05$. Hence the endpoints of the confidence interval for $\mu_1 - \mu_2$ are

$$(57.48 - 66.39) \pm 1.998 \cdot 23.05 \sqrt{(1/30) + (1/35)},$$

or -8.91 ± 11.46. Thus the 95% confidence interval is from -20.37 to 2.55.

Step 3 Interpret the confidence interval.

> **What Does it Mean?** We can be 95% confident that the difference between the mean salaries of faculty in public and private institutions is somewhere between $-\$20{,}370$ and $\$2{,}550$.

◆

WHAT IF THE ASSUMPTIONS ARE NOT SATISFIED?

The pooled t-procedures (pooled t-test and pooled t-interval procedure) provide methods for comparing the means of two populations. As you know, the assumptions for using those procedures are (1) independent samples, (2) normal populations or large samples, and (3) equal population standard deviations. If one or more of these conditions are not satisfied, then the pooled t-procedures should not be used.

If the samples are not independent but instead are paired (i.e., Assumption 1 is violated), then procedures designed for paired samples should be used. We discuss such procedures in Section 10.4.

If you have neither normality nor large samples (i.e., Assumption 2 is violated), then a nonparametric method should be used. For example, if the samples are independent and the two distributions (one for each population) of the variable under consideration have the same shape, then you can use a nonparametric method called the *Mann–Whitney test* to perform a hypothesis test and a nonparametric method called the *Mann–Whitney confidence-interval procedure* to obtain a confidence interval.

If the population standard deviations are not equal (i.e., Assumption 3 is violated) but Assumptions 1 and 2 are satisfied, then you can use the nonpooled t-procedures. We present those procedures in the next section.

The Technology Center

Most statistical technologies have programs that automatically perform pooled t-procedures. In this subsection, we present output and (optional) step-by-step instructions to implement such programs.

Example 10.5 Using Technology to Conduct Pooled t-Procedures

Faculty Salaries Table 10.5 on page 444 displays the annual salaries, in thousands of dollars, for independent samples of 30 faculty members in public institutions and 35 faculty members in private institutions. Use Minitab, Excel, or the TI-83 Plus to perform the hypothesis test in Example 10.3 and obtain the confidence interval required in Example 10.4.

Solution Let μ_1 and μ_2 denote the mean salaries of all faculty in public and private institutions, respectively. The task in Example 10.3 is to perform the hypothesis test

$$H_0: \mu_1 = \mu_2 \text{ (mean salaries are the same)}$$

$$H_a: \mu_1 \neq \mu_2 \text{ (mean salaries are different)}$$

at the 5% significance level; the task in Example 10.4 is to obtain a 95% confidence interval for $\mu_1 - \mu_2$.

Printout 10.1 shows the output obtained by applying the pooled t-procedures to the salary data in Table 10.5.

The outputs in Printout 10.1 reveal that the P-value for the hypothesis test is 0.125. Because the P-value exceeds the specified significance level of 0.05, we do not reject H_0. The outputs in Printout 10.1 also show that a 95% confidence interval for the difference between the means is from -20.38 to 2.55. ◆

Obtaining the Output (Optional)

Printout 10.1 provides output from Minitab, Excel, and the TI-83 Plus for pooled t-procedures based on the samples of salaries in Table 10.5. The following are detailed instructions for obtaining that output. First, we store the two samples of salary data in columns (Minitab), ranges (Excel), or lists (TI-83 Plus) named PUBL and PRIV. Then, we proceed as indicated on page 450.[1]

PRINTOUT 10.1
Pooled t-procedures output for the salary data

MINITAB

```
Two-Sample T-Test and CI: PUBL, PRIV

Two-sample T for PUBL vs PRIV

         N      Mean     StDev    SE Mean
PUBL    30      57.5     24.0       4.4
PRIV    35      66.4     22.3       3.8


Difference = mu PUBL - mu PRIV
Estimate for difference:  -8.91
95% CI for difference: (-20.38, 2.55)
T-Test of difference = 0 (vs not =): T-Value = -1.55  P-Value = 0.125  DF = 63
Both use Pooled StDev = 23.1
```

---

[1] Although Minitab simultaneously performs a hypothesis test and obtains a confidence interval, the type of confidence interval Minitab finds depends on the type of hypothesis test. Specifically, Minitab computes a two-sided confidence interval for a two-tailed test and a one-sided confidence interval for a one-tailed test. In this book, we consider only two-sided confidence intervals. To perform a one-tailed hypothesis test and obtain a two-sided confidence interval, we must apply Minitab's pooled t-procedure twice: once for the one-tailed hypothesis test and once for the confidence interval specifying a two-tailed hypothesis test.

PRINTOUT 10.1 (cont.) Pooled t-procedures output for the salary data

EXCEL

2 Sample t Test Results

Test Results

Conclusion
Fail to reject Ho at alpha = 0.05

Summary Statistics

Diff	Std Error
−8.914	5.736

Test Summary

Test:	Pooled t Test
Ho:	μ1 − μ2 = 0
Ha:	2-tailed: μ1 − μ2 ≠ 0
df:	63
t Statistic:	−1.554
p-value:	0.125

PUBL Summary

n	Mean	Std Dev
30	57.48	23.953

PRIV Summary

n	Mean	Std Dev
35	66.394	22.261

Using **2 Var t Test**

Confidence Interval

Interval Results

Confidence Interval
With 95% Confidence, −20.377 < μ1 − μ2 < 2.549

Interval Summary

Diff	Std Err	df	t*
−8.914	5.736	63	1.998

Using **2 Var t Interval**

TI-83 PLUS

```
2-SampTTest
 μ1≠μ2
 t=-1.554012669
 p=.1251909809
 df=63
 x̄1=57.48
↓x̄2=66.39428571
```

```
2-SampTInt
 (-20.38,2.5488)
 df=63
 x̄1=57.48
 x̄2=66.39428571
 Sx1=23.9528042
↓Sx2=22.2611234
```

```
2-SampTTest
 μ1≠μ2
↑Sx1=23.9528042
 Sx2=22.2611234
 SxP=23.0552569
 n1=30
 n2=35
```

```
2-SampTInt
 (-20.38,2.5488)
↑Sx1=23.9528042
 Sx2=22.2611234
 SxP=23.0552569
 n1=30
 n2=35
```

Using **2-SampTTest**   Using **2-SampTInt**

MINITAB

1. Choose **Stat ▶ Basic Statistics ▶ 2-Sample t...**
2. Select the **Samples in different columns** option button
3. Click in the **First** text box and specify PUBL
4. Click in the **Second** text box and specify PRIV
5. Select the **Assume equal variances** check box
6. Click the **Options...** button
7. Click in the **Confidence level** text box and type 95
8. Click in the **Test mean** text box and type 0
9. Click the arrow button at the right of the **Alternative** drop-down list box and select **not equal**
10. Click **OK**
11. Click **OK**

EXCEL

FOR THE HYPOTHESIS TEST:
1. Choose **DDXL ▶ Hypothesis Tests**
2. Select **2 Var t Test** from the **Function type** drop-down box
3. Specify PUBL in the **1st Quantitative Variable** text box
4. Specify PRIV in the **2nd Quantitative Variable** text box
5. Click **OK**
6. Click the **Pooled** button
7. Click the **Set difference** button, type 0, and click **OK**
8. Click the **0.05** button
9. Click the $\mu1 - \mu2 \neq$ **diff** button
10. Click the **Compute** button

FOR THE CI:
1. Exit to Excel
2. Choose **DDXL ▶ Confidence Intervals**
3. Select **2 Var t Interval** from the **Function type** drop-down box
4. Specify PUBL in the **1st Quantitative Variable** text box
5. Specify PRIV in the **2nd Quantitative Variable** text box
6. Click **OK**
7. Click the **Pooled** button
8. Click the **95%** button
9. Click the **Compute Interval** button

TI-83 PLUS

FOR THE HYPOTHESIS TEST:
1. Press **STAT**, arrow over to **TESTS**, and press 4
2. Highlight **Data** and press **ENTER**
3. Press the down-arrow key
4. Press **2nd ▶ LIST**, arrow down to PUBL, and press **ENTER** twice
5. Press **2nd ▶ LIST**, arrow down to PRIV, and press **ENTER** four times
6. Highlight $\neq \mu2$ and press **ENTER**
7. Press the down-arrow key, highlight **Yes**, and press **ENTER**
8. Press the down-arrow key, highlight **Calculate**, and press **ENTER**

FOR THE CI:
1. Press **STAT**, arrow over to **TESTS**, and press 0
2. Highlight **Data** and press **ENTER**
3. Press the down-arrow key
4. Press **2nd ▶ LIST**, arrow down to PUBL, and press **ENTER** twice
5. Press **2nd ▶ LIST**, arrow down to PRIV, and press **ENTER** four times
6. Type .95 for **C-Level** and press **ENTER**
7. Highlight **Yes**, and press **ENTER**
8. Press the down-arrow key and press **ENTER**

Exercises 10.2

Statistical Concepts and Skills

10.16 Regarding the three conditions required for using the pooled t-procedures:
a. what are they?
b. how important is each condition?

10.17 Why is s_p called the pooled sample standard deviation?

10.18 Independent samples are taken from two populations with the intent of performing a hypothesis test to compare their means. Preliminary data analyses indicate that the variable under consideration is normally distributed on each population. The following table provides summary statistics for the two samples.

Sample 1	Sample 2
$\bar{x}_1 = 468.3$	$\bar{x}_2 = 394.6$
$s_1 = 38.2$	$s_2 = 84.7$
$n_1 = 6$	$n_2 = 14$

Is the use of the pooled *t*-test on these data reasonable? Explain your answer.

Preliminary data analyses indicate that you can reasonably consider the assumptions for using pooled t-procedures satisfied in Exercises 10.19–10.24. For each exercise, perform the required hypothesis test by using either the critical-value approach or the P-value approach.

10.19 Doing Time. The U.S. Bureau of Prisons publishes data in *Statistical Report* on the times served by prisoners released from federal institutions for the first time. Independent random samples of released prisoners in the fraud and firearms offense categories yielded the following information on time served, in months.

Fraud		Firearms	
3.6	17.9	25.5	23.8
5.3	5.9	10.4	17.9
10.7	7.0	18.4	21.9
8.5	13.9	19.6	13.3
11.8	16.6	20.9	16.1

At the 5% significance level, do the data provide sufficient evidence to conclude that the mean time served for fraud is less than that for firearms offenses? (*Note:* $\bar{x}_1 = 10.12$, $s_1 = 4.90$, $\bar{x}_2 = 18.78$, and $s_2 = 4.64$.)

10.20 Sex and Direction. In the paper "The Relation of Sex and Sense of Direction to Spatial Orientation in an Unfamiliar Environment" (*Journal of Environmental Psychology*, 2000, Vol. 20, pp. 17–28), Sholl et al. published the results of examining the sense of direction of 30 male and 30 female students. After being taken to an unfamiliar wooded park, the students were given some spatial orientation tests, including pointing to south, which tested their absolute frame of reference. The students pointed by moving a pointer attached to a 360° protractor. Following are the absolute pointing errors, in degrees, of the participants.

Male					Female				
13	130	39	33	10	14	8	20	3	138
13	68	18	3	11	122	78	69	111	3
38	23	60	5	9	128	31	18	35	111
59	5	86	22	70	109	36	27	32	35
58	3	167	15	30	12	27	8	3	80
8	20	67	26	19	91	68	66	176	15

At the 1% significance level, do the data provide sufficient evidence to conclude that, on average, males have a better sense of direction and, in particular, a better frame of reference than females? (*Note:* $\bar{x}_1 = 37.6$, $s_1 = 38.5$, $\bar{x}_2 = 55.8$, and $s_2 = 48.3$.)

10.21 Getting Taller? *Vital and Health Statistics*, published by the National Center for Health Statistics, provides information on heights and weights of Americans, by age and sex. Independent samples of 10 males aged 25–34 years and 15 males aged 45–54 years yielded the following heights, in inches.

25–34		45–54		
73.3	70.4	73.2	69.5	64.7
64.8	66.8	68.5	74.5	73.0
72.1	70.7	62.4	70.6	66.7
68.9	74.4	65.5	69.3	68.1
68.7	71.8	71.3	67.1	64.3

At the 5% significance level, do the data provide sufficient evidence to conclude that males in the age group 25–34 years are, on average, taller than those in the age group 45–54 years? (*Note:* $\bar{x}_1 = 70.19$, $s_1 = 2.951$, $\bar{x}_2 = 68.58$, and $s_2 = 3.543$.)

10.22 Driving Distances. Data on household vehicle miles of travel (VMT) are compiled annually by the Federal Highway Administration and are published in *National Personal Transportation Survey, Summary of Travel Trends*. Independent samples of 15 midwestern households and 14 southern households provided the following data on last year's VMT, in thousands of miles.

Midwest			South		
16.2	12.9	17.3	22.2	19.2	9.3
14.6	18.6	10.8	24.6	20.2	15.8
11.2	16.6	16.6	18.0	12.2	20.1
24.4	20.3	20.9	16.0	17.5	18.2
9.6	15.1	18.3	22.8	11.5	

At the 5% significance level, does there appear to be a difference in last year's mean VMT for midwestern and southern households? (*Note:* $\bar{x}_1 = 16.23$, $s_1 = 4.06$, $\bar{x}_2 = 17.69$, and $s_2 = 4.42$.)

10.23 Vegetarians and Omnivores. Philosophical and health issues are prompting an increasing number of Taiwanese to switch to a vegetarian lifestyle. A study by Lu et al., published in the *Journal of Nutrition* (2000, Vol. 130, pp. 1591–1596), compared the daily intake of nutrients by vegetarians and omnivores living in Taiwan. Among the nutrients considered was protein. Too little protein stunts growth and interferes with all bodily functions; too much protein puts a strain on the kidneys, can cause diarrhea and dehydration, and can leach calcium from bones and teeth. Independent samples of 51 female vegetarians and 53 female omnivores yielded the following summary statistics, in grams, on daily protein intake.

Vegetarians	Omnivores
$\bar{x}_1 = 39.04$	$\bar{x}_2 = 49.92$
$s_1 = 18.82$	$s_2 = 18.97$
$n_1 = 51$	$n_2 = 53$

Do the data provide sufficient evidence to conclude that the mean daily protein intakes of female vegetarians and female omnivores differ? Perform the required hypothesis test at the 1% significance level.

10.24 Offspring of Diabetic Mothers. Previous research indicates that children borne by diabetic mothers may suffer from obesity, high blood pressure, and glucose intolerance. Independent samples of adolescent offspring of diabetic mothers (ODM) and nondiabetic mothers (ONM) were taken by Cho et al. and evaluated for potential differences in vital measurements, including blood pressure and glucose tolerance. The study was published in *The Journal of Pediatrics* (2000, Vol. 136(5), pp. 587–592). The following summary statistics are for the systolic blood pressures, in mm Hg, of the 99 ODM participants and the 80 ONM participants.

ODM	ONM
$\bar{x}_1 = 118$	$\bar{x}_2 = 110$
$s_1 = 12.04$	$s_2 = 11.25$
$n_1 = 99$	$n_2 = 80$

At the 1% significance level, do the data provide sufficient evidence to conclude that the mean systolic blood pressure of ODM children exceeds that of ONM children?

In Exercises 10.25–10.28, apply Procedure 10.2 on page 446 to obtain the required confidence interval.

10.25 Getting Taller? Refer to Exercise 10.21.
a. Obtain a 90% confidence interval for the difference between the mean height of males in the age group 25–34 years and the mean height of males in the age group 45–54 years.
b. Interpret your result from part (a).

10.26 Driving Distances. Refer to Exercise 10.22.
a. Determine a 95% confidence interval for the difference between last year's mean VMTs by midwestern and southern households.
b. Interpret your result from part (a).

10.27 Vegetarians and Omnivores. Refer to Exercise 10.23.
a. Obtain a 99% confidence interval for the difference between the mean daily protein intakes of female vegetarians and female omnivores.
b. Interpret your answer in part (a).

10.28 Offspring of Diabetic Mothers. Refer to Exercise 10.24.
a. Determine a 98% confidence interval for the difference between the mean systolic blood pressures of ODM and ONM children.
b. Interpret your answer in part (a).

Extending the Concepts and Skills

10.29 In this section, we introduced the pooled *t*-test, which provides a method for comparing two population means. In deriving the pooled *t*-test, we stated that the variable

$$z = \frac{(\bar{x}_1 - \bar{x}_2) - (\mu_1 - \mu_2)}{\sigma \sqrt{(1/n_1) + (1/n_2)}}$$

cannot be used as a basis for the required test statistic because σ is unknown. Why can't that variable be used as a basis for the required test statistic?

10.30 The formula for the pooled variance, s_p^2, is given on page 440. Show that, if the sample sizes, n_1 and n_2, are equal, s_p^2 is the mean of s_1^2 and s_2^2.

10.31 Suppose that we want to perform a hypothesis test to compare the means of two populations, using independent samples. Assume that the two distributions (one for each population) of the variable under consideration are normally distributed and have equal standard deviations.
a. Is it permissible to use the pooled *t*-test to perform the hypothesis test? Explain your answer.
b. Is it permissible to use the Mann–Whitney test to perform the hypothesis test? Explain your answer.
c. Which procedure is preferable, the pooled *t*-test or the Mann–Whitney test? Explain your answer.

10.32 Suppose that we want to perform a hypothesis test to compare the means of two populations, using independent samples. Assume that the two distributions of the variable under consideration have the same shape, but are not normal, and both sample sizes are large.
a. Is it permissible to use the pooled *t*-test to perform the hypothesis test? Explain your answer.
b. Is it permissible to use the Mann–Whitney test to perform the hypothesis test? Explain your answer.
c. Which procedure is preferable, the pooled *t*-test or the Mann–Whitney test? Explain your answer.

Using Technology

10.33 Vegetarians and Omnivores. Refer to Exercises 10.23 and 10.27. We have supplied the raw data on the WeissStats CD. Use the technology of your choice to
a. obtain normal probability plots, boxplots, and the standard deviations for the two samples.
b. perform the required hypothesis test and obtain the desired confidence interval.
c. Is your procedure in part (b) justified? Explain your answer.

10.34 Offspring of Diabetic Mothers. Refer to Exercises 10.24 and 10.28. We have supplied the raw data on the WeissStats CD. Use the technology of your choice to
a. obtain normal probability plots, boxplots, and the standard deviations for the two samples.
b. perform the required hypothesis test and obtain the desired confidence interval.
c. Is your procedure in part (b) justified? Explain your answer.

10.35 Blood Cholesterol and Heart Disease. Numerous studies have shown that high blood cholesterol leads to artery clogging and subsequent heart disease. One such study by Scott et al. was published in the paper "Plasma Lipids as Collateral Risk Factors in Coronary Artery Disease: A Study of 371 Males With Chest Pain" (*Journal of Chronic Diseases*, 1978, Vol. 31, pp. 337–345). The research compared the plasma cholesterol concentrations of independent samples of patients with and without evidence of heart disease. Evidence of heart disease was based on the degree of narrowing in the arteries. The raw data, presented in milligrams/deciliter (mg/dl), are provided on the WeissStats CD.

a. Obtain normal probability plots, boxplots, and the standard deviations of the two samples.
b. At the 1% significance level, do the data provide sufficient evidence to conclude that a difference exists between the mean blood cholesterol concentrations of male patients with and without evidence of heart disease? Use the pooled t-test.
c. Determine and interpret a 99% confidence interval for the difference between the mean blood cholesterol concentrations of male patients with and without evidence of heart disease. Apply the pooled t-interval procedure.
d. Are the procedures in parts (b) and (c) justified? Explain your answer.

10.36 In this exercise, you are to perform a computer simulation to illustrate the distribution of the pooled t-statistic, given in Key Fact 10.2 on page 440.
a. Simulate 1000 random samples of size 4 from a normally distributed variable with a mean of 100 and a standard deviation of 16. Then obtain the sample mean and sample standard deviation of each of the 1000 samples.
b. Simulate 1000 random samples of size 3 from a normally distributed variable with a mean of 110 and a standard deviation of 16. Then obtain the sample mean and sample standard deviation of each of the 1000 samples.
c. Determine the value of the pooled t-statistic for each of the 1000 pairs of samples obtained in parts (a) and (b).
d. Obtain a histogram of the 1000 values found in part (c).
e. Theoretically, what is the distribution of all possible values of the pooled t-statistic?
f. Compare your results from parts (d) and (e).

10.3 INFERENCES FOR TWO POPULATION MEANS, USING INDEPENDENT SAMPLES: STANDARD DEVIATIONS NOT ASSUMED EQUAL

In Section 10.2, we examined methods based on independent samples for performing inferences to compare the means of two populations. The methods discussed, called pooled t-procedures, require that the standard deviations of the two populations be equal.

In this section, we develop inferential procedures based on independent samples to compare the means of two populations that do not require the population standard deviations to be equal, even though they may be. As before, we assume that the population standard deviations are unknown, because that is usually the case in practice.

For our derivation, we also assume that the variable under consideration is normally distributed on each population. As we demonstrate later, the resulting inferential procedures are approximately correct for large samples, regardless of distribution type.

HYPOTHESIS TESTS FOR THE MEANS OF TWO POPULATIONS, USING INDEPENDENT SAMPLES

We begin by finding a test statistic. We know from Key Fact 10.1 on page 436 that, for independent samples, the standardized version of $\bar{x}_1 - \bar{x}_2$,

$$z = \frac{(\bar{x}_1 - \bar{x}_2) - (\mu_1 - \mu_2)}{\sqrt{(\sigma_1^2/n_1) + (\sigma_2^2/n_2)}},$$

has the standard normal distribution. We are assuming that the population standard deviations, σ_1 and σ_2, are unknown, so we cannot use this variable as a basis for the required test statistic. We therefore replace σ_1 and σ_2 with their sample estimates, s_1 and s_2, and obtain the variable

$$\frac{(\bar{x}_1 - \bar{x}_2) - (\mu_1 - \mu_2)}{\sqrt{(s_1^2/n_1) + (s_2^2/n_2)}},$$

which we can use as a basis for the required test statistic. This variable does not have the standard normal distribution, but it does have roughly a t-distribution, as indicated in Key Fact 10.3.

Key Fact 10.3

Distribution of the Nonpooled t-Statistic

Suppose that x is a normally distributed variable on each of two populations. Then, for independent samples of sizes n_1 and n_2 from the two populations, the variable

$$t = \frac{(\bar{x}_1 - \bar{x}_2) - (\mu_1 - \mu_2)}{\sqrt{(s_1^2/n_1) + (s_2^2/n_2)}}$$

has approximately a t-distribution. The degrees of freedom used is obtained from the sample data. It is denoted Δ and given by

$$\Delta = \frac{\left[(s_1^2/n_1) + (s_2^2/n_2)\right]^2}{\dfrac{(s_1^2/n_1)^2}{n_1 - 1} + \dfrac{(s_2^2/n_2)^2}{n_2 - 1}},$$

rounded down to the nearest integer.

In light of Key Fact 10.3, for a hypothesis test that has null hypothesis $H_0: \mu_1 = \mu_2$, we can use the variable

$$t = \frac{\bar{x}_1 - \bar{x}_2}{\sqrt{(s_1^2/n_1) + (s_2^2/n_2)}}$$

as the test statistic and obtain the critical value(s) from the t-table, Table IV. Specifically, we have, on pages 455 and 456, Procedures 10.3A and B, both of which we often refer to as the **nonpooled t-test.**

Before we apply the nonpooled t-test, we need to discuss the assumptions for its use. Assumption 1 (independent samples) is essential; the samples must be independent or the procedure does not apply.

Procedure 10.3A — The Nonpooled t-Test for Two Population Means (Critical-Value Approach)

Assumptions
1. Independent samples
2. Normal populations or large samples

Step 1 The null hypothesis is $H_0: \mu_1 = \mu_2$, and the alternative hypothesis is

$$H_a: \mu_1 \neq \mu_2 \quad \text{or} \quad H_a: \mu_1 < \mu_2 \quad \text{or} \quad H_a: \mu_1 > \mu_2$$
$$\text{(Two-tailed)} \quad\quad\quad \text{(Left-tailed)} \quad\quad\quad \text{(Right-tailed)}$$

Step 2 Decide on the significance level, α.

Step 3 Compute the value of the test statistic

$$t = \frac{\bar{x}_1 - \bar{x}_2}{\sqrt{(s_1^2/n_1) + (s_2^2/n_2)}}.$$

Step 4 The critical value(s) are

$$\pm t_{\alpha/2} \quad \text{or} \quad -t_\alpha \quad \text{or} \quad t_\alpha$$
$$\text{(Two-tailed)} \quad\quad \text{(Left-tailed)} \quad\quad \text{(Right-tailed)}$$

with df = Δ, where

$$\Delta = \frac{[(s_1^2/n_1) + (s_2^2/n_2)]^2}{\dfrac{(s_1^2/n_1)^2}{n_1 - 1} + \dfrac{(s_2^2/n_2)^2}{n_2 - 1}},$$

rounded down to the nearest integer. Use Table IV to find the critical value(s).

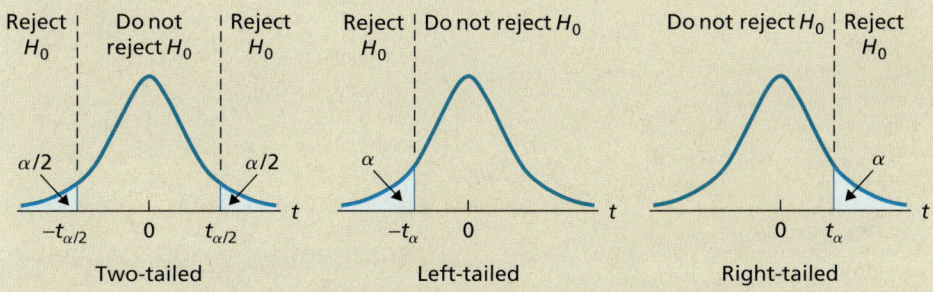

Step 5 If the value of the test statistic falls in the rejection region, reject H_0; otherwise, do not reject H_0.

Step 6 Interpret the results of the hypothesis test.

Procedure 10.3B — The Nonpooled t-Test for Two Population Means (P-Value Approach)

Assumptions

1. Independent samples
2. Normal populations or large samples

Step 1 The null hypothesis is $H_0: \mu_1 = \mu_2$, and the alternative hypothesis is

$$H_a: \mu_1 \neq \mu_2 \quad \text{or} \quad H_a: \mu_1 < \mu_2 \quad \text{or} \quad H_a: \mu_1 > \mu_2$$
$$\text{(Two-tailed)} \qquad \text{(Left-tailed)} \qquad \text{(Right-tailed)}$$

Step 2 Decide on the significance level, α.

Step 3 Compute the value of the test statistic

$$t = \frac{\bar{x}_1 - \bar{x}_2}{\sqrt{(s_1^2/n_1) + (s_2^2/n_2)}}.$$

Denote the value of the test statistic t_0.

Step 4 The t-statistic has df $= \Delta$, where

$$\Delta = \frac{[(s_1^2/n_1) + (s_2^2/n_2)]^2}{\dfrac{(s_1^2/n_1)^2}{n_1 - 1} + \dfrac{(s_2^2/n_2)^2}{n_2 - 1}},$$

rounded down to the nearest integer. Use Table IV to estimate the P-value or obtain it exactly by using technology.

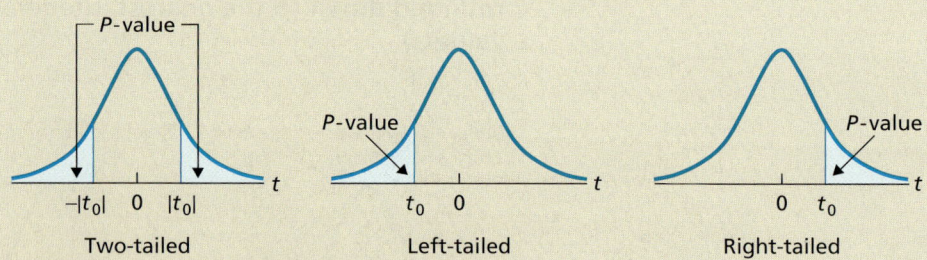

Step 5 If $P \leq \alpha$, reject H_0; otherwise, do not reject H_0.

Step 6 Interpret the results of the hypothesis test.

Regarding Assumption 2, although the nonpooled t-test was derived under the condition that the variable under consideration is normally distributed on each of the two populations (normal populations), it also applies approximately for large samples regardless of distribution type. Actually, the nonpooled

t-test works reasonably well even for small samples or samples of moderate size from nonnormal populations provided the populations are not too nonnormal. In other words, the nonpooled t-test is robust to moderate violations of the normality assumption.

When considering the nonpooled t-test, you must also watch for outliers. Again, the presence of outliers calls into question the normality assumption. Moreover, even for large samples, outliers can sometimes unduly affect a nonpooled t-test because the sample mean and sample standard deviation are not resistant to them.

Example 10.6 illustrates use of the nonpooled t-test.

Example 10.6 The Nonpooled t-Test

Neurosurgery Operative Times Several neurosurgeons wanted to determine whether a dynamic system (Z-plate) reduced the operative time relative to a static system (ALPS plate). R. Jacobowitz, Ph.D., an ASU professor, along with G. Vishteh, M.D., and other neurosurgeons, obtained the data displayed in Table 10.7 on operative times, in minutes, for the two systems. At the 1% significance level, do the data provide sufficient evidence to conclude that the mean operative time is less with the dynamic system than with the static system?

TABLE 10.7
Operative times, in minutes, for dynamic and static systems

Dynamic							Static		
370	360	510	445	295	315	490	430	445	455
345	450	505	335	280	325	500	455	490	535

Solution First, we present in Table 10.8 the required summary statistics for the two samples in Table 10.7. These statistics are obtained in the usual way.

Next, we check the two conditions required for using the nonpooled t-test. The samples are independent, so Assumption 1 is satisfied. Boxplots and normal probability plots (not shown) of the two samples in Table 10.7 reveal no outliers and, keeping in mind that the nonpooled t-test is robust to moderate violations of normality, show that we can consider Assumption 2 satisfied. We can therefore apply the nonpooled t-test, Procedure 10.3, to carry out the hypothesis test.

TABLE 10.8
Summary statistics for the samples in Table 10.7

Dynamic	Static
$\bar{x}_1 = 394.6$	$\bar{x}_2 = 468.3$
$s_1 = 84.7$	$s_2 = 38.2$
$n_1 = 14$	$n_2 = 6$

Step 1 State the null and alternative hypotheses.

Let μ_1 and μ_2 denote the mean operative times for the dynamic and static systems, respectively. Then the null and alternative hypotheses are

H_0: $\mu_1 = \mu_2$ (mean dynamic time is not less than mean static time)

H_a: $\mu_1 < \mu_2$ (mean dynamic time is less than mean static time).

Note that the hypothesis test is left-tailed because a less-than sign ($<$) appears in the alternative hypothesis.

Step 2 Decide on the significance level, α.

The test is to be performed at the 1% significance level, or $\alpha = 0.01$.

Step 3 Compute the value of the test statistic

$$t = \frac{\bar{x}_1 - \bar{x}_2}{\sqrt{(s_1^2/n_1) + (s_2^2/n_2)}}.$$

Referring to Table 10.8, we get

$$t = \frac{394.6 - 468.3}{\sqrt{(84.7^2/14) + (38.2^2/6)}} = -2.681.$$

Critical-Value Approach

Step 4 The critical value for a left-tailed test is $-t_\alpha$ with df $= \Delta$.

From Step 2, $\alpha = 0.01$. Also, from Table 10.8, we see that

$$\text{df} = \Delta = \frac{\left[(84.7^2/14) + (38.2^2/6)\right]^2}{\dfrac{(84.7^2/14)^2}{14-1} + \dfrac{(38.2^2/6)^2}{6-1}},$$

which equals 17 when rounded down. From Table IV with df $= 17$, we find that the critical value is $-t_\alpha = -t_{0.01} = -2.567$, as shown in Fig. 10.3A.

FIGURE 10.3A

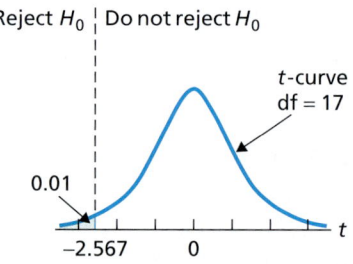

Step 5 If the value of the test statistic falls in the rejection region, reject H_0; otherwise, do not reject H_0.

From Step 3, the value of the test statistic is $t = -2.681$, which, as we see from Fig. 10.3A, falls in the rejection region. Thus we reject H_0. The test results are statistically significant at the 1% level.

P-Value Approach

Step 4 The t-statistic has df $= \Delta$. Use Table IV to estimate the P-value or obtain it exactly by using technology.

From Step 3, the value of the test statistic is $t = -2.681$. The test is left-tailed, so the P-value is the probability of observing a value of t of -2.681 or less if the null hypothesis is true. That probability equals the shaded area shown in Fig. 10.3B.

FIGURE 10.3B

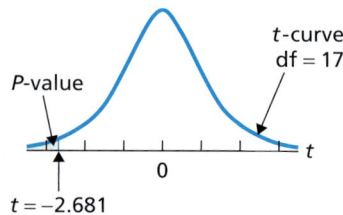

From Table 10.8, we find that

$$\text{df} = \Delta = \frac{\left[(84.7^2/14) + (38.2^2/6)\right]^2}{\dfrac{(84.7^2/14)^2}{14-1} + \dfrac{(38.2^2/6)^2}{6-1}},$$

which equals 17 when rounded down. Referring to Fig. 10.3B and Table IV with df $= 17$, we find that $0.005 < P < 0.01$. (Using technology, we get $P = 0.0079$.)

Step 5 If $P \leq \alpha$, reject H_0; otherwise, do not reject H_0.

From Step 4, $0.005 < P < 0.01$. Because the P-value is less than the specified significance level of 0.01, we reject H_0. The test results are statistically significant at the 1% level and (see Table 9.10 on page 405) provide very strong evidence against the null hypothesis.

Step 6 Interpret the results of the hypothesis test.

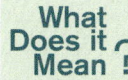

At the 1% significance level, the data provide sufficient evidence to conclude that the mean operative time is less with the dynamic system than with the static system.

◆

CONFIDENCE INTERVALS FOR THE DIFFERENCE BETWEEN THE MEANS OF TWO POPULATIONS, USING INDEPENDENT SAMPLES

We can also use Key Fact 10.3 on page 454 to derive a confidence-interval procedure, Procedure 10.4, for the difference between two means, which we often refer to as the **nonpooled *t*-interval procedure**. We demonstrate its use in Example 10.7.

Procedure 10.4

The Nonpooled *t*-Interval Procedure for Two Population Means

Assumptions
1. Independent samples
2. Normal populations or large samples

Step 1 For a confidence level of $1-\alpha$, use Table IV to find $t_{\alpha/2}$ with df $= \Delta$, where

$$\Delta = \frac{\left[(s_1^2/n_1) + (s_2^2/n_2)\right]^2}{\dfrac{(s_1^2/n_1)^2}{n_1-1} + \dfrac{(s_2^2/n_2)^2}{n_2-1}},$$

rounded down to the nearest integer.

Step 2 The endpoints of the confidence interval for $\mu_1 - \mu_2$ are

$$(\bar{x}_1 - \bar{x}_2) \pm t_{\alpha/2} \cdot \sqrt{(s_1^2/n_1) + (s_2^2/n_2)}.$$

Step 3 Interpret the confidence interval.

Example 10.7 The Nonpooled *t*-Interval Procedure

Neurosurgery Operative Times Use the sample data in Table 10.7 on page 457 to obtain a 99% confidence interval for the difference, $\mu_1 - \mu_2$, between the mean operative times of the dynamic and static systems.

Solution We apply Procedure 10.4.

Step 1 For a confidence level of $1 - \alpha$, use Table IV to find $t_{\alpha/2}$ with df = Δ.

For a 99% confidence interval, $\alpha = 0.01$. From Example 10.6, df = 17. In Table IV, with df = 17, $t_{\alpha/2} = t_{0.01/2} = t_{0.005} = 2.898$.

Step 2 The endpoints of the confidence interval for $\mu_1 - \mu_2$ are

$$(\bar{x}_1 - \bar{x}_2) \pm t_{\alpha/2} \cdot \sqrt{(s_1^2/n_1) + (s_2^2/n_2)}.$$

From Step 1, $t_{\alpha/2} = 2.898$. Referring to Table 10.8 on page 457, we conclude that the endpoints of the confidence interval for $\mu_1 - \mu_2$ are

$$(394.6 - 468.3) \pm 2.898 \cdot \sqrt{(84.7^2/14) + (38.2^2/6)}$$

or -153.4 to 6.0.

Step 3 Interpret the confidence interval.

We can be 99% confident that the difference between the mean operative times of the dynamic and static systems is somewhere between -153.4 minutes and 6.0 minutes.

WHAT IF THE ASSUMPTIONS ARE NOT SATISFIED?

The nonpooled *t*-procedures (nonpooled *t*-test and nonpooled *t*-interval procedure) provide methods for comparing the means of two populations. As you know, the assumptions for using those procedures are (1) independent samples and (2) normal populations or large samples. If one or more of these conditions are not satisfied, then the nonpooled *t*-procedures should not be used.

If the samples are not independent but instead are paired (i.e., Assumption 1 is violated), then procedures designed for paired samples should be used. We discuss such procedures in Section 10.4.

If you have neither normality nor large samples (i.e., Assumption 2 is violated), then a nonparametric method should be used. For example, if the samples are independent and the two distributions (one for each population) of the variable under consideration have the same shape, then you can use the Mann–Whitney test to perform a hypothesis test and the Mann–Whitney confidence-interval procedure to obtain a confidence interval.

POOLED VERSUS NONPOOLED *t*-TESTS

Suppose that we want to perform a hypothesis test based on independent samples to compare the means of two populations. Further suppose that either the variable under consideration is normally distributed on each of the two populations or the sample sizes are large. Then two tests are candidates for the job: the pooled t-test (Procedure 10.1 of Section 10.2) or the nonpooled t-test (Procedure 10.3 of this section).

In theory, the pooled t-test requires that the population standard deviations be equal. What if the pooled t-test is used when in fact the population standard deviations are not equal? The answer to this question depends on several factors. If the population standard deviations are unequal, but not too unequal, and the sample sizes are nearly the same, using the pooled t-test will not cause serious difficulties. If the population standard deviations are quite different, however, using the pooled t-test can result in a significantly larger Type I error probability than the one specified (i.e., α).

In contrast, the nonpooled t-test does not require that the population standard deviations be equal; it applies whether or not they are equal. Then why use the pooled t-test at all? The reason is that, if the population standard deviations are equal or nearly so, then, on average, the pooled t-test is slightly more powerful; that is, the probability of making a Type II error is somewhat smaller.

As emphasized in Key Fact 10.4, the pooled t-test should be used only when the two populations have nearly equal standard deviations; otherwise, the nonpooled t-test should be applied. Similar remarks apply to the pooled t-interval and nonpooled t-interval procedures.

Key Fact 10.4 Choosing Between a Pooled and Nonpooled Procedure

Suppose that you want to use independent samples to compare the means of two populations. When you are deciding between a pooled t-procedure and a nonpooled t-procedure, follow these guidelines: If you are reasonably sure that the populations have nearly equal standard deviations, use a pooled t-procedure; otherwise, use a nonpooled t-procedure.

The Technology Center

Most statistical technologies have programs that automatically perform nonpooled t-procedures. In this subsection, we present output and (optional) step-by-step instructions to implement such programs.

Example 10.8 Using Technology to Conduct Nonpooled t-Procedures

Neurosurgery Operative Times Table 10.7 on page 457 displays samples of neurosurgery operative times, in minutes, for dynamic and static systems. Use Minitab, Excel, or the TI-83 Plus to perform the hypothesis test in Example 10.6 and obtain the confidence interval required in Example 10.7.

Solution Let μ_1 and μ_2 denote, respectively, the mean operative times of the dynamic and static systems. The task in Example 10.6 is to perform the hypothesis test

H_0: $\mu_1 = \mu_2$ (mean dynamic time is not less than mean static time)

H_a: $\mu_1 < \mu_2$ (mean dynamic time is less than mean static time)

at the 1% significance level; the task in Example 10.7 is to obtain a 99% confidence interval for $\mu_1 - \mu_2$.

Printout 10.2 shows the output obtained by applying the nonpooled t-procedures to the data on operative times displayed in Table 10.7.

PRINTOUT 10.2
Nonpooled t-procedures output for the operative-time data

MINITAB

Two-Sample T-Test and CI: DYNA, STAT   [FOR THE HYPOTHESIS TEST]

```
Two-sample T for DYNA vs STAT

        N    Mean    StDev   SE Mean
DYNA   14   394.6     84.7       23
STAT    6   468.3     38.2       16

Difference = mu DYNA - mu STAT
Estimate for difference:  -73.7
99% upper bound for difference: -3.1
T-Test of difference = 0 (vs <): T-Value = -2.68  P-Value = 0.008  DF = 17
```

Two-Sample T-Test and CI: DYNA, STAT   [FOR THE CONFIDENCE INTERVAL]

```
Two-sample T for DYNA vs STAT

        N    Mean    StDev   SE Mean
DYNA   14   394.6     84.7       23
STAT    6   468.3     38.2       16

Difference = mu DYNA - mu STAT
Estimate for difference:  -73.7
99% CI for difference: (-153.4, 6.0)
T-Test of difference = 0 (vs not =): T-Value = -2.68  P-Value = 0.016  DF = 17
```

EXCEL

2 Sample t Test Results	
Test Results	**Test Summary**
Conclusion	Test: 2-Sample t Test
Reject Ho at alpha = 0.01	Ho: μ1 − μ2 = 0
	Ha: Lower tail: μ1 − μ2 < 0
	df: 17
Summary Statistics	t Statistic: −2.68
Diff Std Error	p-value: 0.0079
−73.69 27.492	
DYNA Summary	**STAT Summary**
n Mean Std Dev	n Mean Std Dev
14 394.643 84.75	6 468.333 38.166

Using **2 Var t Test**

PRINTOUT 10.2 (cont.)
Nonpooled *t*-procedures output for the operative-time data

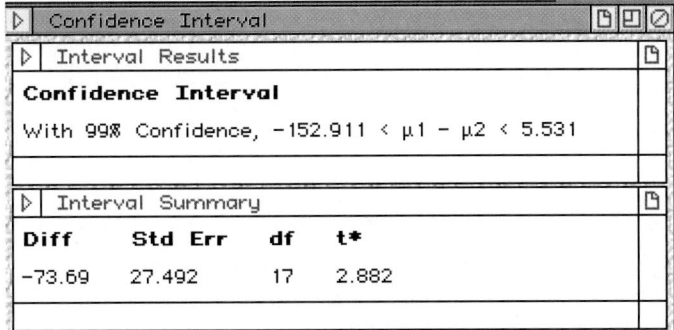

Using **2 Var t Interval**

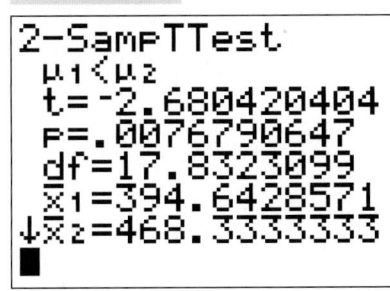

Using **2-SampTTest**   Using **2-SampTInt**

The outputs in Printout 10.2 reveal that the *P*-value for the hypothesis test is 0.008, rounded to three decimal places. As the *P*-value is less than the specified significance level of 0.01, we reject H_0. The outputs in Printout 10.2 also show that a 99% confidence interval for the difference between the means is from -153 to 6, rounded to the nearest integer.

Note that, if we round the endpoints of the confidence interval to one or more decimal places, there are discrepancies among the confidence intervals provided by the three technologies. These differences are due to the fact that some statistical technologies round degrees of freedom, whereas others do not.

Obtaining the Output (Optional)

Printout 10.2 provides output from Minitab, Excel, and the TI-83 Plus for non-pooled t-procedures based on the samples of operative times in Table 10.7. The following are detailed instructions for obtaining that output. First, we store the two samples of operative times in columns (Minitab), ranges (Excel), or lists (TI-83 Plus) named DYNA and STAT. Then, we proceed as follows.[2]

MINITAB

FOR THE HYPOTHESIS TEST:
1. Choose **Stat ➤ Basic Statistics ➤ 2-Sample t...**
2. Select the **Samples in different columns** option button
3. Click in the **First** text box and specify DYNA
4. Click in the **Second** text box and specify STAT
5. Deselect the **Assume equal variances** check box
6. Click the **Options...** button
7. Click in the **Confidence level** text box and type 99
8. Click in the **Test mean** text box and type 0
9. Click the arrow button at the right of the **Alternative** drop-down list box and select **less than**
10. Click **OK**
11. Click **OK**

FOR THE CI:
1. Choose **Edit ➤ Edit Last Dialog**
2. Click the **Options...** button
3. Click the arrow button at the right of the **Alternative** drop-down list box and select **not equal**
4. Click **OK**
5. Click **OK**

EXCEL

FOR THE HYPOTHESIS TEST:
1. Choose **DDXL ➤ Hypothesis Tests**
2. Select **2 Var t Test** from the **Function type** drop-down box
3. Specify DYNA in the **1st Quantitative Variable** text box
4. Specify STAT in the **2nd Quantitative Variable** text box
5. Click **OK**
6. Click the **2-sample** button
7. Click the **Set difference** button, type 0, and click **OK**
8. Click the **0.01** button
9. Click the $\mu 1 - \mu 2 <$ **diff** button
10. Click the **Compute** button

FOR THE CI:
1. Exit to Excel
2. Choose **DDXL ➤ Confidence Intervals**
3. Select **2 Var t Interval** from the **Function type** drop-down box
4. Specify DYNA in the **1st Quantitative Variable** text box
5. Specify STAT in the **2nd Quantitative Variable** text box
6. Click **OK**
7. Click the **2-sample** button
8. Click the **99%** button
9. Click the **Compute Interval** button

TI-83 PLUS

FOR THE HYPOTHESIS TEST:
1. Press **STAT**, arrow over to **TESTS**, and press **4**
2. Highlight **Data** and press **ENTER**
3. Press the down-arrow key
4. Press **2nd ➤ LIST**, arrow down to DYNA, and press **ENTER** twice
5. Press **2nd ➤ LIST**, arrow down to STAT, and press **ENTER** four times
6. Highlight $< \mu 2$ and press **ENTER**
7. Press the down-arrow key, highlight **No**, and press **ENTER**
8. Press the down-arrow key, highlight **Calculate**, and press **ENTER**

FOR THE CI:
1. Press **STAT**, arrow over to **TESTS**, and press **0**
2. Highlight **Data** and press **ENTER**
3. Press the down-arrow key
4. Press **2nd ➤ LIST**, arrow down to DYNA, and press **ENTER** twice
5. Press **2nd ➤ LIST**, arrow down to STAT, and press **ENTER** four times
6. Type .99 for **C-Level** and press **ENTER**
7. Highlight **No** and press **ENTER**
8. Press the down-arrow key and press **ENTER**

---

[2]Although Minitab simultaneously performs a hypothesis test and obtains a confidence interval, the type of confidence interval Minitab finds depends on the type of hypothesis test. Specifically, Minitab computes a two-sided confidence interval for a two-tailed test and a one-sided confidence interval for a one-tailed test. In this book, we consider only two-sided confidence intervals. To perform a one-tailed hypothesis test and obtain a two-sided confidence interval, we must apply Minitab's nonpooled t-procedure twice: once for the one-tailed hypothesis test and once for the confidence interval specifying a two-tailed hypothesis test.

Exercises 10.3

Statistical Concepts and Skills

10.37 Neurosurgery Operative Times. Refer to Example 10.6 on page 457. Explain why using the nonpooled t-test is more appropriate than using the pooled t-test.

10.38 Suppose that you know that a variable is normally distributed on each of two populations. Further suppose that you want to perform a hypothesis test based on independent samples to compare the two population means. In each case, decide whether you would use the pooled or nonpooled t-test and give a reason for your answer.
a. You know that the population standard deviations are equal.
b. You know that the population standard deviations are not equal.
c. The sample standard deviations are 23.6 and 25.2, and each sample size is 25.
d. The sample standard deviations are 23.6 and 59.2.

10.39 What is the difference in assumptions between the pooled and nonpooled t-procedures?

10.40 Discuss the relative advantages and disadvantages of using pooled and nonpooled t-procedures.

Preliminary data analyses indicate that you can reasonably use nonpooled t-procedures in Exercises 10.41–10.46. For each exercise, apply a nonpooled t-test to perform the required hypothesis test, using either the critical-value approach or the P-value approach.

10.41 Political Prisoners. According to the American Psychiatric Association, posttraumatic stress disorder (PTSD) is a common psychological consequence of traumatic events that involve a threat to life or physical integrity. During the Cold War, some 200,000 people in East Germany were imprisoned for political reasons. Many were subjected to physical and psychological torture during their imprisonment, resulting in PTSD. Ehlers, Maercker, and Boos studied various characteristics of political prisoners from the former East Germany and presented their findings in the paper "Posttraumatic Stress Disorder (PTSD) Following Political Imprisonment: The Role of Mental Defeat, Alienation, and Perceived Permanent Change" (*Journal of Abnormal Psychology*, Vol. 109, pp. 45–55). The researchers randomly and independently selected 32 former prisoners diagnosed with chronic PTSD and 20 former prisoners that were diagnosed with PTSD after release from prison but had since recovered (remitted). The ages, in years, at arrest yielded the following summary statistics.

Chronic	Remitted
$\bar{x}_1 = 25.8$	$\bar{x}_2 = 22.1$
$s_1 = 9.2$	$s_2 = 5.7$
$n_1 = 32$	$n_2 = 20$

At the 10% significance level, is there sufficient evidence to conclude that a difference exists in the mean age at arrest of East German prisoners with chronic PTSD and remitted PTSD?

10.42 Nitrogen and Seagrass. The seagrass *Thalassia testudinum* is an integral part of the Texas coastal ecosystem. Essential to the growth of *T. testudinum* is ammonium. Researchers Kun-Seop Lee and Kenneth H. Dunton of the Marine Science Institute of the University of Texas at Austin noticed that the seagrass beds in Corpus Christi Bay (CCB) were taller and thicker than those in Lower Laguna Madre (LLM). They compared the sediment ammonium concentrations in the two locations and published their findings in *Marine Ecology Progress Series* (2000, Vol. 196, pp. 39–48). Following are the summary statistics on sediment ammonium concentrations, in micromoles, obtained by the researchers.

CCB	LLM
$\bar{x}_1 = 115.1$	$\bar{x}_2 = 24.3$
$s_1 = 79.4$	$s_2 = 10.5$
$n_1 = 51$	$n_2 = 19$

At the 1% significance level, is there sufficient evidence to conclude that the mean sediment ammonium concentration in CCB exceeds that in LLM?

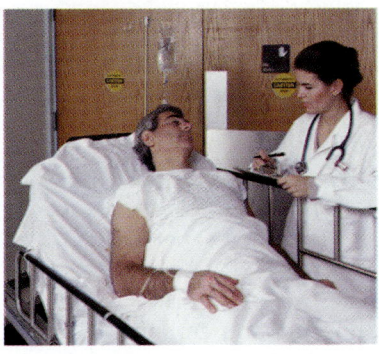

10.43 Acute Postoperative Days. Refer to Example 10.6 on page 457. The researchers also obtained the following data on the number of acute postoperative days in the hospital using the dynamic and static systems.

Dynamic							Static		
7	5	8	8	6	7	7	6	18	9
9	10	7	7	7	7	8	7	14	9

At the 5% significance level, do the data provide sufficient evidence to conclude that the mean number of acute postoperative days in the hospital is smaller with the dynamic system than with the static system? (Note: $\bar{x}_1 = 7.36$, $s_1 = 1.22$, $\bar{x}_2 = 10.50$, and $s_2 = 4.59$.)

10.44 Stressed-Out Bus Drivers. Frustrated passengers, congested streets, time schedules, and air and noise pollution are just some of the physical and social pressures that lead many urban bus drivers to retire prematurely with disabilities such as coronary heart disease and stomach disorders. An intervention program designed by the Stockholm Transit District was implemented to improve the work conditions of the city's bus drivers. Improvements were evaluated by Evans et al. who collected physiological and psychological data for bus drivers who drove on the improved routes (intervention) and for drivers who were assigned the normal routes (control). Their findings were published in the article "Hassles on the Job: a Study of a Job Intervention With Urban Bus Drivers" (*Journal of Organizational Behavior* (1999, Vol. 20, pp. 199–208). Following are data, based on the results of the study, for the heart rates, in beats per minute, of the intervention and control drivers.

Intervention		Control							
68	66	74	52	67	63	77	57	80	
74	58	77	53	76	54	73	54		
69	63	60	77	63	60	68	64		
68	73	66	71	66	55	71	84		
64	76	63	73	59	68	64	82		

a. At the 5% significance level, do the data provide sufficient evidence to conclude that the intervention program reduces mean heart rate of urban bus drivers in Stockholm? (Note: $\bar{x}_1 = 67.90$, $s_1 = 5.49$, $\bar{x}_2 = 66.81$, and $s_2 = 9.04$.)
b. Can you provide an explanation for the somewhat surprising results of the study?
c. Is the study a designed experiment or an observational study? Explain your answer.

10.45 Schizophrenia and Dopamine. Previous research has suggested that changes in the activity of dopamine, a neurotransmitter in the brain, may be a causative factor for schizophrenia. In the paper "Schizophrenia: Dopamine b-Hydroxylase Activity and Treatment Response" (*Science*, 1982, Vol. 216, pp. 1423–1425), Sternberg et al. published the results of their study in which they examined 25 schizophrenic patients who had been classified as either psychotic or not psychotic by hospital staff. The activity of dopamine was measured in each patient by using the enzyme dopamine b-hydroxylase to assess differences in dopamine activity between the two groups. The following are data, in nanomoles per milliliter-hour per milligram (nmol/ml-h/mg).

Psychotic		Not psychotic		
0.0150	0.0222	0.0104	0.0230	0.0145
0.0204	0.0275	0.0200	0.0116	0.0180
0.0306	0.0270	0.0210	0.0252	0.0154
0.0320	0.0226	0.0105	0.0130	0.0170
0.0208	0.0245	0.0112	0.0200	0.0156

At the 1% significance level, do the data suggest that dopamine activity is higher, on average, in psychotic patients? (Note: $\bar{x}_1 = 0.02426$, $s_1 = 0.00514$, $\bar{x}_2 = 0.01643$, and $s_2 = 0.00470$.)

10.46 Potato Yield. The U.S. Department of Agriculture compiles information on acreage, production, and value of potatoes and publishes its findings in *Agricultural Statistics*. Potato yield is measured in hundreds of pounds (cwt) per acre. Independent random samples of forty 1-acre plots of potatoes from Idaho and thirty-two 1-acre plots of potatoes from Nevada gave the following yields.

Idaho					Nevada			
299	337	396	379	301	353	324	398	362
414	380	328	386	311	385	406	448	384
288	354	381	324	287	382	398	342	377
369	336	334	334	360	418	303	424	470
368	375	314	373	369	411	383	379	378
378	330	274	361	312	410	370	386	338
385	316	392	363	353	329	346	341	432
351	337	382	355	399	410	409	370	403

At the 1% significance level, do the data provide sufficient evidence to conclude that Nevada has a larger mean potato yield than Idaho? (Note: $\bar{x}_1 = 349.6$, $s_1 = 34.6$, $\bar{x}_2 = 383.4$, and $s_2 = 37.2$.)

In Exercises 10.47–10.50, apply Procedure 10.4 on page 459 to obtain the required confidence interval.

10.47 Political Prisoners. Refer to Exercise 10.41.
a. Determine a 90% confidence interval for the difference, $\mu_1 - \mu_2$, between the mean ages at arrest of East German prisoners with chronic PTSD and remitted PTSD.
b. Interpret your answer in words.

10.48 Nitrogen and Seagrass. Refer to Exercise 10.42.
a. Determine a 98% confidence interval for the difference, $\mu_1 - \mu_2$, between the mean sediment ammonium concentrations in CCB and LLM.
b. Interpret your answer in words.

10.49 Acute Postoperative Days. Refer to Exercise 10.43.
a. Find a 90% confidence interval for the difference between the mean numbers of acute postoperative days in the hospital with the dynamic and static systems.
b. Interpret your answer in words.

10.50 Stressed-Out Bus Drivers. Refer to Exercise 10.44.
a. Find a 90% confidence interval for the difference between the mean heart rates of urban bus drivers in Stockholm in the two environments.
b. Interpret your answer in words.

Extending the Concepts and Skills

10.51 Acute Postoperative Days. In Exercise 10.43, you conducted a nonpooled t-test to decide whether the mean number of acute postoperative days in the hospital is smaller with the dynamic system than with the static system.
a. Using a pooled t-test, repeat that hypothesis test.
b. Compare your decisions with the pooled and nonpooled t-tests.
c. Which test do you think is more appropriate, the pooled or nonpooled t-test? Explain your answer.

10.52 Neurosurgery Operative Times. In Example 10.6 on page 457, we conducted a nonpooled t-test to decide whether the mean operative time is less with the dynamic system than with the static system.
a. Using a pooled t-test, repeat that hypothesis test.
b. Compare your decisions with the pooled and nonpooled t-tests.
c. Which test do you think is more appropriate, the pooled or nonpooled t-test? Explain your answer.

10.53 Each pair of graphs in Fig. 10.4 shows the distributions of a variable on two populations. Suppose that, in each case, we want to perform a small-sample hypothesis test based on independent samples to compare the means of the two populations. In each case, decide which, if any, of the following tests is preferable: the pooled t-test, the nonpooled t-test, or the Mann–Whitney test.

10.54 Suppose that a variable is normally distributed on each of two populations and that the population standard deviations are equal. Further suppose that we want to conduct a hypothesis test based on independent samples to compare the means of the two populations.
a. Are the assumptions met for use of the pooled t-test? Explain your answer.
b. Are the assumptions met for use of the nonpooled t-test? Explain your answer.
c. Are the assumptions met for use of the Mann–Whitney test? Explain your answer.
d. Which test would be best? Explain your answer.

Using Technology

10.55 Schizophrenia and Dopamine. Refer to Exercise 10.45. Use the technology of your choice to
a. obtain boxplots and normal probability plots for the two samples.
b. perform the required hypothesis test.
c. obtain a 99% confidence interval for the difference between the two population means.
d. Justify the use of your procedure in parts (b) and (c).

10.56 Potato Yield. Refer to Exercise 10.46. Use the technology of your choice to
a. obtain boxplots and normal probability plots for the two samples.
b. perform the required hypothesis test.
c. obtain a 99% confidence interval for the difference between the two population means.
d. Justify the use of your procedure in parts (b) and (c).

FIGURE 10.4
Figure for Exercise 10.53

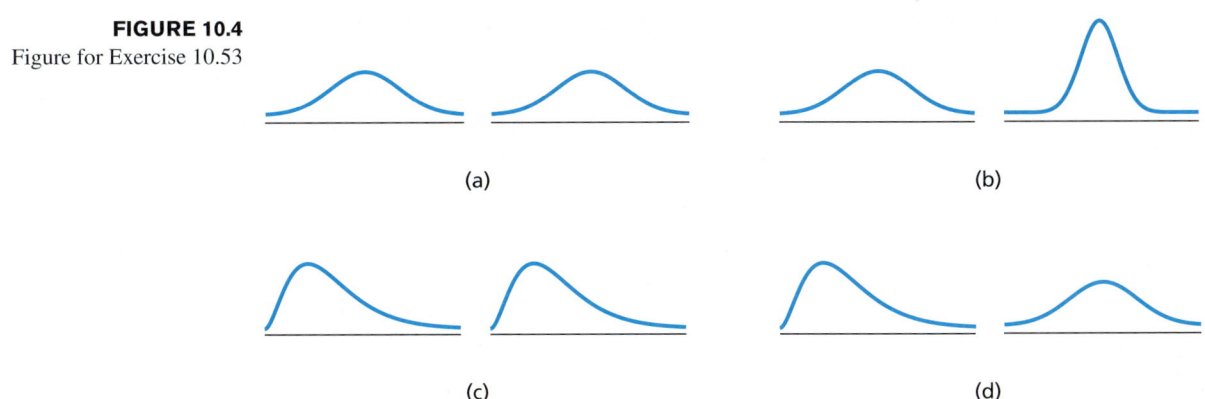

10.4 INFERENCES FOR TWO POPULATION MEANS, USING PAIRED SAMPLES

So far, the methods we have presented for comparing the means of two populations are based on independent samples. In this section, we examine methods based on **paired samples** for comparing the means of two populations. A paired sample may be appropriate when there is a natural pairing of the members of the two populations.

Each pair in a paired sample consists of a member of one population and that member's corresponding member in the other population. With a random paired sample, each possible paired sample is equally likely to be the one selected. Example 10.9 provides an unrealistically simple illustration of paired samples, but it will help you understand the concept.

Example 10.9 Introducing Random Paired Samples

Husbands and Wives Let's consider two small populations, one consisting of five married women and the other of their five husbands, as shown in the following figure. The arrows in the figure indicate that Elizabeth and Karim are married, Carol and Harold are married, and so on. The married couples constitute the pairs for these two populations.

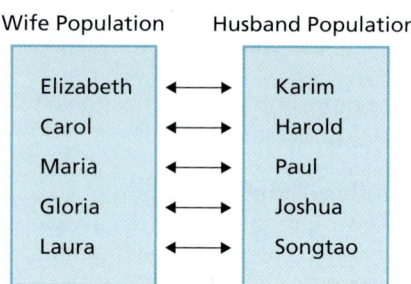

TABLE 10.9
Possible paired samples of size 3 from the wife and husband populations

Paired sample
(E, K), (C, H), (M, P)
(E, K), (C, H), (G, J)
(E, K), (C, H), (L, S)
(E, K), (M, P), (G, J)
(E, K), (M, P), (L, S)
(E, K), (G, J), (L, S)
(C, H), (M, P), (G, J)
(C, H), (M, P), (L, S)
(C, H), (G, J), (L, S)
(M, P), (G, J), (L, S)

Suppose that we take a paired sample of size 3 (i.e., a sample of three pairs) from these two populations.

a. List the possible paired samples.
b. If a paired sample is selected at random, determine the chance that any particular paired sample will be the one obtained.

Solution For convenience, we use the first letter of each name as an abbreviation for the name and use parentheses to designate a wife–husband pair. For example, (E, K) represents the couple Elizabeth and Karim.

a. There are 10 possible paired samples of size 3, as displayed in Table 10.9.
b. For a random paired sample of size 3, each of the 10 possible paired samples listed in Table 10.9 is equally likely to be the one selected. Therefore the chances are $\frac{1}{10}$ (1 in 10) that any particular paired sample of size 3 will be the one obtained. ◆

The purpose of Example 10.9 is to provide a concrete illustration of paired samples and to emphasize that, for random paired samples of any given size, each possible paired sample is equally likely to be the one selected. In practice, we neither obtain the number of possible paired samples nor explicitly compute the chance of selecting a particular paired sample. However, these concepts underlie the methods we do use.

COMPARING TWO POPULATION MEANS, USING A PAIRED SAMPLE

We are now ready to examine a process for comparing the means of two populations based on a paired sample. In Example 10.10, we introduce the ideas underlying this process.

Example 10.10 *Comparing Two Means, Using a Paired Sample*

Gasoline Additive Suppose that we want to decide whether a newly developed gasoline additive increases gas mileage. We first note that we have one variable—gas mileage—and two populations:

Population 1: All cars when the additive is used

Population 2: All cars when the additive is not used

Let μ_1 and μ_2 denote the means of the variable "gas mileage" for Population 1 and Population 2, respectively:

μ_1 = mean gas mileage of all cars when the additive is used.

μ_2 = mean gas mileage of all cars when the additive is not used.

We want to perform the hypothesis test

H_0: $\mu_1 = \mu_2$ (mean gas mileage with additive is not greater)

H_a: $\mu_1 > \mu_2$ (mean gas mileage with additive is greater).

Independent samples could be used to carry out the hypothesis test: Take independent random samples of, say, 10 cars each; have one group driven with the additive (sample from Population 1) and the other group driven without the additive (sample from Population 2); and then apply a pooled or nonpooled *t*-test to the gas mileage data obtained.

However, in this case, a paired sample is probably more appropriate. Here, a pair consists of a car driven with the additive and the same car driven without the additive. The variable we analyze is the difference between the gas mileages of a car driven with and without the additive.

By using a paired sample, we can remove extraneous sources of variation, in this case, the variation in the gas mileages of cars. The sampling error thus made in estimating the difference between the population means will generally be smaller. As a result, we are more likely to detect differences between the population means when such differences exist.

So, suppose that 10 cars are selected at random and that the cars sampled are driven both with and without the additive, yielding a paired sample of size 10. Further suppose that the resulting gas mileages, in miles per gallon (mpg), are as displayed in the second and third columns of Table 10.10.

TABLE 10.10
Gas mileages, with and without additive, for 10 randomly selected cars

Car	Gas mileage with additive	Gas mileage w/o additive	Paired difference d
1	25.7	24.9	0.8
2	20.0	18.8	1.2
3	28.4	27.7	0.7
4	13.7	13.0	0.7
5	18.8	17.8	1.0
6	12.5	11.3	1.2
7	28.4	27.8	0.6
8	8.1	8.2	−0.1
9	23.1	23.1	0.0
10	10.4	9.9	0.5
			6.6

The last column of Table 10.10 contains the difference, d, between the gas mileages with and without the additive for each of the 10 cars sampled. We refer to each difference as a **paired difference** because it is the difference of a pair of observations. For example, the first car got 25.7 mpg with the additive and 24.9 mpg without the additive, giving a paired difference of $d = 25.7 - 24.9 = 0.8$ mpg, an increase in gas mileage of 0.8 mpg with the additive.

If the null hypothesis is true, the paired differences of the gas mileages for the cars sampled should average about zero; that is, the sample mean $\bar{d}$ of the paired differences should be roughly zero. If $\bar{d}$ is too much greater than zero, we would take this as evidence that the null hypothesis is false.

From the last column of Table 10.10, we find that the sample mean of the paired differences is

$$\bar{d} = \frac{\Sigma d}{n} = \frac{6.6}{10} = 0.66 \text{ mpg},$$

a mean increase in gas mileage of 0.66 mpg when the additive is used. The question now is: Can this mean increase in gas mileage be reasonably attributed to sampling error or is it large enough to indicate that, on average, the additive improves gas mileage (i.e., $\mu_1 > \mu_2$)? To answer that question, we need to know the distribution of the variable $\bar{d}$. We discuss that distribution and then return to solve the gas mileage problem. ◆

THE PAIRED t-STATISTIC

Suppose that x is a variable on each of two populations whose members can be paired. For each pair, we let d denote the difference between the values of the variable x on the members of the pair. We call d the **paired-difference variable.**

The mean of the paired differences equals the difference between the two population means. In symbols,

$$\mu_d = \mu_1 - \mu_2.$$

Furthermore, if d is normally distributed, we can apply this equation and our knowledge of the studentized version of a sample mean (Key Fact 8.5 on page 350) to obtain Key Fact 10.5.

Key Fact 10.5 **Distribution of the Paired t-Statistic**

Suppose that x is a variable on each of two populations whose members can be paired. Further suppose that the paired-difference variable d is normally distributed. Then, for paired samples of size n, the variable

$$t = \frac{\bar{d} - (\mu_1 - \mu_2)}{s_d/\sqrt{n}}$$

has the t-distribution with df $= n - 1$.

Note: We use the phrase **normal differences** as an abbreviation of "the paired-difference variable is normally distributed."

HYPOTHESIS TESTS FOR THE MEANS OF TWO POPULATIONS, USING A PAIRED SAMPLE

We now present a hypothesis testing procedure based on a paired sample for comparing the means of two populations when the paired-difference variable is normally distributed. In light of Key Fact 10.5, for a hypothesis test with null hypothesis H_0: $\mu_1 = \mu_2$, we can use the variable

$$t = \frac{\bar{d}}{s_d/\sqrt{n}}$$

as the test statistic and obtain the critical value(s) from the t-table, Table IV. Specifically, we have two procedures, Procedures 10.5A and B, which we often refer to as the **paired t-test.** Note that the paired t-test is just the one-sample t-test applied to the paired-difference variable with null hypothesis H_0: $\mu_d = 0$.

Before applying Procedure 10.5, let's discuss the assumptions for its use. Assumption 1 (paired sample) is essential. The sample must be paired or the procedure does not apply.

Regarding Assumption 2, although the paired t-test is based on the assumption that the paired-difference variable is normally distributed, it also applies approximately for large samples regardless of distribution type, as noted at the bottom of Procedure 10.5. And, like the one-sample t-test, the paired t-test works reasonably well even for small samples or samples of moderate size when the paired-difference variable is not normally distributed, provided that variable is not too far from being normally distributed.

Procedure 10.5A

The Paired t-Test for Two Population Means (Critical-Value Approach)

Assumptions
1. Paired sample
2. Normal differences or large sample

Step 1 The null hypothesis is $H_0: \mu_1 = \mu_2$, and the alternative hypothesis is

$H_a: \mu_1 \neq \mu_2$ or $H_a: \mu_1 < \mu_2$ or $H_a: \mu_1 > \mu_2$
(Two-tailed)   (Left-tailed)   (Right-tailed)

Step 2 Decide on the significance level, α.

Step 3 Calculate the paired differences of the sample pairs.

Step 4 Compute the value of the test statistic

$$t = \frac{\bar{d}}{s_d/\sqrt{n}}.$$

Step 5 The critical value(s) are

$\pm t_{\alpha/2}$ or $-t_\alpha$ or t_α
(Two-tailed)   (Left-tailed)   (Right-tailed)

with df = $n - 1$. Use Table IV to find the critical value(s).

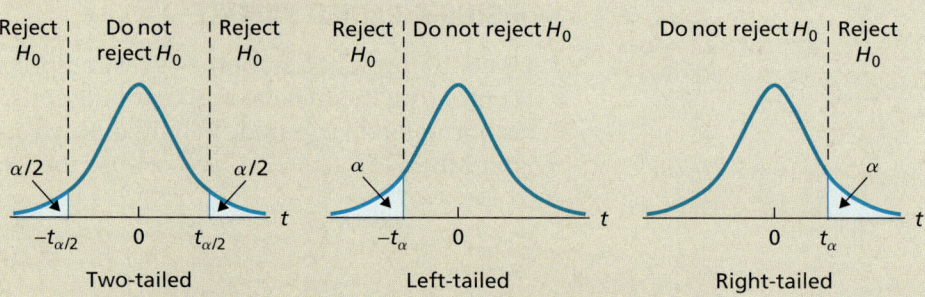

Step 6 If the value of the test statistic falls in the rejection region, reject H_0; otherwise, do not reject H_0.

Step 7 Interpret the results of the hypothesis test.

The hypothesis test is exact when the paired-difference variable is normally distributed (normal differences) and is approximately correct for large samples when the paired-difference variable is not normally distributed (nonnormal differences).

Procedure 10.5B The Paired t-Test for Two Population Means (P-Value Approach)

Assumptions
1. Paired sample
2. Normal differences or large sample

Step 1 The null hypothesis is $H_0: \mu_1 = \mu_2$, and the alternative hypothesis is

$H_a: \mu_1 \neq \mu_2$ or $H_a: \mu_1 < \mu_2$ or $H_a: \mu_1 > \mu_2$
(Two-tailed)   (Left-tailed)   (Right-tailed)

Step 2 Decide on the significance level, α.

Step 3 Calculate the paired differences of the sample pairs.

Step 4 Compute the value of the test statistic

$$t = \frac{\bar{d}}{s_d/\sqrt{n}}$$

and denote that value t_0.

Step 5 The t-statistic has df $= n - 1$. Use Table IV to estimate the P-value or obtain it exactly by using technology.

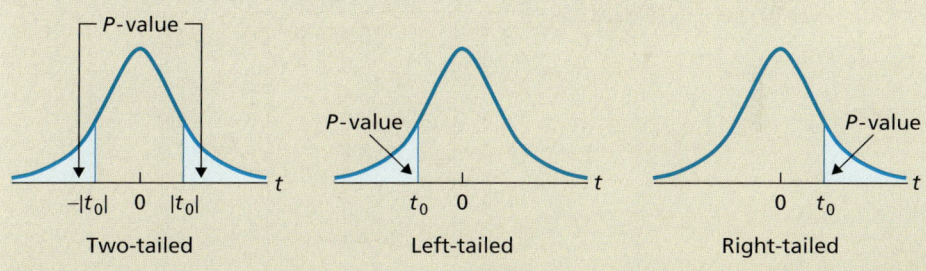

Two-tailed   Left-tailed   Right-tailed

Step 6 If $P \leq \alpha$, reject H_0; otherwise, do not reject H_0.

Step 7 Interpret the results of the hypothesis test.

The hypothesis test is exact when the paired-difference variable is normally distributed (normal differences) and is approximately correct for large samples when the paired-difference variable is not normally distributed (nonnormal differences).

CHAPTER 10 Inferences for Two Population Means

When considering the paired t-test, you must also watch for outliers in the sample of paired differences. Again, the presence of outliers calls into question the normality assumption. Moreover, even for large samples, outliers can sometimes unduly affect a paired t-test because the sample mean and sample standard deviation are not resistant to them.

Practical guidelines for the use of the paired t-test are the same as those given for the one-sample z-test in Key Fact 9.4 on page 390 when applied to paired differences. Always look at the sample of paired differences before applying the paired t-test to ensure that its use is reasonable.

Finally, we emphasize that the normality assumption in Assumption 2 refers to the paired-difference variable. The two distributions of the variable under consideration need not be normally distributed.

Example 10.11 illustrates use of Procedure 10.5.

Example 10.11   The Paired t-Test

Gasoline Additive   We now return to the gas mileage problem posed in Example 10.10. The gas mileages of 10 randomly selected cars, both with and without a new gasoline additive, are displayed in the second and third columns of Table 10.10, which we repeat here as Table 10.11.

TABLE 10.11
Gas mileages, with and without additive, for 10 randomly selected cars

Car	Gas mileage with additive	Gas mileage w/o additive	Paired difference d
1	25.7	24.9	0.8
2	20.0	18.8	1.2
3	28.4	27.7	0.7
4	13.7	13.0	0.7
5	18.8	17.8	1.0
6	12.5	11.3	1.2
7	28.4	27.8	0.6
8	8.1	8.2	−0.1
9	23.1	23.1	0.0
10	10.4	9.9	0.5
			6.6

At the 5% significance level, do the data provide sufficient evidence to conclude that, on average, the gasoline additive improves gas mileage?

Solution   To begin, we check the two conditions required for using the paired t-test. We have a paired sample—each pair consists of a car driven both with and without the additive. So, Assumption 1 is satisfied.

10.4 Inferences for Two Population Means, Using Paired Samples

Because the sample size, $n = 10$, is small, we need to consider questions of normality and outliers. (See the first bulleted item in Key Fact 9.4 on page 390.) To do so, we constructed a normal probability plot (not shown) for the sample of paired differences contained in the last column of Table 10.11. The normal probability plot reveals no outliers and is quite linear, so we can consider Assumption 2 satisfied. Hence we can apply the paired t-test to perform the required hypothesis test.

Step 1 State the null and alternative hypotheses.

Let μ_1 denote the mean gas mileage of all cars when the additive is used and μ_2 denote the mean gas mileage of all cars when the additive is not used. Then the null and alternative hypotheses are

H_0: $\mu_1 = \mu_2$ (mean gas mileage with additive is not greater)

H_a: $\mu_1 > \mu_2$ (mean gas mileage with additive is greater).

Note that the hypothesis test is right-tailed because a greater-than sign (>) appears in the alternative hypothesis.

Step 2 Decide on the significance level, α.

The test is to be performed at the 5% significance level, or $\alpha = 0.05$.

Step 3 Calculate the paired differences of the sample pairs.

We have already done so in the last column of Table 10.11.

Step 4 Compute the value of the test statistic

$$t = \frac{\bar{d}}{s_d/\sqrt{n}}.$$

We first need to determine the sample mean and sample standard deviation of the paired differences listed in the last column of Table 10.11. We do so in the usual manner:

$$\bar{d} = \frac{\Sigma d}{n} = \frac{6.6}{10} = 0.66$$

and

$$s_d = \sqrt{\frac{\Sigma d^2 - (\Sigma d)^2/n}{n-1}} = \sqrt{\frac{6.12 - (6.6)^2/10}{10-1}} = 0.443.$$

Consequently, the value of the test statistic is

$$t = \frac{\bar{d}}{s_d/\sqrt{n}} = \frac{0.66}{0.443/\sqrt{10}} = 4.711.$$

Critical-Value Approach	P-Value Approach
Step 5 The critical value for a right-tailed test is t_α with df = $n-1$.	**Step 5** The t-statistic has df = $n-1$. Use Table IV to estimate the P-value or obtain it exactly by using technology.

We have $n = 10$ and $\alpha = 0.05$. Table IV shows that, for df = $10 - 1 = 9$, $t_{0.05} = 1.833$, as shown in Fig. 10.5A.

FIGURE 10.5A

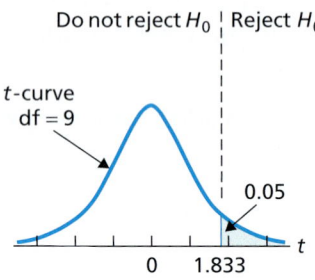

From Step 4, the value of the test statistic is $t = 4.711$. The test is right-tailed, so the P-value is the probability of observing a value of t of 4.711 or greater if the null hypothesis is true. That probability equals the shaded area shown in Fig. 10.5B.

FIGURE 10.5B

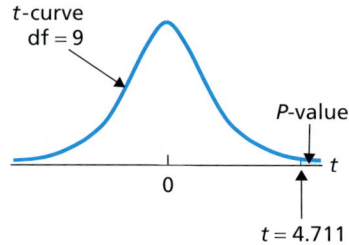

Step 6 If the value of the test statistic falls in the rejection region, reject H_0; otherwise, do not reject H_0.

From Step 4, the value of the test statistic is $t = 4.711$, which falls in the rejection region, as shown in Fig. 10.5A. Hence we reject H_0. The test results are statistically significant at the 5% level.

We have $n = 10$, so df = $10 - 1 = 9$. Referring to Fig. 10.5B and to Table IV with df = 9, we find that $P < 0.005$. (Using technology, we obtain $P = 0.000549$.)

Step 6 If $P \leq \alpha$, reject H_0; otherwise, do not reject H_0.

From Step 5, $P < 0.005$. Because the P-value is less than the specified significance level of 0.05, we reject H_0. The test results are statistically significant at the 5% level and (see Table 9.10 on page 405) provide very strong evidence against the null hypothesis.

Step 7 Interpret the results of the hypothesis test.

 At the 5% significance level, the data provide sufficient evidence to conclude that the mean gas mileage of all cars when the additive is used is greater than the mean gas mileage of all cars when the additive is not used. Evidently, the additive is effective in increasing gas mileage.

10.4 Inferences for Two Population Means, Using Paired Samples

CONFIDENCE INTERVALS FOR THE DIFFERENCE BETWEEN THE MEANS OF TWO POPULATIONS, USING A PAIRED SAMPLE

We can also use Key Fact 10.5 on page 471 to derive a confidence-interval procedure, Procedure 10.6, for the difference between two population means, which we often refer to as the **paired t-interval procedure.**

Procedure 10.6

The Paired t-Interval Procedure for Two Population Means

Assumptions
1. Paired sample
2. Normal differences or large sample

Step 1 For a confidence level of $1 - \alpha$, use Table IV to find $t_{\alpha/2}$ with df $= n - 1$.

Step 2 The endpoints of the confidence interval for $\mu_1 - \mu_2$ are

$$\bar{d} \pm t_{\alpha/2} \cdot \frac{s_d}{\sqrt{n}}.$$

Step 3 Interpret the confidence interval.

The confidence interval is exact when the paired-difference variable is normally distributed (normal differences) and is approximately correct for large samples when the paired-difference variable is not normally distributed (nonnormal differences).

Example 10.12 The Paired t-Interval Procedure

Gasoline Additive Use the sample data in Table 10.11 on page 474 to obtain a 90% confidence interval for the difference, $\mu_1 - \mu_2$, between the mean gas mileage of all cars when the additive is used and the mean gas mileage of all cars when the additive is not used.

Solution We apply Procedure 10.6.

Step 1 For a confidence level of $1 - \alpha$, use Table IV to find $t_{\alpha/2}$ with df $= n - 1$.

For a 90% confidence interval, $\alpha = 0.10$. From Table IV, for df $= n - 1 = 10 - 1 = 9$, $t_{\alpha/2} = t_{0.10/2} = t_{0.05} = 1.833$.

Step 2 The endpoints of the confidence interval for $\mu_1 - \mu_2$ are

$$\bar{d} \pm t_{\alpha/2} \cdot \frac{s_d}{\sqrt{n}}.$$

From Step 1, $t_{\alpha/2} = 1.833$. Also, $n = 10$ and, from Example 10.11, we know that $\bar{d} = 0.66$ and $s_d = 0.443$. Thus the endpoints of the confidence interval for $\mu_1 - \mu_2$ are

$$0.66 \pm 1.833 \cdot \frac{0.443}{\sqrt{10}},$$

or 0.40 to 0.92.

Step 3 **Interpret the confidence interval.**

We can be 90% confident that the difference between the mean gas mileage of all cars when the additive is used and the mean gas mileage of all cars when the additive is not used is somewhere between 0.40 mpg and 0.92 mpg. In particular, we can be confident that, on average, the additive increases gas mileage by at least 0.40 mpg.

WHAT IF THE ASSUMPTIONS ARE NOT SATISFIED?

The paired t-procedures (paired t-test and paired t-interval procedure) provide methods for comparing the means of two populations. As you know, the assumptions for using those procedures are (1) paired sample and (2) normal differences or large sample. If one or more of these conditions are not satisfied, then the paired t-procedures should not be used.

If you have independent samples instead of a paired sample (i.e., Assumption 1 is violated), then procedures designed for independent samples should be used.

In case you have neither normality of the paired-difference variable nor a large sample (i.e., Assumption 2 is violated), then a nonparametric method should be used. For example, if you have a paired sample and the paired-difference variable has a symmetric distribution, then you can use a nonparametric method called the *paired Wilcoxon signed-rank test* to perform a hypothesis test and a nonparametric method called the *paired Wilcoxon confidence-interval procedure* to obtain a confidence interval.

The Technology Center

Most statistical technologies have programs that automatically perform paired t-procedures. In this subsection, we present output and (optional) step-by-step instructions to implement such programs.

Example 10.13 **Using Technology to Conduct Paired t-Procedures**

Gasoline Additive Table 10.11 on page 474 displays the gas mileages, in miles per gallon, of 10 randomly selected cars, both with and without a new gasoline additive. Use Minitab, Excel, or the TI-83 Plus to perform the hypothesis test in Example 10.11 and obtain the confidence interval required in Example 10.12.

10.4 Inferences for Two Population Means, Using Paired Samples

Solution Let μ_1 denote the mean gas mileage of all cars when the additive is used and let μ_2 denote the mean gas mileage of all cars when the additive is not used. The task in Example 10.11 is to perform the hypothesis test

$H_0: \mu_1 = \mu_2$ (mean gas mileage with additive is not greater)

$H_a: \mu_1 > \mu_2$ (mean gas mileage with additive is greater),

at the 5% significance level; the task in Example 10.12 is to obtain a 90% confidence interval for $\mu_1 - \mu_2$.

Printout 10.3 shows the output obtained by applying the paired t-procedures to the mileage data presented in Table 10.11.

PRINTOUT 10.3
Paired t-procedures output for the mileage data

MINITAB

```
Paired T-Test and CI: WITH, WOUT        [FOR THE HYPOTHESIS TEST]

Paired T for WITH - WOUT

                N       Mean      StDev    SE Mean
WITH           10      18.91       7.47       2.36
WOUT           10      18.25       7.42       2.35
Difference     10      0.660      0.443      0.140

90% lower bound for mean difference: 0.466
T-Test of mean difference = 0 (vs > 0): T-Value = 4.71   P-Value = 0.001


Paired T-Test and CI: WITH, WOUT        [FOR THE CONFIDENCE INTERVAL]

Paired T for WITH - WOUT

                N       Mean      StDev    SE Mean
WITH           10      18.91       7.47       2.36
WOUT           10      18.25       7.42       2.35
Difference     10      0.660      0.443      0.140

90% CI for mean difference: (0.403, 0.917)
T-Test of mean difference = 0 (vs not = 0): T-Value = 4.71   P-Value = 0.001
```

TI-83 PLUS

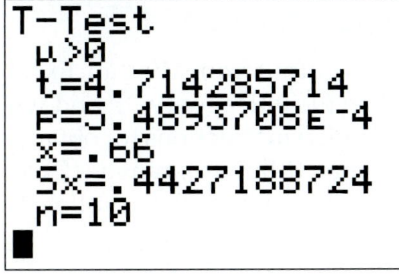

Using **T-Test**

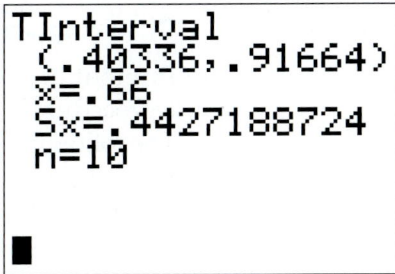

Using **TInterval**

PRINTOUT 10.3 (cont.)
Paired t-procedures output for the mileage data

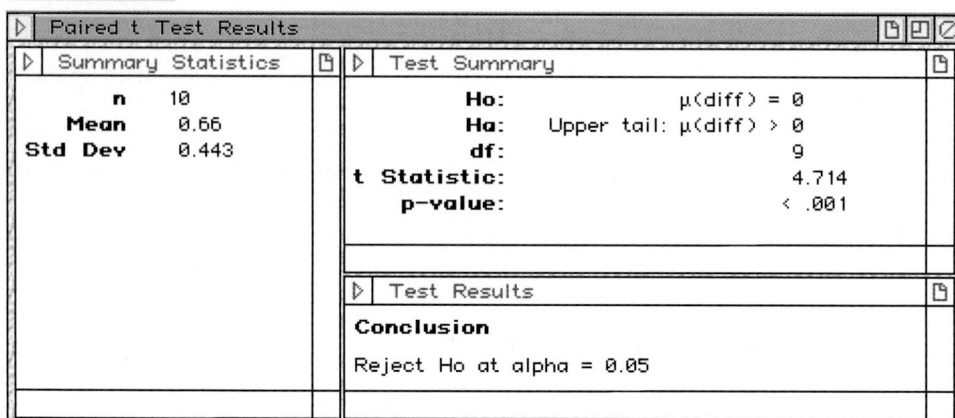

Using **Paired t Test**

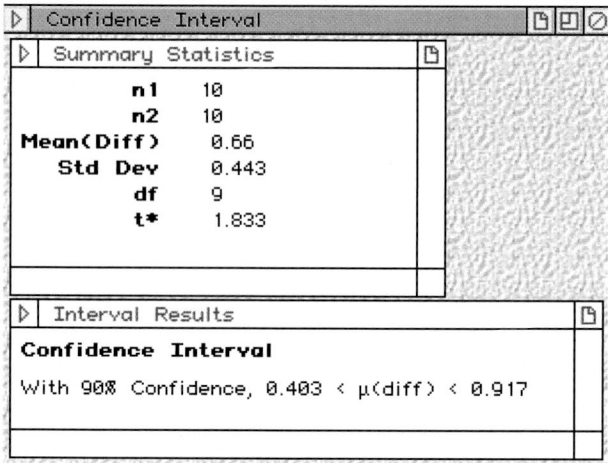

Using **Paired t Interval**

The outputs in Printout 10.3 reveal that the P-value for the hypothesis test is less than 0.001. Because the P-value is less than the significance level of 0.05, we reject H_0. The outputs in Printout 10.3 also show that a 90% confidence interval for the difference between the means is from 0.403 to 0.917. ◆

Obtaining the Output (Optional)

Printout 10.3 provides output from Minitab, Excel, and the TI-83 Plus for paired t-procedures based on the mileages (with and without additive) in Table 10.11. The following are detailed instructions for obtaining that output. First, we store the mileages in columns (Minitab), ranges (Excel), or lists (TI-83 Plus) named WITH and WOUT. Then, we proceed as follows.[3]

---

[3]Minitab computes a two-sided confidence interval for a two-tailed test and a one-sided confidence interval for a one-tailed test. To perform a one-tailed hypothesis test and obtain a two-sided confidence interval, we must apply Minitab's paired t-procedure twice: once for the one-tailed hypothesis test and once for the confidence interval specifying a two-tailed hypothesis test.

MINITAB

FOR THE HYPOTHESIS TEST:
1. Choose **Stat ➤ Basic Statistics ➤ Paired t...**
2. Click in the **First sample** text box and specify WITH
3. Click in the **Second sample** text box and specify WOUT
4. Click the **Options...** button
5. Click in the **Confidence level** text box and type 90
6. Click in the **Test mean** text box and type 0
7. Click the arrow button at the right of the **Alternative** drop-down list box and select **greater than**
8. Click **OK**
9. Click **OK**

FOR THE CI:
1. Choose **Edit ➤ Edit Last Dialog**
2. Click the **Options...** button
3. Click the arrow button at the right of the **Alternative** drop-down list box and select **not equal**
4. Click **OK**
5. Click **OK**

EXCEL

FOR THE HYPOTHESIS TEST:
1. Choose **DDXL ➤ Hypothesis Tests**
2. Select **Paired t Test** from the **Function type** drop-down box
3. Specify WITH in the **1st Quantitative Variable** text box
4. Specify WOUT in the **2nd Quantitative Variable** text box
5. Click **OK**
6. Click the **Set µ(diff)0** button, type 0, and click **OK**
7. Click the **0.05** button
8. Click the **µ(diff) > µ(diff)0** button
9. Click the **Compute** button

FOR THE CI:
1. Exit to Excel
2. Choose **DDXL ➤ Confidence Intervals**
3. Select **Paired t Interval** from the **Function type** drop-down box
4. Specify WITH in the **1st Quantitative Variable** text box
5. Specify WOUT in the **2nd Quantitative Variable** text box
6. Click **OK**
7. Click the **90%** button
8. Click the **Compute Interval** button

TI-83 PLUS

FOR THE PAIRED DIFFERENCES:
1. Press **2nd ➤ LIST**, arrow down to WITH, and press **ENTER**
2. Press −
3. Press **2nd ➤ LIST**, arrow down to WOUT, and press **ENTER**
4. Press **STO ▶**
5. Press **2nd ➤ A-LOCK**, type DIFF, and press **ENTER**

FOR THE HYPOTHESIS TEST:
1. Press **STAT**, arrow over to **TESTS**, and press **2**
2. Highlight **Data** and press **ENTER**
3. Press the down-arrow key, type 0 for μ_0, and press **ENTER**
4. Press **2nd ➤ LIST**, arrow down to DIFF, and press **ENTER** three times
5. Highlight **> μ_0** and press **ENTER**
6. Press the down-arrow key, highlight **Calculate**, and press **ENTER**

FOR THE CI:
1. Press **STAT**, arrow over to **TESTS**, and press **8**
2. Highlight **Data** and press **ENTER**
3. Press the down-arrow key
4. Press **2nd ➤ LIST**, arrow down to DIFF, and press **ENTER** three times
5. Type .9 for **C-Level** and press **ENTER** twice

Exercises 10.4

Statistical Concepts and Skills

10.57 What does each pair in a paired sample consist of?

10.58 State one possible advantage of using paired samples instead of independent samples.

10.59 Ages of Married People. The U.S. Bureau of the Census publishes information on the ages of married people in *Current Population Reports*. Suppose that you want to use a paired sample to compare the mean ages of married men and married women. Identify
a. the variable under consideration.
b. the two populations.
c. the pairs.
d. the paired-difference variable.

10.60 TV Viewing by Married People. The A. C. Nielsen Company collects data on the TV viewing habits of Americans and publishes the information in *Nielsen Report on Television*. Suppose that you want to use a paired sample to compare the mean viewing times of married men and married women. Identify
a. the variable under consideration.
b. the two populations.
c. the pairs.
d. the paired-difference variable.

10.61 State the two conditions required for performing a paired *t*-procedure. How important are those conditions?

10.62 Provide an example (different from those considered in this section) of a procedure based on a paired sample being more appropriate than one based on independent samples.

Preliminary data analyses indicate that use of a paired t-test is reasonable in Exercises 10.63–10.68. Perform each hypothesis test by using either the critical-value approach or the P-value approach.

10.63 Zea Mays. Charles Darwin, author of *Origin of Species*, investigated the effect of cross-fertilization on the heights of plants. In one study he planted 15 pairs of Zea mays plants. Each pair consisted of one cross-fertilized plant and one self-fertilized plant grown in the same pot. The following table gives the height differences, in eighths of an inch, for the 15 pairs. Each difference is obtained by subtracting the height of the self-fertilized plant from that of the cross-fertilized plant.

49	−67	8	16	6
23	28	41	14	29
56	24	75	60	−48

a. Identify the variable under consideration.
b. Identify the two populations.
c. Identify the paired-difference variable.
d. Are the numbers in the table paired differences? Why or why not?
e. At the 5% significance level, do the data provide sufficient evidence to conclude that the mean heights of cross-fertilized and self-fertilized Zea mays differ? (*Note:* $\bar{d} = 20.93$ and $s_d = 37.74$.)
f. Repeat part (e) at the 1% significance level.

10.64 Sleep. In 1908, W. S. Gosset published "The Probable Error of a Mean" (*Biometrika*, Vol. 6, pp. 1–25). In this pioneering paper, published under the pseudonym "Student," he introduced what later became known as Student's t-distribution. Gosset used the following data set, which gives the additional sleep in hours obtained by 10 patients who used laevohysocyamine hydrobromide.

1.9	0.8	1.1	0.1	−0.1
4.4	5.5	1.6	4.6	3.4

a. Identify the variable under consideration.
b. Identify the two populations.
c. Identify the paired-difference variable.
d. Are the numbers in the table paired differences? Why or why not?
e. At the 5% significance level, do the data provide sufficient evidence to conclude that laevohysocyamine hydrobromide is effective in increasing sleep? (*Note:* $\bar{d} = 2.33$ and $s_d = 2.002$.)
f. Repeat part (e) at the 1% significance level.

10.65 Anorexia Treatment. Anorexia nervosa is a serious eating disorder, particularly among young women. The following data provide the weights, in pounds, of 17 anorexic young women before and after receiving a family therapy treatment for anorexia nervosa. [SOURCE: Hand et al. (ed.) *A Handbook of Small Data Sets*, London: Chapman & Hall, 1994. Raw data from B. Everitt (personal communication).]

Before	After	Before	After	Before	After
83.3	94.3	76.9	76.8	82.1	95.5
86.0	91.5	94.2	101.6	77.6	90.7
82.5	91.9	73.4	94.9	83.5	92.5
86.7	100.3	80.5	75.2	89.9	93.8
79.6	76.7	81.6	77.8	86.0	91.7
87.3	98.0	83.8	95.2		

Does family therapy appear to be effective in helping anorexic young women gain weight? Perform the appropriate hypothesis test at the 5% significance level.

10.66 Measuring Treadwear. Stichler, Richey, and Mandel compared two methods of measuring treadwear in their paper "Measurement of Treadwear of Commercial Tires" (*Rubber Age*, Vol. 73:2). Eleven tires were each measured for treadwear by two methods, one based on weight and the other on groove wear. The following are the data, in thousands of miles.

Weight method	Groove method	Weight method	Groove method
30.5	28.7	24.5	16.1
30.9	25.9	20.9	19.9
31.9	23.3	18.9	15.2
30.4	23.1	13.7	11.5
27.3	23.7	11.4	11.2
20.4	20.9		

At the 5% significance level, do the data provide sufficient evidence to conclude that, on average, the two measurement methods give different results?

10.67 Glaucoma and Corneal Thickness. Glaucoma is a leading cause of blindness in the United States. N. Ehlers measured the corneal thickness of eight patients who had glaucoma in one eye but not in the other. The results of the study were published as the paper "On Corneal Thickness and Intraocular Pressure, II" (*Acta Opthalmologica*, Vol. 48, pp. 1107–1112). The following are the data on corneal thickness, in microns.

Patient	Normal	Glaucoma
1	484	488
2	478	478
3	492	480
4	444	426
5	436	440
6	398	410
7	464	458
8	476	460

At the 10% significance level, do the data provide sufficient evidence to conclude that mean corneal thickness is greater in normal eyes than in eyes with glaucoma?

10.68 TV Viewing by Married People. Twenty married couples are randomly selected. Their weekly viewing times, in hours, are as follows.

Husband	Wife	Husband	Wife	Husband	Wife
21	24	38	45	36	35
56	55	27	29	20	34
34	55	30	41	43	32
30	34	31	37	4	13
41	32	30	35	16	9
35	38	32	48	21	23
26	38	15	17		

At the 1% level of significance, do married men appear to watch less TV, on average, than married women? (*Note:* $\bar{d} = -4.4$ and $s_d = 8.15$.)

In Exercises 10.69–10.72, use Procedure 10.6 on page 477 to obtain the required confidence interval.

10.69 Zea Mays. Refer to Exercise 10.63.
a. Determine a 95% confidence interval for the difference between the mean heights of cross-fertilized and self-fertilized Zea mays. Interpret your answer.
b. Repeat part (a) for a 99% confidence level.

10.70 Sleep. Refer to Exercise 10.64.
a. Determine a 90% confidence interval for the additional sleep that would be obtained, on average, by using laevo-hysocyamine hydrobromide. Interpret your answer.
b. Repeat part (a) for a 98% confidence level.

10.71 Anorexia Treatment. Refer to Exercise 10.65. Determine a 90% confidence interval for the weight gain that would be obtained, on average, by using the family therapy treatment. Interpret your answer.

10.72 Measuring Treadwear. Refer to Exercise 10.66. Determine a 95% confidence interval for the mean difference in measurement by the weight and groove methods. Interpret your answer.

Extending the Concepts and Skills

10.73 Explain exactly how a paired *t*-test can be formulated as a one-sample *t*-test. (*Hint:* Work solely with the paired-difference variable.)

10.74 Faculty Salaries. In Example 10.3 on page 444, we performed a hypothesis test based on independent samples to decide whether mean salaries differ for faculty in public and private institutions. Now you are to perform that same hypothesis test based on a paired sample. Pairs are formed by matching faculty in public and private institutions by rank and specialty. A random sample of 30 pairs yields the following annual salaries, in thousands of dollars.

Public	Private	Public	Private	Public	Private
78.1	84.9	34.9	44.2	35.5	39.2
48.3	57.0	29.3	43.2	80.8	90.8
81.7	88.4	84.3	95.6	71.5	78.0
71.5	80.6	56.8	59.5	46.1	60.4
52.8	56.8	60.9	63.4	77.0	78.8
95.6	93.3	81.9	87.2	47.0	53.0
46.2	50.5	69.7	77.0	70.3	79.8
44.3	50.4	38.0	46.4	55.1	66.6
21.9	25.9	60.5	70.3	49.2	54.8
51.2	60.8	61.2	77.4	53.8	62.2

a. Do the data provide sufficient evidence to conclude that mean salaries differ for faculty in public and private institutions? Perform the required hypothesis test at the 5% significance level. (Note: $\bar{d} = -7.367$ and $s_d = 3.992$.)
b. Compare your result in part (a) to the one obtained in Example 10.3.
c. Which test is more appropriate? Explain your answer.
d. Find a 95% confidence interval for the difference between the mean salaries of faculty in public and private institutions.
e. Compare your result in part (d) to the one obtained in Example 10.4 on page 446.

10.75 A hypothesis test is to be performed to compare the means of two populations, using a paired sample. The sample of 15 paired differences contains an outlier but otherwise is roughly bell-shaped. Assuming that it is not legitimate to remove the outlier, which test is better to use—the paired *t*-test or the paired Wilcoxon signed-rank test? Explain your answer.

10.76 Suppose that you want to perform a hypothesis test to compare the means of two populations, using a paired sample. For each part, decide whether you would use the paired *t*-test, the paired Wilcoxon signed-rank test, or neither of these tests, if preliminary data analyses of the sample of paired differences suggest that the distribution of the paired-difference variable is
a. approximately normal.
b. highly skewed; the sample size is 20.
c. symmetric bimodal.

10.77 Suppose that you want to perform a hypothesis test to compare the means of two populations, using a paired sample. For each part, decide whether you would use the paired *t*-test, the paired Wilcoxon signed-rank test, or neither of these tests, if preliminary data analyses of the sample of paired differences suggest that the distribution of the paired-difference variable is
a. uniform.
b. neither symmetric nor normal; the sample size is 132.
c. moderately skewed but otherwise roughly bell-shaped.

10.78 Gasoline Additive. This exercise shows what can happen when a hypothesis testing procedure designed for use with independent samples is applied to perform a hypothesis test on a paired sample. In Example 10.11 on page 474, we applied the paired *t*-test to decide whether a gasoline additive is effective in increasing gas mileage. Specifically, if we let μ_1 and μ_2 denote the mean gas mileages of all cars when the additive is and is not used, respectively, the null and alternative hypotheses are

$$H_0: \mu_1 = \mu_2$$
$$H_a: \mu_1 > \mu_2.$$

a. Apply the nonpooled *t*-test to the sample data in the second and third columns of Table 10.11 on page 474 to perform the hypothesis test. Use $\alpha = 0.05$.
b. Why is performing the hypothesis test the way you did in part (a) inappropriate?
c. Compare your result in part (a) to the one obtained in Example 10.11.

Using Technology

10.79 Anorexia Treatment. Refer to Exercises 10.65 and 10.71. Use the technology of your choice to
a. obtain a normal probability plot of the paired differences.
b. perform the required hypothesis test and obtain the desired confidence interval.
c. Justify the use of your procedure in part (b).

10.80 Measuring Treadwear. Refer to Exercises 10.66 and 10.72. Use the technology of your choice to
a. obtain a normal probability plot of the paired differences.
b. perform the required hypothesis test and obtain the desired confidence interval.
c. Justify the use of your procedure in part (b).

10.81 Tobacco Mosaic Virus. To assess the effects of two different strains of the tobacco mosaic virus, W. Youden and H. Beale randomly selected eight tobacco leaves. Half of each leaf was subjected to one of the strains of tobacco mosaic virus and the other half to the other strain. The researchers then counted the number of local lesions apparent on each half of each leaf. The results of their study were published in the paper "A Statistical Study of the Local Lesion Method for Estimating Tobacco Mosaic Virus" (*Contributions to Boyce Thompson Institute*, 1934, Vol. 6, p. 437). The following are the data.

Leaf	Virus 1	Virus 2
1	31	18
2	20	17
3	18	14
4	17	11
5	9	10
6	8	7
7	10	5
8	7	6

Suppose that you want to perform a hypothesis test to determine whether a difference exists between the mean number of local lesions resulting from the two viral strains. Conduct graphical data analyses to decide whether applying the paired *t*-test is reasonable. Explain your decision.

10.82 Improving Car Emissions? The makers of the MAGNETIZER Engine Energizer System (EES) claim that it improves gas mileage and reduces emissions in automobiles by using magnetic free energy to increase the amount of oxygen in the fuel for greater combustion efficiency. Following are test results, performed under International and U.S. Government agency standards, on a random sample of 14 vehicles. The data give the carbon monoxide (CO) levels, in parts per million, of each vehicle tested, both before installation of EES and after installation. [SOURCE: *Global Source Marketing*.]

Before	After	Before	After
1.60	0.15	2.60	1.60
0.30	0.20	0.15	0.06
3.80	2.80	0.06	0.16
6.20	3.60	0.60	0.35
3.60	1.00	0.03	0.01
1.50	0.50	0.10	0.00
2.00	1.60	0.19	0.00

Suppose that you want to perform a hypothesis test to determine whether, on average, EES reduces CO emissions. Conduct graphical data analyses to decide whether applying the paired *t*-test is reasonable. Explain your decision.

Chapter Review

You Should Be Able To

1. use and understand the formulas presented in this chapter.

2. perform inferences based on independent samples to compare the means of two populations when the population standard deviations are unknown but are assumed to be equal.

3. perform inferences based on independent samples to compare the means of two populations when the population standard deviations are unknown but are not assumed to be equal.

4. perform inferences based on a paired sample to compare the means of two populations.

Key Terms

independent samples, 432
nonpooled *t*-interval procedure, 459
nonpooled *t*-test, 455, 456
normal differences, 471
paired difference, 470
paired-difference variable, 470

paired samples, 468
paired *t*-interval procedure, 477
paired *t*-test, 472, 473
pool, 440
pooled sample standard deviation (s_p), 440

pooled *t*-interval procedure, 446
pooled *t*-test, 442, 443
sampling distribution of the difference between two sample means, 436

Review Test

Statistical Concepts and Skills

1. Discuss the basic strategy for comparing the means of two populations based on independent samples.

2. Discuss the basic strategy for comparing the means of two populations based on a paired sample.

3. Regarding the pooled and nonpooled *t*-procedures,
a. what is the difference in assumptions between the two procedures?
b. how important is the assumption of independent samples for these procedures?
c. how important is the normality assumption for these procedures?
d. Suppose that the variable under consideration is normally distributed on each of the two populations and that you are going to use independent samples to compare the population means. Fill in the blank and explain your answer: Unless you are quite sure that the _____ are equal, the nonpooled *t*-procedures should be used instead of the pooled *t*-procedures.

4. Explain one possible advantage of using a paired sample instead of independent samples.

5. **Grip and Leg Strength.** In the paper, "Sex Differences in Static Strength and Fatigability in Three Different Muscle Groups" (*Research Quarterly for Exercise and Sport*, 1990, Vol 61(3), pp. 238–242), J. Misner et al. published results of a study on grip and leg strength of males and females. The following data, in newtons, is based on their measurements of right-leg strength.

Male			Female		
2632	1796	2256	1344	1351	1369
2235	2298	1917	2479	1573	1665
1105	1926	2644	1791	1866	1544
1569	3129	2167	2359	1694	2799
1977			1868	2098	

Preliminary data analyses indicate that you can reasonably presume leg strength is normally distributed for both males and females and that the standard deviations of leg strength are approximately equal.

a. At the 5% significance level, do the data provide sufficient evidence to conclude that mean right-leg strength of males exceeds that of females? (*Note:* $\bar{x}_1 = 2127$, $s_1 = 513$, $\bar{x}_2 = 1843$, and $s_2 = 446$.)

b. Estimate the P-value of the hypothesis test, and use that estimate and Table 9.10 on page 405 to assess the strength of the evidence against the null hypothesis.

6. **Grip and Leg Strength.** Refer to Problem 5. Obtain a 90% confidence interval for the difference between the mean right-leg strengths of males and females. Interpret your result.

7. **Cottonmouth Litter Size.** A study published by Blem and Blem in the *Journal of Herpetology* (1995, Vol. 29, pp. 391–398) examined the reproductive characteristics of the eastern cottonmouth. Following are data, based on the results of the researchers' study, that give the number of young per litter for 24 female cottonmouths in Florida and 44 female cottonmouths in Virginia.

Florida			Virginia					
8	6	7	5	12	7	7	6	8
7	4	3	12	9	7	4	9	6
1	7	5	12	7	5	6	10	3
6	6	5	10	8	8	12	5	6
6	8	5	10	11	3	8	4	5
5	7	4	7	6	11	7	6	8
6	6	5	8	14	8	7	11	7
5	5	4	5	4				

Preliminary data analyses indicate that you can reasonably presume that litter sizes of cottonmouths in both states are approximately normally distributed. At the 1% significance level, do the data provide sufficient evidence to conclude that, on average, the number of young per litter of cottonmouths in Florida is less than that in Virginia? Do not assume that the population standard deviations are equal. (*Note:* $\bar{x}_1 = 5.46$, $s_1 = 1.59$, $\bar{x}_2 = 7.59$, and $s_2 = 2.68$.)

8. **Cottonmouth Litter Size.** Refer to Problem 7. Find a 98% confidence interval for the difference between the mean litter sizes of cottonmouths in Florida and Virginia. Interpret your result.

9. **Speed Reading.** To compare the effectiveness of two speed-reading programs, 10 pairs of people were randomly selected. Each pair consisted of people whose then current reading speeds were essentially identical. From each pair, one person was randomly selected to take Program 1; the other person to take Program 2. After the 10 pairs of people completed the speed-reading programs, their reading speeds, in words per minute, were as follows.

Pair	Program 1	Program 2
1	1114	1032
2	996	1148
3	979	1074
4	1125	1076
5	910	959
6	1056	1094
7	1091	1091
8	1053	1096
9	996	1032
10	894	1012

At the 10% significance level, can you conclude that there is a difference in effectiveness of the two speed-reading programs? (*Note:* A normal probability plot of the paired differences suggests that it is reasonable to presume that the paired-difference variable is approximately normally distributed.)

10. Speed Reading. Refer to Problem 9. Find a 90% confidence interval for the difference in mean reading speeds for the two programs.

Each of Problems 11–16 provides a type of sampling (independent or paired), sample size(s), and a figure showing the results of preliminary data analyses on the sample(s). For independent samples, the graphs are for the two samples; for a paired sample the graphs are for the paired differences. The intent is to employ the sample data to perform a hypothesis test to compare the means of the two populations from which the data were obtained. In each case, decide which, if any, of the procedures that we have studied should be applied.

11. Paired; $n = 75$; Fig. 10.6

12. Independent; $n_1 = 25$, $n_2 = 20$; Fig. 10.7

13. Independent; $n_1 = 17$, $n_2 = 17$; Fig. 10.8

14. Independent; $n_1 = 40$, $n_2 = 45$; Fig. 10.9

15. Independent; $n_1 = 20$, $n_2 = 15$; Fig. 10.10

16. Paired; $n = 18$; Fig. 10.11

FIGURE 10.6
Results of preliminary data analyses on the data referred to in Problem 11

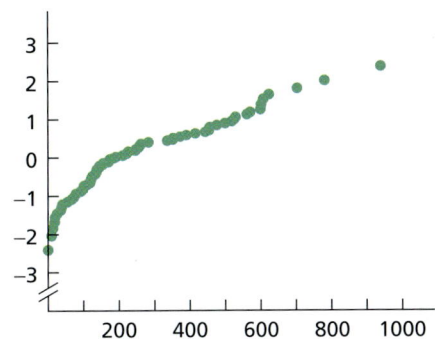
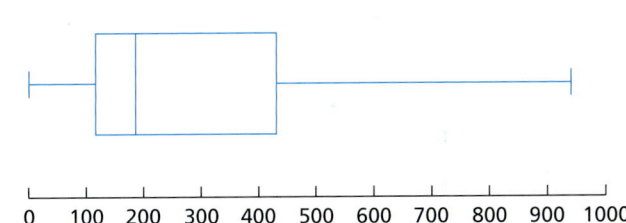

FIGURE 10.7
Results of preliminary data analyses on the data referred to in Problem 12

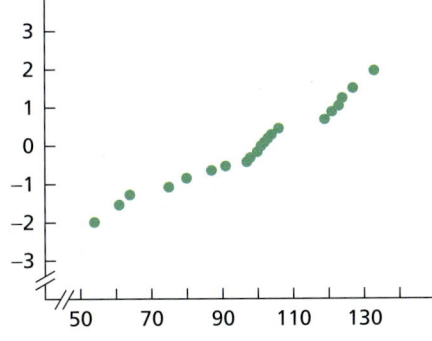
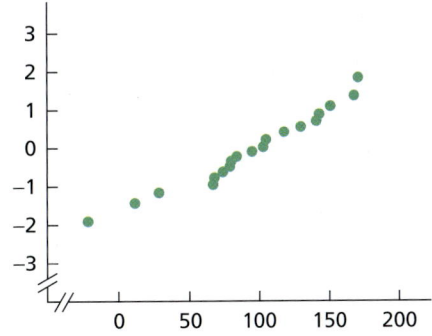
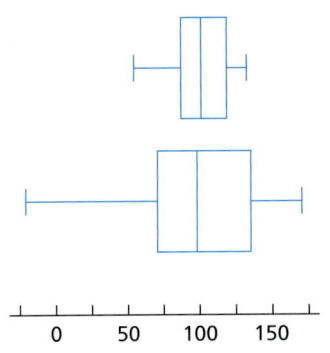

FIGURE 10.8
Results of preliminary data analyses on the data referred to in Problem 13

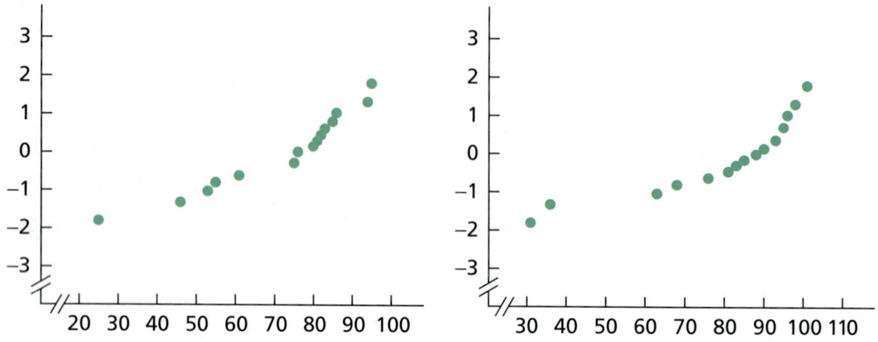

5	2	
	3	1 6
6	4	
5 3	5	
1	6	3 8
6 5 5 5	7	6
6 5 3 2 1 0	8	1 3 5 8
5 4	9	0 3 3 5 5 6 8
	10	1

FIGURE 10.9
Results of preliminary data analyses on the data referred to in Problem 14

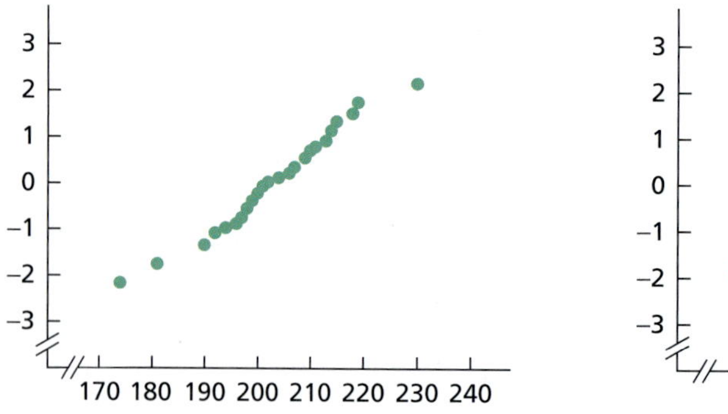

FIGURE 10.10
Results of preliminary data analyses on the data referred to in Problem 15

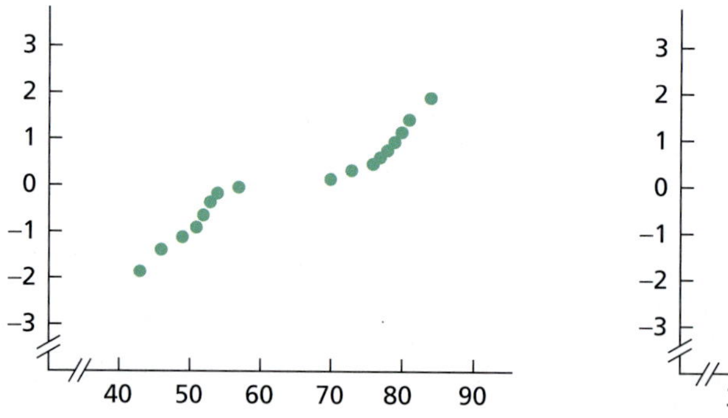

FIGURE 10.11
Results of preliminary data analyses on the data referred to in Problem 16

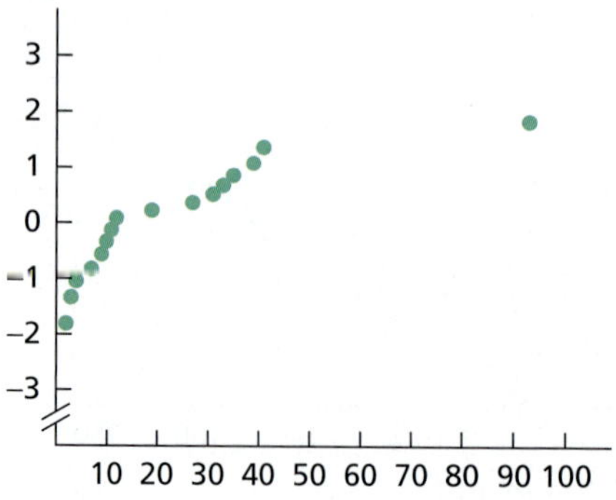

0	2 3 4 7 9 9
1	0 1 1 2 9
2	7
3	1 3 5 9
4	1
5	
6	
7	
8	
9	3

Using Technology

17. Grip and Leg Strength. Refer to Problems 5 and 6. Use the technology of your choice to
a. obtain normal probability plots, stem-and-leaf diagrams, boxplots, and the standard deviations of the two samples.
b. perform the required hypothesis test and obtain the desired confidence interval.
c. Justify the use of your procedures in part (b).

18. Cottonmouth Litter Size. Refer to Problems 7 and 8. Use the technology of your choice to
a. obtain normal probability plots, stem-and-leaf diagrams, boxplots, and the standard deviations of the two samples.
b. perform the required hypothesis test and obtain the desired confidence interval.
c. Justify the use of your procedures in part (b).

19. Speed Reading. Refer to Problems 9 and 10. Use the technology of your choice to
a. obtain a normal probability plot, stem-and-leaf diagram, and boxplot of the paired differences.
b. perform the required hypothesis test and obtain the desired confidence interval.
c. Justify the use of your procedures in part (b).

Internet Project

Women Workers and Equality in the United States

The rise of women in the U.S. labor force has been dramatic. According to the Women's Bureau of the U.S. Department of Labor, women workers made up 46% of the U.S. labor force in 1994. The Bureau predicts that this figure will increase to 48% by 2005.

Although these numbers reflect progress for women in the United States, problems remain. More women are working than in the past, but are they compensated the same as men? Some advocates for equality claim that most of the women in the U.S. work force have jobs that tend to pay less than male occupations. Additionally, these advocates suggest that such women have fewer opportunities for advancement. In this Internet project, you are to explore relevant data and come to your own conclusion.

URL for access to Internet Projects Page: www.aw.com/weiss

Focusing on Data Analysis

SAT SCORES, GPA

Recall from Chapter 1 (see page 34) that the Focus database contains information on 500 randomly selected Arizona State University sophomores. Use the technology of your choice to solve the following problems.

a. Obtain normal probability plots, boxplots, and the sample standard deviations of the SAT math scores of the male sophomores in the sample and the female sophomores in the sample.
b. At the 5% significance level, do the data provide sufficient evidence to conclude that male sophomores at Arizona State University have a higher mean SAT math score than female sophomores? Justify the use of the procedure you chose to carry out the hypothesis test.
c. Obtain a 90% confidence interval for the difference between the mean SAT math scores of male and female sophomores at Arizona State University.
d. Obtain normal probability plots, boxplots, and the standard deviations of the SAT verbal scores of the male sophomores in the sample and the female sophomores in the sample.
e. At the 5% significance level, do the data provide sufficient evidence to conclude that male and female sophomores at Arizona State University have different mean SAT verbal scores? Justify the use of the procedure you selected to perform the hypothesis test.

490   CHAPTER 10 Inferences for Two Population Means

f. Obtain a 95% confidence interval for the difference between the mean SAT verbal scores of male and female sophomores at Arizona State University.

g. Obtain a normal probability plot, a histogram, and a boxplot for the paired differences of the SAT verbal scores and SAT math scores of the sophomores in the sample.

h. Do the data provide sufficient evidence to conclude that the mean SAT verbal score is less than the mean SAT math score for Arizona State University sophomores? Perform the required hypothesis test at the 0.01 significance level. Justify the use of the procedure you employed to conduct the hypothesis test.

i. Find a 98% confidence interval for the difference between the mean SAT math and SAT verbal scores of Arizona State University sophomores.

j. Obtain normal probability plots, boxplots, and the standard deviations of the cumulative GPAs of the sophomores in the sample who are under 21 years of age and those who are 21 years of age or over.

k. Do the data provide sufficient evidence to conclude that, for Arizona State University sophomores, there is a difference between the mean cumulative GPAs of those under 21 years of age and those 21 years of age or older? Perform the required hypothesis test at the 5% significance level. Justify the use of the procedure you chose to carry out the hypothesis test.

case study discussion

Breast Milk and IQ

On page 431 of this chapter, we presented data obtained by five researchers studying the effect of breast feeding on subsequent IQ of preterm babies at age $7\frac{1}{2}$–8 years. Three categories were considered: children whose mothers declined to provide breast milk (Group I); those whose mothers had chosen but were unable to provide breast milk (Group IIa); and those whose mothers had chosen and were able to provide breast milk (Group IIb).

Presuming that IQs are normally distributed in all three categories, solve each of the following problems.

a. Do the data provide sufficient evidence to conclude that, for children age $7\frac{1}{2}$–8 years who are born preterm, a difference exists in mean IQ between those whose mothers decline to provide breast milk and those whose mothers choose but are unable to provide breast milk? Perform the required hypothesis test at the 5% significance level.

b. Do the data provide sufficient evidence to conclude that, for children age $7\frac{1}{2}$–8 years who are born preterm, the mean IQ of those whose mothers decline to provide breast milk is less than that of those whose mothers choose and are able to provide breast milk? Perform the required hypothesis test at the 5% significance level.

c. Do the data provide sufficient evidence to conclude that, for children age $7\frac{1}{2}$–8 years who are born preterm, the mean IQ of those whose mothers choose but are unable to provide breast milk is less than that of those whose mothers choose and are able to provide breast milk? Perform the required hypothesis test at the 5% significance level.

d. Is this study observational, or is it a designed experiment? Explain your answer.

e. Based on your answers in parts (a)–(d), what conclusions do you draw?

The researchers also adjusted the data for such factors as social class, mother's education, and infant's sex, and still reached the same conclusions: "...preterm babies whose mothers provided breast milk had a substantial advantage in subsequent IQ at $7\frac{1}{2}$–8 years over those who did not...." However, the researchers emphasized that they could not exclude the possibility that their findings could be explained by differences in parental behavior or genetic potential between the groups.

Internet Resources: Visit the Weiss Web site www.aw.com/weiss for additional discussion, exercises, and resources related to this case study.

Biography

Gertrude Cox: Spreading the Gospel According to St. Gertrude

GERTRUDE MARY COX was born on January 13, 1900, in Dayton, Iowa, the daughter of John and Emmaline Cox. She graduated from Perry High School, Perry, Iowa, in 1918. Between 1918 and 1925, she prepared to become a deaconess in the Methodist Episcopal Church.

In 1929 and 1931, Cox received a B.S. and an M.S., respectively, from Iowa State College in Ames. Her work there was directed by George W. Snedecor, and her degree was the first master's degree in statistics given by the department of mathematics at Iowa State.

From 1931 to 1933, Cox studied psychological statistics at the University of California at Berkeley. Snedecor meanwhile had established a new Statistical Laboratory at Iowa State, and in 1933 he asked her to be his assistant. This position launched her internationally influential career in statistics. Cox worked in the lab until becoming an Iowa State assistant professor in 1939.

In 1940, the committee in charge of filling a newly created position as head of the department of experimental statistics at North Carolina State College in Raleigh asked Snedecor for recommendations; he first named several male statisticians, then wrote, "…but if you would consider a woman for this position I would recommend Gertrude Cox of my staff." They did consider a woman and Cox accepted their offer.

In 1945, Cox organized and became director of the Institute of Statistics, which combined the teaching of statistics at the University of North Carolina and North Carolina State. Work conferences that Cox organized established the Institute as an international center for statistics. She also developed statistical programs throughout the South, referred to as "spreading the gospel according to St. Gertrude."

Cox's area of expertise was experimental design. She, with W. G. Cochran, wrote *Experimental Designs* (1950), recognized as the classic textbook on design and analysis of replicated experiments.

From 1960–1964, Cox was director of the Statistics Section of the Research Triangle Institute in Durham, North Carolina. She then retired, working only as a consultant. She died of leukemia on October 17, 1978, in Durham.

chapter 11

Inferences for Population Proportions

CHAPTER OUTLINE

11.1 Confidence Intervals for One Population Proportion

11.2 Hypothesis Tests for One Population Proportion

11.3 Inferences for Two Population Proportions, Using Independent Samples

GENERAL OBJECTIVES In Chapters 8–10, we discussed methods for finding confidence intervals and performing hypothesis tests for one or two population means. Now we describe how to conduct those inferences for one or two population proportions.

A *population proportion* is the proportion (percentage) of a population that has a specified attribute. For example, if the population under consideration consists of all Americans and the specified attribute is "retired," the population proportion is the proportion of all Americans who are retired.

In Section 11.1, we first introduce the required notation and terminology for performing proportion inferences and then discuss confidence intervals for one population proportion. Next, in Section 11.2, we examine a method for conducting a hypothesis test for one population proportion.

In Section 11.3, we investigate how to perform a hypothesis test to compare two population proportions and how to construct a confidence interval for the difference between two population proportions.

case study

DOUBLE-DIPPING ATM FEES

Currently, many of the banks in the United States charge customers as much as $3.00 per transaction for using an automated teller machine (ATM). These surcharges earned banks approximately $2.1 billion in 1999.

As explained by the U.S. Public Interest Research Group (PIRG), surcharges paid to banks that operate ATMs are in addition to fees that customers pay to their own banks when they use another bank's ATM—hence the term *double-dipping*. These surcharges have come under fire by many consumer advocate groups that consider the fees excessive and unfair. The surcharges have even prompted a congressional investigation.

Bank representatives defend the fees, claiming that they are outweighed by the 24-hour convenience for customers and that they are necessary to make the ATMs profitable. Nationwide, opponents say the fees are unjustifiable at a time of soaring bank profits, teller layoffs, and bank branch closures. They also contend that the fees hurt competition by inducing customers to switch to larger banks, which have more ATMs.

Although Congress thus far has rejected legislation that would ban the surcharges nationwide, many states and local communities have instituted or are considering instituting such bans. Even the military is getting involved: the Department of Defense recently said that it would consider a ban on ATM fees on U.S. military bases to help financially strapped military personnel.

In southern California, Santa Monica city officials passed an ordinance banning the surcharges. Other California communities, including Los Angeles and San Diego, are considering bans. Connecticut and Iowa have used existing laws to institute statewide bans on surcharges.

The fourth PIRG national survey found that 93% of 336 U.S. banks surcharge nonholders of accounts. Based on this statistic, PIRG stated in an April 1999 news release that "More than nine out of ten [U.S.] banks charge consumers the controversial ATM surcharge…." At the end of this chapter, you are asked to decide whether PIRG was justified, based on the survey data, in making the quoted statement.

11.1 CONFIDENCE INTERVALS FOR ONE POPULATION PROPORTION

Many statistical studies are concerned with obtaining the proportion (percentage) of a population that has a specified attribute. For example, we might be interested in

- the percentage of U.S. adults who have health insurance,
- the percentage of cars in the United States that are imports,
- the percentage of U.S. adults who favor stricter clean air health standards, or
- the percentage of Canadian women in the labor force.

In the first case, the population consists of all U.S. adults and the specified attribute is "has health insurance." For the second case, the population consists of all cars in the United States and the specified attribute is "is an import." The population in the third case is all U.S. adults and the specified attribute is "favors stricter clean air health standards." And, in the fourth case, the population consists of all Canadian women and the specified attribute is "is in the labor force."

Generally, the population under consideration is large, and determining the population proportion by taking a census is therefore usually impractical and often impossible; for instance, imagine trying to interview every U.S. adult for the purpose of ascertaining the proportion who have health insurance. Thus, in practice, we mostly rely on sampling and use the sample data to make inferences about the population proportion. In Example 11.1, we introduce proportion notation and terminology.

Example 11.1 *Proportion Notation and Terminology*

Playing Hooky From Work Many employers are concerned about employees who call in sick when in fact they are not ill. A survey commissioned by the Hilton Hotels Corporation investigated this issue. One question asked of the people taking part in the survey was whether they call in sick at least once a year when they simply need time to relax. For brevity, we use the phrase *play hooky* to refer to that practice.

In the survey, 1010 randomly selected U.S. employees were polled. The proportion of the 1010 employees sampled who play hooky was used to estimate the proportion of all U.S. employees who play hooky. Discuss the statistical notation and terminology used in this and similar studies on proportions.

Solution We use p to denote the proportion of all U.S. employees who play hooky; it represents the **population proportion** and is the parameter whose value is to be estimated. The proportion of the 1010 U.S. employees sampled who play hooky is designated $\hat{p}$ (read "p hat") and represents a **sample proportion;** it is the statistic used to estimate the unknown population proportion, p.

Although unknown, the population proportion, p, is a fixed number. In contrast, the sample proportion, $\hat{p}$, is a variable; its value varies from sample to sample. For instance, if 202 of the 1010 employees sampled play hooky,

$$\hat{p} = \frac{202}{1010} = 0.2 \ (20\%).$$

Whereas, if 184 of the 1010 employees sampled play hooky,

$$\hat{p} = \frac{184}{1010} = 0.182 \ (18.2\%).$$

These two calculations also reveal how to compute a sample proportion: Divide the number of employees sampled who play hooky, denoted x, by the total number of employees sampled, n. In symbols, $\hat{p} = x/n$. ◆

In Example 11.1, we introduced some notation and terminology used when we make inferences about a population proportion. In general, we have the following definitions.

DEFINITION 11.1 **Population Proportion and Sample Proportion**

Consider a population in which each member either has or does not have a specified attribute. Then we use the following notation and terminology.

Population proportion, p: The proportion (percentage) of the entire population that has the specified attribute.

Sample proportion, $\hat{p}$: The proportion (percentage) of a sample from the population that has the specified attribute.

In Example 11.1, the population consists of all U.S. employees, and the specified attribute is "plays hooky." The population proportion, p, is the proportion of all U.S. employees who play hooky; and a sample proportion, $\hat{p}$, is the proportion of employees sampled who play hooky. As demonstrated in Example 11.1, we compute a sample proportion as indicated in Formula 11.1.

FORMULA 11.1 **Sample Proportion**

A sample proportion, $\hat{p}$, is computed by using the formula

$$\hat{p} = \frac{x}{n},$$

where x denotes the number of members in the sample that have the specified attribute and, as usual, n denotes the sample size.

Note: For convenience, we sometimes refer to x (the number of members in the sample that have the specified attribute) as the **number of successes** and to $n - x$ (the number of members in the sample that do not have the specified attribute) as the **number of failures.** But remember that, in this context, the words *success* and *failure* need not have the ordinary meanings of the words.

TABLE 11.1
Correspondence between notations for means and proportions

	Parameter	Statistic
Means	μ	$\bar{x}$
Proportions	p	$\hat{p}$

Before proceeding, let's draw some parallels between proportions and means. Table 11.1 shows the correspondence between the notation for means and the notation for proportions.

Recall that a sample mean, $\bar{x}$, can be used to make inferences about a population mean, μ. Similarly, a sample proportion, $\hat{p}$, can be used to make inferences about a population proportion, p.

THE SAMPLING DISTRIBUTION OF THE SAMPLE PROPORTION

To make inferences about a population mean, μ, we must know the sampling distribution of the sample mean, that is, the distribution of the variable $\bar{x}$. The same is true for proportions: To make inferences about a population proportion, p, we need to know the **sampling distribution of the sample proportion**, that is, the distribution of the variable $\hat{p}$.

Because a proportion can always be regarded as a mean, we can use our knowledge of the sampling distribution of the sample mean to derive the sampling distribution of the sample proportion. (See Exercise 11.33 for details.) In practice, the sample size usually is large, so we concentrate on that case, as presented in Key Fact 11.1.

> **Key Fact 11.1** **The Sampling Distribution of the Sample Proportion**
>
> For samples of size n,
>
> - the mean of $\hat{p}$ equals the population proportion, or $\mu_{\hat{p}} = p$;
> - the standard deviation of $\hat{p}$ equals the square root of the product of the population proportion and one minus the population proportion divided by the sample size, or $\sigma_{\hat{p}} = \sqrt{p(1-p)/n}$; and
> - $\hat{p}$ is approximately normally distributed for large n.
>
> In particular, if n is large, the possible sample proportions for samples of size n have approximately a normal distribution with mean p and standard deviation $\sqrt{p(1-p)/n}$.

The accuracy of the normal approximation depends on n and p. If p is close to 0.5, the approximation is quite accurate, even for moderate n. The farther p is from 0.5, the larger n must be for the approximation to be accurate. As a rule of thumb, we use the normal approximation when np and $n(1-p)$ are both 5 or greater.[1] In this chapter, when we say that n is large, we mean that np and $n(1-p)$ are both 5 or greater.

We can make Key Fact 11.1 plausible through simulation. We do so in Example 11.2 by returning to the situation described in Example 11.1.

---

[1] Another commonly used rule of thumb is that np and $n(1-p)$ are both 10 or greater; still another is that $np(1-p)$ is 25 or greater. However, our rule of thumb, which is less conservative than either of these two, is consistent with the conditions required for performing a chi-square goodness-of-fit test (discussed in Chapter 12).

Example 11.2 Sampling Distribution of the Sample Proportion

Playing Hooky From Work Suppose that, in reality, 19.1% of all U.S. employees play hooky; that is, the population proportion is $p = 0.191$. Then, according to Key Fact 11.1, for samples of size 1010, $\mu_{\hat{p}} = p = 0.191$, $\sigma_{\hat{p}} = \sqrt{p(1-p)/n} = 0.012$, and $\hat{p}$ is approximately normally distributed. Use simulation to make these facts plausible.

Solution We simulated 2000 samples of size 1010 each from the population of all U.S. employees, determined the sample proportion for each of the 2000 samples, and obtained a histogram of those 2000 sample proportions (displayed in Printout 11.1). For purposes of comparison, we have superimposed on the histogram the normal distribution with a mean of 0.191 and a standard deviation of 0.012.

PRINTOUT 11.1
Histogram of the sample proportions for 2000 samples of size 1010 with the approximating normal curve for $\hat{p}$ superimposed

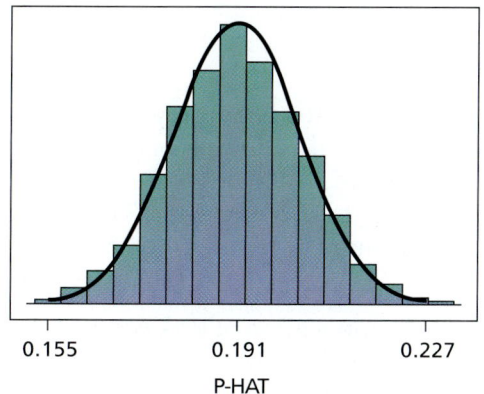

The histogram shown in Printout 11.1 is shaped roughly like a normal curve, specifically like the normal curve with parameters 0.191 and 0.012. This result makes it plausible that $\hat{p}$ is approximately normally distributed with mean 0.191 and standard deviation 0.012, as proposed in Key Fact 11.1. ◆

LARGE-SAMPLE CONFIDENCE INTERVALS FOR A POPULATION PROPORTION

We now present Procedure 11.1, a step-by-step method for obtaining a confidence interval for a population proportion. We often refer to this procedure as the **one-sample z-interval procedure** for a population proportion or, simply, as the **z-interval procedure** for a population proportion. The one-sample z-interval procedure for a population proportion is based on Key Fact 11.1 and is derived in a way similar to the one-sample z-interval procedure for a population mean (Procedure 8.1 on page 335).

> **Procedure 11.1**
>
> **The One-Sample z-Interval Procedure for a Population Proportion**
>
> **Assumption**
>
> The number of successes, x, and the number of failures, $n - x$, are both 5 or greater.
>
> **Step 1** For a confidence level of $1 - \alpha$, use Table II to find $z_{\alpha/2}$.
>
> **Step 2** The confidence interval for p is from
>
> $$\hat{p} - z_{\alpha/2} \cdot \sqrt{\hat{p}(1-\hat{p})/n} \quad \text{to} \quad \hat{p} + z_{\alpha/2} \cdot \sqrt{\hat{p}(1-\hat{p})/n},$$
>
> where $z_{\alpha/2}$ is found in Step 1, n is the sample size, and $\hat{p} = x/n$ is the sample proportion.
>
> **Step 3** Interpret the confidence interval.

Note: As stated at the beginning of Procedure 11.1, the condition for using that procedure is "the number of successes, x, and the number of failures, $n - x$, are both 5 or greater." We can restate this condition as "$n\hat{p}$ and $n(1 - \hat{p})$ are both 5 or greater," which, for an unknown p, corresponds to the rule of thumb for using the normal approximation given after Key Fact 11.1.

In our first application of Procedure 11.1, we obtain a confidence interval for the proportion of all U.S. employees who play hooky. We use the information obtained in the poll commissioned by the Hilton Hotels Corporation.

Example 11.3 The One-Sample z-Interval Procedure

Playing Hooky From Work A poll was taken of 1010 U.S. employees. The employees sampled were asked whether they "play hooky," that is, call in sick at least once a year when they simply need time to relax; 202 responded "yes." Use these data to obtain a 95% confidence interval for the proportion, p, of all U.S. employees who play hooky.

Solution Before we apply Procedure 11.1, we must check whether the condition for its use is satisfied. The attribute in question is "plays hooky," the sample size is 1010, and the number of employees sampled who play hooky is 202. Hence $x = 202$ and $n - x = 1010 - 202 = 808$, both of which are 5 or greater, meeting the condition for using Procedure 11.1.

Step 1 For a confidence level of $1 - \alpha$, use Table II to find $z_{\alpha/2}$.

We want a 95% confidence interval, which means that $\alpha = 0.05$. In Table II or at the bottom of Table IV, we find that $z_{\alpha/2} = z_{0.05/2} = z_{0.025} = 1.96$.

Step 2 The confidence interval for p is from

$$\hat{p} - z_{\alpha/2} \cdot \sqrt{\hat{p}(1-\hat{p})/n} \quad \text{to} \quad \hat{p} + z_{\alpha/2} \cdot \sqrt{\hat{p}(1-\hat{p})/n}.$$

We have $n = 1010$ and, from Step 1, $z_{\alpha/2} = 1.96$. Also, because 202 of the 1010 employees sampled play hooky, $\hat{p} = x/n = 202/1010 = 0.2$. Consequently, a 95% confidence interval for p is from

$$0.2 - 1.96 \cdot \sqrt{(0.2)(1-0.2)/1010} \quad \text{to} \quad 0.2 + 1.96 \cdot \sqrt{(0.2)(1-0.2)/1010},$$

or

$$0.2 - 0.025 \quad \text{to} \quad 0.2 + 0.025,$$

or 0.175 to 0.225.

Step 3 Interpret the confidence interval.

We can be 95% confident that the percentage of all U.S. employees who play hooky is somewhere between 17.5% and 22.5%.

◆

MARGIN OF ERROR

In Section 8.3, we discussed the margin of error in estimating a population mean by a sample mean. In general, the **margin of error** of an estimator represents the precision with which it estimates the parameter in question. The confidence-interval formula in Step 2 of Procedure 11.1 indicates that the margin of error, E, in estimating a population proportion by a sample proportion is $z_{\alpha/2} \cdot \sqrt{\hat{p}(1-\hat{p})/n}$.

DEFINITION 11.2 Margin of Error for the Estimate of p

The *margin of error* for the estimate of p is

$$E = z_{\alpha/2} \cdot \sqrt{\hat{p}(1-\hat{p})/n}.$$

The margin of error is equal to half the length of the confidence interval. It represents the precision with which a sample proportion, $\hat{p}$, estimates the population proportion, p, at the specified confidence level.

In Example 11.3, the margin of error is

$$E = z_{\alpha/2} \cdot \sqrt{\hat{p}(1-\hat{p})/n} = 1.96 \cdot \sqrt{(0.2)(1-0.2)/1010} = 0.025,$$

which can also be obtained by taking one-half the length of the confidence interval: $(0.225 - 0.175)/2 = 0.025$. Therefore we can be 95% confident that the error in estimating the proportion p of all U.S. employees who play hooky by the proportion, 0.2, of those in the sample who play hooky is at most 0.025, that is, plus or minus 2.5 percentage points.

On the one hand, given a confidence interval, we can find the margin of error by taking half the length of the confidence interval. On the other hand, given the sample proportion and the margin of error, we can determine the confidence interval—its endpoints are $\hat{p} \pm E$.

Most newspaper and magazine polls provide the sample proportion and the margin of error associated with a 95% confidence interval. For example, a survey of U.S. women conducted by Gallup for the CNBC cable network stated, "…36% of those polled believe their gender will hurt them; the margin of error for the poll is plus or minus 4 percentage points."

Translated into our terminology, $\hat{p} = 0.36$ and $E = 0.04$. Thus the confidence interval has endpoints $\hat{p} \pm E = 0.36 \pm 0.04$, or 0.32 to 0.40. As a result, we can be 95% confident that the percentage of all U.S. women who believe that their gender will hurt them is somewhere between 32% and 40%.

DETERMINING THE REQUIRED SAMPLE SIZE

The margin of error and confidence level of a confidence interval are often specified in advance. We must then determine the sample size required to meet those specifications. If we solve for n in the formula for the margin of error, we obtain

$$n = \hat{p}(1-\hat{p}) \left(\frac{z_{\alpha/2}}{E} \right)^2. \tag{11.1}$$

This formula cannot be used to obtain the required sample size because the sample proportion, $\hat{p}$, is not known prior to sampling.

There are two ways around this problem. To begin, we examine the graph of $\hat{p}(1-\hat{p})$ versus $\hat{p}$ shown in Fig. 11.1, which reveals that the largest $\hat{p}(1-\hat{p})$ can be is 0.25, or when $\hat{p} = 0.5$. The farther $\hat{p}$ is from 0.5, the smaller will be the value of $\hat{p}(1-\hat{p})$.

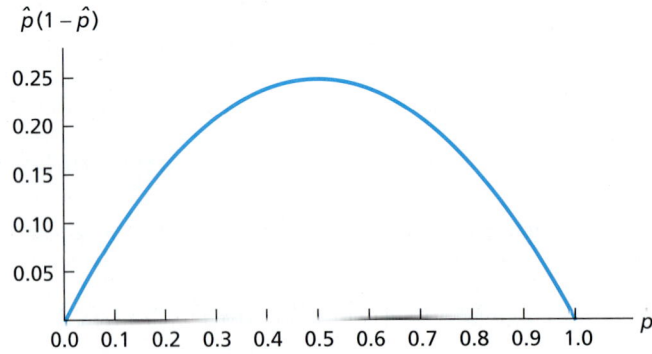

FIGURE 11.1 Graph of $\hat{p}(1-\hat{p})$ versus $\hat{p}$

Because the largest possible value of $\hat{p}(1-\hat{p})$ is 0.25, the most conservative approach for determining sample size is to use that value in Equation (11.1). The sample size obtained then will generally be larger than necessary and the margin of error less than required. Nonetheless, this approach guarantees that the specifications will be met or bettered.

However, because sampling tends to be time-consuming and expensive, we usually do not want to take a larger sample than necessary. If we can make an educated guess for the observed value of $\hat{p}$—say, from a previous study or theoretical considerations—we can use that guess to obtain a more realistic sample size.

In this same vein, if we have in mind a likely range for the observed value of $\hat{p}$, then, in light of Fig. 11.1, we should take as our educated guess for $\hat{p}$ the value in the range closest to 0.5. But, in either case, we should be aware that, if the observed value of $\hat{p}$ is closer to 0.5 than is our educated guess, the margin of error will be larger than desired.

Formula 11.2 summarizes this discussion, and we apply it in Example 11.4.

FORMULA 11.2 Sample Size for Estimating p

A $(1 - \alpha)$-level confidence interval for a population proportion that has a margin of error of at most E can be obtained by choosing

$$n = 0.25 \left(\frac{z_{\alpha/2}}{E}\right)^2,$$

rounded up to the nearest whole number. If we can make an educated guess, $\hat{p}_g$ (g for guess), for the observed value of $\hat{p}$, then we should instead choose

$$n = \hat{p}_g (1 - \hat{p}_g) \left(\frac{z_{\alpha/2}}{E}\right)^2,$$

rounded up to the nearest whole number.

Example 11.4 Sample Size for Estimating p

Playing Hooky From Work Consider again the problem of estimating the proportion of all U.S. employees who play hooky.

a. Obtain a sample size that will ensure a margin of error of at most 0.01 for a 95% confidence interval.
b. Find a 95% confidence interval for p if, for a sample of the size determined in part (a), the proportion of those who play hooky is 0.194.
c. Determine the margin of error for the estimate in part (b) and compare it to the margin of error specified in part (a).
d. Repeat parts (a)–(c) if the proportion of those sampled who play hooky can reasonably be presumed to be somewhere between 0.1 and 0.3.
e. Compare the results obtained in parts (a)–(c) with those obtained in part (d).

Solution a. We apply the first displayed equation in Formula 11.2. To do so, we must identify $z_{\alpha/2}$ and the margin of error, E. The confidence level is stipulated to be 0.95, so $z_{\alpha/2} = z_{0.05/2} = z_{0.025} = 1.96$, and the margin of error is specified at 0.01. Thus a sample size that will ensure a margin of error of at most 0.01 for a 95% confidence interval is

$$n = 0.25 \left(\frac{z_{\alpha/2}}{E}\right)^2 = 0.25 \left(\frac{1.96}{0.01}\right)^2 = 9604.$$

b. We find, by applying Procedure 11.1 (page 498) with $\alpha = 0.05$, $n = 9604$, and $\hat{p} = 0.194$, that a 95% confidence interval for p has endpoints

$$0.194 \pm 1.96 \cdot \sqrt{(0.194)(1 - 0.194)/9604},$$

or 0.194 ± 0.008, or 0.186 to 0.202.

> **What Does it Mean?**
>
> If we take a sample of 9604 U.S. employees, the margin of error for our estimate of the proportion of all U.S. employees who play hooky will be 0.01 or less, that is, at most plus or minus 1 percentage point.

> **What Does it Mean?**
>
> Based on a sample of 9604 U.S. employees, we can be 95% confident that the percentage of all U.S. employees who play hooky is somewhere between 18.6% and 20.2%.

c. The margin of error for the estimate in part (b) is 0.008. Not surprisingly, this is less than the margin of error of 0.01 specified in part (a).

d. If we can reasonably presume that the proportion of those sampled who play hooky will be somewhere between 0.1 and 0.3, we use the second displayed equation in Formula 11.2, with $\hat{p}_g = 0.3$ (the value in the range closest to 0.5), to obtain the sample size:

$$n = \hat{p}_g(1 - \hat{p}_g)\left(\frac{z_{\alpha/2}}{E}\right)^2 = (0.3)(1 - 0.3)\left(\frac{1.96}{0.01}\right)^2 = 8068 \text{ (rounded up)}.$$

Applying Procedure 11.1 with $\alpha = 0.05$, $n = 8068$, and $\hat{p} = 0.194$, we find that a 95% confidence interval for p has endpoints

$$0.194 \pm 1.96 \cdot \sqrt{(0.194)(1 - 0.194)/8068},$$

or 0.194 ± 0.009, or 0.185 to 0.203.

> **What Does it Mean?**
>
> Based on a sample of 8068 U.S. employees, we can be 95% confident that the percentage of all U.S. employees who play hooky is somewhere between 18.5% and 20.3%. The margin of error for the estimate is 0.009.

e. By using the educated guess for $\hat{p}$ in part (d), we reduced the required sample size by more than 1500 (from 9604 to 8068). Moreover, only 0.1% (0.001) of precision was lost—the margin of error rose from 0.008 to 0.009. The risk of using the guess 0.3 for $\hat{p}$ is that, if the observed value of $\hat{p}$ had turned out to be larger than 0.3 (but smaller than 0.7), the achieved margin of error would have exceeded the specified 0.01. ◆

The Technology Center

Most statistical technologies have programs that automatically obtain a confidence interval for a population proportion. In this subsection, we present output and (optional) step-by-step instructions to implement such programs.

Example 11.5 Using Technology to Obtain a z-Interval

Playing Hooky From Work In Example 11.3, we applied Procedure 11.1 to determine a 95% confidence interval for the proportion of all U.S. employees who play hooky. Use Minitab, Excel, or the TI-83 Plus to obtain that confidence interval.

Solution We first recall that the sample size is 1010 and that the number of employees sampled who play hooky is 202. Printout 11.2 shows the output obtained by applying the one-sample z-interval programs to the data.

PRINTOUT 11.2
One-sample z-interval output for the data on playing hooky from work

MINITAB

Test and CI for One Proportion

```
Test of p = 0.5 vs p not = 0.5

Sample      X      N   Sample p         95.0% CI         Z-Value  P-Value
1          202   1010  0.200000   (0.175331, 0.224669)   -19.07    0.000
```

EXCEL

Summary Statistics		Interval Results
n	1010	**Confidence Interval**
p-hat	0.2	With 95% Confidence, 0.175 < p < 0.225
Std Err	0.0126	
z*	1.96	

TI-83 PLUS

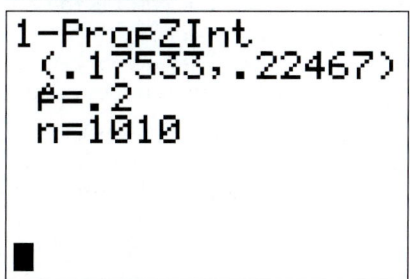

The outputs in Printout 11.2 indicate that the required 95% confidence interval is from 0.175 to 0.225. Thus we can be 95% confident that the percentage of all U.S. employees who play hooky is somewhere between 17.5% and 22.5%.

Obtaining the Output (Optional)

Printout 11.2 provides output from Minitab, Excel, and the TI-83 Plus for a 95% confidence interval for the proportion of all U.S. employees who play hooky. The following are detailed instructions for obtaining that output.

MINITAB
1. Choose **Stat ➤ Basic Statistics ➤ 1 Proportion...**
2. Select the **Summarized data** option button
3. Click in the **Number of trials** text box and type 1010
4. Click in the **Number of successes** text box and type 202
5. Click the **Options...** button
6. Click in the **Confidence level** text box and type 95
7. Select the **Use test and interval based on normal distribution** check box
8. Click **OK**
9. Click **OK**

EXCEL
1. Store the sample size, 1010, and the number of successes, 202, in ranges named n and x, respectively
2. Choose **DDXL ➤ Confidence Intervals**
3. Select **Summ 1 Var Prop Interval** from the **Function type** drop-down list box
4. Specify x in the **Num Successes** text box
5. Specify n in the **Num Trials** text box
6. Click **OK**
7. Click the **95%** button
8. Click the **Compute Interval** button

TI-83 PLUS
1. Press **STAT**, arrow over to **TESTS**, and press **ALPHA ➤ A**
2. Type 202 for **x** and press **ENTER**
3. Type 1010 for **n** and press **ENTER**
4. Type .95 for **C-Level** and press **ENTER** twice

Exercises 11.1

Statistical Concepts and Skills

11.1 In a newspaper or magazine of your choice, find a statistical study that contains an estimated population proportion.

11.2 Why is statistical inference generally used to obtain information about a population proportion?

11.3 Is a population proportion a parameter or a statistic? What about a sample proportion? Explain your answers.

11.4 Answer the following questions about the basic notation and terminology for proportions.
a. What is a population proportion?
b. What symbol is used for a population proportion?
c. What is a sample proportion?
d. What symbol is used for a sample proportion?
e. For what is the phrase "number of successes" an abbreviation? What symbol is used for the number of successes?
f. For what is the phrase "number of failures" an abbreviation?
g. Explain the relationships among the sample proportion, the number of successes, and the sample size.

11.5 This exercise involves the use of an unrealistically small population to provide a concrete illustration for the exact distribution of a sample proportion. A population consists of three men and two women. The first names of the men are Jose, Pete, and Carlo; the first names of the women are Gail and Frances. Suppose that the specified attribute is "female."

a. Determine the population proportion, p.
b. The first column of the following table provides the possible samples of size 2, where each person is represented by the first letter of his or her first name; the second column gives the number of successes—the number of females obtained—for each sample, and the third column shows the sample proportion. Complete the table.

Sample	Number of females x	Sample proportion $\hat{p}$
J, G	1	0.5
J, P	0	0.0
J, C	0	0.0
J, F	1	0.5
G, P		
G, C		
G, F		
P, C		
P, F		
C, F		

c. Construct a dotplot for the sampling distribution of the proportion for samples of size 2. Mark the position of the population proportion on the dotplot.
d. Use the third column of the table to obtain the mean of the variable $\hat{p}$.
e. Compare your answers from parts (a) and (d). Why are they the same?

11.6 Repeat parts (b)–(e) of Exercise 11.5 for samples of size 1.

11.7 Repeat parts (b)–(e) of Exercise 11.5 for samples of size 3. (There are 10 possible samples.)

11.8 Repeat parts (b)–(e) of Exercise 11.5 for samples of size 4. (There are five possible samples.)

11.9 Repeat parts (b)–(e) of Exercise 11.5 for samples of size 5.

11.10 Prerequisite to this exercise are Exercises 11.5–11.9. What do your graphs in parts (c) of those exercises illustrate about the impact of increasing sample size on sampling error? Explain your answer.

11.11 NBA Draft Picks. Since 1966, 45% of the No. 1 draft picks in the National Basketball Association have been centers.
a. Identify the population.
b. Identify the specified attribute.
c. Is the proportion 0.45 (45%) a population proportion or a sample proportion? Explain your answer.

11.12 Staying Single. According to an article in *Time* magazine, women are staying single longer these days, by choice. In 1963, 83% of women in the United States between the ages of 25 and 55 were married compared to 65% in 1997. For 1997,
a. identify the population.
b. identify the specified attribute.
c. Under what circumstances is the proportion 0.65 a population proportion? a sample proportion? Explain your answers.

11.13 Random Drug Testing. A *Harris Poll* conducted in June 2000, asked Americans whether states should be allowed to conduct random drug tests on elected officials. Of 21,355 respondents, 79% said "yes."
a. Determine the margin of error for a 99% confidence interval.
b. Without doing any calculations, indicate whether the margin of error is larger or smaller for a 90% confidence interval. Explain your answer.

11.14 Presidential Ethics. A *USA TODAY/CNN/Gallup Poll*, taken in January 1999, reported that 257 of 1070 respondents said that the terms "honest" and "trustworthy" applied to then-President Clinton.
a. Determine the margin of error for a 90% confidence interval.
b. Without doing any calculations, indicate whether the margin of error is larger or smaller for a 95% confidence interval. Explain your answer.

11.15 In each of parts (a)–(f), we have given a likely range for the observed value of a sample proportion $\hat{p}$. Based on the given range, identify the educated guess that should be used for the observed value of $\hat{p}$ to calculate the required sample size for a prescribed confidence level and margin of error.
a. 0.2 to 0.4   b. 0.4 to 0.7   c. 0.7 or greater
d. 0.2 or less   e. 0.4 or greater   f. 0.7 or less
g. In each of parts (a)–(f), which observed values of the sample proportion will yield a larger margin of error than the

one specified if the educated guess is used for the sample size computation?

In Exercises 11.16–11.19, apply Procedure 11.1 on page 498 to obtain the required confidence interval. Be sure to check the condition for using that procedure.

11.16 Asthmatics and Sulfites. Studies are performed to estimate the percentage of the nation's 10 million asthmatics who are allergic to sulfites. In one survey, 38 of 500 randomly selected U.S. asthmatics were found to be allergic to sulfites.
a. Find a 95% confidence interval for the proportion, p, of all U.S. asthmatics who are allergic to sulfites.
b. Interpret your result from part (a).

11.17 Drinking Habits. A *Reader's Digest/Gallup Survey* on the drinking habits of Americans estimated the percentage of adults across the country who drink beer, wine, or hard liquor, at least occasionally. Of the 1516 adults interviewed, 985 said that they drank.
a. Determine a 95% confidence interval for the proportion, p, of all Americans who drink beer, wine, or hard liquor, at least occasionally.
b. Interpret your result from part (a).

11.18 Factory Farming Funk. The U.S. Environmental Protection Agency recently reported that confined animal feeding operations (CAFOs) dump 2 trillion pounds of waste into the environment annually, contaminating the ground water in 17 states and polluting more than 35,000 miles of our nation's rivers. In a recent survey of 1000 registered voters by Snell, Perry and Associates, 80% favored the creation of standards to limit such pollution and, in general, viewed CAFOs unfavorably.
a. Find a 99% confidence interval for the percentage of all registered voters who favor the creation of standards on CAFO pollution and, in general, view CAFOs unfavorably.
b. Interpret your answer in part (a).

11.19 The Nipah Virus. From fall 1998 through mid 1999, Malaysia was the site of an encephalitis outbreak caused by the Nipah virus, a paramyxovirus that appears to spread from pigs to workers on pig farms. As reported by Goh et al. in the *New England Journal of Medicine* (2000, Vol. 342(17), p. 1229), neurologists from the University of Malaysia found that, among 94 patients infected with the Nipah virus, 30 died from encephalitis.
a. Find a 90% confidence interval for the percentage of Malaysians infected with the Nipah virus who will die from encephalitis.
b. Interpret your answer in part (a).

11.20 Literate Adults. Suppose that you have been hired to estimate the percentage of adults in your state who are literate. You take a random sample of 100 adults and find that 96 are literate. You then obtain a 95% confidence interval of

$$0.96 \pm 1.96 \cdot \sqrt{(0.96)(0.04)/100},$$

or 0.922 to 0.998. From it you conclude that you can be 95% confident that the percentage of all adults in your state who are literate is somewhere between 92.2% and 99.8%. Is anything wrong with this reasoning?

11.21 Infant Mortality. Suppose that you have been commissioned to estimate the infant mortality rate in Norway. From a random sample of 500 live births, you find that 0.8% of them resulted in infant deaths. You then find a 90% confidence interval for the infant mortality rate in Norway of

$$0.008 \pm 1.645 \cdot \sqrt{(0.008)(0.992)/500},$$

or 0.001 to 0.015. You then conclude that, "I can be 90% confident that the proportion of infant deaths in Norway is somewhere between 0.001 and 0.015." How did you do?

11.22 Conservation Funding. Both the 106th Congress and the Clinton administration proposed permanent funding sources for conservation and recreation programs. According to the League of Conservation Voters, in a telephone poll of 1000 registered voters, 780 favored a lands legacy program to provide permanent federal funding for protecting America's natural and historic resources. The margin of error of the poll was plus or minus 3.1 percentage points (for a 0.95 confidence level). Use this information to obtain a 95% confidence interval for the percentage of all registered voters who favor a lands legacy program.

11.23 Online Tax Returns. According to the U.S. Internal Revenue Service, among people entitled to tax refunds, those who file online receive their refunds twice as fast as paper filers. A study conducted by ICR of Media, Pennsylvania, found that 57% of those polled said that they are not worried about the privacy of their financial information when filing their tax returns online. The telephone survey of 1002 people from March 30, 2000, to April 5, 2000, had a margin of error of plus or minus 3 percentage points (for a 0.95 confidence level). Use this information to obtain a 95% confidence interval for the percentage of all people who are not worried about the privacy of their financial information when filing their tax returns online.

11.24 Asthmatics and Sulfites. Refer to Exercise 11.16.
a. Determine the margin of error for the estimate of p.
b. Obtain a sample size that will ensure a margin of error of at most 0.01 for a 95% confidence interval without making a guess for the observed value of $\hat{p}$.
c. Find a 95% confidence interval for p if, for a sample of the size determined in part (b), the proportion of asthmatics sampled who are allergic to sulfites is 0.071.
d. Determine the margin of error for the estimate in part (c) and compare it to the margin of error specified in part (b).
e. Repeat parts (b)–(d) if you can reasonably presume that the proportion of asthmatics sampled who are allergic to sulfites will be at most 0.10.
f. Compare the results you obtained in parts (b)–(d) with those obtained in part (e).

11.25 Drinking Habits. Refer to Exercise 11.17.
a. Find the margin of error for the estimate of p.
b. Obtain a sample size that will ensure a margin of error of at most 0.02 for a 95% confidence interval without making a guess for the observed value of $\hat{p}$.
c. Find a 95% confidence interval for p if, for a sample of the size determined in part (b), 63% of those sampled drink alcoholic beverages.
d. Determine the margin of error for the estimate in part (c) and compare it to the margin of error specified in part (b).
e. Repeat parts (b)–(d) if you can reasonably presume that the percentage of adults sampled who drink alcoholic beverages will be at least 60%.
f. Compare the results you obtained in parts (b)–(d) with those obtained in part (e).

11.26 Factory Farming Funk. Refer to Exercise 11.18.
a. Find the margin of error for the estimate of the percentage.
b. Obtain a sample size that will ensure a margin of error of at most 1.5 percentage points for a 99% confidence interval without making a guess for the observed value of $\hat{p}$.
c. Find a 99% confidence interval for p if, for a sample of the size determined in part (b), 82.2% of the registered voters sampled favor the creation of standards on CAFO pollution and, in general, view CAFOs unfavorably.
d. Determine the margin of error for the estimate in part (c) and compare it to the margin of error specified in part (b).
e. Repeat parts (b)–(d) if you can reasonably presume that the percentage of registered voters sampled who favor the creation of standards on CAFO pollution and, in general, view CAFOs unfavorably will be between 75% and 85%.
f. Compare the results you obtained in parts (b)–(d) with those obtained in part (e).

11.27 The Nipah Virus. Refer to Exercise 11.19.
a. Find the margin of error for the estimate of the percentage.
b. Obtain a sample size that will ensure a margin of error of at most 5 percentage points for a 90% confidence interval without making a guess for the observed value of $\hat{p}$.
c. Find a 90% confidence interval for p if, for a sample of the size determined in part (b), 28.8% of the sampled Malaysians infected with the Nipah virus die from encephalitis.
d. Determine the margin of error for the estimate in part (c) and compare it to the margin of error specified in part (b).
e. Repeat parts (b)–(d) if you can reasonably presume that the percentage of sampled Malaysians infected with the Nipah virus who will die from encephalitis will be between 25% and 40%.
f. Compare the results you obtained in parts (b)–(d) with those obtained in part (e).

11.28 Product Response Rate. A company manufactures goods that are sold exclusively by mail order. The director of market research needed to test market a new product. She planned to send brochures to a random sample of households and use the proportion of orders obtained as an estimate of the true proportion, known as the *product response rate*. The results of the market research were to be utilized as a primary source for advance production planning, so the director wanted the figures she presented to be as accurate as possible. Specifically, she wanted to be 95% confident that the estimate of the product response rate would be accurate to within 1%.
a. Without making any assumptions, determine the sample size required.
b. Historically, product response rates for products sold by this company have ranged from 0.5% to 4.9%. If the director had been willing to assume that the sample product response rate for this product would also fall in that range, find the required sample size.
c. Compare the results from parts (a) and (b).
d. Discuss the possible consequences if the assumption made in part (b) turns out to be incorrect.

11.29 Indicted Governor. On Thursday, June 13, 1996, then-Arizona Governor Fife Symington was indicted on 23 counts of fraud and extortion. Just hours after the federal prosecutors announced the indictment, several polls were conducted of Arizonans asking whether they thought Symington should resign. One poll, conducted by Research Resources, Inc., which appeared in the *Phoenix Gazette*, revealed that 58% of Arizonans felt that Symington should resign; it had a margin of error of plus or minus 4.9 percentage points. Another poll, conducted by Phoenix-based Behavior Research Center and appearing in the *Tempe Daily News*, reported that 54% of Arizonans felt that Symington should resign; it had a margin of error of plus or minus 4.4 percentage points. Can the conclusions of both polls be correct? Explain your answer.

Extending the Concepts and Skills

11.30 What important theorem in statistics implies that, for a large sample size, the possible sample proportions of that size have approximately a normal distribution?

11.31 In discussing the sample size required for obtaining a confidence interval with a prescribed confidence level and margin of error, we made the following statement: "If we have in mind a likely range for the observed value of $\hat{p}$, then, in light of Fig. 11.1, we should take as our educated guess for $\hat{p}$ the value in the range closest to 0.5." Explain why.

11.32 In discussing the sample size required for obtaining a confidence interval with a prescribed confidence level and margin of error, we made the following statement: "…we should be aware that, if the observed value of $\hat{p}$ is closer to 0.5 than is our educated guess, the margin of error will be larger than desired." Explain why.

11.33 Consider a population in which the proportion of members having a specified attribute is p. Let y be the variable whose value is 1 if a member has the specified attribute and 0 if a member does not.
a. If the size of the population is N, how many members of the population have the specified attribute?
b. Use part (a) and Definition 3.11 on page 129 to show that $\mu_y = p$.
c. Use part (b) and the computing formula in Definition 3.12 on page 131 to show that $\sigma_y = \sqrt{p(1-p)}$.
d. Explain why $\bar{y} = \hat{p}$.
e. Use parts (b)–(d) and Key Fact 7.4 on page 316, to justify Key Fact 11.1.

Using Technology

11.34 Asthmatics and Sulfites. Refer to Exercise 11.16.
a. Use the technology of your choice to obtain the confidence interval required in part (a) of Exercise 11.16.
b. Compare your answer to the one you obtained in Exercise 11.16. Explain any discrepancy that you observe.

11.35 Drinking Habits. Refer to Exercise 11.17.
a. Use the technology of your choice to obtain the confidence interval required in part (a) of Exercise 11.17.
b. Compare your answer to the one you obtained in Exercise 11.17. Explain any discrepancy that you observe.

11.2 HYPOTHESIS TESTS FOR ONE POPULATION PROPORTION

In Section 11.1, we showed how to obtain confidence intervals for a population proportion. Now we demonstrate how to perform hypothesis tests for a population proportion. This procedure is actually a special case of the one-sample z-test for a population mean (Procedure 9.1, page 389).

From Key Fact 11.1, on page 496, we can deduce that, for large n, the standardized version of $\hat{p}$,

$$z = \frac{\hat{p} - p}{\sqrt{p(1-p)/n}},$$

has approximately the standard normal distribution. Consequently, to perform a large-sample hypothesis test with the null hypothesis $H_0: p = p_0$, we can use the variable

$$z = \frac{\hat{p} - p_0}{\sqrt{p_0(1-p_0)/n}}$$

Procedure 11.2A — The One-Sample z-Test for a Population Proportion (Critical-Value Approach)

Assumption

Both np_0 and $n(1-p_0)$ are 5 or greater.

Step 1 The null hypothesis is $H_0: p = p_0$, and the alternative hypothesis is

$H_a: p \neq p_0$ (Two-tailed) or $H_a: p < p_0$ (Left-tailed) or $H_a: p > p_0$ (Right-tailed)

Step 2 Decide on the significance level, α.

Step 3 Compute the value of the test statistic

$$z = \frac{\hat{p} - p_0}{\sqrt{p_0(1-p_0)/n}}.$$

Step 4 The critical value(s) are

$\pm z_{\alpha/2}$ (Two-tailed) or $-z_\alpha$ (Left-tailed) or z_α (Right-tailed)

Use Table II to find the critical value(s).

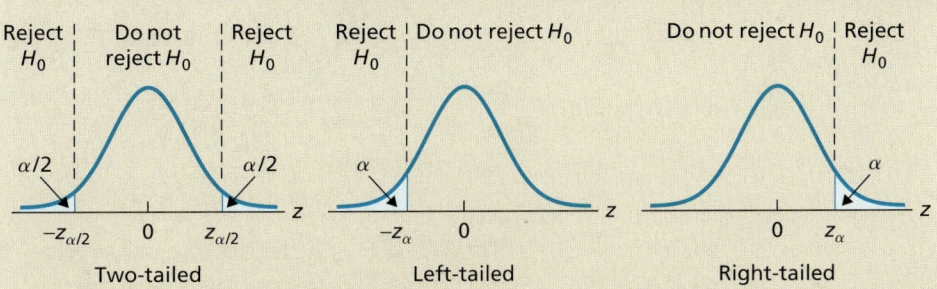

Step 5 If the value of the test statistic falls in the rejection region, reject H_0; otherwise, do not reject H_0.

Step 6 Interpret the results of the hypothesis test.

as the test statistic and obtain the critical value(s) from the standard normal table, Table II. Specifically, we have Procedures 11.2A and B, both of which we call the **one-sample z-test** for a population proportion or, simply, the **z-test** for a population proportion. We demonstrate use of these procedures in Example 11.6.

Procedure 11.2B — **The One-Sample z-Test for a Population Proportion (P-Value Approach)**

Assumption
Both np_0 and $n(1-p_0)$ are 5 or greater.

Step 1 The null hypothesis is H_0: $p = p_0$, and the alternative hypothesis is

H_a: $p \neq p_0$ or H_a: $p < p_0$ or H_a: $p > p_0$
(Two-tailed)   (Left-tailed)   (Right-tailed)

Step 2 Decide on the significance level, α.

Step 3 Compute the value of the test statistic

$$z = \frac{\hat{p} - p_0}{\sqrt{p_0(1-p_0)/n}}$$

and denote that value z_0.

Step 4 Use Table II to obtain the P-value.

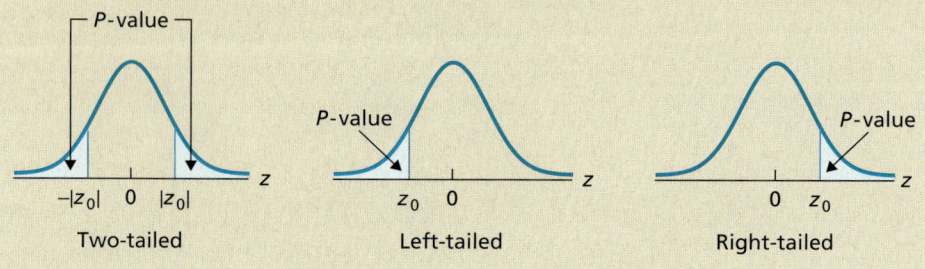

Step 5 If $P \leq \alpha$, reject H_0; otherwise, do not reject H_0.

Step 6 Interpret the results of the hypothesis test.

Example 11.6 The One-Sample z-Test

Gun Control One of the more controversial issues in the United States is gun control; there are many avid proponents and opponents of banning handgun sales. In a survey conducted by Louis Harris of LH Research, 1250 U.S. adults were polled regarding their views on banning handgun sales. Of those sampled, 650 favored a ban. At the 5% significance level, do the data provide sufficient evidence to conclude that a majority of U.S. adults (i.e., more than 50%) favor banning handgun sales?

Solution We apply Procedure 11.2 to perform the required hypothesis test but only after verifying that the condition for its use is met. As $n = 1250$ and $p_0 = 0.50$ (50%),

$$np_0 = 1250 \cdot 0.50 = 625 \quad \text{and} \quad n(1 - p_0) = 1250 \cdot (1 - 0.50) = 625.$$

Both np_0 and $n(1 - p_0)$ are 5 or greater, so we can utilize Procedure 11.2.

Step 1 State the null and alternative hypotheses.

Let p denote the proportion of all U.S. adults that favor banning handgun sales. Then the null and alternative hypotheses are

H_0: $p = 0.50$ (it is not true that a majority favor a ban)

H_a: $p > 0.50$ (a majority favor a ban).

The hypothesis test is right-tailed because a greater-than sign (>) appears in the alternative hypothesis.

Step 2 Decide on the significance level, α.

We are to perform the hypothesis test at the 5% significance level; consequently, $\alpha = 0.05$.

Step 3 Compute the value of the test statistic

$$z = \frac{\hat{p} - p_0}{\sqrt{p_0(1 - p_0)/n}}.$$

We have $n = 1250$ and $p_0 = 0.50$. The number of U.S. adults surveyed who favor banning handgun sales is 650. Therefore the proportion of those surveyed who favor a ban is $\hat{p} = x/n = 650/1250 = 0.520$ (52.0%). Consequently, the value of the test statistic is

$$z = \frac{0.520 - 0.50}{\sqrt{(0.50)(1 - 0.50)/1250}} = 1.41.$$

Critical-Value Approach

Step 4 The critical value for a right-tailed test is z_α.

For $\alpha = 0.05$, the critical value is $z_{0.05} = 1.645$, as shown in Fig. 11.2A.

FIGURE 11.2A

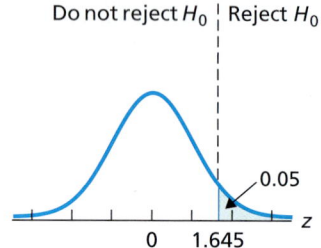

Step 5 If the value of the test statistic falls in the rejection region, reject H_0; otherwise, do not reject H_0.

From Step 3, the value of the test statistic is $z = 1.41$, which, as we see from Fig. 11.2A, does not fall in the rejection region. Thus we do not reject H_0. The test results are not statistically significant at the 5% level.

P-Value Approach

Step 4 Use Table II to obtain the P-value.

From Step 3, the value of the test statistic is $z = 1.41$. The test is right-tailed, so the P-value is the probability of observing a value of z of 1.41 or greater if the null hypothesis is true. That probability equals the shaded area in Fig. 11.2B, which by Table II is 0.0793, or $P = 0.0793$.

FIGURE 11.2B

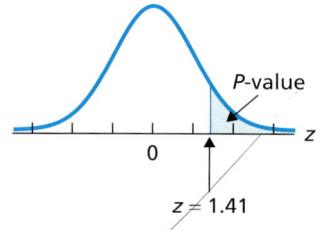

Step 5 If $P \le \alpha$, reject H_0; otherwise, do not reject H_0.

From Step 4, $P = 0.0793$. Because the P-value exceeds the specified significance level of 0.05, we do not reject H_0. The test results are not statistically significant at the 5% level but (see Table 9.10 on page 405) do provide moderate evidence against the null hypothesis.

Step 6 Interpret the results of the hypothesis test.

What Does it Mean? At the 5% significance level, the data do not provide sufficient evidence to conclude that a majority of U.S. adults favor banning handgun sales.

◆

Example 11.6 provides a good illustration of how statistical results are sometimes misstated. The newspaper article that featured the survey had the headline "Fear prompts 52% in U.S. to back pistol-sale ban, poll says." In fact, the poll says no such thing. It says only that 52% of those *sampled* back a pistol-sale ban. And, as we have demonstrated, at the 5% significance level the poll does not provide sufficient evidence to conclude that a majority of U.S. adults back a pistol-sale ban.

11.2 Hypothesis Tests for One Population Proportion

The Technology Center

Most statistical technologies have programs that automatically perform a hypothesis test for a population proportion. In this subsection, we present output and (optional) step-by-step instructions to implement such programs.

Example 11.7 Using Technology to Conduct a z-Test

Gun Control Use Minitab, Excel, or the TI-83 Plus to perform the hypothesis test considered in Example 11.6 on page 510.

Solution Let p denote the proportion of all U.S. adults that favor banning handgun sales. The task is to perform the hypothesis test

H_0: $p = 0.50$ (it is not true that a majority favor a ban)

H_a: $p > 0.50$ (a majority favor a ban)

at the 5% significance level. Note that the hypothesis test is right-tailed because a greater-than sign ($>$) appears in the alternative hypothesis. Also, recall that 1250 U.S. adults were polled and that 650 of those adults favored banning handgun sales. Printout 11.3 shows the output obtained by applying the one-sample z-test programs to the data.

PRINTOUT 11.3
One-sample z-test output for the data on banning handguns

MINITAB

Test and CI for One Proportion

```
Test of p = 0.5 vs p > 0.5

Sample       X       N   Sample p    95.0% Lower Bound   Z-Value   P-Value
1           650    1250  0.520000           0.496757        1.41     0.079
```

EXCEL

x Proportion Test

Summary Statistics		Test Summary	
n	1250	p0:	0.5
p-hat	0.52	Ho:	p = 0.5
Std Dev	0.0141	Ha:	Upper tail: p > 0.5
		z Statistic:	1.414
		p-value:	0.0786

Test Results

Conclusion

Fail to reject Ho at alpha = 0.05

PRINTOUT 11.3 (cont.)
One-sample z-test output for the data on banning handguns

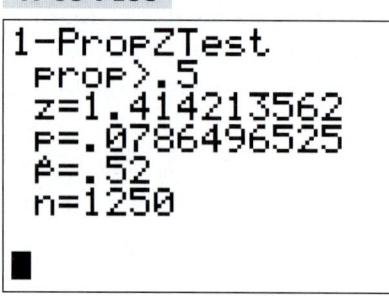

Using **Calculate**

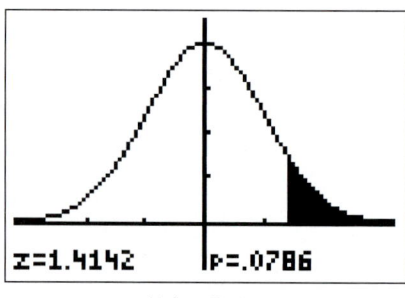

Using **Draw**

The outputs in Printout 11.3 show that the P-value for the hypothesis test is 0.079 (to three decimal places). The P-value exceeds the specified significance level of 0.05, so we do not reject H_0. The test results are not statistically significant at the 5% level; that is, at the 5% significance level, the data do not provide sufficient evidence to conclude that a majority of U.S. adults favor banning handgun sales. ◆

Obtaining the Output (Optional)

Printout 11.3 provides output from Minitab, Excel, and the TI-83 Plus for a one-sample z-test to decide whether a majority of U.S. adults favor banning handgun sales. The following are detailed instructions for obtaining that output.

MINITAB	EXCEL	TI-83 PLUS
1 Choose **Stat ➤ Basic Statistics ➤ 1 Proportion...**	1 Store the sample size, 1250, and the number of successes, 650, in ranges named n and x, respectively	1 Press **STAT**, arrow over to **TESTS**, and press **5**
2 Select the **Summarized data** option button	2 Choose **DDXL ➤ Hypothesis Tests**	2 Type <u>0.50</u> for p_0 and press **ENTER**
3 Click in the **Number of trials** text box and type <u>1250</u>	3 Select **Summ 1 Var Prop Test** from the **Function type** drop-down list box	3 Type <u>650</u> for **x** and press **ENTER**
4 Click in the **Number of successes** text box and type <u>650</u>	4 Specify x in the **Num Successes** text box	4 Type <u>1250</u> for **n** and press **ENTER**
5 Click the **Options...** button	5 Specify n in the **Num Trials** text box	5 Highlight **> p_0** and press **ENTER**
6 Click in the **Test proportion** text box and type <u>0.50</u>	6 Click **OK**	6 Press the down-arrow key, highlight **Calculate** or **Draw**, and press **ENTER**
7 Click the arrow button at the right of the **Alternative** drop-down list box and select **greater than**	7 Click the **Set p0** button	
8 Select the **Use test and interval based on normal distribution** check box	8 Click in the **Hypothesized Population Proportion** text box and type <u>0.50</u>	
9 Click **OK**	9 Click **OK**	
10 Click **OK**	10 Click the **.05** button	
	11 Click the **p > p0** button	
	12 Click the **Compute** button	

Exercises 11.2

Statistical Concepts and Skills

11.36 Of what procedure is Procedure 11.2 a special case? Why do you think that is so?

In Exercises 11.37–11.42, use either the critical-value approach or the P-value approach to perform each hypothesis test. Comment on the practical significance of all tests whose results are statistically significant.

11.37 Generation Y Online. People who were born between 1978 and 1983 are sometimes classified by demographers as belonging to Generation Y. According to a recent Forrester Research survey published in *American Demographics* (2000, Vol. 22(1), p. 12), of 850 Generation Y Web users, 459 reported using the Internet to download music.
a. Determine the sample proportion.
b. At the 5% significance level, do the data provide sufficient evidence to conclude that a majority of Generation Y Web users use the Internet to download music?

11.38 Christmas Presents. The *Arizona Republic* conducted a telephone poll of 758 Arizona adults who celebrate Christmas. The question asked was, "In your family, do you open presents on Christmas Eve or Christmas Day?" Of those surveyed, 394 said they wait until Christmas Day.
a. Determine the sample proportion.
b. At the 5% significance level, do the data provide sufficient evidence to conclude that a majority of Arizona families who celebrate Christmas wait until Christmas Day to open their presents?

11.39 Marijuana and Hashish. The U.S. Substance Abuse and Mental Health Services Administration conducts surveys on drug use by type of drug and age group. Results are published in *National Household Survey on Drug Abuse*. According to that publication, 12.8% of 18–25-year-olds were current users of marijuana or hashish in 1997. A recent poll of 1283 randomly selected 18–25-year-olds revealed that 146 currently use marijuana or hashish. At the 10% significance level, do the data provide sufficient evidence to conclude that the percentage of 18–25-year-olds who currently use marijuana or hashish has changed from the 1997 percentage of 12.8%?

11.40 Families in Poverty. In 1997, 10.3% of all U.S. families had incomes below the poverty level, as reported by the Census Bureau in *Current Population Reports*. During that same year, of 400 randomly selected families whose householder had at least a Bachelor's degree, 11 had incomes below the poverty level. At the 1% significance level, do the data provide sufficient evidence to conclude that, in 1997, the percentage of families that earned incomes below the poverty level was lower among those whose householders had at least a Bachelor's degree than among all U.S. families?

11.41 Environmental President. A poll conducted March 11–14, 1999, by the *Washington Post/ABC News* asked a random sample of adults nationwide the question: "How important will a [presidential] candidate's position on protecting the environment be to you in deciding how to vote in the next presidential election?" Of the 1515 adults polled, 909 said that the candidate's position on protecting the environment is very important. At the 5% significance level, do the data provide sufficient evidence to conclude that
a. a majority of U.S. adults believe that a presidential candidate's position on protecting the environment is very important in deciding how to vote in the next presidential election?
b. less than two-thirds of U.S. adults believe that a presidential candidate's position on protecting the environment is very important in deciding how to vote in the next presidential election?

11.42 An Edge in Roulette? Of the 38 numbers on an American roulette wheel, 18 are red, 18 are black, and 2 are green. If the wheel is balanced, the probability of the ball landing on red is $\frac{18}{38} = 0.474$. A gambler has been studying a roulette wheel. If the wheel is out of balance, he can improve his odds of winning. The gambler observes 200 spins of the wheel and finds that the ball lands on red 93 times. At the 10% significance level, do the data provide sufficient evidence to conclude that the ball is not landing on red the correct percentage of the time for a balanced wheel?

Using Technology

11.43 Marijuana and Hashish. Use the technology of your choice to perform the hypothesis test in Exercise 11.39.

11.44 Families in Poverty. Use the technology of your choice to perform the hypothesis test in Exercise 11.40.

11.3 INFERENCES FOR TWO POPULATION PROPORTIONS, USING INDEPENDENT SAMPLES

In Sections 11.1 and 11.2, you studied inferences for one population proportion. Now we examine inferences for comparing two population proportions. In this case, we have two populations and one specified attribute; the problem is to compare the proportion of one population that has the specified attribute to the proportion of the other population that has the specified attribute. We begin by discussing hypothesis testing in Example 11.8.

Example 11.8 Hypothesis Tests for Two Population Proportions

Eating Out Vegetarian A *Zogby International* poll of 1181 U.S. adults was conducted in March 1999, to gauge the demand for vegetarian meals in restaurants. The study was commissioned by the Vegetarian Resource Group and was published in the September/October 1999 issue of the *Vegetarian Journal*.

In the survey, independent random samples of 747 U.S. men and 434 U.S. women were taken. Of those sampled, 276 men and 195 women said that they sometimes order a dish without meat, fish, or fowl when they eat out. Do the data provide sufficient evidence to conclude that, in the United States, the percentage of men who sometimes order a dish without meat, fish, or fowl is smaller than the percentage of women who sometimes order a dish without meat, fish, or fowl?

Solution The specified attribute is "sometimes orders a dish without meat, fish, or fowl," which we abbreviate as "sometimes orders veg." The two populations are

Population 1: All U.S. men
Population 2: All U.S. women.

Let p_1 and p_2 denote the population proportions for the two populations:

p_1 = proportion of all U.S. men who sometimes order veg

p_2 = proportion of all U.S. women who sometimes order veg.

We want to perform the hypothesis test

H_0: $p_1 = p_2$ (percentage for men is not less than that for women)

H_a: $p_1 < p_2$ (percentage for men is less than that for women).

Roughly speaking, we can carry out the hypothesis test as follows.

1. Compute the proportion of the men sampled who sometimes order veg, $\hat{p}_1$, and the proportion of the women sampled who sometimes order veg, $\hat{p}_2$.
2. If $\hat{p}_1$ is too much smaller than $\hat{p}_2$, reject H_0; otherwise, do not reject H_0.

The first step is easy. Because 276 of the 747 men sampled sometimes order veg and 195 of the 434 women sampled sometimes order veg,

$$\hat{p}_1 = \frac{x_1}{n_1} = \frac{276}{747} = 0.369 \ (36.9\%)$$

and

$$\hat{p}_2 = \frac{x_2}{n_2} = \frac{195}{434} = 0.449 \ (44.9\%).$$

For the second step, we must decide whether the sample proportion $\hat{p}_1 = 0.369$ is less than the sample proportion $\hat{p}_2 = 0.449$ by a sufficient amount to warrant rejecting the null hypothesis in favor of the alternative hypothesis. In other words, we need to decide whether the difference between the two sample proportions can reasonably be attributed to sampling error or whether it indicates that the percentage of men who sometimes order veg is less than the percentage of women who sometimes order veg.

To make that decision, we need to know the distribution of the difference between two sample proportions. We discuss that sampling distribution and then complete the hypothesis test. ◆

THE SAMPLING DISTRIBUTION OF THE DIFFERENCE BETWEEN TWO SAMPLE PROPORTIONS FOR LARGE AND INDEPENDENT SAMPLES

To begin our discussion of the sampling distribution of the difference between two sample proportions, we summarize the required notation in Table 11.2.

TABLE 11.2
Notation for parameters and statistics when two population proportions are being considered

	Population 1	Population 2
Population proportion	p_1	p_2
Sample size	n_1	n_2
Number of successes	x_1	x_2
Sample proportion	$\hat{p}_1$	$\hat{p}_2$

Recall that the *number of successes* refers to the number of members sampled that have the specified attribute. Consequently, we compute the sample proportions by using the formulas

$$\hat{p}_1 = \frac{x_1}{n_1} \quad \text{and} \quad \hat{p}_2 = \frac{x_2}{n_2}.$$

Armed with the notation in Table 11.2, we now describe, in Key Fact 11.2, the **sampling distribution of the difference between two sample proportions.** Recalling Key Fact 11.1 on page 496, which gives the sampling distribution of one sample proportion, helps.

Key Fact 11.2   **The Sampling Distribution of the Difference Between Two Sample Proportions for Independent Samples**

For independent samples of sizes n_1 and n_2 from the two populations,

- $\mu_{\hat{p}_1 - \hat{p}_2} = p_1 - p_2$,
- $\sigma_{\hat{p}_1 - \hat{p}_2} = \sqrt{p_1(1-p_1)/n_1 + p_2(1-p_2)/n_2}$, and
- $\hat{p}_1 - \hat{p}_2$ is approximately normally distributed for large n_1 and n_2.

In particular, for large samples, the possible differences between the two sample proportions have approximately a normal distribution with mean $p_1 - p_2$ and standard deviation $\sqrt{p_1(1-p_1)/n_1 + p_2(1-p_2)/n_2}$.

Key Fact 11.2 provides the necessary basis for deriving inferential procedures to compare two population proportions.

LARGE-SAMPLE HYPOTHESIS TESTS FOR TWO POPULATION PROPORTIONS, USING INDEPENDENT SAMPLES

We now develop a hypothesis-testing procedure for comparing two population proportions. Our immediate goal is to identify a variable that we can use as the test statistic. From Key Fact 11.2, we know that, for large, independent samples, the variable

$$z = \frac{(\hat{p}_1 - \hat{p}_2) - (p_1 - p_2)}{\sqrt{p_1(1-p_1)/n_1 + p_2(1-p_2)/n_2}} \quad (11.2)$$

has approximately the standard normal distribution.

The null hypothesis for a hypothesis test to compare two population proportions is

$H_0: p_1 = p_2$ (population proportions are equal).

If the null hypothesis is true, $p_1 - p_2 = 0$, and the variable in Equation (11.2) becomes

$$z = \frac{\hat{p}_1 - \hat{p}_2}{\sqrt{p(1-p)/n_1 + p(1-p)/n_2}}, \quad (11.3)$$

where p denotes the common value of p_1 and p_2. Factoring $p(1-p)$ out of the denominator of Equation (11.3) yields the variable

$$z = \frac{\hat{p}_1 - \hat{p}_2}{\sqrt{p(1-p)}\sqrt{(1/n_1) + (1/n_2)}}. \quad (11.4)$$

However, because p is unknown, we cannot use this variable as the test statistic.

Consequently, we must estimate p by using sample information. The best estimate of p is obtained by pooling the data to get the proportion of successes in both samples combined; that is, we estimate p by

$$\hat{p}_p = \frac{x_1 + x_2}{n_1 + n_2}.$$

We call $\hat{p}_p$ the **pooled sample proportion**.

Procedure 11.3A The Two-Sample z-Test for Two Population Proportions (Critical-Value Approach)

Assumptions

1. Independent samples
2. x_1, $n_1 - x_1$, x_2, and $n_2 - x_2$ are all 5 or greater

Step 1 The null hypothesis is $H_0: p_1 = p_2$, and the alternative hypothesis is

$$H_a: p_1 \neq p_2 \quad \text{or} \quad H_a: p_1 < p_2 \quad \text{or} \quad H_a: p_1 > p_2$$
$$\text{(Two-tailed)} \quad\quad \text{(Left-tailed)} \quad\quad \text{(Right-tailed)}$$

Step 2 Decide on the significance level, α.

Step 3 Compute the value of the test statistic

$$z = \frac{\hat{p}_1 - \hat{p}_2}{\sqrt{\hat{p}_p(1-\hat{p}_p)}\sqrt{(1/n_1)+(1/n_2)}},$$

where $\hat{p}_p = (x_1 + x_2)/(n_1 + n_2)$.

Step 4 The critical value(s) are

$$\pm z_{\alpha/2} \quad \text{or} \quad -z_\alpha \quad \text{or} \quad z_\alpha$$
$$\text{(Two-tailed)} \quad\quad \text{(Left-tailed)} \quad\quad \text{(Right-tailed)}$$

Use Table II to find the critical value(s).

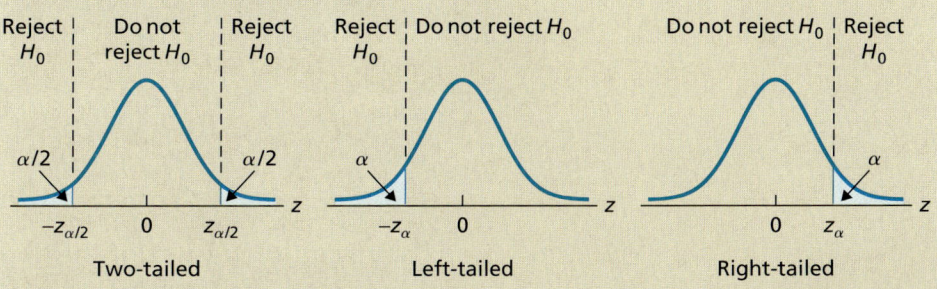

Two-tailed   Left-tailed   Right-tailed

Step 5 If the value of the test statistic falls in the rejection region, reject H_0; otherwise, do not reject H_0.

Step 6 Interpret the results of the hypothesis test.

Replacing p in Equation (11.4) with its estimate $\hat{p}_p$ yields the variable

$$\frac{\hat{p}_1 - \hat{p}_2}{\sqrt{\hat{p}_p(1-\hat{p}_p)}\sqrt{(1/n_1)+(1/n_2)}},$$

Procedure 11.3B — The Two-Sample z-Test for Two Population Proportions (P-Value Approach)

Assumptions

1. Independent samples
2. x_1, $n_1 - x_1$, x_2, and $n_2 - x_2$ are all 5 or greater

Step 1 The null hypothesis is $H_0: p_1 = p_2$, and the alternative hypothesis is

$H_a: p_1 \neq p_2$ or $H_a: p_1 < p_2$ or $H_a: p_1 > p_2$
(Two-tailed)   (Left-tailed)   (Right-tailed)

Step 2 Decide on the significance level, α.

Step 3 Compute the value of the test statistic

$$z = \frac{\hat{p}_1 - \hat{p}_2}{\sqrt{\hat{p}_p(1-\hat{p}_p)}\sqrt{(1/n_1)+(1/n_2)}},$$

where $\hat{p}_p = (x_1 + x_2)/(n_1 + n_2)$. Denote that value z_0.

Step 4 Use Table II to obtain the P-value.

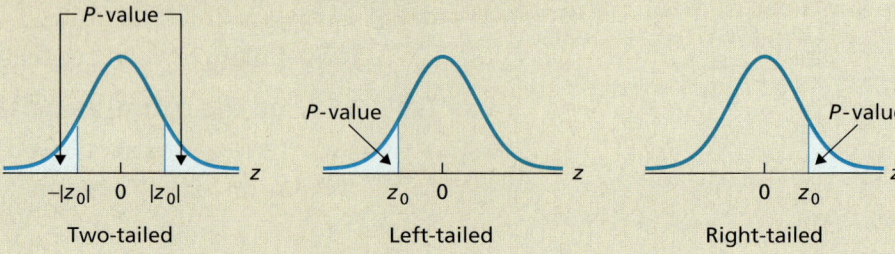

Step 5 If $P \leq \alpha$, reject H_0; otherwise, do not reject H_0.

Step 6 Interpret the results of the hypothesis test.

which can be used as the test statistic and, like the variable in Equation (11.4), has approximately the standard normal distribution for large samples if the null hypothesis is true. Therefore we have Procedures 11.3A and B, both of which we call the **two-sample z-test** for two population proportions. In Example 11.9, we demonstrate use of the procedures.

Example 11.9 The Two-Sample z-Test

Eating Out Vegetarian We now return to the problem posed in Example 11.8. Independent random samples of 747 U.S. men and 434 U.S. women were taken. Of those sampled, 276 men and 195 women said that they sometimes order a dish without meat, fish, or fowl when they eat out. At the 5% significance level, do the data provide sufficient evidence to conclude that, in the United States, the percentage of men who sometimes order a dish without meat, fish, or fowl is smaller than the percentage of women who sometimes order a dish without meat, fish, or fowl?

Solution We first recall that the specified attribute is "sometimes orders a dish without meat, fish, or fowl," abbreviated as "sometimes orders veg." We apply Procedure 11.3, noting first that both assumptions for its use are satisfied.

Step 1 State the null and alternative hypotheses.

Let p_1 and p_2 denote the proportions of all U.S. men and all U.S. women who sometimes order veg, respectively. Then the null and alternative hypotheses are

$H_0: p_1 = p_2$ (percentage for men is not less than that for women)

$H_a: p_1 < p_2$ (percentage for men is less than that for women).

The hypothesis test is left-tailed because a less-than sign (<) appears in the alternative hypothesis.

Step 2 Decide on the significance level, α.

The test is to be performed at the 5% significance level, or $\alpha = 0.05$.

Step 3 Compute the value of the test statistic

$$z = \frac{\hat{p}_1 - \hat{p}_2}{\sqrt{\hat{p}_p(1-\hat{p}_p)}\sqrt{(1/n_1)+(1/n_2)}},$$

where $\hat{p}_p = (x_1 + x_2)/(n_1 + n_2)$.

We first obtain $\hat{p}_1$, $\hat{p}_2$, and $\hat{p}_p$. As 276 of the 747 men sampled and 195 of the 434 women sampled sometimes order veg, $x_1 = 276$, $n_1 = 747$, $x_2 = 195$, and $n_2 = 434$. Therefore

$$\hat{p}_1 = \frac{x_1}{n_1} = \frac{276}{747} = 0.369, \qquad \hat{p}_2 = \frac{x_2}{n_2} = \frac{195}{434} = 0.449,$$

and

$$\hat{p}_p = \frac{x_1 + x_2}{n_1 + n_2} = \frac{276 + 195}{747 + 434} = \frac{471}{1181} = 0.399.$$

Consequently, the value of the test statistic is

$$z = \frac{\hat{p}_1 - \hat{p}_2}{\sqrt{\hat{p}_p(1-\hat{p}_p)}\sqrt{(1/n_1) + (1/n_2)}}$$

$$= \frac{0.369 - 0.449}{\sqrt{(0.399)(1-0.399)}\sqrt{(1/747) + (1/434)}} = -2.71.$$

Critical-Value Approach

Step 4 The critical value for a left-tailed test is $-z_\alpha$.

For $\alpha = 0.05$, we find that the critical value is $-z_{0.05} = -1.645$, as depicted in Fig. 11.3A.

FIGURE 11.3A

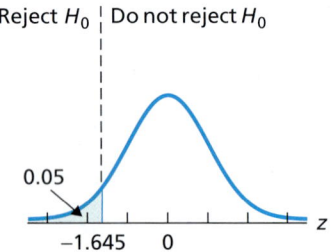

Step 5 If the value of the test statistic falls in the rejection region, reject H_0; otherwise, do not reject H_0.

From Step 3, the value of the test statistic is $z = -2.71$, which, as we see from Fig. 11.3A, falls in the rejection region. Thus we reject H_0. The test results are statistically significant at the 5% level.

P-Value Approach

Step 4 Use Table II to obtain the P-value.

From Step 3, the value of the test statistic is $z = -2.71$. As the test is left-tailed, the P-value is the probability of observing a value of z of -2.71 or less if the null hypothesis is true. That probability equals the shaded area in Fig. 11.3B, which by Table II is 0.0034, or $P = 0.0034$.

FIGURE 11.3B

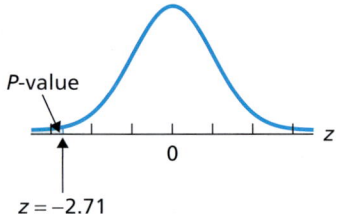

Step 5 If $P \leq \alpha$, reject H_0; otherwise, do not reject H_0.

From Step 4, $P = 0.0034$. Because the P-value is less than the specified significance level of 0.05, we reject H_0. The test results are statistically significant at the 5% level and (see Table 9.10 on page 405) provide very strong evidence against the null hypothesis.

Step 6 Interpret the results of the hypothesis test.

What Does it Mean? At the 5% significance level, the data provide sufficient evidence to conclude that, in the United States, the percentage of men who sometimes order a dish without meat, fish, or fowl is smaller than the percentage of women who sometimes order a dish without meat, fish, or fowl.

LARGE-SAMPLE CONFIDENCE INTERVALS FOR THE DIFFERENCE BETWEEN TWO POPULATION PROPORTIONS

We can also use Key Fact 11.2 on page 518 to derive a confidence-interval procedure, Procedure 11.4, for the difference between two population proportions, which we call the **two-sample z-interval procedure** for two population proportions. We apply the procedure in Example 11.10.

Procedure 11.4

The Two-Sample z-Interval Procedure for Two Population Proportions

Assumptions
1. Independent samples
2. x_1, $n_1 - x_1$, x_2, and $n_2 - x_2$ are all 5 or greater

Step 1 For a confidence level of $1 - \alpha$, use Table II to find $z_{\alpha/2}$.

Step 2 The endpoints of the confidence interval for $p_1 - p_2$ are

$$(\hat{p}_1 - \hat{p}_2) \pm z_{\alpha/2} \cdot \sqrt{\hat{p}_1(1-\hat{p}_1)/n_1 + \hat{p}_2(1-\hat{p}_2)/n_2}.$$

Step 3 Interpret the confidence interval.

Example 11.10 The Two-Sample z-Interval Procedure

Eating Out Vegetarian Refer to Example 11.9 and obtain a 90% confidence interval for the difference, $p_1 - p_2$, between the proportions of U.S. men and U.S. women who sometimes order a dish without meat, fish, or fowl.

Solution We apply Procedure 11.4, noting first that both conditions for its use are met.

Step 1 For a confidence level of $1 - \alpha$, use Table II to find $z_{\alpha/2}$.

For a 90% confidence interval, $\alpha = 0.10$. From Table II, $z_{\alpha/2} = z_{0.10/2} = z_{0.05} = 1.645$.

Step 2 The endpoints of the confidence interval for $p_1 - p_2$ are

$$(\hat{p}_1 - \hat{p}_2) \pm z_{\alpha/2} \cdot \sqrt{\hat{p}_1(1-\hat{p}_1)/n_1 + \hat{p}_2(1-\hat{p}_2)/n_2}.$$

From Step 1, $z_{\alpha/2} = 1.645$. As we found in Example 11.9, $\hat{p}_1 = 0.369$, $n_1 = 747$, $\hat{p}_2 = 0.449$, and $n_2 = 434$. Therefore the endpoints of the 90% confidence interval for $p_1 - p_2$ are

$$(0.369 - 0.449) \pm 1.645 \cdot \sqrt{(0.369)(1-0.369)/747 + (0.449)(1-0.449)/434},$$

or -0.080 ± 0.049, or -0.129 to -0.031.

Step 3 Interpret the confidence interval.

We can be 90% confident that, in the United States, the difference between the proportions of men and women who sometimes order a dish without meat, fish, or fowl is somewhere between -0.129 and -0.031. In other words, we can be 90% confident that the percentage of U.S. women who sometimes order veg exceeds the percentage of U.S. men who sometimes order veg by somewhere between 3.1 and 11.9 percentage points.

◆

MARGIN OF ERROR AND SAMPLE SIZE

We can obtain the **margin of error** in estimating the difference between two population proportions by referring to Step 2 of Procedure 11.4. From the formula for the margin of error, we can determine the sample sizes required to obtain a confidence interval with a specified confidence level and margin of error. In Formula 11.3, we supply the formulas for both the margin of error and sample size.

FORMULA 11.3 **Margin of Error and Sample Size for Estimating $p_1 - p_2$**

The margin of error for the estimate of $p_1 - p_2$ is

$$E = z_{\alpha/2} \cdot \sqrt{\hat{p}_1(1 - \hat{p}_1)/n_1 + \hat{p}_2(1 - \hat{p}_2)/n_2}.$$

It equals half the length of the confidence interval and represents the precision with which the difference between the sample proportions, $\hat{p}_1 - \hat{p}_2$, estimates the difference between the population proportions, $p_1 - p_2$, at the specified confidence level.

A $(1 - \alpha)$-level confidence interval for the difference between two population proportions that has a margin of error of at most E can be obtained by choosing

$$n_1 = n_2 = 0.5 \left(\frac{z_{\alpha/2}}{E} \right)^2,$$

rounded up to the nearest whole number. If we can make educated guesses, $\hat{p}_{1g}$ and $\hat{p}_{2g}$, for the observed values of $\hat{p}_1$ and $\hat{p}_2$, we should instead choose

$$n_1 = n_2 = \left(\hat{p}_{1g}(1 - \hat{p}_{1g}) + \hat{p}_{2g}(1 - \hat{p}_{2g}) \right) \left(\frac{z_{\alpha/2}}{E} \right)^2,$$

rounded up to the nearest whole number.

The second displayed formula in Formula 11.3 provides sample sizes that ensure obtaining a $(1 - \alpha)$-level confidence interval with a margin of error of

11.3 Inferences for Two Population Proportions

at most E, but it may yield sample sizes that are unnecessarily large. The third displayed formula in Formula 11.3 yields smaller sample sizes, but it should not be used unless the guesses for the sample proportions are considered to be reasonably accurate.

If likely ranges for the observed values of the two sample proportions are known, the values in the ranges closest to 0.5 should be taken as the educated guesses. For further discussion of these ideas and for applications of Formula 11.3, see Exercise 11.60.

The Technology Center

Most statistical technologies have programs that automatically perform a hypothesis test for comparing two population proportions and obtain a confidence interval for the difference between two population proportions. In this subsection, we present output and (optional) step-by-step instructions to implement such programs.

Example 11.11 Using Technology to Conduct Two-Sample z-Procedures

Eating Out Vegetarian Use Minitab, Excel, or the TI-83 Plus to perform the hypothesis test in Example 11.9 on page 521 and obtain the confidence interval required in Example 11.10 on page 523.

Solution Let p_1 and p_2 denote the proportions of all U.S. men and all U.S. women who sometimes order veg, respectively. The task in Example 11.9 is to perform the hypothesis test

H_0: $p_1 = p_2$ (percentage for men is not less than that for women)

H_a: $p_1 < p_2$ (percentage for men is less than that for women)

at the 5% significance level; the task in Example 11.10 is to obtain a 90% confidence interval for $p_1 - p_2$.

We recall that the sample sizes for the men and women are 747 and 434, respectively, and that the numbers of men and women sampled who sometimes order veg are 276 and 195, respectively. Printout 11.4 on pages 526 and 527 shows the output obtained by applying the two-sample-z programs to the data.

The outputs in Printout 11.4 reveal that the P-value for the hypothesis test is 0.003 (to three decimal places). The P-value is less than the specified significance level of 0.05, so we reject H_0. The outputs in Printout 11.4 also show that a 90% confidence interval for the difference between the proportions is from -0.129 to -0.031. ◆

Obtaining the Output (Optional)

Printout 11.4 provides output from Minitab, Excel, and the TI-83 Plus for two-sample z-procedures, based on the sample data for the study on sometimes ordering vegetarian. Detailed instructions for obtaining that output are presented on page 528.

PRINTOUT 11.4
Two-sample-z output for the study on ordering vegetarian

MINITAB

Test and CI for Two Proportions   [FOR THE HYPOTHESIS TEST]

```
Sample     X      N    Sample p
1        276    747    0.369478
2        195    434    0.449309
```

Estimate for p(1) - p(2): -0.0798308
90% upper bound for p(1) - p(2): -0.0417711
Test for p(1) - p(2) = 0 (vs < 0):   Z = -2.70   P-Value = 0.003

Test and CI for Two Proportions   [FOR THE CONFIDENCE INTERVAL]

```
Sample     X      N    Sample p
1        276    747    0.369478
2        195    434    0.449309
```

Estimate for p(1) - p(2): -0.0798308
90% CI for p(1) - p(2):   (-0.128680, -0.0309817)
Test for p(1) - p(2) = 0 (vs not = 0):   Z = -2.70   P-Value = 0.007

EXCEL

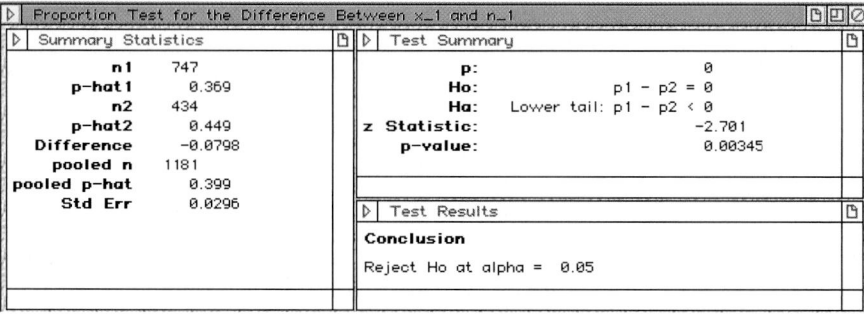

Using **Summ 2 Var Prop Test**

11.3 Inferences for Two Population Proportions

PRINTOUT 11.4 (cont.)
Two-sample-z output for the study on ordering vegetarian

EXCEL

Confidence Interval for the Difference Between x_1 and n_1

Summary Statistics
```
n1         747
p-hat1     0.369
n2         434
p-hat2     0.449
Difference -0.0798
Std Err    0.0297
z*         1.64
```

Interval Results
Confidence Interval
With 90% Confidence, -0.129 < p < -0.031

Using **Summ 2 Var Prop Interval**

TI-83 PLUS

```
2-PropZTest
 p1<p2
 z=-2.701227783
 p=.0034542498
 p̂1=.3694779116
 p̂2=.4493087558
↓p̂=.3988145639
```

```
2-PropZInt
 (-.1287,-.031)
 p̂1=.3694779116
 p̂2=.4493087558
 n1=747
 n2=434
```

Using **2-PropZInt**

```
2-PropZTest
 p1<p2
↑p̂1=.3694779116
 p̂2=.4493087558
 p̂=.3988145639
 n1=747
 n2=434
```

Using **2-PropZTest**

MINITAB

FOR THE HYPOTHESIS TEST:
1. Choose **Stat ➤ Basic Statistics ➤ 2 Proportions...**
2. Select the **Summarized data** option button
3. Click in the **Trials** text box for **First sample** and type 747
4. Click in the **Successes** text box for **First sample** and type 276
5. Click in the **Trials** text box for **Second sample** and type 434
6. Click in the **Successes** text box for **Second sample** and type 195
7. Click the **Options...** button
8. Click in the **Confidence level** text box and type 90
9. Click in the **Test difference** text box and type 0
10. Click the arrow button at the right of the **Alternative** drop-down list box and select **less than**
11. Select the **Use pooled estimate of p for test** check box
12. Click **OK**
13. Click **OK**

FOR THE CI:
1. Choose **Edit ➤ Edit Last Dialog**
2. Click the **Options...** button
3. Click the arrow button at the right of the **Alternative** drop-down list box and select **not equal**
4. Click **OK**
5. Click **OK**

EXCEL

Store the sample sizes, 747 and 434, in ranges named n_1 and n_2, respectively, and store the numbers of successes, 276 and 195, in ranges named x_1 and x_2, respectively.

FOR THE HYPOTHESIS TEST:
1. Choose **DDXL ➤ Hypothesis tests**
2. Select **Summ 2 Var Prop Test** from the **Function type** drop-down list box
3. Specify x_1 in the **Num Successes 1** text box, n_1 in the **Num Trials 1** text box, x_2 in the **Num Successes 2** text box, and n_2 in the **Num Trials 2** text box
4. Click **OK**
5. Click the **Set p** button
6. Click in the **Specify p** text box and type 0
7. Click **OK**
8. Click the **.05** button
9. Click the **p1 − p2 < p** button
10. Click the **Compute** button

FOR THE CI:
1. Choose **DDXL ➤ Confidence Intervals**
2. Select **Summ 2 Var Prop Interval** from the **Function type** drop-down list box
3. Specify x_1 in the **Num Successes 1** text box, n_1 in the **Num Trials 1** text box, x_2 in the **Num Successes 2** text box, and n_2 in the **Num Trials 2** text box
4. Click **OK**
5. Click the **90%** button
6. Click the **Compute Interval** button

TI-83 PLUS

FOR THE HYPOTHESIS TEST:
1. Press **STAT**, arrow over to **TESTS**, and press **6**
2. Type 276 for **x1** and press **ENTER**
3. Type 747 for **n1** and press **ENTER**
4. Type 195 for **x2** and press **ENTER**
5. Type 434 for **n2** and press **ENTER**
6. Highlight **<p2** and press **ENTER**
7. Press the down-arrow key, highlight **Calculate**, and press **ENTER**

FOR THE CI:
1. Press **STAT**, arrow over to **TESTS**, and press **ALPHA ➤ B**
2. Type 276 for **x1** and press **ENTER**
3. Type 747 for **n1** and press **ENTER**
4. Type 195 for **x2** and press **ENTER**
5. Type 434 for **n2** and press **ENTER**
6. Type .90 for **C-Level** and press **ENTER** twice

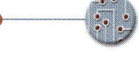

Exercises 11.3

Statistical Concepts and Skills

11.45 Explain the basic idea for performing a hypothesis test, based on independent samples, to compare two population proportions.

11.46 Kids Attending Church. A Roper Starch Worldwide for A.B.C. Global Kids Study conducted surveys in various countries to estimate the percentage of children who attend

church at least once a week. Two of the countries in the survey were the United States and Germany. Considering these two countries only,
a. identify the specified attribute.
b. identify the two populations.
c. What are the two population proportions under consideration?

11.47 Sunscreen Use. Industry Research polled teenagers on sunscreen use. The survey revealed that 46% of teenage girls and 30% of teenage boys regularly use sunscreen before going out in the sun.
a. Identify the specified attribute.
b. Identify the two populations.
c. Are the proportions 0.46 (46%) and 0.30 (30%) sample proportions or population proportions? Explain your answer.

11.48 Consider a hypothesis test for two population proportions with the null hypothesis $H_0: p_1 = p_2$. What parameter is being estimated by the
a. sample proportion $\hat{p}_1$?
b. sample proportion $\hat{p}_2$?
c. pooled sample proportion $\hat{p}_p$?

11.49 Of the quantities $p_1, p_2, x_1, x_2, \hat{p}_1, \hat{p}_2$, and $\hat{p}_p$,
a. which represent parameters and which represent statistics?
b. which are fixed numbers and which are variables?

For Exercises 11.50–11.55, use either the critical-value approach or the P-value approach to perform the required hypothesis test.

11.50 Vasectomies and Prostate Cancer. Approximately 450,000 vasectomies are performed each year in the United States. In this surgical procedure for contraception, the tube carrying sperm from the testicles is cut and tied. Several studies have been conducted to analyze the relationship between vasectomies and prostate cancer. The results of one such study by E. Giovannucci et al. appeared in the paper "A Retrospective Cohort Study of Vasectomy and Prostate Cancer in U.S. Men" (*Journal of the American Medical Association*, 1993, Vol. 269(7), pp. 878–882). Of 21,300 men who had not had a vasectomy, 69 were found to have prostate cancer; of 22,000 men who had had a vasectomy, 113 were found to have prostate cancer.
a. At the 1% significance level, do the data provide sufficient evidence to conclude that men who have had a vasectomy are at greater risk of having prostate cancer?
b. Is this study a designed experiment or an observational study? Explain your answer.
c. In view of your answers to parts (a) and (b), could you reasonably conclude that having a vasectomy causes an increased risk of prostate cancer? Explain your answer.

11.51 Folic Acid and Birth Defects. For several years, evidence had been mounting that folic acid reduces major birth defects. An issue of the *Arizona Republic* reported on a Hungarian study that provided the strongest evidence to date. The results of the study, directed by Drs. Andrew E. Czeizel and Istvan Dudas of the National Institute of Hygiene in Budapest, were published in the paper "Prevention of the First Occurrence of Neural-Tube Defects by Periconceptional Vitamin Supplementation" (*New England Journal of Medicine*, 1992, Vol. 327(26), p. 1832). For the study, the doctors enrolled 4753 women prior to conception. The women were divided randomly into two groups. One group, consisting of 2701 women, took daily multivitamins containing 0.8 mg of folic acid; the other group, consisting of 2052 women, received only trace elements. Major birth defects occurred in 35 cases when the women took folic acid and in 47 cases when the women did not.
a. At the 1% significance level, do the data provide sufficient evidence to conclude that women who take folic acid are at lesser risk of having children with major birth defects?
b. Is this study a designed experiment or an observational study? Explain your answer.
c. In view of your answers to parts (a) and (b), could you reasonably conclude that taking folic acid causes a reduction in major birth defects? Explain your answer.

11.52 Racial Crossover. In the paper "The Racial Crossover in Comorbidity, Disability, and Mortality," (*Demography*, 2000, Vol. 37(3), pp. 267–283), Nan E. Johnson investigated the health of independent random samples of white and African-American elderly (aged 70 or older). Of the 4989 white elderly surveyed, 529 had at least one stroke, whereas 103 of the 906 African-American elderly surveyed reported at least one stroke. At the 5% significance level, do the data suggest that there is a difference in stroke incidence between white and African-American elderly?

11.53 Buckling Up. Response Insurance collects data on seat-belt use among U.S. drivers. Of 1000 drivers 25–34 years old, 27% said that they buckle up, whereas

330 of 1100 drivers 45–64 years old said that they did. At the 10% significance level, do the data suggest that there is a difference in seat-belt use between drivers 25–34 years old and those 45–64 years old? [SOURCE: *USA TODAY Online*.]

11.54 Microsoft Breakup. During late 1999, the computer magazine *PC World* hired Research Results of Fitchburg, Massachusetts, to survey its readers on what they would decide if they had a say in the software giant Microsoft's antitrust case with the United States Justice Department. Of 1853 respondents, 53 were against the proposed breakup of Microsoft. Subsequently, on April 3, 2000, a federal judge ordered the breakup of Microsoft for violating antitrust laws. The following day a *Harris Poll* asked, "Do you agree with the ruling against Microsoft for violation of antitrust laws?" Of 4699 respondents, 1751 said that they did not agree with the ruling. At the 1% significance level, do the data suggest that a higher percentage of people were against the breakup after the judge's decision?

11.55 Overweight Men. A man is considered overweight if he has a body mass index of 27.8 kilograms/meter squared (kg/m^2) or greater. This point is used because it represents the sex-specific 85th percentile for males 20–29 years of age in the 1976–1980 *National Health and Nutrition Examination Survey*. In 1994, of 700 men 20–34 years old, 160 were found to be overweight, whereas, in 1980, of 750 men 20–34 years old, 130 were found to be overweight. At the 5% significance level, do the data provide sufficient evidence to conclude that for men 20–34 years old, a higher percentage were overweight in 1994 than 14 years earlier?

In Exercises 11.56–11.59, apply Procedure 11.4 on page 523 to obtain the required confidence interval.

11.56 Vasectomies and Prostate Cancer. Refer to Exercise 11.50.
a. Determine a 98% confidence interval for the difference between the prostate cancer rates of men who have had a vasectomy and those who have not.
b. Interpret your answer from part (a).

11.57 Folic Acid and Birth Defects. Refer to Exercise 11.51.
a. Determine a 98% confidence interval for the difference between the rates of major birth defects for babies born to women who have taken folic acid and those born to women who have not.
b. Interpret your answer from part (a).

11.58 Racial Crossover. Refer to Exercise 11.52. Determine and interpret a 95% confidence interval for the difference between the stroke incidences of white and African-American elderly.

11.59 Buckling Up. Refer to Exercise 11.53. Determine and interpret a 90% confidence interval for the difference between the proportions of seat-belt users for drivers in the age groups 25–34 years and 45–64 years.

Extending the Concepts and Skills

11.60 Eating Out Vegetarian. In this exercise, apply Formula 11.3 on page 524 to the study on ordering vegetarian considered in Examples 11.8–11.10.
a. Obtain the margin of error for the estimate of the difference between the proportions of men and women who sometimes order veg by taking half the length of the confidence interval found in Example 11.10 on page 523. Interpret your answer in words.
b. Obtain the margin of error for the estimate of the difference between the proportions of men and women who sometimes order veg by applying the first displayed formula in Formula 11.3.
c. Without making a guess for the observed values of the sample proportions, obtain the common sample size that will ensure a margin of error of at most 0.01 for a 90% confidence interval.
d. Find a 90% confidence interval for $p_1 - p_2$ if, for samples of the size determined in part (c), 38.3% of the men and 43.7% of the women sometimes order veg.
e. Determine the margin of error for the estimate in part (d) and compare it to the required margin of error specified in part (c).
f. Repeat parts (c)–(e) if you can reasonably presume that at most 41% of the men sampled and at most 49% of the women sampled will be people who sometimes order veg.
g. Compare the results obtained in parts (c)–(e) to those obtained in part (f).

11.61 Identify the formula in this section that shows that the difference between the two sample proportions is an unbiased estimator of the difference between the two population proportions.

Using Technology

11.62 Racial Crossover. Refer to Exercises 11.52 and 11.58. Use the technology of your choice to conduct the required hypothesis test and obtain the desired confidence interval.

11.63 Folic Acid and Birth Defects. Refer to Exercises 11.51 and 11.57. Use the technology of your choice to conduct the required hypothesis test and obtain the desired confidence interval.

Chapter Review

You Should Be Able To

1. use and understand the formulas presented in this chapter.

2. find a large-sample confidence interval for a population proportion.

3. compute the margin of error for the estimate of a population proportion.

4. understand the relationship between the sample size, confidence level, and margin of error for a confidence interval for a population proportion.

5. determine the sample size required for a specified confidence level and margin of error for the estimate of a population proportion.

6. perform a large-sample hypothesis test for a population proportion.

7. perform large-sample inferences (hypothesis tests and confidence intervals) to compare two population proportions.

8. understand the relationship between the sample sizes, confidence level, and margin of error for a confidence interval for the difference between two population proportions.

9. determine the sample sizes required for a specified confidence level and margin of error for the estimate of the difference between two population proportions.

Key Terms

margin of error, 499, 524
number of failures, 495
number of successes, 495
one-sample z-interval procedure, 498
one-sample z-test, 509, 510
pooled sample proportion ($\hat{p}_p$), 518

population proportion (p), 495
sample proportion ($\hat{p}$), 495
sampling distribution of the difference between two sample proportions, 518

sampling distribution of the sample proportion, 496
two-sample z-interval procedure, 523
two-sample z-test, 519, 520
z-interval procedure, 497
z-test, 509

Review Test

Statistical Concepts and Skills

1. Medical Marijuana? A *Harris Poll* was recently conducted to estimate the proportion of Americans who feel that marijuana should be legalized for medicinal use in patients with cancer and other painful and terminal diseases. Identify the
a. specified attribute.   b. population.
c. population proportion.
d. According to the poll, 80% of the 83,957 respondents said that marijuana should be legalized for medicinal use. Is the proportion 0.80 (80%) a sample proportion or a population proportion? Explain your answer.

2. Why is a sample proportion generally used to estimate a population proportion instead of obtaining the population proportion directly?

3. Explain what each phrase means in the context of inferences for a population proportion.
a. Number of successes   b. Number of failures

4. Fill in the blanks.
a. The mean of all possible sample proportions equals the _____.
b. For large samples, the possible sample proportions have approximately a _____ distribution.
c. A rule of thumb for using a normal distribution to approximate the distribution of all possible sample proportions is that both _____ and _____ are _____ or greater.

5. What does the margin of error for the estimate of a population proportion tell you?

6. Holiday Blues. A poll was conducted by *Opinion Research Corporation* to estimate the proportions of men and women who get the "holiday blues." Identify the
a. specified attribute.   b. two populations.
c. two population proportions.
d. two sample proportions.

e. According to the poll, 34% of men and 44% of women get the "holiday blues." Are the proportions 0.34 and 0.44 sample proportions or population proportions? Explain your answer.

7. Suppose that you are using independent samples to compare two population proportions. Fill in the blanks.
   a. The mean of all possible differences between the two sample proportions equals the _____.
   b. For large samples, the possible differences between the two sample proportions have approximately a _____ distribution.

8. **Young Voter Apathy.** A recent survey conducted by Project Vote Smart found that, of 1326 young Americans (aged 18–25 years), 46% do not plan to vote in the next presidential election because of a lack of trust and interest in government. The margin of error for the poll was plus or minus 4.7 percentage points (for a 0.95 confidence level). Use this information to obtain a 95% confidence interval for the percentage of all young Americans who do not plan to vote in the next presidential election.

9. Suppose that you want to obtain a 95% confidence interval based on independent samples for the difference between two population proportions and that you want a margin of error of at most 0.01.
   a. Without making an educated guess for the observed sample proportions, find the required common sample size.
   b. Suppose that, from past experience, you are quite sure that the two sample proportions will be 0.75 or greater. What common sample size should you use?

10. **Getting a Job.** The National Association of Colleges and Employers sponsors the *Graduating Student and Alumni Survey*. Part of the survey gauges student optimism in landing a job after graduation. According to the survey results, published in the May 2000, issue of *American Demographics*, among the 1218 respondents, 733 said that they expected difficulty finding a job. Use these data to obtain and interpret a 95% confidence interval for the proportion of students who expect difficulty finding a job.

11. **Getting a Job.** Refer to Problem 10.
    a. Find the margin of error for the estimate of p.
    b. Obtain a sample size that will ensure a margin of error of at most 0.02 for a 95% confidence interval without making a guess for the observed value of $\hat{p}$.
    c. Find a 95% confidence interval for p if, for a sample of the size determined in part (b), 58.7% of those surveyed say that they expect difficulty finding a job.
    d. Determine the margin of error for the estimate in part (c) and compare it to the required margin of error specified in part (b).

e. Repeat parts (b)–(d) if you can reasonably presume that the percentage of those surveyed who say that they expect difficulty finding a job will be at least 56%.
f. Compare the results obtained in parts (b)–(d) with those obtained in part (e).

12. **Justice in the Courts?** In an issue of *Parade Magazine*, the editors reported on a national survey on law and order. One question asked of the 2512 U.S. adults who took part was whether they believed that juries "almost always" convict the guilty and free the innocent. Only 578 said that they did. Do the data provide sufficient evidence to conclude that less than one in four Americans believe that juries "almost always" convict the guilty and free the innocent?
    a. Use either the critical-value approach or the P-value approach to perform the appropriate hypothesis test at the 5% significance level.
    b. Assess the strength of the evidence against the null hypothesis by referring to Table 9.10 on page 405.

13. **Height and Breast Cancer.** An article published in an issue of *Annals of Epidemiology* discussed the relationship between height and breast cancer. The study by the National Cancer Institute, which took 5 years and involved more than 1500 women with breast cancer and 2000 women without breast cancer, revealed a trend between height and breast cancer: "…taller women have a 50 to 80 percent greater risk of getting breast cancer than women who are closer to 5 feet tall." But Christine Swanson, a nutritionist who was involved with the study, added that "…height may be associated with the culprit, …but no one really knows" the exact relationship between height and the risk of breast cancer.
    a. Classify this study as either an observational study or a designed experiment. Explain your answer.
    b. Interpret the statement made by Christine Swanson in light of your answer to part (a).

14. **Views on the Economy.** State and local governments often poll their constituents about their views on the economy. In two polls, taken approximately 1 year apart, O'Neil Associates asked 600 Maricopa County, Arizona, residents

whether they thought the state's economy would improve over the next 2 years. In the first poll, 48% said "yes"; in the second poll, 60% said "yes". Do the data provide sufficient evidence to conclude that the percentage of Maricopa County residents who thought that the state's economy would improve over the next 2 years was less during the time of the first poll than during the time of the second?

a. Use either the critical-value approach or the P-value approach to perform the appropriate hypothesis test at the 1% significance level.
b. Assess the strength of the evidence against the null hypothesis by referring to Table 9.10 on page 405.

15. **Views on the Economy.** Refer to Problem 14.
a. Determine a 98% confidence interval for the difference, $p_1 - p_2$, between the proportions of Maricopa County residents who thought that the state's economy would improve over the next 2 years during the time of the first poll and during the time of the second poll.
b. Interpret your answer from part (a).

16. **Views on the Economy.** Refer to Problems 14 and 15.
a. Take half the length of the confidence interval found in Problem 15(a) to obtain the margin of error for the estimate of the difference between the two population proportions. Interpret your result in words.
b. Solve part (a) by applying the first displayed formula in Formula 11.3 on page 524.
c. Obtain the common sample size that will ensure a margin of error of at most 0.03 for a 98% confidence interval without making a guess for the observed values of the sample proportions.
d. Find a 98% confidence interval for $p_1 - p_2$ if, for samples of the size determined in part (c), the sample proportions are 0.475 and 0.603, respectively.
e. Determine the margin of error for the estimate in part (d) and compare it to the required margin of error specified in part (c).

Using Technology

17. **Getting a Job.** Use the technology of your choice to obtain the confidence interval required in Problem 10.

18. **Justice in the Courts?** Use the technology of your choice to conduct the hypothesis test required in Problem 12.

19. **Views on the Economy.** Use the technology of your choice to perform the required hypothesis test in Problem 14 and to obtain the desired confidence interval in Problem 15.

The Salk Polio Vaccine Trial

The Salk vaccine trial is one of the most famous statistical studies ever conducted. This field trial was designed to determine whether a new vaccine, developed by Dr. Jonas Salk of the University of Pittsburgh, would be effective in preventing poliomyelitis, a disease also known as infantile paralysis.

In the late 1940s and early 1950s, polio epidemics tended to come in cyclic waves of ever-increasing severity; children were particularly vulnerable. Thus, in 1954, when the trial was conducted, polio was one of the most feared of all diseases. In this Internet project, you will explore a number of interesting issues about the design of this experiment and competing experiments, and you will analyze the results.

URL for access to Internet Projects Page: www.aw.com/weiss

GPA AND SAT Scores

Recall from Chapter 1 (see page 34) that the Focus database contains information on 500 randomly selected Arizona State University sophomores. Use the technology of your choice to solve the following problems.

a. Obtain a 95% confidence interval for the percentage of all Arizona State University sophomores whose cumulative GPAs are at least 3.00. Interpret your result.
b. Referring to part (a), determine the margin of error for the estimate. Interpret your answer.
c. At the 5% significance level, do the data provide sufficient evidence to conclude that more than 20% of Arizona State University sophomores score 600 or higher on the SAT math?
d. Can you conclude that a difference exists between the proportions of male and female sophomores at Arizona State University who score 500 or higher on the SAT verbal? Perform the required hypothesis test at the 5% significance level.
e. Determine a 95% confidence interval for the difference between the proportions of male and female sophomores at Arizona State University who score 500 or higher on the SAT verbal.

case study discussion

Double-Dipping ATM Fees

At the beginning of this chapter, we discussed a national survey by the U.S. Public Interest Research Group (PIRG). In an April 1999 news release reporting on the survey, PIRG stated that "More than nine out of ten [U.S.] banks charge consumers the controversial ATM surcharge…." This statement was made as a result of the finding that 93% of 336 U.S. banks surveyed surcharge nonholders of accounts.

a. Identify the population and sample in this study.
b. Identify the specified attribute.
c. What is the sample proportion of banks that surcharge nonholders of accounts?
d. At the 5% significance level, do the data provide sufficient evidence to support the claim made by PIRG that "More than nine out of ten [U.S.] banks charge consumers the controversial ATM surcharge…."?
e. Referring to part (d), use Table 9.10 on page 405 to assess the strength of the evidence against the null hypothesis and hence in favor of the alternative hypothesis that more than 9 out of 10 U.S. banks charge consumers the controversial ATM surcharge.

Internet Resources: Visit the Weiss Web site www.aw.com/weiss for additional discussion, exercises, and resources related to this case study.

Biography

Abraham de Moivre: Paving the Way for Proportion Inferences

ABRAHAM DE MOIVRE was born in Vitry-le-François, France, on May 26, 1667, the son of a country surgeon. He was educated in the Catholic school in his village and at the Protestant Academy at Sedan. In 1684, he went to Paris to study under Jacques Ozanam.

In late 1685, de Moivre, a French Huguenot (Protestant), was imprisoned in Paris because of his religion. (In October, 1685, Louis XIV revoked an edict that had allowed Protestantism in addition to the Catholicism favored by the French Court.) The duration of his incarceration is unclear, but de Moivre was probably jailed 1 to 3 years. In any case, upon his release he fled to London where he began tutoring students in mathematics.

In London, de Moivre mastered Sir Isaac Newton's *Principia* and became a close friend of Newton's and of Edmond Halley's, an English astronomer (in whose honor, incidentally, Halley's Comet is named). In Newton's later years, he would refuse to take new students, saying, "Go to Mr. de Moivre; he knows these things better than I do."

De Moivre's contributions to probability theory, mathematics, and statistics range from the definition of statistical independence to analytical trigonometric formulas to his major discovery: the normal approximation to the binomial distribution—of monumental importance in its own right, precursor to the central limit theorem, and fundamental to proportion inferences. The definition of statistical independence appeared in *The Doctrine of Chances*, published in 1718 and dedicated to Newton; the normal approximation to the binomial distribution was contained in a Latin pamphlet published in 1733. Many of his other papers were published in *Philosophical Transactions of the Royal Society*.

De Moivre also did research on the analysis of mortality statistics and the theory of annuities. In 1725, the first edition of his *Annuities on Lives*, in which he derived annuity formulas and addressed other annuity problems, was published.

De Moivre was elected to the Royal Society in 1697, to the Berlin Academy of Sciences in 1735, and to the Paris Academy in 1754. But, despite his obvious talents as a mathematician and his many champions, he was never able to obtain a position in any of England's universities. Instead, he had to rely on his meager earnings as a tutor in mathematics and a consultant on gambling and insurance, supplemented by the sales of his books. De Moivre died in London on November 27, 1754.

chapter 12

Chi-Square Procedures

CHAPTER OUTLINE

12.1 The Chi-Square Distribution

12.2 Chi-Square Goodness-of-Fit Test

12.3 Contingency Tables; Association

12.4 Chi-Square Independence Test

GENERAL OBJECTIVES The statistical-inference techniques presented so far have dealt exclusively with hypothesis tests and confidence intervals for population parameters, such as population means and population proportions. In this chapter, we consider two widely used inferential procedures that are not concerned with population parameters. These two procedures are often referred to as **chi-square procedures** because they rely on a distribution called the *chi-square distribution.*

To prepare for examination of chi-square procedures, we discuss the chi-square distribution in Section 12.1. In Section 12.2, we present the chi-square goodness-of-fit test, a hypothesis test that can be used to make inferences about the distribution of a variable. For instance, we could apply that test to a sample of university students to decide whether the political preference distribution of all university students differs from that of the population as a whole.

In Section 12.3, as a preliminary to the study of a second chi-square procedure, we discuss contingency tables—frequency distributions for bivariate data—and related topics. Then, in Section 12.4, we present the chi-square independence test, a hypothesis test used to decide whether an association exists between two characteristics of a population. For instance, we could apply that test to a sample of U.S. adults to decide whether an association exists between annual income and educational level for all U.S. adults.

case study

ROAD RAGE

The report *Controlling Road Rage: A Literature Review and Pilot Study*, dated June 9, 1999, was prepared for the AAA Foundation for Traffic Safety by Daniel B. Rathbone, Ph.D., and Jorg C. Huckabee, MSCE. The authors discuss the results of a literature review and pilot study on how to prevent aggressive driving and road rage.

Road rage is defined as "…an incident in which an angry or impatient motorist or passenger intentionally injures or kills another motorist, passenger, or pedestrian, or attempts or threatens to injure or kill another motorist, passenger, or pedestrian."

One of the goals of the study was to determine when road rage occurs most often. The table at the right provides the days on which 69 road-rage incidents occurred. For this sample of 69 road-rage incidents, more incidents occurred on Friday than any other day. This information, of course, is a descriptive statistic and, by itself, does not imply that Friday is the mode for all road-rage incidents.

Using the data to make inferences about all road-rage incidents would be more informative. For instance, do the data provide sufficient evidence to conclude that some days are more likely than others for the occurrence of road-rage incidents? We can answer this question by applying one of the chi-square procedures discussed in this chapter—namely, the chi-square goodness-of-fit test. At the end of this chapter, you are asked to apply that test to the road-rage data and obtain the answer to this question.

F	Sa	W	M	Tu	F	Th	M
Tu	F	Tu	F	Su	W	Th	F
Th	W	Th	Sa	W	W	F	F
Tu	Su	Tu	Th	W	Sa	Tu	Th
F	W	F	F	Su	F	Th	Tu
F	Tu	Tu	Tu	Sa	W	W	Sa
F	Sa	Th	W	F	Th	F	M
F	M	F	Su	W	Th	M	Tu
Sa	Th	F	Su	W			

12.1 THE CHI-SQUARE DISTRIBUTION

The statistical-inference procedures discussed in this chapter rely on a distribution called the **chi-square distribution.** A variable is said to have a chi-square distribution if its distribution has the shape of a special type of right-skewed curve, called a **chi-square (χ^2) curve.**

Actually, there are infinitely many chi-square distributions, and we identify the chi-square distribution (and χ^2-curve) in question by stating its number of degrees of freedom, just as we did for t-distributions. Figure 12.1 shows three χ^2-curves and illustrates some basic properties of χ^2-curves, which are presented in Key Fact 12.1.

FIGURE 12.1
χ^2-curves for df = 5, 10, and 19

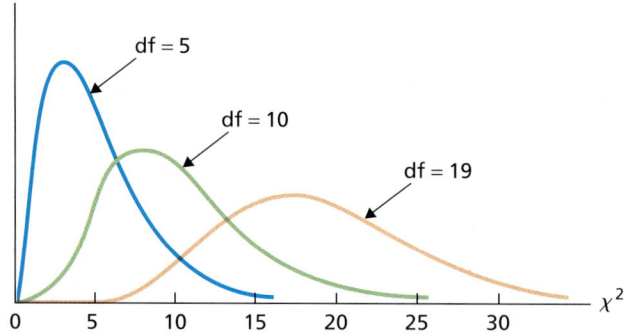

Key Fact 12.1   **Basic Properties of χ^2-Curves**

Property 1: The total area under a χ^2-curve equals 1.

Property 2: A χ^2-curve starts at 0 on the horizontal axis and extends indefinitely to the right, approaching, but never touching, the horizontal axis.

Property 3: A χ^2-curve is right skewed.

Property 4: As the number of degrees of freedom becomes larger, χ^2-curves look increasingly like normal curves.

USING THE χ^2-TABLE

Percentages (and probabilities) for a variable that has a chi-square distribution equal areas under its associated χ^2-curve. To perform a chi-square test, we need to know how to find the χ^2-value that has a specified area to its right. Table V in Appendix A provides χ^2-values that correspond to several areas for various degrees of freedom.

The χ^2-table (Table V) is similar to the t-table (Table IV). The two outside columns of Table V, labeled df, display the number of degrees of freedom. As expected, the symbol χ^2_α denotes the χ^2-value that has area α to its right under a χ^2-curve. Thus the column headed $\chi^2_{0.995}$ contains χ^2-values that have area 0.995 to their right; the column headed $\chi^2_{0.99}$ contains χ^2-values that have area 0.99 to their right; and so on. We illustrate a use of Table V in Example 12.1.

Example 12.1 Finding the χ^2-Value Having a Specified Area to Its Right

For a χ^2-curve with 12 degrees of freedom, find $\chi^2_{0.025}$; that is, find the χ^2-value that has area 0.025 to its right, as shown in Fig. 12.2(a).

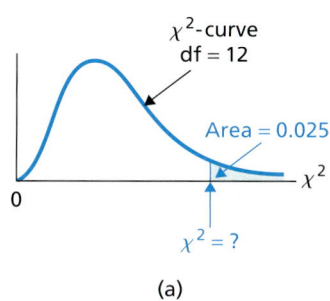
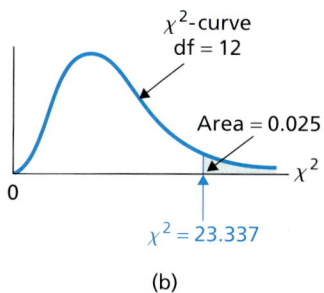

FIGURE 12.2
Finding the χ^2-value that has area 0.025 to its right

(a) (b)

Solution To find this χ^2-value, we use Table V. As the number of degrees of freedom is 12, we first go down the outside columns, labeled df, to "12." Then we go across that row to the column headed $\chi^2_{0.025}$. The number in the body of the table there, 23.337, is the required χ^2-value; that is, for a χ^2-curve with df = 12, the χ^2-value having area 0.025 to its right is $\chi^2_{0.025} = 23.337$, as shown in Figure 12.2(b).

Exercises 12.1

Statistical Concepts and Skills

12.1 What is meant by saying that a variable has a chi-square distribution?

12.2 How do you identify different chi-square distributions?

12.3 Consider two χ^2-curves with degrees of freedom 12 and 20, respectively. Which one more closely resembles a normal curve? Explain your answer.

12.4 The t-table has entries for areas of 0.10, 0.05, 0.025, 0.01, and 0.005. In contrast, the χ^2-table has entries for those areas and for 0.995, 0.99, 0.975, 0.95, and 0.90. Explain why the t-values corresponding to these additional areas can be obtained from the existing t-table, but must be provided explicitly in the χ^2-table.

In Exercises 12.5–12.8, use Table V to find the required χ^2-values. Illustrate your work graphically.

12.5 For a χ^2-curve with 19 degrees of freedom, find the χ^2-value that has area

a. 0.025 to its right. **b.** 0.95 to its right.

12.6 For a χ^2-curve with 22 degrees of freedom, find the χ^2-value that has area
a. 0.01 to its right. **b.** 0.995 to its right.

12.7 For a χ^2-curve with df = 10, determine
a. $\chi^2_{0.05}$. **b.** $\chi^2_{0.975}$.

12.8 For a χ^2-curve with df = 4, determine
a. $\chi^2_{0.005}$. **b.** $\chi^2_{0.99}$.

Extending the Concepts and Skills

12.9 Explain how you would use Table V to find the χ^2-value that has area 0.05 to its left. Obtain this χ^2-value for a χ^2-curve with df = 26.

12.10 Explain how you would use Table V to find the two χ^2-values that divide the area under a χ^2-curve into a middle 0.95 area and two outside 0.025 areas. Find these two χ^2-values for a χ^2-curve with df = 14.

12.2 CHI-SQUARE GOODNESS-OF-FIT TEST

The first chi-square procedure that we discuss is called the **chi-square goodness-of-fit test.** We can use this procedure to perform a hypothesis test about the distribution of a qualitative (categorical) variable or a discrete quantitative variable that has only finitely many possible values.[1] In Example 12.2, we introduce and explain the reasoning behind the chi-square goodness-of-fit test.

Example 12.2 Introduces the Chi-Square Goodness-of-Fit Test

Violent Crimes The U.S. Federal Bureau of Investigation (FBI) compiles data on crimes and crime rates and publishes the information in *Crime in the United States.* A violent crime is classified by the FBI as murder, forcible rape, robbery, or aggravated assault. Table 12.1 provides a relative-frequency distribution for (reported) violent crimes in 1995. For instance, in 1995, 32.3% of violent crimes were robberies.

A random sample of 500 violent-crime reports from last year yielded the frequency distribution shown in Table 12.2. Do the data provide sufficient evidence to conclude that last year's distribution of violent crimes has changed from the 1995 distribution?

TABLE 12.1
Distribution of violent crimes in the United States, 1995

Type of violent crime	Relative frequency
Murder	0.012
Forcible rape	0.054
Robbery	0.323
Agg. assault	0.611
	1.000

TABLE 12.2
Sample results for 500 randomly selected violent-crime reports from last year

Type of violent crime	Frequency
Murder	9
Forcible rape	26
Robbery	144
Agg. assault	321
	500

Solution The population is last year's (reported) violent crimes. The variable under consideration is "type of violent crime," and its possible values are murder, forcible rape, robbery, and aggravated assault. We want to perform the hypothesis test

H_0: Last year's violent-crime distribution is the same as the 1995 distribution.

H_a: Last year's violent-crime distribution is different from the 1995 distribution.

The basic idea behind the chi-square goodness-of-fit test is to compare the **observed frequencies** in the second column of Table 12.2 to the frequencies

---

[1] Actually, the chi-square goodness-of-fit test can be applied to any variable whose possible values have been grouped into a finite number of categories.

12.2 Chi-Square Goodness-of-Fit Test

that would be expected—the **expected frequencies**—if last year's violent-crime distribution is the same as the 1995 distribution. If the observed and expected frequencies match fairly well, we do not reject the null hypothesis; otherwise, we reject the null hypothesis. To transform this idea into a precise procedure, we need to answer two questions.

1. What frequencies should we expect from a random sample of 500 violent-crime reports from last year if last year's violent-crime distribution is the same as the 1995 distribution?
2. How do we decide whether the observed frequencies match reasonably well with those that we would expect?

The first question is easy to answer. If last year's violent-crime distribution is the same as the 1995 distribution, then, for instance, 32.3% of last year's violent crimes were robberies, as shown in Table 12.1. Therefore, in a random sample of 500 violent-crime reports from last year, we would expect about 32.3% of the 500, or 161.5, to be robberies. In general, we compute each expected frequency, denoted E, by using the formula

$$E = np,$$

where n is the sample size and p is the appropriate relative frequency from the second column of Table 12.1. For instance, the expected frequency for robberies is

$$E = np = 500 \cdot 0.323 = 161.5,$$

as we have already demonstrated. Calculations of the expected frequencies for all four types of violent crime are shown in Table 12.3.

TABLE 12.3
Expected frequencies if last year's violent-crime distribution is the same as the 1995 distribution

Type of violent crime	Relative frequency p	Expected frequency $np = E$
Murder	0.012	$500 \cdot 0.012 = 6.0$
Forcible rape	0.054	$500 \cdot 0.054 = 27.0$
Robbery	0.323	$500 \cdot 0.323 = 161.5$
Agg. assault	0.611	$500 \cdot 0.611 = 305.5$

The third column of Table 12.3 provides the answer to the first question. It gives the frequencies that we would expect if last year's violent-crime distribution is the same as the 1995 distribution.

The second question—whether the observed frequencies match reasonably well with the expected frequencies—is harder to answer. We need to calculate a number that measures how good the fit is.

The second column of Table 12.4 on the next page repeats the observed frequencies from the second column of Table 12.2. The third column of Table 12.4 lists the expected frequencies from the third column of Table 12.3.

To measure how well the observed and expected frequencies match, we look at the differences, $O - E$, displayed in the fourth column of Table 12.4. Summing these differences to obtain a "total difference" isn't very useful because the sum

TABLE 12.4
Calculating the goodness of fit

Type of violent crime x	Observed frequency O	Expected frequency E	Difference $O - E$	Square of difference $(O - E)^2$	Chi-square subtotal $(O - E)^2/E$
Murder	9	6.0	3.0	9.00	1.500
Forcible rape	26	27.0	−1.0	1.00	0.037
Robbery	144	161.5	−17.5	306.25	1.896
Agg. assault	321	305.5	15.5	240.25	0.786
	500	500.0	0		4.219

is 0. Instead, we square each difference (fifth column) and then divide by the corresponding expected frequency. Doing so gives the values $(O-E)^2/E$, called **chi-square subtotals,** shown in the sixth column. The sum of the chi-square subtotals,

$$\Sigma(O - E)^2/E = 4.219,$$

is the statistic used to measure how well (or poorly) the observed and expected frequencies match.

If the null hypothesis is true, the observed and expected frequencies should be roughly equal, resulting in a small value of the test statistic, $\Sigma(O - E)^2/E$. In other words, large values of $\Sigma(O - E)^2/E$ provide evidence against the null hypothesis.

As we have shown, $\Sigma(O - E)^2/E = 4.219$. Can this value be reasonably attributed to sampling error, or is it large enough to suggest that the null hypothesis is false? To answer this question, we need to know the distribution of the test statistic $\Sigma(O - E)^2/E$, which is described in Key Fact 12.2. ◆

Key Fact 12.2 — **Distribution of the χ^2-Statistic for a Chi-Square Goodness-of-Fit Test**

For a chi-square goodness-of-fit test, the test statistic

$$\chi^2 = \Sigma(O - E)^2/E$$

has approximately a chi-square distribution if the null hypothesis is true. The number of degrees of freedom is 1 less than the number of possible values for the variable under consideration.

PROCEDURE FOR THE CHI-SQUARE GOODNESS-OF-FIT TEST

We can now present a method for performing a chi-square goodness-of-fit test—Procedures 12.1A and B, which we apply in Example 12.3. The null hypothesis will be rejected only when the test statistic is too large, so the hypothesis test is always right-tailed.

Procedure 12.1A The Chi-Square Goodness-of-Fit Test (Critical-Value Approach)

Assumptions
1. All expected frequencies are 1 or greater.
2. At most 20% of the expected frequencies are less than 5.

Step 1 The null and alternative hypotheses are

H_0: The variable under consideration has the specified distribution.

H_a: The variable under consideration does not have the specified distribution.

Step 2 Calculate the expected frequency for each possible value of the variable under consideration by using the formula $E = np$, where n is the sample size and p is the relative frequency (or probability) given for the value in the null hypothesis.

Step 3 Determine whether the expected frequencies satisfy Assumptions 1 and 2. If they do not, this procedure should not be used.

Step 4 Decide on the significance level, α.

Step 5 Compute the value of the test statistic

$$\chi^2 = \Sigma(O - E)^2 / E,$$

where O and E denote observed and expected frequencies, respectively.

Step 6 The critical value is χ_α^2 with df $= k - 1$, where k is the number of possible values for the variable under consideration. Use Table V to find the critical value.

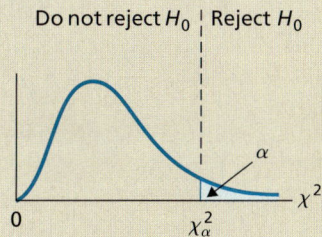

Step 7 If the value of the test statistic falls in the rejection region, reject H_0; otherwise, do not reject H_0.

Step 8 Interpret the results of the hypothesis test.

Procedure 12.1B — The Chi-Square Goodness-of-Fit Test (*P*-Value Approach)

Assumptions
1. All expected frequencies are 1 or greater.
2. At most 20% of the expected frequencies are less than 5.

Step 1 The null and alternative hypotheses are

H_0: The variable under consideration has the specified distribution.

H_a: The variable under consideration does not have the specified distribution.

Step 2 Calculate the expected frequency for each possible value of the variable under consideration by using the formula $E = np$, where n is the sample size and p is the relative frequency (or probability) given for the value in the null hypothesis.

Step 3 Determine whether the expected frequencies satisfy Assumptions 1 and 2. If they do not, this procedure should not be used.

Step 4 Decide on the significance level, α.

Step 5 Compute the value of the test statistic

$$\chi^2 = \Sigma(O-E)^2/E$$

and denote it χ_0^2. Here O and E denote observed and expected frequencies, respectively.

Step 6 The χ^2-statistic has df $= k - 1$, where k is the number of possible values for the variable under consideration. Use Table V to estimate the *P*-value, or obtain it exactly by using technology.

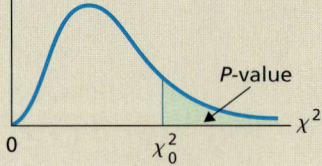

Step 7 If $P \leq \alpha$, reject H_0; otherwise, do not reject H_0.

Step 8 Interpret the results of the hypothesis test.

Note: Regarding Assumptions 1 and 2 of Procedure 12.1, in many texts the rule given is that all expected frequencies be 5 or greater. Research by the noted statistician W. G. Cochran shows that the "rule of 5" is too restrictive.

Example 12.3 The Chi-Square Goodness-of-Fit Test

Violent Crimes We can now complete the hypothesis test introduced in Example 12.2. Table 12.5 repeats the relative-frequency distribution for violent crimes in the United States in 1995.

A random sample of 500 violent-crime reports from last year yielded the frequency distribution shown in Table 12.6. At the 5% significance level, do the data provide sufficient evidence to conclude that last year's violent-crime distribution is different from the 1995 distribution?

Solution We apply Procedure 12.1.

Step 1 State the null and alternative hypotheses.

The null and alternative hypotheses are

H_0: Last year's violent-crime distribution is the same as the 1995 distribution.

H_a: Last year's violent-crime distribution is different from the 1995 distribution.

Step 2 Calculate the expected frequency for each possible value of the variable under consideration by using the formula $E = np$, where n is the sample size and p is the relative frequency given for the value in the null hypothesis.

We have $n = 500$, and the relative frequencies for the null hypothesis are shown in the second column of Table 12.5. The required calculations are summarized in Table 12.3 on page 541.

Step 3 Determine whether the expected frequencies satisfy Assumptions 1 and 2.

1. Are all expected frequencies 1 or greater? Yes, as shown in Table 12.3.
2. Are at most 20% of the expected frequencies less than 5? Yes, in fact, none of the expected frequencies are less than 5, as shown in Table 12.3.

Step 4 Decide on the significance level, α.

We are to perform the test at the 5% significance level, or $\alpha = 0.05$.

Step 5 Compute the value of the test statistic

$$\chi^2 = \Sigma(O - E)^2 / E,$$

where O and E represent observed and expected frequencies, respectively.

The observed frequencies are displayed in the second column of Table 12.6. The calculated value of the test statistic displayed in Table 12.4 on page 542 again is $\chi^2 = \Sigma(O - E)^2/E = 4.219$.

TABLE 12.5
Distribution of violent crimes in the United States, 1995

Type of violent crime	Relative frequency
Murder	0.012
Forcible rape	0.054
Robbery	0.323
Agg. assault	0.611
	1.000

TABLE 12.6
Sample results for 500 randomly selected violent-crime reports from last year

Type of violent crime	Observed frequency
Murder	9
Forcible rape	26
Robbery	144
Agg. assault	321

Critical-Value Approach

Step 6 The critical value is χ_α^2 with df $= k - 1$, where k is the number of possible values for the variable under consideration.

From Step 4, $\alpha = 0.05$. The variable under consideration is "type of violent crime." There are four types of violent crime, so $k = 4$. In Table V, we find that, for df $= k - 1 = 4 - 1 = 3$, $\chi_{0.05}^2 = 7.815$, as shown in Fig. 12.3A.

FIGURE 12.3A

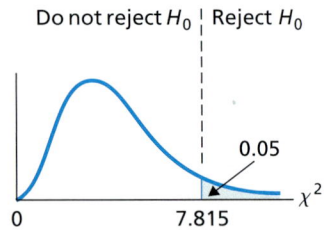

Step 7 If the value of the test statistic falls in the rejection region, reject H_0; otherwise, do not reject H_0.

From Step 5, the value of the test statistic is $\chi^2 = 4.219$. Because it does not fall in the rejection region, as shown in Fig. 12.3A, we do not reject H_0. The test results are not statistically significant at the 5% level.

P-Value Approach

Step 6 The χ^2-statistic has df $= k - 1$, where k is the number of possible values for the variable under consideration. Use Table V to estimate the P-value, or obtain it exactly by using technology.

From Step 5, the value of the test statistic is $\chi^2 = 4.219$. The test is right-tailed, so the P-value is the probability of observing a value of χ^2 of 4.219 or greater if the null hypothesis is true. That probability equals the shaded area in Fig. 12.3B.

FIGURE 12.3B

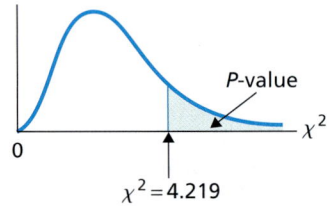

The variable under consideration is "type of violent crime." Because there are four types of violent crime, $k = 4$. Referring to Fig. 12.3B and to Table V with df $= k - 1 = 4 - 1 = 3$, we find that $P > 0.10$. (Using technology, we obtain $P = 0.239$.)

Step 7 If $P \leq \alpha$, reject H_0; otherwise, do not reject H_0.

From Step 6, $P > 0.10$. Because the P-value exceeds the specified significance level of 0.05, we do not reject H_0. The test results are not statistically significant at the 5% level and (see Table 9.10 on page 405) provide essentially no evidence against the null hypothesis.

Step 8 Interpret the results of the hypothesis test.

What Does it Mean? At the 5% significance level, the data do not provide sufficient evidence to conclude that last year's violent-crime distribution differs from the 1995 distribution.

12.2 Chi-Square Goodness-of-Fit Test

The Technology Center

Some statistical technologies have dedicated programs that automatically perform a chi-square goodness-of-fit test, but others do not. For a statistical technology that does not have a dedicated program for a chi-square goodness-of-fit test, you can often use the macro capabilities of the statistical technology to write a program. Refer to the technology manuals for more details.

Exercises 12.2

Statistical Concepts and Skills

12.11 Why is the phrase "goodness of fit" used to describe the type of hypothesis test considered in this section?

12.12 Are the observed frequencies variables? What about the expected frequencies? Explain your answers.

12.13 In each part of this exercise, we have given the relative frequencies for the null hypothesis of a chi-square goodness-of-fit test and the sample size. In each case, decide whether the two assumptions for using that test are satisfied.
a. Sample size: $n = 100$.
   Relative frequencies: 0.65, 0.30, 0.05.
b. Sample size: $n = 50$.
   Relative frequencies: 0.65, 0.30, 0.05.
c. Sample size: $n = 50$.
   Relative frequencies: 0.20, 0.20, 0.25, 0.30, 0.05.
d. Sample size: $n = 50$.
   Relative frequencies: 0.22, 0.21, 0.25, 0.30, 0.02.
e. Sample size: $n = 50$.
   Relative frequencies: 0.22, 0.22, 0.25, 0.30, 0.01.
f. Sample size: $n = 100$.
   Relative frequencies: 0.44, 0.25, 0.30, 0.01.

12.14 Primary Heating Fuel. According to *Current Housing Reports*, published by the U.S. Bureau of the Census, the primary heating fuel for all occupied housing units is distributed as follows.

Primary heating fuel	Percentage
Natural gas	51.3
Fuel oil, kerosene	10.9
Electricity	29.4
Liquid propane gas	5.4
Wood	2.2
Other	0.8

Suppose that you want to decide whether the distribution of primary heating fuel of occupied housing units built after 1974 differs from that of all occupied housing units. To help you decide, you take a random sample of n housing units built after 1974 and obtain a frequency distribution of their primary heating fuel.
a. Identify the population and variable under consideration.
b. For each of the following sample sizes (values of n), decide whether conducting a chi-square goodness-of-fit test is reasonable and explain your answers: 100; 150; 200; 250.

In Exercises 12.15–12.18, use either the critical-value approach or the P-value approach to perform the required hypothesis test.

12.15 On Death Row. The U.S. Bureau of Justice Statistics collects data on characteristics of prisoners under sentence of death and publishes its findings in *Capital Punishment*. Following is the distribution of educational attainment for death row inmates in 1980.

Education	Rel. frequency
8th grade or less	0.257
9th–11th grade	0.370
High school grad/GED	0.295
Any college	0.078

A frequency distribution of educational attainment for 128 randomly sampled prisoners sentenced to death in 1998 is as follows.

Education	Frequency
8th grade or less	18
9th–11th grade	48
High school grad/GED	49
Any college	13

a. Identify the population and variable under consideration.
b. Do the data provide sufficient evidence to conclude that the educational attainment distribution of prisoners sentenced to death in 1998 differs from that of 1980 death-row inmates? Use $\alpha = 0.05$.
c. Repeat part (b), using $\alpha = 0.01$.

12.16 Car Sales. The American Automobile Manufacturers Association compiles data on U.S. car sales by type of car. Following is the 1990 distribution, as reported in the *World Almanac*.

Type of car	Small	Midsize	Large	Luxury
Percentage	32.8	44.8	9.4	13.0

A random sample of last year's U.S. car sales yielded the following data.

Type of car	Small	Midsize	Large	Luxury
Frequency	133	249	47	71

a. Identify the population and variable under consideration.
b. At the 5% significance level, do the data provide sufficient evidence to conclude that last year's type-of-car distribution for U.S. car sales differs from the 1990 distribution?

12.17 M&M Colors. Observing that the proportion of blue M&Ms in his bowl of candy appeared to be less than that of the other colors, Ronald D. Fricker, Jr., decided to compare the color distribution in randomly chosen bags of M&Ms to the theoretical distribution reported by M&M/MARS consumer affairs. Fricker published his findings in the article "The Mysterious Case of the Blue M&Ms" (*Chance*, 1996, Vol. 9(4), pp. 19–22). The following is the theoretical distribution.

Color	Percentage
Brown	30
Yellow	20
Red	20
Orange	10
Green	10
Blue	10

For his study, Fricker bought three bags of M&Ms from local stores and counted the number of each color. The average number of each color in the three bags was distributed as follows.

Color	Frequency
Brown	152
Yellow	114
Red	106
Orange	51
Green	43
Blue	43

Do the data provide sufficient evidence to conclude that the color distribution of M&Ms differs from that reported by M&M/MARS consumer affairs? Use $\alpha = 0.05$.

12.18 An Edge in Roulette? An American roulette wheel contains 18 red numbers, 18 black numbers, and 2 green numbers. The following table shows the frequency with which the ball landed on each color in 200 trials.

Number	Red	Black	Green
Frequency	88	102	10

At the 5% significance level, do the data suggest that the wheel is out of balance?

Extending the Concepts and Skills

12.19 Table 12.4 on page 542 showed the calculated sums of the observed frequencies, the expected frequencies, and their differences. Strictly speaking, those sums are not needed. However, they serve as a check for computational errors.

a. In general, what common value should the sum of the observed frequencies and the sum of the expected frequencies equal? Explain your answer.
b. Fill in the blank. The sum of the differences between each observed and expected frequency should equal _____.
c. Suppose that you are conducting a chi-square goodness-of-fit test. If the sum of the expected frequencies does not equal the sample size, what do you conclude?
d. Suppose that you are conducting a chi-square goodness-of-fit test. If the sum of the expected frequencies equals the sample size, can you conclude that you made no error in calculating the expected frequencies? Explain your answer.

12.20 The chi-square goodness-of-fit test provides a method for performing a hypothesis test about the distribution of a variable that has k possible values. If the number of possible values is 2, that is, $k = 2$, the chi-square goodness-of-fit test is equivalent to a procedure that you studied earlier.
a. Which procedure is that? Explain your answer.
b. Suppose that you want to perform a hypothesis test to decide whether the proportion of a population that has a specified attribute is different from p_0. Discuss the method for performing such a test if you use (1) the one-sample z-test for a population proportion (pages 509–510) or (2) the chi-square goodness-of-fit test.

Using Technology

12.21 On Death Row. Use the technology of your choice to perform the hypothesis test in Exercise 12.15.

12.22 Car Sales. Use the technology of your choice to perform the hypothesis test in Exercise 12.16.

12.23 Credit Card Marketing. According to market research by Brittain Associates, published in the January 1999, issue of *American Demographics*, the income distribution of adult Internet users closely mirrors that of credit card applicants. That is exactly what many major credit card issuers want to hear because they hope to replace direct mail marketing with more efficient Web-based marketing. Following is an income distribution for credit card applicants.

Income ($1000)	< 30	30 < 50	50 < 70	70+
Percentage	28	33	21	18

A random sample of 109 adult Internet users yielded the following income distribution.

Income ($1000)	< 30	30 < 50	50 < 70	70+
Frequency	25	29	26	29

Use the technology of your choice to decide, at the 5% significance level, whether the data do not support the claim by Brittain Associates. What if you use a 10% significance level?

12.24 Incoming College Freshman. The Higher Education Research Institute at UCLA conducts annual surveys on the nation's incoming freshman class and publishes its findings in *The American Freshman: National Norms*. A distribution for average high school grades of the incoming 1990 freshman class follows.

Average grade	A- to A+	B- to B+	C- to C+
Rel. frequency	0.23	0.58	0.19

A random sample of incoming freshman for 1999 gave the following data.

Average grade	A- to A+	B- to B+	C- to C+
Frequency	170	270	60

Use the technology of your choice to decide, at the 5% significance level, whether the data provide sufficient evidence to conclude that the distribution of average high school grades of the incoming 1999 freshman class differs from that of 9 years earlier.

12.3 CONTINGENCY TABLES; ASSOCIATION

The next chi-square procedure that we present is the **chi-square independence test** which is used to decide, based on sample data, whether two variables of a population are statistically related. Before we can do that, however, we need to discuss two prerequisite concepts: *contingency tables* and *association*.

CONTINGENCY TABLES

In Section 2.2, you learned how to group data from one variable into a frequency distribution. Recall that data obtained by observing values of one variable of a population are called **univariate data.**

Now, we show how to simultaneously group data from two variables into a frequency distribution. Data obtained by observing values of two variables of a population are called **bivariate data,** and a frequency distribution for bivariate data is called a **contingency table** or **two-way table.** In Example 12.4, we introduce contingency tables.

Example 12.4 Introducing Contingency Tables

Political Party and Class Level In Example 2.8 on page 50, we considered data on political party affiliation for the students in Professor Weiss's introductory statistics course. These are univariate data obtained by observing values of the single variable "political party affiliation."

Now, we simultaneously consider data on political party affiliation and class level for the students in Professor Weiss's introductory statistics course, as shown in Table 12.7. These are bivariate data, obtained by observing values of the two variables "political party affiliation" and "class level." The task is to group these bivariate data into a contingency table.

TABLE 12.7
Political party affiliation and class level for students in introductory statistics

Student	Political party	Class level	Student	Political party	Class level
1	Democratic	Freshman	21	Democratic	Junior
2	Other	Junior	22	Democratic	Senior
3	Democratic	Senior	23	Republican	Freshman
4	Other	Sophomore	24	Democratic	Sophomore
5	Democratic	Sophomore	25	Democratic	Senior
6	Republican	Sophomore	26	Republican	Sophomore
7	Republican	Junior	27	Republican	Junior
8	Other	Freshman	28	Other	Junior
9	Other	Sophomore	29	Other	Junior
10	Republican	Sophomore	30	Democratic	Sophomore
11	Republican	Sophomore	31	Republican	Sophomore
12	Republican	Junior	32	Democratic	Junior
13	Republican	Sophomore	33	Republican	Junior
14	Democratic	Junior	34	Other	Senior
15	Republican	Sophomore	35	Other	Sophomore
16	Republican	Senior	36	Republican	Freshman
17	Democratic	Sophomore	37	Republican	Freshman
18	Democratic	Junior	38	Republican	Freshman
19	Other	Senior	39	Democratic	Junior
20	Republican	Sophomore	40	Republican	Senior

Solution A contingency table must provide for each possible pair of values for the two variables. In this case, the contingency table has the form shown in Table 12.8.

TABLE 12.8
Form of contingency table for political party affiliation and class level

		Class level				
		Freshman	Sophomore	Junior	Senior	Total
Party	Democratic	|	||||	ＷＨ	|||	
	Republican	||||	ＷＨ |||	||||	||	
	Other	|	|||	|||	||	
	Total					

The small boxes inside the rectangle formed by the heavy lines are called **cells,** which hold the frequencies.

To group the bivariate data in Table 12.7 into the contingency table, we need to determine how many students fall in each cell. We do so by going through the data in Table 12.7 and placing a tally mark in the appropriate cell of Table 12.8 for each student. For instance, the first student is both a Democrat and a freshman, so this combination calls for a tally mark in the upper left cell of Table 12.8. The results of the tallying procedure are shown in Table 12.8.

We now count the tallies in each cell to determine the frequencies. Replacing the tallies in Table 12.8 by the frequencies, we obtain the contingency table for the bivariate data in Table 12.7, as shown in Table 12.9.

TABLE 12.9
Contingency table for political party affiliation and class level

		Class level				
		Freshman	Sophomore	Junior	Senior	Total
Party	Democratic	1	4	5	3	13
	Republican	4	8	4	2	18
	Other	1	3	3	2	9
	Total	6	15	12	7	40

The number 1 in the upper left cell of Table 12.9 indicates that one student in the course is both a Democrat and a freshman. The number 8, diagonally below and to the right of the 1, shows that eight students in the course are both Republicans and sophomores.

The total in the first row indicates that 13 ($1 + 4 + 5 + 3$) of the students are Democrats. Similarly, the total in the third column shows that 12 of the students are juniors. The number 40 in the lower right corner of the table gives the total number of students in the course. That total can be found by summing either the row totals or the column totals; it can also be found by summing the frequencies in the 12 cells. ◆

Grouping bivariate data into a contingency table by hand, as we did in Example 12.4, is useful for purposes of understanding. However, in practice, computers are almost always used to accomplish such tasks.

ASSOCIATION

Next, we need to discuss the concept of **association** for two variables. We do so for variables that are either categorical or quantitative with only finitely many possible values. Roughly speaking, there is an association between two variables of a population if knowing the value of one of the variables imparts information about the value of the other variable. In Example 12.5, we introduce the concept of association.

Example 12.5 Introduces Association

Political Party and Class Level In Example 12.4, we presented data on political party affiliation and class level for the students in Professor Weiss's introductory statistics course. Considering those students a population of interest, decide whether there is an association between the variables "political party affiliation" and "class level."

Solution We first obtain the distribution of political party affiliation within each class level. We do so by dividing each entry in a column of the contingency table in Table 12.9 by its column total. The results are shown in Table 12.10.

TABLE 12.10
Conditional distributions of political party affiliation by class level

Party	Class level				
	Freshman	Sophomore	Junior	Senior	Total
Democratic	0.167	0.267	0.417	0.429	0.325
Republican	0.667	0.533	0.333	0.286	0.450
Other	0.167	0.200	0.250	0.286	0.225
Total	1.000	1.000	1.000	1.000	1.000

The first column of Table 12.10 gives the distribution of political party affiliation for freshman: 16.7% are Democrats, 66.7% are Republicans, and 16.7% are Other. This distribution is called the **conditional distribution** of the variable "political party affiliation" corresponding to the value "freshman" of the variable "class level"; or, more simply, the conditional distribution of political party affiliation for freshmen.

Similarly, the second, third, and fourth columns give the conditional distributions of political party affiliation for sophomores, juniors, and seniors, respectively. The "Total" column provides the (unconditional) distribution of political party affiliation for the entire population which, in this context, is called the **marginal distribution** of the variable "political party affiliation." This distribution is the same as the one we found in Example 2.8 (Table 2.11, page 51).

Table 12.10 shows that there is an association between the variables "political party affiliation" and "class level" because knowing the value of the variable "class level" imparts information about the variable "political party affiliation." For instance, as shown in Table 12.10, if we are given no information about the class level of a student in the course, there is a 32.5% chance that the student is a Democrat. But, if we know that the student is a junior, there is a 41.7% chance that the student is a Democrat.

If there were no association between the variables "political party affiliation" and "class level," the four conditional distributions of political party affiliation would be the same as each other and as the marginal distribution of political party affiliation; in other words, all five columns of Table 12.10 would be identical.

A **segmented bar graph** is helpful for understanding the concept of association. The first four bars in the segmented bar graph in Fig. 12.4 provide the conditional distributions of political party affiliation for freshman, sophomores, juniors, and seniors, respectively, and the fifth bar gives the marginal distribution of political party affiliation.

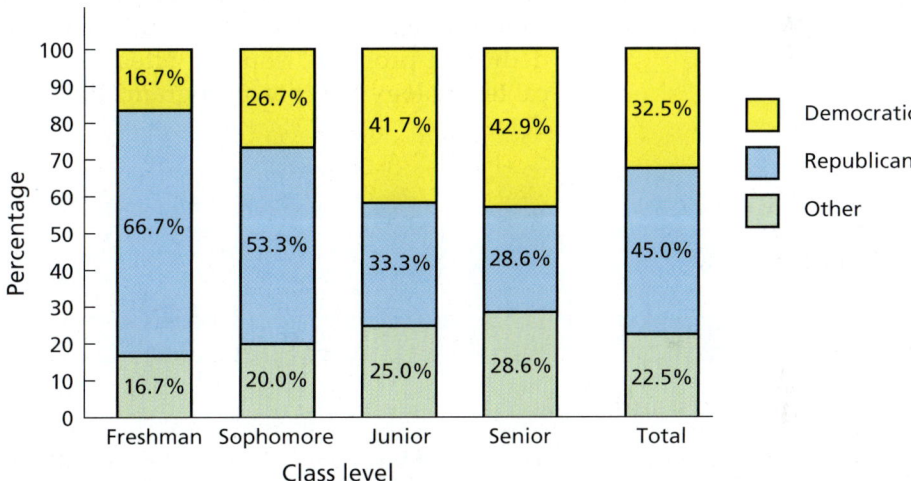

FIGURE 12.4
Segmented bar graph for the conditional distributions and marginal distribution of political party affiliation

If there were no association between political party affiliation and class level, the four bars displaying the conditional distributions of political party affiliation would be the same as each other and as the bar displaying the marginal distribution of political party affiliation; in other words, all five bars in Fig. 12.4 would be identical. That there is in fact an association between political party affiliation and class level is reflected in the segmented bar graph by nonidentical bars.

Alternatively, we could decide whether there is an association between the two variables by obtaining the conditional distribution of class level within each political party affiliation. The conclusion regarding association (or nonassociation) will be the same, regardless of which variable's conditional distributions are obtained. ◆

Keeping in mind the terminology introduced in Example 12.5, we can now define the concept of *association* for two variables.

DEFINITION 12.1 Association

We say that there is an *association* between two variables of a population if the conditional distributions of one variable given the other are not identical.

The phrase **statistically dependent variables** is also used to express the fact that there is an association between two variables. Similarly, the phrase **statistically independent variables** is often used to indicate that there is no association between two variables.

The Technology Center

Some statistical technologies have dedicated programs that automatically group bivariate data into a contingency table and obtain conditional and marginal distributions as well. For a statistical technology that does not have this kind of dedicated program, you can often use the macro capabilities of the statistical technology to write a program. Refer to the technology manuals for more details.

Exercises 12.3

Statistical Concepts and Skills

12.25 Provide an example of univariate data; of bivariate data.

12.26 Identify the type of table that is used to group bivariate data.

12.27 What are the small boxes inside the heavy lines of a contingency table called?

12.28 Suppose that bivariate data are to be grouped into a contingency table. Determine the number of cells that the contingency table will have if the number of possible values for the two variables are
a. two and three.   b. four and three.
c. m and n.

12.29 Identify three ways in which the total number of observations of bivariate data can be obtained from the frequencies in a contingency table.

12.30 U.S. Voting. Congressional Quarterly, Inc., provides information about the popular vote cast for president in the United States, by political party and region, in *America Votes*. According to that publication, in the 1996 presidential election, 40.7% of those voting voted for the Republican candidate, whereas 45.2% of those voting who live in the South did so. For that presidential election, is there an association between the variables "party of presidential candidate voted for" and "region of residence" for those who voted? Explain your answer.

12.31 U.S. Physicians. The American Medical Association compiles information on U.S. physicians in *Physician Characteristics and Distribution in the U.S.* According to that document, in 1996, 15.9% of male physicians specialized in internal medicine and 19.1% of female physicians specialized in internal medicine. Is there an association between the variables "sex" and "specialty" for U.S. physicians practicing medicine in 1996? Explain your answer.

Table 12.11 provides data on sex, class level, and college for the students in one section of the course Introduction to Computer Science in the spring semester of 1998 at Arizona State Univer-

sity. In the table, we have used the abbreviations BUS for Business, ENG for Engineering and Applied Sciences, and LIB for Liberal Arts and Sciences.

TABLE 12.11
Sex, class level, and college for students in introduction to computer science

Sex	Class	College	Sex	Class	College
M	Junior	ENG	F	Soph	BUS
M	Soph	ENG	F	Junior	ENG
F	Senior	BUS	M	Junior	LIB
F	Junior	BUS	F	Junior	BUS
M	Junior	ENG	M	Soph	BUS
F	Junior	LIB	M	Junior	BUS
M	Senior	LIB	M	Soph	ENG
M	Soph	ENG	M	Junior	ENG
M	Junior	ENG	M	Junior	ENG
M	Soph	ENG	M	Soph	LIB
F	Soph	BUS	F	Senior	ENG
F	Junior	BUS	F	Senior	BUS
M	Junior	ENG			

In Exercises 12.32–12.34, use the data in Table 12.11.

12.32 Sex and Class Level. Refer to Table 12.11. Consider the variables "sex" and "class level."
a. Group the bivariate data for these two variables into a contingency table.
b. Determine the conditional distribution of sex within each class level and the marginal distribution of sex.
c. Determine the conditional distribution of class level within each sex and the marginal distribution of class level.
d. Is there an association between the variables "sex" and "class level" for this population? Explain your answer.

12.33 Sex and College. Refer to Table 12.11. Consider the variables "sex" and "college."
a. Group the bivariate data for these two variables into a contingency table.
b. Determine the conditional distribution of sex within each college and the marginal distribution of sex.
c. Determine the conditional distribution of college within each sex and the marginal distribution of college.
d. Is there an association between the variables "sex" and "college" for this population? Explain your answer.

12.34 Class level and College. Refer to Table 12.11. Consider the variables "class level" and "college."
a. Group the bivariate data for these two variables into a contingency table.

b. Determine the conditional distribution of class level within each college and the marginal distribution of class level.
c. Determine the conditional distribution of college within each class level and the marginal distribution of college.
d. Is there an association between the variables "class level" and "college" for this population? Explain your answer.

Table 12.12 provides hypothetical data on political party affiliation and class level for the students in a night-school course.

TABLE 12.12
Political party affiliation and class level for the students in a night-school course (hypothetical data)

Party	Class	Party	Class	Party	Class
Rep	Jun	Rep	Soph	Rep	Jun
Dem	Soph	Other	Jun	Rep	Soph
Dem	Jun	Dem	Soph	Rep	Soph
Other	Jun	Rep	Soph	Rep	Fresh
Dem	Jun	Dem	Sen	Rep	Soph
Dem	Fresh	Rep	Jun	Rep	Jun
Dem	Soph	Dem	Jun	Rep	Sen
Dem	Sen	Dem	Jun	Rep	Jun
Other	Sen	Rep	Sen	Dem	Soph
Dem	Fresh	Rep	Fresh	Rep	Jun
Rep	Jun	Rep	Jun	Other	Jun
Rep	Jun	Dem	Jun	Dem	Jun
Dem	Sen	Rep	Sen	Other	Soph
Rep	Jun	Rep	Sen	Rep	Sen
Dem	Sen	Rep	Sen	Other	Soph
Rep	Jun	Dem	Soph	Rep	Soph
Rep	Soph	Other	Fresh	Other	Soph
Rep	Fresh	Rep	Soph	Other	Sen
Rep	Jun	Other	Jun	Rep	Soph
Dem	Soph	Dem	Jun	Dem	Jun

In Exercises 12.35 and 12.36, use the data in Table 12.12.

12.35 Party and Class. Refer to Table 12.12.
a. Group the bivariate data for the two variables into a contingency table.
b. Determine the conditional distribution of political party affiliation within each class level.
c. Is there an association between the variables "political party affiliation" and "class level" for this population of night-school students? Explain your answer.
d. Without doing any further calculation, determine the marginal distribution of political party affiliation.

e. Without doing further calculation, respond true or false to the following statement and explain your answer. "The conditional distributions of class level within political party affiliations are identical to each other and to the marginal distribution of class level."

12.36 Party and Class. Refer to Table 12.12.
a. If you have not done Exercise 12.35, group the bivariate data for the two variables into a contingency table.
b. Determine the conditional distribution of class level within each political party affiliation.
c. Is there an association between the variables "political party affiliation" and "class level" for this population of night-school students? Explain your answer.
d. Without doing any further calculation, determine the marginal distribution of class level.
e. Without doing further calculation, respond true or false to the following statement and explain your answer. "The conditional distributions of political party affiliation within class levels are identical to each other and to the marginal distribution of political party affiliation."

12.37 AIDS in the United States. According to the Centers for Disease Control in Atlanta, Georgia, acquired immunodeficiency syndrome (AIDS) is a specific group of diseases or conditions that indicate severe immunosuppression related to infection with the human immunodeficiency virus (HIV). According to *HIV/AIDS Surveillance Report* (Vol. 11, No. 2), the number of AIDS cases in the United States for 1999, by gender and race/ethnicity, was as shown in the following contingency table.

		Gender		
		Male	Female	Total
Race/Ethnicity	White	12,855		14,779
	Black	14,946	6,784	21,730
	Hispanic	7,019	1,948	
	Other	439	103	542
	Total		10,759	

a. How many cells does this contingency table have?
b. Fill in the missing entries.
c. What was the total number of AIDS cases in the United States in 1999?
d. How many AIDS cases were Hispanics?
e. How many AIDS cases were males?
f. How many AIDS cases were white females?

12.38 Vehicles in Use. As reported by the Motor Vehicle Manufacturers Association of the United States in *Motor Vehicle Facts and Figures*, the number of cars and trucks in use by age are as shown in the following contingency table. Frequencies are in millions.

		Type		
		Car	Truck	Total
Age (yr)	Under 6	46.2	27.8	74.0
	6–8	26.9		40.0
	9–11	23.3	10.7	
	12 & over	26.8	18.6	45.4
	Total	123.2		

a. How many cells does this contingency table have?
b. Fill in the missing entries.
c. What is the total number of cars and trucks in use?
d. How many vehicles are trucks?
e. How many vehicles are between 6 and 8 years old?
f. How many vehicles are trucks that are between 9 and 11 years old?

12.39 U.S. Physicians. The American Medical Association compiles information on U.S. physicians in *Physician Characteristics and Distribution in the U.S.* Following is a contingency table for U.S. surgeons, cross classified by specialty and base of practice.

		Base of practice			
		Office	Hospital	Other	Total
Specialty	General surgery	24,128	12,225	1,658	38,011
	Obstetrics/ gynecology	24,150	6,734	1,140	32,024
	Orthopedics	13,364	4,248	414	18,026
	Ophthalmology	12,328	2,694	518	15,540
	Total	73,970	25,901	3,730	103,601

a. How many surgeons are office-based?
b. How many surgeons are ophthalmologists?
c. How many surgeons are office-based ophthalmologists?
d. How many surgeons are either office-based or ophthalmologists?
e. How many general surgeons are hospital-based?
f. How many hospital-based surgeons are OB/GYNs?
g. How many surgeons are not hospital-based?

12.40 U.S. Hospitals. The American Hospital Association publishes information about U.S. hospitals and nursing homes in *Hospital Statistics*. The following contingency table provides a cross classification of U.S. hospitals and nursing homes by type of facility and number of beds.

		Number of beds			
		24 or fewer	25–74	75 or more	Total
Facility	General	260	1586	3557	5403
	Psychiatric	24	242	471	737
	Chronic	1	3	22	26
	Tuberculosis	0	2	2	4
	Other	25	177	208	410
	Total	310	2010	4260	6580

In the following questions, the term *hospital* refers to either a hospital or nursing home.
a. How many hospitals have at least 75 beds?
b. How many hospitals are psychiatric facilities?
c. How many hospitals are psychiatric facilities with at least 75 beds?
d. How many hospitals either are psychiatric facilities or have at least 75 beds?
e. How many general facilities have between 25 and 74 beds?
f. How many hospitals with between 25 and 74 beds are chronic facilities?
g. How many hospitals have more than 24 beds?

12.41 AIDS in the United States. Refer to Exercise 12.37. Here, we abbreviate "race/ethnicity" by "race." For AIDS cases in the United States in 1999, answer the following questions.
a. Find and interpret the conditional distribution of gender by race.
b. Find and interpret the marginal distribution of gender.
c. Is there an association between the variables "gender" and "race"? Explain your answer.
d. What percentage of AIDS cases were females?
e. What percentage of AIDS cases among whites were females?
f. Without doing further calculations, respond true or false to the following statement and explain your answer. "The conditional distributions of race by gender are not identical."
g. Find and interpret the marginal distribution of race and the conditional distributions of race by gender.

12.42 Vehicles in Use. Refer to Exercise 12.38. Here, the term "vehicle" refers to either a U.S. car or truck currently in use.

a. Determine the conditional distribution of age group for each type of vehicle.
b. Determine the marginal distribution of age group for vehicles.
c. Is there an association between the variables "type" and "age group" for vehicles? Explain your answer.
d. Find the percentage of vehicles under 6 years old.
e. Find the percentage of cars under 6 years old.
f. Without doing any further calculations, respond true or false to the following statement and explain your answer. "The conditional distributions of type of vehicle within age groups are not identical."
g. Determine and interpret the marginal distribution of type of vehicle and the conditional distributions of type of vehicle within age groups.

12.43 U.S. Physicians. Refer to Exercise 12.39.
a. Find the conditional distribution of specialty within each base-of-practice category.
b. Is there an association between specialty and base of practice for U.S. surgeons? Explain your answer.
c. Determine the marginal distribution of specialty for U.S. surgeons.
d. Construct a segmented bar graph for the conditional distributions of specialty and marginal distribution of specialty that you obtained in parts (a) and (c), respectively. Interpret the graph in light of your answer to part (b).
e. Without doing any further calculations, respond true or false to the following statement and explain your answer. "The conditional distributions of base of practice within specialties are identical."
f. Determine the marginal distribution of base of practice and the conditional distributions of base of practice within specialties.
g. Find the percentage of surgeons that are hospital-based.
h. Find the percentage of OB/GYNs that are hospital-based.
i. Find the percentage of hospital-based surgeons that are OB/GYNs.

12.44 U.S. Hospitals. Refer to Exercise 12.40.
a. Determine the conditional distribution of number of beds within each facility type.
b. Is there an association between facility type and number of beds for U.S. hospitals? Explain your answer.
c. Determine the marginal distribution of number of beds for U.S. hospitals.
d. Construct a segmented bar graph for the conditional distributions and marginal distribution of number of beds. Interpret the graph in light of your answer to part (b).
e. Without doing any further calculations, respond true or false to the following statement and explain your answer. "The conditional distributions of facility type within number-of-beds categories are identical."

f. Obtain the marginal distribution of facility type and the conditional distributions of facility type within number-of-beds categories.
g. What percentage of hospitals are general facilities?
h. What percentage of hospitals that have at least 75 beds are general facilities?
i. What percentage of general facilities have at least 75 beds?

Extending the Concepts and Skills

12.45 In this exercise, you are to consider two variables, x and y, defined on a hypothetical population. Following are the conditional distributions of the variable y corresponding to each value of the variable x.

		\multicolumn{3}{c}{x}	
		A	B	C	Total
y	0	0.316	0.316	0.316	
	1	0.422	0.422	0.422	
	2	0.211	0.211	0.211	
	3	0.047	0.047	0.047	
	4	0.004	0.004	0.004	
	Total	1.000	1.000	1.000	

a. Is there an association between the variables x and y? Explain your answer.
b. Determine the marginal distribution of y.
c. Can you determine the marginal distribution of x? Explain your answer.

12.46 Age and Sex. The U.S. Bureau of the Census publishes census data on the resident population of the United States in *Current Population Reports*. According to that document, 6.8% of male residents are in the age group 20–24 years.
a. If there were no association between age group and sex, what percentage of the resident population would be in the age group 20–24 years? Explain your answer.
b. If there were no association between age group and sex, what percentage of female residents would be in the age group 20–24 years? Explain your answer.
c. There are about 138.2 million female residents of the United States. If there were no association between age group and sex, how many female residents would there be in the age group 20–24 years?
d. In fact there are some 8.7 million female residents in the age group 20–24 years. Given this number and your answer to part (c), what do you conclude?

Using Technology

12.47 Sex, Class Level, and College. Use the technology of your choice to carry out parts (a)–(c) of
a. Exercise 12.32.
b. Exercise 12.33.
c. Exercise 12.34.

12.48 Party and Class. Use the technology of your choice to carry out
a. parts (a) and (b) of Exercise 12.35.
b. part (b) of Exercise 12.36.

12.4 CHI-SQUARE INDEPENDENCE TEST

In Section 12.3, you learned how to determine whether there is an association between two variables of a population if you have the bivariate data for the entire population. However, because, in most cases, data for an entire population are not available, you must usually apply inferential methods to decide whether an association exists between two variables.

One of the most commonly used procedures for making such decisions is the **chi-square independence test**. In Example 12.6, we introduce and explain the reasoning behind the chi-square independence test.

Example 12.6 Introducing the Chi-Square Independence Test

Marital Status and Drinking A national survey was conducted to obtain information on the alcohol consumption patterns of U.S. adults by marital status. A random sample of 1772 residents, 18 years old and older, yielded the data displayed in Table 12.13.[2] For instance, of the 1772 adults sampled, 1173 are married, 590 abstain, and 411 are married and abstain.

TABLE 12.13
Contingency table of marital status and alcohol consumption for 1772 randomly selected U.S. adults

	Drinks per month			
Marital status	Abstain	1–60	Over 60	Total
Single	67	213	74	354
Married	411	633	129	1173
Widowed	85	51	7	143
Divorced	27	60	15	102
Total	590	957	225	1772

We want to use the sample data to decide whether there is an association between marital status and alcohol consumption; that is, we want to perform the hypothesis test

H_0: Marital status and alcohol consumption are not associated.

H_a: Marital status and alcohol consumption are associated.

The idea behind the chi-square independence test is to compare the observed frequencies in Table 12.13 with the frequencies that would be expected if the null hypothesis of nonassociation is true. The test statistic for making the comparison is the same one used for the goodness-of-fit test: $\chi^2 = \Sigma(O-E)^2/E$, where O represents observed frequency and E represents expected frequency.

We now develop a formula for computing the expected frequencies. Consider, for instance, the cell of Table 12.13 corresponding to "Married *and* Abstain," the cell in the second row and first column. To begin, we note that the population proportion of all adults who abstain can be estimated by the sample proportion of the 1772 adults sampled who abstain, that is, by

Number sampled who abstain ↘

$$\frac{590}{1772} = 0.333 \quad \text{or} \quad 33.3\%.$$

Total number sampled ↗

If no association exists between marital status and alcohol consumption (i.e., if H_0 is true), the proportion of married adults who abstain is the same as the proportion of all adults who abstain. Thus, if H_0 is true, the sample proportion 590/1772 is also an estimate of the population proportion of married adults who abstain which, in turn, implies that of the 1173 married adults

---

[2] Adapted from "Alcohol Use and Alcohol Problems among U.S. Adults: Results of the 1979 National Survey" by W. B. Clark and L. Midanik. In National Institute on Alcohol Abuse and Alcoholism, *Alcohol and Health Monograph No. 1, Alcohol Consumption and Related Problems.* DHHS Pub. No. (ADM) 82–1190, 1982.

sampled, we would expect about

$$\frac{590}{1772} \cdot 1173 = 390.6$$

to abstain from alcohol.

Let's rewrite the left side of this expected-frequency computation in a slightly different way. By using algebra and referring to Table 12.13, we obtain

$$\text{Expected frequency} = \frac{590}{1772} \cdot 1173 = \frac{1173 \cdot 590}{1772}$$

$$= \frac{(\text{Row total}) \cdot (\text{Column total})}{\text{Sample size}}.$$

If we let R denote "Row total" and C denote "Column total," we can express this equation compactly as

$$E = \frac{R \cdot C}{n},$$

where, as usual, E denotes expected frequency and n denotes sample size.

Using this simple formula, we can obtain the expected frequencies for all 12 cells in Table 12.13. We have already done that for the cell in the second row and first column. For the cell in the upper right corner of the table, we get

$$E = \frac{R \cdot C}{n} = \frac{354 \cdot 225}{1772} = 44.9.$$

Similar computations give the expected frequencies for the remaining cells.

In Table 12.14, we have modified Table 12.13 by placing the expected frequency for each cell beneath the corresponding observed frequency. Table 12.14 shows, for instance, that of the adults sampled, 74 were observed to be single and consumed more than 60 drinks per month, whereas if there is no association between marital status and alcohol consumption, the expected frequency is 44.9.

TABLE 12.14
Observed and expected frequencies for marital status and alcohol consumption (expected frequencies printed below observed frequencies)

		Drinks per month			
		Abstain	1–60	Over 60	Total
Marital status	Single	67 117.9	213 191.2	74 44.9	354
	Married	411 390.6	633 633.5	129 148.9	1173
	Widowed	85 47.6	51 77.2	7 18.2	143
	Divorced	27 34.0	60 55.1	15 13.0	102
	Total	590	957	225	1772

If the null hypothesis of nonassociation is true, the observed and expected frequencies should be approximately equal, which would result in a relatively small value of the test statistic, $\chi^2 = \Sigma(O - E)^2/E$. Consequently, if χ^2 is too large, we reject the null hypothesis and conclude that an association exists between marital status and alcohol consumption. From Table 12.14 we find that

$$\begin{aligned}\chi^2 &= \Sigma(O - E)^2/E \\ &= (67 - 117.9)^2/117.9 + (213 - 191.2)^2/191.2 + (74 - 44.9)^2/44.9 \\ &\quad + (411 - 390.6)^2/390.6 + (633 - 633.5)^2/633.5 + (129 - 148.9)^2/148.9 \\ &\quad + (85 - 47.6)^2/47.6 + (51 - 77.2)^2/77.2 + (7 - 18.2)^2/18.2 \\ &\quad + (27 - 34.0)^2/34.0 + (60 - 55.1)^2/55.1 + (15 - 13.0)^2/13.0 \\ &= 21.952 + 2.489 + 18.776 + 1.070 + 0.000 + 2.670 \\ &\quad + 29.358 + 8.908 + 6.856 + 1.427 + 0.438 + 0.324 \\ &= 94.269.[3]\end{aligned}$$

Can this value be reasonably attributed to sampling error, or is it large enough to indicate that marital status and alcohol consumption are associated? Before we can answer that question, we must know the distribution of the χ^2-statistic, which is described in Key Fact 12.3. ◆

Key Fact 12.3

Distribution of the χ^2-Statistic for a Chi-Square Independence Test

For a chi-square independence test, the test statistic

$$\chi^2 = \Sigma(O - E)^2/E$$

has approximately a chi-square distribution if the null hypothesis of nonassociation is true. The number of degrees of freedom is $(r-1)(c-1)$, where r and c are the number of possible values for the two variables under consideration.

PROCEDURE FOR THE CHI-SQUARE INDEPENDENCE TEST

We can now present a method for performing a chi-square independence test—Procedures 12.2A and B, which we apply in Example 12.7. Because the null hypothesis will be rejected only when the test statistic is too large, the hypothesis test is always right-tailed.

---

[3] Although we have displayed the expected frequencies to one decimal place and the chi-square subtotals to three decimal places, the calculations were made at full calculator accuracy.

Procedure 12.2A The Chi-Square Independence Test (Critical-Value Approach)

Assumptions
1. All expected frequencies are 1 or greater.
2. At most 20% of the expected frequencies are less than 5.

Step 1 The null and alternative hypotheses are

  H_0: The two variables under consideration are not associated.

  H_a: The two variables under consideration are associated.

Step 2 Calculate the expected frequencies by using the formula

$$E = \frac{R \cdot C}{n},$$

where R = row total, C = column total, and n = sample size. Place each expected frequency below its corresponding observed frequency in the contingency table.

Step 3 Determine whether the expected frequencies satisfy Assumptions 1 and 2. If they do not, this procedure should not be used.

Step 4 Decide on the significance level, α.

Step 5 Compute the value of the test statistic

$$\chi^2 = \Sigma(O-E)^2/E,$$

where O and E represent observed and expected frequencies, respectively.

Step 6 The critical value is χ_α^2 with df $= (r-1)(c-1)$, where r and c are the number of possible values for the two variables under consideration. Use Table V to find the critical value.

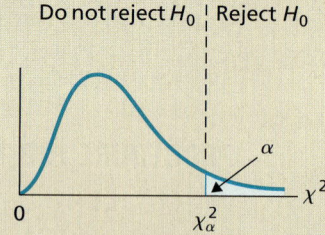

Step 7 If the value of the test statistic falls in the rejection region, reject H_0; otherwise, do not reject H_0.

Step 8 Interpret the results of the hypothesis test.

Procedure 12.2B The Chi-Square Independence Test (P-Value Approach)

Assumptions
1. All expected frequencies are 1 or greater.
2. At most 20% of the expected frequencies are less than 5.

Step 1 The null and alternative hypotheses are

H_0: The two variables under consideration are not associated.

H_a: The two variables under consideration are associated.

Step 2 Calculate the expected frequencies by using the formula

$$E = \frac{R \cdot C}{n},$$

where R = row total, C = column total, and n = sample size. Place each expected frequency below its corresponding observed frequency in the contingency table.

Step 3 Determine whether the expected frequencies satisfy Assumptions 1 and 2. If they do not, this procedure should not be used.

Step 4 Decide on the significance level, α.

Step 5 Compute the value of the test statistic

$$\chi^2 = \Sigma(O-E)^2/E$$

and denote that value χ_0^2. Here O and E denote observed and expected frequencies, respectively.

Step 6 The χ^2-statistic has df = $(r-1)(c-1)$, where r and c are the number of possible values for the two variables under consideration. Use Table V to estimate the P-value, or obtain it exactly by using technology.

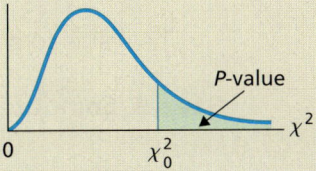

Step 7 If $P \leq \alpha$, reject H_0; otherwise, do not reject H_0.

Step 8 Interpret the results of the hypothesis test.

Example 12.7 The Chi-Square Independence Test

Marital Status and Drinking A random sample of 1772 U.S. adults yielded the data on marital status and alcohol consumption displayed in Table 12.13 on page 559. At the 5% significance level, do the data provide sufficient evidence to conclude that an association exists between marital status and alcohol consumption?

Solution We apply Procedure 12.2.

Step 1 State the null and alternative hypotheses.

The null and alternative hypotheses are

H_0: Marital status and alcohol consumption are not associated.

H_a: Marital status and alcohol consumption are associated.

Step 2 Calculate the expected frequencies by using the formula

$$E = \frac{R \cdot C}{n},$$

where R = row total, C = column total, and n = sample size. Place each expected frequency below its corresponding observed frequency in the contingency table.

We did so earlier and displayed the results in Table 12.14 on page 560.

Step 3 Determine whether the expected frequencies satisfy Assumptions 1 and 2.

1. Are all expected frequencies 1 or greater? Yes, as shown in Table 12.14.
2. Are at most 20% of the expected frequencies less than 5? Yes, in fact, none of the expected frequencies are less than 5, as shown in Table 12.14.

Step 4 Decide on the significance level, α.

The test is to be performed at the 5% significance level, or $\alpha = 0.05$.

Step 5 Compute the value of the test statistic

$$\chi^2 = \Sigma(O-E)^2 / E,$$

where O and E represent observed and expected frequencies, respectively.

The observed and expected frequencies are displayed in Table 12.14. Using them, we compute the value of the test statistic:

$$\chi^2 = (67 - 117.9)^2/117.9 + (213 - 191.2)^2/191.2 + \cdots + (15 - 13.0)^2/13.0$$
$$= 21.952 + 2.489 + \cdots + 0.324 = 94.269.$$

Critical-Value Approach

Step 6 The critical value is χ_α^2 with df = $(r-1)(c-1)$, where r and c are the number of possible values for the two variables under consideration.

The number of marital status categories is four, and the number of drinks per month categories is three. Hence $r = 4$, $c = 3$, and

$$\text{df} = (r-1)(c-1) = 3 \cdot 2 = 6.$$

For $\alpha = 0.05$, Table V reveals that the critical value is $\chi_{0.05}^2 = 12.592$, as depicted in Fig. 12.5A.

FIGURE 12.5A

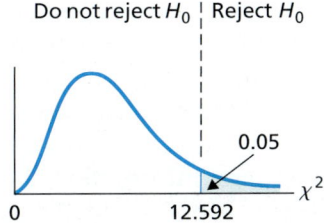

Step 7 If the value of the test statistic falls in the rejection region, reject H_0; otherwise, do not reject H_0.

From Step 5, the value of the test statistic is $\chi^2 = 94.269$, which falls in the rejection region, as shown in Fig. 12.5. Thus we reject H_0. The test results are statistically significant at the 5% level.

P-Value Approach

Step 6 The χ^2-statistic has df = $(r-1)(c-1)$, where r and c are the number of possible values for the two variables under consideration. Use Table V to estimate the P-value, or obtain it exactly by using technology.

From Step 5, the value of the test statistic is $\chi^2 = 94.269$. Because the test is right-tailed, the P-value is the probability of observing a value of χ^2 of 94.269 or greater if the null hypothesis is true. That probability equals the shaded area shown in Fig. 12.5B.

FIGURE 12.5B

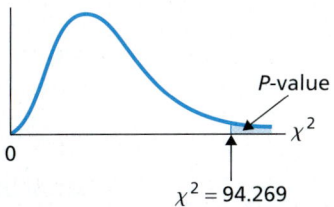

The number of marital status categories is four and the number of drinks per month categories is three. Hence $r = 4$, $c = 3$, and

$$\text{df} = (r-1)(c-1) = 3 \cdot 2 = 6.$$

From Fig. 12.5B and Table V with df = 6, we find that $P < 0.005$. (Using technology, we obtain $P = 0.000$ to three decimal places.)

Step 7 If $P \leq \alpha$, reject H_0; otherwise, do not reject H_0.

From Step 6, $P < 0.005$. Because the P-value is less than the specified significance level of 0.05, we reject H_0. The test results are statistically significant at the 5% level and (see Table 9.10 on page 405) provide very strong evidence against the null hypothesis.

Step 8 Interpret the results of the hypothesis test.

 At the 5% significance level, the data provide sufficient evidence to conclude that there is an association between marital status and alcohol consumption.

CONCERNING THE ASSUMPTIONS

In Procedure 12.2 we made two assumptions about expected frequencies.

1. All expected frequencies are 1 or greater.
2. At most 20% of the expected frequencies are less than 5.

What can we do if one or both of these assumptions are violated? Three approaches are possible. We can combine rows or columns to increase the expected frequencies in those cells in which they are too small; we can eliminate certain rows or columns in which the small expected frequencies occur; or we can increase the sample size.

ASSOCIATION AND CAUSATION

Association does not imply causation!

The chi-square independence test is used to decide whether an association exists between two variables of a population—the null hypothesis is that the two variables are not associated, and the alternative hypothesis is that they are associated. If the null hypothesis is rejected, we can conclude that the two variables are associated, but not that they are causally related.

For instance, in Example 12.7, we rejected the null hypothesis of nonassociation for the variables marital status and alcohol consumption. In other words, knowing the marital status of a person imparts information about the alcohol consumption of that person, and vice versa. It does not necessarily mean, for instance, that being single causes a person to drink more.

Although we must keep in mind that association does not imply causation, we must also note that, if two variables are not associated, there is no point in looking for a causal relationship. In other words, association is a necessary but not sufficient condition for causation.

The Technology Center

Most statistical technologies have programs that automatically perform a chi-square independence test. In this subsection, we present output and (optional) step-by-step instructions to implement such programs for Minitab and the TI-83 Plus. Currently, Excel's program has some technical problems, and DDXL requires raw data (as opposed to contingency-table data); ways to work around these problems are discussed in the *Excel Manual*.

Example 12.8 Using Technology to Perform an Independence Test

Marital Status and Drinking Use Minitab or the TI-83 Plus to perform the chi-square independence test considered in Example 12.7 on page 564.

Solution We want to perform the hypothesis test

H_0: Marital status and alcohol consumption are not associated.

H_a: Marital status and alcohol consumption are associated.

at the 5% significance level. Printout 12.1 shows the output obtained by applying the programs for a chi-square independence test to the data presented in Table 12.13.

The outputs in Printout 12.1 reveal that the *P*-value for the hypothesis test is 0.000 to three decimal places. Because the *P*-value is less than the specified significance level of 0.05, we reject H_0. The test results are statistically significant at the 5% level. That is, at the 5% significance level, the data provide sufficient evidence to conclude that there is an association between marital status and alcohol consumption. ◆

PRINTOUT 12.1
Chi-square independence test output for the data on marital status and alcohol consumption

MINITAB

Chi-Square Test: ABSTAIN, 1-60, OVER 60

Expected counts are printed below observed counts

```
        ABSTAIN      1-60    OVER 60     Total
    1        67       213         74       354
         117.87    191.18      44.95

    2       411       633        129      1173
         390.56    633.50     148.94

    3        85        51          7       143
          47.61     77.23      18.16

    4        27        60         15       102
          33.96     55.09      12.95

Total       590       957        225      1772

Chi-Sq = 21.952 +  2.489 + 18.776 +
          1.070 +  0.000 +  2.670 +
         29.358 +  8.908 +  6.856 +
          1.427 +  0.438 +  0.324 = 94.269
DF = 6, P-Value = 0.000
```

TI-83 PLUS

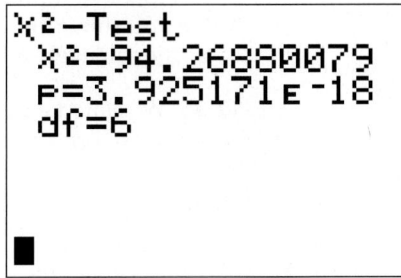

Using **Calculate**

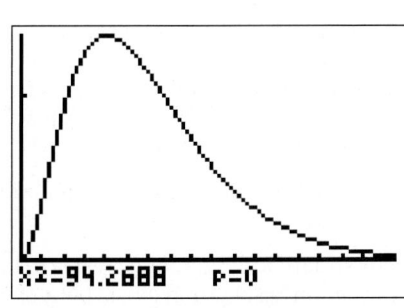

Using **Draw**

Obtaining the Output (Optional)

Printout 12.1 provides output from Minitab and the TI-83 Plus for a chi-square independence test based on the sample data displayed in Table 12.13 on page 559. The following are detailed instructions for obtaining that output.

MINITAB	EXCEL	TI-83 PLUS
1 Store the cell data from Table 12.13 in columns named ABSTAIN, 1-60, and OVER 60. 2 Choose **Stat ➤ Tables ➤ Chi-Square Test...** 3 Specify ABSTAIN, '1-60', and 'OVER 60' in the **Columns containing the table** text box 4 Click **OK**	SEE THE EXCEL MANUAL	1 Press **2nd ➤ MATRIX**, arrow over to **EDIT**, and press **1** 2 Type **4** and press **ENTER** 3 Type **3** and press **ENTER** 4 Enter the cell data from Table 12.13, pressing **ENTER** after each entry 5 Press **STAT**, arrow over to **TESTS**, and press **ALPHA ➤ C** 6 Press **2nd ➤ MATRIX**, press **1**, and press **ENTER** 7 Press **2nd ➤ MATRIX**, press **2**, and press **ENTER** 8 Highlight **Calculate** or **Draw**, and press **ENTER**

Exercises 12.4

Statistical Concepts and Skills

12.49 To decide whether two variables of a population are associated, we usually need to resort to inferential methods such as the chi-square independence test. Why?

12.50 Step 1 of Procedure 12.2 gives generic statements for the null and alternative hypotheses of a chi-square independence test. Use the terms *statistically dependent* and *statistically independent*, introduced on page 554, to restate those hypotheses.

12.51 In Example 12.6, we made the following statement: If no association exists between marital status and alcohol consumption, the proportion of married adults who abstain is the same as the proportion of all adults who abstain. Explain why that statement is true.

12.52 Explain why a chi-square independence test is always right-tailed.

12.53 A chi-square independence test is to be conducted to decide whether an association exists between two variables of a population. One variable has six possible values and the other variable has four. What is the degrees of freedom for the χ^2-statistic?

12.54 Education and Salary. Studies have shown that a positive association exists between educational level and annual salary; in other words, people with more education tend to make more money.
a. Does this finding mean that more education *causes* a person to make more money? Explain your answer.
b. Do you think there is a causal relationship between educational level and annual salary? Explain your answer.

12.55 We stated earlier that, if two variables are not associated, there is no point in looking for a causal relationship. Why?

12.56 Identify three techniques that can be tried as a remedy when one or more of the expected-frequency assumptions for a chi-square independence test are violated.

In Exercises 12.57–12.61, use either the critical-value approach or the P-value approach to perform a chi-square independence test, provided the conditions for using the test are met.

12.57 Siskel and Ebert. In the late Gene Siskel and Roger Ebert's TV show *Sneak Preview,* the two Chicago movie critics reviewed the week's new movie releases and then rated them thumbs up (positive), mixed, or thumbs down (negative). These two critics often saw the merits of a movie differently. But, in general, were the ratings given by Siskel and Ebert associated? The answer to this question was the focus of the paper "Evaluating Agreement and Disagreement Among Movie Reviewers" by Alan Agresti and Larry Winner that appeared in *Chance* (1997, Vol. 10(2), pp. 10–14). Following is a contingency table that summarizes the ratings by Siskel and Ebert for 160 movies.

		Ebert's rating			
		Thumbs down	Mixed	Thumbs up	Total
Siskel's rating	Thumbs down	24	8	13	45
	Mixed	8	13	11	32
	Thumbs up	10	9	64	83
	Total	42	30	88	160

At the 1% significance level, do the data provide sufficient evidence to conclude that an association exists between the ratings of Siskel and Ebert?

12.58 Diabetes in Native Americans. Preventable chronic diseases are increasing rapidly in Native American populations, particularly diabetes. Gilliland et al. examined the diabetes issue in the paper, "Preventative Health Care among Rural American Indians in New Mexico" (*Preventative Medicine*, 1999, Vol. 28, pp. 194–202). Following is a contingency table showing cross classification of educational attainment and diabetic state for a sample of 1273 Native Americans.

		Diabetic state		
		Diabetes	No diabetes	Total
Education	Less than HS	33	218	251
	HS grad	25	389	414
	Some college	20	393	413
	College grad	17	178	195
	Total	95	1178	1273

At the 1% significance level, do the data provide sufficient evidence to conclude that an association exists between educational level and diabetic state for Native Americans?

12.59 Regional Primaries. The Gallup Organization conducts periodic surveys to gauge the support by U.S. adults for regional primary elections. The question asked is, "It has been proposed that four individual primaries be held in different weeks of June during presidential election years. Does this sound like a good idea or a poor idea?" The following contingency table displays responses, by political affiliation, adapted from the results of a *Gallup Poll* appearing in the *Arizona Republic*.

		Response			
		Good idea	Poor idea	No opinion	Total
Affiliation	Rep	266	266	186	718
	Dem	308	250	176	734
	Ind	28	27	21	76
	Total	602	543	383	1528

At the 5% level of significance, do the data suggest that the opinions of U.S. adults on the issue of regional primaries are associated with political affiliation?

12.60 Thoughts of Suicide. A study reported by D. Goldberg in *The Detection of Psychiatric Illness by Questionnaire* (Oxford University, London, p. 126, 1972) examined the relationship between mental-health classification and thoughts of suicide. The mental health of each person in a sample of 295 was classified as normal, mild psychiatric illness, or severe psychiatric illness. Also, each person was asked: "Have you recently found that the idea of taking your own life kept coming into your mind?" Following are the results.

	Mental health			
Response	Normal	Mild illness	Severe illness	Total
Definitely not	90	43	34	167
Don't think so	5	18	8	31
Crossed my mind	3	21	21	45
Definitely yes	1	15	36	52
Total	99	97	99	295

Is there evidence that an association exists between response to the suicide question and mental-health classification? Perform the required hypothesis test at the 5% significance level.

12.61 Lawyers. The American Bar Foundation publishes information on the characteristics of lawyers in *The Lawyer Statistical Report*. The following contingency table cross classifies 307 randomly selected U.S. lawyers by status in practice and the size of the city in which they practice.

	Size of city			
Status in practice	Less than 250,000	250,000–499,999	500,000 or more	Total
Government	12	4	14	30
Judicial	8	1	2	11
Private practice	122	31	69	222
Salaried	19	7	18	44
Total	161	43	103	307

At the 5% significance level, do the data provide sufficient evidence to conclude that size of city and status in practice are statistically dependent for U.S. lawyers?

Extending the Concepts and Skills

12.62 Lawyers. In Exercise 12.61, you couldn't perform the chi-square independence test because the assumptions regarding expected frequencies were not met. As mentioned in the text, three approaches are available for remedying the situation: (1) combine rows or columns; (2) eliminate rows or columns; or (3) increase the sample size.
a. Combine the first two rows of the contingency table in Exercise 12.61 to form a new contingency table.
b. Use the table obtained in part (a) to perform the hypothesis test required in Exercise 12.61, if possible.
c. Eliminate the second row of the contingency table in Exercise 12.61 to form a new contingency table.
d. Use the table obtained in part (c) to perform the hypothesis test required in Exercise 12.61, if possible.

Using Technology

12.63 Siskel and Ebert. Use the technology of your choice to perform the hypothesis test in Exercise 12.57.

12.64 Diabetes in Native Americans. Use the technology of your choice to perform the hypothesis test in Exercise 12.58.

12.65 Job Satisfaction. A *CNN/USA TODAY* poll conducted by Gallup asked a sample of employed Americans the following question: "Which do you enjoy more, the hours when you are on your job, or the hours when you are not on your job?" The responses to this question were cross tabulated against several characteristics, among which were sex, age, type of community, amount of education, income, and type of employer. The following table summarizes the poll's results.

	On the job	Off the job	Don't know
Male	77	263	28
Female	77	215	27
18–29 years	33	136	5
30–49 years	77	274	25
50–64 years	35	56	19
65 and older	9	11	5
Urban	62	197	14
Suburban	47	171	25
Rural	42	109	15
Postgraduate	23	51	10
College graduate	41	126	18
Some college	20	108	5
No college	68	192	21
Under $20,000	40	80	11
$20,000–$29,999	32	116	7
$30,000–$49,999	41	131	8
$50,000 and over	34	138	22
Private	67	326	27
Government	23	82	11
Self	61	69	14

Use the data to decide, at the 5% significance level, whether an association exists between each pair of variables.
a. sex and response (to the question)
b. age and response
c. type of community and response
d. amount of education and response
e. income and response
f. type of employer and response

Chapter Review

You Should Be Able To

1. use and understand the formulas presented in this chapter.

2. identify the basic properties of χ^2-curves.

3. use the chi-square table, Table V.

4. explain the reasoning behind the chi-square goodness-of-fit test.

5. perform a chi-square goodness-of-fit test.

6. group bivariate data into a contingency table.

7. determine and graph marginal and conditional distributions.

8. decide whether an association exists between two variables of a population, given bivariate data for the entire population.

9. explain the reasoning behind the chi-square independence test.

10. perform a chi-square independence test to decide whether an association exists between two variables of a population, given bivariate data for a sample of the population.

Key Terms

association, *554*
bivariate data, *550*
cells, *551*
χ^2_α, *538*
chi-square (χ^2) curve, *538*
chi-square distribution, *538*
chi-square goodness-of-fit test, *543, 544*

chi-square independence test, *562, 563*
chi-square procedures, *536*
chi-square subtotals, *542*
conditional distribution, *552*
contingency table, *550*
expected frequencies, *541*
marginal distribution, *552*

observed frequencies, *540*
segmented bar graph, *553*
statistically dependent variables, *554*
statistically independent variables, *554*
two-way table, *550*
univariate data, *550*

Review Test

Statistical Concepts and Skills

1. How do you distinguish among the infinitely many chi-square distributions and corresponding χ^2-curves?

2. Regarding a χ^2-curve,
a. at what point on the horizontal axis does the curve begin?
b. what shape does it have?
c. As the number of degrees of freedom increases, a χ^2-curve begins to look like another type of curve. What type of curve is that?

3. Recall that the number of degrees of freedom for the t-distribution used in a one-sample t-test for a population mean depends on the sample size.
a. Is that true for the chi-square distribution used in a chi-square goodness-of-fit test? Explain your answer.
b. Is that true for the chi-square distribution used in a chi-square independence test? Explain your answer.

4. Explain why a chi-square goodness-of-fit test or a chi-square independence test is always right-tailed.

5. If the observed and expected frequencies for a chi-square goodness-of-fit test or a chi-square independence test matched perfectly, what would be the value of the test statistic?

6. Regarding the expected-frequency assumptions for a chi-square goodness-of-fit test or a chi-square independence test,
   a. state them.
   b. how important are they?

7. **Getting to Work.** The U.S. Bureau of the Census publishes information on how Americans get to work in *Census of Population and Housing*. According to that document, 5.3% of Americans use public transportation to get to work.
   a. If there were no association between means of transportation to work and region of residence, what percentage of Americans who live in the West would use public transportation to get to work?
   b. There are (roughly) 58.5 million Americans who live in the West. If there were no association between means of transportation to work and region of residence, how many Americans who live in the West would use public transportation to get to work?
   c. In fact, there are (roughly) 2.4 million Americans who live in the West and use public transportation to get to work. Given this and your answer to part (b), what can you conclude?

8. Suppose that you have bivariate data for an entire population.
   a. How would you decide whether there is an association between the two variables under consideration?
   b. Assuming that you make no calculation mistakes, could your conclusion be in error? Explain your answer.

9. Suppose that you have bivariate data for a sample of a population.
   a. How would you decide whether there is an association between the two variables under consideration?
   b. Assuming that you make no calculation mistakes, could your conclusion be in error? Explain your answer.

10. Consider a χ^2-curve with 17 degrees of freedom. Use Table V to determine
    a. $\chi^2_{0.99}$.
    b. $\chi^2_{0.01}$.
    c. the χ^2-value that has area 0.05 to its right.
    d. the χ^2-value that has area 0.05 to its left.
    e. the two χ^2-values that divide the area under the curve into a middle 0.95 area and two outside 0.025 areas.

11. **Educational Attainment.** The U.S. Bureau of the Census compiles census data on educational attainment of Americans. From the document *1990 Census of Population*, we obtained the 1990 percent distribution of educational attainment for U.S. adults 25 years old and older. Here is that distribution.

Highest level	Percentage
Not HS graduate	24.8
HS graduate	30.0
Some college	18.7
Associate's degree	6.2
Bachelor's degree	13.1
Advanced degree	7.2

A random sample of 500 U.S. adults (25 years old and older) taken this year gave the following frequency distribution.

Highest level	Frequency
Not HS graduate	86
HS graduate	169
Some college	86
Associate's degree	37
Bachelor's degree	82
Advanced degree	40

   a. Use either the critical-value approach or *P*-value approach to decide, at the 5% significance level, whether this year's distribution of educational attainment differs from the 1990 distribution.
   b. Estimate the *P*-value of the hypothesis test and use that estimate to assess the evidence against the null hypothesis.

12. **U.S. Governors.** According to the *Statistical Abstract of the United States* and the *World Almanac*, the region and governor's party affiliation for each state in the United States is as follows. Governors who are neither Democratic nor Republican are designated "Ind" (Independent).
    a. Group the bivariate data for the variables "region" and "party of governor" into a contingency table.
    b. Determine the conditional distributions of region by party and the marginal distribution of region.
    c. Determine the conditional distributions of party by region and the marginal distribution of party.
    d. Is there an association between the variables "region" and "party of governor" for the states of the United States? Explain your answer.
    e. What percentage of states have Republican governors?
    f. If there were no association between region and party of governor, determine the percentage of Midwest states that would have Republican governors.
    g. In reality, what percentage of Midwest states have Republican governors?

State	Region	Party	State	Region	Party
AL	SO	Dem	MT	WE	Rep
AK	WE	Dem	NE	MW	Rep
AZ	WE	Rep	NV	WE	Rep
AR	SO	Rep	NH	NE	Dem
CA	WE	Dem	NJ	NE	Rep
CO	WE	Rep	NM	WE	Rep
CT	NE	Rep	NY	NE	Rep
DE	SO	Dem	NC	SO	Dem
FL	SO	Rep	ND	MW	Rep
GA	SO	Dem	OH	MW	Rep
HI	WE	Dem	OK	SO	Rep
ID	WE	Rep	OR	WE	Dem
IL	MW	Rep	PA	NE	Rep
IN	MW	Dem	RI	NE	Rep
IA	MW	Dem	SC	SO	Dem
KS	MW	Rep	SD	MW	Rep
KY	SO	Dem	TN	SO	Rep
LA	SO	Rep	TX	SO	Rep
ME	NE	Ind	UT	WE	Rep
MD	SO	Dem	VT	NE	Dem
MA	NE	Rep	VA	SO	Rep
MI	MW	Rep	WA	WE	Dem
MN	MW	Ind	WV	SO	Rep
MS	SO	Rep	WI	MW	Rep
MO	MW	Dem	WY	WE	Rep

h. What percentage of states are in the Midwest?
i. If there were no association between region and party of governor, determine the percentage of states with Republican governors that would be in the Midwest.
j. In reality, what percentage of states with Republican governors are in the Midwest?

13. U.S. Hospitals. From data in *Hospital Statistics*, published by the American Hospital Association, we obtained the following contingency table for U.S. hospitals and nursing homes, by type of facility and type of control. We used the abbreviations Gov for Government, Prop for Proprietary, and NP for nonprofit.

		Control			
		Gov	Prop	NP	Total
Facility	General	1697	660	3046	5403
	Psychiatric	266	358	113	737
	Chronic	21	1	4	26
	Tuberculosis	3	0	1	4
	Other	59	148	203	410
	Total	2046	1167	3367	6580

In the following questions, the term *hospital* refers to either a hospital or nursing home.
a. How many hospitals are government controlled?
b. How many hospitals are psychiatric facilities?
c. How many hospitals are government controlled psychiatric facilities?
d. How many general facilities are nonprofit?
e. How many hospitals are not under proprietary control?
f. How many hospitals are either general facilities or under proprietary control?

14. U.S. Hospitals. Refer to Problem 13.
a. Obtain the conditional distribution of control type within each facility type.
b. Is there an association between facility type and control type for U.S. hospitals? Explain your answer.
c. Determine the marginal distribution of control type for U.S. hospitals.
d. Construct a segmented bar graph for the conditional distributions and marginal distribution of control type. Interpret the graph in light of your answer to part (b).
e. Without doing any further calculations, respond true or false to the following statement and explain your answer. "The conditional distributions of facility type within control types are identical."
f. Determine the marginal distribution of facility type and the conditional distributions of facility type within control types.
g. What percentage of hospitals are under proprietary control?
h. What percentage of psychiatric hospitals are under proprietary control?
i. What percentage of hospitals under proprietary control are psychiatric hospitals?

15. Hodgkin's Disease. Hodgkin's disease is a malignant, progressive, sometimes fatal disease of unknown cause, and characterized by enlargement of the lymph nodes, spleen, and liver. The following contingency table summarizes data collected during a study by Hancock et al. (*Journal of Clinical Oncology*, 1979, Vol. 5(4), pp. 283–297) of 538 patients with Hodgkin's disease. The table cross classifies the histological types of patients and their responses to treatment three months prior to the study.

		Response			
		Positive	Partial	None	Total
Histological type	Lymphocyte depletion	18	10	44	72
	Lymphocyte predominance	74	18	12	104
	Mixed cellularity	154	54	58	266
	Nodular sclerosis	68	16	12	96
	Total	314	98	126	538

At the 1% significance level, do the data provide sufficient evidence to conclude that histological type and treatment response are statistically dependent?

Using Technology

16. Educational Attainment. Use the technology of your choice to conduct the required chi-square goodness-of-fit test in Problem 11.

17. U.S. Governors. Use the technology of your choice to solve parts (a)–(c) of Problem 12.

18. Hodgkin's Disease. Use the technology of your choice to perform the hypothesis test in Problem 15.

Sex and the Death Penalty

In this Internet project, you are to examine data for men and women on death row to determine whether sex differences exist in the death-row population. Currently, there are 49 women on death row, which accounts for only 1.5% of the total death-row population.

In general, both the death-sentencing rate and the death-row population are very small for women compared to those for men. Additionally, actual execution of female offenders is rare, with only 533 documented instances. Now you can explore these differences yourself in an attempt to understand the many social aspects underlying the numbers.

URL for access to Internet Projects Page: www.aw.com/weiss

Sex and GPA

Recall from Chapter 1 (page 34) that the Focus database contains information on 500 randomly selected Arizona State University sophomores. Three of the variables in the Focus database are sex, high school GPA, and cumulative GPA.

Use the technology of your choice to perform the following two hypothesis tests using the chi-square independence test. Use the coding scheme 1, 2, 3, and 4, respectively, for grade point averages less than 1, at least 1 but less than 2, at least 2 but less than 3, and at least 3.

a. At the 5% significance level, do the data provide sufficient evidence to conclude that sex and high school GPA are statistically dependent for ASU sophomores?
b. Repeat part (a) for sex and cumulative GPA.

case study discussion

Road Rage

At the beginning of this chapter, we discussed the report *Controlling Road Rage: A Literature Review and Pilot Study,* prepared for the AAA Foundation for Traffic Safety by Daniel B. Rathbone, Ph.D., and Jorg C. Huckabee, MSCE. The authors examined the results of a literature review and pilot study on how to prevent aggressive driving and road rage.

One aspect of the study was to investigate road rage as a function of the day of the week. The table on page 537 indicates the day of the week on which road rage occurred for a random sample of 69 road-rage incidents. Use those data to decide, at the 5% significance level, whether road-rage incidents are more likely to occur on some days than on others.

Internet Resources: Visit the Weiss Web site www.aw.com/weiss for additional discussion, exercises, and resources related to this case study.

Biography

Karl Pearson: The Founding Developer of Chi-Square Tests

KARL PEARSON was born on March 27, 1857, in London, the second son of William Pearson, a prominent lawyer, and his wife, Fanny Smith. Karl Pearson's early education took place at home. At the age of 9, he was sent to University College School in London, where he remained for the next 7 years. Because of ill health, Pearson was then privately tutored for a year. He received a scholarship at King's College, Cambridge, in 1875. There he earned a B.A. (with honors) in mathematics in 1879 and an M.A. in law in 1882. He then studied physics and metaphysics in Heidelberg, Germany.

In addition to his expertise in mathematics, law, physics, and metaphysics, Pearson was competent in literature and knowledgeable about German history, folklore, and philosophy. He was also considered somewhat of a political radical because of his interest in the ideas of Karl Marx and the rights of women.

In 1884, Pearson was appointed Goldsmid professor of applied mathematics and mechanics at University College; from 1891–1894, he was also a lecturer in geometry at Gresham College, London. In 1911, he gave up the Goldsmid chair to become the first Galton professor of Eugenics at University College. Pearson was elected to the Royal Society—a prestigious association of scientists—in 1896 and was awarded the society's Darwin Medal in 1898.

Pearson really began his pioneering work in statistics in 1893, mainly through an association with Walter Weldon (a zoology professor at University College), Francis Edgeworth (a professor of logic at University College), and Sir Francis Galton (see the Chapter 14 Biography). An analysis of published data on roulette wheels at Monte Carlo led to Pearson's discovery of the chi-square goodness-of-fit test. He also coined the term *standard deviations,* introduced his amazingly diverse skew curves, and developed the most widely used measure of correlation, the correlation coefficient.

Pearson, Weldon, and Galton cofounded the statistical journal *Biometrika,* of which Pearson was editor (1901–1936) and a major contributor. Pearson retired from University College in 1933. He died in London on April 27, 1936.

chapter 13

Analysis of Variance (ANOVA)

CHAPTER OUTLINE

13.1 The F-Distribution

13.2 One-Way ANOVA: The Logic

13.3 One-Way ANOVA: The Procedure

GENERAL OBJECTIVES In Chapter 10, you studied inferential methods for comparing the means of two populations. Now you will study **analysis of variance,** or **ANOVA,** which provides methods for comparing the means of more than two populations. For instance, you could use ANOVA to compare the mean energy consumption by households among the four U.S. regions. Just as there are several different procedures for comparing two population means, there are several different ANOVA procedures.

In Section 13.1, to prepare for the study of ANOVA, we consider the F-distribution. Then we introduce one-way analysis of variance, the simplest type of ANOVA, and examine the logic behind it in Section 13.2. We discuss the one-way ANOVA procedure in Section 13.3.

case study

HEAVY DRINKING AMONG COLLEGE STUDENTS

Professor Kate Carey of Syracuse University surveyed 78 college students, all of whom were regular drinkers of alcohol. Her purpose was twofold—to identify interpersonal and intrapersonal situations associated with excessive drinking among college students and to detect situations that differentiate heavy drinkers from light and moderate drinkers. She published her findings in the paper "Situational Determinants of Heavy Drinking Among College Students" (*Journal of Counseling Psychology*, 1993, Vol. 40, pp. 217–220).

To assess the frequency of excessive drinking in interpersonal and intrapersonal situations, Carey utilized the short form of the Inventory of Drinking Situations (IDS). The following table gives the sample size, sample mean, and sample standard deviation of IDS scores for each drinking category and situational context.

IDS subscale	Light drinkers ($n_1 = 16$)		Moderate drinkers ($n_2 = 47$)		Heavy drinkers ($n_3 = 15$)	
	$\bar{x}_1$	s_1	$\bar{x}_2$	s_2	$\bar{x}_3$	s_3
Interpersonal situations						
Conflict with others	1.23	0.27	1.53	0.49	1.79	0.49
Social pressure to drink	2.64	0.80	2.91	0.55	3.51	0.51
Pleasant times with others	2.21	0.67	2.53	0.51	3.03	0.38
Intrapersonal situations						
Unpleasant emotions	1.22	0.35	1.61	0.69	1.68	0.46
Physical discomfort	1.03	0.08	1.19	0.29	1.40	0.32
Pleasant emotions	2.09	0.73	2.61	0.58	3.03	0.30
Testing personal control	1.52	0.74	1.56	0.56	1.53	0.48
Urges and temptations	1.80	0.56	1.96	0.51	2.33	0.58

At the end of this chapter, you will analyze these data to decide, for each IDS category, whether a difference exists in mean IDS scores among the three drinker categories.

13.1 THE F-DISTRIBUTION

Analysis-of-variance procedures rely on a distribution called the *F-distribution*, named in honor of Sir Ronald Fisher. See the Biography at the end of this chapter for more information about Fisher.

A variable is said to have an **F-distribution** if its distribution has the shape of a special type of right-skewed curve, called an **F-curve**. There are infinitely many F-distributions, and we identify an F-distribution (and F-curve) by stating its number of degrees of freedom, just as we did for t-distributions and chi-square distributions.

But an F-distribution has two numbers of degrees of freedom instead of one. Figure 13.1 depicts two different F-curves; one has df = (10, 2), and the other has df = (9, 50).

FIGURE 13.1
Two different F-curves

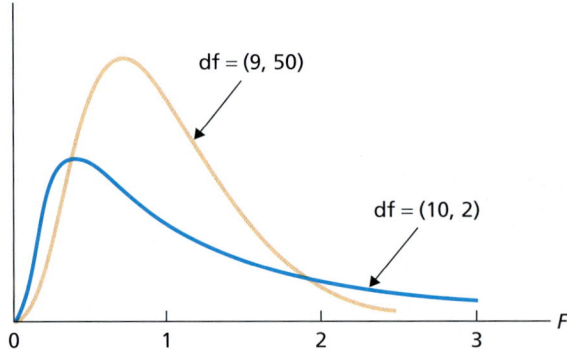

The first number of degrees of freedom for an F-curve is called the **degrees of freedom for the numerator,** and the second is called the **degrees of freedom for the denominator.** (The reason for this terminology will become clear in Section 13.2.) Thus, for the F-curve in Fig. 13.1 with df = (10, 2), we have

$$df = (10, 2)$$

Degrees of freedom for the numerator ↗   ↖ Degrees of freedom for the denominator

Some basic properties of F-curves are presented in Key Fact 13.1.

Key Fact 13.1 Basic Properties of F-Curves

Property 1: The total area under an F-curve equals 1.

Property 2: An F-curve starts at 0 on the horizontal axis and extends indefinitely to the right, approaching, but never touching, the horizontal axis as it does so.

Property 3: An F-curve is right skewed.

13.1 The F-Distribution

USING THE F-TABLE

Percentages (and probabilities) for a variable having an F-distribution equal areas under its associated F-curve. To perform an ANOVA test, we need to know how to find the F-value having a specified area to its right. The symbol F_α is used to denote the F-value having area α to its right.

Table VI in Appendix A provides F-values corresponding to several areas for various degrees of freedom. The degrees of freedom for the denominator (dfd) are displayed in the outside columns of the table, the values of α in the next columns, and the degrees of freedom for the numerator (dfn) along the top. In Example 13.1, we show how to use Table VI.

Example 13.1 Finding the F-Value Having a Specified Area to Its Right

For an F-curve with df = (4, 12), find $F_{0.05}$; that is, find the F-value having area 0.05 to its right, as shown in Fig. 13.2(a).

FIGURE 13.2
Finding the F-value having area 0.05 to its right

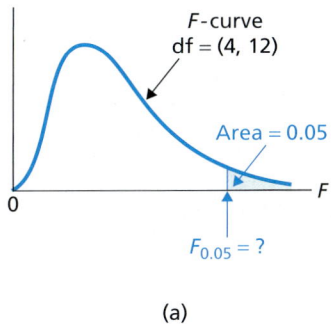
(a)

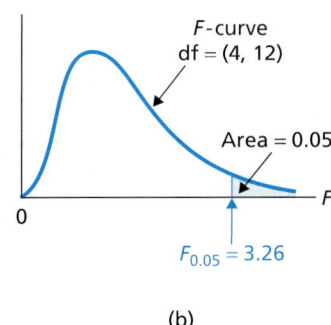
(b)

Solution To obtain the F-value, we use Table VI. In this case, $\alpha = 0.05$, the degrees of freedom for the numerator is 4, and the degrees of freedom for the denominator is 12. We first go down the dfd column to "12." Next, we go across the row for α labeled 0.05 to the column headed "4." The number in the body of the table there, 3.26, is the required F-value; in other words, for an F-curve with df = (4, 12), the F-value having area 0.05 to its right is 3.26: $F_{0.05} = 3.26$, as shown in Fig. 13.2(b).

Exercises 13.1

Statistical Concepts and Skills

13.1 How do you identify an F-distribution and its corresponding F-curve?

13.2 How many degrees of freedom does an F-curve have? What are those degrees of freedom called?

13.3 What symbol is used to denote the F-value having area 0.05 to its right? 0.025 to its right? α to its right?

13.4 Using the F_α-notation, identify the F-value having area 0.975 to its left.

13.5 An F-curve has df = (12, 7). What is the degrees of freedom for the
a. numerator?   b. denominator?

13.6 An F-curve has df = (8, 19). What is the degrees of freedom for the
a. denominator?   b. numerator?

In Exercises 13.7–13.10, use Table VI in Appendix A to find the required F-values. Illustrate your work with graphs similar to that shown in Fig. 13.2 on page 579.

13.7 An F-curve has df = (24, 30). In each case, find the F-value having the specified area to its right.
a. 0.05   b. 0.01   c. 0.025

13.8 An F-curve has df = (12, 5). In each case, find the F-value having the specified area to its right.
a. 0.01   b. 0.05   c. 0.005

13.9 For an F-curve with df = (20, 21), find
a. $F_{0.01}$.   b. $F_{0.05}$.   c. $F_{0.10}$.

13.10 For an F-curve with df = (6, 10), find
a. $F_{0.05}$.   b. $F_{0.01}$.   c. $F_{0.025}$.

Extending the Concepts and Skills

13.11 Refer to Table VI in Appendix A. Because of space restrictions, the numbers of degrees of freedom are not consecutive. For instance, the degrees of freedom for the numerator skips from 24 to 30. If you had only Table VI and you needed to find $F_{0.05}$ for df = (25, 20), how would you do it?

13.2 ONE-WAY ANOVA: THE LOGIC

In Chapter 10, you learned how to compare two populations means, that is, the means of a single variable for two different populations. You studied various methods for making such comparisons, one being the pooled *t*-procedure.

Analysis of variance (ANOVA) provides methods for comparing several population means, that is, the means of a single variable for several populations. In this section and Section 13.3, we present the simplest kind of ANOVA, **one-way analysis of variance**. This type of ANOVA is called *one-way* analysis of variance because it compares the means of a variable for populations that result from a classification by *one* other variable, called the **factor.** The possible values of the factor are referred to as the **levels** of the factor.

For example, suppose that you want to compare the mean energy consumption by households among the four regions of the United States. The variable under consideration is "energy consumption" and there are four populations—households in the Northeast, Midwest, South, and West. The four populations result from classifying households in the United States by the factor "region," whose levels are Northeast, Midwest, South, and West.

One-way analysis of variance is the generalization to more than two populations of the pooled *t*-procedure. As in the pooled *t*-procedure, we make the assumptions listed in Key Fact 13.2.

> **Key Fact 13.2** **Assumptions for One-Way ANOVA**
>
> 1. *Independent samples:* The samples taken from the populations under consideration are independent of one another.
> 2. *Normal populations:* For each population, the variable under consideration is normally distributed.
> 3. *Equal standard deviations:* The standard deviations of the variable under consideration are the same for all the populations.

One-way ANOVA has the same robustness properties as those of the pooled *t*-procedure. The independent samples assumption (Assumption 1) is essential; the samples must be independent or the procedure does not apply. One-way ANOVA is robust to moderate violations of the normality assumption (Assumption 2). It is also reasonably robust to moderate violations of the equal standard deviations assumption (Assumption 3) if the sample sizes are roughly equal.

Generally, normal probability plots are effective in detecting gross violations of the normality assumption. The equal standard deviations assumption is usually more difficult to check. As a rule of thumb, we consider that assumption satisfied if *the ratio of the largest to the smallest sample standard deviation is less than 2*. For convenience, we call this rule of thumb the **rule of 2**.

Additionally, we can assess the normality and equal standard deviations assumptions by performing a residual analysis, in a way similar to what we did in regression. (See Section 14.1 for a discussion of the analysis of residuals.)

In ANOVA, the **residual** of an observation is the difference between the observation and the mean of the sample containing it. If the normality and equal standard deviations assumptions are met, a normal probability plot of (all) the residuals should be roughly linear. Moreover, a plot of the residuals against the sample means should fall roughly in a horizontal band centered on and symmetric about the horizontal axis.

THE LOGIC BEHIND ONE-WAY ANOVA

The reason for the word *variance* in *analysis of variance* is that the procedure for comparing the means analyzes the variation in the sample data. To examine how this procedure works, let's suppose that independent random samples are taken from two populations—say, Populations 1 and 2—having means μ_1 and μ_2. Further, let's suppose that the means of the two samples are $\bar{x}_1 = 20$ and $\bar{x}_2 = 25$. Can we reasonably conclude from these statistics that $\mu_1 \neq \mu_2$, that is, that the population means are different? To answer this question, we must consider the variation within the samples.

Suppose, for instance, that the sample data are as displayed in Table 13.1 and depicted in Fig. 13.3.

TABLE 13.1
Sample data from Populations 1 and 2

Sample from Population 1	21	37	11	20	8	23
Sample from Population 2	24	31	29	40	9	17

FIGURE 13.3
Dotplots for sample data in Table 13.1

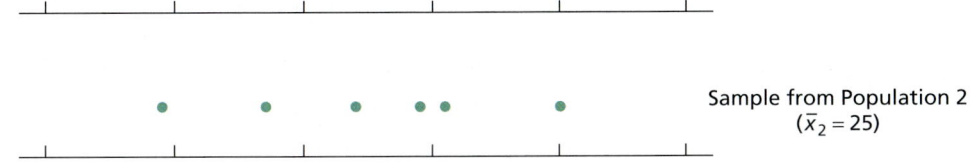

What Does it Mean?

Intuitively speaking, because the variation between the sample means is not large relative to the variation within the samples, we cannot conclude that $\mu_1 \neq \mu_2$.

For these two samples, $\bar{x}_1 = 20$ and $\bar{x}_2 = 25$. But we cannot infer that $\mu_1 \neq \mu_2$ because it is not clear whether the difference between the sample means is due to a difference between the population means or to the variation within the populations.

However, suppose that the sample data are as displayed in Table 13.2 and depicted in Fig. 13.4.

TABLE 13.2
Sample data from Populations 1 and 2

Sample from Population 1	21	21	20	18	20	20
Sample from Population 2	25	28	25	24	24	24

FIGURE 13.4
Dotplots for sample data in Table 13.2

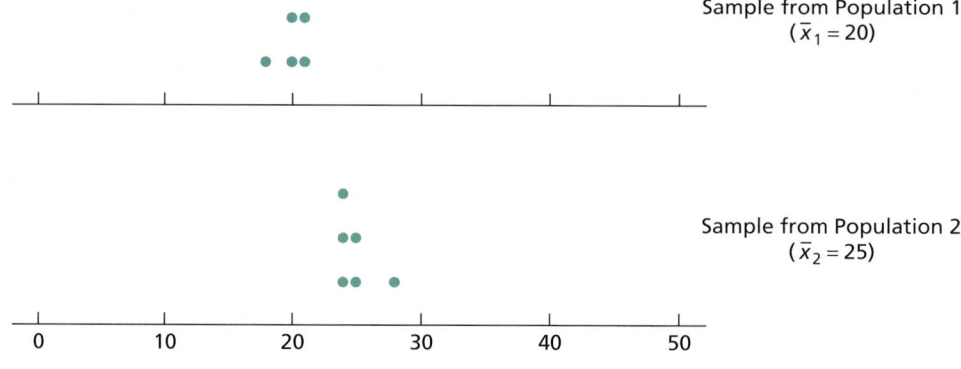

What Does it Mean?

Intuitively speaking, because the variation between the sample means is large relative to the variation within the samples, we can conclude that $\mu_1 \neq \mu_2$.

Again, for these two samples, $\bar{x}_1 = 20$ and $\bar{x}_2 = 25$. But this time, we *can* infer that $\mu_1 \neq \mu_2$ because it seems clear that the difference between the sample means is due to a difference between the population means, not to the variation within the populations.

The preceding two illustrations reveal the basic idea for performing a one-way analysis of variance to compare the means of several populations: (1) take independent random samples from the populations; (2) compute the sample means; and (3) if the variation among the sample means is large relative to the variation within the samples, conclude that the means of the populations are not all equal.

To make this process precise, we need quantitative measures of the variation among the sample means and the variation within the samples. We also need an objective method for deciding whether the variation among the sample means is large relative to the variation within the samples. We address these two issues in Example 13.2.

Example 13.2 Introducing One-Way ANOVA

Energy Consumption The U.S. Energy Information Administration gathers data on residential energy consumption and expenditures and publishes its findings in *Residential Energy Consumption Survey: Consumption and Expenditures*. Suppose that we want to decide whether a difference exists in mean annual energy consumption by households among the four U.S. regions. Let μ_1, μ_2, μ_3, and μ_4 denote last year's mean energy consumptions by households in the Northeast, Midwest, South, and West, respectively. Then the hypotheses to be tested are

$H_0: \mu_1 = \mu_2 = \mu_3 = \mu_4$ (mean energy consumptions are all equal)

H_a: Not all the means are equal.

The basic strategy for carrying out this hypothesis test follows the three steps just mentioned.

1. Independently and randomly take samples of households in the four U.S. regions.
2. Compute last year's mean energy consumptions, $\bar{x}_1, \bar{x}_2, \bar{x}_3$, and $\bar{x}_4$, of the four samples.
3. Reject the null hypothesis if the variation among the sample means is large relative to the variation within the samples; otherwise, do not reject the null hypothesis.

This process is illustrated in Fig. 13.5.

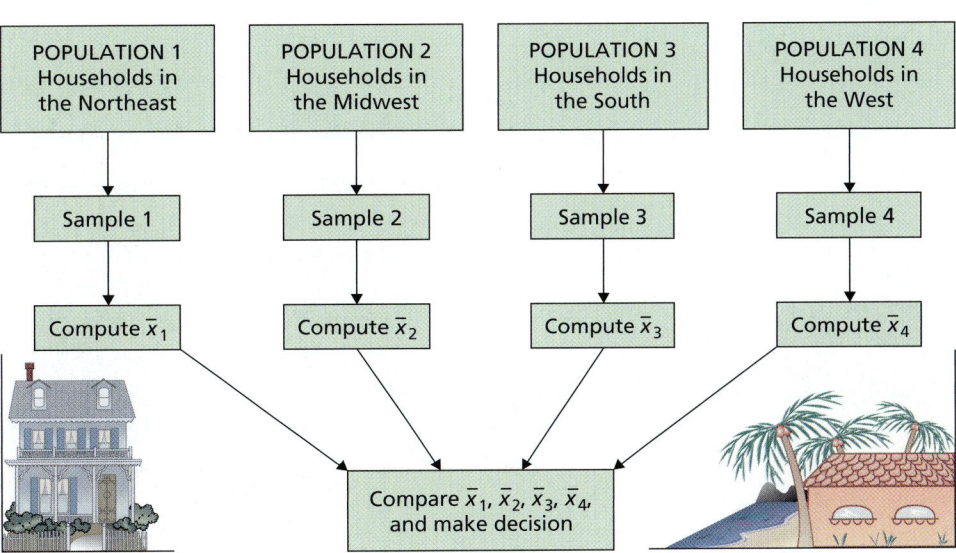

FIGURE 13.5
Process for comparing four population means

In Steps 1 and 2, we obtain the sample data and compute the sample means. Suppose that the results of those steps are as shown in Table 13.3, where the data are displayed to the nearest 10 million BTU.

CHAPTER 13 Analysis of Variance (ANOVA)

TABLE 13.3
Samples and their means of last year's energy consumptions for households in the four U.S. regions

Northeast	Midwest	South	West
15	17	11	10
10	12	7	12
13	18	9	8
14	13	13	7
13	15		9
	12		
13.0	14.5	10.0	9.2	← Means

In Step 3, we compare the variation among the four sample means, shown at the bottom of Table 13.3, to the variation within the samples. Let's first consider the variation among the sample means.

In hypothesis tests for two population means, we measure the variation between the two sample means by calculating their difference, $\bar{x}_1 - \bar{x}_2$. When more than two populations are involved, as in this problem, we cannot measure the variation among the sample means simply by taking a difference. However, we can measure that variation by computing the standard deviation or variance of the sample means or, for that matter, by computing any descriptive statistic that measures variation.

In one-way ANOVA, we measure the variation among the sample means by a weighted average of their squared deviations about the mean, $\bar{x}$, of all the sample data. That measure of variation is called the **treatment mean square, MSTR,** and is defined as

$$MSTR = \frac{SSTR}{k-1},$$

where k denotes the number of populations being sampled and

$$SSTR = n_1(\bar{x}_1 - \bar{x})^2 + n_2(\bar{x}_2 - \bar{x})^2 + \cdots + n_k(\bar{x}_k - \bar{x})^2.$$

The quantity **SSTR** is called the **treatment sum of squares.**

MSTR is similar to the sample variance of the sample means. In fact, if all the sample sizes are identical, *MSTR* equals that common sample size times the sample variance of the sample means.

Let's determine *MSTR* for the sample data in Table 13.3. We have $k = 4$, $n_1 = 5, n_2 = 6, n_3 = 4, n_4 = 5, \bar{x}_1 = 13.0, \bar{x}_2 = 14.5, \bar{x}_3 = 10.0$, and $\bar{x}_4 = 9.2$. To obtain the overall mean, $\bar{x}$, we need to divide the sum of all the observations in Table 13.3 by the total number of observations:

$$\bar{x} = \frac{\Sigma x}{n} = \frac{15 + 10 + 13 + \cdots + 7 + 9}{20} = \frac{238}{20} = 11.9.$$

Therefore

$$SSTR = n_1(\bar{x}_1 - \bar{x})^2 + n_2(\bar{x}_2 - \bar{x})^2 + n_3(\bar{x}_3 - \bar{x})^2 + n_4(\bar{x}_4 - \bar{x})^2$$
$$= 5(13.0 - 11.9)^2 + 6(14.5 - 11.9)^2 + 4(10.0 - 11.9)^2 + 5(9.2 - 11.9)^2$$
$$= 97.5.$$

> **What Does it Mean?**
>
> *MSTR* measures the variation among the sample means.

13.2 One-Way ANOVA: The Logic

Hence

$$MSTR = \frac{SSTR}{k-1} = \frac{97.5}{4-1} = 32.5,$$

which is the measure of variation among the four sample means shown at the bottom of Table 13.3.

Next, we must obtain a measure of variation within the samples. This measure is the pooled estimate of the common population variance, σ^2. It is called the **error mean square, MSE,** and is defined as

$$MSE = \frac{SSE}{n-k},$$

where n denotes the total number of observations and

$$SSE = (n_1 - 1)s_1^2 + (n_2 - 1)s_2^2 + \cdots + (n_k - 1)s_k^2.$$

The quantity *SSE* is called the **error sum of squares.**[1, 2]

For the sample data in Table 13.3, we have $k = 4$, $n_1 = 5$, $n_2 = 6$, $n_3 = 4$, $n_4 = 5$, and $n = 20$. Computing the variance of each sample gives $s_1^2 = 3.5$, $s_2^2 = 6.7$, $s_3^2 = 6.\overline{6}$, and $s_4^2 = 3.7$. Consequently,

$$SSE = (n_1 - 1)s_1^2 + (n_2 - 1)s_2^2 + (n_3 - 1)s_3^2 + (n_4 - 1)s_4^2$$
$$= (5-1) \cdot 3.5 + (6-1) \cdot 6.7 + (4-1) \cdot 6.\overline{6} + (5-1) \cdot 3.7 = 82.3.$$

Hence

$$MSE = \frac{SSE}{n-k} = \frac{82.3}{20-4} = 5.144,$$

which is the measure of variation within the samples.

Finally, we must compare the variation among the sample means, *MSTR*, to the variation within the samples, *MSE*. To do so, we employ the statistic $F = MSTR/MSE$, which we refer to as the **F-statistic.** Large values of F indicate that the variation among the sample means is large relative to the variation within the samples and hence that the null hypothesis of equal population means should be rejected.

For the energy-consumption data, $MSTR = 32.5$ and $MSE = 5.144$. Thus the value of the F-statistic is

$$F = \frac{MSTR}{MSE} = \frac{32.5}{5.144} = 6.32.$$

Is this value of F large enough to conclude that the null hypothesis of equal population means is false? To answer that question, we need to know the distribution of the F-statistic. We discuss that distribution in Section 13.3 and then return to complete the hypothesis test. ◆

> **What Does it Mean?**
> MSE measures the variation within the samples.

> **What Does it Mean?**
> The F-statistic is the ratio of the variation among the sample means to the variation within the samples.

---

[1] The terms **treatment** and **error** arose from the fact that many ANOVA techniques were first developed to analyze agricultural experiments. In any case, the treatments refer to the different populations and the errors pertain to the variation within the populations.

[2] For two populations (i.e., $k = 2$), *MSE* is the pooled variance, s_p^2, defined in Section 10.2 on page 440.

Exercises 13.2

Statistical Concepts and Skills

13.12 State the three assumptions required for one-way ANOVA. How crucial are these assumptions?

13.13 One-way ANOVA is a procedure for comparing the means of several populations. It is the generalization of what procedure for comparing the means of two populations?

13.14 If we define $s = \sqrt{MSE}$, of which parameter is s an estimate?

13.15 Explain the reason for the word *variance* in the phrase *analysis of variance*.

13.16 The null and alternative hypotheses for a one-way ANOVA test are

$$H_0: \mu_1 = \mu_2 = \cdots = \mu_k$$
$$H_a: \text{Not all means are equal.}$$

Suppose that, in reality, the null hypothesis is false. Does that mean that no two of the populations have the same mean? If not, what does it mean?

13.17 In one-way ANOVA, identify the statistic used
a. as a measure of variation among the sample means.
b. as a measure of variation within the samples.
c. to compare the variation among the sample means to the variation within the samples.

13.18 Explain the logic behind one-way ANOVA.

13.19 What does the term *one-way* signify in the phrase *one-way ANOVA*?

13.20 Figure 13.6 shows side-by-side boxplots of independent samples from three normally distributed populations having equal standard deviations. Based on these boxplots, would you be inclined to reject the null hypothesis of equal population means? Explain your answer.

13.21 Figure 13.7 shows side-by-side boxplots of independent samples from three normally distributed populations having equal standard deviations. Based on these boxplots, would you be inclined to reject the null hypothesis of equal population means? Explain your answer.

Extending the Concepts and Skills

13.22 Show that, for two populations, $MSE = s_p^2$, where s_p^2 is the pooled variance defined in Section 10.2 on page 440. Conclude that $\sqrt{MSE}$ is the pooled sample standard deviation, s_p.

13.23 Suppose that the variable under consideration is normally distributed on each of two populations and that the population standard deviations are equal. Further suppose that you want to perform a hypothesis test to decide whether the populations have different means, that is, whether $\mu_1 \neq \mu_2$. If independent samples are used, identify two hypothesis testing procedures that you can use to carry out the hypothesis test.

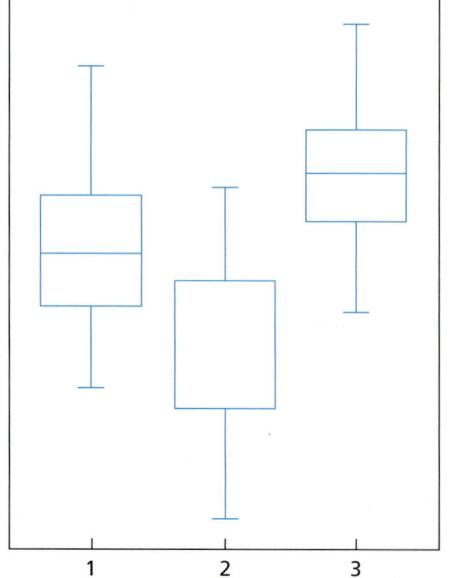

FIGURE 13.6
Side-by-side boxplots for Exercise 13.20

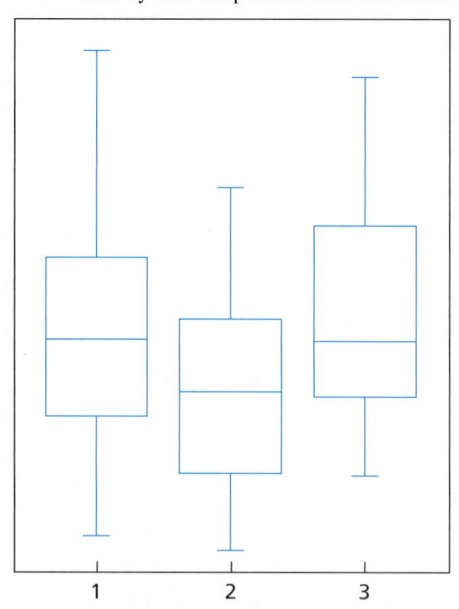

FIGURE 13.7
Side-by-side boxplots for Exercise 13.21

13.3 ONE-WAY ANOVA: THE PROCEDURE

In this section, we present a step-by-step procedure for performing a one-way ANOVA to compare the means of several populations. To begin, we need to identify the distribution of the variable $F = MSTR/MSE$, introduced at the end of Section 13.2. We do that in Key Fact 13.3.

Key Fact 13.3 **Distribution of the F-Statistic for One-Way ANOVA**

Suppose that the variable under consideration is normally distributed on each of k populations and that the population standard deviations are equal. Then, for independent samples from the k populations, the variable

$$F = \frac{MSTR}{MSE}$$

has the F-distribution with df $= (k-1, n-k)$ if the null hypothesis of equal population means is true. Here, n denotes the total number of observations.

We have now covered all the elements required to formulate a procedure for performing a one-way analysis of variance. Before presenting the procedure, however, we need to consider two additional concepts.

ONE-WAY ANOVA IDENTITY

First, we define another sum of squares—one that provides a measure of total variation among all the sample data. It is called the **total sum of squares, SST,** and is defined by

$$SST = \Sigma(x - \bar{x})^2,$$

where the sum extends over all n observations. If we divide SST by $n-1$, we get the sample variance of all the observations. So SST really is a measure of total variation.

For the energy consumption data in Table 13.3 on page 584, $\bar{x} = 11.9$, and therefore

$$SST = \Sigma(x - \bar{x})^2 = (15 - 11.9)^2 + (10 - 11.9)^2 + \cdots + (9 - 11.9)^2$$
$$= 9.61 + 3.61 + \cdots + 8.41 = 179.8.$$

In Section 13.2, we found that, for the energy consumption data, $SSTR = 97.5$ and $SSE = 82.3$. Note that, because $179.8 = 97.5 + 82.3$, $SST = SSTR + SSE$. This equation is always true and is called the **one-way ANOVA identity,** which we emphasize as Key Fact 13.4.

Key Fact 13.4 **One-Way ANOVA Identity**

The total sum of squares equals the treatment sum of squares plus the error sum of squares; that is, $SST = SSTR + SSE$.

The one-way ANOVA identity shows that we can partition the total variation among all the sample data into a component representing variation among the sample means and a component representing variation within the samples. We illustrate this partitioning in Fig. 13.8.

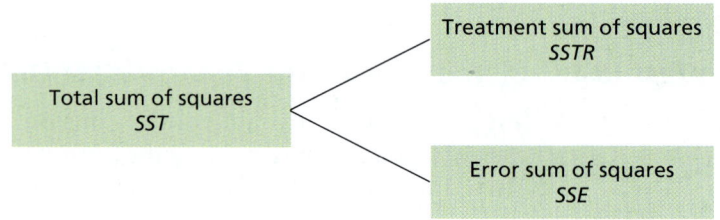

FIGURE 13.8
Partitioning of the total sum of squares into the treatment sum of squares and the error sum of squares

ONE-WAY ANOVA TABLES

One-way ANOVA tables are useful for organizing and summarizing the quantities required for performing a one-way analysis of variance. The general format of a one-way ANOVA table is as shown in Table 13.4.

TABLE 13.4 ANOVA table format for a one-way analysis of variance

Source	df	SS	MS = SS/df	F-statistic
Treatment	$k-1$	SSTR	$MSTR = \dfrac{SSTR}{k-1}$	$F = \dfrac{MSTR}{MSE}$
Error	$n-k$	SSE	$MSE = \dfrac{SSE}{n-k}$	
Total	$n-1$	SST		

For the energy consumption data in Table 13.3, we have already computed all quantities appearing in the one-way ANOVA table. Table 13.5 displays the one-way ANOVA table for those data.

TABLE 13.5 One-way ANOVA table for the energy consumption data

Source	df	SS	MS = SS/df	F-statistic
Treatment	3	97.5	32.500	6.32
Error	16	82.3	5.144	
Total	19	179.8		

PERFORMING A ONE-WAY ANOVA

To perform a one-way ANOVA, we need to obtain the three sums of squares, *SST*, *SSTR*, and *SSE*. We can do so by using the defining formulas introduced earlier. Generally, however, when calculating by hand from the raw data, computing formulas are more accurate and easier to use. Both the defining formulas and their computing equivalents are presented in Formula 13.1.

FORMULA 13.1 **Sums of Squares in One-Way ANOVA**

For a one-way ANOVA of k population means, the defining and computing formulas for the three sums of squares are as follows.

Sum of square	Defining formula	Computing formula
Total, SST	$\Sigma(x - \bar{x})^2$	$\Sigma x^2 - (\Sigma x)^2/n$
Treatment, SSTR	$\Sigma n_j(\bar{x}_j - \bar{x})^2$	$\Sigma(T_j^2/n_j) - (\Sigma x)^2/n$
Error, SSE	$\Sigma(n_j - 1)s_j^2$	$SST - SSTR$

In this table, we used the notation

n = total number of observations
$\bar{x}$ = mean of all n observations;

and, for $j = 1, 2, \ldots, k$,

n_j = size of sample from Population j
$\bar{x}_j$ = mean of sample from Population j
s_j^2 = variance of sample from Population j
T_j = sum of sample data from Population j.

Keep the following facts in mind when you use Formula 13.1.

- Only two of the three sums of squares need ever be calculated; the remaining one can always be determined from the other two by using the one-way ANOVA identity, Key Fact 13.4 on page 587.
- Summations involving no subscripted variables are over all n observations; those involving subscripts are over the k populations.
- When using the computing formulas, the most efficient formula for calculating the sum of all n observations is $\Sigma x = T_1 + T_2 + \cdots + T_k$.

We now present a step-by-step method—Procedures 13.1A and B—that can be used to perform a **one-way ANOVA test.** Note that the hypothesis test is always right-tailed because the null hypothesis is rejected only when the test statistic, F, is too large. We apply the procedure in Example 13.3.

Procedure 13.1A — The One-Way ANOVA Test for k Population Means (Critical-Value Approach)

Assumptions
1. Independent samples
2. Normal populations
3. Equal population standard deviations

Step 1 The null and alternative hypotheses are

$$H_0: \mu_1 = \mu_2 = \cdots = \mu_k$$
$$H_a: \text{Not all the means are equal.}$$

Step 2 Decide on the significance level, α.

Step 3 Obtain the three sums of squares, SST, SSTR, and SSE.

Step 4 Construct a one-way ANOVA table to obtain the value of the F-statistic.

Source	df	SS	MS = SS/df	F-statistic
Treatment	$k-1$	SSTR	$MSTR = \dfrac{SSTR}{k-1}$	$F = \dfrac{MSTR}{MSE}$
Error	$n-k$	SSE	$MSE = \dfrac{SSE}{n-k}$	
Total	$n-1$	SST		

Step 5 The critical value is F_α, with df = $(k-1, n-k)$, where n is the total number of observations. Use Table VI to find the critical value.

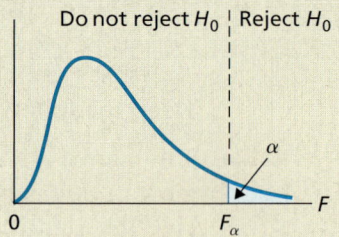

Step 6 If the value of the F-statistic falls in the rejection region, reject H_0; otherwise, do not reject H_0.

Step 7 Interpret the results of the hypothesis test.

Procedure 13.1B — The One-Way ANOVA Test for k Population Means (P-Value Approach)

Assumptions
1. Independent samples
2. Normal populations
3. Equal population standard deviations

Step 1 The null and alternative hypotheses are

$$H_0: \mu_1 = \mu_2 = \cdots = \mu_k$$

$$H_a: \text{Not all the means are equal.}$$

Step 2 Decide on the significance level, α.

Step 3 Obtain the three sums of squares, SST, SSTR, and SSE.

Step 4 Construct a one-way ANOVA table to obtain the value of the F-statistic; denote that value F_0.

Source	df	SS	MS = SS/df	F-statistic
Treatment	$k-1$	SSTR	$MSTR = \dfrac{SSTR}{k-1}$	$F = \dfrac{MSTR}{MSE}$
Error	$n-k$	SSE	$MSE = \dfrac{SSE}{n-k}$	
Total	$n-1$	SST		

Step 5 The F-statistic has df $= (k-1, n-k)$, where n is the total number of observations. Use Table VI to estimate the P-value or obtain it exactly by using technology.

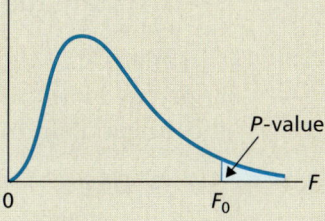

Step 6 If $P \leq \alpha$, reject H_0; otherwise, do not reject H_0.

Step 7 Interpret the results of the hypothesis test.

Example 13.3 The One-Way ANOVA Test

Energy Consumption Recall that independent random samples of households in the four U.S. regions yielded the data on last year's energy consumptions shown in Table 13.6. At the 5% significance level, do the data provide sufficient evidence to conclude that a difference exists in last year's mean energy consumption by households among the four U.S. regions?

TABLE 13.6
Last year's energy consumptions for samples of households in the four U.S. regions

Northeast	Midwest	South	West
15	17	11	10
10	12	7	12
13	18	9	8
14	13	13	7
13	15		9
	12		

Solution First, we check the three conditions required for performing a one-way ANOVA. Because the samples are independent, Assumption 1 is satisfied. Normal probability plots (not shown) of the four samples in Table 13.6 reveal no outliers and are roughly linear, indicating no gross violations of the normality assumption; thus we can consider Assumption 2 to be satisfied.

The sample standard deviations of the four samples in Table 13.6 are 1.87, 2.59, 2.58, and 1.92, respectively. Because the ratio of the largest to the smallest standard deviation is $2.59/1.87 = 1.39$, which is less than 2, we can, in light of the rule of 2, consider Assumption 3 to be satisfied. A residual analysis further indicates that we can reasonably consider Assumptions 2 and 3 to be satisfied.

Therefore we conclude that the one-way ANOVA procedure can be used to carry out the hypothesis test. We proceed as follows.

Step 1 State the null and alternative hypotheses.

Let μ_1, μ_2, μ_3, and μ_4 denote last year's mean energy consumptions for households in the Northeast, Midwest, South, and West, respectively. Then the null and alternative hypotheses are

H_0: $\mu_1 = \mu_2 = \mu_3 = \mu_4$ (mean energy consumptions are equal)

H_a: Not all the means are equal.

Step 2 Decide on the significance level, α.

We are to perform the hypothesis test at the 5% significance level; consequently, $\alpha = 0.05$.

Step 3 Obtain the three sums of squares, SST, SSTR, and SSE.

Although we obtained these sums earlier by using the defining formulas, we determine them again to illustrate use of the computing formulas. Referring to Formula 13.1 on page 589 and Table 13.6, we find that

$$k = 4$$

$$n_1 = 5 \quad n_2 = 6 \quad n_3 = 4 \quad n_4 = 5$$
$$T_1 = 65 \quad T_2 = 87 \quad T_3 = 40 \quad T_4 = 46$$

and

$$n = 5 + 6 + 4 + 5 = 20$$
$$\Sigma x = 65 + 87 + 40 + 46 = 238.$$

Summing the squares of all the data in Table 13.6 yields

$$\Sigma x^2 = (15)^2 + (10)^2 + (13)^2 + \cdots + 7^2 + 9^2 = 3012.$$

Consequently,

$$SST = \Sigma x^2 - (\Sigma x)^2/n = 3012 - (238)^2/20 = 3012 - 2832.2 = 179.8,$$

$$SSTR = \Sigma(T_j^2/n_j) - (\Sigma x)^2/n$$
$$= (65)^2/5 + (87)^2/6 + (40)^2/4 + (46)^2/5 - (238)^2/20$$
$$= 2929.7 - 2832.2 = 97.5,$$

and

$$SSE = SST - SSTR = 179.8 - 97.5 = 82.3.$$

Step 4 Construct a one-way ANOVA table to obtain the value of the F-statistic.

Table 13.5 on page 588 is the one-way ANOVA table for the energy consumption data. We repeat that table here. It reveals that $F = 6.32$.

Source	df	SS	MS = SS/df	F-statistic
Treatment	3	97.5	32.500	6.32
Error	16	82.3	5.144	
Total	19	179.8		

Critical-Value Approach

Step 5 The critical value is F_α, with df = $(k-1, n-k)$, where n is the total number of observations. Use Table VI to find the critical value.

From Step 2, $\alpha = 0.05$. Also, Table 13.6 shows that four populations are under consideration, or $k = 4$, and that the number of observations totals 20, or $n = 20$. Hence df = $(k-1, n-k) = (4-1, 20-4) = (3, 16)$. From Table VI, the critical value is $F_{0.05} = 3.24$, as shown in Fig. 13.9A.

FIGURE 13.9A

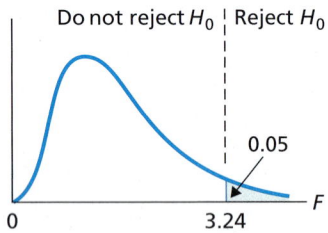

Step 6 If the value of the F-statistic falls in the rejection region, reject H_0; otherwise, do not reject H_0.

From Step 4, the value of the F-statistic is $F = 6.32$, which, as Fig. 13.9A shows, falls in the rejection region. Thus we reject H_0. The test results are statistically significant at the 5% level.

P-Value Approach

Step 5 The F-statistic has df = $(k-1, n-k)$, where n is the total number of observations. Use Table VI to estimate the P-value or obtain it exactly by using technology.

From Step 4, the value of the F-statistic is $F = 6.32$. Because the test is right-tailed, the P-value is the probability of observing a value of F of 6.32 or greater if the null hypothesis is true. That probability equals the shaded area in Fig. 13.9B.

FIGURE 13.9B

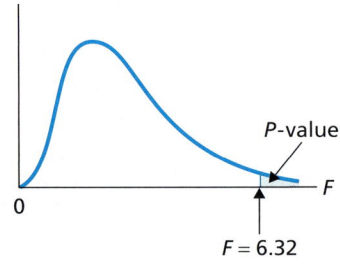

From Table 13.6, four populations are under consideration, or $k = 4$, and the number of observations totals 20, or $n = 20$. Hence df = $(k-1, n-k) = (4-1, 20-4) = (3, 16)$. Referring to Fig. 13.9B and to Table VI with df = $(3, 16)$, we find $P < 0.005$. (Using technology, we obtain $P = 0.00495$.)

Step 6 If $P \leq \alpha$, reject H_0; otherwise, do not reject H_0.

From Step 5, $P < 0.005$. Because the P-value is less than the specified significance level of 0.05, we reject H_0. The test results are statistically significant at the 5% level and (see Table 9.10 on page 405) provide very strong evidence against the null hypothesis.

Step 7 Interpret the results of the hypothesis test.

 At the 5% significance level, the data provide sufficient evidence to conclude that a difference exists in last year's mean energy consumption by households among the four U.S. regions. Evidently, at least two of the regions have different mean energy consumptions.

MULTIPLE COMPARISONS

The results of the one-way ANOVA in Example 13.3 show that (at the 5% significance level) a difference exists in last year's mean energy consumption by households among the four U.S. regions. But the analysis does not tell us which means are different, which mean is largest, or, more generally, the relationship among the four means. Such questions are answered by using techniques called *multiple comparisons*.

Although we do not cover multiple comparisons in this book, many basic statistics texts discuss these techniques. See, for example, *Introductory Statistics*, 6th edition, by Neil A. Weiss (Boston: Addison-Wesley, 2002).

WHAT IF THE ASSUMPTIONS ARE NOT SATISFIED?

One-way ANOVA provides methods for comparing the means of several populations. As you know, the assumptions for using that procedure are (1) independent samples, (2) normal populations, and (3) equal population standard deviations. If one or more of these conditions are not satisfied, then the one-way ANOVA test should not be used.

Which test should be used depends on which conditions are violated and which hold. For example, if the samples are independent and the distributions (one for each population) of the variable under consideration have the same shape, then we can use a nonparametric method called the *Kruskal–Wallis test*, regardless of normality or sample size.

OTHER TYPES OF ANOVA

We can consider one-way ANOVA to be a method for comparing the means of populations classified according to one factor. Put another way, it is a method for analyzing the effect of one factor on the mean of the variable under consideration, called the **response variable.**

For instance, in Example 13.3, we compared last year's mean energy consumption by households among the four U.S. regions (Northeast, Midwest, South, and West). Here, the factor is "region" and the response variable is "energy consumption." One-way ANOVA permits us to analyze the effect of region on mean energy consumption.

Other ANOVA procedures provide methods for comparing the means of populations classified according to two or more factors. Put another way, these are methods for simultaneously analyzing the effect of two or more factors on the mean of a response variable.

For example, suppose that you want to consider the effect of "region" and "home type" (the two factors) on energy consumption (the response variable). Two-way ANOVA permits you to determine simultaneously whether region affects mean energy consumption, whether home type affects mean energy consumption, and whether region and home type interact in their effect on mean energy consumption (e.g., whether the effect of home type on mean energy consumption depends on region).

Two-way ANOVA and other ANOVA procedures, such as randomized block ANOVA, are treated in detail in the chapter *Design of Experiments and Analysis of Variance*, on the WeissStats CD accompanying this book and on the Weiss Web site, www.aw.com/weiss.

The Technology Center

Most statistical technologies have programs that automatically perform a one-way analysis of variance. In this subsection, we present output and (optional) step-by-step instructions to implement such programs.

Example 13.4 Using Technology to Conduct a One-Way ANOVA

Energy Consumption Table 13.6 on page 592 displays last year's energy consumptions for independent samples of households in the four U.S. regions. Use Minitab, Excel, or the TI-83 Plus to perform the hypothesis test in Example 13.3.

Solution Let μ_1, μ_2, μ_3, and μ_4 denote last year's mean energy consumptions for households in the Northeast, Midwest, South, and West, respectively. We want to perform the hypothesis test

H_0: $\mu_1 = \mu_2 = \mu_3 = \mu_4$ (mean energy consumptions are equal)

H_a: Not all the means are equal

at the 5% significance level.

Printout 13.1 shows the output obtained by applying the one-way ANOVA programs to the energy consumption data presented in Table 13.6.

The outputs in Printout 13.1 show that the P-value for the hypothesis test is 0.005 (to three decimal places). Because the P-value is less than the specified significance level of 0.05, we reject H_0. At the 5% significance level, the data provide sufficient evidence to conclude that last year's mean energy consumptions for households in the four U.S. regions are not all the same. See the technology manuals for further interpretation of Printout 13.1. ◆

Obtaining the Output (Optional)

Printout 13.1 provides output from Minitab, Excel, and the TI-83 Plus for a one-way ANOVA based on the samples of energy consumptions in Table 13.6. The following are detailed instructions for obtaining that output. For the TI-83 Plus, store the four samples in Table 13.6 in lists named NE, MW, SO, and WE, respectively.

For Minitab and Excel, first store all 20 energy consumptions from Table 13.6 in a column (Minitab) or range (Excel) named ENERGY. Then, in a column or range named REGION, store the regions corresponding to the energy consumptions in ENERGY. For instance, suppose that you store the sample data for the

PRINTOUT 13.1
One-way ANOVA procedure output for the energy consumption data

MINITAB

One-way ANOVA: ENERGY versus REGION

```
Analysis of Variance for ENERGY
Source      DF        SS        MS        F        P
REGION       3     97.50     32.50     6.32    0.005
Error       16     82.30      5.14
Total       19    179.80
                                    Individual 95% CIs For Mean
                                    Based on Pooled StDev
Level        N      Mean     StDev  -------+---------+---------+---------
Midwest      6    14.500     2.588                        (-----*------)
Northeas     5    13.000     1.871                  (------*-------)
South        4    10.000     2.582        (--------*-------)
West         5     9.200     1.924    (--------*------)
                                    -------+---------+---------+---------
Pooled StDev =    2.268              9.0      12.0      15.0
```

EXCEL

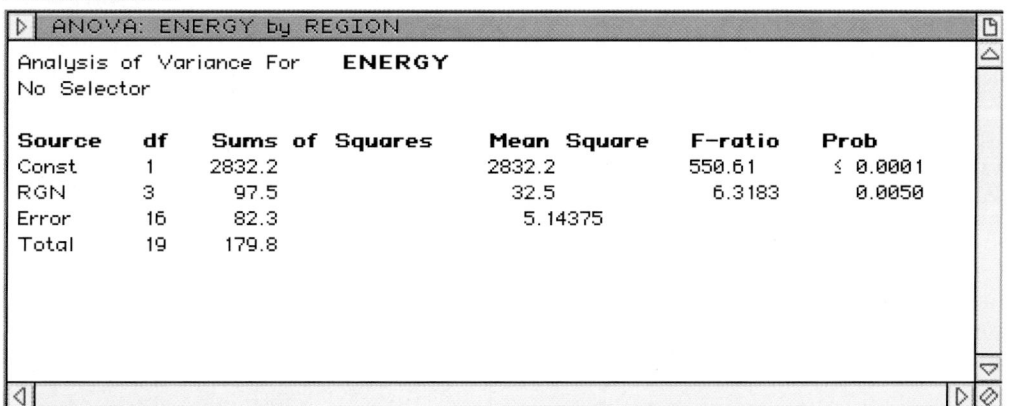

TI-83 PLUS

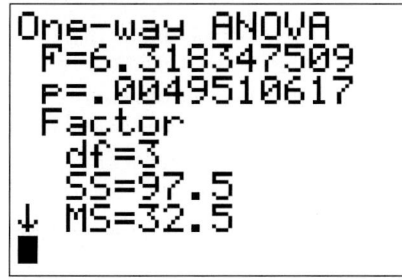

Northeast in the first five rows of ENERGY, that for the Midwest in the next six rows of ENERGY, and so on. Then you would store the word Northeast in the first five rows of REGION, the word Midwest in the next six rows of REGION, and so on.

Now, proceed as follows.

MINITAB	EXCEL	TI-83 PLUS
1 Choose **Stat ➤ ANOVA ➤ One-way...** 2 Specify ENERGY in the **Response** text box 3 Specify REGION in the **Factor** text box 4 Click **OK**	1 Choose **DDXL ➤ Regression** 2 Select **1 Way ANOVA** from the **Function type** drop-down box 3 Specify ENERGY in the **Response Variable** text box 4 Specify REGION in the **Factor Variable** text box 5 Click **OK**	1 Press **STAT**, arrow over to **TESTS**, and press **ALPHA ➤ F** 2 Press **2nd ➤ LIST**, arrow down to NE and press **ENTER** 3 Press **, ➤ 2nd ➤ LIST**, arrow down to MW, and press **ENTER** 4 Press **, ➤ 2nd ➤ LIST**, arrow down to SO, and press **ENTER** 5 Press **, ➤ 2nd ➤ LIST**, arrow down to WE, and press **ENTER** 6 Press **)** and then **ENTER**

Exercises 13.3

Statistical Concepts and Skills

13.24 Suppose that a one-way ANOVA is being performed to compare the means of three populations and that the sample sizes are 10, 12, and 15. Determine the degrees of freedom for the F-statistic.

13.25 We stated earlier that a one-way ANOVA test is always right-tailed because the null hypothesis is rejected only when the test statistic, F, is too large. Why is the null hypothesis rejected only when F is too large?

13.26 Following are the notations for the three sums of squares. State the name of each sum of squares and the source of variation each sum of squares represents.
    a. SSE   b. SSTR   c. SST

13.27 State the one-way ANOVA identity and interpret its meaning with regard to partitioning the total variation in the data.

13.28 True or false: If you know any two of the three sums of squares, SST, SSTR, and SSE, you can determine the remaining one. Explain your answer.

13.29 Fill in the missing entries in the following partially completed one-way ANOVA table.

Source	df	SS	MS = SS/df	F-statistic
Treatment	2		21.652	
Error		84.400		
Total	14			

13.30 Fill in the missing entries in the following partially completed one-way ANOVA table.

Source	df	SS	MS = SS/df	F-statistic
Treatment		2.124	0.708	0.75
Error	20			
Total				

In Exercises 13.31 and 13.32,
a. compute SST, SSTR, and SSE, using the defining formulas.
b. verify that the one-way ANOVA identity holds.
c. compute SST, SSTR, and SSE, using the computing formulas, and compare your answers with those obtained in part (a).

13.31 Use the following three samples.

A	B	C
1	5	2
9	2	8
	4	5
	3	
	1	

13.32 Use the following four samples.

A	B	C	D
6	9	4	8
3	5	4	4
3	7	2	6
	8	2	
	6	3	

In Exercises 13.33 and 13.34, construct the one-way ANOVA table for the data. Compute SSTR and SSE, using the defining formulas given in Formula 13.1 on page 589.

13.33 The Assembly Line. The times required by three workers to perform an assembly-line task were recorded on five randomly selected occasions. Here are the times, to the nearest minute.

Hank	Susan	Joseph
8	8	10
10	9	9
9	9	10
11	8	11
10	10	9

(*Note:* $\bar{x}_1 = 9.6$, $\bar{x}_2 = 8.8$, $\bar{x}_3 = 9.8$, $s_1^2 = 1.3$, $s_2^2 = 0.7$, $s_3^2 = 0.7$, and $\bar{x} = 9.4$.)

13.34 Monthly Rents. The U.S. Bureau of the Census collects data on monthly rents of newly completed apartments and publishes the results in *Current Housing Reports*. Independent random samples of monthly rents for newly completed apartments in the four U.S. regions yielded the following data, in dollars.

Northeast	Midwest	South	West
700	665	706	660
593	543	445	647
643	494	676	725
876	609	851	561
939	516		904
	401		

(*Note:* $\bar{x}_1 = 750.2$, $\bar{x}_2 = 538.0$, $\bar{x}_3 = 669.5$, $\bar{x}_4 = 699.4$, $s_1^2 = 22{,}548.7$, $s_2^2 = 8{,}476.8$, $s_3^2 = 28{,}239.0$, $s_4^2 = 16{,}492.3$, and $\bar{x} = 657.7$.)

Preliminary data analyses indicate that you can reasonably consider the assumptions for one-way ANOVA to be satisfied in Exercises 13.35–13.38. In each exercise, perform the required hypothesis test, using either the critical-value approach or the P-value approach.

13.35 Copepod Cuisine. Copepods are tiny crustaceans that are an essential link in the estuarine food web. Marine scientists G. Weiss, G. McManus, and H. Harvey at the Chesapeake Biological Laboratory in Maryland designed an experiment to determine whether dietary lipid (fat) content is important in the population growth of a Chesapeake Bay copepod. Their findings were published as the paper "Development and Lipid Composition of the Harpacticoid Copepod Nitocra Spinipes Reared on Different Diets" (*Marine Ecology Progress Series*, 1996, Vol. 132, pp. 57–61). Independent random samples of copepods were placed in containers containing lipid-rich diatoms, bacteria, or leafy macroalgae. There were 12 containers total with four replicates per diet. Five gravid (egg-bearing) females were placed in each container. After 14 days, the number of copepods in each container were as follows.

Diatoms	Bacteria	Macroalgae
426	303	277
467	301	324
438	293	302
497	328	272

At the 5% significance level, do the data provide sufficient evidence to conclude that a difference exists in mean number of copepods among the three different diets? (*Note:* $T_1 = 1828$, $T_2 = 1225$, $T_3 = 1175$, and $\Sigma x^2 = 1{,}561{,}154$.)

13.36 In Section 13.2, we considered two hypothetical examples to explain the logic behind one-way ANOVA. Now, you are to further examine those examples.
a. Refer to Table 13.1 on page 581. Perform a one-way ANOVA on the data and compare your conclusion to that stated in the corresponding "What Does it Mean?" box. Use $\alpha = 0.05$.

b. Repeat part (a) for the data displayed in Table 13.2 on page 582.

13.37 Weekly Earnings. The U.S. Bureau of Labor Statistics publishes data on weekly earnings of nonsupervisory workers in *Employment and Earnings*. The following data, in dollars, were obtained from independent random samples of full and part-time nonsupervisory workers in five service-producing industries.

Transp. and Pub. util.	Wholesale trade	Retail trade	Finance Insurance, Real estate	Services
543	524	260	482	408
583	469	188	436	420
544	449	170	518	427
588	518	298	404	343
635	502	185		380
566		279		317

Do the data provide sufficient evidence to conclude that a difference exists in mean weekly earnings of nonsupervisory workers among the five industries? Use $\alpha = 0.05$. (Note: $T_1 = 3459$, $T_2 = 2462$, $T_3 = 1380$, $T_4 = 1840$, $T_5 = 2295$, and $\Sigma x^2 = 5{,}290{,}870$.)

13.38 Driving Golf Balls. Each manufacturer of golf balls always seems to be claiming that its balls go the farthest. A writer for a sports magazine decided to conduct an impartial test. She randomly selected 20 golf professionals and then randomly assigned four golfers to each of five brands. Each golfer drove the assigned brand of ball. The driving distances, in yards, are displayed in the following table.

Brand 1	Brand 2	Brand 3	Brand 4	Brand 5
286	279	270	284	281
276	277	262	271	293
281	284	277	269	276
274	288	280	275	292

At the 5% significance level, do the data provide sufficient evidence to conclude that a difference exists in mean driving distances among the five brands of golf ball? (Note: $T_1 = 1117$, $T_2 = 1128$, $T_3 = 1089$, $T_4 = 1099$, $T_5 = 1142$, and $\Sigma x^2 = 1{,}555{,}185$.)

Extending the Concepts and Skills

13.39 Political Prisoners. Journal articles and other sources frequently provide only summary statistics of data. This exercise gives you practice in working with such data in the context of ANOVA. According to the American Psychiatric Association, posttraumatic stress disorder (PTSD) is a common psychological consequence of traumatic events that involve threat to life or physical integrity. During the Cold War, some 200,000 people in East Germany were imprisoned for political reasons. Many of these prisoners were subjected to physical and psychological torture during their imprisonment, resulting in PTSD. Ehlers, Maercker, and Boos studied various characteristics of political prisoners from the former East Germany and presented their findings in the paper "Posttraumatic Stress Disorder (PTSD) Following Political Imprisonment: The Role of Mental Defeat, Alienation, and Perceived Permanent Change" (*Journal of Abnormal Psychology*, Vol. 109, pp. 45–55). The researchers randomly and independently selected 32 former prisoners diagnosed with chronic PTSD, 20 former prisoners diagnosed with PTSD after release from prison but subsequently recovered (remitted), and 29 diagnosed with no signs of PTSD. The ages, in years, of these people at time of arrest were as follows.

PTSD	n_j	$\bar{x}_j$	s_j
Chronic	32	25.8	9.2
Remitted	20	22.1	5.7
None	29	26.6	9.6

At the 1% significance level, do the data provide sufficient evidence to conclude that a difference exists in mean age at time of arrest among the three types of former prisoners? (Note: Use the formula

$$\bar{x} = \frac{n_1 \bar{x}_1 + n_2 \bar{x}_2 + n_3 \bar{x}_3}{n_1 + n_2 + n_3}$$

to obtain the mean of all the observations.)

Confidence Intervals in One-Way ANOVA. Assume that the conditions for one-way ANOVA are satisfied and let $s = \sqrt{MSE}$. Then we have the following confidence-interval formulas.

- A $(1 - \alpha)$-level confidence interval for any particular population mean, say, μ_i, has endpoints

$$\bar{x}_i \pm t_{\alpha/2} \cdot \frac{s}{\sqrt{n_i}}.$$

- A $(1 - \alpha)$-level confidence interval for the difference between any two particular population means, say, μ_i and μ_j, has endpoints

$$(\bar{x}_i - \bar{x}_j) \pm t_{\alpha/2} \cdot s\sqrt{(1/n_i) + (1/n_j)}.$$

In both formulas, df = $n - k$, where, as usual, k denotes the number of populations and n denotes the total number of observations. Apply these formulas in Exercise 13.40.

13.40 Monthly Rents. Refer to Exercise 13.34.
a. Find and interpret a 99% confidence interval for the mean monthly rent of newly completed apartments in the Midwest.
b. Find and interpret a 99% confidence interval for the difference between the mean monthly rents of newly completed apartments in the Northeast and South.
c. What assumptions are you making in solving parts (a) and (b)?

13.41 Monthly Rents. Refer to Exercise 13.40. Suppose that you have obtained a 99% confidence interval for each of the two differences, $\mu_1 - \mu_2$ and $\mu_1 - \mu_3$. Can you be 99% confident of both results simultaneously, that is, that both differences are contained in their corresponding confidence intervals? Explain your answer.

Using Technology

In Exercises 13.42–13.45, use the technology of your choice to:
a. Obtain individual normal probability plots and the standard deviations of the samples.
b. Perform a residual analysis.
c. Decide whether conducting a one-way ANOVA on the data is reasonable. If so, also do parts (d) and (e).
d. Perform the specified hypothesis test.
e. Interpret the results of your hypothesis test.

13.42 Cuckoo Care. Many species of cuckoos are brood parasites. The females lay their eggs in the nests of smaller bird species who then raise the young cuckoos at the expense of their own young. Data on the lengths, in millimeters, of cuckoo eggs found in the nests of three bird species—the Tree Pipet, Hedge Sparrow, and Pied Wagtail—are provided on the WeissStats CD. These data were collected by the late O. M. Latter in 1902 and used by L. H. C. Tippett in his text *The Methods of Statistics* (New York: Wiley, 1952, p. 176). At the 10% significance level, do the data provide sufficient evidence to conclude that a difference exists in the mean lengths of cuckoo eggs among the three bird species?

13.43 Magazine Ads. Advertising researchers Shuptrine and McVicker wanted to determine whether there were significant differences in the readability of magazine advertisements. Thirty magazines were classified by educational level—high, mid, or low—and then three magazines were randomly selected from each level. From each magazine, six advertisements were randomly chosen and examined for readability. In this particular case, readability was characterized by the numbers of words, sentences, and words of three syllables or more in each ad. The researchers published their findings in the *Journal of Advertising Research* (1981, Vol. 21, p. 47). The number of words of three syllables or more in each ad are provided on the WeissStats CD. At the 5% significance level, do the data provide evidence of a difference in the mean number of words of three syllables or more among the three magazine levels?

13.44 Sickle Cell Disease. A study published by E. Anionwu et al. in the *British Medical Journal* (1981, Vol. 282, pp. 283–286) measured the steady state hemoglobin levels of patients with three different types of sickle cell disease: HB SS, HB ST, and HB SC. The data are presented on the WeissStats CD. At the 5% significance level, do the data suggest a difference in mean steady state hemoglobin levels among the three types of sickle cell disease?

13.45 Prolonging Life. Vitamin C (ascorbate) boosts the human immune system and is effective in preventing a variety of illnesses. In a study by E. Cameron and L. Pauling, published in the *Proceedings of the National Academy of Science USA* (1978, Vol. 75, pp. 4538–4542), patients in advanced stages of cancer were given a Vitamin C supplement. Patients were grouped according to the organ affected by cancer: stomach, bronchus, colon, ovary, or breast. The study yielded the survival times, in days, given on the WeissStats CD. At the 5% significance level, do the data provide sufficient evidence to conclude that, for patients in advanced stages of cancer who are given a Vitamin C treatment, a difference exists in mean survival time among the five different types of cancer?

Chapter Review

You Should Be Able To

1. use and understand the formulas presented in this chapter.

2. use the *F*-table, Table VI in Appendix A.

3. explain the essential ideas behind a one-way analysis of variance.

4. state and check the assumptions required for a one-way ANOVA.

5. obtain the sums of squares for a one-way ANOVA by using the defining formulas.

6. obtain the sums of squares for a one-way ANOVA by using the computing formulas.

7. compute the mean squares and the *F*-statistic for a one-way ANOVA.

8. construct a one-way ANOVA table.

9. perform a one-way ANOVA test.

Key Terms

analysis of variance (ANOVA), 576
degrees of freedom for the denominator, 578
degrees of freedom for the numerator, 578
error, 585
error mean square (*MSE*), 585
error sum of squares (*SSE*), 585
F_α, 579
F-curve, 578
F-distribution, 578
F-statistic, 585
factor, 580
levels, 580
one-way analysis of variance, 580
one-way ANOVA identity, 587
one-way ANOVA tables, 588
one-way ANOVA test, 590, 591
residual, 581
response variable, 595
rule of 2, 581
total sum of squares (*SST*), 587
treatment, 585
treatment mean square (*MSTR*), 584
treatment sum of squares (*SSTR*), 584

Review Test

Statistical Concepts and Skills

1. For what is one-way ANOVA used?

2. State the three assumptions for one-way ANOVA and explain how those assumptions can be checked.

3. On what distribution does one-way ANOVA rely?

4. Suppose that you want to compare the means of three populations by using one-way ANOVA. If the sample sizes are 5, 6, and 6, determine the degrees of freedom for the appropriate *F*-curve.

5. In one-way ANOVA, identify a statistic that measures
a. the variation among the sample means.
b. the variation within the samples.

6. In one-way ANOVA,
a. list and interpret the three sums of squares.
b. state the one-way ANOVA identity and interpret its meaning with regard to partitioning the total variation among all the data.

7. For a one-way ANOVA,
a. identify one purpose of one-way ANOVA tables.
b. construct a generic one-way ANOVA table.

8. Consider an *F*-curve with df = (2, 14).
a. Identify the degrees of freedom for the numerator.
b. Identify the degrees of freedom for the denominator.
c. Determine $F_{0.05}$.
d. Find the *F*-value having area 0.01 to its right.
e. Find the *F*-value having area 0.05 to its right.

9. Consider the following hypothetical samples.

A	B	C
1	0	3
3	6	12
5	2	6
	5	3
	2	

a. Obtain the sample mean and sample standard deviation of each of the three samples.
b. Obtain SST, SSTR, and SSE by using the defining formulas and verify that the one-way ANOVA identity holds.
c. Obtain SST, SSTR, and SSE by using the computing formulas.
d. Construct the one-way ANOVA table.

10. **Losses to Robbery.** The U.S. Federal Bureau of Investigation conducts surveys to obtain information on the value of losses from various types of robberies. Results of the surveys are published in *Population-at-Risk Rates and Selected Crime Indicators*. Independent random samples of reports for three types of robberies—highway, gas station, and convenience store—gave the following data, in dollars, on value of losses.

Highway	Gas station	Convenience store
608	636	476
652	533	553
495	512	512
744	451	338
680	291	234
	618	246

a. What does MSTR measure?
b. What does MSE measure?
c. Suppose that you want to perform a one-way ANOVA to compare the mean losses among the three types of robberies. What conditions are necessary? How crucial are those conditions?

11. **Losses to Robbery.** Refer to Problem 10. At the 5% significance level, do the data provide sufficient evidence to conclude that a difference in mean losses exists among the three types of robberies? Use one-way ANOVA to perform the required hypothesis test. (*Note:* $T_1 = 3179$, $T_2 = 3041$, $T_3 = 2359$, and $\Sigma x^2 = 4{,}700{,}509$.)

Using Technology

12. **Losses to Robbery.** Refer to Problem 10. Use the technology of your choice to
a. obtain normal probability plots for each of the three samples.
b. perform a residual analysis.
c. Does it seem reasonable to consider the assumptions for one-way ANOVA met? Explain your answer.

13. **Losses to Robbery.** Use the technology of your choice to carry out the one-way ANOVA test required in Problem 11.

Internet Project

Brain Damage and the Courts

In this project, you are to examine data collected within the Australian court system. The subjects in the study are plaintiffs: people who suffered brain damage in automobile accidents and sued for monetary damages based on their injuries.

You will be able to decide whether the (mean) amount of money that plaintiffs request differs among age groups—in other words, whether there is a difference in requested compensation based on age. In a second analysis, you will determine whether there is a difference owing to the plaintiffs' gender.

URL for access to Internet Projects Page: www.aw.com/weiss

Focusing on Data Analysis

Age, Sex, GPA, and SAT Scores

Recall from Chapter 1 (see page 34) that the Focus database contains information on 500 randomly selected Arizona State University sophomores. For these database exercises, you should eliminate all cases (students) in which one or more of the four variables, cumulative GPA, high school GPA, SAT math score, and SAT verbal score, equal 0. Use the technology of your choice to solve the following problems.

a. Conduct a one-way ANOVA at the 5% significance level to test for differences among mean cumulative GPAs of Arizona State University sophomores in the three high school GPA categories: under 2, 2–2.99, and 3 or over.
b. Conduct a one-way ANOVA at the 5% significance level to test for differences among mean cumulative GPAs of Arizona State University sophomores in the five SAT math score categories: under 400, 400–499, 500–599, 600–699, and 700 or over.
c. Conduct a one-way ANOVA at the 5% significance level to test for differences among mean cumulative GPAs of Arizona State University sophomores in the four SAT verbal score categories: under 400, 400–499, 500–599, and 600–699. (None of the students under consideration have an SAT verbal score of 700 or above.)
d. Conduct a one-way ANOVA at the 5% significance level to test for differences among mean cumulative GPAs of Arizona State University sophomores in the three age categories: under 20, 20, and over 20.

case study discussion

Heavy Drinking Among College Students

As you learned at the beginning of this chapter, Professor Kate Carey of Syracuse University surveyed 78 college students from an introductory psychology class, all of whom were regular drinkers of alcohol. Her purpose was to identify interpersonal and intrapersonal situations associated with excessive drinking among college students and to detect those situations that differentiate heavy drinkers from light and moderate drinkers.

To quantify drinking patterns, Carey used the time-line follow-back procedure (TLFB). The TLFB is a structured interview that provides reliable estimates of daily drinking. In this case, each student filled in each day of a blank calendar covering the previous month with the number of standard drink equivalents (SDEs) consumed on that day. One SDE is defined to be 1 fluid ounce of hard liquor, 12 fluid ounces of beer, or 4 fluid ounces of wine. Based on the results of the TLFB, the students were divided into three categories according to average quantity of alcohol consumed per drinking day: light drinkers ($\leq$ 3 SDEs), moderate drinkers (4–6 SDEs), and heavy drinkers ($>$ 6 SDEs).

To assess the frequency of excessive drinking in interpersonal and intrapersonal situations, Carey utilized the short form of the Inventory of Drinking Situations (IDS). This form consists of 42 items, each of which is rated on a 4-point scale ranging from (1) never drink heavily in that type of situation to (4) almost always drink heavily in that type of situation. The 42 items are divided into eight subscales, three interpersonal and five intrapersonal, as displayed in the first column of the table on page 577. A subscale score represents the average rating for the items constituting the subscale.

a. For each of the eight IDS subscales, perform a (separate) one-way ANOVA to decide whether a difference exists in mean IDS scores among the three drinker categories. Use $\alpha = 0.05$. (*Note:* For each ANOVA, use the formula

$$\bar{x} = \frac{n_1 \bar{x}_1 + n_2 \bar{x}_2 + n_3 \bar{x}_3}{n_1 + n_2 + n_3}$$

to obtain the mean of all the observations.)
b. Based on the data in the table on page 577, should any of the eight ANOVAs perhaps not been carried out? Explain your answer. (*Hint:* Rule of 2.)

Internet Resources: Visit the Weiss Web site www.aw.com/weiss for additional discussion, exercises, and resources related to this case study.

Biography
Sir Ronald Fisher: Mr. ANOVA

RONALD FISHER was born on February 17, 1890, in London, England; he was a surviving twin in a family of eight children; his father was a prominent auctioneer. Fisher graduated from Cambridge in 1912 with degrees in mathematics and physics.

From 1912 to 1919, Fisher worked at an investment house, did farm chores in Canada, and taught high school. In 1919, he took a position as a statistician at Rothamsted Experimental Station in Harpenden, West Hertford, England. His charge was to sort and reassess a 66-year accumulation of data on manurial field trials and weather records.

Fisher's work at Rothamsted during the next 15 years earned him the reputation as the leading statistician of his day and as a top-ranking geneticist. It was there, in 1925, that he published *Statistics for Research Workers*, a book that remained in print for 50 years. Fisher made important contributions to analysis of variance (ANOVA), exact tests of significance for small samples, and maximum-likelihood solutions. He developed experimental designs to address issues in biological research, such as small samples, variable materials, and fluctuating environments.

Fisher has been described as "slight, bearded, eloquent, reactionary, and quirkish; genial to his disciples and hostile to his dissenters." He was also a prolific writer—over a span of 50 years, he wrote an average of one paper every 2 months!

In 1933, Fisher became Galton professor of Eugenics at University College in London and, in 1943, Balfour professor of genetics at Cambridge. In 1952, he was knighted. Fisher "retired" in 1959, moved to Australia, and spent the last 3 years of his life working at the Division of Mathematical Statistics of the Commonwealth Scientific and Industrial Research Organization. He died in 1962 in Adelaide, Australia.

chapter 14

Inferential Methods in Regression and Correlation

CHAPTER OUTLINE

14.1 The Regression Model; Analysis of Residuals

14.2 Inferences for the Slope of the Population Regression Line

14.3 Estimation and Prediction

14.4 Inferences in Correlation

GENERAL OBJECTIVES In Chapter 4, you studied descriptive methods in regression and correlation. You discovered how to determine the regression equation for a set of data points and how to use that equation to make predictions. You also learned how to compute and interpret the coefficient of determination and the linear correlation coefficient for a set of data points.

In this chapter, you will study inferential methods in regression and correlation. In Section 14.1, we examine the conditions required for performing such inferences and methods for checking whether those conditions are satisfied. In presenting the first inferential method, in Section 14.2, we show how to decide whether a regression equation is useful for making predictions.

In Section 14.3, we investigate methods for estimating the mean of the response variable corresponding to a particular value of the predictor variable and for predicting the value of the response variable for a particular value of the predictor variable. We also discuss, in Section 14.4, the use of the linear correlation coefficient of a set of data points to decide whether the two variables under consideration are linearly correlated and, if so, the nature of the linear correlation.

case study

FAT CONSUMPTION AND PROSTATE CANCER

As you learned in the Chapter 4 Case Study, many investigations have shown a relationship between nutrition and cancer. One dietary factor studied for its relationship with prostate cancer—one of the most virulent forms of cancer—is fat consumption.

In the Chapter 4 Case Study, you also examined data on fat consumption and prostate cancer death rate for various nations of the world. We repeat those data, obtained from a graph in John Robbins's classic book *Diet for a New America* (Walpole, N.H.: Stillpoint, 1987), in the following table.

Country	Dietary fat (grams/day)	Death rate (per 100,000)	Country	Dietary fat (grams/day)	Death rate (per 100,000)
El Salvador	38	0.9	Spain	97	10.1
Philippines	29	1.3	Portugal	73	11.4
Japan	42	1.6	Finland	112	11.1
Mexico	57	4.5	Hungary	100	13.1
Greece	96	4.8	United Kingdom	143	12.4
Colombia	47	5.4	Germany	134	12.9
Bulgaria	67	5.5	Canada	142	13.4
Yugoslavia	72	5.6	Austria	119	13.9
Poland	93	6.4	France	137	14.4
Panama	58	7.8	Netherlands	152	14.4
Israel	95	8.4	Australia	129	15.1
Romania	67	8.8	Denmark	156	15.9
Venezuela	62	9.0	United States	147	16.3
Czechoslovakia	96	9.1	Norway	133	16.8
Italy	86	9.4	Sweden	132	18.4

The regression and correlation analyses conducted on these data in Chapter 4 were descriptive. At the end of this chapter, you will be asked to return to the data to make regression and correlation inferences.

14.1 THE REGRESSION MODEL; ANALYSIS OF RESIDUALS

Before we can perform statistical inferences in regression and correlation, we must know whether the variables under consideration satisfy certain conditions. In this section, we discuss those conditions and examine methods for deciding whether they hold.

THE REGRESSION MODEL

Let's return to the Orion illustration used throughout Chapter 4. In Table 14.1, we reproduce the data on age and price for a sample of 11 Orions.

TABLE 14.1 Age and price data for a sample of 11 Orions

Car	Age (yr) x	Price ($100) y	Car	Age (yr) x	Price ($100) y
1	5	85	7	6	66
2	4	103	8	6	95
3	6	70	9	2	169
4	5	82	10	7	70
5	5	89	11	7	48
6	5	98			

On page 157, we found that the regression equation for these data—with age as the predictor variable and price as the response variable—is $\hat{y} = 195.47 - 20.26x$. Recall that the regression equation can be used to predict the price of an Orion from its age. However, we cannot expect such predictions to be completely accurate because prices vary even for Orions of the same age.

For instance, the sample data in Table 14.1 include four 5-year-old Orions. Their prices are $8500, $8200, $8900, and $9800. This variation in price for 5-year-old Orions should be expected because such cars generally have different mileages, interior conditions, paint quality, and so forth.

We use the population of all 5-year-old Orions to introduce some important regression terminology. The distribution of their prices is called the **conditional distribution** of the response variable "price" corresponding to the value 5 of the predictor variable "age." Likewise, their mean price is called the **conditional mean** of the response variable "price" corresponding to the value 5 of the predictor variable "age." Similar terminology applies to the standard deviation and other parameters.

In general, there is a population of Orions for each age. The distribution, mean, and standard deviation of prices for that population are called the *conditional distribution, conditional mean,* and *conditional standard deviation,* respectively, of the response variable "price" corresponding to the value of the predictor variable "age."

With the preceding discussion in mind, we now state the conditions—as Key Fact 14.1—required for using inferential methods in regression analysis.

Key Fact 14.1 **Assumptions for Regression Inferences**

1. *Population regression line:* There are constants β_0 and β_1 such that, for each value x of the predictor variable, the conditional mean of the response variable is $\beta_0 + \beta_1 x$.
2. *Equal standard deviations:* The conditional standard deviations of the response variable are the same for all values of the predictor variable. We denote this common standard deviation σ.[1]
3. *Normal populations:* For each value of the predictor variable, the conditional distribution of the response variable is a normal distribution.
4. *Independent observations:* The observations of the response variable are independent of one another.

Note: We refer to the straight line $y = \beta_0 + \beta_1 x$—on which the conditional means of the response variable lie—as the **population regression line** and to its equation as the **population regression equation.**

Assumptions 1–3 require that there are constants β_0, β_1, and σ such that, for each value x of the predictor variable, the conditional distribution of the response variable, y, is a normal distribution having mean $\beta_0 + \beta_1 x$ and standard deviation σ. These assumptions are often referred to as the **regression model.**

The inferential procedures in regression are robust to moderate violations of Assumptions 1–3 for regression inferences. In other words, the inferential procedures work reasonably well provided the variables under consideration don't violate any of those assumptions too badly.

In Example 14.1, we further explain and illustrate graphically these assumptions.

Example 14.1 Assumptions for Regression Inferences

Age and Price of Orions Discuss what satisfying the regression-inference Assumptions 1–3 would mean for Orions, with age as the predictor variable and price as the response variable. Display those assumptions graphically.

Solution Satisfying regression-inference Assumptions 1–3 requires that there are constants β_0, β_1, and σ so that for each age, x, the prices of all Orions of that age are normally distributed with mean $\beta_0 + \beta_1 x$ and standard deviation σ. Thus the prices of all 2-year-old Orions must be normally distributed with mean $\beta_0 + \beta_1 \cdot 2$ and standard deviation σ, the prices of all 3-year-old Orions must be normally distributed with mean $\beta_0 + \beta_1 \cdot 3$ and standard deviation σ, and so on.

To display the assumptions for regression inferences graphically, let's first consider Assumption 1. This assumption requires that, for each age, the mean price of all Orions of that age lies on the straight line $y = \beta_0 + \beta_1 x$, as shown in Fig. 14.1.

---

[1] The condition of equal standard deviations is called *homoscedasticity*. When that condition fails, we have what is called *heteroscedasticity*.

610 CHAPTER 14 Inferential Methods in Regression and Correlation

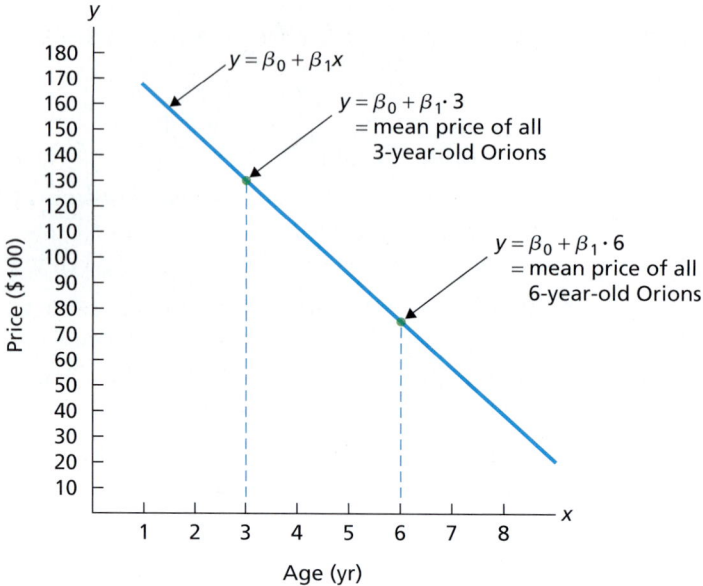

FIGURE 14.1
Population regression line

Next, we present graphs that depict Assumptions 2 and 3. These assumptions require that the price distributions for the various ages of Orions are all normally distributed with the same standard deviation, σ, as illustrated in Fig. 14.2 for the price distributions of 2-year-old, 5-year-old, and 7-year-old Orions. The shapes of the three normal curves in Fig. 14.2 are identical because normal distributions that have the same standard deviation have the same shape.

FIGURE 14.2
Price distributions for 2-, 5-, and 7-year-old Orions under Assumptions 2 and 3 (The means shown for the three normal distributions reflect Assumption 1)

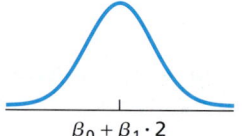
$\beta_0 + \beta_1 \cdot 2$
Prices of 2-year-old Orions

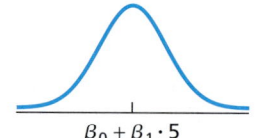
$\beta_0 + \beta_1 \cdot 5$
Prices of 5-year-old Orions

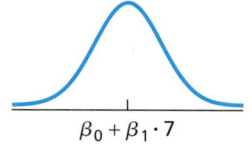
$\beta_0 + \beta_1 \cdot 7$
Prices of 7-year-old Orions

Assumptions 1–3 for regression inferences, as they pertain to the variables age and price of Orions, can be portrayed graphically by combining Figs. 14.1 and 14.2 into a three-dimensional graph, as displayed in Fig. 14.3.

Figure 14.3 depicts the various price distributions for Orions under the condition that Assumptions 1–3 are true for the variables age and price of Orions. Whether this condition is actually the case remains to be seen. ◆

ESTIMATING THE REGRESSION PARAMETERS

Suppose that we are considering two variables, x and y, for which the assumptions for regression inferences are met. Then there are constants β_0, β_1, and σ so that, for each value x of the predictor variable, the conditional distribution

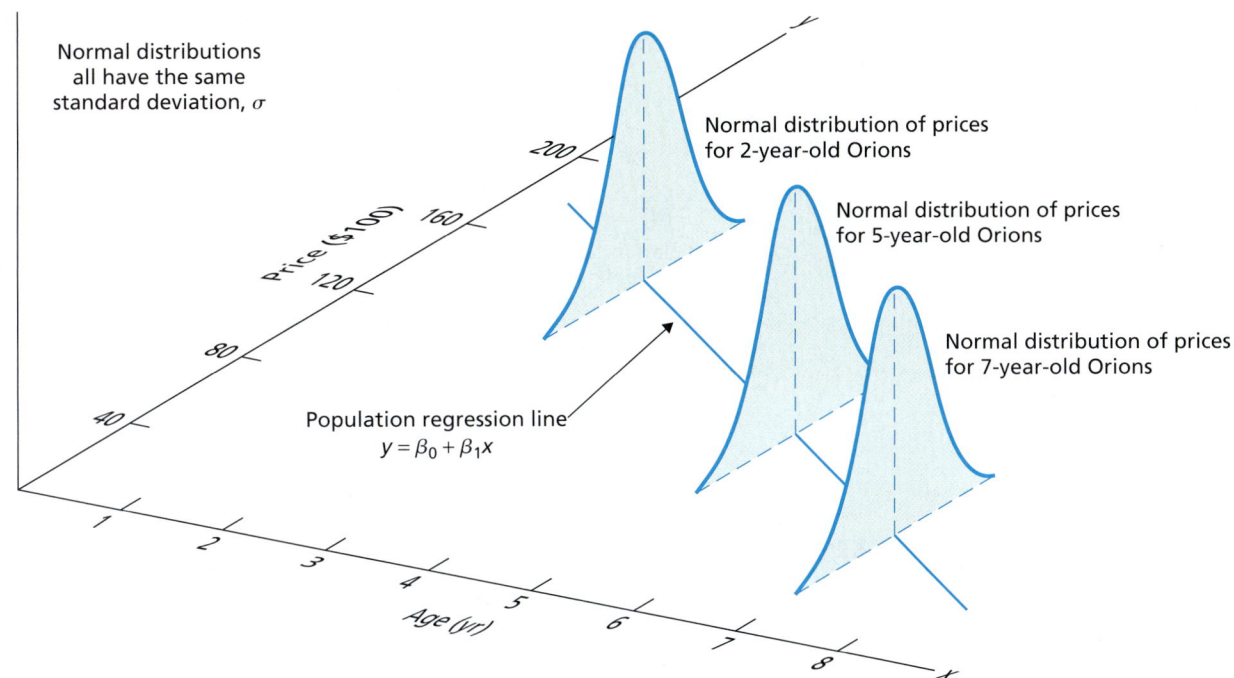

FIGURE 14.3
Graphical portrayal of Assumptions 1–3 for regression inferences pertaining to age and price of Orions

of the response variable is a normal distribution having mean $\beta_0 + \beta_1 x$ and standard deviation σ.

The parameters β_0, β_1, and σ are usually unknown and must therefore be estimated from sample data. Point estimates for the y-intercept, β_0, and slope, β_1, of the population regression line are provided by the y-intercept, b_0, and slope, b_1, respectively, of a sample regression line.

Another way of looking at this situation is that a sample regression line is used to estimate the population regression line. Of course, a sample regression line ordinarily will not be the same as the population regression line, just as a sample mean, $\bar{x}$, generally will not equal the population mean, μ. We illustrate this situation for the Orion example in Fig. 14.4 on the next page. (Although the population regression line is unknown, we have drawn it to illustrate the difference between the population regression line and a sample regression line.)

The solid line in Fig. 14.4 is the population regression line; the dashed line is a sample regression line. This sample regression line is the best approximation that can be made to the population regression line by using the sample data in Table 14.1 on page 608. A different sample of Orions would almost certainly yield a different sample regression line.

The statistic used to obtain a point estimate for the common conditional standard deviation σ is called the **standard error of the estimate** or the **residual standard deviation** and is defined as follows.

FIGURE 14.4
Population regression line and sample regression line for age and price of Orions

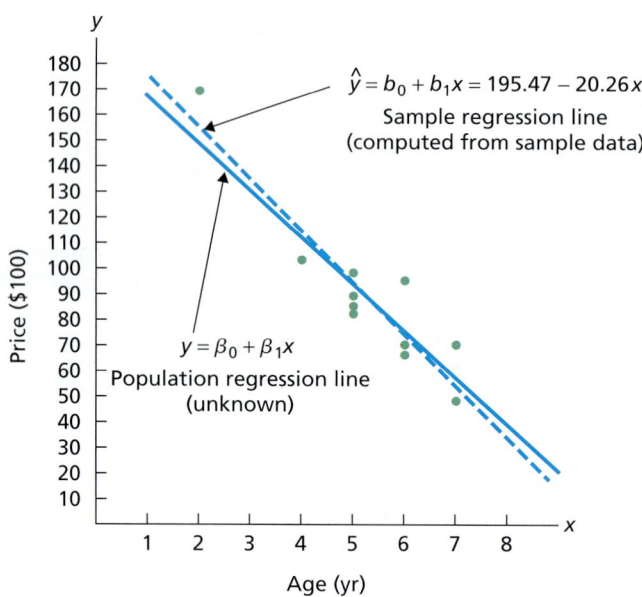

DEFINITION 14.1 **Standard Error of the Estimate**

The *standard error of the estimate*, s_e, is defined by

$$s_e = \sqrt{\frac{SSE}{n-2}},$$

where $SSE = \Sigma(y - \hat{y})^2 = S_{yy} - S_{xy}^2/S_{xx}$.

Recall that SSE is the error sum of squares and equals the sum of squared errors when the regression equation is used to predict the observed values of the response variable. Thus the standard error of the estimate indicates roughly how much, on average, the predicted values of the response variable differ from the observed values of the response variable, as illustrated in Example 14.2.

Example 14.2 **Standard Error of the Estimate**

Age and Price of Orions Refer to the age and price data for a sample of 11 Orions displayed in Table 14.1 on page 608.

a. Compute and interpret the standard error of the estimate.
b. Presuming that the variables age and price for Orions satisfy the assumptions for regression inferences, interpret the result from part (a).

Solution a. We computed the error sum of squares on page 174, finding that $SSE = 1423.5$. So the standard error of the estimate is

$$s_e = \sqrt{\frac{SSE}{n-2}} = \sqrt{\frac{1423.5}{11-2}} = 12.58,$$

or $1258.

> **What Does it Mean?**
>
> Roughly speaking, the predicted price of an Orion in the sample differs, on average, from the observed price by $1258.

b. Presuming that the variables age and price for Orions satisfy the assumptions for regression inferences, the standard error of the estimate, $s_e = 12.58$, or $1258, provides an estimate for the common population standard deviation, σ, of prices for all Orions of any particular age. ◆

ANALYSIS OF RESIDUALS

Now that we have examined the assumptions for regression inferences, we need to discuss how the sample data can be used to decide whether we can reasonably presume that those assumptions are met. We concentrate on Assumptions 1–3; checking Assumption 4—the independence assumption—is more involved and is best left for a second course in statistics.

The method for checking Assumptions 1–3 relies on an analysis of the errors made by using the regression equation to predict the observed values of the response variable, that is, on the differences, $y - \hat{y}$, between the observed and predicted values of the response variable. Each such difference is called a **residual**, generically denoted e. Thus

$$\text{Residual} = e = y - \hat{y}.$$

Figure 14.5 gives a graphical representation for the residual of a single data point.

FIGURE 14.5
Residual, e, of a data point

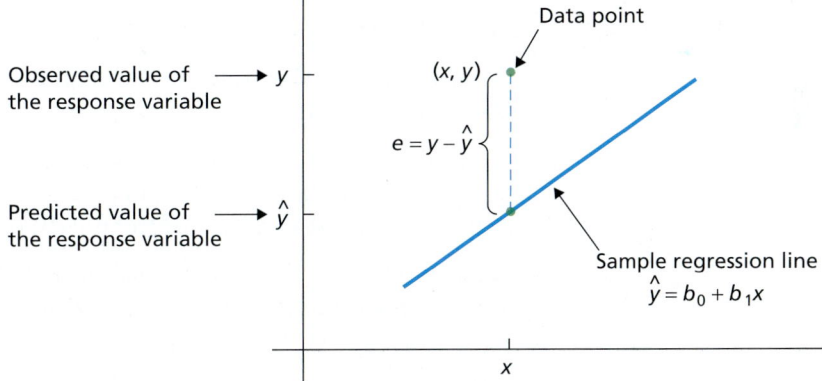

We can express the standard error of the estimate, s_e, in terms of the residuals. Referring to Definition 14.1, we find that the standard error of the estimate can be written as

$$s_e = \sqrt{\frac{SSE}{n-2}} = \sqrt{\frac{\Sigma(y-\hat{y})^2}{n-2}} = \sqrt{\frac{\Sigma e^2}{n-2}}.$$

We can show that the sum of the residuals is always 0, which, in turn, implies that $\bar{e} = 0$. Consequently, the standard error of the estimate is essentially the same as the standard deviation of the residuals.[2] Thus the standard error of the estimate is sometimes called the *residual standard deviation*.

---

[2] The exact standard deviation of the residuals is obtained by dividing by $n-1$ instead of $n-2$.

We can analyze the residuals to decide whether Assumptions 1–3 for regression inferences are met because those assumptions can be translated into conditions on the residuals. To show how, let's consider a sample of data points obtained from two variables that satisfy the assumptions for regression inferences.

In light of Assumption 1, the data points should be scattered about the (sample) regression line, which means that the residuals should be scattered about the x-axis. In light of Assumption 2, the variation of the observed values of the response variable should remain approximately constant from one value of the predictor variable to the next, which means the residuals should fall roughly in a horizontal band. In light of Assumption 3, for each value of the predictor variable, the distribution of the corresponding observed values of the response variable should be approximately bell-shaped, which implies that the horizontal band should be centered and symmetric about the x-axis.

Furthermore, considering all four regression assumptions simultaneously, we can regard the residuals as independent observations of a variable having a normal distribution with mean 0 and standard deviation σ. Thus a normal probability plot of the residuals should be roughly linear.

In summary, we have the criteria presented in Key Fact 14.2 for deciding whether Assumptions 1–3 for regression inferences are met by the two variables under consideration.

Key Fact 14.2 **Residual Analysis for the Regression Model**

If the assumptions for regression inferences are met, the following two conditions should hold.

- A plot of the residuals against the values of the predictor variable should fall roughly in a horizontal band centered and symmetric about the x-axis.
- A normal probability plot of the residuals should be roughly linear.

Failure of either of these two conditions casts doubt on the validity of one or more of the assumptions for regression inferences for the variables under consideration.

A plot of the residuals against the values of the predictor variable, called a **residual plot,** provides approximately the same information as does a scatter diagram of the data points. However, a residual plot makes spotting patterns such as curvature and nonconstant standard deviation easier.

Because the residual plot in Fig. 14.6(a) is roughly linear and the scatter about the line remains roughly constant, it suggests that the linearity assumption (Assumption 1) and the constant-standard-deviation assumption (Assumption 2) appear to be met for the variables under consideration. The residual plot in Fig. 14.6(b) suggests that the relation between the variables appears to be curved, indicating that the linearity assumption may be violated. The residual plot in Fig. 14.6(c) suggests that the conditional standard deviations appear

FIGURE 14.6
Residual plots suggesting (a) no violation of linearity or constant standard deviation, (b) violation of linearity, and (c) violation of constant standard deviation

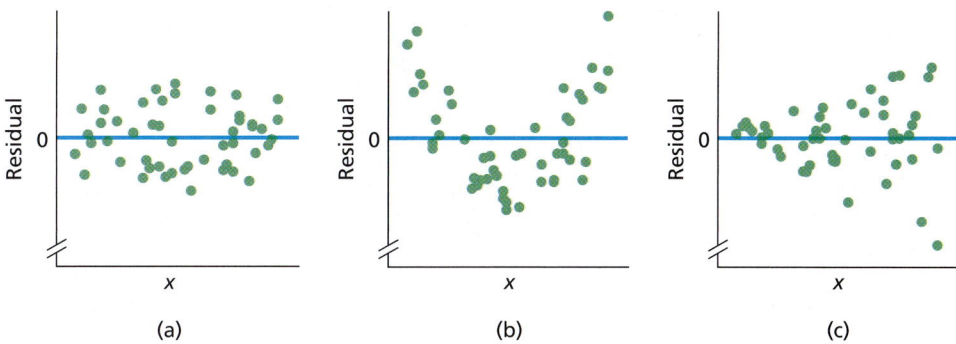

to increase as x increases, indicating that the constant-standard-deviation assumption may be violated.

Our previous data analyses show that deciding on the appropriateness of a model is often difficult when we are dealing with small samples—say, of size 20 or less. The same difficulty holds in regression: For small samples, we must be more liberal in allowing moderate departures from the idealized patterns when analyzing residual plots and normal probability plots to ascertain whether the assumptions for regression inferences are met. There are no definite rules—only judgment based on experience. Example 14.3 illustrates the application of such an analysis.

Example 14.3   Analysis of Residuals

Age and Price of Orions   Perform a residual analysis to decide whether we can reasonably consider the assumptions for regression inferences to be met by the variables age and price of Orions.

Solution   We apply the criteria presented in Key Fact 14.2. The ages and residuals for the Orion data are displayed in the first and fourth columns of Table 4.8, respectively. We repeat that information in Table 14.2.

Figure 14.7(a) shows a plot of the residuals against age, and Fig. 14.7(b) shows a normal probability plot for the residuals.

TABLE 14.2
Age and residual data for Orions

Age x	Residual e	Age x	Residual e
5	−9.16	6	−7.90
4	−11.42	6	21.10
6	−3.90	2	14.05
5	−12.16	7	16.36
5	−5.16	7	−5.64
5	3.84		

FIGURE 14.7
(a) Residual plot; (b) normal probability plot for residuals

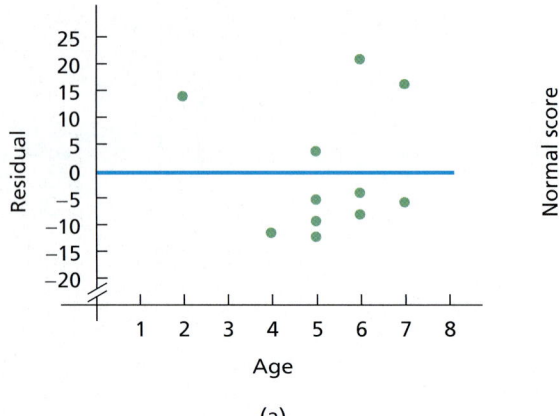
(a)

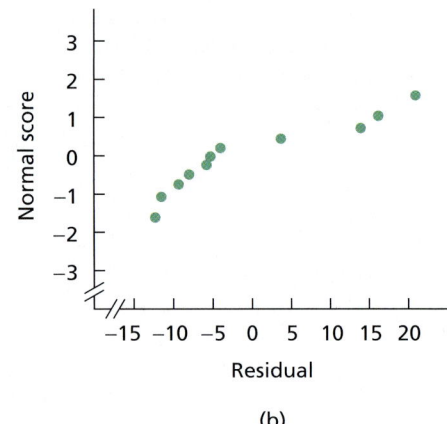
(b)

What Does it Mean?

There are no obvious violations of the assumptions for regression inferences for the variables age and price of Orions (in the age range from 2 to 7 years).

Taking into account the small sample size, we can say that the residuals fall roughly in a horizontal band that is centered and symmetric about the *x*-axis. We can also say that the normal probability plot for the residuals is (very) roughly linear, although the departure from linearity is sufficient for some concern.[3]

The Technology Center

Most statistical technologies, including Minitab and Excel, provide the standard error of the estimate as part of their regression analysis output. For instance, consider the regression output in Printout 4.2 on page 164 for the age and price data of 11 Orions. In the Minitab output, the standard error of the estimate is the first entry in the sixth line: S = 12.58. (Minitab uses S instead of s_e to denote the standard error of the estimate.)

In the Excel output, the standard error of the estimate is the first entry in the fourth line: s = 12.58. (Excel uses s instead of s_e to denote the standard error of the estimate.)

Although the TI-83 Plus does not display the standard error of the estimate, it can easily be obtained after the regression procedure is run. See the *TI-83 Plus Manual* for details.

We can also use statistical technology to obtain a residual plot and a normal probability plot of the residuals. Example 14.4 provides the details for doing so with Minitab, Excel, and the TI-83 Plus.

Example 14.4 Using Technology to Obtain Plots of Residuals

Age and Price of Orions Use Minitab, Excel, or the TI-83 Plus to obtain a residual plot and a normal probability plot of the residuals for the age and price data of Orions given in Table 14.1 on page 608.

---

[3] Recall, though, that the inferential procedures in regression analysis are robust to moderate violations of Assumptions 1–3 for regression inferences.

14.1 The Regression Model; Analysis of Residuals

Solution Printout 14.1 on the following page shows output that results from applying the programs for obtaining a residual plot and a normal probability plot of the residuals for the age and price data.

Note that Excel plots the residuals against the predicted values instead of the observed values of the predictor variable. Nonetheless, that residual plot can be used in the same way as a diagnostic tool to help assess the appropriateness of regression inferences. ◆

Obtaining the Output (Optional)

Printout 14.1 provides output from Minitab, Excel, and the TI-83 Plus for a residual plot and a normal probability plot of the residuals for the age and price data of 11 Orions. The following are detailed instructions for obtaining that output. First, we store the age and price data from Table 14.1 in columns (Minitab), ranges (Excel), or lists (TI-83 Plus) named AGE and PRICE, respectively. Then, we proceed as follows.

MINITAB

1. Choose **Stat ➤ Regression ➤ Regression...**
2. Specify PRICE in the **Response** text box
3. Specify AGE in the **Predictors** text box
4. Click the **Graphs...** button
5. Select the **Regular** option button from the **Residuals for Plots** list
6. Select the **Normal plot of residuals** check box from the **Residual Plots** list
7. Click in the **Residuals versus the variables** text box and specify AGE
8. Click **OK**
9. Click **OK**

EXCEL

1. Choose **DDXL ➤ Regression**
2. Select **Simple Regression** from the **Function type** drop-down list box
3. Specify PRICE in the **Response Variable** text box
4. Specify AGE in the **Explanatory Variable** text box
5. Click **OK**
6. Click the **Check the Residuals** button

TI-83 PLUS

1. Clear the **Y=** screen or turn off any equations located there
2. Press **STAT**, arrow over to **CALC**, and press **8**
3. Press **2nd ➤ LIST**, arrow down to AGE, and press **ENTER**
4. Press **, ➤ 2nd ➤ LIST**, arrow down to PRICE, and press **ENTER** twice
5. Press **2nd ➤ STAT PLOT** and then press **ENTER** twice
6. Arrow to the first graph icon and press **ENTER**
7. Press the down-arrow key
8. Press **2nd ➤ LIST**, arrow down to AGE, and press **ENTER** twice
9. Press **2nd ➤ LIST**, arrow down to RESID, and press **ENTER** twice
10. Press **ZOOM** and then **9** (and then **TRACE**, if desired)
11. Press **2nd ➤ STAT PLOT** and then press **ENTER** twice
12. Arrow to the sixth graph icon and press **ENTER**
13. Press the down-arrow key
14. Press **2nd ➤ LIST**, arrow down to RESID, and press **ENTER** twice
15. Press **ZOOM** and then **9** (and then **TRACE**, if desired)

PRINTOUT 14.1
Residual plots and normal probability plots of the residuals for the age and price data of 11 Orions

MINITAB

Residuals Versus AGE
(response is PRICE)

Normal Probability Plot of the Residuals
(response is PRICE)

EXCEL

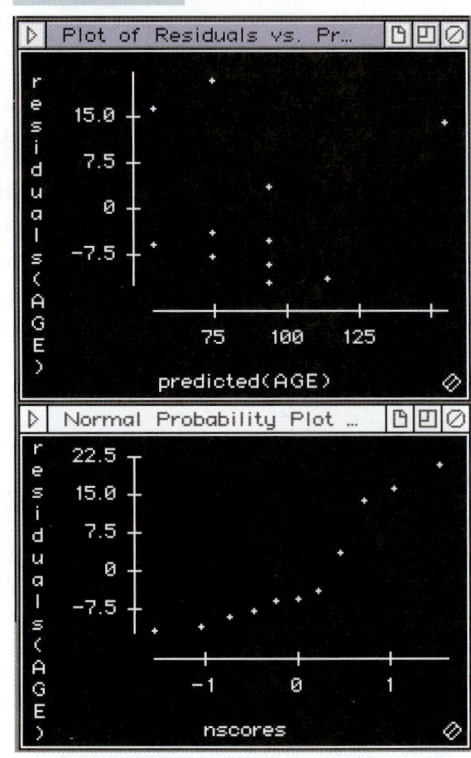

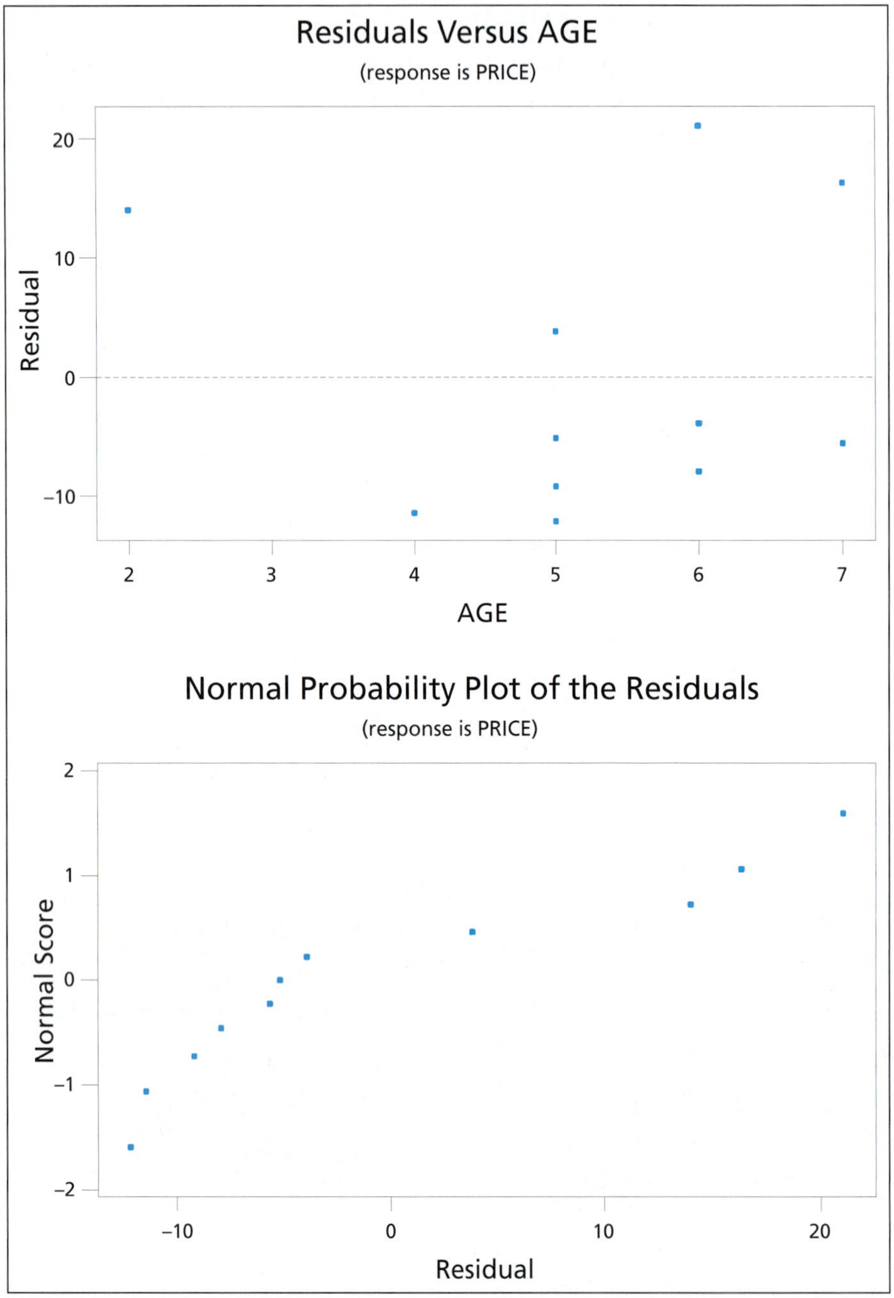

TI-83 PLUS

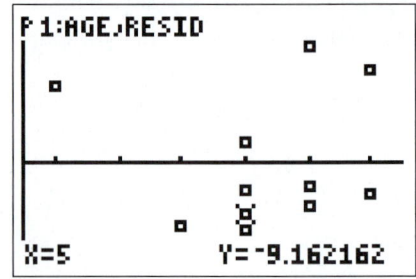

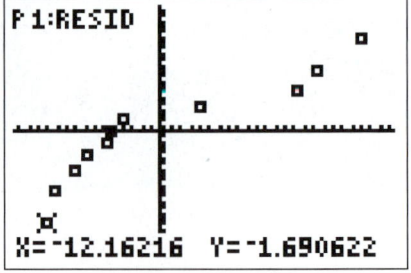

Exercises 14.1

Statistical Concepts and Skills

14.1 Suppose that x and y are predictor and response variables, respectively, of a population. Consider the population that consists of all members of the original population that have a specified value of the predictor variable. The distribution, mean, and standard deviation of the response variable for this population are called the ___, ___, and ___, respectively, corresponding to the specified value of the predictor variable.

14.2 State the four conditions required for making regression inferences.

In Exercises 14.3–14.6, assume that the variables under consideration satisfy the assumptions for regression inferences.

14.3 Fill in the blanks.
a. The straight line $y = \beta_0 + \beta_1 x$ is called the ___.
b. The common conditional standard deviation of the response variable is denoted ___.
c. For $x = 6$, the conditional distribution of the response variable is a ___ distribution having mean ___ and standard deviation ___.

14.4 What statistic is used to estimate
a. the y-intercept of the population regression line?
b. the slope of the population regression line?
c. the common conditional standard deviation, σ, of the response variable?

14.5 Based on a sample of data points, what is the best estimate of the population regression line?

14.6 Regarding the standard error of the estimate,
a. give two interpretations of it.
b. identify another name used for it and explain the rationale for that name.
c. which one of the three sums of squares figures in its computation?

14.7 The difference between an observed value and a predicted value of the response variable is called a ___.

14.8 Identify two graphs used in a residual analysis to check the Assumptions 1–3 for regression inferences and explain the reasoning behind their use.

14.9 Which graph used in a residual analysis provides roughly the same information as a scatter diagram? What advantages does it have over a scatter diagram?

In Exercises 14.10–14.13, we repeat the information from Exercises 4.42–4.45. For each exercise here, discuss what satisfying Assumptions 1–3 for regression inferences by the variables under consideration would mean.

14.10 Tax Efficiency. *Tax efficiency* is a measure—ranging from 0 to 100—of how much tax due to capital gains stock or mutual fund investors pay on their investments each year; the higher the tax efficiency, the lower is the tax. The paper "At the Mercy of the Manager" (*Financial Planning*, 2000, Vol. 30(5), pp. 54–56) by Craig Israelsen examined the relationship between investments in mutual fund portfolios and their associated tax efficiencies. The following table shows percentage of investments in energy securities (x) and tax efficiency (y) for 10 mutual fund portfolios.

x	3.1	3.2	3.7	4.3	4.0	5.5	6.7	7.4	7.4	10.6
y	98.1	94.7	92.0	89.8	87.5	85.0	82.0	77.8	72.1	53.5

14.11 Corvette Prices. The *Kelley Blue Book* provides information on wholesale and retail prices of cars. Following are age and price data for 10 randomly selected Corvettes between 1 and 6 years old. Here, x denotes age, in years, and y denotes price, in hundreds of dollars.

x	6	6	6	2	2	5	4	5	1	4
y	205	195	210	340	299	230	270	243	340	240

14.12 Custom Homes. Hanna Properties specializes in custom-home resales in the Equestrian Estates, an exclusive subdivision in Phoenix, Arizona. A random sample of nine custom homes currently listed for sale provided the following information on size and price. Here, x denotes size, in hundreds of square feet, rounded to the nearest hundred, and y denotes price, in thousands of dollars, rounded to the nearest thousand.

x	26	27	33	29	29	34	30	40	22
y	259	274	294	296	325	380	457	523	215

14.13 Plant Emissions. Plants emit gases that trigger the ripening of fruit, attract pollinators, and cue other physiological responses. N. G. Agelopolous, K. Chamberlain, and J. A. Pickett examined factors that affect the emission of volatile compounds by the potato plant *Solanum tuberosom* and published their findings in the *Journal of Chemical Ecology* (2000, Vol. 26(2), pp. 497–511). The volatile compounds analyzed were hydrocarbons used by other plants and animals. Following are data on plant weight (x), in grams, and quantity of volatile compounds emitted (y), in hundreds of nanograms, for 11 potato plants.

x	57	85	57	65	52	67	62	80	77	53	68
y	8.0	22.0	10.5	22.5	12.0	11.5	7.5	13.0	16.5	21.0	12.0

In Exercises 14.14–14.17,
a. compute the standard error of the estimate and interpret your answer.
b. interpret your result from part (a) if the assumptions for regression inferences hold.
c. obtain a residual plot and a normal probability plot of the residuals.
d. decide whether you can reasonably consider Assumptions 1–3 for regression inferences to be met by the variables under consideration. (The answer here is subjective, especially in view of the extremely small sample sizes.)

14.14 Tax Efficiency. Use the data on percentage of investments in energy securities and tax efficiency from Exercise 14.10.

14.15 Corvette Prices. Use the age and price data for Corvettes from Exercise 14.11.

14.16 Custom Homes. Use the size and price data for custom homes from Exercise 14.12.

14.17 Plant Emissions. Use the data on plant weight and quantity of volatile emissions from Exercise 14.13.

14.18 Figure 14.8 shows three residual plots and a normal probability plot of residuals. For each part, decide whether the graph suggests violation of one or more of the assumptions for regression inferences. Explain your answers.

14.19 Figure 14.9 on page 622 displays three residual plots and one normal probability plot of residuals. For each part, decide whether the graph suggests violation of one or more of the assumptions for regression inferences. Explain your answers.

Using Technology

For Exercises 14.20–14.25, use the technology of your choice to
a. obtain and interpret the standard error of the estimate.
b. obtain a residual plot and a normal probability plot of the residuals.
c. decide whether you can reasonably consider Assumptions 1–3 for regression inferences to be met by the variables under consideration.

14.20 Batting and Scoring. Is the number of runs a baseball team scores in a season related to its team batting average? ESPN compiles end-of-season statistics for Major League Baseball and maintains them on its Web site. The following table provides season team batting averages and total runs scored for a sample of major league baseball teams.

Average	Runs	Average	Runs
.294	968	.267	793
.278	938	.265	792
.278	925	.256	764
.270	887	.254	752
.274	825	.246	740
.271	810	.266	738
.263	807	.262	731
.257	798	.251	708

14.21 Body Fat. In the paper "Total Body Composition by Dual-Photon (^{153}Gd) Absorptiometry" (*American Journal of Clinical Nutrition*, 1984, Vol. 40, pp. 834–839), R. B. Mazess et al. studied methods for quantifying body composition. Eighteen randomly selected adults were measured for percentage of body fat, using dual-photon absorptiometry. The following table shows the results of the measurements and the ages of the adults.

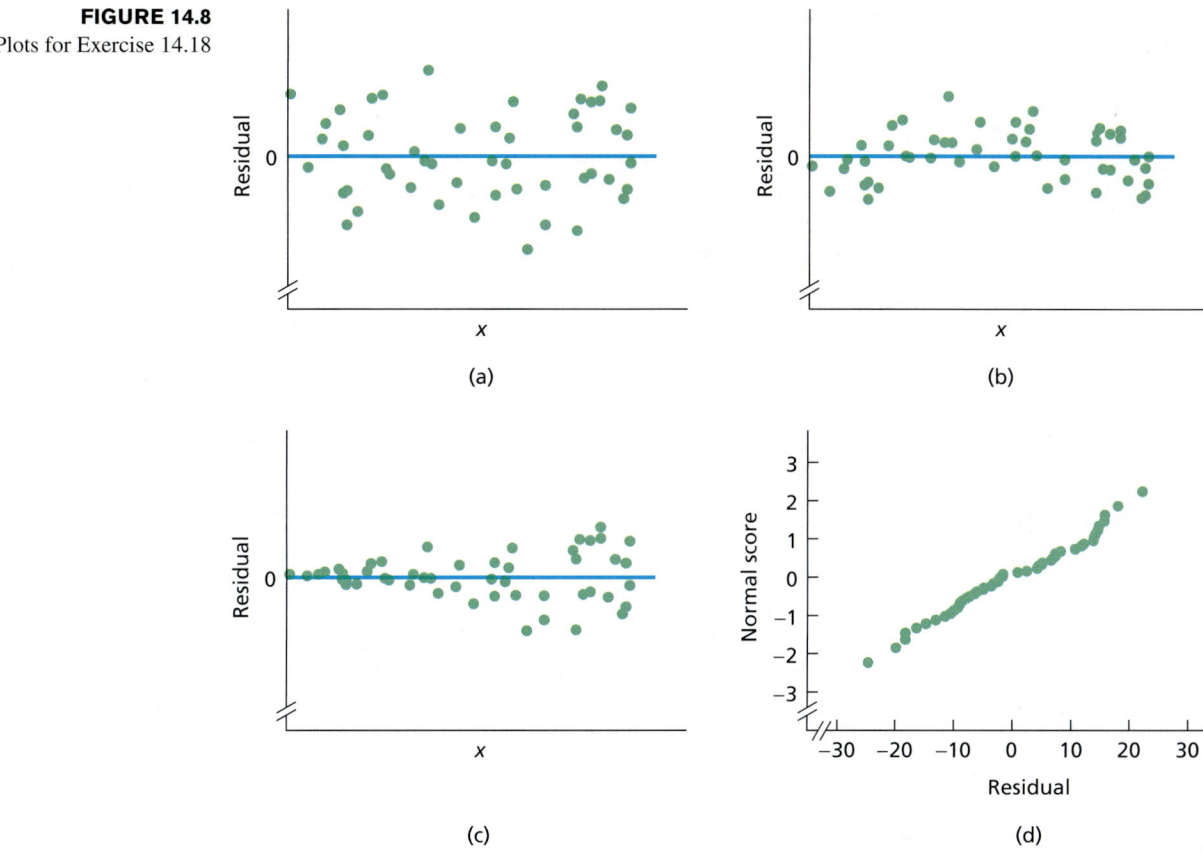

FIGURE 14.8
Plots for Exercise 14.18

Age	%Fat	Age	%Fat	Age	%Fat
23	9.5	45	27.4	56	32.5
23	27.9	49	25.2	57	30.3
27	7.8	50	31.1	58	33.0
27	17.8	53	34.7	58	33.8
39	31.4	53	42.0	60	41.1
41	25.9	54	29.1	61	34.5

14.22 PCBs and Pelicans. Polychlorinated biphenyls (PCBs), an industrial pollutant, are a great danger to natural ecosystems. In a study by R. W. Risebrough titled "Effects of Environmental Pollutants Upon Animals Other Than Man" (*Proceedings of the 6th Berkeley Symposium on Mathematics and Statistics, VI*, University of California Press, 1972, pp. 443–463), 60 Anacapa pelican eggs were collected and measured for their shell thickness, in millimeters (mm), and concentration of PCBs, in parts per million (ppm). The data are presented on the WeissStats CD.

14.23 Gas Guzzlers. The magazine *Consumer Reports* publishes information on automobile gas mileage and variables that affect gas mileage. In the April 1999 issue, data on gas mileage (in mpg) and engine displacement (in liters, L) were published for 121 vehicles. Those data are stored on the WeissStats CD.

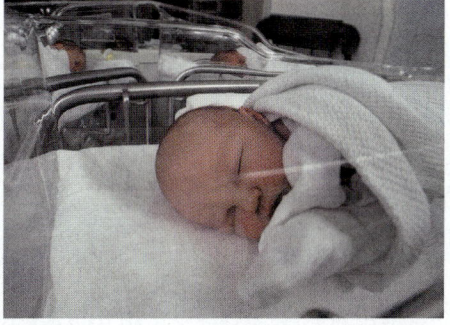

14.24 Estriol Level and Birth Weight. J. Greene and J. Touchstone conducted a study on the relationship between the estriol levels of pregnant women and the birth weights of their children. Their findings, "Urinary Tract Estriol: An Index of Placental Function," were published in the *American Journal of Obstetrics and Gynecology* (1963,

Vol. 85(1), pp. 1–9). The data points are provided on the WeissStats CD, where estriol levels are in mg/24 hr and birth weights are in hectograms (hg).

14.25 Shortleaf Pines. The ability to estimate the volume of a tree based on a simple measurement, such as the diameter of the tree, is important to the lumber industry, ecologists, and conservationists. Data on volume, in cubic feet, and diameter at breast height, in inches, for 70 shortleaf pines was reported in C. Bruce and F. X. Schumacher's *Forest Mensuration* (New York: McGraw-Hill, 1935) and analyzed by A. C. Akinson in the article "Transforming Both Sides of a Tree" (*The American Statistician*, 1994, Vol. 48, pp. 307–312). The data are provided on the WeissStats CD.

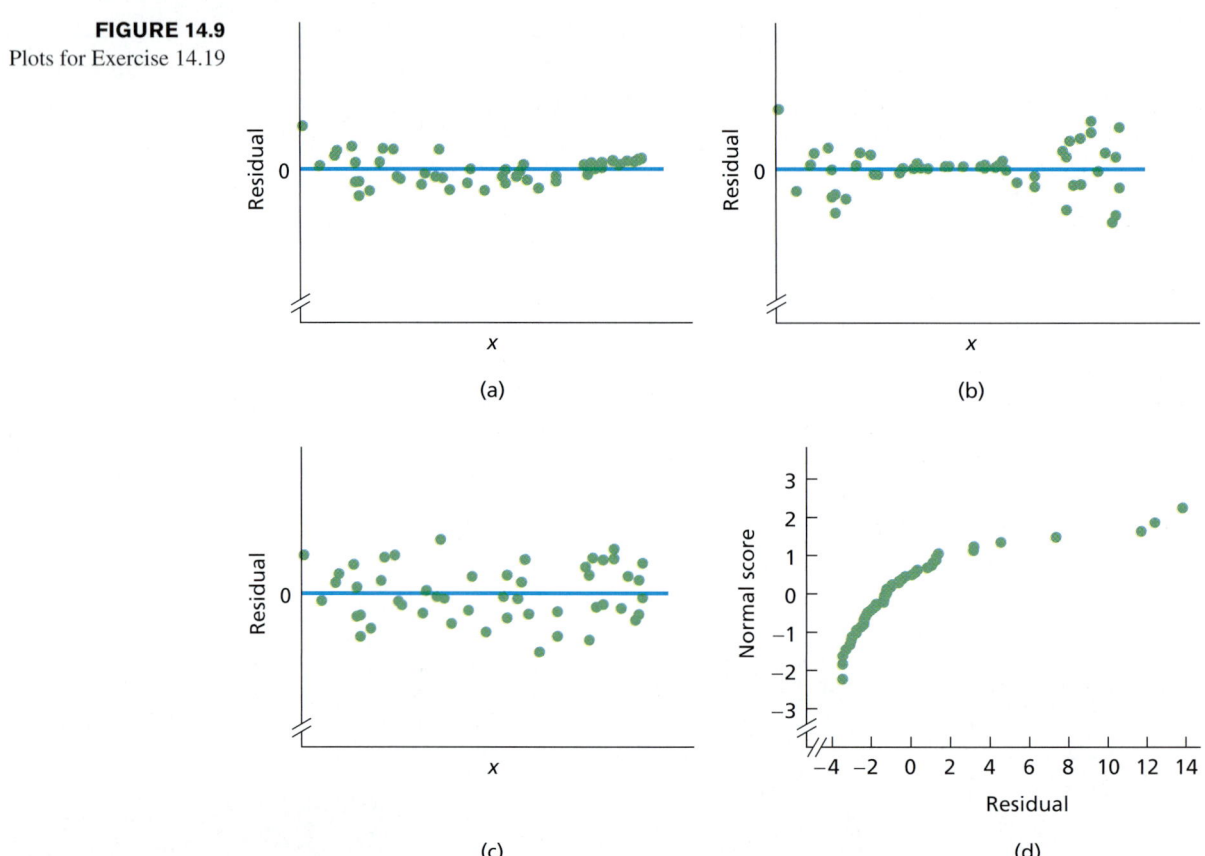

FIGURE 14.9 Plots for Exercise 14.19

14.2 INFERENCES FOR THE SLOPE OF THE POPULATION REGRESSION LINE

In this section and Section 14.3, we examine several inferential procedures used in regression analysis. Strictly speaking, these inferential techniques require that the assumptions for regression inferences given in Key Fact 14.1 on page 609 be satisfied by the variables under consideration. However, as we noted earlier, these techniques are robust to moderate violations of those assumptions.

The first inferential methods we present concern the slope, β_1, of the population regression line. To begin, we consider hypothesis testing.

HYPOTHESIS TESTS FOR THE SLOPE OF THE POPULATION REGRESSION LINE

Suppose that the variables x and y satisfy the assumptions for regression inferences. Then, for each value x of the predictor variable, the conditional distribution of the response variable is a normal distribution with mean $\beta_0 + \beta_1 x$ and standard deviation σ.

Of particular interest is whether the slope, β_1, of the population regression line equals 0. If $\beta_1 = 0$, then, for each value x of the predictor variable, the conditional distribution of the response variable is a normal distribution having mean β_0 ($= \beta_0 + 0 \cdot x$) and standard deviation σ. Because x does not appear in either of those two parameters, it is useless as a predictor of y.[4]

Hence, we can decide whether x is useful as a (linear) predictor of y—that is, whether the regression equation has utility—by performing the hypothesis test

$H_0: \beta_1 = 0$ (x is not useful for predicting y)

$H_a: \beta_1 \neq 0$ (x is useful for predicting y).

We base hypothesis tests for β_1 (the slope of the population regression line) on the statistic b_1 (the slope of a sample regression line). To explain how this method works, let's return to the Orion illustration. The data on age and price for a sample of 11 Orions are repeated in Table 14.3.

TABLE 14.3
Age and price data for a sample of 11 Orions

Car	Age (yr) x	Price ($100) y	Car	Age (yr) x	Price ($100) y
1	5	85	7	6	66
2	4	103	8	6	95
3	6	70	9	2	169
4	5	82	10	7	70
5	5	89	11	7	48
6	5	98			

On page 157, we found that the regression equation for these data—with age as the predictor variable and price as the response variable—is $\hat{y} = 195.47 - 20.26x$. In particular, the slope, b_1, of the sample regression line is -20.26.

We now consider all possible samples of 11 Orions whose ages are the same as those given in the Age columns of Table 14.3. For such samples, the slope, b_1, of the sample regression line varies from one sample to another and is therefore a variable. Its distribution is called the **sampling distribution of the slope of the regression line.** From the assumptions for regression inferences, we can show that this distribution is a normal distribution whose mean

---

[4]Although x alone may not be useful for predicting y, it may be useful in conjunction with another variable or variables. Thus, in this section, when we say that x is not useful for predicting y, we really mean that the regression equation with x as the only predictor variable is not useful for predicting y. Conversely, although x alone may be useful for predicting y, it may not be useful in conjunction with another variable or variables. Thus, in this section, when we say that x is useful for predicting y, we really mean that the regression equation with x as the only predictor variable is useful for predicting y.

is the slope, β_1, of the population regression line. More generally, we have Key Fact 14.3.

Key Fact 14.3   The Sampling Distribution of the Slope of the Regression Line

Suppose that the variables x and y satisfy Assumptions 1–3 for regression inferences. Then, for samples of size n, each with the same values $x_1, x_2, \ldots, x_n$, for the predictor variable, the following properties hold for the slope, b_1, of the sample regression line.

- The mean of b_1 equals the slope of the population regression line, or $\mu_{b_1} = \beta_1$.
- The standard deviation of b_1 is $\sigma_{b_1} = \sigma/\sqrt{S_{xx}}$.
- The variable b_1 is normally distributed.

In other words, the distribution of slopes of all possible sample regression lines is a normal distribution with mean β_1 and standard deviation $\sigma/\sqrt{S_{xx}}$.

As a consequence of Key Fact 14.3, the standardized variable

$$z = \frac{b_1 - \beta_1}{\sigma/\sqrt{S_{xx}}}$$

has the standard normal distribution. But this variable cannot be used as a basis for the required test statistic because the common conditional standard deviation, σ, is unknown. We therefore replace σ with its sample estimate s_e, the standard error of the estimate. As you might suspect, the resulting variable has a t-distribution, as presented in Key Fact 14.4.

Key Fact 14.4 t-Distribution for Inferences for β_1

Suppose that the variables x and y satisfy Assumptions 1–3 for regression inferences. Then, for samples of size n, each with the same values $x_1, x_2, \ldots, x_n$, for the predictor variable, the variable

$$t = \frac{b_1 - \beta_1}{s_e/\sqrt{S_{xx}}}$$

has the t-distribution with df $= n - 2$.

In light of Key Fact 14.4, for a hypothesis test with the null hypothesis $H_0: \beta_1 = 0$, we can use the variable

$$t = \frac{b_1}{s_e/\sqrt{S_{xx}}}$$

as the test statistic and obtain the critical values from the t-table, Table IV in Appendix A. Specifically, we have Procedures 14.1A and B, which we apply in Example 14.5.

14.2 Inferences for the Slope of the Population Regression Line

Procedure 14.1A — **The *t*-Test for the Utility of a Regression (Critical-Value Approach)**

Assumptions
The four assumptions for regression inferences

Step 1 The null and alternative hypotheses are

H_0: $\beta_1 = 0$ (predictor variable is not useful for making predictions)

H_a: $\beta_1 \neq 0$ (predictor variable is useful for making predictions).

Step 2 Decide on the significance level, α.

Step 3 Compute the value of the test statistic

$$t = \frac{b_1}{s_e/\sqrt{S_{xx}}}.$$

Step 4 The critical values are $\pm t_{\alpha/2}$ with $df = n-2$. Use Table IV to find the critical values.

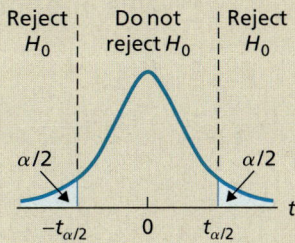

Step 5 If the value of the test statistic falls in the rejection region, reject H_0; otherwise, do not reject H_0.

Step 6 Interpret the results of the hypothesis test.

Example 14.5 The *t*-Test for the Utility of a Regression

Age and Price of Orions The data on age and price for a sample of 11 Orions are displayed in Table 14.3 on page 623. At the 5% significance level, do the data provide sufficient evidence to conclude that age is useful as a (linear) predictor of price for Orions?

Solution As we discovered in Example 14.3, we can reasonably consider the assumptions for regression inferences to be satisfied by the variables age and price for Orions, at least for Orions between 2 and 7 years old. So we apply Procedure 14.1 to carry out the required hypothesis test.

Procedure 14.1B — The t-Test for the Utility of a Regression (P-Value Approach)

Assumptions

The four assumptions for regression inferences

Step 1 The null and alternative hypotheses are

H_0: $\beta_1 = 0$ (predictor variable is not useful for making predictions)

H_a: $\beta_1 \neq 0$ (predictor variable is useful for making predictions).

Step 2 Decide on the significance level, α.

Step 3 Compute the value of the test statistic

$$t = \frac{b_1}{s_e/\sqrt{S_{xx}}}.$$

and denote that value t_0.

Step 4 The t-statistic has df $= n - 2$. Use Table IV to estimate the P-value or obtain it exactly by using technology.

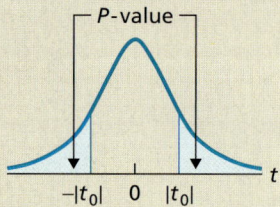

Step 5 If $P \leq \alpha$, reject H_0; otherwise, do not reject H_0.

Step 6 Interpret the results of the hypothesis test.

Step 1 State the null and alternative hypotheses.

Let β_1 denote the slope of the population regression line that relates price to age for Orions. Then the null and alternative hypotheses are

H_0: $\beta_1 = 0$ (predictor variable is not useful for making predictions)

H_a: $\beta_1 \neq 0$ (predictor variable is useful for making predictions).

Step 2 Decide on the significance level, α.

We are to perform the hypothesis test at the 5% significance level, or $\alpha = 0.05$.

Step 3 Compute the value of the test statistic

$$t = \frac{b_1}{s_e/\sqrt{S_{xx}}}.$$

In Example 4.4 on page 157, we found that $b_1 = -20.26$, $\Sigma x^2 = 326$, and $\Sigma x = 58$. Also, in Example 14.2 on page 612, we determined that $s_e = 12.58$. Therefore, because $n = 11$, the value of the test statistic is

$$t = \frac{b_1}{s_e/\sqrt{S_{xx}}} = \frac{b_1}{s_e/\sqrt{\Sigma x^2 - (\Sigma x)^2/n}} = \frac{-20.26}{12.58/\sqrt{326 - (58)^2/11}} = -7.235.$$

Critical-Value Approach

Step 4 The critical values are $\pm t_{\alpha/2}$ with df $= n - 2$.

From Step 2, $\alpha = 0.05$. For $n = 11$, df $= n - 2 = 11 - 2 = 9$. Using Table IV, we find that the critical values are $\pm t_{\alpha/2} = \pm t_{0.025} = \pm 2.262$, as depicted in Fig. 14.10A.

FIGURE 14.10A

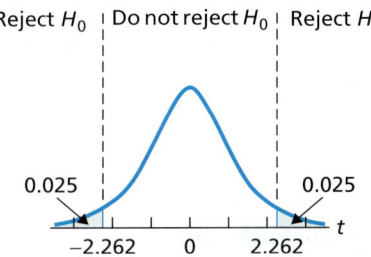

Step 5 If the value of the test statistic falls in the rejection region, reject H_0; otherwise, do not reject H_0.

The value of the test statistic, found in Step 3, is $t = -7.235$. Because this value falls in the rejection region, we reject H_0. The test results are statistically significant at the 5% level.

P-Value Approach

Step 4 The t-statistic has df $= n - 2$. Use Table IV to estimate the P-value or obtain it exactly by using technology.

From Step 3, the value of the test statistic is $t = -7.235$. Because the test is two-tailed, the P-value is the probability of observing a value of t of 7.235 or greater in magnitude if the null hypothesis is true. That probability equals the shaded area shown in Fig. 14.10B.

FIGURE 14.10B

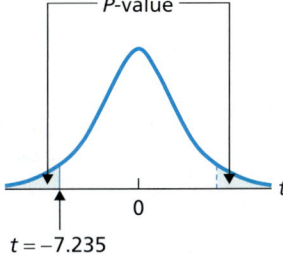

For $n = 11$, df $= 11 - 2 = 9$. Referring to Fig. 14.10B and to Table IV with df $= 9$, we find that $P < 0.01$. (Using technology, we obtain $P = 0.0000488$.)

Step 5 If $P \leq \alpha$, reject H_0; otherwise, do not reject H_0.

From Step 4, $P < 0.01$. Because the P-value is less than the specified significance level of 0.05, we reject H_0. The test results are statistically significant at the 5% level and (see Table 9.10 on page 405) provide very strong evidence against the null hypothesis.

Step 6 Interpret the results of the hypothesis test.

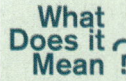

At the 5% significance level, the data provide sufficient evidence to conclude that the slope of the population regression line is not 0 and hence that age is useful as a (linear) predictor of price for Orions.

OTHER PROCEDURES FOR TESTING UTILITY OF THE REGRESSION

We use Procedure 14.1, which is based on the statistic b_1, to perform a hypothesis test to decide whether the slope of the population regression line is not 0 or, equivalently, whether the regression equation is useful for making predictions.

In Section 4.3, we introduced the coefficient of determination, r^2, as a descriptive measure of the utility of the regression equation for making predictions. Thus we should also be able to utilize the statistic r^2 as a basis for performing a hypothesis test to decide whether the regression equation is useful for making predictions—and indeed we can. However, we do not cover the hypothesis test based on r^2 because it is equivalent to the hypothesis test based on b_1.

We can also use the linear correlation coefficient, r, introduced in Section 4.4, as a basis for performing a hypothesis test to decide whether the regression equation is useful for making predictions. That test too is equivalent to the hypothesis test based on b_1 but, because it has other uses, we discuss it in Section 14.4.

CONFIDENCE INTERVALS FOR THE SLOPE OF THE POPULATION REGRESSION LINE

Recall that the slope of a straight line represents the change in the dependent variable, y, resulting from an increase in the independent variable, x, by 1 unit. Also recall that the population regression line, whose slope is β_1, gives the conditional means of the response variable. Therefore β_1 represents the change in the conditional mean of the response variable for each increase in the value of the predictor variable by 1 unit.

For instance, consider the variables age and price of Orions. In this case, β_1 is the amount that the mean price decreases for every increase in age by 1 year. In other words, β_1 is the mean yearly depreciation of Orions.

Consequently, obtaining an estimate for the slope of the population regression line is worthwhile. We know that a point estimate for β_1 is provided by b_1. To determine a confidence-interval estimate for β_1, we apply Key Fact 14.4 on page 624 to obtain Procedure 14.2.

14.2 Inferences for the Slope of the Population Regression Line

Procedure 14.2

The t-Interval Procedure for the Slope of a Population Regression Line

Assumptions

The four assumptions for regression inferences

Step 1 For a confidence level of $1 - \alpha$, use Table IV to find $t_{\alpha/2}$ with df = $n - 2$.

Step 2 The endpoints of the confidence interval for β_1 are

$$b_1 \pm t_{\alpha/2} \cdot \frac{s_e}{\sqrt{S_{xx}}}.$$

Step 3 Interpret the confidence interval.

Example 14.6 The t-Interval Procedure for the Slope of a Population Regression Line

Age and Price of Orions Use the data in Table 14.3 on page 623 to obtain a 95% confidence interval for the slope of the population regression line that relates price to age for Orions.

Solution We apply Procedure 14.2.

Step 1 For a confidence level of $1 - \alpha$, use Table IV to find $t_{\alpha/2}$ with df = $n - 2$.

For a 95% confidence interval, $\alpha = 0.05$. Because $n = 11$, df $= 11 - 2 = 9$. From Table IV, $t_{\alpha/2} = t_{0.05/2} = t_{0.025} = 2.262$.

Step 2 The endpoints of the confidence interval for β_1 are

$$b_1 \pm t_{\alpha/2} \cdot \frac{s_e}{\sqrt{S_{xx}}}.$$

From Example 4.4, $b_1 = -20.26$, $\Sigma x^2 = 326$, and $\Sigma x = 58$. Also, from Example 14.2, $s_e = 12.58$. Hence the endpoints of the confidence interval for β_1 are

$$-20.26 \pm 2.262 \cdot \frac{12.58}{\sqrt{326 - (58)^2/11}},$$

or -20.26 ± 6.33, or -26.59 to -13.93.

Step 3 Interpret the confidence interval.

> **What Does it Mean?** 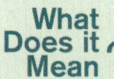 We can be 95% confident that the slope of the population regression line is somewhere between −26.59 and −13.93. In other words, we can be 95% confident that the yearly decrease in mean price for Orions is somewhere between $1393 and $2659.

The Technology Center

Procedure 14.1 provides a step-by-step method for performing a hypothesis test to decide whether the slope of a population regression line is not 0 and hence whether the regression equation is useful for making predictions. Most statistical technologies, including Minitab and Excel, provide the information needed to perform this test as part of their regression analysis output. However, some statistical technologies, such as the TI-83 Plus, require the implementation of a dedicated procedure.

For instance, consider the regression output in Printout 4.2 on page 164 for the age and price data of 11 Orions. In the Minitab output, the value of the t-statistic and the P-value for the hypothesis test appear as the last two entries in the fifth line. In the Excel output, those two items appear as the last two entries in the last line.

For the TI-83 Plus, we implement the hypothesis test to decide whether the slope of a population regression line is not 0 by using the **LinRegTTest** procedure. See the *TI-83 Plus Manual* for details.

Exercises 14.2

Statistical Concepts and Skills

14.26 Explain why the predictor variable is useless as a predictor of the response variable if the slope of the population regression line is 0.

14.27 For two variables satisfying Assumptions 1–3 for regression inferences, the population regression equation is $y = 20 - 3.5x$. For samples of size 10 and given values of the predictor variable, the distribution of slopes of all possible sample regression lines is a _____ distribution with mean _____.

14.28 Consider the standardized variable
$$z = \frac{b_1 - \beta_1}{\sigma/\sqrt{S_{xx}}}.$$

a. Identify its distribution.
b. Why can't it be used as the test statistic for a hypothesis test concerning β_1?
c. What statistic is used? What is the distribution of that statistic?

14.29 In this section, we used the statistic b_1 as a basis for conducting a hypothesis test to decide whether a regression equation is useful for prediction. Identify two other statistics that can be used as a basis for such a test.

In Exercises 14.30–14.33, we repeat information from Exercises 14.10–14.13. Presuming that the assumptions for regression inferences are met, perform the required hypothesis tests, using either the critical-value approach or the P-value approach. (Recall that you previously obtained the sample regression equations in Exercises 4.42–4.45 and the standard errors of the estimate in Exercises 14.14–14.17.)

14.30 Tax Efficiency. Following are the data on percentage of investments in energy securities and tax efficiency from Exercise 14.10.

x	3.1	3.2	3.7	4.3	4.0	5.5	6.7	7.4	7.4	10.6
y	98.1	94.7	92.0	89.8	87.5	85.0	82.0	77.8	72.1	53.5

At the 5% significance level, do the data provide sufficient evidence to conclude that the slope of the population regression line is not 0 and hence that percentage of investments in energy securities is useful as a predictor of tax efficiency for mutual fund portfolios?

14.31 Corvette Prices. Following are the age and price data for Corvettes from Exercise 14.11.

x	6	6	6	2	2	5	4	5	1	4
y	205	195	210	340	299	230	270	243	340	240

At the 10% significance level, do the data provide sufficient evidence to conclude that the slope of the population regression line is not 0 and hence that age is useful as a predictor of price for Corvettes?

14.32 Custom Homes. Following are the size and price data for custom homes from Exercise 14.12.

x	26	27	33	29	29	34	30	40	22
y	259	274	294	296	325	380	457	523	215

Do the data suggest that size is useful as a predictor of price for custom homes in the Equestrian Estates? Perform the required hypothesis test at the 0.01 level of significance.

14.33 Plant Emissions. Following are the data on plant weight and quantity of volatile emissions from Exercise 14.13.

x	57	85	57	65	52	67	62	80	77	53	68
y	8.0	22.0	10.5	22.5	12.0	11.5	7.5	13.0	16.5	21.0	12.0

Do the data suggest that weight is useful as a predictor of quantity of volatile emissions for the potato plant *Solanum tuberosom*? Use $\alpha = 0.05$.

In Exercises 14.34–14.37, apply Procedure 14.2 on page 629 to obtain the required confidence intervals.

14.34 Tax Efficiency. Refer to Exercise 14.30.
a. Find a 95% confidence interval for the slope, β_1, of the population regression line that relates tax efficiency to percent of investments in energy securities.
b. Interpret your answer to part (a).

14.35 Corvette Prices. Refer to Exercise 14.31.
a. Find a 90% confidence interval for the slope, β_1, of the population regression line that relates price to age for Corvettes.
b. Interpret your answer to part (a).

14.36 Custom Homes. Refer to Exercise 14.32.
a. Find a 99% confidence interval for the slope of the population regression line that relates price to size for custom homes in the Equestrian Estates.
b. Interpret your answer to part (a).

14.37 Plant Emissions. Refer to Exercise 14.33.
a. Obtain a 95% confidence interval for the slope, β_1, of the population regression line that relates quantity of volatile emissions to weight for the potato plant *Solanum tuberosom*.
b. Interpret your answer to part (a).

Using Technology

In Exercises 14.38–14.42, use the technology of your choice to
a. *decide at the 5% significance level whether the regression equation is useful for making predictions.*
b. *repeat part (a), but first remove all influential observations and outliers.*
c. *Compare your answers in parts (a) and (b) and state your conclusions.*

14.38 Batting and Scoring. Following are the data on season team batting average and total runs scored for a sample of major league baseball teams from Exercise 14.20.

Average	Runs	Average	Runs
.294	968	.267	793
.278	938	.265	792
.278	925	.256	764
.270	887	.254	752
.274	825	.246	740
.271	810	.266	738
.263	807	.262	731
.257	798	.251	708

14.39 Body Fat. Following are the age and body fat data for 18 randomly selected adults from Exercise 14.21.

Age	%Fat	Age	%Fat	Age	%Fat
23	9.5	45	27.4	56	32.5
23	27.9	49	25.2	57	30.3
27	7.8	50	31.1	58	33.0
27	17.8	53	34.7	58	33.8
39	31.4	53	42.0	60	41.1
41	25.9	54	29.1	61	34.5

14.40 PCBs and Pelicans. Use the data points given on the WeissStats CD for shell thickness and concentration of PCBs for 60 Anacapa pelican eggs referred to in Exercise 14.22.

14.41 Gas Guzzlers. Use the data on the WeissStats CD for gas mileage and engine displacement for 121 vehicles referred to in Exercise 14.23.

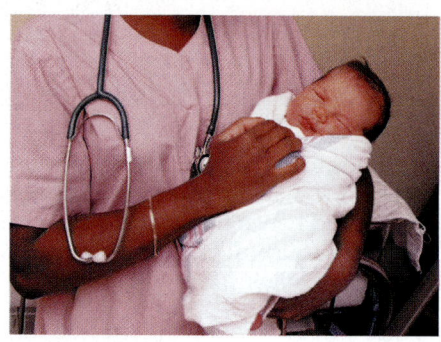

14.42 Estriol Level and Birth Weight. Use the data on the WeissStats CD for estriol levels of pregnant women and birth weights of their children referred to in Exercise 14.24.

14.3 ESTIMATION AND PREDICTION

In this section, we examine how a sample regression equation can be used to make two important inferences:

- estimating the conditional mean of the response variable corresponding to a particular value of the predictor variable; and
- predicting the value of the response variable for a particular value of the predictor variable.

We again use the Orion data, in Example 14.7, to illustrate the pertinent ideas. In doing so, we presume that the assumptions for regression inferences (Key Fact 14.1 on page 609) are satisfied by the variables age and price for Orions. Example 14.3 on page 615 shows that to presume so is not unreasonable.

Example 14.7 Estimating Conditional Means in Regression

Age and Price of Orions The data on age and price for a sample of 11 Orions are repeated in Table 14.4. Use the data to estimate the mean price of all 3-year-old Orions.

Solution By Assumption 1 of the assumptions for regression inferences, the population regression line gives the mean prices for the various ages of Orions. In partic-

TABLE 14.4
Age and price data for a sample of 11 Orions

Car	Age (yr) x	Price ($100) y	Car	Age (yr) x	Price ($100) y
1	5	85	7	6	66
2	4	103	8	6	95
3	6	70	9	2	169
4	5	82	10	7	70
5	5	89	11	7	48
6	5	98			

ular, the mean price of all 3-year-old Orions is $\beta_0 + \beta_1 \cdot 3$. Because β_0 and β_1 are unknown, we estimate the mean price of all 3-year-old Orions—$\beta_0 + \beta_1 \cdot 3$—by the corresponding value—$b_0 + b_1 \cdot 3$—on the sample regression line.

Recalling that the sample regression equation for the age and price data in Table 14.4 is $\hat{y} = 195.47 - 20.26x$, we estimate that the mean price of all 3-year-old Orions is

$$\hat{y} = 195.47 - 20.26 \cdot 3 = 134.69,$$

or $13,469. Note that the estimate for the mean price of all 3-year-old Orions is the same as the predicted price for a 3-year-old Orion. Both are obtained by substituting $x = 3$ into the sample regression equation. ◆

The estimate of $13,469 for the mean price of all 3-year-old Orions is a point estimate. Having some idea of how accurate that point estimate is would be more informative; in other words, providing a confidence-interval estimate for the mean price of all 3-year-old Orions would be better. We now explain how to obtain such confidence-interval estimates.

CONFIDENCE INTERVALS FOR CONDITIONAL MEANS IN REGRESSION

To develop a confidence-interval procedure for conditional means in regression, we must first identify the distribution of the predicted value of the response variable for a particular value of the predictor variable. Let's return to the Orion illustration and consider the particular value 3 of the predictor variable, that is, 3-year-old Orions.

As shown in Example 14.7, based on the sample data in Table 14.4, the predicted price for a 3-year-old Orion is 134.69 ($13,469). We now consider all possible samples of 11 Orions whose ages are the same as those given in the Age columns of Table 14.4.

For such samples, the predicted price of a 3-year-old Orion varies from one sample to another and is therefore a variable. Using the assumptions for regression inferences, we can show that its distribution is a normal distribution with a mean equalling the mean price of all 3-year-old Orions. More generally, we have Key Fact 14.5.

634 CHAPTER 14 Inferential Methods in Regression and Correlation

Key Fact 14.5 **Distribution of the Predicted Value of a Response Variable**

Suppose that the variables x and y satisfy Assumptions 1–3 for regression inferences. Let x_p denote a particular value of the predictor variable and let $\hat{y}_p$ be the corresponding value predicted for the response variable by the sample regression equation; that is, $\hat{y}_p = b_0 + b_1 x_p$. Then, for samples of size n, each with the same values, $x_1, x_2, \ldots, x_n$, for the predictor variable, the following properties hold for $\hat{y}_p$.

- The mean of $\hat{y}_p$ equals the conditional mean of the response variable corresponding to the value x_p of the predictor variable, or $\mu_{\hat{y}_p} = \beta_0 + \beta_1 x_p$.
- The standard deviation of $\hat{y}_p$ is

$$\sigma_{\hat{y}_p} = \sigma \sqrt{\frac{1}{n} + \frac{(x_p - \Sigma x/n)^2}{S_{xx}}}.$$

- The variable $\hat{y}_p$ is normally distributed.

In particular, the distribution of all possible predicted values of the response variable corresponding to x_p is a normal distribution with mean $\beta_0 + \beta_1 x_p$.

In light of Key Fact 14.5, if we standardize the variable $\hat{y}_p$, the resulting variable has the standard normal distribution. However, because the standardized variable contains the unknown parameter σ, it cannot be used as a basis for a confidence-interval formula. So we replace σ by its estimate s_e, the standard error of the estimate. The resulting variable has a t-distribution. More precisely, we have Key Fact 14.6.

Key Fact 14.6 **t-Distribution for Confidence Intervals for Conditional Means in Regression**

Suppose that the variables x and y satisfy Assumptions 1–3 for regression inferences. Then, for samples of size n, each with the same values, $x_1, x_2, \ldots, x_n$, for the predictor variable, the variable

$$t = \frac{\hat{y}_p - (\beta_0 + \beta_1 x_p)}{s_e \sqrt{\frac{1}{n} + \frac{(x_p - \Sigma x/n)^2}{S_{xx}}}}$$

has the t-distribution with df $= n - 2$.

Recalling that $\beta_0 + \beta_1 x_p$ is the conditional mean of the response variable corresponding to the value x_p of the predictor variable, we can apply Key Fact 14.6 to derive a confidence-interval procedure—Procedure 14.3—for means in regression. We then apply it in Example 14.8.

14.3 Estimation and Prediction

Procedure 14.3

The *t*-Interval Procedure for a Conditional Mean of the Response Variable

Assumptions

The four assumptions for regression inferences

Step 1 For a confidence level of $1-\alpha$, use Table IV to find $t_{\alpha/2}$ with df $= n-2$.

Step 2 Compute the point estimate, $\hat{y}_p = b_0 + b_1 x_p$, for the conditional mean of the response variable corresponding to the particular value x_p of the predictor variable.

Step 3 The endpoints of the confidence interval for the conditional mean of the response variable are

$$\hat{y}_p \pm t_{\alpha/2} \cdot s_e \sqrt{\frac{1}{n} + \frac{(x_p - \Sigma x/n)^2}{S_{xx}}}.$$

Step 4 Interpret the confidence interval.

Example 14.8 The *t*-Interval Procedure for a Conditional Mean of the Response Variable

Age and Price of Orions Use the sample data in Table 14.4 on page 633 to obtain a 95% confidence interval for the mean price of all 3-year-old Orions.

Solution We apply Procedure 14.3.

Step 1 For a confidence level of $1-\alpha$, use Table IV to find $t_{\alpha/2}$ with df $= n-2$.

We want a 95% confidence interval, or $\alpha = 0.05$. Because $n = 11$, we have df $= 9$. From Table IV, $t_{\alpha/2} = t_{0.05/2} = t_{0.025} = 2.262$.

Step 2 Compute the point estimate, $\hat{y}_p = b_0 + b_1 x_p$, for the conditional mean of the response variable corresponding to the particular value x_p of the predictor variable.

Here, $x_p = 3$ (3-year-old Orions). From Example 14.7, the point estimate for the mean price of all 3-year-old Orions is

$$\hat{y}_p = 195.47 - 20.26 \cdot 3 = 134.69.$$

Step 3 The endpoints of the confidence interval for the conditional mean of the response variable are

$$\hat{y}_p \pm t_{\alpha/2} \cdot s_e \sqrt{\frac{1}{n} + \frac{(x_p - \Sigma x/n)^2}{S_{xx}}}.$$

In Example 4.4, we found that $\Sigma x = 58$ and $\Sigma x^2 = 326$; in Example 14.2, we determined that $s_e = 12.58$. Also, from Step 1, $t_{\alpha/2} = 2.262$ and, from Step 2, $\hat{y}_p = 134.69$. Consequently, the endpoints of the confidence interval for the conditional mean are

$$134.69 \pm 2.262 \cdot 12.58 \sqrt{\frac{1}{11} + \frac{(3 - 58/11)^2}{326 - (58)^2/11}},$$

or 134.69 ± 16.76, or 117.93 to 151.45.

Step 4 Interpret the confidence interval.

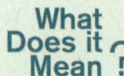

We can be 95% confident that the mean price of all 3-year-old Orions is somewhere between $11,793 and $15,145.

◆

PREDICTION INTERVALS

A primary use of a sample regression equation is to make predictions. The sample regression equation for the Orion data in Table 14.4 is $\hat{y} = 195.47 - 20.26x$. Substituting, for example, $x = 3$ into that equation, we obtain the predicted price for a 3-year-old Orion of 134.69, or $13,469. However, because the prices of such cars vary, finding a **prediction interval** for the price of a 3-year-old Orion makes more sense than giving a single predicted value.

Prediction intervals are similar to confidence intervals. The term *confidence* is usually reserved for interval estimates of parameters, such as the mean price of all 3-year-old Orions. The term *prediction* is used for interval estimates of variables, such as the price of a 3-year-old Orion.

To develop a prediction-interval procedure, we must first identify the distribution of the difference between the observed and predicted values of the response variable for a particular value of the predictor variable. Let's again return to the Orion illustration and consider the particular value 3 of the predictor variable, that is, 3-year-old Orions.

Based on the sample data for 11 Orions displayed in Table 14.4, the predicted price, in hundreds of dollars, for a 3-year-old Orion is 134.69. Suppose that we observe the price of a 3-year-old Orion to be 144.12. Then the difference between the observed price and predicted price is $144.12 - 134.69$, or 9.43.

We now consider all possible samples of 11 Orions whose ages are the same as those given in the second column of Table 14.4. For such samples, the predicted price of a 3-year-old Orion varies from one sample to another and is therefore a variable. The observed price of a 3-year-old Orion is also a variable. Consequently, the difference between the observed price and predicted price is also a variable. Using the assumptions for regression inferences, we can show that its distribution is a normal distribution with a mean of 0. More generally, we have Key Fact 14.7.

14.3 Estimation and Prediction

Key Fact 14.7 **Distribution of the Difference Between the Observed and Predicted Values of the Response Variable**

Suppose that the variables x and y satisfy Assumptions 1–3 for regression inferences. Let x_p denote a particular value of the predictor variable and let $\hat{y}_p$ be the corresponding value predicted for the response variable by the sample regression equation. Furthermore, let y_p be an independently observed value of the response variable corresponding to the value x_p of the predictor variable. Then, for samples of size n, each with the same values, $x_1, x_2, \ldots, x_n$, for the predictor variable, the following properties hold for $y_p - \hat{y}_p$, the difference between the observed and predicted values.

- The mean of $y_p - \hat{y}_p$ equals zero, or $\mu_{y_p - \hat{y}_p} = 0$.
- The standard deviation of $y_p - \hat{y}_p$ is

$$\sigma_{y_p - \hat{y}_p} = \sigma \sqrt{1 + \frac{1}{n} + \frac{(x_p - \Sigma x/n)^2}{S_{xx}}}.$$

- The variable $y_p - \hat{y}_p$ is normally distributed.

In particular, the distribution of all possible differences between the observed and predicted values of the response variable corresponding to x_p is a normal distribution with a mean of 0.

In light of Key Fact 14.7, if we standardize the variable $y_p - \hat{y}_p$, the resulting variable has the standard normal distribution. However, because the standardized variable contains the unknown parameter σ, it cannot be used as a basis for a prediction-interval formula. So we replace σ by its estimate s_e, the standard error of the estimate. The resulting variable has a t-distribution, as presented in Key Fact 14.8.

Key Fact 14.8 **t-Distribution for Prediction Intervals in Regression**

Suppose that the variables x and y satisfy Assumptions 1–3 for regression inferences. Then, for samples of size n, each with the same values, $x_1, x_2, \ldots, x_n$, for the predictor variable, the variable

$$t = \frac{y_p - \hat{y}_p}{s_e \sqrt{1 + \frac{1}{n} + \frac{(x_p - \Sigma x/n)^2}{S_{xx}}}}$$

has the t-distribution with df $= n - 2$.

Using Key Fact 14.8, we can derive a procedure—Procedure 14.4—for obtaining a prediction interval. We then apply it in Example 14.9.

Procedure 14.4 — The *t*-Interval Procedure for a Prediction of the Response Variable

Assumptions

The four assumptions for regression inferences

Step 1 For a prediction level of $1-\alpha$, use Table IV to find $t_{\alpha/2}$ with df $= n-2$.

Step 2 Compute the predicted value, $\hat{y}_p = b_0 + b_1 x_p$, of the response variable corresponding to the particular value x_p of the predictor variable.

Step 3 The endpoints of the prediction interval for the observed value of the response variable are

$$\hat{y}_p \pm t_{\alpha/2} \cdot s_e \sqrt{1 + \frac{1}{n} + \frac{(x_p - \Sigma x/n)^2}{S_{xx}}}.$$

Step 4 Interpret the prediction interval.

Example 14.9 The *t*-Interval Procedure for a Prediction of the Response Variable

Age and Price of Orions Using the sample data in Table 14.4 on page 633, obtain a 95% prediction interval for the price of a 3-year-old Orion.

Solution We apply Procedure 14.4.

Step 1 For a prediction level of $1-\alpha$, use Table IV to find $t_{\alpha/2}$ with df $= n-2$.

We want a 95% prediction interval, or $\alpha = 0.05$. Also, because $n = 11$, we have df $= 9$. From Table IV, $t_{\alpha/2} = t_{0.05/2} = t_{0.025} = 2.262$.

Step 2 Compute the predicted value, $\hat{y}_p = b_0 + b_1 x_p$, of the response variable corresponding to the particular value x_p of the predictor variable.

As previously shown, the sample regression equation for the data in Table 14.4 is $\hat{y} = 195.47 - 20.26x$. Consequently, the predicted price for a 3-year-old Orion is

$$\hat{y}_p = 195.47 - 20.26 \cdot 3 = 134.69.$$

Step 3 The endpoints of the prediction interval for the observed value of the response variable are

$$\hat{y}_p \pm t_{\alpha/2} \cdot s_e \sqrt{1 + \frac{1}{n} + \frac{(x_p - \Sigma x/n)^2}{S_{xx}}}.$$

From Example 4.4, $\Sigma x = 58$ and $\Sigma x^2 = 326$; from Example 14.2, we know that $s_e = 12.58$. Also, $n = 11$, $t_{\alpha/2} = 2.262$, $x_p = 3$, and $\hat{y}_p = 134.69$. Consequently, the endpoints of the prediction interval are

$$134.69 \pm 2.262 \cdot 12.58 \sqrt{1 + \frac{1}{11} + \frac{(3 - 58/11)^2}{326 - (58)^2/11}},$$

or 134.69 ± 33.02, or 101.67 to 167.71.

Step 4 Interpret the prediction interval.

> **What Does it Mean?** We can be 95% certain that the observed price of a 3-year-old Orion will be somewhere between $10,167 and $16,771.

♦

We just demonstrated that a 95% prediction interval for the observed price of a 3-year-old Orion is from $10,167 to $16,771. In Example 14.8, we found that a 95% confidence interval for the mean price of all 3-year-old Orions is from $11,793 to $15,145. We show both intervals in Fig. 14.11.

FIGURE 14.11
Prediction and confidence intervals for 3-year-old Orions

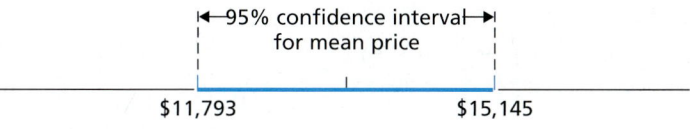

What Does it Mean?

More error is involved in predicting the price of a single 3-year-old Orion than in estimating the mean price of all 3-year-old Orions.

Note that the prediction interval is wider than the confidence interval, an outcome to be expected, for the following reason: The error in the estimate of the mean price of all 3-year-old Orions is due only to the fact that the population regression line is being estimated by a sample regression line, whereas the error in the prediction of the observed price of a 3-year-old Orion is due to the error in estimating the mean price plus the variation in prices of 3-year-old Orions.

The Technology Center

Some statistical technologies (e.g., Minitab) provide dedicated programs to automatically obtain confidence intervals for means and prediction intervals in regression, but others (e.g., Excel, TI-83 Plus) do not. For a statistical technology that does not have such programs, you can often use the macro capabilities of the statistical technology to write programs. Refer to the technology manuals for more details.

Exercises 14.3

Statistical Concepts and Skills

14.43 Without doing any calculations, fill in the blank and explain your answer. Based on the sample data in Table 14.4, the predicted price for a 4-year-old Orion is $11,443. A point estimate for the mean price of all 4-year-old Orions, based on the same sample data, is _____.

In Exercises 14.44–14.47, we repeat information from Exercises 14.10–14.13. Presuming that the assumptions for regression inferences are met, determine the required confidence and prediction intervals. (Recall that you previously obtained the sample regression equations in Exercises 4.42–4.45 and the standard errors of the estimate in Exercises 14.14–14.17.)

14.44 Tax Efficiency. Following are the data on percentage of investments in energy securities and tax efficiency from Exercise 14.10.

x	3.1	3.2	3.7	4.3	4.0	5.5	6.7	7.4	7.4	10.6
y	98.1	94.7	92.0	89.8	87.5	85.0	82.0	77.8	72.1	53.5

a. Obtain a point estimate for the mean tax efficiency of all mutual fund portfolios with 6% of their investments in energy securities.
b. Determine a 95% confidence interval for the mean tax efficiency of all mutual fund portfolios with 6% of their investments in energy securities.
c. Find the predicted tax efficiency of a mutual fund portfolio with 6% of its investments in energy securities.
d. Determine a 95% prediction interval for the tax efficiency of a mutual fund portfolio with 6% of its investments in energy securities.
e. Draw graphs similar to those in Fig. 14.11 on page 639, showing both the 95% confidence interval from part (b) and the 95% prediction interval from part (d).
f. Why is the prediction interval wider than the confidence interval?

14.45 Corvette Prices. Following are the age and price data for Corvettes from Exercise 14.11.

x	6	6	6	2	2	5	4	5	1	4
y	205	195	210	340	299	230	270	243	340	240

a. Obtain a point estimate for the mean price of all 4-year-old Corvettes.
b. Determine a 90% confidence interval for the mean price of all 4-year-old Corvettes.
c. Find the predicted price of a 4-year-old Corvette.
d. Determine a 90% prediction interval for the price of a 4-year-old Corvette.
e. Draw graphs similar to those in Fig. 14.11 on page 639, showing both the 90% confidence interval from part (b) and the 90% prediction interval from part (d).
f. Why is the prediction interval wider than the confidence interval?

14.46 Custom Homes. Following are the size and price data for custom homes from Exercise 14.12.

x	26	27	33	29	29	34	30	40	22
y	259	274	294	296	325	380	457	523	215

a. Obtain a point estimate for the mean price of all 2800-sq-ft Equestrian Estate homes.
b. Find a 99% confidence interval for the mean price of all 2800-sq-ft Equestrian Estate homes.
c. Find the predicted price of a 2800-sq-ft Equestrian Estate home.
d. Determine a 99% prediction interval for the price of a 2800-sq-ft Equestrian Estate home.

14.47 Plant Emissions. Following are the data on plant weight and quantity of volatile emissions from Exercise 14.13.

x	57	85	57	65	52	67	62	80	77	53	68
y	8.0	22.0	10.5	22.5	12.0	11.5	7.5	13.0	16.5	21.0	12.0

a. Obtain a point estimate for the mean quantity of volatile emissions of all (*Solanum tuberosom*) plants that weigh 60 g.
b. Find a 95% confidence interval for the mean quantity of volatile emissions of all plants that weigh 60 g.
c. Find the predicted quantity of volatile emissions for a plant that weighs 60 g.
d. Determine a 95% prediction interval for the quantity of volatile emissions for a plant that weighs 60 g.

Extending the Concepts and Skills

Margin of Error in Regression. In Exercises 14.48 and 14.49, you are asked to examine the magnitude of the margin of error of confidence intervals and prediction intervals in regression as a function of how far the specified value of the predictor variable is from the mean of the observed values of the predictor variable.

14.48 Age and Price of Orions. Refer to the data on age and price of a sample of 11 Orions given in Table 14.4 on page 633.

a. For each age between 2 and 7 years, obtain a 95% confidence interval for the mean price of all Orions of that age. Plot the confidence intervals against age and discuss your results.
b. Determine the margin of error for each confidence interval that you obtained in part (a). Plot the margins of error against age and discuss your results.
c. Repeat parts (a) and (b) for prediction intervals.

14.49 Refer to the confidence interval and prediction interval formulas in Procedures 14.3 and 14.4, respectively.
a. Explain why, for a fixed confidence level, the margin of error for the estimate of the conditional mean of the response variable increases as the value of the predictor variable moves farther from the mean of the observed values of the predictor variable.
b. Explain why, for a fixed prediction level, the margin of error for the estimate of the predicted value of the response variable increases as the value of the predictor variable moves farther from the mean of the observed values of the predictor variable.

Using Technology

Use the technology of your choice in Exercises 14.50–14.54.

14.50 Batting and Scoring. Following are the data on season team batting average and total runs scored for a sample of major league baseball teams from Exercise 14.20.

Average	Runs	Average	Runs
.294	968	.267	793
.278	938	.265	792
.278	925	.256	764
.270	887	.254	752
.274	825	.246	740
.271	810	.266	738
.263	807	.262	731
.257	798	.251	708

a. Obtain a point estimate for the mean total runs scored by all major league teams with a season team batting average of .270.
b. Find a 95% confidence interval for the mean total runs scored by all major league teams with a season team batting average of .270.

c. Find the predicted total runs scored by a major league team with a season team batting average of .270.
d. Determine a 95% prediction interval for the total runs scored by a major league team with a season team batting average of .270.
e. Remove the influential observation and repeat parts (a)–(d). Compare your results with and without the removal of the influential observation.

14.51 Body Fat. Following are the age and body fat data for 18 randomly selected adults from Exercise 14.21.

Age	%Fat	Age	%Fat	Age	%Fat
23	9.5	45	27.4	56	32.5
23	27.9	49	25.2	57	30.3
27	7.8	50	31.1	58	33.0
27	17.8	53	34.7	58	33.8
39	31.4	53	42.0	60	41.1
41	25.9	54	29.1	61	34.5

a. Obtain a point estimate for the mean percentage of body fat of all 30-year-old adults.
b. Find a 95% confidence interval for the mean percentage of body fat of all 30-year-old adults.
c. Find the predicted percentage of body fat of a 30-year-old adult.
d. Determine a 95% prediction interval for the percentage of body fat of a 30-year-old adult.

14.52 PCBs and Pelicans. Use the data points given on the WeissStats CD for shell thickness and concentration of PCBs for 60 Anacapa pelican eggs referred to in Exercise 14.22.

a. Obtain a point estimate for the mean shell thickness of all Anacapa pelican eggs with a PCB concentration of 200 ppm.
b. Find a 95% confidence interval for the mean shell thickness of all Anacapa pelican eggs with a PCB concentration of 200 ppm.
c. Find the predicted shell thickness of an Anacapa pelican egg with a PCB concentration of 200 ppm.
d. Determine a 95% prediction interval for the shell thickness of an Anacapa pelican egg with a PCB concentration of 200 ppm.

14.53 Gas Guzzlers. Use the data on the WeissStats CD for gas mileage and engine displacement for 121 vehicles referred to in Exercise 14.23.
a. Find a 95% confidence interval for the mean gas mileage of all vehicles with an engine displacement of 3.0 L.
b. Determine a 95% prediction interval for the gas mileage of a vehicle with an engine displacement of 3.0 L.
c. Compare and discuss the differences between the confidence interval that you obtained in part (a) and the prediction interval that you obtained in part (b).

14.54 Estriol Level and Birth Weight. Use the data on the WeissStats CD for estriol levels of pregnant women and birth weights of their children referred to in Exercise 14.24.
a. Find a 95% confidence interval for the mean birth weight of all children whose mothers had an estriol level of 18 mg/24 hr.
b. Determine a 95% prediction interval for the birth weight of a child whose mother had an estriol level of 18 mg/24 hr.
c. Compare and discuss the differences between the confidence interval that you obtained in part (a) and the prediction interval that you obtained in part (b).

14.4 INFERENCES IN CORRELATION

Frequently, we want to decide whether two variables are linearly correlated, that is, whether there is a linear relationship between the two variables. In the context of regression, we can make that decision by performing a hypothesis test for the slope of the population regression line, as discussed in Section 14.2.

Alternatively, we can perform a hypothesis test for the **population linear correlation coefficient,** ρ (rho). This parameter measures the linear correlation of all possible pairs of observations of two variables in the same way that a sample linear correlation coefficient, r, measures the linear correlation of a sample of pairs. Thus ρ actually describes the strength of the linear relationship between two variables; r is only an estimate of ρ obtained from sample data.

The population linear correlation coefficient of two variables, x and y, always lies between -1 and 1. Values of ρ near -1 or 1 indicate a strong linear relationship between the variables, whereas values of ρ near 0 indicate a weak linear relationship between the variables.

If $\rho > 0$, the variables are **positively linearly correlated variables,** meaning that y tends to increase linearly as x increases (and vice versa), with the tendency being greater the closer ρ is to 1. If $\rho < 0$, the variables are **negatively linearly correlated variables,** meaning that y tends to decrease linearly as x increases (and vice versa), with the tendency being greater the closer ρ is to -1. If $\rho = 0$, the variables are **linearly uncorrelated variables,** meaning that there is no linear relationship between the variables. If $\rho \neq 0$—that is, the variables are not linearly uncorrelated or, equivalently, are either positively linearly correlated or negatively linearly correlated—the variables are **linearly correlated variables.**

Because a sample linear correlation coefficient, r, is an estimate of the population linear correlation coefficient, ρ, we can use r as a basis for performing a hypothesis test for ρ. For a test with the null hypothesis H_0: $\rho = 0$ (i.e., the variables are linearly uncorrelated), we use Key Fact 14.9.

Key Fact 14.9 **t-Distribution for a Correlation Test**

Suppose that the variables x and y satisfy Assumptions 1–3 for regression inferences. Then, for samples of size n, the variable

$$t = \frac{r}{\sqrt{\dfrac{1 - r^2}{n - 2}}}$$

has the t-distribution with df $= n - 2$ if the null hypothesis $\rho = 0$ is true.

In light of Key Fact 14.9, for a hypothesis test with the null hypothesis H_0: $\rho = 0$, we can use the variable

$$t = \frac{r}{\sqrt{\dfrac{1 - r^2}{n - 2}}}$$

as the test statistic and obtain the critical values from the t-table, Table IV. Specifically, we have Procedures 14.5A and B. We apply them in Example 14.10.

Procedure 14.5A The *t*-Test for Correlation (Critical-Value Approach)

Assumptions

The four assumptions for regression inferences

Step 1 The null hypothesis is $H_0: \rho = 0$, and the alternative hypothesis is

$H_a: \rho \neq 0$ (Two-tailed) or $H_a: \rho < 0$ (Left-tailed) or $H_a: \rho > 0$ (Right-tailed)

Step 2 Decide on the significance level, α.

Step 3 Compute the value of the test statistic

$$t = \frac{r}{\sqrt{\dfrac{1-r^2}{n-2}}}.$$

Step 4 The critical value(s) are

$\pm t_{\alpha/2}$ (Two-tailed) or $-t_{\alpha}$ (Left-tailed) or t_{α} (Right-tailed)

with df $= n-2$. Use Table IV to find the critical value(s).

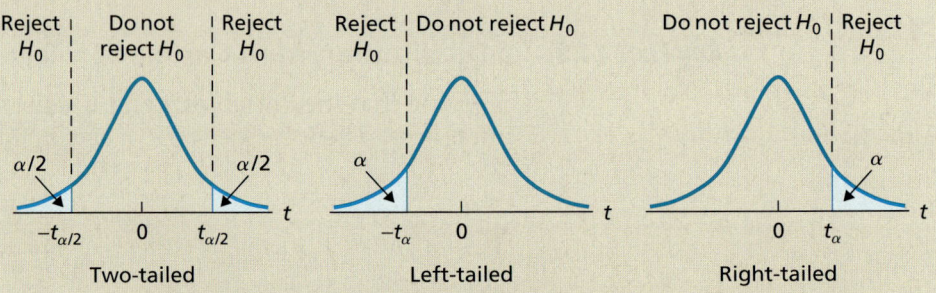

Step 5 If the value of the test statistic falls in the rejection region, reject H_0; otherwise, do not reject H_0.

Step 6 Interpret the results of the hypothesis test.

Procedure 14.5B — The t-Test for Correlation (P-Value Approach)

Assumptions

The four assumptions for regression inferences

Step 1 The null hypothesis is H_0: $\rho = 0$, and the alternative hypothesis is

H_a: $\rho \neq 0$ (Two-tailed) or H_a: $\rho < 0$ (Left-tailed) or H_a: $\rho > 0$ (Right-tailed)

Step 2 Decide on the significance level, α.

Step 3 Compute the value of the test statistic

$$t = \frac{r}{\sqrt{\frac{1-r^2}{n-2}}}$$

and denote that value t_0.

Step 4 The t-statistic has df $= n - 2$. Use Table IV to estimate the P-value or obtain it exactly by using technology.

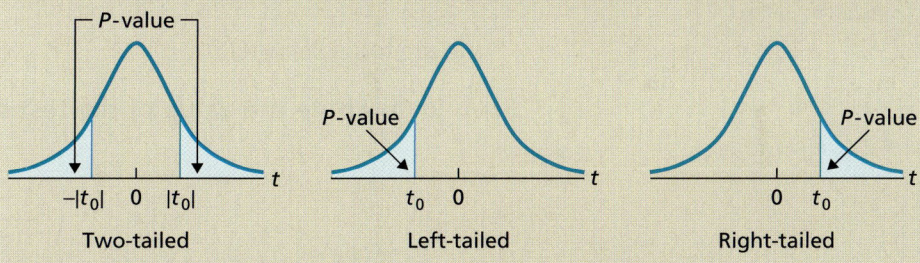

Two-tailed   Left-tailed   Right-tailed

Step 5 If $P \leq \alpha$, reject H_0; otherwise, do not reject H_0.

Step 6 Interpret the results of the hypothesis test.

Example 14.10 The t-Test for Correlation

Age and Price of Orions Refer to the age and price data for a sample of 11 Orions given in Table 14.4 on page 633. At the 5% significance level, do the data provide sufficient evidence to conclude that age and price of Orions are negatively linearly correlated?

Solution As we discovered in Example 14.3 on page 615, considering that the assumptions for regression inferences are met by the variables age and price for Orions is not unreasonable, at least for Orions between 2 and 7 years old. Consequently, we apply Procedure 14.5 to carry out the required hypothesis test.

Step 1 State the null and alternative hypotheses.

Let ρ denote the population linear correlation coefficient for the variables age and price of Orions. Then the null and alternative hypotheses are

H_0: $\rho = 0$ (age and price are linearly uncorrelated)

H_a: $\rho < 0$ (age and price are negatively linearly correlated).

Note that the hypothesis test is left-tailed because a less-than sign (<) appears in the alternative hypothesis.

Step 2 Decide on the significance level, α.

We are to use $\alpha = 0.05$.

Step 3 Compute the value of the test statistic

$$t = \frac{r}{\sqrt{\frac{1-r^2}{n-2}}}.$$

In Example 4.10 on page 181, we computed the sample linear correlation coefficient for the age and price data displayed in Table 14.4. We found that $r = -0.924$, so the value of the test statistic is

$$t = \frac{-0.924}{\sqrt{\frac{1-(-0.924)^2}{11-2}}} = -7.249.$$

Critical-Value Approach

Step 4 The critical value for a left-tailed test is $-t_\alpha$, with df $= n-2$.

For $n = 11$, df $= 9$. Also, $\alpha = 0.05$. From Table IV, for df $= 9$, $t_{0.05} = 1.833$. Thus the critical value is $-t_{0.05} = -1.833$, as shown in Fig. 14.12A.

FIGURE 14.12A

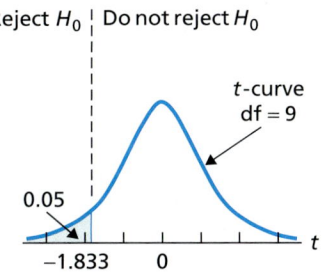

Step 5 If the value of the test statistic falls in the rejection region, reject H_0; otherwise, do not reject H_0.

The value of the test statistic, found in Step 3, is $t = -7.249$. Figure 14.12A shows that this value falls in the rejection region, so we reject H_0. The test results are statistically significant at the 5% level.

P-Value Approach

Step 4 The t-statistic has df $= n-2$. Use Table IV to estimate the P-value or obtain it exactly by using technology.

From Step 3, the value of the test statistic is $t = -7.249$. Because the test is left-tailed, the P-value is the probability of observing a value of t of -7.249 or less if the null hypothesis is true. That probability equals the shaded area shown in Fig. 14.12B.

FIGURE 14.12B

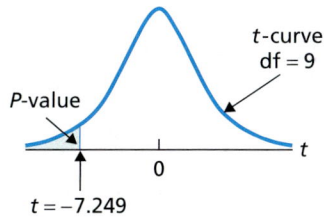

For $n = 11$, df $= 9$. Referring to Fig. 14.12B and Table IV, we find that $P < 0.005$. (Using technology, we obtain $P = 0.0000244$.)

Step 5 If $P \leq \alpha$, reject H_0; otherwise, do not reject H_0.

From Step 4, $P < 0.005$. Because the P-value is less than the specified significance level of 0.05, we reject H_0. The test results are statistically significant at the 5% level and (see Table 9.10 on page 405) provide very strong evidence against the null hypothesis.

Step 6 Interpret the results of the hypothesis test.

What Does it Mean? At the 5% significance level, the data provide sufficient evidence to conclude that age and price of Orions are negatively linearly correlated. Prices for Orions tend to decrease linearly with increasing age, at least for Orions between 2 and 7 years old.

The Technology Center

Some statistical technologies have programs that automatically conduct a correlation test. For instance, the TI-83 Plus program **LinRegTTest**, which we mentioned at the end of Section 14.2, can be used to perform such a test.

Minitab's **Correlation** program, examined at the end of Section 4.4, provides r and the P-value for a two-tailed correlation test but currently doesn't give the P-value for one-tailed tests. Excel's **Correlation** program, also examined at the end of Section 4.4, provides r but not a P-value.

The time-consuming part of conducting a correlation test is computing the sample linear correlation coefficient, r. Most statistical technologies (including Minitab, Excel, and the TI-83 Plus) have programs for automatically obtaining r. See the technology manuals for details of performing a correlation test.

Exercises 14.4

Statistical Concepts and Skills

14.55 Identify the statistic used to estimate the population linear correlation coefficient.

14.56 Suppose that, for a sample of pairs of observations from two variables, the linear correlation coefficient, r, is positive. Does this result necessarily imply that the variables are positively linearly correlated? Explain your answer.

14.57 Fill in the blanks.
a. If $\rho = 0$, the two variables under consideration are linearly _____.
b. If two variables are positively linearly correlated, one of the variables tends to increase as the other _____.
c. If two variables are _____ linearly correlated, one of the variables tends to decrease as the other increases.

In Exercises 14.58–14.61, we repeat information from Exercises 14.10–14.13. Presuming that the assumptions for regression inferences are met, perform the required correlation tests, using either the critical-value approach or the P-value approach. (Recall that you previously obtained the sample linear correlation coefficients in Exercises 4.86–4.89.)

14.58 Tax Efficiency. Following are the data on percentage of investments in energy securities and tax efficiency from Exercise 14.10.

x	3.1	3.2	3.7	4.3	4.0	5.5	6.7	7.4	7.4	10.6
y	98.1	94.7	92.0	89.8	87.5	85.0	82.0	77.8	72.1	53.5

At the 2.5% significance level, do the data provide sufficient evidence to conclude that percentage of investments in energy securities and tax efficiency are negatively linearly correlated for mutual fund portfolios?

14.59 Corvette Prices. Following are the age and price data for Corvettes from Exercise 14.11.

x	6	6	6	2	2	5	4	5	1	4
y	205	195	210	340	299	230	270	243	340	240

At the 5% level of significance, do the data provide sufficient evidence to conclude that age and price of Corvettes are negatively linearly correlated?

14.60 Custom Homes. Following are the size and price data for custom homes from Exercise 14.12.

x	26	27	33	29	29	34	30	40	22
y	259	274	294	296	325	380	457	523	215

At the 0.5% significance level, do the data provide sufficient evidence to conclude that, for custom homes in the Equestrian Estates, size and price are positively linearly correlated?

dence to conclude that the variables student-to-faculty ratio and graduation rate are positively linearly correlated?

Using Technology

17. Graduation Rates. Use the technology of your choice to carry out the residual analysis in Problem 13.

18. Graduation Rates. Refer to Problem 11. Use the technology of your choice to

a. obtain the sample regression equation.
b. determine the standard error of the estimate.

19. Graduation Rates. Use the technology of your choice to do the following.
a. Carry out the hypothesis test in Problem 14(a).
b. Obtain the confidence interval in Problem 15(b) and the prediction interval in Problem 15(d).

20. Graduation Rates. Use the technology of your choice to perform the correlation test in Problem 16.

Assisted Reproductive Technology (Revisited)

In this Internet project, you are to take a deeper look into the data on Assisted Reproductive Technology (ART). In your previous exploration of the data in Chapter 4, you found a linear relationship between the age of the prospective mother who uses ART and her chances for reproductive success. Now you will further analyze the results from that regression.

Another interesting relationship appears in the ART data. When eggs from a donor are implanted (i.e., when the implanted eggs are not the prospective mother's), the relationship between success rate and age changes in a surprising way. This part of the study will encourage you to think about the real situation that the analysis is attempting to explain.

URL for access to Internet Projects Page: www.aw.com/weiss

SAT Scores and GPA

Recall from Chapter 1 (see page 34) that the Focus database contains information on 500 randomly selected Arizona State University sophomores. For these database exercises, you should eliminate all cases (students) in which one or more of the four variables, cumulative GPA, high school GPA, SAT math score, and SAT verbal score, equal 0. Use the technology of your choice to solve the following problems.

First, consider a regression analysis on cumulative GPA with high school GPA as the predictor variable.

a. Determine the sample regression equation.
b. Perform a residual analysis to decide whether considering the assumptions for regression inferences to be satisfied appears reasonable.

Presuming that the assumptions for regression inferences hold for the variables high school GPA and cumulative GPA, solve the following problems.

c. Obtain and interpret the standard error of the estimate.
d. At the 5% significance level, do the data provide sufficient evidence to conclude that high school GPA is useful for predicting cumulative GPA of sophomores at Arizona State University?

b. A residual plot becomes wider with increasing values of the predictor variable.
c. A normal probability plot of the residuals shows extreme curvature.
d. A normal probability plot of the residuals shows outliers but is otherwise roughly linear.

5. Suppose that you perform a hypothesis test for the slope of the population regression line with the null hypothesis $H_0: \beta_1 = 0$ and the alternative hypothesis $H_a: \beta_1 \neq 0$. If you reject the null hypothesis, what can you say about the utility of the regression equation for making predictions?

6. Identify three statistics that can be used as a basis for testing the utility of a regression.

7. For a particular value of a predictor variable, is there a difference between the predicted value of the response variable and the point estimate for the conditional mean of the response variable? Explain your answer.

8. Generally speaking, what is the difference between a confidence interval and a prediction interval?

9. Fill in the blank: $\bar{x}$ is to μ as r is to _____.

10. Identify the relationship between two variables and the terminology used to describe that relationship if
a. $\rho > 0$. **b.** $\rho = 0$. **c.** $\rho < 0$.

11. Graduation Rates. Graduation rate—the percentage of entering freshmen, attending full time and graduating within 5 years—and what influences it have become a concern in U.S. colleges and universities. *U.S. News and World Report*'s "College Guide" provides data on graduation rates for colleges and universities as a function of the percentage of freshmen in the top 10% of their high school class, total spending per student, and student-to-faculty ratio. A random sample of 10 universities gave the following data on student-to-faculty ratio (S/F ratio) and graduation rate (grad rate).

S/F ratio x	Grad rate y
16	45
20	55
17	70
19	50
22	47
17	46
17	50
17	66
10	26
18	60

Discuss what satisfying the assumptions for regression inferences would mean with student-to-faculty ratio as the predictor variable and graduation rate as the response variable.

12. Graduation Rates. Refer to Problem 11.
a. Determine the regression equation for the data.
b. Compute and interpret the standard error of the estimate.
c. Presuming that the assumptions for regression inferences are met, interpret your answer to part (b).

13. Graduation Rates. Refer to Problems 11 and 12. Perform a residual analysis to decide whether considering the assumptions for regression inferences to be met by the variables student-to-faculty ratio and graduation rate is reasonable.

In the remainder of this review test, presume that the variables student-to-faculty ratio and graduation rate satisfy the assumptions for regression inferences.

14. Graduation Rates. Refer to Problems 11 and 12.
a. At the 5% significance level, do the data provide sufficient evidence to conclude that student-to-faculty ratio is useful as a predictor of graduation rate?
b. Determine a 95% confidence interval for the slope, β_1, of the population regression line that relates graduation rate to student-to-faculty ratio. Interpret your answer.

15. Graduation Rates. Refer to Problems 11 and 12.
a. Determine a point estimate for the mean graduation rate of all universities that have a student-to-faculty ratio of 17.
b. Determine a 95% confidence interval for the mean graduation rate of all universities that have a student-to-faculty ratio of 17.
c. Find the predicted graduation rate for a university that has a student-to-faculty ratio of 17.
d. Obtain a 95% prediction interval for the graduation rate of a university that has a student-to-faculty ratio of 17.
e. Explain why the prediction interval in part (d) is wider than the confidence interval in part (b).

16. Graduation Rates. Refer to Problem 11. At the 2.5% significance level, do the data provide sufficient evi-

CHAPTER 14 Inferential Methods in Regression and Correlation

Chapter Review

You Should Be Able To

1. use and understand the formulas presented in this chapter.
2. state the assumptions for regression inferences.
3. understand the difference between the population regression line and a sample regression line.
4. estimate the regression parameters β_0, β_1, and σ.
5. determine the standard error of the estimate.
6. perform a residual analysis to check the assumptions for regression inferences.
7. perform a hypothesis test to decide whether the slope, β_1, of the population regression line is not 0 and hence whether x is useful for predicting y.
8. obtain a confidence interval for β_1.
9. determine a point estimate and a confidence interval for the conditional mean of the response variable corresponding to a particular value of the predictor variable.
10. determine a predicted value and a prediction interval for the response variable corresponding to a particular value of the predictor variable.
11. understand the difference between the population correlation coefficient and a sample correlation coefficient.
12. perform a hypothesis test for a population linear correlation coefficient.

Key Terms

conditional distribution, *608*
conditional mean, *608*
linearly correlated variables, *643*
linearly uncorrelated variables, *643*
negatively linearly correlated
    variables, *643*
population linear correlation
    coefficient (ρ), *642*
population regression equation, *609*
population regression line, *609*
positively linearly correlated
    variables, *643*
prediction interval, *636*
regression model, *609*
residual (e), *613*
residual plot, *614*
residual standard deviation, *611*
sampling distribution of the slope of
    the regression line, *624*
standard error of the estimate (s_e), *612*

Review Test

Statistical Concepts and Skills

1. Suppose that x and y are two variables of a population with x a predictor variable and y a response variable.
   a. The distribution of all possible values of the response variable y corresponding to a particular value of the predictor variable x is called a _____ distribution of the response variable.
   b. State the four assumptions for regression inferences.

2. Suppose that x and y are two variables of a population and that the assumptions for regression inferences are met with x as the predictor variable and y as the response variable.
   a. What statistic is used to estimate the slope of the population regression line?
   b. What statistic is used to estimate the y-intercept of the population regression line?
   c. What statistic is used to estimate the common conditional standard deviation of the response variable corresponding to fixed values of the predictor variable?

3. What two plots did we use in this chapter to decide whether we can reasonably presume that the assumptions for regression inferences are met by two variables of a population? What properties should those plots have?

4. Regarding analysis of residuals, decide in each case which assumption for regression inferences may be violated.
   a. A residual plot—that is, a plot of the residuals against the observed values of the predictor variable—shows curvature.

14.4 Inferences in Correlation

14.61 Plant Emissions. Following are the data on plant weight and quantity of volatile emissions from Exercise 14.13.

x	57	85	57	65	52	67	62	80	77	53	68
y	8.0	22.0	10.5	22.5	12.0	11.5	7.5	13.0	16.5	21.0	12.0

Do the data suggest that, for the potato plant *Solanum tuberosom*, weight and quantity of volatile emissions are linearly correlated? Use $\alpha = 0.05$.

14.62 Height and Score. A random sample of 10 students was taken from an introductory statistics class. The following data were obtained, where x denotes height, in inches, and y denotes score on the final exam.

x	71	68	71	65	66	68	68	64	62	65
y	87	96	66	71	71	55	83	67	86	60

At the 5% significance level, do the data provide sufficient evidence to conclude that, for students in introductory statistics courses, height and final exam score are linearly correlated?

14.63 Is ρ a parameter or a statistic? What about r? Explain your answers.

Using Technology

Use the technology of your choice in Exercises 14.64–14.68.

14.64 Batting and Scoring. Following are the data on season team batting average and total runs scored for a sample of major league baseball teams from Exercise 14.20.

Average	Runs	Average	Runs
.294	968	.267	793
.278	938	.265	792
.278	925	.256	764
.270	887	.254	752
.274	825	.246	740
.271	810	.266	738
.263	807	.262	731
.257	798	.251	708

a. At the 2.5% significance level, do the data provide sufficient evidence to conclude that season team batting average and total runs scored are positively linearly correlated for major league baseball teams?
b. Remove the influential observation and repeat part (a).
c. Compare your results with and without the removal of the influential observation and state your conclusions.

14.65 Body Fat. Following are the age and body fat data for 18 randomly selected adults from Exercise 14.21.

Age	%Fat	Age	%Fat	Age	%Fat
23	9.5	45	27.4	56	32.5
23	27.9	49	25.2	57	30.3
27	7.8	50	31.1	58	33.0
27	17.8	53	34.7	58	33.8
39	31.4	53	42.0	60	41.1
41	25.9	54	29.1	61	34.5

a. Do the data provide sufficient evidence to conclude that, for adults, age and percentage of body fat are positively linearly correlated? Use $\alpha = 0.025$.
b. Remove the potential outlier and repeat part (a).
c. Compare your results with and without the removal of the potential outlier and state your conclusions.

14.66 PCBs and Pelicans. Use the data points given on the WeissStats CD for shell thickness and concentration of PCBs for 60 Anacapa pelican eggs referred to in Exercise 14.22. Do the data provide sufficient evidence to conclude, at the 5% significance level, that concentration of PCBs and shell thickness are linearly correlated for Anacapa pelican eggs?

14.67 Gas Guzzlers. Use the data on the WeissStats CD for gas mileage and engine displacement for 121 vehicles referred to in Exercise 14.23. Do the data provide sufficient evidence to conclude that engine displacement and gas mileage are negatively linearly correlated? Use $\alpha = 0.025$.

14.68 Estriol Level and Birth Weight. Use the data on the WeissStats CD for estriol levels of pregnant women and birth weights of their children referred to in Exercise 14.24.
a. At the 0.05 level of significance, are estriol level and birth weight linearly correlated?
b. At the 0.025 level of significance, are estriol level and birth weight positively linearly correlated?

e. Determine a point estimate for the mean cumulative GPA of all sophomores at Arizona State University who had a high school GPA of 3.0.
f. Find a 95% confidence interval for the mean cumulative GPA of all sophomores at Arizona State University who had a high school GPA of 3.0.
g. Determine the predicted cumulative GPA of a sophomore at Arizona State University who had a high school GPA of 3.0.
h. Obtain a 95% prediction interval for the cumulative GPA of a sophomore at Arizona State University who had a high school GPA of 3.0.
i. Repeat parts (a)–(h) with SAT math score instead of high school GPA as the predictor variable. For the estimation and prediction, use an SAT math score of 500.
j. Repeat parts (a)–(h) with SAT verbal score instead of high school GPA as the predictor variable. For the estimation and prediction, use an SAT verbal score of 450.

case study discussion

Fat Consumption and Prostate Cancer

At the beginning of this chapter, we repeated data on fat consumption and prostate cancer death rate for various nations of the world from Chapter 4. There you used those data to perform some descriptive regression and correlation analyses. Now you are to employ those same data to carry out several inferential procedures in regression and correlation.

a. Obtain the sample regression equation with fat consumption as the predictor variable for prostate cancer death rate.
b. Perform a residual analysis to decide whether considering Assumptions 1–3 for regression inferences to be satisfied by the variables fat consumption and prostate cancer death rate appears reasonable.
c. Obtain and interpret the standard error of the estimate.
d. At the 5% significance level, do the data provide sufficient evidence to conclude that fat consumption is useful for predicting prostate cancer death rate for nations of the world?
e. Find a point estimate for the mean prostate cancer death rate for nations with a fat consumption of 140 g per day.
f. Obtain a 95% confidence interval for the mean prostate cancer death rate for nations with a fat consumption of 140 g per day. Interpret your answer.
g. Determine the predicted prostate cancer death rate of a nation with a fat consumption of 140 g per day.
h. Find a 95% prediction interval for the prostate cancer death rate of a nation with a fat consumption of 140 g per day. Interpret your answer.
i. At the 5% significance level, do the data provide sufficient evidence to conclude that fat consumption and prostate cancer death rate are positively linearly correlated?
j. Use the technology of your choice to solve parts (a)–(i).

Internet Resources: Visit the Weiss Web site www.aw.com/weiss for additional discussion, exercises, and resources related to this case study.

Biography

Sir Francis Galton: Discoverer of Regression and Correlation

FRANCIS GALTON was born on February 16, 1822, into a wealthy Quaker family of bankers and gunsmiths on his father's side and as a cousin of Charles Darwin's on his mother's side. Although his IQ was estimated to be about 200, his formal education was unfinished.

He began training in medicine in Birmingham and London, but quit when, in his words, "A passion for travel seized me as if I had been a migratory bird." After a tour through Germany and southeastern Europe, he went to Trinity College in Cambridge to study mathematics. He left Cambridge in his third year, broken from overwork. He recovered quickly and resumed his medical studies in London. However, his father died before he had finished medical school and left to him, at 22, "a sufficient fortune to make me independent of the medical profession."

Galton held no professional or academic positions; nearly all his experiments were conducted at his home or performed by friends. He was curious about almost everything, and carried out research in fields that included meteorology, biology, psychology, statistics, and genetics.

The origination of the concepts of regression and correlation, developed by Galton as tools for measuring the influence of heredity, are summed up in his work *Natural Inheritance*. He discovered regression during experiments with sweet-pea seeds to determine the law of inheritance of size. He made his other great discovery, correlation, while applying his techniques to the problem of measuring the degree of association between the sizes of two different body organs of an individual.

In his later years, Galton was associated with Karl Pearson, who became his champion and an extender of his ideas. Pearson was the first holder of the chair of eugenics at University College in London, which Galton had endowed in his will. Galton was knighted in 1909. He died in Haslemere, Surrey, England, in 1911.

APPENDIXES

APPENDIX A	Statistical Tables
APPENDIX B	Answers to Selected Exercises

STATISTICAL TABLES

I	Random Numbers A-5
II	Areas under the standard normal curve A-6
III	Normal scores A-8
IV	Values of t_α A-10
V	Values of χ^2_α A-12
VI	Values of F_α A-14

TABLE I
Random numbers

Line number	Column number									
	_00–09_		_10–19_		_20–29_		_30–39_		_40–49_	
_00_	15544	80712	97742	21500	97081	42451	50623	56071	28882	28739
_01_	01011	21285	04729	39986	73150	31548	30168	76189	56996	19210
_02_	47435	53308	40718	29050	74858	64517	93573	51058	68501	42723
_03_	91312	75137	86274	59834	69844	19853	06917	17413	44474	86530
_04_	12775	08768	80791	16298	22934	09630	98862	39746	64623	32768
_05_	31466	43761	94872	92230	52367	13205	38634	55882	77518	36252
_06_	09300	43847	40881	51243	97810	18903	53914	31688	06220	40422
_07_	73582	13810	57784	72454	68997	72229	30340	08844	53924	89630
_08_	11092	81392	58189	22697	41063	09451	09789	00637	06450	85990
_09_	93322	98567	00116	35605	66790	52965	62877	21740	56476	49296
_10_	80134	12484	67089	08674	70753	90959	45842	59844	45214	36505
_11_	97888	31797	95037	84400	76041	96668	75920	68482	56855	97417
_12_	92612	27082	59459	69380	98654	20407	88151	56263	27126	63797
_13_	72744	45586	43279	44218	83638	05422	00995	70217	78925	39097
_14_	96256	70653	45285	26293	78305	80252	03625	40159	68760	84716
_15_	07851	47452	66742	83331	54701	06573	98169	37499	67756	68301
_16_	25594	41552	96475	56151	02089	33748	65289	89956	89559	33687
_17_	65358	15155	59374	80940	03411	94656	69440	47156	77115	99463
_18_	09402	31008	53424	21928	02198	61201	02457	87214	59750	51330
_19_	97424	90765	01634	37328	41243	33564	17884	94747	93650	77668

TABLE II
Areas under the standard normal curve

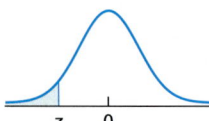

0.09	0.08	0.07	0.06	0.05	0.04	0.03	0.02	0.01	0.00	z
									0.0000†	−3.9
0.0001	0.0001	0.0001	0.0001	0.0001	0.0001	0.0001	0.0001	0.0001	0.0001	−3.8
0.0001	0.0001	0.0001	0.0001	0.0001	0.0001	0.0001	0.0001	0.0001	0.0001	−3.7
0.0001	0.0001	0.0001	0.0001	0.0001	0.0001	0.0001	0.0001	0.0002	0.0002	−3.6
0.0002	0.0002	0.0002	0.0002	0.0002	0.0002	0.0002	0.0002	0.0002	0.0002	−3.5
0.0002	0.0003	0.0003	0.0003	0.0003	0.0003	0.0003	0.0003	0.0003	0.0003	−3.4
0.0003	0.0004	0.0004	0.0004	0.0004	0.0004	0.0004	0.0005	0.0005	0.0005	−3.3
0.0005	0.0005	0.0005	0.0006	0.0006	0.0006	0.0006	0.0006	0.0007	0.0007	−3.2
0.0007	0.0007	0.0008	0.0008	0.0008	0.0008	0.0009	0.0009	0.0009	0.0010	−3.1
0.0010	0.0010	0.0011	0.0011	0.0011	0.0012	0.0012	0.0013	0.0013	0.0013	−3.0
0.0014	0.0014	0.0015	0.0015	0.0016	0.0016	0.0017	0.0018	0.0018	0.0019	−2.9
0.0019	0.0020	0.0021	0.0021	0.0022	0.0023	0.0023	0.0024	0.0025	0.0026	−2.8
0.0026	0.0027	0.0028	0.0029	0.0030	0.0031	0.0032	0.0033	0.0034	0.0035	−2.7
0.0036	0.0037	0.0038	0.0039	0.0040	0.0041	0.0043	0.0044	0.0045	0.0047	−2.6
0.0048	0.0049	0.0051	0.0052	0.0054	0.0055	0.0057	0.0059	0.0060	0.0062	−2.5
0.0064	0.0066	0.0068	0.0069	0.0071	0.0073	0.0075	0.0078	0.0080	0.0082	−2.4
0.0084	0.0087	0.0089	0.0091	0.0094	0.0096	0.0099	0.0102	0.0104	0.0107	−2.3
0.0110	0.0113	0.0116	0.0119	0.0122	0.0125	0.0129	0.0132	0.0136	0.0139	−2.2
0.0143	0.0146	0.0150	0.0154	0.0158	0.0162	0.0166	0.0170	0.0174	0.0179	−2.1
0.0183	0.0188	0.0192	0.0197	0.0202	0.0207	0.0212	0.0217	0.0222	0.0228	−2.0
0.0233	0.0239	0.0244	0.0250	0.0256	0.0262	0.0268	0.0274	0.0281	0.0287	−1.9
0.0294	0.0301	0.0307	0.0314	0.0322	0.0329	0.0336	0.0344	0.0351	0.0359	−1.8
0.0367	0.0375	0.0384	0.0392	0.0401	0.0409	0.0418	0.0427	0.0436	0.0446	−1.7
0.0455	0.0465	0.0475	0.0485	0.0495	0.0505	0.0516	0.0526	0.0537	0.0548	−1.6
0.0559	0.0571	0.0582	0.0594	0.0606	0.0618	0.0630	0.0643	0.0655	0.0668	−1.5
0.0681	0.0694	0.0708	0.0721	0.0735	0.0749	0.0764	0.0778	0.0793	0.0808	−1.4
0.0823	0.0838	0.0853	0.0869	0.0885	0.0901	0.0918	0.0934	0.0951	0.0968	−1.3
0.0985	0.1003	0.1020	0.1038	0.1056	0.1075	0.1093	0.1112	0.1131	0.1151	−1.2
0.1170	0.1190	0.1210	0.1230	0.1251	0.1271	0.1292	0.1314	0.1335	0.1357	−1.1
0.1379	0.1401	0.1423	0.1446	0.1469	0.1492	0.1515	0.1539	0.1562	0.1587	−1.0
0.1611	0.1635	0.1660	0.1685	0.1711	0.1736	0.1762	0.1788	0.1814	0.1841	−0.9
0.1867	0.1894	0.1922	0.1949	0.1977	0.2005	0.2033	0.2061	0.2090	0.2119	−0.8
0.2148	0.2177	0.2206	0.2236	0.2266	0.2296	0.2327	0.2358	0.2389	0.2420	−0.7
0.2451	0.2483	0.2514	0.2546	0.2578	0.2611	0.2643	0.2676	0.2709	0.2743	−0.6
0.2776	0.2810	0.2843	0.2877	0.2912	0.2946	0.2981	0.3015	0.3050	0.3085	−0.5
0.3121	0.3156	0.3192	0.3228	0.3264	0.3300	0.3336	0.3372	0.3409	0.3446	−0.4
0.3483	0.3520	0.3557	0.3594	0.3632	0.3669	0.3707	0.3745	0.3783	0.3821	−0.3
0.3859	0.3897	0.3936	0.3974	0.4013	0.4052	0.4090	0.4129	0.4168	0.4207	−0.2
0.4247	0.4286	0.4325	0.4364	0.4404	0.4443	0.4483	0.4522	0.4562	0.4602	−0.1
0.4641	0.4681	0.4721	0.4761	0.4801	0.4840	0.4880	0.4920	0.4960	0.5000	−0.0

† For $z \leq -3.90$, the areas are 0.0000 to four decimal places.

TABLE II (cont.)
Areas under the standard normal curve

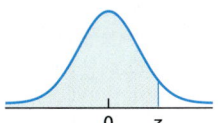

z	Second decimal place in z									
	0.00	0.01	0.02	0.03	0.04	0.05	0.06	0.07	0.08	0.09
0.0	0.5000	0.5040	0.5080	0.5120	0.5160	0.5199	0.5239	0.5279	0.5319	0.5359
0.1	0.5398	0.5438	0.5478	0.5517	0.5557	0.5596	0.5636	0.5675	0.5714	0.5753
0.2	0.5793	0.5832	0.5871	0.5910	0.5948	0.5987	0.6026	0.6064	0.6103	0.6141
0.3	0.6179	0.6217	0.6255	0.6293	0.6331	0.6368	0.6406	0.6443	0.6480	0.6517
0.4	0.6554	0.6591	0.6628	0.6664	0.6700	0.6736	0.6772	0.6808	0.6844	0.6879
0.5	0.6915	0.6950	0.6985	0.7019	0.7054	0.7088	0.7123	0.7157	0.7190	0.7224
0.6	0.7257	0.7291	0.7324	0.7357	0.7389	0.7422	0.7454	0.7486	0.7517	0.7549
0.7	0.7580	0.7611	0.7642	0.7673	0.7704	0.7734	0.7764	0.7794	0.7823	0.7852
0.8	0.7881	0.7910	0.7939	0.7967	0.7995	0.8023	0.8051	0.8078	0.8106	0.8133
0.9	0.8159	0.8186	0.8212	0.8238	0.8264	0.8289	0.8315	0.8340	0.8365	0.8389
1.0	0.8413	0.8438	0.8461	0.8485	0.8508	0.8531	0.8554	0.8577	0.8599	0.8621
1.1	0.8643	0.8665	0.8686	0.8708	0.8729	0.8749	0.8770	0.8790	0.8810	0.8830
1.2	0.8849	0.8869	0.8888	0.8907	0.8925	0.8944	0.8962	0.8980	0.8997	0.9015
1.3	0.9032	0.9049	0.9066	0.9082	0.9099	0.9115	0.9131	0.9147	0.9162	0.9177
1.4	0.9192	0.9207	0.9222	0.9236	0.9251	0.9265	0.9279	0.9292	0.9306	0.9319
1.5	0.9332	0.9345	0.9357	0.9370	0.9382	0.9394	0.9406	0.9418	0.9429	0.9441
1.6	0.9452	0.9463	0.9474	0.9484	0.9495	0.9505	0.9515	0.9525	0.9535	0.9545
1.7	0.9554	0.9564	0.9573	0.9582	0.9591	0.9599	0.9608	0.9616	0.9625	0.9633
1.8	0.9641	0.9649	0.9656	0.9664	0.9671	0.9678	0.9686	0.9693	0.9699	0.9706
1.9	0.9713	0.9719	0.9726	0.9732	0.9738	0.9744	0.9750	0.9756	0.9761	0.9767
2.0	0.9772	0.9778	0.9783	0.9788	0.9793	0.9798	0.9803	0.9808	0.9812	0.9817
2.1	0.9821	0.9826	0.9830	0.9834	0.9838	0.9842	0.9846	0.9850	0.9854	0.9857
2.2	0.9861	0.9864	0.9868	0.9871	0.9875	0.9878	0.9881	0.9884	0.9887	0.9890
2.3	0.9893	0.9896	0.9898	0.9901	0.9904	0.9906	0.9909	0.9911	0.9913	0.9916
2.4	0.9918	0.9920	0.9922	0.9925	0.9927	0.9929	0.9931	0.9932	0.9934	0.9936
2.5	0.9938	0.9940	0.9941	0.9943	0.9945	0.9946	0.9948	0.9949	0.9951	0.9952
2.6	0.9953	0.9955	0.9956	0.9957	0.9959	0.9960	0.9961	0.9962	0.9963	0.9964
2.7	0.9965	0.9966	0.9967	0.9968	0.9969	0.9970	0.9971	0.9972	0.9973	0.9974
2.8	0.9974	0.9975	0.9976	0.9977	0.9977	0.9978	0.9979	0.9979	0.9980	0.9981
2.9	0.9981	0.9982	0.9982	0.9983	0.9984	0.9984	0.9985	0.9985	0.9986	0.9986
3.0	0.9987	0.9987	0.9987	0.9988	0.9988	0.9989	0.9989	0.9989	0.9990	0.9990
3.1	0.9990	0.9991	0.9991	0.9991	0.9992	0.9992	0.9992	0.9992	0.9993	0.9993
3.2	0.9993	0.9993	0.9994	0.9994	0.9994	0.9994	0.9994	0.9995	0.9995	0.9995
3.3	0.9995	0.9995	0.9995	0.9996	0.9996	0.9996	0.9996	0.9996	0.9996	0.9997
3.4	0.9997	0.9997	0.9997	0.9997	0.9997	0.9997	0.9997	0.9997	0.9997	0.9998
3.5	0.9998	0.9998	0.9998	0.9998	0.9998	0.9998	0.9998	0.9998	0.9998	0.9998
3.6	0.9998	0.9998	0.9999	0.9999	0.9999	0.9999	0.9999	0.9999	0.9999	0.9999
3.7	0.9999	0.9999	0.9999	0.9999	0.9999	0.9999	0.9999	0.9999	0.9999	0.9999
3.8	0.9999	0.9999	0.9999	0.9999	0.9999	0.9999	0.9999	0.9999	0.9999	0.9999
3.9	1.0000[†]									

[†] For $z \geq 3.90$, the areas are 1.0000 to four decimal places.

TABLE III Normal scores

Ordered position	|				n				
	5	6	7	8	9	10	11	12	13
1	−1.18	−1.28	−1.36	−1.43	−1.50	−1.55	−1.59	−1.64	−1.68
2	−0.50	−0.64	−0.76	−0.85	−0.93	−1.00	−1.06	−1.11	−1.16
3	0.00	−0.20	−0.35	−0.47	−0.57	−0.65	−0.73	−0.79	−0.85
4	0.50	0.20	0.00	−0.15	−0.27	−0.37	−0.46	−0.53	−0.60
5	1.18	0.64	0.35	0.15	0.00	−0.12	−0.22	−0.31	−0.39
6		1.28	0.76	0.47	0.27	0.12	0.00	−0.10	−0.19
7			1.36	0.85	0.57	0.37	0.22	0.10	0.00
8				1.43	0.93	0.65	0.46	0.31	0.19
9					1.50	1.00	0.73	0.53	0.39
10						1.55	1.06	0.79	0.60
11							1.59	1.11	0.85
12								1.64	1.16
13									1.68

TABLE III (cont.) Normal scores

Ordered position					n				
	14	15	16	17	18	19	20	21	22
1	−1.71	−1.74	−1.77	−1.80	−1.82	−1.85	−1.87	−1.89	−1.91
2	−1.20	−1.24	−1.28	−1.32	−1.35	−1.38	−1.40	−1.43	−1.45
3	−0.90	−0.94	−0.99	−1.03	−1.06	−1.10	−1.13	−1.16	−1.18
4	−0.66	−0.71	−0.76	−0.80	−0.84	−0.88	−0.92	−0.95	−0.98
5	−0.45	−0.51	−0.57	−0.62	−0.66	−0.70	−0.74	−0.78	−0.81
6	−0.27	−0.33	−0.39	−0.45	−0.50	−0.54	−0.59	−0.63	−0.66
7	−0.09	−0.16	−0.23	−0.29	−0.35	−0.40	−0.45	−0.49	−0.53
8	0.09	0.00	−0.08	−0.15	−0.21	−0.26	−0.31	−0.36	−0.40
9	0.27	0.16	0.08	0.00	−0.07	−0.13	−0.19	−0.24	−0.28
10	0.45	0.33	0.23	0.15	0.07	0.00	−0.06	−0.12	−0.17
11	0.66	0.51	0.39	0.29	0.21	0.13	0.06	0.00	−0.06
12	0.90	0.71	0.57	0.45	0.35	0.26	0.19	0.12	0.06
13	1.20	0.94	0.76	0.62	0.50	0.40	0.31	0.24	0.17
14	1.71	1.24	0.99	0.80	0.66	0.54	0.45	0.36	0.28
15		1.74	1.28	1.03	0.84	0.70	0.59	0.49	0.40
16			1.77	1.32	1.06	0.88	0.74	0.63	0.53
17				1.80	1.35	1.10	0.92	0.78	0.66
18					1.82	1.38	1.13	0.95	0.81
19						1.85	1.40	1.16	0.98
20							1.87	1.43	1.18
21								1.89	1.45
22									1.91

TABLE III (cont.)
Normal scores

Ordered position	\(n\)							
	23	24	25	26	27	28	29	30
1	−1.93	−1.95	−1.97	−1.98	−2.00	−2.01	−2.03	−2.04
2	−1.48	−1.50	−1.52	−1.54	−1.56	−1.58	−1.59	−1.61
3	−1.21	−1.24	−1.26	−1.28	−1.30	−1.32	−1.34	−1.36
4	−1.01	−1.04	−1.06	−1.09	−1.11	−1.13	−1.15	−1.17
5	−0.84	−0.87	−0.90	−0.93	−0.95	−0.98	−1.00	−1.02
6	−0.70	−0.73	−0.76	−0.79	−0.82	−0.84	−0.87	−0.89
7	−0.57	−0.60	−0.63	−0.66	−0.69	−0.72	−0.75	−0.77
8	−0.44	−0.48	−0.52	−0.55	−0.58	−0.61	−0.64	−0.67
9	−0.33	−0.37	−0.41	−0.44	−0.48	−0.51	−0.54	−0.57
10	−0.22	−0.26	−0.30	−0.34	−0.38	−0.41	−0.44	−0.47
11	−0.11	−0.15	−0.20	−0.24	−0.28	−0.31	−0.35	−0.38
12	0.00	−0.05	−0.10	−0.14	−0.18	−0.22	−0.26	−0.29
13	0.11	0.05	0.00	−0.05	−0.09	−0.13	−0.17	−0.21
14	0.22	0.15	0.10	0.05	0.00	−0.04	−0.09	−0.12
15	0.33	0.26	0.20	0.14	0.09	0.04	0.00	−0.04
16	0.44	0.37	0.30	0.24	0.18	0.13	0.09	0.04
17	0.57	0.48	0.41	0.34	0.28	0.22	0.17	0.12
18	0.70	0.60	0.52	0.44	0.38	0.31	0.26	0.21
19	0.84	0.73	0.63	0.55	0.48	0.41	0.35	0.29
20	1.01	0.87	0.76	0.66	0.58	0.51	0.44	0.38
21	1.21	1.04	0.90	0.79	0.69	0.61	0.54	0.47
22	1.48	1.24	1.06	0.93	0.82	0.72	0.64	0.57
23	1.93	1.50	1.26	1.09	0.95	0.84	0.75	0.67
24		1.95	1.52	1.28	1.11	0.98	0.87	0.77
25			1.97	1.54	1.30	1.13	1.00	0.89
26				1.98	1.56	1.32	1.15	1.02
27					2.00	1.58	1.34	1.17
28						2.01	1.59	1.36
29							2.03	1.61
30								2.04

TABLE IV
Values of t_α

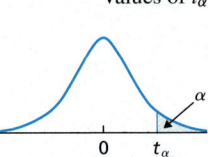

df	$t_{0.10}$	$t_{0.05}$	$t_{0.025}$	$t_{0.01}$	$t_{0.005}$	df
1	3.078	6.314	12.706	31.821	63.657	1
2	1.886	2.920	4.303	6.965	9.925	2
3	1.638	2.353	3.182	4.541	5.841	3
4	1.533	2.132	2.776	3.747	4.604	4
5	1.476	2.015	2.571	3.365	4.032	5
6	1.440	1.943	2.447	3.143	3.707	6
7	1.415	1.895	2.365	2.998	3.499	7
8	1.397	1.860	2.306	2.896	3.355	8
9	1.383	1.833	2.262	2.821	3.250	9
10	1.372	1.812	2.228	2.764	3.169	10
11	1.363	1.796	2.201	2.718	3.106	11
12	1.356	1.782	2.179	2.681	3.055	12
13	1.350	1.771	2.160	2.650	3.012	13
14	1.345	1.761	2.145	2.624	2.977	14
15	1.341	1.753	2.131	2.602	2.947	15
16	1.337	1.746	2.120	2.583	2.921	16
17	1.333	1.740	2.110	2.567	2.898	17
18	1.330	1.734	2.101	2.552	2.878	18
19	1.328	1.729	2.093	2.539	2.861	19
20	1.325	1.725	2.086	2.528	2.845	20
21	1.323	1.721	2.080	2.518	2.831	21
22	1.321	1.717	2.074	2.508	2.819	22
23	1.319	1.714	2.069	2.500	2.807	23
24	1.318	1.711	2.064	2.492	2.797	24
25	1.316	1.708	2.060	2.485	2.787	25
26	1.315	1.706	2.056	2.479	2.779	26
27	1.314	1.703	2.052	2.473	2.771	27
28	1.313	1.701	2.048	2.467	2.763	28
29	1.311	1.699	2.045	2.462	2.756	29
30	1.310	1.697	2.042	2.457	2.750	30
31	1.309	1.696	2.040	2.453	2.744	31
32	1.309	1.694	2.037	2.449	2.738	32
33	1.308	1.692	2.035	2.445	2.733	33
34	1.307	1.691	2.032	2.441	2.728	34
35	1.306	1.690	2.030	2.438	2.724	35
36	1.306	1.688	2.028	2.434	2.719	36
37	1.305	1.687	2.026	2.431	2.715	37
38	1.304	1.686	2.024	2.429	2.712	38
39	1.304	1.685	2.023	2.426	2.708	39
40	1.303	1.684	2.021	2.423	2.704	40
41	1.303	1.683	2.020	2.421	2.701	41
42	1.302	1.682	2.018	2.418	2.698	42
43	1.302	1.681	2.017	2.416	2.695	43
44	1.301	1.680	2.015	2.414	2.692	44
45	1.301	1.679	2.014	2.412	2.690	45
46	1.300	1.679	2.013	2.410	2.687	46
47	1.300	1.678	2.012	2.408	2.685	47
48	1.299	1.677	2.011	2.407	2.682	48
49	1.299	1.677	2.010	2.405	2.680	49

TABLE IV (cont.)
Values of t_α

df	$t_{0.10}$	$t_{0.05}$	$t_{0.025}$	$t_{0.01}$	$t_{0.005}$	df
50	1.299	1.676	2.009	2.403	2.678	50
51	1.298	1.675	2.008	2.402	2.676	51
52	1.298	1.675	2.007	2.400	2.674	52
53	1.298	1.674	2.006	2.399	2.672	53
54	1.297	1.674	2.005	2.397	2.670	54
55	1.297	1.673	2.004	2.396	2.668	55
56	1.297	1.673	2.003	2.395	2.667	56
57	1.297	1.672	2.002	2.394	2.665	57
58	1.296	1.672	2.002	2.392	2.663	58
59	1.296	1.671	2.001	2.391	2.662	59
60	1.296	1.671	2.000	2.390	2.660	60
61	1.296	1.670	2.000	2.389	2.659	61
62	1.295	1.670	1.999	2.388	2.657	62
63	1.295	1.669	1.998	2.387	2.656	63
64	1.295	1.669	1.998	2.386	2.655	64
65	1.295	1.669	1.997	2.385	2.654	65
66	1.295	1.668	1.997	2.384	2.652	66
67	1.294	1.668	1.996	2.383	2.651	67
68	1.294	1.668	1.995	2.382	2.650	68
69	1.294	1.667	1.995	2.382	2.649	69
70	1.294	1.667	1.994	2.381	2.648	70
71	1.294	1.667	1.994	2.380	2.647	71
72	1.293	1.666	1.993	2.379	2.646	72
73	1.293	1.666	1.993	2.379	2.645	73
74	1.293	1.666	1.993	2.378	2.644	74
75	1.293	1.665	1.992	2.377	2.643	75
80	1.292	1.664	1.990	2.374	2.639	80
85	1.292	1.663	1.988	2.371	2.635	85
90	1.291	1.662	1.987	2.368	2.632	90
95	1.291	1.661	1.985	2.366	2.629	95
100	1.290	1.660	1.984	2.364	2.626	100
200	1.286	1.653	1.972	2.345	2.601	200
300	1.284	1.650	1.968	2.339	2.592	300
400	1.284	1.649	1.966	2.336	2.588	400
500	1.283	1.648	1.965	2.334	2.586	500
600	1.283	1.647	1.964	2.333	2.584	600
700	1.283	1.647	1.963	2.332	2.583	700
800	1.283	1.647	1.963	2.331	2.582	800
900	1.282	1.647	1.963	2.330	2.581	900
1000	1.282	1.646	1.962	2.330	2.581	1000

$z_{0.10}$	$z_{0.05}$	$z_{0.025}$	$z_{0.01}$	$z_{0.005}$
1.282	1.645	1.960	2.326	2.576

TABLE V Values of χ_α^2

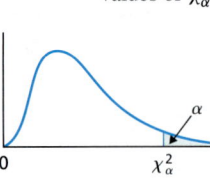

df	$\chi_{0.995}^2$	$\chi_{0.99}^2$	$\chi_{0.975}^2$	$\chi_{0.95}^2$	$\chi_{0.90}^2$
1	0.000	0.000	0.001	0.004	0.016
2	0.010	0.020	0.051	0.103	0.211
3	0.072	0.115	0.216	0.352	0.584
4	0.207	0.297	0.484	0.711	1.064
5	0.412	0.554	0.831	1.145	1.610
6	0.676	0.872	1.237	1.635	2.204
7	0.989	1.239	1.690	2.167	2.833
8	1.344	1.646	2.180	2.733	3.490
9	1.735	2.088	2.700	3.325	4.168
10	2.156	2.558	3.247	3.940	4.865
11	2.603	3.053	3.816	4.575	5.578
12	3.074	3.571	4.404	5.226	6.304
13	3.565	4.107	5.009	5.892	7.042
14	4.075	4.660	5.629	6.571	7.790
15	4.601	5.229	6.262	7.261	8.547
16	5.142	5.812	6.908	7.962	9.312
17	5.697	6.408	7.564	8.672	10.085
18	6.265	7.015	8.231	9.390	10.865
19	6.844	7.633	8.907	10.117	11.651
20	7.434	8.260	9.591	10.851	12.443
21	8.034	8.897	10.283	11.591	13.240
22	8.643	9.542	10.982	12.338	14.041
23	9.260	10.196	11.689	13.091	14.848
24	9.886	10.856	12.401	13.848	15.659
25	10.520	11.524	13.120	14.611	16.473
26	11.160	12.198	13.844	15.379	17.292
27	11.808	12.879	14.573	16.151	18.114
28	12.461	13.565	15.308	16.928	18.939
29	13.121	14.256	16.047	17.708	19.768
30	13.787	14.953	16.791	18.493	20.599
40	20.707	22.164	24.433	26.509	29.051
50	27.991	29.707	32.357	34.764	37.689
60	35.534	37.485	40.482	43.188	46.459
70	43.275	45.442	48.758	51.739	55.329
80	51.172	53.540	57.153	60.391	64.278
90	59.196	61.754	65.647	69.126	73.291
100	67.328	70.065	74.222	77.930	82.358

TABLE V (cont.)
Values of χ_α^2

$\chi_{0.10}^2$	$\chi_{0.05}^2$	$\chi_{0.025}^2$	$\chi_{0.01}^2$	$\chi_{0.005}^2$	df
2.706	3.841	5.024	6.635	7.879	1
4.605	5.991	7.378	9.210	10.597	2
6.251	7.815	9.348	11.345	12.838	3
7.779	9.488	11.143	13.277	14.860	4
9.236	11.070	12.833	15.086	16.750	5
10.645	12.592	14.449	16.812	18.548	6
12.017	14.067	16.013	18.475	20.278	7
13.362	15.507	17.535	20.090	21.955	8
14.684	16.919	19.023	21.666	23.589	9
15.987	18.307	20.483	23.209	25.188	10
17.275	19.675	21.920	24.725	26.757	11
18.549	21.026	23.337	26.217	28.300	12
19.812	22.362	24.736	27.688	29.819	13
21.064	23.685	26.119	29.141	31.319	14
22.307	24.996	27.488	30.578	32.801	15
23.542	26.296	28.845	32.000	34.267	16
24.769	27.587	30.191	33.409	35.718	17
25.989	28.869	31.526	34.805	37.156	18
27.204	30.143	32.852	36.191	38.582	19
28.412	31.410	34.170	37.566	39.997	20
29.615	32.671	35.479	38.932	41.401	21
30.813	33.924	36.781	40.290	42.796	22
32.007	35.172	38.076	41.638	44.181	23
33.196	36.415	39.364	42.980	45.559	24
34.382	37.653	40.647	44.314	46.928	25
35.563	38.885	41.923	45.642	48.290	26
36.741	40.113	43.195	46.963	49.645	27
37.916	41.337	44.461	48.278	50.994	28
39.087	42.557	45.722	49.588	52.336	29
40.256	43.773	46.979	50.892	53.672	30
51.805	55.759	59.342	63.691	66.767	40
63.167	67.505	71.420	76.154	79.490	50
74.397	79.082	83.298	88.381	91.955	60
85.527	90.531	95.023	100.424	104.213	70
96.578	101.879	106.628	112.328	116.320	80
107.565	113.145	118.135	124.115	128.296	90
118.499	124.343	129.563	135.811	140.177	100

TABLE VI
Values of F_α

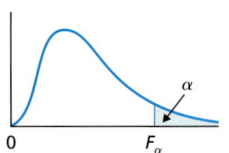

dfd	α	1	2	3	4	5	6	7	8	9
						dfn				
1	0.10	39.86	49.50	53.59	55.83	57.24	58.20	58.91	59.44	59.86
	0.05	161.45	199.50	215.71	224.58	230.16	233.99	236.77	238.88	240.54
	0.025	647.79	799.50	864.16	899.58	921.85	937.11	948.22	956.66	963.28
	0.01	4052.2	4999.5	5403.4	5624.6	5763.6	5859.0	5928.4	5981.1	6022.5
	0.005	16211	20000	21615	22500	23056	23437	23715	23925	24091
2	0.10	8.53	9.00	9.16	9.24	9.29	9.33	9.35	9.37	9.38
	0.05	18.51	19.00	19.16	19.25	19.30	19.33	19.35	19.37	19.38
	0.025	38.51	39.00	39.17	39.25	39.30	39.33	39.36	39.37	39.39
	0.01	98.50	99.00	99.17	99.25	99.30	99.33	99.36	99.37	99.39
	0.005	198.50	199.00	199.17	199.25	199.30	199.33	199.36	199.37	199.39
3	0.10	5.54	5.46	5.39	5.34	5.31	5.28	5.27	5.25	5.24
	0.05	10.13	9.55	9.28	9.12	9.01	8.94	8.89	8.85	8.81
	0.025	17.44	16.04	15.44	15.10	14.88	14.73	14.62	14.54	14.47
	0.01	34.12	30.82	29.46	28.71	28.24	27.91	27.67	27.49	27.35
	0.005	55.55	49.80	47.47	46.19	45.39	44.84	44.43	44.13	43.88
4	0.10	4.54	4.32	4.19	4.11	4.05	4.01	3.98	3.95	3.94
	0.05	7.71	6.94	6.59	6.39	6.26	6.16	6.09	6.04	6.00
	0.025	12.22	10.65	9.98	9.60	9.36	9.20	9.07	8.98	8.90
	0.01	21.20	18.00	16.69	15.98	15.52	15.21	14.98	14.80	14.66
	0.005	31.33	26.28	24.26	23.15	22.46	21.97	21.62	21.35	21.14
5	0.10	4.06	3.78	3.62	3.52	3.45	3.40	3.37	3.34	3.32
	0.05	6.61	5.79	5.41	5.19	5.05	4.95	4.88	4.82	4.77
	0.025	10.01	8.43	7.76	7.39	7.15	6.98	6.85	6.76	6.68
	0.01	16.26	13.27	12.06	11.39	10.97	10.67	10.46	10.29	10.16
	0.005	22.78	18.31	16.53	15.56	14.94	14.51	14.20	13.96	13.77
6	0.10	3.78	3.46	3.29	3.18	3.11	3.05	3.01	2.98	2.96
	0.05	5.99	5.14	4.76	4.53	4.39	4.28	4.21	4.15	4.10
	0.025	8.81	7.26	6.60	6.23	5.99	5.82	5.70	5.60	5.52
	0.01	13.75	10.92	9.78	9.15	8.75	8.47	8.26	8.10	7.98
	0.005	18.63	14.54	12.92	12.03	11.46	11.07	10.79	10.57	10.39
7	0.10	3.59	3.26	3.07	2.96	2.88	2.83	2.78	2.75	2.72
	0.05	5.59	4.74	4.35	4.12	3.97	3.87	3.79	3.73	3.68
	0.025	8.07	6.54	5.89	5.52	5.29	5.12	4.99	4.90	4.82
	0.01	12.25	9.55	8.45	7.85	7.46	7.19	6.99	6.84	6.72
	0.005	16.24	12.40	10.88	10.05	9.52	9.16	8.89	8.68	8.51
8	0.10	3.46	3.11	2.92	2.81	2.73	2.67	2.62	2.59	2.56
	0.05	5.32	4.46	4.07	3.84	3.69	3.58	3.50	3.44	3.39
	0.025	7.57	6.06	5.42	5.05	4.82	4.65	4.53	4.43	4.36
	0.01	11.26	8.65	7.59	7.01	6.63	6.37	6.18	6.03	5.91
	0.005	14.69	11.04	9.60	8.81	8.30	7.95	7.69	7.50	7.34

TABLE VI (cont.)
Values of F_α

10	12	15	20	24	30	40	60	120	α	dfd
60.19	60.71	61.22	61.74	62.00	62.26	62.53	62.79	63.06	0.10	
241.88	243.91	245.95	248.01	249.05	250.10	251.14	252.20	253.25	0.05	
968.63	976.71	984.87	993.10	997.25	1001.41	1005.60	1009.80	1014.02	0.025	1
6055.8	6106.3	6157.3	6208.7	6234.6	6260.6	6286.7	631.9	6339.4	0.01	
24224	24426	24630	24836	24940	25044	25148	25253	25359	0.005	
9.39	9.41	9.42	9.44	9.45	9.46	9.47	9.47	9.48	0.10	
19.40	19.41	19.43	19.45	19.45	19.46	19.47	19.48	19.49	0.05	
39.40	39.41	39.43	39.45	39.46	39.46	39.47	39.48	39.49	0.025	2
99.40	99.42	99.43	99.45	99.46	99.47	99.47	99.48	99.49	0.01	
199.40	199.42	199.43	199.45	199.46	199.47	199.47	199.48	199.49	0.005	
5.23	5.22	5.20	5.18	5.18	5.17	5.16	5.15	5.14	0.10	
8.79	8.74	8.70	8.66	8.64	8.62	8.59	8.57	8.55	0.05	
14.42	14.34	14.25	14.17	14.12	14.08	14.04	13.99	13.95	0.025	3
27.23	27.05	26.87	26.69	26.60	26.50	26.41	26.32	26.22	0.01	
43.69	43.39	43.08	42.78	42.62	42.47	42.31	42.15	41.99	0.005	
3.92	3.90	3.87	3.84	3.83	3.82	3.80	3.79	3.78	0.10	
5.96	5.91	5.86	5.80	5.77	5.75	5.72	5.69	5.66	0.05	
8.84	8.75	8.66	8.56	8.51	8.46	8.41	8.36	8.31	0.025	4
14.55	14.37	14.20	14.02	13.93	13.84	13.75	13.65	13.56	0.01	
20.97	20.70	20.44	20.17	20.03	19.89	19.75	19.61	19.47	0.005	
3.30	3.27	3.24	3.21	3.19	3.17	3.16	3.14	3.12	0.10	
4.74	4.68	4.62	4.56	4.53	4.50	4.46	4.43	4.40	0.05	
6.62	6.52	6.43	6.33	6.28	6.23	6.18	6.12	6.07	0.025	5
10.05	9.89	9.72	9.55	9.47	9.38	9.29	9.20	9.11	0.01	
13.62	13.38	13.15	12.90	12.78	12.66	12.53	12.40	12.27	0.005	
2.94	2.90	2.87	2.84	2.82	2.80	2.78	2.76	2.74	0.10	
4.06	4.00	3.94	3.87	3.84	3.81	3.77	3.74	3.70	0.05	
5.46	5.37	5.27	5.17	5.12	5.07	5.01	4.96	4.90	0.025	6
7.87	7.72	7.56	7.40	7.31	7.23	7.14	7.06	6.97	0.01	
10.25	10.03	9.81	9.59	9.47	9.36	9.24	9.12	9.00	0.005	
2.70	2.67	2.63	2.59	2.58	2.56	2.54	2.51	2.49	0.10	
3.64	3.57	3.51	3.44	3.41	3.38	3.34	3.30	3.27	0.05	
4.76	4.67	4.57	4.47	4.41	4.36	4.31	4.25	4.20	0.025	7
6.62	6.47	6.31	6.16	6.07	5.99	5.91	5.82	5.74	0.01	
8.38	8.18	7.97	7.75	7.64	7.53	7.42	7.31	7.19	0.005	
2.54	2.50	2.46	2.42	2.40	2.38	2.36	2.34	2.32	0.10	
3.35	3.28	3.22	3.15	3.12	3.08	3.04	3.01	2.97	0.05	
4.30	4.20	4.10	4.00	3.95	3.89	3.84	3.78	3.73	0.025	8
5.81	5.67	5.52	5.36	5.28	5.20	5.12	5.03	4.95	0.01	
7.21	7.01	6.81	6.61	6.50	6.40	6.29	6.18	6.06	0.005	

dfn (column header spanning top)

TABLE VI (cont.)
Values of F_α

dfd	α	\multicolumn{9}{c}{dfn}								
		1	2	3	4	5	6	7	8	9
9	0.10	3.36	3.01	2.81	2.69	2.61	2.55	2.51	2.47	2.44
	0.05	5.12	4.26	3.86	3.63	3.48	3.37	3.29	3.23	3.18
	0.025	7.21	5.71	5.08	4.72	4.48	4.32	4.20	4.10	4.03
	0.01	10.56	8.02	6.99	6.42	6.06	5.80	5.61	5.47	5.35
	0.005	13.61	10.11	8.72	7.96	7.47	7.13	6.88	6.69	6.54
10	0.10	3.29	2.92	2.73	2.61	2.52	2.46	2.41	2.38	2.35
	0.05	4.96	4.10	3.71	3.48	3.33	3.22	3.14	3.07	3.02
	0.025	6.94	5.46	4.83	4.47	4.24	4.07	3.95	3.85	3.78
	0.01	10.04	7.56	6.55	5.99	5.64	5.39	5.20	5.06	4.94
	0.005	12.83	9.43	8.08	7.34	6.87	6.54	6.30	6.12	5.97
11	0.10	3.23	2.86	2.66	2.54	2.45	2.39	2.34	2.30	2.27
	0.05	4.84	3.98	3.59	3.36	3.20	3.09	3.01	2.95	2.90
	0.025	6.72	5.26	4.63	4.28	4.04	3.88	3.76	3.66	3.59
	0.01	9.65	7.21	6.22	5.67	5.32	5.07	4.89	4.74	4.63
	0.005	12.23	8.91	7.60	6.88	6.42	6.10	5.86	5.68	5.54
12	0.10	3.18	2.81	2.61	2.48	2.39	2.33	2.28	2.24	2.21
	0.05	4.75	3.89	3.49	3.26	3.11	3.00	2.91	2.85	2.80
	0.025	6.55	5.10	4.47	4.12	3.89	3.73	3.61	3.51	3.44
	0.01	9.33	6.93	5.95	5.41	5.06	4.82	4.64	4.50	4.39
	0.005	11.75	8.51	7.23	6.52	6.07	5.76	5.52	5.35	5.20
13	0.10	3.14	2.76	2.56	2.43	2.35	2.28	2.23	2.20	2.16
	0.05	4.67	3.81	3.41	3.18	3.03	2.92	2.83	2.77	2.71
	0.025	6.41	4.97	4.35	4.00	3.77	3.60	3.48	3.39	3.31
	0.01	9.07	6.70	5.74	5.21	4.86	4.62	4.44	4.30	4.19
	0.005	11.37	8.19	6.93	6.23	5.79	5.48	5.25	5.08	4.94
14	0.10	3.10	2.73	2.52	2.39	2.31	2.24	2.19	2.15	2.12
	0.05	4.60	3.74	3.34	3.11	2.96	2.85	2.76	2.70	2.65
	0.025	6.30	4.86	4.24	3.89	3.66	3.50	3.38	3.29	3.21
	0.01	8.86	6.51	5.56	5.04	4.69	4.46	4.28	4.14	4.03
	0.005	11.06	7.92	6.68	6.00	5.56	5.26	5.03	4.86	4.72
15	0.10	3.07	2.70	2.49	2.36	2.27	2.21	2.16	2.12	2.09
	0.05	4.54	3.68	3.29	3.06	2.90	2.79	2.71	2.64	2.59
	0.025	6.20	4.77	4.15	3.80	3.58	3.41	3.29	3.20	3.12
	0.01	8.68	6.36	5.42	4.89	4.56	4.32	4.14	4.00	3.89
	0.005	10.80	7.70	6.48	5.80	5.37	5.07	4.85	4.67	4.54
16	0.10	3.05	2.67	2.46	2.33	2.24	2.18	2.13	2.09	2.06
	0.05	4.49	3.63	3.24	3.01	2.85	2.74	2.66	2.59	2.54
	0.025	6.12	4.69	4.08	3.73	3.50	3.34	3.22	3.12	3.05
	0.01	8.53	6.23	5.29	4.77	4.44	4.20	4.03	3.89	3.78
	0.005	10.58	7.51	6.30	5.64	5.21	4.91	4.69	4.52	4.38

TABLE VI (cont.)
Values of F_α

10	12	15	20	24	30	40	60	120	α	dfd
2.42	2.38	2.34	2.30	2.28	2.25	2.23	2.21	2.18	*0.10*	
3.14	3.07	3.01	2.94	2.90	2.86	2.83	2.79	2.75	*0.05*	
3.96	3.87	3.77	3.67	3.61	3.56	3.51	3.45	3.39	*0.025*	9
5.26	5.11	4.96	4.81	4.73	4.65	4.57	4.48	4.40	*0.01*	
6.42	6.23	6.03	5.83	5.73	5.62	5.52	5.41	5.30	*0.005*	
2.32	2.28	2.24	2.20	2.18	2.16	2.13	2.11	2.08	*0.10*	
2.98	2.91	2.85	2.77	2.74	2.70	2.66	2.62	2.58	*0.05*	
3.72	3.62	3.52	3.42	3.37	3.31	3.26	3.20	3.14	*0.025*	10
4.85	4.71	4.56	4.41	4.33	4.25	4.17	4.08	4.00	*0.01*	
5.85	5.66	5.47	5.27	5.17	5.07	4.97	4.86	4.75	*0.005*	
2.25	2.21	2.17	2.12	2.10	2.08	2.05	2.03	2.00	*0.10*	
2.85	2.79	2.72	2.65	2.61	2.57	2.53	2.49	2.45	*0.05*	
3.53	3.43	3.33	3.23	3.17	3.12	3.06	3.00	2.94	*0.025*	11
4.54	4.40	4.25	4.10	4.02	3.94	3.86	3.78	3.69	*0.01*	
5.42	5.24	5.05	4.86	4.76	4.65	4.55	4.45	4.34	*0.005*	
2.19	2.15	2.10	2.06	2.04	2.01	1.99	1.96	1.93	*0.10*	
2.75	2.69	2.62	2.54	2.51	2.47	2.43	2.38	2.34	*0.05*	
3.37	3.28	3.18	3.07	3.02	2.96	2.91	2.85	2.79	*0.025*	12
4.30	4.16	4.01	3.86	3.78	3.70	3.62	3.54	3.45	*0.01*	
5.09	4.91	4.72	4.53	4.43	4.33	4.23	4.12	4.01	*0.005*	
2.14	2.10	2.05	2.01	1.98	1.96	1.93	1.90	1.88	*0.10*	
2.67	2.60	2.53	2.46	2.42	2.38	2.34	2.30	2.25	*0.05*	
3.25	3.15	3.05	2.95	2.89	2.84	2.78	2.72	2.66	*0.025*	13
4.10	3.96	3.82	3.66	3.59	3.51	3.43	3.34	3.25	*0.01*	
4.82	4.64	4.46	4.27	4.17	4.07	3.97	3.87	3.76	*0.005*	
2.10	2.05	2.01	1.96	1.94	1.91	1.89	1.86	1.83	*0.10*	
2.60	2.53	2.46	2.39	2.35	2.31	2.27	2.22	2.18	*0.05*	
3.15	3.05	2.95	2.84	2.79	2.73	2.67	2.61	2.55	*0.025*	14
3.94	3.80	3.66	3.51	3.43	3.35	3.27	3.18	3.09	*0.01*	
4.60	4.43	4.25	4.06	3.96	3.86	3.76	3.66	3.55	*0.005*	
2.06	2.02	1.97	1.92	1.90	1.87	1.85	1.82	1.79	*0.10*	
2.54	2.48	2.40	2.33	2.29	2.25	2.20	2.16	2.11	*0.05*	
3.06	2.96	2.86	2.76	2.70	2.64	2.59	2.52	2.46	*0.025*	15
3.80	3.67	3.52	3.37	3.29	3.21	3.13	3.05	2.96	*0.01*	
4.42	4.25	4.07	3.88	3.79	3.69	3.58	3.48	3.37	*0.005*	
2.03	1.99	1.94	1.89	1.87	1.84	1.81	1.78	1.75	*0.10*	
2.49	2.42	2.35	2.28	2.24	2.19	2.15	2.11	2.06	*0.05*	
2.99	2.89	2.79	2.68	2.63	2.57	2.51	2.45	2.38	*0.025*	16
3.69	3.55	3.41	3.26	3.18	3.10	3.02	2.93	2.84	*0.01*	
4.27	4.10	3.92	3.73	3.64	3.54	3.44	3.33	3.22	*0.005*	

(dfn across the top)

TABLE VI (cont.)
Values of F_α

| dfd | α | \multicolumn{9}{c}{dfn} |
		1	2	3	4	5	6	7	8	9
17	0.10	3.03	2.64	2.44	2.31	2.22	2.15	2.10	2.06	2.03
	0.05	4.45	3.59	3.20	2.96	2.81	2.70	2.61	2.55	2.49
	0.025	6.04	4.62	4.01	3.66	3.44	3.28	3.16	3.06	2.98
	0.01	8.40	6.11	5.18	4.67	4.34	4.10	3.93	3.79	3.68
	0.005	10.38	7.35	6.16	5.50	5.07	4.78	4.56	4.39	4.25
18	0.10	3.01	2.62	2.42	2.29	2.20	2.13	2.08	2.04	2.00
	0.05	4.41	3.55	3.16	2.93	2.77	2.66	2.58	2.51	2.46
	0.025	5.98	4.56	3.95	3.61	3.38	3.22	3.10	3.01	2.93
	0.01	8.29	6.01	5.09	4.58	4.25	4.01	3.84	3.71	3.60
	0.005	10.22	7.21	6.03	5.37	4.96	4.66	4.44	4.28	4.14
19	0.10	2.99	2.61	2.40	2.27	2.18	2.11	2.06	2.02	1.98
	0.05	4.38	3.52	3.13	2.90	2.74	2.63	2.54	2.48	2.42
	0.025	5.92	4.51	3.90	3.56	3.33	3.17	3.05	2.96	2.88
	0.01	8.18	5.93	5.01	4.50	4.17	3.94	3.77	3.63	3.52
	0.005	10.07	7.09	5.92	5.27	4.85	4.56	4.34	4.18	4.04
20	0.10	2.97	2.59	2.38	2.25	2.16	2.09	2.04	2.00	1.96
	0.05	4.35	3.49	3.10	2.87	2.71	2.60	2.51	2.45	2.39
	0.025	5.87	4.46	3.86	3.51	3.29	3.13	3.01	2.91	2.84
	0.01	8.10	5.85	4.94	4.43	4.10	3.87	3.70	3.56	3.46
	0.005	9.94	6.99	5.82	5.17	4.76	4.47	4.26	4.09	3.96
21	0.10	2.96	2.57	2.36	2.23	2.14	2.08	2.02	1.98	1.95
	0.05	4.32	3.47	3.07	2.84	2.68	2.57	2.49	2.42	2.37
	0.025	5.83	4.42	3.82	3.48	3.25	3.09	2.97	2.87	2.80
	0.01	8.02	5.78	4.87	4.37	4.04	3.81	3.64	3.51	3.40
	0.005	9.83	6.89	5.73	5.09	4.68	4.39	4.18	4.01	3.88
22	0.10	2.95	2.56	2.35	2.22	2.13	2.06	2.01	1.97	1.93
	0.05	4.30	3.44	3.05	2.82	2.66	2.55	2.46	2.40	2.34
	0.025	5.79	4.38	3.78	3.44	3.22	3.05	2.93	2.84	2.76
	0.01	7.95	5.72	4.82	4.31	3.99	3.76	3.59	3.45	3.35
	0.005	9.73	6.81	5.65	5.02	4.61	4.32	4.11	3.94	3.81
23	0.10	2.94	2.55	2.34	2.21	2.11	2.05	1.99	1.95	1.92
	0.05	4.28	3.42	3.03	2.80	2.64	2.53	2.44	2.37	2.32
	0.025	5.75	4.35	3.75	3.41	3.18	3.02	2.90	2.81	2.73
	0.01	7.88	5.66	4.76	4.26	3.94	3.71	3.54	3.41	3.30
	0.005	9.63	6.73	5.58	4.95	4.54	4.26	4.05	3.88	3.75
24	0.10	2.93	2.54	2.33	2.19	2.10	2.04	1.98	1.94	1.91
	0.05	4.26	3.40	3.01	2.78	2.62	2.51	2.42	2.36	2.30
	0.025	5.72	4.32	3.72	3.38	3.15	2.99	2.87	2.78	2.70
	0.01	7.82	5.61	4.72	4.22	3.90	3.67	3.50	3.36	3.26
	0.005	9.55	6.66	5.52	4.89	4.49	4.20	3.99	3.83	3.69

TABLE VI (cont.)
Values of F_α

dfn										
10	*12*	*15*	*20*	*24*	*30*	*40*	*60*	*120*	α	dfd
2.00	1.96	1.91	1.86	1.84	1.81	1.78	1.75	1.72	0.10	
2.45	2.38	2.31	2.23	2.19	2.15	2.10	2.06	2.01	0.05	
2.92	2.82	2.72	2.62	2.56	2.50	2.44	2.38	2.32	0.025	17
3.59	3.46	3.31	3.16	3.08	3.00	2.92	2.83	2.75	0.01	
4.14	3.97	3.79	3.61	3.51	3.41	3.31	3.21	3.10	0.005	
1.98	1.93	1.89	1.84	1.81	1.78	1.75	1.72	1.69	0.10	
2.41	2.34	2.27	2.19	2.15	2.11	2.06	2.02	1.97	0.05	
2.87	2.77	2.67	2.56	2.50	2.44	2.38	2.32	2.26	0.025	18
3.51	3.37	3.23	3.08	3.00	2.92	2.84	2.75	2.66	0.01	
4.03	3.86	3.68	3.50	3.40	3.30	3.20	3.10	2.99	0.005	
1.96	1.91	1.86	1.81	1.79	1.76	1.73	1.70	1.67	0.10	
2.38	2.31	2.23	2.16	2.11	2.07	2.03	1.98	1.93	0.05	
2.82	2.72	2.62	2.51	2.45	2.39	2.33	2.27	2.20	0.025	19
3.43	3.30	3.15	3.00	2.92	2.84	2.76	2.67	2.58	0.01	
3.93	3.76	3.59	3.40	3.31	3.21	3.11	3.00	2.89	0.005	
1.94	1.89	1.84	1.79	1.77	1.74	1.71	1.68	1.64	0.10	
2.35	2.28	2.20	2.12	2.08	2.04	1.99	1.95	1.90	0.05	
2.77	2.68	2.57	2.46	2.41	2.35	2.29	2.22	2.16	0.025	20
3.37	3.23	3.09	2.94	2.86	2.78	2.69	2.61	2.52	0.01	
3.85	3.68	3.50	3.32	3.22	3.12	3.02	2.92	2.81	0.005	
1.92	1.87	1.83	1.78	1.75	1.72	1.69	1.66	1.62	0.10	
2.32	2.25	2.18	2.10	2.05	2.01	1.96	1.92	1.87	0.05	
2.73	2.64	2.53	2.42	2.37	2.31	2.25	2.18	2.11	0.025	21
3.31	3.17	3.03	2.88	2.80	2.72	2.64	2.55	2.46	0.01	
3.77	3.60	3.43	3.24	3.15	3.05	2.95	2.84	2.73	0.005	
1.90	1.86	1.81	1.76	1.73	1.70	1.67	1.64	1.60	0.10	
2.30	2.23	2.15	2.07	2.03	1.98	1.94	1.89	1.84	0.05	
2.70	2.60	2.50	2.39	2.33	2.27	2.21	2.14	2.08	0.025	22
3.26	3.12	2.98	2.83	2.75	2.67	2.58	2.50	2.40	0.01	
3.70	3.54	3.36	3.18	3.08	2.98	2.88	2.77	2.66	0.005	
1.89	1.84	1.80	1.74	1.72	1.69	1.66	1.62	1.59	0.10	
2.27	2.20	2.13	2.05	2.01	1.96	1.91	1.86	1.81	0.05	
2.67	2.57	2.47	2.36	2.30	2.24	2.18	2.11	2.04	0.025	23
3.21	3.07	2.93	2.78	2.70	2.62	2.54	2.45	2.35	0.01	
3.64	3.47	3.30	3.12	3.02	2.92	2.82	2.71	2.60	0.005	
1.88	1.83	1.78	1.73	1.70	1.67	1.64	1.61	1.57	0.10	
2.25	2.18	2.11	2.03	1.98	1.94	1.89	1.84	1.79	0.05	
2.64	2.54	2.44	2.33	2.27	2.21	2.15	2.08	2.01	0.025	24
3.17	3.03	2.89	2.74	2.66	2.58	2.49	2.40	2.31	0.01	
3.59	3.42	3.25	3.06	2.97	2.87	2.77	2.66	2.55	0.005	

TABLE VI (cont.)
Values of F_α

| dfd | α | \multicolumn{9}{c}{dfn} |
		1	2	3	4	5	6	7	8	9
25	0.10	2.92	2.53	2.32	2.18	2.09	2.02	1.97	1.93	1.89
	0.05	4.24	3.39	2.99	2.76	2.60	2.49	2.40	2.34	2.28
	0.025	5.69	4.29	3.69	3.35	3.13	2.97	2.85	2.75	2.68
	0.01	7.77	5.57	4.68	4.18	3.85	3.63	3.46	3.32	3.22
	0.005	9.48	6.60	5.46	4.84	4.43	4.15	3.94	3.78	3.64
26	0.10	2.91	2.52	2.31	2.17	2.08	2.01	1.96	1.92	1.88
	0.05	4.23	3.37	2.98	2.74	2.59	2.47	2.39	2.32	2.27
	0.025	5.66	4.27	3.67	3.33	3.10	2.94	2.82	2.73	2.65
	0.01	7.72	5.53	4.64	4.14	3.82	3.59	3.42	3.29	3.18
	0.005	9.41	6.54	5.41	4.79	4.38	4.10	3.89	3.73	3.60
27	0.10	2.90	2.51	2.30	2.17	2.07	2.00	1.95	1.91	1.87
	0.05	4.21	3.35	2.96	2.73	2.57	2.46	2.37	2.31	2.25
	0.025	5.63	4.24	3.65	3.31	3.08	2.92	2.80	2.71	2.63
	0.01	7.68	5.49	4.60	4.11	3.78	3.56	3.39	3.26	3.15
	0.005	9.34	6.49	5.36	4.74	4.34	4.06	3.85	3.69	3.56
28	0.10	2.89	2.50	2.29	2.16	2.06	2.00	1.94	1.90	1.87
	0.05	4.20	3.34	2.95	2.71	2.56	2.45	2.36	2.29	2.24
	0.025	5.61	4.22	3.63	3.29	3.06	2.90	2.78	2.69	2.61
	0.01	7.64	5.45	4.57	4.07	3.75	3.53	3.36	3.23	3.12
	0.005	9.28	6.44	5.32	4.70	4.30	4.02	3.81	3.65	3.52
29	0.10	2.89	2.50	2.28	2.15	2.06	1.99	1.93	1.89	1.86
	0.05	4.18	3.33	2.93	2.70	2.55	2.43	2.35	2.28	2.22
	0.025	5.59	4.20	3.61	3.27	3.04	2.88	2.76	2.67	2.59
	0.01	7.60	5.42	4.54	4.04	3.73	3.50	3.33	3.20	3.09
	0.005	9.23	6.40	5.28	4.66	4.26	3.98	3.77	3.61	3.48
30	0.10	2.88	2.49	2.28	2.14	2.05	1.98	1.93	1.88	1.85
	0.05	4.17	3.32	2.92	2.69	2.53	2.42	2.33	2.27	2.21
	0.025	5.57	4.18	3.59	3.25	3.03	2.87	2.75	2.65	2.57
	0.01	7.56	5.39	4.51	4.02	3.70	3.47	3.30	3.17	3.07
	0.005	9.18	6.35	5.24	4.62	4.23	3.95	3.74	3.58	3.45
60	0.10	2.79	2.39	2.18	2.04	1.95	1.87	1.82	1.77	1.74
	0.05	4.00	3.15	2.76	2.53	2.37	2.25	2.17	2.10	2.04
	0.025	5.29	3.93	3.34	3.01	2.79	2.63	2.51	2.41	2.33
	0.01	7.08	4.98	4.13	3.65	3.34	3.12	2.95	2.82	2.72
	0.005	8.49	5.79	4.73	4.14	3.76	3.49	3.29	3.13	3.01
120	0.10	2.75	2.35	2.13	1.99	1.90	1.82	1.77	1.72	1.68
	0.05	3.92	3.07	2.68	2.45	2.29	2.18	2.09	2.02	1.96
	0.025	5.15	3.80	3.23	2.89	2.67	2.52	2.39	2.30	2.22
	0.01	6.85	4.79	3.95	3.48	3.17	2.96	2.79	2.66	2.56
	0.005	8.18	5.54	4.50	3.92	3.55	3.28	3.09	2.93	2.81

TABLE VI (cont.)
Values of F_α

10	12	15	20	24	30	40	60	120	α	dfd
1.87	1.82	1.77	1.72	1.69	1.66	1.63	1.59	1.56	0.10	
2.24	2.16	2.09	2.01	1.96	1.92	1.87	1.82	1.77	0.05	
2.61	2.51	2.41	2.30	2.24	2.18	2.12	2.05	1.98	0.025	25
3.13	2.99	2.85	2.70	2.62	2.54	2.45	2.36	2.27	0.01	
3.54	3.37	3.20	3.01	2.92	2.82	2.72	2.61	2.50	0.005	
1.86	1.81	1.76	1.71	1.68	1.65	1.61	1.58	1.54	0.10	
2.22	2.15	2.07	1.99	1.95	1.90	1.85	1.80	1.75	0.05	
2.59	2.49	2.39	2.28	2.22	2.16	2.09	2.03	1.95	0.025	26
3.09	2.96	2.81	2.66	2.58	2.50	2.42	2.33	2.23	0.01	
3.49	3.33	3.15	2.97	2.87	2.77	2.67	2.56	2.45	0.005	
1.85	1.80	1.75	1.70	1.67	1.64	1.60	1.57	1.53	0.10	
2.20	2.13	2.06	1.97	1.93	1.88	1.84	1.79	1.73	0.05	
2.57	2.47	2.36	2.25	2.19	2.13	2.07	2.00	1.93	0.025	27
3.06	2.93	2.78	2.63	2.55	2.47	2.38	2.29	2.20	0.01	
3.45	3.28	3.11	2.93	2.83	2.73	2.63	2.52	2.41	0.005	
1.84	1.79	1.74	1.69	1.66	1.63	1.59	1.56	1.52	0.10	
2.19	2.12	2.04	1.96	1.91	1.87	1.82	1.77	1.71	0.05	
2.55	2.45	2.34	2.23	2.17	2.11	2.05	1.98	1.91	0.025	28
3.03	2.90	2.75	2.60	2.52	2.44	2.35	2.26	2.17	0.01	
3.41	3.25	3.07	2.89	2.79	2.69	2.59	2.48	2.37	0.005	
1.83	1.78	1.73	1.68	1.65	1.62	1.58	1.55	1.51	0.10	
2.18	2.10	2.03	1.94	1.90	1.85	1.81	1.75	1.70	0.05	
2.53	2.43	2.32	2.21	2.15	2.09	2.03	1.96	1.89	0.025	29
3.00	2.87	2.73	2.57	2.49	2.41	2.33	2.23	2.14	0.01	
3.38	3.21	3.04	2.86	2.76	2.66	2.56	2.45	2.33	0.005	
1.82	1.77	1.72	1.67	1.64	1.61	1.57	1.54	1.50	0.10	
2.16	2.09	2.01	1.93	1.89	1.84	1.79	1.74	1.68	0.05	
2.51	2.41	2.31	2.20	2.14	2.07	2.01	1.94	1.87	0.025	30
2.98	2.84	2.70	2.55	2.47	2.39	2.30	2.21	2.11	0.01	
3.34	3.18	3.01	2.82	2.73	2.63	2.52	2.42	2.30	0.005	
1.71	1.66	1.60	1.54	1.51	1.48	1.44	1.40	1.35	0.10	
1.99	1.92	1.84	1.75	1.70	1.65	1.59	1.53	1.47	0.05	
2.27	2.17	2.06	1.94	1.88	1.82	1.74	1.67	1.58	0.025	60
2.63	2.50	2.35	2.20	2.12	2.03	1.94	1.84	1.73	0.01	
2.90	2.74	2.57	2.39	2.29	2.19	2.08	1.96	1.83	0.005	
1.65	1.60	1.55	1.48	1.45	1.41	1.37	1.32	1.26	0.10	
1.91	1.83	1.75	1.66	1.61	1.55	1.50	1.43	1.35	0.05	
2.16	2.05	1.94	1.82	1.76	1.69	1.61	1.53	1.43	0.025	120
2.47	2.34	2.19	2.03	1.95	1.86	1.76	1.66	1.53	0.01	
2.71	2.54	2.37	2.19	2.09	1.98	1.87	1.75	1.61	0.005	

ANSWERS TO SELECTED EXERCISES

Note: Most of the numerical answers presented here were obtained by using a computer. If you solve a problem by hand and do some intermediate rounding or use provided summary statistics, your answer may differ slightly from the one given in this appendix.

CHAPTER 1

EXERCISES 1.1

1.1 See Definition 1.2 on page 5.

1.2 The two major types of statistics are descriptive statistics and inferential statistics. For more details, see Definition 1.1 on page 4 and Definition 1.3 on page 5, respectively.

1.3 Descriptive statistics includes the construction of graphs, charts, and tables, and the calculation of various descriptive measures such as averages, measures of variation, and percentiles.

1.4 Descriptive statistics is often used to organize and summarize information from a sample prior to conducting an inferential analysis. Preliminary descriptive analyses of a sample sometimes reveal features of the data that lead to reconsideration of the method for the inferential analysis.

1.5 Inferential

1.6 Descriptive

1.7 Inferential

1.8 Inferential

1.9 Descriptive

1.10 Inferential

EXERCISES 1.3

1.13 Conducting a census is generally time-consuming and costly, frequently impractical, and sometimes impossible.

1.14 Sampling and experimentation

1.15 Obtaining a representative sample is important because the sample will be used to draw conclusions about the entire population.

1.16 The online poll has a built-in bias. Because it was taken over the Memorial Day weekend, most of those who responded were people who stayed at home and had access to their computers. Generally, people vacationing outdoors over the weekend would not have carried computers with them and therefore would not have been able to respond.

1.17 Dentists form a high-income group whose incomes are not representative of the incomes of Seattle residents in general.

1.18 Answers will vary.

1.19
a. In probability sampling a random device, such as tossing a coin or consulting a random-number table, is used to decide which members of the population will constitute the sample instead of leaving such decisions to human judgement.
b. No. Because probability sampling uses a random device, it is possible to obtain a nonrepresentative sample.
c. Probability sampling eliminates unintentional selection bias and permits the researcher to control the chance of obtaining a nonrepresentative sample. Also, use of probability sampling guarantees that the techniques of inferential statistics can be applied.

1.20
a. Simple random sampling is a sampling procedure for which each possible sample of a given size is equally likely to be the one obtained.

b. A simple random sample is one obtained by a simple random sampling procedure.

c. Simple random sampling may be done with or without replacement. In the former case, it is possible for a member of the population to be chosen more than once; in the latter case, it is not possible.

1.21 Simple random sampling

1.22 Answers will vary.

1.23

a.

G, L, S	G, L, A	G, L, T	G, S, A	G, S, T
G, A, T	L, S, A	L, S, T	L, A, T	S, A, T

b. $\frac{1}{10}, \frac{1}{10}, \frac{1}{10}$

1.24

a.

E, M	E, P	E, L	E, B	E, F
M, P	M, L	M, B	M, F	P, L
P, B	P, F	L, B	L, F	B, F

b. Write the initials of the six artists on separate pieces of paper, place the six slips of paper in a box, and then, while blindfolded, pick two of the slips of paper.

c. $\frac{1}{15}, \frac{1}{15}$

1.25

a.

E, M, P, L	E, M, P, B	E, M, P, F	E, M, L, B	E, M, L, F
E, M, B, F	E, P, L, B	E, P, L, F	E, P, B, F	E, L, B, F
M, P, L, B	M, P, L, F	M, P, B, F	M, L, B, F	P, L, B, F

b. Write the initials of the six artists on separate pieces of paper, place the six slips of paper in a box, and then, while blindfolded, pick four of the slips of paper.

c. $\frac{1}{15}, \frac{1}{15}$

1.26

a.

E, M, P	E, M, L	E, M, B	E, M, F	E, P, L
E, P, B	E, P, F	E, L, B	E, L, F	E, B, F
M, P, L	M, P, B	M, P, F	M, L, B	M, L, F
M, B, F	P, L, B	P, L, F	P, B, F	L, B, F

b. Write the initials of the six artists on separate pieces of paper, place the six slips of paper in a box, and then, while blindfolded, pick three of the slips of paper.

c. $\frac{1}{20}, \frac{1}{20}$

1.27 Answers will vary.

1.28 Answers will vary.

EXERCISES 1.4

1.33

a. The population under consideration consists of the 500 firms from *Fortune Magazine*'s list of "The International 500." The sample consists of 10 of those firms. From Procedure 1.1 on page 18, the method is as follows. Step 1: Divide the population size, 500, by the sample size, 10, which gives 50 (rounding down is unnecessary in this case). Step 2: Use a random number table (or a similar device) to obtain a number, k, between 1 and 50. Step 3: Select for the sample those firms on the "The International 500" that are numbered $k, k + 50, k + 100$, and so on. For example, if $k = 6$, the firms in the sample will be those numbered 6, 56, 106, ...

b. Systematic random sampling

c. Answers will vary.

1.34

a. The population under consideration consists of the 80 keno balls. The sample consists of 20 of those balls. From Procedure 1.1 on page 18, the method is as follows. Step 1: Divide the population size, 80, by the sample size, 20, which gives 4 (rounding down is unnecessary in this case). Step 2: Use a random number table (or a similar device) to obtain a number, k, between 1 and 4. Step 3: The keno balls obtained are those numbered $k, k + 4, k + 8$, and so on. For example, if $k = 3$, the keno balls obtained will be those numbered 3, 7, 11, ...

b. Systematic random sampling

c. No. In keno, each collection of 20 balls should have the same chance of being chosen. Systematic sampling would give each of four collections of 20 balls a 1/4 chance of occurring, whereas each of the other possible collections of 20 balls would have no chance of occurring. Here simple random sampling is the appropriate sampling procedure.

1.35

a. Number the suites from 1 to 48, use a table of random numbers to randomly select 3 of the 48 suites, and take as the sample the 24 dormitory residents living in the 3 suites obtained.

b. Probably not, because friends often have similar opinions.

c. Proportional allocation dictates that the number of freshmen, sophomores, juniors, and seniors selected be 8, 7, 6, and 3, respectively. Thus a stratified sample of 24 dormitory residents can be obtained as follows: Number the freshman dormitory residents from 1 through 128 and use a table of random numbers to randomly select 8 of the 128 freshman dormitory residents; number the sophomore dormitory residents from 1 through 112 and use a table of random numbers to randomly select 7 of the 112 sophomore dormitory residents; and so on.

EXERCISES 1.5

1.38
a. In an observational study, researchers simply observe characteristics and take measurements, as in a sample survey.
b. In a designed experiment, researchers impose treatments and controls and then observe characteristics and take measurements.

1.39 Causation (cause and effect)

1.40 See Key Fact 1.1 on page 24.

1.41 Here is one of several methods that could be used: Number the women from 1 to 4753; use a table of random numbers or a random-number generator to obtain 2376 different numbers between 1 and 4753; the 2376 women with those numbers are in one group, the remaining 2377 women are in the other group.

1.42
a. To make the study a designed experiment, a researcher could start with a randomly chosen group of men who have not had vasectomies. The men would then be randomly divided into two groups. In one group—the treatment group—all the men would be forced to have vasectomies. In the other group—the control group—all the men would be forbidden to have vasectomies.
b. The designed experiment described in part (a) is infeasible because, in the treatment group, there would be men who did not want a vasectomy and, in the control group, there would be men who wanted one.

1.43 Designed experiment

1.44 Observational study

1.45
a. The individuals or items on which the experiment is performed
b. Subject

1.46
a. The 2444 patients who took Prozac
b. The 1331 patients who were given placebo
c. Prozac and placebo

1.47
a. The 20 flashlights
b. Lifetime of a battery in a flashlight
c. Battery brand
d. Four brands of batteries
e. Four brands of batteries

1.48
a. The perishable items in the study
b. A measure of deterioration of such items
c. Storage time and storage temperature
d. Storage time has five levels: the five storage times. Storage temperature has three levels: the three storage temperatures.
e. The 15 different possible combinations of the five storage times and the three storage temperatures

1.49
a. Batches of the product being sold (Some might say that the stores are the experimental units.)
b. Unit sales of the product
c. Display type and pricing scheme
d. Display type has three levels: normal display space interior to an aisle, normal display space at the end of an aisle, and enlarged display space. Pricing scheme has three levels: regular price, reduced price, and cost.
e. Each treatment is a combination of a level of display type and a level of pricing scheme.

1.50
a. The fields of oats in the study
b. Oat yield
c. Oat variety and manure concentration
d. Oat variety has three levels: the three varieties of oats. Manure concentration has four levels: 0, 0.2, 0.4, and 0.6 cwt per acre.
e. The 12 different possible combinations of the three oat varieties and the four manure concentrations

1.51 Completely randomized design

1.52 Randomized block design

REVIEW TEST FOR CHAPTER 1

1. Answers will vary.
2. It is almost always necessary to invoke techniques of descriptive statistics to organize and summarize the information obtained from a sample before carrying out an inferential analysis.
3. Descriptive
4. Descriptive
5. A literature search
6. a. A representative sample is a sample that reflects as closely as possible the relevant characteristics of the population under consideration.
   b. In probability sampling, a random device, such as tossing a coin or consulting a table of random numbers, is used to decide which members of the population will constitute the sample instead of leaving such decisions to human judgement.

c. Simple random sampling is a sampling procedure for which each possible sample of a given size is equally likely to be the one obtained from the population.

7. No, because parents of students at Yale tend to have higher incomes than parents of college students in general.

8. Only (b)

9. a.

SW, AA, DL	SW, AA, US	SW, AA, AK
SW, DL, US	SW, DL, AK	SW, US, AK
AA, DL, US	AA, DL, AK	AA, US, AK
DL, US, AK		

b. $\frac{1}{10}, \frac{1}{10}, \frac{1}{10}$

10. a. Number the athletes from 1 to 100, use Table I to obtain 15 different numbers between 1 and 100, and take as the sample the 15 athletes who are numbered with the numbers obtained.
b. 082, 008, 016, 001, 047, 094, 097, 074, 052, 076, 098, 003, 089, 041, 063

11. See Section 1.4 and, in particular, (a) Procedure 1.1 on page 18, (b) Procedure 1.2 on page 19, and (c) Procedure 1.3 on page 21.

12. a. The population under consideration consists of the top 100 North American athletes of the twentieth century. The sample consists of 15 of those athletes. From Procedure 1.1 on page 18, the method is as follows. Step 1: Divide the population size, 100, by the sample size, 15, and round the result down, which gives 6. Step 2: Use a random number table (or a similar device) to obtain a number between 1 and 6; call it k. Step 3: Select for the sample those athletes who are numbered $k, k+6, k+12$, and so on. For example, if $k=4$, then the athletes in the sample will be those numbered 4, 10, 16, ...
b. Yes, unless for some reason there is a cyclical pattern in the listing of the athletes.

13. a. Proportional allocation dictates that 10 full professors, 16 associate professors, 12 assistant professors, and 2 instructors be selected.
b. The procedure is as follows: Number the full professors from 1 to 205, and use Table I to randomly select 10 of the 205 full professors; number the associate professors from 1 to 328, and use Table I to randomly select 16 of the 328 associate professors; and so on.

14. The statement under the vote tally is a disclaimer as to the validity of the survey. Because the results reflect only responses of Internet users, they cannot be regarded as representative of the public in general. Moreover, because the sample was not chosen at random from Internet users—but rather was obtained only from volunteers—the results cannot even be considered representative of Internet users.

15. a. In an observational study, researchers simply observe characteristics and take measurements. In a designed experiment, researchers impose treatments and controls and then observe characteristics and take measurements.
b. Observational studies can reveal only association, whereas designed experiments can help establish causation (cause and effect).

16. Observational study

17. a. Designed experiment
b. The treatment group consists of the 158 patients who took AVONEX. The control group consists of the 143 patients who were given placebo. The treatments are AVONEX and placebo.

18. See Key Fact 1.1 on page 24.

19. a. The batches of doughnuts
b. Amount of fat absorbed
c. Fat type
d. Four types of fat
e. Four types of fat

20. a. The tomato plants in the study (Some might say the plots of land are the experimental units.)
b. Yield of tomato plants
c. Tomato variety and planting density
d. Different tomato varieties and different planting densities
e. Each treatment is a combination of a level of tomato variety and a level of planting density.

21. a. Completely randomized design
b. Randomized block design; the six different car models
c. The randomized block design in part (b)

22. Answers will vary.

CHAPTER 2

EXERCISES 2.1

2.1 Answers will vary.

2.2 See Definition 2.1 on page 40.

2.3 See Definition 2.2 on page 41.

2.4 It may serve as an aid in the choice of the correct statistical method.

2.5 Qualitative variable

2.6
a. Quantitative, discrete; rank of language by number of speakers
b. Qualitative; language that a person speaks
c. Quantitative, discrete; number of people who speak a given language

2.7
a. Quantitative, discrete; rank of U.S. cities by highest temperature
b. Quantitative, continuous; highest temperature, in degrees Fahrenheit, for U.S. cities
c. Qualitative; state in which a U.S. city is located

2.8
a. Quantitative, discrete; rank of a TV program by ratings
b. Quantitative, continuous; ratings for a TV program

2.9
a. Quantitative, discrete; number of albums sold, in millions, in 1999
b. Qualitative; artist/group of an album

EXERCISES 2.2

2.11 Grouping can help to make a large and complicated set of data more compact and easier to understand.

2.12 No. Cutpoints and midpoints make sense only for numerical data (for which doing arithmetic is meaningful).

2.13 See 1–3 on pages 45–46.

2.14
a. The frequency of a class is the number of observations in the class, whereas the relative frequency of a class is the ratio of the class frequency to the total number of observations.
b. The percentage of a class equals 100 times the relative frequency of the class. Equivalently, the relative frequency of a class is the percentage of the class expressed as a decimal.

2.15 Relative-frequency distributions are better than frequency distributions when two data sets are being compared because relative frequencies are always between 0 and 1 and hence provide a standard for comparison.

2.16 Classes, frequencies, relative frequencies, and midpoints

2.18
a. (1)   b. (3)

2.19 Because each class is based on a single value, the midpoint of each class is the same as the class.

2.20

Consumption (mil. BTU)	Frequency	Relative frequency	Midpoint
40 < 50	1	0.02	45
50 < 60	7	0.14	55
60 < 70	7	0.14	65
70 < 80	3	0.06	75
80 < 90	6	0.12	85
90 < 100	10	0.20	95
100 < 110	5	0.10	105
110 < 120	4	0.08	115
120 < 130	2	0.04	125
130 < 140	3	0.06	135
140 < 150	0	0.00	145
150 < 160	2	0.04	155
	50	1.00	

2.21

Speed (mph)	Frequency	Relative frequency	Midpoint
52 < 54	2	0.057	53
54 < 56	5	0.143	55
56 < 58	6	0.171	57
58 < 60	8	0.229	59
60 < 62	7	0.200	61
62 < 64	3	0.086	63
64 < 66	2	0.057	65
66 < 68	1	0.029	67
68 < 70	0	0.000	69
70 < 72	0	0.000	71
72 < 74	0	0.000	73
74 < 76	1	0.029	75
	35	1.001	

2.22

Consumption (mil. BTU)	Frequency	Relative frequency	Mark
40–49	1	0.02	44.5
50–59	7	0.14	54.5
60–69	7	0.14	64.5
70–79	3	0.06	74.5
80–89	6	0.12	84.5
90–99	10	0.20	94.5
100–109	5	0.10	104.5
110–119	4	0.08	114.5
120–129	2	0.04	124.5
130–139	3	0.06	134.5
140–149	0	0.00	144.5
150–159	2	0.04	154.5
	50	1.00	

2.23

Speed (mph)	Frequency	Relative frequency	Mark
52–53.9	2	0.057	52.95
54–55.9	5	0.143	54.95
56–57.9	6	0.171	56.95
58–59.9	8	0.229	58.95
60–61.9	7	0.200	60.95
62–63.9	3	0.086	62.95
64–65.9	2	0.057	64.95
66–67.9	1	0.029	66.95
68–69.9	0	0.000	68.95
70–71.9	0	0.000	70.95
72–73.9	0	0.000	72.95
74–75.9	1	0.029	74.95
	35	1.001	

2.24

Number of persons	Frequency	Relative frequency
1	7	0.175
2	13	0.325
3	9	0.225
4	5	0.125
5	4	0.100
6	1	0.025
7	1	0.025
	40	1.000

2.25

Number of pups	Frequency	Relative frequency
3	2	0.025
4	5	0.063
5	10	0.125
6	11	0.138
7	17	0.213
8	17	0.213
9	11	0.138
10	4	0.050
11	2	0.025
12	1	0.013
	80	1.003

2.26

Day	Frequency	Relative frequency
Su	5	0.072
M	5	0.072
Tu	11	0.159
W	12	0.174
Th	11	0.159
F	18	0.261
Sa	7	0.101
	69	0.998

2.27

Network	Frequency	Relative frequency
ABC	5	0.25
CBS	8	0.40
NBC	7	0.35
	20	1.00

EXERCISES 2.3

2.37 A frequency histogram displays the class frequencies on the vertical axis, whereas a relative-frequency histogram displays the class relative frequencies on the vertical axis.

2.38 Answers will vary.

2.39 To avoid confusing bar graphs and histograms, the bars in a bar graph are positioned so that they do not touch each other.

2.40 Answers will vary.

2.41
a. The heights of the bars in the histogram would be comparable to the heights of the columns of dots in the dotplot.
b. No. Each bar in the histogram would represent a range of possible values, whereas, in the dotplot, each column of dots represents one possible value.

2.42
a.
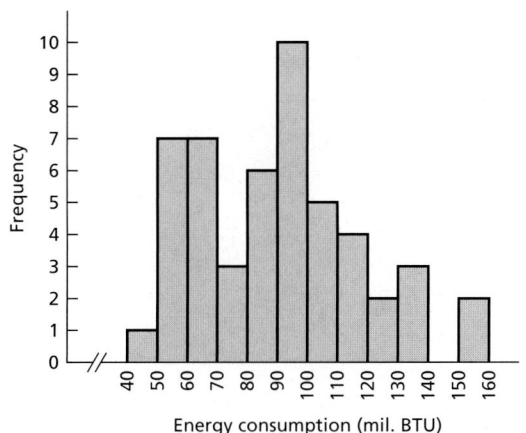

b.
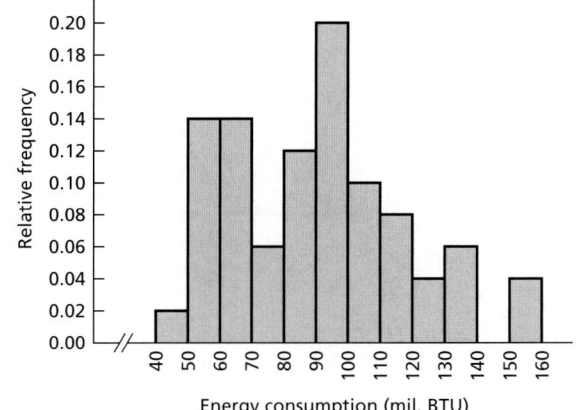

2.43
a.
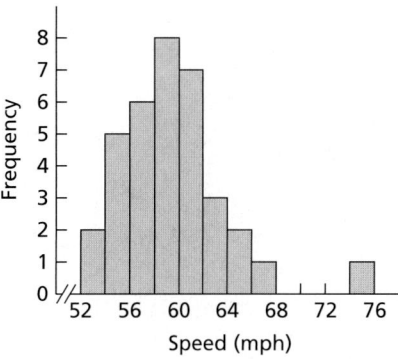

b.
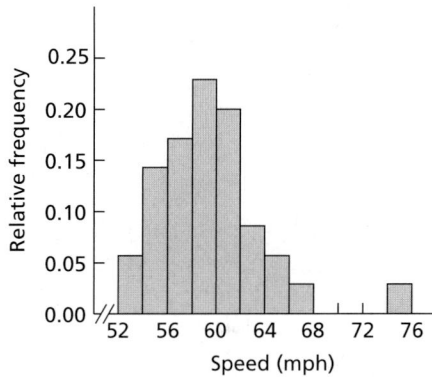

2.44
a.
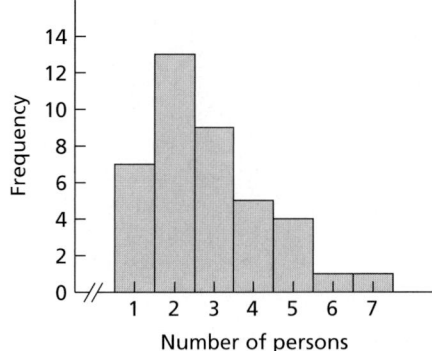

b.

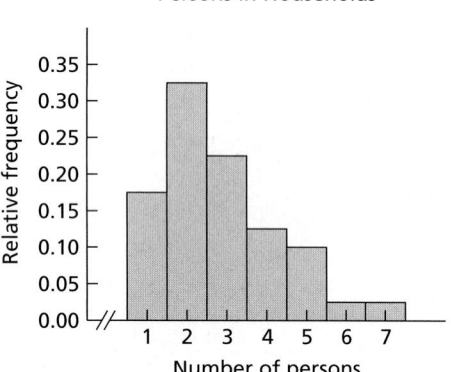

2.45
a.

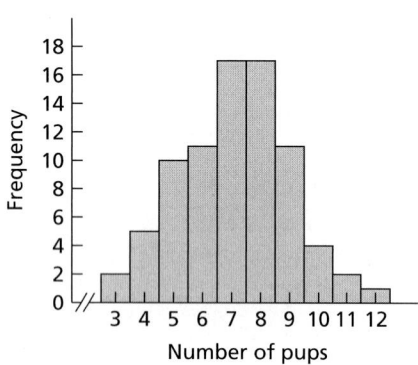

b.

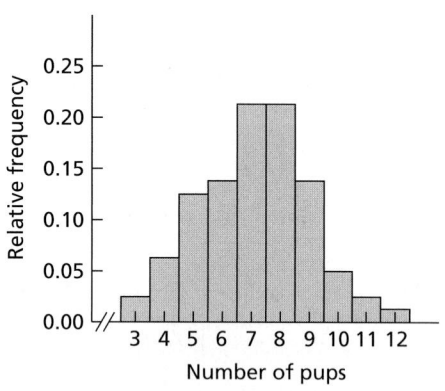

2.46

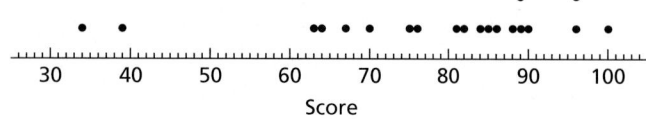

2.47

2.48
a.

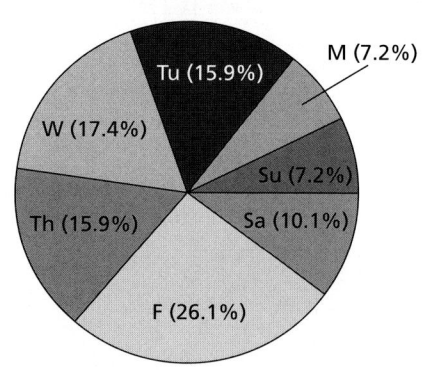

b.

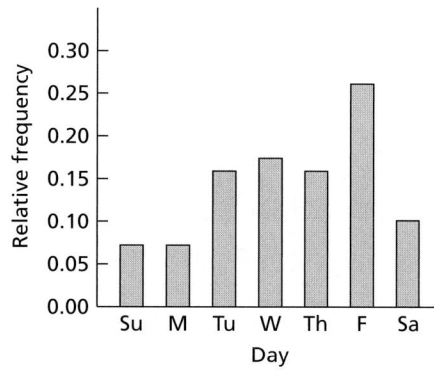

2.49
a.

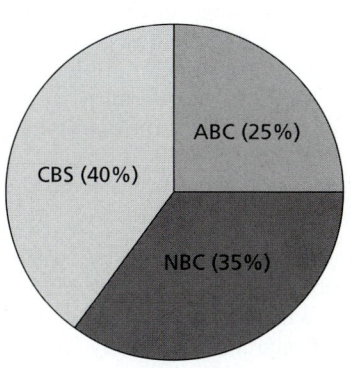

Networks of Top TV Programs

b.

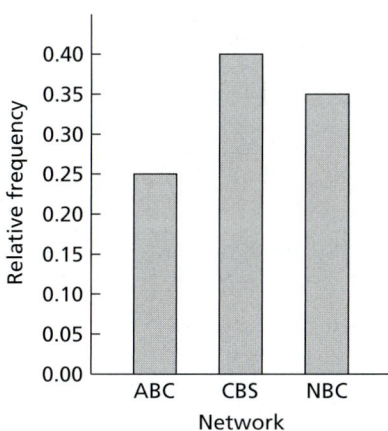

Networks of Top TV Programs

2.50
a. 27.5%   **b.** 84.0%   **c.** 14,388,480

2.51
a. 20%   **b.** 25%   **c.** 7

EXERCISES 2.4

2.59 Histogram. Stem-and-leaf diagrams are generally not useful with large data sets.

2.60 If each class represents a range of possible values, it is not possible to know which of those values contributed to the frequency of a class. If, however, each class represents only a single possible value (single-value grouping), the raw data can be recovered.

2.61 Reconstruct the stem-and-leaf diagram, using more lines per stem.

2.62

a.
```
 91 | 4
 92 |
 93 |
 94 | 6
 95 | 9 7
 96 | 4
 97 | 7 5 4 7
 98 | 6 9 4 8 7
 99 | 0 6 1 9 5 7
100 | 1
101 | 4 8 0 7
102 | 5 8
103 | 0 1
104 |
105 |
106 | 0
```

b.
```
 91 | 4
 92 |
 93 |
 94 | 6
 95 | 7 9
 96 | 4
 97 | 4 5 7 7
 98 | 4 6 7 8 9
 99 | 0 1 5 6 7 9
100 | 1
101 | 0 4 7 8
102 | 5 8
103 | 0 1
104 |
105 |
106 | 0
```

2.63

a.
```
5 | 2 7 3 4 4 5 9
6 | 7 3 0 3 0 8 4 6 6 3 8 4
7 | 4 7 7 6 3 7 1 1 3
8 | 0 4 2
```

b.
```
5 | 2 3 4 4 5 7 9
6 | 0 0 3 3 3 4 4 6 6 7 8 8
7 | 1 1 3 3 4 6 7 7 7
8 | 0 2 4
```

c.
```
5 | 2 3 4 4        5 | 2 3 4 4
5 | 5 7 9          5 | 5 7 9
6 | 3 0 3 0 4 3 4  6 | 0 0 3 3 3 4 4
6 | 7 8 6 6 8      6 | 6 6 7 8 8
7 | 4 3 1 1 3      7 | 1 1 3 3 4
7 | 7 7 6 7        7 | 6 7 7 7
8 | 0 4 2          8 | 0 2 4
```

2.64
a.
```
7 | 9 7 8 9 7 9 7 8 6
8 | 2 0 4 5 4 2 0 5 3 4 4 8 9 7 5 6 5 9 3 9 8 9 4 7 0 2 1 4 6 5 6 4 1 6 9 7 3 8
9 | 1 0 2 0
```

b.
```
7 | 9 7 8 9 7 9 7 8 6
8 | 2 0 4 4 2 0 3 4 4 3 4 0 2 1 4 4 1 3
8 | 5 5 8 9 7 5 6 5 9 9 8 9 7 6 5 6 6 9 7 8
9 | 1 0 2 0
```

c.
```
7 | 7 7 7 6
7 | 9 8 9 9 8
8 | 0 0 0 1 1
8 | 2 2 3 3 2 3
8 | 4 5 4 5 4 4 5 5 4 4 5 4
8 | 7 6 7 6 6 6 7
8 | 8 9 9 9 8 9 9 8
9 | 1 0 0
9 | 2
```

d. The stem-and-leaf diagram of part (c) is the most useful.

2.65

a.
```
2 | 6 7 8 5
3 | 9 8 1 1 7 9 4 7 2 9 7
4 | 9 7 9 7 0 5 6 9 4 6 8 4 3 1 5 1
5 | 2 1 8 1 7 5 5 5 5 9
6 | 0 4 0 9 3 1 0
7 | 2 3
```

b.
```
2 | 6 7 8 5
3 | 1 1 4 2
3 | 9 8 7 9 7 9 7
4 | 0 4 4 3 1 1
4 | 9 7 9 7 5 6 9 6 8 5
5 | 2 1 1
5 | 8 5 5 5 5 9 7
6 | 0 4 0 3 1 0
6 | 9
7 | 2 3
```

c.
```
2 | 5
2 | 6 7
2 | 8
3 | 1 1
3 | 2
3 | 4
3 | 7 7 7
3 | 9 8 9 9
4 | 0 1 1
4 | 3
4 | 5 4 4 5
4 | 7 7 6 6
4 | 9 9 9 8
5 | 1 1
5 | 2
5 | 5 5 5 5
5 | 7
5 | 8 9
6 | 0 0 1 0
6 | 3
6 | 4
6 |
6 | 9
7 |
7 | 2 3
```

d. The stem-and-leaf diagram of part (b) is the most useful. That in part (a) is also useful.

EXERCISES 2.5

2.71

a. The *distribution of a data set* is a table, graph, or formula that provides the values of the observations and how often they occur.

b. *Sample data* is a data set obtained by observing the values of a variable for a sample of the population.
c. *Population data* is the data set obtained by observing the values of a variable for an entire population.
d. *Census data* is another name for population data.
e. A *sample distribution* is the distribution of sample data.
f. The *population distribution* is the distribution of population data.
g. *Distribution of a variable* is another name for population distribution.

2.72 The use of smooth curves makes it easier to visualize the shape of a distribution. It also permits you to concentrate on overall patterns, which, in turn, allows you to classify most distributions by designating relatively few shapes.

2.73 Roughly a bell shape

2.74
a. Yes, roughly reverse J-shaped
b. Yes

2.75 Answers will vary.

2.76
a. Right skewed   **b.** Right skewed

2.77
a. Bell-shaped   **b.** Symmetric

2.78
a. Reverse J-shaped   **b.** Right skewed

2.79
a. Left skewed   **b.** Left skewed

2.80
a. Bell-shaped   **b.** Symmetric

2.81
a. Right skewed   **b.** Right skewed

EXERCISES 2.6

2.86 Graphs and charts are frequently constructed in a manner that causes them to be misleading.

2.87
a. Part of the vertical axis of the graph has been cut off, or truncated.
b. It may be done to present a clearer picture of the ups and downs in a data pattern rather than to mislead the reader.
c. You should start the axis at 0 and put slashes in the axis to indicate that part of the axis is missing.

2.89
c. They give the misleading impression that the district average is much greater relative to the national average than it actually is.

2.90
a. A break is shown in the first bar to warn the reader that part of it has been removed.
b. The graph was constructed with a broken bar to enable the reader to see differences among the other three bars.
c. The graph was constructed with a broken bar to help avoid misinterpretation.

2.91
a. It is a truncated graph.
b.
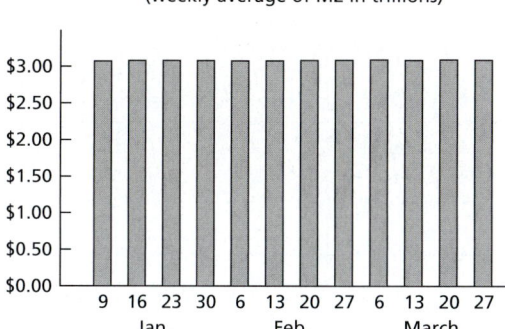
c.
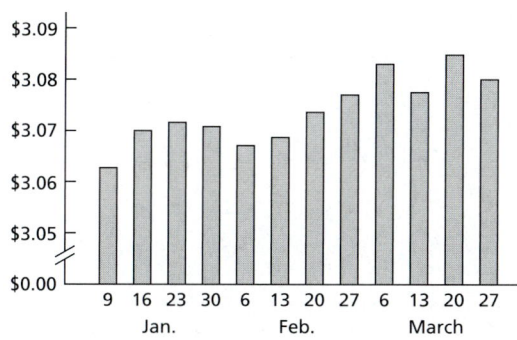

REVIEW TEST FOR CHAPTER 2

1. a. A variable is a characteristic that varies from one person or thing to another.
   b. Quantitative variables and qualitative (or categorical) variables
   c. Discrete variables and continuous variables
   d. The information obtained by observing the values of a variable
   e. By the type of variable being observed

2. It helps organize the data, making them much simpler to comprehend.

3. Qualitative data. It makes no sense to look for cutpoints or midpoints for nonnumerical data (or for numerical data obtained by coding nonnumerical data).

4. a. 6 and 14   b. 18   c. 22 and 30
   d. The third class

5. a. 10   b. 20   c. 25 and 35

6. When grouping discrete data in which there are only relatively few distinct observations

7. a. The bar for each class extends from the lower cutpoint of the class to the upper cutpoint of the class.
   b. The bar for each class is centered over the midpoint of the class.

8. Pie charts and bar graphs

9. Histogram. Stem-and-leaf diagrams are generally not useful with large data sets.

10. See Fig. 2.9 on page 73.

12. a. Left skewed. The distribution of a random sample taken from a population approximates the population distribution. The larger the sample, the better the approximation tends to be.
    b. No. Sample distributions vary from sample to sample.
    c. Yes. Left skewed. The overall shapes of the two sample distributions should be similar to that of the population distribution and hence to each other.

13. a. Discrete quantitative
    b. Continuous quantitative
    c. Qualitative

14. a.

Age at inauguration	Frequency	Relative frequency	Mark
40–44	2	0.048	42
45–49	6	0.143	47
50–54	12	0.286	52
55–59	12	0.286	57
60–64	7	0.167	62
65–69	3	0.071	67
	42	1.001	

b. 40 and 45   c. 5

d.

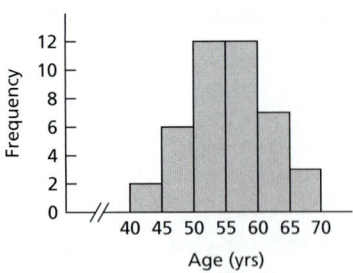

Ages at Inauguration for First 42 U.S. Presidents

b.

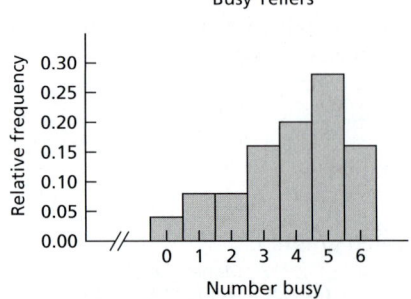

Busy Tellers

15.

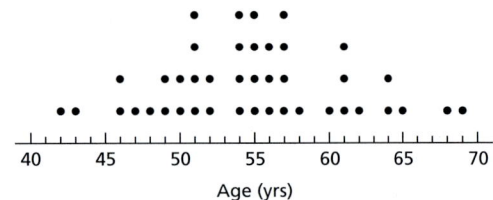

Ages at Inauguration for First 42 U.S. Presidents

16. a.
```
4 | 2 3 6 6 7 8 9 9
5 | 0 0 1 1 1 1 2 2 4 4 4 4 5 5 5 5 6 6 6 7 7 7 7 8
6 | 0 1 1 1 2 4 4 5 8 9
```

b.
```
4 | 2 3
4 | 6 6 7 8 9 9
5 | 0 0 1 1 1 1 2 2 4 4 4 4
5 | 5 5 5 5 6 6 6 7 7 7 7 8
6 | 0 1 1 1 2 4 4
6 | 5 8 9
```

c. The one in part (b)

17. a.

Number busy	Frequency	Relative frequency
0	1	0.04
1	2	0.08
2	2	0.08
3	4	0.16
4	5	0.20
5	7	0.28
6	4	0.16
	25	1.00

18. a.

Class level	Frequency	Relative frequency
Freshman	6	0.150
Sophomore	15	0.375
Junior	12	0.300
Senior	7	0.175
	40	1.000

b.

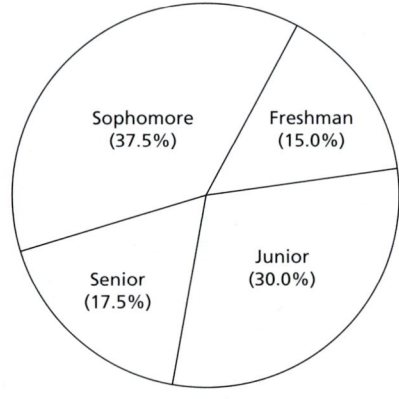

Class Levels for Statistics Students

c.

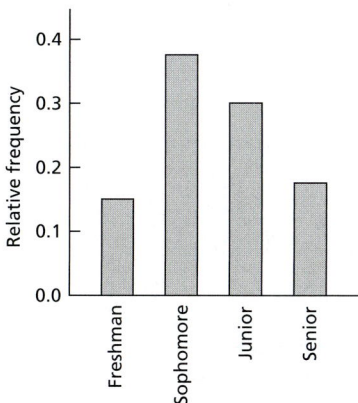

Class Levels for Statistics Students

b.

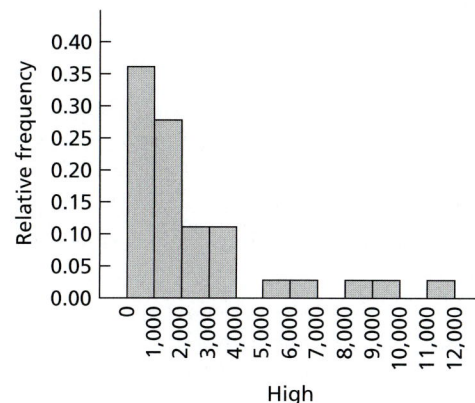

Dow Jones Highs, 1964 – 1999*

* Data from the *World Almanac*

19. a.

High	Freq.	Relative frequency	Midpoint
0 ⩽ 1000	13	0.361	500
1000 ⩽ 2000	10	0.278	1500
2000 ⩽ 3000	4	0.111	2500
3000 ⩽ 4000	4	0.111	3500
4000 ⩽ 5000	0	0.000	4500
5000 ⩽ 6000	1	0.028	5500
6000 ⩽ 7000	1	0.028	6500
7000 ⩽ 8000	0	0.000	7500
8000 ⩽ 9000	1	0.028	8500
9000 ⩽ 10000	1	0.028	9500
10000 ⩽ 11000	0	0.000	10500
11000 ⩽ 12000	1	0.028	11500
	36	1.001	

20. a. Bell-shaped **b.** Left skewed

21. Answers will vary, but here is one possibility:

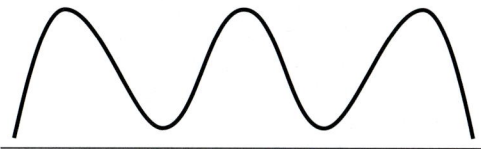

22. b. Having followed the directions in part (a), you might conclude that the percentage of women in the labor force for 2000 is about 3.5 times that for 1960.
 c. Not covering up the vertical axis, you would find that the percentage of women in the labor force for 2000 is about 1.8 times that for 1960.
 d. The graph is potentially misleading because it is truncated. Note that the vertical axis begins at 30 rather than at 0.
 e. To make the graph less potentially misleading, start it at 0 instead of at 30.

CHAPTER 3

EXERCISES 3.1

3.1 To indicate where the center or most typical value of a data set lies

3.2 The three most important measures of center are the mean, the median, and the mode. See Definitions 3.1–3.3 for details.

3.3 The mode

3.4 True

3.5
a. Mean = 5; median = 5
b. Mean = 15; median = 5. The median is a better measure of center because it is not influenced by the one unusually large value, 99.
c. Resistance

3.6 It is not sensitive to the influence of a few extreme observations.

3.7 Median. Unlike the mean, the median is not affected strongly by the relatively few homes that have extremely large or small floor spaces.

3.8 Median. Unlike the mean, the median is not affected strongly by the relatively few households with extremely high net worth.

3.9 Mean = 193.0 thousand volumes; median = 79.0 thousand volumes; no mode.

3.10 Mean = 120.0 kg per hectare per year; median = 131.5 kg per hectare per year; modes = 147 kg per hectare per year and 154 kg per hectare per year.

3.11 Mean = 118.1 tornadoes; median = 77.0 tornadoes; mode = 72 tornadoes.

3.12 Mean = 14.0 days; median = 9.0 days; mode = 12 days.

3.13
a. CBS
b. No; neither the mean nor the median can be used as a measure of center for qualitative data.

3.14
a. F (Friday)
b. No; neither the mean nor the median can be used as a measure of center for qualitative data.

EXERCISES 3.2

3.21 Mathematical notation allows you to express mathematical definitions and other mathematical relationships much more concisely.

3.22
a. Σ is an abbreviation for the phrase "the sum of" and indicates that you should sum the values that follow it.
b. n represents the number of observations.
c. $\bar{x}$ denotes a sample mean.

3.23 No; the population mean is a constant. Yes; the sample mean is a variable because it varies from sample to sample.

3.24
a. 27   b. 5   c. 5.4

3.25
a. 46   b. 4   c. 11.5

3.26
a. 108 days   b. 12   c. 9.0 days

3.27
a. 23.3 hours   b. 10   c. 2.33 hours

3.28
a. 10.5 days
b. 767 days^2; 0 days; 105.50 days^2

3.29
a. 81.0 inches
b. 32,835 inches^2; 0 inches; 30 inches^2

EXERCISES 3.3

3.33 To indicate the amount of variation in a data set

3.34 One reason is that the standard deviation takes into account all the observations, whereas the range considers only the largest and smallest ones.

3.35 The mean

3.36 It is not resistant.

3.37
a. 2.7   b. 31.6   c. Resistance

3.38
a. 5
b. The amount of variation within each data set differs among the data sets.
c. Data Set III; Data Set II   d. 8, 8, 0, 8
e. 3.3, 4.2, 0, 2.7   f. The standard deviation

3.39
a. 16.1   b. 16.1

3.40
a. 0   b. 0   c. 0
d. All observations in the data set are equal.

3.41
a. 501 thousand volumes
b. 205.5 thousand volumes
c. 205.5 thousand volumes

3.42
a. 118 kg per hectare per year
b. 41.2 kg per hectare per year
c. 41.2 kg per hectare per year

3.43
a. 367 tornadoes   b. 113.4 tornadoes
c. 113.4 tornadoes

3.44
a. 52 days   b. 16.1 days   c. 16.1 days

EXERCISES 3.4

3.52 Deciles, quintiles, and quartiles

3.53 The median and interquartile range are resistant measures, whereas the mean and standard deviation are not.

3.54 The three quartiles by themselves don't provide information about the variation of the first and fourth quarters of the data.

3.55 No. It may, for example, be an indication of skewness.

3.56 When the data set is large

3.57
a. A measure of variation
b. Roughly, the range of the middle 50% of the observations

3.58 To identify potential outliers

3.59 If the data set has no potential outliers, its boxplot and modified boxplot are identical. This is the case when both the minimum and maximum observations lie within the lower and upper limits; in other words, when the minimum and maximum values are also the adjacent values.

3.60
a. Standard deviation   b. Interquartile range

3.61 $Q_1 = 21.5$ miles, $Q_2 = 29.5$ miles, $Q_3 = 36.5$ miles

3.62 $Q_1 = \$198$, $Q_2 = \$205.0$, $Q_3 = \$212$

3.63 $Q_1 = 4$ days, $Q_2 = 7$ days, $Q_3 = 12$ days

3.64 $Q_1 = 11.0$ thousand miles, $Q_2 = 12.2$ thousand miles, $Q_3 = 14.2$ thousand miles

Note: If you use technology to obtain your results for the remaining answers in this section, they may differ from those presented here because different technologies often use different rules for computing quartiles.

3.65
a. 15 miles
b. 13, 21.5, 29.5, 36.5, 51 miles
c. No potential outliers
d. Figure A.1 shows a boxplot.

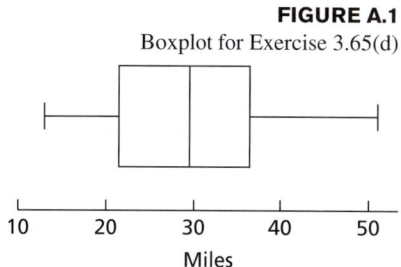

FIGURE A.1
Boxplot for Exercise 3.65(d)

3.66
a. $14
b. $180, $198, $205.0, $212, $225
c. No potential outliers
d. Figure A.2 shows a boxplot.

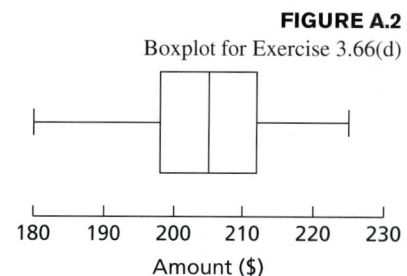

FIGURE A.2
Boxplot for Exercise 3.66(d)

3.67
a. 8 days
b. 1, 4, 7, 12, 55 days
c. 55 days is a potential outlier.
d. Figure A.3(a) shows a boxplot. Figure A.3(b) shows a modified boxplot.

3.68
a. 3.2 thousand miles
b. 3.3, 11.0, 12.2, 14.2, 16.7 thousand miles
c. 3.3 thousand miles is a potential outlier.
d. Figure A.4(a) shows a boxplot. Figure A.4(b) shows a modified boxplot.

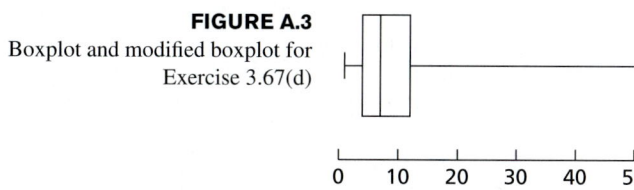
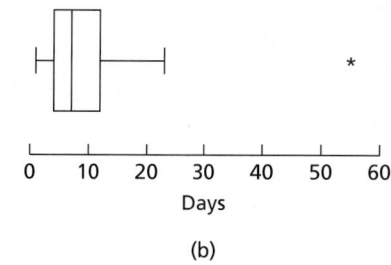

FIGURE A.3
Boxplot and modified boxplot for Exercise 3.67(d)

(a)   (b)

FIGURE A.4
Boxplot and modified boxplot for Exercise 3.68(d)

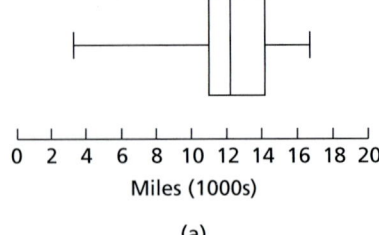
(a)

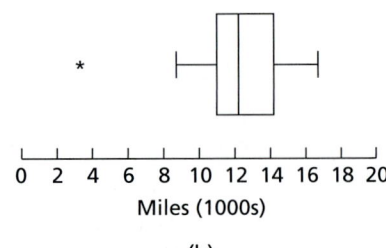
(b)

3.69
a. $Q_1 = 8$ cigs/day, $Q_2 = 9$ cigs/day, $Q_3 = 10$ cigs/day
b. The quartiles for this data set are not particularly useful because of its small range and the relatively large number of identical values. Note, for instance, that Q_3 and Max are equal.

EXERCISES 3.5

3.78
a. Parameter **b.** Statistic
c. Statistic **d.** Parameter

3.79 To describe the entire population

3.80 0; 1

3.81
a. The number of standard deviations that the observation is from the mean, that is, how far the observation is from the mean in units of standard deviation
b. Above (greater than); below (less than)

3.82
a. The sample mean, $\bar{x}$
b. The sample standard deviation, s

3.83 Parameter. A parameter is a descriptive measure of a population.

3.84
a. $\bar{x} = 75.0$ in. **b.** $s = 6.2$ in.
c. $\mu = 75.0$ in. **d.** $\sigma = 5.6$ in.
e. $\bar{x}$ and μ are computed in the same way: Sum the observations and then divide by the total number of observations.
f. s and σ are computed differently: In the defining formula for s, we divide by 1 less than the total number of observations, but in the defining formula for σ, we divide by the total number of observations.

3.85
a. $\mu = 105.4$ mph **b.** $\sigma = 41.7$ mph
c. $\eta = 107.5$ mph **d.** Modes: 60, 140, 155 mph
e. IQR $= 85$ mph

3.86
a. $\mu = 7.83$ thousand acres
b. $\sigma = 2.98$ thousand acres

3.87
a. $z = (x - 16.3)/17.9$ **b.** 0; 1
c. 2.70; −0.68
d. The time served of 64.7 months is 2.70 standard deviations above the mean time served of 16.3 months; the time served of 4.2 months is 0.68 standard deviations below the mean time served of 16.3 months.

3.88
a. $z = (y - 266)/16$ **b.** 0; 1
c. −2.44; 3.06
d. The gestation period of 227 days is 2.44 standard deviations below the mean gestation period of 266 days; the gestation period of 315 days is 3.06 standard deviations above the mean gestation period of 266 days.

3.89 Yes, quite well. Your z-score is 3.50, meaning that your score of 350 points is 3.50 standard deviations above the mean score of 280 points. Applying the three-standard-deviations rule (Key Fact 3.2), almost all the exam scores lie within three standard deviations to either side of the mean. So, your score of 350 points is greater than almost all the other scores on the exam.

REVIEW TEST FOR CHAPTER 3

1. a. Numbers that are used to describe data sets are called descriptive measures.
b. Descriptive measures that indicate where the center or most typical value of a data set lies are called measures of center.
c. Descriptive measures that indicate the amount of variation, or spread, in a data set are called measures of variation.

2. Mean and median. The median is a resistant measure, whereas the mean is not. The mean takes into account the actual numerical value of all observations, whereas the median does not.

3. The mode
4. a. Standard deviation   b. Interquartile range
5. a. $\bar{x}$ b. s c. μ d. σ
6. a. Not necessarily true   b. Necessarily true
7. Three
8. a. Minimum, quartiles, and maximum; that is, Min, Q_1, Q_2, Q_3, Max
   b. Q_2 can be used to describe center. Max − Min, Q_1 − Min, Max − Q_3, Q_2 − Q_1, Q_3 − Q_2, and Q_3 − Q_1 are all measures of variation for different portions of the data.
   c. Boxplot
9. a. An outlier is an observation that falls well outside the overall pattern of the data.
   b. First, determine the lower and upper limits—the numbers 1.5 IQRs below the first quartile and 1.5 IQRs above the third quartile, respectively. Observations that lie outside the lower and upper limits—either below the lower limit or above the upper limit—are potential outliers.
10. a. Subtract from x its mean and then divide by its standard deviation.
    b. The z-score of an observation gives the number of standard deviations that the observation is from the mean, that is, how far the observation is from the mean in units of standard deviation.
    c. The observation is 2.9 standard deviations above the mean. It is larger than most of the other observations.
11. a. 2.35 drinks; 2.0 drinks; 1, 2 drinks
    b. Answers will vary.
12. The median, because it is resistant to outliers and other extreme values.
13. The mode; neither the mean nor the median can be used as a measure of center for qualitative data.
14. a. $\bar{x} = 45.7$ kg   b. Range = 17 kg
    c. $s = 5.0$ kg
15. a.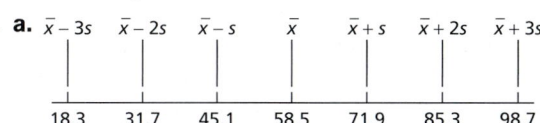
    b. 18.3 yr, 98.7 yr
16. a. $Q_1 = 48.0$ yr, $Q_2 = 59.5$ yr, $Q_3 = 68.5$ yr
    b. 20.5 yr; roughly speaking, the middle 50% of the ages has a range of 20.5 yr.
    c. 31, 48.0, 59.5, 68.5, 79 yr
    d. Lower limit: 17.25 yr. Upper limit: 99.25 yr.
    e. No potential outliers

f.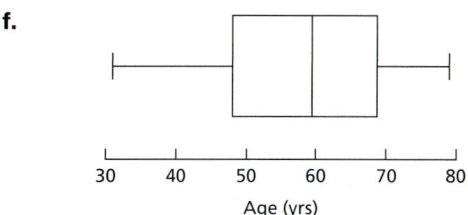

17. a. $\mu = 19.26$ thousand students
    b. $\sigma = 9.64$ thousand students
    c. $z = (x - 19.26)/9.64$ d. 0; 1
    f. 1.72; −0.90. The enrollment at Los Angeles is 1.72 standard deviations above the UC campuses' mean enrollment of 19.26 thousand students; the enrollment at Riverside is 0.90 standard deviations below the UC campuses' mean enrollment of 19.26 thousand students.
18. a. A sample mean. It is the mean price per gallon for the sample of 10,000 service stations.
    b. $\bar{x}$
    c. A statistic. It is a descriptive measure of a sample.

CHAPTER 4

EXERCISES 4.1

4.1
a. $y = b_0 + b_1 x$
b. b_0 and b_1 represent constants; x and y represent variables
c. x is the independent variable; y is the dependent variable

4.2 Straight line

4.3
a. The number b_0 is the y-intercept. It is the y-value at which the straight-line graph of the linear equation intersects the y-axis.
b. The number b_1 is the slope. It measures the steepness of the straight line; more precisely, b_1 indicates how much the y-value on the straight line changes (increases or decreases) when the x-value increases by 1 unit.

4.4
a. False. The straight-line graph of a linear equation slopes downward if the slope is negative.
b. True.

4.5
a. $y = 120 + 0.25x$
b. $b_0 = 120$, $b_1 = 0.25$
c.

x	50	100	250
y	132.5	145.0	182.5

d.

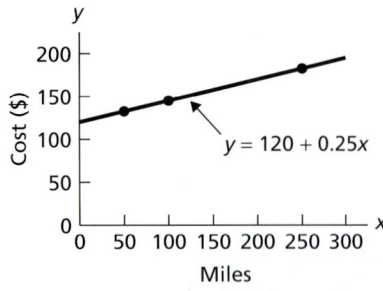

e. About $155; exact cost is $157.50

4.6
a. $y = 30 + 36x$
b. $b_0 = 30, b_1 = 36$
c.

x	0.5	1	2.25
y	48	66	111

d.

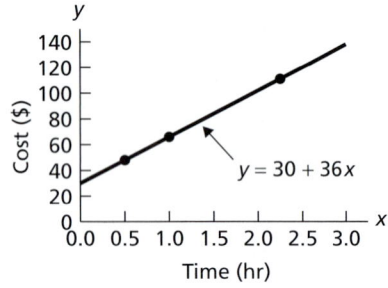

e. About $90; exact cost is $93

4.7
a. $b_0 = 32, b_1 = 1.8$ **b.** $-40, 32, 68, 212$
c.

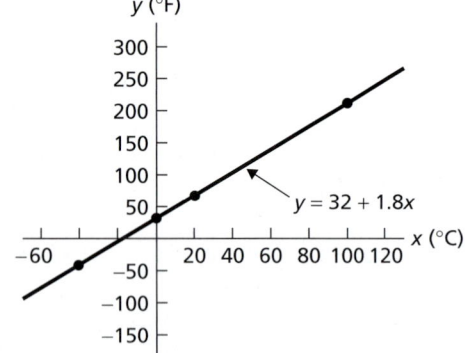

d. About 80° F; exact temperature is 82.4° F

4.8
a. $b_0 = 64, b_1 = -32$ **b.** $32, 0, -32, -64$

c.

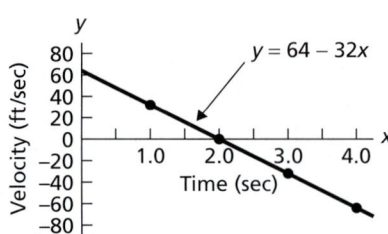

d. About 15 ft/sec; exact velocity is 16 ft/sec

4.9
a. $b_0 = 120, b_1 = 0.25$
b. The y-intercept, $b_0 = 120$, gives the y-value at which the straight line, $y = 120 + 0.25x$, intersects the y-axis. The slope, $b_1 = 0.25$, indicates that the y-value increases by 0.25 unit for every increase in x of 1 unit.
c. The y-intercept, $b_0 = 120$, is the cost (in dollars) for driving the car 0 miles. The slope, $b_1 = 0.25$, represents the fact that the cost per mile is $0.25; it is the amount the total cost increases for each additional mile driven.

4.10
a. $b_0 = 30, b_1 = 36$
b. The y-intercept, $b_0 = 30$, gives the y-value at which the straight line, $y = 30 + 36x$, intersects the y-axis. The slope, $b_1 = 36$, indicates that the y-value increases by 36 units for every increase in x of 1 unit.
c. The y-intercept, $b_0 = 30$, is the service charge, that is, the cost (in dollars) for a repair job that takes 0 hours. The slope, $b_1 = 36$, represents the fact that the cost per hour is $36; it is the amount the total cost of the repair job increases for each additional hour that it takes to complete the job.

4.11
a. $b_0 = 32, b_1 = 1.8$
b. The y-intercept, $b_0 = 32$, gives the y-value at which the straight line, $y = 32 + 1.8x$, intersects the y-axis. The slope, $b_1 = 1.8$, indicates that the y-value increases by 1.8 units for every increase in x of 1 unit.
c. The y-intercept, $b_0 = 32$, is the Fahrenheit temperature corresponding to 0° C. The slope, $b_1 = 1.8$, represents the fact that the Fahrenheit temperature increases by 1.8° for every increase of the Celsius temperature of 1°.

4.12
a. $b_0 = 64, b_1 = -32$
b. The y-intercept, $b_0 = 64$, gives the y-value at which the straight line, $y = 64 - 32x$, intersects the y-axis. The slope, $b_1 = -32$, indicates that the y-value decreases by 32 units for every increase in x of 1 unit.
c. The y-intercept, $b_0 = 64$, is the initial velocity of the ball, that is, the velocity (in feet per second) of the ball at time 0. The slope, $b_1 = -32$, represents the fact that the velocity of the ball decreases by 32 ft/sec every second.

4.13
a. $b_0 = 3, b_1 = 4$ **b.** Slopes upward
c.
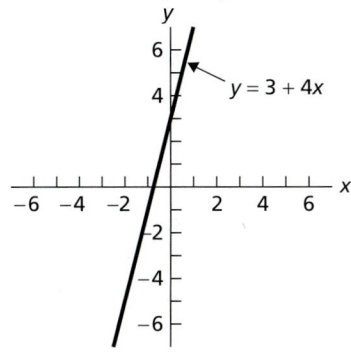

4.14
a. $b_0 = -1, b_1 = 2$ **b.** Slopes upward

4.15
a. $b_0 = 6, b_1 = -7$ **b.** Slopes downward
c.
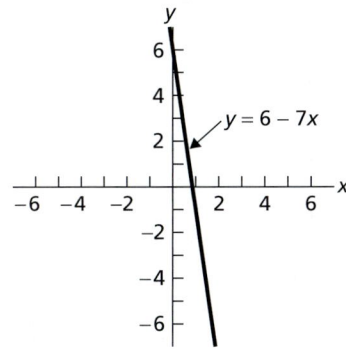

4.16
a. $b_0 = -8, b_1 = -4$ **b.** Slopes downward

4.17
a. $b_0 = -2, b_1 = 0.5$ **b.** Slopes upward

4.18
a. $b_0 = -5, b_1 = -0.75$ **b.** Slopes downward

4.19
a. $b_0 = 2, b_1 = 0$ **b.** Horizontal

4.20
a. $b_0 = 0, b_1 = -3$ **b.** Slopes downward

4.21
a. $b_0 = 0, b_1 = 1.5$ **b.** Slopes upward

4.22
a. $b_0 = -3, b_1 = 0$ **b.** Horizontal

4.23
a. Slopes upward **b.** $y = 5 + 2x$
c.
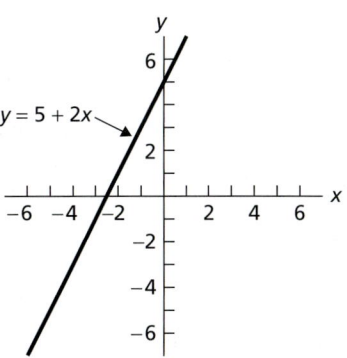

4.24
a. Slopes upward **b.** $y = -3 + 4x$

4.25
a. Slopes downward **b.** $y = -2 - 3x$
c.
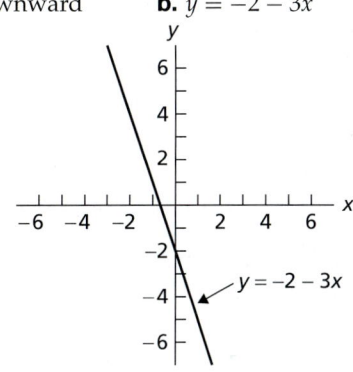

4.26
a. Slopes upward **b.** $y = 0.4 + x$

4.27
a. Slopes downward **b.** $y = -0.5x$

4.28
a. Horizontal **b.** $y = -1.5$

4.29
a. Horizontal **b.** $y = 3$

4.30
a. Slopes upward **b.** $y = 3x$

EXERCISES 4.2

4.32
a. A scatter diagram helps you visualize any apparent relationship between the two variables under consideration.
b. The points should be scattered about a straight line.

4.33
a. Least-squares criterion
b. The straight line that best fits a set of data points is the one having the smallest possible sum of squared errors.

4.34
a. Regression line **b.** Regression equation

4.35
a. Response variable
b. Predictor variable, or explanatory variable

4.36 Extrapolation

4.37
a. Outlier
b. Influential observation

4.38
a.

Line A: $y = 1.5 + 0.5x$

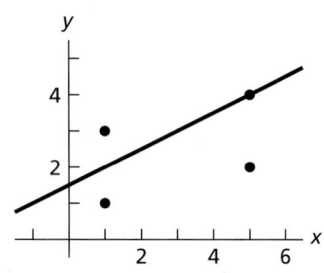

Line B: $y = 1.125 + 0.375x$

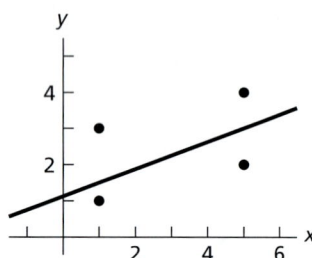

b. Line A: $y = 1.5 + 0.5x$

x	y	$\hat{y}$	e	e^2
1	1	2	−1	1
1	3	2	1	1
5	2	4	−2	4
5	4	4	0	0
				6

Line B: $y = 1.125 + 0.375x$

x	y	$\hat{y}$	e	e^2
1	1	1.5	−0.5	0.25
1	3	1.5	1.5	2.25
5	2	3.0	−1.0	1.00
5	4	3.0	1.0	1.00
				4.50

c. Line B

4.39
a.

Line A: $y = 3 - 0.6x$

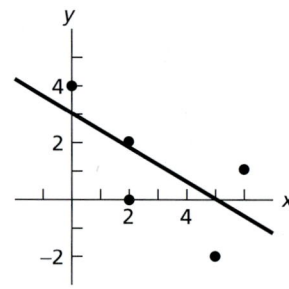

Line B: $y = 4 - x$

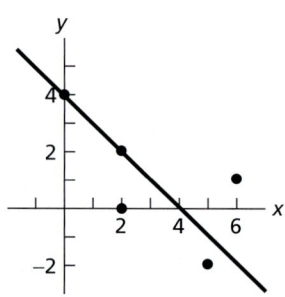

b. Line A: $y = 3 - 0.6x$

x	y	$\hat{y}$	e	e^2
0	4	3.0	1.0	1.00
2	2	1.8	0.2	0.04
2	0	1.8	−1.8	3.24
5	−2	0.0	−2.0	4.00
6	1	−0.6	1.6	2.56
				10.84

Line B: $y = 4 - x$

x	y	$\hat{y}$	e	e^2
0	4	4	0	0
2	2	2	0	0
2	0	2	−2	4
5	−2	−1	−1	1
6	1	−2	3	9
				14

c. Line A

4.40
a. $\hat{y} = 1.75 + 0.250x$
b.
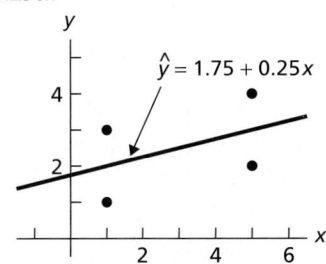

4.41
a. $\hat{y} = 2.875 - 0.625x$
b.
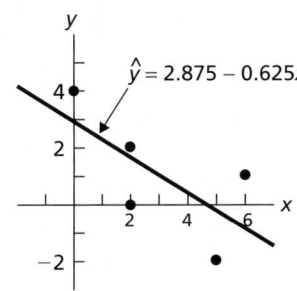

4.42
a. $\hat{y} = 112.68 - 5.26x$
b.
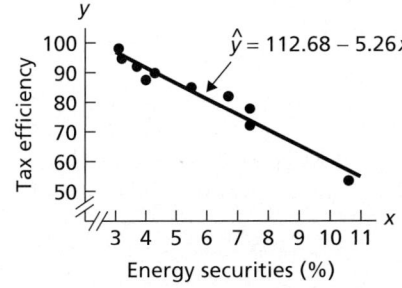

c. Tax efficiency tends to decrease as the percentage of investments in energy securities increases.
d. The tax efficiency of mutual fund portfolios decreases an estimated 5.26 for each increase in the percentage of investments in energy securities of 1%.
e. 86.36; 73.72 (see the note at the top of page A-23)
f. The predictor variable is percentage of investments in energy securities; the response variable is tax efficiency.
g. (10.6, 53.5) is a potential influential observation.

4.43
a. $\hat{y} = 371.6 - 27.9x$

b.
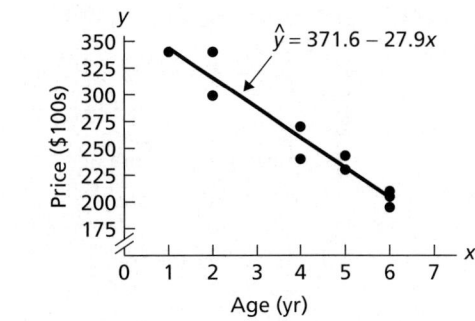

c. Price tends to decrease as age increases.
d. Corvettes depreciate an estimated $2790 per year, at least in the 1- to 6-year-old range.
e. $31,580; $28,789 (see the note at the top of page A-23)
f. The predictor variable is age (in years); the response variable is price (in hundreds of dollars).
g. None

4.44
a. $\hat{y} = -140.9 + 15.9x$
b.
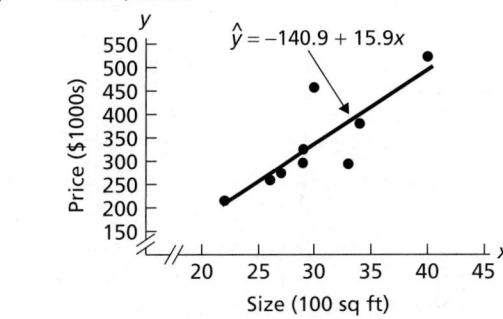

c. Price tends to increase as size increases.
d. Prices of custom homes in the Equestrian Estates increase an estimated $15,900 for each increase in size of 100 square feet.
e. $272,300 (see the note at the top of page A-23)
f. The predictor variable is size (in hundreds of square feet); the response variable is price (in thousands of dollars).
g. (30, 457) is a (mild) outlier; no potential influential observations.

4.45
a. $\hat{y} = 3.52 + 0.16x$
b.
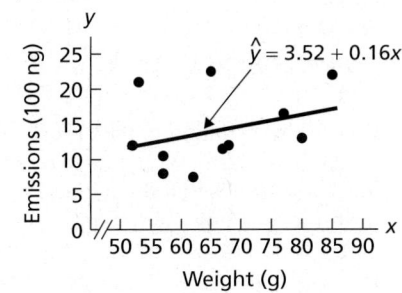

c. Quantity of volatile compounds emitted tends to increase as potato plant weight increases.
d. The quantity of volatile compounds emitted increases an estimated 16 nanograms for each increase in potato plant weight of 1 g.
e. 1574 nanograms (see the note at the top of page A-23)
f. The predictor variable is potato plant weight (in grams); the response variable is quantity of volatile compounds emitted (in hundreds of nanograms).
g. None

4.46 Only the first one

4.47 Only the second one

4.48
a. It is acceptable to use the regression equation to predict the tax efficiency of a mutual fund portfolio with 6.4% of its investments in energy securities because that percentage lies within the range of the percentages in the sample data. It is not acceptable (and would be extrapolation) to use the regression equation to predict the tax efficiency of a mutual fund portfolio with 15% of its investments in energy securities because that percentage lies outside the range of the percentages in the sample data.
b. Percentages between 3.1 and 10.6, inclusive.

4.49
a. It is acceptable to use the regression equation to predict the price of a 4-year-old Corvette because that age lies within the range of ages in the sample data. It is not acceptable (and would be extrapolation) to use the regression equation to predict the price of a 10-year-old Corvette because that age lies outside the range of the ages in the sample data.
b. Ages between 1 and 6 years, inclusive.

4.50 Answers will vary.

EXERCISES 4.3

4.59
a. The coefficient of determination, r^2
b. The proportion of variation in the observed values of the response variable explained by the regression

4.60
a. Total sum of squares; SST
b. Regression sum of squares; SSR
c. Error sum of squares; SSE

4.61
a. $r^2 = 0.920$, 92.0% of the variation in the observed values of the response variable is explained by the regression. The fact that r^2 is near 1 indicates that the regression equation is extremely useful for making predictions.
b. 664.4

4.62
a. $SST = 5$, $SSR = 1$, $SSE = 4$
b. $5 = 1 + 4$ **c.** $r^2 = 0.2$
d. 20%   **e.** Only somewhat useful

4.63
a. $SST = 20$, $SSR = 9.375$, $SSE = 10.625$
b. $20 = 9.375 + 10.625$ **c.** $r^2 = 0.469$
d. 46.9%   **e.** Moderately useful

4.64
a. $SST = 1532.9$, $SSR = 1456.7$, $SSE = 76.2$
b. 0.950
c. 95.0%; 95.0% of the variation in the tax efficiency data is explained by percentage of investments in energy securities.
d. Extremely useful

4.65
a. $SST = 25{,}681.6$, $SSR = 24{,}057.9$, $SSE = 1623.7$
b. 0.937
c. 93.7%; 93.7% of the variation in the price data is explained by age.
d. Extremely useful

4.66
a. $SST = 79{,}444.9$, $SSR = 54{,}562.4$, $SSE = 24{,}882.5$
b. 0.687
c. 68.7%; 68.7% of the variation in the price data is explained by size (square footage).
d. Moderately useful

4.67
a. $SST = 296.68$, $SSR = 32.52$, $SSE = 264.16$
b. 0.110
c. 11.0%; 11.0% of the variation in the quantity of volatile emissions is explained by potato plant weight.
d. Not very useful

EXERCISES 4.4

4.76 To provide a descriptive measure of the strength of the linear relationship between two variables

4.77 Pearson product moment correlation coefficient

4.78
a. r **b.** Strong   **c.** 0

4.79
a. ± 1 **b.** Not very useful

4.80
a. Positively   **b.** Negatively   **c.** Uncorrelated

4.81 False. Correlation does not imply causation.

4.82
a. Positive. The sign of r is the same as the sign of the slope of the regression line.
b. $r^2 = 0.716$

4.83 $r = -0.842$

4.84 $r = 0.447$

4.85 $r = -0.685$

4.86
a. $r = -0.975$
b. Suggests an extremely strong negative linear relationship between percentage of investments in energy securities and tax efficiency.
c. Data points are clustered closely about the regression line.
d. $r^2 = 0.951$. From Exercise 4.64(b), $r^2 = 0.950$. The discrepancy is due to the error resulting from rounding r to three decimal places before squaring.

4.87
a. $r = -0.968$
b. Suggests an extremely strong negative linear relationship between age and price of Corvettes.
c. Data points are clustered closely about the regression line.
d. $r^2 = 0.937$. This value of r^2 is the same as the one obtained in Exercise 4.65(b).

4.88
a. $r = 0.829$
b. Suggests a moderately strong positive linear relationship between size and price of custom homes in the Equestrian Estates.
c. Data points are clustered moderately closely about the regression line.
d. $r^2 = 0.687$. This value of r^2 is the same as the one obtained in Exercise 4.66(b).

4.89
a. $r = 0.331$
b. Suggests a weak positive linear relationship between potato plant weight and quantity of volatile emissions.
c. Data points are scattered widely about the regression line.
d. $r^2 = 0.110$. This value of r^2 is the same as the one obtained in Exercise 4.67(b).

4.90
a. A value close to 0
b. 0.087

4.91
a. $r = 0$
b. No. Only that there is no *linear* relationship between the variables.
d. No. Because the data points are not scattered about a straight line.
e. For each data point (x, y), the relation $y = x^2$ holds.
f. $r = 0.930$
g. No. A high correlation does not imply a linear relationship between two variables.
i. No. Because the data points are not scattered about a straight line.
j. For each data point (x, y), the relation $y = x^3$ holds.

4.92
a. Approximately 0   b. Negative   c. Positive

REVIEW TEST FOR CHAPTER 4

1. a. x b. y c. b_1 d. b_0
2. a. $y = 4$ b. $x = 0$ c. -3
   d. -3 units   e. 6 units
3. a. True. The y-intercept indicates only where the line crosses the y-axis; that is, it is the y-value when $x = 0$.
   b. False. Its slope is 0.
   c. True. This is equivalent to saying: If a line has a positive slope, then y-values on the line increase as the x-values increase.
4. Scatter diagram (or scatterplot)
5. A regression equation can be used to predict the response variable for values of the predictor variable within the range of the observed values of the predictor variable.
6. a. Predictor variable, or explanatory variable
   b. Response variable
7. a. Smallest   b. Regression   c. Extrapolation
8. a. An outlier is a data point that lies far from the regression line, relative to the other data points.
   b. An influential observation is a data point whose removal causes the regression equation (and line) to change considerably.
9. It is a descriptive measure of the utility of the regression equation for making predictions.
10. a. SST is the total sum of squares. It measures the variation in the observed values of the response variable.
    b. SSR is the regression sum of squares. It measures the variation in the observed values of the response variable explained by the regression.
    c. SSE is the error sum of squares. It measures the variation in the observed values of the response variable not explained by the regression.
11. a. Linear   b. Increases
    c. Negative   d. 0
12. True
13. a. $y = 72 - 12x$ b. $b_0 = 72$, $b_1 = -12$
    c. The line slopes downward because $b_1 < 0$.
    d. $4800; $1200

e.

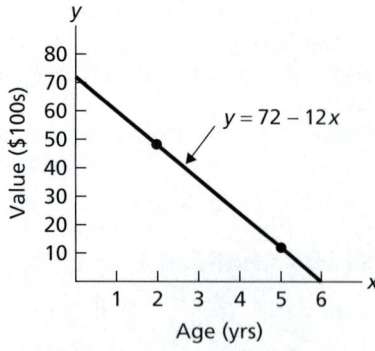

f. About $2500; exact value is $2400.

14. a.

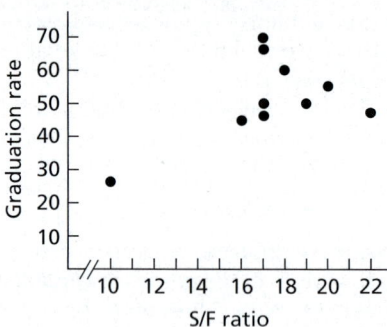

b. It is reasonable to find a regression line for the data because the data points appear to be scattered about a straight line.

c. $\hat{y} = 16.4 + 2.03x$

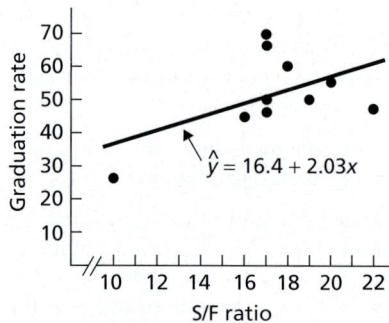

d. Graduation rate tends to increase as student-to-faculty ratio increases.

e. Graduation rate increases by an estimated 2.03 percentage points for each increase of 1 in the student-to-faculty ratio.

f. 50.9%

g. There are no outliers. The data point (10, 26) is a potential influential observation.

15. a. $SST = 1384.50$; $SSR = 361.66$; $SSE = 1022.84$
b. $r^2 = 0.261$ **c.** 26.1%
d. Not very useful

16. a. $r = 0.511$
b. Suggests a moderately weak positive linear relationship between student-to-faculty ratio and graduation rate.
c. Data points are rather widely scattered about the regression line.
d. $r^2 = (0.511)^2 = 0.261$

CHAPTER 5

EXERCISES 5.1

5.1 An experiment is an action whose outcome cannot be predicted with certainty. An event is some specified result that may or may not occur when an experiment is performed.

5.2
a. The experiment has a finite number of possible outcomes, all equally likely.
b. The probability of an event equals the ratio of the number of ways that the event can occur to the total number of possible outcomes.

5.3 There is no difference.

5.4 Percentages (or relative frequencies)

5.5 The probability of an event is the proportion of times it occurs in a large number of repetitions of the experiment.

5.6
a. In a large number of births, the baby born will be a girl roughly 48.7% of the time.
b. If you purchase one lottery ticket many times, you will win a prize about 2.9% of the time.
c. If the experiment of tossing a balanced dime three times is repeated many times, the percentage of experiments in which all three tosses come up heads will be approximately 12.5%.

5.7 (b) and (e) because the probability of an event must always be between 0 and 1, inclusive.

5.8
a.

G, L, S	G, L, A	G, L, T	G, S, A	G, S, T
G, A, T	L, S, A	L, S, T	L, A, T	S, A, T

b. 0.1 **c.** 0.3 **d.** 0.6

5.9
a. 0.209 **b.** 0.670 **c.** 0.017
d. 0 **e.** 1

5.10
a. 0.105 **b.** 0.747 **c.** 0.156 **d.** 0.474

5.11
a. 0.152   b. 0.352   c. 0.958

5.12
a. 0.009   b. 0.192   c. 0.576

5.13
a. 0.139   b. 0.500   c. 0.222   d. 0.111

5.14
a. 0.375   b. 0.250   c. 0.250   d. 0.500

5.15 The event in part (e) is certain; the event in part (d) is impossible.

EXERCISES 5.2

5.21 Venn diagrams

5.23 Two or more events are mutually exclusive if at most one of them can occur when the experiment is performed. Thus two events are mutually exclusive if they do not have outcomes in common. Three events are mutually exclusive if no two of them have outcomes in common.

5.24
a. False. Event C could have outcomes in common with event A or event B.
b. True. Event A and event B have outcomes in common.

5.25
A = [3] [5] [6]

B = [4] [5] [6]

C = [1] [6]

D = [3]

5.26 A: #3, #4; B: #6, #7, #8; C: #1, #2, #3; D: #2, #5

5.27
a. (not A) = [1] [3] [5]

The event that the die comes up odd

b. (A & B) = [4] [6]

The event that the die comes up 4 or 6

c. (B or C) = [1] [2] [4] [5] [6]

The event that the die does not come up 3

5.28
a. (not C): #4, #5, #6, #7, #8; the event that the winning horse has a number above 3.
b. (C & D): #2; the event that the winning horse is number 2.
c. (A or C): #1, #2, #3, #4; the event that the winning horse has a number below 5.

5.29
a. (not A) is the event the unit has at least five rooms. There are 75,232 thousand units that have at least five rooms.
b. (A & B) is the event the unit has two, three, or four rooms. There are 36,653 thousand units that have two, three, or four rooms.
c. (C or D) is the event the unit has at least five rooms. There are 75,232 thousand units that have at least five rooms. (*Note:* From part (a), (not A) = (C or D).)

5.30
a. (not B) is the event that the tree has less than 20% seed damage. There are 21 such trees.
b. (C & D) is the event that the tree has at least 50% seed damage but less than 60% seed damage. There are 2 such trees.
c. (A or D) is the event that the tree has either less than 40% seed damage or at least 50% seed damage. There are 33 such trees.
d. (not C) is the event that the tree has either less than 30% seed damage or at least 60% seed damage. There are 28 such trees.
e. (A & D) is the event that the tree has less than 40% seed damage and at least 50% seed damage, which is impossible. There are no such trees.

5.31
a. No   b. Yes   c. No
d. Yes, events B, C, and D. No.

5.32
a. Mutually exclusive   b. Mutually exclusive
c. Not mutually exclusive   d. Mutually exclusive
e. Not mutually exclusive

5.33 A and C; A and D; C and D; A, C, and D

5.34 A and D

EXERCISES 5.3

5.38 0.040; $P(G) = 0.040$

5.39
a. 0.56   b. $S = (A$ or B or $C)$
c. 0.01, 0.14, 0.41   d. 0.56

5.40
a. 0.545   b. 0.728   c. 0.645

A-48 APPENDIX B Answers to Selected Exercises

d. 54.5% of households with home Internet access only have incomes under $75,000; 72.8% have incomes of $50,000 or above; 64.5% have incomes between $50,000 and $150,000.

5.41
a. 0.070   **b.** 0.120   **c.** 0.698

5.42 Because sometimes computing the probability that an event does not occur is easier than computing the probability that it does occur.

5.43
a. 0.99   **b.** 0.56

5.44 0.728

5.45
a. 0.167, 0.056, 0.028, 0.056, 0.028, 0.139, 0.167
b. 0.223   **c.** 0.112   **d.** 0.278   **e.** 0.278

5.46
a. 0.510, 0.071, 0.041
b. 0.540; 54.0% of U.S. adults are either female or divorced (or both).
c. 0.490

5.47
a. No, because $P(A \text{ or } B) \neq P(A) + P(B)$.
b. 0.083

5.48 0.267

EXERCISES 5.4

5.51
a. Probability   **b.** Probability

5.52 Answers will vary.

5.53 $\{X = 3\}$ is the event that the student has three siblings; $P(X = 3)$ is the probability of the event that the student has three siblings.

5.54 1

5.55 The probability distribution of the random variable

5.56 The special addition rule

5.57
a. 2, 3, 4, 5, 6, 7, 8   **b.** $\{X = 7\}$
c. 0.021. 2.1% of the shuttle missions between April 1981 and July 2000 had a crew size of 4.
d.

x	2	3	4	5	6	7	8
$P(X = x)$	0.042	0.010	0.021	0.375	0.188	0.344	0.021

e.

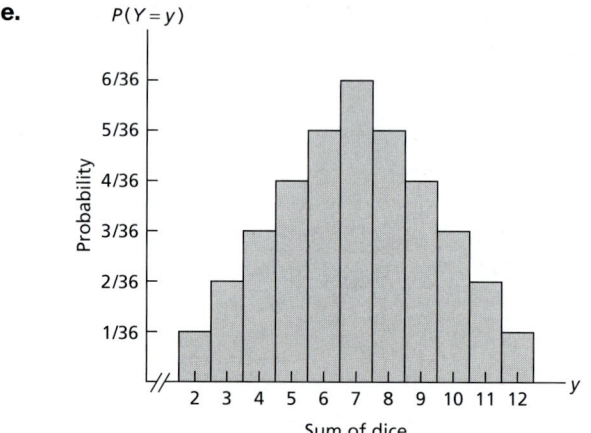

5.58
a. 2, 3, 4, 5, 6, 7, 8, 9, 10, 11, 12
b. $\{Y = 7\}$ **c.** $\frac{1}{6}$
d.

y	2	3	4	5	6	7	8	9	10	11	12
$P(Y = y)$	$\frac{1}{36}$	$\frac{1}{18}$	$\frac{1}{12}$	$\frac{1}{9}$	$\frac{5}{36}$	$\frac{1}{6}$	$\frac{5}{36}$	$\frac{1}{9}$	$\frac{1}{12}$	$\frac{1}{18}$	$\frac{1}{36}$

e.

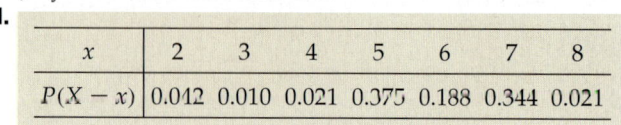

5.59
a. $\{X = 4\}$ **b.** $\{X \geq 2\}$ **c.** $\{X < 5\}$
d. $\{2 \leq X < 5\}$ **e.** 0.212   **f.** 0.922
g. 0.523   **h.** 0.445

5.60
a. No; it is a continuous random variable.
b. Yes, because its possible values are finite (or countably infinite).

EXERCISES 5.5

5.65 The mean of a variable of a finite population (population mean)

5.66
a. No; because the means of the two corresponding random variables are equal, the returns of the two investments are identical, on average.
b. The investment corresponding to Y is more conservative because it has less variation in return and hence less risk.

5.67
a. 5.8 crew members   **b.** 1.3 crew members

5.68
a. 7   **b.** 2.4

5.69
b. −0.052   **c.** 5.2¢   **d.** $5.20, $52

5.70
a.

v	$P(V=v)$
6,000	1

w	$P(W=w)$
15,000	0.4
5,000	0.6

x	$P(X=x)$
33,000	0.4
−17,000	0.6

y	$P(Y=y)$
5,500	0.4
10,000	0.6

b. $6000, $9000, $3000, $8200
c. Office complex; land speculation

5.71
a. $\mu_W = 0.25$, $\sigma_W = 0.536$ **b.** 0.25   **c.** 62.5

EXERCISES 5.6

5.73 Answers will vary.

5.74 Two

5.75 6; 5040; 40,320; 362,880

5.76
a. 4   **b.** 15   **c.** 56   **d.** 84

5.77
a. 10   **b.** 1   **c.** 1   **d.** 126

5.78
a. Each trial consists of observing whether a child with pinworm is cured by treatment with pyrantel and has two possible outcomes: cured or not cured. The trials are independent. The success probability is 0.9; that is, $p = 0.9$.

b.

Outcome	Probability
sss	(0.9)(0.9)(0.9) = 0.729
ssf	(0.9)(0.9)(0.1) = 0.081
sfs	(0.9)(0.1)(0.9) = 0.081
sff	(0.9)(0.1)(0.1) = 0.009
fss	(0.1)(0.9)(0.9) = 0.081
fsf	(0.1)(0.9)(0.1) = 0.009
ffs	(0.1)(0.1)(0.9) = 0.009
fff	(0.1)(0.1)(0.1) = 0.001

d. *ssf*, *sfs*, *fss*
e. 0.081. Because each probability is obtained by multiplying two success probabilities of 0.9 and one failure probability of 0.1.
f. 0.243
g.

x	0	1	2	3
$P(X=x)$	0.001	0.027	0.243	0.729

5.79
a. $p = 0.2$
b.

Outcome	Probability
ssss	(0.2)(0.2)(0.2)(0.2) = 0.0016
sssf	(0.2)(0.2)(0.2)(0.8) = 0.0064
ssfs	(0.2)(0.2)(0.8)(0.2) = 0.0064
ssff	(0.2)(0.2)(0.8)(0.8) = 0.0256
sfss	(0.2)(0.8)(0.2)(0.2) = 0.0064
sfsf	(0.2)(0.8)(0.2)(0.8) = 0.0256
sffs	(0.2)(0.8)(0.8)(0.2) = 0.0256
sfff	(0.2)(0.8)(0.8)(0.8) = 0.1024
fsss	(0.8)(0.2)(0.2)(0.2) = 0.0064
fssf	(0.8)(0.2)(0.2)(0.8) = 0.0256
fsfs	(0.8)(0.2)(0.8)(0.2) = 0.0256
fsff	(0.8)(0.2)(0.8)(0.8) = 0.1024
ffss	(0.8)(0.8)(0.2)(0.2) = 0.0256
ffsf	(0.8)(0.8)(0.2)(0.8) = 0.1024
fffs	(0.8)(0.8)(0.8)(0.2) = 0.1024
ffff	(0.8)(0.8)(0.8)(0.8) = 0.4096

d. *sssf*, *ssfs*, *sfss*, *fsss*
e. 0.0064. Because each probability is obtained by multiplying three success probabilities of 0.2 and one failure probability of 0.8.
f. 0.0256

g.

y	P(Y = y)
0	0.4096
1	0.4096
2	0.1536
3	0.0256
4	0.0016

5.80 The appropriate binomial probability formula is

$$P(X = x) = \binom{3}{x}(0.9)^x(0.1)^{3-x}.$$

Applying this formula for $x = 0, 1, 2,$ and 3, gives the same result as in part (g) of Exercise 5.30.

5.81 The appropriate binomial probability formula is

$$P(Y = y) = \binom{4}{y}(0.2)^y(0.8)^{4-y}.$$

Applying this formula for $y = 0, 1, 2, 3,$ and 4, gives the same result as in part (g) of Exercise 5.31.

5.82
a. $p = 0.5$ **b.** $p < 0.5$

5.83
a. 0.161 **b.** 0.332 **c.** 0.468 **d.** 0.821
e.

x	P(X = x)
0	0.004
1	0.040
2	0.161
3	0.328
4	0.332
5	0.135

f. Left skewed
g.

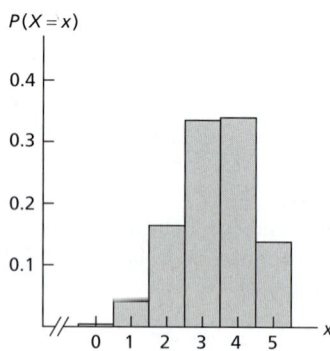

h. $\mu = 3.35$ times; $\sigma = 1.05$ times.
i. $\mu = 3.35$ times; $\sigma = 1.05$ times.

j. On average, the favorite will finish in the money 3.35 times for every 5 races.

5.84
a. 0.188 **b.** 0.946 **c.** 0.644 **d.** 0.643
e.

y	P(Y = y)
0	0.000
1	0.000
2	0.007
3	0.047
4	0.188
5	0.401
6	0.356

Note: To three significant digits, the first four probabilities in the table are 1.56×10^{-5}, 4.97×10^{-4}, 0.00663, and 0.0471, respectively.

f. $\mu = 5.052$ VCRs; on average, 5.052 of every 6 households have a VCR.
g. $\sigma = 0.893$ VCR
h. The probability distribution is only approximately correct because sampling is without replacement; a hypergeometric distribution.

5.85
a. 0.201 **b.** 0.666 **c.** 0.046 **d.** 0.954

REVIEW TEST FOR CHAPTER 5

1. It enables you to evaluate and control the likelihood that a statistical inference is correct. More generally, probability theory provides the mathematical basis for inferential statistics.

2. **a.** The experiment has a finite number of possible outcomes, all equally likely.
   b. The probability of an event equals the ratio of the number of ways that the event can occur to the total number of possible outcomes.

3. It is the proportion of times the event occurs in a large number of repetitions of the experiment.

4. (b) and (c), because the probability of an event must always be between 0 and 1, inclusive.

5. Venn diagrams

6. Two or more events are said to be mutually exclusive if at most one of them can occur when the experiment is performed, that is, if no two of them have outcomes in common.

7. **a.** $P(E)$ **b.** $P(E) = 0.436$

8. **a.** False **b.** True

9. It is sometimes easier to compute the probability that an event does not occur than the probability that it does occur.
10. **a.** 0.231 **b.** 0.363
    c. 0.231, 0.201, 0.147, 0.106, 0.080, 0.177, 0.059
11. **a.** (not J) is the event that the return shows an AGI of at least $100K. There are 7186 thousand such returns.
    b. (H & I) is the event that the return shows an AGI of between $20K and $50K. There are 40,765 thousand such returns.
    c. (H or K) is the event that the return shows an AGI of at least $20K. There are 69,586 thousand such returns.
    d. (H & K) is the event that the return shows an AGI of between $50K and $100K. There are 21,635 thousand such returns.
12. **a.** Not mutually exclusive
    b. Mutually exclusive
    c. Mutually exclusive
    d. Not mutually exclusive
13. **a.** 0.510, 0.765, 0.941, 0.235
    b. $H = (C \text{ or } D \text{ or } E \text{ or } F)$
    $I = (A \text{ or } B \text{ or } C \text{ or } D \text{ or } E)$
    $J = (A \text{ or } B \text{ or } C \text{ or } D \text{ or } E \text{ or } F)$
    $K = (F \text{ or } G)$
    c. 0.510, 0.765, 0.942, 0.236
14. **a.** 0.059, 0.333, 0.568, 0.177
    b. 0.941 **c.** 0.568 **d.** They are the same.
15. **a.** Random variable
    b. Finite; countably infinite
16. The possible values and corresponding probabilities of the discrete random variable
17. Probability histogram
18. 1
19. **a.** $P(X = 2) = 0.386$ **b.** 38.6%
    c. 19.3; 193
20. 3.6
21. X, because it has a smaller standard deviation, therefore less variation.
22. Each trial has the same two possible outcomes; the trials are independent; the probability of a success remains the same from trial to trial.
23. The binomial distribution is the probability distribution for the number of successes in a finite sequence of Bernoulli trials.
24. 120

25. Substitute the binomial probability formula into the formulas for the mean and standard deviation of a discrete random variable and then simplify mathematically.
26. **a.** Binomial distribution
    b. Hypergeometric distribution
    c. When the sample size does not exceed 5% of the population size because, under this condition, there is little difference between sampling with and without replacement.
27. **a.** 1, 2, 3, 4 **b.** $\{X = 3\}$
    c. 0.2521; 25.2% of undergraduates at ASU are juniors.
    d.

x	1	2	3	4
$P(X = x)$	0.191	0.210	0.252	0.347

e.

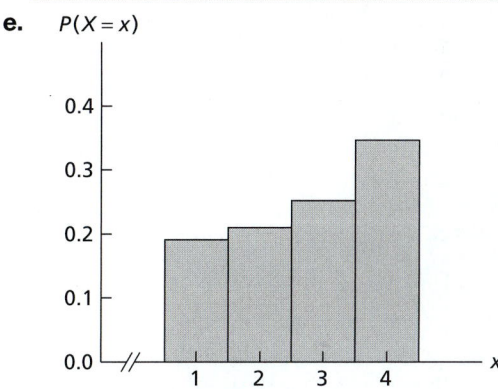

28. **a.** $\{Y = 4\}$ **b.** $\{Y \geq 4\}$ **c.** $\{2 \leq Y \leq 4\}$
    d. $\{Y \geq 1\}$ **e.** 0.174 **f.** 0.322
    g. 0.646 **h.** 0.948
29. **a.** 2.817 lines **b.** 2.817 lines **c.** 1.504 lines
30. 1, 6, 24, 5040
31. **a.** 56 **b.** 56 **c.** 1 **d.** 45
    e. 91,390 **f.** 1
32. **a.** $p = 0.4$
    b.

Outcome	Probability
sss	$(0.4)(0.4)(0.4) = 0.064$
ssf	$(0.4)(0.4)(0.6) = 0.096$
sfs	$(0.4)(0.6)(0.4) = 0.096$
sff	$(0.4)(0.6)(0.6) = 0.144$
fss	$(0.6)(0.4)(0.4) = 0.096$
fsf	$(0.6)(0.4)(0.6) = 0.144$
ffs	$(0.6)(0.6)(0.4) = 0.144$
fff	$(0.6)(0.6)(0.6) = 0.216$

d. ssf, sfs, fss

e. 0.096. Each probability is obtained by multiplying two success probabilities of 0.4 and one failure probability of 0.6.
f. 0.288
g.

y	0	1	2	3
$P(Y=y)$	0.216	0.432	0.288	0.064

h. Binomial with parameters $n = 3$ and $p = 0.4$

33. a. 0.3456   **b.** 0.4752   **c.** 0.8704
d.

x	$P(X=x)$
0	0.0256
1	0.1536
2	0.3456
3	0.3456
4	0.1296

e. Left skewed
f.

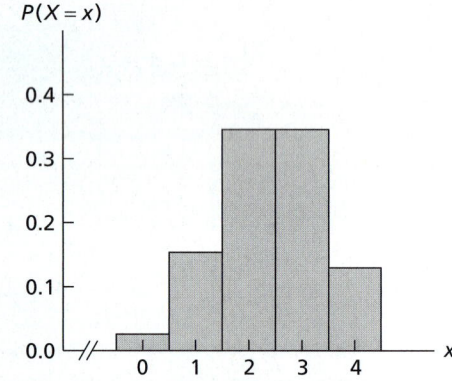

g. The probability distribution is only approximately correct because the sampling is without replacement; a hypergeometric distribution.
h. 2.4 households; on average, 2.4 of every 4 U.S. households live with one or more pets.
i. 0.98 households

34. a. $p > 0.5$ **b.** $p = 0.5$

CHAPTER 6

EXERCISES 6.1

6.1 Roughly bell-shaped

6.2 If a variable of a population is normally distributed and is the only variable under consideration, common practice is to say that the population is normally distributed.

6.3 They are the same. A normal distribution is completely determined by the mean and standard deviation.

6.4 The first one has a wider spread because its standard deviation is larger.

6.5
a. True. They have the same shape because their standard deviations are equal.
b. False. A normal distribution is centered at its mean, which is different for these two distributions.

6.6 True. The shape of a normal distribution is completely determined by its standard deviation.

6.7 The mean μ and standard deviation σ

6.8
a.

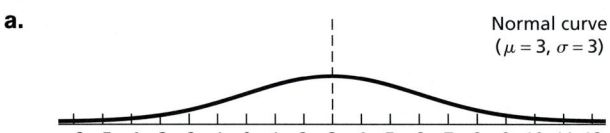

b.

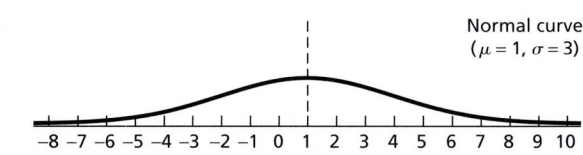

c.

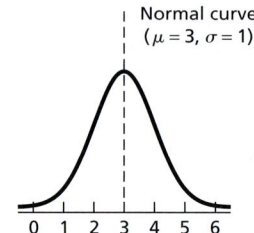

6.9 They are equal. They are approximately equal.

6.10 68.74%

6.11
a. 55.70%
b. 0.5570; This is only an estimate because the distribution of heights is only approximately normally distributed.

6.12
a. 7.83%   **b.** 7.84%

6.13
a.

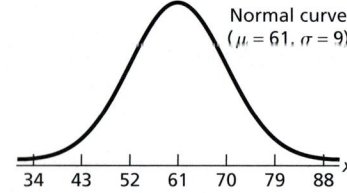

b. $z = (x - 61)/9$
c. Standard normal distribution

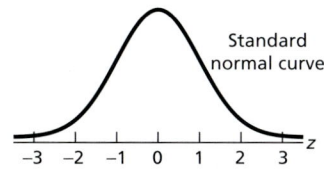

d. $-1.22; 1$ **e.** right; 1.56

6.14
a.

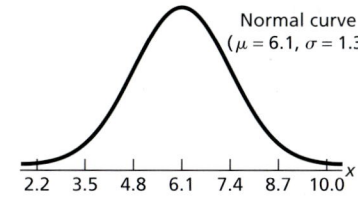

b. $z = (x - 6.1)/1.3$
c. Standard normal distribution; see the graph in the answer to Exercise 6.13(c)
d. 0.69; 1.46   **e.** Left; -2.38

EXERCISES 6.2

6.19 For a normally distributed variable, you can obtain the percentage of all possible observations that lie within any specified range by first converting to z-scores and then determining the corresponding area under the standard normal curve.

6.20 The normal distribution with a mean of 0 and a standard deviation of 1

6.21 The total area under the standard normal curve equals 1, and the standard normal curve is symmetric about 0. So the area to the right of 0 is one-half of 1, or 0.5.

6.22 By symmetry, it equals 0.0188.

6.23 0.3336. The total area under the curve is 1, so the area to the right of 0.43 equals 1 minus the area to its left, which is $1 - 0.6664 = 0.3336$.

6.24 0.025. By symmetry, the area under the standard normal curve that lies to the left of -1.96 equals that to the right of 1.96. Because the total area under the standard normal curve equals 1, this latter area equals $1 - 0.975 = 0.025$.

6.25 99.74%

6.26 Because the standard normal curve is the associated normal curve for a standardized normally distributed variable and a standardized variable is labeled z

6.27
a. Read the area directly from the table.
b. Subtract the table area from 1.
c. Subtract the smaller table area from the larger.

6.28 0; 1

6.29
a. 0.9875   **b.** 0.0594   **c.** 0.5
d. 0.0000 (to four decimal places)

6.30
a. 0.8577   **b.** 0.2743   **c.** 0.5
d. 0.0000 (to four decimal places)

6.31
a. 0.9105   **b.** 0.0440   **c.** 0.2121   **d.** 0.1357

6.32
a. 0.0645   **b.** 0.7975

6.33
a. 0.7994   **b.** 0.8990   **c.** 0.0500   **d.** 0.0198

6.34
a. 0.6826

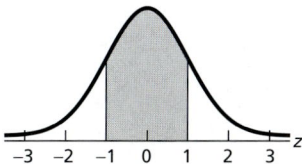

b. 0.9544

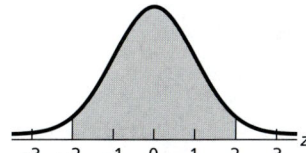

c. 0.9974

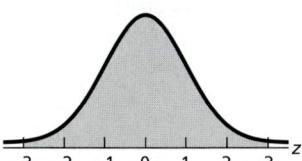

6.35
a. 0.0013; 0.0215; 0.1359; 0.3413; 0.3413; 0.1359; 0.0215; 0.0013
b. The entries in the second column of the table are the same as those given in the answer to part (a). The entries in the third column of the table are obtained from those in the second column by multiplying by 100.

6.36 -1.96

6.37 0.67

6.38 −1.645

6.39 0.44

6.40
a. 1.88 **b.** 2.575

6.41 ±1.645

6.42 The four missing entries are 1.645, 1.96, 2.33, and 2.575.

EXERCISES 6.3

6.45 First express the range in terms of z-scores and then determine the corresponding area under the standard normal curve.

6.46 The z-scores corresponding to the x-values that lie two standard deviations below and above the mean are −2 and 2, respectively.

6.47
a. 76.47% **b.** 0.03%

6.48
a. 17.82% **b.** 96.56%

6.49
a. 0.0594 **b.** 0.2699

6.50
a. 0.0087 **b.** 0.5572

6.51
a. 68.26% **b.** 95.44% **c.** 99.74%

6.52
a. 18.27; 30.73 **b.** 12.04; 36.96
c. 5.81; 43.19 **d.** See the graphs shown in Fig. A.5.

FIGURE A.5 Graphs for Exercise 6.52(d)

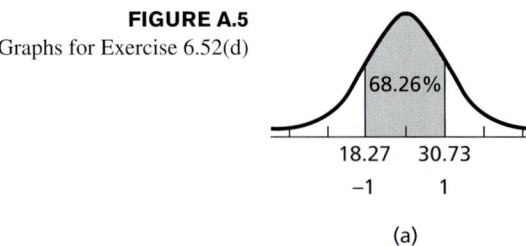
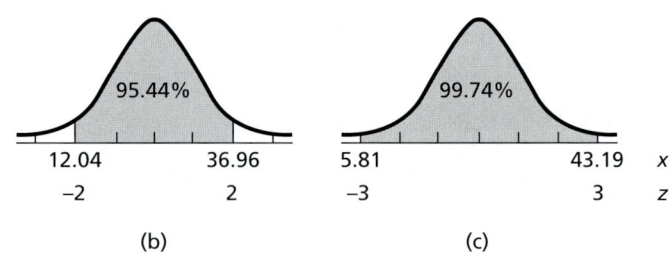

(a) (b) (c)

6.53
a. 266.76 yd, 272.20 yd, 277.64 yd
b. 285.56 yd **c.** 267.98 yd
d. For tee shots on the 1999 men's PGA tour: 25% were less than 266.76 yd, 25% were between 266.76 and 272.20 yd, 25% were between 272.20 and 277.64 yd, 25% were greater than 277.64 yd, 95% were less than 285.56 yd, and 30% were less than 267.98 yd.

6.54
a. 1.33 kg, 1.40 kg, 1.47 kg **b.** 1.31 kg **c.** 1.46 kg
d. For brain weights of Swedish males: 25% are less than 1.33 kg, 25% are between 1.33 and 1.40 kg, 25% are between 1.40 and 1.47 kg, 25% are greater than 1.47 kg, 20% are less than 1.31 kg, and 70% are less than 1.46 kg.

EXERCISES 6.4

6.62 Decisions about whether a variable is normally distributed often are important in subsequent analyses—from percentage or percentile calculations to statistical inferences.

6.63 When sample sizes are relatively small

6.64
a. A normal probability plot is a plot of the observed values of the variable versus the normal scores—the observations expected for a variable having the standard normal distribution. If the variable is normally distributed, the normal probability plot should be roughly linear and vice versa.
b. In a normal probability plot, outliers lie outside the overall pattern formed by the other points in the plot.

6.65
a.

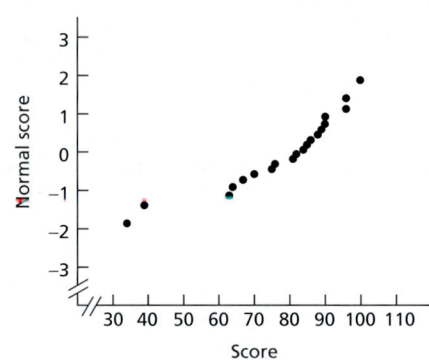

b. 34 and 39 are outliers.
c. Final-exam scores in this introductory statistics class appear not to be normally distributed.

6.66
a.

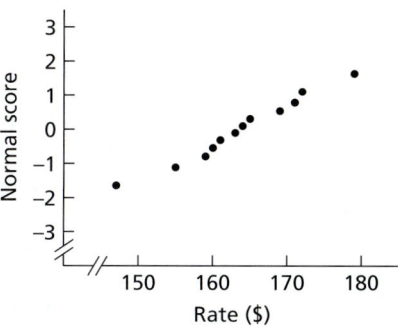

b. No outliers
c. 1998 subscription rates to law periodicals appear to be (approximately) normally distributed.

6.67
a.

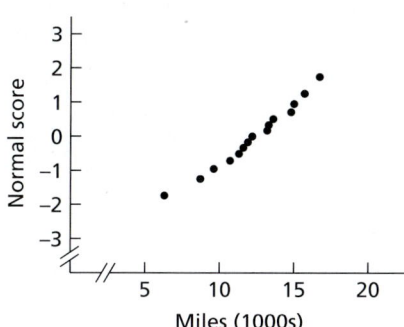

b. No outliers
c. It appears plausible that the number of miles cars were driven last year is (approximately) normally distributed.

6.68
a.

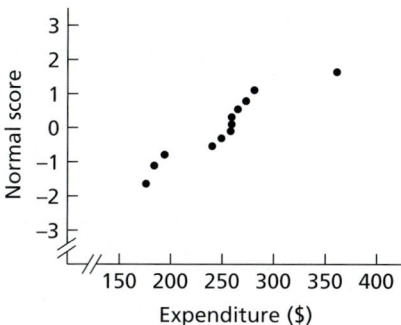

b. 361 is an outlier.
c. Last year's expenditures by consumers on nonalcoholic beverages appear not to be normally distributed.

REVIEW TEST FOR CHAPTER 6

1. It appears again and again in both theory and practice.
2. **a.** A variable is said to be normally distributed if its distribution has the shape of a normal curve.
   b. If a variable of a population is normally distributed and is the only variable under consideration, common practice is to say that the population is a normally distributed population.
   c. The parameters for a normal curve are the corresponding mean and standard deviation of the variable.
3. **a.** False
   b. True. A normal distribution is completely determined by its mean and standard deviation.
4. They are the same when areas are expressed as percentages.
5. Standard normal distribution
6. **a.** True **b.** True
7. **a.** The second curve
   b. The first and second curves
   c. The first and third curves
   d. The third curve **e.** The fourth curve
8. Key Fact 6.2, which states that the standardized version of a normally distributed variable has the standard normal distribution
9. **a.** Read the area directly from the table.
   b. Subtract the table area from 1.
   c. Subtract the smaller table area from the larger.
10. **a.** Locate the table entry closest to the specified area and read the corresponding z-score.
    b. Locate the table entry closest to 1 minus the specified area and read the corresponding z-score.
11. The z-score having area α to its right under the standard normal curve
12. See Key Fact 6.4.
13. The observations expected for a sample of the same size from a variable that has the standard normal distribution
14. Linear
15. **a.**

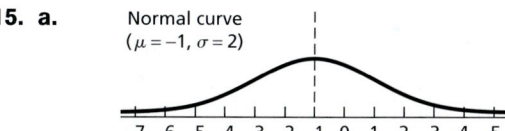

b.

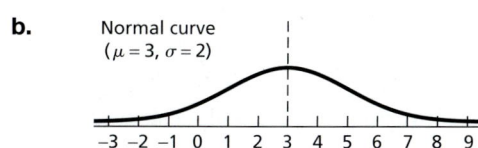

A-56 APPENDIX B Answers to Selected Exercises

c.

Normal curve ($\mu = -1$, $\sigma = 0.5$)

16. a.

Normal curve ($\mu = 18.8$, $\sigma = 1.1$)

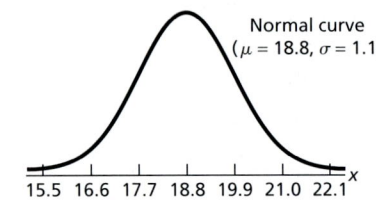

b. $z = (x - 18.8)/1.1$
c. Standard normal distribution
d. 0.8115   **e.** Left; -2.55

17. a. 0.1469   **b.** 0.1469   **c.** 0.7062
18. a. 0.0013   **b.** 0.2709   **c.** 0.1305
  d. 0.9803   **e.** 0.0668   **f.** 0.8426
19. a. -0.52 **b.** 1.28   **c.** 1.96; 1.645; 2.33; 2.575
  d. ± 2.575
20. a. 82.76%   **b.** 89.44%   **c.** 99.38%
21. a. 400, 600   **b.** 300, 700   **c.** 200, 800
22. a. 433, 500, 567. Thus 25% of GRE scores are below 433, 25% are between 433 and 500, 25% are between 500 and 567, and 25% are above 567.
  b. 733. Thus 99% of GRE scores are below 733 and 1% are above 733.

23. a.

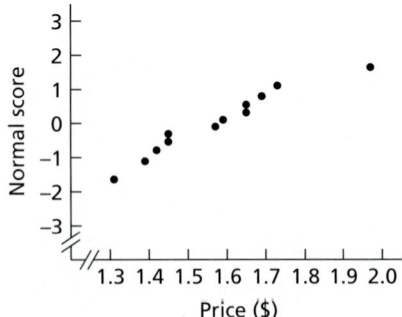

b. No outliers
c. It appears plausible that, for June 2000, gas prices were (approximately) normally distributed.

CHAPTER 7

EXERCISES 7.1

7.1 Generally, sampling is less costly and can be done more quickly than a census.

7.2 Because a sample from a population provides data for only a portion of the entire population, the sample cannot be expected to yield perfectly accurate information about the population. Sampling error.

7.3
a. $\mu = 81$ inches
b.

Sample	Heights (in.)	$\bar{x}$
HG, BG	78, 79	78.5
HG, HF	78, 82	80.0
HG, GF	78, 81	79.5
HG, OC	78, 85	81.5
BG, HF	79, 82	80.5
BG, GF	79, 81	80.0
BG, OC	79, 85	82.0
HF, GF	82, 81	81.5
HF, OC	82, 85	83.5
GF, OC	81, 85	83.0

c. See Fig. A.6.

FIGURE A.6 Dotplot for Exercise 7.3(c)

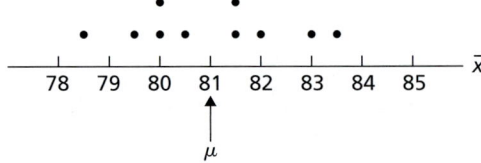

d. 0
e. 0.6. If a random sample of two players is taken, there is a 60% chance that the mean height of the two players selected will be within 1 inch of the population mean height.

7.4
b.

Sample	Height (in.)	$\bar{x}$
HG	78	78
BG	79	79
HF	82	82
GF	81	81
OC	85	85

c. See Fig. A.7.

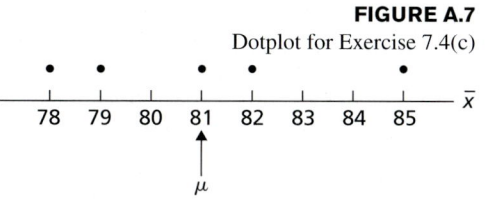

FIGURE A.7
Dotplot for Exercise 7.4(c)

d. 0.2
e. 0.4. If a random sample of one player is taken, there is a 40% chance that the (mean) height of the player selected will be within 1 inch of the population mean height.

7.5
b.

Sample	Heights (in.)	$\bar{x}$
HG, BG, HF	78, 79, 82	79.7
HG, BG, GF	78, 79, 81	79.3
HG, BG, OC	78, 79, 85	80.7
HG, HF, GF	78, 82, 81	80.3
HG, HF, OC	78, 82, 85	81.7
HG, GF, OC	78, 81, 85	81.3
BG, HF, GF	79, 82, 81	80.7
BG, HF, OC	79, 82, 85	82.0
BG, GF, OC	79, 81, 85	81.7
HF, GF, OC	82, 81, 85	82.7

c. See Fig. A.8.

FIGURE A.8
Dotplot for Exercise 7.5(c)

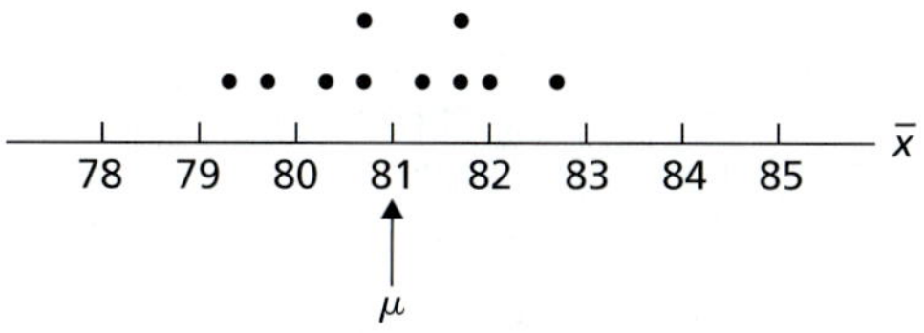

d. 0
e. 0.7. If a random sample of three players is taken, there is a 70% chance that the mean height of the three players selected will be within 1 inch of the population mean height.

7.6
b.

Sample	Heights (in.)	$\bar{x}$
HG, BG, HF, GF	78, 79, 82, 81	80.00
HG, BG, HF, OC	78, 79, 82, 85	81.00
HG, BG, GF, OC	78, 79, 81, 85	80.75
HG, HF, GF, OC	78, 82, 81, 85	81.50
BG, HF, GF, OC	79, 82, 81, 85	81.75

c. See Fig. A.9.

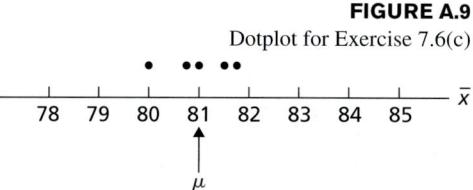

FIGURE A.9
Dotplot for Exercise 7.6(c)

d. 0.2
e. 1. If a random sample of four players is taken, it is certain (a 100% chance) that the mean height of the four players selected will be within 1 inch of the population mean height.

7.7
b.

Sample	Heights (in.)	$\bar{x}$
HG, BG, HF, GF, OC	78, 79, 82, 81, 85	81.0

c. See Fig. A.10.

FIGURE A.10
Dotplot for Exercise 7.7(c)

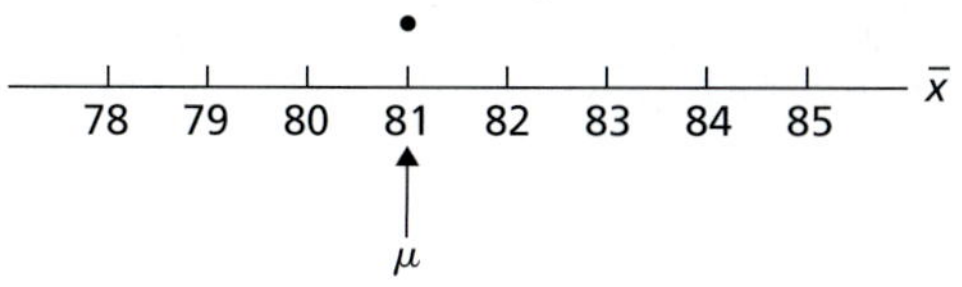

d. 1
e. 1. If a random sample of five players is taken, it is certain (a 100% chance) that the mean height of the five players selected will be within 1 inch of the population mean height.

7.8
b. Sampling error tends to be smaller for large samples than for small samples.
c. Answers will vary.

7.9
a. $\mu = \$36$ billion

b.

Sample	Wealth ($billions)	$\bar{x}$
G, E	60, 47	53.5
G, K	60, 30	45.0
G, A	60, 28	44.0
G, B	60, 28	44.0
G, N	60, 23	41.5
E, K	47, 30	38.5
E, A	47, 28	37.5
E, B	47, 28	37.5
E, N	47, 23	35.0
K, A	30, 28	29.0
K, B	30, 28	29.0
K, N	30, 23	26.5
A, B	28, 28	28.0
A, N	28, 23	25.5
B, N	28, 23	25.5

d. 0

e. 0.2. If a random sample of two of the six richest people is taken, there is a 20% chance that the mean wealth of the two people selected will be within 2 (i.e., $2 billion) of the population mean wealth.

7.10
b.

Sample	Wealth ($billions)	$\bar{x}$
G	60	60
E	47	47
K	30	30
A	28	28
B	28	28
N	23	23

d. 0

e. 0. If a random sample of one of the six richest people is taken, it is impossible (a 0% chance) that the (mean) wealth of the person selected will be within 2 (i.e., $2 billion) of the population mean wealth.

7.11
b.

Sample	Wealth ($billions)	$\bar{x}$
G, E, K	60, 47, 30	45.7
G, E, A	60, 47, 28	45.0
G, E, B	60, 47, 28	45.0
G, E, N	60, 47, 23	43.3
G, K, A	60, 30, 28	39.3
G, K, B	60, 30, 28	39.3
G, K, N	60, 30, 23	37.7
G, A, B	60, 28, 28	38.7
G, A, N	60, 28, 23	37.0
G, B, N	60, 28, 23	37.0
E, K, A	47, 30, 28	35.0
E, K, B	47, 30, 28	35.0
E, K, N	47, 30, 23	33.3
E, A, B	47, 28, 28	34.3
E, A, N	47, 28, 23	32.7
E, B, N	47, 28, 23	32.7
K, A, B	30, 28, 28	28.7
K, A, N	30, 28, 23	27.0
K, B, N	30, 28, 23	27.0
A, B, N	28, 28, 23	26.3

d. 0

e. 0.3. If a random sample of three of the six richest people is taken, there is a 30% chance that the mean wealth of the three people selected will be within 2 (i.e., $2 billion) of the population mean wealth.

7.12
b.

Sample	Wealth ($billions)	$\bar{x}$
G, E, K, A	60, 47, 30, 28	41.25
G, E, K, B	60, 47, 30, 28	41.25
G, E, K, N	60, 47, 30, 23	40.00
G, E, A, B	60, 47, 28, 28	40.75
G, E, A, N	60, 47, 28, 23	39.50
G, E, B, N	60, 47, 28, 23	39.50
G, K, A, B	60, 30, 28, 28	36.50
G, K, A, N	60, 30, 28, 23	35.25
G, K, B, N	60, 30, 28, 23	35.25
G, A, B, N	60, 28, 28, 23	34.75
E, K, A, B	47, 30, 28, 28	33.25
E, K, A, N	47, 30, 28, 23	32.00
E, K, B, N	47, 30, 28, 23	32.00
E, A, B, N	47, 28, 28, 23	31.50
K, A, B, N	30, 28, 28, 23	27.25

d. 0

e. 0.267. If a random sample of four of the six richest people is taken, there is a 26.7% chance that the mean wealth of the four people selected will be within 2 (i.e., $2 billion) of the population mean wealth.

7.13
b.

Sample	Wealth ($billions)	$\bar{x}$
G, E, K, A, B	60, 47, 30, 28, 28	38.6
G, E, K, A, N	60, 47, 30, 28, 23	37.6
G, E, K, B, N	60, 47, 30, 28, 23	37.6
G, E, A, B, N	60, 47, 28, 28, 23	37.2
G, K, A, B, N	60, 30, 28, 28, 23	33.8
E, K, A, B, N	47, 30, 28, 28, 23	31.2

d. 0
e. 0.5. If a random sample of five of the six richest people is taken, there is a 50% chance that the mean wealth of the five people selected will be within 2 (i.e., $2 billion) of the population mean wealth.

7.14
b.

Sample	Wealth ($billions)	$\bar{x}$
G, E, K, A, B, N	60, 47, 30, 28, 28, 23	36.0

d. 1
e. 1. If a random sample of six of the six richest people is taken, it is certain (a 100% chance) that the mean wealth of the six people selected will be within 2 (i.e., $2 billion) of the population mean wealth.
They are the same.

7.15 Sampling error tends to be smaller for large samples than for small samples.

EXERCISES 7.2

7.18 A normal distribution

7.19 A normal distribution is determined by the mean and standard deviation. Hence a first step in learning how to approximate the sampling distribution of the mean by a normal distribution is to obtain the mean and standard deviation of the variable $\bar{x}$.

7.20 No. The mean of all possible sample means (i.e., of the variable $\bar{x}$) always equals the population mean.

7.21 Yes. The standard deviation of all possible sample means (i.e., of the variable $\bar{x}$) gets smaller as the sample size gets larger.

7.22 The larger the sample size, the smaller is the standard deviation of $\bar{x}$; the smaller the standard deviation of $\bar{x}$, the more closely the possible values of $\bar{x}$ (the possible sample means) cluster around the mean of $\bar{x}$; the mean of $\bar{x}$ equals the population mean.

7.23 Standard error (SE) of the mean. Because the standard deviation of $\bar{x}$ determines the amount of sampling error to be expected when a population mean is estimated by a sample mean.

7.25
a. $\mu = 81$ inches   **b.** $\mu_{\bar{x}} = 81$ inches
c. $\mu_{\bar{x}} = \mu = 81$ inches

7.26
b. $\mu_{\bar{x}} = 81$ inches   **c.** $\mu_{\bar{x}} = \mu = 81$ inches

7.27
b. $\mu_{\bar{x}} = 81$ inches   **c.** $\mu_{\bar{x}} = \mu = 81$ inches

7.28
b. $\mu_{\bar{x}} = 81$ inches   **c.** $\mu_{\bar{x}} = \mu = 81$ inches

7.29
b. $\mu_{\bar{x}} = 81$ inches   **c.** $\mu_{\bar{x}} = \mu = 81$ inches

7.30
a. The population consists of all self-employed persons with home-based businesses. The variable is time worked per week at home.
b. 23 hr; 1.0 hr   **c.** 23 hr; 0.3 hr

7.31
a. The population consists of all babies born in 1991. The variable is birth weight.
b. 3369 g; 41.1 g   **c.** 3369 g; 29.1 g

7.32
a. $\mu_{\bar{x}} = 5.8$ days, $\sigma_{\bar{x}} = 0.50$ days. For samples of 75 female patients, the mean and standard deviation of all possible sample mean lengths of stay are 5.8 days and 0.50 day, respectively.
b. $\mu_{\bar{x}} = 5.8$ days, $\sigma_{\bar{x}} = 0.19$ day. For samples of 500 female patients, the mean and standard deviation of all possible sample mean lengths of stay are 5.8 days and 0.19 day, respectively.

7.33
a. $\mu_{\bar{x}} = \$43{,}800$, $\sigma_{\bar{x}} = \$1018.2$. For samples of 50 new mobile homes, the mean and standard deviation of all possible sample mean prices are $43,800 and $1018.2, respectively.
b. $\mu_{\bar{x}} = \$43{,}800$, $\sigma_{\bar{x}} = \$720.0$. For samples of 100 new mobile homes, the mean and standard deviation of all possible sample mean prices are $43,800 and $720.0, respectively.

7.34
a. 437 days   **b.** ±598.5 days

EXERCISES 7.3

7.39
a. Approximately normally distributed with a mean of 100 and a standard deviation of 4
b. None
c. No. Because the distribution of the variable under consideration is not specified, a sample size of at least 30 is needed to apply Key Fact 7.4.

7.40
a. Normally distributed with a mean of 35 and a standard deviation of 14
b. No. Because, if the distribution of the variable under consideration is unknown, a sample size of at least 30 is needed to apply Key Fact 7.4.
c. Yes. Because, under these circumstances, Key Fact 7.4 can be applied to conclude that the sampling distribution of the sample mean is approximately a normal distribution.

7.41
a. Normal with mean μ and standard deviation $\sigma/\sqrt{n}$
b. No. Because the variable under consideration is normally distributed.
c. μ and $\sigma/\sqrt{n}$
d. Essentially, no. For any variable, the mean of $\bar{x}$ equals the population mean, and the standard deviation of $\bar{x}$ equals (at least approximately) the population standard deviation divided by the square root of the sample size.

7.42
a. Approximately normal with mean μ and standard deviation $\sigma/\sqrt{n}$
b. Yes. Because, if the distribution of the variable under consideration is unknown, a sample size of at least 30 is needed to apply Key Fact 7.4.
c. μ and $\sigma/\sqrt{n}$
d. Essentially, no. For any variable, the mean of $\bar{x}$ equals the population mean, and the standard deviation of $\bar{x}$ equals (at least approximately) the population standard deviation divided by the square root of the sample size.

7.43
a. All four graphs are centered at the same place because $\mu_{\bar{x}} = \mu$ and normal distributions are centered at their means.
b. Because $\sigma_{\bar{x}} = \sigma/\sqrt{n}$, $\sigma_{\bar{x}}$ decreases as n increases. This fact results in a diminishing of the spread because the spread of a distribution is determined by its standard deviation. As a consequence, the larger the sample size, the greater is the likelihood for small sampling error.
c. If the variable under consideration is normally distributed, so is the sampling distribution of the mean, regardless of sample size.
d. The central limit theorem indicates that, if the sample size is relatively large, the sampling distribution of the mean is approximately a normal distribution, regardless of the distribution of the variable under consideration.

7.44
a. $n \geq 30$.
b. Roughly speaking, the farther the variable under consideration is from being normally distributed, the larger the sample size must be for a normal distribution to provide an adequate approximation to the distribution of $\bar{x}$. Usually, however, a sample size of 30 or more ($n \geq 30$) is large enough.

7.45
a. A normal distribution with a mean of 1.40 and a standard deviation of 0.064. Thus, for samples of three Swedish men, the distribution of all possible sample mean brain weights is a normal distribution with a mean of 1.40 kg and a standard deviation of 0.064 kg.
b. A normal distribution with a mean of 1.40 and a standard deviation of 0.032. Thus, for samples of 12 Swedish men, the distribution of all possible sample mean brain weights is a normal distribution with a mean of 1.40 kg and a standard deviation of 0.032 kg.
c.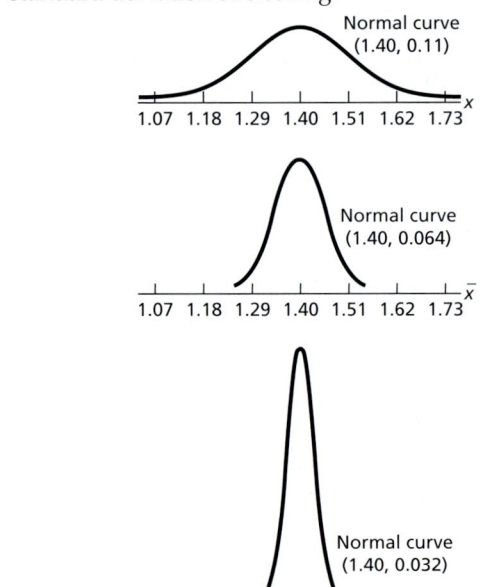

7.46
a. Approximately a normal distribution with a mean of 40,133 and a standard deviation of 1000. Thus, for samples of 64 classroom teachers in the public school system, the distribution of all possible sample mean annual salaries is approximately normally distributed with a mean of $40,133 and a standard deviation of $1000.

b. Approximately a normal distribution with a mean of 40,133 and a standard deviation of 500. Thus, for samples of 256 classroom teachers in the public school system, the distribution of all possible sample mean annual salaries is approximately normally distributed with a mean of $40,133 and a standard deviation of $500.
c. No. Because, in each case, the sample size exceeds 30.

7.47
a. Approximately a normal distribution with a mean of 272.2 and a standard deviation of 0.812.
b. Approximately a normal distribution with a mean of 272.2 and a standard deviation of 0.574.
c. No. Because, in each case, the sample size exceeds 30.

7.48
a. A normal distribution with a mean of 61 and a standard deviation of 4.5. Thus, for samples of four finishers in the New York City 10 km run, the distribution of all possible sample means is a normal distribution with a mean of 61 minutes and a standard deviation of 4.5 minutes.
b. A normal distribution with a mean of 61 and a standard deviation of 3.0. Thus, for samples of nine finishers in the New York City 10 km run, the distribution of all possible sample means is a normal distribution with a mean of 61 minutes and a standard deviation of 3.0 minutes.
c.

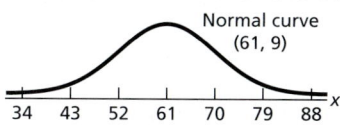

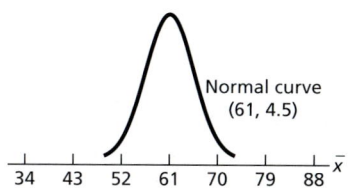

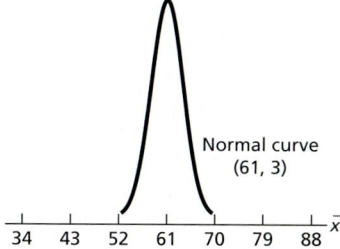

7.49
a. 88.12%. Chances are 88.12% that the sampling error made in estimating the mean brain weight of all Swedish men by that of a sample of three Swedish men will be at most 0.1 kg.

b. 99.82%. Chances are 99.82% that the sampling error made in estimating the mean brain weight of all Swedish men by that of a sample of 12 Swedish men will be at most 0.1 kg.

7.50
a. 68.26%. Chances are 68.26% that the sampling error made in estimating the mean annual salary of all classroom teachers in the public school system by that of a sample of 64 such teachers will be at most $1000.
b. 95.44%. Chances are 95.44% that the sampling error made in estimating the mean annual salary of all classroom teachers in the public school system by that of a sample of 256 such teachers will be at most $1000.

7.51
a. 0.7814 **b.** 0.9182

7.52
a. 0.7330 **b.** 0.9050

7.53 0.9522

REVIEW TEST FOR CHAPTER 7

1. Sampling error is the error resulting from using a sample to estimate a population characteristic.

2. The distribution of a statistic (i.e., of all possible observations of the statistic for samples of a given size) is called the sampling distribution of the statistic.

3. Sampling distribution of the mean; distribution of the variable $\bar{x}$

4. The possible sample means cluster closer around the population mean as the sample size increases. Thus the larger the sample size, the smaller the sampling error tends to be in estimating a population mean, μ, by a sample mean, $\bar{x}$.

5. **a.** The error resulting from using the mean income tax, $\bar{x}$, of the 125,000 tax returns selected as an estimate of the mean income tax, μ, of all 1998 tax returns.
   b. $88
   c. No, not necessarily. However, increasing the sample size from 125,000 to 250,000 would increase the likelihood for small sampling error.
   d. Increase the sample size.

A-62 APPENDIX B Answers to Selected Exercises

6. a. $\mu = \$18$ thousand
b. The completed table is as follows.

Sample	Salaries	$\bar{x}$
A, B, C, D	8, 12, 16, 20	14
A, B, C, E	8, 12, 16, 24	15
A, B, C, F	8, 12, 16, 28	16
A, B, D, E	8, 12, 20, 24	16
A, B, D, F	8, 12, 20, 28	17
A, B, E, F	8, 12, 24, 28	18
A, C, D, E	8, 16, 20, 24	17
A, C, D, F	8, 16, 20, 28	18
A, C, E, F	8, 16, 24, 28	19
A, D, E, F	8, 20, 24, 28	20
B, C, D, E	12, 16, 20, 24	18
B, C, D, F	12, 16, 20, 28	19
B, C, E, F	12, 16, 24, 28	20
B, D, E, F	12, 20, 24, 28	21
C, D, E, F	16, 20, 24, 28	22

c.

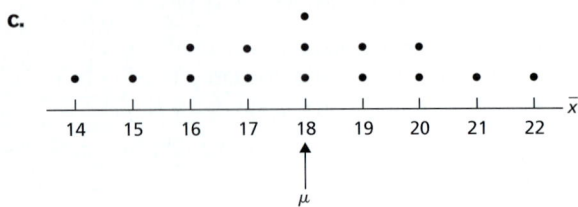

d. $\frac{7}{15}$
e. $18 thousand. For samples of four officers from the six, the mean of all possible sample mean monthly salaries equals $18 thousand.
f. Yes. Because $\mu_{\bar{x}} = \mu$ and, from part (a), $\mu = \$18$ thousand.

7. a. The population consists of all new cars and trucks sold in the United States in 1999. The variable is the amount spent on a new car or truck.
b. $21,022; $1442.5
c. $21,022; $1020.0
d. Smaller, because $\sigma_{\bar{x}} = \sigma/\sqrt{n}$ and hence $\sigma_{\bar{x}}$ decreases with increasing sample size.

8. a. False   **b.** Not possible to tell   **c.** True

9. a. False   **b.** True   **c.** True

10. a. See the first graph that follows.
b. Normal distribution with a mean of 40 mm and a standard deviation of 6.0 mm, as shown in the second graph that follows.

c. Normal distribution with a mean of 40 mm and a standard deviation of 4.0 mm, as shown in the third graph that follows.

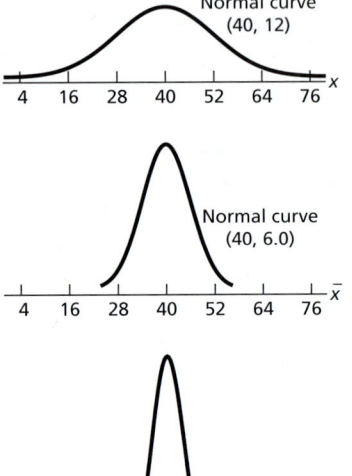

11. a. 86.64%   **b.** 0.8664
c. The probability that the sampling error will be at most 9 mm in estimating the population mean length of all krill by the mean length of a random sample of four krill is 0.8664.
d. 97.56%. 0.9756. The probability that the sampling error will be at most 9 mm in estimating the population mean length of all krill by the mean length of a random sample of nine krill is 0.9756.

12. a. For a normally distributed variable, the sampling distribution of the mean is a normal distribution, regardless of the sample size. Also, we know that $\mu_{\bar{x}} = \mu$. Consequently, because the normal curve for a normally distributed variable is centered at the mean, all three curves are centered at the same place.
b. Curve B. Because $\sigma_{\bar{x}} = \sigma/\sqrt{n}$, the larger the sample size, the smaller is the value of $\sigma_{\bar{x}}$ and hence the smaller is the spread of the normal curve for $\bar{x}$. Thus Curve B, which has the smaller spread, corresponds to the larger sample size.
c. Because $\sigma_{\bar{x}} = \sigma/\sqrt{n}$ and the spread of a normal curve is determined by the standard deviation, different sample sizes result in normal curves with different spreads.
d. Curve B. The smaller the value of $\sigma_{\bar{x}}$, the smaller the sampling error tends to be.

e. Because the variable under consideration is normally distributed and, hence, so is the sampling distribution of the mean, regardless of sample size.

13. a. 0.6212
    b. No. Because the sample size is large and therefore $\bar{x}$ is approximately normally distributed, regardless of the distribution of life insurance amounts. Yes.
    c. 0.9946

14. a. No. If the manufacturer's claim is correct, the probability that the paint life for a randomly selected house painted with this paint will be 4.5 years or less is 0.1587; that is, such an event would occur roughly 16% of the time.
    b. Yes. If the manufacturer's claim is correct, the probability that the mean paint life for 10 randomly selected houses painted with this paint will be 4.5 years or less is 0.0008; that is, such an event would occur less than 0.1% of the time.
    c. No. If the manufacturer's claim is correct, the probability that the mean paint life for 10 randomly selected houses painted with this paint will be 4.9 years or less is 0.2643; that is, such an event would occur roughly 26% of the time.

CHAPTER 8

EXERCISES 8.1

8.1 Point estimate

8.2 A confidence-interval estimate of a parameter consists of an interval of numbers obtained from a point estimate of the parameter and a percentage that specifies how confident we are that the parameter lies in the interval. The confidence percentage is called the confidence level.

8.3
a. $18,943.9
b. No. It is unlikely that a sample mean, $\bar{x}$, will exactly equal the population mean, μ; some sampling error is to be anticipated.

8.4
a. 7.6 young
b. No. It is unlikely that a sample mean, $\bar{x}$, will exactly equal the population mean, μ; some sampling error is to be anticipated.

8.5
a. $15,321.5 to $22,566.3
b. We can be 95.44% confident that the mean cost, μ, of all recent U.S. weddings is somewhere between $15,321.5 and $22,566.3.

c. It may or may not, but we can be 95.44% confident that it does.

8.6
a. 6.9 to 8.3 young
b. We can be 95.44% confident that the mean number of young per litter, μ, of all female eastern cottonmouths is somewhere between 6.9 and 8.3.
c. As litter size for eastern cottonmouths is a discrete variable, it cannot be exactly normally distributed.

8.7
a. 1187.7 miles. Based on the sample data, the mean number of miles traveled per business flight in 1999 is estimated to be 1187.7.
b. 1023.4 to 1352.0 miles. We can be 95.44% confident that the mean number of miles traveled per business flight in 1999 is somewhere between 1023.4 and 1352.0.
c. Obtain a normal probability plot of the data.
d. No. Because the sample size is large.

8.8
a. $2885.5. Based on the sample data, the mean budget, μ, of home improvement jobs is estimated to be $2885.5.
b. $2483.0 to $3288.0. We can be 95.44% confident that the population mean budget, μ, of home improvement jobs is somewhere between $2483.0 and $3288.0.
c. Obtain a normal probability plot of the data.
d. No. Because the sample size is large.

EXERCISES 8.2

8.11
a. Confidence level = 0.90; α = 0.10.
b. Confidence level = 0.99; α = 0.01.

8.12
a. Saying that the CI is exact means that the true confidence level is equal to $1 - \alpha$.
b. Saying that the CI is approximately correct means that the true confidence level is only approximately equal to $1 - \alpha$.

8.13
a. To ensure that the variable $\bar{x}$ is normally distributed.
b. Because, for large samples, the variable $\bar{x}$ is approximately normally distributed, regardless of the distribution of the variable under consideration.

8.14 The variable under consideration is normally distributed on the population of interest.

8.15
a. Assumption 1 of the z-interval procedure read in full means that the variable under consideration is normally distributed or that the sample size is large. Assumption 2 is that the standard deviation of the variable under consideration is known.

b. Actually, the z-interval procedure works reasonably well even when the variable is not normally distributed and the sample size is small or moderate, provided the variable is not too far from being normally distributed.

8.16 A statistical procedure is said to be *robust* if it is insensitive to departures from the assumptions on which it is based.

8.17 Key Fact 8.1 yields the following answers.
a. Reasonable   **b.** Reasonable
c. Not reasonable **d.** Reasonable
e. Not reasonable **f.** Reasonable

8.18 Look at the data by obtaining one or more graphical displays. If any of the conditions required for using the contemplated statistical-inference procedure appear to be violated, the procedure should not be applied. Instead a different, more appropriate procedure should be used. In difficult cases, consult a statistician.

8.19 a 95% confidence level

8.20
a. 456.4 to 608.0 tongue flicks per 20 minutes
b. We can be 90% confident that the mean number of tongue flicks per 20 minutes for all juvenile common lizards is somewhere between 456.4 and 608.0.

8.21
a. $5.39 million to $7.27 million
b. We can be 95% confident that the mean amount, μ, of all venture capital investments in the fiber optics business sector is somewhere between $5.39 million and $7.27 million.

8.22 18.8 to 48.0 months. We can be 95% confident that the mean duration of imprisonment, μ, of all East German political prisoners with chronic PTSD is somewhere between 18.8 and 48.0 months.

8.23 $2.03 million to $2.51 million. We can be 99% confident that the mean gross earnings of all Rolling Stones concerts is somewhere between $2.03 million and $2.51 million.

8.24
a. 413.5 to 650.9 tongue flicks per 20 minutes
b. It is longer because the confidence level is greater.
c.

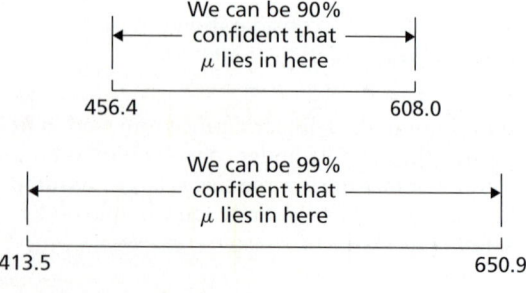

d. The 90% CI is a more precise estimate of μ because it is narrower than the 99% CI.

8.25
a. $5.72 million to $6.95 million
b. It is shorter because the confidence level is smaller.
c.

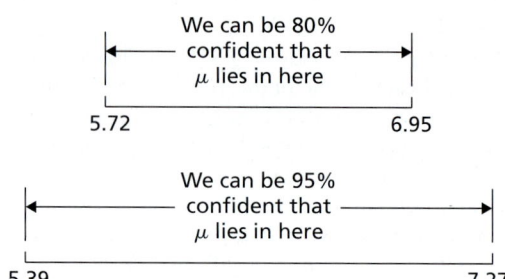

d. The 80% CI is a more precise estimate of μ because it is narrower than the 95% CI.

EXERCISES 8.3

8.33 The margin of error equals the standard error of the mean multiplied by $z_{\alpha/2}$.

8.34 Because the margin of error equals half the length of a CI, it determines the precision with which a sample mean estimates a population mean.

8.35
a. Increases the margin of error and hence decreases the precision
b. Decreases the margin of error and hence increases the precision

8.36
a. 6.8   **b.** 49.4 to 56.2

8.37
a. 10   **b.** 50 to 70

8.38
a. True. Because the margin of error is half the length of a CI, you can determine the length of a CI by doubling the margin of error.
b. True. By taking half the length of a CI, you can determine the margin of error.
c. False. You need to know the sample mean as well.
d. True. Because the CI is from $\bar{x} - E$ to $\bar{x} + E$, you can obtain a CI by knowing only the margin of error, E, and the sample mean, $\bar{x}$.
e. False. To determine the margin of error, you also need the population standard deviation and the sample size.

f. False. To determine the confidence level, you also need the population standard deviation and the sample size.
g. True.   **h.** True.

8.39
a. The sample size (number of observations) cannot be fractional; it must be a whole number.
b. The number resulting from Formula 8.1 is the smallest value that will provide the required margin of error. If that value were rounded down, the sample size thus obtained would be insufficient to ensure the required margin of error.

8.40 If σ is unknown, which is usually the case in practice, and you want to apply Formula 8.1, you must first estimate σ. One way to do so is to take a preliminary large sample, say, of size 30 or more. The sample standard deviation, s, of the sample obtained provides an estimate of σ and can be used in place of σ in Formula 8.1.

8.41 $0.49

8.42
a. 75.8 tongue flicks per 20 minutes
b. 75.8 tongue flicks per 20 minutes

8.43
a. $0.94 million   **b.** $0.94 million

8.44
a. 14.6 months
b. We can be 95% confident that the error made in estimating μ by $\bar{x}$ is at most 14.6 months.
c. 82 prisoners   **d.** 24.3 to 48.1 months

8.45
a. $0.24 million
b. We can be 99% confident that the error made in estimating μ by $\bar{x}$ is at most $0.24 million.
c. 97 concerts   **d.** $2.25 million to $2.45 million

EXERCISES 8.4

8.50 The difference in the formulas lies in their denominators. The denominator of the standardized version of $\bar{x}$ uses the population standard deviation, σ, whereas the denominator of the studentized version of $\bar{x}$ uses the sample standard deviation, s.

8.51 When the population standard deviation is unknown, the confidence-interval procedure for a population mean cannot be based on the standardized version of $\bar{x}$. The best that can be done is to replace the population standard deviation, σ, by the sample standard deviation, s, in the formula for the standardized version of $\bar{x}$. The result is the studentized version of $\bar{x}$.

8.52
a. $z = 1$ **b.** $t = 1.333$

8.53
a. The one-sample z-interval procedure
b. The one-sample t-interval procedure

8.54
a. The standard normal distribution
b. t-distribution with df $= 19$

8.55 The variation in the possible values of the standardized version is due solely to the variation of sample means, whereas that of the studentized version is due to the variation of both sample means and sample standard deviations.

8.56 The t-curve with df $= 20$ because, as the number of degrees of freedom becomes larger, t-curves look increasingly like the standard normal curve.

8.57
a. 1.440   **b.** 2.447   **c.** 3.143

8.58
a. 1.740   **b.** 2.110   **c.** 2.898

8.59
a. 1.323   **b.** 2.518   **c.** -2.080 **d.** ± 1.721

8.60
a. 1.860   **b.** 1.397   **c.** -2.896 **d.** ± 2.306

8.61 Yes. Because the sample size exceeds 30 and there are no outliers.

8.62 No. Because the sample size is moderate and there is an outlier.

8.63
a. $141.95 to $160.13
b. We can be 95% confident that the mean cost for a family of four to spend the day at an American amusement park is somewhere between $141.95 and $160.13.

8.64
a. 24.85 to 31.08 minutes
b. We can be 90% confident that the mean commute time of all commuters in Washington, D.C., is somewhere between 24.85 and 31.08 minutes.

8.65
a. 14.46 to 15.64 cm
b. We can be 90% confident that the mean depth of all subterranean coruro burrows is somewhere between 14.46 and 15.64 cm.

8.66
a. 0.90 to 3.76 hr
b. It appears so because, based on the confidence interval, we can be 95% confident that the mean additional sleep is somewhere between 0.90 and 3.76 hours and that, in particular, the mean is positive.

REVIEW TEST FOR CHAPTER 8

1. A point estimate of a parameter is the value of a statistic that is used to estimate the parameter; it consists of a single number, or point. A confidence-interval estimate of a parameter consists of an interval of numbers obtained from a point estimate of the parameter and a percentage that specifies how confident we are that the parameter lies in the interval.

2. False. The mean of the population may or may not lie somewhere between 33.8 and 39.0, but we can be 95% confident that it does.

3. No. See the guidelines in Key Fact 8.1.

4. Roughly 950 intervals would actually contain μ.

5. Look at graphical displays of the data to ascertain whether the conditions required for using the procedure appear to be satisfied.

6. **a.** The precision of the estimate would decrease because the CI would be wider for a sample of size 50.
   b. The precision of the estimate would increase because the CI would be narrower for a 90% confidence level.

7. **a.** Because the length of a CI is twice the margin of error, the length of the CI is 21.4.
   b. 64.5 to 85.9

8. **a.** 6.58
   b. The sample mean, $\bar{x}$

9. **a.** $z = -0.77$ **b.** $t = -0.605$

10. **a.** Standard normal distribution
    b. t-distribution with 14 degrees of freedom

11. From Property 4 of Key Fact 8.6, as the number of degrees of freedom becomes larger, t-curves look increasingly like the standard normal curve. So the curve that is closer to the standard normal curve has the larger degrees of freedom.

12. **a.** t-interval procedure
    b. z-interval procedure
    c. z-interval procedure
    d. Neither procedure
    e. z-interval procedure
    f. Neither procedure

13. 54.3 to 62.8 yr

14. Part (c) provides the correct interpretation of the statement in quotes.

15. **a.** 11.7 to 12.1 mm
    b. We can be 90% confident that the mean length, μ, of all *N. trivittata* is somewhere between 11.7 and 12.1 mm.
    c. A normal probability plot of the data should fall roughly in a straight line.

16. **a.** 0.2 mm
    b. We can be 90% confident that the error made in estimating μ by $\bar{x}$ is at most 0.2 mm.
    c. $n = 1692$ **d.** 11.9 to 12.1 mm

17. **a.** 2.101 **b.** 1.734
    c. -1.330 **d.** ± 2.878

18. **a.** 81.7 to 90.7 mm Hg
    b. We can be 95% confident that the mean arterial blood pressure for all children of diabetic mothers is somewhere between 81.7 and 90.7 mm Hg.

CHAPTER 9

EXERCISES 9.1

9.1 A hypothesis is a statement that something is true.

9.2 The decision criterion provides an objective method for deciding whether the null hypothesis should be rejected in favor of the alternative hypothesis.

9.3
a. The population mean, μ, equals some specified number, μ_0; H_0: $\mu = \mu_0$
b. Two-tailed: The population mean, μ, differs from μ_0; H_0: $\mu \neq \mu_0$.
Left-tailed: The population mean, μ, is less than μ_0; H_0: $\mu < \mu_0$.
Right-tailed: The population mean, μ, is greater than μ_0; H_0: $\mu > \mu_0$.

9.4
a. H_0: $\mu \neq \mu_0$; two-tailed
b. H_0: $\mu < \mu_0$; left-tailed
c. H_0: $\mu > \mu_0$; right-tailed

9.5 Let μ denote the mean cadmium level in *Boletus pinicola* mushrooms.
a. H_0: $\mu = 0.5$ ppm **b.** H_a: $\mu > 0.5$ ppm
c. Right-tailed test

9.6 Let μ denote the mean body temperature of all healthy humans.
a. H_0: $\mu = 98.6°F$ **b.** H_a: $\mu \neq 98.6°F$
c. Two-tailed test

9.7 Let μ denote last year's mean local monthly bill for cell phone users.
a. H_0: $\mu = \$47.70$ **b.** H_a: $\mu < \$47.70$
c. Left-tailed test

9.8 Let μ denote the mean daily iron intake of all adult females under the age of 51.
a. H_0: $\mu = 18$ mg **b.** H_a: $\mu < 18$ mg
c. Left-tailed test

9.9 Let μ denote the mean annual consumption of beer per person for the nation's capital.
a. H_0: $\mu = 22.0$ gal **b.** H_a: $\mu \neq 22.0$ gal
c. Two-tailed test

9.10 Let μ denote the 1997 mean cost to community hospitals per patient per day in Ohio.
a. H_0: $\mu = \$1033$ **b.** H_a: $\mu > \$1033$
c. Right-tailed test

EXERCISES 9.2

9.14
a. True. Because the significance level, α, is the probability of making a Type I error, it is unlikely that a true null hypothesis will be rejected if the hypothesis test is conducted at a small significance level.
b. True. By Key Fact 9.1, for a fixed sample size, the smaller you specify the significance level, α, the larger will be the probability, β, of not rejecting a false null hypothesis.

9.15 The two types of incorrect decisions are a Type I error (rejection of a true null hypothesis) and a Type II error (nonrejection of a false null hypothesis). The probabilities of these two errors are denoted α and β, respectively.

9.16
a. $z \geq 1.645$ **b.** $z < 1.645$ **c.** $z = 1.645$
d. $\alpha = 0.05$
e.

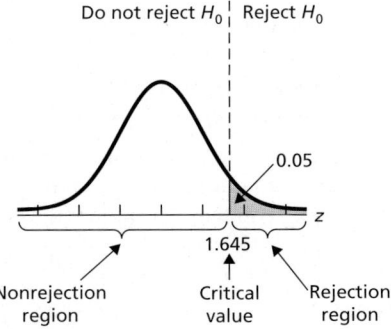

f. Right-tailed test

9.17
a. $z \leq -1.96$ or $z \geq 1.96$
b. $-1.96 < z < 1.96$
c. $z = \pm 1.96$
d. $\alpha = 0.05$

e.

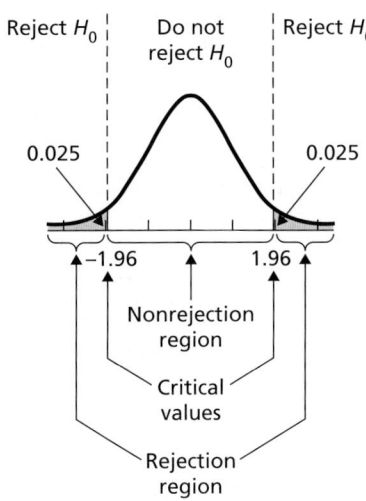

f. Two-tailed test

9.18
a. $z \leq -2.33$ **b.** $z > -2.33$ **c.** $z = -2.33$
d. $\alpha = 0.01$
e.

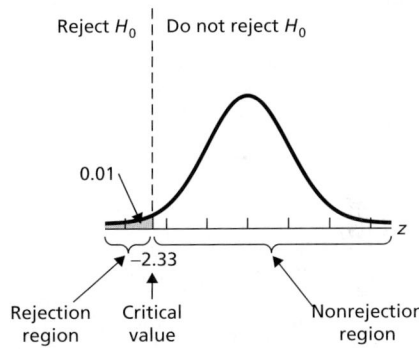

f. Left-tailed test

9.19
a. A Type I error would occur if in fact $\mu = 0.5$ ppm, but the results of the sampling lead to the conclusion that $\mu > 0.5$ ppm.
b. A Type II error would occur if in fact $\mu > 0.5$ ppm, but the results of the sampling fail to lead to that conclusion.
c. A correct decision would occur if in fact $\mu = 0.5$ ppm and the results of the sampling do not lead to the rejection of that fact; or if in fact $\mu > 0.5$ ppm and the results of the sampling lead to that conclusion.
d. Correct decision **e.** Type II error

9.20
a. A Type I error would occur if in fact $\mu = 98.6°F$, but the results of the sampling lead to the conclusion that $\mu \neq 98.6°F$.

b. A Type II error would occur if in fact $\mu \neq 98.6°F$, but the results of the sampling fail to lead to that conclusion.
c. A correct decision would occur if in fact $\mu = 98.6°F$ and the results of the sampling do not lead to the rejection of that fact; or if in fact $\mu \neq 98.6°F$ and the results of the sampling lead to that conclusion.
d. Type I error   **e.** Correct decision

9.21
a. A Type I error would occur if in fact $\mu = \$47.70$, but the results of the sampling lead to the conclusion that $\mu < \$47.70$.
b. A Type II error would occur if in fact $\mu < \$47.70$, but the results of the sampling fail to lead to that conclusion.
c. A correct decision would occur if in fact $\mu = \$47.70$ and the results of the sampling do not lead to the rejection of that fact; or if in fact $\mu < \$47.70$ and the results of the sampling lead to that conclusion.
d. Correct decision   **e.** Type II error

9.22
a. A Type I error would occur if in fact $\mu = 18$ mg, but the results of the sampling lead to the conclusion that $\mu < 18$ mg.
b. A Type II error would occur if in fact $\mu < 18$ mg, but the results of the sampling fail to lead to that conclusion.
c. A correct decision would occur if in fact $\mu = 18$ mg and the results of the sampling do not lead to the rejection of that fact; or if in fact $\mu < 18$ mg and the results of the sampling lead to that conclusion.
d. Type I error   **e.** Correct decision

9.23
a. A Type I error would occur if in fact $\mu = 22.0$ gal, but the results of the sampling lead to the conclusion that $\mu \neq 22.0$ gal.
b. A Type II error would occur if in fact $\mu \neq 22.0$ gal, but the results of the sampling fail to lead to that conclusion.
c. A correct decision would occur if in fact $\mu = 22.0$ gal and the results of the sampling do not lead to the rejection of that fact; or if in fact $\mu \neq 22.0$ gal and the results of the sampling lead to that conclusion.
d. Type I error   **e.** Correct decision

9.24
a. A Type I error would occur if in fact $\mu = \$1033$, but the results of the sampling lead to the conclusion that $\mu > \$1033$.
b. A Type II error would occur if in fact $\mu > \$1033$, but the results of the sampling fail to lead to that conclusion.
c. A correct decision would occur if in fact $\mu = \$1033$ and the results of the sampling do not lead to the rejection of that fact; or if in fact $\mu > \$1033$ and the results of the sampling lead to that conclusion.
d. Correct decision   **e.** Type II error

EXERCISES 9.3

9.31 Critical value: $-z_{0.05} = -1.645$

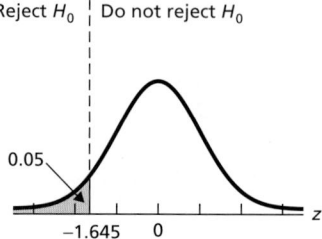

9.32 Critical value: $z_{0.01} = 2.33$

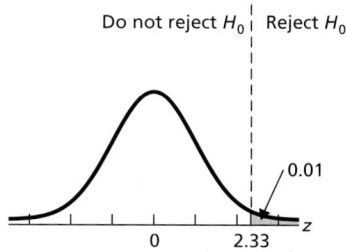

9.33 Critical values: $\pm z_{0.025} = \pm 1.96$

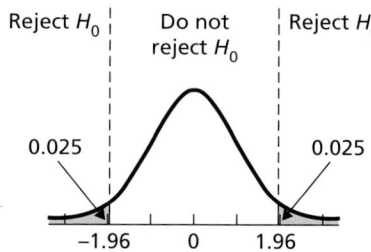

9.34 The presence of outliers calls into question the normality assumption and, even for large samples, outliers can sometimes unduly affect a z-test because the sample mean is not resistant to outliers.

9.35 H_0: $\mu = 0.5$ ppm, H_a: $\mu > 0.5$ ppm; $\alpha = 0.05$; $z = 0.24$; critical value $= 1.645$; do not reject H_0; at the 5% significance level, the data do not provide sufficient evidence to conclude that the mean cadmium level in *Boletus pinicola* mushrooms is greater than the government's recommended limit of 0.5 ppm.

9.36 H_0: $\mu = 98.6°F$, H_a: $\mu \neq 98.6°F$; $\alpha = 0.01$; $z = -7.29$; critical values $= \pm 2.575$; reject H_0; at the 1% significance level, the data provide sufficient evidence to conclude that the mean body temperature of healthy human beings differs from 98.6°F.

9.37 H_0: $\mu = \$47.70$, H_a: $\mu < \$47.70$; $\alpha = 0.01$; $z = -1.78$; critical value $= -2.33$; do not reject H_0; at the 1% significance level, the data do not provide sufficient evidence to conclude that last year's mean local monthly bill for cell phone users has decreased from the 1996 mean of $47.70.

9.38 H_0: $\mu = 18$ mg, H_a: $\mu < 18$ mg; $\alpha = 0.01$; $z = -5.30$; critical value $= -2.33$; reject H_0; at the 1% significance level, the data provide sufficient evidence to conclude that adult females under the age of 51 are, on average, getting less than the RDA of 18 mg of iron.

9.39 H_0: $\mu = 22.0$ gal, H_a: $\mu \neq 22.0$ gal; $\alpha = 0.10$; $z = 1.83$; critical values $= \pm 1.645$; reject H_0; at the 10% significance level, the data provide sufficient evidence to conclude that the mean annual consumption of beer per person for the nation's capital differs from the national mean.

9.40 H_0: $\mu = \$1033$, H_a: $\mu > \$1033$; $\alpha = 0.05$; $z = 1.41$; critical value $= 1.645$; do not reject H_0; at the 5% significance level, the data do not provide sufficient evidence to conclude that, in 1997, the mean cost in Ohio hospitals exceeded the national mean of $1033.

EXERCISES 9.4

9.44 The P-value is the probability of observing a value of the test statistic as extreme or more extreme than that observed if the null hypothesis is true. A small P-value (i.e., close to 0) provides evidence against the null hypothesis.

9.45 The two different approaches to hypothesis testing are the critical-value approach and the P-value approach. For a comparison of the two approaches, see Table 9.11.

9.47 True

9.48
a. Do not reject the null hypothesis.
b. Reject the null hypothesis.
c. Reject the null hypothesis.

9.49 A P-value of 0.02 provides stronger evidence against the null hypothesis because it reflects an observed value of the test statistic that is more inconsistent with the null hypothesis.

9.50
a. Moderate   **b.** Weak or none
c. Strong   **d.** Very strong

9.51
a. 0.0212   **b.** 0.6217

9.52
a. 0.0329   **b.** 0.8944

9.53
a. 0.0020   **b.** 0.0156

9.54
a. 0.1075   **b.** 0.7549

9.55 H_0: $\mu = 0.5$ ppm, H_a: $\mu > 0.5$ ppm; $\alpha = 0.05$; $z = 0.24$; $P = 0.4052$; do not reject H_0; at the 5% significance level, the data do not provide sufficient evidence to conclude that the mean cadmium level in *Boletus pinicola* mushrooms is greater than the government's recommended limit of 0.5 ppm. The evidence against the null hypothesis is weak or none.

9.56 H_0: $\mu = 98.6°$F, H_a: $\mu \neq 98.6°$F; $\alpha = 0.01$; $z = -7.29$; $P = 0.0000$ (to four decimal places); reject H_0; at the 1% significance level, the data provide sufficient evidence to conclude that the mean body temperature of healthy humans differs from 98.6°F. The evidence against the null hypothesis is very strong.

9.57 H_0: $\mu = \$47.70$, H_a: $\mu < \$47.70$; $\alpha = 0.01$; $z = -1.78$; $P = 0.0375$; do not reject H_0; at the 1% significance level, the data do not provide sufficient evidence to conclude that last year's mean local monthly bill for cell phone users has decreased from the 1996 mean of $47.70. The evidence against the null hypothesis is strong.

9.58 H_0: $\mu = 18$ mg, H_a: $\mu < 18$ mg; $\alpha = 0.01$; $z = -5.30$; $P = 0.0000$ (to four decimal places); reject H_0; at the 1% significance level, the data provide sufficient evidence to conclude that adult females under the age of 51 are, on average, getting less than the RDA of 18 mg of iron. The evidence against the null hypothesis is very strong.

9.59 H_0: $\mu = 22.0$ gal, H_a: $\mu \neq 22.0$ gal; $\alpha = 0.10$; $z = 1.83$; $P = 0.0672$; reject H_0; at the 10% significance level, the data provide sufficient evidence to conclude that the mean annual consumption of beer per person for the nation's capital differs from the national mean. The evidence against the null hypothesis is moderate.

9.60 H_0: $\mu = \$1033$, H_a: $\mu > \$1033$; $\alpha = 0.05$; $z = 1.41$; $P = 0.0793$; do not reject H_0; at the 5% significance level, the data do not provide sufficient evidence to conclude that, in 1997, the mean cost in Ohio hospitals exceeded the national mean of $1033. The evidence against the null hypothesis is moderate.

EXERCISES 9.5

9.68 σ-unknown versus σ-known

9.69 H_0: $\mu = \$1729$, H_a: $\mu \neq \$1729$; $\alpha = 0.05$; $t = -1.056$; critical values $= \pm 2.030$; $P > 0.20$; do not reject H_0; at the 5% significance level, the data do not provide sufficient evidence to conclude that the 1997 mean annual expenditure on apparel and services for consumer units in the Midwest differed from the national mean of $1729.

9.70 H_0: $\mu = 80$ mm Hg, H_a: $\mu > 80$ mm Hg; $\alpha = 0.10$; $t = 1.089$; critical value $= 1.303$; $P > 0.10$; do not reject H_0; at the 10% significance level, the data do not provide sufficient evidence to conclude that the mean diastolic blood pressure of bus drivers in Stockholm, Sweden exceeds the normal diastolic blood pressure of 80 mm Hg.

9.71 $H_0: \mu = 2.30\%$, $H_a: \mu > 2.30\%$; $\alpha = 0.01$; $t = 4.251$; critical value $= 2.821$; $P < 0.005$; reject H_0; at the 1% significance level, the data provide sufficient evidence to conclude that the mean available limestone in soil treated with 100% MMBL effluent exceeds 2.30%.

9.72 $H_0: \mu = 463$ min, $H_a: \mu < 463$ min; $\alpha = 0.01$; $t = -3.408$; critical value $= -2.426$; $P < 0.005$; reject H_0; at the 1% significance level, the data provide sufficient evidence to conclude that, during the time slot from 8:00 P.M. to 11:00 P.M., women in the age group 18–24 years watched less TV, on average, than people in general.

9.73 $H_0: \mu = 51.0¢/\text{lb}$, $H_a: \mu \neq 51.0¢/\text{lb}$; $\alpha = 0.05$; $t = 2.655$; critical values $= \pm 2.145$; $0.01 < P < 0.02$; reject H_0; at the 5% significance level, the data provide sufficient evidence to conclude that the current mean retail price for bananas is different from the 1998 mean of 51.0 cents per pound.

9.74 $H_0: \mu = \$2528$, $H_a: \mu < \$2528$; $\alpha = 0.05$; $t = -0.886$; critical value $= -1.653$; $P > 0.10$; do not reject H_0; at the 5% significance level, the data do not provide sufficient evidence to conclude that, on average, AML reduces the cost of having a baby in a U.S. hospital.

9.75 z-test

9.76 z-test

9.77 t-test

9.78 Neither

9.79 Neither

9.80 Neither

9.81 Neither

9.82 Neither

REVIEW TEST FOR CHAPTER 9

1. a. The null hypothesis is a hypothesis to be tested.
  b. The alternative hypothesis is a hypothesis to be considered as an alternate to the null hypothesis.
  c. The test statistic is the statistic used as a basis for deciding whether the null hypothesis should be rejected.
  d. The rejection region is the set of values for the test statistic that leads to rejection of the null hypothesis.
  e. The nonrejection region is the set of values for the test statistic that leads to nonrejection of the null hypothesis.
  f. The critical values are the values of the test statistic that separate the rejection and nonrejection regions. The critical values are considered part of the rejection region.

2. a. The weight of a package of Tide is a variable. A particular package may weigh slightly more or less than the marked weight. The mean weight of all packages produced on any specified day (the population mean weight for that day) exceeds the marked weight.
  b. The null hypothesis would be that the population mean weight for a specified day equals the marked weight; the alternative hypothesis would be that the population mean weight for the specified day exceeds the marked weight.
  c. The null hypothesis would be that the population mean weight for a specified day equals the marked weight of 76 oz; the alternative hypothesis would be that the population mean weight for the specified day exceeds the marked weight of 76 oz. In statistical terminology, the hypothesis test would be $H_0: \mu = 76$ oz and $H_a: \mu > 76$ oz, where μ is the mean weight of all packages produced on the specified day.

3. a. Obtain the data from a random sample of the population or from a designed experiment. If the data are consistent with the null hypothesis, do not reject the null hypothesis; if the data are inconsistent with the null hypothesis, reject the null hypothesis and conclude that the alternative hypothesis is true.
  b. We establish a precise criterion for deciding whether to reject the null hypothesis prior to obtaining the data.

4. Two-tailed test, $H_a: \mu \neq \mu_0$. Used when the primary concern is deciding whether a population mean, μ, is different from a specified value μ_0.

Left-tailed test, $H_a: \mu < \mu_0$. Used when the primary concern is deciding whether a population mean, μ, is less than a specified value μ_0.

Right-tailed test, $H_a: \mu > \mu_0$. Used when the primary concern is deciding whether a population mean, μ, is greater than a specified value μ_0.

5. a. A Type I error is the incorrect decision of rejecting a true null hypothesis. A Type II error is the incorrect decision of not rejecting a false null hypothesis.
  b. α and β, respectively
  c. A Type I error
  d. A Type II error

6. It must be chosen so that, if the null hypothesis is true, the probability equals 0.05 that the test statistic will fall in the rejection region, in this case, to the right of the critical value.

7. a. Assumptions: normal population or large sample; σ unknown. Test statistic: $t = (\bar{x} - \mu_0)/(s/\sqrt{n})$.
  b. Assumptions: normal population or large sample; σ known. Test statistic: $z = (\bar{x} - \mu_0)/(\sigma/\sqrt{n})$.

8. a. The true significance level equals α.
  b. The true significance level only approximately equals α.

9. The results of a hypothesis test are statistically significant if the null hypothesis is rejected at the specified significance level. Statistical significance means that the data provide sufficient evidence to conclude that the truth is different from the stated null hypothesis. It does not necessarily mean that the difference is important in any practical sense.

10. It increases.

11. a. The P-value is the probability, calculated under the assumption that the null hypothesis is true, of observing a value of the test statistic as extreme or more extreme than that observed. By *extreme* we mean "far from what we would expect to observe if the null hypothesis is true."
  b. True   **c.** True
  d. Because it is the smallest significance level for which the observed sample data result in rejection of the null hypothesis.

13. Let μ denote last year's mean cheese consumption by Americans.
  a. H_0: $\mu = 28.0$ lb   **b.** H_a: $\mu > 28.0$ lb
  c. Right-tailed

14. a. $z \geq 1.28$ **b.** $z < 1.28$
  c. $z = 1.28$ **d.** $\alpha = 0.10$
  e.

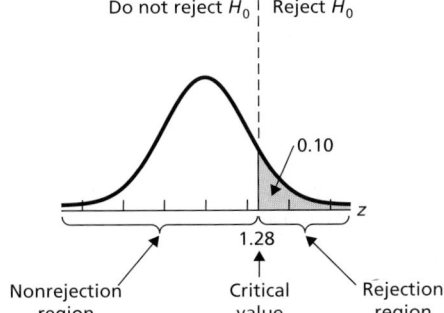

  f. Right-tailed

15. a. A Type I error would occur if in fact $\mu = 28.0$ lb, but the results of the sampling lead to the conclusion that $\mu > 28.0$ lb.
  b. A Type II error would occur if in fact $\mu > 28.0$ lb, but the results of the sampling fail to lead to that conclusion.
  c. A correct decision would occur if in fact $\mu = 28.0$ lb and the results of the sampling do not lead to the rejection of that fact; or if in fact $\mu > 28.0$ lb and the results of the sampling lead to that conclusion.

  d. Correct decision   **e.** Type II error

16. a. H_0: $\mu = 28.0$ lb, H_a: $\mu > 28.0$ lb; $\alpha = 0.10$; $z = 0.69$; critical value $= 1.28$; do not reject H_0; at the 10% significance level, the data do not provide sufficient evidence to conclude that last year's mean cheese consumption for all Americans has increased over the 1997 mean of 28.0 lb.
  b. A Type II error because, given that the null hypothesis was not rejected, the only error that could be made is the error of not rejecting a false null hypothesis.

17. a. H_0: $\mu = 28.0$ lb, H_a: $\mu > 28.0$ lb; $\alpha = 0.10$; $z = 0.69$; $P = 0.2451$; do not reject H_0; at the 10% significance level, the data do not provide sufficient evidence to conclude that last year's mean cheese consumption for all Americans has increased over the 1997 mean of 28.0 lb.
  b. The data provide at most weak evidence against the null hypothesis.

18. H_0: $\mu = \$362$, H_a: $\mu < \$362$; $\alpha = 0.05$; $t = -1.909$; critical value $= -1.796$; $0.025 < P < 0.05$; reject H_0; at the 5% significance level, the data provide sufficient evidence to conclude that last year's mean value lost to purse snatching has decreased from the 1998 mean of \$362.

19. a. 0 points
  b. H_0: $\mu = 0$ points, H_a: $\mu \neq 0$ points; $\alpha = 0.05$; $t = -0.843$; critical values $= \pm 1.96$; $P > 0.20$; do not reject H_0.
  c. At the 5% significance level, the data do not provide sufficient evidence to conclude that the population mean point-spread error differs from 0. In fact, because $P > 0.20$, there is virtually no evidence against the null hypothesis that the population mean point-spread error equals 0.

20. It is probably okay to use the z-test because the sample size is large and σ is known. However, it does appear from the normal probability plot that there may be outliers, so one should proceed cautiously in using the z-test.

21. It appears that the variable under consideration is far from being normally distributed and, in fact, has a left-skewed distribution. However, the sample size is large and the plots reveal no outliers. Keeping in mind that σ is unknown, it is probably reasonable to use the t-test.

CHAPTER 10

EXERCISES 10.1

10.1
a. Age
b. Population 1 consists of buyers of new domestic cars; Population 2 consists of buyers of new imported cars.
c. Let μ_1 and μ_2 denote the mean ages of buyers of new domestic cars and new imported cars, respectively. The null and alternative hypotheses are H_0: $\mu_1 = \mu_2$ and H_a: $\mu_1 > \mu_2$, respectively.

10.2
a. amount spent (at the shopping mall)
b. Population 1 consists of teens who go to some shopping mall; Population 2 consists of adults who go to some shopping mall.
c. Let μ_1 and μ_2 denote the mean amounts spent at the shopping mall by teens and adults, respectively. The null and alternative hypotheses are H_0: $\mu_1 = \mu_2$ and H_a: $\mu_1 < \mu_2$, respectively.

10.3 Answers will vary.

10.4 *Independent samples* means that the sample selected from one of the populations has no effect or bearing on the sample selected from the other population.

10.5
a. μ_1, σ_1, μ_2, and σ_2 are parameters; $\bar{x}_1, s_1, \bar{x}_2$, and s_2 are statistics.
b. μ_1, σ_1, μ_2, and σ_2 are fixed numbers; $\bar{x}_1, s_1, \bar{x}_2$, and s_2 are variables.

10.6 For a two-tailed test, the basic strategy is as follows: (1) independently and randomly take samples from the two populations under consideration; (2) compute the sample means, $\bar{x}_1$ and $\bar{x}_2$; and (3) reject the null hypothesis if the sample means differ by too much—otherwise, do not reject the null hypothesis. The process is the same for a one-tailed test except that, for a left-tailed test, the null hypothesis is rejected only when $\bar{x}_1$ is too much smaller than $\bar{x}_2$, and, for a right-tailed test, the null hypothesis is rejected only when $\bar{x}_1$ is too much larger than $\bar{x}_2$.

10.7 So that you can determine whether the observed difference between the two sample means can be reasonably attributed to sampling error or whether that difference suggests that the null hypothesis of equal population means is false and the alternative hypothesis is true.

10.8 The assumption that the population standard deviations, σ_1 and σ_2, are known.

10.9
a. 0 and 5   b. No.   c. No.

10.10
a. 0 and 5   b. Yes, by Key Fact 10.1.
c. 95.44%

EXERCISES 10.2

10.16
a. Independent samples, normal populations or large samples, and equal population standard deviations
b. Independent samples is an essential assumption. Moderate violations of the normality assumption are permissible even for small or moderate size samples. Moderate violations of the equal standard deviations requirement are not serious provided the two sample sizes are roughly equal.

10.17 Because it is obtained by combining (pooling) information on variation from the individual samples into one estimate of the common population standard deviation.

10.18 No. One sample standard deviation is more than twice the other—a good indication that the two population standard deviations are not equal—and the two sample sizes are not roughly equal.

10.19 H_0: $\mu_1 = \mu_2$, H_a: $\mu_1 < \mu_2$; $\alpha = 0.05$; $t = -4.058$; critical value $= -1.734$; $P < 0.005$; reject H_0; at the 5% significance level, the data provide sufficient evidence to conclude that the mean time served for fraud is less than that for firearms offenses.

10.20 H_0: $\mu_1 = \mu_2$, H_a: $\mu_1 < \mu_2$; $\alpha = 0.01$; $t = -1.615$; critical value $= -2.392$; $0.05 < P < 0.10$; do not reject H_0; at the 1% significance level, the data do not provide sufficient evidence to conclude that, on average, males have a better sense of direction and, in particular, a better frame of reference than females.

10.21 H_0: $\mu_1 = \mu_2$, H_a: $\mu_1 > \mu_2$; $\alpha = 0.05$; $t = 1.186$; critical value $= 1.714$; $P > 0.10$; do not reject H_0; at the 5% significance level, the data do not provide sufficient evidence to conclude that males in the age group 25–34 years are, on average, taller than those in the age group 45–54 years.

10.22 H_0: $\mu_1 = \mu_2$, H_a: $\mu_1 \neq \mu_2$; $\alpha = 0.05$; $t = -0.927$; critical values $= \pm 2.052$; $P > 0.20$; do not reject H_0; at the 5% significance level, the data do not provide sufficient evidence to conclude that a difference exists in last year's mean VMT for midwestern and southern households.

10.23 H_0: $\mu_1 = \mu_2$, H_a: $\mu_1 \neq \mu_2$; $\alpha = 0.01$; $t = -2.935$; critical values $= \pm 2.625$; $P < 0.01$; reject H_0; at the 1% significance level, the data provide sufficient evidence to conclude that the mean daily protein intakes of female vegetarians and female omnivores differ.

10.24 $H_0: \mu_1 = \mu_2$, $H_a: \mu_1 > \mu_2$; $\alpha = 0.01$; $t = 4.551$; critical value = 2.348; $P < 0.005$; reject H_0; at the 1% significance level, the data provide sufficient evidence to conclude that the mean systolic blood pressure of ODM children exceeds that of ONM children.

10.25
a. −0.72 to 3.94 inches
b. We can be 90% confident that the difference between the mean height of males in the age group 25–34 years and the mean height of males in the age group 45–54 years is somewhere between −0.72 and 3.94 inches.

10.26
a. −4.69 to 1.77 thousand miles
b. We can be 95% confident that the difference between last year's mean VMTs by midwestern and southern households is somewhere between −4.69 and 1.77 thousand miles.

10.27
a. −20.61 to −1.15 grams
b. We can be 99% confident that the difference between the mean daily protein intakes of female vegetarians and female omnivores is somewhere between −20.61 and −1.15 g.

10.28
a. 3.87 to 12.13 mm Hg
b. We can be 98% confident that the difference between the mean systolic blood pressures of ODM and ONM children is somewhere between 3.87 and 12.13 mm Hg.

EXERCISES 10.3

10.37 The sample standard deviations are 84.7 minutes and 38.2 minutes. These two sample standard deviations provide a fairly clear indication that the two population standard deviations are not equal and thus that the nonpooled *t*-test is more appropriate than the pooled *t*-test.

10.38
a. Pooled *t*-test   **b.** Nonpooled *t*-test
c. Pooled *t*-test   **d.** Nonpooled *t*-test

10.39 The pooled *t*-test requires equal population standard deviations, whereas the nonpooled *t*-test does not.

10.41 $H_0: \mu_1 = \mu_2$, $H_a: \mu_1 \neq \mu_2$; $\alpha = 0.10$; $t = 1.791$; critical values = ±1.677; $0.05 < P < 0.10$; reject H_0; at the 10% significance level, the data provide sufficient evidence to conclude that a difference exists in the mean age at arrest of East German prisoners with chronic PTSD and remitted PTSD.

10.42 $H_0: \mu_1 = \mu_2$, $H_a: \mu_1 > \mu_2$; $\alpha = 0.01$; $t = 7.982$; critical value = 2.397; $P < 0.005$; reject H_0; at the 1% significance level, the data provide sufficient evidence to conclude that the mean sediment ammonium concentration in CCB exceeds that in LLM.

10.43 $H_0: \mu_1 = \mu_2$, $H_a: \mu_1 < \mu_2$; $\alpha = 0.05$; $t = -1.651$; critical value = −2.015; $0.05 < P < 0.10$; do not reject H_0; at the 5% significance level, the data do not provide sufficient evidence to conclude that the mean number of acute postoperative days in the hospital is smaller with the dynamic system than with the static system.

10.44
a. $H_0: \mu_1 = \mu_2$, $H_a: \mu_1 < \mu_2$; $\alpha = 0.05$; $t = 0.460$; critical value = −1.708; $P > 0.10$; do not reject H_0; at the 5% significance level, the data do not provide sufficient evidence to conclude that the intervention program reduces mean heart rate of urban bus drivers in Stockholm.
b. The fact that the mean heart rate for Intervention exceeded that for Control might be due to the fact that the intervention drivers were stressed because of the new environment.
c. Designed experiment

10.45 $H_0: \mu_1 = \mu_2$, $H_a: \mu_1 > \mu_2$; $\alpha = 0.01$; $t = 3.863$; critical value = 2.552; $P < 0.005$; reject H_0; at the 1% significance level, the data provide sufficient evidence to conclude that dopamine activity is higher, on average, in psychotic patients.

10.46 $H_0: \mu_1 = \mu_2$, $H_a: \mu_1 < \mu_2$; $\alpha = 0.01$; $t = -3.952$; critical value = −2.386; $P < 0.005$; reject H_0; at the 1% significance level, the data provide sufficient evidence to conclude that Nevada has a larger mean potato yield than Idaho.

10.47
a. 0.2 to 7.2 years
b. We can be 90% confident that the difference between the mean ages at arrest of East German prisoners with chronic PTSD and remitted PTSD is somewhere between 0.2 and 7.2 yr.

10.48
a. 63.5 to 118.1 micromoles
b. We can be 98% confident that the difference between the mean sediment ammonium concentrations in CCB and LLM is somewhere between 63.5 and 118.1 micromoles.

10.49
a. −6.97 to 0.69 days
b. We can be 90% confident that the difference between the mean number of acute postoperative days in the hospital with the dynamic and static systems is somewhere between −6.97 and 0.69 days.

10.50
a. −2.96 to 5.15 beats per minute
b. We can be 90% confident that the difference between the mean heart rates of urban bus drivers in Stockholm in the two environments is somewhere between −2.96 and 5.15 beats per minute.

EXERCISES 10.4

10.57 Each pair in a paired sample consists of a member of one population and that member's corresponding member in the other population.

10.58 By using a paired sample, extraneous sources of variation can be removed. The sampling error thus made in estimating the difference between the population means will generally be smaller. As a result, detecting differences between the population means is more likely when such differences exist.

10.59
a. Age   b. Married men and married women
c. Married couples
d. The difference between the ages of a married couple

10.60
a. TV viewing time
b. Married men and married women
c. Married couples
d. The difference between the TV viewing times of a married couple

10.61 Paired sample, and normal differences or large sample. The paired-sample assumption is essential. Moderate violations of the normal-differences assumption are permissible even for small or moderate size samples.

10.62 Answers will vary.

10.63
a. Height (of Zea mays)
b. Cross-fertilized Zea mays and self-fertilized Zea mays
c. The difference between the heights of a cross-fertilized Zea may and a self-fertilized Zea may grown in the same pot
d. Yes. Because each number is the difference between the heights of a cross-fertilized Zea may and a self-fertilized Zea may grown in the same pot.
e. H_0: $\mu_1 = \mu_2$, H_a: $\mu_1 \neq \mu_2$; $\alpha = 0.05$; $t = 2.148$; critical values = ± 2.145; $0.02 < P < 0.05$; reject H_0; at the 5% significance level, the data provide sufficient evidence to conclude that the mean heights of cross-fertilized and self-fertilized Zea mays differ.
f. H_0: $\mu_1 = \mu_2$, H_a: $\mu_1 \neq \mu_2$; $\alpha = 0.01$; $t = 2.148$; critical values = ± 2.977; $0.02 < P < 0.05$; do not reject H_0; at the 1% significance level, the data do not provide sufficient evidence to conclude that the mean heights of cross-fertilized and self-fertilized Zea mays differ.

10.64
a. Sleep time
b. All people when laevohysocyamine hydrobromide is used and all people when laevohysocyamine hydrobromide is not used
c. The difference between the sleep time of a person with and without the use of laevohysocyamine hydrobromide

d. Yes. Because each number is the difference between the sleep time of a person with and without the use of laevohysocyamine hydrobromide.
e. H_0: $\mu_1 = \mu_2$, H_a: $\mu_1 > \mu_2$; $\alpha = 0.05$; $t = 3.680$; critical value = 1.833; $P < 0.005$; reject H_0; at the 5% significance level, the data provide sufficient evidence to conclude that laevohysocyamine hydrobromide is effective in increasing sleep.
f. H_0: $\mu_1 = \mu_2$, H_a: $\mu_1 > \mu_2$; $\alpha = 0.01$; $t = 3.680$; critical value = 2.821; $P < 0.005$; reject H_0; at the 1% significance level, the data provide sufficient evidence to conclude that laevohysocyamine hydrobromide is effective in increasing sleep.

10.65 H_0: $\mu_1 = \mu_2$, H_a: $\mu_1 < \mu_2$; $\alpha = 0.05$; $t = -4.185$; critical value = -1.746; $P < 0.005$; reject H_0; at the 5% significance level, the data provide sufficient evidence to conclude that family therapy is effective in helping anorexic young women gain weight.

10.66 H_0: $\mu_1 = \mu_2$, H_a: $\mu_1 \neq \mu_2$; $\alpha = 0.05$; $t = 3.866$; critical values = ± 2.228; $P < 0.01$; reject H_0; at the 5% significance level, the data provide sufficient evidence to conclude that, on average, the two measurement methods give different results.

10.67 H_0: $\mu_1 = \mu_2$, H_a: $\mu_1 > \mu_2$; $\alpha = 0.10$; $t = 1.053$; critical value = 1.415; $P > 0.10$; do not reject H_0; at the 10% significance level, the data do not provide sufficient evidence to conclude that mean corneal thickness is greater in normal eyes than in eyes with glaucoma.

10.68 H_0: $\mu_1 = \mu_2$, H_a: $\mu_1 < \mu_2$; $\alpha = 0.01$; $t = -2.416$; critical value = -2.539; $0.01 < P < 0.025$; do not reject H_0; at the 1% significance level, the data do not provide sufficient evidence to conclude that married men watch less TV, on average, than married women.

10.69
a. 0.03 to 41.84 eighths of an inch
b. -8.08 to 49.94 eighths of an inch

10.70
a. 1.17 to 3.49 hr
b. 0.54 to 4.12 hr

10.71 -10.30 to -4.23 lb. We can be 90% confident that the weight gain that would be obtained, on average, by using the family therapy treatment is somewhere between 4.23 and 10.30 lb.

10.72 1.59 to 5.92 thousand miles. We can be 95% confident that the mean difference in measurement by the weight and groove methods is somewhere between 1.59 and 5.92 thousand miles.

REVIEW TEST FOR CHAPTER 10

1. Independently and randomly take samples from the two populations; compute the two sample means; compare the two sample means; and make the decision.

2. Randomly take a paired sample from the two populations; calculate the paired differences of the sample pairs; compute the mean of the sample of paired differences; compare that sample mean to 0; and make the decision.

3. **a.** The pooled t-test requires equal population standard deviations, whereas the nonpooled t-test does not.
   b. It is essential that the assumption of independence be satisfied.
   c. For very small sample sizes, the normality assumption is essential for both t-procedures. However, for larger samples, the normality assumption is less important.
   d. Population standard deviations

4. By using a paired sample, extraneous sources of variation can be removed. As a consequence, the sampling error made in estimating the difference between the population means will generally be smaller. This fact, in turn, makes it more likely that differences between the population means will be detected when such differences exist.

5. **a.** $H_0: \mu_1 = \mu_2$, $H_a: \mu_1 > \mu_2$; $\alpha = 0.05$; $t = 1.538$; critical value $= 1.708$; $0.05 < P < 0.10$; do not reject H_0; at the 5% significance level, the data do not provide sufficient evidence to conclude that the mean right-leg strength of males exceeds that of females.
   b. $0.05 < P < 0.10$; the evidence against the null hypothesis is moderate.

6. -31.3 to 599.3 newtons (N). We can be 90% confident that the difference between the mean right-leg strengths of males and females is somewhere between -31.3 and 599.3 N.

7. $H_0: \mu_1 = \mu_2$, $H_a: \mu_1 < \mu_2$; $\alpha = 0.01$; $t = -4.118$; critical value $= -2.385$; $P < 0.005$; reject H_0; at the 1% significance level, the data provide sufficient evidence to conclude that, on average, the number of young per litter of cottonmouths in Florida is less than that in Virginia.

8. -3.4 to -0.9 young per litter. We can be 98% confident that the difference between the mean litter sizes of cottonmouths in Florida and Virginia is somewhere between -3.4 and -0.9. With 98% confidence, we can say that, on average, cottonmouths in Virginia have somewhere between 0.9 and 3.4 more young per litter than those in Florida.

9. $H_0: \mu_1 = \mu_2$, $H_a: \mu_1 \neq \mu_2$; $\alpha = 0.10$; $t = -1.766$; critical values $= \pm 1.833$; $0.10 < P < 0.20$; do not reject H_0; at the 10% significance level, the data do not provide sufficient evidence to conclude that there is a difference in effectiveness of the two speed-reading programs.

10. -81.5 to 1.5 words per minute
11. paired t-test
12. nonpooled t-test
13. none that we have studied
14. nonpooled t-test
15. none that we have studied
16. none that we have studied

CHAPTER 11

EXERCISES 11.1

11.1 Answers will vary.

11.2 Generally, the population under consideration is large, and determining the population proportion by taking a census is therefore usually impractical and often impossible.

11.3 A population proportion is a parameter because it is a descriptive measure for a population. A sample proportion is a statistic because it is a descriptive measure for a sample.

11.4
a. The proportion (percentage) of the entire population that has the specified attribute.
b. p
c. The proportion (percentage) of a sample from the population that has the specified attribute.
d. $\hat{p}$
e. The number of members in the sample that have the specified attribute; x
f. The number of members in the sample that do not have the specified attribute
g. The sample proportion equals the number of successes divided by the sample size, that is, $\hat{p} = x/n$.

11.5
a. $p = 0.4$

b.

Sample	No. of females x	Sample proportion $\hat{p}$
J, G	1	0.5
J, P	0	0.0
J, C	0	0.0
J, F	1	0.5
G, P	1	0.5
G, C	1	0.5
G, F	2	1.0
P, C	0	0.0
P, F	1	0.5
C, F	1	0.5

c.

d. 0.4

e. They are the same because the mean of the variable $\hat{p}$ equals the population proportion; in symbols, $\mu_{\hat{p}} = p$.

11.6
b.

Sample	No. of females x	Sample proportion $\hat{p}$
J	0	0.0
P	0	0.0
C	0	0.0
G	1	1.0
F	1	1.0

c.

d. 0.4

e. They are the same because the mean of the variable $\hat{p}$ equals the population proportion; in symbols, $\mu_{\hat{p}} = p$.

11.7
b.

Sample	No. of females x	Sample proportion $\hat{p}$
J, P, C	0	0.00
J, P, G	1	0.33
J, P, F	1	0.33
J, C, G	1	0.33
J, C, F	1	0.33
J, G, F	2	0.67
P, C, G	1	0.33
P, C, F	1	0.33
P, G, F	2	0.67
C, G, F	2	0.67

c.

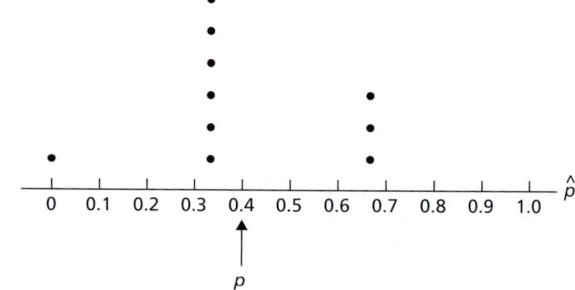

d. 0.4

e. They are the same because the mean of the variable $\hat{p}$ equals the population proportion; in symbols, $\mu_{\hat{p}} = p$.

11.8
b.

Sample	No. of females x	Sample proportion $\hat{p}$
J, P, C, G	1	0.25
J, P, C, F	1	0.25
J, P, G, F	2	0.50
J, C, G, F	2	0.50
P, C, G, F	2	0.50

c.

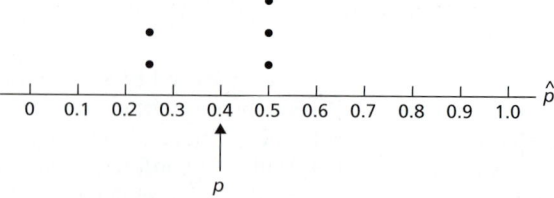

d. 0.4

e. They are the same because the mean of the variable $\hat{p}$ equals the population proportion; in symbols, $\mu_{\hat{p}} = p$.

11.9
b.

Sample	No. of females x	Sample proportion $\hat{p}$
J, P, C, G, F	2	0.4

c.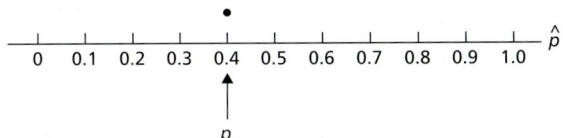

d. 0.4
e. They are the same because the mean of the variable $\hat{p}$ equals the population proportion; in symbols, $\mu_{\hat{p}} = p$.

11.10 Sampling error tends to be smaller for large samples than for small samples.

11.11
a. The No. 1 draft picks in the NBA since 1966.
b. Being a center
c. Population proportion. It is the proportion of the population of No. 1 draft picks in the NBA since 1996 who are centers.

11.12
a. All women in the United States between the ages of 25 and 55 in 1997.
b. Being married
c. The proportion 0.65 is a population proportion if it was obtained from a census of all women in the United States between the ages of 25 and 55 in 1997. It is a sample proportion if it was obtained from a sample of women in the United States between the ages of 25 and 55 in 1997.

11.13
a. 0.00718   b. Smaller

11.14
a. 0.0215   b. Larger

11.15
a. 0.4   b. 0.5   c. 0.7
d. 0.2   e. 0.5   f. 0.5
g. (a) $0.4 < \hat{p} < 0.6$ (b) None (c) $0.3 < \hat{p} < 0.7$
(d) $0.2 < \hat{p} < 0.8$ (e) None (f) None

11.16
a. 0.0528 to 0.0992
b. We can be 95% confident that the proportion of all U.S. asthmatics who are allergic to sulfites is somewhere between 0.0528 and 0.0992.

11.17
a. 0.626 to 0.674

b. We can be 95% confident that the percentage of Americans who drink beer, wine, or hard liquor, at least occasionally, is somewhere between 62.6% and 67.4%.

11.18
a. 76.7% to 83.3%
b. We can be 99% confident that the percentage of all registered voters who favor the creation of standards on CAFO pollution and, in general, view CAFOs unfavorably is somewhere between 76.7% and 83.3%.

11.19
a. 24.0% to 39.8%
b. We can be 90% confident that the percentage of Malaysians infected with the Nipah virus who will die from encephalitis is somewhere between 24.0% and 39.8%.

11.20 Yes! Procedure 11.1 was applied without checking the assumptions for its use; namely, that the number of successes, x, and the number of failures, $n - x$, are both 5 or greater. Because the number of failures here is only 4, Procedure 11.1 should not have been used.

11.21 Not very well! Procedure 11.1 was applied without checking the assumptions for its use; namely, that the number of successes, x, and the number of failures, $n - x$, are both 5 or greater. Because the number of successes here is $0.008 \cdot 500 = 4$, Procedure 11.1 should not have been used.

11.22 74.9% to 81.1%

11.23 54.0% to 60.0%

11.24
a. 0.0232   b. 9604   c. 0.0659 to 0.0761
d. 0.0051, which is less than 0.01
e. 3458; 0.0624 to 0.0796; 0.0086, which is less than 0.01
f. By using the guess for $\hat{p}$ in part (e), the required sample size is reduced by 6146. Moreover, only 0.35% of precision is lost—the margin of error rises from 0.0051 to 0.0086.

11.25
a. 0.024   b. 2401   c. 0.611 to 0.649
d. 0.019, which is less than 0.02
e. 2305; 0.610 to 0.650; 0.02
f. By using the guess for $\hat{p}$ in part (e), the required sample size is reduced by 96. Moreover, only 0.1% of precision is lost—the margin of error rises from 0.019 to 0.020.

11.26
a. 3.3% (i.e., 3.3 percentage points)   b. 7368
c. 0.811 to 0.833
d. 0.011, which is less than 0.015 (1.5%)
e. 5526; 0.809 to 0.835; 0.013, which is less than 0.015 (1.5%)
f. By using the guess for $\hat{p}$ in part (e), the required sample size is reduced by 1842. Moreover, only 0.2% of precision is lost—the margin of error rises from 0.011 to 0.013.

11.27
a. 7.9% (i.e., 7.9 percentage points)   b. 271
c. 0.243 to 0.333

d. 0.045, which is less than 0.05 (5%)
e. 260; 0.242 to 0.334; 0.046, which is less than 0.05 (5%)
f. By using the guess for $\hat{p}$ in part (e), the required sample size is reduced by 11. Moreover, only 0.1% of precision is lost—the margin of error rises from 0.045 to 0.046.

11.28
a. 9604 **b.** 1791
c. By using the guess for $\hat{p}$ in part (b), the required sample size is reduced by 7813.
d. If the observed value of $\hat{p}$ turns out to be larger than 0.049 (but smaller than 0.951), the achieved margin of error will exceed the specified 0.01.

11.29 Yes. Because the two confidence intervals, 53.1% to 62.9% and 49.6% to 58.4%, overlap.

EXERCISES 11.2

11.36 The one-sample z-test for a population mean. Because proportions can be regarded as means. Indeed, define the variable y to equal 1 or 0 according to whether a member of the population has or does not have the specified attribute. Then $p = \mu_y$ and $\hat{p} = \bar{y}$.

11.37
a. 0.54
b. H_0: $p = 0.5$, H_a: $p > 0.5$; $\alpha = 0.05$; $z = 2.33$; critical value $= 1.645$; $P = 0.0099$; reject H_0; at the 5% significance level, the data provide sufficient evidence to conclude that a majority of Generation Y Web users use the Internet to download music.

11.38
a. 0.520
b. H_0: $p = 0.5$, H_a: $p > 0.5$; $\alpha = 0.05$; $z = 1.09$; critical value $= 1.645$; $P = 0.1379$; do not reject H_0; at the 5% significance level, the data do not provide sufficient evidence to conclude that a majority of Arizona families who celebrate Christmas wait until Christmas Day to open their presents.

11.39 H_0: $p = 0.128$, H_a: $p \neq 0.128$; $\alpha = 0.10$; $z = -1.52$; critical values $= \pm 1.645$; $P = 0.1286$; do not reject H_0; at the 10% significance level, the data do not provide sufficient evidence to conclude that the percentage of 18–25-year-olds who currently use marijuana or hashish has changed from the 1997 percentage of 12.8%.

11.40 H_0: $p = 0.103$, H_a: $p < 0.103$; $\alpha = 0.01$; $z = -4.97$; critical value $= -2.33$; $P = 0.0000$ (to four decimal places); reject H_0; at the 1% significance level, the data provide sufficient evidence to conclude that, in 1997, the percentage of families that earned incomes below the poverty level was lower among those whose householders had at least a Bachelor's degree than among all U.S. families.

11.41
a. H_0: $p = 0.5$, H_a: $p > 0.5$; $\alpha = 0.05$; $z = 7.78$; critical value $= 1.645$; $P = 0.0000$ (to four decimal places); reject H_0; at the 5% significance level, the data provide sufficient evidence to conclude that a majority of U.S. adults believe that a presidential candidate's position on protecting the environment is very important in deciding how to vote in the next presidential election.
b. H_0: $p = 2/3$, H_a: $p < 2/3$; $\alpha = 0.05$; $z = -5.50$; critical value $= -1.645$; $P = 0.0000$ (to four decimal places); reject H_0; at the 5% significance level, the data provide sufficient evidence to conclude that less than two-thirds of U.S. adults believe that a presidential candidate's position on protecting the environment is very important in deciding how to vote in the next presidential election.

11.42 H_0: $p = 0.474$, H_a: $p \neq 0.474$; $\alpha = 0.10$; $z = -0.25$; critical values $= \pm 1.645$; $P = 0.8026$; do not reject H_0; at the 10% significance level, the data do not provide sufficient evidence to conclude that the ball is not landing on red the correct percentage of the time for a balanced wheel.

EXERCISES 11.3

11.45 For a two-tailed test, the basic strategy is as follows: (1) independently and randomly take samples from the two populations under consideration; (2) compute the sample proportions, $\hat{p}_1$ and $\hat{p}_2$; and (3) reject the null hypothesis if the sample proportions differ by too much—otherwise, do not reject the null hypothesis. The process is the same for a one-tailed test except that, for a left-tailed test, the null hypothesis is rejected only when $\hat{p}_1$ is too much smaller than $\hat{p}_2$, and, for a right-tailed test, the null hypothesis is rejected only when $\hat{p}_1$ is too much larger than $\hat{p}_2$.

11.46
a. Attend church at least once a week
b. Children in the United States and children in Germany
c. The proportion of children in the United States who attend church at least once a week and the proportion of children in Germany who attend church at least once a week

11.47
a. Uses sunscreen before going out in the sun
b. Teenage girls and teenage boys
c. Sample proportions. Industry Research acquired those proportions by polling samples of the populations of all teenage girls and all teenage boys.

11.48
a. p_1 **b.** p_2
c. The common population proportion, presuming that the null hypothesis is true

11.49
a. p_1 and p_2 are parameters, and the other quantities are statistics.
b. p_1 and p_2 are fixed numbers, and the other quantities are variables.

11.50
a. $H_0: p_1 = p_2$, $H_a: p_1 < p_2$; $\alpha = 0.01$; $z = -3.05$; critical value $= -2.33$; $P = 0.0011$; reject H_0; at the 1% significance level, the data provide sufficient evidence to conclude that men who have had a vasectomy are at greater risk of having prostate cancer.
b. Observational study
c. No. Because, for an observational study, it is not reasonable to interpret statistical significance as a causal relationship.

11.51
a. $H_0: p_1 = p_2$, $H_a: p_1 < p_2$; $\alpha = 0.01$; $z = -2.61$; critical value $= -2.33$; $P = 0.0045$; reject H_0; at the 1% significance level, the data provide sufficient evidence to conclude that women who take folic acid are at lesser risk of having children with major birth defects.
b. Designed experiment
c. Yes. Because for a designed experiment, it is reasonable to interpret statistical significance as a causal relationship.

11.52 $H_0: p_1 = p_2$, $H_a: p_1 \neq p_2$; $\alpha = 0.05$; $z = -0.68$; critical values $= \pm 1.96$; $P = 0.4966$; do not reject H_0; at the 5% significance level, the data do not provide sufficient evidence to conclude that there is a difference in stroke incidence between white and African-American elderly.

11.53 $H_0: p_1 = p_2$, $H_a: p_1 \neq p_2$; $\alpha = 0.10$; $z = -1.52$; critical values $= \pm 1.645$; $P = 0.1286$; do not reject H_0; at the 10% significance level, the data do not provide sufficient evidence to conclude that there is a difference in seat-belt use between drivers 25–34 years old and those 45–64 years old.

11.54 $H_0: p_1 = p_2$, $H_a: p_1 < p_2$; $\alpha = 0.01$; $z = -28.08$; critical value $= -2.33$; $P = 0.0000$ (to four decimal places); reject H_0; at the 1% significance level, the data provide sufficient evidence to conclude that a higher percentage of people were against the breakup after the judge's decision.

11.55 $H_0: p_1 = p_2$, $H_a: p_1 > p_2$; $\alpha = 0.05$; $z = 2.63$; critical value $= 1.645$; $P = 0.0043$; reject H_0; at the 5% significance level, the data provide sufficient evidence to conclude that for men 20–34 years old, a higher percentage were overweight in 1994 than 14 years earlier.

11.56
a. 0.000456 to 0.00334
b. We can be 98% confident that the difference between the prostate cancer rates of men who have had a vasectomy and those who have not is somewhere between 0.000456 and 0.00334.

11.57
a. -0.0191 to -0.000746, or about -0.019 to -0.001
b. Roughly, we can be 98% confident that the rate of major birth defects for babies born to women who have not taken folic acid is somewhere between 1 per 1000 and 19 per 1000 higher than for babies born to women who have taken folic acid.

11.58 -0.0300 to 0.0147. We can be 95% confident that the difference between the stroke incidences of white and African-American elderly is somewhere between -0.0300 and 0.0147.

11.59 -0.0624 to 0.00240. We can be 90% confident that the difference between the proportions of seat-belt users for drivers in the age groups 25–34 years and 45–64 years is somewhere between -0.0624 and 0.00240.

REVIEW TEST FOR CHAPTER 11

1. a. Feeling that marijuana should be legalized for medicinal use in patients with cancer and other painful and terminal diseases
   b. Americans
   c. Proportion of all Americans who feel that marijuana should be legalized for medicinal use in patients with cancer and other painful and terminal diseases
   d. Sample proportion; it is the proportion of Americans sampled who feel that marijuana should be legalized for medicinal use in patients with cancer and other painful and terminal diseases

2. Generally, obtaining a sample proportion can be done more quickly and is less costly than obtaining the population proportion. Sampling is often the only practical way to proceed.

3. a. The number of members in the sample that have the specified attribute
   b. The number of members in the sample that do not have the specified attribute

4. a. Population proportion   b. Normal
   c. np, $n(1-p)$, 5

5. The precision with which a sample proportion, $\hat{p}$, estimates the population proportion, p, at the specified confidence level

6. a. Getting the "holiday blues"
   b. All men, all women
   c. The proportion of all men who get the "holiday blues" and the proportion of all women who get the "holiday blues"
   d. The proportion of all sampled men who get the "holiday blues" and the proportion of all sampled women who get the "holiday blues"

e. Sample proportions. The poll used samples of men and women to obtain the proportions.

7. a. Difference between the population proportions **b.** Normal

8. 41.3% to 50.7%

9. a. 19,208   **b.** 14,406

10. 0.574 to 0.629. We can be 95% confident that the percentage of students who expect difficulty finding a job is somewhere between 57.4% and 62.9%.

11. a. 0.028   **b.** 2401   **c.** 0.567 to 0.607
d. 0.020, which is the same as that specified in part (b)
e. 2367; 0.567 to 0.607; 0.020
f. By using the guess for $\hat{p}$ in part (e), the required sample size is reduced by 34 with (virtually) no sacrifice in precision.

12. a. H_0: $p = 0.25$, H_a: $p < 0.25$; $\alpha = 0.05$; $z = -2.30$; critical value $= -1.645$; $P = 0.0107$; reject H_0; at the 5% significance level, the data provide sufficient evidence to conclude that less than one in four Americans believe that juries "almost always" convict the guilty and free the innocent.
b. The data provide strong evidence against the null hypothesis and hence in favor of the alternative hypothesis that less than one in four Americans believe that juries "almost always" convict the guilty and free the innocent.

13. a. Observational study
b. Being observational, the study established only an association between height and breast cancer; no causal relationship can be inferred, although there may be one.

14. a. H_0: $p_1 = p_2$, H_a: $p_1 < p_2$; $\alpha = 0.01$; $z = -4.17$; critical value $= -2.33$; $P = 0.0000$ (to four decimal places); reject H_0; at the 1% significance level, the data provide sufficient evidence to conclude that the percentage of Maricopa County residents who thought Arizona's economy would improve over the next 2 years was less during the time of the first poll than during the time of the second poll.
b. The data provide very strong evidence against the null hypothesis and hence in favor of the alternative hypothesis that the percentage of Maricopa County residents who thought Arizona's economy would improve over the next 2 years was less during the time of the first poll than during the time of the second poll.

15. a. −0.186 to −0.054
b. We can be 98% confident that the difference between the percentages of Maricopa County residents who thought Arizona's economy would improve over the next 2 years during the time of the first poll and during the time of the second poll is somewhere between −18.6% and −5.4%.

16. a. 0.066; we can be 98% confident that the error in estimating the difference between the two population proportions, $p_1 - p_2$, by the difference between the two sample proportions, −0.12, is at most 0.066.
b. 0.066   **c.** 3006   **d.** −0.158 to −0.098
e. 0.03, which is the same as that specified in part (c)

CHAPTER 12

EXERCISES 12.1

12.1 A variable is said to have a chi-square distribution if its distribution has the shape of a special type of right-skewed curve, called a chi-square curve.

12.2 By their degrees of freedom

12.3 The χ^2-curve with 20 degrees of freedom more closely resembles a normal curve. As the number of degrees of freedom becomes larger, χ^2-curves look increasingly like normal curves.

12.4 Because a t-curve is symmetric (about 0), whereas a χ^2-curve is not.

12.5
a. 32.852   **b.** 10.117

12.6
a. 40.290   **b.** 8.643

12.7
a. 18.307   **b.** 3.247

12.8
a. 14.860   **b.** 0.297

EXERCISES 12.2

12.11 Because the hypothesis test is carried out by determining how well the observed frequencies fit the expected frequencies.

12.12 The observed frequencies are variables, as they vary from sample to sample. The expected frequencies are not variables, as they are determined by the sample size and the distribution specified in the null hypothesis.

12.13
a. Both assumptions are satisfied.
b. Assumption 1 is satisfied, but Assumption 2 fails because 33.3% of the expected frequencies are less than 5.

c. Both assumptions are satisfied. Note that 20% of the expected frequencies are less than 5.
d. Both assumptions are satisfied. Note that 20% of the expected frequencies are less than 5.
e. Assumption 2 is satisfied because only 20% of the expected frequencies are less than 5, but Assumption 1 fails because there is an expected frequency of 0.5 which is less than 1.
f. Assumption 1 is satisfied, but Assumption 2 fails because 25% of the expected frequencies are less than 5.

12.14
a. The population consists of occupied housing units built after 1974; the variable is primary heating fuel.
b. In the following table, the first column gives the sample size, the second column shows the number of expected frequencies less than 1 and parenthetically whether Assumption 1 is satisfied, the third column shows the percentage of expected frequencies less than 5 and parenthetically whether Assumption 2 is satisfied, and the fourth column states whether both assumptions for a chi-square goodness-of-fit test are satisfied.

Sample size	Number less than 1	Percentage less than 5	Both satisfied?
100	1 (No)	33.3 (No)	No
150	0 (Yes)	33.3 (No)	No
200	0 (Yes)	33.3 (No)	No
250	0 (Yes)	16.7 (Yes)	Yes

12.15
a. The population consists of all U.S. prisoners sentenced to death in 1998; the variable is educational attainment.
b. H_0: The educational attainment distribution of prisoners sentenced to death in 1998 is the same as that of 1980 death-row inmates. H_a: The educational attainment distribution of prisoners sentenced to death in 1998 differs from that of 1980 death-row inmates. $\alpha = 0.05$; $\chi^2 = 11.011$; critical value = 7.815; $0.01 < P < 0.025$; reject H_0; at the 5% significance level, the data provide sufficient evidence to conclude that the educational attainment distribution of prisoners sentenced to death in 1998 differs from that of 1980 death-row inmates.
c. H_0: The educational attainment distribution of prisoners sentenced to death in 1998 is the same as that of 1980 death-row inmates. H_a: The educational attainment distribution of prisoners sentenced to death in 1998 differs from that of 1980 death-row inmates. $\alpha = 0.01$; $\chi^2 = 11.011$; critical value = 11.345; $0.01 < P < 0.025$; do not reject H_0; at the 1% significance level, the data do not provide sufficient evidence to conclude that the educational attainment distribution of prisoners sentenced to death in 1998 differs from that of 1980 death-row inmates.

12.16
a. The population consists of all last year's U.S. car sales; the variable is type of car.
b. H_0: Last year's type-of-car distribution for U.S. car sales is the same as the 1990 distribution; H_a: Last year's type-of-car distribution for U.S. car sales differs from the 1990 distribution. $\alpha = 0.05$; $\chi^2 = 9.204$; critical value = 7.815; $0.025 < P < 0.05$; reject H_0; at the 5% significance level, the data provide sufficient evidence to conclude that last year's type-of-car distribution for U.S. car sales differs from the 1990 distribution.

12.17 H_0: The color distribution of M&Ms is that reported by M&M/MARS consumer affairs. H_a: The color distribution of M&Ms differs from that reported by M&M/MARS consumer affairs. $\alpha = 0.05$; $\chi^2 = 4.091$; critical value = 11.070; $P > 0.10$; do not reject H_0; at the 5% significance level, the data do not provide sufficient evidence to conclude that the color distribution of M&Ms differs from that reported by M&M/MARS consumer affairs.

12.18 H_0: The wheel is not out of balance. H_a: The wheel is out of balance. $\alpha = 0.05$; $\chi^2 = 1.062$; critical value = 5.991; $P > 0.10$; do not reject H_0; at the 5% significance level, the data do not provide sufficient evidence to conclude that the wheel is out of balance.

EXERCISES 12.3

12.25 Answers will vary.

12.26 Contingency table, or two-way table

12.27 Cells

12.28
a. 6   **b.** 12   **c.** mn

12.29 Summing the row totals, summing the column totals, or summing the frequencies in the cells

12.30 Yes. If there were no association between "party of the presidential candidate voted for" and "region of residence," the percentage of voters in the South who voted for the Republican candidate would be the same as the percentage of all voters who voted for the Republican candidate. As that is not the case, there is an association between the two variables.

12.31 Yes. If there were no association between "sex" and "specialty," the percentages of male physicians and female physicians who specialized in internal medicine would be identical. As that is not the case, there is an association between the two variables.

12.32

a.
	Class			
Sex	Soph	Junior	Senior	Total
Male	6	8	1	15
Female	2	5	3	10
Total	8	13	4	25

b.
	Class			
Sex	Soph	Junior	Senior	Total
Male	0.750	0.615	0.250	0.600
Female	0.250	0.385	0.750	0.400
Total	1.000	1.000	1.000	1.000

c.
	Class			
Sex	Soph	Junior	Senior	Total
Male	0.400	0.533	0.067	1.000
Female	0.200	0.500	0.300	1.000
Total	0.320	0.520	0.160	1.000

d. Yes. The tables in parts (b) and (c) show that the conditional distributions of one variable given the other are not identical.

12.33

a.
	College			
Sex	Bus.	Engr.	Lib. Arts	Total
Male	2	10	3	15
Female	7	2	1	10
Total	9	12	4	25

b.
	College			
Sex	Bus.	Engr.	Lib. Arts	Total
Male	0.222	0.833	0.750	0.600
Female	0.778	0.167	0.250	0.400
Total	1.000	1.000	1.000	1.000

c.
	College			
Sex	Bus.	Engr.	Lib. Arts	Total
Male	0.133	0.667	0.200	1.000
Female	0.700	0.200	0.100	1.000
Total	0.360	0.480	0.160	1.000

d. Yes. The tables in parts (b) and (c) show that the conditional distributions of one variable given the other are not identical.

12.34

a.
	College			
Class	Bus.	Engr.	Lib. Arts	Total
Soph	3	4	1	8
Junior	4	7	2	13
Senior	2	1	1	4
Total	9	12	4	25

b.
	College			
Class	Bus.	Engr.	Lib. Arts	Total
Soph	0.333	0.333	0.250	0.320
Junior	0.444	0.583	0.500	0.520
Senior	0.222	0.083	0.250	0.160
Total	1.000	1.000	1.000	1.000

c.
	College			
Class	Bus.	Engr.	Lib. Arts	Total
Soph	0.375	0.500	0.125	1.000
Junior	0.308	0.538	0.154	1.000
Senior	0.500	0.250	0.250	1.000
Total	0.360	0.480	0.160	1.000

d. Yes. The tables in parts (b) and (c) show that the conditional distributions of one variable given the other are not identical.

12.35

a.

	Class				
Party	Fresh.	Soph.	Junior	Senior	Total
Republican	3	9	12	6	30
Democrat	2	6	8	4	20
Other	1	3	4	2	10
Total	6	18	24	12	60

b.

	Class			
Party	Fresh.	Soph.	Junior	Senior
Republican	0.500	0.500	0.500	0.500
Democrat	0.333	0.333	0.333	0.333
Other	0.167	0.167	0.167	0.167
Total	1.000	1.000	1.000	1.000

c. No. The table in part (b) shows that the conditional distributions of political party affiliation within class levels are identical.
d. Republican 0.500, Democrat 0.333, Other 0.167, Total 1.000
e. True. From part (c), political party affiliation and class level are not associated. Therefore the conditional distributions of class level within political party affiliations are identical to each other and to the marginal distribution of class level.

12.36
a. See the answer to Exercise 12.35(a).
b.

	Class				
Party	Fresh.	Soph.	Junior	Senior	Total
Republican	0.1	0.3	0.4	0.2	1.0
Democrat	0.1	0.3	0.4	0.2	1.0
Other	0.1	0.3	0.4	0.2	1.0

c. No. The table in part (b) shows that the conditional distributions of class level within political party affiliations are identical.
d. Freshman 0.1, Sophomore 0.3, Junior 0.4, Senior 0.2, Total 1.0
e. True. From part (c), political party affiliation and class level are not associated. Therefore the conditional distributions of political party affiliation within class levels are identical to each other and to the marginal distribution of political party affiliation.

12.37
a. 8
b. The missing entries, from top to bottom and left to right, are: 1,924; 8,967; 35,259; and 46,018
c. 46,018   **d.** 8967   **e.** 35,259   **f.** 1924

12.38
a. 8
b. The missing entries, from top to bottom and left to right, are: 13.1, 34.0, 70.2, and 193.4
c. 193.4 million   **d.** 70.2 million
e. 40.0 million   **f.** 10.7 million

12.39
a. 73,970   **b.** 15,540   **c.** 12,328   **d.** 77,182
e. 12,225   **f.** 6734   **g.** 77,700

12.40
a. 4260   **b.** 737   **c.** 471   **d.** 4526
e. 1586   **f.** 3   **g.** 6270

12.41
a.

		Gender		
		Male	Female	Total
Race/Ethnicity	White	0.870	0.130	1.000
	Black	0.688	0.312	1.000
	Hispanic	0.783	0.217	1.000
	Other	0.810	0.190	1.000

b. Male 0.766; Female 0.234; Total 1.000
c. Yes. Because the conditional distributions of gender within races are not identical.
d. 23.4%   **e.** 13.0%
f. True. Because by part (c), there is an association between the variables "gender" and "race."
g.

		Gender		
		Male	Female	Total
Race/Ethnicity	White	0.365	0.179	0.321
	Black	0.424	0.631	0.472
	Hispanic	0.199	0.181	0.195
	Other	0.012	0.010	0.012
	Total	1.000	1.000	1.000

12.42

a.

	Type	
Age (yr)	Car	Truck
Under 6	0.375	0.396
6–8	0.218	0.187
9–11	0.189	0.152
12 & over	0.218	0.265
Total	1.000	1.000

b. Under 6: 0.383; 6–8: 0.207; 9–11: 0.176; 12 & over: 0.235; Total: 1.000
c. Yes. Because the conditional distributions of age group within vehicle types are not identical.
d. 38.3%   **e.** 37.5%
f. True. Because by part (c), there is an association between the variables "vehicle type" and "age group."
g.

	Type		
Age (yr)	Car	Truck	Total
Under 6	0.624	0.376	1.000
6–8	0.672	0.328	1.000
9–11	0.685	0.315	1.000
12 & over	0.590	0.410	1.000
Total	0.637	0.363	1.000

12.43

a.

	Base of practice		
Specialty	Office	Hospital	Other
General	0.326	0.472	0.445
Ob/Gyn	0.326	0.260	0.306
Orthopedics	0.181	0.164	0.111
Ophthalmology	0.167	0.104	0.139
Total	1.000	1.000	1.000

b. Yes. Because the conditional distributions of specialty within base of practice categories are not identical.
c. General 0.367; Ob/Gyn 0.309; Orthopedics 0.174; Ophthalmology 0.150; Total 1.000

d.

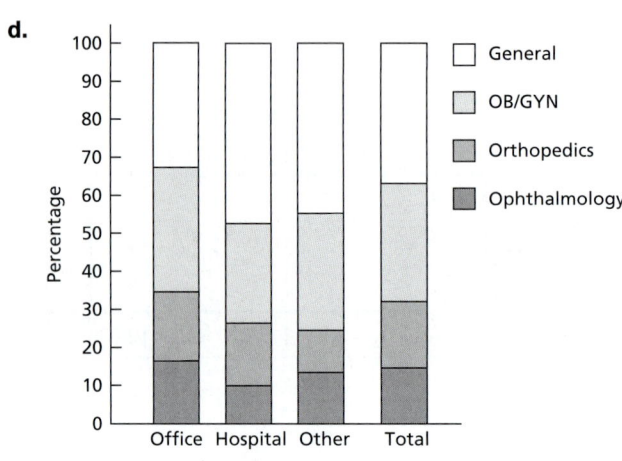

That the bars are not identical reflects the fact that there is an association between specialty and base of practice.
e. False. Because by part (b), there is an association between specialty and base of practice.
f.

	Base of practice			
Specialty	Office	Hospital	Other	Total
General	0.635	0.322	0.044	1.000
Ob/Gyn	0.754	0.210	0.036	1.000
Orthopedics	0.741	0.236	0.023	1.000
Ophthalmology	0.793	0.173	0.033	1.000
Total	0.714	0.250	0.036	1.000

g. 25.0%   **h.** 21.0%   **i.** 26.0%

12.44

a.

	Number of beds			
Facility	24 or fewer	25–74	75 or more	Total
General	0.048	0.294	0.658	1.000
Psychiatric	0.033	0.328	0.639	1.000
Chronic	0.038	0.115	0.846	1.000
Tuberculosis	0.000	0.500	0.500	1.000
Other	0.061	0.432	0.507	1.000

b. Yes. Because the conditional distributions of number of beds within facility types are not identical.

c. 24 or fewer: 0.047; 25–74: 0.305; 75 or more: 0.647; Total: 1.000

d.

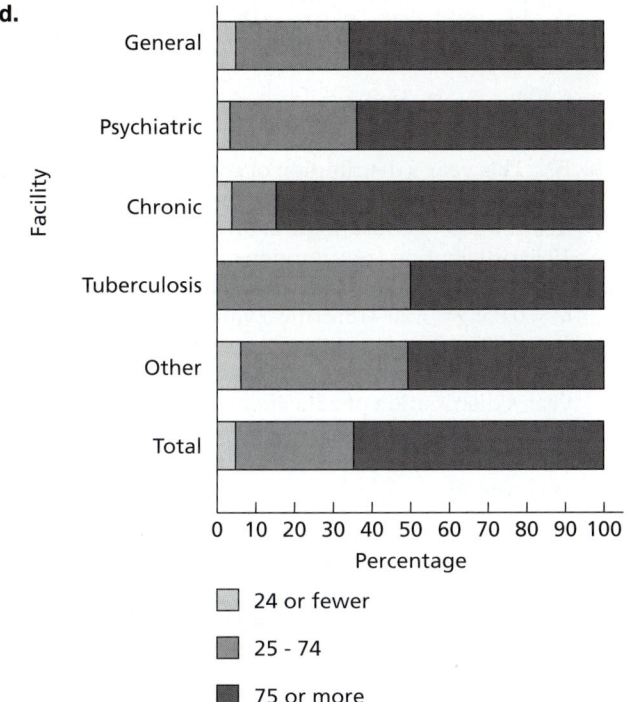

That the bars are not identical reflects the fact that there is an association between facility type and number of beds.

e. False. By part (b), there is an association between facility type and number of beds.

f.

	Number of beds			
	24 or fewer	25–74	75 or more	Total
General	0.839	0.789	0.835	0.821
Psychiatric	0.077	0.120	0.111	0.112
Chronic	0.003	0.001	0.005	0.004
Tuberculosis	0.000	0.001	0.000	0.001
Other	0.081	0.088	0.049	0.062
Total	1.000	1.000	1.000	1.000

g. 82.1% **h.** 83.5% **i.** 65.8%

EXERCISES 12.4

12.49 In most cases, data for an entire population are not available. Therefore inferential methods must usually be applied to decide whether an association exists between two variables.

12.50 H_0: The two variables under consideration are statistically independent. H_a: The two variables under consideration are statistically dependent.

12.51 If no association exists between marital status and alcohol consumption, the (conditional) distribution of alcohol consumption for married adults is the same as the (marginal) distribution of alcohol consumption for all adults.

12.52 Because the null hypothesis is rejected only when the observed and expected frequencies do not match well, that is, only when the test statistic, χ^2, is too large.

12.53 15

12.54
a. No. Association in observational studies does not imply causation.
b. Answers will vary.

12.55 If there is a causal relationship between two variables, they are necessarily associated. In other words, if there is no association between two variables, they could not possibly be causally related.

12.56 (1) Combine rows or columns to increase the expected frequencies in those cells in which they are too small. (2) Eliminate certain rows or columns in which the small expected frequencies occur. (3) Increase the sample size.

12.57 H_0: An association does not exist between the ratings of Siskel and Ebert. H_a: An association exists between the ratings of Siskel and Ebert. Assumptions 1 and 2 are satisfied because all expected frequencies are 5 or greater. $\alpha = 0.01$; $\chi^2 = 45.357$; critical value $= 13.277$; $P < 0.005$; reject H_0; at the 1% significance level, the data provide sufficient evidence to conclude that an association exists between the ratings of Siskel and Ebert.

12.58 H_0: An association does not exist between educational level and diabetic state for Native Americans. H_a: An association exists between educational level and diabetic state for Native Americans. Assumptions 1 and 2 are satisfied because all expected frequencies are 5 or greater. $\alpha = 0.01$; $\chi^2 = 17.512$; critical value $= 11.345$; $P < 0.005$; reject H_0; at the 1% significance level, the data provide sufficient evidence to conclude that an association exists between educational level and diabetic state for Native Americans.

12.59 H_0: Response and political affiliation are not associated. H_a: Response and political affiliation are associated. Assumptions 1 and 2 are satisfied because all expected frequencies are 5 or greater. $\alpha = 0.05$; $\chi^2 = 4.017$; critical value $= 9.488$; $P > 0.10$; do not reject H_0; at the 5% significance level, the data do not provide sufficient evidence to conclude that the opinions of U.S. adults on the issue of regional primaries are associated with political affiliation.

12.60 H_0: An association does not exist between response to the suicide question and mental-health classification. H_a: An association exists between response to the suicide question and mental-health classification. Assumptions 1 and 2 are satisfied because all expected frequencies are 5 or greater. $\alpha = 0.05$; $\chi^2 = 91.253$; critical value = 12.592; $P < 0.005$; reject H_0; at the 5% significance level, the data provide sufficient evidence to conclude that an association exists between response to the suicide question and mental-health classification.

12.61 H_0: Size of city and status in practice are statistically independent for U.S. lawyers. H_a: Size of city and status in practice are statistically dependent for U.S. lawyers. Assumption 1 is satisfied, but Assumption 2 is not because 25% (3 of 12) of the expected frequencies are less than 5. The chi-square independence test should not be applied here.

REVIEW TEST FOR CHAPTER 12

1. By their degrees of freedom
2. **a.** 0 **b.** Right skewed **c.** Normal curve
3. **a.** No. The degrees of freedom for the chi-square goodness-of-fit test depends on the number of possible values for the variable under consideration, not on the sample size.
   b. No. The degrees of freedom for the chi-square independence test depends on the number of possible values for the two variables under consideration, not on the sample size.
4. For both tests, the null hypothesis is rejected only when the observed and expected frequencies match up poorly, which corresponds to large values of the chi-square test statistic. Thus both tests are always right-tailed.
5. 0
6. **a.** (1) All expected frequencies are 1 or greater. (2) At most 20% of the expected frequencies are less than 5.
   b. They are very important. If the assumptions are not met, the results could be invalid.
7. **a.** 5.3% **b.** Roughly 3.1 million
   c. There is an association between means of transportation to work and region of residence.
8. **a.** Obtain the conditional distribution of one of the variables for each possible value of the other variable. If all these conditional distributions are identical, there is no association between the two variables; otherwise, there is an association between the two variables.
   b. No. Because the data are for an entire population, no inference is being made from a sample to the population. The conclusion is a fact.
9. **a.** Perform a chi-square independence test.
   b. Yes. As in any inference, it is always possible that the conclusion is in error.
10. **a.** 6.408 **b.** 33.409 **c.** 27.587
    d. 8.672 **e.** 7.564, 30.191
11. **a.** H_0: This year's distribution of educational attainment is the same as the 1990 distribution. H_a: This year's distribution of educational attainment differs from the 1990 distribution. Assumptions 1 and 2 are satisfied because all expected frequencies are 5 or greater. $\alpha = 0.05$; $\chi^2 = 20.416$; critical value = 11.070; $P < 0.005$; reject H_0; at the 5% significance level, the data provide sufficient evidence to conclude that this year's distribution of educational attainment differs from the 1990 distribution.
    b. $P < 0.005$. The evidence against the null hypothesis is very strong

12. **a.**

	Party of governor			
Region	Rep	Dem	Ind	Total
Northeast	6	2	1	9
Midwest	8	3	1	12
South	9	7	0	16
West	8	5	0	13
Total	31	17	2	50

b.

	Party of governor			
Region	Rep	Dem	Ind	Total
Northeast	0.194	0.118	0.500	0.180
Midwest	0.258	0.176	0.500	0.240
South	0.290	0.412	0.000	0.320
West	0.258	0.294	0.000	0.260
Total	1.000	1.000	1.000	1.000

c.

Party of governor

Region	Rep	Dem	Ind	Total
Northeast	0.667	0.222	0.111	1.000
Midwest	0.667	0.250	0.083	1.000
South	0.563	0.438	0.000	1.000
West	0.615	0.385	0.000	1.000
Total	0.620	0.340	0.040	1.000

d. Yes. Because the conditional distributions of party of governor within regions are not identical.
e. 62.0%   **f.** 62.0%   **g.** 66.7%
h. 24.0%   **i.** 24.0%   **j.** 25.8%

13. a. 2046   **b.** 737   **c.** 266
d. 3046   **e.** 5413   **f.** 5910

14. a.

Control

Facility	Gov	Prop	NP	Total
General	0.314	0.122	0.564	1.000
Psychiatric	0.361	0.486	0.153	1.000
Chronic	0.808	0.038	0.154	1.000
Tuberculosis	0.750	0.000	0.250	1.000
Other	0.144	0.361	0.495	1.000

b. Yes. Because the conditional distributions of control type within facility types are not identical.
c. Gov 0.311, Prop 0.177, NP 0.512, Total 1.000
d. See Fig. A.11. That the bars are not identical reflects the fact that there is an association between facility type and control type.
e. False. By part (b) there is an association between facility type and control type.
f.

Control

Facility	Gov	Prop	NP	Total
General	0.829	0.566	0.905	0.821
Psychiatric	0.130	0.307	0.034	0.112
Chronic	0.010	0.001	0.001	0.004
Tuberculosis	0.001	0.000	0.000	0.001
Other	0.029	0.127	0.060	0.062
Total	1.000	1.000	1.000	1.000

g. 17.7%   **h.** 48.6%   **i.** 30.7%

15. H_0: Histological type and treatment response are statistically independent. H_a: Histological type and treatment response are statistically dependent. Assumptions 1 and 2 are satisfied because all expected frequencies are 5 or greater. $\alpha = 0.01$; $\chi^2 = 75.890$; critical value $= 16.812$; $P < 0.005$; reject H_0; at the 1% significance level, the data provide sufficient evidence to conclude that histological type and treatment response are statistically dependent.

FIGURE A.11
Segmented bar graph for Problem 14(d)

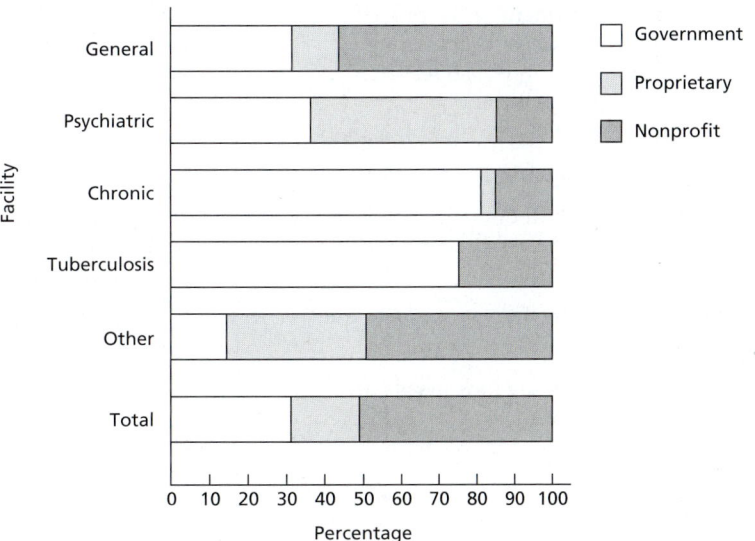

CHAPTER 13

EXERCISES 13.1

13.1 By stating its two numbers of degrees of freedom

13.2 An F-distribution has two numbers of degrees of freedom. The first is called the degrees of freedom for the numerator and the second the degrees of freedom for the denominator.

13.3 $F_{0.05}, F_{0.025}, F_\alpha$

13.4 $F_{0.025}$

13.5
a. 12   b. 7

13.6
a. 19   b. 8

13.7
a. 1.89   b. 2.47   c. 2.14

13.8
a. 9.89   b. 4.68   c. 13.38

13.9
a. 2.88   b. 2.10   c. 1.78

13.10
a. 3.22   b. 5.39   c. 4.07

EXERCISES 13.2

13.12 The three assumptions required for one-way ANOVA are independent samples, normal populations, and equal standard deviations. The independent samples assumption is essential; the samples must be independent or the procedure does not apply. One-way ANOVA is robust to moderate violations of the normality assumption. It is also reasonably robust to moderate violations of the equal standard deviations assumption if the sample sizes are roughly equal.

13.13 The pooled t-procedure of Section 10.2

13.14 The common population standard deviation, σ, of the variable under consideration on the populations under consideration

13.15 The procedure for comparing the means analyzes the variation in the sample data.

13.16 No. It means that not all the populations means are identical; that is, at least two of the populations have different means.

13.17
a. The treatment mean square, $MSTR$
b. The error mean square, MSE
c. The F-statistic, $F = MSTR/MSE$

13.18 Reject the null hypothesis of equal population means if the variation among the sample means is large relative to the variation within the samples because, under those circumstances, attributing the variation among the sample means to sampling error is not reasonable. Rather, it must be considered due to a difference among the population means.

13.19 It signifies that the ANOVA compares the means of a variable for populations that result from a classification by *one* other variable (called the *factor*).

13.20 Yes. Because the variation among the sample means is large relative to the variation within the samples.

13.21 No. Because the variation among the sample means is not large relative to the variation within the samples.

EXERCISES 13.3

13.24 df $= (2, 34)$

13.25 A small value of F results when $SSTR$ is small relative to SSE, that is, when the variation among sample means is small relative to the variation within samples. This result describes what is expected when the null hypothesis is true; thus it doesn't constitute evidence against the null hypothesis. Only when the variation among sample means is large relative to the variation within samples (i.e., only when F is large), is there evidence that the null hypothesis is false.

13.26
a. SSE is the error sum of squares; it represents the variation within the samples.
b. $SSTR$ is the treatment sum of squares; it represents the variation among the sample means.
c. SST is the total sum of squares; it represents the total variation among all the sample data.

13.27 $SST = SSTR + SSE$. The total variation among all the sample data can be partitioned into a component representing variation among the sample means and a component representing variation within the samples.

13.28 True, as shown by the one-way ANOVA identity.

13.29 The missing entries are as follows: In the first row, they are 43.304 and 3.08; in the second row, they are 12 and 7.033; and in the third row, it is 127.704.

13.30 The missing entries are as follows: In the first row, it is 3; in the second row, they are 18.880 and 0.944; and in the third row, they are 23 and 21.004.

13.31
a. $SST = 70, SSTR = 10, SSE = 60$
b. $70 = 10 + 60$
c. $SST = 70, SSTR = 10, SSE = 60$

13.32
a. $SST = 74, SSTR = 46, SSE = 28$

b. $74 = 46 + 28$
c. $SST = 74, SSTR = 46, SSE = 28$

13.33

Source	df	SS	MS	F
Treatment	2	2.8	1.4	1.56
Error	12	10.8	0.9	
Total	14	13.6		

13.34

Source	df	SS	MS	F
Treatment	3	138,001.2	46,000.400	2.60
Error	16	283,265.0	17,704.063	
Total	19	421,266.2		

13.35 $H_0: \mu_1 = \mu_2 = \mu_3$, H_a: Not all the means are equal. $\alpha = 0.05$; $SST = 71{,}488.667$, $SSTR = 66{,}043.167$, $SSE = 5{,}445.50$; $F = 54.58$; critical value $= 4.26$; $P < 0.005$; reject H_0; at the 5% significance level, the data provide sufficient evidence to conclude that a difference exists in mean number of copepods among the three different diets.

13.36
a. $H_0: \mu_1 = \mu_2$, $H_a: \mu_1 \neq \mu_2$; $\alpha = 0.05$; $SST = 1197$, $SSTR = 75$, $SSE = 1122$; $F = 0.67$; critical value $= 4.96$; $P > 0.10$; do not reject H_0; at the 5% significance level, the data do not provide sufficient evidence to conclude that the two population means differ. This conclusion is the same as the informal one made in the "What Does it Mean?" box.
b. $H_0: \mu_1 = \mu_2$, $H_a: \mu_1 \neq \mu_2$; $\alpha = 0.05$; $SST = 93$, $SSTR = 75$, $SSE = 18$; $F = 41.67$; critical value $= 4.96$; $P < 0.005$; reject H_0; at the 5% significance level, the data provide sufficient evidence to conclude that the two population means differ. This conclusion is the same as the informal one made in the "What Does it Mean?" box.

13.37 $H_0: \mu_1 = \mu_2 = \mu_3 = \mu_4 = \mu_5$, H_a: Not all the means are equal. $\alpha = 0.05$; $SST = 447{,}088.667$, $SSTR = 404{,}258.467$, $SSE = 42{,}830.200$; $F = 51.91$; critical value $= 2.82$; $P < 0.005$; reject H_0; at the 5% significance level, the data provide sufficient evidence to conclude that a difference exists in mean weekly earnings among nonsupervisory workers in the five industries.

13.38 $H_0: \mu_1 = \mu_2 = \mu_3 = \mu_4 = \mu_5$, H_a: Not all the means are equal. $\alpha = 0.05$; $SST = 1153.75$, $SSTR = 458.50$, $SSE = 695.25$; $F = 2.47$; critical value $= 3.06$; $0.05 < P < 0.10$; do not reject H_0; at the 5% significance level, the data do not provide sufficient evidence to conclude that a difference exists in mean driving distances among the five brands of golf ball.

REVIEW TEST FOR CHAPTER 13

1. To compare the means of a variable for populations that result from a classification by one other variable (called the *factor*)

2. *Independent samples:* Check by carefully studying the way the sampling was done. *Normal populations:* Check by constructing normal probability plots. *Equal standard deviations:* As a rule of thumb, this assumption is considered to be satisfied if the ratio of the largest sample standard deviation to the smallest sample standard deviation is less than 2.

   Also, the normality and equal-standard-deviations assumptions can be assessed by performing a residual analysis.

3. The F-distribution

4. $df = (2, 14)$

5. **a.** $MSTR$ (or $SSTR$) **b.** MSE (or SSE)

6. **a.** The total sum of squares, SST, represents the total variation among all the sample data; the treatment sum of squares, $SSTR$, represents the variation among the sample means; and the error sum of squares, SSE, represents the variation within the samples.
   b. $SST = SSTR + SSE$; the one-way ANOVA identity shows that the total variation among all the sample data can be partitioned into a component representing variation among the sample means and a component representing variation within the samples.

7. **a.** For organizing and summarizing the quantities required for performing a one-way analysis of variance
   b.

Source	df	SS	MS = SS/df	F
Treatment	$k-1$	SSTR	$MSTR = \dfrac{SSTR}{k-1}$	$F = \dfrac{MSTR}{MSE}$
Error	$n-k$	SSE	$MSE = \dfrac{SSE}{n-k}$	
Total	$n-1$	SST		

8. **a.** 2 **b.** 14 **c.** 3.74
   d. 6.51 **e.** 3.74

9. **a.** The sample means are 3, 3, and 6, respectively; the sample standard deviations are 2, 2.449, and 4.243, respectively.
   b. $SST = 110$, $SSTR = 24$, $SSE = 86$; $110 = 24 + 86$
   c. $SST = 110$, $SSTR = 24$, $SSE = 86$

d.

Source	df	SS	MS = SS/df	F
Treatment	2	24	12.000	1.26
Error	9	86	9.556	
Total	11	110		

10. a. The variation among the sample means.
b. The variation within the samples.
c. Independent samples, normal populations, and equal (population) standard deviations. The independent samples assumption is essential; the samples must be independent or the procedure does not apply. One-way ANOVA is robust to moderate violations of the normality assumption. It is also reasonably robust to moderate violations of the equal standard deviations assumption if the sample sizes are roughly equal.

11. $H_0: \mu_1 = \mu_2 = \mu_3$, H_a: Not all the means are equal. $\alpha = 0.05$; $SST = 371,141.882$, $SSTR = 160,601.416$, $SSE = 210,540.467$; $F = 5.34$; critical value $= 3.74$; $0.01 < P < 0.025$; reject H_0; at the 5% significance level, the data provide sufficient evidence to conclude that a difference in mean losses exists among the three types of robberies.

CHAPTER 14

EXERCISES 14.1

14.1 Conditional distribution, conditional mean, conditional standard deviation

14.2 See Key Fact 14.1.

14.3
a. Population regression line   **b.** σ
c. Normal; $\beta_0 + 6\beta_1$; σ

14.4
a. b_0 **b.** b_1 **c.** s_e

14.5 The sample regression line, $\hat{y} = b_0 + b_1 x$

14.6
a. The standard error of the estimate indicates roughly how much, on average, the predicted values of the response variable differ from the observed values of the response variable. It also provides a point estimate for the common population standard deviation, σ.
b. The standard error of the estimate is sometimes called the residual standard deviation because it essentially equals the standard deviation of the residuals.
c. The error sum of squares, SSE.

14.7 Residual

14.8 A plot of the residuals against the values of the predictor variable and a normal probability plot of the residuals.

14.9 A residual plot, that is, a plot of the residuals against the values of the predictor variable. A residual plot makes it easier to spot patterns such as curvature and nonconstant standard deviation than does a scatter diagram.

14.10 There are constants, β_0, β_1, and σ, such that, for each percentage of investments in energy securities, x, the tax efficiencies of all mutual fund portfolios with that percentage of investments in energy securities are normally distributed with mean $\beta_0 + \beta_1 x$ and standard deviation σ.

14.11 There are constants, β_0, β_1, and σ, such that, for each age, x, the prices of all Corvettes of that age are normally distributed with mean $\beta_0 + \beta_1 x$ and standard deviation σ.

14.12 There are constants, β_0, β_1, and σ, such that, for each size (square footage), x, the prices of all custom homes in the Equestrian Estates of that size are normally distributed with mean $\beta_0 + \beta_1 x$ and standard deviation σ.

14.13 There are constants, β_0, β_1, and σ, such that, for each weight, x, the quantities of volatile compounds emitted by all potato plants of that weight are normally distributed with mean $\beta_0 + \beta_1 x$ and standard deviation σ.

14.14
a. $s_e = 3.09$; very roughly speaking, on average, the predicted tax efficiency of a mutual fund portfolio in the sample differs from the observed tax efficiency by about 3.09.
b. Presuming that, for mutual fund portfolios, the variables percentage of investments in energy securities (x) and tax efficiency (y) satisfy the assumptions for regression inferences, the standard error of the estimate, $s_e = 3.09$, provides an estimate for the common population standard deviation, σ, of tax efficiencies for all mutual fund portfolios with any particular percentage of investments in energy securities.
c. See Fig. A.12.
d. It appears reasonable.

14.15
a. $s_e = 14.25$; very roughly speaking, on average, the predicted price of a Corvette in the sample differs from the observed price by about $1425.
b. Presuming that, for Corvettes, the variables age (x) and price (y) satisfy the assumptions for regression inferences, the standard error of the estimate, $s_e = 14.25$, provides an estimate for the common population standard deviation, σ, of prices (in hundreds of dollars) for all Corvettes of any particular age.
c. See Fig. A.13.
d. It appears reasonable.

FIGURE A.12
(a) Residual plot and (b) normal probability plot of residuals for Exercise 14.14(c)

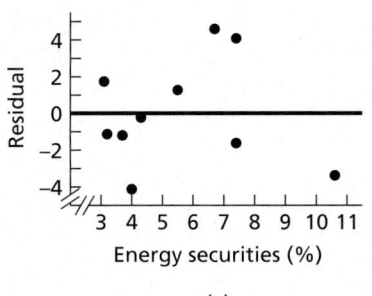
(a)

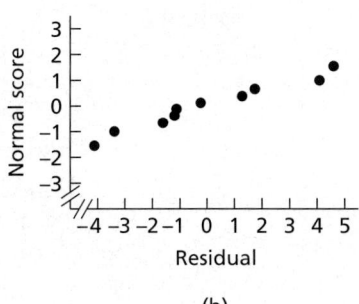
(b)

FIGURE A.13
(a) Residual plot and (b) normal probability plot of residuals for Exercise 14.15(c)

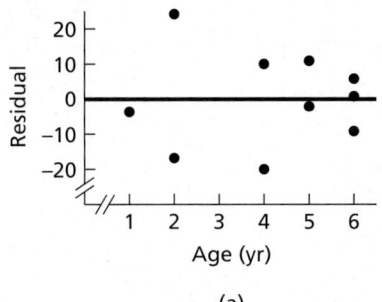
(a)

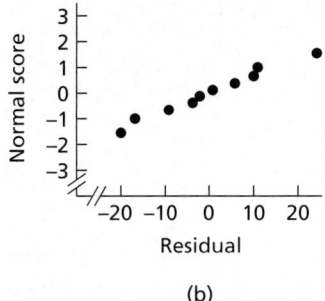
(b)

14.16
a. $s_e = 59.6$; very roughly speaking, on average, the predicted price of a custom home in the Equestrian Estates in the sample differs from the observed price by about $59,600.
b. Presuming that, for custom homes in the Equestrian Estates, the variables size (x) and price (y) satisfy the assumptions for regression inferences, the standard error of the estimate, $s_e = 59.6$, provides an estimate for the common population standard deviation, σ, of prices (in thousands of dollars) for all custom homes in the Equestrian Estates of any particular size.
c. See Fig. A.14.
d. The normality assumption (Assumption 3) is in question because of the outlier and the curvature in the normal probability plot of the residuals, as shown in Fig. A.14(b).

14.17
a. $s_e = 5.42$; very roughly speaking, on average, the predicted quantity of volatile compounds emitted by a potato plant in the sample differs from the observed quantity by about 542 nanograms.
b. Presuming that, for potato plants, the variables weight (x) and quantity of volatile compounds emitted (y) satisfy the assumptions for regression inferences, the standard error of the estimate, $s_e = 5.42$, provides an estimate for the common population standard deviation, σ, of quantities of volatile compounds emitted (in hundreds of nanograms) for all potato plants of any particular weight.
c. See Fig. A.15.
d. Although Fig. A.15(b) shows some curvature, it is probably not sufficiently curved to call into question the validity of the normality assumption (Assumption 3).

14.18 In part (b), it appears that the assumption of linearity (Assumption 1) is violated. In part (c), it appears that the assumption of equal standard deviations (Assumption 2) is violated.

14.19 Part (a) is a tough call, but the assumption of linearity (Assumption 1) may be violated, as may be the assumption of equal standard deviations (Assumption 2). In part (b), it appears that the assumption of equal standard deviations (Assumption 2) is violated. In part (d), it appears that the normality assumption (Assumption 3) is violated.

FIGURE A.14
(a) Residual plot and (b) normal probability plot of residuals for Exercise 14.16(c)

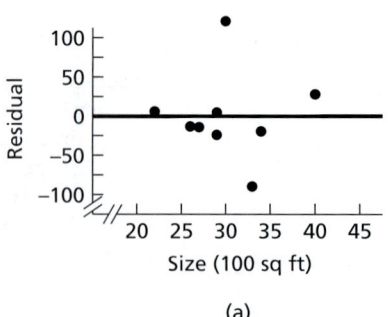
(a)

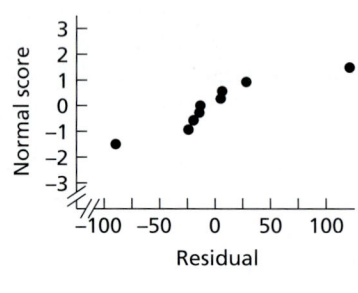
(b)

FIGURE A.15
(a) Residual plot and (b) normal probability plot of residuals for Exercise 14.17(c)

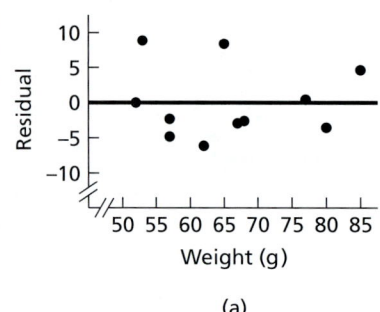
(a)

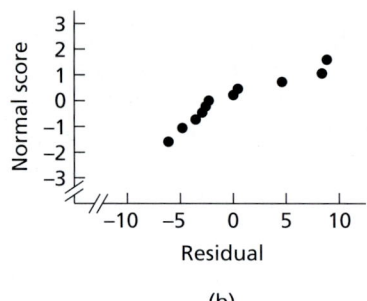
(b)

EXERCISES 14.2

14.26 If $\beta_1 = 0$, then, for each value x of the predictor variable, the conditional distribution of the response variable is a normal distribution having mean β_0 ($= \beta_0 + 0 \cdot x$) and standard deviation σ. Because x does not appear in either of those two parameters, it is useless as a predictor of y.

14.27 normal, -3.5

14.28
a. Standard normal distribution
b. Because σ is unknown
c. The statistic used is

$$t = \frac{b_1 - \beta_1}{s_e/\sqrt{S_{xx}}},$$

which has the t-distribution with df $= n - 2$.

14.29 r^2, r

14.30 $H_0: \beta_1 = 0$, $H_a: \beta_1 \neq 0$; $\alpha = 0.05$; $t = -12.369$; critical values $= \pm 2.306$; $P < 0.01$; reject H_0; at the 5% significance level, the data provide sufficient evidence to conclude that the slope of the population regression line is not 0 and hence that percentage of investments in energy securities is useful as a predictor of tax efficiency for mutual fund portfolios.

14.31 $H_0: \beta_1 = 0$, $H_a: \beta_1 \neq 0$; $\alpha = 0.10$; $t = -10.887$; critical values $= \pm 1.860$; $P < 0.01$; reject H_0; at the 10% significance level, the data provide sufficient evidence to conclude that the slope of the population regression line is not 0 and hence that age is useful as a predictor of price for Corvettes.

14.32 $H_0: \beta_1 = 0$, $H_a: \beta_1 \neq 0$; $\alpha = 0.01$; $t = 3.918$; critical values $= \pm 3.499$; $P < 0.01$; reject H_0; at the 1% significance level, the data provide sufficient evidence to conclude that size is useful as a predictor of price for custom homes in the Equestrian Estates.

14.33 $H_0: \beta_1 = 0$, $H_a: \beta_1 \neq 0$; $\alpha = 0.05$; $t = 1.053$; critical values $= \pm 2.262$; $P > 0.20$; do not reject H_0; at the 5% significance level, the data do not provide sufficient evidence to conclude that weight is useful as a predictor of quantity of volatile emissions for the potato plant *Solanum tuberosom*.

14.34
a. -6.25 to -4.28
b. We can be 95% confident that, for mutual fund portfolios, the decrease in mean tax efficiency per 1% increase in percentage of investments in energy securities is somewhere between 4.28 and 6.25.

14.35
a. -32.7 to -23.1
b. We can be 90% confident that, for Corvettes, the decrease in mean price per 1-year increase in age (i.e., the mean annual depreciation) is somewhere between $2310 and $3270.

14.36
a. 1.70 to 30.09
b. We can be 99% confident that, for custom homes in the Equestrian Estates, the increase in mean price per increase of 100 square feet in size is somewhere between $1,700 and $30,090.

14.37
a. −0.19 to 0.51
b. We can be 95% confident that, for the potato plant *Solanum tuberosom*, the change in the mean quantity of volatile emissions per 1-gram increase of weight is somewhere between −19 and 51 nanograms.

EXERCISES 14.3

14.43 $11,443. A point estimate for the mean price is the same as the predicted price.

14.44
a. 81.09
b. 78.81 to 83.38. We can be 95% confident that the mean tax efficiency of all mutual fund portfolios with 6% of their investments in energy securities is somewhere between 78.81 and 83.38.
c. 81.09
d. 73.62 to 88.57. We can be 95% certain that the observed tax efficiency of a mutual fund portfolio with 6% of its investments in energy securities will be somewhere between 73.62 and 88.57.
e. See Fig. A.16.
f. The error in the estimate of the mean tax efficiency of all mutual fund portfolios with 6% of their investments in energy securities is due only to the fact that the population regression line is being estimated by a sample regression line. In contrast, the error in the prediction of the observed tax efficiency of a mutual fund portfolio with 6% of its investments in energy securities is due to the error in estimating the mean tax efficiency plus the variation in tax efficiencies of mutual fund portfolios with 6% of their investments in energy securities.

14.45
a. 259.99 ($25,999)
b. 251.60 to 268.38. We can be 90% confident that the mean price of all 4-year-old Corvettes is somewhere between $25,160 and $26,838.
c. 259.99 ($25,999)
d. 232.20 to 287.78. We can be 90% certain that the observed price of a 4-year-old Corvette will be somewhere between $23,220 and $28,778.
e. See Fig. A.17.
f. The error in the estimate of the mean price of all 4-year-old Corvettes is due only to the fact that the population regression line is being estimated by a sample regression line. In contrast, the error in the prediction of the observed price of a 4-year-old Corvette is due to the error in estimating the mean price plus the variation in prices of 4-year-old Corvettes.

FIGURE A.16
95% confidence and prediction intervals for Exercise 14.44(e)

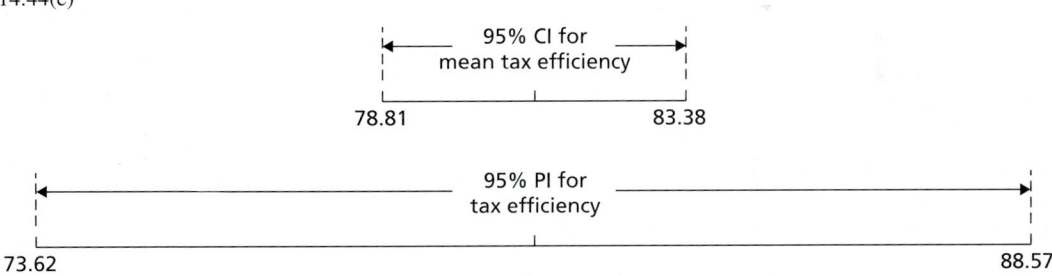

FIGURE A.17
90% confidence and prediction intervals for Exercise 14.45(e)

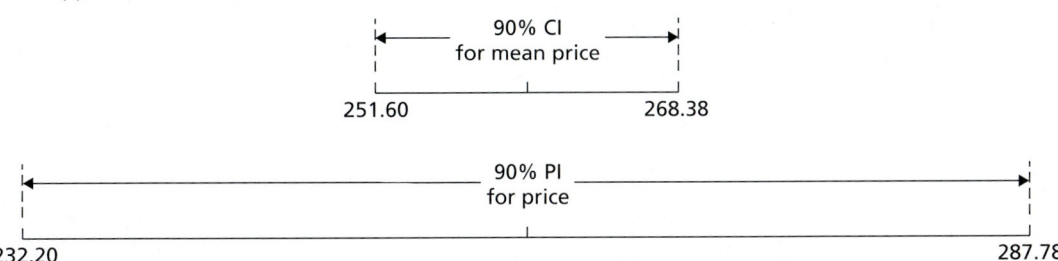

14.46
a. 304.1 ($304,100)
b. 229.0 to 379.2. We can be 99% confident that the mean price of all 2800-sq-ft Equestrian Estates homes is somewhere between $229,000 and $379,200.
c. 304.1 ($304,100)
d. 82.3 to 525.9. We can be 99% certain that the observed price of a 2800-sq-ft Equestrian Estates home will be somewhere between $82,300 and $525,900.

14.47
a. 13.29 (1329 ng)
b. 9.09 to 17.50. We can be 95% confident that the mean quantity of volatile emissions of all plants that weigh 60 g is somewhere between 909 and 1750 ng.
c. 13.29 (1329 ng)
d. 0.34 to 26.25. We can be 95% certain that the observed quantity of volatile emissions of a plant that weighs 60 g will be somewhere between 34 and 2625 ng.

EXERCISES 14.4

14.55 The (sample) linear correlation coefficient, r

14.56 No. Because of sampling error, it is possible for $\rho \leq 0$ (i.e., for the two variables to not be positively linearly correlated) but yet have $r > 0$ for a sample.

14.57
a. Uncorrelated **b.** Increases **c.** Negatively

14.58 $H_0: \rho = 0$, $H_a: \rho < 0$; $\alpha = 0.025$; $t = -12.369$; critical value $= -2.306$; $P < 0.005$; reject H_0; at the 2.5% significance level, the data provide sufficient evidence to conclude that, for mutual fund portfolios, percentage of investments in energy securities and tax efficiency are negatively linearly correlated.

14.59 $H_0: \rho = 0$, $H_a: \rho < 0$; $\alpha = 0.05$; $t = -10.887$; critical value $= -1.860$; $P < 0.005$; reject H_0; at the 5% significance level, the data provide sufficient evidence to conclude that, for Corvettes, age and price are negatively linearly correlated.

14.60 $H_0: \rho = 0$, $H_a: \rho > 0$; $\alpha = 0.005$; $t = 3.918$; critical value $= 3.499$; $P < 0.005$; reject H_0; at the 0.5% significance level, the data provide sufficient evidence to conclude that, for custom homes in the Equestrian Estates, size and price are positively linearly correlated.

14.61 $H_0: \rho = 0$, $H_a: \rho \neq 0$; $\alpha = 0.05$; $t = 1.053$; critical values $= \pm 2.262$; $P > 0.20$; do not reject H_0; at the 5% significance level, the data do not provide sufficient evidence to conclude that, for the potato plant *Solanum tuberosom*, weight and quantity of volatile emissions are linearly correlated.

14.62 $H_0: \rho = 0$, $H_a: \rho \neq 0$; $\alpha = 0.05$; $t = 0.248$; critical values $= \pm 2.306$; $P > 0.20$; do not reject H_0; at the 5% significance level, the data do not provide sufficient evidence to conclude that, for students in introductory statistics courses, height and final exam score are linearly correlated.

14.63 ρ is a parameter; r is a statistic

REVIEW TEST FOR CHAPTER 14

1. **a.** Conditional
   b. See Key Fact 14.1.
2. **a.** b_1 **b.** b_0 **c.** s_e
3. A residual plot (i.e., a plot of the residuals against the observed values of the predictor variable) and a normal probability plot of the residuals. A plot of the residuals against the observed values of the predictor variable should fall roughly in a horizontal band, centered and symmetric about the x-axis. A normal probability plot of the residuals should be roughly linear.
4. **a.** Assumption 1 **b.** Assumption 2
   c. Assumption 3 **d.** Assumption 3
5. The regression equation is useful for making predictions.
6. b_1, r, r^2
7. No. Both equal the number obtained by substituting the specified value of the predictor variable into the sample regression equation.
8. The term *confidence* is usually reserved for interval estimates of parameters, whereas the term *prediction* is used for interval estimates of variables.
9. ρ
10. **a.** The variables are positively linearly correlated, meaning that y tends to increase linearly as x increases (and vice versa), with the tendency being greater the closer that ρ is to 1.
    b. The variables are linearly uncorrelated, meaning that there is no linear relationship between the variables.
    c. The variables are negatively linearly correlated, meaning that y tends to decrease linearly as x increases (and vice versa), with the tendency being greater the closer that ρ is to -1.
11. There are constants, β_0, β_1, and σ, such that, for each student-to-faculty ratio, x, the graduation rates for all universities with that student-to-faculty ratio are normally distributed with mean $\beta_0 + \beta_1 x$ and standard deviation σ.
12. **a.** $\hat{y} = 16.4 + 2.03x$
    b. $s_e = 11.31\%$; very roughly speaking, on average, the predicted graduation rate for a university in the sample differs from the observed graduation rate by about 11.31 percentage points.

c. Presuming that, for universities, the variables student-to-faculty ratio (x) and graduation rate (y) satisfy the assumptions for regression inferences, the standard error of the estimate, $s_e = 11.31\%$, provides an estimate for the common population standard deviation, σ, of graduation rates for all universities with any particular student-to-faculty ratio.

13.

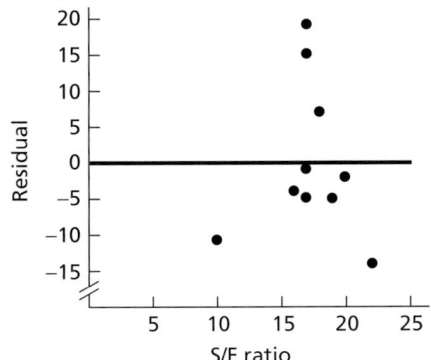

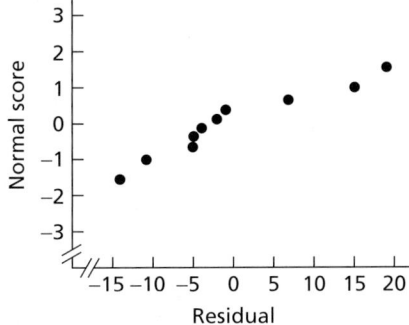

It appears reasonable.

14. a. $H_0: \beta_1 = 0$, $H_a: \beta_1 \neq 0$; $\alpha = 0.05$; $t = 1.682$; critical values $= \pm 2.306$; $0.10 < P < 0.20$; do not reject H_0; at the 5% significance level, the data do not provide sufficient evidence to conclude that, for universities, student-to-faculty ratio is useful as a predictor of graduation rate.

b. -0.75% to 4.80%. We can be 95% confident that, for universities, the change in mean graduation rate per increase by 1 in the student-to-faculty ratio is somewhere between -0.75 and 4.80 percentage points.

15. a. 50.9%

b. 42.6% to 59.2%. We can be 95% confident that the mean graduation rate of all universities that have a student-to-faculty ratio of 17 is somewhere between 42.6% and 59.2%.

c. 50.9%

d. 23.5% to 78.3%. We can be 95% certain that the observed graduation rate of a university that has a student-to-faculty ratio of 17 will be somewhere between 23.5% and 78.3%.

e. The error in the estimate of the mean graduation rate of all universities that have a student-to-faculty ratio of 17 is due only to the fact that the population regression line is being estimated by a sample regression line, whereas the error in the prediction of the observed graduation rate of a university that has a student-to-faculty ratio of 17 is due to the error in estimating the mean graduation rate plus the variation in graduation rates of universities that have a student-to-faculty ratio of 17.

16. $H_0: \rho = 0$, $H_a: \rho > 0$; $\alpha = 0.025$; $t = 1.682$; critical value $= 2.306$; $0.05 < P < 0.10$; do not reject H_0; at the 2.5% significance level, the data do not provide sufficient evidence to conclude that, for universities, the variables student-to-faculty ratio and graduation rate are positively linearly correlated.

INDEX

Acceptance region, 378
Adjacent values, 122
Alternative hypothesis, 370
   choice of, 371
Analysis of residuals, 613
Analysis of variance, 576
   one way, 580
ANOVA, see Analysis of variance
Approximately normally distributed, 258
Assessing normality, 284
Association, 552, 554
   and causation, 566
   hypothesis test for, 562, 563
At random, 200

Bar graph, 60
   segmented, 553
Bernoulli trials, 235
   and binomial coefficients, 238
Biased estimator, 310
Bimodal, 73
Binomial coefficients, 235
   and Bernoulli trials, 238
Binomial distribution, 236, 239
   as an approximation to the hypergeometric distribution, 244
   by computer, 244
   shape of, 241
Binomial probability formula, 239
   procedure for finding, 240
Binomial random variable, 239
   mean of, 242
   standard deviation of, 242
Bivariate data, 55, 550
Box-and-whisker diagram, 121

Boxplot, 121
   by computer, 125
   modified, 121
   procedure for construction of, 122

Categorical variable, 40
Cells
   of a contingency table, 551
Census, 11
Census data, 74
Central limit theorem, 314
Certain event, 202
Chebychev's rule, 112
χ_α^2, 538
Chi-square curve, 538
Chi-square curves
   basic properties of, 538
Chi-square distribution, 538
   for a goodness-of-fit test, 542
   for an independence test, 561
Chi-square goodness-of-fit test, 540, 543, 544
   by computer, 547
Chi-square independence test, 558, 562, 563
   by computer, 566
   concerning the assumptions for, 566
   distribution of test statistic for, 561
Chi-square procedures, 536
Chi-square subtotals, 542
Chi-square table
   use of, 538
CI, 329
Class
   frequency of, 46, 47
   lower cutpoint of, 46, 47
   lower limit of, 49
   mark of, 49
   midpoint of, 47

   percentage of, 46
   relative frequency of, 46, 47
   upper cutpoint of, 46, 47
   upper limit of, 49
   width of, 47
Class count, 46
Class cutpoint
   lower, 46, 47
   upper, 46, 47
Class frequency, 46, 47
Class limit
   lower, 49
   upper, 49
Class mark, 49
Class midpoint, 47
Class percentage, 46
Class relative frequency, 46, 47
Class width, 47
Classes, 45, 47
Cluster sampling, 18
Cochran, W. G., 544
Coefficient of determination
   by computer, 177
   interpretation of, 175
   relation to linear correlation coefficient, 183
Complement, 207
Complementation rule, 215
Completely randomized design, 27
Conditional distribution, 552, 608
   by computer, 554
Conditional mean, 608
Confidence interval
   length of, 339
   relation to hypothesis testing, 396, 397, 438

I-1

Confidence interval for one population
    mean
  by computer in regression, 640
  by computer when σ is known, 339
  by computer when σ is unknown, 357
  in one-way analysis of variance, 600
  in regression, 635
  σ known, 335
  σ unknown, 353
  which procedure to use, 356
Confidence interval for one population
    proportion, 498
  by computer, 503
Confidence interval for the difference
    between two population means
  by computer for a paired sample, and
    normal differences or a large sample,
    478
  by computer for independent samples,
    and normal populations or large
    samples, 461
  by computer for independent samples,
    normal populations or large samples,
    and equal but unknown standard
    deviations, 447
  in one-way analysis of variance, 600
  independent samples, and normal
    populations or large samples, 459
  independent samples, normal
    populations or large samples, and
    equal but unknown standard
    deviations, 446
  paired sample, and normal differences or
    a large sample, 477
Confidence interval for the difference
    between two population proportions,
    523
  by computer for large and independent
    samples, 525
Confidence interval for the slope of a
    population regression line, 629
Confidence level, 329
  and precision, 339
Confidence-interval estimate, 329
Contingency table, 55, 550
  by computer, 554
Continuous data, 41
Continuous variable, 40
Control, 24
Control group, 25
Correlation, 146
Count
  of a class, 46

Cox, Gertrude Mary
  biographical sketch, 491
Critical values, 378, 379
  choice of for a specified significance level,
    386
Critical-value approach, 398
Cumulative frequency, 65
Cumulative probability, 279
  inverse, 280
Cumulative relative frequency, 65
Curvilinear regression, 162

Data, 41
  bivariate, 55, 550
  continuous, 41
  discrete, 41
  grouping of, 44
  qualitative, 41
  quantitative, 41
  univariate, 55, 550
Data analysis
  a fundamental principle of, 337
Data classification
  and the choice of a statistical method, 43
Data set, 41
de Moivre, Abraham
  biographical sketch, 534
Deciles, 116
Degrees of freedom, 350
  for an F-curve, 578
Degrees of freedom for the denominator,
    578
Degrees of freedom for the numerator, 578
Descriptive measure
  resistant, 93
Descriptive measures, 88
  of center, 90
  of central tendency, 90
  of spread, 103
  of variation, 103
Descriptive statistics, 4
Designed experiment, 22
Deviations from the mean, 105
Discrete data, 41
Discrete random variable, 220
  mean of, 229
  probability distribution of, 221
  standard deviation of, 231
  variance of, 231
Discrete variable, 40
Distribution
  conditional, 552, 608

  marginal, 552
  normal, 256
  of a data set, 71
  of a population, 74
  of a variable, 74
  of the difference between the observed
    and predicted values of a response
    variable, 637
  of the predicted value of a response
    variable, 634
Dotplot, 59
Double blinding, 30

Empirical rule, 112, 277
Equal-likelihood model, 202
Error, 585
Error mean square, 585
Error sum of squares, 174
  by computer, 177
  computing formula for in regression, 176
  in one-way analysis of variance, 585
  in regression, 174
Estimator
  biased, 310
  unbiased, 310
Event, 199, 205, 206
  (A & B), 207
  (A or B), 207
  certain, 202
  complement of, 207
  impossible, 202
  (not E), 207
Events, 205
  mutually exclusive, 210
  notation and graphical display for, 206
  relationships among, 207
Expectation, 229
Expected frequencies, 541
Expected value, 229
Experiment, 199
Experimental design, 22
  principles of, 24
Experimental units, 25
Experimentation, 11
Explanatory variable, 158
Exploratory data analysis, 38, 145
Exponential distribution, 319
Exponentially distributed variable, 319
Extrapolation, 159

Factor, 25, 26, 580
Factorials, 234

Failure, 235
F_α, 579
F-curve, 578
   basic properties of, 578
F-distribution, 578
First quartile, 117
Fisher, Ronald, 8, 578
   biographical sketch, 605
Five-number summary, 119
f/N rule, 198
Focus database, 34
Frequency
   cumulative, 65
   of a class, 46, 47
Frequency distribution, 46, 47
   for qualitative data, 50
Frequency histogram, 56, 57
Frequentist interpretation of probability, 201
F-statistic, 585
   in one-way analysis of variance, 587
F-table
   use of, 579

Galton, Francis
   biographical sketch, 654
Gauss, Carl Friedrich
   biographical sketch, 295
General addition rule, 216
Geometric distribution, 248
Gosset, William Sealy, 350
   biographical sketch, 367
Graph
   bar, 60
   improper scaling of, 80
   truncated, 79
Grouped data
   formulas for the sample mean and sample standard deviation, 114
Grouped-data table, 47
Grouping, 44
   by computer, 51
   terms used in, 47
   using classes based on a single value, 49

Heteroscedasticity, 609
Histogram
   for single-value grouping, 58
   frequency, 56, 57
   probability, 221
   relative-frequency, 57
Homoscedasticity, 609

Hypergeometric distribution, 243, 248
   binomial approximation to, 244
Hypothesis, 370
Hypothesis test, 368, 370
   choosing the hypotheses, 370
   logic of, 373
   possible conclusions for, 383
Hypothesis test for a population linear correlation coefficient, 644, 645
   by computer, 648
Hypothesis test for association of two variables of a population, 562, 563
Hypothesis test for one population mean
   by computer for σ known, 405
   by computer for σ unknown, 417
   σ known, 389, 403
   σ unknown, 413, 414
Hypothesis test for one population proportion, 509, 510
   by computer, 513
Hypothesis test for the slope of a population regression line, 625, 626
   by computer, 630
Hypothesis test for the utility of a regression, 625, 626
Hypothesis test for two population means
   by computer for a paired sample, and normal differences or a large sample, 478
   by computer for independent samples, and normal populations or large samples, 461
   by computer for independent samples, normal populations or large samples, and equal but unknown standard deviations, 447
   independent samples, and normal populations or large samples, 455, 456
   independent samples, normal populations or large samples, and equal but unknown standard deviations, 442, 443
   paired sample, and normal differences or a large sample, 472, 473
Hypothesis test for two population proportions, 519, 520
   by computer for large and independent samples, 525
Hypothesis testing
   critical-value approach to, 398

   P-value approach to, 398
   relation to confidence intervals, 396, 397, 438

Impossible event, 202
Improper scaling, 80
Independent samples, 432
Inferences for two population means
   choosing between a pooled and a nonpooled t-procedure, 461
Inferential statistics, 4, 5
Influential observation, 160
Intercept, 150
Interquartile range, 118, 119
Inverse cumulative probability, 280
IQR, 118

Kolmogorov, A. N.
   biographical sketch, 255
Kruskal–Wallis test, 595

Laplace, Pierre-Simon
   biographical sketch, 323
Law of averages, 230
Law of large numbers, 230
Least-squares criterion, 154, 156
Leaves, 67
Left skewed, 74
Left-tailed test, 371
   rejection region for, 379
Legendre, Adrien-Marie
   biographical sketch, 192
Levels, 25, 26, 580
Linear correlation coefficient, 179, 180
   and causation, 184
   by computer, 185
   relation to coefficient of determination, 183
   warning on the use of, 184
Linear equation, 148
   with one independent variable, 148
Linear regression, 146
   by computer, 162
   warning on the use of, 161
Linearly correlated variables, 643
Linearly uncorrelated variables, 643
Lower cutpoint, 46, 47
Lower limit, 49, 120

Mann–Whitney confidence-interval procedure, 447, 460

Mann–Whitney test, 447, 460
Margin of error
　for the estimate of μ, 344, 345
　for the estimate of p, 499
　for the estimate of $p_1 - p_2$, 524
Marginal distribution, 552
　by computer, 554
Mark
　of a class, 49
Maximum error of the estimate, 344
Mean, 90
　conditional, 608
　deviations from, 105
　interpretation for random variables, 230
　of a binomial random variable, 242
　of a discrete random variable, 229
　of a population, see Population mean
　of a sample, see Sample mean
　of a variable, 95, 129
　of $\bar{x}$, 306
　trimmed, 94, 99
　using technology, 95
Mean of a random variable, 229
Mean of a variable, 95, 129
Measures of center, 90
　comparison of, 93
Measures of central tendency, 90
Measures of spread, 103
Measures of variation, 103
Median, 91
　using technology, 95
Midpoint
　of a class, 47
Mode, 92
Modified boxplot, 121
　procedure for construction of, 122
Multimodal, 73
Multiple comparisons, 595
Multistage sampling, 21
Mutually exclusive events, 210
　and the special addition rule, 214

Negatively linearly correlated variables,
　　181, 643
Neyman, Jerzy
　biographical sketch, 429
Nightingale, Florence
　biographical sketch, 35
Nonparametric methods, 356
Nonpooled t-interval procedure, 459
Nonpooled t-test, 454
Nonrejection region, 378, 379

Normal curve, 258
　equation of, 258
　parameters of, 258
　standard, 261
Normal differences, 471
Normal distribution, 256, 258
　approximate, 258
　assessing using normal probability plots,
　　284
　by computer, 278
　standard, 261
Normal probability plots, 284
　use in detecting outliers, 285
Normal scores, 284
Normally distributed population, 258
Normally distributed variable, 258
　68.26-95.44-99.74 rule for, 276
　procedure for finding a range, 277
　procedure for finding percentages for, 274
　standardized version of, 262
Not statistically significant, 383
Null hypothesis, 370
　choice of, 370
Number of failures, 495
Number of successes, 495

Observation, 41
Observational study, 22
Observed frequencies, 540
Observed significance level, 398
Occurs, 206
Odds, 204
Ogive, 65
One-sample t-interval procedure, 353
One-sample t-test, 410
One-sample Wilcoxon confidence-interval
　procedure, 356
One-sample Wilcoxon signed-rank test, 417
One-sample z-interval procedure, 335
　for a population proportion, 497
One-sample z-test, 388
　for a population proportion, 509
One-tailed test, 371
One-way analysis of variance, 580
　assumptions for, 580
　by computer, 596
　distribution of test statistic for, 587
　procedure for, 590, 591
One-way ANOVA identity, 587
One-way ANOVA table, 588
One-way ANOVA test, 590, 591

Ordinal data, 44
　measures of center for, 98
Outlier, 99, 120
　detection of with normal probability
　　plots, 285
　effect on the standard deviation, 114
　identification of, 120
　in regression, 159

Paired difference, 470
Paired samples, 468
Paired t-interval procedure, 477
Paired t-test, 471
Paired Wilcoxon confidence-interval
　procedure, 478
Paired Wilcoxon signed-rank test, 478
Parameter, 133
Parameters
　of a normal curve, 258
Parametric methods, 356
Pearson product moment correlation
　coefficient, see Linear correlation
　coefficient
Pearson, Karl, 8, 654
　biographical sketch, 575
Percentage
　of a class, 46
Percentiles, 116
　of a normally distributed variable, 283
Pictogram, 80
Pie chart, 60
Placebo effect, 24
Point estimate, 328, 329
Poisson distribution, 249
Poisson, Simeon, 249, 323
Pool, 440
Pooled sample proportion, 518
Pooled sample standard deviation, 440
Pooled t-interval procedure, 446
Pooled t-test, 441
Population, 5
　distribution of, 74
　normally distributed, 258
Population data, 74, 95
Population distribution, 74
Population linear correlation coefficient, 642
Population mean, 95, 129
Population median
　notation for, 137
Population proportion, 492, 494, 495
Population regression equation, 609
Population regression line, 609

Population standard deviation, 131
 computing formula for, 131
Population variance, 131
Positively linearly correlated variables, 181, 643
Power, 382
Practical significance
 versus statistical significance, 395
Prediction interval, 636
 by computer, 640
 procedure for, 638
Predictor variable, 158
Probability
 basic properties of, 202
 cumulative, 279
 equally likely outcomes, 199
 frequentist interpretation of, 201
 inverse cumulative, 280
 model of, 202
 notation for, 213
 rules of, 213
Probability distribution
 binomial, 239
 geometric, 248
 hypergeometric, 243, 248
 interpretation of, 225, 226
 of a discrete random variable, 221
 Poisson, 249
Probability histogram, 221
Probability model, 202
Probability sampling, 12
Probability theory, 196
Probability value, 398
Proportion
 population, *see* Population proportion
 sample, *see* Sample proportion
 sampling distribution of, 496
Proportional allocation, 21
P-value, 398
 as the observed significance level, 402
 general procedure for obtaining, 409
 use in assessing the evidence against the null hypothesis, 405
 use of as a decision criterion for a hypothesis test, 402
P-value approach, 398

Qualitative data, 41
 frequency and relative-frequency distributions for, 50
 graphical displays for, 60
Qualitative variable, 40

Quantitative data, 41
Quantitative variable, 40
Quartile
 first, 117
 second, 117
 third, 117
Quartiles, 116, 117
 of a normally distributed variable, 283
Quetelet, Adolphe
 biographical sketch, 87
Quintiles, 116

Random sampling, 12
 systematic, 17
Random variable, 220
 binomial, 239
 discrete, *see* Discrete random variable
 interpretation of mean of, 230
 notation for, 221
Randomization, 24
Randomized block design, 27
Random-number table, 13
Range, 104
 by computer, 113
Regression equation
 definition of, 156
 determination of using the sample covariance, 169
 formula for, 157
Regression identity, 175
Regression inferences
 assumptions for in simple linear regression, 609
Regression line
 criterion for finding, 161
 definition of, 156
Regression model, 609
Regression sum of squares, 172
 by computer, 177
 computing formula for, 176
Rejection region, 378, 379
Relative frequency
 cumulative, 65
 of a class, 46, 47
Relative-frequency distribution, 46, 47
 for qualitative data, 50
Relative-frequency histogram, 57
Relative-frequency polygon, 65
Replication, 24
Representative sample, 11
Research hypothesis, 370

Residual, 613
 in ANOVA, 581
Residual plot, 614
 by computer, 616
Residual standard deviation, 611
Resistant measure, 93
Response variable, 25, 26, 595
 in regression, 158
Right skewed, 74
 property of a χ^2-curve, 538
 property of an F-curve, 578
Right-tailed test, 371
 rejection region for, 379
Robust, 336
Rounding error, 48
Roundoff error, 48
Rule of 2, 581

Sample, 5
 distribution of, 74
 representative, 11
 simple random, 12
 size of, 101
 stratified, 20
Sample covariance, 169
Sample data, 74, 95
Sample distribution, 74
Sample mean, 95, 101
 as an estimate for a population mean, 130
 formula for grouped data, 114
 sampling distribution of, 299
 standard error of, 309
Sample proportion, 494, 495
 formula for, 495
 pooled, 518
Sample size, 101
 and sampling error, 301, 309
 for estimating a population mean, 346
 for estimating a population proportion, 501
 for estimating the difference between two population proportions, 524
Sample space, 205, 206
Sample standard deviation, 105, 107
 as an estimate of a population standard deviation, 132
 by computer, 113
 computing formula for, 110
 defining formula for, 108, 110
 formula for grouped data, 114
 pooled, 440

Sample variance, 107
Samples
   independent, 432
   paired, 468
Sampling, 11
   cluster, 18
   multistage, 21
   simple random, 12
   stratified, 20
   with replacement, 243
   without replacement, 243
Sampling distribution, 298
Sampling distribution of the difference between two sample means, 436
Sampling distribution of the difference between two sample proportions, 518
Sampling distribution of the sample mean, 299
   for a normally distributed variable, 312
Sampling distribution of the sample proportion, 496
Sampling distribution of the slope of the regression line, 623, 624
Sampling error, 298
   and sample size, 301, 309
Scatter diagram, 154
   by computer, 162
Scatterplot, 154
Second quartile, 117
Segmented bar graph, 553
Significance level, 381, 382
Simple random sample, 12
Simple random sampling, 12
   with replacement, 12
   without replacement, 12
Simpson's paradox, 86
Single-value grouping, 49
   histograms for, 58
Skewed
   to the left, 74
   to the right, 74
Slope, 150
   graphical interpretation of, 152
Special addition rule, 214
Squared deviations
   sum of, 106
Standard deviation
   of a binomial random variable, 242
   of a discrete random variable, 231
   of a population, *see* Population standard deviation
   of a sample, *see* Sample standard deviation
   of $\bar{x}$, 308
Standard deviation of a random variable, 231
   computing formula for, 231
Standard deviation of a variable, 131
Standard error, 309
Standard error of the estimate, 611, 612
   by computer, 616
Standard error of the sample mean, 309
Standard normal curve, 261
   areas under, 266
   basic properties of, 266
   finding the z-score(s) for a specified area, 269
Standard normal distribution, 261
Standard score, 135
Standardized variable, 134
Standardized version
   of a variable, 134
   of $\bar{x}$, 349
Standard-normal table
   use of, 266
Statistic, 133
   sampling distribution of, 298
Statistical significance
   versus practical significance, 395
Statistically dependent variables, 554
Statistically independent variables, 554
Statistically significant, 383
Statistics
   descriptive, 4
   inferential, 4, 5
Stem-and-leaf diagram, 66, 67
   ordered, 67
   shaded, 67
   using rounded observations, 70
   using truncated observations, 70
Stemplot, 66
Stems, 67
Straight line, 148
Strata, 20
Stratified random sampling with proportional allocation, 21
Stratified sampling, 20
   proportional allocation in, 21
   with proportional allocation, 21
Student's t-distribution, *see* t-distribution
Studentized version of $\bar{x}$, 349
   distribution of, 350, 410
Subject, 25
Subscripts, 100

Success, 235
Success probability, 235
Sum of squared deviations, 106
Summation notation, 100
Symmetric, 74
   property of a t-curve, 351
   property of the standard normal curve, 266
Symmetric distribution, 74
Systematic random sampling, 17

t_α, 351
t-curve, 350
   basic properties of, 351
t-distribution, 350, 410, 440, 454, 471, 624, 634, 637, 643
Technology Center, 10
Test statistic, 378, 379
Third quartile, 117
t-interval procedure, 353
Total sum of squares
   by computer, 177
   computing formula for in regression, 176
   in one-way analysis of variance, 587
   in regression, 174
Treatment, 24, 585
Treatment group, 25
Treatment mean square
   in one-way analysis of variance, 584
Treatment sum of squares
   in one-way analysis of variance, 584
Tree diagram, 237
Trial, 233
Trimmed mean, 93, 99
Truncated graph, 79
t-test, 410
Tukey, John, 66, 121
   biographical sketch, 145
Two-sample z-interval procedure, 437, 438
   for the difference between two population proportions, 523
Two-sample z-procedures, 438
Two-sample z-test, 437, 438
   for two population proportions, 520
Two-tailed test, 371
   rejection region for, 379
Two-way table, 550
Type I error, 380
   probability of, 382
Type II error, 380
   probability of, 382
Type II error probabilities
   calculation of, 385

Unbiased estimator, 310
Uniform distribution, 322
Uniformly distributed variable, 322
Unimodal, 73
Univariate data, 55, 550
Upper cutpoint, 46, 47
Upper limit, 49, 120

Variable, 40
    approximately normally distributed, 258
    assessing normality, 284
    categorical, 40
    continuous, 40
    discrete, 40
    distribution of, 74
    exponentially distributed, 319
    mean of, 95, 129
    normally distributed, 258
    qualitative, 40
    quantitative, 40
    standard deviation of, 131
    standardized, 134
    standardized version of, 134
    uniformly distributed, 322
Variance
    of a discrete random variable, 231
    of a population, *see* Population variance
    of a sample, *see* Sample variance
Variance of a random variable, 231
Venn diagrams, 207
Venn, John, 207

Whiskers, 122
Width
    of a class, 47

Wilcoxon confidence-interval procedure, 356
    paired, 478
Wilcoxon signed-rank test, 417
    paired, 478

y-intercept, 150

z_α, 270, 334
z-curve, 266
    see also Standard normal curve
z-interval procedure, 335
    for a population proportion, 497
z-score, 135
    as a measure of relative standing, 137
z-test, 388
    for a population proportion, 509, 510

DATA SOURCES

A.C. Nielsen Company
AAA Daily Fuel Gauge Report
AAA Foundation for Traffic Safety
Academy of Medicine Cleveland Survey
Acta Opthalmologica
Administration for Children and Families
Advances in Cancer Research
African Entomology
Agency for International Development
Alan Guttmacher Institute
American Association for the Advancement of Science
American Association of University Professors
American Banker
American Bar Foundation
American College Testing Program
American Council of Life Insurance
American Demographics
American Elasmobranch Society
American Film Institute
American Hospital Association
American Journal of Clinical Nutrition
American Journal of Obstetrics and Gynecology
American Medical Association
Amusement Business
Annals of Epidemiology
Appetite
Arizona Republic
Arizona State University Focus Student Database
Arizona State University Main Facts Book
Arthritis Today
Association of Community Organizations for Reform Now
ASU Insight

Austin360.com
Auto Trader
Barron's National Business and Financial Weekly
Behavior Research Center
Biometrika
Board of Governors of the Federal Reserve System
Boston Globe
Bottom Line
Bride's Magazine
British Medical Journal
Bureau of Economic Analysis
Bureau of Justice Statistics
Bureau of Labor Statistics
Bureau of Prisons
Business Failure Record
Buyers of New Cars
CBS Sportsline
Cellular Telecommunications Industry Association
Census Bureau
Center for Disease Control
Center for Housing Policy
Chance
Cheetah Conservation of Southern Africa
Chesapeake and Ohio Railroad Company
Chicago Title Insurance Company
CNN/Sports Illustrated Online
Coleman & Associates, Inc.
College Entrance Examination Board
Computer Industry Almanac Inc., 1999
Congressional Directory
Congressional Quarterly Inc.
Consumer Reports
Contribution to Boyce Thompson Institute
Crain's Cleveland Business

Daily Racing Form
Demography
Department of Agriculture
Department of Commerce
Department of Housing and Urban Development
Department of Justice
Dictionary of Scientific Biography
Diet for a New America
Directory of Governors of the American States, Commonwealths & Territories
Edinburgh Medical and Surgical Journal
Employment and Training Administration
Energy Information Administration
Entertainment Weekly
Environmental Pollution (Series A)
Environmental Protection Agency
Environmental Science and Technology
Euromonitor Publications Limited, London
Excite Sports
Excite.com
Experimental Agriculture
Federal Bureau of Investigation
Federal Highway Administration
Financial Planning
Florida Museum of Natural History
Food and Nutrition Board of the National Academy of Sciences
Forbes Magazine
Forest Mensuration
Fortune Magazine
Gallup Organization
Giving and Volunteering in the U.S.
Greg D. Adams and Chris Fastnow
Handbook of Small Data Sets
Hanna Properties

Harris Poll
Higher Education Research Institute
Human Nutrition and Metabolism
Hydrobiologia
Information Please Almanac
Internal Revenue Service
International Civil Aviation Organization
International Journal for Quality in Health Care
International Waterpower and Dam Construction Handbook
Journal of Abnormal Psychology
Journal of Advertising Research
Journal of Agricultural Sciences
Journal of Applied Ecology
Journal of Athletic Training
Journal of Business
Journal of Chemical Ecology
Journal of Chronic Diseases
Journal of Clinical Oncology
Journal of Counseling Psychology
Journal of Environmental Psychology
Journal of Environmental Science and Health
Journal of Herpetology
Journal of Nutrition
Journal of Organizational Behavior
Journal of Pediatrics
Journal of Studies on Alcohol
Journal of the American Medical Association
Journal of the American Public Health Association
Journal of Tropical Ecology
Journal of Zoology, London
Kelley Blue Book
Library Journal
Literary Digest
Limnology and Oceanography
Los Angeles Times
M Street Corporation
Marine Ecology Progress Series
Marine Mammal Science
Mediamark Research Inc.
Medical College of Wisconsin Eye Institute
Merck Manual
Monthly Labor Review
Motor Vehicle Manufacturers Association
National Association for Gardening
National Basketball Association
National Center for Education Statistics
National Center for Health Statistics
National Council of the Churches of Christ
National Football League
National Gardening Association
National Geographic
National Institute on Alcohol Abuse and Alcoholism
National Institute of Mental Health
National Oceanic and Atmospheric Administration
National Opinion Research Center
National Science Foundation
National Sporting Goods Association
National Survey of Salaries and Wages in Public Schools
New England Journal of Medicine
New York Times
Newsweek
Northwestern Endicott-Lindquist Report
Northwestern University Placement Center
Office of Juvenile Justice and Delinquency Prevention
O'Neil Associates
Parade Magazine
Patent and Trademark Office
PC World
Pediatrics
Peterson's Annual Survey
Peterson's Guide to Four-Year Colleges, 2000
Physician's Handbook
Pollstar
Preventative Medicine
Proceedings of the 6th Berkeley Symposium on Mathematics and Statistics, VI
Proceeding of the National Academy of Science USA
Public Health Reports
Public Interest Research Group
R. R. Bowker Company of New York
Radio Advertising Bureau of New York
Reader's Digest
Reader's Digest/Gallup Survey
Real Estate Research Corp.
Recording Industry Association of America, Inc.
Research Quarterly for Exercise and Sport
Research Resources, Inc.
Rubber Age
Runner's World
Salt River Project
Science
Science News
Scientific American
Social Forces
Sports Illustrated
Statistical Abstract of the United States, 1999
Substance Abuse and Mental Health Services Administration
Technometrics
TELENATION/Market Facts Inc.
Television Bureau of Advertising
Tempe Daily News
The American Midland Naturalist
The American Statistician
The Beer Institute
The Detection of Psychiatric Illness by Questionnaire
The Earth: Structure, Composition and Evolution
The History of Statistics
The Lancet
The Marathon: Physiological, Medical, Epidemiological and Psychological Studies
The Method of Statistics
The Morgan Horse
The Phoenix Gazette
The World Fact Book
TIME
Tropical Biodiversity
Truck Trader
U.S. News & World Report
University of Michigan Institute for Social Research
USA TODAY
USA TODAY/CNN/Gallup Poll
USA WEEKEND
Vegetarian Journal
VentureOne Corporation
Wall Street Journal
Washington Post/ABC News Poll
Webster's New World Dictionary
Western Journal of Medicine
Western North American Naturalist
Wichita Eagle
World Almanac, 1999
World of Wireless Communication
Zero Population Growth
Zogby American Poll

Photo Credits

Pages 3 and 35, photo from "Citizen Kane" © Bettman/CORBIS; page 5, photo of Harry Truman © Bettman/CORBIS; pages 16 and 44, photo of the Eagles © Henry Diltz/CORBIS; page 29, photo of iron lung © Hulton-Deutsch Collection/CORBIS; page 35, image of Florence Nightingale from www.spartucus.schoolnet.co.uk/REnightingale.htm; pages 39 and 86, photo of infants © 2001 PhotoDisc, Inc.; page 41, photo of marathon runner © Reuters New Media Inc./CORBIS; page 53, photo of cheetahs © 2001 PhotoDisc, Inc.; page 54, photo of great white shark, Corbis Royalty-free; page 55, photo of stockbrokers © 2001 PhotoDisc, Inc.; page 87, image of Adolphe Quetelet courtesy St. Andrews University; pages 89 and 144, New York Yankees photo © Bettman/CORBIS; page 97, photo of tornado damage © FreeStockPhotos.com; page 98, photo of driver courtesy AAA Foundation for Traffic Safety; page 103, photo of Los Angeles Lakers © AFP/CORBIS; page 114, photo of hurricane damage © 2001 PhotoDisc, Inc.; page 129, photo of U.S. Women's Soccer team © Reuters NewMedia Inc./CORBIS; page 138, photo of hurricane eye © 2001 PhotoDisc, Inc.; page 141, photo of party © 2001 PhotoDisc, Inc.; page 145, image of John Tukey courtesy St. Andrews University; pages 147 and 192, photo of fatty food © 2001 PhotoDisc, Inc.; page 153, photo of thermometers © 2001 PhotoDisc, Inc.; page 169, photo of baseball player © Reuters New Media Inc./CORBIS; page 178, photo of Corvette courtesy of CorvetteMagazine.com; page 179, photo of pelicans © 2001 PhotoDisc, Inc.; page 192, image of Adrien Legendre courtesy St. Andrews University; pages 197 and 254, Powerball logo ® the Multi-State Lottery Association; page 205, photo of racehorse © AFP/CORBIS; page 218, photo of oil spill courtesy of NOAA; page 223, photo of elementary school students © 2001 PhotoDisc, Inc.; page 226, photo of space shuttle courtesy of NASA; page 227, photo of eclipse © 2001 PhotoDisc, Inc.; page 233, photo of factory © 2001 PhotoDisc, Inc.; page 240, photo of couple © 2001 PhotoDisc, Inc.; page 251, photo of meeting © 2001 PhotoDisc, Inc.; page 255, image of Andrei Kolmogorov courtesy of St. Andrews University; pages 257 and 294, photo of Scottish militiamen courtesy of Beth Anderson; page 282, photo of Jingdong black gibbon © Rod Williams/Bruce Coleman, PictureQuest; page 295, image of Carl Friedrich Gauss courtesy of St. Andrews University; pages 297 and 323, photo of Chesapeake & Ohio railroad car © Karen Huntt Mason/CORBIS; page 303, photo of Los Angeles Lakers © AP/Wide World Photos; page 304, photo of Bill Gates © Reuters NewMedia Inc./CORBIS; page 310, photo of earthquake damage © 2001 CARE photo; page 317, image of brain scans © 2001 PhotoDisc, Inc.; page 320, photo of tax return © 2001 PhotoDisc, Inc.; page 323, image of Pierre-Simon Laplace courtesy St. Andrews University; page 332, wedding photo courtesy of Aaron and Carla Weiss; page 342, photo of the Rolling Stones © Lynn Goldsmith/CORBIS; page 348, photo of fiber optic wires © 2001 PhotoDisc, Inc.; page 359, photo of amusement park ride © Neil Rabinowitz/CORBIS; page 363, photo of seashell © 2001 PhotoDisc, Inc.; page 367, image of William Gosset courtesy of St. Andrews University; pages 369 and 428, photo of park © 2001 PhotoDisc, Inc.; page 377, photo of cell phone user © 2001 PhotoDisc, Inc.; page 384, photo of child © 2001 PhotoDisc, Inc.; page 385, photo of trial, Corbis Royalty-free; page 415, photo of water © 2001 PhotoDisc, Inc.; page 420, photo of mother and newborn, Corbis Royalty-free; page 426, photo of an arrest © Jonathan Blair/CORBIS; page 429, image of Jerzy Neyman courtesy St. Andrews University; pages 431 and 490, photo of reader, Corbis Royalty-free; page 465, photo of patient © 2001 PhotoDisc, Inc.; page 482, photo of person sleeping, Corbis Royalty-free; page 482, photo of tires, Corbis Royalty-free; page 486, photo of snake, Corbis Royalty-free; page 491, image of Gertrude Cox courtesy of Research Triangle Institute; pages 493 and 534, photo of ATM © 2001 PhotoDisc, Inc.; page 505, photo of women, Corbis Royalty-free; page 506, photo of a toast © 2001 PhotoDisc, Inc.; page 515, photo of a family opening presents © 2001 PhotoDisc, Inc.; page 529, photo of "Buckle Up" highway sign © 2001 PhotoDisc, Inc.; page 532, photo of jurors, Corbis Royalty-free; page 534, image of Abraham de Moivre courtesy of St. Andrews University; pages 537 and 575, photo of angry driver © 2001 PhotoDisc, Inc.; page 547, photo of jail © Bettman/CORBIS; page 569, photo of Siskel and Ebert © AP Photo/Buena Vista Television; page 573, photo of hospital © David H. Wells/CORBIS; page 575, image of Karl Pearson © Brown Brothers; pages 577 and 604, photo of college students © 2001 PhotoDisc, Inc.; page 599, photo of couple in new apartment, Corbis Royalty-free; page 601, photo of cuckoo © Roger Tidman/CORBIS; page 601, photo of Linus Pauling with Vitamin C molecule © Roger Ressmeyer/CORBIS; page 605, image of Sir Ronald Fisher courtesy St. Andrews University; pages 607 and 653, photo of hamburger and potato chips © 2001 PhotoDisc, Inc.; page 619, photo of mutual fund statement © 2001 PhotoDisc, Inc.; page 619, photo of Corvette courtesy of CorvetteMagazine.com; page 621, photo of newborn, Corbis Royalty-free; page 631, photo of potato plants © Patrick Johns/CORBIS; page 632, photo of newborn © 2001 PhotoDisc, Inc.; page 651, photo of graduate courtesy of Greg Weiss; page 654, image of Sir Francis Galton courtesy of St. Andrews University.

Indexes for Internet Projects, Biographical Sketches and Case Studies

Internet Projects

The Titanic Disaster *34*
Simpson's Paradox *86*
Old Faithful Geyser and a Survey of Wages *143*
Assisted Reproductive Technology *191*
The Space Shuttle Challenger *253*
IQ of Boys and Girls *293*
Simulations *322*
Famous Data Sets *365*
The Ozone Hole *428*
Women Workers and Equality in the United States *489*
The Salk Polio Vaccine Trial *533*
Sex and the Death Penalty *574*
Brain Damage and the Courts *603*
Assisted Reproductive Technology (Revisited) *652*

Biographical Sketches

Florence Nightingale *35*
Adolphe Quetelet *87*
John Tukey *145*
Adrien Legendre *192*
Andrei Kolmogorov *255*
Carl Friedrich Gauss *295*
Pierre-Simon Laplace *323*
William Gosset *367*
Jerzy Neyman *429*
Gertrude Cox *491*
Abraham de Moivre *534*
Karl Pearson *575*
Sir Ronald Fisher *605*
Sir Francis Galton *654*

Case Studies

Top Films of All Time *3, 35*
Preventing Infant Mortality *39, 86*
New York Yankees Y2K Salaries *89, 144*
Fat Consumption and Prostate Cancer *147, 192*
The Powerball *197, 254*
Chest Sizes of Scottish Militiamen *257, 294*
The Chesapeake and Ohio Freight Study *297, 323*
The Chips Ahoy! 1,000 Chips Challenge *327, 366*
Sex and Sense of Direction *369, 428*
Breast Milk and IQ *431, 490*
Double-Dipping ATM Fees *493, 534*
Road Rage *537, 575*
Heavy Drinking Among College Students *577, 604*
Fat Consumption and Prostate Cancer *607, 653*

Procedure Index

Following is an index that provides page-number references for the various statistical procedures discussed in the book.

Binomial Distribution Binomial probability formula, *240*

Boxplots To construct a boxplot, *122* To construct a modified boxplot, *122*

Chi-Square Tests Goodness-of-fit test, *543, 544* Independence test, *562, 563*

Correlation Inferences Linear correlation test, *644, 645*

Generic Hypothesis Tests Critical-value approach, *405* P-value approach, *405*

Inferences for One Mean
Hypothesis tests
  One-sample z-test, *389, 403*
  One-sample t-test, *413, 414*
Confidence intervals
  One-sample z-interval procedure, *335*
  One-sample t-interval procedure, *353*

Inferences for Two Means
Hypothesis tests
  Pooled t-test, *442, 443*
  Nonpooled t-test, *455, 456*
  Paired t-test, *472, 473*
Confidence intervals
  Pooled t-interval procedure, *446*
  Nonpooled t-interval procedure, *459*
  Paired t-interval procedure, *477*

Inferences for Several Means One-way ANOVA, *590, 591*

Inferences for One or Two Proportions
One proportion
  One-sample z-interval procedure, *498*
  One-sample z-test, *509, 510*
Two proportions
  Two-sample z-test, *519, 520*
  Two-sample z-interval procedure, *523*

Normally Distributed Variables To determine a percentage or probability, *274* To determine the observations corresponding to a specified percentage or probability, *277*

Regression Inferences
Slope of the population regression line
  Hypothesis tests, *625, 626*
  Confidence intervals, *629*
Confidence intervals for means, *635*
Prediction intervals, *638*